# West Bromwich Albion

## A Complete Record

Tony Matthews

The Breedon Books
Publishing Company
Derby

First published in Great Britain by
The Breedon Books Publishing Company Limited
44 Friar Gate, Derby DE1 1DA
1993

ISBN 1 873626 47 9

Printed and bound by Hillmans Printers, Frome, Somerset.
Covers printed by BDC Printing Services Ltd of Derby.

# Contents

# Acknowledgements

Foremost, I have to acknowledge the splendid co-operation of my friend Colin Mackenzie, a civil servant based at Birmingham International Airport, who has provided so much valuable assistance in the past and whose help in checking and re-checking the statistical information has been of tremendous value.

Colin, an Albion supporter for 40 years, has painstakingly, fingered through the many old newspapers and periodicals available at libraries in Birmingham and London, clarifying hundreds of facts and figures in an effort to make this book what it is — A *Complete Record* of *West Bromwich Albion* Football Club. Thank you sincerely, Colin.

Grateful acknowledgement is also made to my wife, Margaret, for her unstinted effort in proof-reading the manuscript and for putting up with the continuous tapping of the typewriter as well as having heaps of pages scattered round the living room, bedroom, ante-room and bathroom.

Also I have to say thank you to Anton Rippon and the staff at Breedon Books, Derby; to professional photographers Bill Goulding (Peerless Photography), Geoff Wright (*Express & Star*), and Dale Martin; to amateur photographers Barry Marsh and Lawrie Rampling; Dave Shaw, Barry Swash and Donald Seely for use of old pictures and newspaper cuttings; to former players Harold Pearson, Johnny Nicholls, Jim Sanders and the late Bill Richardson; to the *Birmingham Post and Mail;* the Provincial Press Agency (Southport); the *Express and Star* (Wolverhampton); Kevin Grice and Kevin Powell, and the Universal Pictorial Press & Agency (London), whose pictures of past and present Albion players and match-action have proved so very useful in this publication.

There must be some people, somewhere, who have given their assistance in a small way, and who I have failed to mention here. But take it from me your work has been appreciated — thank you all.

TONY MATTHEWS
August 1993

# Introduction

THIS second edition of *Albion: A Complete Record* is probably the most comprehensive work ever compiled on a particular football club as far as facts and figures are concerned.

There are literally thousands upon thousands of statistics throughout the pages of this 'Complete Record' of West Bromwich Albion Football club — a club which is now 114 years old, having been formed by an enthusiastic group of young cricketers, all of whom worked at the George Salter Spring Factory in the town.

Initially it took Colin Mackenzie and myself three full years to get everything 'right' for publication, and believe me, it was hard work, but extremely interesting and fascinating for all that.

Football statistics can be a nightmare for anyone who cares to dabble in them and, during the compilation of this book, all the vital statistics have been diligently researched, using every possible source available. It is known that over the years, a number of major errors have occurred and been passed down, errors, I might add, which have been a constant thorn in my side since I became Albion's statistician some 28 years ago. These, I sincerely hope, have now been rectified thanks to my colleague, Colin, and the help of material at hand from various archives. Indeed, frequent reference has been made to the club's official organ, the *Albion News and Record* which began in 1905 and which today is one of the top programmes in the country; and to the 'History of West Bromwich Albion Football Club' which was serialised in the club's programme from 1911 to 1930 inclusive and gave, on the whole, an excellent account of Albion's earlier years.

A variety of local and national newspapers have also been methodically scrutinised and exhaustively read, particularly copies of the *Sport Argus*, the *Free Press*, the *Weekly News*, the *Birmingham Daily Gazette*, *Saturday Night* and the *Midland Athlete* to name but a few.

Here I would like to point out that, in a number of these older publications, the details of certain Albion scorers vary considerably, especially during the Victorian era, but every conceivable effort has been made to produce accurate statistics from what is an extremely complicated subject, bearing in mind that some goals were reported as being scored by the result of a 'scrimmage,' and that in the days before World War Two, players did not wear numbered jerseys, hence another worrying jigsaw to solve whereby in some team line-ups players were inserted 'out of position' (defenders in a forward role, and vice versa). But we've conquered these infuriating points, and each and every League and senior Cup game played by the Albion club since 1883 (when they first entered the FA Cup) has been detailed in full, with team line-ups in the League competition given in easy-to-read, 1-11 formation with the substitutes included only when they were used.

Attendances are from official Albion records, and not from newspapers or magazines. The information set out in other sections speaks for itself and with regard to transfer fees, these have been given in 'round' figures in most cases, and many differ with what the reader may have seen previously printed in other football annuals. The category featuring 'star' players has had to be restricted to a certain number and these have been chosen by myself, with no guidance from other people. And under Players' Records I have given the actual year of signing for Albion, when the man first put pen to paper, either as an amateur, an apprentice or as a full-time professional.

Colin and I have covered the complete history of West Bromwich Albion Football Club in this book. Very little, if anything, has been overlooked. Many photographs have been used, some of which have never been published before. Much of the information in this unique book has been updated from my previous Albion publications, and all the statistical records included are up to the end of season 1992-93. Entries in this book, however small or insignificant, supersede all previous statistical records appertaining to West Bromwich Albion FC. Colin and I sincerely believe that the contents in this latest Albion book will act as a permanent encyclopaedia of The Hawthorns' club for many years to come. It is indeed a COMPLETE RECORD.

As a final note, I would like to stress that all the views expressed in this publication are those of myself and Colin, and not necessarily those of West Bromwich Albion Football Club.

**TONY MATTHEWS**
August 1993

# The Albion Story

WEST Bromwich Albion Football Club owes its existence to a group of working-class youths who, not relishing the prospect of yet another long winter with little to occupy themselves, looked to football as a way of passing the months until the cricket season came around again.

The lads were all from George Salter Spring Works in West Bromwich, where they played for the works cricket team. What they could not have known, especially in those formative years of the game itself, was that their fledgeling would grow into one of the most famous names in soccer.

They had heard good reports of the game from their pals in Wednesbury which, at that time, boasted no fewer than four football teams, the Old Athletic Club, Wednesbury Town, the Strollers, and Elwell's Works side. The lads from Salter's works believed they could raise a team capable of playing matches against anyone who cared to take them on.

Initially, 12 youngsters formed the new club. A seven-man committee comprised James Stanton, George Bell, his brother Harry Bell, John Stokes, Arthur Eld, George Timmins and Billy Bisseker.

A ball was needed — and as football had not been introduced to the folk of West Bromwich, none of the local shops stocked such an item. Committee members had to walk to Wednesbury where the necessary equipment was purchased after each individual member had donated sixpence to the club's funds. The committee decided unanimously on a weekly subscription of twopence, which met all requirements as there was no rent to pay.

Anybody who wanted to join the team had to pay an introductory fee of sixpence. At the outset, wearing all types of coloured clothing, and various designs of footwear, the newly-formed Strollers kicked around on a piece of enclosed ground known as Cooper's Hill, adjacent to Dartmouth Park.

Until recently it was generally accepted that the decision to form a club was taken on a mid-September afternoon — either the 13th or 20th — in the year 1879, and that the name of West Bromwich Strollers was adopted soon afterwards. Reference to local newspaper archives has, however, since revealed that a team going under the name of West Bromwich Strollers played out a goalless draw with a works team called Hudson's on 23 September 1878. Several of the Strollers players on that occasion had subsequent connections with the 1879-80 team and it may be the case that the Strollers club was in existence earlier than previously thought. However, this might have been a trial game to see if there was sufficient interest in forming the club whose activities began in earnest the following year.

On 13 December 1879, the team celebrated a 1-0 victory over Black Lake Victoria, watched by 500 people, and this is the first recorded game in the 1879-80 season.

A week later Strollers played a another match, this time against the Bullock's Club. The venue was an excellent stretch of turf in Dartmouth Park, near the Beeches Road entrance, and again the Strollers excelled, winning convincingly by four clear goals.

Harry Aston hit two more, and Harry Evans notched the others. The attendance this time was around 1,000 and in the Strollers side at left-back was big Bob Roberts, later to become Albion's first international.

Roberts was nothing if not keen, and although he failed consistently wherever he played, he still managed to find his way into the side in some other position. Eventually he was persevered with in goal. It was a brilliant move, for Roberts became known as the 'Prince of Goalkeepers' and played three times for England.

Everything appeared to be running smoothly for the Strollers, and there is no record of them having lost a game in the 1879-80 season.

The annual general meeting of the club was held in July 1880 — and the following season the Strollers chalked up a record 14-0 win over Oakfield. In the same season Strollers suffered their first defeat.

Yet 1880-81 was a good season, and it seemed to justify a little enterprise. At the annual meeting of 1881 three decisions were made. The name 'Albion' was adopted in place of Strollers (the title coming from the same district in West Bromwich); George Bell was appointed club captain, in succession to Jimmy Stanton, who had hitherto held the post with Billy Bisseker. Bisseker was made 'sub-captain'; and a new ground, Bunn's Fied, Walsall Street, was acquired on a 12-month lease.

The players and officials levelled and rolled the ground and put the fences in reasonably good order so that they might charge an entrance fee. They eventually called their new headquarters The Birches, and this ground was officially opened on 10 September 1881. Oldbury FC were Albion's guests and a crowd numbering about 300 paid 15s.2d to see Albion triumph 5-1 with Billy Bisseker grabbing two of the goals.

And that money taken at the turnstile — yes only one — was wealth indeed to the youthful enthusiasts of the Albion club.

Within three years of playing their first match, West Bromwich Albion, as they had now become, had beaten Aston Villa and were being talked about as a club with a great future.

That win over Villa, who were to become Albion's keenest rivals down the years, was achieved in 1882 and the forecast about great times ahead came from the secretary of the Birmingham County FA.

Albion had entered the Birmingham Cup for the first time in 1881 and it was their 3-2 win over Calthorpe that moved Mr J.H.Cofield, secretary of the County FA, to write a three-page letter congratulating the club on their performance. The game itself was played on Calthorpe's Bristol Road ground and in a cleanly fought tie, Albion won 3-2.

From that time forward Albion's yellow and white quartered jerseys, with the Staffordshire knot embroidered neatly on the front, became familiar on local grounds.

Albion went on to oust Elwell's in the second round (2-1), Fallings Heath (3-1) in the third, and Notts Rangers (5-2) in the quarter-final, but were then narrowly pipped for a Final place by the favourites, Wednesbury Old Athletic 3-2. Old Athletic went on to win the trophy that year, but Albion were becoming a power in Midland football circles.

The 1882-3 season found Albion competing for the Birmingham, Wednesbury and Staffordshire Cups, and Mr George Salter was made an enthusiastic president of the club.

Unfortunately Albion could not hold on to their Bunn's Field arena, yet luckily they were handed the Four Acres Cricket Ground by the local Dartmouth club, whose football section had been very much eclipsed by the rising performances of the Albion.

The tenancy agreement was dated 20 September 1882 and in view of the improved conditions, the club entrance fee was raised to five shillings with an annual subscription of 2s.6d. Season tickets were issued at three shillings but these were not valid for cup-ties.

Albion's first season at the Four Acres saw them now running a useful second team and the fight for first-team places was beginning to hot up.

At the end of the campaign the annual report stated, in bold print, that the first team had played 39 matches, won 27, drawn seven and lost only five, scoring 177 goals and conceding 60. Harry Aston and George Bell were chief marksmen, each scoring over 40 goals.

The report added: 'Every club of importance in Birmingham has during the past season, succumbed to the prowess of the Albion, who even beat the famous Aston Villa by a goal to nil.'

It finished with the prophetic words: 'We hope the time is not far distant when even the English Cup (*the FA Cup*) will find a home in West Bromwich.'

In the 1882-3 Birmingham Cup, Albion ran up a mammoth score of 26-0 against Coseley in a first round tie on 11 November. Every player, except goalkeeper Bob Roberts, scored and the victory is still Albion's highest.

Violence and hooliganism at football matches is nothing new and was very much in evidence the first time Albion met Villa, at Perry Barr in November 1882 in the Staffordshire Cup.

The Albion party had to run a gauntlet of stones and clods of earth as they travelled to the ground. Villa, who had been established for eight years to Albion's mere three, reckoned they were on to an easy win and fielded an under-strength team. They got a nasty shock when Albion, brimming with confidence and backed by some 3,000 fans, held on for a 3-3 draw.

Villa were still confident and sent an unchanged side to Albion for the replay. They paid the penalty as Albion overturned the form book with a 1-0 win, thanks to George 'Drake' Timmins' solitary goal in the second half. A record crowd of 10,447 packed the Four Acres for that Christmastide replay, producing gate receipts of over £400.

Albion went on to lift the Staffordshire Cup with victory over Stoke in the Final. Thus, in less than five years, the boys who collected their sixpences to play were the proud holders of this sparkling silver prize. If anyone had any doubts about the position of Albion in the hearts of the locals, this was the occasion to dispell them.

In 1883, Albion entered the FA Cup for the first time. But any dreams they might have had of a spectacular triumph

# *Albion on the Football Map*

## STOKE 2    ALBION 3

VICTORY over Stoke in the 1883 Staffordshire Cup Final at the Victoria Ground on 21 April did much to put West Bromwich Albion on the football map and make the likes of Aston Villa and Wolverhampton Wanderers sit up and take notice. It was Albion's first appearance in any kind of Cup Final and their performance that day did them proud.

On the way to their meeting with Stoke, Albion had ousted Bloxwich after a replay, and then removed Aston Villa, also at the second attempt. The win over Villa was indeed a feather in the Throstles' cap and it gave them a quarter-final match with another useful team, Mitchell St George's, who were eliminated by default. In the semi-final, Leek White Star were whipped 8-0.

There was a great deal of excitement in the Black Country as Albion prepared to meet a well-balanced, efficient Stoke team which had scored 42 goals on their way to the Final. A cheap-day railway excursion was run from West Bromwich and more than 1,500 fans too advantage of it, decking themselves out in Albion favours for the big occasion.

Albion, who had trained at Malvern in the week before the big game, were able to select their strongest team, but they were still the underdogs when the game got underway — and when Johnson put Stoke ahead after only 15 minutes, it appeared that West Brom's second-best status was justified.

The Throstles, however, fought back hard and in a four-minute spell they scored twice through George 'Darkie' Timmins and Fred Bunn. Before the interval, Stoke drew level when Johnson notched his second of the match, making Stanton and While pay for their hesitancy.

Both sides went close in the opening period of the second half, but with 15 minutes remaining, it looked as though the issue would not be resolved that afternoon. Then Albion got a cross deep into the Stoke penalty area, up went winger George Bell to steer a powerful header past goalkeeper Wildin, and Albion were back in front.

When the final whistle sounded, West Brom's players and spectators alike were ecstatic. The fans chaired their heroes off the pitch and the celebrations in West Bromwich went on for three days after the team's triumphant homecoming. The *Athletic* reported: 'The atmosphere throughout the game was terrific and Albion thoroughly deserved their success.'

**Stoke:** Wildin; Stanford, Mellor, Brown, Bettany, Johnson, Brown, Shutt, Fennall, Myatt, Bennett.
**Albion:** Roberts; H.Bell, Stanton, E.Horton, Bunn, While, Aston, Whitehouse, Timmins, Bisseker, G.Bell.
*Ref: Mr L.King (Leicester).*                    *Att: 6,150.*

**Albion's team which won the 1883 Staffordshire Cup, pictured with the trophy. Back row (left to right): A.Eld (secretary), H.Bell, R.Roberts, J.Stanton, J.Noons (umpire). Middle: R.Biddulph (reserve), J.While, Mr G.Salter (president), F.Bunn, E.Horton, H.Green (reserve). Front: G.Bell, G.Timmins, W.Bisseker, H.Aston, J.Whitehouse. Timmins, Bunn and Bell scored the goals which gave Albion victory in their first-ever Cup Final appearance.**

Early action involving Albion in 1882, perhaps a practice match.

were rudely shattered when they were beaten 2-0 at home by Wednesbury Town.

Albion progressed in each of the other three cup competitions in which they participated in 1883-4 but carried off only one prize — the Birmingham Cup, beating Wolverhampton Wanderers in the Final, 2-1 after a replay.

In a friendly that season, Albion played Preston North End at home on Boxing Day and beat the country's top team 2-1 in front of a 3,600 crowd. It was only the second meeting between the clubs, Preston having won the previous encounter 3-1 in Lancashire earlier in the season.

In the 1884-5 FA Cup, Albion came into their own, and reached the sixth round before losing to high-riding Blackburn Rovers 2-0 before a record 16,393 crowd at the Four Acres. In a Birmingham Cup second round tie that season, Albion hammered Bloxwich 15-0.

With Tom Smith now club secretary and Joey Law the first-team trainer, Albion began season 1885-6 at another new ground — Stoney Lane — part of which is still there today. A 15-year lease was taken at £25 per annum. A total of

£150 was spent on improving parts of the popular enclosure and helping towards the cost of a stand.

The year 1886 provided Albion with another landmark when they reached the FA Cup Final for the first time. Luck smiled on the club all the way. Every round brought a home draw until the semi-final where they beat Small Heath 4-1 at Aston to become the first Midlands team to reach the Final.

Blackburn Rovers, were Albion's opponents in the Final at the Kennington Oval, which was jammed full with 15,156 people paying receipts of £650.

They saw a goalless draw, with Albion giving a good account of themselves despite being the underdogs. But in the Derby replay, which was witnessed by a crowd bigger than the initial game, 16,144, Rovers, who had won the trophy in the past two seasons, came out winners 2-0.

Albion had the consolations of winning both the Birmingham and Staffordshire Cups in 1886, beating Walsall Swifts and Stoke in the respective Finals.

Within 12 months they were back in the FA Cup Final again, this time facing

local rivals, Aston Villa. And again Albion crashed — this time 2-0.

After defeats in successive FA Cup Finals, Albion were determined to make amends and in 1888 they won the Cup, beating the famous Preston 'Invincibles' in the Final.

The Black Country was aflame with enthusiasm for weeks, for never before had there been such football heroes — not even back in 1883 when Albion captured their first prize.

In 1888, Albion were invited to be one of the original 12 members of the Football League but there were no spectacular achievements for the Throstles in those early days, although they did have the honour of being the first club to top the League table. After just one match, a 2-0 away victory over Stoke, they headed the other 11 teams.

The FA Cup was still their 'lucky' competition. Twice they reached the semi-finals, only to lose out to old rivals Preston in 1888-9 and Blackburn Rovers in 1890-91.

In 1891-2, however, a golden page was written in Albion's history. After three games to get rid of Nottingham Forest in the semi-final — Geddes getting a hat-trick in a fierce snowstorm at Derby — Albion met Aston Villa in the Final where they triumphed 3-0 to take the trophy for the second time. Villa goalkeeper, Jim Warner returned home after the game to find all the windows in his Spring Hill Public House smashed.

Mr Louis Ford was directing Albion's fortunes in the early 1890s and his net was cast far wider than his predecessor. His team included Scots and Irish, as well as Englishmen. One 'Irishman' who deserves a special mention was John Reynolds and owing to his lack of hair, he soon become known as 'Baldy' Reynolds.

He played for Ireland five times but Albion then found out that he was an Englishman, having been born in Blackburn, and thus he went on to play for England. A player of many moods, he won a Cup-winner's medal with Albion, against Villa and later a winner's medal for Villa against Albion.

One of the Scots was Willie Groves, once Celtic's centre-forward and winner of three full caps. Two years earlier Everton protested to the Football League that Groves had signed for them, although he never played. Groves was suspended. Albion then converted him into a highly efficient half-back and he was a key figure in their 1892 FA Cup win.

Curiously enough there was again trouble when in 1893, Aston Villa signed Groves while Albion were negotiating for his transfer to Everton. Villa were fined £25 for approaching him without Albion's consent.

In 1892, Albion set a Football League scoring record by thumping Darwen 12-0, on 4 April. Tom Pearson (4) and Billy Bassett (3) led the scoring. This record still stands, although it was equalled by Nottingham Forest, against Leicester Fosse, in 1909.

The League had now been increased

The Albion team for the opening of the Stoney Lane ground on 5 September 1885, for a match against Third Lanark Rifle Volunteers. Albion won 4-1. Back row (left to right): H.Green, H.Bell. Centre row: T.Green, T.Lavender, R.Roberts, E.Horton, G.Bell, G.Timmins, A.Loach. Front row: G.Woodhall, J.M.Bayliss, F.Bunn.

Albion team group showing ten of the players who contested the 'Championship of the World'. Back row (left to right): Mr Birch, Mr Jas Raybould, Mr George Slater, Mr Tom Smith, Mr H.Jackson, Mr Louis Ford. Middle: A.Aldridge, C.Perry, E.Horton, R.Roberts, G.Timmins, H.Green. Front: G.Woodhall, W.I.Bassett, J.M.Bayliss (captain), T.Pearson, J.J.Wilson. Tom Pearson scored for Albion, but Renton were soon on top.

# *World Championship*

IN 1887-8, West Brom played a grand total of 58 first-team matches. They won 43 of them, drew seven and lost only eight, scoring 195 goals and conceding 62 in the process.

They reached four Cup Finals, winning two and losing two, and one of those triumphs came in the FA Cup against 'Proud' Preston, whom they defeated 2-1 at The Oval.

Following this victory, Albion were asked to play for the 'Championship of the United Kingdom'. The game, which was also dubbed the 'Championship of the World', took place at Hampden Park on 19 May 1888, and Albion's opponents were the Scottish Cup holders, Renton, then one of the top teams North of the Border. The outcome was a 4-1 win for the Scots.

The football correspondent of the *Lennox Herald*, who rejoiced in the name of 'Saint Crispin', noted: 'Champions of the World is no doubt a very big title, nevertheless there is a club now holding that honour, and that club is Renton, as whoever are the Champions of the United Kingdom, can quite easily single themselves conquerors of the World.'

The match itself was an exciting affair. The rainy, windy weather was not conducive to footballing skill and it kept the crowd down to little over 6,000.

Renton defended stoutly at first, withstanding heavy pressure from Albion, whose right-wing pairing of Woodhall and Bassett went close on three occasions. 'Jock' Lindsay, the Renton goalkeeper, also saved a tremendous shot from 'Jem' Bayliss and then, seconds later, dived at the feet of the same player.

But in the 25th minute, in a breakaway, McNee put Renton ahead totally against the run of play, when he cashed in on

a slip by Timmins to score from close range. Albion struck back fiercely, and held the upper hand right up until the break, yet their efforts failed to produce a goal.

Tom Pearson did equalise soon after the restart in a goalmouth mêlée, but within five minutes Renton had touched peak form and rattled in three goals in the space of a quarter of an hour to knock the stuffing out of the Baggies.

McNee rifled in his second goal from 20 yards, McCall sneaked in a third and after Charlie Perry had failed to clear a free-kick, Johnny Campbell slotted in a fourth, the ball hitting both uprights before crossing the line.

Albion tried to make the scoreline a little more respectable but as the rain poured down, so the saturated surface made ground football virtually impossible, and that was no use to Albion who were renowned for their quick man-to-man soccer.

Indeed, the weather became so bad that Mr Sinclair, the Irish referee, almost abandoned the game with ten minutes remaining. He was perhaps persuaded to carry on by the expressions displayed on the Rentonians' faces.

The final whistle sounded and Renton were deserved winners and thus 'World Champions'. Two weeks later they confirmed their status by beating another top English club, Preston North End.

The teams for the first-ever World Championship game were:
**Renton:** Lindsay; Hannah, McCall, Kelso, Kelly, McKechnie, H.Campbell, McColl, J.Campbell, McCallan, McNee.
**Albion:** Roberts; C.Mason, H.Green, E.Horton, C.Perry, Timmins, Woodhall, Bassett, Bayliss, Pearson, Wilson.

# The Throstles Win the FA Cup

## ALBION 2   PRESTON NORTH END 1

FOR two successive seasons Albion had fallen at the last hurdle in their attempt to win the FA Cup. In 1886, Blackburn Rovers had beaten them in the Final, and the following year it was the turn of arch-rivals Aston Villa to lift the Cup at Albion's expense.

When Albion reached the Final again in 1888, they opposed Preston North End, and once more it looked as though the Throstles were going to end up as runners-up, for Proud Preston were the favourites.

Indeed, Preston were so confident that they asked to be photographed with the trophy before the start. 'Had you not better win it first?' was the brisk response from referee Major Marindin.

The game certainly caught the imagination of the football public and the gates at The Oval on 24 March 1888 were closed by kick-off time — the first time this had happened for a soccer match. It is a matter of history that almost 19,000 spectators saw Albion win the Cup 2-1, and there have been few more gallant, or popular, victories than the Throstles' success that afternoon.

Albion's team was comprised entirely of Englishmen and the club's weekly wage bill was no more than £10, yet they outfought mighty Preston with all their stars. And remember that 12 months later North End would become the first club to lift the double of League and Cup.

Albion played the long-passing game, backed up by a tremendous enthusiasm which swept aside the artistry of the Lancashire team. The man who proved Albion's greatest inspiration was 19-year-old Billy Bassett, who later that evening was selected for England and who was on the threshold of a great career.

Albion went ahead after only 20 minutes when Bassett collected a poor clearance from Preston goalkeeper, Mills-Roberts. Bassett sprinted away down the right before laying on an inch-perfect cross for Jim Bayliss to score from close range.

Preston clawed back and after 50 minutes of cut and thrust they equalised through Dewhurst, although West Brom complained that the ball had not crossed the line.

Undeterred, the Midlanders bounced back and in the 83rd minute, George 'Spry' Woodhall grabbed the winner amidst wild cheering from the Black Country fans who had made the trip south.

**Albion:** Roberts; Aldridge, Green, E.Horton, C.Perry, Timmins, Woodhall, Bassett, Bayliss, Pearson, Green.
**Preston North End:** Mills-Roberts; Howarth, Holmes, N.Ross, Russell, Gordon, J.Ross, Goodall, Dewhurst, Drummond, Graham.
*Ref: Major Marindin (London).*               *Att: 18,904*
                                        *(receipts £827.13s.0d).*

# Into the Football League

## STOKE 0   ALBION 2

WHEN the Football League was formed in 1888, West Bromwich Albion were one of the founder members. The Throstles' first match in the new competition was against Stoke at the Victoria Ground on 8 September 1888 and Albion went into the match brimming with confidence after friendly match victories over Sheffield Wednesday and Wolves.

Some 4,000 spectators — a good crowd for the first day of the brand-new competition — included a fair number of Albion supporters and their hopes of an early success were soon fulfilled as West Brom ran the match from the first whistle.

They pushed Stoke back into their own half from the onset and dominated the early exchanges, causing the home goalkeeper, Rowley, some anxious moments. Yet the goal which Albion threatened to score was a long time coming considering their territorial supremacy.

Woodhall twice went close, as did the forceful Pearson, and Hendry had a shot kicked off the line by Shutt, Stoke's almighty defender.

Stoke, to their credit, hit back purposefully and Albion 'keeper, Bob Roberts, had to be on his toes to keep out fine efforts from Staton and Tunnicliffe. Thus, although Albion had most of the first half, Stoke were still very much in with a chance as the 45 minutes ended.

Indeed, as the minutes ticked away in the second-half, Albion's play became sloppy and on one occasion Roberts had to be at his international best to keep out a stinging shot from Sayer.

But with only six minutes left to play, the Albion got the breakthrough they had been waiting for. Rowley was under intense pressure and was forced to clear his lines hurriedly by throwing the ball away. Joe Wilson, as quick as lightning, snapped up the ball and fired it straight back past the startled Stoke goalkeeper for Albion's first-ever goal in the Football League.

In the final minute they made absolutely certain of both points when George Woodhall headed a second goal from Billy Bassett's centre, and although it counted for little at this stage, the Throstles had the pleasure of topping the table on goal-average from Preston who, of course, were to win the Championship and the FA Cup that season.

**Stoke:** Rowley, Clare, Underwood, Ramsey, Shutt, Smith, Sayer, McSkimming, Staton, Edge, Tunnicliffe.
**Albion:** Roberts; J.Horton, J.Green, E.Horton, C.Perry, J.Bayliss, Bassett, Woodhall, Hendry, Pearson, Wilson.
*Ref: Mr S.Swann (Sheffield)*                    *Att: 4,524.*

to 14 clubs, and Albion's place at the end of 1891-2 was a moderate 11th with only 18 points.

In 1894-5, Albion again fought their way through to the FA Cup Final — their fifth appearance in 11 years — but trailed after only 40 seconds. That is how long

it took for Villa to score the only goal of the game. As some consolation, Albion carried off the Birmingham Senior Cup the same season, beating Aston Villa 1-0 in the Final.

As soccer — and Albion — grew in popularity, it became obvious that the

club's Stoney Lane ground was not large enough. Enclosed by buildings and streets, it could not be expanded in any direction. So new, more spacious premises were sought. A keen member of the board from June 1896 had been Mr Harry Keys. Accompanied by secretary Frank

Albion line-up in 1899-1900. Back row (left to right): J.Paddock (trainer), W.Walker, J.Reader, C.Simmons, T.Brennand (director), H.Powell (director), F.Heaven (secretary), H.Hadley, R.J.Roberts, B.Garfield. Front row: A.Dunn, J.Paddock, T.Perry, W.Richards, J.Banks. Seated on ground: A.Adams, A.Jones, W.Williams.

Joe Wilson, who scored Albion's first-ever League goal.

Heaven, he began negotiating the lease of a 10-acre site situated on the corner of Halfords Lane and the main Birmingham Road. The area was named 'The Hawthorns' on Ordnance Survey maps and this title seemed as good as any for the new home of the 'Throstles', as Albion were now called.

Albion played their first match on their new ground against Derby County on 3 September 1900. It ended 1-1 and over 20,000 fans turned out. But Albion had a disastrous first season at The Hawthorns and they were relegated to Division Two for the first time.

Some of the more established stars were nearing the end of their playing days. Goalkeeper Joe Reader was considering retirement, and Billy Williams, one of the club's best-ever left-backs, saw his career ended by injury at the age of 24. Former Villa inside-forward Freddie Wheldon, a brilliant star in his day, was a shadow of his former self. And Tom Perry was also past his best. Albion's slump into the Second Division, plus a 4-0 FA Cup semi-final defeat by Tottenham Hotspur, meant drastic action.

New players were sought as Albion's directors decided unanimously on reorganisation. With few funds available they still managed to sign men who became some of the finest players the Albion had ever possessed.

Chief among these was Dan Nurse, a right-half from Wolverhampton Wanderers, who was immediately made club captain. A man who led by example, Nurse was to serve Albion for many years, both on and off the field.

Ike Webb, from Small Heath, took Reader's place in goal. His courageous dives at the feet of oncoming forwards were a feature of his play and after many seasons in the game, it was discovered that he had been playing with a fractured skull.

Jack Kifford, another defender of the Williams calibre, who had played for Derby County and Portsmouth, was signed from Bristol Rovers to partner Amos Adams, a local lad, who had worked at George Salters.

Another local man, Abe Jones, the 'hard man' of the defence, who for several seasons had been a tower of strength at centre-half, had begun to put on too much weight. He was replaced by Scot Jimmy Stevenson, signed from Preston North End the previous season as a centre-forward. Harry Hadley, a polished wing-half, completed the middle trio.

The usual forward line in 1901-02 was: Jimmy McLean, a sturdy product of Walsall junior football; 'Chippy' Simmons; Billy Lee, another bustling centre-forward from Bournville; Tommy Worton, who came with Dan

# Another Cup Final Victory

## ALBION 3    ASTON VILLA 0

THE 1892 FA Cup Final was the last to be played at the Kennington Oval ground where the Surrey cricket authorities were becoming increasingly alarmed at the large crowds now being attracted to the showpiece game of the English football season. The honour of completing the end of an era fell to Midlands rivals, West Brom and Aston Villa, who took the field there on 19 March.

Throughout the season, Albion's form had been erratic and Villa supporters felt that all their team had to do was simply turn up and the Cup was theirs for the taking. Albion, naturally, had other ideas and the result was a brilliant display by the Throstles.

Villa began brightly on a warm, sunny and cloudless day which had helped swell the attendance to almost 33,000, but Albion had an early surprise in store and after only four minutes they took the lead.

A sudden break down the right by Bassett saw the England winger end a top-speed dash by curling over a perfect centre. Geddes was correctly positioned and the Albion left-winger fired the ball past the startled Warner in the Villa goal.

Villa certainly fought back hard but they found Albion goalkeeper Joe Reader in tremendous form. The Villains' efforts to find an early equaliser were in vain and gradually the complexion of the game changed.

Albion's half-backs, Groves, Perry and Reynolds, took a tight grip on the midfield exchanges and another brilliant run by Bassett, and fine work between McLeod and Geddes, led to Sammy Nicholl making it 2-0 after 27 minutes.

Ten minutes into the second half, Villa's last hopes disappeared when Reynolds scored Albion's third with a spectacular 25-yard shot which flew past poor Warner. Thereafter, Albion's determined defenders held Villa in tight rein and the Cup was on its way to Stoney Lane for the second time.

**Albion's Cup-winning team with the trophy. From left to right: Bassett, Nicholson, Reynolds, McLeod, Reader, Nicholls, Perry, Pearson, Groves, McCulloch, Geddes.**

The *Athletic News* reported that Albion's defence was 'simply superb' and praised goalkeeper Reader, saying he was 'cool, tall and calculating and 133,000 would not have upset his nerves.' Reynolds, said the newspaper, had a 'marvellous game', and Nicholls, Pearson and Geddes all played 'splendidly', as did Bassett, 'a master winger'.

**Albion:** Reader; Nicholson, McCulloch, Reynolds, C.Perry, Groves, Bassett, McLeod, Nicholls, Pearson, Geddes.
**Aston Villa:** Warner; Evans, Cox, D.Devey, Cowan, Baird, Athersmith, J.Devey, Dickson, Campbell, Hodgetts.
*Ref: J.C.Clegg (London).        Att: 32,710 (receipts £1,757).*

# A Record Victory

## ALBION 12    DARWEN 0

THIS was the day that Albion created a little piece of football history, becoming the first team to score more than ten goals in a Football League game. And today, their achievement still holds good, being the joint biggest win in the First Division.

Against the team from the Lancashire cotton town of Darwen, Albion were quite magnificent. They attacked from the first whistle and might well have claimed another five or six goals, had chances been put away.

Tom Pearson fired them ahead after only two minutes, his shot rocketing high past McOwen's outstretched right hand. Billy Bassett's effort struck the bar, then Nicholls chipped the ball inches over before John Reynolds steered home Jasper Geddes' corner.

Bassett netted number-three, Reynolds diverted Geddes' low cross home for the fourth goal, and on the stroke of half-time, Pearson assisted by Roddy McLeod, claimed Albion's fifth. Joe Reader made the for dressing-room to reflect that he had not been called upon to make a save in the first half.

The second half saw Albion in much the same hungry mood, although few could have forgiven them for slackening the pace in a game they had already won. Following a desperate scramble in the Darwen penalty area, Bassett made it 6-0 and the same player completed his hat-trick one minute later.

For 20 minutes Albion eased back, but the crowd were not content and urged them forward. The Throstles responded and Pearson scored their eighth. Darwen's Hunt obliged with an own-goal for the ninth and Pearson was on target again to take Albion into double figures.

Geddes made it 11-0 and in the dying moments of the game, Sammy Nicholls rounded things off with the twelfth goal to write West Brom into the record books.

**Albion:** Reader; J.Horton, McCulloch, Reynolds, C.Perry, Groves, Bassett, McLeod, Nicholls, Pearson, Geddes.
**Darwen:** McOwen; Hunt, Aspin, Entwistle, Owen, McEvoy, Wad, Nightingale, Fish, Alexander, Craven.
*Ref: Mr S.Lockett (Derby).                    Att: 1,109.*

# Unlucky Cup Final Losers

## ALBION 0    ASTON VILLA 1

ALBION were desperately unlucky to lose this superbly-fought Cup Final on 20 April 1895, one of the finest ever staged up to that time. Although what proved to be the match-winning goal was scored after only 39 seconds, the result was in doubt right up to the final whistle

A huge crowd of almost 43,000 packed the Crystal Palace ground at Sydenham and several thousands of them never saw the vital goal. They were still finding their places when Villa went ahead.

From the kick-off the Villa forwards rushed at the Albion defence and after a hectic scramble in the Baggies' penalty area involving Chatt, opposing full-back Jack Horton and Villa's great star, Jack Devey, Chatt's low cross struck Devey on the thigh and flew between the Albion posts. The goal is believed to be one of the fastest-ever in the Cup Final.

To their great credit, Albion battled hard after that, with Higgins and Taggart doing extremely well. Reynolds, playing against his former club, steadied Villa in the centre and sent in one rocket of a shot which grazed the Albion crossbar with Reader well beaten.

In the Villa goal, Wilkes was in fine form and saved from Richards and McLeod as Albion tried to force their way back into the game. There was action at both ends as first Bassett shot wide, then Richards headed over and Chatt and Athersmith both went close for Villa.

Just before half-time, Devey and Higgins collided in midfield and the Albion player was missing when the teams came out after the interval. When he did reappear, head swathed in a bandage, he was greeted with sympathetic applause from both sets of fans.

Thereafter, Higgins played a courageous game and certainly deserved more success for his brave effort. All he had to show for it was a losers' medal and a five-pound note, given to him after the game by the Villa chairman for his 'spirited performance'.

Albion slogged away looking for the equaliser but Villa held on to go 2-1 ahead over Albion in Cup Final victories.

**Albion:** Reader; J.Horton, Williams, T.Perry, Higgins, Taggart, Bassett, McLeod, Richards, Hutchinson, Banks.
**Aston Villa:** Wilkes; Spencer, Walford, Reynolds, Cowan, Russell, Athersmith, Chatt, Devey, Hodgetts, Smith.
*Ref: Mr J.Lewis (Blackburn).*      *Att: 42,652*
*(receipts £1,545 10s 0d).*

**Albion in 1901-02. Back row (left to right):** W.Brierley (trainer), B.Garfield, J.Lowe, I.Webb, F.Hobson, H.Cole, A.Green, Mr.G.W.East (director), W.Rogers, O.Taylor, J.Westwood, W.Barber (assistant trainer). **Middle row:** S.Brett, T.Evans, J.Stevenson, E.Smith, A.Randle, H.Hadley, G.Williams, Mr F.Heaven (secretary), Dr I.Pitt (director), Mr S.Makepeace (director), C.Simmons, W.Harper, J.Kifford, Mr F.Everiss (assistant secretary). **Front row:** P.Gollings, S.Edwards, A.Adams, W.Lee, D.Nurse, H.Keys (chairman), J.Chadburn, T.Jones, W.Walker, G.Dorsett. **On ground:** J.McLean, A.Smith, F.Buck, T.Worton, W.Poynton, B.Appleby. The trophies are the Second Division championship shield, Staffordshire Cup and Birmingham & District League championship shield.

Nurse from Wolves; and George 'Sos' Dorsett, who was found performing admirably with Brownhills Albion. Andrew 'Scottie' Smith was the standby utility forward.

In November 1900, Albion had signed, from Stafford Rangers, a diminutive forward named Freddy Buck. He made one or two first-team appearances that season but some time was to elapse before the chant of 'Have you seen Buck?', became commonly used as an Albion war cry.

The 1901-02 season started off ominously. Glossop, the Derbyshire club who were financed by a wealthy businessman

who later became identified with Arsenal, won the opening match at The Hawthorns 1-0.

But after that setback, Albion got into their stride and took the division apart with some devastating and consistent football. The next ten matches saw Albion undefeated and during this successful run Gainsborough were hammered 7-0 and Chesterfield 4-0. After a lapse at Doncaster on 23 November where they were beaten 2-0, Albion went 17 more League games without losing, to pull well clear at the head of the table.

In this undefeated sequence — a club

record — Albion played some sparkling football and 14 wins were recorded. Attendances began to rise, touching 23,697 for the Christmas game against Stockport. Even a 5-1 defeat by Bury in the opening round of the FA Cup did not stop Albion's romp — and they finished off the season in tremendous style, chalking up successive wins over Burton Swifts, Woolwich Arsenal and Barnsley, to end with this record:

| P | W | D | L | F | A | P |
|---|---|---|---|---|---|---|
| 35 | 25 | 5 | 4 | 82 | 29 | 55 |

Albion finished four points ahead of

# *Throstles Hammer the Magpies*

## ALBION 6    NEWCASTLE UNITED 1

NEWCASTLE, one of the finest teams in the country during the early Edwardian era, had started the 1902-03 season in style — three wins out of three games and a goals record of 9-0. Albion, newly promoted to Division One, had won two of their opening four matches and everyone at The Hawthorns on 27 September 1902 was looking forward to the prospect of a cracking game.

Newcastle fielding former Albion winger Dick Roberts and the famous Scottish international Bob McColl, found themselves under intense pressure from the start and after only three minutes they were a goal down after Billy Lee netted from close-range following a miscued clearance from goalkeeper Kingsley.

Thereafter, Albion were in irrepressible form and after 19 minutes, Freddie Buck made it 2-0. Only 60 seconds later, Albion found themselves three goals ahead. Again Kingsley was at fault. The Magpies' goalkeeper mishandled an inswinging corner from Dorsett and there was 'Chippy' Simmons to bundle both ball and 'keeper over the line.

Before half-time, United pulled a goal back when the unmarked McColl headed Roberts' looping cross past Ike Webb, but it was only a temporary fightback and four minutes into the second half, Albion restored their three-goal advantage.

Buck raced clear to crack a scorcher over Kingsley's head from 18 yards and then another piledriver — this time from Jim Stevenson — made it 5-1.

There were still 20 minutes to go and Albion tore the Magpies' defence to shreds. They could even afford to miss a penalty — Jack Kifford was the culprit — before Jimmy McLean rounded off a fine performance by clipping in the sixth goal with barely three minutes remaining.

One report said: 'The score carries on its lop-sided face all that is necessary in the way of comment — Albion deserved to win by six goals to one. They played so manfully, skilfully, untiringly and dashingly that they would have beaten any team, past, present or to come, on the form they displayed.'

**Albion:** Webb; Kifford, Adams, Nurse, Stevenson, Hadley, McLean, Simmons, Lee, Buck, Dorsett.
**Newcastle United:** Kingsley; Agnew, Davidson, Gardner, Aitken, Carr, Stewart, Orr, McColl, Rutherford, Roberts.
*Ref: Mr J.Campbell (Blackburn).    Att: 22,160 (receipts £520).*

second-placed Middlesbrough. The total of 55 points gained was then a League record, and Stoke were beaten 3-0 in the Staffordshire Cup Final.

Frank Heaven resigned as Albion secretary in 1902 — so opening the way for Fred Everiss, who was to stay with the club for 55 years. His early days were fraught with difficulties. There were internal quarrels about policy and half the board had given up their positions. The club's bank balance was at a very low ebb — this despite a promotion-winning season in the Second Division — and there was an inevitable lowering in overall standards. However, under Everiss' shrewd guidance, things turned themselves out and in time Albion became a side respected and feared by almost every team in the land.

Indeed, Albion seemed right in line for the First Division title in 1902-03. Up to mid-January they had obtained 32 points out of a possible 44 and were heading the table. Crowds were good — around the 18,000 mark — and some terrific wins had been registered. For instance, Newcastle, a fine side around this time, were slammed 6-1 at The Hawthorns, Aston Villa were clipped 3-0 at Villa Park, Blackburn Rovers were beaten 5-3, Liverpool 2-0 and Wolves 2-1.

Jack Kifford was firing in penalty-kicks at a fine rate and Billy Lee was also scoring fluently, as were George Dorsett and 'Chippy' Simmons. But then everything went wrong. Poor Albion picked up a mere four points from their remaining 12 games to end in seventh position with 36 points.

The turning point could well have been their 2-0 home FA Cup defeat by Tottenham Hotspur in February. Directly after this slip Albion drew 3-3 with Sheffield United and then proceeded to lose eight League games in succession — and with them the title.

To help ease the pain, Albion carried off the 1903 Staffordshire Cup beating Stoke 2-0 in the Final at Aston, with Freddy Buck hitting both goals. And the Throstles' average home League attendance in 1902-03 was 15,657 — the fourth best in the division.

Yet Albion's next campaign was a complete disaster. They were relegated for a second time, finishing bottom of the table with 24 points out of a possible 68. It was Albion's rearguard which took most of the blame with 60 goals conceded.

Albion players out for a 'training walk' in 1905. From left to right: Fred Shinton, Eli Bradley, Bill Barber (trainer), Jim Stringer, Jesse Pennington, Jack Manners, 'Chippy' Simmons, George Young and Adam Haywood.

Albion in 1905-06. Standing (left to right): Mr W.I.Bassett (director), W.Barber (trainer), J.Pennington, G.Young, J.Stringer, A.Adams, A.Randle, Mr F.Everiss (secretary). Seated: F.Haycock, C.Simmons, E.Pheasant, F.Shinton, A.Haywood, E.Perkins. On ground: E.Bradley, W.Law.

Albion were back in the Second Division in 1904, with problems mounting all the time. There was little money in the bank. And on Bonfire Night that year, the old stand, transferred from Stoney Lane, joined in the activities and burned down — the cause was put down to an errant sky-rocket.

Meanwhile, Albion's creditors hammered at the door and the whole board resigned. Harry Keys returned as chairman. Billy Bassett joined the board with local businessmen, and two years' grace was obtained so that Albion could carry on.

Twelve months later Albion were able to report a profit of £240 before charging depreciation, though £965 had been spent in transfer fees to strengthen the team.

One new player was Ted 'Cock' Pheasant, a half-back or centre-forward, who had rendered good service to Wolves. Another was Jack Manners, a pit lad from Morpeth Harriers in the North-East.

Dan Nurse had suffered a leg injury which eventually ended his career and to replace him, Albion introduced Arthur Randle, a talented Oldbury youngster.

Lawrie Bell, Albert Lewis — who scored a hat-trick on his debut at Burnley — Fred Haycock and Jimmy Williams were other newcomers in 1904-05, as were Jack Dawes, Llewellyn Davies — later to become a prominent Welsh international — goalkeeper Jim Stringer and centre-half Tom Hayward. Right at the end of the season Fred Shinton was signed from Hednesford Town.

Shinton was a player renowned for his aggressive all-action displays at centre-forward. His weight and strength made him a danger to any defence and he was second-highest scorer in his first full season (1905-06) with 18 goals. The following campaign he netted 28 goals in 30 matches, including four in one game on three separate occasions — against Clapton Orient, Glossop and Grimsby Town.

He suffered a nasty knock in the return game against Clapton in 1906-07 and never really recovered. He was transferred to Leicester Fosse after scoring 46 goals in only 64 League games in Albion colours.

Another player drafted into the first team in the early 1900s was a young man called Jesse Pennington. Pennington became one of the greatest of all England left-backs, a man spoken of in high regard all over the country as 'Peerless Pennington'.

A tendency to drop points at home is not a fault that is new to Albion — they had the same trouble early in the century. For three successive seasons they finished no higher than fourth and no lower than fifth in Division Two — and each time it was dropped home points that cost them promotion.

They did keep their fans happy in 1907 when they reached the FA Cup semi-final — and the man mainly responsible was Oxford University undergraduate, Billy Jordan. Jordan, a member of a well-known Oldbury family, won a Blue and two amateur caps as a striker — and once scored six goals in a 15-0 win for England over France.

Albion could have done with a couple of those goals in 1908-09, when they missed promotion by one fifty-sixth of a goal. And Albion claimed that they were robbed by a referee's decision at Blackpool when Charlie Hewitt's shot hit the underside of the bar and rebounded out. Bill Garraty, the centre-forward, did not bother to tap it into the net because he thought Albion had scored, but the referee ruled the ball had not crossed the line and although Albion still won the match, they always reckoned that the decision cost them promotion.

It was during the years between 1906 and 1909 that several fine players first appeared for Albion, including Hubert Pearson, David Walker, Bill Davies, and a player who broke his leg four times in his career, Albert Evans. Tommy Dilly signed in 1907 and was the last Scottish-born player to join Albion for 30 years.

Season 1909-10 saw the Albion finish 11th in Division Two — their lowest position in League football at that time — and for 1910-11 the Throstles gambled and practically rebuilt their side, many of the new players never having played League football before.

The move paid off and Albion won the Second Division championship with one of the youngest sides they have ever fielded. The team that season usually read — Pearson; Smith, Pennington, Baddeley, Waterhouse, McNeal, Wollaston, Bowser, Pailor, Buck, Lloyd.

Hubert Pearson served Albion for over 20 years, making more than 370 appearances and was followed into The Haw-

*Above:* Albion in 1914. Back row: Richardson, Riddle, Crutchley, Shore, Pearson, Wright, Moorwood, Waterfall, Paddock (assistant trainer). Second row: W.Barber (trainer), Reed, Deacey, Morris, Poulton, Lewis, Steer, Jackson, Wood, Buck, Baddeley, Harrison (groundsman). Seated: McNeal, Cook, Waterhouse, Bentley, Pennington (captain), Smith, Gregory, Shearman. On ground: Jephcott, Hackett, Swift, Lloyd, Mann, Donald, Newall. *Opposite:* Action from January 1914: Division 1, Albion 0 Liverpool 1. Pearson goes out for a high ball.

thorns team by his son, Harold. Joe Smith, who was signed from Cradley St Luke's, was capped three times for England and played 470 games for Albion. Another England player was Bobby McNeal, who was converted from an inside-forward and turned out more than 400 times for Albion. And former Wattville Road schoolboy, Sid Bowser, played for England at centre-half after starting his career as a centre-forward.

Albion clinched the title with a 1-0 win over Huddersfield in the last game of the season — the vital goal coming from a Freddie Buck penalty that went through the Huddersfield 'keeper's legs.

Back in the First Division, Albion finished a respectable ninth, but it was their Cup run that made the news, as the Throstles once more stormed through to the Final. En route they beat some good sides. Indeed only one goal had been conceded in seven matches and Albion were favourites to beat Barnsley in the Final But they failed and a row blew up over the replaying of the FA Cup Final in 1912. Albion lost the argument and lost the match too.

The original game at The Crystal Palace was drawn 0-0. When the FA announced that the replay was to be held at Sheffield, Albion protested. Their objections were overruled and the huge majority of the 38,500 crowd were

Yorkshiremen urging Barnsley to victory. A 119th-minute goal by Tufnell beat Albion.

On the way to that Final there had been a crowd of 45,000 — with mounted police in attendance — when Albion beat Sunderland in the quarter-final on Wearside, and a goal by Pailor a minute from the end of extra-time won a replayed semi-final against Blackburn Rovers.

But the Cup run cost Albion dearly. They were so far behind with their League matches that they had to play 12 games in April, including one spell of seven games in ten days either side of the

Final and the replay. Albion were fined by the League for fielding a weakened side in one of those games.

Albion's average League attendance of 18,042 was one of the highest in the First Division. The cash from these 'gates' allowed the club to buy the freehold of The Hawthorns in June 1913, for £5,350. A year later they were able to finish work on the grandstand.

World War One broke out in August 1914 but League football continued for a season and was then broken down into regional competitions. One player to emerge from the conflict was Tommy

War memorial at The Hawthorns, unveiled by Colonel John V.Campbell VC, ADC, on 4 February 1922.

Magee, the 'Pocket Hercules' who was to serve the Albion so well for 15 years. Magee, a soldier serving on the Western Front, was recommended to Albion by one of his army colleagues, Tom Brewer.

But if the war produced a great Albion player, it took away another when Lt Harold Bache was killed in action on 15 February 1916.

Peace in 1918 was followed by the resumption of League football and that brought extra joy to Albion in the shape of their very first League Championship. They finished 1919-20 nine points clear of runners-up Burnley with 60 points from 28 wins and 104 goals. Just to cap the season Albion made a profit of £7,432.

Yet the 'Roaring Twenties' were depressing times for Albion after such a fine first season following the war. There were only a few moments of glory as the team struggled to recapture the exciting flair and method of that Championship-winning season.

They managed to finish runners-up to Huddersfield Town in 1924-5, but two years later, finished bottom with 30 points and went back into Division Two.

It was said that a 'weakness in defence' was the cause of relegation — despite a rearguard that included Harold Pearson (in goal in place of his father), George Shaw, signed from Huddersfield Town halfway through the term, and newcomer Bob Finch.

Those years are best glossed over, but there were one or two moments to remember. Like the match in 1922-3 in which Freddie Morris scored four times in a 7-0 win over Arsenal. And the emergence of Stan Davies, the utility forward, who played in six different positions in 19 appearances for Wales.

There was also the flourishing wing partnership of Tommy Glidden and Joe

# *Fred Morris' Five-Goal Rampage*

## ALBION 8    NOTTS COUNTY 0

ALBION had already achieved some major scoring feats before this match against Notts County at The Hawthorns in the first League season after World War One, but no one could have foreseen this performance when poor Notts were slammed for eight goals without reply on 25 October 1919.

Indeed, Albion's fans were worrying about the absence of Pearson, Smith, Bowser and Jephcott, all regular first-teamers. Their fears were groundless and the Throstles' goals rained home, six of them coming in a splendid second half when County hardly got out of their own penalty area.

Freddie Morris netted twice in the first 45 minutes, both goals coming from fine moves which involved four and five players. After the interval, Morris completed his hat-trick and then Notts' Foster turned Jack Crisp's centre past his own goalkeeper, the great Albert Iremonger.

Morris added two more to put Albion 6-0 ahead and take his own personal tally to five. His fourth was laid on by a superb piece of creative football from Tommy Magee, the

'Mighty Atom', and his fifth followed some splendid wing play from Crisp.

Howard Gregory darted in to slip home goal number seven, and Magee capped a fine display by claiming the eighth when he scored from close range after Morris' shot hit the bar.

Albion's forwards had been absolutely brilliant and there had been some remarkable individual displays as well as some great team-work. Nothing seemed to go amiss and it was the club's misfortune to meet Albion when the Throstles were in such rampant form.

Seven days later, however, Albion went to Meadow Lane and lost 2-0, just to underline the unpredictability of football.

**Albion:** Moorwood; Cook, Pennington, Richardson, Reed, McNeal, Crisp, Magee, A.W.Smith, Morris, Gregory.
**Notts County:** Iremonger; Tasker, Marriott, Flint, Pembleton, Foster, Cooke, Cook, McLeod, Hill, Henshall.
*Ref: Mr J.W.D.Fowler (Sunderland).*          *Att: 36,086.*

First Division champions. Here are the men who brought the League title to The Hawthorns in 1919-20. **Back row (left to right):** W.Barber (trainer), Pearson, W.Gopsill (assistant trainer), E.Smith (assistant secretary). **Third row:** Mr F.Everiss (secretary), Mr D.G.Nurse (director), Cook, Mr.W.I.Bassett (vice-chairman), Mr H.Keys (chairman), Jephcott, Mr Seymour (director), Lieut-Col Ely (director). **Seated:** Crisp, A.Smith, McNeal, Pennington, Bowser, Morris, Gregory. **On ground:** J.Smith, Magee, Bentley, Richardson. The trophies are for the League Championship and the FA Charity Shield.

# League Champions 1919-1920

ALBION have won the Football League Championship only once, in 1919-20 — the first post-war season — when they coasted home with 60 points, nine clear of second-placed Burnley. Albion recorded 28 wins, drew only four of their 42 games, and scored a record 104 goals, conceding 47.

They clinched the title on Saturday, 10 April 1920, when Bradford were defeated 3-1 at The Hawthorns in front of nearly 30,000 spectators

The Throstles' season had started on 30 August 1919 with a 3-1 home win over Oldham. Freddy Morris scored twice and Tommy Magee made his League debut.

A 2-0 win at Newcastle followed, with Pearson saving a penalty, and then Oldham turned the tables, winning the return 2-1.

Four successive wins sent Albion storming on. They triumphed 3-0 over Newcastle, beat Everton 4-3 at home and 5-2 away, and defeated Bradford City 4-1, with centre-half Sid Bowser claiming a hat-trick, including two penalties.

City, however, grabbed revenge and won the return 3-0 on the first Saturday in October.

Three more successive wins boosted Albion's confidence. Bolton were beaten 4-1 at The Hawthorns and 2-1 at Burnden Park, and an 8-0 hammering of Notts County saw Morris score five splendid goals to cheer the 36,086 crowd.

County, though, caused a major upset by beating Albion 2-0 in the return, and then Villa smashed West Brom's unbeaten home record with a 2-1 win on the 10 November. Yet that defeat was soon forgotten when Albion went to Villa Park and won the return 4-2 in front of 60,202 fans.

A second home lapse — a 3-1 defeat by Sheffield Wednesday — was followed by a great run of six consecutive victories, with the double coming over Manchester City (3-2 and 2-0), and Derby (4-0 and 3-0), plus victories over Wednesday (3-0), and Sunderland (4-0).

At the season's halfway stage Albion were one point clear at the top of the table with 32 to Burnley's 31. Newcastle were third and Sunderland fourth. At this point Albion had still to draw a game.

Into 1920, Albion continued to prosper. After a 4-1 setback at Sunderland, they hammered Blackburn for ten goals in two games, winning 5-1 away and 5-2 at home. A 2-1 success over Manchester United saw a five-point gap open up over Burnley and the Championship prize was in sight.

Sheffield United jolted Albion by completing the double over them (2-0 and 1-0), before a run of eight games without defeat sent the Throstles' hopes soaring. They beat Middlesbrough, Manchester United, Burnley, Preston (twice) and Bradford, and drew with Middlesbrough and Burnley to pull six points clear of Burnley who had only four games left.

A 1-0 Easter defeat at Arsenal was avenged the following day when the Gunners were pipped by a Morris goal, and on 10 April, the title came to West Bromwich.

The run-in brought two draws against Liverpool (1-1 and 0-0), a 2-0 defeat at Chelsea and then a tremendous 4-0 finale against Chelsea at home when the Championship trophy was presented to Jesse Pennington in front of 35,668 cheering supporters.

Fred Morris, with 37 goals (a new club record), topped the scoring charts. Alf Bentley (15), Howard Gregory (12), Bowser (10 including eight penalties), Jack Crisp (eight), Magee and Andy Smith (seven each), Claude Jephcott (five), Bobby McNeal (two) and an own-goal made up the total of 104.

Only McNeal was an ever-present in the side (42 games); Bowser made 41 appearances, Sam Richardson and Joe Smith each 40, followed by Hubert Pearson and Morris 39 each), Crisp (38), Pennington (37), Gregory (34), Andy Smith (29), Magee (24), Bentley (24), Jephcott (21), Cook (seven), Len Moorwood (three), Frank Waterhouse (two), Fred Reed and Sam Hatton (one each).

The average League attendance at The Hawthorns in 1919-20 was 30,532, and, for the record, Albion were knocked out of the FA Cup in the first round by Barnsley, but then that hardly mattered.

# The Gunners Hit for Seven

## ALBION 7    ARSENAL 0

WITH 18 minutes remaining in this First Division game at The Hawthorns on 14 October 1922, Albion led Arsenal 2-0 and there was a slim possibility that the Gunners might yet sneak their way back into the match. Then came a sensational finale — five goals by a vintage Albion display which produced some quite astonishing attacking play.

A week earlier, Arsenal had beaten Albion 3-1 at Highbury and for the return match in the Black Country, West Brom fielded the same team whilst Arsenal made only one change, at full-back.

In the opening quarter of the game, both goals came under threat. Jones and Morris went close for Albion — Arsenal 'keeper Dunn making two good saves — and Rutherford and Voysey had chances for the Gunners.

After 29 minutes it was Albion who drew first blood when Smith, Jones and Stan Davies combined down the right to give Davies a chance. Dunn blocked the Albion man's effort but the ball ran loose for the ever-alert Morris to slam the ball home.

Two minutes later, Morris added a second, cashing in on a slip by Turnbull. And on the stroke of half-time, Davies had a 'goal' disallowed for offside, although the Albion man disputed the decision fiercely.

Arsenal began the second half in rampant form, pressing the Throstles back, but Albion's defence held firm — one report said that the home defenders 'lay low like Brer Rabbit'

as the Gunners chased the goal that would have put them back in contention.

Young and White both had half-chances but this time it was the turn of Albion goalkeeper, Pearson, to produce two fine saves. Pearson's alertness proved the turning point of the game for, after soaking up the pressure, Albion returned to the attack in no uncertain terms.

The Throstles crashed home five hammer blows in less than 15 minutes. After 71 minutes, Jack Crisp netted from Davies' clever cross; five minutes later, Morris completed his hat-trick when he cracked home a short pass from Jones; less than 60 seconds later, Crisp made it 5-0 with a close-range shot.

And so Albion continued: Morris set up Howard for their sixth goal after 78 minutes, then Morris himself rounded off a splendid afternoon's work by grabbing his fourth and Albion's seventh goal with six minutes remaining.

In the final seconds, Davies came within inches of making it 8-0 and then the whistle blew to leave Albion only four points behind the First Division leaders, Liverpool.

**Albion:** Pearson; Smith, Adams, Magee, Bowser, McNeal, Crisp, Jones, Davies, Morris, Gregory.
**Arsenal:** Dunn; Bradshaw, Turnbull, Baker, Voysey, Graham, Rutherford, White, Young, Boreham, Dr Patterson.
*Ref: Mr W.F.Bunnell (Preston).*                    *Att: 21,730.*

---

Carter, who set up many chances for the goalscoring combination of George James and Charlie Wilson. James had topped the 1924-5 scoring charts with 30 goals.

By the end of the decade there were already signs of an Albion recovery. The starting point of this resurgence in the Throstles' fortunes can be traced back to the day they signed Jimmy Cookson from Chesterfield in June 1927.

Cookson had been released by Manchester City, and Chesterfield converted him from a defender into a forward with instant success. He smashed the Chesterfield scoring record in his first season and a host of clubs chased his signature.

Albion won the race and as soon as Cookson arrived at The Hawthorns he found the net. At the end of his first season Freddie Morris' scoring record had gone as 'Cooky' netted 38 League goals, including six in the home game against Blackpool.

Indeed, three seasons in Division Two saw Albion involved in some big score-lines. They beat Grimsby 6-0 in January 1928, and the following Christmas hammered Wolves 7-3.

In 1929-30 they scored 105 League goals — a club record that still stands. Cookson scored 33 of those goals to take his tally for three seasons to 92. Tommy Glidden hit 54 over the same period and Joe Carter 46.

Other new faces had joined up now — Bert Trentham was at full-back, Len Darnell at left-half, Frank Cresswell at inside-left and Stan Wood his wing partner.

Undoubtedly the most significant

**Albion on their way to Wembley and FA Cup glory in 1931.**

arrivals shared the same name — and they were to be household names for years to come. The William Richardsons turned out at centre-half and centre-forward respectively in the same Albion side in the early 1930s.

The problem of identification was solved by the centre-forward's hair colouring. He was renamed 'W.G.' — for 'Ginger' Richardson.

Billy Richardson, the centre-half, was a local lad who had just won his place

in the side when his namesake arrived from Hartlepools United, who were playing in the Third Division North.

'W.G.' was to lead the Albion attack for the next 16 years, achieving many scoring feats. Incredibly, he was capped only once for England — a 1-0 win over Holland in 1935.

The team was settled and success arrived again, but there was controversy over Albion's 1931 FA Cup Final win that set up the famous 'double' of Cup success

# Cookson's Double Hat-Trick

## ALBION 6    BLACKPOOL 3

WHEN a useful Blackpool team visited The Hawthorns for a Second Division match on 17 September 1927, Albion centre-forward Jimmy Cookson turned the occasion into a personal triumph, scoring all six goals against the Seasiders.

From the first kick of the game it was evident that both teams were hungry for goals and the 20,000 crowd saw nine go into the net. Indeed, they would have been treated to a dozen or more but for some fine goalkeeping from both Ashmore and Hobbs.

Albion went ahead in the sixth minute when Cookson flicked home Glidden's measured pass. Blackpool hit back, then it was Albion's turn to counter-attack. It was action all the way and in the 33rd minute, a misunderstanding between Evans and Fryer allowed Tuffnell to nip in and equalise.

Two minutes into the second half, Albion were awarded a penalty when Thorpe handled Fitton's cross. Cookson thumped the spot kick past Hobbs and ten minutes later completed his hat-trick, cooly gliding home the ball to make it 3-1.

Tuffnell was on hand to reduce the arrears but if Blackpool then harboured thoughts of another equaliser, they were to be bitterly disappointed. Cookson, who was playing absolutely brilliantly, scored a second hat-trick, his trio of goals coming in the space of only seven minutes.

In the 63rd minute Glidden and Carter combined for Albion's hero of the day to net his fourth; his fifth came after his own initial effort had rebounded off the 'keeper; and after 70 minutes Fitton and Wilson set him up and then watched as the centre-forward lashed home a rocket of a shot from 10 yards.

Blackpool, to their credit, never gave up and ten minutes from time, Williams reduced the arrears with a long-range shot which dropped over Ashmore's head from fully 35 yards.

Right on the final whistle, Cookson thought he had scored a seventh goal but his delight was short-lived as an upraised linesman's flag robbed him. Nevertheless, Jimmy Cookson's feat went into the record books, for no other Albion player has equalled his tally of six goals in a single League or Cup game for the club.

**Albion:** Ashmore; Finch, Shaw, Magee, Evans, Fryer, Glidden, Carter, Cookson, Wilson, Fitton.
**Blackpool:** Hobbs; Thorpe, Tilford, Watson, Grimwood, Benton, Meredith, Browell, Williams, Tuffnell, Downes.
*Ref: Mr G.N.Watson (West Bridgford).*          *Att: 20,203.*

**Tottenham goalkeeper Cyril Spiers punches clear from Albion's Tommy Glidden in the FA Cup tie at The Hawthorns in January 1931. Albion won 1-0.**

and promotion from the Second Division.

The row surrounded a 'goal that wasn't' for Birmingham. It came in the first-half when Gregg headed the ball past Harold Pearson. The linesman flagged for offside and the referee, Mr Kingscott from Derby, agreed. Blues fans maintained that their side were robbed, but a man who was close to the action, Tommy Magee, said later, "Gregg was a yard offside — he was in front of me and I was the last Albion defender apart from 'Pop' Pearson."

'W.G.'Richardson had put Albion into the lead after 25 minutes. Joe Bradford equalised for Birmingham, but it was not to last. Straight from the kick-off 'W.G.' prodded home Albion's second.

Tommy Glidden took the trophy from the Duke of Gloucester and 150,000 people lined the streets of West Bromwich when the team returned in triumph.

The Cup victory came at the end of a season that included great League wins

Albion and Wolves players, along with the match officials, on 11 October 1930 participating in a minute's silence in memory of those men who lost their lives in the Norton Canes pit disaster earlier that month.

Tommy Glidden (centre) holds the FA Cup after Albion's Wembley victory in 1931.

Albion's double-winning side. Back row (left to right): Mr F.Everiss (secretary), W.Richardson, Carter, Pearson, Trentham, Sandford, F.Reed (trainer). Front row: Shaw, Magee, W.G.Richardson, Mr W.I.Bassett (chairman), Edwards, Wood, Glidden.

# Double-Winners

ALBION created history in 1930-31 when they won promotion from the Second Division and carried off the FA Cup, beating neighbours Birmingham 2-1 in the Final at Wembley.

Albion clinched their place in the First Division by winning their final League game of the season, 3-2 at home to Charlton Athletic before a record 52,415 crowd.

They finished runners-up, seven points behind Everton and three ahead of third-placed Spurs. In the Cup Final, seven days before that last vital League game, Albion went 1-0 ahead in the 25th minute through a W.G. Richardson goal. Twenty minutes into the second half, Joe Bradford equalised for the Blues, but within a matter of seconds, Albion were back in front with W.G.'s winning goal.

Wherever they went, Albion entertained with their forceful attacking football. They scored 99 goals in 52 competitive games and five players — W.G.Richardson, Glidden, Wood, Cookson and Carter — each reached double-figures.

— 4-0 and 6-3 at Charlton and Cardiff respectively, 6-1 at Nottingham Forest, 4-0 over Stoke and 5-0 against Barnsley.

The men who played in most of the matches were Harold Pearson, George Shaw, Bert Trentham, Tommy Magee, Billy Richardson, Jimmy Edwards, Tommy Glidden, Joe Carter, 'W.G.'Richardson, Teddy Sandford and Stanley Wood.

Saturday, 2 May 1931 was the proudest day in the history of Albion and the day a new page was written in the story of English football. It was the afternoon that Albion won promotion from Division Two, adding to their FA Cup win of a week before and so completing a 'double' never achieved before or since.

The scenes at The Hawthorns after the victory over Charlton were never to be forgotten. Even when the players managed to reach the dressing-room they had to go out again and again to acknowledge their supporters, who refused to go home until due homage had been paid.

The historic double had a profitable spin-off for Albion. It allowed ground improvements to be carried out at The Hawthorns, including the provision of tip-up seats in the Halfords Lane stand and new surfacing on the terracing. Later that year, the Great Western Railway opened a railway station less than 200 yards from the main entrance to the ground.

Albion had arrived. More than 55,000 people turned up to see the Throstles' first match back in Division One. Arsenal were the hosts but Albion were the winners, a goal from Stan Wood earning them both points in London.

Albion had little trouble holding their own in the top flight, finishing sixth in the first season and fourth the next year. New faces arrived at The Hawthorns. Jimmy Murphy replaced Tommy Magee; Walter Robbins, the man with 'tree-trunk' legs and thumping shot, came

# A Unique Double

## ALBION 3   CHARLTON ATHLETIC 2

WEST Bromwich Albion's defeat of Charlton on 2 May 1931 ended a magnificent season for the Throstles, leaving them with the unique double of FA Cup and promotion from Division Two in the same season.

Albion went into their game against Charlton knowing that victory was the only certain way back to Division One after an absence of four years. A draw might be sufficient, but then they would have to rely on the results of other promotion contenders.

Albion also knew that their task would not be an easy one, for Charlton had given the Throstles a tough battle in three FA Cup matches on Albion's road to Wembley that season. Still, the Black Country team had the boost of an FA Cup Final victory over neighbours Birmingham, and a 1-0 win at Stoke just two days before they met Charlton.

A huge crowd saw Charlton dominate the early exchanges and it was no surprise when Dai Astley shot the Londoners in front after only eight minutes. After 37 minutes, Teddy Sandford equalised for Albion, only for Astley to restore Charlton's lead almost immediately.

Back bounced Albion once more and before half-time, skipper Tommy Glidden had levelled the scores again. The teams walked to the dressing-rooms with the game — and Albion's immediate future — still agonisingly poised.

In the 68th minute, The Hawthorns erupted when W.G.Richardson, a player not renowned for his heading ability — rose to nod the ball home following fine work by Glidden and Carter.

Albion hung on to that slender lead and when the whistle blew, spectators swarmed on to the pitch, overwhelming the last few Albion players to leave the stage of this great victory. They battled hard to join their colleagues in the Directors' Box to acknowledge the rapturous cheers of the fans.

**Albion:** Pearson; Finch, Shaw, Magee, W.Richardson, Edwards, Glidden, Carter, W.G.Richardson, Sandford, Wood.
**Charlton Athletic:** Robertson; Smith, Langford, Pitcairn, Pritchard, Pugsley, Wyper, McKay, Astley, McLeod, Horton.
*Ref: Mr W.E.Russell (Northampton).*          *Att: 52,415*
*(receipts £3,155.9s.0d).*

# Four Goals in Five Minutes for 'W.G.'

## WEST HAM 1   ALBION 5

'W.G.' RICHARDSON — Albion's supreme marksman of the 1930s — entered the record books on 7 November 1931, when he scored four goals in five minutes at West Ham in a First Division match. This terrific bout of goal-grabbing certainly stirred to majority of the 18,000 plus crowd for his foursome came right at the start.

Albion 'roasted' West Ham in the opening 15 minutes and might have scored six or seven. They had to settle for four — all claimed by centre-forward Richardson. The first came after five minutes when 'W.G.' fired home from close range after Stan Wood's precise lob had deceived Hammers' centre-half Wally St Pier.

Two minutes later 'W.G.' met Harry Raw's low cross to score from eight yards — and 45 seconds later he grabbed his hat-trick, banging the ball home from 12 yards after good work by Teddy Sandford. On nine minutes it was 4-0 to Albion when Tommy Glidden got away down the right and from his pin-point centre, 'W.G.' tucked the ball past Ted Hufton.

West Ham came into the game more during the latter stages of the first half but Albion's defence was never really troubled and on 63 minutes Sandford headed in Wood's cross to make it 5-0. Seconds later the same player hammered the crossbar and then a shot from 'W.G.' went inches wide.

The Hammers managed a consolation goal 15 minutes from time, Jimmy Ruffell scoring after a mistake by George Shaw. But Albion came back again and both 'W.G.' and Wood almost added to the Baggies' scoreline.

Richardson's feat of four goals in five minutes equalled Jim McIntyre's individual League scoring record and still stands.

Amazingly, on the same day, at The Hawthorns, Albion Reserves beat Liverpool 10-0 in a Central League match and Jimmy Cookson, the player replaced in the first team by 'W.G.'Richardson, scored seven.

**West Ham United:** Goodacre; Cox, Collins, St Pier, Barrett, Wood, Earle, Watson, Weldon, Ruffell.
**Albion:** Pearson; Shaw, Trentham, Magee, W.Richardson, Murphy, Glidden, Raw, 'W.G.'Richardson, Sandford, Wood.
*Referee: Mr.L.Boulstridge (Tamworth)*          *Att: 18,134*

from Cardiff; and schoolteacher Arthur Gale was appearing at either centre-forward or outside-right.

Between 1931 and 1935, Albion were involved in some more high-scoring games. There was a 6-5 defeat by Grimsby, at home, a 4-4 draw at Blackburn, a 7-2 win at Maine Road over Manchester City, 6-5 and 6-4 scorelines against Sunderland, and a 4-4 draw with Aston Villa at Villa Park. All this brought the crowds flocking back to The Hawthorns. Attendances were averaging well over 20,000 — good figures for those days.

Four years after their 1931 Wembley triumph, Albion were back at the Empire Stadium, but this time they were not successful, as the management took a gamble on the day of the 1935 FA Cup Final — and lost both the gamble and the Cup.

The right-wing pair of Tommy Glidden and Joe Carter both had knee injuries in the weeks before the Final against Sheffield Wednesday. Glidden had had a cartilage operation but was playing again before the Final. Carter was still receiving treatment right until the eve of the big game.

Secretary Fred Everiss had talks with Glidden, the captain, and after Carter had also assured him that he was fit, the board included both men in the team. After only ten minutes Carter was limping; Glidden was far from match fit and faded in the second-half when his side needed him most.

Wednesday finished 4-2 victors of a fine game in which Albion were twice behind but each time pulled back, first through Boyes and then through Sandford. Injuries apart, Albion had a good chance of pulling off a victory against the odds but 'W.G.'Richardson, of all people, missed a 'sitter' when the scores were level at 2-2.

Albion's bid for Central League honours in the 1930s attracted bigger crowds than some first-team matches. In March 1934, there were 22,372 people at The Hawthorns to watch Albion and Aston Villa in a Central League game. A week later, for the first-team match against Huddersfield Town, the turn-out was only just over 16,000.

In those days Albion reserves were making history. Between 1932 and 1935 they won the Central League Championship three times in succession. To mark the feat, Albion were presented with an inscribed silver salver by the League.

New faces arriving on the scene at The Hawthorns in the late 1930s included Jimmy 'Doc' Adams, the goalkeeper who was to assist Albion throughout the war, 'Sandy' McNab, a Scotsman from Sunderland, Cecil Shaw, who made 119 consecutive appearances for Wolves, and Gilbert Alsop, the hero of Walsall's sensational FA Cup win over Arsenal in 1933.

There were goals galore in 1935-6 when Albion scored 89 and conceded 88. Among their wins was one of 7-0 at Villa Park which helped send Villa into the Second Division for the first time — 'W.G.'Richardson scored four that day.

March 1937 was a sad month for Albion. They lost an FA Cup semi-final and much more tragically also lost a grand servant in Mr William Isaiah Bassett. Billy Bassett, one-time player and long-term official of the club, died just two days before Albion took on Preston North End at Highbury. His death seemed to affect the team who were three goals down inside half-an-hour and finally lost 4-1.

The following year Albion were relegated, finishing bottom of the table and conceding 91 goals. The club's annual report stated: 'Injuries to key players at a vital period of the season undoubtedly prejudiced our position. However, we offer no excuses, and our mission is to get back to the First Division at the earliest possible moment.'

That job was interrupted when League football was suspended upon the outbreak of World War Two but one of the players to emerge from the dark days of World War Two was Billy Elliott, signed from Bournemouth in 1938 after previously having a spell with Wolves.

Elliott marked his return to the Midlands with a series of dazzling wing displays that would have won him many more England caps but for the presence of Stanley Matthews. In all, Elliott played 329 senior matches for Albion and scored 155 goals. During the war alone, he scored 116 times in 147 games — including a few hat-tricks.

Elliott was the 'local' star of an Albion wartime line-up that often included famous names when players were loaned

Vic Watson of West Ham darts between Albion full-back Bert Trentham and goalkeeper Harold Pearson in the League game at Upton Park on 7 November 1931.

For many years during the 1930s, a thrush (throstle) was kept in a cage at The Hawthorns. Here, trainer Fred Reed shows off the Baggies mascot.

Albion's Central League championship team of 1932-3. Back row (left to right): Mr F.Everiss (secretary), Sammy Short (trainer), Arthur Gale, Ted Crowe, Jimmy Cookson, Sam Guest, Eph Smith (assistant secretary). Front row: Eli Postin, Wally Boyes, Bob Finch, Mr W.I.Bassett (chairman), Jack Sankey, Hugh Foulkes, Stan Horrocks. On ground: Wally Lambeth, 'Bos' Trevis.

# *Albion Go Goal Crazy at Maine Road*

## MANCHESTER CITY 2    ALBION 7

IT WASN'T very often that big Frank Swift conceded seven goals in one game, especially in front of his own supporters. But on the first day of 1934, 'Swifty' had backache after Albion thrashed Manchester City at Maine Road in a First Division game.

It must be said that Albion's defence was like a colander that season, conceding 72 goals altogether as they finished fifth in Division One, yet on New Year's Day, Albion would probably have netted a hatful against most teams. Their performance on a pitch made treacherous by a combination of frost and heavy rain was certainly one of their very best.

City's rearguard was frequently caught square by a quite brilliant Albion forward line for whom Walter Robbins had his best game in a Throstles shirt. Outside-right Tommy Glidden also played superbly until he was injured with 20 minutes to play.

The *Manchester Guardian* said: 'Robbins was the forward of the match; Glidden too was brilliant, and W.G.Richardson took his chances in great style. City's Gregory met his master in W.Richardson, and Pearson, in goal, maintained the family reputation with a fine performance. Full-backs Trentham and Shaw kicked with wonderful accuracy and length. Albion were a magnificent team in every department.'

Strangely, it was City who took the lead, through Herd in the 20th minute, but before the interval Robbins, with two swift efforts, pushed Albion 2-1 ahead. Then it was W.G.Richardson's turn and between the 56th and 78th minutes he scored a grand hat-trick.

Wing-half Jackie Bray, a hobbling injured passenger on the left wing, pulled a goal back for City almost immediately, but late in the game, Joe Carter and Teddy Sandford added further goals for Albion to complete the Maine Road club's humiliation.

**Manchester City:** Swift; Barnett, Dale, Percival, Marshall, Bray, Toseland, Herd, Gregory, Busby, Book.
**Albion:** Pearson; Shaw, Trentham, Murphy, W.Richardson, Edwards, Glidden, Carter, W.G.Richardson, Sandford, Robbins.
*Ref: Mr W.R.Jennings (York).*                    *Att: 20,996.*

**Harold Pearson punches clear from a corner during the FA Cup tie against Sheffield United at The Hawthorns in 1935. The other Albion players are (from left to right) Bert Trentham, George Shaw, Bill Richardson and Joe Carter.**

# So Sweet Victory Over Villa

## ASTON VILLA 0    ALBION 7

VICTORY at Villa Park always tastes especially sweet for Albion fans. Whether it comes in League, Cup or even in friendly matches, the flavour is always good.

But Albion's defeat of Villa on 19 October 1935 caused a sensation. It was the talking point of Midlands soccer fans for months afterwards — and it created a record as the biggest scoreline for a match between these two old Midlands rivals.

The hero of the day was undoubtedly W.G.Richardson who scored four of Albion's seven goals, and who would have made it a double hat-trick had he accepted the two simple 'tap-in' chances in the later stages.

It should be remembered that Villa were a poor side this season and destined for relegation. Albion, on the other hand, were a useful team, having reached the FA Cup Final the previous season. Ten thousand Albion fans had made the short journey to Villa Park and they had something to celebrate as early as the seventh minute when W.G.Richardson scored from Jack Mahon's low cross.

Thus inspired, Albion struck again less than a minute later, 'W.G.' this time setting up a simple chance for Stan Wood. Playing with a gale-force wind at their backs, Villa tried to rally, but they found Albion's defence in splendid form, with goalkeeper Harold Pearson having an outstanding afternoon.

Helped by the wind, Villa were having more of the play, but after 25 minutes they found themselves 3-0 down when 'W.G.' netted a beauty from another pin-point cross from Mahon. Before the break, Mahon himself made it 4-0, after Wood had robbed Blair inside Villa's penalty area.

In the second half Albion eased up, yet still proved far too good for Villa. Further goals came from Jack Sankey (75 minutes) and 'W.G.' (77 and 78). Wood then had a goal disallowed, 'W.G.' missed those two simple chances, and Carter's shot hit the bar as Villa were swept away.

**Aston Villa:** Biddlestone; Beeson, Blair, Gibson, Allen, McLuckie, Houghton, Brocklebank, Broome, Astley, Cunliffe.
**Albion:** Pearson; Shaw, Trentham, Murphy, W.Richardson, Sankey, Mahon, Carter, W.G.Richardson, Sandford, Wood.
*Ref: Mr G.Hewitt (St Helens).*                    *Att: 38,037.*

Albion's 1935 FA Cup Final squad. Back row (left to right): F.Reed (trainer), Mr W.H.Keys (director), H.Trentham, H.Pearson, J.Carter, Mr J.Round (director), Mr C.Jephcott (director). Middle row: Mr L.Nurse (director), W.Richardson, W.G.Richardson, W.I.Bassett (chairman), T.Glidden, E.Sandford, Mr F.Everiss (secretary). Front row: A.Gale, J.Edwards, G.Shaw, J.Murphy, W.Boyes, J.Sankey.

out to clubs. Some of the guests who played for Albion included George Hardwick (Middlesbrough), Gil Merrick and Don Dearson (Birmingham), Eddie Hapgood (Arsenal), Peter Doherty (Manchester City), Les Smith (Brentford) and Jack Acquaroff (Norwich City).

Acquaroff, in fact, helped Albion to their only major prize in almost 300 wartime matches. He scored two goals in the second leg of the Midland War Cup Final in 1944 when Albion beat Nottingham Forest 6-5 on aggregate.

But it was another Jack who was to make a bigger impact on Albion's history. Jack Smith had guested for the Throstles from Chelsea during the war and he was soon to become the club's first-ever team manager.

Fred Everiss was secretary of Albion for 46 years, and when he resigned in 1948

# *Albion Slump to Heaviest Defeat*

## STOKE CITY 10    ALBION 3

ALBION'S heaviest defeat in any senior competition came amidst the most amazing circumstances, with the Throstles' goalkeeper, Billy Light, literally rooted to the spot for almost all the game because of injury.

It was certainly an astonishing game and, whilst Stoke merited their victory at the Victoria Ground on 4 February 1937, adapting much better to the pitch which was quite literally a quagmire, the Potters were greatly indebted to the fact that Albion persisted with the injured Light in goal.

Light's injury was sustained in the 11th minute, as Stoke took the lead. The goalkeeper hurt his ankle and was forced to leave the field. Inside-right Harry Jones donned the goalkeeper's sweater until Light returned with his ankle and foot heavily bandaged. He went back in goal, but from that moment could hardly move.

W.G.Richardson had managed to grab an equaliser whilst Albion were down to ten men, but with Light now returned, Stoke began to rain shots on his goal. By half-time they were 4-1 in front after Freddie Steele had completed a hat-trick and Turner had slotted home a penalty.

Joe Johnson made it 5-1 before Wally Boyes pulled back a goal for Albion, then Steele added two more to give Stoke a 7-2 lead with 22 minutes still to play. Johnson made it 8-2, and George Antonio scored Stoke's ninth and tenth goals before Walter Robbins flicked home Albion's third with eight minutes remaining.

Albion were left to reflect that they might have left Jones in goal, and to wonder what might have happened had centre-half Bill Richardson not been feeling unwell. Things then might have been different. As it was, the Throstles went crashing to a record defeat.

**Stoke City:** D.Westland; Brigham, Harbot, Tutin, Turner, Kirton, Matthews, Antonio, Steele, J.Westland, Johnson.
**Albion:** Light; Finch, C.Shaw, Murphy, W.Richardson, Boyes, Mahon, Jones, W.G.Richardson, Sandford, Robbins.
*Ref: Mr H.E.Hull (Stockport).*          *Attendance: 15,230.*

**Action from the 3-2 win over Birmingham at The Hawthorns in September 1936. 'W.G.' Richardson and Teddy Sandford are the Albion players.**

the club had over 100 applications for the new job of team manager. The man appointed was Jack Smith, who had played several games for Albion as a full-back during the years 1942 to 1944, and within nine months he had guided the team back to Division One.

In that promotion-winning side were two classy Irishmen — Dave Walsh and Jack Vernon. Walsh had been signed from Linfield in the summer of 1946 and scored at least once in each of his first six League outings for the club — a record.

Vernon came to Albion from Belfast Celtic for £9,500 in February 1947 but it was sometime before he got a first-team game. When he did, it was a day he wanted to forget — Albion were beaten 3-2 by West Ham United with the 'Hammers' Neary scoring a hat-trick.

**Don Dearson (right) scores for Birmingham against West Brom at St Andrew's on Good Friday 1938. The Blues won 2-1.**

# *Record Crowd Pack The Hawthorns*

## ALBION 3    ARSENAL 1

NEVER again will a near 65,000 crowd pack The Hawthorns. The record attendance for the ground was set in 1937 when mighty Arsenal, the team of the 1930s and one of the greatest of any era, visited West Brom for a sixth-round FA Cup tie. Gates were shut half-an-hour before kick-off and the 64,815 fans lucky enough to gain entrance saw a quite brilliant game of football, despite ice-cold conditions and a snowy pitch.

At the time Albion were languishing in the bottom five of Division One whilst Arsenal were in second place, two points behind Charlton. The odds on an Albion victory were high and a draw against the mighty Gunners was as much as most people hoped for.

But what a grand display the Throstles put on, matching Arsenal man for man, in effort, enthusiasm and, on the day, outright skill. They ran and ran, and in the end deserved their place in the semi-finals.

Albion went ahead in the tenth minute when ace goalscorer W.G.Richardson capitalised on a slip by 'keeper Frank Boulton, whipping the ball home from six yards after Mahon's effort had been initially parried.

As the snow eased, so the pitch began to churn up and

soon mud was flying. This did not deter the Throstles and they stormed forward at every opportunity. One minute from the interval, Mahon grabbed a second goal when Boyes rolled a free-kick to him some 20 yards out. Mahon's shot flew into the Arsenal net off Roberts.

The Gunners looked demoralised as they trooped off and in the second half, after losing Milne just after the break, they looked dead and buried. Yet true to their great fighting tradition, Arsenal fought back with a goal from Cliff Bastin who was played through by Alex James's shrewd free-kick with Albion appealing for offside.

Jimmy Adams made three important saves in the Albion goal before Mahon relieved the tension. The outside-right rose high to head home his second goal and West Brom were victors of a memorable match they had not expected to win.

**Albion:** Adams; Finch, C.Shaw, Murphy, Sandford, Sankey, Mahon, Jones, Richardson, Boyes, Coen.
**Arsenal:** Boulton; Male, Hapgood, Crayston, Roberts, Copping, Milne, Bowden, Kirchen, James, Bastin.
*Ref: Mr J.Rennie (Oldham).      Att: 64,815 (receipts £3,913).*

**Manager Jack Smith (extreme left) discusses tactics with some of his players and coaching staff in 1948.**

But Vernon went on to skipper the side, his country and to play for Great Britain against the Rest of Europe at Hampden Park in 1947. He played in 200 League and Cup games for Albion in a five-year spell that earned him the tag from no less a judge than Fred Everiss as the best centre-half Albion ever had.

So it was back to the First Division after a break of 11 years for Albion, who were watched by an average home 'gate' of well over 33,000. The biggest attendance was to see the match against other promotion candidates, Southampton, in November when 47,000 turned up.

Goalkeeper Jim Sanders, who had been wounded in the war, while flying a bomber, played in all 42 League games and Len Millard and Dave Walsh 41 each. Walsh was the leading scorer with 23 League and five Cup goals.

Debates on who is the finest player Albion have had since the war go on long into the night among the fans. But the man who gets many votes is Ronnie Allen. Allen came into the side in the first season after Albion had returned to Division One after signing from Port Vale for £20,000 — then a club record fee.

He started his Albion career as an outside-right and was later converted to centre-forward. But wherever he played he scored goals. In fact, he started the habit straight away. In his first match, in front of 61,000 people at The Hawthorns against Wolves, he popped in Albion's goal in a 1-1 draw.

It was the following year that Allen

# Albion's Wartime Cup Marathon

## NOTTINGHAM FOREST 3    ALBION 4

SENSATION followed sensation in the second leg of the Wartime Cup Final at the City Ground on 6 May 1944. It was a marathon affair, lasting only a minute short of two hours, during which time the 14,500 crowd, who included a small but vociferous band of Albion fans who had overcome transport difficulties, were kept in electrifying suspense.

When Forest scored their third goal late in extra-time, a large section of the crowd invaded the pitch and began to carry the home players towards the main stand where the trophy was awaiting the victors. They thought the match was over but Warwick referee Mr Dutton insisted that the police clear the pitch so that the remaining two minutes could be played.

The match restarted and from the kick-off, Albion's Jack Acquaroff sprinted away to score, so levelling the scores at 3-3 and the aggregate at 5-5.

With extra-time exhausted — and players of both sides also drained — the match continued only until another goal was scored. The match became a sudden-death affair and it was Albion who clinched it, 'Ike' Clarke netting the decisive goal after a further nine minutes. Albion were Cup winners with a 6-5 aggregate victory.

In the early stages of the game, Albion had been in a strangely subdued mood and Forest, with guest players Freddie Steele (Stoke) and goalkeeper Ray Middleton (Chesterfield), went ahead with goals from Johnston and Steele.

As half-time approached, Albion's old cup-fighting spirit began to assert itself and in the second period a dogged rally brought a goal from Acquaroff. Soon afterwards Frank Hodgetts headed a brilliant equaliser from Clarke's cross. Dulson got Forest's third and the stage was set for that thrilling finale.

West Brom skipper 'Sandy' McNab received the Cup from the Lord Mayor of Nottingham and all the players — winners and losers — were presented with savings certificates instead of medals.

**Nottingham Forest:** Middleton; McCall, Hutchinson, Baxter, Blagg, Elliott, Davies, Steele, Dulson, Johnston, Allen.
**Albion:** Heath; Southam, J.Smith, Millard, Gripton, McNab, Heaselgrave, Acquaroff, Clarke, C.Evans, Hodgetts. Ref: Mr G.Dutton (Warwick).    Att: 14,438 (receipts £1,331).

# Back to the First Division

## LEICESTER CITY 0    ALBION 3

WITH two games of the 1948-9 season, remaining, Albion needed two points to ensure a return to Division One after a break of 11 years. Both the Throstles' remaining matches were away from home and the first, at Leicester, looked particularly difficult.

Leicester were on the brink of relegation and Albion knew they faced a side desperate for success. They also lined up against a team which, despite its lowly League position, had still been good enough to reach that season's FA Cup Final. Five days earlier they had lost 3-1 to Wolves at Wembley.

Thus, Albion needed two points to go up, City required at least one point to stay up, and the prospect attracted over 34,000 fans to Filbert Street. When the teams ran out, the atmosphere was electric.

Jack Smith, Albion's manager, gambled by playing two big men — Ray Barlow and Joe Kennedy — in the forward line either side of centre-forward Dave Walsh. Smith's gamble paid off as Barlow, Kennedy and Walsh scored the goals which put Albion back into Division One.

It was a hectic game. Albion began cautiously and then stepped up a gear so that after 26 minutes they led 2-0. Leicester refused to give up immediately and for a period

in the second half Albion had to thank some fine goalkeeping by Jim Sanders for their continued two-goal lead.

Albion's first goal came after 12 minutes. Reg Ryan planted a free-kick deep into the Leicester penalty area where Kennedy rose high above 'keeper Major, nodding the ball down for Walsh to steer into an empty net.

In the 26th minute, a corner from Smith on the left was beautifully glided home by the raven-haired Kennedy. It was his first goal for the club and what an important one it proved, extending the Throstles' lead at a crucial time.

Barlow grabbed Albion's third goal in the 64th minute, striking a clean shot just inside a post from the narrowest of angles.

When the final whistle shrilled, hundreds of delighted Albion fans ran on to the pitch and carried their heroes shoulder-high from the scene of their triumph.

**Leicester City:** Major; Jelly, Scott, Harrison, Plummer, Johnston, Griffiths, Lee, King, Chisholm, Adam.
**Albion:** Sanders; Pemberton, Millard, Ryan, Vernon, Hood, Elliott, Kennedy, Walsh, Barlow, Smith.
*Ref: Mr E.Plinston (Warrington)*            *Att: 34,585*

switched from the right-wing to centre-forward and was an immediate success, scoring ten goals. In 1951-2 he netted 35 goals in League and Cup games, a figure bettered only by Newcastle United's George Robledo, who hit 39.

In the mid-1950s Allen, with Ray Barlow, was the kingpin of perhaps the finest side Albion have ever had. Allen's ability to elude or beat a close-marking opponent, his quickness at reading the game and his speed off the mark allowed

him to play deep, well away from the defensive area and set up openings for the strikers who thrived on the gaps he created. He was capped for England only five times, but to many he was the complete footballer.

Albion's great season of 1953-4 got off to a flying start when they played the first nine League games without defeat. The highlight of this tremendous spell was a memorable 7-3 win at St James' Park over Newcastle United, and there

was also a fine 4-2 win over Sheffield Wednesday after being two goals down.

All season it was neck and neck at the top of Division One between Wolverhampton Wanderers, Albion and Huddersfield Town. At the turn of the year, with all three sides having played 26 games, Wolves had 39 points, Albion 38 points and Huddersfield 33 points.

The turning point in Albion's Championship chase came in the match against Sunderland at Roker Park. Albion were

# *Victors in a Nine-Goal Christmas Box*

## SHEFFIELD WEDNESDAY 4    ALBION 5

SUPPORTERS love to see goals, preferably scored by their own team, of course. Albion's visit to Hillsborough on Boxing Day 1952 was witnessed by almost 60,000 fans who saw nine goals — six of them scored by home players — yet Albion still emerged the victors.

At this stage of the season Albion were lying second in Division One, behind neighbours Wolves. Wednesday were in a comfortable mid-table position but they began at a terrific pace and inside five minutes were a goal ahead through outside-left Dennis Woodhead.

Albion bounced straight back and after ten minutes they were level when Ray Barlow, cool as you like, slotted home past Owls' goalkeeper, Capewell. Wednesday went straight back downfield to regain the lead through Redfern Froggatt. And five minutes later, Norman Curtis netted an own-goal to bring Albion level for a second time.

Before the interval Woodhead struck again for Wednesday and the teams trooped off the field to a standing ovation from both sets of supporters, appreciative of a superb, breathtaking 45 minutes football.

The second half was only two minutes old when Derek Dooley, the centre-forward who was later to tragically lose a leg after a football accident, darted in to send Wednesday 4-2 ahead as Albion's defence hesitated following a dead-ball situation.

Still Albion came back and within five minutes, the Owls' lead was reduced to a single goal once more when Eddie Gannon, under pressure from Allen and Nicholls, gave away another own-goal. Albion were firmly back in the hunt.

For the next 30 minutes play swung from end to end and there were thrills and spills in front of both goals before Albion struck two killer blows, first through Johnny Nicholls (80 minutes) and then a goal from England international Ronnie Allen (87 minutes) which put the game beyond Wednesday's reach.

It was a sensational finish to a rousing match and Albion were the first to admit that the Owls had been unlucky to lose such a magnificent game of football. Twenty-four hours later, however, Wednesday had their revenge with a 1-0 victory at The Hawthorns in front of over 52,600 spectators.

**Sheffield Wednesday:** Capewell; Kenny, Curtis, Gannon, Turton, Witcomb, Marriott, Sewell, Dooley, Froggatt, Woodhead.
**Albion:** Heath; Rickaby, Millard, Dudley, Kennedy, Barlow, Griffin, Nicholls, Allen, Ryan, Lee.
*Ref: Mr R.P.Hartley (Burnley).*                    *Att: 59,398.*

hard hit by injuries and England calls — yet their troubles had only just begun. The game was not very old before Norman Heath was injured in a goal-mouth clash with Ted Purdon — so badly in fact that he never played again. Ray Barlow went into goal and played a 'blinder' but Albion went down 2-1 and with it went the real hopes of the title.

The decider was a meeting with Wolves at The Hawthorns in front of nearly 50,000 people. Wolves won 1-0 and picked up the Championship, pushing Albion into second place. With only one win in

their last six League games Albion's form had taken a turn for the worst.

Two of the most exciting matches in the club's history were the semi-final and Final of the FA Cup in 1954.

Albion had reached the last four with wins over Chelsea, Rotherham United, Newcastle United and Tottenham Hotspur and they had scored 13 goals and conceded only two.

They were favourites to beat Port Vale, from the Third Division, in front of a crowd of 68,000 packed into Villa Park. But Vale, who had given away only 19

goals in 40 League games, defied Albion's efforts for long periods. In fact, they took a half-time lead.

Goalkeeper King was Vale's hero, aided by a quick covering defence. But he missed a curling centre from Jimmy Dudley and Albion were level. In the last quarter of an hour Albion piled on even greater pressure and when George Lee was up-ended they were awarded a penalty. And the man who took it was the former Port Vale forward, Ronnie Allen, who duly knocked his former team out of the Cup.

**Ronnie Allen's opening goal in the 1954 FA Cup Final against Preston North End at Wembley.**

# Albion's Crowning Glory

## NEWCASTLE UNITED 3    ALBION 7

SOME 40 years ago, in the Coronation Year of 1953, West Bromwich Albion reached the crowning glory of football perfection at Newcastle United's St James' Park.

On the evening of 16 September, under a dulling Tyneside sky, Albion swept aside the famous Geordies with a remarkable display of attacking football which conjured up a 7-3 scoreline in the Throstles' favour to stun the home supporters in a massive 58,000 crowd.

One man who has special reason to remember that great occasion is former Albion favourite Johnny Nicholls who celebrated his 50th game for the club by scoring a hat-trick. And the team's overall performance was arguably the best ever given by a Throstles side.

Those who saw it will still argue that there have been few better displays — and that includes the magical Hungarians of the same period, the Tottenham of the 1960s, or the Liverpool of more recent times. On the night Albion were simply unstoppable. No wonder Nicholls remembered: "The crowd just stood and applauded us off at the end of the game."

Albion got off to a flying start. They had a goal disallowed inside five minutes, were denied what most people thought was an obvious penalty, and had two shots cleared off the line. They had to wait until the 32nd minute, however, for their first breakthrough when Ronnie Allen crashed home a blockbuster from 30 yards.

Nicholls made it 2-0, darting between Cowell and goalkeeper Simpson, and after 42 minutes Albion led 3-0 when another Allen thunderbolt hit the back of the net.

Newcastle stormed back after the interval and first Vic Keeble (42 minutes) and then Bobby Mitchell (60) brought the Magpies right back into the game, only to see Albion simply step up a gear to go 4-2 in front through Nicholls after 65 minutes.

With 15 minutes to go, Mitchell scored his second but Albion were now in full flood and Nicholls completed his hat-trick. Reg Ryan netted number six and with barely five minutes remaining, Frank Griffin elegantly swept home Albion's seventh goal.

In the dying seconds only a brave save by Simpson at the feet of Allen prevented Albion from scoring an eighth goal. It did not matter though as the Throstles completed one of the finest victories in their history.

**Manager Vic Buckingham with Ronnie Allen and Reg Ryan.**

**Newcastle United:** Simpson; Cowell, Batty, Scoular, Brennan, Crowe, Milburn, Davies, Keeble, Hannah, Mitchell.
**Albion:** Heath; Rickaby, Millard, Dudley, Dugdale, Barlow, Griffin, Ryan, Allen, Nicholls, Lee.
*Ref: Mr T.Seymour (Wakefield).*                    *Att: 58,075.*

---

Allen was to repeat his ice-cool kicking in the Final against Preston North End. He scored from the spot to pull Albion back to 2-2 after they had led 1-0. Allen had glided home a Lee centre to open the scoring after 21 minutes. Morrison headed an equaliser 60 seconds later and then Wayman scored a controversial second for Preston after 51 minutes as Albion appealed for offside.

The winner did not come until three minutes from time when Joe Kennedy, Reg Ryan and Frank Griffin linked down the right for Griffin to roll the ball under Thompson's body and give Albion the FA Cup for the fourth time.

Albion started the 1954-5 season in great style, winning seven out of their first ten games before beginning to slide. They drew 3-3 with the eventual League Champions, Chelsea, at Stamford Bridge, then went abroad to take on the crack Hungarian club, Honved, in a challenge match in Brussels.

Honved fielded seven current internationals including goalkeeper Grosics and forwards Kocsis, Czibor and Ferenc Puskas.

Hundreds of Albion fans had travelled to Belgium to see the game and it turned out to be a real thriller — Albion losing a classic match 5-3 after they had held a 3-1 lead.

In a packed stadium, Albion were coasting to success with goals by Allen and Nicholls (2). Then Ray Barlow was hurt and the Throstles were reduced to ten men.

After this match it was back to the 'bread and butter' of the League and Albion gradually slipped down the table to finish 17th. They picked up only 40 points from a possible 84 and conceded no fewer than 96 goals — their worst deficit since 1936-7. The crowds, however, did not fade away from The Hawthorns, Albion averaged 30,732 at their 21 home League games.

Ronnie Allen was leading scorer with 32 goals in all games, Johnny Nicholls hit 14, George Lee 12 and Wilf Carter nine.

New recruits were Don Howe, a stylish young full-back from Wolverhampton Schools football, who was destined to play 23 times for England, and big Derek 'The Tank' Kevan from Bradford. He was signed by Vic Buckingham, who was once his manager at Park Avenue. Another future England international, Kevan became a tremendous hit with the Albion fans and went on to score 157 League goals in 262 outings.

# *On the Road to Wembley*

## ALBION 3    NEWCASTLE UNITED 2

ALBION had a magnificent Cup run in season 1953-4, a run which ended in style with a Wembley triumph over Preston North End, but perhaps the team's best performance in that FA Cup campaign was their fifth-round victory over those redoubtable Cup fighters, Newcastle United, at The Hawthorns on 20 February 1954.

A bumper crowd of over 61,000 squeezed into the Albion ground and gates were closed an hour before the kick-off with an estimated 20,000 locked outside. The atmosphere was electric and the 15,000 Geordie fans who had made the long journey to the Midlands made themselves heard with a rousing and continuous rendering of 'Bladon Races'.

Albion, playing in an unfamiliar change strip of red shirts, played to their full potential, as did Newcastle, and the result was a superb Cup match full of excitement. Both sides' desire to play attacking football led to many goalmouth skirmishes at both ends of the field and two of the afternoon's five goals were absolute beauties.

Albion scored twice in a thrilling first half — this after both Lee and Dudley had fluffed easy chances. Allen was Albion's scorer each time, his first coming from a classy right-foot shot that flew between Stokoe and Cowell, his second from a rebound after Nicholls had fired a shot against the crossbar.

Mitchell made it 2-1 early in the second half, and then came a goal of sheer genius. George Lee whipped over a corner from the left and Allen, moving to the edge of the box, met the ball shoulder-high with his left foot to send it screaming into the net past Simpson's right arm. It was a goal of stunning brilliance which brought the crowd to their toes and gave Allen his hat-trick.

Jackie Milburn gave United hope with a second goal but Albion were in no mood to relinquish their lead and strode further along the road to Wembley's twin towers. Stan Rickaby, Barlow — and Allen, of course — were the key figures in this dazzling Albion performance which many rated as one of the best they had ever given in front of their own fans.

**Albion:** Heath; Rickaby, Millard, Dudley, Dugdale, Barlow, Griffin, Ryan, Allen, Nicholls, Lee.
**Newcastle United:** Simpson; Cowell, McMichael, Scoular, Brennan, Stokoe, Foulkes, Broadis, Milburn, Hannah, Mitchell.
*Ref: Mr B.M.Griffiths (Newport).*              *Att: 61,088.*

**The 1954 FA Cup winners. Albion parade the trophy around Wembley after their victory over Preston.**

**West Brom pictured with the FA Cup in 1954. Back row (left to right): Joe Kennedy, Jimmy Dugdale, Ray Barlow, Jim Sanders, Jimmy Dudley, Len Millard, George Lee. Front row: Reg Ryan, Ronnie Allen, Frank Griffin, Johnny Nicholls.**

Maurice Setters a tough, bandy-legged wing-half, was signed from Exeter City for £3,000; Graham Williams was brought down from Rhyl in the Welsh League; and a goalkeeper, big Fred Brown, was signed from Aldershot as cover for Jim Sanders.

Among those who left Albion were Reg Ryan, to Derby County after ten years at The Hawthorns, and Stan Rickaby, to Poole Town as player-manager.

Albion went through season 1955-6 tentatively and they eventually finished 13th. They were knocked out of the FA Cup by Birmingham City, 1-0 in front of a packed 57,381 Hawthorns crowd. Peter Murphy struck the winning goal and it helped send the Blues on to Wembley, where they lost 3-1 to Manchester City.

During this campaign, centre-half Jimmy Dugdale was transferred to Aston Villa for a reported £25,000 fee.

Albion's average home League gate in 1955-6 was 27,400, the lowest at The Hawthorns since 1946-7. Yet towards the end of the season over 55,000 turned up when Albion staged a testimonial match for their former goalkeeper, Norman Heath, who was seriously injured against Sunderland in 1954.

An All-Star International XI came to West Bromwich and drew 5-5 with Albion before an all-ticket crowd of 55,497 (who paid £6,500). On the pitch that night were some great footballers including Trevor Ford, Billy Wright, Danny Blanchflower,

**Don Howe goes after the ball against Charlton Athletic in 1956, watched by Len Millard and Jim Sanders.**

Alf Sherwood and Charlie 'Cannonball' Fleming.

The 1956-7 season saw Albion reach their 15th FA Cup semi-final — and come within two minutes of playing in their tenth Final. They were joined in the last-four by West Midlands neighbours, Aston Villa and Birmingham City.

Albion were paired with Villa at Wolverhampton. Blues met Manchester United at Hillsborough. A Molineux crowd of 55,549 witnessed the Albion-Villa tie and twice Albion were in front — only for Peter McParland to pull Villa level each time. Whitehouse hit the two Albion goals, and Villa's second equaliser came

Albion's 1958 first-team squad. Back row (left to right): V.Buckingham (manager), D.Hogg, E.Robinson, D.Howe, C.Jackman, J.Dudley, S.Williams, J.Kennedy, R.Graham (trainer). Centre: R.Allen, R.Robson, C.Drury, M.Setters, R.Barlow, B.Whitehouse, F.Griffin. Front: J.Carvin, D.Burnside, J.Campbell, A.Jackson, R.Horobin. Brian Whitehouse had come in for injured England international star Ronnie Allen and he played a major role as Albion whipped Forest with only ten men.

# *That Wembley Look Again*

## NOTTINGHAM FOREST 1    ALBION 5

ALBION'S victory at the City Ground in this FA Cup match was outstanding by any measure — but the fact that it was achieved with only ten men makes the Throstles' performance on 28 January 1958 even more remarkable.

Cyril Chapman (*Birmingham Post*) and Bill Holden (*Daily Mirror*) both described the win as 'a miracle' and everyone present agreed with the overall assessment of the press that Albion 'had that Wembley look written all over them'.

Brilliant Albion baffled and blinded their rivals in this fourth round replay with a display straight out of the soccer science manual. The only people who were not impressed were the thousands of Forest fans who began streaming out of the ground with some 20 minutes still to play. Those fickle Forest supporters left to Albion chants of "We want six," ringing in their ears.

Yet Albion, a goal down after only 12 minutes, had been reduced to ten men when tough-guy Maurice Setters was stretchered off with a suspected fractured ankle just after his team had equalised in the 24th minute. Manager Vic Buckingham came down to the touchline, sat Setters alongside him, and began to urge his team to an epic victory.

Eddie Baily crossed for Tom Wilson to head home Forest's early goal before Robson's leap to Roy Horobin's centre levelled the issue. In the 33rd minute Albion went in front when Frank Griffin fired in a cracking shot and that was the state of play as the players went off at half-time.

Brian Whitehouse, playing in place of the injured Allen, made it 3-1 in the 57th minute and a joyous Derek Kevan rapped home Albion's fourth only four minutes later, almost ripping the back out of the net with a 20-yard piledriver. A Don Howe penalty in the 70th minute ended the scoring and that was the signal for the exodus of those disgruntled Forest fans.

After the final whistle, Forest manager Billy Walker said, 'We've seen the Cup winners today — Albion were brilliant.' Alas, Albion fell at the quarter-final stage, beaten 1-0 by Manchester United in a replay at Old Trafford.

**Nottingham Forest:** Thomson; Ware, Thomas, Morley, McKinlay, Burkitt, Gray, Quigley, Wilson, Baily, Imlach.
**Albion:** Sanders; Howe, S.Williams, Setters, Kennedy, Barlow, Griffin, Whitehouse, Robson, Kevan, Horobin.
*Ref: Mr A.E.Ellis (Halifax).*     *Att: 46,455 (receipts £6,967).*

two minutes from time. The replay was at St Andrew's where Albion had Ronnie Allen injured early on and lost 1-0.

In the summer of 1957 the Football Association invited Albion to visit the Soviet Union where they won two and drew one of their three matches to become the first British professional club to score a victory in Russia.

Back home there was a festival of goals in the 1957-8 season, and Albion were deeply involved.

They beat Manchester City 9-2 in the League and 5-1 in the FA Cup, hammered Nottingham Forest 5-1 in the Cup, and

then hit six against Leicester City and five each against both Birmingham City and Burnley.

The biggest goals bonanza was a rain-soaked game against the Russian Red Army that ended in a 6-5 win for Albion before 52,805 packed into The Hawthorns.

Three Albion men scored more than 20 goals that season: Ronnie Allen (28), Derek Kevan (23) and new man Bobby Robson (27). Robson was signed from Fulham for £25,000.

That 5-1 win at Forest was an incredible performance. Albion were trailing

when Maurice Setters retired injured, yet they managed to score five times with ten men. Another great win with ten men was against Sheffield United in the FA Cup at The Hawthorns after Frank Griffin had broken a leg. Albion won 4-1 and that gave them a tie against Manchester United, just after the Munich air disaster had destroyed Busby's great team.

A crowd of 57,574 saw a 2-2 draw, with Albion scoring in the last two minutes. There were only 30 seconds remaining of the emotional replay at Old Trafford when Colin Webster scored the goal that knocked out Albion.

The following season of 1958-9 Albion won ten away League games including a 6-0 hammering of Birmingham City and a 6-2 win at Portsmouth. This was also the season that Aston Villa crashed back into Division Two, after Ronnie Allen's 25-yard drive earned his side a 1-1 draw against Villa in the last match of the season.

That summer Albion went to North America where they won seven of their nine games and were beaten only once. In a 15-0 win over Alberta All-Stars, Bobby Robson scored six times to equal the record set by Jimmy Cookson and 'W.G.'Richardson.

On their return to England, Vic Buckingham resigned as manager and went to Amsterdam to take charge of Ajax. Gordon Clark took over. The saddest note, however, was the sudden death of 'W.G.'Richardson who collapsed while playing in a charity match on 27 March 1959, aged 49.

The 1960s were a time of constant

**Goal! Derek Kevan scores for Albion against Arsenal at The Hawthorns on 21 February 1959.**

**One of Derek Kevan's four goals in the 7-1 win over Blackpool on the last day of the 1961-62 season.**

change at The Hawthorns, both on and off the field. Gordon Clark was followed as Albion manager by Archie Macaulay, who in only a short time was succeeded by Jimmy Hagan. Hagan's period in charge is perhaps best remembered for the players' 'strike' when several of them refused to train without tracksuit trousers on a bitterly cold day.

Already Derek Kevan had moved to Chelsea for £50,000 much to the consternation of supporters, Ronnie Allen went to Crystal Palace on a free transfer, Joe Kennedy went to Chester, Bobby Robson back to Fulham, Ray Barlow to Blues, David Burnside and Stuart Williams to Southampton and Don Howe to Arsenal.

On the credit side, John Kaye arrived from Scunthorpe, for a then club record fee of £44,750. Doug Fraser came from Aberdeen for £25,000, and a similar fee was paid to Notts County for Jeff Astle.

Youngsters Tony Brown, Bobby Hope and Ken Foggo appeared in the attack and Bobby Cram and Graham Williams were the full-backs in front of goalkeeper Ray Potter. Other teenagers, Ray Wilson, Mickey Fudge, Graham Lovett, Gerry Howshall and Ian Collard, were also pressing for places as Albion rebuilt.

It was in 1962, in the FA Cup fifth round against Tottenham Hotspur, that the last crowd of over 50,000 — it was actually almost 55,000 — was seen on the ground. Times indeed were changing.

Cup fever broke out in a big way in the second half of the 1960s as Albion reached three Finals in four seasons, the first when they won the League Cup at

Terry Simpson (centre) is challenged by Arsenal's Geoff Strong during the League game at Highbury in August 1963. The Gunners won 3-2, but Albion gained revenge a week later, winning 4-0 at The Hawthorns.

*Left:* Stan Jones and Bobby Cram combine to thwart a Chelsea raid at Stamford Bridge in April 1965. *Right:* Albion forwards John Kaye and Clive Clark battle for the ball with Wolves defender Bobby Thomson in March 1965.

# Albion's League Cup Glory

## ALBION 4    WEST HAM UNITED 1

THIS was 'part two' of Albion's first major Cup Final for 12 years — the Football League Cup Final. In those days the competition was in its infancy. There was no sponsorship and no Wembley finale, simply a two-legged affair, the victors of which would enjoy European soccer the following season.

The first leg at Upton Park had ended in a 2-1 win for the Hammers. Now Albion knew that victory by at least two goals at The Hawthorns on 23 February 1966 would mean European competition for the first time, not to mention the Throstles' first major honour since 1954.

The implications were not lost on the fans either, and over 32,000 crowded into the Albion ground on a chilly evening. They were treated to a night to remember as Albion produced some scintillating football in the first 45 minutes to demoralise and finally destroy West Ham.

John Kaye, who a week earlier had played for the Football League, was in splendid form and he levelled the aggregate score with a brilliant goal after only ten minutes, driving home Bobby Cram's measured cross in emphatic style.

After Astle and Kaye had gone close, Tony Brown netted number two in 19 minutes, inching Albion ahead over the two legs. Clive Clark grabbed a third goal after 28 minutes. The nippy winger darted forward to head home after Hammers' goalkeeper, Jim Standen, hesitated following a shot from Kaye which was blocked by Burnett.

Astle again went close and then Brown saw his snap header saved on the line. It was all Albion as West Ham back-pedalled. In the 35th minute, Throstles' skipper Graham Williams went forward to drill home goal number four from fully 30 yards after Astle had played the ball back to him from the edge of the penalty area.

West Ham rallied a little in the second half and stole a consolation goal through Martin Peters after 75 minutes, but one minute from time Albion went back upfield and emphasized their superiority when first Kaye hit the crossbar and then Brown's header was stopped on the line.

Albion were 5-3 aggregate winners and looked forward to a place in the 1966-7 Fairs Cup competition. Throstles' manager Jimmy Hagan said afterwards: 'We won well, we played well, and I'm proud of the lads. That first-half performance was one of the best I've seen from a club side for years.'

**Albion:** Potter; Cram, Fairfax, Fraser, Campbell, Williams, T.Brown, Astle, Kaye, Hope, Clark.
**West Ham United:** Standen; Burnett, Peters, Bovington, K.Brown, Moore, Brabrook, Boyce, Byrne, Hurst, Sissons.
*Ref: Mr J.Mitchell (Whiston, Lancs).*          *Att: 32,013*
                                                 *(receipts £8,217).*

the first attempt, in 1965-6, beating West Ham in a two-legged Final.

Albion's first taste of competitive European soccer was in Holland when they met DOS Utrecht in the Fairs Cup, drawing 1-1 with Bobby Hope scoring their first-ever 'Euro-goal'. The second-leg saw the Throstles coast to a 5-2 victory with Brown hitting a hat-trick.

That set-up a tie with Bologna, who were much too experienced. The Italians won 3-0 in their own country and 3-1 at The Hawthorns. The second-leg defeat came four days after Albion had been beaten in the 1967 League Cup Final.

Albion lost at Wembley after they had led Third Division Queen's Park Rangers 2-0 at half-time, with both goals from Clive Clark who was playing against his old team. After the break Rangers came storming back and scored through Morgan, Marsh, and Lazarus after Albion goalkeeper Rick Sheppard had been floored in a tangle with Hunt.

Perhaps the decision to play Kaye deep alongside the inexperienced Dennis Clarke cost Albion the trophy. But whatever the reason, Bobby Cram never played for the club again and manager Jimmy Hagan left within a month.

Tears were to turn to cheers within a year, however, as Albion returned to Wembley. Their 1968 FA Cup success

**Sheffield Wednesday goalkeeper Ron Springett is beaten at The Hawthorns in September 1965. Albion won 4-2 with Jeff Astle grabbing a hat-trick.**

The 1968 FA Cup winners. Back row (left to right): Stuart Williams (trainer), Jeff Astle, John Talbut, John Osborne, John Kaye, Graham Lovett, Doug Fraser. Front: Ian Collard, Tony Brown, Graham Williams, Alan Ashman (manager), Bobby Hope, Clive Clark.

grew from very humble beginnings — and a referee's controversial decision.

It was at Layer Road, the home of Fourth Division Colchester United — where Leeds were later to be humbled — that the story began. Most of the crowd of just under 16,000 were convinced that referee Arthur Jones was wrong when he disallowed a goal by United's Micky Bullock only 90 seconds from the end, with the teams level at 1-1. Tony Brown's penalty had kept Albion in the game and the Throstles won the replay 4-0.

Their stuttering path to Wembley continued with two attempts to beat Southampton, with Graham Williams taking over in goal in the replay after Osborne was injured — and Astle hitting the winner in the last minute.

Alan Ashman had taken over as manager, and coached by former player Stuart Williams, Albion took a gamble by moving striker Johnny Kaye to half-back at a crucial time. It was a master-stroke, Kaye figured prominently in the sixth round tie against Liverpool.

The first two meetings were drawn, with only two goals scored after three-and-a-half hours of football. The second replay was at Maine Road, with Kaye in defence in place of Colquhoun, who

Asa Hartford (8) scores against QPR in October 1968. Albion won 3-1.

broke a leg at Newcastle. Kaye took a blow on the head, but continued playing with a bandage around the wound which needed 12 stitches. Tony Hateley equalised an early goal by Astle, but Clive Clark, the winger with a reputation for

scoring important Cup goals, knocked in the winner.

Kaye was ready for the semi-final at Villa Park against Birmingham City. Albion, fated for success, had only four shots at goal and scored twice — through

Astle and Brown. Blues had 12 shots and did not score at all, so Albion were on the way to their tenth Final.

The only question for manager Ashman before the Wembley meeting with Everton was who to play at outside-right. The choice lay between Kenny Stephens, Dennis Clarke and Graham Lovett, the man who had suffered terrible injuries in a road accident only 17 months before. Alan Ashman and coach Stuart Williams chose Lovett.

At Wembley, Everton pinned Albion back for long periods especially in the second half, but the scoreline remained blank until the end of 90 minutes. Extra-time was only two minutes old when Astle took a pass from Fraser, went past one defender and slammed a right-footed shot against Harvey. As the rebound came back to him, Astle hit it with his left and it flew high past West for the winner.

More than 250,000 people lined the streets of West Bromwich to welcome back the Cup winners and crown a great season for Ashman. To add to the Wembley victory there was an 8-1 win over Burnley and a 6-3 thrashing of Manchester United. Jeff Astle topped the First Division scoring lists with 35 goals.

Albion's second venture into Europe, in 1968-9, took them to the quarter-finals of the Cup-winners' Cup, but not before an exciting chapter in Bruges, against the Belgian Cup-holders. Albion lost 3-1 and had Jeff Astle taken to hospital after being

Albion's playing staff pictured in 1969. Back row (left to right): R.Potter, L.Hughes, J.Holton, L.Cantello, G.Johnson, C.Suggett, S.Woolgar, D.Findlater, J.Honour, R.Krzywicki, K.Morton, D.Hogg. Third row: A.McPherson (coach), D.Martin, P.Freeman, J.Talbut, J.Kaye, S.Williams (trainer), P.Latchford, J.Osborne, G.Nisbet, H.MacLean, G.Lovett, H.Reed, J.Dunn (trainer). Seated: R.A.Harford, J.Astle, T.Brown, D.Fraser, R.Hope. A.Ashman (manager), G.Williams, R.Wilson, D.Hegan, A.Glover, A.Merrick. On ground: B.Collard, S.Bell, S.McLaren, R.Minton, A.Robertson, D.Butler.

Leeds United v West Brom in April 1971. Irate fans invade the pitch as referee Ray Tinkler gets his book out.

attacked by home supporters. But that away goal, scored by Asa Hartford, helped see them through when they won 2-0 at The Hawthorns.

Yet their troubles had only just begun. In Bucharest, Hartford again scored, Ronnie Rees was sent off and players and officials had to duck a hail of stones as they left the stadium.

Albion had no problem in the second-leg — sweeping through 4-0 to win a place against Dunfermline in the last eight.

A goalless draw in Scotland made Albion favourites for The Hawthorns leg. But on a bitterly cold night, the Scots grabbed an early goal and held out to win.

Albion's defence of the FA Cup was sunk by a great goal from former Throstles supporter, Allan Clarke, with three minutes left of the semi-final against Leicester City at Hillsborough, after Albion had beaten three London clubs, Arsenal, Fulham and Chelsea, together with Norwich City, to reach that stage.

Many Albion fans believe that Jeff Astle's seventh-minute goal in the 1969-70 League Cup Final against Manchester City actually cost them yet another triumph. The goal, headed by the big England striker, tended to relax Albion and spur on City. Mike Doyle grabbed a second-half equaliser for Joe Mercer's team and when the match went into extra-time, City lasted the pace better. Glyn Pardoe hit the winner on a pitch saturated by melting snow.

In the League, Albion were away to a bad start, losing their first three home games, and it was not until the eighth match of the season, against Manchester United at home, that they managed their first victory.

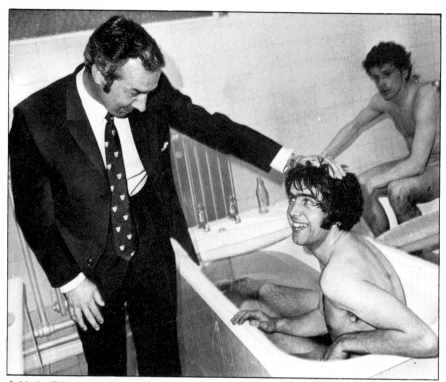

**Athletic Bilbao manager Ronnie Allen ruffles the hair of Albion's Bobby Hope after a testimonial game for the Scottish international at The Hawthorns.**

A 45,120 crowd saw them win 2-1 and in the side for the first time was Alistair Robertson, one of seven new players introduced that season.

After a disappointing season in 1970-71, the Albion board replaced Alan Ashman with Don Howe. It looked the correct move when the side won their first two games of the season, but after that they began to slip down the table until they beat Liverpool and climbed back to safety.

New faces in the side included Willie Johnston, signed for a club record fee of £138,000 from Rangers, John Wile, from Peterborough United, and Ally Brown from Leicester City.

All three settled in quickly, as did Bobby Gould from Wolves. But success did not materialise and the following season Albion were relegated for the first time in 24 years. They won only eight home matches and lost their last four fixtures in a row to go down with Crystal

# *Unstoppable Albion Hammer United*

## ALBION 6   MANCHESTER UNITED 3

JUST forty-eight hours before Manchester United were due to meet Albion in this crucial League game on 29 April 1968, the Throstles had fought through to the FA Cup Final. United were still in with a chance of taking the League Championship, and five days earlier they had taken a 1-0 lead from the first leg of their European Cup semi-final match against Real Madrid.

The stage was set for a great game at The Hawthorns — and what a game it turned out to be. Almost 46,000 fans paid to get into the ground, another 5,000 simply forced their way in free of charge, and 5,000 more were left stranded outside. It was the match everyone wanted to see.

Albion were on a 'high' following their 2-0 win over Birmingham City in the previous Saturday's FA Cup semi-final, yet their overall League form had been disappointing. Indeed, they had won only one of their last four home games and Everton had thumped them 6-2 at The Hawthorns.

On this occasion, however, the Throstles played brilliantly and destroyed this great United team in style. Every pass made by an Albion player seemed to drop into place whereas United's efforts largely went astray. Roared on by their fans, Albion, it seemed, could do no wrong.

Bobby Hope, Albion's Scottish inside-forward, remem-

bered later: "The final result could have resembled a cricket score. Denis Law missed a few, including a sitter, and George Best was also way off target. We, too, spurned one or two chances — but we still managed to get six."

Albion stormed into a 4-0 lead inside an hour through Jeff Astle (nine and 59 minutes), Ronnie Rees (39) and a Tony Brown penalty (57). Law pulled one back for United with a spot kick, but Asa Hartford and Astle again gave Albion a comprehensive 6-1 scoreline with 10 minutes to play.

United, to their credit, never gave up, such was the skill and character of that great team, and two late goals from Brian Kidd gave the scoreline a more respectable look.

Albion went on to win the FA Cup that season, whilst United became the first English team to lift the European Cup. The Reds were pipped by neighbours City for the League title and no doubt looked back to that defeat at The Hawthorns when Albion were unstoppable.

**Albion:** Osborne; Clarke, Williams, Brown, Talbut, Kaye, Rees, Collard, Astle, Hope, Hartford.
**Manchester United:** Stepney; Dunne, Burns, Crerand, Sadler, Stiles, Best, Law, Charlton, Kidd, Aston.
*Ref: Mr H.Davey (Verwood, Dorset).      Attendance: 45,992.*

**Ally Brown's first goal for West Brom, on his debut against Crystal Palace at The Hawthorns in March 1972. It earned Albion a 1-1 draw.**

Palace, after managing to score only 38 goals — their lowest total for 70 years.

At one stage it looked as if Albion were going to make a quick return but an FA Cup defeat by Newcastle United in the fifth round at The Hawthorns was followed by League setbacks against Hull City and Middlesbrough and from then on their form was erratic and they ended the season in eighth place. A League Cup knockout by Fourth Division Exeter City did not help morale.

One bright spot in that season was the attendance for the Boxing Day match at The Hawthorns against Aston Villa. It was the biggest Second Division attendance of the season — 43,119.

During the same season Albion were involved in an off the field drama when Asa Hartford was due to move to Leeds United. Terms had been agreed between the clubs and with the player when' a medical examination revealed a heart condition and Leeds backed out.

The signing of Johnny Giles as player-manager was perhaps the shrewdest deal Albion have ever pulled off. The little Irishman was persuaded to leave Leeds United in the summer of 1975, although

he had plans to continue with the Yorkshire club.

He came to The Hawthorns after the sacking of Don Howe following Albion's second season in Division Two, when their promotion run-in faded in the latter half of the campaign. Successive defeats at Easter, by Villa and Blackpool, finally killed off their faint hopes.

But there was a sign of better times ahead in the young players coming through the ranks — Bob Ward, Bryan Robson, John Trewick, David Rushbury, Ian Edwards and Trevor Thompson. Joe Mayo had been signed from Walsall for £8,000, and Giles took over a side which had twice gone so close to promotion, only to fail at the last hurdle.

Giles signed Geoff Hurst, Mick Martin and Paddy Mulligan and immediately set about shaping the side into a First Division outfit. It took time though, and after 12 matches of the 1975-6 compaign Albion were just five points off the bottom of the Division.

Then Albion's fortunes began to prosper as the players started to believe in themselves. Performances were workmanlike and the support, at home and away, was tremendous. Not since 1973 had there been regular attendances of over 20,000 — and on six occasions this season that figure was topped as Albion went for promotion.

The issue was in doubt right up to the last Saturday. Sunderland and Bristol City were already up and with one promotion place remaining, Albion had to go north to Oldham on 24 April and win to regain their First Division status. Tony Brown's left-foot shot early in the second-half gave Albion victory and promotion.

# *Back to the First Division*

## OLDHAM ATHLETIC 0    ALBION 1

THIS was probably Albion's most vital match for six years. Consider the situation — with one game left of their Second Division programme, the Throstles had to take both points to win promotion. A draw at Oldham's Boundary Park on 24 April 1976 would not be good enough. Albion had to come out fighting from the first whistle.

Upwards of 15,000 dedicated Albion fans made the 100-mile trip up the M6 to make Boundary Park look more like The Hawthorns revisited. Bolton Wanderers, Albion's nearest challengers,were on their way south to meet Charlton at The Valley. The Trotters had to take four points from their remaining two matches to pip Albion at the post — if the Baggies failed to win at Oldham.

Albion arrived at the ground some 90 minutes before kick-off in order to avoid the traffic jams, and when strikers Joe Mayo and Ally Brown walked on to the pitch for a pre-match look at the surface they were astounded by the vast bank of Albion supporters behind one goal. 'It was unbelievable,' said Mayo, 'The atmosphere resembled a Cup Final.'

Oldham had former Albion favourite, David Shaw, in their ranks, while Johnny Giles was able to field a full side for what he described as a 'mini Cup Final'.

Play in the first half was somewhat restrained. Both teams had chances but nerves played their part as a taut Albion

struggled to get their game together. At half-time news filtered through that Bolton were winning at Charlton. Victory for Albion was vital.

In the second half Giles began to look far more convincing and the Albion boss was soon spraying passes from midfield; Tony Brown was looking more menacing and Willie Johnston was also turning on some of his old magic.

In the 54th minute Albion found the goal they had been looking for — and appropriately it came at the end of the ground occupied by thousands of Baggies supporters.

The move developed on the right where Martin, Mulligan and Ally Brown created space. When the cross came over, it found ace striker Tony Brown some 18 yards from goal. Brown got the ball under control before hooking it wide of 'keeper Ogden. It was no more than Albion deserved and after a few heart-stopping moments near the final whistle, the Throstles celebrated their return to Division One.

**Oldham Athletic:** Ogden; Wood, Whittle, Bell, Edwards, Hicks, Blair, Shaw, Robins, Chapman(Branagan), Groves.
**Albion:** Osborne; Mulligan, Cantello, T.Brown, Wile, Robertson, Martin, A.Brown, Mayo, Giles, Johnston. Sub: Robson.
*Ref: Mr R.Tinkler (Boston).*                                    *Att: 22,356.*

The Goal of the Seventies? 'Bomber' Brown volleys the goal at Boundary Park that won Albion promotion in 1976.

Peter Barnes and Gary Owen in training in 1979.

John Osborne was an ever-present between the Albion posts, and he capped a grand season by keeping a blank sheet in no fewer than 22 League games, a club record. Alistair Robertson was also an ever-present in the first-team, while Tony Brown topped the scoring charts with eight goals in the League and four in the FA Cup.

The top of Division Two for 1975-6 ended thus:

| | P | W | D | L | F | A | P |
|---|---|---|---|---|---|---|---|
| 1 Sunderland | 42 | 24 | 8 | 10 | 67 | 36 | 56 |
| 2 Bristol C | 42 | 19 | 15 | 8 | 59 | 35 | 53 |
| 3 West Brom A | 42 | 20 | 13 | 9 | 50 | 33 | 53 |
| 4 Bolton W | 42 | 20 | 12 | 10 | 64 | 38 | 52 |

To crown a great season, Albion's Youth team carried off the FA Youth Cup for the first time in the club's history, beating Wolves 5-0 on aggregate in the two-legged Final, and the Central League side finished runners-up to Liverpool, failing by just four points to overtake the seemingly invincible Reds from Anfield.

Back in the First Division, Albion soon began to show their skills, picking up a creditable point in their opening game at Leeds. They hung around the middle of the table for a good four months, registering some fine wins including successive ones of — 4-2 over Tottenham (after being 2-0 down) and 4-0 over Manchester United, both at home.

After 21 games Albion were in ninth place with 22 points — 11 behind leaders Liverpool. Ten matches later, after Laurie Cunningham had been signed from Orient for £110,000 and Tony Godden had replaced John Osborne in goal, they lay seventh, one rung off a UEFA Cup place for 1978. But a tough Easter programme, coupled with future England skipper Bryan Robson fracturing a leg for the third time in less than a year, meant that Albion had to be content with that seventh place. Yet it was indeed a happy return to the top-flight for the club, players and of course supporters, who pushed the average Hawthorns attendance for the season up from 16,000 to 24,500.

Those same fans were shocked and dismayed in the summer of 1977 when Giles left Albion. He was replaced initially by former favourite Ronnie Allen, but Allen decided to gamble on taking a job in Saudi Arabia and that left the way clear for Ron Atkinson to step into The Hawthorns.

Atkinson arrived in January 1978 and he made an immediate impact. His flamboyant approach rubbed off on everyone and in a matter of weeks Albion were again looking a useful side. Brendon Batson was signed from Atkinson's old club, Cambridge United, and with Cyrille Regis, snapped up by Allen from non-Leaguers Hayes for £5,000, plus the skills of Laurie Cunningham and the wing play of Willie Johnston, Albion were becoming a force with which to be reckoned.

They powered on in the FA Cup and after knocking out Blackpool, Manchester United, Derby County and then the favourites Nottingham Forest, a place in

# *Cantello's Goal of the Season*

## MANCHESTER UNITED 3    ALBION 5

NOT many teams have gone to Old Trafford and put five goals past Manchester United, but on 30 December 1978, under Ron Atkinson's managership, Albion went there and whipped United 5-3 in front of a 45,000 crowd. And to rub salt into United's wounds, television cameras were there to record the action.

At the time Albion were riding on the crest of a wave, unbeaten in ten matches and pushing strongly at the top of the First Division table. United, on the other hand, were going through a bad patch, having lost three of their last six matches including two successive 3-0 defeats, one of them against struggling Bolton Wanderers.

The game itself was a magnificent advertisement for British football. A thrill-a-minute match with goalmouth action at both ends, the game also provided plenty of midfield cut and thrust — and eight goals, several of them absolute beauties.

United struck the first blow, Brian Greenhoff smashing in a shot from 20 yards following a left-wing corner. Tony Brown equalised, then Len Cantello, latching on to a deft back-heel from Cyrille Regis, scored with a classic effort which won him ITV's 'Goal of the Season'.

Gordon McQueen headed in United's equaliser from another left-wing corner, then Sammy McIlroy weaved his way through to put United 3-2 ahead. Right on the half-time whistle, Tony Brown nudged in Albion's third to make it all-square.

The action continued thick, fast and furious in the second period. Bailey made two superb saves from Regis, and then Laurie Cunningham raced away to put Albion 4-3 ahead with less than 15 minutes to play.

Regis made absolutely certain with a fantastic goal for Albion in the dying minutes, collecting Ally Brown's inside pass to rifle a fierce right-foot shot past the groping Bailey. It was a fitting end to Albion's best away performance for years.

**Manchester United:** Bailey; B.Greenhoff, Houston, McIlroy, McQueen, Buchan, Coppell, J.Greenhoff(Sloan), Ritchie, McCreery, Thomas.
**Albion:** Godden; Batson, Statham, T.Brown, Wile, Roberston, Robson, A.Brown, Regis, Cantello, Cunningham. Sub: Johnston.
*Ref: Mr G.P.Owen (Anglesey).*                    *Att: 45,091*

the Wembley Final looked a distinct possibility. At Highbury in the semi-final against Ipswich Town, however, everything went wrong. John Wile was injured early on, Johnston was carrying a damaged shoulder and then Mick Martin was sent-off as Ipswich won 3-1.

In 1977-8 Albion finished sixth in the First Division and so won a place in the UEFA Cup, their first taste of European football for ten years. Atkinson got his team geared up with some useful early season displays and they knocked out Galatasaray, Braga, and the crack Span-ish outfit, Valencia, before losing the first-leg of the quarter-final against Red Star, 1-0 in Belgrade. European inexperience cost Albion a place in the semi-final when they allowed the Yugoslavs a late strike and so eventually went out on that away goal.

David Mills, Britain's first £500,000 footballer, was signed from Middlesbrough, and Martyn Bennett was given his Football League debut as Albion earned a second season in European competition by finishing third in Division One in 1978-9. Indeed, they might

have won the Championship had not the dreadful English winter disrupted their form and programme at a crucial time in the campaign.

Fine wins over Manchester United (5-3 at Old Trafford), Coventry (7-1) and Manchester City (4-0, both at The Hawthorns) were just three magnificent displays from Albion this season, and Tony Brown created a new club record by passing Ronnie Allen's total of 208 League goals.

Despite going out of the fifth round of the FA Cup, Albion always looked

Albion's first-team squad before the start of the club's centenary season of 1979-80. Back row (left to right): Derek Statham, Cyrille Regis, Tony Godden, David Stewart, Ally Brown, John Trewick, Bryan Robson. Front row: Tony Brown; Ally Robertson, Brendon Batson, George Wright (physiotherapist), John Wile, Ron Atkinson (manager), David Mills, Gary Owen, Peter Barnes.

capable of finishing at least second in the table and they would have done but for a last match defeat, at home to European Cup champions, Nottingham Forest.

Nevertheless, Albion — and Atkinson — had done exceptionally well and West Bromwich was back on the footballing map.

The club's centenary season of 1979-80 was somewhat subdued. Albion took tenth place in the League, went out of the FA Cup in round three, lost to Norwich in the fourth round of the League Cup. They failed at the first hurdle in the UEFA Cup, going under to the East German club, Carl Zeiss Jena.

John Deehan (from Aston Villa), Gary Owen and Peter Barnes (from Manchester City), and Garry Pendrey (Birmingham) were added to the first-team pool as Cunningham (to Real Madrid for almost £1 million), and Johnston left The Hawthorns.

In 1980-81, Albion played some neat soccer but they still lacked that vital spark. Atkinson was being 'eyed-up' by Manchester United and as soon as the season ended he packed his bags and left The Hawthorns for Old Trafford.

Early in the 1981-2 season he paid out over £2 million and took both Bryan Robson and Remi Moses away from The Hawthorns. Their departure destroyed Albion's midfield.

Ronnie Allen returned to replace Atkinson and although he helped Albion to the semi-finals of both the FA and League Cup competitions in 1981-2, his

stay was short-lived, and somewhat tempestuous. Ron Wylie the former Aston Villa and Birmingham City player, was appointed to take over from Allen in 1983 but he never really settled at The Hawthorns, despite making several changes, including the signing of Ken McNaught and Tony Morley (from Villa)

By this time, Regis had moved to Coventry in a deal which caused quite a stir among the fans. Garry Thompson had been bought from Coventry, Clive Whitehead from Bristol City and Peter Eastoe from Everton, along with Paul Barron from Crystal Palace and the two Dutch internationals Romeo Zondervan and Martin Jol, plus midfielder Steve Mackenzie from Manchester City. John Wile had moved on to become player-manager of Peterborough.

On paper Albion looked a useful side but their overall performances where mediocre, to say the least. Albion brought back Johnny Giles as manager in February 1984. At that time, the club was at a particularly low ebb. Home attendances had slumped to 11,000 and generally speaking the standard of play had dropped alarmingly.

When Giles arrived at The Hawthorns, Albion were still in the FA Cup but his first match back in charge ended in disaster as Plymouth, from the Third Division, bundled Albion out of the competition in front of 24,000 fans at The Hawthorns.

It was now an uphill battle all the way for Giles and his back-up crew of Nobby

Stiles and Norman Hunter. Albion struggled painfully on. There were regular internal disputes but Giles remained right through the 1984-5 campaign and although he signed Jimmy Nicholl, Carl Valentine, and David Cross (for a second spell) to play alongside Steve Hunt and Tony Grealish (secured on the transfer-deadline of 1984), Albion never looked a good side.

Garry Thompson was sold — to the dismay of the supporters — to Sheffield Wednesday, but when Imre Varadi, Garth Crooks, Gerry Armstrong, Colin Anderson, Paul Bradshaw and Robbie Dennison, arrived, things looked brighter.

But the promise was not sustained and Albion slumped to the foot of the First Division soon after the start of that 1985-6 campaign. Giles left following a 3-0 defeat at Coventry in September, handing over his duties to Nobby Stiles. But relegation, even at this early stage, was staring Albion in the face.

Stiles carried on, but he was fighting a losing battle. Albion needed a miracle. George Reilly was signed from Newcastle but matters did not improve and the Albion board went for experience and appointed former Villa and Birmingham manager, Ron Saunders, in a last-gasp effort to prevent relegation.

Albion improved somewhat but it was too late and Second Division football became inevitable. New signings were made — Paul Dyson from Stoke, Stuart Naylor from Lincoln, Craig Madden from Bury, Darren Bradley from Aston

**Albion in 1984. Back row (left to right): Mick Perry, Garry Thompson, Martin Bennett, Paul Barron, Tony Godden, Ken McNaught, Barry Cowdrill, Mickey Forsyth, Gary Robson. Middle row: Gary Leonard, Joey Tortolano, Clive Whitehead, Cyrille Regis, Steve Mackenzie, Nicky Cross, Wayne Ebanks, Mickey Lewis. Front: Nobby Stiles (coach), Ally Robertson, Derek Statham, Gary Owen, Johnny Giles (manager), Steve Hunt, Tony Grealish, Tony Morley, George Wright (physiotherapist).**

# Albion's Worst Season In Division One 1985-86

WITHOUT doubt the 1985-86 campaign was Albion's worst-ever in Division One. They started badly, deteriorated, and subsequently suffered relegation for the sixth time since the Football League was formed in 1888. Albion set up several unwanted records and had statistically-minded supporters thumbing through the record books. These are the facts about the sad season of 1985-86 campaign: (Previous record totals in brackets)

- Fewest League wins — four (nine).
- Record number of defeats — 26 (23).
- Least number of away wins — just one (equalling previous low).
- Fewest home wins in season — three (six).
- Most home defeats in 21-match programme — 10 (equalling previous high).
- Least number of home points gained in season — 17 (22).
- Fewest home League goals scored — 21 (22).
- Lowest number of points gained in 42-match programme — 24 (28).
- Nine consecutive League games lost (previous record eight).
- Most players utilised in season (League & Cup games) — 34 (33).
- Most home goals conceded by a First Division club in 1985-86 — 36.
- Most away League goals conceded by a First Division club in 1985-86 — 53.
- Five goalkeepers used during season (League and Cup competitions).

- Nineteen players made their senior debuts for Albion in 1985-6.
- Albion dropped to the bottom of the First Division table after their third game — and stayed there.
- There were three managers at The Hawthorns during the season — Johnny Giles, Nobby Stiles and Ron Saunders (appointed February 1986).
- And to cap it all, Albion's reserve side suffered relegation from the Central League Division One.

Some supporters never saw Albion win a match in 1985-86. Others were so disgruntled after the first two months of the season that they stayed away for the rest of the campaign, which resulted in Albion having their lowest average League attendance (just over 12,000) for more than 70 years.

Players came and went. At the start of the season, Garth Crooks and Imre Varadi were paired together to replace Garry Thompson; later, big George Reilly arrived from Newcastle. None of them sparkled although Reilly did perform a lot better during the last month of the season.

The midfield was switched around throughout the season with Steve Hunt, Mickey Thomas, Tony Grealish, Steve Mackenzie, Martin Dickinson, Andy Thompson and Darren Bradley all having spells in the team. Paul Dyson was signed from Stoke City to replace long-serving Ally Robertson in the back-four, and goalkeeper Stuart Naylor was recruited from Lincoln City to become Ron Saunders' first signing — on St Valentine's Day.

---

Villa and Martin Dickinson from Leeds, all to no avail.

After such a dismal start to the 1985-6 season — easily the worst in Albion's League history — the supporters, players and directors of the club were looking for a vast improvement in 1986-7. But, alas, things were basically unchanged and Albion were lucky not to suffer relegation for the second season running, finishing in their lowest-ever League position (15th).

They had a reasonable start to the campaign; dropped off somewhat in mid-September; had a fair October; a respectable November and a so-and-so December. But once into 1987 things started to go drastically wrong.

From 1 January to 9 May inclusive, Albion played a total of 20 Second Division games and one FA Cup tie, away to Fourth Division Swansea (lost 3-2). Out of those League fixtures they managed to win only four and plummeted deep into the relegation zone. Thankfully there were one or two other teams struggling around the same time and Albion survived the drop — and the play-offs — by the skin of their teeth.

Manager Ron Saunders' job was made more difficult by a series of injuries to key players and began he the season with Derek Statham, Darren Bradley and striker George Reilly all side-lined. During the course of the campaign Martyn Bennett, Martin Dickinson, Steve Mackenzie, Gary Robson and new-signing Robert Hopkins (from Manchester City) were also under treatment. Saunders signed strikers Bobby Williamson (from Rangers) and Stewart Evans

(Wimbledon) at the start. Later on, after securing Hopkins, he snapped up Martin Singleton and Don Goodman from Bradford City, former Hawthorns apprentice Steve Lynex (from Leicester City), who returned 'home' ten years after leaving the club, and Kevin Steggles, a defender from Ipswich Town. There were also 12 players sold during the season: Irishman Jimmy Nicholl was exchanged for Williamson, going on to win a Scottish Premier Division Championship medal with Rangers; Mickey Thomas (Wichita Wings, NASL) and Gary Owen (Panionios, Greece); Tony Godden signed permanently for Chelsea; Imre Varadi and Tony Grealish both joined Manchester City; Steve Ball, Andy Thompson, Robbie Dennison and the long-serving Ally Robertson all joined Wolves, Robertson leaving Albion after 18 years service and more than 600 senior games; Craig Madden went to Blackpool (£50,000); Stewart Evans (Plymouth, £50,000) and striker Garth Crooks was sold to Charlton for £75,000.

Goalkeeper Stuart Naylor and skipper Paul Dyson were both ever-presents with Naylor being voted 'Player of the Year'. Crooks was top-scorer, closely followed by Williamson. The average League attendance at The Hawthorns was under 10,000 — the lowest figure since 1905-06.

Albion, a club with a great history, approached 1987-8 with the knowledge that they had not won a major honour since 1968, and they had a new secretary, Gordon Bennett from Bristol Rovers, who later switched to Norwich City as youth development officer, and a new

commercial manager Alan Stevenson, the former Burnley goalkeeper.

There were new shirt sponsors as well — Apollo 2000 Limited, the largest gas and electrical-appliance retailers in the West Midlands. Apollo agreed a three-year contract and at the time things certainly looked much brighter than they had been during the previous two rather dismal and disappointing campaigns.

But alas nothing changed. In fact, things got progressively worse in 1987-8 and for the third season running, Albion's form was quite abysmal. They finished in their lowest-ever League position — 20th in Division Two — only five points clear of automatic relegation and a mere one point and goal-difference away from having to battle it out in the play-offs.

Ron Saunders began the season as manager but was replaced after the first month by Ron Atkinson, who returned to The Hawthorns for a second spell, his first term in office having lasted from 1978 to 1981.

Atkinson faced a big task in refloating a sinking ship, and with coach Colin Addison, also back at the club for a second time, set about a difficult job with confidence. But the players simply weren't good enough, and the results, both at home and away, were sometimes quite awful.

Players came and went, and Atkinson was never really able to field a settled side, injuries and suspensions proving the biggest headaches. Yet The Hawthorns loyalists were always behind the team and the manager and, indeed, the average attendance for home League matches was over 10,000, almost 800 up on the previous season's figure.

Some horrid home performances saw Albion crash 4-1 to both Millwall — perhaps the best footballing side to visit The Hawthorns during the season — and Leeds United. They also went down disastrously to Swindon Town, when Tony Kelly was sent off, Blackburn Rovers and Reading, the latter certainly being Albion's worst display of a sad, sad campaign.

Quite surprisingly away from The Hawthorns, Albion should have won at Aston Villa, Middlesbrough and Ipswich,

three of the better sides in the Second Division, and they were unlucky not to reap greater rewards at Plymouth, where they fought back from 3-1 down to draw 3-3, and at Leicester where, in the end, they lost 3-0. But, in truth, the side was simply not good enough.

In all, a total of 30 players were utilised during the season — the figure had been 28 in 1986-7 and 34 in 1985-6 — and there lay the trouble because Albion were unable to field a settled, balanced side. Atkinson also knew that he had to strengthen his squad. He had some useful youngsters and one or two experienced

and dedicated senior professionals, but he desperately needed new blood to reinforce his team.

Former Ipswich, Arsenal and England midfielder Brian Talbot was signed from Stoke City for £15,000 in January. Talbot arrived too late to make any real impact on the team's overall position, but he certainly added something to the centre of the field, where before Albion had been so lacking.

It was anticipated that Talbot would be the key figure in 1988-9, with defenders Paul Dyson and Stacey North.

Atkinson also believed that his defence,

**John Paskin scores Albion's third goal from Gary Robson's pass as Stoke are hammered at The Hawthorns.**

# *Talbot's Men Hit Stoke for Six*

## ALBION 6    STOKE CITY 0

THIS demolition of Stoke City on 18 December 1988 turned out to be Albion's best win of the season and shot them into third place in the Second Division as well as bringing a great deal of satisfaction to player-manager Brian Talbot, who had left the Victoria Ground to join Albion for a bargain £15,000 the previous January and had been in charge of team affairs for only two months.

Albion celebrated Christmas with a thrilling display of attacking football which had the home supporters in the 17,634 crowd — the biggest Hawthorns turnout for two seasons — in raputres, chanting, 'Going up! Going up!'

It was the eighth win in 11 games for a revitalised Baggies, who, under Talbot's guidance, had shot up from 18th to within striking distance of promotion.

Talbot had some pre-match worries with Robert Hopkins and Carlton Palmer ruled out of the midfield. Talbot himself was nursing a knee injury but decided to play and seemed to be involved in everything in midfield. And but for his unselfishness in aiming to create an opening for a colleague, he might well have figured on the scoresheet himself. Albion ran Stoke ragged and the visitors had Tony Ford (later to join Albion) sent off after 67 minutes following a bad tackle on star man Colin Anderson.

Albion scored after only 90 seconds when Anderson's corner was flicked on by Chris Whyte for Gary Robson to head home from six yards. On 32 minutes, Talbot and

Anderson linked up in midfield and the latter's pass found Goodman in space to make it 2-0.

The second half was one-way traffic as Albion tore Stoke to shreds. In the 70th minute, after a series of near-misses, South African-born striker John Paskin made it 3-0, turning in Robson's pass after another flowing move started by Talbot and carried on by Anderson. Six minutes later, after good work by Goodman and Anderson, the same player banged in number four.

After 84 minutes, Goodman weighed in with the fifth following an excellent pass from Wayne Dobbins. And to round things off, Robson left Stoke in utter despair with a sixth goal two minutes later. Talbot said later: "Strange that a year ago I wasn't good enough to get into that Stoke side — and I was fit then!"

Alas, Albion's mid-season flourish in 1988-9 fizzled out after their FA Cup exit at Everton and they had to settle for ninth place in the table, ten points behind runners-up Manchester City and two wins short of the play-offs.

**Albion:** Naylor; Hodson, Albiston, Talbot, Whyte, North, Dobbins, Goodman, Robson, Paskin, Anderson. Subs: Phillips, Patterson.
**Stoke City:** Fox; Gidman, Carr, Kamara, Henry, Berry, Hackett, Ware, Shaw, Ford, Beagrie. Subs: Hemming, Fowler.
*Ref: Mr G.Alpin (Kendal).*                    *Att: 17,634.*

and to a certain extent, his midfield, was easily sorted out. It was up front where the problems lay and he desperately wanted to improve the strike force.

As the 1987-8 campaign ended, Ron said, "It can only get better — and I believe it will."

One consolation this term was that Albion's reserve side gained promotion from Division Two of the Central League.

Consequently, after John Silk had taken over as chairman from Sid Lucas, there was a great deal of optimism around The Hawthorns prior to the start of 1988-9 — and when Albion went to the top of the Second Division on 2 January, following a splendid 6-0 home win over Stoke City, a 3-1 triumph at Boundary Park and a confident 4-0 home success over Shrewsbury Town, they looked a good bet for promotion.

A run of eight games without defeat had shot them six places up the table and attendances had risen to over 18,000.

But then it all went wrong, once 1989 set in. After going out of the FA Cup to Everton, the eventual Finalists, in a replay, Albion's form dipped dramatically and in the second half of the season they gained only 28 points out of a possible 66, having collected 44 from their first 24 matches, and eventually finished well down the ladder in ninth place, three places below the promotion play-off line.

Perhaps the crucial talking points, certainly inside the club and amongst the fans, following that second-half collapse surrounded the injuries suffered by two key players in those Cup games against Everton.

Don Goodman, the leading scorer who up until then had been quite brilliant, and left-sided midfielder Colin Anderson, were both side-lined for important matches. And indeed, during their absence Albion's form nose-dived considerably. Goodman, in fact, never regained full fitness. There is no doubt that manager Brian Talbot, who took over the hot seat in mid-October and took charge on a permanent basis later — following Atkinson's hasty departure to Spain, where he became boss of Atletico Madrid — did an excellent job in his first season in charge — and he quickly signed a new three-year contract.

When Talbot was asked to take charge of team affairs, Albion were lying 13th in the table — and struggling to get their game together. But Talbot's experience and commitment out on the park was a breath of fresh air to the team, and inside three months performances changed around completely. Admittedly, he sold young defender David Burrows to Liverpool for £650,000 and midfielder Carlton Palmer to Sheffield Wednesday for £450,000 plus striker Colin West, but he did recruit other players who he thought would do the job for the club.

Speedy Kevin Bartlett arrived from Cardiff, winger Tony Ford from Stoke, midfield 'hardman' Ian Banks and the defensive duo of Paul Raven and Ronnie Robinson from Doncaster all came on the scene, as well as some shrewd loan-signings, all of whom helped the team tick over nicely through a rather difficult period when injuries and suspensions crept in.

Talbot moulded Albion's defence into the best in the Second Division, in terms of goals conceded, but credit here must go to the two experienced figures of former Scottish international left-back Arthur Albiston, who was signed on a free transfer from Manchester United, and centre-back Chris Whyte, who was brought back to England after a good stint in America on the recommendation of Talbot, both players in effect, being signed by Atkinson. Goalkeeper Stuart Naylor and Stacey North also did well, the latter being the only ever-present in the side.

Albion's problem, in hindsight, was that they drew far too many matches — a club record 18 — and they failed to score at all against relegated Walsall. But Talbot certainly learnt a lot from his first season as manager, and he wanted to go one better in 1989-90, hoping to steer Albion back into the First Division. But before that could be achieved, he desperately wanted to strengthen his squad to have any chance of making that dream become a reality. But money was in short supply.

As so often happens in football, things failed to take off and 1989-90 turned out to be another very disappointing season for Albion, who, by finishing 20th in Division Two, equalled their lowest-ever position in League history — and it was also the second time in three years that

# *Albion's Great Littlewoods Comeback*

## BRADFORD CITY 3    ALBION 5

THIS second-round second-leg Littlewoods Cup clash at Valley Parade on 4 October 1989 saw one of the greatest comebacks in Albion's history.

It had been four years since the Baggies had won their opening tie of any major Cup tournament and few people gave them much hope of reaching the next round of this competition after they had been beaten 3-1 in the first leg at The Hawthorns.

Brian Talbot travelled to Yorkshire with six of his regular players out injured and he later revealed that he had told the team: "Go out and play football, enjoy yourselves, you've nothing to lose!" Albion did just that — and the drama which unfolded, was pure theatre.

The undoubed star was stand-in 31-year-old striker John Thomas, who was playing in only his second full game for the club since his £30,000 transfer from Bolton in the summer. 'Thommo' claimed a hat-trick — he might have had a couple of more — but the whole team deserved the standing ovation they received from the ardent Baggies supporters who made the trip.

Mark Barham rediscovered some of the skills which had earned him an England place whilst with Norwich City and he played his part in two of the goals, whilst defender Chris Whyte provided the 55th-minute strike just when the cause seemed lost.

And what a night it was for Brian Talbot. He netted on 38 minutes. It was the 100th goal of his career and what a crucial one this turned out to be.

Thomas gave Albion the lead after ten minutes, then Talbot made it 2-0 before Bradford hit back with two goals in a minute, from full-back Greg Abbott and midfielder Paul Jewell, to bring the scores level on the night as Albion's back-four suddenly relaxed. But 60 seconds from half-time, the sprightly Thomas edged Albion back in front with a beautifully judged lob, only for Bradford to equalise again through Jimmy Quinn on 48 minutes.

Still Albion refused to lie down and following Barham's deft corner, the alert Whyte cracked in number four. And there was more to come as a surging run from Bartlett spread open the home defence to leave Thomas free to complete his hat-trick with the game's best goal.

Still Bradford came back and Stuart Naylor pulled off three fine saves to take the tie into extra-time. It was nerve-tingling stuff throughout those extra 30 minutes, but Talbot's men held firm to record a famous victory on the away goals rule from a game which was truly a great advert for British football.

**Bradford City:** Tomlinson; Abbott, Tinnion, Oliver, Sinnott, Jackson, Megson, Campbell, Leonard(Costello), Quinn, Jewell. Other Sub: Duxbury.
**Albion:** Naylor; Bradley, Burgess, Talbot, Whyte, North, Barham, Goodman, Thomas, McNally, Bartlett. Subs: Foster, Allardyce.
*Ref: Mr.R.Dixon (West Kirby).*                    *Att: 5,731.*

**Don Goodman scores against Swindon Town at The Hawthorns during the 1988-9 season.**

they had to battle against relegation to the Third.

A quite dreadful home record was mainly responsible for Albion's poor showing — only six wins in 23 matches at The Hawthorns, losing nine and conceding 37 goals, the most by any club at home in the League throughout the campaign.

Over 30 players were again used in major competitions, including four goalkeepers, all of whom figured in the side before the end of September. Five players were utilised at right-back, five in the centre of the defence (at number-five) and no fewer than eight occupied the left-wing berth. Injuries did cause a lot of problems for Talbot and he was hardly ever able to field an unchanged team. Over 20 players were in for treatment at various times during the campaign, three recovering from broken legs.

But the reason for Albion's dismal season could be summed up in one word — inconsistency.

They managed no more than two League wins on the trot and indeed, Third Division football looked on the cards after only one victory was registered between early January and mid-March,

during which time two First Division clubs, Wimbledon and Charlton Athletic, were dumped out of the FA Cup by Albion. Perhaps the two crucial wins from Albion's point of view were those against Watford and Bradford City (both at home) in March, and then two more, at Hull and Brighton. At the time, three of these teams were also deep in relegation trouble and Albion collected vital points which, in the end, saved them.

Despite the influx of a number of new players — left-back Graham Harbey (from Ipswich Town) in November, and then later former Walsall midfielder Craig Shakespeare (from Sheffield Wednesday), striker Gary Bannister (from Coventry City) and winger Gary Hackett (from Stoke City) — Albion had a really awful first four and a half months of 1990. They won only six of their 22 League matches, and, all-told, bagged a mere 25 points out of a possible 66. Again the supporters were surprisingly tolerant and the average attendance at The Hawthorns was a shade over 11,300.

Two players called it a day at the end of the season. Defender Martyn Bennett was told to quit League football on medical advice because of a niggling back

injury — he joined his former colleague Ally Robertson at Worcester City — and Brian Talbot decided to finish, although he did play occasionally the following term.

Bernard McNally, the Northern Ireland international midfielder, signed from Shrewsbury Town for £385,000, was voted 'Player of the Year' at the Supporters' Club annual dinner, where it was said that 'things can only improve at The Hawthorns'.

During the summer of 1990, Chris Whyte signed for Leeds United after a tribunal fixed his fee at £450,000, the Hawthorns pitch was completely returfed — the first time since 1911 that the whole surface had been replaced — and it was hoped that Albion would be able to put on some worthwhile performances on their new grass to celebrate the ground's 90th birthday and, hopefully, win back their First Division status.

Instead of the glory days returning to the club, however, disaster befell the Baggies and their die-hard, long-suffering but dedicated supporters. There were tears when, at 4.44pm on Saturday 11 May 1991, West Bromwich Albion were relegated to the Third Division for the first time in their history after their worst-ever season. Chairman John Silk admitted that it was, indeed, a black day, but he confidently predicted that the team would bounce back.

That was no consolation to their loyal supporters who had backed them every inch of the way in a quite disastrous campaign.

It was amazing to think that the Throstles ended the 1990-91 campaign with a nine-match unbeaten run, includ- ing seven draws. But they had won only four League games out of 23 since 1 January. That was relegation form in anyone's language. Halfway through the season, Albion were humiliated 4-2 in the FA Cup by non-Leaguers Woking

Colin West's powerful header gives Albion a half-time lead against the non-Leaguers, Woking.

# *Albion's FA Cup Woe*

## ALBION 2    WOKING 4

THIS result will never be forgotten by Albion supporters — whether they attended The Hawthorns to witness the third-round FA Cup tie in person on 5 January 1991, or stayed at home listening to it on local radio. Nor will it be erased from the memories of the players who were outplayed by little Woking from the Vauxhall League, the side who pulled off a sensational victory against all the odds.

Tim Buzaglo, a cricketing-footballer, was Woking's match-winner with a stunning second-half hat-trick after Colin West had headed Albion in front after 35 minutes.

Despite that early lead, beleaguered boss Brian Talbot was on his way out, only a year or so after steering Albion to the top of the Second Division.

He knew this as soon as the final whistle sounded, as the fans showed their disapproval, booing the Baggies' players and jeering at the management and the board before cheering and then carrying off, shoulder-high in front of the TV cameras, the Woking stars who had caused a major Cup upset.

Albion, who gave Mel Rees his debut in goal, looked to have the game under control following West's powerful header from Craig Shakespeare's right-wing corner ten minutes before half-time.

But after the break it all went wrong for Talbot's men as the part-timers tore through Albion's defence. After a couple of close calls in the Woking penalty area, and a near miss at the other end, Albion's defence was caught square after 59 minutes when Biggins played the ball through to Brown, who in turn helped it on for Buzaglo to send a low left-foot shot wide of Rees and into the net.

Albion replied with a snap-shot by McNally, but six minutes later Buzaglo whipped in a dramatic second goal for the non-Leaguers. He raced on to a long clearance from goalkeeper Read, which had been headed on by Brown. Rees blocked his first shot but Buzaglo carried on to nod the bouncing ball home from close range.

Albion were stunned and, with a quarter of an hour remaining, the irrepressible Buzaglo grabbed a sensational third goal to complete his hat-trick. His powerful left-foot drive whipped past Rees after Biggins and Cowler had set him free on the left side of the penalty area. It was all too much for some Albion fans and an irate few had to be escorted from the field.

Albion were shell-shocked and it was no surprise when, with time running out, Woking substitute Worsfield charged in to head home his side's fourth goal from a right-wing cross by Biggins. Amazingly, inside the last three minutes Albion created five good chances but West (twice), Bannister and Ford all missed before Bradley reduced the deficit.

It was a sad, sad day for everyone associated with West Brom. Several hundred fans vented their frustration by staying inside the ground for 45 minutes and, shortly after this humiliating defeat, manager Talbot was dismissed, being replaced by his assistant Stuart Pearson, who took charge on a caretaker basis before Bobby Gould came into the hot seat.

**Albion:** Rees; Shakespeare, Harbey(L.Palmer), Roberts, Bradley, Strodder, Ford, West, Bannister, McNally, Robson. Other sub: Hodson.
**Woking:** Read; Mitchell, Cowler, Pratt, Baron, S.Wye, Brown, Biggins, Franks(Worsfield), Buzaglo, L.Wye. Other sub: Russell.
*Ref: Mr R.L.Hamer(Bristol).*                    *Att: 14,516.*

Former Albion players and coaches who attended the opening of a new restaurant at The Hawthorns. From left to right are Cyrille Regis, Stuart Pearson, Sam Allardyce, John Wile, John Osborne, Jeff Astle, Ally Robertson, Campbell Crawford, Johnny Nicholls, Ronnie Allen, Graham Williams and Bobby Hope.

at The Hawthorns — a defeat which was by far the most shattering result suffered by the club this century. Within a matter of days, manager Brian Talbot was dismissed.

His right-hand man, Stuart Pearson, took over as caretaker boss and Albion's performances improved. But then the directors appointed former player Bobby Gould as the new manager.

Gould's first game in charge saw Albion draw 0-0 with West Ham, but there followed a dismal run of six successive defeats, and from that moment, relegation was staring the Baggies in the face. With nine games remaining, Albion were sitting on the edge of disaster, just one place above the trapdoor to Division Three.

On the transfer deadline, in an effort to stave off the threat of relegation, Gould splashed out on two Fourth Division players — striker Paul Williams from Stockport County for £250,000, and midfielder Winston White from Burnley for £35,000, plus taking Kwamo Ampadu on loan from Arsenal. The gamble failed miserably. Hartlepool reject Williams didn't score in any of the remaining games and was a big disappointment, especially considering the large fee placed on his head, although he was capped by Northern Ireland.

From the final 27 points, Albion mustered a meagre 13, drawing each of their last five games, all 1-1. They even missed two penalties in the home game against Port Vale, and perhaps relegation was on the cards after they failed to beat

fellow relegation battlers Watford and Hull City.

Consequently, following their 18th draw of the season — on the last Saturday at Twerton Park against Bristol Rovers (Gould's former club) in a game which Albion had to win to stay up — Third Division football came to West Brom for the first time in 112 years, and it was a real stunner for everyone associated with this famous old club.

On reflection, Albion's home form let them down badly — they picked up only 32 points out of a possible 69, winning just seven of their 23 matches. Conceding late goals also proved to be catastrophic, and in the end they got what they deserved.

It was shattering to think that in 1991-2, Albion would be playing the likes of Chester City, Darlington (briefly a non-League team two years earlier), Exeter City, Hartlepool United, Peterborough and Wigan Athletic, when ten years earlier, under Ron Atkinson's reign, they had finished fourth in the First Division and qualified for the UEFA Cup. During the next season they had reached two major Cup semi-finals. How times had changed.

The 1991-2 season turned out to be the most turbulent in club's history — and it ended in sheer frustration and total disappointment as Albion missed out on the play-offs, finishing seventh in Division Three, their lowest-ever League position.

Manager Bobby Gould attempted to win promotion with the same band of

players who had been relegated from the Second Division the season before. Alas, for a number of reasons, including selling star striker Don Goodman to Sunderland for £900,000 in December, Gould did not prove popular and although Albion went top of the table in early February, following an emphatic 3-0 win at Birmingham, there followed a shattering demise with the fans calling for both the manager and the board to resign.

Results during the second half of the season were, in the main, disastrous. Indeed, Albion won only seven of their last 23 matches (only five in 21 before the final two games) and after a humiliating home defeat at the hands of Hartlepool United, one disgruntled fan summed the situation up thus: "We've reached rock bottom now . . .let's pack 'em all off and start again." The team simply fell apart under pressure and when Gould sacked his coach, Stuart Pearson, there was uproar amongst the supporters. Things went from bad to worse and although Bob Taylor, a £300,000 capture from Bristol City, and Wayne Fereday, signed from AFC Bournemouth, added a little bit of extra bite, Albion could not stay in contention with the leading group.

They had been the bookies' favourites to regain their Second Division status at the first attempt — and, indeed, they got off to a flying start, beating Exeter City 6-3 at The Hawthorns on the opening Saturday. And even an early exit from the Rumbelows Cup (when they were knocked out by Swindon Town) hardly

# Setting off in Style

## ALBION 6   EXETER CITY 3

ALBION'S first-ever game in the Third Division produced nine goals, two penalties and a feast of attacking football, all witnessed by a sun-drenched crowd of almost 13,000 on 17 August 1991.

Albion boss Bobby Gould gave goalkeeper Allan Miller, a loan signing from Arsenal, his debut in place of the injured Stuart Naylor. The Albion boss preferred Adrian Foster to big Paul Williams in an attack which also contained Gary Bannister and Don Goodman. Gary Robson was also ruled out through injury.

Albion had most of the early play and Kwame Ampadu went close with a shot which hit the legs of the Exeter 'keeper. Then three corners came Albion's way in the space of seven minutes. From the second, Goodman had a half-chance but was foiled by a strong tackle from Daniels.

Then, approaching the 15-minute mark, with Exeter under pressure, Darren Bradley got in a shot which was quickly followed by a forceful header from Goodman.

With Craig Shakespeare dictating things in midfield, Albion continued to press forward and Goodman went close yet again with a curling shot towards the far corner before hammering the rebound against Malloy's legs.

On 29 minutes, Albion deservedly took the lead. Adrian Foster broke clear, only to be floored by the 'keeper inside the area, and Shakespeare stepped up to slam home the spot-kick.

Daniels and Goodman were both booked as the contest hotted up and then, totally against the run of play, Exeter grabbed an equaliser on 43 minutes when Mark Cooper (soon to join Birmingham City) crashed in a superb volley from Steve Moran's right-wing cross. But within 30 seconds, Albion regained the lead, thanks to another Shakespeare penalty after O'Donnell had brought down the dangerous Goodman.

At the start of the second half, Bernard McNally replaced Ampadu and was soon in the action, setting up first Tony Ford and then Goodman. Albion, now well in command, stepped up a gear and on 62 minutes, Goodman latched on to Graham Harbey's pin-point pass to drill a shot wide of Malloy.

Two minutes later, the lethal striker leapt head and shoulders above the Exeter defence to nod Foster's cross home to make it 4-1.

Exeter were under siege and with 15 minutes remaining, Foster tapped in substitute Williams' unselfish pass. Foster soon returned to compliment, Williams scoring his first goal for the club with a powerful header to make it six.

All credit to Alan Ball's Exeter side, though. They never gave up and pulled two goals back right at the death as Albion's back-four dozed. First Moran chipped the ball over Miller, then Marshall rammed home a left-foot rocket from fully 30 yards out on the right.

Albion, though, had started their Third Division campaign off in style and the signs were good, especially up front where Goodman looked so sharp and decisive.

**Don Goodman claims Albion's fourth goal against the Grecians.**

**Paul Williams heads number six against Exeter. It was his first goal for Albion.**

**Albion:** Miller; Bradley, Harbey, Ford, Strodder, Burgess, Bannister, Goodman(P.Williams), Foster, Shakespeare, Ampadu(McNally).
**Exeter City:** Malloy; Hiley, Brown, S.Williams, Daniels, O'Donnell, Rowbotham, Cooper, Moran, Kelly, Marshall. Subs: Cole and Shaughnessy.
*Ref: Mr.K.Breen (Liverpool).*          *Att: 12,892.*

mattered as League results remained favourable.

Albion headed the table in mid-October and made progress in both the Autoglass Trophy and the FA Cup, hammering Marlow 6-0 in the latter competition. But then came that collapse! The fans were devastated — yet they stayed loyal to the end and the average attendance at The Hawthorns that season was almost 13,000 — 1,000 up on the previous campaign.

A staggering 34 players were used by Gould during the campaign with only one ever-present, left-back Graham Harbey who was subsequently transferred to Stoke City.

Craig Shakespeare top-scored with 12 goals in League and Cup; Gary Robson netted 11 and Taylor hit eight (in 19 games), giving a clear indication that he was to become the star man in Albion's attack in 1992-3.

At the end of the season, Gould and

club chairman John Silk both resigned, being replaced by the former Tottenham Hotspur and Argentinian World Cup star Ossie Ardiles and Trevor Summers respectively. Ardiles also brought in Keith Burkinshaw (who had been his manager at White Hart Lane) and physiotherapist Danny Thomas, another former Spurs player.

Before he had settled into his office seat, Ardiles set about the task of sifting through his squad — and he decided to unload a fair proportion of his professional players. Out went proven goalscorer Gary Bannister, who was eventually signed by Nottingham Forest and moved on to Stoke City in May 1993, where he teamed up with his former Albion colleague, left-back Graham Harbey, who had left West Brom for the Victoria Ground shortly after the 1991-2 campaign had ended.

Utility man Steve Parkin was transferred to Mansfield Town; centre-back Darren Rogers was taken on a free transfer by Birmingham City; goalkeeper Jonathon Gould moved to Coventry City, where his father was manager; experienced defender and former England international Graham Roberts was released and later joined non-League Enfield; striker Adrian Foster went south to Torquay United; midfielder Dave Pritchard was secured by Telford United; utility forward Les Palmer was taken on by non-Leaguers Kidderminster Harriers; and little winger Stewart Bowen also went to Coventry City (on trial) and later played for Telford United.

Within a matter of days, the former Argentinian World Cup star had recruited four new players, one from outside the Football League. He brought in midfielder Ian Hamilton from Scunthorpe United for £160,000, left-back Steve Lilwall from Kidderminster Harriers for £70,000, Blackburn Rovers' champion goalscorer Simon Garner, who cost a bargain £30,000, and goalkeeper Tony Lange on a free transfer from neighbours Wolverhampton Wanderers, who took over from Naylor during the last quarter of the season.

There was certainly an air of anticipation — and, indeed, optimism — surrounding The Hawthorns as the start of the 1992-3 season approached. So enthusiastic were the fans that the three home friendly matches against FA Premier League opposition in Sheffield Wednesday, Tottenham Hotspur and Blackburn Rovers attracted a total of almost 20,000 supporters.

The scene was set then for Albion — and Ardiles — to embark on a new venture, that of trying to win promotion, and a sun-drenched crowd of over 16,500 saw the Baggies get off to a flying start, beating Blackpool 3-1 at home on the first Saturday of the new League campaign when Ardiles fielded the following team: Stuart Naylor (who reached the milestone of 300 senior appearances for the club during the course of the season); Wayne Fereday, 'rookie' Steve Lilwall; teenager Roy Hunter (in for the suspended Darren Bradley), Gary Strodder, Craig Shakespeare; Simon Garner, Ian Hamilton, Bob Taylor (who scored twice against the Seasiders), Bernard McNally and Gary Robson. Kwame Ampadu and Simeon Hodson were on the bench, the latter teaming up with Mansfield Town (via Doncaster Rovers) during the course of the season.

Bob Taylor went from strength to strength, having a fabulous time, grabbing almost 40 goals in beating the club's post-war scoring record of 35 in a season,

held jointly by Ronnie Allen and Jeff Astle.

Although knocked out of the Coca-Cola Cup at the first hurdle — beaten 2-1 on aggregate by Plymouth Argyle — Albion prospered in the League and they hit top spot on the second Saturday after winning 1-0 at Huddersfield, thanks to Garner's first goal for the club. In fact, the Baggies, playing terrific football, remained unbeaten in their first seven League games, Stoke City finally ending their fine opening run with a 4-3 win in a cracking contest at the Victoria Ground in mid-September.

Albion then had a poor spell, winning only one of their next five games, suffering defeats at home to Port Vale and away at lowly Wigan and mid-table Burnley, all by narrow margins.

They relinquished top spot to Stoke for a while, but regained pole position in November after beating Hull City and Hartlepool United in quick succession. And, in fact, that was the last time Albion topped the Second Division table during 1992-3.

Around this juncture, former England striker Luther Blissett was taken on loan from Watford; young full-back Stacey Coldicott was contesting the number-two position with Fereday and Daryl Burgess, who was slowly regaining fitness after injury problems, and Paul Raven had lodged himself firmly into a central defensive role, alongside Strodder.

Albion, despite a few hiccups here and there, maintained their overall form, and they started their FA Cup campaign with a crushing 8-0 home win over luckless Aylesbury United with new midfield signing Kevin Donovan (bought from Huddersfield Town) scoring a hat-trick on his debut in the competition for the Baggies.

Four successive League draws followed that Cup triumph before Wycombe Wanderers were ousted in the second round, Albion going through 1-0 after a replay, having been held 2-2 by the GMVC champions-elect in the first game in front of the live TV cameras.

Before the turn of the year, Alan Dickens (from Chelsea) had replaced Blissett as the on-loan signing and not a single goal was conceded in five matches as Ardiles seemed to have sorted out his defence.

An exit from the FA Cup was eventually suffered at the hands of a skilful West Ham United side, who won a third-round tie 2-0 at The Hawthorns in front of a near-26,000 crowd. But Albion quickly got over that set-back and duly whipped Walsall 4-0 at home in their first Autoglass Trophy game of the season. They followed up with a vital 3-1 home win over promotion-chasing Bolton Wanderers in the League and a 3-2 success at Exeter — this after the Baggies had been 2-0 down with time fast running out.

Almost 30,000 spectators (paying new record receipts of over £182,000) saw the return home League game against Stoke City, but it was the travelling fans from the Potteries who went away happy, Albion losing 2-1 to the eventual Second Division champions.

The former Scottish international forward David Speedie, once of Chelsea, Coventry City, Liverpool and Bir-

**Bob Taylor celebrates his second and Albion's third goal against Stoke early in the season. But the Potters won 4-3 and eventually went up as champions whilst Albion made it via the play-offs.**

mingham City, signed on loan from Southampton, was now in the side, and he went on to score twice in nine games, including the match-winner at Bournemouth as Albion bounced back after that defeat by Stoke. Speedie, of course, was to move on, enjoying promotion to the Premier League as a loan player with West Ham United.

A few indifferent results interrupted Albion's progress, though, and they went out of the Autoglass Trophy to the holders, Stoke City. This defeat was followed by a 5-1 hammering at Stockport County, for whom Paul Williams scored, this after he had returned to Edgeley Park for just £25,000 after his disappointing spell with Albion. And Port Vale also completed the double over the Baggies, winning 2-1 at Vale Park in a game that had sunshine, showers and snow — and a cracking goal from Ian Hamilton.

Nicky Reid, the former Manchester City player, was now bedded in at The Hawthorns, having moved south from Blackburn Rovers, and just before that débâcle at Stockport, Ardiles had signed (initially on loan, finally completing the £100,000 transfer in the summer) the tall Newcastle United striker Andy Hunt — and what a great start he made to his career with Albion, scoring on his first outing (at Bradford City on 28 March) and then claiming a rapid-fire seven-minute hat-trick on his home debut against Brighton six days later — the first Baggies player to achieve this feat for almost 80 years!

Thankfully in-form, and now the fans' favourite son, Bob Taylor, was also continuing to hit the target, and in their last 15 League games of 1992-3 — when the pressure was really on — Albion lost only twice, one of them a 5-2 humiliation at home to their 'bogey' side Plymouth over Easter. This result shook everyone rigid at The Hawthorns, but gutsy Albion hit back immediately and easily clinched fourth place in the table behind Stoke City, Bolton Wanderers and Port Vale, thus qualifying for the end-of-season promotion play-offs.

Albion were paired with Swansea City in the 'semi-final', playing the first leg away at a rainswept Vetch Field on Sunday, 16 May. A fair-sized crowd of almost 14,000, including around 4,500 Albion followers (plus another 2,750 at the National Indoor Arena in Birmingham where the game was beamed back live on a giant TV screen) witnessed the contest, which the Swans deservedly won 2-1.

Albion simply failed to adapt to the conditions and in truth, did not perform anywhere near their best. The home side led 2-0 at one stage, but an own-goal by Andy McFarlane, after Daryl Burgess had lobbed on to the crossbar, gave Albion a fighting chance in the return leg.

Thus the scene was set for an intriguing battle at The Hawthorns three days later, and in front of a vociferous 26,000-plus crowd, Albion, without the injured Burgess (replaced by Gary Strodder) stormed through to Wembley, beating the Swans 2-0.

**Andy Hunt's first goal in the second-leg play-off game against Swansea.**

**Ian Hamilton, scorer of the second goal, Bob Taylor and Andy Hunt celebrate the victory over Swansea that put West Brom through to Wembley.**

Andy Hunt fired home Bob Taylor's low cross on ten minutes and Ian Hamilton brilliantly conjured up a second nine minutes later. Both goals coming in front of a packed Brummie Road End as Albion attacked non-stop in a thrilling first half. Despite the sending-off of Micky Mellon soon after the interval it was Albion who still pressed forward and Swansea goalkeeper Roger Freestone pulled off a string of excellent saves to keep his side in the game.

Swansea substitute Colin West, a former Albion player, was then dismissed for stamping on Hamilton as the pace hotted up and both Hunt and skipper Darren Bradley missed easy one-on-one chances to sew things up for the Baggies. With the crowd chanting, "Wember-ley, Wember-ley, Wember-ley," and Albion still driving forward, referee Allan Gunn sounded the final whistle amidst scenes of jubilation — Albion were at Wembley for the first time in 23 years, and the celebrations continued long into the night.

Port Vale won through to meet Albion

at Wembley Stadium on Sunday, 30 May — to decide who would gain a place in the First Division in 1993-4.

The atmosphere at Wembley was quite stupendous with some 42,000 Albion supporters completely outnumbering the Vale fans in the 53,471 crowd.

And what a terrific 'May Day' it turned out to be for Albion, their 41-year-old manager and, indeed, the vast army of supporters who celebrated long into the night — and for the next couple of days — after Port Vale, who had a man sent off, were beaten 3-0 for the Baggies to clinch a place in the First Division.

Ardiles said: "The sky's the limit now. We're going places. My next step is to win a place in the Premier League — and then lift a European trophy."

Trevor Summers, the bouyant Albion chairman who was a terrace supporter the last time the Baggies played at Wembley, said: "I've been on cloud ten ever since we beat Swansea in the play-off semi-final. I'm so proud to be chairman of such a great club, a club with such a marvellous history, a band of super supporters and the best management

# *Wembley Winners Again*

## ALBION 3 PORT VALE 0

PRIOR to this Second Division Play-off Final on Sunday, 30 May 1993, Albion had visited Wembley on six previous occasions and their sequence of results was quite coincidental: 1931 Won, 1935 Lost, 1954 Won, 1967 Lost, 1968 Won, 1970 Lost!

Consequently, every Baggies' supporter in the land believed that this was again Albion's year — and around 42,000 fans made the trip to the Empire Stadium for this great day out, by far the biggest army of supporters ever to watch Albion play away. Indeed, it was the fourth-best following ever recorded for a club side at Wembley.

Port Vale had been to Wembley — and won — eight days previously, beating Stockport County 2-1 in the Autoglass Trophy Final. And they had finished one place and four points higher than Albion in the Second Division table. Thus, they were the bookies' favourites, but Albion boss Ossie Ardiles and his players — along with the travelling fans — were confident that they would be victors on the day. And so it proved.

Ardiles was forced to make one change from the team which beat Swansea City in the second leg of the play-off semi-final, the experienced Nicky Reid replacing the suspended Micky Mellon, with Bernard McNally switching from right-back to midfield to accommodate the former Manchester City and Blackburn defender.

The atmosphere inside the stadium was electric, with Albion's colourful band of supporters outnumbering their Vale counterparts by almost four to one. The chant of "Boing, Boing, Baggies, Baggies" echoed around the ground for an hour before the teams appeared and the encouragement for Albion never wavered once the game had started.

Vale, with a strong wind behind them, shaded the first-half. They looked more forceful than Albion and certainly had more of the possession. Yet Tony Lange and his defenders were rarely troubled. Paul Kerr had two shots at goal: Morten Foyle got in one weak effort; Bernie Slaven managed a tame effort which went wide, and Andy Porter's long-range drive flew high over the bar.

Surprisingly, Albion had the two best chances of the half, both of them falling to Kevin Donovan, who shot high and wide after being put through by Andy Hunt and then saw his overhead kick on 44 minutes drop agonisingly wide.

It was Donovan who had the first clear-cut opening of the second half but his shot was too close to 'keeper Paul Musselwhite after he had been set up by the hard-working Bob Taylor.

Paul Raven had a header saved by Musselwhite as Albion stepped up the pace, but then came the turning point when Vale defender Peter Swan was sent off for a professional foul on Taylor in the 58th minute.

Ian Hamilton's superb flighted pass sent Taylor racing clear between Neil Aspin and Swan, and as he approached the edge of the penalty area he was tripped from behind by Swan. Referee Roger Milford, after consulting his linesman, had no alternative but to produce the red card. After this incident Albion never looked back — they had, in fact, been in control since the 46th minute — and the vital breakthrough arrived eight minutes after Swan's dismissal.

Hamilton's precise left-wing cross was headed powerfully against a post by Gary Strodder. Bob Taylor collected the rebound before switching the ball to Reid, whose cross was headed home by Hunt — his 11th goal of the season in only his 13th match for Albion.

Albion were now hungry for more and they drove forward at will, but Steve Lilwall had to be alert to get in an excellent tackle to prevent Slaven breaking free.

Bob Taylor missed an easy chance on 75 minutes, shooting straight at the goalkeeper, but seven minutes later Albion went 2-0 up when the impressive Nicky Reid rifled in his first goal for the Baggies, latching on to a pin-point pass from Donovan to bury a right-foot shot high into the net from 20 yards after having made a tremendous 50-yard run from his own half.

Substitute Nicky Cross had two efforts saved by Lange as Vale made a late, desperate surge on the Albion goal, but it was Donovan who drove the final nail into their coffin when he netted a third goal in the last minute. 'Man of the Match' Reid made another surging run down the right flank and from his low centre, Taylor got the ball out from between Dean Glover's feet for Donovan to nip in to do the business.

Darren Bradley was a proud man when he went up to collect the trophy at the end of the game — and how the fans celebrated. Albion were back . . .and over 200,000 cheered their heroes as they toured the town in an open-decked bus en route to a civic reception on the Tuesday evening after the triumph at Wembley.

**Albion:** Lange; Reid, Lilwall, Bradley, Raven, Strodder, Hunt(Garner), Hamilton, R.Taylor, McNally, Donovan. Sub: Robson (not used).
**Port Vale:** Musselwhite; Aspin, Kent(Billing), Porter, Swan, Glover, Slaven, Van der Laan(Cross), Foyle, Kerr, I.Taylor.
*Ref: Mr R.Milford (Bristol)    Att: 53,471 (Receipts £856,000)*

**Manager Ossie Ardiles with the Wembley goalscorers Nicky Reid, Andy Hunt and Kevin Donovan.**

team in the country. I see no reason why Ossie and Keith Burkinshaw can't be with us for many years to come."

Summers said that there was money available for Ardiles to strengthen the squad for 1993-4, as Albion looked forward to mouth-watering clashes with Birmingham City and Wolves, as well as other Midlands derby games against Leicester, Stoke, Derby and the two Nottingham clubs.

Alas, on 19 June, Ardiles announced that he was accepting an offer to manage Spurs in the wake of the Sugar-Venables turmoil. Albion appointed Keith Burkinshaw in his place, whilst threatening to seek £1 million compensation for the loss of Ardiles.

# Albion's Grounds — Past and Present

## The Hawthorns

DURING the summer of 1898, the Albion board set in motion the activities which were to eventually lead to the transfer of the club to The Hawthorns two years later.

The directors found a number of pitfalls in front of them before a piece of land was finally located at the corner of Halford's Lane and the adjoining Birmingham Road. Local tradesmen got wind of the news via two Albion directors, Tom Brennand and Harry Powell, who were themselves traders. Representations were made to Albion because shopkeepers feared that they would lose business on match days. Meanwhile, the board secured an option on a piece of ground on the Birmingham Road but this option was later withdrawn.

In May 1899, a meeting of shareholders was convened to consider the club's position, and a syndicate offered to put up enough money to improve the existing facilities at Stoney Lane. Nothing came of this scheme and the Albion board, under the wise leadership of Harry Keys, pressed on with their plans.

The lease on Stoney Lane expired in 1899 and by that year it was one of the worst grounds in the First Division. Because it was rented, the directors were unwilling to spend much money on it. Nevertheless, the lease was renewed for a further year while the ground committee searched around for a suitable site and on 14 May 1900, the club's seal was affixed to a 14-year lease on the field that was to become known as The Hawthorns.

Why was the new ground called The Hawthorns? It was the suggestion of the then club secretary, Frank Heaven, who noted that the area was shown on the surveyor's map as The Hawthorns Estate. As a hawthorn copse had apparently flourished there at one time, it seemed an obvious choice of name.

The field had a marshy appearance because of the presence of a brook which formed the boundary between Smethwick, Handsworth and West Bromwich but this did not deter the Albion management who forged ahead. It was a tremendous gamble but the alternative was stagnation and probable extinction at Stoney Lane.

A number of ground improvements have been made to The Hawthorns down the years. Successive Albion boards have not been slow to improve facilities at the ground but even more could have been achieved but for the crippling entertainments tax which was introduced during World War One and which was not abolished until 1959; in ten years after World War Two, Albion had to pay out £134,038 in this iniquitous tax, £17,600 in season 1954-5 alone.

### Calendar 1900-1993

**1900** Opening match played at The Hawthorns between Albion and Derby County (1-1). Steve Bloomer scored the first goal recorded at The Hawthorns.
**1904** The old Stoney Lane stand, the 'Noah's Ark', was burnt down on Guy Fawkes' Night.
**1906** A new stand was constructed at the Smethwick End.
**1911** Main stand overhauled. Banking increased on Handsworth side.
**1913** Freehold purchased for £5,350.
**1914** Halford's Lane stand extended.
**1920** Concrete terracing constructed. A concrete wall replaced wooden fencing around the playing area.
**1923** Handsworth embankment extended further back and stand heightened.
**1931** Terracing finally completed. Tip-up seats installed in wing stands. The Hawthorns Halt station on the Great Western Railway was opened on Christmas Day.
**1934** A new stand was completed at the Smethwick corner in Halford's Lane (750 extra seats).
**1935** New oak panelled tea-room constructed.
**1939** The wooden roof of the Halford's Lane stand was dismantled and replaced by asbestos sheets resting on five steel stanchions. The roof was also extended to the front of the terraces.
**1939-45** Only the bare necessities were done to the ground because building licenses could not be obtained. Even directly after the war, repairs were difficult to put into effect because of the shortage of building materials.
**1947** A new block of turnstiles erected on the Handsworth side behind the Woodman Inn.
**1949** The wooden terraces in front of the Main Stand were replaced with the extension of the front of the stand, providing 750 extra seats. First

electronic turnstile aggregator to be installed on any British sports ground was housed at The Hawthorns.
**1950** New directors' box was provided and offices and dressing-rooms were remodelled.
**1951** Eight new turnstiles introduced at the Smethwick End.
**1957** Installation of floodlights at a cost of £18,000.
**1958** A wing was added to the Main Stand at the West Bromwich end of the ground.
**1961** A new car park, for 600 cars, was opened in Middlemore Road. By September 1964 there were four car parks within 800 yards of the ground.
**1964** Rainbow Stand erected on the Handsworth side, containing over 4,000 tip-up seats, paid for with funds from the Development Association. The Handsworth Stand was re-erected on the previously uncovered bank at the Birmingham Road End.
**1965** First Throstle Club opened at The Hawthorns.
**1967** Buffet bars renovated at a cost of £20,000.
**1968** The Hawthorns Halt used for the last time in April.
**1969** First 'open' day for supporters.
**1970** Renovation of floodlights — illumination increased four-fold for colour TV transmissions.
**1976** Fourteen executive boxes erected on Handsworth side. An extra 750 paddock seats also constructed.
**1977** Executive box complex completed. Terracing reconstructed at Smethwick and Birmingham Road ends of ground. New crush barriers erected.
**1979** Commencement of new £2 million stand on the Halford's Lane side of ground (built in two phases, 1979-82).
**1983** Closure of The Hawthorns Throstle Club, situated next to The Woodman public house on the Handsworth side of the ground. Electronic scoreboard erected at Smethwick End (removed 1985).
**1985** Smethwick End stand reroofed. New safety measures installed at ground.
**1986** Crowd control video cameras installed.
**1988-92** Major safety work carried out in all areas of the ground following the tragedies at Valley Parade and Hillsborough.
**1989** Sponsors' lounge opened on the corner of the Halford's Lane Stand and Birmingham Road terracing.
**1990** During the summer the Hawthorns pitch was completely resurfaced, the old turf being sold off to supporters.
**1991** In February, a major water-pipe burst causing several thousands of pounds worth of damage to the Halford's Lane complex. In December, television pictures of Albion's FA Cup second-round tie at Leyton Orient were beamed live to The Hawthorns, two giant screens being erected in front of the Main Stand.
**1992** Roof removed above Smethwick End terracing.

## Cooper's Hill

West Bromwich Strollers (later Albion) contested their earliest kick-abouts on open land at Cooper's Hill between Walsall Street and Beeches Road, now occupied by St Philip's Church. Coats and hats were originally used as goal-posts and then a crude form of woodwork was erected with a piece of string tied to the top serving as a crossbar.

A local cricket club also played here so, to save wear and tear on the ground, the Strollers also used a pitch in Dartmouth Park. When the players went there they carried their goal-posts with them, erecting them as best as they could, with the aid of bricks. Sometimes the pitch they intended to use was already occupied on arrival

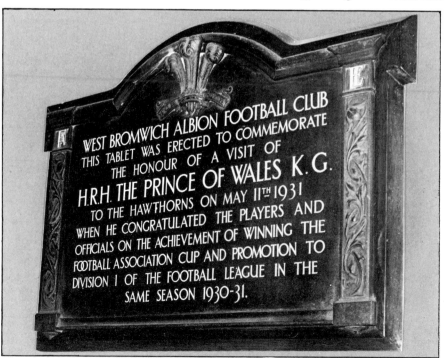

**Plaque commemorating a visit by the Prince of Wales, later King Edward VIII, to The Hawthorns.**

The Hawthorns pictured in 1904.

General view of The Hawthorns from the Woodman Corner in 1958.

so the posts had to be taken back to Beeches Road.

Albion's first recorded match at Cooper's Hill was on 20 December 1879 when Bullock's Club were overcome 4-0 by this team: S.Biddlestone; H.Bell, R.Roberts, H.Twist, E.Turner, E.T.Smith, W.Bisseker, H.Evans, J.Stanton, H.Aston, J.Round, J.Armstrong. Billy Bisseker was captain.

## Dartmouth Park

Albion played at Dartmouth Park on a regular basis in 1880-81 under skipper Jimmy Stanton. Their regular pitch was on a square near to the main entrance to the park, although occasionally a pitch was utilized at the Herbert Street end of Dartmouth Park. The teams changed at the Glebe Inn in Reform Street.

Even after Albion had transferred to Bunn's Field and The Four Acres, the occasional pre-season friendly was played in Dartmouth Park, usually against Wednesbury Old Athletic to celebrate the opening of the West Bromwich Flower Show.

## Bunn's Field

Albion's first enclosed ground was at Bunn's Field in Walsall Street (now Alfred Street), West Bromwich. The move here was made in August 1881 when a nine-month lease was taken out, and the Albion players equipped the field themselves, levelling and rolling it and then erecting goal-posts which were linked by a nailed tape which served as a crossbar. The entrance to the field was opposite Christ Church School where so many of the earliest Albion players were educated. The field was so muddy at times that supporters used to bring their own

planks to stand on in wet weather. There was no covered accommodation of any sort; indeed, one of the original Albion pioneers, Jimmy Stanton, once told the founder of the Football League, William McGregor, that the only thing resembling a grandstand was a manure heap.

The new headquarters of Albion was known as The Birches, and it was here that the club was able to charge admission to their matches for the first time. Not everyone paid to witness those early contests, however, as one of Albion's first season ticket holders, Joe Stringer, recalled many years later:

*"As a youth in those days I did not have many coppers to spend in paying for admission to football matches. But I was one of the privileged few who had the pleasure of going into the yard of Mr W.Ward's candle factory . . . fronting New*

**The Hawthorns in 1968, showing the Main Stand.**

*Street, and by standing on a wagon was able to overlook the ground and see the match for nothing."*

The players dressed at the White Hart public house which stood at the junction of Herbert Street, Bull Street and Walsall Street and for some obscure reason the changing-rooms were known as 'Charlie Lamper's'. Once they were togged out, the players went through a back-yard of the pub, over a wall and on to the pitch. More suitable dressing-rooms were subsequently found at the Roebuck Inn, at the corner of New Street and Walsall Street.

Albion's first match at The Birches is believed to be the 5-1 victory over Oldbury on 10 September 1881. Although a full fixture list for the only season at Bunn's Field is not available, it appears that Albion were a difficult side to beat on their own patch. Among the results at The Birches were a 12-0 defeat of Milton on 8 October, a 9-1 destruction of Nechells on 3 December, a 6-1 defeat of West Bromwich Rovers on 4 February, a 5-0 win over Fallings Heath Rovers on 25 February, and a 10-0 victory against St Luke's on 4 March.

Albion's colours in the only season at The Birches were yellow and white quartered jerseys with the Staffordshire knot embroidered on the front and also chocolate and blue halves. By the end of a successful first season, in which Albion reached the semi-final of the Birmingham Cup, it was found that the Dartmouth Cricket Club were willing to share their much more comfortable accommodation with the Albion and so Bunn's Field faded into the history books as Albion transferred to the Four Acres.

## The Four Acres

In September 1882, Albion moved from their primitive ground at Walsall Street to more comfortable accommodation at The Four Acres, the home of West Bromwich Dartmouth Cricket Club who played there for over 80 years after their formation in 1834.

The Four Acres was a well-known local centre

where athletics races were held at festivals and on public holidays; it was originally dedicated by William, fourth Earl of Dartmouth, for the recreation of local inhabitants.

One of the conditions Albion had imposed upon them by the Dartmouth club was that football matches could be played there on two days of the week only — Saturdays and Mondays. Season tickets at 2s 6d (12p) were issued at the start of the first season at The Four Acres. The opening fixture played there by Albion was a friendly against Stourbridge Standard on 7 October 1882 and the Throstles celebrated in style, winning 10-0 with goals from Billy Bisseker (6), John Stokes and Harry Aston (3). The Albion team was: Roberts; H.Bell, Stanton, Horton, Bunn, While, Whitehouse, Aston, Bisseker, Stokes, G.Bell.

Some improvements were made to The Four Acres in the summer of 1883 when the playing pitch was enclosed by a form of tubing instead of by ropes and wooden racks were laid around the reserve portion of the ground so that spectators could stand on them. At the Albion AGM in July 1883 it was disclosed that the Dartmouth club had agreed to let The Four Acres for a further two years at a rental of £15 per annum and to pay a third of the cost of a new ticket office and pavilion.

Albion's biggest match at The Four Acres was a sixth round FA Cup tie against Blackburn Rovers on 21 February 1885 when a crowd of 16,393 saw a thrilling confrontation. According to *The Athlete*, the spectators were 'thickly packed round the field of play, in stands temporary and stands permanent, on the walls and house-tops, everywhere, in fact, where a footing could be obtained . . .'

The optimistic Albion supporters wore in their hats a funeral card with a black border inscribed thus: 'In memoriam. Blackburn Rovers defeated in the English Cup competition, West Bromwich, February 21, 1885'. Rovers had other ideas, however, and took the lead just before half-time, whereupon (according to the Birmingham *Daily Gazette*) 'the supporters of

the West Bromwich team immediately upon this ascended a small balloon, bearing the inscription 'Play up Albion'. This aerial injunction passed slowly over the field and was observed by the home players, who, as if in answer to its bidding, played up strenuously . . .'

At the interval, pigeons were dispatched to various Black Country locations to announce the news that Albion were trailing to the FA Cup holders. Rovers were 2-0 winners at the conclusion of the game which prompted *Saturday Night* to surround their report of the match with black lines — as if a royal personage had passed away.

Even as this Cup tie was being played, the Albion committee were on the look-out for new premises as The Four Acres (now part of Park Crescent in Seager Street) was already too small for the club's requirements. The last senior match Albion contested at The Four Acres before the move to Stoney Lane in the summer of 1885 was against Wednesbury Old Athletic on 6 April 1885, when this team wore the cardinal and blue halves: Roberts; H.Bell, Green, Horton, Bunn, Bradbury, Woodhall, Aston, Smith, Loach, G.Bell. Albion were 3-2 winners.

**The Four Acres Facts and Figures**
**Record Victory** 26-0 v Coseley, Birmingham Cup 1st round, 11 Nov 1882.
**Record defeat** 5-1 v Stoke, Friendly, 20 Oct 1882.
**Most goals by one player** Six, by W.Bisseker (v Stourbridge Standard, 1882) and by H.Aston (v Birmingham Junior Association, 1883).

Complete playing record:

| P | W | D | L | F | A |
|---|---|---|---|---|---|
| 61 | 48 | 6 | 7 | 268 | 56 |

In three seasons Albion played 22 Cup ties at the ground, in the FA Cup, Staffordshire, Birmingham and Wednesbury Charity Cups. Albion were defeated only twice.

## Stoney Lane

In the playing sense Stoney Lane was the headquarters of the Albion club from 1885 to

1900, but the Throstles' administration was dealt with at the nearby Plough & Harrow public house and afterwards at offices in High Street, West Bromwich.

The move from The Four Acres to Stoney Lane came about in 1885 because the Albion committee wanted more spacious accommodation in keeping with the growing reputation of the club. A ground committee was established and a number of sites were inspected before it was decided to lease a field at the back of the Sandwell Brewery in Stoney Lane.

It was not far from the Four Acres and close to the club's headquarters at the Plough & Harrow. On 27 February 1885 the committee were authorized to secure the tenancy of the field which belonged to the local undertaker, Mr Webb. The lease was for a seven-year term at an annual rent of £28 and work was begun almost immediately to convert the field into a suitable home for Albion.

The field was returfed and levelled and ashes were laid around the ground which was 120 yards long by 82 yards wide, the playing area being 110 yards by 78. A wooden grandstand was erected with planking serving as seats and it became affectionately known as the 'Noah's Ark'. It was on the Sandwell Road side of the ground (the brewery side) and the centre, which was covered, allowed for 600 people. The uncovered portions at each end accommodated a further 1,500 spectators. The opposite side of the ground was covered in ash and it was gradually raised towards the back so that everyone had a good view although it had no covered accommodation of any sort. Fencing and a boundary wall were also put in place and two simply furnished brick 'dressing tents', sporting corrugated iron roofs, were also constructed. Three refreshment stalls were added. Wagonettes and other vehicles were permitted to drive into the ground and were stationed behind the bank at the Stoney Lane entrance.

The pitch had a pronounced slope towards the Stoney Lane end of the ground and the sight of Albion's attack in full cry down the gradient gave many a goalkeeper the jitters. At first there were five pay boxes situated in Stoney Lane but these were found to be inefficient, so admission was gained by purchasing tickets through openings in the walls. On the opposite side of the road from the ground, tickets could also be purchased at the Plough & Harrow and, on important match-days, neighbouring houses were utilized to sell tickets. The cost of equipping the ground was £370 and to help pay for the cost, Albion arranged a series of home friendlies in September 1885.

In future years the standards slumped at Stoney Lane because the directors were reluctant to spend much money on a ground which was only rented and in time it became the poorest Division One ground for amenities.

The first season-tickets at Stoney Lane cost five shillings (25p) and Albion's total gate receipts in their opening campaign there amounted to £1,190. The first groundsman was a Mr Russell who was paid the princely sum of five shillings (25p) a week. The usual admission charge to matches at Stoney Lane was sixpence in old money.

The opening fixture at Stoney Lane was a friendly against Third Lanark Rifle Volunteers of Glasgow on 5 September 1885 and the Albion selection was: Roberts; H.Bell, H.Green, Horton, Bunn, Timmins, Woodhall, Bayliss, T.Green, Lavender, G.Bell. Albion were 4-1 winners with goals from T.Green (3) and Woodhall. Tom Green was the scorer of the first goal on the ground after five minutes play.

The first team to win at Stoney Lane was Burnley (3-0) on 23 November 1885 and the same club took part in the first Football League fixture there, on 29 September 1888. Albion said goodbye to Stoney Lane on 16 April 1900, defeating Nottingham Forest 8-0 in a Division One game. Preston North End were the most successful visitors to the ground in League matches, winning six times. Aston Villa and Sunderland were also rather successful with five wins apiece.

Albion played over 350 games at Stoney Lane, winning 223 of them and losing only 70. They scored almost 900 goals and were undefeated in 14 consecutive FA Cup games between 1885 and 1893.

# Attendances at The Hawthorns

FIGURES given in this section have been taken from the official records of the club and may differ from those published in certain newspapers. Today, for safety reasons, the official capacity of The Hawthorns is a shade under 32,000. Yet before World War Two it was said that 70,000 fans could have been packed into the ground.

However, obvious and necessary ground improvements, including the insertion of extra seats — there are now 10,865 — have cut the official capacity quite dramatically, especially over the last 25 years.

The biggest attendance for a soccer match at The Hawthorns was on Saturday, 6 March 1937, when Albion beat Arsenal 3-1 in a sixth round FA Cup tie. That day 64,815 spectators paid £3,914 in receipts to see the action. The top League 'gate' at The Hawthorns — 60,945 — gathered on Saturday, 4 March 1950, for the Albion-Wolves First Division game. The best Second Division audience was the 52,415 for the Albion-Charlton Athletic match on 2 May 1931 — the day Albion clinched that wonderful Cup and promotion double. In the Football League Cup, Walsall were Albion's visitors for a second round tie on 22 September 1965, when a record 41,188 supporters flocked to The Hawthorns to see Albion win 3-1 under floodlights.

**These are the 'top ten' crowds at The Hawthorns:**

| | | | |
|---|---|---|---|
| 1. 64,815 v Arsenal | FA Cup | 6 Mar 1937 |
| 2. 64,612 v Aston Villa | FA Cup | 21 Feb 1925 |
| 3. 61,088 v Newcastle United | FA Cup | 20 Feb 1954 |
| 4. 60,945 v Wolves | Div One | 4 Mar 1950 |
| 5. 59,674 v Aston Villa | Div One | 14 Nov 1931 |
| 6. 59,448 v Portsmouth | FA Cup | 28 Jan 1956 |
| 7. 58,163 v Nottingham Forest | FA Cup | 25 Jan 1958 |
| 8. 57,843 v Chelsea | FA Cup | 12 Feb 1949 |
| 9. 57,574 v Manchester United | FA Cup | 1 Mar 1958 |
| 10. 57,503 v Sheffield United | FA Cup | 19 Feb 1958 |

**And the ten lowest 'gates' at The Hawthorns:**

| | | | |
|---|---|---|---|
| 1. 1,050 v Sheffield United | Div One | 30 Apr 1901 |
| 2. 1,206 v Burton United | Div Two | 5 Apr 1902 |
| 3. 1,495 v Nottingham Forest | Div Two | 19 Mar 1930 |
| 4. 2,072 v Gainsborough T | Div Two | 28 Jan 1905 |
| 5. 2,366 v Bradford City | Div Two | 25 Mar 1905 |
| 6. 2,533 v Leeds City | Div Two | 6 Jan 1906 |
| 7. 2,675 v Barnsley | Div Two | 17 Dec 1904 |
| 8. 3,103 v Blackpool | Div Two | 16 Apr 1910 |
| 9. 3,104 v Leicester Fosse | Div Two | 8 Apr 1905 |
| 10. 3,109 v Norwich City | Div Two | 29 Apr 1939 |

**This table shows how The Hawthorns crowd record has been broken down the years.**

| | | | |
|---|---|---|---|
| 20,104 | Albion v Derby County | 3 Sep 1900 | Div One |
| 35,417 | Albion v Aston Villa | 8 Sep 1900 | Div One |
| 35,529 | Albion v Derby County | 23 Feb 1907 | FAC Rd 3 |
| 36,727 | Albion v Birmingham | 11 Jan 1908 | FAC Rd 1 |
| 38,049 | Albion v Birmingham | 26 Dec 1908 | Div Two |
| 45,203 | Albion v Aston Villa | 30 Sep 1911 | Div One |
| 48,057 | Albion v Aston Villa | 4 Oct 1913 | Div One |
| 49,488 | Albion v Birmingham | 26 Dec 1921 | Div One |
| 56,474 | Albion v Sunderland | 3 Feb 1923 | FAC Rd 2 |
| 64,612 | Albion v Aston Villa | 21 Feb 1925 | FAC Rd 3 |
| 64,815 | Albion v Arsenal | 6 Mar 1937 | FAC Rd 6 |

**Crowd Facts & Figures**
The lowest FA Cup crowd for an Albion home tie is 5,230, v Leicester Fosse on 14 January 1905 (Intermediate Round).

In the League Cup, before the competition was sponsored, the smallest turnout is the 8,294 v Millwall on 10 September 1974.

A total of 6,288 fans witnessed Albion's Milk Cup clash with Port Vale at The Hawthorns on 24 September 1985.

The lowest attendance for an Albion home game in the Littlewoods Cup is 4,264 v Peterborough United on 31 August 1988.

In the Rumbelows Cup, the lowest Hawthorns crowd figure is that of 8,522 v Swindon Town on 28 August 1991.

Coca-Cola Cup attendances are, of course, so far restricted to the games played in the 1992-93 season — 8,264 for the first-round first-leg game at home to Plymouth Argyle on 19 August 1992, and 7,880 for the return leg at Home Park on 25 August that year.

There were only 1,841 fans present at Boundary Park for the Oldham-Albion Simod Cup game in November 1987 and 1,861 saw the Autoglass Trophy game at Lincoln on 4 December 1991.

Only 987 fans watched Albion's Full Members' Cup game at Millwall on 21 October 1986. And there were only 405 to see the Albion-Derby County Football League game at Stoney Lane on 29 November 1890. This is the lowest attendance ever to watch Albion, home or away, in a senior competitive match.

The lowest European attendance at The Hawthorns — 16,745 — was on 30 September 1981, when Albion played hosts to Grasshopper Zürich in the UEFA Cup.

Albion's best wartime home crowd was 38,077, against Wolverhampton Wanderers, in the Football League South on 23 April 1946 although, of course, the war had ended some months before but League football proper had not resumed.

In non-competitive football, Albion's top home gate is 55,497 against an Invitation XI for Norman Heath's benefit match on 25 April 1956.

In the Central League, Albion Reserves boast a record home crowd of 22,372, versus Aston Villa on 3 March 1934.

The attendance of 15,613 for the Albion versus Sunderland 1969 FA Youth Cup Final (first leg) is the highest below reserve team level at The Hawthorns.

**Top Twelve 'Away' Crowds**

| | | | |
|---|---|---|---|
| 1. 99,852 v Preston NE | FAC Final | 1 May 1954 |
| 2. 99,665 v Everton | FAC Final | 18 May 1968 |
| 3. 97,963 v Manchester C | FLC Final | 7 Mar 1970 |
| 4. 97,952 v Queen's Park R | FLC Final | 4 Mar 1967 |
| 5. 95,300 v Red Star Belgrade | UEFA Cup | 7 Mar 1979 |
| 6. 93,204 v Sheffield Wed | FAC Final | 27 Apr 1935 |
| 7. 90,368 v Birmingham | FAC Final | 25 Apr 1931 |
| 8. 89,400 v China XI | friendly | 19 May 1978 |
| 9. 80,500 v CDSA (USSR) | friendly | 12 Jun 1957 |
| 10. 80,000 v Peking XI | friendly | 16 May 1978 |
| 11. 80,000 v Zenit Leningrad | friendly | 1 Jun 1957 |
| 12. 71,853 v Tottenham H | FAC Rd 4 | 24 Jan 1948 |

Albion's best average home League attendance for a single season is 38,819 — set in 1949-50. The aggregate total of fans who saw the 21 home First Division matches was 815,217.

**The attendance figure was broken at the following grounds when Albion played there. The list is given in chronological order.**

*The Oval.* FA Cup Final, 1885-86, v Blackburn Rovers — 15,156

*Derby (County Ground).* FA Cup Final Replay, 1885-86, v Blackburn Rovers — 16,144

*Trent Bridge.* FA Cup semi-final, 1886-87, v Preston NE — 16,068

*The Oval.* FA Cup Final, 1886-87, v Aston Villa — 15,534

*Cape Hill, Smethwick.* FA Cup Rd 2, 1887-88, v Mitchell's St George — 7,805

*The Oval.* FA Cup Final, 1887-88, v Preston North End — 18,904

*Bramall Lane, Sheffield.* FA Cup semi-final, 1888-89, v Preston North End — 22,688

*The Links, Chatham.* FA Cup Rd 3, 1888-89, v Chatham — 17,092

*Victoria Ground, Stoke.* FA Cup semi-final, 1890-91, v Blackburn Rovers — 21,774

*Edgbaston.* Birmingham Cup, 1890-91, v Aston Villa — 12,000

*Molineux Grounds.* FA Cup Semi-final, 1891-92 v Nottingham Forest — 21,076

*The Oval.* FA Cup Final, 1891-92, v Aston Villa — 32,710

*Goodison Park.* FA Cup Rd 1, 1892-93, v Everton — 23,867

*The Crystal Palace.* FA Cup Final, 1894-95, v Aston Villa — 42,652

*Derby (County Ground).* FA Cup Semi-final, 1894-95, v Sheffield Wednesday — 25,013

*Blundell Park.* FA Cup Rd 2, 1895-96, v Grimsby Town — 7,108

*Dallow Lane, Luton.* FA Cup Rd 1, 1896-97, v Luton Town — 6,898

*Home Park, Plymouth.* Friendly, 1897-98, v Devon County — 4,000

*Baseball Ground.* Div One, 1902-03, v Derby County — 21,909

*Elland Road.* Div Two, 1905-06, v Leeds City — 6,802

*Stamford Bridge.* Div Two, 1905-06, v Chelsea — 10,123

*The Dell.* FA Cup Rd 2, 1907-08, v Southampton — 18,728

*Elland Road.* FA Cup Rd 2, 1911-12, v Leeds City — 21,320

*Roker Park.* FA Cup Rd 3, 1911-12, v Sunderland — 43,383

*Villa Park.* Div One, 1912-3, v Aston Villa — 55,064

*Elland Road.* FA Cup Rd 2, 1913-4, v Leeds City — 29,733

*Villa Park.* Div One, 1919-20, v Aston Villa — 58,273

*St James' Park, Newcastle.* Div One, 1920-21, v Newcastle United — 61,080

*Villa Park.* Div One, 1920-21, v Aston Villa — 66,094

*Goodison Park.* Div One, 1920-21, v Everton — 59,964

*Meadow Lane.* FA Cup Rd 1, 1920-21, v Notts County — 32,995

*Bowerford.* FA Cup Rd 1, 1922-23, v Stalybridge Celtic — 9,753

*The Den.* FA Cup Rd 1, 1923-24, v Millwall — 30,922

*Bramall Lane.* FA Cup Rd 4, 1924-25, v Sheffield United — 57,197

*Racecourse Ground, Wrexham.* FA Cup Rd 3 1929-30, v Wrexham — 16,570

*Old Trafford.* FA Cup Semi-final, 1930-31, v Everton — 69,241

*St Andrew's.* Div One, 1931-32, v Birmingham — 57,806

*Edgeley Park.* FA Cup Rd 5, 1934-35, v Stockport County — 24,684

*Victoria Ground, Stoke.* FA Cup semi-final, 1934-35, v Bolton Wanderers — 49,110

*Highfield Road.* FA Cup Rd 5, 1936-37, v Coventry City — 44,492

*Bootham Crescent.* FA Cup Rd 4, 1937-38, v York City — 18,795

*Sincil Bank.* FA Cup Rd 3, 1948-49, v Lincoln City — 19,602

*Redheugh Park.* FA Cup Rd 4, 1948-49, v Gateshead — 16,885

*The Dell.* Div Two, 1948-49, v Southampton — 30,856

*King's Lynn.* Benefit Match, 1952-53, v King's Lynn — 9,200

*Dean Court.* FA Cup Rd 3, 1954-55, v Bournemouth — 19,498

*City Ground.* Div One, 1957-58, v Nottingham Forest — 41,675

*City Ground.* FA Cup Rd 4, 1957-58, v Nottingham Forest — 46,455

*Tiflis, Russia.* Friendly, 1957, Dinamo Tblisi — 35,000

*National Stadium, Peking.* Friendly, 1977-78, v China XI — 89,400

*St Martin's Ground, Guernsey.* Friendly, 1978-79, v Birmingham City — 4,400

*Marriott's Close Stadium, Witney.* Benefit Match, 1978-79, v Nottingham Forest — 3,558

On 26 December 1933, Albion's 'A' team played a home game at The Hawthorns against Cheltenham Town in a Birmingham Combination fixture — and a record crowd of 3,340 turned up to see it.

In their 1957-58 FA Cup run, Albion were watched by a total of 227,263 spectators in four home ties — which gave an average of 56,816 per game.

Albion played four away games against Tottenham Hotspur between January 1947 and January 1949 — three in the League and one in the FA Cup. The four-match crowd total was a staggering 226,459, and at the time both teams were in the Second Division.

The best attendance figure for an-opening-of-season match at The Hawthorns is 49,596 (receipts £5,133) for Albion's First Division 'return' match against Charlton Athletic on 20 August 1949.

The lowest 'opening day' crowd is 4,123 — Albion v Grimsby, Div Two, 10 September 1904.

The lowest attendance figure for any Albion home League game (September 1888 to date) is a mere 405 — for the visit of Derby County to Stoney Lane in a First Division match on 29 November, 1890.

Albion's average home Football League 'gate' (September 1888 to May 1993) is 19,136 (aggregate 35,650,383 from 1,863 matches excluding Test Matches and Play-Offs).

The average home League attendance at The Hawthorns (September 1900 to May 1993 is 20,493 (1,693 matches, aggregate 34,695,898).

In the FA Cup, Albion's average home 'gate' (1883 to 1993) is 27,547 (159 ties, aggregate 4,380,051).

And in the Football League Cup (including all its sponsored forms to 1993) the average crowd for an Albion game at The Hawthorns is 18,141 (50 matches, aggregate 907,062).

**Albion's home League attendances 1888 to 1993 inclusive:**

| Season | P | Ave | Agg | Largest | Smallest |
| --- | --- | --- | --- | --- | --- |
| 1888-99 | 11 | 4,582 | 50,409 | 8,515 | 2,079 |
| 1889-90 | 11 | 5,241 | 57,650 | 10,122 | 1,550 |
| 1890-91 | 11 | 4,418 | 48,605 | 8,537 | 405 |
| 1891-92 | 13 | 7,162 | 93,114 | 14,185 | 1,109 |
| 1892-93 | 15 | 4,620 | 69,301 | 11,239 | 607 |
| 1893-94 | 15 | 5,123 | 76,852 | 13,997 | 2,024 |
| 1894-95 | 15 | 6,921 | 103,818 | 19,720 | 2,535 |
| 1895-96 | 15 | 5,711 | 85,671 | 17,510 | 560 |
| 1896-97 | 15 | 5,857 | 87,855 | 10,291 | 1,105 |
| 1897-98 | 15 | 7,006 | 105,102 | 12,244 | 3,455 |
| 1898-99 | 17 | 4,879 | 82,955 | 15,896 | 1,571 |
| 1899-1900 | 17 | 5,491 | 93,353 | 14,905 | 1,717 |
| 1900-01 | 17 | 11,938 | 202,950 | 35,417 | 1,050 |
| 1901-02 | 17 | 7,822 | 132,974 | 23,697 | 1,206 |
| 1902-03 | 17 | 15,657 | 266,176 | 28,536 | 4,148 |
| 1903-04 | 17 | 12,651 | 215,057 | 31,418 | 4,467 |
| 1904-05 | 17 | 4,884 | 83,032 | 10,105 | 2,072 |
| 1905-06 | 19 | 8,637 | 164,093 | 23,021 | 2,533 |
| 1906-07 | 19 | 12,126 | 230,397 | 25,562 | 5,034 |
| 1907-08 | 19 | 11,100 | 210,902 | 30,026 | 4,140 |
| 1908-09 | 19 | 17,845 | 339,061 | 38,049 | 4,982 |
| 1909-10 | 19 | 11,705 | 222,398 | 30,104 | 3,103 |
| 1910-11 | 19 | 15,601 | 296,427 | 30,135 | 3,577 |
| 1911-12 | 19 | 18,042 | 342,803 | 46,203 | 3,122 |
| 1912-13 | 19 | 17,047 | 323,908 | 40,589 | 6,565 |
| 1913-14 | 19 | 20,629 | 391,948 | 48,057 | 12,057 |
| 1914-15 | 19 | 10,823 | 205,657 | 19,492 | 4,410 |
| 1919-20 | 21 | 30,532 | 641,187 | 43,579 | 19,058 |
| 1920-21 | 21 | 27,802 | 583,835 | 44,023 | 17,242 |
| 1921-22 | 21 | 21,691 | 455,514 | 49,488 | 11,026 |
| 1922-23 | 21 | 18,817 | 395,152 | 39,576 | 5,520 |
| 1923-24 | 21 | 17,381 | 365,010 | 42,096 | 8,003 |
| 1924-25 | 21 | 20,596 | 432,522 | 41,990 | 9,892 |
| 1925-26 | 21 | 18,595 | 390,507 | 52,322 | 8,287 |
| 1926-27 | 21 | 21,710 | 455,919 | 50,392 | 10,043 |
| 1927-28 | 21 | 19,596 | 411,517 | 37,342 | 8,116 |
| 1928-29 | 21 | 13,220 | 277,263 | 24,902 | 6,994 |
| 1929-30 | 21 | 14,023 | 294,501 | 25,221 | 1,495 |
| 1930-31 | 21 | 21,722 | 456,179 | 52,415 | 11,037 |
| 1931-32 | 21 | 24,251 | 509,284 | 59,674 | 7,796 |
| 1932-33 | 21 | 22,799 | 478,781 | 45,038 | 8,933 |
| 1933-34 | 21 | 20,078 | 421,647 | 32,660 | 10,493 |
| 1934-35 | 21 | 22,350 | 469,342 | 44,503 | 10,420 |
| 1935-36 | 21 | 23,064 | 484,345 | 42,402 | 7,893 |
| 1936-37 | 21 | 21,707 | 455,855 | 33,962 | 7,022 |
| 1937-38 | 21 | 23,246 | 488,183 | 55,444 | 8,028 |
| 1938-39 | 21 | 18,467 | 387,828 | 30,943 | 3,109 |
| 1946-47 | 21 | 24,642 | 517,498 | 42,031 | 10,506 |
| 1947-48 | 21 | 30,856 | 647,985 | 51,945 | 13,349 |
| 1948-49 | 21 | 33,379 | 700,961 | 47,028 | 13,009 |
| 1949-50 | 21 | 38,819 | 815,217 | 60,945 | 16,780 |
| 1950-51 | 21 | 31,082 | 652,741 | 44,543 | 17,912 |
| 1951-52 | 21 | 29,712 | 623,962 | 47,782 | 18,903 |
| 1952-53 | 21 | 31,527 | 662,063 | 54,480 | 16,250 |
| 1953-54 | 21 | 38,279 | 803,852 | 53,210 | 20,306 |
| 1954-55 | 21 | 31,247 | 656,201 | 51,853 | 7,764 |
| 1955-56 | 21 | 26,922 | 565,361 | 45,306 | 16,141 |
| 1956-57 | 21 | 23,343 | 490,217 | 37,255 | 6,397 |
| 1957-58 | 21 | 32,558 | 683,717 | 56,904 | 16,518 |
| 1958-59 | 21 | 31,547 | 662,495 | 48,898 | 17,071 |
| 1959-60 | 21 | 27,504 | 577,595 | 40,739 | 12,204 |
| 1960-61 | 21 | 24,707 | 518,840 | 41,903 | 15,099 |
| 1961-62 | 21 | 20,998 | 440,953 | 39,071 | 13,894 |
| 1962-63 | 21 | 18,637 | 391,381 | 32,450 | 10,759 |
| 1963-64 | 21 | 20,552 | 431,601 | 37,189 | 10,715 |
| 1964-65 | 21 | 19,405 | 407,508 | 28,504 | 10,511 |
| 1965-66 | 21 | 19,781 | 415,414 | 29,669 | 13,079 |
| 1966-67 | 21 | 23,352 | 490,393 | 37,969 | 16,832 |
| 1967-68 | 21 | 25,837 | 542,580 | 45,992 | 15,490 |
| 1968-69 | 21 | 25,091 | 526,924 | 38,299 | 16,483 |
| 1969-70 | 21 | 27,871 | 585,309 | 45,120 | 18,512 |
| 1970-71 | 21 | 25,691 | 539,526 | 41,134 | 12,684 |
| 1971-72 | 21 | 25,784 | 541,471 | 46,992 | 16,702 |
| 1972-73 | 21 | 21,438 | 450,207 | 39,209 | 12,215 |
| 1973-74 | 21 | 16,001 | 336,023 | 43,119 | 11,456 |
| 1974-75 | 21 | 12,679 | 266,260 | 29,614 | 7,812 |
| 1975-76 | 21 | 17,233 | 361,900 | 26,640 | 10,496 |
| 1976-77 | 21 | 24,523 | 514,995 | 41,867 | 16,434 |
| 1977-78 | 21 | 24,133 | 506,798 | 36,067 | 17,053 |
| 1978-79 | 21 | 26,702 | 560,745 | 35,166 | 17,499 |
| 1979-80 | 21 | 22,735 | 477,442 | 35,093 | 11,735 |
| 1980-81 | 21 | 20,382 | 428,038 | 34,195 | 14,833 |
| 1981-82 | 21 | 16,851 | 353,874 | 23,378 | 11,733 |
| 1982-83 | 21 | 15,260 | 320,460 | 25,331 | 9,221 |
| 1983-84 | 21 | 14,620 | 307,037 | 27,954 | 10,313 |
| 1984-85 | 21 | 13,958 | 293,132 | 26,401 | 7,423 |
| 1985-86 | 21 | 12,194 | 256,076 | 25,068 | 6,021 |
| 1986-87 | 21 | 9,280 | 194,893 | 15,329 | 6,198 |
| 1987-88 | 22 | 10,126 | 222,780 | 22,072 | 7,303 |
| 1988-89 | 23 | 12,766 | 293,618 | 21,316 | 7,248 |
| 1989-90 | 23 | 11,313 | 260,199 | 21,316 | 8,017 |
| 1990-91 | 23 | 12,001 | 276,023 | 28,495 | 7,657 |
| 1991-92 | 23 | 12,707 | 292,263 | 26,168 | 8,439 |
| 1992-93 | 23 | 15,174 | 349,016 | 29,341 | 12,305 |

# England at The Hawthorns

England have played two full international matches at The Hawthorns — in 1922 and 1924 — and one Victory international in 1945. Here are details of those three internationals on Albion soil, with team line-ups, results, scorers and attendances.

## England 2 Ireland 0 - 21 October 1922

*Attendance: 20,173     Goalscorer: Chambers 2*

**ENGLAND:** Taylor (Huddersfield Town); Smith (West Bromwich Albion), Harrow (Chelsea), Moss (Aston Villa), Wilson (Sheffield Wednesday), Grimsdell (Tottenham Hotspur), Mercer (Sheffield United), Seed (Tottenham Hotspur), Osborne (Fulham), Chambers (Liverpool), Williams (Clapton Orient).

**IRELAND:** Harland (Linfield); Rollo (Blackburn Rovers), Curran (Pontypridd), Emerson (Burnley), Smith (Cardiff City), Morgan (Linfield), Lyner (Manchester United), Irvine (Everton), Nellis (Nottingham Forest), Gillespie (Sheffield United), Burns (Glenavon).

Both goals came in the second-half after an even first 45 minutes. The deadlock was broken in the 66th minute when Harry Chambers, who later played for Albion, forced home Mercer's right-wing corner. Six minutes from time the same player, put through by Williams, netted past Harland's right hand with a sweetly struck shot from 15 yards.

## England 4 Belgium 0 - 8 December 1924

*Attendance: 15,405 Goalscorers: Bradford 2, Walker 2*

**ENGLAND:** Hardy (Stockport County); Ashurst (Notts County), Bower (Corinthians), Magee (West Bromwich Albion), Butler (Arsenal), Ewer (The Casuals), Osborne (Tottenham Hotspur), Roberts (Manchester City), Bradford (Birmingham), Walker (Aston Villa), Dorrell (Aston Villa).

**BELGIUM:** Debie (R.Racing C.B.); Swartenbroeks (Daring C.B.), Baes (C.S. Brugge), Cnudde (Union St.Gilliose), Augustus (Antwerp), Braine (Beerschot), Dries (Berchen), Gillis (Stannard), Adams (Anderlecht), Grimonprez (R.C.Gand), Bastin (Antwerp).

Although the scoreline suggests that this was an easy victory for England, the Belgians put up a tremendous fight and deserved better reward for their efforts. But England took their chances well, despite a missed penalty by Villa's Billy Walker.

It was Walker, in fact, who set up England's first goal in the 17th minute, his pass finding Joe Bradford who netted from fully 25 yards. On the hour Bradford set up Walker for goal number-two and immediately afterwards Bradford ran on to Ewer's through ball to make it 3-0. Ten minutes from time Osborne and Roberts linked well down the right and Walker finished off in style.

## England 0 Wales 1 - 20 October 1945

*Attendance: 54,611          Goalscorer: Powell*

**ENGLAND:** Williams (Wolves); Scott (Arsenal), Kinsell (West Bromwich Albion), Soo (Leicester City), Franklin (Stoke City), Mercer (Everton), Matthews (Stoke City), Fenton (Middlesbrough), Stubbins (Newcastle United), Barrass (Bolton Wanderers), Watson (Huddersfield Town).

**WALES:** Sidlow (Wolves); Winter (Bolton Wanderers), Hughes (Birmingham), Dearson (Birmingham), Davies (Nottingham Forest), Burgess (Tottenham Hotspur), Powell (Leeds United), Astbury (Chester), Lowrie (Coventry City), Lucas (Swindon Town), Edwards (Birmingham).

This was a tough international with two players, Harry Kinsell (England) and George Lowrie (Wales), often at loggerheads and were lucky not to be sent off. The winning goal was scored by the Leeds United outside-right, Powell, in the first-half following some good work on the left by George Edwards.

The gate receipts of £8,573 created a new record for The Hawthorns.

### International and Representative Matches at The Hawthorns

| | | |
|---|---|---|
| 7 Oct 1914 | Football League 2 Irish League 1 | (9,250) |
| 9 Feb 1920 | England 2 The South 1 | (14,427) |
| 21 Oct 1922 | England 2 Ireland 0 | (20,173) |
| 8 Dec 1924 | England 4 Belgium 0 | (15,405) |
| 23 Jan 1928 | England 5 The Rest 1 | (9,345) |
| 27 Feb 1935 | England 2 The Rest 2 | (12,845) |
| 20 Oct 1945 | England 0 Wales 1 | (54,611) |

### Other Representative Matches at The Hawthorns

| | | |
|---|---|---|
| 4 Apr 1908 | England Juniors 4 Scotland Juniors 0 | |
| 18 Apr 1925 | England Juniors 4 Scotland Juniors 1 | |
| 13 Apr 1935 | England Juniors 3 Scotland Juniors 1 | |
| 15 Mar 1972 | England Schools 1 Northern Ireland Schools 1 | |
| 9 Jan 1974 | England Youth 1 Wales Youth 0 | |
| 13 Feb 1974 | England Youth 1 Holland Youth 1 | |
| 9 Mar 1977 | England Youth 1 Wales Youth 0 | |
| 1 May 1978 | England Schools 6 Wales Schools 0 | |
| 13 May 1983 | Scotland Youth 3 USSR Youth 0 | |
| 21 Mar 1986 | England Schools 4 Scotland Schools 2 | |
| 10 Nov 1986 | England Youth 3 Sweden Youth 3 | |

### Cup Semi-finals at The Hawthorns

15 Mar 1902  Derby County 1 Sheffield United 1
FA Cup                                          (33,603)
26 Mar 1960  Wolverhampton Wanderers 1 Aston Villa 1
FA Cup                                          (55,596)
5 Apr 1967  Hendon Town 1 Skelmersdale United 3
FA Amateur Cup                                  (5,225)
18 Dec 1968  Swindon Town 3 Burnley 2
FL Cup replay                                   (20,155)
3 Apr 1971  Telford United 3 Yeovil Town 1
FA Trophy                                       (9,058)

### FA Trophy Final Replays

12 May 1987  Burton Albion 1 Kidderminster Harriers 2
(15,865)
12 May 1988  Enfield 3 Telford United 2 (6,916)

### The Hawthorns Facts and Figures

**First Match** Albion 1 Derby County 1 (Football League, Div One) 3 September 1900. Albion team: J.Reader; A.Adams, W.Williams, A.Dunn, A.Jones, H.Hadley, J.Chadburn, T.Pickering, C.Simmons, F.Wheldon, R.Roberts.
**First Albion goalscorer** 'Chippy' Simmons, against Derby County, 3 September 1900.
**First Albion League win** 3-2 v Manchester City, 6 October 1900.
**Record League victory** 9-2 v Manchester City, 21 September 1957.
**Record League defeat** 1-6 v Nottingham Forest, 20 October 1900, and v Sunderland, 23 October 1937.
**Highest attendance** 64,815 v Arsenal (FA Cup 6th round), 6 March 1937.
**Highest League attendance** 60,945 v Wolverhampton Wanderers, 4 March 1950.
**Lowest attendance** 1,050 v Sheffield United, 30 April 1901.
**Record receipts** The record receipts for a League game at The Hawthorns, of £182,293.10, came from the Second Division game against Stoke City on 23 January 1993.

**Spectators perch on top of the stand at The Hawthorns for the England-Wales wartime international.**

The record takings for an FA Cup tie are £162,705.30 v West Ham United (third round), 2 January 1993. Top League Cup receipts are £79,494.76 v Tottenham Hotspur (semi-final 1st leg), 3 February 1982.

**Points of Interest**
It is believed that The Hawthorns is the highest Football League ground, lying about 550 feet above sea-level. The next highest appear to be those of Port Vale (just two or three feet lower than Albion's) and Oldham Athletic (500 feet).

In the 1919-20 season Wolverhampton Wanderers were permitted to play two Second Division matches at The Hawthorns after Molineux had been closed because of crowd disturbances. On 6 December 1919 Wolves drew 2-2 with Stockport County and on 29 November 1919 they lost 4-2 to Barnsley.

On 11 May 1931, HRH The Prince of Wales (later King Edward VIII and then Duke of Windsor) called in at The Hawthorns while on a visit to the Midlands. He offered his congratulations on the unique double achievement and posed for a photograph with the FA Cup winning team.

On 7 August 1944, American and Canadian army teams staged a baseball match at The Hawthorns before a crowd of over 5,000 spectators.

The Hawthorns staged the Telford United-Leeds United FA cup third-round game on 11 January 1987. A crowd of 6,460 saw Leeds win 2-1.

# Albion Managers

THE post of Albion team manager was first created in the 1948 close season when Fred Everiss retired as secretary-manager after 46 years' unstinting service to the club. It was considered that the post was now too demanding for one man, so the position of team manager was advertised. Below are the career details of all the men to have held the job since then.

### JACK SMITH
*22 June 1948 to 17 April 1952*

Career: ALBION trialist, Wolverhampton Wanderers, Swindon Town, Chelsea, ALBION wartime guest, Wolverhampton Wanderers (coach), ALBION (manager), Reading (manager).

### JESSE CARVER
*18 April 1952 to 9 December 1952*

Career: England Schoolboy international, Blackburn Rovers, Newcastle United, Bury, Huddersfield Town (assistant trainer), Dutch FA (coach), Marzotto

(coach), Lazio (coach), Juventus (coach), Valdagno (coach), ALBION (manager), Torino (coach), AS Roma (manager), Coventry City (joint manager), Lazio (coach), Tottenham Hotspur (trainer-coach), Portugal (coach).

### VIC BUCKINGHAM
*2 February 1953 to 18 June 1959*

Career: Tottenham Hotspur, Middlesex County (FA coach), Oxford University (coach), Pegasus (coach), Bradford (manager), ALBION (manager), Ajax Amsterdam (manager), Plymouth Argyle (coach), Sheffield Wednesday (manager), Ajax Amsterdam (manager), Fulham (manager), Ethnikos (coach), Barcelona (coach), Seville (caoch).
England wartime international.

### GORDON CLARK
*6 July 1959 to 11 October 1961*

Career: Goldthorpe United, Southend United, Manchester City, Waterford,

Hyde United (player-manager), Distillery (manager), Aldershot (manager), ALBION (chief scout 1955, then assistant manager and manager), Sheffield Wednesday (assistant manager), Peterborough United (manager), Arsenal (chief scout), Fulham (assistant manager), Philadelphia Fury (coach).

### ARCHIE MACAULAY
*19 October 1961 to 2 April 1963*

Career: Camelon Juniors, Glasgow Rangers, West Ham United, Brentford, Arsenal, Fulham, Guildford City (manager), Dundee (coach), Norwich City (manager), ALBION (manager), Brighton and Hove Albion (manager).
13 Scotland caps.

### JIMMY HAGAN
*10 April 1963 to 3 May 1967*

Career: England Schoolboy international, ALBION trialist, Washington

Colliery, Liverpool, Derby County, Sheffield United, Peterborough United (manager), ALBION (manager), Manchester City (scout), Benfica (manager), Kuwait (coach), Sporting Lisbon (manager).

1 England cap, plus 16 in wartime.

### ALAN ASHMAN
*23 May 1967 to 2 July 1971*

Career: Sheffield United, Nottingham Forest, Carlisle United, Penrith (coach), Carlisle United (manager), ALBION (manager), Olympiakos (manager), Carlisle United (manager), Workington (manager), Manchester United (scout), Walsall (manager), Derby County (chief scout, then assistant manger), Hereford United (assistant manager), then scouting for Plymouth Argyle, Mansfield Town and Derby County.

### DON HOWE
*9 July 1971 to 6 April 1975*

Career: St Peter's School, Wolverhampton Wanderers, ALBION (player 1950-64), Arsenal (player-coach and assistant

manager), ALBION (manager), Galatasaray (coach), Leeds United (coach), Arsenal (chief coach, then manager), England 'B' (coach), England (chief coach), Saudi Arabia (coach), Bristol Rovers (coach), Wimbledon (coach, then manager), QPR (coach), Barnet (coach), Coventry City (coach, then manager), Chelsea (assistant manager).

23 England caps.

### JOHNNY GILES
*19 June 1975 to 27 May 1977 and 13 December 1983 to 29 September 1985*

Career: Republic of Ireland Schoolboy international, St Columbus, Dublin City, Munster Victoria, The Leprechauns, Stella Maris, Home Farm, Manchester United, Leeds United, ALBION (player-manager), Shamrock Rovers (player-manager), Philadelphia Fury (coach), Vancouver Whitecaps (coach), Republic of Ireland (manager), ALBION (manager).

60 caps for the Republic of Ireland.

### RONNIE ALLEN
*22 June 1977 to 22 December 1977 and 26 July 1981 to 30 June 1982 (as general manager)*

Career: Bucknall Boys Brigade, Wellington SC, Northwood Mission, Port Vale, ALBION (player), Crystal Palace (player and coach), Wolverhampton Wanderers (coach and manager), Athletic Bilbao (coach), Sporting Lisbon (manager), Walsall (manager), ALBION (scout, then manager), Saudi Arabia national team (manager), Panathinaikos (manager), ALBION (scout, then manager, later coach).

5 England caps.

### RON ATKINSON
*12 January 1978 to 9 June 1981 and 3 September 1987 to 12 October 1988*

Career: Lea Village School, BSA Tools, Wolverhamtpon Wanderers, Aston Villa, Headington United/Oxford United, Kettering Town (player-manager), Cambridge United (manager), ALBION (manager 1978-81), Manchester United (manager), Bolton Wanderers (coach), ALBION (manager 1987-88) Atlético Madrid (coach), Sheffield Wednesday (manager), Aston Villa (manager).

### RON WYLIE
*27 July 1982 to 13 December 1983*

Career: Clydesdale Juniors, Scotland Schoolboys, Notts County, Aston Villa, Birmingham City, Aston Villa (coach), Coventry City (coach then assistant manager). Cyprus (coach), Bulova Hong Kong (manager), ALBION (manager), Aston Villa (coach), Aston Villa (community liaison officer), Aston Villa (youth development & football in the community officer).

## NOBBY STILES
*15 October 1985 to 14 February 1986*

Career: St Patrick's School, Lancashire Schools, England Schoolboys, Manchester United, Middlesbrough, Preston North End (player, then manager), Vancouver Whitecaps (coach), ALBION (coach-assistant manager 1983, then manager, coach 1986-87), Manchester United (coach).
28 caps for England.

## RON SAUNDERS
*14 February 1986 to 1 September 1987*

Career: Birkenhead and Liverpool District Schools, Everton, Tonbridge, Gil-

lingham, Portsmouth, Watford, Charlton Athletic, Yeovil Town (manager), Oxford United (manager), Norwich City (manager), Manchester City (manager), Aston Villa (manager), Birmingham City (manager), ALBION (manager).

## BRIAN TALBOT
*2 November 1988 to 8 January 1991*
*(Caretaker manager 13 October 1988 to 1 November 1988)*

Career: Ipswich & Suffolk County Schools, Ipswich Town, Arsenal, Watford, Stoke City, ALBION (£15,000, January 1988 as player, manager November 1988), Fulham, Aldershot (manager).

Career: Coventry City, Arsenal, Wolverhampton Wanderers, ALBION (£66,666, September 1971 as player), Bristol City, West Ham United, Wolverhampton Wanderers, Bristol Rovers (player-coach), Aalsund Norway (coach), Hereford United, Charlton Athletic (coach), Chelsea, Wimbledon, Aldershot, Bristol Rovers (manager), Coventry City (manager), Bristol Rovers (manager), Wimbledon (manager), ALBION (manager), Coventry City (manager).

## OSSIE ARDILES
*8 May 1992-18 June 1993*

Career: Instituto de Cordoba. Huracán. Tottenham Hotspur, Paris St-Germain (loan), Blackburn R (loan), QPR, Swindon Town (manager), Newcastle U (manager), ALBION (manager). Tottenham Hotspur manager.

---

## Albion's other Caretaker Managers

### BRIAN WHITEHOUSE
*7 April 1975 to 14 June 1975*

### JOHN WILE
*23 December 1977 to 11 January 1978*

### BRIAN TALBOT
*13 October 1988 to 1 November 1988*

### STUART PEARSON
*9 January 1991 to 25 February 1991*

## BOBBY GOULD
*26 February 1991 to 5 May 1992*

# Albion's Coaches, Trainers & Physiotherapists

## Coaches

ALBION'S first officially appointed coach was the former Aston Villa defender Albert Evans, whose career was terminated by a broken leg. He was at The Hawthorns as coach in 1910-11. A number of other former players have since held coaching positions at Albion, among them Jesse Pennington, (1922-23), Tommy Glidden (1936-38), 'W.G.'Richardson (assistant trainer-coach, 1946-59) George Lee (trainer-coach, 1959-63), Graham Williams (1970-72), Brian Whitehouse (1971-81), Tony Brown (1985-86).

Other coaches employed by Albion in recent times have included Albert McPherson (trainer-coach 1964-84), Geoff Hudson (1970-72), Bill Asprey (1972-74), Jimmy Dunn (also trainer, 1965-71), Colin Addison (1979), Mick Brown (1980), and since then Mike Kelly, Norman Hunter, Nobby Stiles, Keith Leonard, Colin Addison, Stuart Pearson, Sam Allardyce, Keith Burkinshaw, Tony Brown, Dennis Mortimer and Cyril Lea.

## Trainers

Albion appointed their first trainer in March 1883. He was Dick Oxenbould of Birchfield Harriers Athletic Club. Later that year, another Harrier, Joey Law, an old George Salter's employee, was engaged as a permanent trainer at the fee of 2s 6d (12p) per week, which was later increased to five shillings (25p) and then 7s 6d (37p). For a time Law was assisted by Billy Nicholls but in August 1886 he was joined by Jack Paddock who was subsequently confirmed as sole trainer of Albion in 1888 when Law joined Burnley for a brief spell.

### Albion's first-team trainers 1883-1993

Joe Law (1883-88), Jack Paddock (1888-1901), Bill Brierley (1901-04), Jimmy Millar (1904-05), Bill Barber (1905-22), T.H. 'Bill' Gopsill (1922-27), Fred Reed (1927-50), Arthur Fitton (1950-56), 'Dick' Graham (1956-60), George Lee (1960-61), Wilf Dixon (1961-64), John Jarman (1964-65), Albert McPherson (1965-67), Stuart Williams (1967-69), Jimmy Dunn (1969-71), George Wright (1971-79), Richard Roberts (1979-83), Colin Saunders (1983-84), George Wright (1984-86), Graham Doig (1986-89), John MacGowan (1989-92) and Danny Thomas (1992-93).

#### Assistant trainers have included:-
Bill Nicholls, Jimmy Painter (from 1888), Bill Barber (1900-05), Harry Bell (1906-07), Eddie Jones (1907-08), Bob Crone (1908-09), Ted Paddock (1909-10), Jim Stevenson (1914-15), Sam Guest (1919-39), Sammy Short (1930-46), 'W.G.'Richardson (1946-48), Arthur Fitton (1948-50), Fred Pedley (1950), Wilf Dixon (1959-60) and John Jarman (1961-64).

Albion have not officially appointed an assistant trainer since 1964-65. Several people have, however, done the job on a temporary basis.

## Masseurs & Physiotherapists

Albion's first masseur was T.H.'Bill' Gopsill, when the Football League Championship was won in 1919-20. He died, prematurely, in 1927.

Since the last war, Fred Pedley (from 1950 to 1965), Tom Jones (1966-71), George Wright (1971-79 and 1984-86), Richard Roberts (1971-72 and 1979-83), Colin Saunders (1983-84), Graham Doig (1986-89), John MacGowan (1989-92) and Danny Thomas (1992-93) have been physiotherapists at Albion.

### Training 'Honours'

J.Paddock, Football League v Irish League, 1896-97.
W.Barber, Football League v Scottish League, 1908-09.
W.Barber, Football League v Irish League, 1914-15.
T.H.Gopsill, FA XI v Oxford University, 1922-23.

T.H.Gopsill, England v Belgium, 1924-25.
S.Guest, Belgium v England, 1924-25.
S.Guest, FA XI v Staffordshire, 1926-27.
S.Guest, The Rest v England, 1927-28, 1934-35.
F.Reed, England v The Rest, 1927-28, 1934-35.
F.Reed, Football League v Irish League, 1934-35.
F.Reed, England v Wales, 1945-46.

**Jack Paddock, Albion's trainer 1888-1901.**

**Albert McPherson, trainer 1965-7, coach 1964-84.**

## AMOS ADAMS

*Born: West Bromwich, June 1880. Died: January 1941.*
*Career: West Bromwich Baptist and Bratt Street Schools. Geo. Salter Works. Springfields FC. ALBION (June 1897-April 1910). Retired to become sportsmaster at a local school (West Bromwich). Later coached the Amiens Club (France), becoming manager in 1926-7.*

*Amos Adams*

Amos Adams was an intelligent, versatile and stylish full-back, accurate in kicking, strong in the tackle and an excellent clubman. He spent 12 seasons with Albion and during that time appeared in well over 200 senior games. He won a Second Division championship medal in 1902 and if Albion had been a more fashionable club in the First Division, then Adams would have surely won international honours in the early 1900s. He arrived at the club in 1897 and after a year or so in the reserves, made his first-team debut at centre-forward. But it was at full-back where he made good, and after Billy Williams had been forced to quit football in 1901, Adams made the left-back slot his own until Jesse Pennington came along, when he switched to the right-hand side.
*Albion debut v Notts County (away) Division One, 9 March 1899.*

## JIMMY ADAMS

*Born: Norton Canes, Cannock, January 1908. Died: Birmingham, 1983.*
*Career: Cannock Schools. Cannock Chase Colliery. Cannock Town. ALBION (July 1929-May 1945). Retired.*
'Doc' Adams was a fine, competent goalkeeper, hefty but extremely mobile, whose career at Albion coincided with those of Harold Pearson, George Ashmore and Billy Light. He was one of the

*Jimmy Adams*

club's heaviest players, tipping the scales at 14st 10lb during World War Two when he played most of his 221 matches for the Throstles.
*Albion debut v Notts County (home) Division Two, 23 November 1929.*

## RONNIE ALLEN

*Born: Fenton, Stoke-on-Trent, January 1929.*
*Career: Hanley High School. Bucknall Boys' Brigade. Wellington Scouts. Northwood Mission. Port Vale (1944). RAF. ALBION (March 1950-May 1961). Crystal Palace (£4,500). Wolves (coach, later manager). Athletic Bilbao (manager). Sporting Lisbon (manager). Walsall (manager). ALBION (January 1977 as scouting advisor, then manager June 1977-December 1977). Panathinaikos, (Greece). ALBION (manager, July 1981-May 1982, then general manager until 1983). Later coach at The Hawthorns 1991-3.*
The 'complete footballer' and the king-pin of Albion's wonderful attack of the 1950s, Ronnie Allen filled every forward position for the club, with centre-forward undoubtedly his favourite. He possessed a powerful shot in both feet, was a superb volleyer of the ball and an ace penalty-taker. Winner of five England caps (1952-54) he also represented the Football League, the England 'B' team, the FA XI and the RAF. Allen gained an FA Cup winners' medal in 1954, when his two goals helped Albion beat Preston North End 3-2 at Wembley, and in 1967 he led Wolves back into the First Division. Two years later he was with Bilbao when they won the Spanish Cup. For Albion alone, Allen appeared in 415 League games (all in Division One, 306 of them at centre-forward) and scored 208 goals — a club

*Ronnie Allen*

record until passed by Tony Brown in 1978. He also played in 42 FA Cup-ties (23 goals) and hit a hat-trick for Albion in the 1954 FA Charity Shield match against Wolves. In his magnificent career, Allen amassed a grand total of 637 League appearances (276 goals) and in all matches he played over 800 times and scored 354 goals. Allen holds the honour of being the only player to have scored in each of the first 20 post-war seasons (1945-6 to 1964-5 inclusive). He was the First Division's leading marksman in 1954-5 with 27 goals.
*Albion debut v Wolves (home) Division One, 4 March 1950.*

## GEORGE ASHMORE

*Born: Plymouth, May 1898. Died: Birmingham, May 1973.*
*Career: South Devon & District Schools.*

*George Ashmore*

*Nineveh Wesley. ALBION (November 1919-October 1931). Chesterfield. Retired 1935.*

An agile, daring goalkeeper, George Ashmore was in the shadows of Hubert Pearson for a number of seasons at The Hawthorns. 'Cap', as he was known, played for England in 1926 and appeared in 268 senior games for the Throstles. A loyal clubman, he worked for the Midlands Electricity Board for several years after announcing his retirement from football at the age of 37.

*Albion debut v Blackburn Rovers (away) Division One, 9 October 1920.*

## JEFF ASTLE

*Born: Eastwood, Nottinghamshire, May 1942.*
*Career: Devonshire Drive and Walker Street Schools. Holy Trinity YC. West Notts Boys. John Player FC (Nottingham). Notts County. ALBION (September 1964-July 1974). Hellenic (South Africa). Dunstable Town. Weymouth. Atherstone Town. Hillingdon Borough. WBA All Stars. Retired 1977.*

*Jeff Astle*

Jeff Astle proved a real bargain-buy for Albion, manager Jimmy Hagan paying £25,000 for this superb striker in 1964. Nicknamed the 'King', Astle was, indeed, a brilliant centre-forward, exceptional in the air and good on the ground as well. He won five England caps (1969-70), had outings for the Football League and England 'B' teams and collected an FA Cup winners' medal in 1968, when his extra-time special beat Everton at Wembley. Two years earlier, he gained a League Cup winners' tankard and was in Albion's side in both the 1967 and 1970 League Cup Finals, scoring in the latter, against Manchester City, which gave him the record of becoming the first player to find the net in both the FA and League Cup Final at Wembley. In 1968 he was vote Midlands Footballer of the Year. Altogether, in a truly wonderful career, Astle accumulated more than 450 appearances in senior football — 361 of them with Albion. He scored 168 League goals, with 25 coming in 1969-70 when he topped the First Division charts. His tally for Albion in the League was 137, which included six hat-tricks — two in a week in September 1965 and two in 72 hours at the end of the 1967-8 campaign. In August 1986, Astle returned to Albion in the capacity of president of the club's newly-formed Challenge Club.

*Albion debut v Leicester City (away) Division One, 30 September 1964.*

## HAROLD BACHE

*Born: Churchill, Nr Kidderminster, August 1889. Died: France (killed in action), February 1916.*
*Career: King Edward's Grammar School, Birmingham. Cambridge University. The Corinthians. West Bromwich Springfield. Staffordshire Youths. Eastbourne. ALBION (February 1914-February 1916).*

*Harold Bache*

Harold Bache was a quite brilliant amateur international centre-forward, who looked destined for all the major soccer honours until tragedy struck when he was serving with the Lancashire Fusiliers in France in 1916, when he was only 26 years of age. Standing 5ft 8in tall and weighing barely 10st, Bache was so skilful and positive in everything he did that his slight build was insignificant. Because war interrupted League football, he played in only 14 games for Albion, scoring four goals, but had been an England amateur international long before he moved to The Hawthorns in 1914. He collected seven caps (1910-13) and in one game, against France at Ipswich in 1910, he scored seven of England's goals in their 20-0 victory. Bache also played for the Football League in 1914 and besides being a superb soccer player, he excelled at Rugby Union, cricket (with Worcestershire), tennis and athletics. He was a grand sportsman in every sense of the word, a man who was respected throughout the sporting world.

*Albion debut v Aston Villa (away), FA Cup, 21 February 1914.*
*League debut v Newcastle United (away) 2 September 1914.*

## GEORGE BADDELEY

*Born: Fegg Hayes, Staffs, May 1874. Died: West Bromwich, July 1952.*
*Career: Pitshill FC. Biddulph FC. Stoke. ALBION (June 1908-May 1914). Retired cs 1914.*

*George Baddeley*

George Baddeley was strong in all aspects of half-back play — being safe, difficult to pass and, above all, a fine feeder of the attack. He was captain of Stoke for several years before moving to The Hawthorns. As an Albion man he made over 150 first-team appearances and won a Second Division championship medal in 1911 and an FA Cup runners-up medal a year later. After his retirement he became a publican in West Bromwich.

*Albion debut v Grimsby Town (away) Division Two, 5 September 1908.*

## RAY BARLOW

*Born: Swindon, August 1926.*
*Career: Sandford Street School, Swindon.*
*Swindon Town (trial). Garrards FC.*
*ALBION (June 1944-June 1960). Bir-*
*mingham City, Stourbridge. Retired*
*1962. Guested for Swindon Town in*
*World War Two and played for WBA All*
*Stars (1969-81).*

*Ray Barlow*

A tall, rangy player, who was poised, elegant, skilful, fast over 20 yards, wholehearted and with heaps of energy, Ray Barlow was converted successfully by Albion from an inside-forward into a classy international left-half where he developed a sound tackle. He strutted across the field majestically, sending passes straight to his man from distances of up to 40 yards. His powerful runs into the opposing penalty-areas caused all sorts of trouble and it was his forward dash into the box in the 1954 FA Cup Final that resulted in a penalty being awarded to Albion as they strove to beat Preston. Barlow also turned out occasionally in the centre-half and centre-forward positions, but it was at left-half that he is best remembered. He was extremely unlucky not to win more than one cap for England (gained against Northern Ireland in 1954), but he did play for the 'B' team, the Football League XI and the FA representative side on many occasions, as well as being a regular England reserve. He skippered Albion during the late 1950s and during his professional career, with Albion and Birmingham City, amassed a total of 490 competitive appearances in 17 years. He toured South America with the FA in 1953. After ending his playing career, Barlow went into the newsagents' and tobacconists'

trade in West Bromwich, and later at Stourbridge.
*Albion debut v Walsall (home) Wartime League Cup, 3 February 1945.*
*League debut v Newport County (away) Division Two, 28 September 1946 (scored in a 7-2 Albion win).*

## PETER BARNES

*Born: Manchester, June 1957.*
*Career: Chorlton Park Juniors. Chorlton High Grammar School. Whitehall. Gatley Rangers. Manchester & District Boys. Manchester City (1972, professional 1974). ALBION (July 1979-July 1981). Leeds United. Real Betis (Spain). Leeds United. West Ham United. Coventry City. Manchester United. Manchester City. Bolton Wanderers. Port Vale. Hull City. Sporting Ferense (Portugal). Bolton Wanderers. Sunderland. Drogheda United. Wrexham. Northwich Victoria. Radcliffe Borough.*

Peter Barnes was a highly skilled outside-left, winner of 22 full England caps, one at 'B' level, nine at Under-21, and a former Schoolboy and Youth International. He cost Albion a club record £748,000 when they signed him from Manchester City in the summer of 1979. When he left The Hawthorns for Elland Road in 1981, Albion collected £930,000, a record incoming fee. A player who flitted in and out of the game, Barnes had speed, a fine body swerve and powerful shot. He scored

*Peter Barnes*

a splendid goal for Manchester City in the 1976 League Cup Final against Newcastle United, when City won the trophy for the second time. Barnes had a wonderful first season with Albion (1979-80), when he scored 15 goals, including a hat-trick against Bolton at The Hawthorns in March. After leaving Albion, he never really settled again and although he had a good spell in Spain, his career slowly wound down until in 1986-7, when he was basically a reserve at Old Trafford.
*Albion debut v Derby County (home) Division One, 18 August 1979.*

## BILLY BASSETT

*Born: West Bromwich, January 1869.*
*Died: West Bromwich, April 1937.*
*Career: Christ Church School. Oak Villa. West Bromwich Strollers (not Albion). Old Church Club. ALBION (August 1886-April 1899). Retired. Became Albion director (September 1905) and elected chairman in 1908, serving in that capacity until his untimely death in 1937, hours before Albion met Preston North End in the FA Cup semi-final at Highbury. League Management Committee (1930-37) and a member of the England International Selection Committee (1936-7). He was also a JP (appointed in 1935).*

*Billy Bassett*

One of the great names in Albion's history, Billy (William Isaiah) Bassett was a brilliant footballer. Fast and clever, determined and dedicated, he played mostly at outside-right, hugging the touch-line and putting in many darting runs. His centres were immaculate and he possessed a fierce shot. He was a wonderful clubman who gained 16 England caps (eight against Scotland) as well as performing regularly for the Football League representative side and the FA XI. He played in three FA Cup Finals — 1888, 1892 and 1895 — picking up winners' medals in the first two. He was associated with the Albion club for 51 years.
*Albion debut v Wednesbury Old Athletic (home) FA Cup, 15 October 1887.*
*League debut v Stoke (away) 8 September 1888.*

## BRENDON BATSON

*Born: St George's, Grenada, West Indies, February 1953.*
*Career: St Mary's Junior School, Tilbury.*

*Brendon Batson*

*McEntee Technical College, Waltham-stow. Waltham Forest Boys. Arsenal. Cambridge United. ALBION (February 1978-May 1984). Retired. Assisted WBA All Stars 1984-87. PFA assistant secretary* Brendon Batson was a highly efficient right-back who began his playing career with Arsenal as either a midfielder or central defender. Steady, easy-going and sincere, Batson was Ron Atkinson's first signing for Albion — and he turned out to be one of his best — a £30,000 bargain. With Arsenal he won an FA Youth Cup winners' medal in 1971 and later, as Cambridge United's captain, he helped his team win the Fourth Division championship in 1977. He gained England 'B' recognition (three caps) in 1980 — his only representative honours. Sadly in 1984, he was forced to retire from competitive football through injury and Albion granted him a testimonial to say 'thank you' for his magnificent service to the club. Batson, an intelligent, articulate man, became assistant secretary of the PFA in 1984-5.
*Albion debut v Birmingham City (away) Division One, 28 February 1978.*

### 'JEM' BAYLISS

*Born: Tipton, August 1863. Died: West Bromwich, August 1933.*
*Career: Great Bridge and Horseley Heath Schools. Great Bridge Unity. Tipton Providence. Wednesbury Old Athletic. ALBION (August 1884, professional August 1885-March 1892). Guested for Walsall Town. Retired. Albion director, a post he initially held whilst an active player with the club, (1891-1905).*

'Jem' Bayliss — a nickname taken from three of his Christian names (Edward James Matthias) — was a grand all-round footballer, always full of running, always willing to work and always likely to score a spectacular goal. He played at wing-half, inside-right and centre-forward for Albion and gained one England cap in 1891. He was Albion's centre-forward in the 1886, 1887 and 1888 FA Cup Finals, scoring the first goal in the latter tie against Preston North End. He made his Albion debut at the start of the 1884-5 season, against Aston Villa at Villa Park, scoring 20 goals in his first year with the club. In 1885-6 he notched another 20, including a hat-trick in the FA Cup tie against Old Westminsters; his 1886-7 haul was around the 40 mark and in 1887-8 he topped the charts with 50.

*'Jem' Bayliss*

Bayliss was a real 'gem' when it came to finding a way past the 'keeper — and for Albion his goal total was in excess of 150 (all competitions and friendlies). He had virtually retired in 1891 but was recalled for an FA Cup semi-final replay against Nottingham Forest, his last appearance for Albion. A real gentleman in more ways than one, Bayliss read his own obituary notice in a local newspaper in 1897. He had gone on holiday to Gibraltar and whilst away from his Great Bridge home, rumours gained currency that he had died. He returned and proved he was alive and kicking and quickly had the notice framed for posterity. He lived for another 36 years.
*Albion debut v Derby Junction Street School (away) FA Cup, 25 October 1884 (scored twice in a 7-1 Albion win).*
*League debut v Stoke (away) 8 September 1888.*

### MARTYN BENNETT

*Born: Birmingham, August 1961.*
*Career: Pheasey Junior School, Birmingham. Aldridge Comprehensive School. Aston Schools. Aldridge and*

Brownhills Schools. Walsall Schools. *West Midlands County Schools. ALBION (August 1977, professional August 1978-May 1990). Worcester City (player, then player-manager 1991).*

*Martyn Bennett*

A talented defender, tall, dominant and quick, Martyn Bennett won nine School-boy caps for England. He understudied John Wile and Ally Robertson for a number of years before establishing himself in Albion's first team during the 1980-81 season. Injuries have troubled him from time to time and have twice prevented him from representing his country. When Bennett was called up by England in 1982-3, he was described by Jimmy Greaves as 'the fastest covering defender I've ever seen'. Bennett, who was appointed Albion club captain at the start of the 1986-7 season, was forced to quit League football through injury in 1990.
*Albion debut v Everton (home) Division One, 7 September 1979*

### ALF BENTLEY

*Born: Alfreton, Derbyshire, September 1887. Died: Derby, April 1940.*
*Career: Church of England School (Alfreton). Alfreton Town. Derby County. Bolton Wanderers. ALBION (June 1913-May 1922), Burton Town. Alfreton Town. Retired 1926.*
Alf Bentley was an 'eager-beaver' type of centre-forward who cost Albion £650

*Alf Bentley*

*Bobby Blood*

Richmond. Willenhall. Birmingham (trial). ALBION (July 1908-April 1913). Belfast Distillery. ALBION (February 1914-August 1924). Walsall. Retired 1927. Guested for Southport Vulcan and Notts County during World War One.

A tenacious, resilient and hard-working player, Sid Bowser divided his immense talents between two widely differing roles, those of inside-forward and centre-half. A big, strong fellow, Bowser had two spells with Albion and in each of them he achieved personal success. In 1910-11 he helped Albion win the Second Division championship and a year later played for them in the FA Cup Final. On his return he was a key member of the League Championship-winning side of 1919-20, helping himself to eight penalties and a hat-trick from centre-half against Bradford City. A sterling performer, Bowser won an England cap, against Ireland in 1919 and represented the Irish League whilst a Distillery player.

*Albion debut v Grimsby Town (home) Division Two, 2 January 1909 (scored twice in Albion's 7-2 win).*

when he signed from Bolton shortly before World War One. 'Nobby' or 'Snobby', as he was called by colleagues and supporters, made an immediate impact when he scored four goals on his Albion debut, against Burnley at The Hawthorns in September 1913. He was dangerous around the penalty area, always ready to take a shot at goal, and his League striking record was good — over 160 goals in 265 appearances. For Derby alone he scored 99 goals in 151 League games, twice breaking the Rams' individual scoring record for a season. Derby needed his goals, too, for they had parted company with the great Steve Bloomer. Bentley won a League Championship medal with Albion in 1919-20, when his 15 goals were bettered only by the prolific Freddie Morris with whom he had drawn up a fine understanding.

*Albion debut v Burnley (home) Division One, 6 September 1913 (scored four goals in a 4-1 Albion win).*

## BOBBY BLOOD

*Born: Harpur Hill, near Buxton, March 1894. Died: Buxton, August 1988.*
*Career: Harpur Hill School, Buxton. Buxton Lime Firms. Leek Alexandra. Port Vale. ALBION (February 1921-December 1924). Stockport County. Winsford United. Mossley. Ashton National. Retired 1931.*
Bobby Blood was a dynamic centre-forward, renowned for his 'cannonball' shooting. He stood only 5ft 7in tall but was a brave player. A real terrier around goal, he scored well over 70 goals in less than 150 League matches during his career. In all types of football, after leaving school until his retirement in 1931, Blood claimed somewhere in the region of 400 goals, including 100 in two seasons immediately prior to joining Port

Vale. For Vale, he hit 44 goals in only 53 League games, including 24 in his first season, 1919-20. He lived in a Salvation Army Hostel in Buxton right up until his death at the age of 96.

*Albion debut v Tottenham Hotspur (home) Division One, 19 February 1921 (scored a penalty in Albion's 3-1 win).*

## SID BOWSER

*Born: Handsworth, Birmingham, January 1892. Died: Birmingham, February 1961.*
*Career: Wattville Road School. Astbury*

*Sid Bowser*

## WALLY BOYES

*Born: Killamarsh, Sheffield, January 1913. Died: September 1960.*
*Career: Netherthorpe Council School. Sheffield Boys. Woodhouse Mills United. ALBION (February 1931-February 1938). Everton. Notts County (player-coach). Scunthorpe United (player-trainer). Retford Town (manager). Hyde United (manager). Swansea Town (trainer). Retired (ill-health) 1960. Guested for Aldershot, Brentford, Clapton Orient, Leeds United, Manchester United, Middlesbrough, Millwall, Newcastle United, Preston North End and Sunderland during World War Two.*

*Wally Boyes*

A spirited little footballer who was perhaps best-known as an orthodox outside-left, Wally Boyes also competed ably at left-half and inside-left. He was a purposeful player with an accurate shot which he allied to quickness off the mark.

A schoolboy prodigy in Sheffield — where he once scored 17 goals in one game — Boyes took over from Stan Wood in the Albion team and scored in the 1935 FA Cup Final against Sheffield Wednesday at Wembley. After leaving The Hawthorns, he gained a League Championship medal with Everton in 1938-9, netting four goals in 36 appearances for the Merseysiders. He won four full international caps (two with Albion, two with Everton) and at 5ft 3in tall was one of the smallest players to represent England. Boyes' career was even more remarkable when one remembers that he had one leg shorter than the other.

*Albion debut v Aston Villa (home) Division One, 14 November 1931 (in front of a near-60,000 attendance).*

## DARREN BRADLEY

*Born: Kings Norton, South Birmingham, November 1965.*
*Career: St Thomas Aquinas School. King's Norton Boys. West Midlands County Schools. South Birmingham Boys. Broadmeadow All Stars. Aston Villa (apprentice July 1982, professional November 1983), ALBION (March 1986 in player/exchange deal involving Steve Hunt and £90,000). Guested for Capetown Spurs in South Africa (summer 1988).*

*Darren Bradley*

As a youth-team player at Villa Park, Bradley occupied three different positions — centre-half, central midfield and centre-forward — but always preferred the defensive role, and it was from there he skippered both Aston Villa and England Youth teams, winning six caps. After failing to establish himself in Villa's League side, he was delighted to move to The Hawthorns and there continued his versatility, appearing at full-back, wing-half, centre-half, inside-forward

and on the wing. A hard-working professional, Bradley never gives up and although he has suffered his fair share of injuries over the past few years, he has always bounced back. He was bitterly disappointed when Albion went down to Division Three in 1991, having been one of the mainstays during that sad campaign. In 1992 he passed the 200 appearances mark for the club and in 1993 became the first Albion skipper for 25 years to lead the Baggies to a Wembley victory when they won the play-off Final against Port Vale.

*Albion debut v Leicester City (home) Division One, 15 March 1986.*

## ALLY BROWN

*Born: Musselburgh, Scotland, April 1951.*
*Career: Musselburgh and Edinburgh District Schools. Leicester City. ALBION (March 1972-March 1983). Crystal Palace. Walsall. Port Vale. Retired 1986. Played for Portland Timbers (NASL) May-August 1981, WBA All Stars.*

*Ally Brown*

Ally Brown cost Albion the unusual fee of £61,111 when he signed from Leicester City on the 1972 transfer deadline. He scored on each of his first two outings in Albion's senior side and went on to prove a good professional for the rest of his 15-year career with the Throstles, finishing leading marksman in 1975-6 and 1978-9. He had a couple of lean seasons (1973-4 and 1974-5), when Don Howe was manager, but overall he served the club consistently in all competitions. When he retired in the summer of 1986, Brown became a publican in West Bromwich. He scored a total of 157

League and Cup goals for his five English clubs and was Leicester's leading scorer when they won the Second Division title in 1970-71.

*Albion debut v Crystal Palace (home) Division One, 11 March 1972.*

## TONY BROWN

*Born: Oldham, Lancashire, October 1945.*
*Career: Columba RC School (Manchester). St Peter's (Wythenshawe) and St Clare's (Blakely) Schools. Manchester and District Boys. Lancashire Boys. ALBION (April 1961, professional October 1963-October 1981). Torquay United. Stafford Rangers. Played for New England Teamen and Jacksonville Teamen (NASL, 1980-1981). WBA All Stars. Returned to The Hawthorns as coach (1984-6). Birmingham City (coach 1987-1989).*

*Tony Brown*

The man who made more League appearances for Albion than any other player, Tony 'The Bomber' Brown enjoyed 20 wonderful years with the Throstles, during which time he gave many sparkling displays in many different positions. A wholehearted player, Brown packed a deadly shot in his right foot and was no slouch with his left either. He converted over 50 penalties for Albion and created many club records. When he netted at Leeds on 14 October 1978, he overtook Ronnie Allen's record of 208 League goals, ending his Albion career with 218 goals in a record 574 League games. In all first-team games (including friendlies) he made 819 appearances and scored 312 goals. His 459 First Division appearances is also an Albion record, as is his 146 senior Cup appearances. Brown gained a League Cup winners' tankard (1966) and an FA Cup winners' medal

(1968) as well as playing in the 1967 and 1970 League Cup Finals at Wembley. He played for the England Youth team and gained one full cap, against Wales in 1971. Brown also represented the Football League, was Midlands Footballer of the Year in 1969, 1971 and 1979, and topped the First Division goalscoring list with 28 goals in 1970-71. He returned to the Hawthorns as coach under Johnny Giles' managership but lost the job when Ron Saunders was appointed. He still plays regularly for the WBA All Stars.

*Albion debut v Ipswich Town (away) Division One, 28 September 1963 (scored in Albion's 2-1 win).*

## FRED BUCK

*Born: Newcastle-under-Lyme, Staffs, July 1880. Died: June 1952.*
*Career: Newcastle-under-Lyme District Schools. Stafford Wesleyans. Stafford Rangers. ALBION (November 1900-May 1903). Liverpool. Plymouth Argyle. ALBION (April 1906-May 1914). Swansea Town. Retired 1917.*

*Fred Buck*

One of the great little players Albion have had on their books, Fred Buck, of slight physique, was fast and dangerous, possessed wonderful judgement and was ever-dangerous in front of goal. He began his career as an inside-forward and spent his first three years with Albion in the forward line. During his second spell with the club he was converted into a safe, solid centre-half and, despite his size — he stood only 5ft 4in but weighed 11st — he was regarded as one of the finest in the country. Buck represented the Football League in 1911, won a Second Division championship medal the same year and was Albion's centre-half in the 1912 FA Cup Final against Barnsley. Buck was a brilliant footballer who made well over 500 appearances during his lengthy career with four different clubs.

*Albion debut v Bolton Wanderers (home) Division One, 8 December 1900 (scored once in Albion's 7-2 win).*

## DAVY BURNSIDE

*Born: Bristol, December 1939.*
*Career: Kingswood School. Bristol & District Boys. Bristol City (amateur). ALBION (December 1955, professional February 1957-September 1962). Southampton (£17,000). Crystal Palace. Wolves. Plymouth Argyle. Bristol City. Colchester United. Bath City (manager). Walsall (assistant manager). Cadbury Heath. Bridgwater Town. (player-manager). Taunton Town. Retired May 1980. Later FA coach and appointed England youth-team manager 1983.*

*Davy Burnside*

Davy Burnside was a talented inside-forward with exceptional ball skills which he displayed to capture the acclaim of the paying customers. In 1957, during the half-time interval of the Albion v CDSA (Russia) friendly, he showed off his individual artistry live on TV and afterwards was offered a lucrative contract to appear regularly on shows all over the world. He turned the offer down to concentrate on football. In 1960, Burnside entered the *Sunday Despatch* 'Get-a-Header' contest, which was organised to find out whether Britain possessed a footballer capable of capturing the world's heading record which at the time was held by the Austrian George Kaul, aged 19. Burnside managed 495 clean headers without a break; Kaul's record was 3,025. In 135 games for Albion, he scored 42 goals. He represented England Youth and the Under-23s (two caps), as well playing for an FA XI. He was in Wolves' 1966-7 promotion-winning side.

*Albion debut v Leeds United (away) Division One, 19 October 1957.*

## JACK BYERS

*Born: Selby, Yorkshire, January 1897.*
*Died: November 1931.*
*Career: Selby Schools. Knaresborough*

*Jack Byers*

*(Harrogate). Huddersfield Town. Blackburn Rovers. ALBION (January 1924-July 1928). Worcester City. Torquay United. Kidderminster Harriers. Retired close season 1931.*

An outstandingly quick and dangerous outside-left, who had loads of skill and a powerful shot, Jack Byers joined Albion as cover for Howard Gregory (who was looking to retire) and Arthur Fitton. Byers went immediately into Albion's League side but he suffered a number of injuries and during the second half of the 1923-4 season he was in and out of the side. The following campaign he was a consistent performer but then began to lose his form, and flair and subsequently found himself 'recovering' in the Reserves. During his League career — with Huddersfield, Blackburn and Albion — he made a total of 143 appearances.

*Albion debut v Burnley (away) Division One, 26 January 1924.*

## LEN CANTELLO

*Born: Newton Heath, Manchester, September 1951.*
*Career: Albert Memorial School. Manchester & Lancashire Boys. Newton Heath Schools. ALBION (July 1967, professional October 1968-May 1979). Bolton Wanderers. Burnley (trial). Altrincham. Eastern FC (Hong Kong). Hereford United (non-contract). Bury (non-contract). SC Cambuur (Holland, player-coach). Peterborough United (trial). Retired 1986. Assisted Dallas Tornados (NASL, May-August 1978). Stockport County (assistant manager/coach 1987-9). Radcliffe Borough (manager 1989-90). Peterborough (scout 1991-2).*

Len Cantello carried out many duties for Albion during his professional career at

The Hawthorns, donning ten different numbered shirts in the first team and performing with style and artistry, mainly as a midfielder. He certainly had flair and he drew up an excellent understanding, first with Asa Hartford and afterwards with Johnny Giles and Bryan Robson. As a defender, lining up at left-back, Cantello tackled hard and was always eager to attack down the flank. He gained international honours for England at Schoolboy (six caps), Youth (four caps) and Under-23 (eight

*Len Cantello*

caps). He played in well over 360 games for Albion including an appearance in the 1970 League Cup Final, at the age of 18. He left Albion for Bolton immediately after his testimonial in 1979.
*Albion debut v Ipswich Town (away) Division One, 7 December 1968 (as substitute).*

## JOE CARTER

*Born: Aston, Birmingham, April 1901. Died: Handsworth, Birmingham, January 1977.*
*Career: Farm Street and Hockley Hill Schools (Birmingham). Westbourne Celtic. ALBION (April 1921-May 1936). Sheffield Wednesday (for six days). Tranmere Rovers. Walsall. Vono Sports FC (player-manager). Retired 1940.*
Joe Carter gave Albion 15 years of loyal service at inside-right. He was upright, had a grand dribbling technique, a magnificent body-swerve, expert positional sense and a pretty useful goalscoring record. He formed a wonderful partnership with outside-right Tommy Glidden and the 'twins', as they were called by The Hawthorns' faithful, performed together on Albion's right flank in well over 350 senior matches.

*Joe Carter*

Carter made over 450 appearances for Albion, scoring 155 goals. He won three England caps (1926-9), and represented the Football League. He was a key figure in Albion's 'double-winning' team of 1930-31, and played in both of Albion's FA Cup Finals in the 1930s, collecting a winners' medal in 1931. He left Albion for Sheffield Wednesday in 1936 but was rejected by the Hillsborough club on medical grounds owing to complications with his right leg which resulted him having a cartilage operation prior to switching his transfer to Tranmere. Carter had a particularly sad death, of dehydration, at his Handsworth home in 1977.
*Albion debut v Bolton Wanderers (away) Division One, 9 December 1922.*

## WILF CARTER

*Born: Wednesbury, Staffs, October 1933.*
*Career: Wednesbury High School. SE Staffs Boys. Birmingham & District Schools. Birmingham County Youths. ALBION (April 1949, professional January 1951-May 1957). Plymouth Argyle. Exeter City. Bath City. Retired 1970.*
Wilf Carter was initially an inside-forward at The Hawthorns and therefore had to battle it out for a first-team place with some pretty useful players — Allen, Nicholls, Kevan and Robson amongst them. All told, he made only 61 senior appearances for the club, 11 of them in the left-back position during 1956-7 when he replaced the injured Len Millard. After leaving Albion in 1957, Carter went on to perform majestically for Plymouth and in 252 League games for the Devon club he scored 133 goals. He was Argyle's leading marksman for five successive seasons (1957-62) and helped his club win

*Wilf Carter*

the Third Division South title in 1959. In 1957, Carter was selected for the Third Division South representative side but had to miss the game through injury.
*Albion debut v Fulham (away) Division One, 22 September 1951.*

## HARRY CHAMBERS

*Born: Willington Quay, Nr Newcastle upon Tyne, February 1896. Died: June 1949.*
*Career: Percy Main School (Tynemouth). Willington United Methodists. North Shields Athletic. Liverpool. Distillery*

*Harry Chambers*

*and Glentoran (wartime guest). Liverpool. ALBION (March 1928-July 1929). Oakengates Town (player-manager). Retired June 1948 after playing his last game at the age of 52.*

'Smiler' Chambers was a player of ice-cool temperament who had a brilliant football brain. Bow-legged, he could 'bend' a ball at will and occasionally surprised opponents with a fierce left-foot shot. He played inside-left for most of his career but during his spell at Albion reverted to centre-half with good effect. He moved to Anfield just before World War One and during the war guested for Irish League clubs, Distillery and Glentoran, playing in the latter club's losing 1919 Irish Cup Final team. He returned to Liverpool and became an immediate success with the fans. When the Merseysiders won the League Championship in successive seasons (1921-2 and 1922-3), Chambers netted 41 goals in 72 League matches. In all he netted 151 goals for the Reds (338 appearances) for an average of a goal almost every two games. He topped Liverpool's scoring charts in each of the first five post-war seasons. Chambers won eight England caps (scoring four goals) and played five times for the Football League.

*Albion debut v Fulham (home) Division Two, 10 March 1928 (scored in a 4-0 win).*

## CLIVE CLARK

*Born: Leeds, December 1940.*
*Career: Harehills and Leeds City Schools. Ashley Road Methodists Club. Huddersfield Town (trial). Leeds United. QPR. ALBION (January 1961-June 1969). QPR. Preston North End. Southport. Telford United. Washington Diplomats (NASL). Dallas Tornado (NASL). Philadelphia Fury (NASL). Skegness Town. Retired during 1976-7.*

*Clive Clark*

'Chippy' Clark was an accomplished left-winger, fast, direct and courageous — and a great goalscorer. He cost Albion £17,000 in 1961, the year he won an England Under-23 cap, and repaid the Throstles with 98 goals in over 350 games, a figure

which made him Albion's greatest goal-scoring winger after Tommy Glidden. He took over the number-11 shirt from Derek Hogg and was a virtual ever-present until injury sidelined him in 1968, soon after he had helped Albion win the FA Cup. A year earlier, in March 1967, he scored two goals in the first-half of the League Cup Final against his old club, QPR, but after the break Third Division Rangers fought back to take the trophy in the first Final of that competition to be staged at Wembley. In 1966, Clark was in Albion's League Cup-winning side against West Ham United. In the 1966-7 competition he became the first player to score in every round up to and including the Final. He helped Preston win the Third Division North title in 1970-71 and his League career spanned 447 matches and 98 goals. Today he lives in London.

*Albion debut v Preston North End (home) Division One, 14 January 1961.*

## IKE CLARKE

*Born: Tipton, January 1915.*
*Career: Prince's End Baptists. Coseley Juniors. Toll End Wesley. ALBION (January 1937-November 1947). Portsmouth (£5,000). Sittingbourne (manager). Yeovil Town (manager). Canterbury City (manager). Ashford Town (manager). Retired from football 1973, aged 58. Guested for Walsall and Nottingham Forest during World War Two.*

*Ike Clarke*

Ike Clarke was a fearless competitor with a strong kick, boundless energy and a solid frame able to take the fiercest of challenges. A former England Junior international (capped in 1937), he played inside or centre-forward for Albion for ten years, either side of World War Two, appearing in 213 games and scoring almost 100 goals. A true Black Country

man, born and bred in the industrial area near West Bromwich and Dudley, Clarke was a great favourite of The Hawthorns fans and they were in uproar when Albion sold him to Pompey in 1947. He prospered at Fratton Park, and helped Portsmouth win the First Division championship in successive seasons, 1949 and 1950, scoring 49 goals in 116 League matches. In 1951, at the tail-end of his playing career, he toured Australia with the FA and appeared in five 'internationals' against the Aussies.

*Albion debut v Charlton Athletic (away) Division Two, 11 September 1937.*

## IAN COLLARD

*Born: South Hetton, County Durham, August 1947.*
*Career: South Hetton Primary and Senior Schools. Durham Boys. ALBION (June 1962, professional November 1964-May 1969). Ipswich Town. Portsmouth (on loan, 1975). Retired 1976. Coach to the Kuwait Sporting Club 1978-9.*

Ian Collard was a player who always put maximum effort into his performances. He started off as a talented inside-forward and later did splendid work as a left-half and left-back. He joined Ipswich in a player-exchange deal involving Danny Hegan plus £55,000. Collard played in the 1967 League Cup Final and in the 1968 FA Cup Final for Albion, gaining a winners' medal in the latter when he

*Ian Collard*

lined up in midfield with Bobby Hope and Tony Brown. Brother of Bruce Collard, the former Scunthorpe United defender, he made over 90 appearances for Albion, almost 100 for Ipswich and just one for Pompey. Returned to live in Ipswich area 1982.

*Albion debut v Burnley (home) Division One, 26 September 1964.*

## JIMMY COOKSON

*Born: Manchester, December 1904. Died: December 1970.*
*Career: Johnston Street School, Manchester. South Salford Lads' Club. Clayton FC. Manchester North End. Manchester City. Southport (trial). Chesterfield. ALBION (June 1927-August 1933). Plymouth Argyle. Swindon Town. Retired 1938. Became a publican, but still played local football in Swindon up to 1952.*

*Jimmy Cookson*

A powerful and most prolific goalscoring inside or centre-forward, Jimmy Cookson notched 92 goals in only 103 League appearances for Albion in just three full seasons (1927-30), including a club record six-goal haul in a Second Division match against Blackpool at The Hawthorns in September 1927. In his 15 years in top-class football, 'Cooky' scored 255 League goals — 85 for Chesterfield, 103 for Albion, 37 for Argyle and 30 for Swindon — and he appeared in only 290 matches — a magnificent record for a truly remarkable striker. He was leading scorer in Division Three North in 1925-6 and in Division Two in 1927-8. The 100th League goal of his career came in only his 89th match — playing for Albion v South Shields in December 1927 — which is the quickest individual century of goals in League history from the start of a player's career. He also scored more Second Division goals than anyone else in Albion's history. Cookson eventually lost his place in Albion's front line to another great marksman, W.G. Richardson.
*Albion debut v Oldham Athletic (away) Division Two, 27 August 1927 (scored in a 3-1 Albion defeat).*

## BOBBY CRAM

*Born: Hetton-le-Hole, County Durham, November 1939.*
*Career: Hetton-le-Hole Schools. Durham*
*& District Boys. ALBION (September 1955, professional January 1957-August 1967). Bromsgrove Rovers. Vancouver Royals. Vancouver All Stars. Paul Taylor's (coach). Colchester United. Royal Canada FC. Bath City. Canada (coach). Retired 1974.*

*Bobby Cram*

Bobby Cram was a determined and versatile footballer who played at right-back, wing-half and inside or centre-forward during his 12 years with Albion. He wore the number-two shirt in the 1967 League Cup Final at Wembley — his last game for Albion — and, all-told, appeared in 163 senior games for the club, scoring 26 goals, one-third of which came from penalty-kicks. Cram is one of only two players to have scored hat-tricks in League football from the full-back position — his treble coming against Stoke City in Albion's home First Division game on 12 September 1964. He is the uncle of athlete Steve Cram.
*Albion debut v Bolton Wanderers (away) Division One, 17 October 1959.*

## JACK CRISP

*Born: Hamstead, Birmingham, November 1896. Died: February 1939.*
*Career: Hamstead School. Leicester Fosse. Ordnance FC. ALBION (May 1914-May 1923). Blackburn Rovers. Coventry City. Birmingham. Cheltenham Town. Retired 1935.*
Jack Crisp played on both wings for Albion and gained a League Championship medal in 1920, when he missed only four matches. He preferred the right wing and this was where most of his better displays came. He had rapid acceleration and a useful shot, but was inconsistent. He represented the Football League in 1919-20 and during his career, with Albion, Blackburn, Coventry and Bir-

*Jack Crisp*

mingham, he made well over 250 senior appearances and scored 40 goals.
*Albion debut v Everton (away) Division One, 5 December 1914 (scored his side's goal in a 2-1 defeat).*

## JIM CUMBES

*Born: East Didsbury, Manchester, May 1944.*
*Career: Didsbury Grammar School. Didsbury & Manchester Boys. Whalley Range FC. Runcorn. Tranmere Rovers.*

*Jim Cumbes*

*ALBION (August 1969-November 1971). Aston Villa (£36,000). Portland Timbers (NASL). Coventry City. Runcorn. Southport. Worcester City. WBA All Stars. Kidderminster Harriers. Retired 1984. Played county cricket for Lancashire, Surrey, Worcestershire and Warwickshire; Lancashire CCC commercial manager 1987.*

Jim Cumbes was a tall goalkeeper, acrobatic, with a safe pair of hands, but who sometimes lacked total concentration. He cost Albion £33,350 when signed from Tranmere in 1969. Later he won a League Cup tankard with Aston Villa in 1975, against Norwich City. A friend of former Albion goalkeeper John Osborne, he went into business with Osborne in the sports outfitting trade in 1978. Cumbes made well over 400 League and Cup appearances during a splendid career.

*Albion debut v Arsenal (home) Division One, 16 August 1969.*

## LAURIE CUNNINGHAM

*Born: Archway, London, March 1956; Died: near Madrid, July 1989.*
*Career: Stroud Green School. Highgate Wood Boys. Haringey Schools. SE Counties Schools. Orient. ALBION (March 1977-June 1979). Real Madrid. Olympique Marseilles. Manchester United. Sporting Gijon. Leicester City. Rayo Vallecano (1986-7). FC Betis. RSC Charleroi (Belgium). Wimbledon (1988). Rayo Vallecano (1988).*

*Laurie Cunningham*

Laurie Cunningham, who joined the Throstles for £110,000, was called the 'second Pele' when he starred for Albion in the late 1970s. Nicknamed the 'Black Pearl' and 'Black Beauty' by the Baggies' supporters who idolised him, Cunningham had pace, intricate footwork, fine finishing technique, power, expert

reflexes, determination and wonderful balance. He became the first coloured footballer to wear an England international jersey in a major representative match, when he lined up against Scotland in an Under-21 game in 1977. Later he added a further five Under-21 caps, a 'B' cap, and six full caps to his collection. He left Albion, for the Spanish giants, Real Madrid, for a Albion club record fee of £995,000, and at once assumed the nickname 'El Negrito'. He appeared in the 1981 European Cup Final with Real and was in their team which won the Spanish League and Cup double in 1979-80. Cunningham attempted a comeback in English football with Manchester United and Leicester City in the mid 1980s, after a series of niggling leg injuries, but sadly failed to re-establish himself, although he gained an FA Cup winners' medal, as substitute, with Wimbledon in 1988. He was killed in a motoring accident.

*Albion debut v Tottenham Hotspur (away) Division One, 12 March 1977.*

## STAN DAVIES

*Born: Chirk, March 1898. Died: Birmingham, January 1972.*
*Career: Chirk Schools. Rochdale. Preston North End. Everton. ALBION (November 1921-November 1927). Barnsley. Manchester Central. Dudley Town. Chelmsford City (trainer). Retired 1936. Became a publican in West Bromwich 1937-46.*

*Stan Davies*

Stan Davies was a Welsh international who skippered his country twice and who won a total of 19 caps in six different positions — an indication of his wonderful versatility. Big and strong, Davies, who cost Albion £3,300, possessed a good shot, he could head a ball hard and true and he had lots of stamina. He joined

Albion in 1921, when the centre-forward position was becoming something of a problem at The Hawthorns, and stayed with the Baggies for six years, during which time he became a big hit with the fans, scoring 83 goals in 159 League and Cup games. During his career he scored 110 goals in almost 250 senior appearances for seven League clubs (1919-31). In World War One he distinguished himself with the Welsh Fusiliers and was awarded the Military Medal and the Croix de Guerre.

*Albion debut v Manchester City (home) Division One, 26 November 1921.*

## GEORGE DORSETT

*Born: Brownhills, August 1881: Died: April 1943.*
*Career: Brownhills & District Shools. Shireoaks Athletic. Small Heath (trial). Brownhills Albion. ALBION (November 1901-December 1904). Manchester City. Retired 1912 (injury).*

George Dorsett was an excellent ball-playing outside-left. He had splendid control and an unflurried demeanour which certainly graced his game. He was clever and altogether a cultured performer who, when sold to Manchester City in 1904, cost £400, then a record transfer fee for a winger. Dorsett played in exactly 100 senior games for Albion, scoring 22 goals. He won a Second Division championship medal in 1902, when he was part of a excellent front line which also included McLean, Simmons, Smith, Worton and Lee. That season Dorsett netted seven important goals in 32 outings and he went a long way in helping Albion regain their First Div-

*George Dorsett*

ision status after only one season in the lower division. Nicknamed 'Sos' and brother of Joe, also an Albion player, he

was converted into a classy left-half by City and in 1910 helped himself to another Second Division championship prize. In 1905-06, he represented the Football League, his only international honour. A penalty expert, he replaced Ben Garfield as Albion's regular outside-left.
*Albion debut v Preston North End (away) Division Two, 4 January 1902.*

## CHARLES 'CHUCK' DRURY

*Born: Darlaston, July 1937.*
*Career: Darlaston & Wednesbury Schools. SE Staffs Boys. F.H. Lloyds FC. ALBION (September 1954, professional February 1955-June 1964). Bristol City (£7,500). Bradford. Tamworth. Warley. Broms-grove Rovers. Retired 1974. Now living at Acton Trussell, Staffs.*

*Charles 'Chuck' Drury*

An England Youth international, capped in 1955, 'Chuck' Drury was a hard-working, dour, solidly-built half-back and a hard tackler. He was a regular in the Albion side for four seasons (1959-63), linking up with such players as Bobby Robson and Stan Jones in the middle line. After leaving The Haw-thorns he helped Bristol City win pro-motion to the Second Division in 1964-5, and when he retired from com-petitive football in 1969, he had made over 250 League and Cup appearances, including 160 for Albion.
*Albion debut v Bolton Wanderers (away) Division One, 22 February 1958.*

## JIMMY DUDLEY

*Born: Gartcosh, Glasgow, August 1928.*
*Career: Hill Top Schools (West Brom-wich). Walsall Conduits FC. Albright YC. ALBION (August 1944, professional 1945-December 1959). Walsall (£4,000). Stourbridge. Guest Motors FC. Retired 1966.*

Originally an inside-forward, Scotsman Jimmy Dudley became a competent footballer in all aspects of half-back play, performing diligently and without fuss in Albion's number-four shirt for a number of years, and chalking up 166 consecutive League appearances for the club (1952-56), a record beaten later by Ally Robertson, another Scot. In 1954, Dudley won an FA Cup winners' medal with Albion (after scoring a vital goal in the semi-final against Port Vale), as well as a Scottish 'B' cap — his only representative honour. He made a total of 320 senior appearances for Albion and later, with Walsall, added another 175, helping the Saddlers win the Fourth Division title in 1960 and promotion to Division Two in 1961. Whilst at The

*Jimmy Dudley*

Hawthorns, Dudley was part of a wond-erful half-back line which included Joe Kennedy or Jimmy Dugdale and big Ray Barlow. His brother, George, was with Albion from 1937 to 1946 and Jim himself is the cousin of the late Jimmy 'Iron' Edwards, a left-half with Albion before World War Two. Jim Dudley still works for Guest Motors in West Bromwich.
*Albion debut v Manchester City (away) Division One, 10 December 1949.*

## JIMMY DUGDALE

*Born: Liverpool, January, 1932.*
*Career: Liverpool Collegiate FC. Har-rowby FC. ALBION (January 1950-February 1956). Aston Villa. QPR. Retired 1963.*

Jimmy Dugdale was an outstanding centre-half who could control the heart of the defence with efficiency and author-ity. Unfortunately, he had Joe Kennedy as a rival pivot at Albion, and eventually he opted for a transfer and moved to neighbours Aston Villa for a fee of £25,000 in 1956 — this after helping Albion win the FA Cup in 1954. In 1957 he went to Wembley again — with Villa — and collected another winners' medal as Manchester United, with goalkeeper Ray Wood injured, were pipped 2-1 by a Peter McParland-inspired side. In 1960, a Second Division championship medal came Dugdale's way and a year later he added a League Cup winners' tankard to his silverware. He also won three Eng-land 'B' caps and represented the Football League. He is the uncle of former Coventry City, Charlton and Barnsley

*Jimmy Dugdale*

defender, Alan Dugdale. After retiring, he became a publican, first in Aston, then in Moseley and later in Halesowen. Alas, through illness he had a leg amputated in 1989.
*Albion debut v Bolton Wanderers (home) Division One, 13 December 1952.*

## CLIFF EDWARDS

*Born: Chase Terrace, Nr Cannock, March 1921. Died: March 1989.*
*Career: Rawnsley School. Chase Terrace United. Cannock Town. ALBION (October 1938, professional May 1948). Bristol City. Gravesend & Northfleet. Albion director 1971, retired 1986. Guested for Bath City, Blackpool and Carlisle United during World War Two.*
A short, thick-set half-back of natural ability, quick in the tackle and eminently solid in defence, where he usually occupied

*Cliff Edwards*

the centre-half berth, Cliff Edwards was a reliable performer, who always gave a good account of himself despite being only 5ft 7in tall. His career was obviously disrupted by the war and when Albion recruited the services of Irish international Jack Vernon in 1947, Edwards' days were numbered at The Hawthorns. He left the club in a player-exchange deal with Cyril Williams from Bristol City in the summer of 1948. He made 33 League appearances for the Bristol club before dropping into non-League soccer to join Gravesend & Northfleet in 1950. He returned to The Hawthorns in 1971, when he was elected to the board of directors, staying in office until his retirement in 1986 at the age of 65.
*Albion debut v Blackburn Rovers (away) Wartime League Cup, 25 May 1940.*
*League debut v Birmingham City (away) Division Two, 25 September 1946.*

## JIMMY EDWARDS

*Born: Tipton, December 1905. Died: April 1982.*

*Jimmy Edwards*

*Career: Horseley Bridge and Tipton Schools. Great Tipton Park. Newport Foundry FC. Stourbridge. Bridge Celtic. Stourbridge. ALBION (May 1926-May 1937). Norwich City. Bilston. Kingswinford. Dudley Town. Retired 1944.*
Jimmy Edwards — nicknamed 'Iron' — was converted by Albion from an aggressive inside-forward into an indefatigable, solid and highly efficient left-half. He was well-built and possessed a formidable tackle. A grand clubman, Edwards appeared in over 200 first-team games for Albion in his 11 years at The Hawthorns. He was a member of Albion's 1931 and 1935 FA Cup Final teams, collecting a winners' medal in the former. Also in 1931 he represented the Football League. When he played alongside his centre-half partner, Bill Richardson, the pair were often referred to as 'Iron' and 'Steel.'
*Albion debut v Hull City (away) Division Two, 31 March 1928.*

## BILLY ELLIOTT

*Born: Harrington, Cumberland, August 1919. Died: November 1966, holidaying in the Canary Islands.*
*Career: Carlisle Grammar School. Carlisle United. Wolves. Bournemouth. ALBION (December 1938-July 1951). Bilston United (player-manager). Retired 1954.*

*Billy Elliott*

A brilliant outside-right, fast with incredible close ball-control and a powerful shot in his right foot, Billy Elliott might have had a good international career had he not played at the same time as Stanley Matthews. Both Elliott's England appearances came in wartime soccer. He had one particularly smart trick — that of checking when running at top speed, by drawing his foot quickly over the top of the ball. An Achilles' tendon injury finished his career with Albion when he was only 32 and still an active member of the First Division side. After a brief association with Bilston, he became a publican in Handsworth, Birmingham, and was still a licensee when he died on holiday in 1966. For Albion he played in 330 senior matches and scored 157 goals, most of his strikes coming during the wartime period. He was a qualified FA coach and a member of the Players' Union committee. In season 1941-2, Elliott scored in 11 successive games for Albion and thus equalled Harry Jones' club record.
*Albion debut v Luton Town (away) Division Two, 24 December 1938.*

## RAY FAIRFAX

*Born: Smethwick, November 1941.*
*Career: Corbett Street Junior and James Watt Technical Schools, Smethwick. Smethwick and Birmingham Boys. Staffs County FA. Staff Boys. ALBION (May 1959, professional August 1959-June 1968). Northampton Town. Wellingborough. Olney Town. WBA All Stars. Retired 1979. Albion commercial assistant May 1974, assistant secretary 1976. Port Vale club secretary 1985. Worked in Aston Villa's ticket office (1988-92).*

*Ray Fairfax*

Fierce tackling distinguished Ray Fairfax's displays at full-back, his kicking being strong and safe. He had some good defenders with him at The Hawthorns and consequently had his work cut out to establish himself in the senior side. He battled through, however, and managed almost 100 outings for the first team in his nine professional seasons with the club. Later, he played 116 League games for Northampton Town. He won a League Cup winners' tankard with Albion in 1966, and scored one goal, a blockbuster against the Italian club, Bologna, in a Fairs Cup game at The Hawthorns in 1967.
*Albion debut v Liverpool (away) Division One, 20 March 1963.*

## RONNIE FENTON

*Born: South Shields, September 1940.*
*Career: South Shields Schools. Durham Boys. ALBION (trial 1955). South Shields. Burnley. ALBION (November 1962-January 1965). Birmingham City (£7,500). Brentford. Notts County. Later coach at Meadow Lane, then manager (1975-77). Nottingham Forest assistant manager-coach (October 1977-to date).*

*Ronnie Fenton*

An inside-forward, Ronnie Fenton cost Albion £15,000 when secured from Burnley in 1962. His performances for Albion were assertive, yet occasionally he struggled to make an impression. He scored 18 goals in 66 outings for the Throstles and after leaving The Hawthorns he netted 26 goals in League football for Birmingham and Brentford. During his League career, Fenton made a total of 195 appearances and scored 43 goals. He then spent 16 seasons as Brian Clough's assistant at Nottingham Forest.
*Albion debut v West Ham United (away) Division One, 1 December 1962.*

## BOB FINCH

*Born: Hednesford, Staffs. August 1908.*
*Career: Hill Top and West Hill School, Hednesford. Hednesford Prims. Hednesford Town. ALBION (April 1925, professional September 1925-May 1939). Swansea Town. Hednesford Town. Tamworth. Retired 1947. Joined police force in Hereford 1942, serving as a constable until 1956.*

*Bob Finch*

Bob Finch was a fine full-back, who was quick to spot danger. He gave Albion 14 years' splendid service, playing in 234 League and Cup matches without ever scoring a goal. He had to contest the full-back positions with some useful players, including internationals Bill Ashurst and George Shaw, Bert Trentham and Hughie Foulkes (Wales) and later Cecil Shaw, amongst others. He was a first-team regular for three seasons (1927-30), missing only ten out of 126 League games. During the 1930s, he won three Central League championship medals with Albion, skippering the Reserves on many occasions. In 1927-8, he had played in two international trials for England.
*Albion debut v Leicester City (home) Division One, 27 February 1926.*

## ARTHUR FITTON

*Born: Melton Mowbray, May 1902.*
*Career: Edgecliff School (Kinver). Kinver Swifts. Cookley St Peter's. Kidderminster Harriers. ALBION (October 1922-March 1932). Manchester United. Preston North End. Coventry City. Kidderminster Harriers. Retired June 1939. Albion assistant trainer-coach (October 1948-July 1950), then first-team trainer (August 1951-June 1956). Became game warden at Kinver National Trust Park.*

*Arthur Fitton*

'Mother' Fitton was a penetrative left winger who gave Albion great service both on and off the field, for the reserve side and first team alike. A very popular character indeed, he had 99 first-team outings and 261 for the Central League side (56 goals), still a club record. He won three Central League championship medals with Albion (1923, 1924 and 1927), and in September 1954 was trainer to the Football League side which met the League of Ireland in Dublin. Four months earlier he had seen Albion win the FA Cup at Wembley. At Preston he helped the Deepdale club win promotion from Division Two in 1934 and assisted Coventry City to the Third Division South title in 1936. Outside soccer, Fitton was a fine cricketer, keeping wicket for Stourbridge CC, West Bromwich Dartmouth and Staffordshire in the Minor Counties. During World War One, he worked in a factory which produced hand-grenades.
*Albion debut v Manchester City (away) Division One, 11 November 1922.*

## KEN FOGGO

*Born: Perth, Scotland, November 1943.*
*Career: Peebles High School. Peebleshire & Scotland Schools. Peebles YMCA. St Johnstone (trial). ALBION (August, 1959, professional November 1960-October 1967). Norwich City (15,000). Portsmouth. Brentford (loan). Southend United. Chelmsford City. Brereton Social. Retired 1982 and began working in a London market.*
A diminutive outside-right often roughly treated by the bigger defenders, Ken Foggo was a clever footballer whose accurate crosses on the run were a feature of his play. He came from Scotland to

*Ken Foggo*

*Doug Fraser*

A fast, direct and forceful outside-right or centre-forward, Arthur Gale was an 'unlucky' stand-in for Tommy Glidden during Albion's 1935 FA Cup run. Gale, a schoolteacher by profession, had played in every round of that season's competition, including the semi-final, and had scored in four ties, one goal being a brilliant diving header in the sixth round against Preston at The Hawthorns. Glidden, however, was brought back for the Wembley meeting with Sheffield Wednesday, only to break down injured as Gale sat on the bench, virtually in tears.

*Arthur Gale*

The Hawthorns with fellow schoolboys Bobby Hope, Campbell Crawford and Bobby Murray, following their performances for Scotland Boys against England Boys in 1959. He had earlier represented Scotland Boys at Rugby Union. Foggo took over from Alec Jackson on Albion's right wing in 1963 and went on to make in excess of 130 senior appearances for the club, scoring 29 goals. After leaving Albion, he had 187 League games for Norwich City (54 goals), 60 for Portsmouth (three goals) and 30 for Southend United (six goals) which gave him a career record of 406 League appearances and 92 goals.
*Albion debut v Fulham (home) 8 September 1962 (assisted in three goals in Albion's 6-1 victory).*

## DOUG FRASER

*Born: Busby, Lanarkshire, December 1941. Career: Busby Junior and Senior Schools. Rolls Royce FC. Eaglesham Amateurs. Blantyre Celtic. Aberdeen. ALBION (September 1963-January 1971). Nottingham Forest (£35,000). Walsall. Manager at Fellows Park (1975). Retired from football 1977 to become a prison warder at Nottingham.*

A fine, compact wing-half, who cost Albion £23,000, Doug Fraser was remarkably quick in gathering the ball and passing it, almost in one smooth movement. He had a fine tackle and was a stylish player. He did good work in the right-back position in later years. He played for Albion in the 1966, 1967 and 1970 League Cup Finals, skippering the team in the latter. And in 1968 he was in Albion's FA Cup-winning team against Everton. After appearing in 325 games for Albion, he added a further 120 to his tally with Forest and Walsall. He had 70 outings for Aberdeen (1960-63). A Scottish international, he won two caps, in the mid-1960s, against Holland and Cyprus.
*Albion debut v Birmingham City (home) Division One, 18 September 1963.*

## ARTHUR GALE

*Born: Salford, November 1904. Died: May 1976.
Career: Salford & District Schools. South Salford Lads' Club. Sedgley Park (Salford). Bury. Chester. ALBION (June 1931-December 1936). Chester. Macclesfield. Altrincham (coach 1939). Northern Nomads (manager 1967-8.)*

Albion lost the Final 4-2 to the Owls. He managed only 29 first-team appearances (12 goals), yet won three Central League championship medals in the 1930s and for the Reserves his record was quite remarkable — 136 matches and 146 goals, 41 coming in season 1934-5 when Albion's second team netted 121 goals in winning the title for the third season running. It was unfortunate for Gale that he understudied such fine players as Glidden and W.G. Richardson during his five and a half years at The Hawthorns.
*Albion debut v Newcastle United (home) Division One, 2 April 1932.*

## ALF 'JASPER' GEDDES

*Born: West Bromwich, April 1871. Died: October 1927.
Career: Christ Church and Bratt Street Schools (West Bromwich). Causeway Green Villa. ALBION (May 1891-March 1894). Clapham Rovers. Millwall Athletic. ALBION (April-May 1895). Millwall Athletic. Bedminster. Bristol City. Retired 1908.*

A mercurial outside-left, fast, enthusiastic and able to centre in splendid style, Jasper Geddes was also a temperamental player. A little greedy at times, he nevertheless

*Alf 'Jasper' Geddes*

had some outstanding games for Albion. He served them in two separate spells, the second at a crucial stage in the season whereby Albion had to win their remaining two matches to stay in Division One. Albion won those two fixtures, and Geddes scored in both of them. He then returned to Millwall. Only 5ft 4in tall and barely 10st in weight, he won an FA Cup winners' medal with Albion in 1892 and was reputedly Millwall's first professional footballer, skippering the Lions in their two Southern League championship winning seasons of 1894-5 and 1895-6. He played over 100 times for Albion, including friendlies.
*Albion debut v Everton (away), 7 November 1891.*

## JOHNNY GILES

*Born: Cabra, Dublin, November 1940.*
*Career: Brunswick Street School (Dublin). St Colombus FC. Dublin Schools. Dublin City FC (later Munster Victoria). Stella Maris. Home Farm. Manchester United. Leeds United. ALBION (as player-manager June 1975-May 1977). Shamrock Rovers (player-manager). Philadelphia Fury (NASL). Vancouver Whitecaps (NASL, coach). ALBION (manager, February 1984-September 1985). Republic of Ireland player-manager (1973-80). WBA All Stars.*
Arguably one of the most brilliant midfield players Albion have ever had, Johnny Giles combined his magnificent ball skills with vision and thought. He possessed a useful shot and was a great asset to Albion when he arrived at the club in 1975, in a £48,000 deal from Leeds.

*Johnny Giles*

In his first season at The Hawthorns he saw Albion win promotion from the Second Division and then set them firmly back among the big boys before leaving to return home to his native Ireland. He came back to Albion as manager in 1984, but this time things went wrong and he left as the team were heading back into Division Two. With Leeds, Giles won First and Second Division championship medals, FA Cup, Football League Cup and Fairs Cup winners' prizes, and appeared in several other Finals including the 1975 European Cup, which was to be his last game for Leeds. Earlier, with Manchester United, he had gained an FA Cup winners' medal in 1963. In all, he played in 11 FA Cup semi-finals (including replays) and shares the record for most FA Cup Final appearances (five). In fact, he played in six, counting the 1970 replay. He played for the Republic of Ireland Schools against England and was the first Eire player to win 50 full caps for his country; his final tally was 60. He was played in 'The Three' v 'The Six' game at Wembley in 1973, for the Irish XI v Brazil in the same year, and for an Eire XI v Manchester United in 1974. Giles won an FAI Cup winners' medal with Shamrock Rovers in 1978. In a truly wonderful playing career from 1959 to 1977, he amassed 554 League appearances and scored 99 goals. In all competitions, his playing record was 863 appearances and 125 goals. For Albion he netted five times in 88 games.
*Albion debut v Chelsea (home) Division Two, 20 August 1975.*

## TOMMY GLIDDEN

*Born: Coxlodge, Newcastle-upon-Tyne, July 1902. Died: West Bromwich, July 1974.*
*Career: Castletown School. Sunderland Schools. Durham Boys. Sunderland*
(amateur). Bristol City (trial). Colliery Old Boys. Bolden Villa. Sunderland West End. ALBION (April 1922-May 1936). Retired summer 1936. Became coach at The Hawthorns (1936-9), director (1951 until his death).

*Tommy Glidden*

An outside or inside-right and one of Albion's celebrities during the 1930s, Tommy Glidden was an extremely nimble player, a fine ball-artist who was always on hand to cash in on a half-chance. He had the knack of scoring direct from corner-kicks. Glidden skippered Albion in both the 1931 and 1935 FA Cup Finals, collecting the trophy in 1931 after Albion had pipped arch-rivals Birmingham 2-1 at Wembley. During his long and loyal association with Albion, he appeared in 479 competitive matches, scoring 140 goals. He got into the senior side in 1922, at the expense of Jack Crisp, and, but for a few games, was Albion's first-choice outside-right for 14 years. He represented England Schoolboys in 1914 and figured in a full international trial in 1925-6. He received a special award in April 1972, when celebrating 50 years' association with Albion. He died after a heart attack.
*Albion debut v Everton (away) Division One, 25 November 1922.*

## TONY GODDEN

*Born: Gillingham, August 1955.*
*Career: Napier Secondary Modern School. Gillingham. Leonard Star FC. Eastcourt United. Gillingham & District Schools. Gillingham (amateur). Ashford Town. Wolves (trial). ALBION (August 1975-May 1986). Chelsea. Birmingham City. Bury (on*

*loan). Sheffield Wednesday. Peterborough United. Colchester United (on loan). Wivenhoe Town. Warboys Town (manager 1991). Also on loan to Preston North End, Luton Town (March 1982), Walsall (October 1983) Chelsea (March 1986), and Torquay Utd (non-contract).*

*Tony Godden*

In October 1981, goalkeeper Tony Godden set an Albion record which will take some beating — he appeared in his 228th consecutive first-team game. He then lost his place in the side to Mark Grew. Four and a half years earlier, Godden had made his Albion debut against Tottenham and immediately was said to have a bright future ahead of him. He went from strength to strength and when he had his testimonial match at The Hawthorns in May 1986 he had 360 senior games to his name, 329 of them for Albion. A safe 'keeper with fine reflexes, Godden appeared in the 1978 FA Cup semi-final. Eventually he became disillusioned with life at The Hawthorns and towards the end of 1985-6, his loan period to Chelsea ended with a permanent transfer to Stamford Bridge.
*Albion debut v Tottenham Hotspur (away) Division One, 12 March 1977.*

## DON GOODMAN

*Born: Leeds, May 1966.*
*Career: Leeds City Schools. Collingham FC. Bradford City. ALBION (£50,000, March 1987). Sunderland (£900,000, December 1991).*
An exciting striker, fast, alert, eager to pounce, always willing to chase and harass opponents, Goodman had four and a half seasons with Albion during which time he scored 62 goals in 148/18 League and Cup appearances, and became the idol of the 'Brummie Road End' fans. In 1989-90 he became the first Albion player since Tony Brown in 1971

*Don Goodman*

to score more than 20 goals in a season, but injuries plagued him during that season and the following campaign. When fully fit he was a handful for any defender. A very dangerous customer inside the box, where his quickness and ability to get in a shot made him such an asset, Goodman eventually left The Hawthorns for Second Division Sunderland only some six months after seeing Albion relegated to the Third Division, moving to Roker Park as a replacement for Marco Gabbiadini. Some Albion supporters were not at all pleased with the chairman John Silk or his board for allowing their star man to leave. Goodman quickly became a favourite on Wearside.
*Albion debut v Oldham Athletic (away) Division Two, 28 March 1987.*

## HOWARD GREGORY

*Born: Aston Manor, Birmingham, May 1894, Died: August 1954.*
*Career: Gower Street and Aston Schools. Aston Manor FC. Birchfield Trinity. ALBION (May 1911-May 1926). Retired through injury. Licensee of the Woodman Inn, (Handsworth) 1927-32, and remained in trade until 1953.*
Howard Gregory was a quick-witted outside-left, fast and plucky, who was always likely to produce something out of the ordinary. He formed a tremendous left-wing partnership with that fine goal-grabber, Freddie Morris, and in

*Howard Gregory*

Albion's Championship-winning season of 1919-20 they scored between them a total of 49 First Division goals. Nicknamed the 'Express Man', Gregory once struck a soaking-wet ball so hard, playing against Wolves at Molineux, that en route to goal, the casing split, the bladder going into the net and the casing itself over the bar. He took some time to get into Albion's first team but when he did, he performed consistently well, making a total of 181 senior appearances and scoring 45 goals before announcing his retirement, through injury, in 1926.
*Albion debut v Everton (away) Division One, 22 April 1912.*

## FRANK GRIFFIN

*Born: Pendlebury, Manchester, March 1928.*
*Career: Pendlebury Central School. St Augustine's Youth Club. Newton Heath. Hull City (trial). Bolton Wanderers (amateur 1944-48). Eccles Town. Shrewsbury Town. ALBION (April 1951-June 1959). Northampton Town. Wellington Town. Sankey's FC. Worthen United (manager). Retired 1966.*
Frank Griffin was the toast of West Bromwich back in 1954 when he scored the winning goal for Albion against Preston in the FA Cup Final. A right winger, he was worth every penny of the £9,500 transfer fee Albion paid Shrewsbury Town in 1951. Albion signed Griffin to replace Billy Elliott and he was an instant success in the number-seven shirt. Fast and clever, and always eager to try a shot at goal, he appeared in 275 senior games for Albion, scoring 52 goals, in his eight years with the club. He was showing international form in 1958 when he broke his right leg in a collision with Sheffield United's Joe Shaw in an FA Cup tie at The Hawthorns. He failed to regain

*Frank Griffin*

his form and wound down his career slowly with Northampton (18 appearances) and then with a handful of non-League teams.
*Albion debut v Sunderland (away) Division One, 28 April 1951.*

## BILLY GRIPTON

*Born: Prince's End, Tipton, July 1920.*
*Died: July 1981.*
*Career: Prince's End and Tipton Schools. Dartmouth Vics. Bush Rangers Brownhills Albion. ALBION (June 1935, professional November 1937-June 1948).*

*Billy Gripton*

*Luton Town (£3,000). Bournemouth. Worcester City. Retired 1956 to become local works' groundsman in Tipton.*
Billy Gripton was a hard but fair centre-half who was a dominant force at the heart of Albion's defence for a number of years. A great tactician, he managed to total more than 200 first-team appearances, despite the fact that his career was interrupted by war. In 1945 he was replaced in the Albion side by George Tranter who, in turn, lost his place to Jack Vernon.
*Albion debut v Millwall (home) Division Two, 8 April 1939.*

## WILLIE GROVES

*Born: Leith, Scotland, February 1869.*
*Died: February, 1908, Longmore.*
*Career: Thistle Club (Edinburgh). Hibernian. Celtic. Everton (for 2 days). Celtic again. ALBION (October 1890-September 1893). Aston Villa. Hibernian. Rushden FC. Retired 1902.*

*Willie Groves*

An exciting footballer who, although having no claims to greatness in heading and goalscoring, was second to none in foraging and distribution skills. A play-anywhere performer, Groves had immense enthusiasm and dedication for the game. In a splendid career, which saw him converted by Albion from a centre-forward to a wing-half, he won three Scottish caps, in 1888, 1889 and 1890, scoring a hat-trick against Ireland in his second game. He also represented the Football League (1891-2) and played for Edinburgh in an inter-city match. In his first spell with Hibernian he won a Scottish Cup winners' medal in 1887, and a runners-up medal in the same competition in 1896. With Celtic he gained a Cup runners-up medal in 1889 and for Albion he made two of the three goals in the 1892 FA Cup Final, when Aston Villa were beaten 3-0 at the Crystal Palace.

Later, as a Villa player, Groves gained a First Division championship medal (1894). He scored ten goals in 67 League and Cup games for Albion. In his career (with Hibs, Albion and Villa) he scored over 30 goals in almost 200 matches. He did not appear in Everton's first team, the FA declaring his transfer void.
*Albion debut v Wolverhampton Wanderers (home) Division One, 13 December 1890.*

## HARRY HADLEY

*Born: Barrow-in-Furness, April 1878.*
*Died: West Bromwich, September 1942.*
*Career: Cradley Heath & District Schools. Colley Gate United. Halesowen. ALBION (February 1897-February 1905). Aston Villa. Nottingham Forest. Southampton. Croydon Common. Halesowen. Merthyr Town (manager on four separate occasions commencing May 1919 and ending September 1931). Chesterfield (manager). Aberdare Athletic (manager). Gillingham (manager). Bangor City (manager). Retired 1936.*

*Harry Hadley*

Harry Hadley was a good player, cool, calculated, energetic and a half-back who was keen in the tackle, forceful in attack and determined to win. Capped by England once (in 1903) he gained a Second Division championship medal with Albion in 1902, and in his eight years with the club appeared in some 181 games. Normally he filled in at left-half, and at the turn of the century figured in a useful middle-line comprising himself, right-half Dan Nurse and centre-half Jim Stevenson. Brother of Ben Hadley, another Albion player, Harry became a successful manager after retiring as a player, and was sought by many leading clubs. He preferred to remain in the lower divisions and did exceptionally well, particularly with Merthyr Town.
*Albion debut v Notts County (away) Division One, 19 March 1898.*

## ASA HARTFORD

*Born: Clydebank, Scotland, October 1950.*
*Career: Faifley Primary School. Clydebank High School. Dunbartonshire Boys.*

Drumchapel Amateurs. ALBION (April 1966, professional October 1967-November 1971). Leeds United (for 24 hours). ALBION (November 1971-August 1974). Manchester City (for £225,000; a club record sale at the time). Nottingham Forest. Everton. Manchester City. Fort Lauderdale Sun. Norwich City. Bolton Wanderers. Stockport County (player-manager). Oldham Athletic (player-coach). Shrewsbury Town (player-coach). Blackburn Rovers (coach).

*Asa Hartford*

Richard Asa Hartford was a midfield dynamo, a player who darted and danced all over the park each and every time he donned a football jersey. Full of energy, always buzzing around in search of an opening, he was the player who, on medical advice, was rejected by Leeds United in 1971 because of a 'hole in the heart' condition. At the time Albion and Leeds had agreed on a £170,000 fee. Three years later, Hartford moved from The Hawthorns to Maine Road for £225,000. His transfer from City to Forest in 1979 cost £450,000; and it was a £400,000 deal which took him from the City Ground to Goodison Park in that same year before Manchester City paid £350,000 to Everton to recall him to Maine Road in 1981. A Scottish international at Youth, Under-21, Under-23 and full levels, Hartford won a total of 50 senior caps for his country. He played for Albion in the 1970 League Cup Final, won a League Cup winners' medal with Manchester City in 1976, and a Milk Cup medal with Norwich City in 1985, when his deflected shot beat Sunderland. Hartford amassed well over 900 appearances in all competitions, including his spell in America and on the international front. He was named Asa by his parents after the celebrated American singer Al (Asa) Jolson.
*Albion debut v Sheffield United (away) Division One, 10 February 1968 (aged 17).*

## SAMMY HEASELGRAVE

*Born: Smethwick, October 1916. Died: Birmingham, April 1975.*
*Career: Smethwick & District Schools. Bearwood Swifts. Warley Lions. Smethwick Highfield. Brierley Hill Alliance. ALBION (October 1934-October 1945). Northampton Town. Retired 1947-8. Guested for Walsall in 1945-6. All-England Bowls champion in 1963.*

*Sammy Heaselgrave*

Sammy Heaselgrave was a hard-working, seemingly tireless, utility forward, constantly on target with his powerful shooting. A Junior international in 1936, he broke into Albion's first team in March 1937 and from then until his departure, to Northampton Town in 1945, he appeared in well over 160 senior games, scoring 57 goals — an extremely creditable record. Initially he had to bide his time before establishing himself in the League side but, once in, he stayed put and did a splendid job, especially during the wartime period when he played alongside such great players as Len Duns, Jack Acquaroff, 'W.G.' Richardson, Ike Clarke and Billy Elliott, to name but a few. Indeed, Heaselgrave was one of only four Albion players to represent the club in each of the seven wartime seasons (1939-46 inclusive). After his playing days were over he became a solicitor in Bearwood, a business which is still in the family today.
*Albion debut v Brentford (home) Division One, 27 March 1937.*

## NORMAN HEATH

*Born: Wolverhampton, January 1924. Died: Great Barr, Birmingham, November 1983.*

*Career: Bushbury Hill School. Wolverhampton Boys. Henry Meadows FC. ALBION (May 1942, professional October 1943-June 1955). Forced to retire following serious spinal injury suffered in League match at Sunderland in March 1954. Manager of junior side Great Barr Gunners (1971-3).*

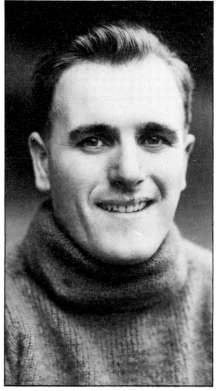

*Norman Heath*

In his time, Norman Heath was a fine, courageous goalkeeper whose agility and brilliant reflexes were key features of his splendid displays between the posts in 169 senior matches for Albion. He came to The Hawthorns during the war and understudied Jimmy Sanders for a number of years before that tragic injury in 1954. It was Sanders who stepped into goal for that year's FA Cup Final against Preston.
*Albion League debut v Sheffield Wednesday (away) Division Two, 13 December 1947.*

## FRANK HODGETTS

*Born: Oakham, Dudley, September 1924.*
*Career: Rowley Regis School. St Mary's Sunday School FC. Accles & Pollock Works FC. ALBION (September 1939, professional October 1942-May 1949). Millwall (£6,000). Worcester City. Retired through injury. Returned to Albion as coach (1958-62). Currently chairman of the Herefordshire and Worcestershire County Tennis Association and chief organiser of coaching.*
Winger Frank Hodgetts was only 16 years, 26 days old when he made his first appearance for Albion's senior team against Notts County in a wartime game at The Hawthorns in October 1940. That made him the youngest-ever player to don Albion's first-team jersey — still a record. Nominally an outside-left, Hodgetts was

*Frank Hodgetts*

likely to bob up anywhere in the attack — sometimes to the annoyance of his colleagues. A cheerful character with a fierce shot, he played well over 200 competitive matches during his career with Albion and Millwall between 1940 and 1953), and scored 44 goals. Most of his outings for Albion were during World War Two. Today he lives in retirement at Hagley, near Kidderminster.
*Albion debut v Notts County (home) Wartime League, 26 October 1940.*
*League debut v Swansea Town (away) Division Two, 31 August 1946 (scored in his side's 3-2 win).*

## DEREK HOGG

*Born: Stockton-on-Tees, November 1930.*
*Career: Middleforth C of E School. Preston North End (trial). Lostock Hall FC. Chorley. Leicester City. ALBION (£20,000 April 1958-October 1960). Car-*

*Derek Hogg*

*diff City (£12,500). Kettering Town. Retired 1965.*
A tricky and fleet-footed outside-left who responded best to a ball-playing inside partner, Derek Hogg had the marked tendency to over-elaborate with his footwork. He arrived at The Hawthorns to replace George Lee and was then himself dislodged by both Geoff Carter and Andy Aitken before leaving Albion for Cardiff City. Hogg, who had occasional game on the right flank, received Football League recognition in 1955-6 and the following season helped Leicester City win the Second Division title. During his League career he appeared in 283 matches (44 goals); his Albion record was 81 outings and 11 goals.
*Albion debut v Luton Town (away) Division One, 23 August 1958.*

## BOBBY HOPE

*Born: Bridge of Allan, Stirlingshire, September 1943.*
*Career: Clydebank High and Dunbartonshire West Schools. Drumchapel Amateurs. Scotland Boys. Sunderland (trial). ALBION (August 1959, professional September 1960-May 1972). Birmingham City (£66,666). Philadelphia Atoms (NASL). Dallas Tornados (NASL). Sheffield Wednesday. Bromsgrove Rovers (player-coach, appointed manager 1983). Burton Albion (manager). Bromsgrove Rovers (manager 1989). WBA All Stars (1979-92).*

*Bobby Hope*

Bobby Hope was a player who displayed a masterly generalship in midfield. His superb ball skills and telling passes were highlights of a wonderful association with Albion for whom he won a League Cup winners' tankard in 1966 and an FA Cup winners' medal in 1968, as well as runners-up prizes in the League Cup in 1967 and 1970. Capped by Scotland at Schoolboy, Under-23 and full levels, he

appeared in over 400 senior games for Albion scoring 42 goals, one of which was Albion's first in Europe — against DOS Utrecht (Holland) in 1966-7. For Albion, Blues and Wednesday, Hope's League record was 407 matches and 45 goals. Today, besides looking after non-Leaguers Bromsgrove Rovers, Hope runs a Post Office in Boldmere near Sutton Coldfield as well as turning out in various charity matches for WBA All Stars.
*Albion debut v Arsenal (home) Division One, 30 April 1960, aged 16.*

## EZRA HORTON

*Born: West Bromwich, August 1861.*
*Died: West Bromwich, July 1939.*
*Career: Christ Church and Beeches Road Schools. George Salter Works FC. West Bromwich FC. ALBION (August 1882, professional August 1885-June 1891). Retired. Became a referee in 1895. Guested for Aston Villa in 1884-5 season. In later years he turned out for the West Bromwich hockey team as a centre-half and became only the second Midlander to play for England at this sport.*

*Ezra Horton*

As a footballer, Ezra Horton — nicknamed 'Ironsides' — was a very sporting player, a largely defensive right-half who was good at heading, strong at kicking and fearsome in the tackle — hence his nickname. He played in three successive FA Cup Finals for Albion (1886-7-8), being on the winning side at the third attempt. He skippered Albion in 1884-5 and had the distinction of playing in each of Albion's first 36 FA Cup-ties. He played in around 300 matches for the Baggies (all competitions including friendlies) during his nine years with the club. Brother of John Horton, Ezra was a member of the first League side fielded by Albion, at Stoke, in September 1888.
*Albion debut v St George's (away), 1882.*
*FA Cup debut v Wednesday Town (home), 10 November 1883.*
*League debut v Stoke (away), 8 September 1888.*

## JOHN HORTON

*Born: West Bromwich, February 1866.*
*Died: January 1947.*
*Career: Dartmouth School. Oak Villa. Burslem Port Vale. Wednesbury Old Athletic. ALBION (October 1882, professional September 1885-May 1899). Retired summer 1899.*

*John Horton*

A schoolteacher by profession, 'Jack' Horton was a grand full-back who could never be faulted when it came to resolute tackling and clearing his lines, which he did in fine style. A magnificent clubman — 17 seasons with Albion — he clocked up over 250 games for the Throstles (all competitions, including friendlies). He was right-back in Albion's first-ever League match, against Stoke in 1888, and during his association with the club he was always one of its greatest supporters. He came back in 1895 to play in the FA Cup Final against Aston Villa after missing all the previous rounds. 'Jack' also put in appearances as a half-back and as a centre-forward, but it was in the full-back position where he excelled best of all. Brother of Ezra Horton, who played in the same team for a number of seasons up to 1891.
*Albion debut v Wednesbury Old Athletic (home) FA Cup, 6 December 1884.*
*League debut v Stoke (away), 8 September 1888.*

## DON HOWE

*Born: Wolverhampton, October 1935.*
*Career: St Peter's School (Wolverhampton). Wolverhampton Boys. Wolves (trial). ALBION (December 1950, professional November 1952-April 1964). Arsenal (£40,000). Retired 1967, to become coach at Highbury, then assistant manager 1969. Albion manager (July 1971-April 1975). Galatasaray (coach). Leeds United (coach). Arsenal (coach, then manager). England 'B' team coach, then chief coach. Saudi Arabia (coach 1986-7). Bristol Rovers (coach 1987). Wimbledon (coach, then assistant manager). QPR (assistant manager 1989, manager November 1989-91). Wimbledon (chief scout). Barnet (coach). Coventry City (manager 1991-2), Chelsea (assistant manager/coach).*

*Don Howe*

Deft positioning and reliability were the hallmarks of Don Howe's play at right-back for Albion and England. Although in later years he did play at right-half and inside-right, the right-back spot was always his favourite — and best. He took over at Albion from Stuart Williams after making his debut early in the 1955-6 season. Howe held his place and went on to make over 375 appearances for Albion, besides winning 23 consecutive caps for England. He also collected six Under-23 caps, played for England 'B', represented the Football League and turned out for the FA XI in 1956 and 1962. He was club captain at Albion for a number of years. With Arsenal he fractured his leg in March 1966 and the injury ended his playing career. He coached the Gunners when they lifted the League and FA Cup double in 1970-71. Howe came back to Albion as manager in the summer of 1971 but disaster struck in 1973 and the Throstles were relegated. Perhaps Howe's best day as Albion boss was when he signed Willie Johnston from Rangers. When he returned to Highbury, Howe coached Arsenal to three successive FA Cup Finals (1978-9-80).
*Albion debut v Everton (home) Division One, 24 August 1955.*

## ALEC JACKSON

*Born: Tipton, May 1937.*
*Career: Park Lane Secondary Modern School. Tipton St John's FC. W.G.Allen's FC. ALBION (May 1954, professional September 1954-June 1964). Birmingham City (£12,500). Walsall. Nuneaton Borough. Kidderminster Harriers. Warley. Oldbury Town. Warley Borough. Darlaston. Blakenhall. Gornal. Rushall Olympic. Bush Rangers. WBA All Stars. Retired 1985. Coach to Coseley Rovers Youth Club 1980-82.*

*Alec Jackson*

Alec Jackson was a pluckily little utility forward, fleet of foot and able to perform in any position with a great deal of success. A brilliant dribbler at times, 'Jacko' chose the right-wing berth as his best and represented the Football League against the Scottish League in 1962, wearing the number-seven shirt. He made his Albion debut as a 17-year-old and was still playing charity football for the WBA All Stars in 1985, at the age of 48. He scored a goal on average every four games for Albion, and during his League career with Albion, Birmingham City and Walsall, he amassed 307 appearances and hit 67 goals. Jackson broke his leg playing against Spurs at White Hart Lane in 1958.
*Albion debut v Charlton Athletic (away) Division One, 6 November 1954 (scored in a 3-1 Albion victory).*

## GEORGE JAMES

*Born: Oldbury, February 1899. Died: December 1976.*
*Career: Oldbury & District Schools. Bilston United. ALBION (January 1920-May 1929). Reading. Watford. Retired 1933 to become a West Bromwich licensee.*

A shortish, heavily-built inside or centre-forward of the bustling type, George James was a player who was fearless, with a telling shot and big heart. He was a chatterbox both on and off the field, but he certainly gave Albion good service during his stay at The Hawthorns. He scored 57 goals in 116 matches for Albion, including a quick-fire effort against Nottingham Forest in December 1924 which was reputedly timed at five seconds from the kick-off. James scored four of Albion's five goals that afternoon —and he finished the season with 30 under his belt for a personal record. He linked up

*George James*

wonderfully well with Joe Carter, 'Tug' Wilson and Stan Davies, and was forever searching for an opening. He played in an England trial in 1925.
*Albion debut v Bolton Wanderers (away) Division One, 12 November 1921.*

## CLAUDE JEPHCOTT

*Born: Smethwick, October 1891. Died: October 1950.*

*Claude Jephcott*

*Career: West Smethwick School. Olive Mount FC. Brierley Hill Alliance. Stourbridge. Brierley Hill Alliance. ALBION (April 1911-May 1923). Retired. Albion director (January 1934 until his death).*
A brilliant outside-right who made full use of his tremendous pace, Claude Jephcott was wonderfully consistent and always rose to the big occasion. A Junior international in 1911, he suffered a fractured leg in 1922, against Aston Villa, which ended his career a shade prematurely — this after he had played in almost 200 first-team matches for the Throstles (16 goals). He appeared in the 1912 FA Cup Final against Barnsley, and in 1919-20 won a First Division championship medal with Albion, his form on the right wing during this campaign being quite superb. He represented the Football League and an England XI between 1913 and 1919.
*Albion debut v Sunderland (away) Division One, 9 December 1911.*

## JOE JOHNSON

*Born: Grimsby, April 1911. Died: West Bromwich, August 1983.*
*Career: Grimsby junior football. Scunthorpe United. Bristol City. Stoke City. ALBION (November 1937-May 1946). Northwich Victoria. Hereford United. Retired 1949-50. Guested for Notts County, Leicester City and Crewe Alexandra during the war.*
An excellent little player who achieved a useful record as a goal-scoring left-winger, most of Joe Johnson's good work was done with Stoke when he had Stan Matthews on the opposite flank. He gave Albion splendid service, too, before and during the war, appearing in 145 senior games and scoring 47 goals. Capped by England on five occasions (1936-7), he won a Second Division championship

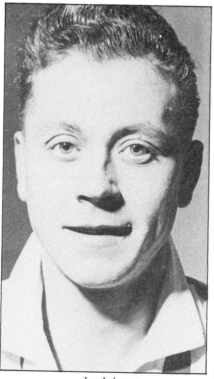

*Joe Johnson*

medal with Stoke in 1933. He ran the Dartmouth Park cafe-restaurant in West Bromwich for a number of years after retiring.
*Albion debut v Huddersfield Town (away) Division One, 11 December 1937.*

## WILLIE JOHNSTON

*Born: Glasgow, December 1946.*
*Career: Lochore Welfare. Rangers. ALBION (£138,000, December 1972-March 1979). Vancouver Whitecaps (NASL, £100,000). Birmingham City (loan). Vancouver Whitecaps. Rangers. Vancouver Whitecaps. Hearts (player, then player-coach). East Fife (coach). Raith Rovers (coach). Falkirk (coach 1987). Now a publican in Kirkcaldy.*

*Willie Johnston*

With his ability to beat a defence with either footwork or speed, and to cap a move with a fierce shot, Willie Johnston was a welcome acquisition to Albion in a defence-orientated game. On the debit side, Johnston's tendency to hold the ball a shade too long, and a short, fiery temper that had him in trouble on several occasions (he was sent off 15 times during his career), often went against him. Nevertheless, he was a fine winger. For Rangers (two spells) he played in over 400 games (160-plus goals) and collected medals galore in League, Cup, League Cup and European competitions. In 1971 he scored a hat-trick of penalties for Rangers against St Johnstone after coming on as substitute, and a year later hit two goals against Moscow Dynamo in the European Cup-winners' Cup Final. For Albion his appearances tally topped 250 and he added further games

with Blues, Hearts and East Fife, ending with almost 700 appearances at club level. As a Scottish international, Johnston won 22 full caps — 13 with Albion, nine with Rangers. He made two appearances for the Scottish League side. and two at Under-23 level, as well as winning Youth recognition. At his best, nobody was faster than Willie Johnston over 30 to 40 yards.
*Albion debut v Liverpool (home) Division One, 9 December 1972.*

## HARRY JONES

*Born: Haydock, October 1911. Died: February 1957.*
*Career: Haydock Schools. Haydock & District Junior Leagues. Preston North End. ALBION (May 1933-August 1943). Retired through injury and illness. Albion scout (1946-7).*

*Harry Jones*

Harry 'Popeye' Jones was a jovial character, able to play equally well in any forward role although he particularly enjoyed the centre-forward spot. He had an aggressive style and would often bundle the ball and goalkeeper over the line as he tore in from deep positions. A big favourite with The Hawthorns crowd, he had an appetite for goals and during his career with Albion he netted no fewer than 104 in only 169 senior outings. In 1939-40 he rattled home 50 goals in only 40 matches (League, Cup and friendlies) including six hat-tricks and a goal in each of 11 consecutive matches — a club record equalled later by winger Billy Elliott. During the war, Jones guested for Everton (in goal) and for Blackburn Rovers. In earlier years he

was awarded a Royal Humane Society medal after he had dived into a canal to save a child from drowning.
*Albion debut v Sheffield Wednesday (away) Division One, 1 January 1935.*

## IVOR JONES

*Born: Merthyr, Wales, July 1899. Died: Birmingham, November 1974.*
*Career: Merthyr Schools. Merthyr Town. Caerphilly. Swansea Town. ALBION (April 1922-May 1926). Swansea Town. Aldershot. Thames FC. Aberystwyth (coach). Retired 1935.*

*Ivor Jones*

A grand little inside-forward with good control, Ivor Jones was difficult to dispossess, yet was erratic at times with his shooting. A Welsh international (ten caps won between 1920 and 1926), he also played for the Welsh League against the Southern League at Aberdare in 1921. Jones played 67 times for Albion. He got into the first team immediately and spread his games out evenly in the inside-left and inside-right positions, forming a fine link with wingers Howard Gregory, Jack Byers and Tommy Glidden. His son, Cliff Jones, is the former Tottenham Hotspur and Wales winger of the 1960s
*Albion debut v Newcastle United (away) Division One, 15 April 1922.*

## STAN JONES

*Born: Highley, Shropshire, November 1938.*
*Career: Highley Council and Bridgnorth Grammar Schools. Staffordshire Youths. Kidderminster Harriers. Wolves (ama-*

*teur). Walsall. ALBION (£7,000, May 1960-March 1968). Walsall. Burton Albion. Kidderminster Harriers. Hednesford Town. Coleshill Town (coach). Walsall (trainer). WBA All Stars.*

*Stan Jones*

An inspiring defender, big and strong, who rarely put a foot wrong, Stan Jones was a cool player, extremely useful in the air. He played 267 games for Albion's senior team and over 250 for Walsall. However, in one five-match spell in the mid-1960s he had the dubious record of scoring three own-goals. Bought by Albion to replace Joe Kennedy, he largely held on to the centre-half shirt up to 1967 when Eddie Colquhoun and John Talbut arrived at The Hawthorns. He missed the 1966 League Cup Final through injury and was dropped for the 1967 Final, playing in only one more first-team game after that.
*Albion debut v Birmingham City (away) Division One, 31 August 1960.*

## JOHN KAYE

*Born: Goole, March 1940.*
*Career: Goole & District Schools. Goole Boys. Goole United. Goole Dockers FC. Hull City (amateur). Goole Town. Scunthorpe United. ALBION (£44,750, May 1963-November 1971). Hull City (£28,000, player, thereafter coach and manager). Scunthorpe United (assistant manager). Retired to go into hotel business.*

*John Kaye*

John Kaye, known as 'Yorky', was a goalscoring inside-right when he was signed by Albion manager Jimmy Hagan in 1963 for a club record fee. He was converted into a defensive half-back during Albion's successful season of 1967-8 and in the number-six shirt, he performed with steadiness, dedication and wholehearted endeavour, committing himself 100 per cent to the game. He gained a League Cup winners' tankard in 1966, a runners-up prize in the same competition a year later, and added an FA Cup winners' medal in 1968, following that with another League Cup runners-up award in 1970. Kaye represented the Football League twice, in 1965-6, and was voted Midland Footballer of the Year in 1966 and 1970. He played in more than 360 games for Albion and during his League career he made 433 appearances and scored 79 goals — 25 for Scunthorpe, 45 for Albion and nine for Hull.
*Albion debut v Leicester City (home) Division One, 24 August 1963.*

## JOE KENNEDY

*Born: Cleator Moor, Nr Whitehaven, November 1925. Died: West Bromwich, September 1986.*
*Career: St Patrick's School (Whitehaven). Whitehaven & District Boys. Cleator Moor Celtic. Brentford (trial). Millwall (trial). Gravesend League football with Freelands FC. Altrincham. ALBION (December 1948-June 1961). Chester. Stourbridge (1962). Brockhouse Works FC. Retired 1966.*
Joe Kennedy began his career as an inside-right, developed into a steady, reliable right-half and ended up as a solid centre-half, tremendous in the air, so sound and sure on the ground. Raven-haired

*Joe Kennedy*

Kennedy seemed destined for full international honours with England after being a permanent reserve during the early 1950s, but injury forced him out of action at crucial times in his career and the only representative calls he received were to skipper England 'B' on three occasions, and play for the FA XI. He played at right-back in Albion's Cup-winning side of 1954 after being out of the team with leg trouble since January. Jack Vernon was in control of the centre-half spot when Kennedy first arrived at Albion. Then Jimmy Dugdale came along and Kennedy was the regular from 1955 to 1960, with the occasional exception when Ray Barlow filled the position. Kennedy appeared in a total of 397 senior games for Albion in his 12 years at the club, playing in a wonderful middle line with Dudley and Barlow. He collapsed and died at his workplace (Brockhouse Ltd), aged only 60.
*Albion debut v Luton Town (away) Division Two, 9 April 1949.*

## DEREK KEVAN

*Born: Ripon, March 1935.*
*Career: Ripon Secondary Modern School. Harrogate & District Schools. Ripon City. Ripon YMCA. Sheffield United (trial). Bradford. ALBION (£3,000, July 1953-March 1963). Chelsea (£50,000). Manchester City. Crystal Palace. Peterborough United. Luton Town. Stockport County. Macclesfield Town. Boston United. Stourbridge. Ansells FC. WBA All Stars (1972-85). Now manager of the All Stars XI. Was with Albion's lottery department in the early 1980s.*
Big Derek Kevan was an Albion 'great'. Standing 6ft tall and weighing 13st, he had power in every department: a big heart, stamina and a lust for goals. He could head a ball as hard as some players could kick one, and he possessed a fierce

*Derek Kevan*

shot in his right foot — and a good one in his left, too. A marvellous competitor, Kevan won 14 full caps for England (eight goals scored), played four times for the Under-23s and had a outing with the Football League XI. In ten years at The Hawthorns he hit 173 goals in 291 League and Cup appearances, including one 'five' against Everton (home) in 1960. After leaving Albion amid some controversy, he won a Fourth Division championship medal with Stockport in 1967, and created a new post-war scoring record for Manchester City in 1963-4 with 30 League goals. In his League career, Kevan scored 235 goals in 440 games and he topped the First Division scoring charts in 1961-2 with 33. A little clumsy when he first set out with Albion, he developed into one of the greatest strikers the club has ever seen.
*Albion debut v Everton (home) Division One, 24 August 1955 (scored both goals in a 2-0 win).*

## HARRY KINSELL

*Born: Cannock, May 1921.*
*Career: Cannock Central & Cannock Senior Schools. ALBION (May 1935, professional June 1938-June 1949). Bolton Wanderers (£12,000). Reading. West Ham United. Bedford Town. Retired 1957, aged 36. Guested for Blackpool, Mansfield, Middlesbrough, and Southport during World War Two, playing left-back in the 1944 League War Cup Final for Blackpool v Aston Villa.*
In his day Harry Kinsell was a wonderful left-back, fast, intelligent, a good footballer who loved to overlap. He partnered Idris Bassett, Cecil Shaw and Jim Pemberton during his stay at The Hawthorns and with all three he performed admirably, winning for himself international

*Harry Kinsell*

recognition in 1945, when he played for England in two Victory internationals and for the FA XI. In 1939, he had gained a Junior cap for his country. A key member of Albion's promotion team of 1948-9 — a season when he lined up once in the outside-left berth — Kinsell played in 158 senior matches for the Throstles and his transfer to Bolton in 1949 realised a record fee for the Lancashire club.
*Albion debut v Walsall (home) Wartime League, 14 May 1940.*
*FA Cup debut v Cardiff City (away), 5 January 1946.*
*League debut v Swansea Town (away) Division Two, 31 August 1946.*

## PETER LATCHFORD

*Born: King's Heath, Birmingham, September 1952.*
*Career: Broadmeadow Juniors and Brandwood Secondary Modern School. South Birmingham Boys. Monyhull Hospital FC. Redditch Town. Sutton Coldfield Town. ALBION (May 1969, professional October 1969-February 1975). Celtic (initially on loan, February 1975, signing full-time July 1975 for £35,000). Clyde (1987). Retired 1988.*
A goalkeeper of exceptional agility for a big man, Peter Latchford became rather inconsistent during the latter part of his stay with Albion. He comes from a footballing family with brothers Dave and Bob perhaps better known nationally. Peter Latchford was at The Hawthorns at a time when the club had some good 'keepers on their books and therefore his stay was short-lived. He went to Celtic, did very well at first, but then dropped into the Reserves, and by the time he had a testimonial in 1985 he was a permanent fixture in Celtic's second team. He won two England Under-23 caps in 1973-4 and appeared in 104 senior games for Albion. With Celtic he gained considerable European experience as well as winning medals in

*Peter Latchford*

League and Cup competitions. He was voted Celtic's 'Player of the Year' in 1977-8 and as a lad represented England at basketball.
*Albion debut v Sheffield United (home) Division One, 26 August 1972.*

## GEORGE LEE

*Born: York, June 1920; Died: Norwich, April 1991.*
*Career: York City Schools. Yorkshire County Boys. Acomb FC. Scarborough.*

*George Lee*

*York City. Nottingham Forest. ALBION (July 1949-June 1958). Lockheed Leamington. Vauxhall Motors FC. ALBION (trainer-coach 1959-63). Norwich City (trainer-coach). Remained with Norwich for a number of years, acting as scout.*
'Ada' Lee was a wholehearted outside-left who varied his game, and style judiciously. Strongly built, he had powerful legs, a useful turn of speed and a good left-foot shot. He came to Albion when their outside-left position was causing some concern and got into the side immediately to hold on to the number-11 shirt well into the late 1950s, apart from an occasional lapse of form. Lee helped Albion win the FA Cup in 1954, laying on the first goal. He scored 65 goals for the Throstles in close on 300 outings. After leaving The Hawthorns for a second time, Lee was trainer to Norwich when they lifted the Second Division crown in 1971-2.
*Albion debut v Charlton Athletic (home) Division One, 20 August 1949.*

## BILLY LEE

*Born: West Bromwich, August 1878.*
*Died: November 1934.*
*Career: West Bromwich Baptist. West Bromwich Standard. Bournville Athletic. ALBION (September 1901-September 1904). Bournemouth Wanderers (loan). Portsmouth. Chesterfield Town. New Brompton. Darlaston. Retired 1911-12.*
Billy Lee's unerring marksmanship made him a consistent scorer from the centre-forward position. He arrived at Albion soon after the club had dropped into the Second Division for the first time, but his presence in the side, plus his goals-scoring expoits, soon had the fans cheering — and promotion was gained imme-

*Billy Lee*

diately. He played in three Junior internationals for England (1899-1900) and scored 25 goals in 76 games for Albion.

*Albion debut v Chesterfield (away) Division Two, 28 September 1901*

## GRAHAM LOVETT

*Born: Sheldon, Birmingham, August 1947.*
*Career: Cockshutt Hill. Sheldon Heath and Camp Lane Schools Birmingham. Birmingham & County Schoolboys. ALBION (February 1964, professional November 1964-June 1972). Southampton (loan). Worcester City. Solihull Borough. Greaves FC. WBA All Stars (1979-85). Retired 1986.*

In the mid-1960s Graham Lovett — nicknamed 'Shuv' — was being talked of as the 'new Duncan Edwards' of Midlands' soccer. A skilful inside-forward or wing-half, he plied his fellow forwards with scoring chances, displaying clever, close ball control in the

*Graham Lovett*

process. He was solidly built, strong in the tackle and had stamina to match. Lovett won an FA Cup winners' medal with Albion in 1968, after he had survived two horrific car crashes. Sadly, the injuries he received in those collisions eventually forced him to give up League soccer at the early age of 26, although he did play some football until 1986. He made 156 appearances for Albion and was showing international form when tragedy struck. In 1973, at Birmingham Crown Court, Lovett was awarded £14,000 damages against the West Midlands Passenger Transport Executive, after one of the accidents, in Quinton, Birmingham.

*Albion debut v Chelsea (home) Division One, 5 December 1964.*

## STEVE MACKENZIE

*Born: Romford, Essex, November 1961.*
*Career: Byron Red Star (Romford). Havering and Essex Schools. Crystal Palace. Manchester City. ALBION (£650,000, July 1981-June 1987). Charlton Athletic. Sheffield Wednesday. Shrewsbury Town (on loan) December 1991 then permanent 1992.*
Steve Mackenzie joined Albion almost immediately after scoring one of the most spectacular goals seen in a Wembley FA Cup Final — for Manchester City against Spurs. Yet his first move in professional football — from Palace to Maine Road — caused something of a stir, because the £250,000 splashed out by Malcolm Allison was for a player who had not featured in a senior League or Cup game. He had been a key figure in Palace's youth team of 1977 and 1978 but was a novice as far as playing in the big time was concerned. However, Mackenzie pulled through. He made over 75 appearances for City and then carried on the good work with Albion, 148 League appear-

*Steve Mackenzie*

ances, although he missed virtually all of the 1982-3 season because of a serious pelvic injury. A midfielder, powerful and with good skills, he preferred a central role at The Hawthorns which enabled him to come forward and unleash one of his thunderbolt shots. On the international front he won caps for England at Youth, (15), Under-23 (three) and 'B' (one) team levels. He collected an FA Youth Cup winners' medal in 1978.

*Albion debut v Manchester City (away) Division One, 29 August 1981.*

## RODDY McLEOD

*Born: Kilsyth, Stirlingshire, February 1872. Died: December 1931.*
*Career: Kilsyth School. Partick Thistle. ALBION (January 1891-April 1897). Leicester Fosse. Brighton United. Southampton. Brentford. Retired 1905-06.*

*Roddy McLeod*

Roddy McLeod was a grand little player, occupying the inside-right position most of the time. He had intricate footwork and his passing and shooting ability were outstanding. He was the perfect foil to Billy Bassett with whom he performed, so wonderfully well in many games for Albion during the 1890s. McLeod's own record for Albion was a useful one — 65 goals in over 180 major appearances. He played in the 1892 and 1895 FA Cup Finals and helped Brentford win the Southern League Division Two title in 1901.

*Albion debut v Sheffield Wednesday (away) FA Cup, 14 February 1891*
*League debut v Accrington (home) Division One, 7 March 1891.*

## SANDY McNAB

*Born: Glasgow, December 1911. Died: September 1962.*
*Career: Glasgow Schools. Tuesday Waverley. Pollok FC (Glasgow). Sunderland. ALBION (March 1938-April 1946). Newport County (£1,000). Dudley Town.*

*Sandy McNab*

Northwich Victoria. Retired 1952 to take a pub in West Bromwich. Guested for Newport County, Nottingham Forest, Northampton Town and Walsall during World War Two.

A marvellous 'pint-sized' left-half whose tackling was done judiciously without him losing his poise, Sandy McNab was the brave and seemingly tireless redhead who rallied Sunderland to victory in the 1937 FA Cup Final, a year after he had helped the Wearsiders win the First Division championship. McNab gained two caps for Scotland (1937 and 1939), represented the Football League, toured Canada and USA with the Scottish FA party in 1939, and all-told amassed almost 190 first-team appearances for Albion, the majority of which came during wartime when he skippered the club for a short while.
*Albion debut v Derby County (home) Division One, 12 March 1938.*

## BERNARD McNALLY

*Born: Shrewsbury, February 1963.*
*Career: Shrewsbury and District Schools. Shrewsbury Town. ALBION (£385,000, June 1989).*
A hard-working, skilful midfielder, Bernard McNally made well over 300 appearances for Shrewsbury Town before his transfer to Albion. Unfortunately he did not seem to fit in with manager Bobby Gould's plans at The Hawthorns, but when Ossie Ardiles took over, McNally bounced back and played some of his best football in season 1992-3. He earlier represented Northern Ireland whilst at Gay Meadow. He also helped the Shrews win the Welsh Cup in 1985, in the same side as Gary Hackett. McNally skippered Albion for a while in 1991-2 and 1992-3.
*Albion debut v Sheffield United (home) Division Two, 19 August 1989.*

*Bernard McNally*

## BOBBY McNEAL

*Born: Hobson Village, County Durham, January 1891. Died: May 1956.*
*Career: Hobson Wanderers. ALBION (June 1910-May 1925). Retired through injury. Albion coach. Guested for Port Vale, Notts County and Middlesbrough during World War One. Later became a publican in West Bromwich.*
Bobby McNeal was a stylish left-half with a footballing brain. He distributed the

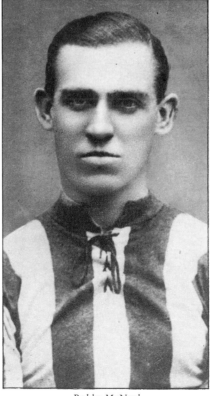

*Bobby McNeal*

ball accurately and defended with commendable steadiness. He came to Albion as a 19-year-old and made his debut in the inside-left position, but was switched to wing-half almost immediately and remained in that position until injuries began to plague him in 1924-5. An English international (two caps), Bobby McNeal also represented the Football League five times (1912-14) and won three medals with Albion — League Championship 1919-20, Division Two title 1910-11 and FA Cup runners-up in 1911-12. He was a penalty-expert, stood only 5ft 6in tall and appeared in more than 400 games for Albion. All in all, he was a magnificent clubman who went into the licensed trade after retiring.
*Albion debut v Leeds City (home) Division Two, 8 October 1910.*

## TOMMY MAGEE

*Born: Widnes, May 1899. Died: May 1974. Career: St Mary's School Widnes. Appleton Hornets (Rugby League). St Helen's Recs (Rugby League). Widnes Athletic (amateur). ALBION (January 1919-May 1934). Crystal Palace (player-coach). Runcorn (player-manager, later coach). Retired 1947.*
Tommy Magee was a 'midget' right-half who was formerly an outside-right or inside-right. He played with evident enjoyment, tenacity, wonderful consistency and constructiveness. Nicknamed 'Pocket Hercules' and the 'Mighty Atom' by players and supporters alike — for he stood only 5ft 2ins tall and weighed 10st — he was a great favourite at The Hawthorns, and for Albion 'wee Tummy' played in over 400 senior games in 15 splendid years. He was initially signed-up whilst serving in the trenches in France during World War One, sending the appropriate papers back to Albion by air. He won five England caps (as a wing-half), toured Canada with the FA party in 1926 and again in 1931, and is the only Albion player to have won a First Division championship medal (1920) and an FA Cup winners' medal (1931). Magee is reputedly the smallest player ever to

*Tommy Magee*

wear an England shirt — and he was certainly the smallest first-team player Albion had fielded until the arrival of Stuart Bowen in 1991.
*Albion debut v Derby County (home) Midland Victory League, 5 April 1919 League debut v Oldham Athletic (home) Division One, 30 August 1919.*

## JACK MAHON

*Born: Gillingham, December 1911.*
*Career: Doncaster Grammar School. New Brompton Excelsior. Doncaster Rovers. Leeds United. ALBION (September 1935-September 1938). Huddersfield Town. York City. Leeds United (coach). Guest for Aldershot, Bradford City, Chelsea, Halifax Town, Leeds United, Millwall, QPR, Reading, Torquay United and West Ham during World War Two. After the war he coached in Denmark and Sweden. Hull City (coach, 1953-4).*

*Jack Mahon*

A resourceful and swift outside-right with a good shot, Jack Mahon never used robust tactics. He came to Albion as a replacement for Tommy Glidden and appeared in well over 120 games (44 goals scored) before switching to Huddersfield. He made a sad start with his new club, however, breaking his right leg in his debut game. Mahon bounced back, though, and toured South Africa with the FA party in 1939, playing in one Test Match. He amassed around 250 senior appearances during his playing career.
*Albion debut v Liverpool (away) Division One, 28 September 1935.*

## JACK MANNERS

*Born: Morpeth, March 1878. Died: May 1946.*
*Career: Morpeth YMCA. Morpeth Harriers. ALBION (May 1904-June 1913). Hartlepools United (player, then manager).*

*Jack Manners*

Jack Manners was a useful half-back, usually found on the left-hand side. He had a biting tackle, good powers of distribution and maintained a consistent level of performance during his nine years at The Hawthorns. He played in a total of 209 League and Cup games for Albion (7 goals scored) and was a mainstay of the side for five seasons (1905-10), forming a solid middle line with first 'Cock' Pheasant and Arthur Randle, and then with George Baddeley and Sammy Timmins. Manners also appeared at outside-left and centre-half for Albion but it was as a left-half that he became a formidable performer, winning a Second Division championship medal in season 1910-11.
*Albion debut v Burnley (away) Division Two, 3 September 1904.*

## MICK MARTIN

*Born: Dublin, July, 1951.*
*Career: Whitehall School. St Vincent's CBS (Football & Hurling Club). Reds United. Home Farm. Greenfields-in-*

*Santry FC. Home Farm. Bohemians. Manchester United. ALBION (loan October 1975; signed for £30,000 December 1975-December 1978). Newcastle United (£100,000). Vancouver Whitecaps (NASL). Wolves. Cardiff City. Peterborough United. Rotherham United. Preston North End. Newcastle United (coach 1987). Celtic (coach 1991).*

*Mick Martin*

Son of Con Martin, the former Aston Villa and Republic of Ireland player, Mick Martin was a versatile performer, who preferred a midfield role. He spent almost five years at Old Trafford without really establishing himself in the United first team. Then Johnny Giles brought him to The Hawthorns, and he developed into a classy player, helping Albion win promotion to the First Division in 1976. In later years he did wonderfully well at Newcastle (over 160 apps), and then dropped down into the lower divisions before retiring after well over 500 games as a professional footballer. He made 52 appearances for the Republic of Ireland (1971-83), collected one cap at Under-23 level and also received one as an amateur while a Bohemians player. He also represented the League of Ireland. Martin had a testimonial match at Dalymount Park in August 1983.
*Albion debut v Oldham Athletic (home) Division Two, 4 October 1975.*

## LEN MILLARD

*Born: Coseley, Nr Wolverhampton, March 1919.*
*Career: Christ Church School. Coseley FC. Wallbrook FC. Coseley Town. Bilston Town. Sunbeam FC. ALBION (May 1937, professional September 1942-June 1958). Stafford Rangers (manager). Retired 1961. Guested for Bilston Borough in 1938.*

*Len Millard*

'Len the Dependable' was Albion's left-back for a number of years, skippering the side to success in the 1954 FA Cup Final. A defender who stuck to his task, he gave fine service to several wing-halves and outside-lefts he played behind, always being fair in the challenge, strong with his kicks and honest in his approach to the game. Millard began as a centre-forward, scoring two hat-tricks; he then had a spell as a wing-half before finally settling down in the No.3 berth in 1949, following the departure of Harry Kinsell. Nicknamed the 'Agitator', he appeared in 645 first team games for Albion, including friendlies, with 436 coming in the League alone. Without doubt he was a truly great servant to West Bromwich Albion for 21 years, and missed only 13 games in the first ten post-war League seasons. Sadly, he had a leg amputated in 1988. He still lives in his birthplace.
*Albion debut v Northampton Town (away) Wartime League, 29 August 1942. League debut v Swansea Town (away) Division Two, 31 August 1946.*

## DAVID MILLS

*Born: Robin Hood's Bay, Nr Whitby, North Yorkshire, December 1951.*
*Career: Whitby Schools. North Yorks Boys. Scarborough & District Youths. Middlesbrough. ALBION (£516,000, January 1979-January 1983). Newcastle United (loan). Sheffield Wednesday. Newcastle United. Middlesbrough, Darlington (n/c 1986-7). Middlesbrough (coach). Whitby Town (player-coach). Retired 1986.*

*David Mills*

David Mills was Britain's costliest footballer when he joined Ron Atkinson at West Bromwich in 1979, but he never lived up to the big price-tag which Albion had placed on his head. An inside-forward, hard-working with a distinctive goalscoring flair, Mills had netted 76 goals in 295 League games for 'Boro before switching to the West Midlands. After some four years and 76 matches for Albion he moved to Sheffield Wednesday, then to Newcastle with whom he had served on loan a year earlier. When he retired, through a series of niggling injuries, Mills had assembled a useful set of statistics — 126 goals in 515 competitive matches for his four major clubs. He gained eight England Under-23 caps whilst with 'Boro, and also collected a Second Division championship medal in 1974.
*Albion debut v Liverpool (away) Division One, 3 February 1979 (as substitute).*

## FRED MORRIS

*Born: Tipton, August 1893; Died: Great Bridge, July 1962.*
*Career: Great Bridge Primary School. Ball Street Primitives. Tipton Victoria. Redditch. ALBION (May 1911-August 1924). Coventry City. Oakengates Town (1925). Retired 1930. Guested for Fulham, Watford and Tipton Excelsior during World War One.*
Fred Morris was a strongly built, courageous centre or inside-forward who displayed glorious talents, neat control, rapid acceleration, dynamic shooting powers and intelligent off-the-ball running. He formed a tremendous left-wing duo with Howard Gregory just after World War One. A Junior international (1911) and winner of two England caps in 1920, as well as receiving Football League and FA recognition, Morris scored a then record 37 League goals when Albion won the First Division Championship in 1919-20, and in 287 appearances for The Baggies he

*Fred Morris*

notched 118 goals. In 1922 he became the first player to reach 100 League goals for Albion — and he is one of only three men to have scored five goals in a League match for the club, doing so against Notts County in October 1919.
*Albion debut v Sunderland (home) Division One, 30 April 1912, scoring in a 1-0 win.*

## PADDY MULLIGAN

*Born: Dublin, March 1945.*
*Career: Dublin Schools. Stella Maris. Home Farm. Bohemians. Shamrock Rovers. Boston Beacons (NASL). Shamrock Rovers. Chelsea. Crystal Palace. ALBION (September 1975-August 1979). Shamrock Rovers. Panathinaikos (Greece, assistant manager). Retired 1982, to become an insurance agent.*
An attacking right-back, an expert at overlapping, steady and thoughtful, and a player with ability who was never completely dominated by a winger, Paddy Mulligan was a wonderful capture by Albion player-manager Johnny Giles and his presence in the defence went a long way in helping the side gain promotion in 1976. A Republic of Ireland Schoolboy international (1960-61), Mulligan went on to gain a total of 51 full caps for his country (1969-80) and he also served the League of Ireland (1965-69). He collected four FAI Cup winners' medals (1965, 66, 67 & 69); and was a member of Chelsea's League Cup Final team which lost to Stoke in 1972. He appeared as substitute for the Londoners in the European Cup-winners' Cup Final of 1971, against Real Madrid in Athens. For Albion, Mulligan

*Paddy Mulligan*

*Jimmy Murphy*

*Stuart Naylor*

made 132 senior appearances and during his professional career in England amassed in excess of 250 League and Cup games for his three clubs.
*Albion debut v Fulham (home) Football League Cup, 9 September 1975.*
*League debut v Blackburn Rovers (away) Division Two, 11 October 1975.*

## JIMMY MURPHY
*Born: Ton Pentre, South Wales, August 1908; Died: November 1989.*
*Career: Ton Pentre Village School. Ton Pentre Boys. Treorchy Thursday FC. Treorchy Juniors. Mid-Rhondda Boys. ALBION (February 1928-March 1939). Swindon Town. Morris Commercial FC. Manchester United (coach and later assistant manager, caretaker manager 1958, scout and adviser at Old Trafford to 1982). Welsh international team manager October 1956 to June 1963, taking Wales to the 1958 World Cup finals in Sweden.*
'Spud' or 'Twinkletoes' Murphy, as he was so aptly called around The Hawthorns, was a vigorous attacking wing-half, skilled in tackling and a glutton for hard work. He had already gained Welsh schoolboy honours (1924 against England at Cardiff) when he joined Albion and he went on to total 15 full interna-

tionals for his country as well as playing in 223 games for Albion, including the 1935 FA Cup Final. He replaced the 'Mighty Midget' Tommy Magee in Albion's middle-line — and did a splendid job. Murphy served overseas during World War Two, with the Eighth Army, and here he met Matt Busby, in Bari, Italy, in 1945 when he was asked to join United as Busby's assistant in rebuilding the club. United won the League title three times, finished runners-up on four occasions, carried off the FA Cup, and twice won the FA Charity Shield — all inside ten seasons before the Munich air disaster destroyed the team. Murphy took over from Busby and when the boss returned, together they reached further heights — more Championships, further Cup success, all culminating in that great triumph in 1968 when the European Cup came to Old Trafford. Murphy resigned in 1971 but remained loyal to the club for a number of years afterwards.
*Albion debut v Blackpool (away) Division Two, 5 March 1930.*

## STUART NAYLOR
*Born: Leeds, December 1962.*
*Career: Wetherby Schools. Leeds City Amateurs. Leeds United (trial). Yorkshire Amateurs. Lincoln City. Peterborough United. Crewe Alexandra (on 13 month loan). Kettering Town (on loan). ALBION (£110,000, February 1986).*
Stuart Naylor was manager, Ron Saunders' first signing for Albion, costing a club record fee for a goalkeeper early in 1986 when he moved from Sincil Bank to The Hawthorns after having languished in the lower reaches of the Football League for a good six seasons. A big man, well built, with huge hands, big heart and big left-footed kick, Naylor replaced Tony Godden and, apart from a niggling knee injury, he retained his place, reaching the

milestone of 300 senior appearances for the Baggies during 1992-3, when he lost his place to Tony Lange. Capped by England at Youth level (1980), he added three 'B' caps in 1989. In October 1982, he had played at centre-forward in a League game for Lincoln against Newport County. Naylor made 65 appearances for the Imps, eight for the Posh and 68 for Crewe. His father, Bill, and uncle, Tommy, both played for Oldham Athletic between 1948 and 1959.
*Albion debut v Manchester United (away) Division One, 22 Feburary 1986 (beaten by two Jesper Olsen's penalties in United's 3-0 win).*

## JOHNNY NICHOLLS
*Born: Wolverhampton, April 1931.*
*Career: Prestwood Road. Holy Trinity and Springfield Road Schools (Wolverhampton). Heath Town FC. ALBION (trial 1946-7). Heath Town Wesley. Heath Town United. Wolvers (trial 1949). ALBION (August 1950, professional August 1951-May 1957). Cardiff City. Exeter City. Worcester City. Wellington Town. Oswestry Town. Sankeys Works FC. H.Meadows FC (technical advisor). Red Dragon FC (West Bromwich League). WBA All Stars (1969-73). Retired June 1973.*
One of the greatest goal 'poachers' of his day, Johnny Nicholls was a player who could run into the right spot instinctively, unleash a cracking shot or delicately place the ball into the net with either foot or with his head. Nicholls formed a magnificent scoring partnership with his Albion 'twin' Ronnie Allen in the mid-1950s and in two successive seasons (1953-55) they scored 105 goals between them in League and Cup. He gained two England caps (with Allen) in 1954, collected a 'B' cap and one at Under-23 level (against Italy). He was a key performer in Albion's wonderful 1953-4

*Johnny Nicholls*

season when they came so close to achieving the double, collecting for himself an FA Cup winners' medal against Preston. His record for Albion was 64 goals in 145 League and Cup appearances. For Albion's reserves he netted 46 goals, notched another 50 for the intermediates and 40 for the juniors. In his entire career — with Albion, Cardiff and Exeter — Nicholls scored 95 goals in 225 games.

*Albion debut v Blackburn Rovers (away) FA Cup, 23 February 1952.*
*League debut v Chelsea (home) Division One, 1 March 1952.*

## SAMMY NICHOLLS

*Born: West Bromwich, January 1871. Died: October 1912.*
*Career: Spon Lane School (West Bromwich). Kidderminster Olympic. West Bromwich Victoria. ALBION (February 1890-June 1892). London CBC. ALBION (July 1893-July 1894). Retired through injury.*

Any lack of ball finesse was more than atoned for by Sammy Nicholls' dashing, fearless displays in and around the opponents' penalty-area. He had two spells with Albion, and during his first helped the team win the 1892 FA Cup Final, scoring once in the 3-0 win over Villa. Perhaps he found it hard to settle into the team early on, but once he had made the breakthrough, he was an eager player, always wanting to be in the thick of the action. He lined up in all three central forward positions for Albion, but seemed to prefer to be leader of the attack. He left football for a year (1892-3) to work for the London County Borough Council, and a serious knee injury ended his career at the early age of 24.

*Albion debut v Everton (away) Division One, 8 March 1890.*

*Sammy Nicholls*

## MAGNUS 'MARK' NICHOLSON

*Born: Oakengates, Shropshire, June 1871. Died: c.1943.*
*Career: Oakengates Fellowship School. Oswestry Town. ALBION (May 1891-May 1894). Luton Town. Cairo. Vienna (when he became associated with the Austrian FA, coaching their national team in 1899-1900); first president of the Austrian Football Union, and had a team named after him (Nicholson FC) in 1900. Was one of the pioneers of Austrian football, playing for Cricket FC and Vienna FC.*

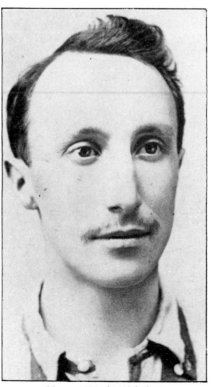

*Magnus 'Mark' Nicholson*

Magnus Nicholson was a fine full-back, whose footwork and speed in recovery were outstanding features of his consistent play. His three seasons with Albion coincided with those of Tom McCulloch, Seth Powell, Jack Horton and Bob Crone, and he had to be in tip-top form to hold on to his senior position. He won an FA Cup winners' medal in 1892, against Aston Villa.

*Albion debut v Everton (home) Division One, 5 September 1891.*

## GORDON NISBET

*Born: Wallsend, September 1951.*
*Career: Wallsend Grammar School. Wallsend & Northumberland Boys. Willington Boys' Club. ALBION (August 1968, professional September 1968-September 1976). Hull City. Plymouth Argyle. Exeter City (August 1987). Ottery St Mary. Plymouth Argyle (coach 1992). Had trials with Blackpool, Leicester City, Preston North End and Sunderland before signing for Albion.*

*Gordon Nisbet*

An always thoughtful and composed right-back, Gordon Nisbet actually started his League career as a First Division goalkeeper. He played reserve-team football with Albion in a number of positions, including right-half and centre-forward, but then under Don Howe's management he was converted into a full-back. He gained one England Under-23 cap in 1972 and when he left The Hawthorns in 1976, following the arrival of Paddy Mulligan, he had accumulated in excess of 160 senior appearances. Nisbet was a member of Plymouth's FA Cup semi-final team in 1984 and he led the Pilgrims to promotion from Division Three in 1985-6.

*Albion debut v Coventry City (away) Division One, 12 August 1969.*

## DAN NURSE

*Born: Prince's End, Tipton, June 1873.
Died: West Bromwich, April 1959.
Career: Prince's End School. Princes's
End FC (Sunday). Coseley FC. Wolverhampton Wanderers. ALBION (May
1901-April 1905). Retired through injury.
Became an Albion director (August 1910),
staying in office until May 1927). Elected
a life member of the club in 1920 in
recognition of his sterling efforts to help
keep Albion in existence during the
summer of 1910.*

*Dan Nurse*

A powerful right-half who was instrumental in helping Albion win promotion, at the first attempt in 1901-02, Dan
Nurse was not always at ease when faced
with intricate dribblers, but he was
mighty efficient in going forward and
breaking up attacks aimed down the
right-hand side of the defence. He
skippered Albion for three years after
having made over 40 appearances for
Wolves in eight years. Nurse made 88
senior appearances for Albion (four
goals) and in 1902-03 represented the
Football League. He was a player who
led by example.
*Albion debut v Glossop (home) Division
Two, 2 September 1901.*

## JOHN OSBORNE

*Born: Barlborough, Derbyshire,
December 1940.
Career: Staveley Netherthorpe Grammar
School. Chesterfield Boys. Derbyshire &
District Schools. Barlborough Colliery
Miners' Welfare. North-East Derbyshire
Boys. Netherthorpe FC. Chesterfield &
District Youths. Bolton Wanderers (ama-
teur). Chesterfield. ALBION (£10,000
January 1967-June 1972). Retired.
Rejoined ALBION (January 1973-July
1978). Walsall (loan). Shamrock Rovers.
Preston North End (non-contract). Tel-
ford United (non-contract). Coventry
City (non-contract). BPM Rangers.
Walsall (amateur). Corinthians FC*

*John Osborne*

*(manager). WBA All Stars (1982-7).
Currently commercial manager of Worcestershire CCC.*
John Osborne was nicknamed the 'bionic
goalkeeper' after having a plastic joint
inserted into his finger. He served Albion
magnificently over a period of some ten
years, divided into two spells. A product
of Chesterfield's famous goalkeeping
'academy' Osborne occasionally performed miracles between the posts for
Albion and was undoubtedly one of the
club's finest post-war 'keepers. Standing
6ft 2in tall, he had a safe pair of hands,
was alert in positioning, and a courageous and dedicated clubman. Initially an
outfield player, he won England Schoolboy honours and appeared in the FA Cup
Final of 1968 and the 1970 League Cup
for Albion, as well as helping the team
win promotion in 1976. He replaced Ray
Potter and Dick Sheppard at Albion, and
but for a brief spell in the 1970s when
Peter Latchford and Jim Cumbes took
over in goal, he was Albion's first-choice
'keeper playing in 312 competitive
matches for the club. He made over 420
appearances during his career. He loves
ornithology, sports quizzes and cricket,
and once ran a sports oufitters' business
with his fellow 'keeper Jim Cumbes. In
later years he worked in the promotions
department of the *Sandwell & Birmingham Evening Mail*. His testimonial
in 1978, realised £32,000, then a record
for a Midlands player.
*Albion debut v Nottingham Forest
(home) Division One, 7 January 1967.*

## GARY OWEN

*Born: St Helens, Lancashire, July 1958.
Career: Warrington & District Schools.
Manchester City. ALBION (£465,000,*

*Gary Owen*

*May 1979-July 1986). Panionios (Greece,
two-year contract). Sheffield Wednesday
(August 1987). Apoel Nicosia. Retired
1989 to become an art dealer.*
Skilful midfielder Gary Owen's career
with Albion was ruined by a series of
injuries, including a fractured shin and
a gashed calf which required a skin graft.
There was no doubting Owen's ability.
He was a fine ball-player, with vision and
craft, but his days at Albion were
numbered when Ron Saunders took over
as manager in 1986, after Owen had been
a permanent fixture in the side for five
years (1979-84). Earlier, with Manchester
City, he won England recognition at
Youth, 'B', and Under-21 levels, and
holds the record for most England Under-
21 caps (22). He also played for the
Football League. Owen appeared in 123
games for City (23 goals) and in 229 for
Albion (26 goals). He opted for a move
to Greece when released by Albion at the
end of the 1985-6 season.
*Albion debut v Derby County (home)
Division One, 18 August 1979.*

## BOB PAILOR

*Born: Stockton-on-Tees, July 1887. Died:
Hartlepool, January 1976.
Career: Galley's Field School. St Oswald's
FC. West Hartlepool. ALBION (October
1908-July 1914). Newcastle United.
Retired 1915 because of a kidney
complaint.*
Bob Pailor was a player made for scoring
goals. His hefty weight, allied with pace
and agility, made him such an effective
centre-forward. He averaged a goal every
two games for Albion, and helped his side
reach the 1912 FA Cup Final with an
extra-time winner in the semi-final
against Blackburn Rovers. He topped
Albion's scoring charts in 1911-12 and
1912-13, and during his six year stay at

*Bob Pailor*

The Hawthorns, won many friends. He made his Newcastle debut against Albion in September 1914. After his footballing days were over he became a successful bookmaker in Hartlepool, later having to give up his license when he became blind. *Albion debut v Bradford (away) Division Two, 30 January 1909.*

## CARLTON PALMER

*Born: Rowley Regis, Warley, West Midlands, December 1965.*
*Career: Whiteheath Infants & St Michael's Junior Schools (Oldbury). Rowley Regis & District Boys. Newton Albion. Netherton. Dudley Town. ALBION (YTS July 1983, professional October 1984). Sheffield Wednesday.*
Carlton Palmer is a tall, long striding workhorse who developed through Albion's youth and reserve teams to

*Carlton Palmer*

become one of the best midfielders in the country in the late 1980s. Palmer, who can play at full-back, centre-half or in midfield as well as up front, went on to play over 100 games for Albion but always seemed to be performing in a struggling side. His form, however, remained good and it wasn't long before Sheffield Wednesday boss, Ron Atkinson, who had seen Palmer in action during his second spell at The Hawthorns, made the Black Country-born player one of his first signings, taking him to Hillsbrough in a deal that cost the Owls £750,000 plus striker Colin West. Palmer quickly settled in and was the driving force in Wednesday's promotion-winning team of 1991 and, indeed, he was instrumental in helping Wednesday reach the Rumbelows League Cup Final that same year, although he was suspended and subsequently missed the 1-0 win over Manchester United at Wembley. Capped by England at Under-21, 'B' and full levels, Palmer was valued at £2 million in 1993, when he played in the FA Cup and Coca-Cola Cup Finals for the Owls, being Man of the Match in the FA Cup Final replay. *Albion debut v Newcastle United (away) Division One, 14 September 1985 (as sub).*

## HAROLD PEARSON

*Born: Tamworth, May 1908.*
*Career: Tamworth & Amington Schools. Glascote United. Glascote Methodists. Belgrave YMCA. Belgrave United. Two Gates FC. Nuneaton Borough. Tam-*

*Harold Pearson*

*worth Castle. ALBION (April 1925, professional May 1927-August 1937). Millwall. Retired 1940 after guesting for West Ham. Returned to Albion as coach (1948-52).*
For a man who stood 6ft 2in tall and weighed 13st 12lb, Harold Pearson made goalkeeping look so simple. Equally adept with high or low crosses, he had a tremendous reach and kicked vast distances out of his hands; and he could throw the ball a fair way, too. 'Algy', as he was known, was on Albion's books along with his father Hubert (1925) and went on to make a grand total of 303 senior appearances for the Throstles, winning an FA Cup winners' medal in 1931 and a runners-up prize in 1935, and later collecting a Third Division South championship medal with Millwall (1938). Earlier in his career he gained a Junior international cap (1927) and added a full cap in 1932, playing against Scotland. Pearson replaced George Ashmore in Albion's first team and was himself dislodged by Billy Light, briefly, and then Jimmy Adams in 1937.
*Albion debut v South Shields (home) Division Two, 17 December 1927.*

## HUBERT PEARSON

*Born: Kettlebrook, Tamworth, May 1886.*
*Died: Tamworth, October 1955.*
*Career: Kettlebrook Oakfield. Tamworth Castle. Tamworth Athletic. ALBION (February 1906-May 1926). Retired 1926. Guested for Oldbury Town 1915-16.*
A board-shouldered goalkeeper, Hubert Pearson was efficient, sound and dependable, a player whose usefulness was not confined to his goal-line. He would advance some distance to avert danger, flykicking to safety if need be, although he was never reckless. A Junior international for England in 1907, Pearson was selected to play for the full England side against France in 1923 but was forced to withdraw

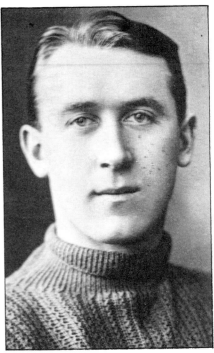

*Hubert Pearson*

through injury. He never got another chance. Nicknamed 'Joe', he won a Second Division championship medal in 1911, added a First Division winners' medal to his collection in 1920 and in between played for Albion in the 1912 FA Cup Final against Barnsley. He represented the Football League in 1914 and 1922, and played in more League games than any other Albion 'keeper. In all Pearson made over 377 appearances for the Throstles, and took over the goalkeeper's jersey in 1909-10 from big Joe Stringer. His son, Harold Pearson, was another fine Albion custodian. Scored two penalties for Albion in 1911-12.

*Albion debut v Birmingham City (away) FA Cup, 15 January 1908.*

*League debut v Clapton Orient (away) Division One, 18 January 1908.*

## TOM PEARSON

*Born: West Bromwich, 1866. Died: West Bromwich, July 1918.*
*Career: Christ Church School. Oak Villa. West Bromwich Sandwell. ALBION (April 1886-May 1894). Retired through injury.*

Albion's first really great marksman, Tom Pearson, was the club's leading scorer in each of the first five Football League seasons, 1888-1893. He was a wonderful inside-left, with endurance, resolution, shooting power in both feet and a distinctive short gait. He was certainly a natural goal-getter, whose alertness and presence of mind brought him well over 100 goals during his Albion career. He played in the 1887, 1888 and 1892 FA Cup Finals, picking up winners' medals in the last two. It was a sad day when he was forced to quit the game, through injury, in 1894 at the relatively

*Tom Pearson*

young age of 28. He was a cripple by the age of 30.

*Albion debut v Halliwell (away), April 1886.*

*Senior debut v Notts County (away), FA Cup, 19 February 1887.*

*League debut v Stoke (away), 8 September 1888.*

## JIM PEMBERTON

*Born: Wolverhampton, April 1916.*
*Career: Willenhall Road School. Wolverhampton Boys. Ward Street Clinic FC. Round Oak FC. Brownhills Albion. Birmingham (amateur). ALBION (September 1937, professional August 1938-March 1951). Retired through injury and ill-health. He later went blind.*

*Jim Pemberton*

Jim Pemberton was a strong, confident right-back, hard and wiry, who had a fine physique, solid kick and good positional sense. A member of Albion's 1948-9 promotion side, he was virtually an ever-present in the team for the first four post-war seasons and was then injured playing against Aston Villa on the opening day of the 1950-51 campaign. Sadly, he never played again. He chalked up 172 League and Cup appearances for the Throstles, all at right-back.

*Albion debut v Swansea Town (away) Division Two, 31 August 1946.*

## JESSE PENNINGTON

*Born: West Bromwich, August 1883. Died: Kidderminster, September 1970. Career: Smethwick Schools. Summit Star. Smethwick Centaur. Langley Villa. Langley St Michael's. Dudley Town. Aston Villa (amateur). Dudley Town. ALBION (March 1903-May 1922). Oldbury Town (guest). Notts County. Retired to become Albion coach until August 1923; Kidderminster Harriers (coach). Malvern College (coach). Wolves (scout). Albion (scout).*

One of the greatest names in the annals of West Bromwich Albion Football Club, Jesse 'Peerless' Pennington was a superbly equipped left-back, and scrupulously fair. Notably quick in recovery and a player with beautiful balance, a keen eye and lovely kick out of defence, he was a magnificent captain, wonderful sportsman and a grand clubman who played in 455 League games for Albion, plus 39 FA Cup-ties and one FA Charity Shield match. He held the club appearances record for 44 years before losing it to Tony Brown in 1976. Pennington won 25 England caps (1907-20), represented the Football League XI on nine occasions, played for an England XI five times and also appeared in five international trials (1910-12). He skippered England twice and the League XI once, all in 1920 when aged 36. He guided Albion to the Second

*Jesse Pennington*

Division title in 1911, led them in the FA Cup Final a year later and in 1920 captained the team that won the First Division championship for the only time to date. In his entire footballing career, Pennington never scored a goal. He was dropped from Albion's team only once and he was universally regarded as the *nonpareil* of Albion and England left-backs. He formed a superb duo in international circles with Blackburn's Bob Crompton, lining up as Crompton's partner in 23 of his 25 matches for his country. Pennington played his first and last League games for Albion against the same team, Liverpool. In 1910 he had a minor dispute with Albion regarding pay and signed for Kidderminster Harriers. That dispute was soon sorted out and the forms cancelled, when he returned to The Hawthorns. In 1913 he was the subject of a bribe scandal when he was approached with cash to 'fix' a League game between Albion and Everton. Pennington informed the police, the culprit was apprehended and later got six months' imprisonment. In November 1969, Pennington was made a life member of West Bromwich Albion at the age of

86, a fitting tribute to a most wonderful footballer, one of Albion's greatest.
*Albion League debut v Liverpool (away) Division One, 26 September 1903.*

## CHARLIE PERRY

*Born: West Bromwich, January 1866. Died: West Bromwich, July 1927. Career: Christ Church School (West Bromwich). West Bromwich Strollers (not Albion). ALBION (March 1884, professional August 1885-May 1896). Retired. Albion director (1902).*

*Charlie Perry*

Charlie Perry was a superb player and a great captain. He had a polished style, was determined in everything he did, cool under pressure, and a man who marshalled his defence magnificently from the centre-half position, which was undoubtedly his best. Brother of Tom and Walter, he won three England caps (1890-93), had two outings for the Football League XI and appeared in four international trials (1889-91). He was Albion's pivot in the 1886, 1887, 1888 and 1892 FA Cup Finals, collecting winners' medals in the last two. He missed the 1895 Final through injury, which eventually forced him to retire from top-class football. Tall and strong, Perry was Albion's first 'great' centre-half and served the club in more than 200 senior games.
*Albion debut v Blackburn Rovers (The Oval) FA Cup Final, 3 April 1886.*
*League debut v Stoke (away), 8 September 1888.*

## TOM PERRY

*Born: West Bromwich, August 1871. Died: West Bromwich, July 1927. Career: Christ Church School. Christ Church FC. West Bromwich Baptist FC. Stourbridge. ALBION (July 1890-*

*Tom Perry*

*October 1901). Aston Villa (for four months). Retired 1902-03.*
A stalwart right-half for Albion during the ten years leading up to the club's move to The Hawthorns, Tom Perry was a capable, efficient and enthusiastic performer, wholehearted in every way, whose hard-working approach to the game made him such a key figure in the 1890s. He made his Albion bow in the outside-left position but soon became noted for his displays in the middle-line where he served alongside his elder brother, Charlie. Tom won one England cap (1898); he played three games for the Football League (1894-98); and turned out for the League XI against Aston Villa in 1894. He was Albion's right-half in the 1895 FA Cup Final and appeared in 277 League and Cup matches for the Throstles, lining up at full-back, and inside-forward as well as his best role. He died two weeks after brother Charlie, and his older brother Walter (also an Albion player) passed on a year later, in 1928.
*Albion debut v Preston North End (away) Division One, 13 September 1890.*

## TED PHEASANT

*Born: Darlaston, February 1877. Died: Leicester, July 1910. Career: Joseph Edward Cox School (Wednesbury). Wednesbury Excelsior. Wednesbury Old Athletic. Wolves. ALBION (November 1904-July 1910). Leicester Fosse. Died of peritonitis two weeks after leaving The Hawthorns.*
'Cock' Pheasant was 6ft 2in tall and weighed almost 15st. He could play centre-half or centre-forward. As hard as nails, 'Cock' made over 150 senior appearances for Albion (22 goals) and when taking penalties, his powerhouse

*Ted Pheasant*

shooting was done almost without a run at the ball. A fearless player, he skippered Albion from 1906 to 1908 after moving to The Hawthorns from nearby Molineux. For Wolves he appeared in well over 150 League and Cup matches (17 goals) between 1896 and 1904, and missed only one League game in three seasons (1899-1902 inclusive). He was once selected to play for the Football League but refused the honour because he wanted to play for Wolves the same day. He died in a Leicester hospital soon after leaving Albion, at the age of 33.
*Albion debut v Manchester United (home) Division Two, 5 November 1904.*

## RAY POTTER

*Born: Beckenham, May 1936. Career: Beckenham & District Schools. Beckenham Boys. Kent Schools XI. Millwall (amateur). Beckenham FC. Crystal Palace. ALBION (June 1958-May 1967). Portsmouth. Colchester United (assistant commercial manager). Bournemouth (assistant commercial manager and secretary). Portsmouth (administration).*
Goalkeeper Ray Potter gave Albion excellent service between the posts for a number of years. Never flashy, he did his job professionally and well. He arrived at The Hawthorns at a time when there was a goalkeeping problem, with Jackman having been injured. Yet Potter, plunged in at the deep end, made the position his own from his first game and went on to appear in over 230 senior games for the Throstles, including the 1966 League Cup Final against West Ham. When he retired at the end of the 1969-70 season, he had amassed a tally

*Ray Potter*

of 264 League appearances — 217 with Albion.
*Albion debut v West Ham United (home) Division One, 18 October 1958.*

## ARTHUR RANDLE

*Born: West Bromwich, December 1880. Died: West Bromwich, September 1913. Career: Springfield School (West Bromwich). Lyng Rovers. Oldbury Town. Darlaston. ALBION (April 1901-May 1908). Leicester Fosse. Retired May 1912, aged 32 (ill-health).*

*Arthur Randle*

The perfect right-half, always foraging and possessing superb close control, excellent passing ability and an accurate shot, Arthur Randle's forté was probably his tactical genius. A Junior interna-

tional in 1901, he joined Albion just as the team were relegated for the first time in the club's history. He spent practically two seasons in the reserves but in 1903-04 began to force himself forward, making 17 League appearances. He finally settled into the senior side in 1904-05 and held his place for three complete terms before handing over his jersey to Sammy Timmins at the start of the 1907-08 season. He had 143 first-team outings for Albion.
*Albion debut v Newton Heath (away) Division Two, 9 November 1901.*

## JOE READER

*Born: West Bromwich, February 1866. Died: West Bromwich, March 1954. Career: Beeches Road and St Phillip's School (West Bromwich). ALBION (January 1885, professional August 1885-April 1901). Retired to become trainer-coach at The Hawthorns, later steward until 1950. His association with Albion spanned 65 years.*

Joe Reader was a goalkeeper to rank with the finest the game has produced. Superb in handling and with marvellous reflexes, Reader used his feet as much as anything else to divert goalbound shots or headers. He appeared in over 350 games for Albion, his only club. He played in the 1892 and 1895 FA Cup Finals, won one England cap, against Ireland in 1894, represented the Football League three times and played for a League XI once. A dedicated clubman, he turned out in one match with his arm in a sling. Nicknamed 'Kicker', he is the only player to have served Albion on three different home grounds — The Four Acres, Stoney Lane and The Hawthorns. He was Albion's goalkeeper for

*Joe Reader*

16 years and he was forced to give up the game through illness rather than injury, yet he was still a keen and active member of the club during his spell as coach till shortly before World War One. It is believed that Reader was the last of the 'keepers to discard the customary long white trousers, doing so in the mid-1890s. He took over between the posts from the great Bob Roberts, and was himself replaced by Ike Webb in 1901.
*Albion debut v Aston Villa (away) Division One, 26 October 1889.*

## FRED REED

*Born: Scotswood-on-Tyne, March 1894. Died: West Bromwich, December 1967. Career: Scotswood School. Newburn FC. Wesley Hall. Benwell FC. Lintz Institute. ALBION (February 1913-July 1927). Newcastle United (guest 1919). Retired to become trainer at The Hawthorns until 1950.*

*Fred Reed*

Fred Reed's performances at centre-half for Albion were typical of a rugged North-Easterner, especially in the tackle where he was solid, determined and so efficient. When he arrived at Albion he understudied Frank Waterhouse and Sid Bowser and had to wait almost ten years before claiming a regular first-team place. Indeed, Reed amassed well over 150 reserve appearances before establishing himself in the senior side as captain. He stayed in the League side for three and a half seasons, during which time he made 138 League appearances before giving way to a younger man in 1927. As Albion's trainer he saw them win the FA Cup in 1931, lose to Sheffield Wednesday in the 1935 Final and win promotion from the Second Division in 1948-9. He was 'sponge-man' to the Football League in 1934-5 and trainer for the England-Rest trial matches in 1927-8 and 1934-5. During the mid-1930s he was masseur to Warwickshire CCC. He was succeeded by Arthur 'Mother' Fitton as Albion's trainer.
*Albion debut v Tottenham Hotspur (home) Division One, 6 April 1915.*

## CYRILLE REGIS

*Born: Maripiasoula, French Guyana, February 1958.*
*Career: Cardinal Hinsley School (Harlesden). Harlesden Borough Boys. Brent Valley. Mosley FC. Chelsea (trial). Hayes. ALBION (May 1977-October 1984). Coventry City (£300,000). Aston Villa (July 1991).*

*Cyrille Regis*

Big Cyrille Regis had seven good years at The Hawthorns, scoring 140 goals in 370 matches (including friendlies). A big favourite with the fans, he scored twice on his debut in 1977 and netted some quite spectacular goals in League and Cup football. Indeed, he created a record by scoring on his debuts for Albion in each of five different competitions. Strong, muscular and aggressive, 'Smokin Joe' had terrific pace, a powerful shot and superb heading ability. He would often collect a ball 40 yards from goal and head towards his target with devastating pace and mobility before unleashing a fierce shot. He was certainly a bargain buy at £5,000 when Albion snapped him up after he had scored 40 goals in two seasons of non-League football. Capped by England at full, 'B' and Under-21 levels, Regis was voted PFA Young Footballer of the Year in 1979 and was runner-up to Footballer of the Year Steve Perryman (Spurs) in 1982. His transfer to Coventry was a shock to all Albion fans and Regis himself found it a big wrench to leave The Hawthorns. He scored five for Coventry against Chester in a Milk Cup game in October 1985.
*Albion debut v Rotherham United (home) Football League Cup, 31 August 1977.*
*League debut v Middlesbrough (home) Division One, 3 September 1977.*

## JOHN REYNOLDS

*Born: Blackburn, February 1869. Died: 1917.*
*Career: Park Road FC (Blackburn).*

*Witton FC. Blackburn Rovers. Park Road FC. East Lancashire Regiment. Distillery. Ulster. ALBION (March 1891-April 1893). Aston Villa. Celtic. Southampton. Bristol St George. New Zealand (as coach). Stockport County. Willesden Town. Retired close season 1905. Guested for Droitwich Town (1891-2).*

'Baldy' Reynolds was a marvellous wing-half who sometimes bewildered his team-mates as well as the opposition. He mastered every trick in the book and aided by some quite remarkable ball skills, his footwork was at times exceptionally brilliant. Reynolds played international football for both Ireland and England, winning a total of 13 full caps — five for Ireland. He also played for the Football League on four occasions, for the Professionals XI three times and appeared in one England trial in 1894. As Albion's right-half he gained an FA Cup winners' medal in 1892, scoring a

*John Reynolds*

fine goal in the 3-0 defeat of Aston Villa, and in 1895 he helped Villa beat Albion 1-0 in the Final. The following year he won a First Division Championship medal and in 1897 was a member of Villa's League and Cup double-winning team. He helped Celtic win the Scottish First Division Championship in 1898, and won an Irish Cup winners' medal, in 1891. Reynolds had the pleasure of scoring Albion's first penalty-kick, against Nottingham Forest in April 1893. He left Albion after falling out with the committee. His League debut for Villa was against Albion on 2 September 1893.
*Albion debut v Blackburn Rovers (home) Division One, 3 October 1891.*

## SAMMY RICHARDSON

*Born: West Bromwich, February 1892. Died: September 1959.*
*Career: Whitehall Road School. Greets Green Prims. Great Bridge Juniors. Great Bridge Celtic. ALBION (February 1913-August 1927). Newport County. Aldershot. Retired 1931. Guested for Oldbury Town and Coventry City during World War One.*

*Sammy Richardson*

A wing-half mainly noted for his work-manlike displays as a defensive rather than an attacking player, Sammy Richardson was a physically strong and dominant player in the air, and an accurate passer of the ball and biting in the tackle. He was a key member of Albion's League Championship-winning team in 1919-20, and was virtually a permanent fixture in the side during the first three campaigns after World War One. He lost his place to Tommy Magee in 1923 but returned as a left-half in seasons 1924-5 and 1925-6. Brother of Bill Richardson, Albion's centre-half, Sammy played in well over 200 games for Albion and he represented the Football League and the FA in 1921.
*Albion debut v Sheffield United (away) Division One, 16 January 1915.*

## BILLY 'G' RICHARDSON

*Born: Framwellgate Moor, County Durham, May 1909. Died: Birmingham, March 1959.*
*Career: Framwellgate Moor and Easington Colliery Schools. Durham Schools. Horden Wednesday FC. United Bus Company (Hartlepool). Hartlepools United. ALBION (June 1929-November 1945). Shrewsbury Town. ALBION (assistant trainer-coach, June 1946. Was still on Albion's training staff when he collapsed and died playing in a charity match). Guested for Derby County and Walsall during World War Two.*

On his day 'W.G.' Richardson had few

*Billy 'G' Richardson*

equals and no superiors at snapping up the half-chance, especially those which flew hard and low across the face of the goal from either wing. A truly dynamic centre-forward who depended largely on his alertness rather than his weight, he was quick, assertive and so sharp inside the box. During the 1930s, 'W.G.' was seemingly always hitting the headlines — and the net. He scored both goals in the 1931 FA Cup Final; secured the match-winning goal against Charlton at The Hawthorns in 1931 which clinched Albion's Cup and promotion double; he grabbed four goals in five minutes against West Ham at Upton Park in November 1931; hit three in six minutes past Derby County in 1933; set an Albion record (which still stands) with 40 League and Cup goals in season 1935-6; and claimed a total of 14 League and Cup hat-tricks, including four 'fours' (1933-5). During World War Two he continued to crack in the goals and twice he netted six times in a match — against Luton Town and the RAF (1941-2) — and he notched up five against Swansea in 1941 and five versus Aston Villa in 1943. His wartime goalscoring exploits were exceptional — 123 in 106 games, including friendlies. For Shrewsbury in 1945-6 he netted 55 goals in only 40 outings before returning to The Hawthorns as a trainer-coach. In his brilliant scoring career, 'W.G.' surprisingly won only one England cap, against Holland in 1935. He weighed in with 202 League goals for Albion, a further 26 in the FA Cup, plus those he netted during the war. His career total was around 450 (all matches) and his

appearance record was not far short of 500 games. He scored 50 Central League goals in his first season in Albion's reserves, including eight hat-tricks. The 'G' was for 'Ginger', added to help distinguish him from the other W.Richardson who was on Albion's books at the same time.
*Albion debut v Millwall (home) Division Two, 26 December 1929 (scored in a 6-1 Albion victory).*

## BILL RICHARDSON

*Born: Great Bridge, Tipton, February 1908. Died: West Bromwich, June 1985. Career: Whitehall Road Schools. Greets Green Boys. Greets Green Prims. Great Bridge Celtic. ALBION (November 1926-May 1937). Swindon Town. Dudley Town. Vono Sports. Retired June 1941.*

*Bill Richardson*

Bill Richardson, no relation to 'W.G' but brother to Sammy, although a shade casual at times, was a splendid pivot, unflagging and especially good in the air. He gave Albion grand service for almost 11 years, making over 350 appearances. He first set foot inside The Hawthorns when the centre-half and wing-half positions were causing some concern, and settled down in the middle line halfway through the 1928-9 campaign, with little Tommy Magee on one side and Len Darnell on the other. From then on Richardson played steadily and was always a popular and reliable servant in the Albion ranks. From December 1928 (his debut) to February 1937, Albion played a total of 347 League matches and Richardson appeared in 319 of them — testament to his tremendous dedication and consistency.
*Albion debut v Middlesbrough (away) Division Two, 1 December 1928.*

## STAN RICKABY

*Born: Stockton-on-Tees, March 1924. Career: Stockton & District Schools. South Bank FC. Middlesbrough. ALBION (£7,500, February 1950-June*

*Stan Rickaby*

*1955). Poole Town (player-manager). Weymouth. Newton Abbot Spurs. Retired July 1964. Went into insurance business, emigrating to Australia in 1969.*
Rickaby was a strong, accomplished right-back, good in the tackle, a player who was never flustered. He arrived at The Hawthorns as cover for Jim Pemberton but inside six months he had replaced him when injury forced the full-back to quit the game. Rickaby himself was lucky with injuries during his stay at Albion — that is until the FA Cup semi-final against Port Vale in 1954. He was hurt in that tie and had to miss the Cup Final against Preston. Capped once by England, against Northern Ireland in 1953, he appeared in 205 senior games for Albion, all of them at right-back. He left the club in 1955 after a disagreement.
*Albion debut v Manchester City (home) Division One, 29 April 1950.*

## WALTER ROBBINS

*Born: Cardiff, November 1910. Died: Swansea, February 1979.*
*Career: Cardiff Boys. Ely Brewery FC. Ely United. Cardiff City. ALBION (April 1932-May 1939). Newport County. Cardiff City (trainer). Swansea (trainer, then assistant manager until 1971, then chief scout). During the 1950s was trainer to the Welsh national team.*
Walter Robbins was a competent outside-left with 'tree-trunk' legs which enabled him to release a thunderbolt shot. He once hit five goals from the left-wing for Cardiff City against Thames at Ninian Park on 6 February 1932 — a League record. A former motor engineer and brewery lorry driver, he came to Albion

*Walter Robbins*

as deputy to Stan Wood but had to contest the left-wing berth with Wally Boyes as well. Robbins had a few outings at inside forward before finally settling for a more controlled role in centre-field. He even played at centre-half twice in 1938. He made over 90 appearances for Albion (including one at centre-half in 1938), and gained 11 caps for Wales (1930-35). In 1929 he toured Canada with the Welsh FA and collected three Central League championship medals with Albion in successive seasons (1932-35). As Swansea's trainer he was on the bench in the 1964 FA Cup semi-final against Preston North End and also won honours when doing the same job at Cardiff, with whom he gained a Welsh Cup-winners' medal in 1929-30. He also played in three divisions of the League with the Welsh club. Robbins had a testimonial match against Albion in May 1971 after spending ten years at Vetch Field.
*Albion debut v Chelsea (away) Division One, 23 April 1932.*

## BOB ROBERTS

*Born: West Bromwich, April 1859. Died: October 1929.*
*Career: Christ Church School. Salters Works. ALBION (Strollers) (professional August 1885-May 1890). Sunderland Albion. ALBION (May 1891-May 1892). Aston Villa. Retired June 1893.*
Albion's first international, goalkeeper Bob Roberts was a giant of a man, measuring 6ft 4in in height and weighing 13st. He was so well built that he could deal comfortably with any player who dared brush with him. He had a tremendous reach, a safe pair of hands, wore size-13 boots (which helped him kick enormous distances), and above all had a wonderful temperament. He started his footballing career as an outfield player, occupying many different positions, before settling down between the posts. He won three England caps, his first against Scotland in 1886-7, and also played for the Football Alliance and in

*Bob Roberts*

three international trials. Roberts was Albion's 'custodian' in the 1886, 1887 and 1888 FA Cup Finals, collecting a winners' medal in the latter against Preston North End when he played superbly. He had two spells with Albion — the second being for only a season — and during his 12 years' association with the club he amassed around 400 appearances including 84 in League and Cup action.
*Albion debut v Wednesbury Town (home) FA Cup, 10 November 1883.*
*League debut v Stoke (away), 8 September 1888.*

## ALLY ROBERTSON

*Born: Philpstoun, Lothian, Scotland, September 1952.*
*Career: Bridgend Junior and East Lothian Schools. Linlithgow Academy. Uphall Saints. ALBION (July 1968, professional September 1969-September 1986). Wolves. Worcester City (player-manager). Cheltenham Town (manager 1991-2)*
After 18 years and more than 700 first-team games, Ally Robertson said farewell to West Bromwich Albion at the beginning of the 1986-7 season, following the arrival at The Hawthorns of manager Ron Saunders, who said that there was no room for the likeable Scot in his long-term plans for the club. It was a sad occasion for Robertson, who had made his debut as a 17-year-old in 1969 against high-flying Manchester United before a 45,000 crowd in the First Division. Since that initial outing, Robertson had served in Albion's defence as a steady, centre-back, solidly built with powerful shoulders, a crunching tackle and

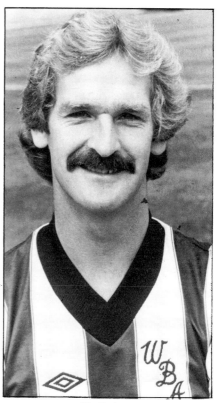

*Ally Robertson*

dogged determination. A real 'toughnut', he drew up a splendid understanding with co-defender, John Wile, and together they appeared in 573 games, helping Albion win promotion in 1975-6, reach three Cup semi-finals, as well as containing some exciting European forwards during Albion's exploits in the UEFA Cup. In 1979, Robertson passed Jimmy Dudley's record of 166 consecutive League appearances for Albion, and when he left the club he was one of only three players to have made over 500 League appearances for Albion (the others being Wile and Tony Brown). In fact, Ally Robertson's grand total of 718 plus 11 as a substitute for Albion (all matches, including friendlies) makes him the second-highest appearance maker in the club's history behind Tony Brown. When only 18, Robertson had the misfortune to break a leg playing against Charlton in a League Cup-tie, but he bounced back to become one of Albion's finest defenders. As a lad he won four Scottish Schoolboy international caps, and added six Youth caps between 1968 and 1970. One disappointment was that he never made an impression on the full Scottish team selectors. In five seasons (1975-80) he missed only seven League games out of 210 as Albion returned to the First Division and established themselves as one of the country's top sides.
*Albion debut v Manchester United (home) Division One, 25 October 1969.*

## BRYAN ROBSON OBE

*Born: Witton Gilbert, County Durham, January 1957.*
*Career: Chester-le-Street Junior and Birtley Comprehensive Schools. Chester-le-Street Cubs. Washington Schoolboys.*

*Bryan Robson OBE*

Chester-le-Street Boys. ALBION (September 1972, professional August 1974-October 1981). Manchester United (£1.5 million). Had trials with Burnley, Coventry City and Newcastle United before joining Albion.

Bryan Robson became Britain's costliest footballer when he left The Hawthorns for Manchester United soon after the start of the 1981-2 season. The deal, worth around £2 million included Remi Moses, rated at the time in the £500,000 class. Regarded by many as the best midfielder since the war, Robson has been plagued by injury over a number of years and after starting England's World Cup challenge in Mexico in 1986 he had to sit out the rest of the tournament with a damaged shoulder. 'Pop' as he is known by players and fans alike, has great stamina, aggression and an abundant supply of skill. He suffered three broken legs in 1976-7 when trying to establish himself in Albion's first team. He recovered full fitness and helped the Throstles into the UEFA Cup. Robson won Youth honours for England and added Under-21, 'B' and 90 full caps to his collection as he became one of the most gifted players in European football during the 1980s. He skippered United to FA Cup glory in 1983, 1985 and 1990 and their European Cup-winners' Cup winning side in 1991 and gained a Premier League Championship Medal in 1993. Has captained his country on many occasions. He was Sports Argus-Sportsco Footballer of the Year 1979; Midland Footballer of the Year and Midland Sportswriters' Player of the Year 1980. He scored the fastest-ever goal in the World Cup finals, for England against France, 27 seconds after kick-off on June 1982. Brother of Gary Robson who joined Albion in 1981, Bryan was awarded the OBE in the 1990 honours list.
*Albion debut v York City (away) Division Two, 12 April 1975.*

# BOBBY ROBSON

*Born: Sacriston, County Durham, February 1933.*
*Career: Waterhouses Secondary Modern School. Langley Park Juniors. Chester-le-Street. Middlesbrough. Southampton (trial). Fulham. ALBION (£25,000 March 1956-August 1962). Fulham (£20,000). Oxford University (trainer-coach). Vancouver Royals (player-manager). Fulham (manager). Chelsea (scout). Ipswich Town (manager). England manager 1982-90. PSV Eindhoven (manager 1990-92). Sporting Lisbon (manager 1992-3). Was England 'B' team manager, January 1978-July 1982.*

*Bobby Robson*

During his Fulham days, Bobby Robson was part of a useful inside trio which included Bedford Jezzard and Johnny Haynes. After leaving Craven Cottage for The Hawthorns in 1956 he was converted from a goalscoring inside-right into an international right-half by manager Vic Buckingham, going on to win 20 full caps (1957-62) before returning to Fulham where he ended his League career in 1967 after 585 appearances. A model competitor whose play oozed confidence, Robson's temperament was a shining example to his colleagues. A hard-worker, always full of fight, he inspired his fellow team-mates and proved a tireless wing-half and inside-forward. Besides his score of full caps, Robson played five times for the League XI, once for the Under-23s, once for the 'B' team, and represented the FA XI on tour to South Africa in 1956. He was in the 1958 and 1962 World Cup finals squads and netted twice on his England debut, against France at Wembley in 1957. He played for the FA XI against Tottenham in the 1962 FA Charity Shield game and as manager of Ipswich, saw the Portman Road club celebrate success in the FA Cup (1978)

and UEFA Cup (1981), as well as winning the Texaco Cup in 1973. He was also Town manager when they were pipped for the League title by Aston Villa in 1981. During his playing career (for Fulham, Albion and England at all levels) Robson made 673 senior appearances and scored 151 goals. For Albion his record was 257 games and 61 goals. He was a good cricketer too, playing for Sacriston, Worcester Park (London), and for West Bromwich Dartmouth. As England team manager, Robson was in charge during the 1986 World Cup Finals in Mexico and led England to World Cup semi-finals in 1990 before handing over to Graham Taylor after over 90 matches in charge.
*Albion debut v Manchester City (home) Division One, 10 March 1956.*

# GARY ROBSON

*Born: Chester-le-Street, County Durham, July 1965.*
*Career: Pelaw Church of England and Roseberry Comprehensive Schools, Chester-le-Street. Lumley Juniors. Whitehill Boys. Chester-le-Street Boys. Newcastle United (trial). ALBION (apprentice July 1981, professional April 1983).*

Gary Robson was the longest-serving player

*Gary Robson*

at The Hawthorns in 1992, but although a dedicated clubman, he has always lived in the shadow of his more famous brother, Bryan. The Robsons were at The Hawthorns together, in 1981, before Manchester United swooped and Bryan went off to Old Trafford and glory with both United and England. Gary took time to establish himself in Albion's first team and it wasn't until 1987-8 that he was able to hold down a regular place in the League side. A determined, hard-working footballer, he has appeared in several positions for Albion, including full-back, wing-half, midfield and centre-forward. But wherever he's lined up, he has always given 100 per cent. Troubled by injuries on many occasions, including breaking a leg in the FA Cup tie with Aston Villa in 1990 — he had to have a pin inserted before the limb heeled

— he has always bounced back and in 1992 he duly passed his brother's total of senior appearances for the Baggies before being given a free transfer in June 1993. Both Gary & Bryan played for the Football League XI in May 1989 (v Skol Northern League).
*Albion debut v Southampton (home) Division One, 7 May 1983 (as sub).*

## REG RYAN

*Born: Dublin, October 1925.*
*Career: Merino School (Gaelic Football). Claremont School (Blackpool). Blackpool Boys. S.S.Cars FC. Sheffield United (trial). Jaguar Cars FC. Nuneaton Borough. Nottingham Forest (trial). Coventry City. ALBION (April 1945-June 1955). Derby County (£3,000). Coventry City. Retired November 1960. Coventry City FC pools organiser. Rejoined Albion (December 1961) on similar basis; became club's chief scout September 1962-October 1976. Later acted as scout for Hereford United, Leeds United and Aston Villa.*

*Reg Ryan*

A stocky, mobile player who gave many impressive displays from both wing-half positions and as an inside-forward for clubs and country, 'Paddy' Ryan took time to stake a claim in Albion's senior side, but once in he was a consistent performer, helping them win promotion from Division Two in 1949 and gaining an FA Cup winners' medal in 1954, when he linked up tremendously well in midfield with Jimmy Dudley and Ray Barlow. After leaving Albion he inspired Derby County to the Third Division North championship in 1956-7, when he skippered the Rams. On the international front, Ryan won 17 caps, 16 for the Republic of Ireland and one for Northern Ireland. He amassed 432 League appearances (234 for Albion) and netted a combined figure of 70 goals in the

competition. In 1955, he played left-half for the Third Division North team against the Third Division South side and scored a penalty. He still follows football and is always eager to attend reunions of old players at his former clubs.
*Albion League debut v Chesterfield (away) Division Two, 4 September 1947.*

## JIM SANDERS

*Born: Hackney, London, July 1920.*
*Career: Hackney Grammar and North London Schools. Longlands FC. Liverpool (trial). Charlton Athletic. ALBION (£2,250, November 1945-June 1958). Coventry City. Hinckley Athletic. Retired 1960. Guested for Albion, Southampton, Chelsea, West Ham United, Fulham and Liverpool during World War Two.*

*Jim Sanders*

Jim Sanders was a very consistent goalkeeper, never acrobatic but always steady and capable. He was something of an expert at stopping penalties, preventing some 25 from entering the net in his 19-year career. He was invalided out of the RAF during the war after many operational flights as an air-gunner, but recovered full fitness and acted as Albion's last line of defence in 391 games, including the 1954 FA Cup Final when he came into the team as a late replacement for the injured Norman Heath. He was a key member of Albion's 1948-9 promotion-winning side and at The Valley was understudy to the great Sam Bartram. Sanders was Albion's first-choice 'keeper for the period 1948 to 1951 and again from 1954 to 1958, when he handed over the duties to Clive Jackman, before moving

to nearby Coventry. After his footballing days were over, Sanders became a publican, first in Derby, then in Birmingham. Today he lives in Tamworth and can still be seen sporting his bow-tie and FA Cup-winners' medal, which hangs proudly on a chain around his neck.
*Albion debut v Millwall (away), Wartime League, 10 November 1945.*
*FA Cup debut v Cardiff City (away), 5 January 1946.*
*League debut v Swansea Town (away) Division Two, 31 August 1946.*

## TEDDY SANDFORD

*Born: Handsworth, Birmingham, October 1910.*
*Career: Wattville Road School. Tantany Athletic. Overend Wesley. Birmingham Carriage Works FC. Smethwick Highfield. ALBION (October 1929-March 1939). Sheffield United. Morris Commercial FC. Retired 1943. Albion coach during 1950s, scout 1961-67.*

*Teddy Sandford*

Teddy Sandford had ten fine years at The Hawthorns. He arrived at the club when Albion were reasonably well-off for inside-forwards, and spent a season in the Reserves before making his first-team debut in 1930-31, the season which ended in triumph with that Cup and promotion double. Sandford was a quiet type of player, never flashy, but nevertheless an excellent goalscoring inside-left who was exceedingly quick to pounce and dispossess an opponent who in turn found it hard to dispossess him. He had an enviable physique which held him in good stead later in his career when he lined up to good effect at centre-half. He won an FA Cup winners' medal with Albion in 1931 and collected a loser's prize in 1935 after scoring a goal in his side's 4-2 defeat by Sheffield Wednesday. He won one England cap, against Wales in 1932, and appeared 317 games for Albion, scoring 75 goals. He is one of the youngest players

ever to win an FA Cup medal with Albion, being only 20 years, six months old when the Throstles took the trophy in 1931.
*Albion debut v Preston North End (away) Division Two, 15 November 1930 (scored in a 3-2 Albion victory).*

## JACK SANKEY

*Born: Moulton, March 1912. Died: Handsworth, Birmingham, January 1985.*
*Career: Moulton C of E School. Moulton Wanderers. Winsford United. ALBION (November 1930-October 1945). Northampton Town. Walsall (guest 1945-6). Hereford United (player, then assistant trainer). ALBION (coach 1955-64, then scout 1965-6).*

*Jack Sankey*

Jack Sankey was an industrious and highly efficient wing-half or inside-forward whose overall play was characterised by some powerful long-range shooting. He spent three and a half seasons playing for Albion's reserve team before making the major breakthrough into the first team in 1933-4, taking over from Jimmy Edwards. From then until the outbreak of World War Two, Sankey's senior outings were frequent and by 1939 his Albion appearances had reached the 150 mark. During the hostilities he added over 120 more competitive matches to his tally and ended his career at The Hawthorns in 1945 with a record of 290 first-team games and 27 goals. He had a testimonial match in 1954 when 4,500 fans saw Hereford United beat Albion 10-5.
*Albion debut v Chelsea (away) FA Cup, 13 January 1934.*
*League debut v Blackburn Rovers (home), Division One, 20 January 1934.*

## MAURICE SETTERS

*Born: Honiton, Devon, December 1936.*
*Career: Honiton & Cullompton Schools. Exeter City. ALBION (£3,000, January 1955-January 1960). Manchester United (£30,000). Stoke City. Coventry City.*

Charlton Athletic. Doncaster Rovers (manager). Sheffield Wednesday (coach). Rotherham United (assistant manager). Newcastle United (chief scout). Republic of Ireland assistant manager (1986 to date).

*Maurice Setters*

Appearances did not deceive with Maurice Setters, whose bandy-legs and crew-cut hair made him look just what he was on the field of play — a real terrier, as hard as nails, determined and fearless, despite standing only 5ft 6in tall. After winning Schoolboy recognition, he went on to gain one Youth cap and 16 at Under-23 level for England. He also played twice for the FA XI and represented Young England in 1958. He appeared in 132 League and Cup games for Albion and 186 for United. For Exeter City, Stoke City, Coventry City and Charlton Athletic, his senior outings totalled 170 — and he finished his League career with 434 games to his name. Setters gained an FA Cup winners' medal with Manchester United in 1963. A tremendous competitor, Setters tasted major football in seven different outfield positions but was at his best in midfield.
*Albion debut v Huddersfield Town (away) Division One, 26 November 1955.*

## CECIL SHAW

*Born: Mansfield, June 1911. Died: Handsworth, Birmingham, January 1977.*
*Career: Mansfield Schools. Mansfield*

Invicta. Blidworth Juniors. Rainworth Church FC. Rufford Colliery FC. Wolves (1930). ALBION (£7,500, December 1936-June 1947). Hereford United. Retired 1949. Guested for Nottingham Forest and Blackpool during World War Two. Refereed in Oldbury & District Leagues 1950-60. Albion scout 1961-4.

*Cecil Shaw*

Cecil Shaw was a tough full-back, a resolute and robust tackler who played some 200 games for Wolves (176 in the League) before transferring to Albion in 1936 for a record fee of £7,500, paid in two instalments. He gained a first-team place with Wolves late in 1932 and played with such consistency and reliability that up to the middle of September 1936 he had missed only one match in the senior side, making 126 consecutive appearances. He was Wolves' skipper and their penalty expert. Alas, Shaw missed the first spot-kick he took for Albion, in an FA Cup-tie at Coventry in February 1937. Standing 5ft 9ins tall and weighing 12st 7lb, he went straight into Albion's League team, holding his place at left-back until the war and partly through it. He is one of only a handful of players who served Albion before, during and after World War Two. Towards the end of 1936-7 and at the start of 1937-8, he lined up alongside his namesake, George, in the full-back position in 15 League matches for Albion. Shaw made 251 appearances for Albion (League, Cup and wartime competitions) and he scored 14 goals. He represented the Football League in 1935 when a Wolves player.
*Albion debut v Liverpool (away) Division One, 28 December 1936.*

## GEORGE SHAW

*Born: Swinton, October 1899. Died: March 1973.*
*Career: Swinton Schools. Bolton-on-Deane FC. Rossington Main Colliery. Doncaster Rovers. Gillingham. Doncas-*

*ter Rovers. Huddersfield Town. ALBION (November 1926-May 1938). Stalybridge Celtic. Worcester City (player-manager). FC Floriana (Malta, player-manager-coach 1948-51). Retired cs 1951, returning to Hamworth Colliery, Doncaster.*

George Shaw

Like several of his comtemporaries, George 'Cocky' Shaw — nicknamed 'Teapot' — gave long and loyal service to Albion. Admirably built for a full-back, he was dominant in the air, strong on the ground and decidedly safe with his kicking. He was a grand volleyer of the ball and a useful penalty-taker. Shaw was an occasional member of Huddersfield's League Championship-winning teams of 1923-4, 1924-5 and 1925-6, making 24 appearances in three seasons. With Albion he won an FA Cup winners' medal in 1931, a runners-up award at Wembley in 1935, one England cap, against Scotland in 1932, and had an outing with the Football League XI. He went on two FA tours, to Belgium, France and Spain in 1929, and to Canada in 1931. After making his Albion debut, he missed only five of the next 300 League games to Janaury 1934, and when he left The Hawthorns, shortly after the end of the 1937-8 campaign, he had amassed 425 senior appearances for the Baggies. Shaw cost Albion £4,100 when signed from Huddersfield — a club record at the time. An ex-naval man, he was a useful singer and his hobby was mat-making.
*Albion debut v Sheffield United (away) Division One, 4 December 1926.*

## BEN SHEARMAN

*Born: Lincoln, June 1884. Died: October 1958.*
*Career: Attercliffe. High Hazels (Sheffield Amateur League). Worksop. Rotherham Town. Bristol City. ALBION (June 1911-August 1919). Nottingham Forest. Gainsborough Trinity. Norton Woodseats. Retired 1938.*
Ben Shearman was an elusive outside-left,

Ben Shearman

quick off the mark and strikingly accurate with his crosses, whether hit high or low. He replaced Amos Lloyd on Albion's left wing and was a consistent performer in that position until Howard Gregory and Jack Crisp came along immediately after World War One to contest the outside-left spot, Shearman rejoined Nottingham Forest. He appeared in 143 games for Albion, and was in their 1912 FA Cup Final side against Barnsley. He played for the Football League XI on two occasions in 1911, and during his career in League football amassed more than 180 appearances.
*Albion debut v Notts County (home) Division One, 2 September 1911 (scored in a 2-1 Albion win).*

## FRED SHINTON

*Born: Wednesbury, March 1883. Died: Leicester, April 1923.*
*Career: St James' School (Wednesbury). Hawthorn Villa. Moxley White Star. Wednesbury Old Athletic. Hednesford Town. ALBION (April 1905-December 1907). Leicester Fosse. Bolton Wanderers. Leicester Fosse. Retired (ill-health) 1912.*
Fred Shinton was a deadly marksman who scored 46 goals in only 64 League games for Albion in two and a half years with the club. A very sporting character, he played with dash and tenacity; he had a never-say-die attitude and thoroughly enjoyed scoring goals. Nicknamed 'Appleyard' and 'Tickler' by his colleagues, he had perhaps one of the best overall scoring records in terms of goals-per-matches, than any other player. In the first half of the 1906-07 campaign he

Fred Shinton

scored 26 goals in 21 matches, including three 'fours'. He had a remarkable knack of finding the net. He was recruited by Albion following the problem of filling the centre-forward spot in 1904-05 when no fewer than six different players were tried. Shinton stepped in and made such an impact that when he left, upset fans caused a rumpus at the ground. His place as leader of the attack was taken by a number of players — yet again — until finally Bob Pailor arrived to fit the bill in 1908.
*Albion debut v Bolton Wanderers (home) Division Two, 22 April 1905.*

## 'CHIPPY' SIMMONS

*Born: West Bromwich, September 1878. Died: Wednesbury, December 1937.*
*Career: Beeches Road School. Trinity Victoria. Oldbury Town. Worcester Rovers. ALBION (April 1898-July 1904). West Ham United. ALBION (May 1905-March 1907). Chesterfield Town. Wellington Town. Royal Rovers (Canada). Retired 1922, returning to West Bromwich where he became a publican, having learnt the trade in 1909.*
Charlie Simmons, always known as 'Chippy', was a regular scorer from the inside-right or centre-forward positions. He teamed up well with first Billy Bassett, and then Jimmy McLean and Fred Buck, and later with Fred Shinton after he had returned to West Bromwich following a brief association with West Ham. A player with a cracking shot, Simmons had plenty of pace and craft. He was a big favourite with the fans, especially the

*'Chippy' Simmons*

ladies, and scored 81 goals in 193 first-team games for the Throstles. He gained a Second Division championship medal in 1902 when he top-scored with 23 League goals, and it was in this same year that he figured in an England international trial, later representing the Professionals of the South v The Amateurs of the South in 1905. He was an England reserve on three occasions during the 1901-02 season.
*Albion debut v. Burnley (away) Division One, 19 November 1898.*

## JOE SMITH

*Born: Darby End, Nr Dudley, April 1890.*
*Died: June 1956.*
*Career: Halesowen Road Council School. Netherton St Andrew's. Darby End Victoria. Cradley Heath St Luke's. ALBION (May 1910-May 1926). Birmingham. Worcester City (player-manager). Retired 1933. Guested for Everton and Notts County in World War One.*
Joe Smith was a right-back strategist who more than balanced any deficiency in speed by good positional sense. He often cleared his lines with long, telling kicks and was sound in the tackle for a relatively small man. His remarkably high level of performance over a long period is illustrated by the number of League appearances he made from 1919-20 to 1924-25 inclusive: 247 out of a possible 252, and all in the First Division. Joe Smith formed fine partnerships at full-back with Jesse Pennington and later with Billy Adams and Arthur Perry. A Junior international in 1909, Smith obtained two full England caps, in 1919-20 and 1922-3, and gained a Second Division championship medal in 1911 and a First Division winners' medal in 1920. He also played for England in a 1919 Victory international. A wonderful clubman, a studious performer, Joe

*Joe Smith*

Smith made more than 470 senior appearances for Albion — 434 in the League alone.
*Albion debut v Bolton Wanderers (away) Division Two, 5 September 1910.*

## DEREK STATHAM

*Born: Whitmore Reams, Wolverhampton, March 1959.*
*Career: St Mary's Primary and St Edmund's Junior Schools (Wolverhampton). ALBION (July 1975, professional April 1976-September 1987). Southampton. Stoke City. Walsall.*
Derek Statham was one of the finest left-backs in England in the early 1980s, but he had Arsenal's Kenny Sansom to contest the left-back shirt with on the international front and won only three full caps, in 1982-3 against Wales and Australia (twice). A cheerful, buoyant character who tackles tigerishly and loves to go forward, Derek Statham scored against one of the finest 'keepers in the country when making his Albion debut in 1976 — that man being Peter Shilton, then

*Derek Statham*

with Stoke. Earlier, Statham had gained an FA Youth Cup winners' medal with Albion and went on to win seven Youth caps for his country, following up with more at Under-21 and 'B' team levels before breaking into the senior side in 1983 after former Albion man, Bobby Robson, had taken over as team manager. Statham has had injury problems (in 1986-7 a proposed move to Liverpool fell through on medical grounds) but when fit he showed tremendous talent. His weaving, darting runs from deep in his own half directly into the opposing penalty area have highlighted his displays.
*Albion debut v Stoke City (away) Division One, 18 December 1976 (scored once).*

## JIM STEVENSON

*Born: Bonhill, Dumbarton, August 1875.*
*Died: Dumbarton, March 1925.*
*Career: Bonhill St Augustine's School. Dumbarton Fereday. Dumbarton. Preston North End. Bristol St George. Preston North End. ALBION (October 1900-June 1904). Dumbarton. Retired cs 1910. Died following an accident at Leven Shipyard.*
Jim Stevenson was a resilient, strong-tackling centre-half who also played and performed admirably at centre-forward. He was aided by his height (6ft 2in) and qualities of coolness and precise judgement. Signed by Albion at a time when the team was at a low ebb, he failed to save them from relegation but was instrumental in helping them regain their First Division status the following season, when he appeared in all 34

*Jim Stevenson*

League matches, lining up in the middle of wing-halves Dan Nurse and Harry Hadley. Stevenson commanded the defence and had a wonderful spell at The Hawthorns, making 129 League and Cup appearances and winning a Second Division championship medal in 1902. He gained one minor representative honour — a game for the Anglo-Scots v Scotland in 1902-03.
*Albion debut v Stoke (home) Division One, 3 November 1900.*

## JIM STRINGER

*Born: Netherton, May 1878. Died: Dudley, December 1933.*
*Career: Netherton & District Schools. Netherton Rovers. Wolves. ALBION (April 1905-October 1910). Dudley Town. Port Talbot (trainer). Retired.*

*Jim Stringer*

Jim Stringer was a sound, vigilant goalkeeper, whose height and weight enabled him to dominate when high crosses looped over, or there was a tight situation near his goal. Albion secured him from neighbouring Wolves to take over between the posts from Ike Webb. Stringer did well, holding his place in the side for four and a half seasons before handing over to Hubert Pearson halfway through the 1909-10 campaign.
*Albion debut v Leicester Fosse (home) Division Two, 8 April 1905.*

## COLIN SUGGETT

*Born: Washington, County Durham, December, 1948.*
*Career: Washington Grammar School. Chester-le-Street and County Durham Schools. Sunderland. ALBION (£100,000, July 1969-February 1973). Norwich City. Newcastle United (August 1978). Retired 1979 to become coach at St James' Park.*
Colin Suggett was Albion's first £100,000 signing, in 1969, and he got off to a flying start, scoring twice on his debut against Southampton at The Dell at the start of the 1969-70 season. He arrived at The Hawthorns with a big reputation as a goal-getter and left as a highly efficient midfielder who cost Norwich £70,000. He made his League debut for Sunderland in March 1967 as an 18-year-old, and whilst at Roker Park played in the 1966 and 1967 FA Youth Cup Finals. He won England Schoolboy and Youth honours

*Colin Suggett*

(1963-4 and 1966-7 respectively) and was in Albion's 1970 League Cup Final team at Wembley. He played for Norwich in the 1975 League Cup Final against Aston Villa, and during his career amassed a grand total of 440 League games, scoring 65 goals. For Norwich he netted 21 times in 203 League matches; and for Sunderland his record was 24 goals in 86 League games. He was a keen pigeon fancier and also enjoyed a wager on the horses and dogs, owning a greyhound while an Albion player.
*Albion debut v Southampton (away) Division One, 9 August 1969 (scored two goals in Albion's 2-0 victory.*

## JOHN TALBUT

*Born: Headington, Oxford, October 1940.*
*Career: South Shields Grammar School. South Shields Schools. Durham Boys. Burnley. ALBION (December 1966-May 1971). KV Mechelen (Belgium, player-manager). Retired 1974 to become a licensee in Belgium, taking the 'Kup Winna' bar in Mechelen. Later a hotelier.*
John Talbut was already an experienced centre-half when he came to Albion halfway through the 1966-7 season, having played in 138 League games for Burnley, besides gaining England caps at Schoolboy (1955) and Under-23 levels (seven appearances). He was recruited to Albion by manager Jimmy Hagan as a replacement for Stan Jones and repaid every penny of the £30,000 fee placed on his head, by appearing in well over 190 senior games for Albion, including the 1968 FA Cup and 1970 League Cup Finals. He broke into League football

*John Talbut*

with Burnley in December 1958, against Leicester, and during the first four months of his Albion career had to sit and watch the team battle through to Wembley in the League Cup, having already played for Burnley in that season's competition. Twelve months later, however, he gained a winners' medal as Albion beat Everton 1-0 in extra-time to take the FA Cup.
*Albion debut v Tottenham Hotspur (home) Division One, 26 December 1966.*

## BOB TAYLOR

*Born: Easington, County Durham, February 1967.*
*Career: Hordon CW. Leeds United. Bristol City. ALBION (January 1992, £300,000).*

*Bob Taylor*

Bob Taylor became the 'star man' at The Hawthorns in 1992-3, when his supreme marksmanship went a long way in helping Albion's challenge for promotion to the First Division. He certainly repaid a big chunk of the £300,000 fee paid by Albion for his services early in 1992, producing some quite superb performances, not only as a goalscorer, but also as a grafter, helping out in midfield and defence when required. He started his League career with Leeds in 1985-6 and scored 13 goals in 54 games whilst at Elland Road. He then proceeded to net another 60 goals for Bristol City, in more than 120 outings for the Ashton Gate club, before moving to The Hawthorns where he grabbed over 40 goals in his first 70 matches for the Baggies.
*Albion debut v Brentford (home) Division Three, 1 February 1992 (scored in a 2-0 Albion win).*

## BERT TRENTHAM

*Born: Chirbury, Salop, April 1908. Died: Birmingham, June, 1979.*
*Career: Chirbury St John's School. Knighton Town. Knighton Victoria. Knighton United. Hereford United. Aston Villa (trial). ALBION (April 1929-May 1937). Hereford United. Darlaston. Retired 1942. Went into ironmongers business in Ward End, Birmingham.*

*Bert Trentham*

'Corker' Trentham was a useful full-back, able and willing to play in either the right or left-hand berth. A model of consistency, he was sound rather than brilliant and always carried a handkerchief in his withered right hand. He drew up a fine relationship on the field with his co-partner, George Shaw, and they played together in over 230 games for Albion during the 1930s, including appearances in both the 1931 and 1935 FA Cup Finals. Trentham was a member of Albion's 'double' team of 1930-31, and during his splendid career he won a Junior international cap (1929) and represented the Football League in 1933. He never scored a goal in more than 270 senior appearances for Albion.
*Albion debut v Blackpool (away) Division Two, 5 March 1930.*

## JACK VERNON

*Born: Belfast, September 1919. Died: Belfast, August 1981.*
*Career: St Paul's School (Belfast). Springfield Road Juniors. Dundela Juniors. Liverpool (trial, 1937). Belfast Celtic. ALBION (February 1947-July 1952). Crusaders. Retired June 1954, to continue his father's butchers business in Belfast, a job he did until his untimely death.*
Jack Vernon was unquestionably among the greatest of West Bromwich Albion

centre-halves, supreme in the air and masterful on the ground —a true sportsman of the highest calibre. Albion signed Vernon on a five-year agreement in 1947, handing over a then club record fee of £9,500 to Belfast Celtic. He had to wait five weeks for his Albion debut due to the atrocious weather which gripped England that winter — and when he did finally step out for his Albion baptism, at Upton Park, he was on the receiving end of a hat-trick from the home striker Neary as the Hammers won 3-2. But Vernon soon settled into the routine of commanding the back division — a job he did so successfully, not only for Albion

*Jack Vernon*

but for Northern Ireland as well. He collected 22 full caps (two with the Republic) and skippered Northern Ireland on 17 occasions. He also captained the United Kingdom side against Wales in 1951 and was at centre-half for the Great Britain XI v the Rest of the World at Hampden Park in 1947, an honour which confirmed him as the game's top pivot at that time. Before he arrived at The Hawthorns, Vernon — nicknamed 'Twinkletoes' because of his small size-5 feet — won Irish Cup winners' medals in 1941, 1943 and 1944, and Irish League Championship medals in 1939 and 1940, as well as playing for the Irish Select XI on three occasions and the Irish League 12 times between 1941 and 1946. He led Albion to promotion in 1948-9 and played in exactly 200 League and Cup matches for the Baggies, scoring just one goal — against Sheffield Wednesday on Christmas morning 1948.
*Albion debut v West Ham United (away) Division Two, 15 March 1947.*

## DAVE WALSH

*Born: Waterford, April 1924.*
*Career: St Joseph's (Waterford). The Corinthians. Shelbourne of Waterford. Glen Rovers. Limerick. Shelbourne of Dublin (on loan). Linfield. ALBION (£3,500, May 1946-December 1950). Aston Villa (£25,000). Walsall. Worcester City. Retired June 1957. Ran successful sports outfitters in Droitwich before retiring to Torquay in 1984.*

*Dave Walsh*

Dave Walsh had an ideal build for a centre-forward, a job he did so well with speed and thrust. He was a consistent scorer throughout his career which saw him win 11 caps for Northern Ireland and 20 for the Republic. He also represented the Irish League twice in 1946, and helped Albion win promotion in 1949, when he scored 23 goals. As keen as mustard in and around the 'box', he had netted over 60 goals for Linfield in 1945-6 when they won the Irish League Championship. He also scored two in the Irish Cup Final against Distillery — and this record prompted Albion boss Fred Everiss to travel to Ireland and secure Walsh's services. Walsh had scored well over 120 goals in Irish football, winning other Cup medals in 1944 (runners-up) and 1945 (winners), and in each of his first six League matches in England he scored at least once to create an Albion record. He notched exactly 100 goals in 174 games for Albion and his record with Villa and Walsall sent his statistics in League football up to 137 goals in 293 outings before he drifted into non-League soccer with Worcester in 1956.
*Albion debut v Swansea Town (away) Division Two, 31 August 1946, when he scored twice in a 3-2 Albion win.*

## IKE WEBB

*Born: Worcester, October 1874. Died: March 1950.*
*Career: Worcester Park School. St Cle-*

*ment's Rangers. Berwick Rangers (Worcester League). Evesham Town. Mansfield Town. Lincoln City. Small Heath. ALBION (May 1901-December 1904). Sunderland. QPR. Retired 1910. Made a comeback for Albion's first team in August 1918, at the age of 43 in a 'wartime' game.*

*Ike Webb*

Ike Webb was a goalkeeper of outstanding reflexes and quickness off his line. Spectacularly agile at times, his actions were usually so perfectly timed, although occasionally he tended to be rather casual. He is believed to have played with a fractured skull during an interesting career which took him to all parts of the country. He was secured by Albion to replace the retiring Joe Reader and he did a wonderful job between the posts for three and a half seasons, making 101 senior appearances. He gained a Second Division championship medal in 1902 and was in terrific form during that campaign, his first with Albion.
*Albion debut v Glossop (home) Division Two, 2 September 1901.*

## CLIVE WHITEHEAD

*Born: Northfield, Birmingham, November 1955.*
*Career: Alston Junior School. Waverley Grammar School. Bordesley Green. Northfield Juniors. Wolves (trial). Bristol City. ALBION (£100,000, November 1981). Wolves (on loan). Portsmouth. Exeter City. Yeovil Town (manager).*
Former England Youth international, Clive Whitehead is a good professional, gritty, unselfish and a player who will do a worthwhile job in any position. Whitehead's Albion career was revitalised following the appointment of manager Ron Saunders in February 1986. He had been on loan to Wolves, but had a new lease of life when told by the boss that

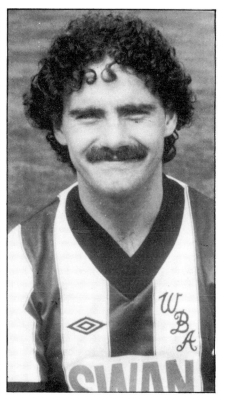
*Clive Whitehead*

he was Albion's best right-back and the position was his, if he put his mind to it. He played 256 games for Bristol City prior to joining Albion and whilst at Ashton Gate had a long spell on the left wing and another one in the left-back berth. He helped City win promotion to Division One in 1975-6, scoring the promotion-winning goal against Portsmouth. In 1982-3, he was used in six different positions by Albion, but always preferred a full-back role. In May 1987, Whitehead's career at The Hawthorns was finally over when he was given a free-transfer.
*Albion debut v Tottenham Hotspur (away) Division One, 7 November 1981.*

## CHRIS WHYTE

*Born: Islington, London, September 1961.*
*Career: Highbury Hill & District Schools. Highbury Grove FC. Islington Boys & Inner London Schools. Arsenal. Crystal Palace (on loan). Los Angeles Lazers. Los Angeles Aztecs. ALBION (free transfer, August 1988), Leeds United (£450,000, tribunal-set fee, July 1990).*
After a dismal 1987-8 season, when Albion finished 20th in Division Two, conceded 76 goals in 49 games overall and utilised seven different centre-backs, manager Ron Saunders, after taking advice from Brian Talbot, secured the services of former Arsenal defender Chris Whyte on a free transfer from the American team, Los Angeles Aztecs. Whyte, who had played with Talbot in the Gunners' side in the early 1980s, desperately wanted to return to Britain and when Albion came in with an offer, he had no hesitation in joining The Hawthorns staff. He quickly slotted into the back-line, playing alongside Stacey

*Chris Whyte*

North and Whyte went on to serve the Baggies admirably for two whole seasons, amassing 94 League and Cup appearances and scoring seven goals. Cool and controlled under pressure, good at set pieces, Whyte was voted Albion's Player of the Year in 1989 but when his contract expired at the end of the 1989-90 campaign, he decided to leave The Hawthorns, teaming up with Leeds United for a vastly reduced fee after Albion had demanded £800,000. Capped four times by England at Under-21 level whilst at Highbury, Whyte became a star performer in the Leeds side and he helped Howard Wilkinson's side to establish itself back in the top flight, performing exceedingly well alongside Chris Fairclough and winning a League Championship medal in 1991-2. In May 1993, however, he was given a free transfer by Leeds.

*Albion debut v Peterborough United (away) Littlewoods Cup, 7 September, 1988.*

## JOHN WILE

*Born: Sherburn, County Durham, March 1947.*
*Career: Sherburn Secondary Modern School. Eppleton Juniors (Hetton). Durham City. Peterborough United (trial). Sunderland. Peterborough United. ALBION (£32,000, December 1970-June 1983). Peterborough United (player-manager, retiring as a player in 1986). Played in the NASL with Vancouver Whitecaps 1982. Later involved in indoor cricket at Walsall and Solihull.*

John Wile's last game for Albion, against his former club, Sunderland, at Roker Park on 14 May 1983, was his 500th in

League competition for the Baggies. It crowned a magnificent 13 years with The Throstles, during which time he made many friends, both inside and outside football; he was a fine 'ambassador' in China in 1978. He was an astute, reliable, commanding and powerful centre-half. Indeed, he was acknowledged by the fans as being one of Albion's finest-ever pivots. He had the will to win and certainly gave Albion everything each time he pulled on the club jersey. Fans still recall his tremendous display in the 1978 FA Cup semi-final against Ipswich Town at Highbury when he played on with his head swathed in blood-stained bandages, albeit to no avail as Albion lost 3-1. But that was the essence of John Wile. He was a born fighter, a true battler and a great sportsman. He retired from first-class football at the end of the 1985-6

*John Wile*

season. He took over the number-five shirt at Albion from John Talbut in 1970 and was succeeded by Ken McNaught in 1983. During his reign at The Hawthorns, Albion fulfilled 525 League fixtures, and Wile played in 500 of them. He missed only one Cup-tie, and in 1978-9, Albion played a total of 76 first team matches, and Wile turned out in 75 of them — the most games played by an Albion footballer in a single season. He played more matches at centre-half than any other Albion player — 616 plus one as substitute (two at left-half). And in the League alone he played in the number-five position on 497 occasions, plus once as a substitute. He is the third-highest appearance maker for Albion with 714 (plus one) games. Sadly, he never won a major honour, despite playing played in three FA Cup semi-finals with Albion, reaching the quarter-finals of the UEFA Cup in 1979 and being a dominant

figure in Albion's promotion-winning side in 1975-6. He was an ever-present for Albion in seven seasons — a club record. Former manager Johnny Giles once said of John Wile: "If he could play football from nine in the morning till nine at night, seven days a week, 52 weeks a year, he still wouldn't be satisfied."

*Albion debut v Blackpool (home) Division One, 19 December 1970.*

## BILLY WILLIAMS

*Born: West Smethwick, June 1875. Died: West Bromwich, January 1929.*
*Career: Oldbury Road School (Smethwick). West Smethwick FC. Old Hill Wanderers. ALBION (May 1894-June 1901). Forced to quit the game after a cartilage injury. Became Albion trainer for a while, later acting as coach at The Hawthorns (1910), before taking over a pub in West Bromwich.*

*Billy Williams*

Billy Williams was a brilliant full-back, stylish, dedicated and above all safe and sure under pressure. He possessed a long, raking kick and scored a few goals from far distances including one from fully 60 yards against Nottingham Forest (FAC) in February 1898. He was also an expert with penalty-kicks. He gained six England caps and played for the Football League and the Professionals in representative matches. He collected a runners-up medal with Albion in the 1895 FA Cup Final and made 208 senior appearances for the Baggies. Williams' enforced retirement was a bitter blow to Albion who suffered relegation for the first time at the end of his farewell season.

*Albion debut v Sheffield United (away) Division One, 1 September 1894.*

## CYRIL WILLIAMS

*Born: Bristol, November 1921. Died: Bristol, January 1980.*
*Career: Luckwell Road School (Bristol). Bristol Boys. Bristol City. ALBION (June 1948-August 1951). Bristol City (£4,500). Chippenham Town (manager). Gloucester City (manager). Guested for Reading and Tottenham Hotspur during World War Two.*

*Cyril Williams*

*Graham Williams*

## STUART WILLIAMS

*Born: Wrexham, July 1930.*
*Career: Aston Park and Grove Park Grammar Schools (Wrexham). Victoria Youth Club. Wrexham. ALBION (November 1950-September 1962). Southampton (£15,000). ALBION (trainer 1967-69). Aston Villa (trainer). Payhaan, (Holland, manager). Morton (trainer-coach). Southampton (coach and assistant manager). Carlisle United (scout). Stavanger (Norway, manager).*

*Stuart Williams*

Cyril Williams was a capable and efficient inside-forward who had enthusiasm as well as skill. A goalscorer who found the net 20 times in 77 League and Cup games for Albion, he was a key figure in the 1948-9 promotion team and later shone at left-half for Bristol City, for whom he played in nearly 300 League matches (68 goals), winning a Third Division South Championship medal in 1954-5. He came to The Hawthorns in a player-exchange deal involving Cliff Edwards plus £500. Cyril Williams was killed in a car crash on 21 January 1980.
*Albion debut v West Ham United (away) Division Two, 4 September 1948.*

## GRAHAM WILLIAMS

*Born: Hellan, North Wales, April 1938.*
*Career: Emmanuel Secondary Modern School. Flintshire Boys. Burnley (trial 1953). Rhyl Athletic. ALBION (September 1954, professional April 1955-April 1972). Weymouth (player-manager). Sports Klub Kuwait. OFI (Greece, coach). Poole Town (manager). Cardiff City (coach, then manager). Newport County (scout). Leopards FC. Nigeria (coach). FC Rovaniemen. Finland (manager to 1990).*

Graham Williams had 18 years' association with Albion, first as an outside-left and later as a powerful left-back. He also put in a few enterprising displays at left-half but it was in the number-three shirt where he blossomed, skippering Albion to FA Cup Final success in 1968, after having led his team to a League Cup triumph two years earlier. He also played in the 1967 League Cup Final (gaining a runners-up medal) but missed the 1970 Final despite playing four times in earlier rounds including the first leg of the semi-final against Carlisle United. He was capped 26 times by Wales and had two outings for the Under-23s. For Albion, his only League club as a player, he appeared in well over 350 competitive matches, including 314 in the First Division. It was not until 1962-3 that he became a firm fixture in Albion's senior team — this after his namesake, Stuart, had left for Southampton. It is interesting to note that Graham and Stuart Williams played together as full-backs for both Albion and Wales. In 1981, Graham Williams took Poole Town to the Final of the Anglo-Italian Tournament. Today he lives in Oswestry with his wife and family.
*Albion debut v Blackpool (home) Division One, 19 November 1955.*

One-time inside-right Stuart Williams was converted by Albion into a grand full-back who gave the Baggies 12 years' yeoman service. He had a sure kick, splendid positional sense and a first-rate temperament. Whilst at The Hawthorns he gained 33 Welsh caps (an Albion record for most-capped player) and after leaving for The Dell, he added another ten to his total. He had 246 senior outings for Albion (nine goals scored) and for the Saints, whom he helped win promotion to the First Division in 1966, his appearance tally topped the 175 mark, 147 coming in the League. He looked likely to replace Stan Rickaby in Albion's 1954 FA Cup Final side but was left out in favour of the more experienced Joe Kennedy.
*Albion debut v Huddersfield Town (away) Division One, 16 February 1952.*

## CHARLIE WILSON

*Born: Heeley, Sheffield, July 1905. Died: Kidderminster, 1985.*
*Career: Netherthorpe School. Stonehouse FC. Chesterfield (trial). Sheffield United (trial). Hallam FC. ALBION (December 1920, professional November 1922-February 1928). Sheffield Wednesday. Grimsby Town. Aston Villa. Coventry City. Kidderminster Harriers. Worcester City. Kidderminster Harriers. Guested for Charlton Athletic and Aldershot during World War Two and played for Kidder-*

*Charlie Wilson*

*Joe Wilson*

*Ray Wilson*

minster Police in 1946. Became a publican in 1947, retiring in 1971.

Charlie Wilson was an opportunist inside or centre-forward, who had an unquenchable thirst for goals — he hit 45 in 133 games for Albion. 'Tug', with his film-star looks, was a constant threat to opposing defenders; he could shoot from any angle and from seemingly any distance with either foot — and he usually hit the target. He had the reputation of keeping himself clean on the muddiest of pitches, yet he was still a 'grafter' who moved to left-half late in his career. He has the distinction of being the youngest player ever to appear in a League game for Albion — his debut coming at Oldham in October 1921 when he was 16 years 63 days old. In the 1920s he gained three Central League championship medals with Albion and assisted Sheffield Wednesday during their First Division title-winning seasons of 1928-9 and 1929-30. He linked superbly up front for Albion with Stan Davies, George James, Joe Carter, and both Arthur Fitton and Jack Byers, his left wingers.

*Albion debut v Oldham Athletic (away) Division One, 1 October 1921.*

## JOE WILSON

*Born: Handsworth, Birmingham, January 1861. Died: Acocks Green, Birmingham, October 1952.*
*Career: Hamstead Swifts. Aston Unity. Stoke. Walsall Town. Aston Villa. Walsall Town. ALBION (September 1887-May 1890). Kidderminster Harriers. Birmingham St George's. Retired. Became Football League referee (1894-1910). Was a goldsmith by trade.*

Joe Wilson had the distinction of scoring Albion's first-ever League goal — at Stoke

on 8 September 1888. Six months earlier he had helped Albion win the FA Cup at The Oval after scoring half-a-dozen goals in the earlier rounds. An aggressive outside-left of dashing style, he kept defences alert with his wing play. He formed a fine partnership with Tom Pearson and was virtually an ever-present in Albion's first two League campaigns. After playing the game he took up refereeing, and did a fine job for 16 seasons, officiating in most divisions, in the FA Cup and at non-League level. He played 53 League and Cup matches for Albion and scored 20 goals.

*Albion debut in September 1887.*
*FA Cup debut v Wednesbury Old Athletic (home), 15 October 1887 (scored twice in Albion's 7-1 victory).*
*League debut v Stoke (away), 8 September 1888.*

## RAY WILSON

*Born: Grangemouth, Stirlingshire, April 1947.*
*Career: Dundas Primary and Grangemouth High Schools. Stirlingshire Boys. Woodburn Athletic. ALBION (July 1963, professional May 1964-March 1977). Forced to retire through serious knee injury.*

Ray Wilson began with Albion as an outside-left but made a big name for himself as a steady left-back, who gained Scottish Under-23 recognition in 1970. A good covering player, who tackled hard, he had exceptional speed which enabled him to recover quickly. He loved to overlap and was a fine 'chipper' of the ball, left-footed down the touchline. He appeared in the 1970 League Cup Final for Albion — one of 284 senior games for the club. He established himself in the first team (at left-back) in the late 1960s, taking over initially from Graham

Williams. His last game in Albion's colours was at Luton during the promotion season of 1975-6. He had a testimonial at The Hawthorns in May 1975 when Albion met Villa.

*Albion debut v Chelsea (home) Division One, 2 October 1965.*

## DOUG WITCOMB

*Born: Cwm Nr Ebbw Vale, Gwent, April 1918.*
*Career: Ebbw Vale Schools. Cwm Villa. Tottenham Hotspur (amateur). Northfleet FC. Enfield. ALBION (October*

*Doug Witcomb*

*1937-February 1947). Sheffield Wednesday (£6,500). Newport County. Llandudno. Retired June 1965, later played works football with H.D.Alloys and Alkamatic in South Wales. Guested for Grimsby Town, Leicester City, Swansea Town, Lovells Athletic and Newport County during World War Two. Later living in Redditch, Worcestershire.*

Doug Witcomb was a wing-half or inside-forward of enormous talent; a quick and cunning distributor of timely passes, and a player with a powerful shot in his right foot. He had almost ten years at The Hawthorns, during which time he appeared in a total of 122 games (55 in the League). He won ten Welsh caps, including wartime internationals, and in 1939 represented the All-British XI v The Football League at Wolverhampton. His career in League football earned him a total of 303 matches, 223 for Wednesday whom he assisted to promotion from Division Two in 1950 and again in 1952.
*Albion debut v Burnley (away) Division Two, 17 September 1938.*

## STAN WOOD

*Born: Winsford, July 1905. Died: Halifax, February 1967.*
*Career: Meadow Bank School (Winsford).Whitegate Victoria. Winsford United. ALBION (April 1928-May 1938). Halifax Town (player, then trainer). Retired 1949. Guested for Huddersfield Town during World War Two.*

Stan Wood nicknamed 'Splinter' and the 'Singing Winger,' was a wiry, slippery outside-left whose cleverness stood him in good stead for ten fine seasons with Albion. He made 280 League and Cup appearances for Albion, scoring 66 goals. He starred in the 1931 FA Cup Final and a year later represented the Football League. Wood staked a claim in the

*Stan Wood*

Albion side in 1928 and eventually took over the mantle from Arthur Fitton, holding the position on the left-wing until Wally Boyes came along in 1934. He was in and out of the side during the latter part of the 1930s, but always gave 100 per cent effort when he did play. A fine footballer.
*Albion debut v Notts County (home) Division Two, 3 September 1928.*

## GEORGE WOODHALL

*Born: West Bromwich, September 1863. Died: West Bromwich, September 1924. Career: Hateley Heath School. West Bromwich All Saints. Churchfield Foresters. ALBION (May 1883, professional August 1885-July 1892). Wolves. Berwick Rangers (Birmingham League). Oldbury Town. Retired 1898.*

'Spry' Woodhall was singularly well-nicknamed, for he was indeed a sprightly outside or inside-right, centering with great accuracy and combining especially well with Billy Bassett. A regular member of Albion's front line for nine seasons,

*George Woodhall*

he won two England caps in 1888, the same year he gained an FA Cup winners' medal after scoring the clinching goal against Preston in the Final. He also played in the 1886 and 1887 Finals and scored 20 goals in 74 senior games for Albion. With his delightful personality. Woodhall was one of the most popular players of 'the old brigade', being remembered as a generous and whole-hearted sportsman by the older generation who lived to tell the tales of his fine play on Albion's right flank.
*Albion debut v Blackburn Rovers (away), November 1883.*
*FA Cup debut v Derby Junction St School (away), 25 October 1884.*
*League debut v Stoke (away), 8 September 1888.*

## HARRY WRIGHT

*Born: West Bromwich October 1888; Died: West Bromwich, September 1950. Career: Beeches Road and St Phillips' schools (West Bromwich). West Bromwich St Mark's. West Bromwich Wednesbury Athletic. ALBION (November 1906-May 1909). Stourbridge. ALBION (June 1910-November 1919). Wolverhampton Wanderers (£500). Newport County (September 1920). Retired cs 1922. Guested for Oldbury Town and Bilston during World War One.*

*Harry Wright*

Harry was an energetic forward, who could play, if required, in any position but preferred an inside berth. A gritty performer, he had two spells with Albion, the first as a raw-boned youngster, the second a much more compact and studious footballer. He helped Albion win the Second Division championship in 1910-11 and the following season played for them in the FA Cup Final, collecting a loser's medal. He had a good scoring record of a goal in every five games for the Baggies, ending up with 20 in 105 senior appearances.

# Albion's Record Against Other League Clubs

*Albion have played a total of 87 clubs in League competition since 1888. Some clubs have modified their names over the years (eg Small Heath to Birmingham to Birmingham City; Clapton Orient to Leyton Orient to Orient and back to Leyton Orient). In all cases the last name used by each club covers all games under previous appellations. Since season 1981-82 three points have been awarded for a win.*

| | HOME | | | | | | | AWAY | | | | | | | TOTAL | | | | | | |
|---|---|---|---|---|---|---|---|---|---|---|---|---|---|---|---|---|---|---|---|---|---|
| | P | W | D | L | F | A | Pts | P | W | D | L | F | A | Pts | P | W | D | L | F | A | Pts |
| Accrington | 5 | 4 | 1 | 0 | 18 | 5 | 9 | 5 | 0 | 1 | 4 | 7 | 12 | 1 | 10 | 4 | 2 | 4 | 25 | 17 | 10 |
| AFC Bournemouth | 5 | 3 | 2 | 0 | 11 | 3 | 11 | 5 | 1 | 1 | 3 | 6 | 8 | 4 | 10 | 4 | 3 | 3 | 17 | 11 | 15 |
| Arsenal | 52 | 21 | 12 | 19 | 76 | 65 | 54 | 52 | 9 | 13 | 30 | 63 | 112 | 32 | 104 | 30 | 25 | 49 | 139 | 177 | 86 |
| Aston Villa | 62 | 28 | 15 | 19 | 100 | 85 | 74 | 62 | 15 | 8 | 39 | 74 | 118 | 38 | 124 | 43 | 23 | 58 | 174 | 203 | 112 |
| Barnsley | 17 | 9 | 5 | 3 | 45 | 28 | 23 | 17 | 6 | 6 | 5 | 22 | 21 | 18 | 34 | 15 | 11 | 8 | 67 | 49 | 41 |
| Birmingham City | 43 | 19 | 14 | 10 | 62 | 42 | 55 | 43 | 18 | 12 | 13 | 60 | 48 | 51 | 86 | 37 | 26 | 23 | 122 | 90 | 106 |
| Blackburn Rovers | 48 | 25 | 13 | 10 | 95 | 59 | 65 | 48 | 11 | 7 | 30 | 54 | 103 | 32 | 96 | 36 | 20 | 40 | 149 | 162 | 97 |
| Blackpool | 37 | 21 | 6 | 10 | 86 | 46 | 49 | 37 | 12 | 6 | 19 | 43 | 60 | 30 | 74 | 33 | 12 | 29 | 129 | 106 | 79 |
| Bolton Wanderers | 55 | 25 | 7 | 13 | 105 | 77 | 68 | 55 | 14 | 14 | 27 | 60 | 105 | 43 | 110 | 39 | 31 | 40 | 165 | 182 | 111 |
| Bradford | 13 | 8 | 2 | 3 | 30 | 9 | 18 | 13 | 4 | 3 | 6 | 27 | 30 | 11 | 26 | 12 | 5 | 9 | 57 | 39 | 29 |
| Bradford City | 16 | 9 | 6 | 1 | 34 | 15 | 24 | 16 | 3 | 7 | 6 | 17 | 31 | 14 | 32 | 12 | 13 | 7 | 51 | 46 | 38 |
| Brentford | 6 | 6 | 0 | 0 | 13 | 5 | 13 | 6 | 2 | 2 | 2 | 7 | 6 | 7 | 12 | 8 | 2 | 2 | 20 | 11 | 20 |
| Brighton & HA | 9 | 5 | 4 | 0 | 14 | 3 | 15 | 8 | 3 | 3 | 2 | 8 | 7 | 11 | 16 | 7 | 7 | 2 | 22 | 10 | 26 |
| Bristol City | 15 | 7 | 6 | 2 | 23 | 13 | 21 | 15 | 5 | 3 | 7 | 16 | 19 | 13 | 30 | 12 | 9 | 9 | 39 | 32 | 34 |
| Bristol Rovers | 3 | 2 | 1 | 0 | 8 | 3 | 6 | 3 | 0 | 2 | 1 | 3 | 4 | 2 | 6 | 2 | 3 | 1 | 11 | 7 | 8 |
| Burnley | 55 | 28 | 11 | 16 | 112 | 65 | 68 | 55 | 18 | 11 | 26 | 69 | 100 | 47 | 110 | 46 | 22 | 42 | 181 | 165 | 115 |
| Burton United | 4 | 4 | 0 | 0 | 14 | 2 | 8 | 4 | 2 | 1 | 1 | 11 | 5 | 5 | 8 | 6 | 1 | 1 | 25 | 7 | 13 |
| Bury | 19 | 10 | 4 | 5 | 41 | 21 | 24 | 19 | 3 | 4 | 12 | 22 | 48 | 10 | 38 | 13 | 8 | 17 | 63 | 69 | 34 |
| Cardiff City | 19 | 11 | 3 | 5 | 40 | 23 | 25 | 19 | 7 | 4 | 8 | 32 | 32 | 18 | 38 | 18 | 7 | 13 | 72 | 55 | 43 |
| Carlisle United | 2 | 1 | 1 | 0 | 4 | 1 | 3 | 2 | 1 | 1 | 0 | 2 | 1 | 3 | 4 | 2 | 2 | 0 | 6 | 2 | 6 |
| Charlton Athletic | 14 | 6 | 6 | 2 | 24 | 17 | 19 | 14 | 5 | 3 | 6 | 24 | 27 | 13 | 28 | 11 | 9 | 8 | 48 | 44 | 32 |
| Chelsea | 50 | 21 | 13 | 16 | 89 | 56 | 55 | 50 | 14 | 14 | 22 | 72 | 98 | 42 | 100 | 35 | 27 | 38 | 161 | 154 | 97 |
| Chester City | 2 | 1 | 1 | 0 | 3 | 1 | 4 | 2 | 2 | 0 | 0 | 4 | 1 | 6 | 4 | 3 | 1 | 0 | 7 | 2 | 10 |
| Chesterfield | 10 | 7 | 2 | 1 | 23 | 8 | 16 | 10 | 3 | 4 | 3 | 14 | 10 | 10 | 20 | 10 | 6 | 4 | 37 | 18 | 26 |
| Coventry City | 20 | 10 | 7 | 3 | 41 | 18 | 29 | 20 | 7 | 4 | 9 | 25 | 30 | 21 | 40 | 17 | 11 | 12 | 76 | 48 | 50 |
| Crystal Palace | 10 | 6 | 2 | 2 | 16 | 12 | 16 | 10 | 4 | 2 | 4 | 12 | 13 | 10 | 20 | 10 | 4 | 6 | 28 | 25 | 26 |
| Darlington | 1 | 1 | 0 | 0 | 3 | 1 | 3 | 1 | 1 | 0 | 0 | 1 | 0 | 3 | 2 | 2 | 0 | 0 | 4 | 1 | 6 |
| Darwen | 2 | 1 | 1 | 0 | 14 | 2 | 3 | 2 | 0 | 1 | 1 | 2 | 3 | 1 | 4 | 1 | 2 | 1 | 16 | 5 | 4 |
| Derby County | 44 | 24 | 12 | 8 | 78 | 44 | 61 | 44 | 6 | 12 | 26 | 54 | 101 | 24 | 88 | 30 | 24 | 34 | 132 | 145 | 85 |
| Doncaster Rovers | 3 | 1 | 1 | 1 | 9 | 6 | 3 | 3 | 1 | 0 | 2 | 2 | 4 | 2 | 6 | 2 | 1 | 3 | 11 | 10 | 5 |
| Everton | 66 | 35 | 17 | 14 | 135 | 79 | 88 | 66 | 14 | 14 | 38 | 84 | 147 | 42 | 132 | 49 | 31 | 52 | 219 | 226 | 130 |
| Exeter City | 2 | 2 | 0 | 0 | 8 | 3 | 6 | 2 | 1 | 1 | 0 | 4 | 3 | 4 | 4 | 3 | 1 | 0 | 12 | 6 | 10 |
| Fulham | 26 | 17 | 3 | 6 | 70 | 32 | 38 | 26 | 11 | 6 | 9 | 26 | 37 | 28 | 52 | 28 | 9 | 15 | 96 | 69 | 66 |
| Gainsborough Trinity | 8 | 7 | 0 | 1 | 29 | 5 | 14 | 8 | 2 | 2 | 4 | 12 | 16 | 6 | 16 | 9 | 2 | 5 | 41 | 21 | 20 |
| Glossop | 9 | 5 | 3 | 1 | 20 | 7 | 13 | 9 | 4 | 2 | 3 | 15 | 11 | 10 | 18 | 9 | 5 | 4 | 35 | 18 | 23 |
| Grimsby Town | 16 | 12 | 1 | 3 | 50 | 24 | 25 | 16 | 4 | 3 | 9 | 26 | 33 | 11 | 32 | 16 | 4 | 12 | 76 | 57 | 36 |
| Hartlepool United | 2 | 1 | 0 | 1 | 4 | 3 | 3 | 2 | 0 | 2 | 0 | 2 | 2 | 2 | 4 | 1 | 2 | 1 | 6 | 5 | 5 |
| Huddersfield Town | 27 | 15 | 6 | 6 | 52 | 34 | 39 | 26 | 6 | 7 | 14 | 31 | 51 | 21 | 54 | 21 | 13 | 20 | 83 | 85 | 60 |
| Hull City | 19 | 9 | 7 | 3 | 32 | 17 | 28 | 19 | 4 | 4 | 11 | 17 | 33 | 15 | 38 | 13 | 11 | 14 | 49 | 50 | 43 |
| Ipswich Town | 23 | 9 | 4 | 10 | 43 | 35 | 23 | 23 | 5 | 5 | 13 | 21 | 49 | 16 | 46 | 14 | 9 | 23 | 64 | 84 | 39 |
| Leeds City | 6 | 6 | 0 | 0 | 15 | 3 | 12 | 6 | 2 | 1 | 3 | 7 | 8 | 5 | 12 | 8 | 1 | 3 | 22 | 11 | 17 |
| Leeds United | 35 | 18 | 5 | 12 | 58 | 43 | 45 | 35 | 8 | 9 | 18 | 37 | 61 | 25 | 70 | 26 | 14 | 30 | 95 | 104 | 70 |
| Leicester City | 42 | 25 | 9 | 8 | 90 | 44 | 62 | 42 | 14 | 10 | 18 | 60 | 75 | 39 | 84 | 39 | 19 | 26 | 150 | 119 | 101 |
| Leyton Orient | 14 | 11 | 2 | 1 | 31 | 8 | 25 | 14 | 5 | 6 | 3 | 16 | 12 | 16 | 28 | 16 | 8 | 4 | 47 | 20 | 41 |

| | HOME | | | | | | | AWAY | | | | | | | TOTAL | | | | | | |
|---|---|---|---|---|---|---|---|---|---|---|---|---|---|---|---|---|---|---|---|---|---|
| | P | W | D | L | F | A | Pts | P | W | D | L | F | A | Pts | P | W | D | L | F | A | Pts |
| Lincoln City | 8 | 6 | 2 | 0 | 23 | 6 | 14 | 8 | 6 | 0 | 2 | 15 | 5 | 12 | 16 | 12 | 2 | 2 | 38 | 11 | 26 |
| Liverpool | 54 | 19 | 16 | 19 | 79 | 63 | 54 | 54 | 9 | 17 | 28 | 48 | 94 | 35 | 108 | 28 | 33 | 47 | 127 | 157 | 89 |
| Luton Town | 15 | 12 | 1 | 2 | 35 | 9 | 28 | 15 | 5 | 4 | 6 | 13 | 20 | 15 | 30 | 17 | 5 | 8 | 48 | 29 | 43 |
| Manchester City | 55 | 29 | 16 | 10 | 105 | 57 | 75 | 55 | 15 | 7 | 33 | 85 | 133 | 37 | 110 | 44 | 23 | 43 | 190 | 190 | 112 |
| Manchester United | 50 | 26 | 11 | 13 | 98 | 72 | 65 | 50 | 11 | 13 | 26 | 65 | 102 | 35 | 100 | 37 | 24 | 39 | 163 | 174 | 100 |
| Mansfield Town | 1 | 1 | 0 | 0 | 2 | 0 | 3 | 1 | 1 | 0 | 0 | 3 | 0 | 3 | 2 | 2 | 0 | 0 | 5 | 0 | 6 |
| Middlesbrough | 35 | 20 | 8 | 7 | 59 | 32 | 49 | 35 | 5 | 9 | 21 | 27 | 58 | 19 | 70 | 25 | 17 | 28 | 86 | 90 | 68 |
| Millwall | 11 | 4 | 3 | 4 | 17 | 16 | 11 | 11 | 3 | 3 | 5 | 15 | 18 | 10 | 22 | 7 | 6 | 9 | 32 | 34 | 21 |
| Newcastle United | 49 | 24 | 15 | 10 | 100 | 60 | 64 | 49 | 14 | 11 | 24 | 70 | 101 | 39 | 98 | 38 | 26 | 34 | 170 | 161 | 103 |
| Newport County | 1 | 0 | 1 | 0 | 2 | 2 | 1 | 1 | 1 | 0 | 0 | 7 | 2 | 2 | 2 | 1 | 1 | 0 | 9 | 4 | 3 |
| Northampton Town | 1 | 0 | 1 | 0 | 1 | 1 | 1 | 1 | 1 | 0 | 0 | 4 | 3 | 2 | 2 | 1 | 1 | 0 | 5 | 4 | 3 |
| Norwich City | 11 | 5 | 4 | 2 | 15 | 8 | 15 | 11 | 3 | 3 | 5 | 14 | 16 | 10 | 22 | 8 | 7 | 7 | 29 | 24 | 25 |
| Nottingham Forest | 50 | 27 | 9 | 14 | 107 | 77 | 66 | 50 | 19 | 11 | 20 | 77 | 82 | 50 | 100 | 46 | 20 | 34 | 184 | 159 | 116 |
| Notts County | 28 | 15 | 9 | 4 | 68 | 39 | 40 | 28 | 6 | 7 | 15 | 29 | 51 | 20 | 56 | 21 | 16 | 19 | 97 | 90 | 60 |
| Oldham Athletic | 22 | 8 | 10 | 4 | 23 | 17 | 28 | 22 | 4 | 5 | 13 | 20 | 36 | 14 | 44 | 12 | 15 | 17 | 43 | 53 | 42 |
| Oxford United | 7 | 6 | 1 | 0 | 15 | 5 | 17 | 7 | 3 | 3 | 1 | 9 | 6 | 11 | 14 | 9 | 4 | 1 | 24 | 11 | 28 |
| Peterborough United | 1 | 1 | 0 | 0 | 4 | 0 | 3 | 1 | 0 | 1 | 0 | 0 | 0 | 1 | 2 | 1 | 1 | 0 | 4 | 0 | 4 |
| Plymouth Argyle | 2 | 4 | 3 | 5 | 18 | 22 | 12 | 12 | 1 | 4 | 7 | 13 | 23 | 6 | 24 | 5 | 7 | 12 | 31 | 45 | 18 |
| Portsmouth | 24 | 18 | 2 | 4 | 58 | 20 | 40 | 24 | 9 | 9 | 6 | 37 | 39 | 27 | 48 | 27 | 11 | 10 | 95 | 59 | 67 |
| Port Vale | 10 | 5 | 2 | 3 | 20 | 10 | 12 | 10 | 3 | 0 | 7 | 13 | 25 | 7 | 20 | 8 | 2 | 10 | 33 | 35 | 19 |
| Preston North End | 43 | 19 | 11 | 13 | 71 | 57 | 51 | 43 | 12 | 12 | 19 | 51 | 77 | 36 | 86 | 31 | 23 | 32 | 126 | 134 | 87 |
| Queen's Park Rangers | 8 | 3 | 3 | 2 | 10 | 7 | 9 | 8 | 3 | 1 | 4 | 10 | 8 | 7 | 16 | 6 | 4 | 6 | 20 | 15 | 16 |
| Reading | 7 | 6 | 0 | 1 | 18 | 5 | 14 | 7 | 3 | 3 | 1 | 16 | 11 | 10 | 14 | 9 | 3 | 2 | 34 | 16 | 24 |
| Rotherham United | 1 | 0 | 1 | 0 | 2 | 2 | 1 | 1 | 1 | 0 | 0 | 2 | 0 | 3 | 2 | 1 | 1 | 0 | 4 | 2 | 4 |
| Sheffield United | 41 | 20 | 8 | 13 | 70 | 47 | 50 | 41 | 8 | 14 | 19 | 36 | 60 | 30 | 82 | 28 | 22 | 32 | 106 | 107 | 80 |
| Sheffield Wednesday | 48 | 15 | 16 | 17 | 78 | 71 | 46 | 48 | 12 | 6 | 30 | 69 | 104 | 30 | 96 | 27 | 22 | 47 | 147 | 175 | 76 |
| Shrewsbury Town | 4 | 3 | 0 | 1 | 9 | 3 | 9 | 4 | 2 | 1 | 1 | 6 | 4 | 7 | 8 | 5 | 1 | 2 | 15 | 7 | 16 |
| Southampton | 25 | 16 | 4 | 5 | 38 | 21 | 38 | 25 | 2 | 10 | 13 | 25 | 44 | 14 | 50 | 18 | 14 | 18 | 63 | 65 | 52 |
| South Shields | 1 | 1 | 0 | 0 | 3 | 0 | 2 | 1 | 1 | 0 | 0 | 3 | 2 | 2 | 2 | 2 | 0 | 0 | 6 | 2 | 4 |
| Stockport County | 9 | 7 | 1 | 1 | 19 | 5 | 17 | 9 | 5 | 2 | 2 | 11 | 11 | 12 | 18 | 12 | 3 | 3 | 30 | 16 | 29 |
| Stoke City | 52 | 28 | 9 | 15 | 109 | 61 | 70 | 52 | 9 | 17 | 26 | 54 | 97 | 36 | 104 | 37 | 26 | 41 | 163 | 158 | 106 |
| Sunderland | 59 | 31 | 15 | 13 | 113 | 82 | 80 | 59 | 8 | 18 | 33 | 61 | 132 | 36 | 118 | 39 | 33 | 46 | 174 | 214 | 116 |
| Swansea City | 10 | 6 | 3 | 1 | 30 | 13 | 17 | 10 | 1 | 3 | 6 | 11 | 21 | 5 | 20 | 7 | 6 | 7 | 41 | 34 | 22 |
| Swindon Town | 5 | 3 | 0 | 2 | 9 | 6 | 8 | 5 | 0 | 1 | 4 | 2 | 7 | 1 | 10 | 3 | 1 | 6 | 11 | 13 | 9 |
| Torquay United | 1 | 1 | 0 | 0 | 1 | 0 | 3 | 1 | 0 | 0 | 1 | 0 | 1 | 0 | 2 | 1 | 0 | 1 | 1 | 1 | 3 |
| Tottenham Hotspur | 53 | 32 | 8 | 13 | 114 | 68 | 73 | 53 | 14 | 14 | 25 | 56 | 91 | 45 | 106 | 46 | 22 | 38 | 170 | 159 | 118 |
| Tranmere Rovers | 1 | 1 | 0 | 0 | 2 | 0 | 2 | 1 | 0 | 0 | 1 | 1 | 3 | 0 | 2 | 1 | 0 | 1 | 3 | 3 | 2 |
| Walsall | 1 | 0 | 1 | 0 | 0 | 0 | 1 | 1 | 0 | 1 | 0 | 0 | 0 | 1 | 2 | 0 | 2 | 0 | 0 | 0 | 2 |
| Watford | 7 | 4 | 1 | 2 | 11 | 7 | 13 | 7 | 2 | 1 | 4 | 7 | 14 | 7 | 14 | 6 | 2 | 6 | 18 | 21 | 20 |
| West Ham United | 33 | 20 | 5 | 8 | 65 | 35 | 47 | 33 | 10 | 4 | 19 | 45 | 71 | 27 | 66 | 30 | 9 | 27 | 110 | 106 | 74 |
| Wigan Athletic | 2 | 1 | 1 | 0 | 6 | 2 | 4 | 2 | 1 | 0 | 1 | 1 | 1 | 3 | 4 | 2 | 1 | 1 | 7 | 3 | 7 |
| Wolverhampton W | 60 | 26 | 18 | 16 | 107 | 84 | 71 | 60 | 16 | 14 | 30 | 86 | 118 | 47 | 120 | 42 | 32 | 46 | 193 | 202 | 118 |
| York City | 2 | 1 | 1 | 0 | 4 | 2 | 3 | 2 | 2 | 0 | 0 | 4 | 1 | 4 | 4 | 3 | 1 | 0 | 8 | 3 | 7 |

# Albion's Football League Record 1888-89 to 1992-93

| | P | W | D | L | F | A | Pts | Pos |
|---|---|---|---|---|---|---|---|---|
| | DIVISION ONE | | | | | | | |
| 1888-89 | 22 | 19 | 2 | 19 | 49 | 46 | 22 | 6th |
| 1889-90 | 22 | 11 | 3 | 8 | 47 | 50 | 25 | 5th |
| 1890-91 | 22 | 5 | 2 | 15 | 34 | 57 | 12 | 12th |
| 1891-92 | 26 | 6 | 6 | 14 | 51 | 58 | 18 | 12th |
| 1892-93 | 30 | 12 | 5 | 13 | 58 | 69 | 29 | 8th |
| 1893-94 | 30 | 14 | 4 | 12 | 66 | 59 | 32 | 8th |
| 1894-95 | 30 | 10 | 4 | 16 | 51 | 66 | 24 | 13th |
| 1895-96 | 30 | 6 | 7 | 17 | 30 | 59 | 19 | 16th |
| 1896-97 | 30 | 10 | 6 | 14 | 33 | 56 | 26 | 12th |
| 1897-98 | 30 | 11 | 10 | 9 | 44 | 45 | 32 | 7th |
| 1898-99 | 34 | 12 | 6 | 16 | 42 | 57 | 30 | 14th |
| 1899-1900 | 34 | 11 | 8 | 15 | 43 | 51 | 30 | 13th |
| 1900-01 | 34 | 7 | 8 | 19 | 35 | 62 | 22 | 18th |
| | DIVISION TWO | | | | | | | |
| 1901-02 | 34 | 25 | 5 | 4 | 82 | 29 | 55 | 1st |
| | DIVISION ONE | | | | | | | |
| 1902-03 | 34 | 16 | 4 | 14 | 54 | 53 | 36 | 7th |
| 1903-04 | 34 | 7 | 10 | 17 | 36 | 60 | 24 | 18th |
| | DIVISION TWO | | | | | | | |
| 1904-05 | 34 | 13 | 4 | 17 | 56 | 48 | 30 | 10th |
| 1905-06 | 38 | 22 | 8 | 8 | 79 | 36 | 52 | 4th |
| 1906-07 | 38 | 21 | 5 | 12 | 83 | 45 | 47 | 4th |
| 1907-08 | 38 | 198 | 9 | 10 | 61 | 39 | 47 | 5th |
| 1908-09 | 38 | 19 | 13 | 6 | 56 | 27 | 51 | 3rd |
| 1909-10 | 38 | 16 | 5 | 17 | 58 | 56 | 37 | 11th |
| 1910-11 | 38 | 22 | 9 | 7 | 67 | 41 | 53 | 1st |
| | DIVISION ONE | | | | | | | |
| 1911-12 | 38 | 15 | 9 | 14 | 43 | 47 | 39 | 9th |
| 1912-13 | 38 | 13 | 12 | 13 | 57 | 50 | 38 | 10th |
| 1913-14 | 38 | 15 | 13 | 19 | 46 | 42 | 43 | 5th |
| 1914-15 | 38 | 15 | 10 | 13 | 49 | 43 | 40 | 11th |
| Competition abandoned (1915-19) during World War One | | | | | | | | |
| 1919-20 | 42 | 28 | 4 | 10 | 104 | 47 | 60 | 1st |
| 1920-21 | 42 | 13 | 14 | 15 | 54 | 58 | 40 | 14th |
| 1921-22 | 42 | 15 | 10 | 17 | 51 | 63 | 40 | 13th |
| 1922-23 | 42 | 17 | 11 | 14 | 58 | 49 | 45 | 7th |
| 1923-24 | 42 | 12 | 14 | 16 | 51 | 62 | 38 | 16th |
| 1924-25 | 42 | 23 | 10 | 9 | 58 | 34 | 56 | 2nd |
| 1925-26 | 42 | 16 | 8 | 18 | 79 | 78 | 40 | 13th |
| 1926-27 | 42 | 11 | 8 | 23 | 65 | 86 | 30 | 22nd |
| | DIVISION TWO | | | | | | | |
| 1927-28 | 42 | 17 | 12 | 13 | 90 | 70 | 46 | 8th |
| 1928-29 | 42 | 19 | 8 | 15 | 80 | 79 | 46 | 7th |
| 1929-30 | 42 | 21 | 5 | 16 | 105 | 73 | 47 | 6th |
| 1930-31 | 42 | 22 | 10 | 10 | 83 | 49 | 54 | 2nd |
| | DIVISION ONE | | | | | | | |
| 1931-32 | 42 | 20 | 6 | 16 | 77 | 55 | 46 | 6th |
| 1932-33 | 42 | 20 | 9 | 13 | 83 | 70 | 49 | 4th |
| 1933-34 | 42 | 17 | 10 | 15 | 78 | 70 | 44 | 7th |
| 1934-35 | 42 | 17 | 10 | 15 | 83 | 83 | 44 | 9th |
| 1935-36 | 42 | 16 | 6 | 20 | 89 | 88 | 38 | 18th |
| 1936-37 | 42 | 16 | 6 | 20 | 77 | 98 | 38 | 16th |
| 1937-38 | 42 | 14 | 8 | 20 | 74 | 91 | 36 | 22nd |
| | DIVISION TWO | | | | | | | |
| 1938-39 | 42 | 18 | 9 | 15 | 89 | 72 | 45 | 10th |
| Competition abandoned (1939-46) during World War Two | | | | | | | | |
| 1946-47 | 42 | 20 | 8 | 14 | 88 | 75 | 48 | 7th |
| 1947-48 | 42 | 18 | 9 | 15 | 63 | 58 | 45 | 7th |
| 1948-49 | 42 | 24 | 8 | 10 | 69 | 39 | 56 | 2nd |
| | DIVISION ONE | | | | | | | |
| 1949-50 | 42 | 14 | 12 | 16 | 47 | 53 | 40 | 14th |
| 1950-51 | 42 | 13 | 11 | 18 | 53 | 61 | 37 | 16th |
| 1951-52 | 42 | 14 | 13 | 15 | 74 | 77 | 41 | 13th |
| 1952-53 | 42 | 21 | 8 | 13 | 66 | 60 | 50 | 4th |
| 1953-54 | 42 | 22 | 9 | 11 | 86 | 63 | 53 | 2nd |
| 1954-55 | 42 | 16 | 8 | 18 | 76 | 96 | 40 | 17th |
| 1955-56 | 42 | 18 | 5 | 19 | 58 | 70 | 41 | 13th |
| 1956-57 | 42 | 14 | 14 | 14 | 59 | 61 | 42 | 11th |
| 1957-58 | 42 | 18 | 14 | 10 | 92 | 70 | 50 | 4th |
| 1958-59 | 42 | 18 | 13 | 11 | 88 | 68 | 49 | 5th |
| 1959-60 | 42 | 19 | 11 | 12 | 83 | 57 | 49 | 4th |
| 1960-61 | 42 | 18 | 5 | 19 | 67 | 71 | 41 | 10th |
| 1961-62 | 42 | 15 | 13 | 14 | 83 | 67 | 43 | 9th |
| 1962-63 | 42 | 16 | 7 | 19 | 71 | 79 | 39 | 14th |
| 1963-64 | 42 | 16 | 11 | 15 | 70 | 61 | 43 | 10th |
| 1964-65 | 42 | 13 | 13 | 16 | 70 | 65 | 39 | 14th |
| 1965-66 | 42 | 19 | 12 | 11 | 91 | 69 | 50 | 6th |
| 1966-67 | 42 | 16 | 7 | 19 | 77 | 73 | 39 | 13th |
| 1967-68 | 42 | 17 | 12 | 13 | 75 | 62 | 46 | 8th |
| 1968-69 | 42 | 16 | 11 | 15 | 64 | 67 | 43 | 10th |
| 1969-70 | 42 | 14 | 9 | 19 | 58 | 66 | 37 | 16th |
| 1970-71 | 42 | 10 | 15 | 17 | 58 | 75 | 35 | 17th |
| 1971-72 | 42 | 12 | 11 | 19 | 42 | 54 | 35 | 16th |
| 1972-73 | 42 | 9 | 10 | 23 | 38 | 62 | 28 | 22nd |
| | DIVISION TWO | | | | | | | |
| 1973-74 | 42 | 14 | 16 | 12 | 48 | 45 | 44 | 8th |
| 1974-75 | 42 | 18 | 9 | 15 | 54 | 42 | 45 | 6th |
| 1975-76 | 42 | 20 | 13 | 9 | 50 | 33 | 53 | 3rd |
| | DIVISION ONE | | | | | | | |
| 1976-77 | 42 | 16 | 13 | 13 | 62 | 56 | 45 | 7th |
| 1977-78 | 42 | 18 | 14 | 10 | 62 | 53 | 50 | 6th |
| 1978-79 | 42 | 24 | 11 | 7 | 72 | 35 | 59 | 3rd |
| 1979-80 | 42 | 11 | 19 | 12 | 54 | 50 | 41 | 10th |
| 1980-81 | 42 | 20 | 12 | 10 | 60 | 42 | 52 | 4th |
| 1981-82 | 42 | 11 | 11 | 20 | 46 | 57 | 44 | 17th |
| 1982-83 | 42 | 15 | 12 | 15 | 51 | 49 | 57 | 11th |
| 1983-84 | 42 | 14 | 9 | 19 | 48 | 62 | 51 | 17th |
| 1984-85 | 42 | 16 | 7 | 19 | 58 | 62 | 55 | 12th |
| 1985-86 | 42 | 4 | 12 | 26 | 35 | 89 | 24 | 22nd |
| | DIVISION TWO | | | | | | | |
| 1986-87 | 42 | 13 | 12 | 17 | 51 | 49 | 51 | 15th |
| 1987-88 | 44 | 12 | 11 | 21 | 50 | 69 | 47 | 20th |
| 1988-89 | 46 | 18 | 18 | 10 | 65 | 41 | 72 | 9th |
| 1989-90 | 46 | 12 | 15 | 19 | 67 | 71 | 51 | 20th |
| 1990-91 | 46 | 10 | 18 | 18 | 47 | 61 | 48 | 23rd |
| | DIVISION THREE | | | | | | | |
| 1991-92 | 46 | 19 | 14 | 13 | 64 | 49 | 71 | 7th |
| | DIVISION TWO (New Structure) | | | | | | | |
| 1992-93 | 46 | 25 | 10 | 11 | 88 | 54 | 85 | 4th |

# *Albion in the*
# *Football League*

## 1888-89

### Football League

| Date | | Opponent | Result | Scorers | Att | Roberts R | Horton J | Green H | Horton E | Perry C | Bayliss J | Bassett W | Woodhall G | Hendry W | Pearson T | Wilson J | Timmins G | Walker L | Perry W | Shaw C | Millard A | Oliver H | Haynes G | Ramsay A | Crabtree F |
|---|---|---|---|---|---|---|---|---|---|---|---|---|---|---|---|---|---|---|---|---|---|---|---|---|---|
| Sep 8 | (a) | Stoke C | W 2-0 | Wilson, Woodhall | 4,524 | 1 | 2 | 3 | 4 | 5 | 6 | 7 | 8 | 9 | 10 | 11 | | | | | | | | | |
| 15 | (a) | Derby C | W 2-1 | Bassett, Pearson | 3,700 | 1 | 2 | 3 | | 5 | 4 | 8 | 7 | 9 | 10 | 11 | 6 | | | | | | | | |
| 22 | (a) | Blackburn R | L 2-6 | Pearson, Bayliss | 3,700 | 1 | 3 | 2 | 4 | 5 | 8 | 7 | | 9 | 10 | 11 | 6 | | | | | | | | |
| 29 | (h) | Burnley | W 4-3 | W.Perry, Bassett, Hendry, Shaw | 2,100 | 1 | 2 | | | 5 | 4 | 7 | | 9 | 10 | | 6 | 3 | 8 | 11 | | | | | |
| Oct 6 | (h) | Derby C | W 5-0 | W.Perry, Pearson 2, Bassett, Hendry | 5,500 | 1 | 2 | 3 | | 5 | 4 | 7 | | 9 | 10 | 11 | 6 | | 8 | | | | | | |
| 13 | (a) | Preston NE | L 0-3 | | 10,200 | 1 | 2 | 3 | | 5 | 4 | 8 | 7 | 9 | 10 | 11 | 6 | | | | | | | | |
| 20 | (h) | Notts C | W 4-2 | Pearson 2, Wilson, Woodhall | 3,448 | 1 | 3 | 2 | | | 4 | 7 | 8 | 9 | 10 | 11 | 6 | | | 5 | | | | | |
| Nov 11 | (h) | Accrington | D 2-2 | Wilson, Bassett | 3,000 | 1 | 3 | | 4 | 5 | 8 | 7 | | 9 | 10 | 11 | 6 | 2 | | | | | | | |
| 5 | (h) | Bolton W | L 1-5 | Bassett | 4,000 | 1 | 3 | | 4 | 5 | 8 | 7 | | 9 | 10 | 11 | 6 | 2 | | | | | | | |
| 10 | (a) | Burnley | L 0-2 | | 5,000 | 1 | | | 4 | 5 | 2 | 7 | | 9 | 10 | 11 | 6 | | | 3 | | | | | |
| 17 | (a) | Bolton W | W 2-1 | Hendry, Pearson | 4,230 | 1 | 2 | | | 5 | 4 | 7 | | 9 | 10 | 11 | 6 | 3 | 8 | | | | | | |
| 24 | (a) | Accrington | L 1-2 | W.Perry | 3,000 | 1 | 3 | | | 5 | 4 | 7 | | 9 | 10 | | 6 | 2 | 8 | | | | 11 | | |
| Dec 1 | (h) | Everton | W 4-1 | W.Perry, Bassett 2, Hendry | 5,700 | 1 | 3 | | | 5 | 4 | 7 | | 9 | 10 | 11 | 6 | 2 | 8 | | | | | | |
| 15 | (a) | Wolves | L 1-2 | Pearson | 8,600 | 1 | 2 | | | 5 | 4 | 7 | 8 | | 10 | 11 | 6 | 3 | 9 | | | | | | |
| 22 | (h) | Blackburn R | W 2-1 | Bassett, Pearson | 4,100 | 1 | 3 | | | 5 | 4 | 8 | 7 | 9 | | 11 | 6 | | | | | | 10 | | |
| 26 | (h) | Preston NE | L 0-5 | | 5,150 | 1 | 2 | | | 5 | 4 | 8 | 7 | 9 | | 11 | 6 | 3 | | | | | 10 | | |
| 29 | (h) | Stoke C | W 2-0 | Bassett, Wilson | 4,896 | 1 | | | | 5 | 4 | 8 | 7 | 9 | | 11 | 6 | 3 | | | | | 10 | 2 | |
| Jan 5 | (h) | Wolves | L 1-3 | Woodhall | 4,000 | 1 | 2 | | | 5 | 4 | 8 | 7 | 9 | 10 | 11 | 6 | 3 | | | | | | | |
| 12 | (a) | Notts C | L 1-2 | Bassett | 1,500 | 1 | 2 | | 4 | 5 | 9 | 7 | 8 | | 10 | 11 | 6 | 3 | | | | | | | |
| 19 | (a) | Aston Villa | L 0-2 | | 10,000 | 1 | 2 | 3 | 4 | | 9 | 7 | 8 | 5 | 10 | 11 | 6 | | | | | | | | |
| 26 | (h) | Aston Villa | D 3-3 | Bassett, Pearson 2 | 8,515 | 1 | | 3 | 4 | 5 | 9 | 7 | | 2 | 10 | 11 | 6 | | 8 | | | | | | |
| Feb 23 | (a) | Everton | W 1-0 | Crabtree | 2,100 | 1 | | 3 | 4 | 5 | 9 | | | 2 | 10 | 11 | 6 | | 8 | | | | | | 7 |
| | | | | | App | 22 | 18 | 9 | 9 | 20 | 22 | 21 | 10 | 18 | 22 | 20 | 21 | 12 | 9 | 1 | 1 | 1 | 4 | 1 | 1 |
| | | | | | Goals | | | | | | 1 | 11 | 3 | 4 | 11 | 4 | | | 4 | 1 | | | | | 1 |

## 1889-90

### Football League

| Date | | Opponent | Result | Scorers | Att | Roberts R | Horton J | Green H | Horton E | Perry C | Timmins G | Bassett W | Evans G | Bayliss J | Pearson T | Wilson J | Woodhall G | Millard A | Pittaway J | Walker L | Nicholls J | Reader J | Haynes G | Johnstone W | Donnachie C | Powell S | Nicholls S |
|---|---|---|---|---|---|---|---|---|---|---|---|---|---|---|---|---|---|---|---|---|---|---|---|---|---|---|---|
| Sep 14 | (a) | Derby C | L 1-3 | Bayliss | 6,000 | 1 | 2 | 3 | 4 | 5 | 6 | 7 | 8 | 9 | 10 | 11 | | | | | | | | | | | |
| 21 | (a) | Notts C | W 2-1 | Pearson, Bayliss | 6,200 | 1 | 2 | 3 | 4 | 5 | 6 | 8 | | 9 | 10 | 11 | 7 | | | | | | | | | | |
| 28 | (h) | Aston Villa | W 3-0 | Woodhall, Wilson, Bayliss | 10,122 | 1 | 2 | 3 | 4 | 5 | 6 | 8 | | 9 | 10 | 11 | 7 | | | | | | | | | | |
| Oct 5 | (a) | Preston NE | L 0-5 | | 10,000 | 1 | 2 | 3 | 4 | 5 | 6 | 8 | | 9 | 10 | 11 | 7 | | | | | | | | | | |
| 12 | (a) | Burnley | W 2-1 | Wilson, Pittaway | 6,000 | 1 | 2 | 3 | 4 | 5 | | 8 | | | 10 | 11 | 7 | 6 | 9 | | | | | | | | |
| 19 | (h) | Wolves | L 1-4 | Evans | 1,550 | 1 | | 3 | 4 | 5 | | | 8 | 9 | 10 | 11 | 7 | | | 2 | 6 | | | | | | |
| 26 | (a) | Aston Villa | L 0-1 | | 8,000 | | | 3 | 4 | 5 | | | 8 | 9 | 10 | 11 | 7 | 6 | | 2 | | 1 | | | | | |
| Nov 4 | (h) | Bolton W | W 6-3 | Pearson 4, Bassett, Woodhall | 4,813 | | | 3 | 4 | 5 | 6 | 8 | 9 | | 10 | | 7 | | | 2 | | 1 | | | | | |
| 9 | (h) | Derby C | L 2-3 | Wilson, Bassett | 5,100 | | 2 | 3 | 4 | 5 | 6 | 8 | | 9 | 10 | 11 | 7 | | | | | 1 | | | | | |
| 16 | (a) | Stoke C | W 3-1 | Pearson, Perry, Evans | 3,900 | 1 | 2 | | 4 | 5 | 6 | 7 | 9 | 8 | 10 | 11 | | | | 3 | | | | | | | |
| 23 | (h) | Burnley | W 6-1 | Bayliss 2, Haynes, Bassett, Evans, Pearson | 7,100 | 1 | 2 | 3 | 4 | 5 | 6 | 7 | 9 | 8 | 10 | | | | | | | | 11 | | | | |
| 30 | (a) | Blackburn R | L 0-5 | | 6,600 | 1 | 2 | 3 | 4 | 5 | 6 | 7 | 9 | 8 | 10 | | | | | | | | | | | | |
| Dec 7 | (a) | Bolton W | L 0-7 | | 3,500 | 1 | | 3 | 4 | 5 | 6 | | 8 | | 10 | | 7 | | | 2 | | | | 11 | 9 | | |
| 21 | (h) | Accrington | W 4-1 | Pearson 3, Bayliss | 3,500 | 1 | 2 | 3 | 4 | 5 | | 7 | | 8 | 10 | 11 | | | | | | | | 9 | 6 | | |
| 26 | (h) | Preston NE | D 2-2 | Evans, Pearson | 10,065 | 1 | 2 | 3 | 4 | 5 | 6 | 7 | 9 | 8 | 10 | 11 | | | | | | | | | | | |
| 2⁰ | (a) | Wolves | D 1-1 | Pearson | 8,500 | 1 | 2 | | 4 | 5 | 6 | 7 | 9 | 8 | 10 | 11 | | | | | | | | | 3 | | |
| Jan 4 | (h) | Notts C | W 4-2 | Bayliss, Pearson 3 | 4,700 | 1 | 2 | 3 | 4 | 5 | 6 | 7 | 9 | 8 | 10 | 11 | | | | | | | | | 3 | | |
| 11 | (h) | Blackburn R | W 3-2 | Evans 2, Bayliss | 5,100 | 1 | 2 | 3 | 4 | 5 | | 7 | 9 | 8 | 10 | 11 | | | | | 6 | | | | | | |
| Feb 8 | (a) | Accrington | D 0-0 | | 2,100 | 1 | 2 | | 4 | 5 | | 7 | | | 10 | 11 | 8 | | | | 6 | | | 9 | 3 | | |
| Mar 8 | (a) | Everton | L 1-5 | Pearson | 8,400 | 1 | | 3 | 4 | 5 | | 7 | 9 | 6 | 10 | 11 | | | | 2 | | | | | | | 8 |
| 15 | (n) | Stoke C | W 2-1 | Woodhall, Bayliss | 1,600 | | 2 | 3 | 4 | | | 9 | 8 | | 10 | 11 | 7 | | | 5 | 1 | | | | 6 | | |
| 22 | (h) | Everton | W 4-1 | Evans 2, Pearson, Wilson | 4,000 | 1 | | 3 | 4 | 5 | | 7 | 9 | 6 | 10 | 11 | | | | | | | | | | 2 | 8 |
| | | | | | App | 18 | 17 | 18 | 22 | 21 | 12 | 19 | 13 | 19 | 22 | 20 | 11 | 2 | 1 | 6 | 4 | 4 | 2 | 3 | 2 | 4 | 2 |
| | | | | | Goals | | | | | 1 | | 3 | 8 | 9 | 17 | 4 | 3 | | 1 | | | | | 1 | | | |

# 1890-91

## Football League

| Date | | Venue | Opponent | Result | Scorers | Att. | Reader J | Green H | Powell S | Horton E | Perry C | Bayliss J | Bassett W | Nicholls S | Dyer F | Pearson T | Roberts H | Woodhall G | Perry T | Burns J | Horton J | Roberts T | Haynes E | Riley J | Groves W | Timmins G | McCulloch T | McCullum W | McLeod R |
|---|---|---|---|---|---|---|---|---|---|---|---|---|---|---|---|---|---|---|---|---|---|---|---|---|---|---|---|---|---|
| Sep | 6 | (h) | Everton | L 1-4 | Pearson | 5,600 | 1 | 2 | 3 | 4 | 5 | 6 | 7 | 8 | 9 | 10 | 11 | | | | | | | | | | | | |
| | 13 | (a) | Preston NE | L 0-3 | | 8,500 | 1 | 2 | 3 | 4 | 5 | | | 8 | 9 | 6 | | 10 | 7 | 11 | | | | | | | | | |
| | 20 | (h) | Sunderland | L 0-4 | | 8,537 | 1 | | 3 | 2 | | 5 | 4 | | | 9 | | 6 | 10 | 7 | 8 | 11 | | | | | | | |
| | 27 | (a) | Aston Villa | W 4-0 | Dyer, Bayliss, Pearson, Burns | 12,000 | 1 | | | 3 | 4 | 5 | 9 | 7 | | 6 | | 10 | | 8 | 11 | 2 | | | | | | | |
| Oct | 4 | (h) | Burnley | W 3-1 | Pearson, Burns 2 | 6,000 | 1 | | | 3 | 4 | 5 | 9 | 7 | | 6 | | 10 | | 8 | 11 | 2 | | | | | | | |
| | 11 | (a) | Notts C | L 2-3 | T.Perry, Woodhall | 4,900 | 1 | | | 3 | 4 | 5 | | 7 | | 6 | | 10 | 9 | 8 | 11 | 2 | | | | | | | |
| | 18 | (h) | Notts C | D 1-1 | Pearson | 7,367 | 1 | | | 3 | 4 | 5 | 9 | 7 | | 6 | | 10 | 8 | | 11 | 2 | | | | | | | |
| | 25 | (a) | Everton | W 3-2 | Dyer, Nicholls, Burns | 9,200 | 1 | | | 3 | 4 | 5 | | 7 | 8 | 6 | | 10 | 9 | | 11 | 2 | | | | | | | |
| Nov | 1 | (h) | Aston Villa | L 0-3 | | 8,000 | 1 | | | 3 | 4 | 5 | | 7 | 8 | 6 | | 10 | 9 | | 11 | 2 | | | | | | | |
| | 3 | (h) | Bolton W | L 2-4 | Pearson 2 | 1,506 | 1 | 3 | | 4 | | | | 7 | 8 | 6 | | 10 | 9 | | 11 | 2 | 5 | | | | | | |
| | 8 | (a) | Sunderland | D 1-1 | Woodhall | 3,400 | 1 | | 3 | 4 | 5 | | | 7 | 8 | 6 | | 10 | 9 | | 2 | | | 11 | | | | | |
| | 22 | (a) | Derby C | L 1-3 | Pearson | 4,000 | 1 | | 3 | 4 | 5 | | | 7 | | 6 | | 10 | 9 | 8 | 11 | 2 | | | | | | | |
| | 29 | (h) | Derby C | L 3-4 | Bayliss, Pearson, Nicholls | 405 | 1 | | 3 | 4 | 5 | 9 | | 8 | 6 | 10 | | | 7 | | 11 | 2 | | | | | | | |
| Dec | 6 | (h) | Burnley | L 4-5 | C.Perry, Riley, Pearson 2 | 5,500 | 1 | 2 | 3 | 4 | 9 | | 8 | 5 | 10 | | | 7 | | 11 | | | | 6 | | | | | |
| | 13 | (h) | Wolves | L 0-1 | | 3,400 | 1 | | 2 | | 5 | 8 | | 6 | 10 | | | 7 | | 11 | 3 | | | 4 | 9 | | | | |
| | 20 | (a) | Blackburn R | L 1-2 | Pearson | 5,500 | 1 | 3 | | 4 | 5 | 8 | | 2 | 10 | | | 7 | | 11 | | | | 9 | 6 | | | | |
| Jan | 3 | (a) | Wolves | L 0-4 | | 9,300 | 1 | | | 4 | 5 | 7 | | 3 | 10 | | | 8 | | 11 | 2 | | | 9 | 6 | | | | |
| Feb | 7 | (h) | Preston NE | L 1-3 | Burns | 4,300 | 1 | | | | 5 | 6 | 8 | 4 | 10 | | | 7 | | 11 | | | | 9 | | 2 | 3 | | |
| Mar | 7 | (h) | Accrington | W 5-1 | Nicholls 2, Pearson 2, Groves | 800 | 1 | | | | | 8 | 4 | 11 | 7 | | | 3 | | | | | | 6 | 9 | | 2 | 5 | 10 |
| | 9 | (h) | Blackburn R | W 1-0 | McLeod | 2,700 | 1 | | | | 5 | | 7 | 8 | 6 | 11 | | | 2 | | | | | | 9 | | 3 | 4 | 10 |
| | 14 | (a) | Bolton W | L 1-7 | Gardiner (og) | 5,200 | 1 | | 2 | 4 | 5 | | 7 | 8 | 6 | 10 | | | | | | | | | 9 | | 3 | | 11 |
| Apr | 18 | (a) | Accrington | L 0-1 | | 3,300 | 1 | | 3 | | 5 | 4 | 7 | 8 | 6 | 10 | | | | | 2 | | | 11 | 9 | | | | |
| | | | | | **App** | | 22 | 6 | 16 | 16 | 20 | 8 | 17 | 14 | 22 | 22 | 1 | 16 | 6 | 15 | 15 | 1 | 2 | 3 | 8 | 2 | 4 | 3 | 3 |
| | | | | | **Goals** | | | | | | 1 | 2 | | 4 | 2 | 13 | | 2 | 1 | 5 | | | | 1 | 1 | | | | 1 |

# 1891-92

## Football League

| Date | | Venue | Opponent | Result | Scorers | Att. | Roberts R | Nicholson M | Powell S | Bayliss J | Perry C | Dyer F | Bassett W | Nicholls S | Groves W | McLeod R | Pearson T | McCulloch T | Reynolds J | Woodhall G | Reader J | Haynes G | Geddes A | Charsley C | Castle C | Horton J | Wheldon S | Millard A | Perry T |
|---|---|---|---|---|---|---|---|---|---|---|---|---|---|---|---|---|---|---|---|---|---|---|---|---|---|---|---|---|---|
| Sep | 5 | (h) | Everton | W 4-0 | Nicholls, Groves, McLeod 2 | 6,000 | 1 | 2 | 3 | 4 | 5 | 6 | 7 | 8 | 9 | 10 | 11 | | | | | | | | | | | | |
| | 12 | (a) | Aston Villa | L 1-5 | Pearson | 12,100 | 1 | 2 | 3 | 4 | 5 | 6 | 7 | 8 | 9 | 10 | 11 | | | | | | | | | | | | |
| | 19 | (h) | Wolves | W 4-3 | Groves 2, Nicholls, C.Perry | 10,000 | 1 | 2 | 3 | | 5 | 6 | 7 | 8 | 9 | 10 | 11 | 4 | | | | | | | | | | | |
| Oct | 3 | (h) | Blackburn R | D 2-2 | Pearson, Nicholls | 4,700 | 1 | 2 | 3 | | 5 | 6 | | 8 | 9 | 10 | 11 | 4 | 7 | | | | | | | | | | |
| | 10 | (a) | Notts C | L 0-4 | | 4,000 | | 2 | 3 | 4 | | 6 | 7 | | 9 | 10 | 11 | 5 | 8 | | 1 | | | | | | | | |
| | 17 | (h) | Sunderland | L 2-5 | McLeod, Bassett | 5,500 | 1 | 2 | 3 | 4 | 5 | 6 | 7 | 8 | 9 | 10 | 11 | | | | | | | | | | | | |
| | 24 | (a) | Sunderland | L 0-4 | | 6,000 | 1 | 2 | 3 | | 5 | 6 | 7 | 8 | 9 | 10 | 11 | 4 | | | | | | | | | | | |
| | 31 | (h) | Notts C | D 2-2 | Pearson 2 | 5,200 | | 2 | | 4 | 5 | 6 | 7 | 8 | 9 | | 10 | 3 | | | 1 | | 11 | | | | | | |
| Nov | 2 | (h) | Bolton W | L 0-2 | | 6,700 | | 2 | | 9 | 5 | 6 | 7 | 8 | 4 | | 10 | 3 | | | 1 | | 11 | | | | | | |
| | 7 | (a) | Everton | L 3-4 | Bassett 2, Pearson | 8,100 | 1 | 2 | 3 | | 5 | 6 | 7 | 8 | 9 | | 10 | 4 | | | | | 11 | | | | | | |
| | 14 | (h) | Aston Villa | L 0-3 | | 14,085 | 1 | 2 | | 9 | 5 | | 7 | 8 | 6 | | 10 | 3 | 4 | | | | 11 | | | | | | |
| | 21 | (h) | Preston NE | L 1-2 | Geddes | 13,000 | | | 3 | | 5 | 6 | 7 | | 8 | | 10 | 2 | 9 | | | | 11 | 1 | 4 | | | | |
| | 28 | (a) | Burnley | L 2-3 | Bassett, Geddes | 8,000 | | | | | 5 | | 7 | | 6 | 10 | 8 | 3 | 9 | | | | 11 | 4 | 2 | | | | |
| Dec | 5 | (h) | Accrington | W 3-1 | Woodhall, Pearson, Geddes | 6,000 | | 2 | | | 5 | | 7 | | 8 | 10 | 3 | 6 | 9 | 1 | | | 11 | 4 | | | | | |
| | 12 | (h) | Derby C | W 4-2 | Woodhall, Pearson, Geddes 2 | 5,800 | | 2 | | | 5 | | 7 | | 8 | 10 | 3 | 6 | 9 | 1 | | | 11 | 4 | | | | | |
| | 19 | (a) | Bolton W | D 1-1 | McLeod | 7,000 | | 2 | | | 5 | 6 | 7 | | 9 | 8 | 10 | 3 | 4 | 1 | | | 11 | | | | | | |
| | 26 | (h) | Burnley | W 1-0 | Pearson | 5,000 | | 2 | | | 5 | 6 | 7 | | 8 | 10 | 3 | 4 | 9 | 1 | | | 11 | | | | | | |
| | 28 | (a) | Wolves | L 1-2 | Rose (og) | 7,200 | | 2 | | | 5 | 6 | 7 | | 8 | 10 | 3 | 4 | 9 | 1 | | | 11 | | | | | | |
| Jan | 9 | (a) | Preston NE | L 0-1 | | 6,400 | | | | | 5 | 6 | 7 | | 9 | 8 | 10 | 3 | 4 | 1 | | | 11 | | | 2 | | | |
| | 23 | (a) | Accrington | L 2-4 | Nicholls, Pearson | 4,200 | | | | | | 6 | 7 | 9 | | 8 | 10 | | 5 | | 1 | | 11 | | | 3 | 2 | 4 | |
| Feb | 6 | (a) | Derby C | D 1-1 | Nicholls | 7,300 | | 2 | | | | 5 | 7 | 9 | 6 | 8 | 10 | 3 | 4 | | 1 | | 11 | | | | | | |
| Mar | 12 | (a) | Blackburn R | L 2-3 | McLeod 2 | 6,000 | | 2 | | | 5 | | 7 | 9 | 6 | 8 | 10 | 3 | 4 | | 1 | | 11 | | | | | | |
| Apr | 4 | (a) | Darwen | W 12-0 | Pearson 4, Reynolds 2, Bassett 3, Hunt(og), Geddes, Nicholls | 1,109 | | | | | 5 | | 7 | 9 | 6 | 8 | 10 | 3 | 4 | | 1 | | 11 | | | 2 | | | |
| | 11 | (h) | Stoke C | D 2-2 | T.Perry 2 | 10,000 | 1 | | | | 5 | 6 | | 9 | | 8 | | 3 | | 7 | | | 11 | | | 2 | | 4 | 10 |
| | 16 | (a) | Darwen | D 1-1 | Nicholls | 3,000 | | 2 | | | 5 | 6 | 7 | 9 | 10 | 8 | | 3 | 4 | | 1 | | 11 | | | | | | |
| | 23 | (a) | Stoke C | L 0-1 | | 5,400 | | 3 | | | 5 | 6 | 7 | 9 | 8 | | 10 | 4 | | | 1 | | 11 | | | 2 | | | |
| | | | | | **App** | | 9 | 19 | 10 | 7 | 24 | 19 | 24 | 17 | 20 | 20 | 24 | 19 | 17 | 7 | 16 | 3 | 15 | 1 | 4 | 6 | 1 | 2 | 2 |
| | | | | | **Goals** | | | | | | 1 | | 7 | 7 | 3 | 6 | 13 | | 2 | 2 | | | 6 | | | | | | 2 |

# 1892-93

## Division 1

| Date | V | Opponent | Res | Scorers | Att | Reader J | Horton J | McCulloch T | Reynolds J | Perry C | Groves W | Bassett W | McLeod R | Bostock A | Pearson T | Geddes A | Nicholson M | Perry T | Wood H | Hadley B | Fellows E | Boyd H | Crone R | Taggart J | Neale W |
|---|---|---|---|---|---|---|---|---|---|---|---|---|---|---|---|---|---|---|---|---|---|---|---|---|---|
| Sep 10 | (a) | Bolton W | L 1-3 | Geddes | 4,100 | 1 | 2 | 3 | 4 | 5 | 6 | 7 | 8 | 9 | 10 | 11 | | | | | | | | | |
| 17 | (h) | Wolves | W 2-1 | Bassett, Bostock | 4,000 | 1 | | 3 | 4 | 5 | 6 | 7 | 8 | 9 | 10 | 11 | 2 | | | | | | | | |
| 19 | (a) | Aston Villa | W 3-2 | McLeod, Pearson 2 | 11,239 | 1 | 2 | 3 | 4 | 5 | 6 | 7 | 8 | 9 | 10 | 11 | | | | | | | | | |
| 24 | (a) | Derby C | D 1-1 | Pearson | 7,000 | 1 | | 3 | 4 | 5 | 6 | 7 | 8 | 9 | 10 | 11 | 2 | | | | | | | | |
| Oct 1 | (h) | Newton Heath | D 0-0 | | 4,000 | 1 | | 3 | 4 | 5 | 6 | 7 | 8 | 9 | 10 | | 2 | 11 | | | | | | | |
| 8 | (a) | Newton Heath | W 4-2 | McLeod, Bassett, Bostock 2 | 4,600 | 1 | | 3 | 4 | 5 | 6 | 7 | 8 | 9 | 10 | 11 | 2 | | | | | | | | |
| 15 | (h) | Everton | W 3-0 | Wood, Pearson 2 | 4,800 | 1 | | 3 | 4 | 5 | 6 | 7 | 8 | 9 | 10 | | 2 | | 11 | | | | | | |
| 22 | (a) | Sunderland | L 1-8 | Bassett | 8,000 | 1 | | 3 | 4 | 5 | 6 | 7 | 8 | 9 | 10 | 11 | 2 | | | | | | | | |
| 29 | (h) | Notts C | W 4-2 | Geddes, Pearson, Bassett, Bostock | 3,000 | 1 | | 3 | 4 | 5 | 6 | 7 | 8 | 9 | 10 | 11 | 2 | | | | | | | | |
| Nov 5 | (a) | Aston Villa | L 2-5 | Geddes 2 | 12,100 | 1 | | 3 | 4 | 9 | 6 | 7 | 8 | | 10 | 11 | 2 | 5 | | | | | | | |
| 7 | (h) | Bolton W | W 1-0 | Geddes | 4,000 | 1 | 2 | 3 | 4 | 5 | 9 | 7 | 8 | | 10 | 11 | | 6 | | | | | | | |
| 12 | (a) | Accrington | W 4-0 | Groves 2, McLeod, Bostock | 4,000 | 1 | 2 | 3 | 4 | 5 | 9 | 7 | 8 | | 10 | 11 | | 6 | | | | | | | |
| 19 | (a) | Notts C | L 1-8 | McLeod | 8,000 | 1 | 2 | 3 | 4 | 5 | 9 | 7 | 8 | | 10 | 11 | | 6 | | | | | | | |
| 26 | (h) | Stoke C | L 1-2 | Pearson | 607 | 1 | | 3 | | 5 | 6 | 7 | 8 | 9 | 10 | 11 | 2 | 4 | | | | | | | |
| Dec 10 | (h) | Preston NE | L 0-1 | | 4,000 | 1 | | 3 | | 5 | 6 | 7 | 8 | 9 | 10 | 11 | 2 | 4 | | | | | | | |
| 17 | (a) | Accrington | L 4-5 | McLeod, Pearson, Bostock 2 | 3,000 | 1 | 2 | 3 | | 5 | 6 | 7 | 8 | 9 | 10 | 11 | | | | | 4 | | | | |
| 24 | (h) | Sunderland | L 1-3 | Bassett | 8,000 | 1 | 2 | 3 | 4 | 5 | 6 | 7 | 8 | 9 | 10 | 11 | | | | | | | | | |
| 26 | (h) | Blackburn R | L 1-2 | Pearson | 7,000 | 1 | 2 | 3 | 4 | 5 | 6 | 7 | 8 | 9 | 10 | 11 | | | | | | | | | |
| 27 | (a) | Wolves | D 1-1 | McLeod | 8,000 | 1 | 2 | 3 | 4 | 5 | 6 | 7 | 8 | | 10 | 11 | | | | | | 9 | | | |
| 31 | (a) | Burnley | L 0-5 | | 3,500 | 1 | 2 | 3 | | 5 | 6 | 7 | 8 | | 10 | 11 | | 4 | | | | 9 | | | |
| Jan 2 | (a) | Sheffield W | L 0-6 | | 15,000 | 1 | 2 | 3 | | 5 | 6 | 7 | 8 | | 10 | 11 | | 4 | | | | 9 | | | |
| 7 | (h) | Burnley | W 7-1 | Geddes, McLeod 3, Bassett 2, Pearson | 1,000 | 1 | 2 | 3 | | 5 | 6 | 7 | 8 | | 10 | 11 | | 4 | | | | 9 | | | |
| 14 | (a) | Everton | L 0-1 | | 10,000 | 1 | 2 | 3 | | 5 | 6 | 7 | 8 | | 10 | 11 | | 4 | | | | 9 | | | |
| 28 | (a) | Blackburn R | L 1-2 | Geddes | 2,300 | 1 | 2 | 3 | | 5 | 6 | 7 | 8 | | | 11 | | 4 | | | 10 | 9 | | | |
| Feb 11 | (a) | Stoke C | W 2-1 | Bassett 2 | 6,000 | 1 | 2 | 3 | 4 | 5 | 6 | 7 | 8 | | 10 | 11 | | | | | | 9 | | | |
| Mar 2 | (a) | Nottingham F | W 4-3 | Geddes, Bassett 2, Groves | 4,100 | 1 | | 3 | 2 | 5 | 6 | 7 | 8 | | 10 | 11 | | 4 | | | | 9 | | | |
| 18 | (h) | Sheffield W | W 3-0 | McLeod, Pearson, Boyd | 5,000 | 1 | | | 4 | 5 | 6 | 7 | 8 | | 10 | 11 | 2 | | | | | 9 | 3 | | |
| Apr 1 | (h) | Derby C | W 3-1 | C.Perry 2, Geddes | 3,655 | 1 | | | | 5 | | 7 | 8 | | 10 | 11 | 2 | 4 | | | | | 3 | 6 | 9 |
| 3 | (h) | Nottingham F | D 2-2 | C.Perry, Reynolds (pen) | 5,000 | 1 | | | 4 | 5 | 11 | 7 | 8 | | 10 | | 2 | 6 | | | | | 3 | | 9 |
| 13 | (a) | Preston NE | D 1-1 | C.Perry | 8,200 | 1 | | 3 | 4 | 2 | | 7 | 8 | | 10 | 11 | | 5 | | | | | 9 | 6 | |
| App | | | | | | 30 | 19 | 23 | 20 | 30 | 30 | 29 | 30 | 18 | 25 | 27 | 13 | 16 | 1 | 1 | 4 | 7 | 3 | 2 | 2 |
| Goals | | | | | | | | | 1 | 4 | 3 | 11 | 10 | 7 | 11 | 9 | | | 1 | | | 1 | | | |

# 1893-94

## Division 1

| Date | V | Opponent | Res | Scorers | Att | Reader J | Nicholson M | Crone R | Perry T | Perry C | Taggart J | Norman O | McLeod R | Nicholls S | Pearson T | Geddes A | Bassett W | Hadley B | Horton J | Bostock A | Burns J | Neale W | Roberts T | Williams O | Banks J | Humpage W |
|---|---|---|---|---|---|---|---|---|---|---|---|---|---|---|---|---|---|---|---|---|---|---|---|---|---|---|
| Sep 2 | (a) | Aston Villa | L 2-3 | Geddes, Cowan (og) | 15,100 | 1 | 2 | 3 | 4 | 5 | 6 | 7 | 8 | 9 | 10 | 11 | | | | | | | | | | |
| 9 | (h) | Newton Heath | W 3-1 | Pearson, McLeod, Nicholls | 4,500 | 1 | 2 | 3 | 4 | 5 | 6 | | 8 | 9 | 10 | 11 | 7 | | | | | | | | | |
| 16 | (h) | Derby C | W 3-2 | McLeod 2, Nicholls | 7,000 | 1 | 2 | 3 | 4 | 5 | 6 | | 8 | 9 | 10 | 11 | 7 | | | | | | | | | |
| 23 | (h) | Burnley | D 1-1 | McLeod | 3,000 | 1 | 2 | 3 | 4 | 5 | 6 | | 8 | 9 | 10 | 11 | 7 | | | | | | | | | |
| 25 | (a) | Sheffield W | W 4-2 | Bassett 2, Geddes 2 | 6,000 | 1 | | 3 | 4 | 2 | 6 | | 8 | 9 | 10 | 11 | 7 | 5 | | | | | | | | |
| 30 | (a) | Nottingham F | W 3-2 | McLeod 2, Bassett | 5,000 | 1 | 2 | | 4 | 5 | 6 | | 8 | | 10 | 11 | 7 | | 3 | 9 | | | | | | |
| Oct 7 | (h) | Wolves | D 0-0 | | 10,000 | 1 | 2 | | 4 | 5 | 6 | 9 | 8 | | 10 | 11 | 7 | | 3 | | | | | | | |
| 14 | (a) | Newton Heath | L 1-4 | Norman | 8,000 | 1 | 2 | | 4 | 5 | 6 | 7 | | | 10 | 11 | | | 3 | 9 | 8 | | | | | |
| 21 | (h) | Aston Villa | L 3-6 | C.Perry, Geddes, McLeod | 14,000 | 1 | 2 | | 4 | 5 | 6 | | 8 | | 10 | 11 | 7 | | 3 | 9 | | | | | | |
| 28 | (a) | Sheffield U | W 2-0 | Bassett, Neale | 6,000 | 1 | 2 | 3 | 4 | 5 | 6 | | 8 | | 10 | 11 | 7 | | | | | 9 | | | | |
| Nov 4 | (h) | Stoke C | W 4-2 | C.Perry 2, McLeod, Nicholls | 3,000 | 1 | 2 | 3 | 4 | 5 | 6 | | 8 | 9 | 10 | 11 | 7 | | | | | | | | | |
| 6 | (h) | Bolton W | W 5-2 | Neale, Pearson 4 | 4,000 | 1 | 2 | 3 | 4 | 5 | 6 | | 8 | | 10 | 11 | 7 | | | | | 9 | | | | |
| 11 | (a) | Darwen | L 1-2 | Neale | 2,000 | 1 | 2 | 3 | 4 | 5 | 6 | | 8 | | 10 | 11 | 7 | | | | | 9 | | | | |
| 25 | (a) | Sunderland | L 1-2 | Bassett | 9,500 | 1 | 2 | 3 | 4 | 5 | 6 | | 8 | 9 | 10 | 11 | 7 | | | | | | | | | |
| 27 | (h) | Sheffield W | D 2-2 | Bostock, McLeod (pen) | 4,828 | 1 | 2 | | 4 | 5 | 6 | | 8 | | 10 | 11 | 7 | | 3 | 9 | | | | | | |
| Dec 4 | (h) | Preston NE | W 2-0 | Norman 2 | 2,000 | 1 | | 3 | 4 | 2 | 6 | 9 | | 8 | 10 | 11 | 7 | 5 | | | | | | | | |
| 9 | (h) | Burnley | L 0-3 | | 5,000 | 1 | 2 | 3 | 4 | 5 | | | 8 | 9 | 10 | 11 | 7 | | | | | | 6 | | | |
| 16 | (h) | Darwen | D 2-2 | McLeod, Bassett | 2,000 | 1 | 2 | 3 | 4 | 5 | 6 | | 8 | | 10 | 11 | 7 | | | | | | | 9 | | |
| 23 | (h) | Sunderland | L 2-3 | Geddes 2 | 7,500 | 1 | 2 | 3 | 4 | 5 | 6 | | 8 | 9 | 10 | 11 | 7 | | | | | | | | | |
| 26 | (h) | Sheffield U | W 3-1 | Bassett, Pearson, Norman | 7,000 | 1 | 2 | 3 | 4 | 5 | 6 | | 8 | 9 | 10 | 11 | 7 | | | | | | | | | |
| 27 | (h) | Wolves | W 8-0 | McLeod 3, C.Perry, Bassett 3, Williams | 8,000 | 1 | 2 | | 4 | 5 | 6 | | 8 | 9 | | 11 | 7 | | 3 | | | | | 10 | | |
| 30 | (a) | Everton | L 1-7 | Williams | 14,000 | 1 | 2 | 3 | 4 | 5 | 6 | | 8 | 9 | | 11 | 7 | | | | | | | 10 | | |
| Jan 6 | (h) | Blackburn R | W 2-1 | Williams, Hadley | 2,024 | 1 | 2 | 3 | | | 6 | | 8 | 9 | | 11 | 7 | 5 | | | | | | 10 | 4 | |
| 13 | (a) | Blackburn R | L 0-3 | | 6,000 | 1 | 2 | 3 | 4 | 5 | | | 8 | 9 | | 11 | 7 | | | | | | | 10 | 6 | |
| 20 | (a) | Stoke C | L 1-3 | Bassett | 3,000 | 1 | 2 | 3 | | 5 | | | 8 | | 10 | | 7 | 4 | | | | 9 | | 11 | 6 | |
| Feb 3 | (h) | Everton | W 3-1 | Williams 2, Pearson | 3,000 | 1 | 2 | 3 | 4 | 5 | 6 | | 8 | | 10 | 11 | 7 | | | | | | | 9 | | |
| Mar 3 | (a) | Preston NE | L 1-3 | McLeod | 5,000 | | 2 | 3 | | 5 | 6 | | 8 | 9 | | 11 | 7 | | | | | | | 10 | 4 | 1 |
| 24 | (h) | Derby C | L 0-1 | | 3,000 | 1 | | 3 | 4 | 2 | 6 | | 8 | | | 11 | 7 | 5 | | 9 | | | | 10 | | |
| 26 | (h) | Nottingham F | W 3-0 | Bostock, Williams 2 | 7,000 | 1 | | 3 | 4 | 5 | 6 | | 8 | | | 11 | 7 | | 2 | 9 | | | | 10 | | |
| Apr 7 | (a) | Bolton W | W 3-0 | Geddes, Bostock 2 | 3,500 | 1 | 2 | 3 | 4 | 5 | 6 | 7 | 8 | 9 | | 11 | | | | 10 | | | | | | |
| App | | | | | | 29 | 24 | 26 | 27 | 29 | 27 | 12 | 29 | 8 | 23 | 28 | 27 | 5 | 7 | 8 | 1 | 4 | 1 | 10 | 4 | 1 |
| Goals | | | | | | | | | | 4 | | 4 | 14 | 3 | 7 | 7 | 11 | 1 | | 4 | | 3 | | 7 | | |

# 1894-95

## Division 1

| Date | Opponent | Result | Scorers | Att | Reader J | Williams W | Crone R | Perry T | Perry C | Taggart J | Bassett W | McLeod R | Hutchinson T | Williams O | Newall W | Richards W | Higgins T | Fellows E | Horton J | Norman O | Banks J | Rea J | Paddock J | Perry W | Parry J | Green T | Roberts F | Geddes A |
|---|---|---|---|---|---|---|---|---|---|---|---|---|---|---|---|---|---|---|---|---|---|---|---|---|---|---|---|---|
| Sep 1 | (a) Sheffield U | L 1-2 | McLeod | 12,000 | 1 | 2 | 3 | 4 | 5 | 6 | 7 | 8 | 9 | 10 | 11 | | | | | | | | | | | | | |
| 8 | (h) Wolves | W 5-1 | McLeod, Richards, Bassett, Newall, Hutchinson | 5,100 | 1 | 2 | 3 | 4 | 5 | 6 | 7 | 8 | 9 | | 11 | 10 | | | | | | | | | | | | |
| 15 | (h) Liverpool | W 5-0 | Bassett, Williams, Richards, McLeod, Hutchinson | 6,951 | 1 | 2 | 3 | 4 | 5 | 6 | 7 | 8 | 9 | | 11 | 10 | | | | | | | | | | | | |
| 22 | (a) Sunderland | L 0-3 | | 7,150 | 1 | 2 | 3 | 4 | 5 | 6 | 7 | 8 | 9 | | 11 | 10 | | | | | | | | | | | | |
| 29 | (a) Everton* | L 1-4 | Bassett | 19,900 | 1 | 2 | 3 | 4 | 5 | 6 | 7 | 8 | 9 | | 11 | | | | | | | | | | | | | |
| Oct 13 | (a) Aston Villa | L 1-3 | McLeod | 15,000 | 1 | 2 | 3 | 4 | 5 | 6 | 7 | 8 | 9 | | 11 | | 10 | | | | | | | | | | | |
| 20 | (h) Derby C | D 2-2 | Newall, Hutchinson | 5,000 | 1 | 2 | 3 | 4 | 5 | 6 | 7 | 8 | 9 | | 11 | | | 10 | | | | | | | | | | |
| 27 | (a) Derby C | D 1-1 | Bassett | 1,990 | 1 | 2 | | 4 | 5 | 6 | 7 | | 9 | | 11 | | | | 3 | 8 | 10 | | | | | | | |
| Nov 3 | (h) Sheffield U | W 1-0 | Hutchinson | 3,250 | 1 | 2 | | 4 | 5 | 6 | 7 | 8 | 9 | | 11 | | | | 3 | | 10 | | | | | | | |
| 5 | (h) Bolton W | D 1-1 | Hutchinson | 3,500 | 1 | 2 | 3 | 4 | 5 | 6 | 7 | | 9 | | 11 | | | | | 8 | 10 | | | | | | | |
| 10 | (h) Small Heath | W 4-1 | Bassett, Richards, Hutchinson, C.Perry | 4,523 | 1 | 2 | | 4 | 5 | 6 | 7 | 8 | 9 | | 11 | 10 | | | 3 | | | | | | | | | |
| 17 | (h) Aston Villa | W 3-2 | Hutchinson, Richards 2 | 12,000 | 1 | 2 | | 4 | 5 | 6 | 7 | 8 | 9 | | 11 | 10 | | | 3 | | | | | | | | | |
| 24 | (a) Burnley | L 0-2 | | 6,000 | 1 | 2 | | 4 | 5 | 6 | | 8 | 9 | | | 10 | | | 3 | 7 | | 11 | | | | | | |
| Dec 1 | (h) Everton | L 1-4 | Hutchinson | 6,000 | 1 | 2 | | 4 | 5 | 6 | 7 | 8 | 9 | | 11 | 10 | | | 3 | | | | | | | | | |
| 8 | (a) Nottingham F | L 3-5 | T.Perry, McLeod, Bassett | 5,800 | 1 | 2 | | 4 | 5 | 6 | 7 | 8 | 9 | | | 10 | | | 3 | | 11 | | | | | | | |
| 15 | (h) Stoke C | W 3-2 | Hutchinson 2, Taggart | 4,400 | 1 | 2 | 3 | 4 | 5 | 6 | 7 | 8 | 9 | | | 10 | | | | | | | 11 | | | | | |
| 22 | (a) Blackburn R | L 0-3 | | 1,200 | 1 | 2 | | 4 | 5 | 6 | 7 | 8 | 9 | | | 10 | | | 3 | | 11 | | | | | | | |
| 26 | (h) Sunderland | L 0-2 | | 15,086 | 1 | 2 | 3 | 4 | 5 | 6 | 7 | 8 | 9 | | 11 | | 10 | | | | | | | | | | | |
| 27 | (a) Wolves | L 1-3 | Hutchinson | 6,500 | 1 | 2 | | 4 | 5 | | 7 | | 8 9 | | | | 6 | 10 | 3 | | | 11 | | | | | | |
| 29 | (h) Burnley | L 0-1 | | 2,535 | 1 | 2 | 8 | | | 6 | 7 | | 10 | | | | 9 | 5 | 3 | | 11 | | | 4 | | | | |
| Jan 1 | (a) Liverpool | L 0-4 | | 19,720 | 1 | 2 | 8 | | | 6 | 7 | | 10 | | | | 9 | 5 | 3 | | 11 | | | 4 | | | | |
| 5 | (h) Preston NE | L 4-5 | Bassett, Hutchinson 2, Richards | 19,700 | 1 | 2 | | 4 | 5 | 6 | 7 | 8 | 10 | | | | 9 | | 3 | | 11 | | | | | | | |
| 26 | (h) Blackburn R | W 2-0 | Hutchinson, Banks | 3,200 | 1 | 2 | | 4 | 3 | 6 | 7 | 8 | 10 | | | | 9 | 5 | | | 11 | | | | | | | |
| Feb 23 | (a) Small Heath | W 2-1 | Taggart 2 | 8,100 | 1 | | | 4 | 2 | 6 | | | 10 | | | | 9 | 5 | 3 | 7 | 11 | | | | | 8 | | |
| 26 | (a) Preston NE | L 0-5 | | 6,400 | 1 | | | 4 | 2 | 6 | | | 10 | | | | 9 | 5 | | 7 | 11 | | | | | 8 | 3 | |
| Mar 25 | (a) Stoke C | D 1-1 | McLeod | 5,100 | 1 | 2 | | 4 | | 6 | 7 | 8 | 9 | 10 | | | 5 | | 3 | | 11 | | | | | | | |
| Apr 1 | (a) Sheffield W | L 2-3 | McLeod 2 | 14,150 | 1 | | 2 | 4 | | 6 | 7 | 8 | 10 | | | | 5 | | | | 11 | | | | | 9 | 3 | |
| 13 | (a) Bolton W | L 0-5 | | 10,200 | 1 | 3 | | 4 | | 6 | 7 | 8 | 10 | | | | 9 | 5 | 2 | | | | | | | | | 11 |
| 15 | (h) Nottingham F | W 1-0 | Geddes | 4,355 | 1 | 3 | | 4 | | 6 | 7 | 8 | 10 | | | | 9 | 5 | 2 | | | | | | | | | 11 |
| 22 | (h) Sheffield W | W 6-0 | Geddes 2, Green, Hutchinson, McLeod, T.Perry | 8,217 | 1 | 3 | | 4 | | 6 | 7 | 8 | 10 | | | | 5 | | 2 | | | | | | | 9 | | 11 |
| **App** | | | | | 30 | 27 | 11 | 30 | 24 | 29 | 27 | 24 | 30 | 3 | 14 | 18 | 11 | 3 | 17 | 5 | 13 | 1 | 1 | 1 | 1 | 4 | 2 | 3 |
| **Goals** | | | | | | 1 | | 2 | 1 | 3 | 7 | 9 | 15 | | 2 | 6 | | | | | 1 | | | | | 1 | | 3 |

* Albion played with ten players in this game.

**The Albion team which beat Oxford University at Oxford in November 1894. Back row (left to right): Mr Clement Keys, T.Roberts, T.Perry, Mr J.Shilton, J.Reader, J.Taggart, R.Crone, Mr C.B.Fry (referee). Front row: W.Perry, W.I.Bassett, R.McLeod, T.Hutchinson, W.Richards, J.Banks**

# 1895-96

## Division 1

| Date | | Opponents | Result | Scorers | Att | Reader J | Perry C | Williams W | Perry T | Higgins T | Banks J | Bassett W | McLeod R | Green T | Hutchinson T | Saunders S | Richards W | Horton J | Williams O | Paddock J | Norman O | Kelsey A | Humpage W | Fellows E | Spooner J | Richards J | Wright F | Hadley B | Hayward A | Taggart J | Flewitt A | Cave G |
|---|---|---|---|---|---|---|---|---|---|---|---|---|---|---|---|---|---|---|---|---|---|---|---|---|---|---|---|---|---|---|---|
| Sep 2 | (a) | Aston Villa | L 0-1 | | 18,000 | 1 | 2 | 3 | 4 | 5 | 6 | 7 | 8 | 9 | 10 | 11 | | | | | | | | | | | | | | | | |
| 7 | (h) | Burnley | L 0-2 | | 5,000 | 1 | 2 | 3 | 4 | 5 | 6 | 7 | 8 | 9 | 10 | | | 11 | | | | | | | | | | | | | | |
| 14 | (h) | Preston NE | L 1-2 | Hutchinson | 4,250 | 1 | | 3 | 4 | 5 | 6 | 7 | 8 | 9 | 10 | 11 | | 2 | | | | | | | | | | | | | | |
| 21 | (a) | Stoke C | L 1-3 | Green | 12,000 | 1 | | 3 | 4 | 5 | 6 | 7 | 8 | 9 | | | 10 | 2 | 11 | | | | | | | | | | | | | |
| 28 | (h) | Nottingham F | W 3-1 | Paddock 2, Bassett | 3,000 | 1 | | 3 | 4 | 5 | 6 | 7 | 8 | | 9 | | 10 | 2 | | 11 | | | | | | | | | | | | |
| Oct 5 | (a) | Sheffield W | L 3-5 | Hutchinson 2, Richards | 8,000 | 1 | | 3 | 4 | 5 | 6 | | 8 | | 9 | | 10 | 2 | | 11 | 7 | | | | | | | | | | | |
| 12 | (h) | Aston Villa | D 1-1 | Paddock | 17,510 | 1 | | 3 | 4 | 5 | 6 | 7 | 8 | | 9 | | | 2 | | 11 | | 10 | | | | | | | | | | |
| 19 | (a) | Everton | D 1-1 | McLeod | 18,900 | 1 | | 3 | 4 | 5 | 6 | 7 | 8 | | 9 | | | 2 | | 11 | | 10 | | | | | | | | | | |
| 26 | (h) | Sheffield W | L 2-3 | Paddock, Banks | 5,550 | 1 | | 3 | 4 | 5 | 6 | 7 | 8 | | 9 | | | 2 | | 11 | | 10 | | | | | | | | | | |
| Nov 2 | (a) | Bury | L 0-3 | | 8,000 | 1 | | 3 | 4 | 5 | 6 | 7 | 8 | | 9 | | | 2 | | 11 | | 10 | | | | | | | | | | |
| 4 | (h) | Bolton W | L 2-3 | McLeod, Sutcliffe (og) | 3,500 | 1 | 2 | 3 | 4 | 5 | 6 | 7 | 8 | | 9 | | | | | 11 | | 10 | | | | | | | | | | |
| 9 | (h) | Stoke C | W 1-0 | McLeod | 3,500 | | | 3 | 4 | 5 | 6 | 7 | 8 | | 9 | | | 2 | | | | 10 | 1 | 11 | | | | | | | | |
| 16 | (a) | Nottingham F | L 0-2 | | 6,000 | | | 3 | 4 | 5 | 6 | 7 | 8 | | 9 | | | 2 | | 11 | | 10 | 1 | | | | | | | | | |
| 23 | (h) | Everton | L 0-3 | | 3,950 | | | 3 | 4 | 5 | 6 | 7 | 8 | | 9 | | | 2 | | | | 10 | 1 | 11 | | | | | | | | |
| 30 | (h) | Wolves | W 2-1 | Richards, McLeod | 3,000 | 1 | | 3 | 4 | 5 | 6 | 7 | 8 | | | | 10 | 2 | | 11 | | | | | | 9 | | | | | | |
| Dec 14 | (a) | Derby C | L 1-4 | Richards | 8,000 | 1 | | 3 | 4 | 5 | | 7 | 8 | | | | 10 | 2 | | 11 | 6 | | | | | 9 | | | | | | |
| 21 | (a) | Small Heath | D 2-2 | McLeod, Banks | 6,000 | 1 | | 3 | 4 | 5 | 11 | 7 | 8 | | | | 10 | 2 | | | | | | | | 9 | | 6 | | | | |
| 26 | (h) | Sunderland | D 1-1 | Bassett | 15,124 | 1 | | 3 | 4 | 5 | 11 | 7 | 8 | | | | 10 | 2 | | | | | | | | 9 | | | 6 | | | |
| Jan 4 | (a) | Sheffield U | L 0-2 | | 5,000 | 1 | | 3 | 4 | 5 | 11 | 7 | 8 | | | | 10 | 2 | | | | | | | | 9 | | | 6 | | | |
| 11 | (a) | Burnley | L 0-3 | | 5,500 | 1 | | 3 | 4 | 5 | | 7 | 8 | | | | 10 | 2 | | | | | | | | 9 | | | 6 | 11 | | |
| 18 | (h) | Derby C | D 0-0 | | 8,877 | 1 | | 3 | 4 | 5 | | 7 | 8 | | | | 10 | 2 | | | | | | | | 9 | | | 11 | 6 | | |
| 25 | (a) | Sunderland | L 1-7 | McLeod | 10,500 | 1 | | 3 | 4 | 5 | | 7 | 8 | | | | 10 | 2 | | | | | | | | 9 | | | 11 | 6 | | |
| Feb 17 | (a) | Blackburn R | L 0-1 | | 5,700 | 1 | | 3 | 4 | 5 | | 7 | 9 | | | | 10 | | | | | 11 | | | | | | | 6 | 8 | 2 | |
| 22 | (h) | Sheffield U | W 1-0 | W.Richards | 3,900 | 1 | | 3 | 4 | 5 | | 7 | 8 | | | | 10 | 2 | | | | 11 | | | | | | | 6 | 9 | | |
| Mar 7 | (a) | Wolves | W 2-1 | W.Richards, Flewitt | 8,114 | 1 | | 3 | 4 | 5 | | 7 | | | 8 | | 10 | 2 | | | | 11 | | | | | | | 6 | 9 | | |
| 9 | (h) | Bury | L 1-3 | Flewitt | 4,200 | 1 | | 3 | 4 | 5 | | 7 | 8 | | | | 10 | 2 | | | | 11 | | | | | | | 6 | 9 | | |
| Apr 3 | (a) | Preston NE | D 0-0 | | 6,700 | 1 | | 3 | 4 | 5 | | 7 | | | 8 | | 10 | 2 | | | | 11 | | | | | | | 6 | 9 | | |
| 4 | (a) | Bolton W | L 1-2 | Banks | 7,000 | 1 | | 3 | 4 | 5 | 11 | | 8 | | | | 10 | 2 | | | | 7 | | | | | | | 6 | 9 | | |
| 6 | (h) | Small Heath | D 0-0 | | 3,750 | 1 | | 3 | 4 | 5 | | 7 | 8 | | | | 10 | 2 | | | | 11 | | | | | | | 6 | 9 | | |
| 29 | (h) | Blackburn R | W 3-2 | W.Richards, Hutchinson, Taggart | 560 | 1 | | 3 | 4 | 5 | 11 | | 8 | 9 | | | 10 | | | | | 7 | | | | | | | 6 | | 2 | |
| App | | | | | | 27 | 3 | 30 | 30 | 30 | 20 | 25 | 30 | 4 | 15 | 2 | 20 | 25 | 1 | 10 | 1 | 11 | 3 | 2 | 2 | 14 | 2 | 1 | 3 | 10 | 7 | 2 |
| Goals | | | | | | | | | | | 3 | 2 | 6 | 1 | 4 | | 6 | | | 4 | | | | | | | | | | 1 | 2 | |

## TEST MATCHES

Albion, by virtue of finishing at the foot of the First Division in 1895-6, were required, along with Small Heath, to meet Liverpool and Manchester City from Division Two to contest a series of Test Matches to see who would be playing in what Division in 1896-7. Both First Division clubs had to play the Second Division clubs twice. Albion, along with Liverpool, gained five points from their four games, and thus remained in Division One. Small Heath and Manchester City each acquired three points and were forced to play in the lower Division.

| Date | | Opponents | Result | Scorers | Att | 1 | 2 | 3 | 4 | 5 | 6 | 7 | 8 | 9 | 10 | 11 |
|---|---|---|---|---|---|---|---|---|---|---|---|---|---|---|---|---|
| Apr 18 | (a) | Manchester C | D 1-1 | T.Perry | 8,000 | Reader | J.Horton | W.Williams | T.Perry | Higgins | Taggart | J.Richards | McLeod | Flewitt | Hutchinson | W.Richards |
| 20 | (h) | Manchester C | W 6-1 | Flewitt 2, Higgins, J.Richards, W.Williams, Johnson | 8,000 | .. | .. | .. | .. | .. | .. | .. | .. | .. | Johnson | .. |
| 25 | (a) | Liverpool | L 0-2 | | 20,100 | .. | .. | .. | Banks | .. | .. | .. | .. | .. | W.Richards | Hutchinson |
| 27 | (h) | Liverpool | W 2-0 | W.Williams (pen), W.Richards | 15,000 | .. | .. | .. | T.Perry | .. | .. | .. | .. | .. | .. | Banks |

Albion in 1895-96. Players only (left to right): T.Higgins, T.Perry, W.I.Bassett, C.Perry, R.McLeod, W.Williams, W.Richards, J.Reader, T.Hutchinson, J.Taggart, J.Banks.

# 1896-97

## Division 1

| Date | V | Opponent | Res | Score | Scorers | Att | Reader J | Evans T | Williams W | Perry T | Higgins T | McManus P | Bassett W | McLeod R | Ford W | Richards W | Garfield B | Banks J | Watson A | Flewitt A | Vigrow S | Cameron J | Horton J | Cave G | Dean A | Law A | Flavell A | Fellows E |
|---|---|---|---|---|---|---|---|---|---|---|---|---|---|---|---|---|---|---|---|---|---|---|---|---|---|---|---|---|
| Sep 1 | (a) | Blackburn R | W | 2-1 | Richards, McLeod | 3,000 | 1 | 2 | 3 | 4 | 5 | 6 | 7 | 8 | 9 | 10 | 11 | | | | | | | | | | | |
| Sep 5 | (h) | Aston Villa | W | 3-1 | Garfield 2, Williams (pen) | 10,000 | 1 | 3 | 2 | 4 | 5 | | 7 | 8 | 9 | 10 | 11 | 6 | | | | | | | | | | |
| Sep 12 | (a) | Sheffield W | L | 1-3 | Ford | 6,800 | 1 | 3 | 2 | 4 | 5 | | 7 | 8 | 9 | 10 | 11 | 6 | | | | | | | | | | |
| Sep 19 | (h) | Preston NE | D | 1-1 | Watson | 9,500 | 1 | 2 | 3 | 4 | 5 | | 7 | 8 | 9 | | 11 | 6 | 10 | | | | | | | | | |
| Sep 26 | (a) | Liverpool | D | 0-0 | | 15,100 | 1 | 2 | 3 | 4 | 5 | 6 | 7 | | 9 | | 11 | | 10 | 8 | | | | | | | | |
| Oct 3 | (h) | Sheffield W | L | 0-2 | | 10,291 | 1 | 2 | 3 | 4 | 5 | 6 | 7 | 8 | 9 | 10 | 11 | | | | | | | | | | | |
| Oct 10 | (a) | Aston Villa | L | 0-2 | | 15,500 | 1 | 2 | 3 | 4 | 5 | | 7 | 8 | 9 | | 11 | 6 | 10 | | | | | | | | | |
| Oct 17 | (h) | Wolves | W | 1-0 | McLeod | 6,000 | 1 | 2 | 3 | 4 | 5 | 6 | 7 | 8 | | 9 | 11 | | | | 10 | | | | | | | |
| Oct 24 | (h) | Bury | D | 0-0 | | 5,000 | 1 | 2 | 3 | 4 | 5 | | 7 | | 9 | 10 | 11 | 6 | | 8 | | | | | | | | |
| Oct 31 | (h) | Liverpool | L | 0-1 | | 6,100 | 1 | | 3 | 2 | 5 | | 7 | | 4 | 9 | 11 | 6 | | 8 | 10 | | | | | | | |
| Nov 2 | (a) | Bolton W | W | 1-0 | Bassett | 5,200 | 1 | 2 | 3 | 4 | 5 | | 7 | | 9 | 10 | 11 | 6 | | 8 | | | | | | | | |
| Nov 14 | (h) | Sheffield U | L | 0-1 | | 5,700 | 1 | 2 | 3 | 4 | 5 | | 7 | | 9 | 10 | 11 | 6 | | 8 | | | | | | | | |
| Nov 21 | (a) | Stoke C | D | 2-2 | Flewitt, Garfield | 6,200 | 1 | 2 | 3 | 4 | 5 | | 7 | | 10 | | 11 | 6 | | 8 | | 9 | | | | | | |
| Nov 28 | (h) | Sunderland | W | 1-0 | Cameron | 4,000 | 1 | 2 | 3 | 4 | 5 | 6 | 7 | | 10 | | 11 | | | 8 | | 9 | | | | | | |
| Dec 5 | (a) | Sheffield U | W | 1-0 | Bassett | 6,000 | 1 | 2 | | 4 | 5 | 6 | 7 | | 10 | | 11 | | | 8 | | 9 | | | | | | |
| Dec 12 | (a) | Stoke C | L | 1-2 | Garfield | 1,105 | 1 | 2 | 3 | 4 | 5 | 6 | 7 | | 10 | | 11 | | | 8 | | 9 | | | | | | |
| Dec 19 | (a) | Bolton W | D | 2-2 | Flewitt, Cameron | 7,000 | 1 | 2 | 3 | 4 | 5 | 6 | 7 | | 10 | | 11 | | | 8 | | 9 | | | | | | |
| Dec 25 | (a) | Derby C | L | 1-8 | Flewitt | 8,000 | 1 | 2 | 3 | 4 | 5 | 6 | 7 | | 10 | | 11 | | | 8 | | 9 | | | | | | |
| Dec 26 | (h) | Blackburn R | W | 1-0 | Flewitt | 9,909 | 1 | | 3 | 4 | 5 | 6 | 7 | | 10 | | 11 | | | 8 | | 9 | 2 | | | | | |
| Dec 28 | (a) | Wolves | L | 1-6 | Bassett | 11,561 | 1 | | 3 | 4 | 5 | 6 | 7 | | 10 | | 11 | | | 8 | | 9 | 2 | | | | | |
| Jan 2 | (a) | Nottingham F | W | 1-0 | Dean | 5,300 | 1 | | 3 | 4 | 5 | 6 | | 8 | 10 | | 11 | | | | | 9 | 2 | | 7 | | | |
| Jan 16 | (h) | Everton | L | 1-4 | Perry | 3,950 | 1 | 2 | 3 | 4 | 5 | | | 8 | 10 | | 11 | 6 | | | | 9 | | | 7 | | | |
| Jan 23 | (h) | Nottingham F | W | 4-0 | Richards 3, Williams | 2,000 | 1 | 2 | 3 | 4 | 5 | | 7 | | 10 | | 11 | 6 | | 8 | | 9 | | | | | | |
| Feb 6 | (h) | Derby C | L | 1-4 | Garfield | 6,000 | | | 3 | 4 | 5 | | 7 | | 10 | | 11 | 6 | | 8 | | 9 | 2 | | | | 1 | |
| Mar 6 | (a) | Sunderland | L | 1-2 | Richards | 4,600 | | 2 | 3 | 4 | 5 | 6 | | | 10 | | 11 | | 7 | 8 | | 9 | | | | | 1 | |
| Mar 13 | (a) | Bury | L | 0-3 | | 8,000 | | 2 | 3 | 4 | 5 | | 7 | | | | 11 | 6 | | 8 | | 9 | | | | | 1 | 10 |
| Apr 3 | (h) | Burnley | W | 3-0 | McLeod, Williams, Flewitt | 3,100 | 1 | | 3 | 4 | 5 | | | 9 | | 10 | 11 | 6 | 7 | 8 | | | | 2 | | | | |
| Apr 10 | (a) | Burnley | L | 0-5 | | 4,900 | 1 | | 3 | 4 | 5 | | | 9 | | 10 | 11 | 6 | 7 | 8 | | | | 2 | | | | |
| Apr 16 | (a) | Preston NE | D | 0-0 | | 8,000 | 1 | | 3 | 4 | 5 | | | 9 | | 10 | 11 | 6 | 7 | 8 | | | | 2 | | | | |
| Apr 17 | (a) | Everton | L | 3-6 | Perry, Flewitt, McLeod | 9,700 | 1 | | 3 | 4 | 5 | | | 9 | | 10 | 11 | 6 | 7 | 8 | | | | 2 | | | | |
| **App** | | | | | | | 27 | 21 | 29 | 30 | 26 | 17 | 23 | 13 | 12 | 9 | 22 | 17 | 22 | 23 | 1 | 13 | 4 | 5 | 2 | 1 | 2 | 1 |
| **Goals** | | | | | | | | 3 | 2 | | | | 3 | 4 | 1 | 5 | 5 | | 1 | 6 | | 2 | | | 1 | | | |

# 1897-98

## Division 1

| Date | V | Opponent | Res | Score | Scorers | Att | Reader J | Cave G | Williams W | Perry T | McManus P | Banks J | Watson A | Flewitt A | Higgins T | McKenzie A | Garfield B | Bassett W | Richards W | Jones A | Dean A | Reid G | Knowles J | Nock J | Hadley H | Connor J | Horton J |
|---|---|---|---|---|---|---|---|---|---|---|---|---|---|---|---|---|---|---|---|---|---|---|---|---|---|---|---|
| Sep 4 | (a) | Aston Villa | L | 3-4 | McKenzie, Higgins, McManus | 20,950 | 1 | 2 | 3 | 4 | 5 | 6 | 7 | 8 | 9 | 10 | 11 | | | | | | | | | | |
| Sep 11 | (h) | Nottingham F | W | 2-0 | Garfield 2 | 5,000 | 1 | 2 | 3 | 4 | 5 | 6 | 7 | 8 | 9 | 10 | 11 | | | | | | | | | | |
| Sep 18 | (a) | Derby C | L | 2-3 | Watson, Higgins | 6,700 | 1 | 2 | 3 | 4 | 5 | 6 | 7 | 8 | 9 | 10 | 11 | | | | | | | | | | |
| Sep 25 | (h) | Stoke C | W | 2-0 | Flewitt, Higgins | 8,200 | 1 | 2 | 3 | 4 | 5 | 6 | 7 | 8 | 9 | 10 | 11 | | | | | | | | | | |
| Oct 2 | (a) | Bury | L | 2-3 | Bassett, Higgins | 4,500 | 1 | 2 | 3 | 4 | 5 | 6 | | 8 | 9 | 10 | 11 | 7 | | | | | | | | | |
| Oct 9 | (h) | Aston Villa | D | 1-1 | Garfield | 12,244 | 1 | 2 | 3 | 4 | 5 | 6 | | 8 | 9 | 10 | 11 | 7 | | | | | | | | | |
| Oct 16 | (a) | Sunderland | W | 2-0 | McNeill (og), Bassett | 6,500 | 1 | 2 | 3 | 4 | 5 | 6 | | 8 | 9 | 10 | 11 | 7 | | | | | | | | | |
| Oct 23 | (h) | Wolves | D | 2-2 | Flewitt, Garfield | 11,750 | 1 | 2 | 3 | 4 | 5 | 6 | 7 | 8 | | 10 | 11 | | | 9 | | | | | | | |
| Oct 30 | (a) | Stoke C | D | 0-0 | | 6,400 | 1 | 2 | 3 | 4 | 5 | 6 | 7 | 8 | 9 | 10 | 11 | | | | | | | | | | |
| Nov 1 | (h) | Bolton W | W | 2-0 | Dean, Jones | 8,200 | 1 | 2 | 3 | 4 | | 6 | | 8 | 9 | 10 | 11 | | | 5 | 7 | | | | | | |
| Nov 6 | (h) | Everton | D | 2-2 | Garfield, Dean | 5,750 | 1 | 2 | 3 | 4 | | 6 | | 8 | 9 | 10 | 11 | | | 5 | 7 | | | | | | |
| Nov 13 | (h) | Liverpool | W | 2-1 | Williams, Jones | 8,200 | 1 | 2 | 3 | 4 | | 6 | | 8 | | 10 | 11 | | | 5 | 7 | 9 | | | | | |
| Nov 20 | (h) | Derby C | W | 3-1 | Garfield, Flewitt, Reid | 10,500 | 1 | 2 | 3 | 4 | | 6 | | 8 | | 10 | 11 | | | 5 | 7 | 9 | | | | | |
| Nov 27 | (a) | Everton | L | 1-6 | Flewitt | 15,700 | 1 | 2 | 3 | 4 | | 6 | | 8 | | 10 | 11 | | | 5 | 7 | 9 | | | | | |
| Dec 11 | (a) | Nottingham F | W | 1-0 | Perry | 10,400 | 1 | 2 | 3 | 4 | | 6 | | 8 | | 10 | 11 | | | 5 | | 9 | 7 | | | | |
| Dec 18 | (h) | Bury | W | 1-0 | Garfield | 6,303 | 1 | 2 | 3 | 4 | | 6 | | 8 | | 10 | 11 | | | 5 | | 9 | 7 | | | | |
| Dec 27 | (h) | Blackburn R | D | 1-1 | Williams (pen) | 5,300 | 1 | 2 | 3 | 4 | | 6 | | 8 | | 10 | 11 | | 7 | 5 | | 9 | | | | | |
| Dec 28 | (a) | Wolves | D | 1-1 | Reid | 8,100 | 1 | 2 | 3 | 4 | | 6 | | 8 | | 10 | 11 | | 7 | 5 | | 9 | | | | | |
| Jan 1 | (a) | Liverpool | D | 1-1 | Flewitt | 10,000 | 1 | 2 | 3 | 4 | | 6 | | 8 | | 10 | | | 7 | 5 | | 9 | 11 | | | | |
| Jan 15 | (h) | Preston NE | W | 3-1 | Garfield 2, Flewitt | 7,000 | 1 | 2 | 3 | 4 | | 6 | | 8 | | 10 | 11 | | 7 | 5 | | 9 | | | | | |
| Feb 5 | (a) | Blackburn R | W | 3-1 | Reid, Flewitt, Bassett | 4,000 | 1 | 2 | 3 | 4 | | 6 | | 8 | | 10 | 11 | | 7 | 5 | | 9 | | | | | |
| Feb 19 | (h) | Sunderland | D | 2-2 | McKenzie 2 | 5,000 | 1 | 2 | 3 | 4 | | 6 | | 8 | | 10 | 11 | | 7 | 5 | | 9 | | | | | |
| Mar 12 | (h) | Sheffield W | L | 0-2 | | 3,455 | 1 | 2 | 3 | 4 | | 6 | | 8 | | 10 | 11 | | 7 | 9 | 5 | | | | | | |
| Mar 19 | (h) | Notts C | D | 2-2 | Garfield, Jones | 3,600 | 1 | 2 | 3 | 4 | | | | | | 10 | 11 | | 7 | 9 | | 5 | | | 6 | 8 | |
| Mar 26 | (h) | Sheffield U | W | 2-0 | Garfield, Richards | 4,200 | 1 | 2 | 3 | 4 | | 6 | | | | 10 | 11 | | 7 | 9 | | 5 | | | | 8 | |
| Mar 31 | (a) | Preston NE | D | 1-1 | Garfield | 5,900 | 1 | 2 | 3 | 4 | | 6 | | | | 10 | 11 | | 7 | 9 | | 5 | | | | 8 | |
| Apr 2 | (a) | Bolton W | L | 0-2 | | 3,650 | 1 | 2 | | 4 | 5 | 6 | | | | 10 | 11 | | 7 | 9 | 3 | | | | | 8 | |
| Apr 4 | (h) | Notts C | L | 0-3 | | 4,000 | 1 | 2 | 3 | 4 | | | | | | 10 | | | 7 | 9 | | 5 | 11 | | 6 | 8 | |
| Apr 9 | (a) | Sheffield W | L | 0-3 | | 3,200 | 1 | 2 | | | 4 | 11 | | | | 10 | | | 7 | 9 | | 5 | | | 6 | 8 | 3 |
| Apr 11 | (a) | Sheffield U | L | 0-2 | | 2,800 | 1 | 2 | 3 | 4 | | 6 | | | | 10 | 11 | | 7 | 9 | | 5 | | | | 8 | |
| **App** | | | | | | | 30 | 30 | 28 | 29 | 11 | 27 | 6 | 23 | 11 | 30 | 27 | 17 | 9 | 21 | 5 | 11 | 2 | 2 | 3 | 7 | 1 |
| **Goals** | | | | | | | | | 2 | 1 | 1 | | 1 | 7 | 4 | 3 | 12 | 3 | | 1 | 3 | 2 | 3 | | | | |

# 1898-99

## Division 1

| Date | | Opponent | Result | Scorers | Att. | Reader J | Cave G | Williams W | Perry T | Jones A | Banks J | Bassett W | Flewitt A | Brett R | Richards W | Garfield B | Dunn A | Connor J | McKenzie A | Foster J | Turner I | Simmons C | Nock J | Hadley H | Brett S | Adams A | Smith A | Fellows E |
|---|---|---|---|---|---|---|---|---|---|---|---|---|---|---|---|---|---|---|---|---|---|---|---|---|---|---|---|---|
| Sep | 3 | (a) Bolton W | D 3-3 | Brett, Garfield 2 | 6,300 | 1 | 2 | 3 | 4 | 5 | 6 | 7 | 8 | 9 | 10 | 11 | | | | | | | | | | | | |
| | 10 | (h) Derby C | D 1-1 | Brett | 7,026 | 1 | 2 | 3 | 4 | 5 | 6 | 7 | 8 | 9 | 10 | 11 | | | | | | | | | | | | |
| | 17 | (h) Bury | W 2-0 | Garfield, Flewitt | 5,521 | 1 | 2 | 3 | 4 | 5 | 6 | 7 | 8 | 9 | 10 | 11 | | | | | | | | | | | | |
| | 24 | (a) Blackburn R | L 1-4 | Garfield | 4,600 | 1 | 2 | | 4 | 5 | 6 | 7 | 8 | 9 | 10 | 11 | 3 | | | | | | | | | | | |
| Oct | 1 | (h) Sheffield W | W 2-0 | Perry, McKenzie | 6,767 | 1 | 2 | | 4 | 5 | | | 8 | 9 | 6 | 11 | | 3 | 7 | 10 | | | | | | | | |
| | 8 | (a) Sunderland | L 0-2 | | 15,000 | 1 | 2 | 3 | 4 | 5 | | | | 9 | 6 | 11 | | | 8 | | 7 | 10 | | | | | | |
| | 15 | (h) Wolves | L 1-2 | Bassett | 6,457 | | 2 | 3 | 4 | 5 | 6 | 7 | | 9 | | 11 | | | 8 | 10 | | 1 | | | | | | |
| | 22 | (a) Everton | L 0-1 | | 9,000 | 1 | 2 | 3 | 4 | 5 | 6 | 7 | | 9 | 10 | 11 | | | 8 | | | | | | | | | |
| | 29 | (h) Notts C | W 2-0 | McKenzie, Richards | 4,286 | 1 | 2 | 3 | 4 | 5 | 6 | 7 | | 9 | 10 | 11 | | | 8 | | | | | | | | | |
| Nov | 5 | (a) Stoke C | L 1-2 | Richards | 7,500 | 1 | 2 | | 4 | 5 | 6 | 7 | | 9 | 10 | 11 | 3 | | 8 | | | | | | | | | |
| | 7 | (h) Everton | W 3-0 | Richards 2, Brett | 6,686 | 1 | 2 | 3 | 4 | 5 | 6 | 7 | | 9 | 10 | 11 | | | 8 | | | | | | | | | |
| | 12 | (a) Aston Villa | L 0-1 | | 15,896 | 1 | 2 | 3 | 4 | 5 | 6 | 7 | 9 | | 10 | 11 | | | 8 | | | | | | | | | |
| | 19 | (a) Burnley | D 1-1 | Williams (pen) | 7,500 | 1 | 2 | 3 | 4 | | | 6 | 7 | | 9 | | 5 | | 10 | | | 8 | 11 | | | | | |
| | 26 | (h) Sheffield U | W 3-0 | Nock, Thickett (og), Richards | 1,999 | 1 | 2 | 3 | 4 | 5 | 6 | 7 | | | 10 | | | | 9 | | | 8 | 11 | | | | | |
| Dec | 3 | (a) Newcastle U | L 0-3 | | 16,200 | 1 | 2 | 3 | 4 | 5 | 6 | 7 | | | 10 | | | | 9 | | | 8 | 11 | | | | | |
| | 10 | (h) Preston NE | W 2-0 | Dunn, McKenzie | 2,433 | 1 | 2 | 3 | 4 | 5 | 6 | 7 | | | 10 | | | | 9 | | | 8 | 11 | | | | | |
| | 17 | (a) Liverpool | D 2-2 | Nock 2 | 5,100 | 1 | 2 | 3 | 4 | 5 | 6 | 7 | | | 10 | | | | 9 | | | 8 | 11 | | | | | |
| | 24 | (h) Nottingham F | W 2-0 | Nock 2 | 2,578 | 1 | 2 | 3 | 4 | 5 | | 7 | | | 10 | | | | 9 | | | 8 | 11 | 6 | | | | |
| | 26 | (h) Liverpool | L 0-1 | | 8,483 | 1 | 2 | 3 | 4 | 5 | | 7 | | | 10 | | | | 9 | | | 8 | 11 | 6 | | | | |
| | 27 | (a) Wolves | L 1-5 | McKenzie | 12,052 | 1 | 2 | | 4 | 3 | | 7 | | | 10 | | | | 5 | | | 8 | 11 | 6 | 9 | | | |
| | 31 | (h) Bolton W | W 1-0 | Nock | 1,571 | 1 | 2 | 3 | 4 | 5 | | 7 | 8 | 9 | 10 | | 6 | | | | | | 11 | | | | | |
| Jan | 7 | (a) Derby C | L 1-4 | Richards | 3,200 | 1 | 2 | 3 | 4 | 5 | | 7 | 8 | 9 | 10 | | 6 | | | | | | 11 | | | | | |
| | 14 | (a) Bury | D 1-1 | Richards | 1,500 | 1 | 2 | 3 | 4 | 5 | | 7 | | 9 | 10 | | 6 | | | | | 8 | 11 | | | | | |
| | 21 | (h) Blackburn R | W 6-2 | Flewitt 2, McKenzie 2, Garfield, Bassett | 1,957 | 1 | 2 | | 4 | 3 | | 7 | 9 | | 5 | 11 | 6 | | 10 | | | 8 | | | | | | |
| Feb | 4 | (h) Sunderland | W 1-0 | Richards | 4,947 | 1 | 2 | 3 | 4 | 5 | 6 | 7 | | 9 | 10 | 11 | | | 8 | | | | | | | | | |
| | 14 | (a) Sheffield W | W 2-1 | Richards 2 | 3,503 | 1 | 2 | 3 | 4 | 5 | | 7 | | 9 | 10 | 11 | 6 | | 8 | | | | | | | | | |
| Mar | 4 | (h) Stoke C | L 0-1 | | 1,714 | 1 | 2 | 3 | 4 | 5 | | 7 | | 9 | 10 | 11 | 6 | | 8 | | | | | | | | | |
| | 9 | (a) Notts C | D 0-0 | | 2,488 | 1 | 2 | 3 | 4 | 5 | | 7 | | | 10 | | | | 11 | | | 8 | | 6 | | 9 | | |
| | 18 | (h) Burnley | L 0-1 | | 2,330 | 1 | 2 | 3 | 4 | 5 | | 7 | | 9 | 10 | 11 | 6 | | 8 | | | | | | | | | |
| | 25 | (a) Sheffield U | L 0-5 | | 3,996 | 1 | 2 | 3 | 4 | 5 | | 7 | | | | | | | 8 | | | 11 | 6 | | | 9 | 10 | |
| Apr | 1 | (h) Newcastle U | W 2-0 | Smith, Bassett | 2,304 | 1 | 2 | | 8 | 5 | | | | | 11 | 4 | | | 6 | | | 3 | | 9 | | | 10 | |
| | 8 | (a) Preston NE | L 0-4 | | 2,976 | 1 | 2 | | 8 | 5 | 6 | 7 | | | 10 | 11 | | | | | | 4 | | 9 | | | 3 | |
| | 22 | (a) Nottingham F | L 0-3 | | 3,015 | 1 | 2 | | 8 | 5 | | 7 | | | 10 | 11 | 4 | | | | | 6 | | | | | 3 | 9 |
| | 24 | (a) Aston Villa | L 1-7 | Perry | 10,000 | 1 | 2 | | 9 | 5 | | 7 | | | 10 | | 4 | | | | | 8 | 11 | 6 | | | 3 | |
| | | App | | | | 33 | 34 | 25 | 34 | 33 | 17 | 32 | 12 | 12 | 31 | 20 | 21 | 3 | 21 | 1 | 1 | 9 | 13 | 9 | 2 | 5 | 3 | 2 |
| | | Goals | | | | | | 1 | 2 | | | 3 | 3 | 3 | 10 | 5 | 1 | | 6 | | | | 6 | | | | 1 | |

# 1899-1900

## Division 1

| Date | | Opponent | Result | Scorers | Att. | Reader J | Cave G | Williams W | Dunn A | Jones A | Banks J | Paddock J | Perry T | Simmons C | Richards W | Garfield B | Adams A | Hadley H | Walker W | Gollings P | Roberts R | Brett S | Chadburn J | Smith A |
|---|---|---|---|---|---|---|---|---|---|---|---|---|---|---|---|---|---|---|---|---|---|---|---|---|
| Sep | 2 | (h) Newcastle U | D 1-1 | Simmons | 6,135 | 1 | 2 | 3 | 4 | 5 | 6 | 7 | 8 | 9 | 10 | 11 | | | | | | | | |
| | 9 | (a) Aston Villa | W 2-0 | Garfield, Simmons | 17,482 | 1 | 2 | 3 | 4 | 5 | 6 | 7 | 8 | 9 | 10 | 11 | | | | | | | | |
| | 16 | (h) Liverpool | W 2-0 | Garfield 2 | 6,431 | 1 | 2 | 3 | 4 | 5 | 6 | 7 | 8 | 9 | 10 | 11 | | | | | | | | |
| | 23 | (a) Burnley | L 0-2 | | 10,027 | 1 | 2 | 3 | 4 | 5 | 6 | 7 | 8 | 9 | 10 | 11 | | | | | | | | |
| | 30 | (h) Preston NE | W 1-0 | Simmons | 4,684 | 1 | | 3 | 4 | 5 | | 7 | 8 | 9 | 10 | 11 | 2 | 6 | | | | | | |
| Oct | 7 | (a) Nottingham F | L 1-6 | Perry | 17,106 | 1 | | 3 | 4 | 5 | | 7 | 8 | 9 | | | 2 | 6 | 10 | | | | | |
| | 14 | (h) Glossop | D 3-3 | Williams, Richards 2 | 5,629 | 1 | | 3 | 4 | 5 | | 7 | 8 | 9 | 10 | 11 | 2 | 6 | | | | | | |
| | 21 | (a) Stoke C | L 0-1 | | 3,603 | 1 | | 3 | | 5 | | 7 | 9 | 8 | 11 | | 2 | 6 | 10 | 4 | | | | |
| | 28 | (h) Sunderland | W 1-0 | Garfield | 6,117 | 1 | | 3 | 4 | 5 | 6 | 7 | 8 | 9 | | 11 | 2 | | 10 | | | | | |
| Nov | 4 | (a) Wolves | L 0-2 | | 10,089 | 1 | | 3 | 4 | 5 | 6 | 7 | 8 | 9 | | 11 | 2 | | 10 | | | | | |
| | 6 | (h) Sheffield U | L 1-2 | Perry | 14,905 | 1 | | 3 | 4 | 5 | 6 | 7 | 8 | 9 | | 11 | 2 | | 10 | | | | | |
| | 11 | (a) Everton | W 3-1 | Paddock, Richards 2 | 8,996 | 1 | | 5 | 3 | 6 | 7 | 4 | 8 | 9 | | 11 | 2 | | 10 | | | | | |
| | 25 | (a) Derby C | L 1-4 | Richards | 6,520 | 1 | | 3 | 6 | 5 | 7 | 4 | 8 | 9 | | 11 | 2 | | 10 | | | | | |
| Dec | 2 | (h) Bury | L 0-1 | | 3,729 | 1 | | 3 | | 5 | 2 | 6 | 4 | 8 | 9 | 11 | | | 10 | 7 | | | | |
| | 9 | (h) Notts C | W 2-1 | Garfield 2 | 4,186 | 1 | | 3 | 4 | 5 | 6 | 7 | 8 | 9 | | 11 | 2 | | 10 | | | | | |
| | 16 | (h) Manchester C | D 0-0 | | 2,429 | 1 | | 3 | 6 | 5 | | 7 | 4 | 8 | 9 | 11 | 2 | | 10 | | | | | |
| | 23 | (a) Sheffield U | D 1-1 | Garfield | 3,492 | 1 | | 3 | 4 | 5 | 6 | 7 | 8 | 9 | 10 | 11 | 2 | | | | | | | |
| | 26 | (h) Everton | D 0-0 | | 8,509 | 1 | | 3 | | 5 | | | 7 | 8 | 9 | | 2 | 4 | 10 | 6 | | | | |
| | 30 | (a) Newcastle U | L 2-4 | Simmons 2 | 10,887 | 1 | | 3 | | 5 | | | 7 | 8 | 9 | 10 | 2 | 4 | | | 6 | 11 | | |
| Jan | 6 | (h) Aston Villa | L 0-2 | | 6,575 | 1 | | 3 | | 5 | 6 | 7 | 8 | 9 | 10 | | 2 | 4 | | | | 11 | | |
| | 13 | (a) Liverpool | L 0-2 | | 12,531 | 1 | | 3 | | 5 | 6 | 7 | | 9 | 10 | | 2 | 4 | 8 | | | 11 | | |
| | 20 | (h) Burnley | W 2-0 | Hadley, Brett | 3,427 | 1 | | 3 | 4 | 5 | | | | 9 | 10 | | 2 | 6 | | | 11 | 8 | 7 | |
| Feb | 3 | (a) Preston NE | L 2-5 | Jones, Simmons | 4,612 | 1 | | 3 | 4 | 5 | | | 8 | 9 | 10 | | 2 | 6 | | | 11 | | 7 | |
| Mar | 3 | (a) Sunderland | L 1-3 | Perry | 10,490 | 1 | | 3 | 4 | 5 | | | 8 | 9 | 10 | | 2 | 6 | | | 11 | | 7 | |
| | 10 | (h) Wolves | W 3-2 | Simmons 2, Richards | 6,680 | 1 | | 3 | 4 | 5 | | | 8 | 9 | 10 | | 2 | 6 | | | 11 | | 7 | |
| | 19 | (h) Stoke C | W 4-0 | Jones, Brett, Chadburn, Simmons | 1,717 | 1 | | 3 | | 5 | | | 4 | 9 | 10 | | 2 | 6 | | | 11 | 8 | 7 | |
| | 24 | (a) Blackburn R | L 0-2 | | 5,026 | 1 | | 3 | | 5 | | | 4 | 9 | 10 | | 2 | 6 | | | 11 | 8 | 7 | |
| | 31 | (h) Derby C | D 0-0 | | 4,603 | 1 | | 3 | 8 | 5 | | | 4 | 9 | 10 | | 2 | 6 | | | 11 | | 7 | |
| Apr | 2 | (h) Blackburn R | W 1-0 | Roberts | 3,342 | 1 | | 3 | | 5 | | | 4 | 9 | 10 | | 2 | 6 | | 8 | 11 | | 7 | |
| | 7 | (a) Bury | L 0-1 | | 2,978 | 1 | | 3 | 4 | 5 | | | | 9 | 10 | | 2 | 6 | | 8 | 11 | | 7 | |
| | 14 | (h) Notts C | D 0-0 | | 3,254 | 1 | | 3 | 4 | 5 | | | | 9 | 8 | | 2 | 6 | 10 | | 11 | | 7 | |
| | 16 | (h) Nottingham F | W 8-0 | Walker 3, Roberts 2, Simmons 2, Chadburn | 5,187 | 1 | | 3 | 4 | 5 | | | | 9 | | | 2 | 6 | 10 | | 11 | | 7 | 8 |
| | 21 | (a) Manchester C | L 0-4 | | 9,960 | 1 | | 3 | 4 | 5 | | | | 9 | | | 2 | 6 | 10 | | 11 | | 7 | 8 |
| | 24 | (a) Glossop | D 1-1 | Simmons | 2,025 | 1 | | 3 | 4 | 5 | | | | 9 | | | 2 | 6 | 10 | | 11 | | 7 | 8 |
| | | App | | | | 34 | 4 | 33 | 30 | 30 | 13 | 20 | 27 | 33 | 25 | 18 | 29 | 21 | 18 | 3 | 16 | 6 | 11 | 3 |
| | | Goals | | | | | | 1 | | 2 | | 1 | 3 | 12 | 6 | 7 | | 1 | 3 | | 3 | 2 | 2 | |

# 1900-01

## Division 1

| Date | | Opponent | Result | Scorers | Att | Reader J | Adams A | Williams W | Dunn A | Jones A | Hadley H | Chadburn J | Pickering T | Simmons C | Wheldon F | Roberts R | Gollings P | Walker W | Garfield B | Richards W | Banks J | Knowles J | Perry T | Smith A | Stevenson J | Williams G | Lowe J | Cave G | Buck F |
|---|---|---|---|---|---|---|---|---|---|---|---|---|---|---|---|---|---|---|---|---|---|---|---|---|---|---|---|---|---|
| Sep 1 | (a) | Wolves | D 0-0 | | 12,000 | 1 | 2 | 3 | 4 | 5 | 6 | 7 | 8 | 9 | 10 | 11 | | | | | | | | | | | | | |
| 3 | (h) | Derby C | D 1-1 | Simmons | 20,104 | 1 | 2 | 3 | 4 | 5 | 6 | 7 | 8 | 9 | 10 | 11 | | | | | | | | | | | | | |
| 8 | (h) | Aston Villa | L 0-1 | | 35,417 | 1 | 2 | 3 | 4 | 5 | 6 | 7 | 8 | 9 | 10 | 11 | | | | | | | | | | | | | |
| 15 | (a) | Liverpool | L 0-5 | | 15,000 | 1 | 2 | 3 | 4 | 5 | 6 | 7 | 8 | 9 | 10 | 11 | | | | | | | | | | | | | |
| 22 | (h) | Newcastle U | L 0-1 | | 11,859 | 1 | 2 | 3 | 4 | 5 | 6 | 7 | 8 | 9 | 10 | 11 | | | | | | | | | | | | | |
| 29 | (a) | Sheffield U | D 1-1 | Simmons | 10,000 | 1 | 2 | | 3 | 5 | 6 | 7 | | 9 | 10 | | 4 | 8 | 11 | | | | | | | | | | |
| Oct 6 | (h) | Manchester C | W 3-2 | Jones, Richards, Garfield | 11,183 | 1 | 2 | | 3 | 5 | 6 | 7 | | | 10 | | 4 | 8 | 11 | 9 | | | | | | | | | |
| 13 | (a) | Bury | L 1-6 | Simmons | 7,000 | 1 | 2 | | 3 | 5 | 6 | 7 | | 9 | 10 | | | 8 | 11 | | 4 | | | | | | | | |
| 20 | (h) | Nottingham F | L 1-6 | Adams | 9,535 | 1 | 2 | 3 | 4 | 5 | 6 | 7 | | 9 | | | | 8 | 11 | | | 10 | | | | | | | |
| 27 | (a) | Blackburn R | D 1-1 | Smith | 9,000 | 1 | 2 | 3 | | 5 | 6 | 7 | | | 10 | | | 8 | 11 | | | | 4 | 9 | | | | | |
| Nov 3 | (h) | Stoke C | D 2-2 | Dunn, Garfield | 11,052 | 1 | 2 | 3 | 5 | | 6 | 7 | | | 10 | | | 8 | 11 | | | | 4 | 9 | | | | | |
| 5 | (h) | Notts C | W 1-0 | Chadburn | 10,492 | 1 | 2 | | 3 | | 6 | 7 | | 8 | 10 | | | | 11 | | | | 4 | 9 | 5 | | | | |
| 10 | (h) | Sheffield W | D 1-1 | Stevenson | 10,338 | 1 | 2 | | 3 | | 6 | | | 8 | 10 | 7 | | | 11 | | | | 4 | 9 | 5 | | | | |
| 17 | (a) | Everton | L 0-1 | | 20,000 | 1 | 2 | | 3 | | 6 | 7 | | 8 | 10 | 11 | | | | | | | 4 | 9 | 5 | | | | |
| 24 | (h) | Sunderland | W 1-0 | Stevenson | 10,045 | 1 | 2 | | 3 | 5 | 6 | 7 | | 8 | 10 | 11 | | | | | | | | 9 | 4 | | | | |
| Dec 1 | (a) | Derby C | L 0-4 | | 11,700 | | 2 | | 3 | | 6 | 7 | | 8 | 10 | 11 | | | | | | | 4 | 9 | 5 | | 1 | | |
| 8 | (h) | Bolton W | W 7-2 | Banks, Roberts 3, Wheldon, Garfield, Buck | 8,157 | 1 | 2 | | | | 6 | | | | 10 | 7 | | | 11 | | 4 | | | 9 | 5 | | | 3 | 8 |
| 15 | (a) | Notts C | L 0-1 | | 6,500 | 1 | | 3 | | | 6 | | | | 10 | 7 | | | 11 | | 4 | | | 9 | 5 | | | 2 | 8 |
| 22 | (h) | Preston NE | L 0-1 | | 7,997 | 1 | 2 | 3 | | | 6 | | | 8 | 10 | 7 | | | 11 | | | | 4 | 9 | 5 | | | | |
| 29 | (h) | Wolves | L 1-2 | Simmons | 18,188 | 1 | 2 | 3 | | | 6 | | | 8 | 10 | 7 | | | 11 | | | | 4 | 9 | 5 | | | | |
| Jan 5 | (a) | Aston Villa | W 1-0 | Simmons | 30,000 | 1 | 2 | | 3 | | 6 | | | 8 | 10 | 7 | | | 11 | | | | 4 | | 5 | 9 | | | |
| 19 | (a) | Newcastle U | D 1-1 | Garfield | 10,500 | 1 | 2 | | 3 | | 6 | | | 8 | 10 | 7 | | | 11 | | | | 4 | | 5 | 9 | | | |
| Feb 16 | (h) | Bury | L 1-2 | Wheldon | 9,691 | 1 | 2 | | 3 | | 6 | | | 8 | 10 | 7 | | | 11 | | | | 4 | | 5 | 9 | | | |
| Mar 2 | (h) | Blackburn R | D 1-1 | Wheldon | 11,876 | 1 | 2 | | 3 | | 6 | | | 8 | 10 | 7 | | | 11 | | | | 4 | | 5 | 9 | | | |
| 9 | (a) | Stoke C | L 0-2 | | 12,000 | 1 | 2 | | 3 | 5 | 6 | | | 8 | 10 | 7 | | | 11 | | | | 4 | | | 9 | | | |
| 13 | (a) | Nottingham F | W 3-2 | Walker, Stevenson, Roberts | 3,500 | 1 | 2 | | 3 | 5 | 6 | | | | | 7 | | 8 | 11 | | | | 4 | | 10 | 9 | | | |
| 16 | (a) | Sheffield W | L 1-2 | Roberts | 9,000 | 1 | 2 | | 3 | 5 | 6 | | | | | 7 | | 8 | 11 | | | | 4 | | 10 | 9 | | | |
| 30 | (a) | Sunderland | L 0-3 | | 10,500 | 1 | 2 | | 3 | 5 | 6 | | | | | 7 | | 8 | 11 | | | | 4 | | 10 | 9 | | | |
| Apr 6 | (a) | Manchester C | L 0-1 | | 11,400 | 1 | 2 | | 3 | 5 | 6 | | | | | 7 | | 8 | 11 | | | | 4 | | | 9 | | | |
| 13 | (h) | Bolton W | L 2-3 | Adams (pen), Smith | 6,000 | 1 | 2 | | 3 | | 6 | | | 8 | 10 | 7 | | | 11 | | | | 4 | 9 | 5 | | | | |
| 15 | (a) | Preston NE | W 3-2 | Walker, Pickering, Perry | 7,500 | 1 | 2 | | 3 | 5 | 6 | | 8 | | | 7 | | 10 | 11 | | | | 4 | | | 9 | | | |
| 22 | (h) | Everton | L 1-2 | Pickering | 6,992 | 1 | 2 | | 3 | 5 | 6 | | 8 | | | 7 | | 10 | 11 | | | | 4 | | | 9 | | | |
| 29 | (h) | Liverpool | L 0-1 | | 8,974 | 1 | 2 | | 3 | 5 | 6 | | | 8 | 10 | 7 | | | 11 | | | | 4 | | | 9 | | | |
| 30 | (h) | Sheffield U | L 0-2 | | 1,050 | 1 | 2 | | 3 | 5 | 6 | | | 8 | 10 | 7 | | | 11 | | | | 4 | | | 9 | | | |
| **App** | | | | | | 33 | 34 | 8 | 20 | 20 | 34 | 24 | 10 | 20 | 26 | 27 | 2 | 14 | 18 | 1 | 8 | 1 | 17 | 8 | 24 | 15 | 1 | 2 | 7 |
| **Goals** | | | | | | | 2 | | 1 | 1 | | 1 | 2 | 5 | 3 | 5 | | 2 | 4 | 1 | 1 | | 1 | 2 | 3 | | | | 1 |

# 1901-02

## Division 2

| Date | | Opponent | Result | Scorers | Att | Webb I | Adams A | Kifford J | Nurse D | Stevenson J | Hadley H | McLean J | Buck F | Appleby B | Worton T | Walker W | Simmons C | Smith A | Garfield B | Taylor O | Lee W | Williams G | Randle A | Harper A | Chadburn J | Dorsett G | Smith E | Poynton W |
|---|---|---|---|---|---|---|---|---|---|---|---|---|---|---|---|---|---|---|---|---|---|---|---|---|---|---|---|---|
| Sep 2 | (h) | Glossop | L 0-1 | | 5,064 | 1 | 2 | 3 | 4 | 5 | 6 | 7 | 8 | 9 | 10 | 11 | | | | | | | | | | | | |
| 7 | (h) | Preston NE | W 3-1 | McLean, Garfield, Simmons | 8,132 | 1 | 3 | 2 | 4 | 5 | 6 | 7 | | | 10 | | 8 | 9 | 11 | | | | | | | | | |
| 9 | (h) | Chesterfield | W 4-0 | Simmons 2 (1 pen), Worton, Smith | 10,845 | | 3 | 2 | 4 | 5 | 6 | 7 | | | 10 | | 8 | 9 | 11 | 1 | | | | | | | | |
| 14 | (a) | Burnley | D 0-0 | | 4,992 | 1 | 3 | 2 | 4 | 5 | 6 | 7 | | | 10 | | 8 | 9 | 11 | | | | | | | | | |
| 21 | (h) | Burslem P.Vale | W 3-1 | Worton 2, Smith | 5,096 | 1 | 3 | 2 | 4 | 5 | 6 | 7 | | | 10 | | 8 | 9 | 11 | | | | | | | | | |
| 28 | (a) | Chesterfield | W 3-0 | Hadley, Worton, Thacker (og) | 3,201 | 1 | 3 | 2 | 4 | 5 | 6 | 7 | | | 10 | | 8 | | 11 | | 9 | | | | | | | |
| Oct 5 | (h) | Gainsborough T | W 7-0 | Worton 2, Simmons 2, McLean, Smith, Lee | 5,368 | 1 | 3 | 2 | 4 | 5 | 6 | 7 | | | 10 | | 8 | | 11 | | 9 | | | | | | | |
| 12 | (a) | Middlesbrough | W 2-1 | Lee, Simmons | 15,117 | 1 | 3 | 2 | 4 | 5 | 6 | 7 | | | 10 | | 8 | | 11 | | 9 | | | | | | | |
| 19 | (h) | Bristol C | D 2-2 | Lee, McLean | 7,829 | 1 | 3 | 2 | 4 | 5 | 6 | 7 | | | 10 | | 8 | | 11 | | 9 | | | | | | | |
| 26 | (a) | Blackpool | D 2-2 | Nurse, Simmons | 3,626 | 1 | 3 | 2 | 4 | | | 7 | | | 10 | 6 | 8 | | 11 | | 9 | | | | | | | |
| Nov 9 | (a) | Newton Heath | W 2-1 | Simmons 2 | 13,029 | 1 | 3 | 2 | 4 | 5 | 6 | 7 | | | 10 | | 8 | | 11 | | 9 | | | | | | | |
| 23 | (a) | Doncaster R | L 0-2 | | 8,370 | 1 | 2 | | 4 | 5 | 6 | 7 | | | 10 | | 8 | | | | 9 | | | 11 | 3 | | | |
| Dec 7 | (a) | Burton U | W 3-1 | Worton, Lee, Simmons | 2,955 | 1 | 3 | 2 | 4 | 5 | 6 | 7 | | | 10 | | 8 | | | | 9 | | | 11 | | | | |
| 9 | (h) | Lincoln C | W 4-1 | Simmons 2, Lee, Harper | 6,224 | 1 | 3 | 2 | 4 | 5 | 6 | 7 | | | 10 | | 8 | | | | 9 | | | 11 | | | | |
| 14 | (h) | Middlesbrough | W 2-0 | Simmons, Lee | 6,868 | 1 | 3 | 2 | 4 | 5 | 6 | 7 | | | 10 | | 8 | | | | 9 | | | 11 | | | | |
| 21 | (h) | Barnsley | W 3-1 | Worton 2, Simmons | 5,577 | 1 | 2 | | 4 | 5 | 6 | 7 | | | 10 | | 8 | | | | 9 | | | 11 | 3 | | | |
| 26 | (h) | Stockport C | W 3-0 | Simmons, Lee 2 | 23,697 | 1 | 2 | | 4 | 5 | 6 | 7 | | | 10 | | 8 | | | | 9 | | | 11 | 3 | | | |
| 28 | (a) | Leicester F | W 3-0 | Simmons 2, McLean | 2,034 | 1 | 2 | | 4 | 5 | 6 | 7 | | | 10 | 11 | 8 | | | | 9 | | | | 3 | | | |
| Jan 4 | (a) | Preston NE | W 2-1 | McLean, Lee | 11,397 | 1 | 3 | 2 | 4 | 5 | 6 | 7 | | | 10 | | 8 | | | | 9 | | | 11 | | | | |
| 6 | (h) | Leicester F | W 1-0 | Nurse | 6,483 | 1 | 2 | | 4 | 5 | 6 | 7 | | | 10 | | 8 | | | | 9 | | | | 3 | 11 | | |
| 11 | (h) | Burnley | W 3-0 | Lee 2, Dorsett | 9,149 | 1 | 3 | 2 | 4 | 5 | 6 | 7 | | | 10 | | 8 | | | | 9 | | | | | 11 | | |
| 18 | (a) | Burslem P.Vale | W 3-2 | Simmons, Lee, Worton | 2,861 | 1 | 3 | 2 | 4 | 5 | 6 | 7 | | | 10 | | 8 | | | | 9 | | | | | 11 | | |
| Feb 1 | (a) | Gainsborough T | D 1-1 | Worton | 2,016 | 1 | 3 | 2 | 4 | 5 | 6 | 7 | | | 10 | | 8 | | | | 9 | | | | | 11 | | |
| 15 | (a) | Bristol C | W 2-1 | Worton, Simmons | 14,175 | 1 | 3 | 2 | 4 | 5 | 6 | 7 | | | 10 | | 8 | | | | 9 | | | | | 11 | | |
| 22 | (a) | Blackpool | W 7-2 | Kifford, Worton 2, Stevenson, Simmons 3 | 6,249 | 1 | 3 | 2 | 4 | 5 | 6 | 7 | | | 10 | | 8 | | | | 9 | | | | | 11 | | |
| Mar 1 | (a) | Stockport C | W 2-0 | Lee, Smith | 5,049 | 1 | 3 | 2 | 4 | 5 | 6 | 7 | | | 10 | | | 8 | | | 9 | | | | | 11 | | |
| 8 | (h) | Newton Heath | W 4-0 | Worton 3, McLean | 10,206 | 1 | 3 | 2 | 4 | 5 | 6 | 7 | | | 10 | | 8 | | | | 9 | | | | | 11 | | |
| 15 | (a) | Glossop | W 2-1 | A.Smith, E.Smith | 1,658 | 1 | 3 | 2 | 4 | 5 | 6 | 7 | | | 10 | | | 9 | | | | | | | | 11 | 8 | |
| 22 | (h) | Doncaster R | D 2-2 | Smith, Worton | 6,103 | 1 | 3 | 2 | 4 | 5 | 6 | 7 | | | 10 | | | 8 | | | 9 | | | | | 11 | | |
| 29 | (a) | Lincoln C | L 0-1 | | 4,460 | 1 | 3 | 2 | 4 | 5 | 6 | 7 | | | 10 | | 8 | | | | 9 | | | | | 11 | | |
| 31 | (a) | W Arsenal | L 1-2 | Worton | 15,762 | 1 | 3 | 2 | 4 | 5 | 6 | 7 | | | 10 | | 8 | | | | 9 | | | | | 11 | | |
| Apr 5 | (h) | Burton U | W 2-1 | Poynton, Buck | 1,206 | 1 | 3 | 2 | 4 | 5 | 6 | | 8 | | 10 | | | | | | 9 | | | | | 11 | | 7 |
| 12 | (h) | W Arsenal | W 2-1 | Simmons, Lee | 8,878 | 1 | 3 | 2 | 4 | 5 | 6 | 7 | | | 10 | | 8 | | | | 9 | | | | | 11 | | |
| 19 | (a) | Barnsley | W 2-0 | Poynton, Stevenson | 4,014 | 1 | 3 | 2 | 4 | 5 | 6 | | | | 10 | | 8 | | | | 9 | | | | | 11 | | 7 |
| **App** | | | | | | 33 | 31 | 32 | 34 | 34 | 32 | 32 | 2 | 1 | 34 | 2 | 28 | 13 | 4 | 1 | 28 | 1 | 1 | 7 | 5 | 16 | 1 | 2 |
| **Goals** | | | | | | | | 1 | 2 | 2 | 1 | 6 | 1 | | 19 | 1 | 23 | 6 | 1 | | 14 | | | 1 | | 1 | | 2 |

# 1902-03

## Division 1

| Date | | Opposition | Res | Scorers | Att | Webb I | Kifford J | Adams A | Nurse D | Stevenson J | Hadley H | McLean J | Simmons C | Lee W | Worton T | Dorsett G | Smith A | Buck F | Randle A | Hobson F | Smith E | Harper W | Taylor O | Chadburn J | Cole HJ | Elmore G | Lowe J | Smith W | Brittain J | Farrington S |
|---|---|---|---|---|---|---|---|---|---|---|---|---|---|---|---|---|---|---|---|---|---|---|---|---|---|---|---|---|---|---|
| Sep | 1 | (h) Everton | W 2-1 | McLean, Simmons | 16,051 | 1 | 2 | 3 | 4 | 5 | 6 | 7 | 8 | 9 | 10 | 11 | | | | | | | | | | | | | | |
| | 6 | (a) Notts C | L 1-3 | Kifford (pen) | 12,339 | 1 | 2 | 3 | 4 | 5 | 6 | 7 | 8 | 9 | 10 | 11 | | | | | | | | | | | | | | |
| | 13 | (h) Bolton W | W 2-1 | Simmons, Dorsett | 12,263 | 1 | 2 | 3 | 4 | 5 | 6 | 7 | 8 | | 10 | 11 | | 9 | | | | | | | | | | | | |
| | 20 | (a) Middlesbrough | D 1-1 | Blackett (og) | 20,157 | 1 | 2 | 3 | 4 | 5 | 6 | 7 | 8 | 9 | 10 | 11 | | | | | | | | | | | | | | |
| | 27 | (h) Newcastle U | W 6-1 | Lee, Buck 2, Simmons, Stevenson, McLean | 22,160 | 1 | 2 | 3 | 4 | 5 | 6 | 7 | 8 | 9 | | 11 | | 10 | | | | | | | | | | | | |
| Oct | 4 | (a) Wolves | W 2-1 | Dorsett, Simmons | 14,072 | 1 | 2 | 3 | 4 | 5 | 6 | 7 | 8 | 9 | | 11 | | 10 | | | | | | | | | | | | |
| | 11 | (h) Liverpool | L 1-2 | McLean | 20,210 | 1 | 2 | 3 | | 5 | 6 | 7 | 8 | 9 | | 11 | | 10 | 4 | | | | | | | | | | | |
| | 18 | (a) Sheffield U | W 2-1 | Simmons 2 | 11,863 | 1 | 2 | 3 | 4 | 5 | 6 | 7 | 8 | 9 | 10 | 11 | | | | | | | | | | | | | | |
| | 25 | (h) Grimsby T | W 1-0 | Lee | 18,047 | 1 | 2 | 3 | 4 | 5 | 6 | 7 | 8 | 9 | | 11 | | 10 | | | | | | | | | | | | |
| Nov | 1 | (a) Aston Villa | W 3-0 | Kifford 2 (1 pen), Lee | 35,128 | 1 | 2 | 3 | 4 | 5 | 6 | | 8 | 9 | 10 | 11 | | | 7 | | | | | | | | | | | |
| | 8 | (h) Nottingham F | W 2-0 | Kifford (pen), Dorsett | 12,612 | 1 | 2 | 3 | 4 | 5 | 6 | | 8 | 9 | 10 | 11 | | | 7 | | | | | | | | | | | |
| | 15 | (a) Bury | W 2-1 | Lee, Dorsett | 13,498 | 1 | 2 | 3 | 4 | 5 | 6 | | 8 | 9 | 10 | 11 | | | 7 | | | | | | | | | | | |
| | 22 | (h) Blackburn R | W 5-3 | Lee, Simmons, Kifford (pen), Stevenson, Worton | 12,134 | 1 | 2 | 3 | 4 | 5 | 6 | 7 | 8 | 9 | 10 | | | | 11 | | | | | | | | | | | |
| | 29 | (a) Sunderland | D 0-0 | | 10,457 | 1 | 2 | 3 | 4 | 5 | 6 | 7 | | 9 | 10 | 11 | | | | 8 | | | | | | | | | | |
| Dec | 6 | (h) Stoke C | W 2-1 | McLean, Smith | 11,235 | 1 | 2 | 3 | 4 | 5 | 6 | 7 | | 9 | 10 | | | | | | 8 | 11 | | | | | | | | |
| | 13 | (a) Everton | L 1-3 | Lee | 14,854 | 1 | 2 | 3 | 4 | 5 | 6 | 7 | | 9 | 10 | 11 | | | 8 | | | | | | | | | | | |
| | 20 | (a) Sheffield W | L 2-3 | Simmons, Dorsett | 14,560 | 1 | 2 | 3 | 4 | 5 | 6 | 7 | 8 | 9 | 10 | 11 | | | | | | | | | | | | | | |
| | 27 | (a) Derby C | L 0-1 | | 21,909 | 1 | 2 | 3 | 4 | 5 | 6 | 7 | 8 | 9 | 10 | 11 | | | | | | | | | | | | | | |
| Jan | 1 | (a) Liverpool | W 2-0 | Dorsett, Lee | 35,731 | | 2 | 3 | 4 | 5 | 6 | 7 | 8 | 9 | 10 | 11 | | | | | | | 1 | | | | | | | |
| | 3 | (h) Notts C | W 3-2 | Lee 2, Worton | 16,785 | | | 3 | 4 | 5 | 6 | 7 | 8 | 9 | 10 | 11 | | | | | | | 1 | 2 | | | | | | |
| | 10 | (a) Bolton W | W 1-0 | Lee | 15,442 | 1 | 2 | 3 | 4 | 5 | 6 | 7 | | 9 | 10 | 11 | | | | | | | | | 8 | | | | | |
| | 17 | (h) Middlesbrough | W 1-0 | Worton | 18,033 | 1 | 2 | 3 | 4 | 5 | 6 | 7 | | 9 | 10 | 11 | | | | | | | | | 8 | | | | | |
| | 24 | (a) Newcastle U | L 0-1 | | 20,156 | 1 | 2 | 3 | 4 | 5 | 6 | 7 | | 9 | 10 | 11 | | | | | | | | | 8 | | | | | |
| | 31 | (h) Wolves | D 2-2 | Kifford (pen), Cole | 26,081 | 1 | 2 | 3 | 4 | 5 | 6 | 7 | | 9 | 10 | 11 | | | | | | | | | 8 | | | | | |
| Feb | 14 | (a) Sheffield U | D 3-3 | Stevenson, Dorsett, Elmore | 17,122 | 1 | 2 | 3 | 4 | 5 | | 7 | | 9 | 10 | 11 | | | | | 6 | | | | | 8 | | | | |
| | 28 | (h) Aston Villa | L 1-2 | Buck | 28,536 | 1 | 2 | 3 | 4 | 5 | 6 | 7 | 8 | 9 | | 11 | | 10 | | | | | | | | | | | | |
| Mar | 7 | (a) Nottingham F | L 1-3 | Buck | 7,052 | 1 | 2 | 3 | 4 | 5 | | | 8 | 9 | 10 | 11 | | 7 | 6 | | | | | | | | | | | |
| | 21 | (a) Blackburn R | L 0-1 | | 10,354 | 1 | 2 | 3 | 4 | 5 | 6 | 7 | | 9 | 10 | 11 | | | | | | | | | 8 | | | | | |
| | 28 | (a) Sunderland | L 0-3 | | 10,517 | 1 | 2 | 3 | 4 | 5 | 6 | 7 | | 9 | 10 | 11 | 8 | | | | | | | | | | | | | |
| Apr | 4 | (a) Stoke C | L 0-3 | | 5,540 | | 2 | 3 | 4 | 5 | 6 | | | 9 | 10 | 11 | 8 | | | | | | 1 | | | 7 | | | | |
| | 10 | (a) Grimsby T | L 0-4 | | 10,514 | | 2 | 3 | 4 | 5 | 6 | | 8 | 9 | 10 | 11 | 7 | | | | | | 1 | | | | | | | |
| | 18 | (a) Sheffield W | L 1-3 | Smith | 19,000 | | 2 | | 4 | 5 | 6 | | 8 | 9 | | 11 | | | | | 10 | | | 3 | | | 1 | 7 | | |
| | 20 | (h) Bury | L 1-3 | Kifford (pen) | 5,682 | | 2 | | 4 | 5 | 6 | | 8 | 9 | | 11 | | | | | 10 | | | 3 | | | 1 | 7 | | |
| | 25 | (h) Derby C | W 3-0 | Smith, Simmons, Farrington | 4,148 | | 2 | | | 5 | 6 | | 8 | | | 11 | 4 | | | | 10 | | | | | | 1 | 7 | 3 | 9 |
| | | App | | | | 27 | 33 | 31 | 32 | 34 | 32 | 25 | 23 | 32 | 26 | 32 | 2 | 13 | 4 | 1 | 4 | 1 | 4 | 3 | 4 | 3 | 3 | 3 | 1 | 1 |
| | | Goals | | | | | 7 | | | 3 | | 4 | 9 | 10 | 3 | 7 | | 4 | | | 3 | | | | 1 | 1 | | | | 1 |

# 1903-04

## Division 1

| Date | | Opposition | Res | Scorers | Att | Webb I | Kifford J | Adams A | Nurse D | Stevenson J | Hadley H | Smith W | Simmons C | Lee W | Smith E | Dorsett G | Clements H | Worton T | Pennington J | Hobson F | Cole HJ | Cook F | Fenton F | Brown H | Randle A | Smith A | Corfield S | Owen A | Aston H | Folks W |
|---|---|---|---|---|---|---|---|---|---|---|---|---|---|---|---|---|---|---|---|---|---|---|---|---|---|---|---|---|---|---|
| Sep | 2 | (h) Sheffield W | L 0-1 | | 8,995 | 1 | 2 | 3 | 4 | 5 | 6 | 7 | 8 | 9 | 10 | 11 | | | | | | | | | | | | | | |
| | 5 | (h) Newcastle U | L 1-2 | Nurse | 10,352 | 1 | 2 | 3 | 4 | 5 | 6 | 7 | 8 | 9 | 10 | 11 | | | | | | | | | | | | | | |
| | 12 | (a) Aston Villa | L 1-3 | Simmons | 38,920 | 1 | 2 | 3 | 4 | 5 | 6 | | 8 | 9 | | 11 | 7 | 10 | | | | | | | | | | | | |
| | 19 | (h) Middlesbrough | D 0-0 | | 14,130 | 1 | 2 | 3 | 4 | 5 | 6 | | 8 | 9 | | 11 | 7 | 10 | | | | | | | | | | | | |
| | 26 | (a) Liverpool | W 3-1 | Simmons, Hobson, Dorsett | 15,578 | 1 | | 2 | 4 | 5 | 6 | | 8 | | | 11 | 7 | 10 | 3 | 9 | | | | | | | | | | |
| Oct | 3 | (h) Bury | W 3-2 | Hobson 2, Cole | 14,381 | 1 | | 2 | 4 | 5 | 6 | | 8 | | | 11 | 7 | 10 | 3 | 9 | 8 | | | | | | | | | |
| | 10 | (a) Blackburn R | L 0-2 | | 10,057 | 1 | | 2 | 4 | 5 | 6 | | 8 | | | 11 | 7 | 10 | 3 | 9 | 8 | | | | | | | | | |
| | 17 | (h) Nottingham F | D 1-1 | Stevenson | 14,276 | 1 | | 2 | 4 | 5 | 6 | | 8 | | | 11 | 7 | 10 | 3 | 9 | | | | | | | | | | |
| | 24 | (a) Sheffield W | L 0-1 | | 12,000 | 1 | | 2 | 4 | 5 | 6 | | 8 | | | 11 | 7 | 10 | 3 | 9 | | | | | | | | | | |
| | 31 | (h) Sunderland | D 1-1 | Worton | 10,128 | 1 | | 2 | 4 | 5 | 6 | | 8 | | | 11 | 7 | 10 | 3 | 9 | | | | | | | | | | |
| Nov | 7 | (a) Wolves | L 0-1 | | 12,431 | 1 | | 2 | 4 | 5 | 6 | | 8 | | | 11 | 7 | 10 | 3 | 9 | | | | | | | | | | |
| | 14 | (a) Small Heath | W 1-0 | Nurse | 12,563 | | | 2 | 4 | 5 | 6 | | 8 | | | 11 | | 10 | 3 | 9 | | 1 | 7 | | | | | | | |
| | 21 | (h) Everton | D 0-0 | | 10,190 | | | 2 | 4 | 5 | 6 | | 8 | | | 11 | | 10 | 3 | | | 1 | 7 | 9 | | | | | | |
| | 28 | (a) Stoke C | L 0-5 | | 3,724 | | | 2 | 4 | 5 | 6 | | 8 | | | 11 | | 10 | 3 | | | 1 | | 9 | | | | | | |
| Dec | 12 | (a) Manchester C | L 3-6 | Fenton, Simmons, Dorsett | 14,471 | | | 2 | 4 | 5 | 6 | | 8 | | 10 | | 7 | | 3 | | | 1 | 11 | 9 | | | | | | |
| | 14 | (h) Derby C | D 0-0 | | 13,525 | | | 2 | | 5 | 6 | | 8 | | 10 | | 7 | | 3 | | | 1 | 11 | 9 | 4 | | | | | |
| | 19 | (h) Notts C | D 0-0 | | 8,188 | | | 2 | 4 | 5 | 6 | | 8 | | 10 | | 7 | | 3 | | | 1 | 11 | 9 | | | | | | |
| | 26 | (a) Sheffield U | L 0-4 | | 10,227 | | 2 | | 4 | 5 | 6 | 9 | | | | | 7 | | 3 | | 10 | 1 | 11 | 8 | | | | | | |
| | 28 | (h) Blackburn R | W 2-1 | Brown, Simmons | 19,554 | | 2 | | | 5 | 6 | | 8 | | | 11 | | | 3 | 9 | | 1 | | 10 | 4 | 7 | | | | |
| Jan | 2 | (a) Newcastle U | L 0-1 | | 13,376 | 1 | 2 | | | 5 | 6 | | 8 | | | 11 | | | 3 | 9 | | | | 10 | 4 | 7 | | | | |
| | 9 | (h) Aston Villa | L 1-3 | Simmons | 31,418 | 1 | 2 | | | 5 | 6 | | 8 | | | 11 | | | 3 | 9 | | | | 10 | 4 | 7 | | | | |
| | 16 | (a) Middlesbrough | D 2-2 | Hobson, Dorsett | 18,021 | 1 | 2 | 3 | | | 6 | | 8 | | | 11 | | | | 9 | | | | 10 | 4 | 7 | 5 | | | |
| | 23 | (h) Liverpool | D 2-2 | Randle, Smith | 10,740 | 1 | | 2 | | | 6 | | 8 | 9 | | 11 | | | 3 | | | | | 10 | 4 | 7 | | | | |
| | 30 | (a) Bury | L 1-2 | Adams | 7,193 | 1 | | 2 | | 5 | 6 | | 8 | | | 11 | | | 3 | | 8 | | | 10 | 4 | 7 | | | | |
| Feb | 20 | (a) Notts C | W 3-2 | Brown, Lee, Dorsett | 5,991 | 1 | 2 | 3 | | | 6 | 7 | 8 | 9 | | 11 | | | | | | | | 10 | 4 | | 5 | | | |
| | 27 | (a) Sunderland | D 1-1 | Smith | 5,632 | 1 | 2 | 3 | | | 6 | 7 | 8 | 9 | | 11 | | | | | | | | 10 | 4 | | 5 | | | |
| Mar | 5 | (h) Wolves | L 1-2 | Dorsett | 6,338 | 1 | 2 | 3 | 4 | | 7 | | | 9 | | 11 | | | | | 10 | | 6 | 8 | 5 | | | | | |
| | 12 | (h) Small Heath | L 0-1 | | 22,760 | 1 | 2 | | 4 | | 7 | | 8 | 9 | | 11 | | | 3 | | 10 | | 6 | | | | | | | |
| | 25 | (h) Stoke C | W 3-0 | Simmons, Dorsett, Brown | 8,107 | 1 | 2 | 3 | | 9 | 6 | | 8 | | | 11 | | | | | 10 | | 4 | | | 5 | 7 | | | |
| | 30 | (a) Nottingham F | L 0-2 | | 2,624 | 1 | 2 | 3 | | 9 | 6 | | 8 | 10 | | 11 | | | | | | | 4 | | | 7 | 5 | | | |
| Apr | 2 | (a) Derby C | L 2-4 | Simmons 2 | 18,140 | 1 | 2 | 3 | | 5 | 6 | | 8 | | | 11 | | | | | 10 | | 4 | | | 7 | 9 | | | |
| | 9 | (h) Manchester C | W 2-1 | Aston, Owen | 7,508 | | 2 | 3 | | 5 | 6 | | 8 | | | 11 | | | | | 1 | | 10 | 4 | | 7 | 9 | | | |
| | 18 | (a) Everton | L 0-4 | | 12,025 | | 2 | 3 | | 5 | 6 | | 8 | | | 11 | | | | | 1 | | 10 | 4 | | 7 | 9 | | | |
| | 23 | (h) Sheffield U | D 2-2 | Cole, Dorsett (pen) | 4,467 | | 2 | 3 | | | 6 | | | 11 | | | 8 | | 1 | | 10 | 4 | | 5 | | | 9 | 7 | | |
| | | App | | | | 23 | 19 | 29 | 19 | 28 | 32 | 7 | 28 | 11 | 5 | 34 | 10 | 12 | 20 | 12 | 5 | 11 | 6 | 21 | 17 | 8 | 8 | 4 | 4 | 1 |
| | | Goals | | | | | 1 | 2 | 1 | | | | 8 | 1 | 1 | 7 | | 1 | | 4 | 2 | | 1 | 3 | 1 | 1 | | 1 | 1 | |

# 1904-05
## Division 2

| Date | | Opponent | Result | Scorers | Att |
|---|---|---|---|---|---|
| Sep 3 | (a) | Burnley | W 4-1 | Lewis 3, Dorsett | 5,389 |
| 10 | (h) | Grimsby T | L 0-2 | | 4,123 |
| 17 | (a) | Blackpool | D 0-0 | | 3,852 |
| 24 | (h) | Doncaster R | W 6-1 | Dorsett 3, Lewis, Jack 2 | 5,261 |
| Oct 1 | (a) | Gainsborough T | L 2-4 | Jack, Aston | 4,523 |
| 8 | (h) | Burton U | W 4-0 | Dorsett 3 (1 pen), Bell | 4,873 |
| 15 | (a) | Liverpool | L 2-3 | Jack, Brown | 16,147 |
| 29 | (a) | Brsitol C | L 1-2 | Jack | 10,795 |
| Nov 5 | (h) | Manchester U | L 0-2 | | 5,578 |
| 7 | (h) | Blackpool | W 4-2 | Aston, Pheasant, Manners, Birkett (og) | 4,951 |
| 19 | (h) | Chesterfield T | L 0-2 | | 3,753 |
| 26 | (a) | Bradford C | L 1-3 | Aston | 11,854 |
| Dec 3 | (h) | Lincoln C | W 2-0 | Smith, Davies | 3,124 |
| 15 | (a) | Leicester F | L 1-3 | Aston | 7,890 |
| 17 | (h) | Barnsley | W 4-1 | Aston, Smith, Brown, Pheasant (pen) | 2,675 |
| 24 | (a) | Bolton W | L 1-2 | Bell | 7,341 |
| 26 | (h) | Burslem P.Vale | L 0-1 | | 7,166 |
| 31 | (h) | Burnley | D 1-1 | Aston | 7,374 |
| Jan 7 | (a) | Grimsby T | W 3-1 | Pheasant, Bell, Aston | 6,105 |
| 21 | (a) | Doncaster R | W 1-0 | Bell | 4,761 |
| 28 | (h) | Gainsborough TW | 4-3 | Jack, Bell 2, Aston | 2,072 |
| Feb 11 | (h) | Liverpool | L 0-2 | | 8,788 |
| 18 | (a) | Burslem P.Vale | L 2-3 | Jack 2 | 3,550 |
| 25 | (h) | Bristol C | D 0-0 | | 4,172 |
| Mar 4 | (a) | Manchester U | L 0-2 | | 9,950 |
| 7 | (a) | Glossop | L 1-2 | Jack | 2,765 |
| 11 | (h) | Glossop | W 1-0 | Lewis | 3,547 |
| 18 | (h) | Chesterfield T | L 0-1 | | 3,568 |
| 25 | (h) | Bradford C | L 0-2 | | 2,366 |
| Apr 1 | (a) | Lincoln C | W 2-0 | Jack 2 | 4,138 |
| 8 | (h) | Leicester F | W 2-0 | Pheasant 2 | 3,104 |
| 15 | (a) | Barnsley | D 1-1 | Haycock | 5,661 |
| 21 | (a) | Burton U | W 6-0 | Williams, Jack 2, Lewis, Pheasant, Haycock | 2,820 |
| 22 | (h) | Bolton W | L 0-1 | | 10,105 |

Player appearances and goals:

| Player | App | Goals |
|---|---|---|
| Webb I | 13 | |
| Kifford J | 12 | |
| Adams A | 25 | |
| Randle A | 33 | |
| Manners J | 31 | 1 |
| Hadley H | 4 | |
| Bell L | 16 | 6 |
| Jack W | 25 | 13 |
| Brown H | 14 | 2 |
| Lewis A | 27 | 6 |
| Dorsett G | 13 | 7 |
| Pennington J | 23 | |
| Davies A | 12 | 1 |
| Bowden J | 8 | |
| Aston H | 21 | 8 |
| Miller J | 1 | |
| Edwards S | 1 | |
| Pheasant E | 24 | 6 |
| Davies L | 3 | |
| Smith W | 11 | 2 |
| Cook F | 17 | |
| Dawes J | 1 | |
| Brittain J | 4 | |
| Turner I | 1 | |
| Owen A | 3 | |
| Haycock F | 7 | 2 |
| Bradley C | 3 | |
| Bamford A | 3 | |
| Burton E | 1 | |
| Haywood T | 6 | |
| Williams J | 6 | 1 |
| Stringer J | 4 | |
| Shinton F | 1 | |

# 1905-06
## Division 2

| Date | | Opponent | Result | Scorers | Att |
|---|---|---|---|---|---|
| Sep 2 | (h) | Burnley | L 1-2 | Shinton | 7,223 |
| 9 | (a) | Leeds C | W 2-0 | Haycock 2 | 6,802 |
| 16 | (h) | Burton U | W 3-0 | Simmons, Shinton, Haycock | 6,500 |
| 23 | (a) | Chelsea | L 0-1 | | 10,123 |
| 30 | (h) | Gainsborough TW | 4-0 | Haycock, A.Haywood 2, Shinton | 5,300 |
| Oct 7 | (a) | Bristol C | L 0-1 | | 8,000 |
| 14 | (h) | Manchester U | W 1-0 | Haywood | 7,024 |
| 21 | (a) | Glossop | W 3-1 | Shinton, Haywood 2 | 5,000 |
| 28 | (h) | Stockport C | W 3-1 | Haywood, Pheasant (pen), Shinton | 8,200 |
| Nov 4 | (a) | Blackpool | W 3-0 | Peters, Shinton, Simmons | 5,000 |
| 11 | (h) | Bradford C | W 6-1 | Shinton 3, Haywood, Simmons 2 | 9,000 |
| 25 | (a) | Leicester F | D 0-0 | | 6,500 |
| Dec 2 | (h) | Hull C | D 1-1 | Pheasant (pen) | 11,203 |
| 9 | (a) | Lincoln C | W 2-1 | Pheasant, Haywood | 4,000 |
| 16 | (h) | Chesterfield T | W 3-0 | Haywood, Simmons, Shinton | 12,554 |
| 23 | (a) | Burslem P.Vale W | 1-0 | Simmons | 3,500 |
| 25 | (h) | Clapton O | D 1-1 | Simmons | 18,048 |
| 26 | (h) | Barnsley | W 5-3 | Simmons 3, Shinton 2 | 23,021 |
| 30 | (a) | Burnley | W 2-0 | Simmons, Shinton | 6,500 |
| Jan 5 | (h) | Leeds C | W 2-1 | Haywood, Pheasant (pen) | 2,553 |
| 20 | (a) | Burton U | D 2-2 | Bradley, Shinton | 4,000 |
| 27 | (h) | Chelsea | D 1-1 | Manners | 5,000 |
| Feb 3 | (a) | Grimsby T | L 2-3 | Pheasant, Simmons | 5,100 |
| 10 | (h) | Bristol C | L 1-3 | Pheasant (pen) | 6,400 |
| 17 | (a) | Manchester U | D 0-0 | | 8,000 |
| 24 | (h) | Glossop | W 6-0 | Rankin, Bradley, Simmons 2, Pheasant (pen), Haywood | 7,200 |
| Mar 3 | (a) | Stockport C | D 2-2 | Manners, Perkins | 4,000 |
| 10 | (h) | Blackpool | W 5-0 | Simmons 2, Haywood 2, Bradley | 6,500 |
| 17 | (h) | Bradford C | W 1-0 | Haywood | 5,106 |
| 24 | (h) | Grimsby T | W 2-0 | Rankin, Pheasant | 7,500 |
| 31 | (h) | Leicester F | W 3-0 | Shinton, Haycock 2 | 10,067 |
| Apr 7 | (a) | Hull C | L 0-4 | | 9,033 |
| 13 | (a) | Barnsley | L 0-3 | | 3,120 |
| 14 | (h) | Lincoln C | D 1-1 | Haywood | 6,000 |
| 16 | (a) | Clapton O | W 2-0 | Shinton, Haywood | 3,517 |
| 18 | (a) | Gainsborough T | L 1-2 | Haywood | 4,223 |
| 21 | (h) | Chesterfield T | W 3-0 | Manners, Haywood, Shinton | 5,558 |
| 28 | (h) | Burslem P.Vale W | 4-1 | Pheasant (pen), Shinton, Haywood 2 | 4,800 |

Player appearances and goals:

| Player | App | Goals |
|---|---|---|
| Stringer J | 36 | |
| Young G | 16 | |
| Pennington J | 31 | |
| Randle A | 36 | |
| Pheasant E | 38 | 8 |
| Manners J | 32 | 3 |
| Williams J | 10 | |
| Simmons C | 30 | 16 |
| Shinton F | 31 | 18 |
| Haywood A | 37 | 21 |
| Perkins E | 20 | 1 |
| Haycock F | 8 | 6 |
| Adams A | 16 | |
| Haywood T | 2 | |
| Peters S | 6 | 1 |
| Varney H | 5 | |
| Brittain J | 4 | |
| Nicholls F | 7 | |
| Law W | 10 | |
| Bradley E | 15 | 3 |
| Lewis A | 2 | |
| Rankin B | 15 | 2 |
| Dilly T | 8 | |
| Picken T | 2 | |
| Buck F | 1 | |

# 1906-07

## Division 2

| | Date | | Opponent | Res | Score | Scorers | Att | Stringer J | Betteley R | Pennington J | Randle A | Pheasant E | Manners J | Rankin B | Buck F | Shinton F | Haywood A | Dilly T | Perkins E | Broad T | Simmons C | Timmins S | Haywood T | Legge S | Williams J | Jones H | Bradley E | Jordan W | Bourne R | Parkes H | Adams A |
|---|---|---|---|---|---|---|---|---|---|---|---|---|---|---|---|---|---|---|---|---|---|---|---|---|---|---|---|---|---|
| Sep | 1 | (a) | Burnley | W | 1-0 | Buck | 7,500 | 1 | 2 | 3 | 4 | 5 | 6 | 7 | 8 | 9 | 10 | 11 | | | | | | | | | | | | | |
| | 8 | (h) | Leeds C | W | 5-0 | Shinton 2, Buck 2, Pheasant | 15,500 | 1 | 2 | 3 | 4 | 5 | 6 | 7 | 8 | 9 | 10 | 11 | | | | | | | | | | | | | |
| | 10 | (a) | Burslem P.Vale | L | 1-2 | Shinton | 5,500 | 1 | 2 | 3 | 4 | 5 | 6 | 7 | 8 | 9 | 10 | 11 | | | | | | | | | | | | | |
| | 15 | (a) | Barnsley | W | 1-0 | Shinton | 6,000 | 1 | 2 | 3 | 4 | 5 | 6 | 7 | 8 | 9 | 10 | | 11 | | | | | | | | | | | | |
| | 22 | (h) | Chelsea | L | 1-2 | Haywood | 25,562 | 1 | 2 | 3 | 4 | 5 | 6 | 7 | 8 | 9 | 10 | | 11 | | | | | | | | | | | | |
| | 29 | (a) | Wolves | W | 3-0 | Shinton, Haywood, Buck | 25,000 | 1 | 2 | 3 | 4 | 5 | 6 | | 8 | 9 | 10 | | 11 | 7 | | | | | | | | | | | |
| Oct | 6 | (h) | Clapton O | W | 5-0 | Shinton 4, Buck | 10,482 | 1 | 2 | 3 | 4 | 5 | 6 | | 8 | 9 | | | 11 | 7 | 10 | | | | | | | | | | |
| | 13 | (a) | Gainsborough TW | W | 4-2 | Shinton 3, Buck | 3,500 | 1 | 2 | 3 | 4 | 5 | 6 | | 8 | 9 | 10 | | 11 | 7 | | | | | | | | | | | |
| | 20 | (h) | Stockport C | D | 1-1 | Buck (pen) | 12,300 | 1 | 2 | 3 | 4 | 5 | 6 | | 8 | 9 | 10 | | 11 | 7 | | | | | | | | | | | |
| | 27 | (a) | Hull C | W | 1-0 | Buck | 6,140 | 1 | 2 | 3 | 4 | 5 | 6 | | 8 | 9 | 10 | | 11 | 7 | | | | | | | | | | | |
| Nov | 3 | (h) | Glossop | W | 5-1 | Shinton 4, Buck | 13,000 | 1 | 2 | 3 | 4 | 5 | 6 | | 8 | 9 | 10 | | 11 | 7 | | | | | | | | | | | |
| | 10 | (a) | Blackpool | L | 1-2 | Pheasant | 5,772 | 1 | 2 | 3 | 4 | 5 | | | 8 | 9 | 10 | 11 | | 7 | | 6 | | | | | | | | | |
| | 17 | (h) | Bradford C | W | 3-0 | Buck 3 | 9,000 | 1 | 2 | 3 | 4 | | | | 8 | 9 | 10 | 11 | | 7 | | 6 | | | 5 | | | | | | |
| | 24 | (h) | Chesterfield T | W | 5-2 | Rankin, Dilly 3, Shinton | 11,335 | 1 | 2 | 3 | 4 | | | 7 | 8 | 9 | 10 | 11 | | | | 6 | | | 5 | | | | | | |
| Dec | 1 | (a) | Leicester F | L | 0-3 | | 19,820 | 1 | 2 | 3 | 4 | | | 7 | 8 | 9 | 10 | 11 | | | | 6 | | | 5 | | | | | | |
| | 8 | (h) | Nottingham F | W | 3-1 | Rankin, Shinton, Legge | 17,000 | 1 | 2 | 3 | 4 | 5 | | 7 | 8 | 9 | 10 | | | | | 6 | | 11 | | | | | | | |
| | 15 | (a) | Lincoln C | L | 1-2 | Haywood | 5,240 | 1 | 2 | 3 | 4 | | | 7 | | 9 | 10 | | | | 8 | 6 | | 11 | 5 | | | | | | |
| | 22 | (h) | Burton U | W | 5-1 | Legge, Simmons 2, Shinton 2 | 5,300 | 1 | 2 | 3 | 4 | 5 | | 7 | | 9 | 10 | | | | 8 | 6 | | 11 | | | | | | | |
| | 25 | (h) | Grimsby T | W | 6-1 | Dilly, Haywood, Shinton 4 | 19,047 | 1 | 2 | 3 | 4 | 5 | | 7 | | 9 | 10 | | | | 8 | 6 | | 11 | | | | | | | |
| | 26 | (a) | Burslem P.Vale | W | 3-0 | Rankin, Dilly, Shinton | 17,000 | | 2 | 3 | 4 | 5 | | 7 | | 9 | 10 | | | | 8 | 6 | | 11 | | 1 | | | | | |
| | 29 | (h) | Burnley | W | 3-2 | Dilly (pen), Shinton, Legge | 12,000 | | 2 | 3 | 4 | 5 | | 7 | | 9 | 10 | | | | 8 | 6 | | 11 | | 1 | | | | | |
| Jan | 5 | (a) | Leeds C | L | 2-3 | Shinton 2 | 10,330 | 1 | 2 | 3 | 4 | 5 | | 7 | | 9 | 10 | | | | 8 | 6 | | 11 | | | | | | | |
| | 26 | (a) | Chelsea | L | 0-2 | | 41,168 | 1 | 2 | 3 | 4 | 5 | 6 | 11 | 8 | | 10 | | 7 | | | | | | | | 9 | | | | |
| Feb | 9 | (a) | Clapton O | D | 1-1 | Dilly | 3,700 | 1 | 2 | 3 | 4 | 5 | 6 | | | 9 | 10 | 11 | 7 | 8 | | | | | | | | | | | |
| | 16 | (h) | Gainsborough TW | W | 5-0 | Buck 2, Jordan 3 | 8,112 | 1 | 2 | 3 | 4 | 5 | 6 | | 8 | | 10 | | 7 | | | | | | | | | 9 | 11 | | |
| Mar | 2 | (h) | Hull C | W | 3-0 | Jordan 2, Buck | 10,130 | 1 | 3 | | 4 | 5 | 6 | | 8 | | 10 | 11 | 7 | | | 2 | | | | | | 9 | | | |
| | 16 | (h) | Blackpool | W | 3-0 | Buck 2, Jordan | 5,500 | 1 | | 3 | 4 | | | | 8 | | 10 | 11 | | | 6 | 2 | | | | | 5 | 9 | | 7 | |
| | 29 | (a) | Grimsby T | L | 1-2 | Jordan | 8,202 | 1 | | 3 | 4 | 5 | 6 | | 8 | 9 | | | | | | 2 | | | | | 10 | 11 | 7 | | |
| | 30 | (a) | Chesterfield T | D | 2-2 | Bradley, Buck | 8,000 | 1 | | 3 | 4 | | | | 8 | 9 | 10 | | | | 6 | | | | | | 5 | 11 | 7 | 2 | |
| Apr | 1 | (h) | Wolves | D | 1-1 | Buck | 22,000 | 1 | | 3 | 4 | 5 | 6 | | 8 | | 10 | | | | | | | | | | 9 | 11 | 7 | 2 | |
| | 6 | (h) | Leicester F | L | 0-1 | | 5,034 | 1 | | | 4 | 5 | 6 | | 8 | | 10 | 11 | | | | 3 | | | | | 9 | | 7 | 2 | |
| | 8 | (a) | Stockport C | W | 1-0 | Parkes | 5,623 | 1 | | | 4 | | 6 | | 8 | | 10 | | | | | 3 | | | | | 5 | 9 | 11 | 7 | 2 |
| | 13 | (a) | Nottingham F | L | 1-3 | Bradley | 7,174 | 1 | | 3 | 4 | | 6 | | 8 | 9 | | 11 | | | | 2 | 10 | | | | 5 | 10 | | 7 | |
| | 16 | (a) | Glossop | D | 0-0 | | 3,121 | 1 | | 3 | 4 | | 6 | | 8 | 9 | | 11 | | | | 2 | 10 | | | | 5 | | | 7 | |
| | 20 | (h) | Lincoln C | W | 2-1 | Parkes, Bourne | 6,995 | 1 | | | 4 | | 6 | | 8 | | | | | | 10 | 3 | 5 | | | | 9 | 11 | 7 | 2 | |
| | 23 | (a) | Bradford C | L | 0-4 | | 6,220 | 1 | | 3 | 4 | | 6 | | 8 | 9 | 10 | | | | | 2 | 5 | | | | | 11 | 7 | | |
| | 25 | (h) | Barnsley | W | 3-1 | Parkes, Jordan, Buck | 5,100 | 1 | | 3 | 4 | | 6 | | 8 | 10 | | 11 | | | | 5 | | | | | 9 | | 7 | 2 | |
| | 27 | (a) | Burton U | L | 0-2 | | 3,580 | 1 | | | 4 | | 6 | | 8 | 9 | | 11 | | | | 10 | 3 | | | | | 5 | 7 | 2 | |
| | | | App | | | | | 36 | 26 | 33 | 38 | 25 | 25 | 14 | 32 | 30 | 24 | 21 | 13 | 11 | 6 | 20 | 7 | 7 | 5 | 2 | 7 | 10 | 7 | 12 | 7 |
| | | | Goals | | | | | | | | | 2 | | 3 | 20 | 28 | 4 | 7 | | | 2 | | | 3 | | | 2 | 8 | 1 | 3 | |

**West Brom in 1906-07. Back row (left to right): H.A.Parkes, A.Randle, F.Buck, J.Manners. Middle row: H.Bell (trainer), J.Williams, W.Barber (trainer), J.Stringer, Mr.W.I.Basett (director), J.Pennington, Mr F.Everiss (secretary). Front row: W.C.Jordan, E.Pheasant, Mr H.Keys (chairman), A.Heywood, T.Dilly.**

# 1907-08

## Division 2

| Date | | Opponent | Res | Score | Scorers | Att | Stringer J | Betteley R | Pennington J | Timmins S | Pheasant E | Manners J | Garratt G | Buck F | Jordan W | Walker D | Brooks J | Williams J | Evenson I | Shinton F | Dilly T | Bowser W | Randle A | Haywood A | Adams A | Bradley E | Parkes H | Bourne R | Evans A | Young W | Wright H | Wilcox H | Owers E | Pearson H | Thompson W | Hewitt C |
|---|---|---|---|---|---|---|---|---|---|---|---|---|---|---|---|---|---|---|---|---|---|---|---|---|---|---|---|---|---|---|---|---|---|---|
| Sep 2 | (a) | Wolves | W | 2-1 | Buck (pen), Walker | 24,000 | 1 | 2 | 3 | 4 | 5 | 6 | 7 | 8 | 9 | 10 | 11 | | | | | | | | | | | | | | | | | | | |
| 7 | (h) | Burnley | W | 5-0 | Buck 2, Pheasant, Garratt, Jordan | 16,032 | 1 | | 3 | 4 | 5 | 6 | 7 | 8 | 9 | 10 | 11 | 2 | | | | | | | | | | | | | | | | | | |
| 14 | (a) | Oldham A | L | 1-2 | Garratt | 11,000 | 1 | | 3 | 4 | 5 | | 7 | 8 | 9 | 10 | 11 | 2 | 6 | | | | | | | | | | | | | | | | | |
| 21 | (h) | Clapton O | W | 3-0 | Jordan, Walker, Buck | 12,336 | 1 | | 3 | 4 | 5 | 6 | 7 | 8 | 9 | 10 | 11 | 2 | | | | | | | | | | | | | | | | | | |
| 28 | (a) | Leeds C | L | 0-1 | | 19,058 | 1 | | 3 | 4 | 5 | 6 | 7 | 8 | 9 | 10 | 11 | 2 | | | | | | | | | | | | | | | | | | |
| Oct 5 | (h) | Wolves | W | 1-0 | Brooks | 30,026 | 1 | 2 | 3 | 4 | 5 | 6 | 7 | 8 | | 10 | 11 | | | 9 | | | | | | | | | | | | | | | | |
| 12 | (a) | Gainsborough TW | 2-1 | | Dilly 2 | 4,900 | 1 | 2 | 3 | 4 | 5 | 6 | 7 | 8 | | 10 | 11 | | | | 9 | | | | | | | | | | | | | | | |
| 19 | (h) | Stockport C | W | 2-0 | Walker 2 | 14,000 | 1 | 2 | 3 | 4 | 5 | 6 | 7 | 8 | | 9 | 11 | | | 10 | | | | | | | | | | | | | | | | |
| 26 | (a) | Glossop | L | 1-2 | Buck (pen) | 1,828 | 1 | | 3 | 2 | 5 | 6 | 7 | 8 | | 9 | 11 | | | | | | 4 | 10 | | | | | | | | | | | | |
| Nov 2 | (h) | Leicester F | D | 1-1 | Bradley | 17,000 | 1 | | 3 | 4 | 5 | 6 | 7 | 8 | | 10 | 11 | | | | | | 2 | | | 9 | | | | | | | | | | |
| 4 | (h) | Oldham A | L | 1-2 | Walker | 10,500 | 1 | | 3 | 4 | 5 | 6 | | 8 | | 10 | | | | | | | 2 | | 9 | 7 | 11 | | | | | | | | | |
| 9 | (a) | Blackpool | W | 1-0 | Buck (pen) | 9,145 | 1 | | 2 | 6 | 5 | | | 8 | | 10 | 11 | | | | | | | | 9 | | 7 | | 3 | 4 | | | | | | |
| 16 | (h) | Stoke C | W | 1-0 | Young | 10,000 | 1 | | 2 | 6 | 5 | | 7 | 8 | | 10 | 11 | | | | | | | | | | | | 3 | 4 | 9 | | | | | |
| 23 | (a) | Grimsby T | D | 2-2 | Walker, Buck | 4,552 | 1 | | 2 | 6 | 9 | | 7 | 8 | | 10 | 11 | | 5 | | | | | | | | | | 3 | 4 | | | | | | |
| 30 | (a) | Bradford C | D | 0-0 | | 18,025 | 1 | | 2 | 9 | 5 | | 7 | 8 | | 10 | 11 | | 6 | | | | | | | | | | 3 | 4 | | | | | | |
| Dec 7 | (h) | Hull C | W | 1-0 | Buck | 15,500 | 1 | | 2 | 4 | 5 | | 7 | 8 | | 10 | 11 | | 6 | | | | | | | | | | 3 | | | 9 | | | | |
| 14 | (a) | Derby C | L | 0-2 | | 8,000 | 1 | 2 | 3 | 6 | 5 | | 7 | 8 | | 10 | 11 | | | | | | | | | | | | | 4 | | 9 | | | | |
| 21 | (h) | Lincoln C | W | 5-2 | Buck (pen), Walker 2 (1 pen), Jordan, Wilcox | 7,000 | 1 | 2 | 3 | 6 | | | 7 | | 10 | 9 | 11 | | 5 | | | | | | | | | | | 4 | | 8 | | | | |
| 25 | (h) | Chesterfield T | W | 4-0 | Walker 2, Buck, Wilcox | 12,478 | 1 | 2 | 3 | 6 | 5 | | 7 | 8 | | 10 | 11 | | | | | | | | 4 | | | | | | | 9 | | | | |
| 26 | (a) | Barnsley | W | 3-1 | Buck 3 (1 pen) | 5,520 | 1 | | 2 | 6 | 5 | | 7 | 8 | | 10 | 11 | | | | | | | | 4 | | | | 3 | | | 9 | | | | |
| 28 | (h) | Fulham | D | 1-1 | Wilcox | 20,063 | 1 | 2 | 3 | 6 | 5 | | 7 | 8 | | 10 | 11 | | | | | | | | | | | | | 4 | | 9 | | | | |
| Jan 4 | (a) | Burnley | D | 1-1 | Walker | 10,146 | 1 | 2 | | | 5 | 6 | 7 | 8 | | 10 | 11 | | | | | | | | | | | | 3 | 4 | | 9 | | | | |
| 18 | (a) | Clapton O | D | 2-2 | Buck, Evenson | 15,252 | | 2 | | | 5 | 6 | | 11 | 9 | 10 | | | 8 | | | | | | | 7 | | | 3 | 4 | | | | 1 | | |
| 25 | (h) | Leeds C | W | 1-0 | Young | 8,000 | | 2 | 3 | | | 6 | | 8 | | 10 | | | 5 | | | | | | | | 7 | 11 | | 4 | 9 | | | 1 | | |
| Feb 8 | (h) | Gainsborough T | L | 0-1 | | 7,500 | 1 | | 2 | | 5 | 6 | | | | 10 | | | | | | | | | | | 7 | | 3 | 4 | | 8 | | 9 | | |
| 15 | (a) | Stockport C | W | 2-1 | Walker, Garratt | 4,000 | | 2 | | | 5 | 6 | 7 | 8 | | 10 | 11 | | | | | | | | | | | | 3 | 4 | | 9 | 1 | | | |
| 22 | (h) | Glossop | D | 1-1 | Parkes | 4,140 | | | 3 | | 5 | 6 | 7 | 8 | | 10 | | | 2 | | | | | | | | 11 | | | 4 | | 9 | 1 | | | |
| 29 | (a) | Leicester F | L | 0-3 | | 6,337 | 1 | | 3 | | 5 | 6 | 7 | 8 | | 10 | 11 | 2 | | | | | | | | | | | | 4 | | 9 | | | | |
| Mar 7 | (h) | Blackpool | W | 3-0 | Walker 2, Timmins | 7,000 | | | 2 | 8 | 5 | 6 | | | | 10 | 11 | | | | | | | | | | 7 | | 3 | 4 | | | | 9 | 1 | |
| 17 | (a) | Stoke C | D | 1-1 | Jordan | 3,224 | | | 2 | 8 | 5 | 6 | | | 9 | | 11 | | | | | | | | | | 7 | | 3 | 4 | 10 | | | 1 | | |
| 21 | (h) | Grimsby T | L | 1-2 | Pheasant | 5,400 | | | 2 | 8 | 5 | 6 | | | 9 | 10 | 11 | | | | | | | | | | 7 | | 3 | 4 | | | | 1 | | |
| 28 | (h) | Bradford C | W | 3-2 | Wilcox, Buck, Walker | 7,000 | 1 | | 2 | | 5 | 6 | 7 | | 11 | 9 | 10 | 4 | | | | | | | | | | | 3 | | | 8 | | | | |
| Apr 4 | (a) | Hull C | L | 2-4 | Pheasant, Timmins | 6,080 | | | 2 | 9 | 5 | 6 | 7 | | | 10 | 11 | | | | | | | | | | | | 3 | 4 | | 8 | | 1 | | |
| 11 | (h) | Derby C | W | 1-0 | Wilcox | 10,000 | | | 2 | 4 | 5 | 6 | 7 | | 9 | 10 | 11 | | | | | | | | | | | | 3 | | | 8 | | 1 | | |
| 17 | (a) | Chesterfield T | L | 0-1 | | 5,539 | | | 2 | 4 | 5 | 6 | 7 | | 9 | 10 | 11 | | | | | | | | | | | | 3 | | | 8 | 9 | 1 | | |
| 18 | (a) | Lincoln C | W | 2-0 | Buck 2 | 6,850 | 1 | | 2 | 4 | 5 | 6 | 7 | | 9 | 10 | 11 | | | | | | | | | | | | 3 | | | 8 | | | | |
| 20 | (h) | Barnsley | D | 1-1 | Buck (pen) | 10,000 | 1 | | 2 | 4 | | | 6 | 7 | 9 | 10 | 11 | | | | | | | | | | 5 | | 3 | | | 8 | | | | |
| 25 | (h) | Fulham | W | 3-1 | Jordan, Wright, Thompson | 6,990 | 1 | | 3 | 4 | 5 | 6 | | | 9 | | 11 | 2 | | | | | | | | | | | 7 | | | | | 8 | 10 | |
| **App** | | | | | | | 28 | 12 | 35 | 30 | 35 | 27 | 29 | 38 | 14 | 36 | 21 | 10 | 8 | 2 | 1 | 1 | 3 | 1 | 2 | 3 | 7 | 2 | 19 | 18 | 3 | 17 | 4 | 10 | 1 | 1 |
| **Goals** | | | | | | | | | | 2 | 3 | | 3 | 18 | 5 | 15 | 1 | | 1 | | 2 | | | | | | 1 | 1 | | 2 | 1 | 5 | | | 1 | |

**Isaac Evenson**

**Albert Evans**

# 1908-09

### Division 2

| Date | | Opponent | Result | Scorers | Att. | Pearson H | Pennington J | Evans A | Baddeley G | Pheasant E | Timmins S | Davies W | Thompson W | Jordan W | Legge S | Buck F | Manners J | Hewitt C | Stringer J | Brown F | Fielding R | Wright H | Betteley R | Dorsett J | Garraty W | Bowser S | Harris G | Pailor R | Hancock H | Burton H | Simpson G |
|---|---|---|---|---|---|---|---|---|---|---|---|---|---|---|---|---|---|---|---|---|---|---|---|---|---|---|---|---|---|---|---|
| Sep 5 | (a) | Grimsby T | D 1-1 | Buck (pen) | 6,000 | 1 | 2 | 3 | 4 | 5 | 6 | 7 | 8 | 9 | 10 | 11 | | | | | | | | | | | | | | | |
| 7 | (h) | Wolves | L 0-2 | | 28,600 | 1 | 2 | 3 | | 5 | 4 | 7 | 8 | 9 | 10 | 11 | 6 | | | | | | | | | | | | | | |
| 12 | (h) | Fulham | D 1-1 | Skene (og) | 14,529 | | 2 | 3 | | 5 | 4 | 7 | 8 | | | 11 | 6 | 10 | 1 | 9 | | | | | | | | | | | |
| 15 | (a) | Bolton W | D 1-1 | Buck (pen) | 5,500 | | 2 | 3 | 4 | 5 | 6 | 11 | 7 | | | 10 | | 8 | 1 | 9 | | | | | | | | | | | |
| 19 | (a) | Burnley | W 2-0 | Buck, Hewitt | 11,340 | | 2 | 3 | 4 | 5 | 6 | 11 | | | | 10 | | 8 | 1 | 9 | 7 | | | | | | | | | | |
| 26 | (h) | Bradford | W 1-0 | Hewitt | 21,496 | | 2 | 3 | 4 | 5 | 6 | 11 | | | | 10 | | 8 | 1 | 9 | 7 | | | | | | | | | | |
| Oct 3 | (a) | Wolves | W 1-0 | Davies | 20,000 | | 2 | 3 | 4 | 5 | | 11 | | | | 10 | 6 | 8 | 1 | 9 | | | 7 | | | | | | | | |
| 10 | (h) | Oldham A | W 1-0 | Hewitt | 18,190 | | 2 | 3 | 4 | 5 | | 11 | 7 | | | 10 | 6 | 8 | 1 | 9 | | | | | | | | | | | |
| 17 | (a) | Clapton O | L 0-1 | | 10,500 | | 2 | 3 | | 5 | 4 | 11 | 7 | | | 10 | 6 | 8 | 1 | 9 | | | | | | | | | | | |
| 24 | (h) | Leeds C | W 2-1 | Thompson, Buck | 13,554 | | | 3 | 4 | 5 | | | 9 | | | 10 | 6 | 8 | 1 | | | 7 | 2 | 11 | | | | | | | |
| 31 | (a) | Barnsley | W 2-0 | Hewitt, Dorsett | 7,000 | | 2 | 3 | 4 | | 5 | 7 | | | | 10 | 6 | 8 | 1 | | | | | 11 | 9 | | | | | | |
| Nov 2 | (h) | Chesterfield T | D 2-2 | Garraty, Buck (pen) | 9,540 | | 2 | 3 | 4 | | 5 | 7 | | | | 10 | 6 | 8 | 1 | | | | | 11 | 9 | | | | | | |
| 7 | (h) | Tottenham H | W 3-0 | Hewitt 2, Garraty | 27,224 | | 2 | 3 | 4 | | 5 | 7 | | | | 10 | 6 | 8 | 1 | | | | | 11 | 9 | | | | | | |
| 14 | (a) | Hull C | D 2-2 | Garraty 2 | 10,000 | | 2 | 3 | 4 | | 5 | 7 | | | | 10 | 6 | 8 | 1 | | | | | 11 | 9 | | | | | | |
| 21 | (h) | Derby C | W 2-0 | Buck, Thompson | 13,241 | | 2 | 3 | 4 | | 5 | 11 | 7 | | | 10 | 6 | 8 | 1 | | | | | | 9 | | | | | | |
| 28 | (a) | Blackpool | W 2-0 | Buck (pen), Timmins | 5,500 | | 2 | 3 | 4 | | 5 | 11 | 7 | | | 10 | 6 | 8 | 1 | | | | | | 9 | | | | | | |
| Dec 12 | (a) | Glossop | W 3-1 | Buck 2, Hewitt | 3,074 | | 2 | 3 | 4 | | 5 | 11 | 7 | | | 10 | 6 | 8 | 1 | | | | | | 9 | | | | | | |
| 19 | (h) | Stockport C | W 2-0 | Hewitt, Garraty | 6,240 | | 2 | 3 | 4 | | 5 | 11 | 7 | | | 10 | 6 | 8 | 1 | | | | | | 9 | | | | | | |
| 25 | (h) | Gainsborough T | W 2-0 | Thompson, Buck | 18,250 | | 2 | 3 | 4 | | 5 | 11 | 7 | | | 10 | 6 | 8 | 1 | | | | | | 9 | | | | | | |
| 26 | (h) | Birmingham | D 1-1 | Buck (pen) | 38,049 | | | 3 | 4 | | 5 | 11 | 7 | | | 10 | 6 | 8 | 1 | | | | 2 | | 9 | | | | | | |
| 28 | (a) | Birmingham | D 0-0 | | 30,035 | | | 3 | 4 | | 5 | 11 | 7 | 10 | | 8 | 6 | | 1 | | | | 2 | | 9 | | | | | | |
| Jan 2 | (h) | Grimsby T | W 7-0 | Bowser 2, Garraty 2, Buck, Manners, Thompson | 5,177 | | | 3 | 4 | | 5 | 11 | 7 | | | 8 | 6 | | 1 | | | | 2 | | 9 | 10 | | | | | |
| 9 | (a) | Fulham | L 0-2 | | 25,000 | | | | 4 | | 5 | 11 | 7 | | | 8 | 6 | | 1 | | | | 2 | | 9 | 10 | 3 | | | | |
| 23 | (h) | Burnley | D 0-0 | | 18,220 | | 2 | | 4 | | 5 | 11 | 7 | | | 8 | 6 | | 1 | | | | | | 9 | 10 | 3 | | | | |
| 30 | (a) | Bradford | D 0-0 | | 17,600 | | 2 | | 4 | | 5 | 11 | 7 | | | 8 | 6 | | 1 | | | | | | | 10 | 3 | 9 | | | |
| Feb 13 | (a) | Oldham A | L 0-2 | | 22,000 | | | 3 | 4 | | 5 | 11 | 7 | | | 10 | | | 1 | | | | 2 | | 8 | | 6 | 9 | | | |
| 20 | (h) | Clapton O | W 1-0 | Davies | 14,565 | | | | 4 | | 5 | 11 | | | | 8 | 6 | | 1 | | 7 | | 2 | | 9 | | 3 | | 10 | | |
| 27 | (a) | Leeds C | D 1-1 | Garraty | 12,140 | | | 3 | 4 | | 5 | 11 | | | | 8 | 6 | | 1 | | 7 | | 2 | | 9 | | | | 10 | | |
| Mar 13 | (a) | Tottenham H | W 3-1 | Garraty, Hewitt 2 (1 pen) | 35,532 | | | 3 | 4 | | 5 | 11 | | | | 10 | | 8 | 1 | | 7 | | 2 | | 9 | | 6 | | | | |
| 20 | (h) | Hull C | W 1-0 | Buck | 17,602 | | | 3 | 4 | | 5 | 11 | 7 | | | 10 | | 8 | 1 | | | | 2 | | 9 | | 6 | | | | |
| 24 | (h) | Barnsley | D 1-1 | Hewitt | 4,982 | | | 3 | 4 | | 5 | 11 | 7 | | | 10 | | 8 | 1 | | | | 2 | | 9 | | 6 | | | | |
| Apr 3 | (h) | Blackpool | W 5-1 | Hewitt 2 (1 pen), Miller (og), Fielding, Garraty | 17,426 | | | | 4 | | 5 | 11 | | | | 10 | | 8 | 1 | | 7 | | 2 | | 9 | | 6 | | | 3 | |
| 9 | (a) | Gainsborough T | L 0-2 | | 7,149 | | | 3 | 4 | | 5 | 7 | | | | 10 | | 8 | 1 | | | | 2 | | 9 | | 6 | | | 2 | 11 |
| 10 | (a) | Chesterfield T | D 2-2 | Davies, Garraty | 5,033 | | | 3 | 4 | | | 11 | | | | 10 | 6 | 8 | 1 | | 7 | | 2 | | 9 | | 5 | | | | |
| 12 | (h) | Bolton W | W 2-0 | Jordan, Hewitt | 34,012 | | | 3 | 4 | | | 11 | | 9 | | 10 | 6 | 8 | 1 | | 7 | | 2 | | 5 | | | | | | |
| 17 | (h) | Glossop | W 1-0 | Hewitt | 18,344 | | | 3 | 4 | | | 11 | 7 | 9 | | 10 | | 8 | 1 | | | | 2 | | 5 | | 6 | | | | |
| 24 | (a) | Stockport C | D 0-0 | | 7,424 | | | 3 | 4 | | | 11 | | 9 | | 10 | 6 | 8 | 1 | | 7 | | 2 | | 5 | | | | | | |
| 26 | (a) | Derby C | L 1-2 | Garraty | 6,508 | | | 3 | 4 | | 5 | 11 | 7 | 9 | | 10 | 6 | | 1 | | | | 2 | | 8 | | | | | | |
| **App** | | | | | | 2 | 35 | 18 | 35 | 9 | 32 | 33 | 27 | 7 | 2 | 38 | 27 | 27 | 36 | 7 | 9 | 2 | 14 | 5 | 26 | 4 | 13 | 2 | 2 | 5 | 1 |
| **Goals** | | | | | | | | 1 | | 1 | 3 | 4 | | 1 | | 13 | 1 | 15 | | 1 | | | | 1 | 11 | 2 | | | | | |

Albion in 1908-09. Back row (left to right): Mr R.Fellows (director), E.Pheasant, J.Stringer, Mr.H.Keys (director), J.Pennington, Mr.F.Everiss (secretary), W.Thompson, J.Manners. Front row: R.Fielding, S.Timmins, C.Hewitt, F.Brown, A.Evans, F.Buck, W.C.Davies, G.Baddeley.

# 1909-10

## Division 2

| | Date | | Opponent | Res | Score | Scorers | Att | Pearson H | Burton H | Pennington J | Baddeley G | Garraty W | Harris G | Dorsett J | Hewitt C | Rouse F | Buck F | Simpson G | Thompson W | Stringer J | Betteley R | Timmins S | Manners J | Davies W | Pheasant E | Dicken H | Young W | Bowser S | Waterhouse F | Pailor R | Corbett R | Crump A | Price G | Brown F |
|---|---|---|---|---|---|---|---|---|---|---|---|---|---|---|---|---|---|---|---|---|---|---|---|---|---|---|---|---|---|---|---|---|---|
| Sep | 1 | (a) | Stockport C | W | 2-0 | Rouse, Hewitt | 6,000 | 1 | 2 | 3 | 4 | 5 | 6 | | 7 | 8 | 9 | 10 | 11 | | | | | | | | | | | | | | | |
| | 4 | (h) | Bradford | W | 1-0 | Rouse | 18,990 | 1 | 2 | 3 | 4 | 5 | 6 | | 8 | 9 | 10 | 11 | 7 | | | | | | | | | | | | | | | |
| | 6 | (h) | Stockport C | L | 0-1 | | 14,883 | 1 | 2 | 3 | 4 | 5 | 6 | | 8 | 9 | 10 | 11 | 7 | | | | | | | | | | | | | | | |
| | 11 | (a) | Oldham A | W | 2-1 | Manners, Garraty | 12,000 | | | 3 | 4 | 9 | | | 8 | | 10 | | 7 | 1 | 2 | 5 | 6 | 11 | | | | | | | | | | |
| | 18 | (h) | Barnsley | W | 4-3 | Garraty, Hewitt 2, Buck | 10,520 | | | 3 | 4 | 9 | | | 8 | | 10 | | 7 | 1 | 2 | 5 | 6 | 11 | | | | | | | | | | |
| | 25 | (a) | Fulham | W | 2-0 | Thompson, Buck | 18,100 | | | 3 | 4 | 9 | | | 8 | | 10 | | 7 | 1 | 2 | | 6 | 11 | 5 | | | | | | | | | |
| | 29 | (a) | Lincoln C | W | 3-0 | Pheasant, Buck, Garraty | 6,500 | | | 3 | 4 | 9 | | | 8 | | 10 | | 7 | 1 | 2 | | 6 | 11 | 5 | | | | | | | | | |
| Oct | 2 | (h) | Burnley | L | 1-2 | Garraty | 15,175 | | | 3 | 4 | 9 | | | 8 | | 10 | | 7 | 1 | 2 | | 6 | 11 | 5 | | | | | | | | | |
| | 9 | (a) | Leeds C | W | 1-0 | Buck (pen) | 17,500 | | | 3 | 4 | 9 | | | 8 | | 10 | | 7 | 1 | 2 | | 6 | 11 | | 5 | | | | | | | | |
| | 16 | (a) | Wolves | L | 1-3 | Buck | 24,000 | | | 3 | 4 | 9 | 5 | | 8 | | 10 | | 7 | 1 | 2 | | 6 | 11 | | | | | | | | | | |
| | 23 | (a) | Gainsborough T | L | 1-3 | Buck (pen) | 3,500 | | | 3 | 5 | 9 | | 11 | 8 | | 10 | | 7 | 1 | 2 | | 6 | | | | 4 | | | | | | | |
| | 30 | (h) | Grimsby T | W | 4-3 | Hewitt 2, Buck 2 (1 pen) | 7,225 | | | 3 | 4 | 8 | | 11 | 9 | | 10 | | 7 | 1 | 2 | 5 | 6 | | | | | | | | | | | |
| Nov | 6 | (a) | Manchester C | L | 2-3 | Hewitt, Dorsett | 29,800 | | | 3 | 4 | | | 11 | 9 | 8 | | | 7 | 1 | 2 | 6 | | | 5 | | | 10 | | | | | | |
| | 13 | (h) | Leicester F | L | 1-2 | Hewitt | 9,040 | | | 3 | 4 | | | 11 | 9 | 8 | | | 7 | 1 | 2 | | | | 5 | | | 10 | 6 | | | | | |
| | 27 | (h) | Clapton O | W | 3-0 | Davies, Buck, Hewitt | 12,167 | | | 3 | 4 | 8 | | | 9 | | 10 | | 7 | 1 | 2 | | 6 | 11 | 5 | | | | | | | | | |
| Dec | 4 | (a) | Blackpool | L | 1-2 | Hewitt | 7,700 | | | 3 | 4 | 8 | | | 9 | | 10 | | 7 | 1 | 2 | | 6 | 11 | 5 | | | | | | | | | |
| | 11 | (h) | Hull C | L | 0-2 | | 8,208 | | 2 | 3 | 4 | 8 | | | 9 | | 10 | | 7 | 1 | | | 6 | 11 | 5 | | | | | | | | | |
| | 18 | (a) | Derby C | L | 1-2 | Bowser | 10,400 | | 2 | 3 | 4 | | | | | 8 | 10 | 11 | 7 | 1 | | | 5 | 6 | | | | 9 | | | | | | |
| | 25 | (h) | Wolves | L | 0-1 | | 24,899 | | 2 | 3 | 4 | | | | | 8 | 10 | 11 | 7 | 1 | | | 5 | 6 | | | | 9 | | | | | | |
| | 27 | (h) | Birmingham | W | 3-1 | Simpson, Bowser, Manners | 12,104 | | 2 | 3 | | | | | 10 | 8 | | 11 | | 1 | | 4 | 6 | 7 | 5 | | | 9 | | | | | | |
| Jan | 1 | (a) | Birmingham | W | 1-0 | Simpson | 15,500 | | 2 | 3 | | | 8 | | | | 10 | 11 | | 1 | | 5 | 6 | 7 | | | | 9 | | | | | | |
| | 8 | (a) | Bradford | L | 0-1 | | 7,980 | | 2 | 3 | 4 | | | | | | 10 | 11 | | 1 | | 5 | 6 | 7 | | | | 8 | 9 | | | | | |
| | 22 | (h) | Oldham A | D | 1-1 | Pailor | 7,901 | | | 3 | 4 | | | | | | 10 | 11 | | 1 | 2 | 5 | 6 | 7 | | | | 8 | 9 | | | | | |
| Feb | 12 | (a) | Burnley | W | 3-2 | Garraty 3 | 6,000 | 1 | 2 | 3 | 4 | 9 | | | | 7 | 10 | | | | | | 6 | | | 11 | | 8 | 5 | | | | | |
| Mar | 5 | (h) | Gainsborough T | W | 5-0 | Bowser, Simpson 2, Buck, Garraty | 10,155 | 1 | 2 | 3 | 4 | 9 | | | | 7 | 10 | 11 | | | | | 6 | | | | | 8 | 5 | | | | | |
| | 7 | (h) | Leeds C | W | 3-1 | Buck 2, Bowser | 6,664 | 1 | 2 | 3 | 4 | 9 | | | | 7 | 10 | 11 | | | | | 6 | | | | | 8 | 5 | | | | | |
| | 12 | (a) | Grimsby T | L | 0-3 | | 5,800 | 1 | 2 | 3 | 4 | 9 | | | | 7 | 10 | 11 | | | | | 6 | | | | | 8 | 5 | | | | | |
| | 19 | (h) | Manchester C | D | 0-0 | | 13,042 | 1 | 2 | 3 | 4 | | | | | 7 | 10 | 11 | | | | | | 6 | | | | 8 | 5 | 9 | | | | |
| | 26 | (a) | Leicester F | L | 1-2 | Bowser | 7,000 | 1 | | 3 | 4 | | | | | 8 | 10 | 11 | | | 2 | | 6 | | | 7 | | 9 | 5 | | | | | |
| | 28 | (h) | Glossop | D | 0-0 | | 12,360 | 1 | | 3 | 4 | | | 11 | 8 | | 10 | | | | 2 | | 6 | | | 7 | | 9 | 5 | | 2 | | | |
| | 29 | (h) | Fulham | W | 3-2 | Waterhouse, Buck, Hewitt | 11,714 | 1 | | 3 | 4 | 9 | | 11 | 7 | | 10 | | | | | | 6 | | | | | 8 | 5 | | 2 | | | |
| Apr | 2 | (h) | Lincoln C | D | 1-1 | Garraty | 12,150 | 1 | | | 4 | 9 | | 11 | 7 | | 10 | | | | | | 6 | | | | | 8 | 5 | | 3 | 2 | | |
| | 9 | (a) | Clapton O | W | 3-1 | Dorsett, Buck, Hewitt | 15,000 | 1 | | 3 | 4 | 8 | 6 | 7 | 9 | | 11 | | | | | 2 | 5 | | | | | 10 | | | | | | |
| | 14 | (a) | Barnsley | L | 1-2 | Buck (pen) | 16,105 | 1 | | 3 | 4 | 8 | 6 | 7 | | | 10 | 11 | | | | 2 | 5 | | | | | | | | | | 9 | |
| | 16 | (h) | Blackpool | L | 0-3 | | 6,103 | 1 | | 3 | 4 | | | | 9 | 8 | 11 | | | | | 2 | 6 | | | 7 | | 10 | 5 | | | | | |
| | 23 | (a) | Hull C | L | 1-5 | Simpson | 18,744 | 1 | | 3 | | 4 | | | 9 | 7 | 11 | | | | | 2 | 6 | | | | | 10 | 5 | | | | | 8 |
| | 26 | (a) | Glossop | L | 2-3 | Bowser, Buck (pen) | 5,225 | 1 | | 3 | 4 | | | 11 | 8 | | 10 | | | | | 2 | 6 | | | 7 | | 9 | 5 | | | | | |
| | 30 | (h) | Derby C | D | 0-0 | | 9,098 | 1 | | 3 | 4 | | | | | 8 | 10 | 11 | | | | 2 | 6 | | | 7 | | 9 | 5 | | | | | |
| | | | | | | App | | 18 | 27 | 24 | 33 | 27 | 6 | 13 | 32 | 5 | 37 | 18 | 18 | 20 | 21 | 22 | 22 | 21 | 20 | 9 | 1 | 22 | 14 | 3 | 3 | 1 | 1 | 1 |
| | | | | | | Goals | | | | | | 9 | | 2 | 11 | 2 | 16 | 5 | 1 | | | | 2 | 1 | 1 | | | 16 | 1 | 1 | | | | |

**Action from Albion's game at Barnsley in April 1910.**

# 1910-11

### Division 2

| Date | | Opponent | Result | Scorers | Att | Pearson H | Betteley R | Timmins S | Baddeley G | Waterhouse F | Manners J | Wollaston W | Bowser S | Pailor R | Buck F | Lloyd A | Richards A | Smith J | Pennington J | Nevin J | McNeal R | Hibbert J | Wright H | Deacey C | Walker W | Moorwood L | Thompson W |
|---|---|---|---|---|---|---|---|---|---|---|---|---|---|---|---|---|---|---|---|---|---|---|---|---|---|---|---|
| Sep | 3 | (a) Hull C | D 1-1 | Buck | 10,400 | 1 | 2 | 3 | 4 | 5 | 6 | 7 | 8 | 9 | 10 | 11 | | | | | | | | | | | |
| | 5 | (a) Bolton W | L 1-3 | Buck | 8,500 | 1 | | | 6 | 4 | 5 | 7 | 8 | 9 | 10 | 11 | | 2 | 3 | | | | | | | | |
| | 10 | (h) Fulham | W 2-1 | Bowser 2 | 10,144 | 1 | 2 | | 6 | 4 | 5 | 7 | 8 | 9 | 10 | 11 | | | 3 | | | | | | | | |
| | 17 | (a) Bradford | D 3-3 | Bowser, Pailor 2 | 9,500 | 1 | 2 | | 4 | 5 | 6 | 7 | 8 | 9 | 10 | 11 | | | 3 | | | | | | | | |
| | 24 | (h) Burnley | W 2-1 | Waterhouse, Wollaston | 15,280 | 1 | 2 | | 4 | 5 | 6 | 7 | 8 | 9 | 10 | 11 | | | 3 | | | | | | | | |
| Oct | 1 | (a) Gainsborough T | D 1-1 | Bowser | 3,600 | 1 | 2 | | 4 | 5 | | 7 | 8 | 9 | 10 | 11 | | | 3 | 6 | | | | | | | |
| | 8 | (h) Leeds C | W 2-0 | Bowser, Pailor | 13,149 | 1 | 2 | | 6 | 4 | 5 | 7 | 8 | 9 | | 11 | | | 3 | | | | | | | | |
| | 15 | (a) Stockport C | W 1-0 | Bowser | 6,000 | 1 | 2 | | 6 | 4 | 5 | 7 | 8 | 9 | | 11 | | | 3 | | 10 | | | | | | |
| | 22 | (h) Derby C | D 1-1 | Pailor | 18,488 | 1 | 2 | | 6 | 4 | 5 | 7 | 8 | 9 | | 11 | | | 3 | | 10 | | | | | | |
| | 29 | (a) Barnsley | D 1-1 | Lloyd | 10,000 | 1 | | | 4 | 5 | | 7 | 8 | 9 | | 11 | | 2 | 3 | | 6 | 10 | | | | | |
| Nov | 5 | (h) Leicester F | W 5-1 | Bowser, Lloyd 2, Wollaston, Buck (pen) | 15,200 | 1 | | | 4 | 5 | | 7 | 8 | 9 | 10 | 11 | | 2 | 3 | | 6 | | | | | | |
| | 12 | (a) Wolves | W 3-2 | Pailor 2 (1 pen), Bowser | 18,500 | 1 | | | 4 | 5 | | | 8 | 9 | 10 | 11 | | 2 | 3 | | 6 | | 7 | | | | |
| | 19 | (h) Chelsea | L 1-3 | Bowser | 21,305 | 1 | | | 4 | 5 | | | 8 | 9 | 10 | 11 | | 2 | 3 | | 6 | | 7 | | | | |
| | 26 | (a) Clapton O | D 0-0 | | 7,000 | 1 | | | 4 | 5 | | | 8 | | 10 | 11 | | 2 | 3 | | 6 | | 7 | 9 | | | |
| Dec | 3 | (h) Blackpool | L 0-1 | | 8,840 | 1 | | | 4 | 5 | | | 8 | | 10 | 11 | | 2 | 3 | | 6 | | 7 | 9 | | | |
| | 10 | (a) Glossop | W 2-0 | Baddeley, Pailor | 4,000 | 1 | | | 4 | 5 | | 7 | 8 | 9 | 10 | 11 | | 2 | 3 | | 6 | | | | | | |
| | 17 | (h) Lincoln C | W 3-0 | Buck 2 (1 pen), Walker | 3,577 | 1 | | | 4 | 5 | | 7 | 8 | | 10 | 11 | | 2 | 3 | | 6 | | | | 9 | | |
| | 24 | (a) Huddersfield T | W 2-0 | Waterhouse, Bowser | 20,700 | 1 | | | 4 | 5 | | 7 | 8 | 9 | 10 | 11 | | 2 | 3 | | 6 | | | | | | |
| | 26 | (h) Bolton W | W 2-0 | Bowser, Lloyd | 20,301 | 1 | | | 4 | 5 | | 7 | 8 | 9 | 10 | 11 | | 2 | 3 | | 6 | | | | | | |
| | 27 | (a) Birmingham | D 1-1 | Pailor | 37,520 | 1 | | | 4 | 5 | | 7 | 8 | 9 | 10 | 11 | | 2 | 3 | | 6 | | | | | | |
| | 31 | (h) Hull C | L 0-2 | | 11,790 | 1 | | | 4 | 5 | | 7 | 8 | 9 | 10 | 11 | | 2 | 3 | | 6 | | | | | | |
| Jan | 7 | (a) Fulham | W 1-0 | Lloyd | 16,000 | 1 | | | 4 | 5 | | 7 | 8 | 9 | 10 | 11 | | 2 | 3 | | 6 | | | | | | |
| | 21 | (h) Bradford | W 3-0 | Buck, Pailor, Lloyd | 6,952 | 1 | | | 4 | 5 | | 7 | 8 | 9 | 10 | 11 | | 2 | 3 | | 6 | | | | | | |
| | 28 | (a) Burnley | L 0-2 | | 8,300 | 1 | | | 4 | 5 | | | 8 | 9 | 10 | 11 | | 2 | 3 | | 6 | | 7 | | | | |
| Feb | 11 | (a) Leeds C | L 1-3 | Wright | 10,700 | | 2 | | 4 | 5 | | | 10 | 9 | | 11 | | | 3 | | 6 | | 8 | | | 1 | 7 |
| | 18 | (h) Stockport C | W 4-2 | Buck 2 (1 pen), Bowser 2 | 6,107 | | | | 4 | 5 | | | 8 | 9 | 10 | 11 | | 2 | 3 | | 6 | | | | | 1 | 7 |
| Mar | 1 | (a) Derby C | W 3-1 | Bowser, Pailor, Wright | 21,640 | | | | 4 | 5 | | | 8 | 9 | | 11 | | 2 | 3 | | 6 | | 10 | | | 1 | 7 |
| | 4 | (h) Barnsley | D 3-3 | Bowser, Wright, Pailor | 7,770 | | 2 | 7 | 4 | 5 | 6 | | 8 | 9 | | 11 | | | 3 | | | | 10 | | | 1 | |
| | 11 | (a) Leicester F | W 3-2 | Bowser 2, Wright | 10,547 | 1 | | | 4 | 5 | 6 | | 8 | 9 | 10 | 11 | | 2 | 3 | | | | 7 | | | | |
| | 18 | (h) Wolves | W 2-1 | Buck (pen), Pailor | 20,303 | 1 | | | 4 | 5 | | | 8 | 9 | 10 | 11 | | 2 | 3 | | 6 | | 7 | | | | |
| | 29 | (a) Chelsea | L 1-2 | Wright | 12,640 | 1 | | | 4 | 5 | | | 8 | | 10 | 11 | | 2 | 3 | | 6 | | | 9 | | | 7 |
| Apr | 1 | (h) Clapton O | W 3-0 | Waterhouse, McNeal, Wright | 12,852 | 1 | 2 | | 4 | 5 | 6 | | 8 | | 10 | 11 | | | 3 | | 9 | | 7 | | | | |
| | 8 | (a) Blackpool | D 0-0 | | 6,100 | 1 | | | 4 | 5 | 6 | | 8 | | 10 | 11 | | 2 | 3 | | 9 | | 7 | | | | |
| | 15 | (h) Glossop | W 3-1 | Lloyd, Wright, Bowser | 13,404 | 1 | | | | 5 | 6 | | 9 | | 10 | 11 | | 2 | 3 | | 4 | | 8 | | | | 7 |
| | 17 | (h) Birmingham | W 1-0 | Bowser | 27,042 | 1 | | | | 5 | 6 | | 8 | 9 | 10 | 11 | | 2 | 3 | | 4 | | 7 | | | | |
| | 18 | (h) Gainsborough T | W 2-1 | Bowser 2 | 23,788 | 1 | | | | 5 | 6 | | 9 | | 10 | 11 | | 2 | 3 | | 4 | | 7 | | | | 8 |
| | 22 | (a) Lincoln C | W 2-1 | Lloyd, Bowser | 8,000 | 1 | | | | 5 | 6 | | 9 | | 10 | 11 | | 2 | 3 | | 4 | | 7 | | | | 8 |
| | 29 | (h) Huddersfield T | W 1-0 | Buck (pen) | 30,135 | 1 | | | | 5 | 6 | | 9 | | 10 | 11 | | 2 | 3 | | 4 | | 7 | | | | 8 |
| | | | | | App | 34 | 11 | 7 | 33 | 38 | 12 | 19 | 38 | 28 | 34 | 35 | 1 | 30 | 33 | 2 | 29 | 1 | 18 | 2 | 1 | 4 | 8 |
| | | | | | Goals | | | | 1 | 3 | | 2 | 22 | 12 | 10 | 8 | | | | | 1 | | 7 | | 1 | | |

Albion's line-up against Bolton Wanderers at Burnden Park in September 1910. Back row (left to right): A.Evans (coach), E.Paddock (assistant trainer), S.Timmins, A.Richards, H.Pearson, R.Pailor, Mr F.Everiss (secretary), G.Baddeley, J.Manners, Mr D.Nurse (director). Middle row: W.Barber (trainer), W.Wollaston, F.Buck, J.Smith, F.Waterhouse. On ground: S.Bowser, A.Lloyd. Insets: B.Shearman, J.Pennington and J.Nevin.

# 1911-12

## Division 1

| Date | | Venue | Opponent | Res | Score | Scorers | Att | Pearson H | Smith J | Pennington J | Baddeley G | Waterhouse F | McNeal R | Wright H | Bowser S | Allan S | Buck F | Shearman B | Manners J | Pailor R | Wollaston W | Jephcott C | Cook A | Moorwood L | Deacey C | Lloyd A | Hibbert J | Morris F | Wood M | Gregory H | Betteley R |
|---|---|---|---|---|---|---|---|---|---|---|---|---|---|---|---|---|---|---|---|---|---|---|---|---|---|---|---|---|---|---|---|
| Sep | 2 | (h) | Notts C | W | 2-1 | Buck, Shearman | 26,638 | 1 | 2 | 3 | 4 | 5 | 6 | 7 | 8 | 9 | 10 | 11 | | | | | | | | | | | | | |
| | 4 | (a) | Aston Villa | W | 3-0 | Allan, Shearman, Bowser | 31,884 | 1 | 2 | 3 | 4 | | 6 | 7 | 8 | 9 | 10 | 11 | 5 | | | | | | | | | | | | |
| | 9 | (a) | Tottenham H | L | 0-1 | | 31,100 | 1 | 2 | 3 | 4 | | 6 | 7 | 8 | 9 | 10 | 11 | 5 | | | | | | | | | | | | |
| | 16 | (h) | Manchester U | W | 1-0 | Allan | 34,921 | 1 | 2 | 3 | 4 | | 6 | 7 | 8 | 9 | 10 | 11 | 5 | | | | | | | | | | | | |
| | 23 | (a) | Liverpool | W | 3-1 | Shearman, Bowser, Allan | 18,000 | 1 | 2 | 3 | 4 | | 6 | 7 | 8 | 9 | 10 | 11 | 5 | | | | | | | | | | | | |
| | 30 | (h) | Aston Villa | D | 2-2 | Shearman 2 | 46,203 | 1 | 2 | 3 | 4 | | 6 | 7 | 8 | 9 | 10 | 11 | 5 | | | | | | | | | | | | |
| Oct | 7 | (a) | Newcastle U | D | 0-0 | | 28,000 | 1 | 2 | 3 | 4 | | 6 | 7 | 8 | 9 | 10 | 11 | 5 | | | | | | | | | | | | |
| | 14 | (h) | Sheffield U | L | 0-1 | | 18,595 | 1 | 2 | 3 | 4 | 5 | 6 | 7 | 8 | 9 | 10 | 11 | | | | | | | | | | | | | |
| | 21 | (a) | Oldham A | L | 1-3 | Pailor | 13,000 | 1 | 2 | 3 | 4 | 5 | 6 | 7 | 8 | | 10 | 11 | | | 9 | | | | | | | | | | |
| | 28 | (h) | Bolton W | D | 0-0 | | 14,377 | 1 | 2 | 3 | 4 | 5 | 6 | 7 | 8 | 9 | 10 | 11 | | | | | | | | | | | | | |
| Nov | 4 | (a) | Bradford C | L | 1-4 | Allan | 19,800 | 1 | 2 | 3 | 4 | | 6 | 7 | 10 | 8 | 11 | 5 | | | 9 | | | | | | | | | | |
| | 11 | (h) | W Arsenal | D | 1-1 | Shearman | 13,900 | 1 | 2 | 3 | 4 | | 6 | | 8 | | 10 | 11 | 5 | | 9 | 7 | | | | | | | | | |
| | 18 | (a) | Manchester C | W | 2-0 | Bowser 2 | 12,000 | 1 | 2 | 3 | 4 | | 6 | | 8 | 10 | | 11 | 5 | 9 | | 7 | | | | | | | | | |
| | 25 | (h) | Everton | W | 1-0 | Pailor | 12,240 | 1 | 2 | 3 | 4 | | 6 | | 8 | 10 | | 11 | 5 | 9 | | 7 | | | | | | | | | |
| Dec | 2 | (a) | Preston NE | D | 1-1 | Bowser | 19,000 | 1 | 2 | 3 | 4 | | 6 | | 8 | 10 | | 11 | 5 | 9 | | 7 | | | | | | | | | |
| | 9 | (a) | Sunderland | L | 2-3 | Pailor 2 | 10,000 | 1 | 2 | 3 | 4 | | 6 | | 8 | 10 | | 11 | 5 | 9 | | 7 | | | | | | | | | |
| | 16 | (h) | Blackburn R | W | 2-0 | Bowser, Pailor | 13,176 | 1 | 2 | 3 | | | 6 | | 8 | 10 | | 4 | 11 | 5 | 9 | 7 | | | | | | | | | |
| | 23 | (a) | Sheffield W | L | 1-4 | Bowser | 13,000 | 1 | 2 | 3 | | | 6 | | 8 | 10 | | 4 | 11 | 5 | 9 | 7 | | | | | | | | | |
| | 26 | (h) | Bury | W | 2-0 | Wright, Pearson (pen) | 10,133 | 1 | 2 | 3 | | 5 | 6 | | 8 | 10 | | 4 | 11 | | 9 | 7 | | | | | | | | | |
| | 30 | (a) | Notts C | L | 0-2 | | 10,000 | 1 | | 3 | | 5 | 6 | | 8 | 10 | 9 | 4 | 11 | | | 7 | 2 | | | | | | | | |
| Jan | 1 | (a) | Bury | L | 0-1 | | 12,000 | | | 3 | | 5 | 6 | 7 | 10 | 8 | 4 | 11 | | | 9 | | 2 | 1 | | | | | | | |
| | 20 | (a) | Manchester U | W | 2-1 | Wright 2 | 11,000 | 1 | | 3 | 4 | | 6 | 8 | 10 | | 5 | 11 | | 9 | | 7 | 2 | | | | | | | | |
| | 27 | (h) | Liverpool | W | 1-0 | Wright | 16,057 | 1 | 2 | | 4 | | 6 | 8 | 10 | | 5 | 11 | | 9 | | 7 | 3 | | | | | | | | |
| Feb | 10 | (h) | Newcastle U | W | 3-1 | Pailor 3 | 30,252 | 1 | 2 | | 4 | | 6 | 8 | 10 | | 5 | 11 | | 9 | | 7 | 3 | | | | | | | | |
| | 17 | (a) | Sheffield U | D | 1-1 | Pailor | 15,000 | 1 | 2 | | 4 | | 6 | 8 | 10 | | 5 | 11 | | 9 | | 7 | 3 | | | | | | | | |
| Mar | 2 | (a) | Bolton W | L | 0-2 | | 12,000 | 1 | | 3 | 4 | | 6 | 8 | 10 | | 5 | | | | | 7 | 2 | | 9 | 11 | | | | | |
| | 13 | (h) | Tottenham H | W | 2-0 | Jephcott 2 | 17,406 | 1 | 2 | | 4 | | 6 | 8 | 10 | | 5 | 11 | | 9 | | 7 | 3 | | | | | | | | |
| | 16 | (a) | W Arsenal | W | 2-0 | Bowser, Pailor | 15,000 | 1 | | 3 | 4 | | 6 | 8 | 10 | | 5 | 11 | | 9 | | 7 | 2 | | | | | | | | |
| | 23 | (h) | Manchester C | D | 1-1 | Shearman | 12,331 | 1 | 2 | | 4 | | 6 | 8 | 10 | | 5 | 11 | | 9 | | 7 | 3 | | | | | | | | |
| Apr | 5 | (a) | Middlesbrough | L | 0-1 | | 12,000 | 1 | 2 | 3 | | 4 | 6 | 8 | | | 10 | | 11 | 5 | | 7 | | | 9 | | | | | | |
| | 8 | (h) | Middlesbrough | W | 3-1 | Pearson (pen), Jephcott 2 | 25,027 | 1 | | 3 | 4 | | 6 | 8 | | | 10 | 5 | 11 | | | 7 | 2 | | 9 | | | | | | |
| | 9 | (h) | Preston NE | L | 0-2 | | 8,240 | 1 | 2 | 3 | | | 6 | 8 | | | 10 | | 11 | 5 | | 7 | | | 9 | 4 | | | | | |
| | 13 | (h) | Sunderland | W | 1-0 | Morris | 20,117 | 1 | 2 | | 4 | | 6 | | | | 8 | 5 | 11 | | | 7 | 3 | | 9 | | 10 | | | | |
| | 22 | (a) | Everton | L | 0-3 | | 7,000 | | 2 | | | 5 | | | | | | 6 | | 7 | | 1 | 9 | 11 | 4 | 10 | 3 | 8 | | | |
| | 25 | (a) | Blackburn R | L | 1-4 | Morris | 12,000 | 1 | 2 | 3 | | 4 | 6 | 8 | | | 5 | 11 | | 9 | | 7 | | | 10 | | | | | | |
| | 26 | (h) | Bradford C | D | 0-0 | | 10,663 | 1 | 2 | 3 | 4 | | 6 | | | | 8 | 5 | 11 | | 9 | 7 | | | 10 | | | | | | |
| | 27 | (h) | Sheffield W | L | 1-5 | Morris | 9,405 | 1 | 2 | | 4 | | 6 | 8 | | | 5 | 11 | | | | 7 | | | 9 | 3 | 10 | | | | |
| | 29 | (h) | Oldham A | D | 0-0 | | 3,122 | 1 | 3 | | | 4 | 6 | | | | 8 | | 5 | 7 | | | | | 11 | 9 | | 10 | 2 | | |
| | | | | | App | | | 36 | 32 | 29 | 28 | 11 | 37 | 34 | 27 | 19 | 30 | 34 | 18 | 20 | 6 | 20 | 12 | 2 | 6 | 3 | 2 | 6 | 2 | 3 | 1 |
| | | | | | Goals | | | 2 | | | | | | 4 | 8 | 4 | 1 | 7 | | 10 | | 4 | | | | | | 3 | | | |

Albion's 1912 FA Cup Final side. Players only (back row, left to right): G.Baddeley, H.Pearson, S.Bowser, R.Pailor. Front row: A.Cook, J.Pennington, R.McNeal, F.Buck. On ground: C.Jephcott, B.Shearman, H.Wright.

# 1912-13

## Division 1

| Date | Match | Res | Score | Scorers | Att | Pearson H | Cook A | Pennington J | Baddeley G | Buck F | McNeal R | Jephcott C | Wright H | Pailor R | Bowser S | Shearman B | Waterhouse F | Smith J | Moorwood L | Gregory H | Morris F | Varty J | Wood M | Deacey C | Jackson W | Lloyd A |
|---|---|---|---|---|---|---|---|---|---|---|---|---|---|---|---|---|---|---|---|---|---|---|---|---|---|---|
| Sep 4 | (h) Middlesbrough | W | 2-0 | Buck (pen), Pailor | 15,085 | 1 | 2 | 3 | 4 | 5 | 6 | 7 | 8 | 9 | 10 | 11 | | | | | | | | | | |
| 7 | (a) Notts C | D | 1-1 | Wright | 13,000 | 1 | 2 | 3 | 4 | | 6 | 7 | 8 | 9 | 10 | 11 | 5 | | | | | | | | | |
| 14 | (a) Manchester U | L | 1-2 | Bowser | 26,140 | 1 | 2 | 3 | | 5 | 6 | 7 | 8 | 9 | 10 | 11 | 4 | | | | | | | | | |
| 21 | (a) Aston Villa | W | 4-2 | Wright, Pailor 3 | 55,064 | 1 | | 3 | | 5 | 6 | 7 | 10 | 9 | 8 | 11 | 4 | 2 | | | | | | | | |
| 28 | (h) Liverpool | W | 3-1 | Pailor, Shearman, McNeal | 21,908 | 1 | | 3 | | 5 | 6 | 7 | 10 | 9 | 8 | 11 | 4 | 2 | | | | | | | | |
| Oct 5 | (a) Bolton W | L | 1-2 | Morris | 24,000 | | | 3 | | 5 | 6 | 7 | 10 | | | 11 | 4 | 2 | 1 | 8 | 9 | | | | | |
| 12 | (h) Sheffield U | W | 3-1 | Morris 2, Wright | 18,040 | 1 | | 3 | | 5 | 6 | 7 | 10 | 9 | | 11 | 4 | 2 | | | 8 | | | | | |
| 19 | (a) Newcastle U | D | 1-1 | Bowser | 30,000 | 1 | | 3 | | 5 | 6 | 7 | 10 | | 8 | 11 | 4 | 2 | | | 9 | | | | | |
| 26 | (h) Oldham A | L | 2-3 | Wright, Shearman | 15,101 | 1 | | 3 | | 5 | 6 | 7 | 10 | 9 | 8 | 11 | 4 | 2 | | | | | | | | |
| Nov 2 | (a) Chelsea | W | 2-0 | Jephcott, Pailor | 35,100 | 1 | | 3 | | 5 | 6 | 7 | 10 | 9 | 8 | 11 | 4 | 2 | | | | | | | | |
| 9 | (h) W Arsenal | W | 2-1 | Morris 2 | 15,980 | 1 | | 3 | | 5 | | 7 | 10 | | 8 | 11 | 4 | 2 | | 9 | 6 | | | | | |
| 16 | (a) Bradford C | D | 1-1 | Torrance (og) | 13,000 | 1 | | 3 | | 5 | | 7 | 10 | | 8 | 11 | 4 | 2 | | 9 | 6 | | | | | |
| 23 | (h) Manchester C | L | 0-2 | | 16,799 | 1 | | 3 | | 5 | | 7 | 10 | | 8 | 11 | 4 | 2 | | 9 | 6 | | | | | |
| 30 | (h) Sunderland | W | 3-1 | Morris, Pailor, Buck (pen) | 13,529 | | | | 4 | 5 | | 7 | 10 | 9 | | 11 | 6 | 2 | 1 | | 8 | 3 | | | | |
| Dec 7 | (a) Everton | W | 3-1 | Pailor 2, Jephcott | 25,000 | | | 3 | 4 | 5 | | 7 | 10 | 9 | | 11 | 6 | 2 | 1 | | 8 | | | | | |
| 14 | (h) Sheffield W | D | 1-1 | Pailor | 15,258 | | | 3 | 4 | 5 | | 7 | 10 | 9 | | 11 | 6 | 2 | 1 | | 8 | | | | | |
| 21 | (a) Blackburn R | W | 4-2 | Pailor 3, Morris | 22,000 | | | 3 | | 5 | 6 | 7 | | 9 | 10 | 11 | 4 | 2 | 1 | | 8 | | | | | |
| 25 | (a) Derby C | W | 2-1 | Buck, Shearman | 21,000 | | | 3 | 4 | 5 | | 7 | | 9 | 10 | 11 | 6 | 2 | 1 | | 8 | | | | | |
| 26 | (h) Derby C | D | 0-0 | | 22,567 | | | 3 | 4 | 5 | 6 | 7 | 8 | | 10 | 11 | | 2 | 1 | | 9 | | | | | |
| 28 | (h) Notts C | W | 2-0 | Gregory, Morris | 21,041 | | | 3 | | | 6 | 7 | | | 10 | 11 | 4 | 2 | 1 | 8 | 9 | | | 5 | | |
| Jan 1 | (a) Middlesbrough | L | 1-3 | Buck | 18,000 | | | | | 5 | 6 | 7 | | 9 | 10 | 11 | 4 | 2 | 1 | | 8 | 3 | | | | |
| 4 | (a) Manchester U | D | 1-1 | Bowser | 15,000 | | | 3 | | 5 | 6 | 7 | 8 | | 10 | 11 | 4 | 2 | 1 | | 9 | | | | | |
| 18 | (h) Aston Villa | D | 2-2 | Morris, Gregory | 40,589 | | | 3 | 4 | 5 | 6 | 7 | | | 10 | 11 | | 2 | 1 | 8 | 9 | | | | | |
| 25 | (a) Liverpool | L | 1-2 | Bowser | 30,400 | | | 3 | 4 | 5 | 6 | 7 | | | 10 | 11 | | 2 | 1 | 8 | 9 | | | | | |
| Feb 8 | (h) Bolton W | D | 2-2 | Waterhouse, Shearman | 18,225 | 1 | | 3 | | 5 | 6 | 7 | 10 | | | 11 | 4 | 2 | | | 8 | | 9 | | | |
| 15 | (a) Sheffield U | L | 0-1 | | 12,000 | 1 | | 3 | | 5 | 6 | 7 | 8 | | 10 | 11 | 4 | 2 | | | | | 9 | | | |
| Mar 1 | (a) Oldham A | D | 0-0 | | 10,500 | 1 | | 3 | | 5 | 6 | 7 | 8 | | 10 | 11 | 4 | 2 | | | | | | 9 | | |
| 8 | (h) Chelsea | L | 0-1 | | 16,293 | 1 | | 3 | 4 | 8 | | 7 | | | | | 6 | 2 | | 10 | | | | 5 | 9 | 11 |
| 15 | (a) W Arsenal | L | 0-1 | | 6,800 | 1 | | 3 | | 5 | 6 | 7 | | 9 | 10 | 11 | 4 | 2 | | 8 | | | | | | |
| 21 | (a) Tottenham H | L | 1-3 | Shearman | 31,500 | 1 | | 3 | | 5 | 6 | 7 | | 9 | 10 | 11 | 4 | 2 | | | 8 | | | | | |
| 22 | (h) Bradford C | D | 1-1 | Pailor | 6,565 | 1 | | 3 | | 5 | 6 | 7 | | 9 | 10 | 11 | 4 | 2 | | | 8 | | | | | |
| 24 | (h) Tottenham H | W | 4-1 | Bowser, Shearman, Pailor 2 | 13,882 | | | 3 | | 5 | 6 | 7 | | 9 | 10 | 11 | 4 | 2 | 1 | | 8 | | | | | |
| 29 | (a) Manchester C | L | 1-2 | Bowser | 21,500 | | | 3 | | 5 | 6 | 7 | | 9 | 10 | 11 | 4 | 2 | 1 | | 8 | | | | | |
| Apr 5 | (a) Sunderland | L | 1-3 | Gregory | 33,700 | | | 3 | | 5 | 6 | 7 | | 9 | 10 | 11 | 4 | 2 | 1 | 8 | | | | | | |
| 9 | (h) Newcastle U | W | 1-0 | Shearman | 8,277 | | | 3 | | 5 | 6 | 7 | | 9 | 10 | 11 | 4 | 2 | 1 | | 8 | | | | | |
| 12 | (h) Everton | D | 0-0 | | 10,795 | | | 3 | | 5 | 6 | 7 | | 9 | 8 | 11 | 4 | 2 | 1 | | | | | 10 | | |
| 19 | (a) Sheffield W | L | 2-3 | Shearman, Gregory | 11,400 | | | 3 | | 5 | 6 | 7 | | 9 | 10 | 11 | 4 | 2 | 1 | 8 | | | | | | |
| 26 | (h) Blackburn R | D | 1-1 | Waterhouse | 11,834 | | | 3 | | 5 | 6 | 7 | | 9 | 10 | 11 | 4 | 2 | 1 | | 8 | | | | | |
| **App** | | | | | | 19 | 8 | 31 | 10 | 36 | 30 | 38 | 20 | 24 | 32 | 37 | 34 | 35 | 19 | 13 | 19 | 3 | 2 | 4 | 3 | 1 |
| **Goals** | | | | | | | | | | 4 | 1 | 2 | 4 | 16 | 6 | 8 | 2 | | | 4 | 9 | | | | | |

Albion in 1912-13. Back row (left to right): A.Lloyd, J.Steer, L.Moorwood, G.Snead, J.Varty, M.Wood, C.Crutchley, B.Millward, S.Jones, A.Graham, J.Mann. Second row: E.Smith (assistant secretary), T.Fletcher, G.Baddeley, H.Pearson, S.Bowser, J.Manners, Mr W.I.Bassett (chairman), F.Waterhouse, C.Deacey, R.Pailor, F.Morris, H.Lane, Mr F.Everiss (secretary). Seated: Mr D.Nurse (director), A.Cook, Mr H.Keys (director), J.Pennington, R.McNeal, Sir E.J.Spencer (president), F.Buck, W.Barber (trainer). On ground: C.Jephcott, W.Jackson, B.Shearman, J.Smith, H.Wright, J.Smart, J.Donald, H.Gregory.

# 1913-14

## Division 1

| Date | Opponent | Result | Scorers | Att | Pearson H | Smith J | Pennington J | Waterhouse F | Buck F | McNeal R | Jephcott C | Morris F | Bentley A | Lewis A | Shearman B | Newall T | Gregory H | Baddeley G | Deacey C | Pailor R | Wright H | Edwards E | Cook A | Nicholls H | Swift A | Bowser S | Wood M | Lloyd A |
|---|---|---|---|---|---|---|---|---|---|---|---|---|---|---|---|---|---|---|---|---|---|---|---|---|---|---|---|---|
| Sep 6 | (h) Burnley | W 4-1 | Bentley 4 | 27,014 | 1 | 2 | 3 | 4 | 5 | 6 | 7 | 8 | 9 | 10 | 11 | | | | | | | | | | | | | |
| 8 | (a) Chelsea | D 1-1 | Morris | 21,000 | 1 | 2 | 3 | 4 | 5 | 6 | 7 | 8 | 9 | 10 | 11 | | | | | | | | | | | | | |
| 13 | (a) Preston NE | W 2-0 | Lewis, Morris | 15,000 | 1 | 2 | 3 | 4 | 5 | 6 | 7 | 8 | 9 | 10 | 11 | | | | | | | | | | | | | |
| 20 | (h) Newcastle U | D 1-1 | Newall | 29,147 | 1 | 2 | 3 | 4 | 5 | 6 | 7 | 8 | | 10 | 11 | 9 | | | | | | | | | | | | |
| 27 | (a) Liverpool | D 0-0 | | 25,000 | 1 | 2 | 3 | 4 | 5 | 6 | 7 | 8 | | 10 | 11 | 9 | | | | | | | | | | | | |
| Oct 4 | (h) Aston Villa | W 1-0 | Lewis | 48,057 | 1 | 2 | 3 | 4 | 5 | 6 | 7 | 8 | 9 | 10 | 11 | | | | | | | | | | | | | |
| 11 | (a) Middlesbrough | L 0-3 | | 15,000 | 1 | 2 | 3 | 4 | 5 | 6 | 7 | 8 | 9 | | 11 | 10 | | | | | | | | | | | | |
| 18 | (h) Sheffield U | W 2-1 | Morris, Bentley | 15,282 | 1 | 2 | 3 | | 5 | 6 | 7 | 8 | 9 | 10 | 11 | | | 4 | | | | | | | | | | |
| 25 | (a) Derby C | W 2-1 | Morris, Bentley | 12,000 | 1 | 2 | 3 | | 5 | 6 | 7 | 8 | 9 | 10 | 11 | | | 4 | | | | | | | | | | |
| Nov 1 | (h) Manchester C | D 0-0 | | 17,443 | 1 | 2 | 3 | | 5 | 6 | 7 | 8 | | 10 | 11 | 9 | | 4 | | | | | | | | | | |
| 8 | (a) Bradford C | L 0-1 | | 10,000 | 1 | 2 | 3 | 4 | | 6 | 7 | 8 | | | | | | | 5 | 9 | | | | | | | | |
| 15 | (h) Blackburn R | W 2-0 | Shearman, Buck | 32,524 | 1 | 2 | 3 | 4 | 5 | 6 | 7 | 8 | 9 | 10 | 11 | | | | | | | | | | | | | |
| 22 | (a) Sunderland | D 0-0 | | 39,700 | 1 | 2 | 3 | 4 | 5 | 6 | 7 | 8 | 9 | 10 | 11 | | | | | | | | | | | | | |
| 29 | (h) Everton | D 1-1 | Lewis | 16,627 | 1 | 2 | 3 | 4 | 5 | 6 | 7 | | 9 | 10 | 11 | | | | | | 8 | | | | | | | |
| Dec 6 | (a) Tottenham H | L 0-3 | | 26,000 | 1 | 2 | 3 | 4 | 5 | 6 | 7 | | | 10 | 11 | 9 | 8 | | | | | | | | | | | |
| 13 | (a) Sheffield W | W 4-1 | Edwards 2, Morris, Pailor | 17,000 | 1 | 2 | 3 | 4 | 5 | 6 | 7 | 10 | | | 11 | | | | | 9 | | 8 | | | | | | |
| 20 | (h) Bolton W | D 1-1 | McNeal | 21,311 | 1 | 2 | 3 | 4 | 5 | 6 | 7 | 10 | 9 | | 11 | | | | | | | 8 | | | | | | |
| 25 | (a) Oldham A | L 0-2 | | 12,000 | 1 | 2 | 3 | 4 | 5 | 6 | 7 | 10 | 9 | | 11 | | | | | | | 8 | | | | | | |
| 26 | (h) Oldham A | D 2-2 | Bentley 2 (2 pens) | 30,294 | 1 | | 3 | 4 | | 6 | 7 | 10 | 9 | | 11 | | | | 5 | | | 8 | 2 | | | | | |
| 27 | (a) Burnley | D 0-0 | | 15,100 | 1 | | 3 | 4 | | 6 | 7 | 10 | 9 | | | | | | 5 | | | 8 | 2 | 11 | | | | |
| Jan 1 | (a) Manchester U | L 0-1 | | 16,400 | 1 | | 3 | 4 | | 6 | 7 | 10 | 9 | | | | | | 5 | | | 8 | 2 | 11 | | | | |
| 3 | (h) Preston NE | W 1-0 | Buck (pen) | 13,659 | 1 | 2 | | 4 | 5 | 6 | 7 | 8 | | 10 | 11 | | | | | | | | 3 | 9 | | | | |
| 17 | (a) Newcastle U | D 3-3 | Edwards, Shearman, Bentley | 18,200 | 1 | 2 | 3 | 4 | | 6 | 7 | 10 | 9 | | 11 | | | | 5 | | | 8 | | | | | | |
| 24 | (h) Liverpool | L 0-1 | | 13,582 | 1 | 2 | 3 | 4 | | 6 | 7 | 10 | 9 | | 11 | 8 | | | 5 | | | | | | | | | |
| Feb 7 | (a) Aston Villa | L 0-2 | | 48,000 | 1 | 2 | 3 | 4 | 5 | 6 | 7 | 8 | 9 | | | | | | | | | | | | 10 | | | |
| 14 | (h) Middlesbrough | W 2-1 | McNeal, Bentley | 15,692 | 1 | 2 | | 4 | 5 | 6 | 7 | | 9 | 10 | 11 | | | | | | | | | | 8 | 3 | | |
| 28 | (h) Derby C | W 2-1 | Bentley, Swift | 14,746 | 1 | 2 | 3 | 4 | | 6 | 7 | 8 | 10 | | | | | | | | | | | | 9 | 5 | | 11 |
| Mar 7 | (a) Bolton W | L 0-1 | | 20,000 | 1 | 2 | 3 | 4 | | 6 | 7 | 8 | 10 | | | | | | | | | | | | 9 | 5 | | 11 |
| 12 | (h) Bradford C | W 2-1 | Bentley 2 | 12,057 | 1 | 2 | 3 | 4 | | 6 | 7 | 10 | 8 | | | | | | | | | | | | 9 | 5 | | 11 |
| 19 | (a) Sheffield U | D 1-1 | Morris | 10,120 | 1 | 2 | | 4 | 5 | 6 | 7 | 10 | 8 | | | | | | | | | | | | 9 | | 3 | 11 |
| 21 | (a) Blackburn R | L 0-2 | | 22,126 | 1 | 2 | | | | 6 | 11 | 8 | | | | | 10 | 4 | | | 7 | | | | 9 | 5 | 3 | |
| 25 | (a) Manchester C | W 3-2 | Swift, Bentley, Gregory | 16,700 | 1 | 2 | | 4 | | 6 | 7 | 8 | | | | | 10 | | | | | | | 11 | 9 | 5 | 3 | |
| 28 | (h) Sunderland | W 2-1 | Gregory 2 | 23,366 | 1 | 2 | 3 | 4 | | 6 | 7 | 8 | | | | | 10 | | | | | | | 11 | 9 | 5 | | |
| Apr 4 | (a) Everton | L 0-2 | | 21,000 | 1 | 2 | | | | 6 | 7 | 10 | 8 | | | | 11 | 4 | | | | | | | 9 | 5 | 3 | |
| 11 | (h) Tottenham H | D 1-1 | Swift | 13,627 | 1 | 2 | 3 | 4 | | 6 | 7 | 8 | | | | 11 | | | | | 10 | | | | 9 | 5 | | |
| 13 | (a) Manchester U | W 2-1 | Wright, Bentley | 16,907 | 1 | 2 | 3 | 4 | | 6 | 7 | 8 | | | | 11 | | | | | 10 | | | | 9 | 5 | | |
| 14 | (h) Chelsea | W 3-1 | Jephcott 2, Swift | 16,479 | 1 | 2 | 3 | 4 | | 6 | 7 | 8 | | | | | | | 10 | | | | | | 9 | 5 | | 11 |
| 18 | (h) Sheffield W | D 1-1 | Bentley | 14,134 | 1 | 2 | 3 | | | 6 | 7 | 8 | | | | | | | 10 | | | | | | 9 | 5 | | 11 |
| | | | App | | 38 | 35 | 32 | 37 | 19 | 36 | 37 | 26 | 31 | 18 | 27 | 7 | 5 | 6 | 6 | 2 | 4 | 7 | 4 | 4 | 13 | 13 | 5 | 6 |
| | | | Goals | | | | | | 2 | 2 | 2 | 6 | 16 | 3 | 2 | 1 | 3 | | | 1 | 1 | 3 | | | 4 | | | |

**Action from the win over Derby County at the Baseball Ground in October 1913.**

# 1914-15

## Division 1

| Date | Venue | Opponent | Result | Score | Scorers | Att. | Pearson H | Smith J | Pennington J | Waterhouse F | Bowser S | McNeal R | Wright H | Bentley A | Poulton A | Bache H | Bookman L | Shearman B | Moorwood L | Swift A | Morris F | Wood M | Newall T | Mann J | Jephcott C | Crisp J | Richardson S | Parkes H | Shore E | Bowen W | Gregory H | Reed F |
|---|---|---|---|---|---|---|---|---|---|---|---|---|---|---|---|---|---|---|---|---|---|---|---|---|---|---|---|---|---|---|---|---|
| Sep 2 | (a) | Newcastle U | W | 2-1 | Bentley, Bookman | 15,000 | 1 | 2 | 3 | 4 | 5 | 6 | 7 | 8 | 9 | 10 | 11 | | | | | | | | | | | | | | | |
| 5 | (a) | Middlesbrough | L | 0-2 | | 14,500 | 1 | 2 | 3 | 4 | 5 | 6 | 7 | 8 | 9 | 10 | | 11 | | | | | | | | | | | | | | |
| 12 | (h) | Sheffield U | D | 1-1 | Poulton | 6,481 | 1 | 2 | 3 | 4 | 5 | 6 | 7 | 8 | 9 | 10 | 11 | | | | | | | | | | | | | | | |
| 19 | (a) | Aston Villa | L | 1-2 | Swift | 29,000 | | 2 | 3 | 4 | 5 | 6 | | 8 | | 10 | 11 | | | 7 | 1 | 9 | | | | | | | | | | |
| 26 | (h) | Liverpool | W | 4-0 | Bentley 2, Morris 2 | 18,026 | 1 | 2 | 3 | 4 | 5 | 6 | | 8 | | 9 | 11 | | | 7 | | | 10 | | | | | | | | | |
| 28 | (a) | Tottenham H | L | 0-2 | | 22,000 | 1 | 2 | 3 | 4 | 5 | 6 | | 8 | | 11 | 7 | | | 9 | 10 | | | | | | | | | | | |
| Oct 3 | (a) | Bradford | W | 4-1 | Bentley, Bache, Morris 2 | 19,000 | 1 | | 3 | 4 | 5 | 6 | | 8 | | 9 | 11 | 7 | | | | | 10 | 2 | | | | | | | | |
| 10 | (h) | Oldham A | D | 0-0 | | 15,768 | 1 | 2 | 3 | 4 | 5 | 6 | | 8 | | 11 | 7 | | | | | | 10 | 9 | | | | | | | | |
| 17 | (a) | Manchester U | D | 0-0 | | 13,200 | 1 | 2 | 3 | 4 | 5 | 6 | | | 9 | 11 | 7 | | | | | | 10 | 8 | | | | | | | | |
| 24 | (h) | Bolton W | W | 3-0 | Bentley, Shearman, Bache | 7,817 | 1 | 2 | 3 | 4 | 5 | 6 | 8 | 9 | 11 | 7 | | | | 10 | | | | | | | | | | | | |
| 31 | (a) | Blackburn R | L | 1-2 | Morris | 8,005 | 1 | 2 | | 4 | 5 | 6 | 8 | 9 | | 11 | 10 | 3 | | | 7 | | | | | | | | | | | |
| Nov 7 | (h) | Notts C | W | 4-1 | Morris 2, Bentley, Bache | 10,368 | 1 | 2 | | 4 | 5 | 6 | 8 | 9 | | 11 | 10 | 3 | | | 7 | | | | | | | | | | | |
| 14 | (a) | Sunderland | W | 2-1 | Jephcott, Bentley | 15,000 | 1 | 2 | 3 | 4 | 5 | 6 | 8 | 9 | | 11 | 10 | | | | 7 | | | | | | | | | | | |
| 21 | (h) | Sheffield W | D | 0-0 | | 11,254 | 1 | 2 | 3 | 4 | 5 | 6 | 8 | 9 | | 11 | 10 | | | | 7 | | | | | | | | | | | |
| 28 | (h) | Manchester C | L | 0-1 | | 9,398 | 1 | 2 | 3 | 4 | 5 | 6 | 8 | 9 | 11 | | 10 | | | | 7 | | | | | | | | | | | |
| Dec 5 | (a) | Everton | L | 1-2 | Crisp | 22,000 | 1 | 2 | 3 | 4 | 5 | 6 | 8 | 9 | 11 | | 10 | | | | | | | 7 | | | | | | | | |
| 12 | (h) | Chelsea | W | 2-0 | Jephcott, Swift | 6,421 | 1 | 2 | 3 | 4 | 5 | 6 | | | 11 | | 9 | 10 | | | | | | 7 | 8 | | | | | | | |
| 19 | (a) | Bradford C | L | 0-5 | | 5,300 | 1 | 2 | 3 | 4 | 5 | 6 | | | 11 | | 9 | 10 | | | | | | 7 | 8 | | | | | | | |
| 25 | (a) | Burnley | W | 2-0 | Morris, Swift | 10,000 | 1 | 2 | 3 | 4 | 5 | 6 | | | 11 | | 9 | 10 | | | | | | 7 | 8 | | | | | | | |
| 26 | (h) | Burnley | W | 3-0 | Swift 2, Crisp | 15,853 | 1 | 2 | 3 | 4 | 5 | 6 | | | 11 | | 9 | 10 | | | | | | 7 | 8 | | | | | | | |
| Jan 2 | (h) | Middlesbrough | W | 1-0 | Bache | 10,914 | 1 | 2 | 3 | 4 | 5 | 6 | | 9 | 11 | | | 10 | | | | | | 7 | 8 | | | | | | | |
| 16 | (a) | Sheffield U | L | 0-2 | | 7,800 | 1 | 2 | 3 | | 5 | 6 | | | 11 | | 9 | 10 | | | | | | 7 | 8 | 4 | | | | | | |
| 23 | (h) | Aston Villa | W | 2-0 | Swift, Morris | 19,492 | 1 | 2 | 3 | 4 | 5 | 6 | | | 11 | | 9 | 10 | | | | | | 7 | 8 | | | | | | | |
| Feb 6 | (h) | Bradford | W | 1-0 | Bowser (pen) | 7,466 | 1 | 2 | 3 | 4 | 5 | 6 | | | 11 | | 9 | 10 | | | | | | 7 | 8 | | | | | | | |
| 20 | (h) | Manchester U | D | 0-0 | | 10,169 | 1 | 2 | 3 | 4 | 5 | 6 | | | 11 | | 9 | 10 | | | | | | 7 | 8 | | | | | | | |
| 27 | (a) | Bolton W | D | 1-1 | Crisp | 8,900 | 1 | 2 | 3 | 4 | 5 | 6 | | | 11 | | 9 | 10 | | | | | | | 8 | 7 | | | | | | |
| Mar 6 | (h) | Blackburn R | D | 0-0 | | 15,168 | 1 | 2 | 3 | 4 | 5 | 6 | 8 | | 11 | | 9 | 10 | | | | | | | | 7 | | | | | | |
| 9 | (a) | Oldham A | D | 1-1 | Crisp | 11,400 | 1 | 2 | 3 | 4 | 5 | 6 | | 9 | 11 | | | 10 | | | | | | 8 | | 7 | | | | | | |
| 13 | (a) | Notts C | D | 1-1 | Morris | 28,000 | 1 | 2 | 3 | 4 | 5 | 6 | | 9 | 11 | | | 10 | | | | | | 8 | | 7 | | | | | | |
| 20 | (h) | Sunderland | L | 1-2 | Morris | 10,233 | 1 | 2 | 3 | 4 | 5 | | 9 | | 11 | | | 10 | | | | | | 8 | 6 | 7 | | | | | | |
| 24 | (a) | Liverpool | L | 1-3 | Newall | 16,000 | 1 | | 3 | 4 | | 6 | | | 11 | | | | | 9 | 8 | | | | | 7 | 2 | 5 | 10 | | | |
| 27 | (a) | Sheffield W | D | 0-0 | | 9,000 | 1 | | 3 | 5 | | 6 | 9 | | 11 | | | | 8 | | 4 | | | | | 7 | 2 | | 10 | | | |
| Apr 3 | (a) | Manchester C | L | 0-4 | | 8,400 | 1 | | | 5 | | 6 | 9 | | 11 | | | | 8 | 3 | 4 | | 7 | | | | 2 | | 10 | | | |
| 5 | (h) | Newcastle U | W | 2-0 | Bentley 2 | 11,858 | 1 | | | 5 | 3 | 6 | 9 | | 11 | | | | | 2 | 4 | | 7 | 8 | | | | | 10 | | | |
| 6 | (h) | Tottenham H | W | 3-2 | Gregory 3 | 5,813 | | | | 3 | 6 | 10 | | | 11 | 1 | 9 | | | 2 | 4 | | 7 | | | | | | | | 8 | 5 |
| 10 | (h) | Everton | L | 1-2 | Swift | 8,748 | 1 | | | 4 | 3 | 6 | 10 | | 11 | | 9 | | | 2 | | | 7 | 8 | | | | | | | | 5 |
| 17 | (a) | Chelsea | L | 1-4 | McNeal | 6,000 | 1 | | | 3 | 6 | 8 | | | 11 | | 9 | | | 4 | | | | | | 7 | 2 | | 10 | | | 5 |
| 24 | (h) | Bradford C | W | 3-0 | Gregory, Newall, McNeal | 4,410 | 1 | | 4 | 5 | 6 | 8 | | | 11 | | | 3 | 9 | | | 7 | | | | 2 | | 10 | | | | |
| **App** | | | | | | | 36 | 29 | 30 | 35 | 35 | 37 | 7 | 19 | 9 | 12 | 16 | 28 | 2 | 15 | 28 | 8 | 8 | 2 | 18 | 18 | 2 | 8 | 5 | 1 | 7 | 3 |
| **Goals** | | | | | | | | | | | 1 | 2 | | 9 | 1 | 4 | 1 | 1 | | 7 | 11 | | 2 | | 2 | 4 | | | | | 4 | |

**West Brom's first and reserve-team players pictured before the start of the 1914-15 season, the last before the League was suspended due to war.**

# 1919-20

## Division 1

| Date | | Opponent | Result | Scorers | Att. | Pearson H | Smith J | Pennington J | Richardson S | Bowser S | McNeal R | Crisp J | Magee T | Smith A | Morris F | Gregory H | Jephcott C | Moorwood L | Cook A | Reed F | Bentley A | Hatton S | Waterhouse F |
|---|---|---|---|---|---|---|---|---|---|---|---|---|---|---|---|---|---|---|---|---|---|---|---|
| Aug 30 | (h) | Oldham A | W 3-1 | Morris 2, Gregory | 19,058 | 1 | 2 | 3 | 4 | 5 | 6 | 7 | 8 | 9 | 10 | 11 | | | | | | | |
| Sep 3 | (a) | Newcastle U | W 2-0 | Magee, Gregory | 50,000 | 1 | 2 | 3 | 4 | 5 | 6 | 7 | 8 | 9 | 10 | 11 | | | | | | | |
| 6 | (a) | Oldham A | L 1-2 | Bowser (pen) | 16,000 | 1 | 2 | 3 | 4 | 5 | 6 | 7 | 8 | 9 | 10 | 11 | | | | | | | |
| 8 | (h) | Newcastle U | W 3-0 | A.Smith, Bowser (pen), Morris | 20,082 | 1 | 2 | 3 | 4 | 5 | 6 | 7 | 8 | 9 | 10 | 11 | | | | | | | |
| 15 | (h) | Everton | W 4-3 | Magee, Morris, Gregory, Crisp | 31,245 | 1 | 2 | 3 | 4 | 5 | 6 | 7 | 8 | 9 | 10 | 11 | | | | | | | |
| 20 | (a) | Everton | W 5-2 | Jephcott, Crisp 2, A.Smith 2 | 25,000 | 1 | 2 | 3 | 4 | 5 | 6 | 11 | 8 | 9 | 10 | | 7 | | | | | | |
| 27 | (h) | Bradford C | W 4-1 | Bowser 3 (2 pens), Morris | 29,680 | 1 | 2 | 3 | 4 | 5 | 6 | 11 | 8 | 9 | 10 | | 7 | | | | | | |
| Oct 4 | (a) | Bradford C | L 0-3 | | 17,000 | 1 | 2 | 3 | 4 | 5 | 6 | 11 | 8 | 9 | 10 | | 7 | | | | | | |
| 11 | (h) | Bolton W | W 4-1 | Magee, Bowser (pen), Crisp, A.Smith | 35,227 | 1 | 2 | 3 | 4 | 5 | 6 | 11 | 8 | 9 | 10 | | 7 | | | | | | |
| 18 | (a) | Bolton W | W 2-1 | Morris, Gregory | 24,000 | | | 3 | 4 | 5 | 6 | 11 | 8 | | 9 | 10 | 7 | 1 | 2 | | | | |
| 25 | (h) | Notts C | W 8-0 | Morris 5, Foster (og), Gregory, Magee | 36,086 | | | 3 | 4 | | 6 | 7 | 8 | 9 | 10 | 11 | | 1 | 2 | 5 | | | |
| Nov 1 | (a) | Notts C | L 0-2 | | 12,050 | | 2 | 3 | 4 | 5 | 6 | 7 | 8 | 9 | 10 | 11 | | 1 | | | | | |
| 10 | (h) | Aston Villa | L 1-2 | Gregory | 43,121 | 1 | 2 | 3 | 4 | 5 | 6 | 7 | 8 | 9 | 10 | 11 | | | | | | | |
| 15 | (a) | Aston Villa | W 4-2 | Gregory 2, Morris 2 | 58,273 | 1 | 2 | 3 | 4 | 5 | 6 | | 8 | 9 | 10 | 11 | 7 | | | | | | |
| 22 | (h) | Sheffield W | L 1-3 | A.Smith | 22,193 | 1 | 2 | 3 | 4 | 5 | 6 | | 8 | 9 | 10 | 11 | 7 | | | | | | |
| 29 | (a) | Sheffield W | W 3-0 | Bowser (pen), Bentley, Morris | 25,000 | 1 | 2 | 3 | 4 | 5 | 6 | 11 | 8 | | 10 | | 7 | | | | 9 | | |
| Dec 6 | (a) | Manchester C | W 3-2 | Bowser (pen), Morris 2 | 26,000 | 1 | 2 | 3 | 4 | 5 | 6 | 11 | 8 | | 10 | | 7 | | | | 9 | | |
| 13 | (h) | Manchester C | W 2-0 | Morris 2 | 25,040 | 1 | 2 | 3 | 4 | 5 | 6 | 7 | 8 | | 10 | 11 | | | | | 9 | | |
| 20 | (a) | Derby C | W 4-0 | Bentley, Morris 2, Gregory | 21,000 | 1 | 2 | 3 | 4 | 5 | 6 | 7 | 8 | | 10 | 11 | | | | | 9 | | |
| 26 | (h) | Sunderland | W 4-0 | Magee, Morris 2, Bentley | 43,579 | 1 | 2 | 3 | 4 | 5 | 6 | 7 | 8 | | 10 | 11 | | | | | 9 | | |
| 27 | (h) | Derby C | W 3-0 | Morris 2, Magee | 34,167 | 1 | 2 | 3 | 4 | 5 | 6 | 7 | 8 | | 10 | 11 | | | | | 9 | | |
| Jan 1 | (a) | Sunderland | L 1-4 | Morris | 32,500 | 1 | 2 | 3 | 4 | 5 | 6 | 7 | 8 | | 10 | 11 | | | | | 9 | | |
| 3 | (a) | Blackburn R | W 5-1 | Bentley 3, Morris, Gregory | 18,000 | 1 | 2 | 3 | 4 | 5 | 6 | 7 | 8 | | 10 | 11 | | | | | 9 | | |
| 17 | (h) | Blackburn R | W 5-2 | Magee, Bentley, Morris, Crisp, Gregory | 23,360 | 1 | 2 | 3 | 4 | 5 | 6 | 7 | 8 | | 10 | 11 | | | | | 9 | | |
| 24 | (h) | Manchester U | W 2-1 | Bowser, Morris | 30,192 | 1 | 2 | 3 | 4 | 5 | 6 | 7 | 8 | 9 | 10 | 11 | | | | | | | |
| Feb 7 | (h) | Sheffield U | L 0-2 | | 28,975 | 1 | 2 | 3 | 4 | 5 | 6 | 7 | 8 | | 10 | 11 | | | | | | 9 | |
| 14 | (a) | Sheffield U | L 0-1 | | 39,850 | 1 | 2 | 3 | 4 | 5 | 6 | | 8 | | 10 | 11 | 7 | | | | 9 | | |
| 21 | (h) | Middlesbrough | W 4-1 | Bentley 2, Morris 2 | 24,955 | 1 | 2 | 3 | 4 | 5 | 6 | | 8 | | 10 | 11 | 7 | | | | 9 | | |
| 25 | (a) | Manchester U | W 2-1 | Bentley 2 | 21,000 | 1 | 2 | | 4 | 5 | 6 | 11 | 8 | | 10 | | 7 | | 3 | | 9 | | |
| 28 | (a) | Middlesbrough | D 0-0 | | 16,500 | 1 | 2 | 3 | | 5 | 6 | 11 | 8 | | 10 | | 7 | | | | 9 | | 4 |
| Mar 6 | (a) | Burnley | D 2-2 | Jephcott, Crisp | 30,200 | 1 | 2 | 3 | | 5 | 6 | 11 | 8 | | 10 | | 7 | | | | 9 | | 4 |
| 13 | (h) | Burnley | W 4-1 | Bentley, Morris 2, Crisp | 32,213 | 1 | 2 | 3 | 4 | 5 | 6 | 11 | 8 | | 10 | | 7 | | | | 9 | | |
| 20 | (a) | Preston NE | W 1-0 | Crisp | 20,000 | 1 | 2 | | 4 | 5 | 6 | 11 | 8 | | 10 | | 7 | | 3 | | 9 | | |
| 27 | (h) | Preston NE | W 4-1 | Jephcott 2, Morris 2 | 24,186 | 1 | 2 | 3 | 4 | 5 | 6 | 11 | 8 | | 10 | | 7 | | | | 9 | | |
| Apr 3 | (a) | Bradford | W 4-0 | Bentley, Morris, McNeal (pen), A.Smith | 9,000 | 1 | 2 | 3 | 4 | 5 | 6 | 11 | 8 | | 10 | | 7 | | | | 9 | | |
| 5 | (a) | Arsenal | L 0-1 | | 38,000 | 1 | 2 | 3 | 4 | 5 | 6 | 11 | 8 | | 10 | | 7 | | | | 9 | | |
| 6 | (h) | Arsenal | W 1-0 | Morris | 39,397 | 1 | 2 | | 4 | 5 | 6 | | 8 | 9 | 10 | 11 | 7 | | 3 | | | | |
| 10 | (h) | Bradford | W 3-1 | Jephcott, Bentley, Bowser (pen) | 29,414 | 1 | 2 | | 4 | 5 | 6 | 11 | 8 | | 10 | | 7 | | 3 | | 9 | | |
| 17 | (a) | Liverpool | D 0-0 | | 45,100 | 1 | 2 | 3 | 4 | 5 | 6 | 7 | 8 | | 10 | 11 | | | | | 9 | | |
| 24 | (h) | Liverpool | D 1-1 | Morris | 33,349 | 1 | 2 | | 4 | 5 | 6 | 7 | 8 | | 10 | 11 | | | 3 | | 9 | | |
| 26 | (a) | Chelsea | L 0-2 | | 39,902 | 1 | 2 | 3 | 4 | 5 | 6 | 7 | 8 | | 10 | 11 | | | | | 9 | | |
| May 1 | (h) | Chelsea | W 4-0 | McNeal, Gregory, A.Smith, Bentley | 35,668 | 1 | 2 | 3 | 4 | 5 | 6 | 7 | 8 | | 10 | 11 | | | | | 9 | | |
| | | | | App | | 39 | 40 | 37 | 40 | 41 | 42 | 38 | 24 | 29 | 39 | 34 | 21 | 3 | 7 | 1 | 24 | 1 | 2 |
| | | | | Goals | | | | | | 10 | 2 | 8 | 7 | 7 | 37 | 12 | 5 | | | | 15 | | |

**Jesse Pennington, skipper of the League Championship side, pictured here after his playing days had ended.**

# 1920-21

## Division 1

| Date | V | Opponent | Result | Scorers | Att | Pearson H | Smith J | Pennington J | Richardson S | Bowser S | McNeal R | Crisp J | Smith A | Bentley A | Morris F | Gregory H | Jephcott C | Magee T | Cook A | Taylor H | Adams W | James R | Ashmore G | Hatton S | Clark B | Long W | Newall T | Reed F | Blood R | Bedford L |
|---|---|---|---|---|---|---|---|---|---|---|---|---|---|---|---|---|---|---|---|---|---|---|---|---|---|---|---|---|---|---|
| Aug 28 | (a) | Newcastle U | D 1-1 | Morris | 61,080 | 1 | 2 | 3 | 4 | 5 | 6 | 7 | 8 | 9 | 10 | 11 | | | | | | | | | | | | | | |
| Sep 1 | (h) | Liverpool | D 1-1 | Gregory | 32,475 | 1 | 2 | 3 | 4 | 5 | 6 | 11 | 9 | | | 10 | 7 | 8 | | | | | | | | | | | | |
| 4 | (h) | Newcastle U | D 0-0 | | 29,202 | 1 | 2 | 3 | 4 | 5 | 6 | 11 | 9 | | | 10 | 7 | 8 | | | | | | | | | | | | |
| 6 | (a) | Liverpool | D 0-0 | | 27,550 | 1 | | 3 | 4 | 5 | 6 | 11 | 9 | | | 10 | 7 | 8 | 2 | | | | | | | | | | | |
| 11 | (a) | Bolton W | L 0-3 | | 18,000 | 1 | | 3 | 4 | 5 | 6 | 11 | | 9 | | 10 | 7 | 8 | 2 | | | | | | | | | | | |
| 18 | (h) | Bolton W | W 2-1 | Crisp, Bentley | 34,865 | 1 | 2 | 3 | 4 | 5 | 6 | 7 | | 8 | 10 | 11 | | | | 9 | | | | | | | | | | |
| 25 | (a) | Derby C | D 1-1 | Morris | 18,300 | 1 | 2 | | 4 | 5 | | 7 | | 8 | 10 | 11 | | | | 9 | 3 | 6 | | | | | | | | |
| Oct 2 | (h) | Derby C | W 3-0 | McNeal, Morris, Bowser (pen) | 26,893 | 1 | 2 | | 4 | 5 | 6 | | | 8 | 10 | 11 | 7 | | | 9 | 3 | | | | | | | | | |
| 9 | (a) | Blackburn R | L 1-5 | Taylor | 15,300 | | 2 | | 4 | 5 | | | | 8 | 10 | | 7 | | | 9 | 3 | | 1 | 6 | 11 | | | | | |
| 16 | (h) | Blackburn R | D 1-1 | Morris | 35,025 | 1 | 2 | | 4 | 5 | | | | 8 | 10 | 11 | | | | 9 | 3 | | | 6 | | 7 | | | | |
| 23 | (a) | Huddersfield T | L 1-5 | Taylor | 25,100 | 1 | 2 | | 4 | 5 | | | | 10 | 8 | | 11 | | | 9 | 3 | | | 6 | | 7 | | | | |
| 30 | (h) | Huddersfield T | W 3-0 | Bowser (pen), A.Smith, Morris | 44,049 | 1 | 2 | 3 | 4 | 5 | 6 | | | 8 | 10 | 11 | 7 | | | 9 | | | | | | | | | | |
| Nov 6 | (a) | Aston Villa | D 0-0 | | 66,094 | 1 | 2 | 3 | 4 | 5 | 6 | | | 8 | 10 | 11 | 7 | | | 9 | | | | | | | | | | |
| 13 | (h) | Aston Villa | W 2-1 | A.Smith, Bowser (pen) | 42,334 | 1 | 2 | 3 | 4 | 5 | 6 | | | 8 | 10 | 11 | 7 | | | 9 | | | | | | | | | | |
| 27 | (h) | Bradford C | W 2-0 | Morris, Gregory | 22,068 | 1 | 2 | 3 | 4 | 5 | 6 | | 8 | 9 | 10 | 11 | 7 | | | | | | | | | | | | | |
| Dec 4 | (h) | Sunderland | W 4-1 | Bentley, Gregory, Bowser 2 (1 pen) | 23,726 | 1 | 2 | 3 | 4 | 5 | 6 | | 8 | 9 | 10 | 11 | 7 | | | | | | | | | | | | | |
| 11 | (a) | Sunderland | L 0-3 | | 20,000 | 1 | 2 | 3 | 4 | 5 | 6 | | 8 | 9 | 10 | 11 | 7 | | | | | | | | | | | | | |
| 18 | (h) | Everton | L 1-2 | Crisp | 19,932 | 1 | 2 | 3 | 4 | 5 | 6 | 7 | 8 | 9 | 10 | 11 | | | | | | | | | | | | | | |
| 25 | (a) | Manchester C | L 0-4 | | 22,306 | 1 | 2 | 3 | 4 | 5 | 6 | 7 | 8 | 9 | 10 | 11 | | | | | | | | | | | | | | |
| 27 | (h) | Manchester C | D 2-2 | A.Smith, Morris | 32,147 | 1 | 2 | 3 | 4 | 5 | 6 | | 8 | 9 | 10 | 11 | 7 | | | | | | | | | | | | | |
| Jan 1 | (a) | Everton | D 2-2 | Morris, James | 59,964 | 1 | 2 | | 4 | 5 | 6 | 7 | | 8 | 10 | 11 | | | 3 | | | 9 | | | | | | | | |
| 15 | (a) | Manchester U | W 4-1 | James 2, A.Smith, Morris | 40,100 | 1 | 2 | 3 | | 5 | 6 | | | 8 | 10 | 11 | 7 | | | | | 9 | | | | | 4 | | | |
| 22 | (h) | Manchester U | L 0-2 | | 26,826 | 1 | 2 | 3 | | 5 | 6 | | | 8 | 10 | 11 | 7 | | | | | 9 | | | | | 4 | | | |
| 29 | (a) | Middlesbrough | W 1-0 | A.Smith | 25,500 | 1 | 2 | 3 | | 5 | 6 | | | 8 | 10 | 11 | 7 | | | | | 9 | | | | | 4 | | | |
| Feb 5 | (h) | Middlesbrough | L 0-1 | | 24,920 | 1 | 2 | 3 | | 5 | 6 | | | 8 | 10 | 11 | 7 | | | | | 9 | | | | | 4 | | | |
| 9 | (a) | Bradford C | D 1-1 | James | 42,000 | 1 | 2 | | 4 | 5 | 6 | | | 8 | 10 | | 7 | | 3 | | | 9 | | | | | | | | |
| 12 | (a) | Chelsea | L 0-3 | | 15,000 | 1 | 2 | 3 | 4 | | 6 | | 11 | 8 | | 10 | 7 | | | | | 9 | | | | | | 5 | | |
| 19 | (h) | Tottenham H | W 3-1 | Crisp, Bentley, Blood (pen) | 31,753 | 1 | 2 | 3 | 4 | 5 | 6 | 11 | | 8 | 10 | | 7 | | | | | | | | | | | | 9 | |
| 26 | (a) | Tottenham H | L 0-1 | | 35,000 | 1 | 2 | 3 | 4 | 5 | | | 11 | 8 | 10 | | 7 | | | | | | | 6 | | | | | 9 | |
| Mar 12 | (a) | Oldham A | W 3-0 | Blood, Morris 2 | 13,000 | 1 | 2 | 3 | 4 | 5 | 6 | | | 8 | 10 | 11 | 7 | | | | | | | | | | | | 9 | |
| 14 | (h) | Chelsea | D 1-1 | Blood | 28,140 | 1 | 2 | 3 | 4 | 5 | 6 | | | 8 | 10 | 11 | 7 | | | | | | | | | | | | 9 | |
| 19 | (h) | Oldham A | D 0-0 | | 23,908 | 1 | 2 | | 4 | 5 | 6 | | | 8 | 10 | 11 | 7 | | 3 | | | | | | | | | | 9 | |
| 25 | (h) | Preston NE | L 0-3 | | 23,511 | 1 | 2 | 3 | 4 | 5 | 6 | | | 8 | 10 | 11 | 7 | | | | | | | | | | | | 9 | |
| 28 | (a) | Arsenal | L 1-2 | Crisp | 20,152 | 1 | 2 | | 4 | 5 | 6 | 11 | | 8 | 10 | | 7 | | 3 | | | | | | | | | | 9 | |
| 29 | (h) | Arsenal | L 3-4 | A.Smith, Bowser (pen), Morris | 23,650 | 1 | 2 | 3 | 4 | 5 | 6 | 7 | | 8 | 10 | | | | | | | | | | | | | | 9 | 11 |
| Apr 2 | (a) | Preston NE | L 1-2 | Blood | 18,052 | 1 | 2 | 3 | 4 | 5 | 6 | 7 | | 8 | 10 | | | | | | | | | | | | | | 9 | 11 |
| 9 | (h) | Burnley | W 2-0 | Crisp, Morris | 17,242 | | 2 | 3 | 4 | 5 | 6 | 11 | | 8 | 10 | | 7 | | | | | | 1 | | | | | | 9 | |
| 16 | (a) | Burnley | D 1-1 | A.Smith | 13,700 | | 2 | 3 | 4 | 5 | 6 | 11 | | 8 | 10 | | 7 | | | | | | 1 | | | | | | 9 | |
| 23 | (h) | Sheffield U | D 1-1 | Blood | 23,697 | | 2 | 3 | 4 | 5 | 6 | 11 | | 8 | 10 | | 7 | | | | | | 1 | | | | | | 9 | |
| 30 | (h) | Sheffield U | W 2-0 | Morris, Blood | 21,000 | | 2 | 3 | 4 | 5 | 6 | 11 | | 8 | 10 | | 7 | | | | | | 1 | | | | | | 9 | |
| May 2 | (h) | Bradford | L 0-1 | | 17,472 | | 2 | 3 | 4 | 5 | 6 | 11 | | 8 | 10 | | 7 | | | | | | 1 | | | | | | 9 | |
| 7 | (a) | Bradford | W 3-0 | Morris 2 (1 pen), Blood | 8,105 | | 2 | 3 | 4 | | 6 | | 5 | 8 | 10 | 11 | | 7 | | | | | 1 | | | | | | 9 | |
| **App** | | | | | | 35 | 40 | 33 | 38 | 40 | 37 | 27 | 28 | 18 | 37 | 29 | 31 | 5 | 4 | 9 | 7 | 8 | 7 | 4 | 1 | 2 | 4 | 1 | 15 | 2 |
| **Goals** | | | | | | | | | | 6 | 1 | 5 | 7 | 3 | 16 | 3 | | | | 2 | | 4 | | | | | | | 7 | |

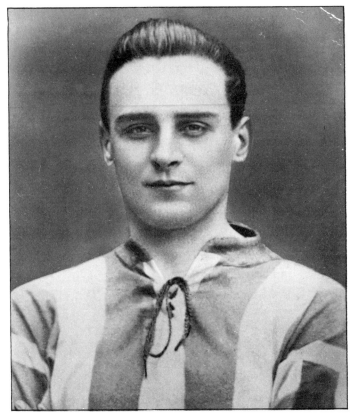

**Albion's utility forward Jack Crisp who scored five goals in 27 League games in 1920-21.**

# 1921-22

## Division 1

| Date | | Opponent | Result | Scorers | Att | Ashmore G | Smith J | Adams W | Richardson S | Bowser S | McNeal R | Jephcott C | Smith A | Blood R | Morris F | Crisp J | Magee T | Bedford L | Cook A | Bentley A | Gregory H | Pennington J | Newall T | Wilson C | Blagden J | Savage G | James G | Pearson H | Hatton S | Davies S | Reed F | James R | Jones I | Watson E |
|---|---|---|---|---|---|---|---|---|---|---|---|---|---|---|---|---|---|---|---|---|---|---|---|---|---|---|---|---|---|---|---|---|---|---|
| Aug 27 | (h) | Middlesbrough | D 0-0 | | 24,880 | 1 | 2 | 3 | 4 | 5 | 6 | 7 | 8 | 9 | 10 | 11 | | | | | | | | | | | | | | | | | | |
| 29 | (a) | Manchester U | W 3-2 | Brett (og), Blood 2 | 20,000 | 1 | 2 | 3 | 4 | 5 | 6 | 7 | 8 | 9 | 10 | 11 | | | | | | | | | | | | | | | | | | |
| Sep 3 | (a) | Middlesbrough | L 2-3 | Blood, A.Smith | 15,000 | 1 | 2 | 3 | 4 | 5 | 6 | 7 | 8 | 9 | 10 | 11 | | | | | | | | | | | | | | | | | | |
| 7 | (h) | Manchester U | D 0-0 | | 20,557 | 1 | 2 | 3 | 4 | 5 | 6 | | 8 | 9 | 10 | 11 | 7 | | | | | | | | | | | | | | | | | |
| 10 | (h) | Blackburn R | L 0-2 | | 20,160 | 1 | 2 | 3 | 4 | 5 | 6 | | 8 | 9 | 10 | | | 7 | 11 | | | | | | | | | | | | | | | |
| 17 | (a) | Blackburn R | W 3-2 | Crisp, Bentley | 13,000 | 1 | 2 | | 4 | 5 | 6 | | | 9 | 10 | 7 | | | 3 | 8 | 11 | | | | | | | | | | | | | |
| 24 | (h) | Oldham A | L 0-1 | | 19,840 | 1 | 2 | | 4 | 5 | 6 | | | 9 | 10 | 7 | | | 3 | 8 | 11 | | | | | | | | | | | | | |
| Oct 1 | (a) | Oldham A | L 0-1 | | 10,107 | 1 | 2 | | | 5 | 6 | | 8 | | 10 | 7 | | | | | 11 | 3 | 4 | 9 | | | | | | | | | | |
| 8 | (h) | Aston Villa | L 0-1 | | 45,077 | 1 | 2 | | 4 | 5 | 6 | | | 9 | 10 | 7 | | | | 8 | 11 | 3 | | | | | | | | | | | | |
| 15 | (a) | Aston Villa | W 1-0 | Blood | 55,000 | 1 | 2 | | 4 | 5 | 6 | | 8 | 9 | 10 | 7 | | | | | 11 | 3 | | | | | | | | | | | | |
| 22 | (h) | Cardiff C | D 2-2 | Gregory, A.Smith | 20,969 | 1 | 2 | | 4 | 5 | 6 | | 8 | 9 | 10 | 7 | | | | | 11 | 3 | | | | | | | | | | | | |
| 29 | (a) | Cardiff C | L 0-2 | | 16,000 | 1 | 2 | | 4 | 5 | 6 | | | 9 | 10 | 7 | | | | 8 | 11 | 3 | | | | | | | | | | | | |
| Nov 5 | (h) | Bolton W | L 0-1 | | 15,502 | 1 | 2 | | | 5 | 6 | | | 9 | | | 7 | | | | 11 | 3 | 4 | | 8 | 10 | | | | | | | | |
| 12 | (a) | Bolton W | L 0-2 | | 13,514 | 1 | 2 | | 4 | 5 | 6 | | 8 | | | | 7 | | | | 11 | 3 | | 9 | | | 10 | | | | | | | |
| 19 | (a) | Manchester C | L 1-6 | Bentley | 18,000 | | 2 | | | 5 | 6 | | | 9 | | | 7 | | | 8 | 11 | 3 | | | | | 10 | 1 | 4 | | | | | |
| 26 | (h) | Manchester C | W 2-0 | Blagden, Morris | 14,145 | | 2 | | 4 | 5 | 6 | | | | 10 | | 7 | | | | 11 | 3 | | | 8 | | | 1 | | 9 | | | | |
| Dec 3 | (a) | Everton | W 2-1 | Morris, Reed | 21,000 | | 2 | | 4 | | 6 | | | | 10 | | 7 | | | | 11 | 3 | | | 8 | | | 1 | | 9 | 5 | | | |
| 10 | (h) | Everton | D 1-1 | Morris | 16,606 | | 2 | | 4 | 5 | 6 | | | | 10 | | 7 | | | | 11 | 3 | | | 8 | | | 1 | | 9 | | | | |
| 17 | (h) | Sunderland | W 2-1 | Morris, Davies | 18,251 | | 2 | | 4 | 5 | 6 | | | | 10 | | 7 | | | | 11 | 3 | | | 8 | | | 1 | | 9 | | | | |
| 24 | (a) | Sunderland | L 0-5 | | 10,522 | | 2 | | 4 | 5 | 6 | | | | 10 | | 7 | | | | 11 | 3 | | | 8 | | | 1 | | 9 | | | | |
| 26 | (h) | Birmingham | W 1-0 | Davies | 49,488 | | 2 | | 4 | | 6 | | | | 10 | | 7 | | | | 11 | 3 | | | 8 | | | 1 | | 9 | 5 | | | |
| 27 | (a) | Birmingham | W 2-0 | Magee, Morris | 44,500 | | 2 | | 4 | | 6 | | | | 10 | | 7 | | | | 11 | 3 | | | 8 | | | 1 | | 9 | 5 | | | |
| 31 | (h) | Huddersfield T | W 3-2 | Morris, Blagden, Gregory | 25,036 | | 2 | | 4 | | 6 | | | | 10 | | 7 | | | | 11 | 3 | | | 8 | | | 1 | | 9 | 5 | | | |
| Jan 14 | (a) | Huddersfield T | L 0-2 | | 6,000 | | 2 | | 4 | 10 | 6 | | | | | 11 | 7 | | | | | 3 | | | 8 | | | 1 | | 9 | 5 | | | |
| 21 | (h) | Tottenham H | W 3-0 | Davies 2, Magee | 21,498 | | 2 | | 4 | | 6 | | | | 10 | 11 | 7 | | | | | 3 | | | 8 | | | 1 | | 9 | 5 | | | |
| 30 | (a) | Tottenham H | L 0-2 | | 20,400 | | 2 | 3 | 4 | | | | | | 10 | 11 | 7 | | | | | | | | 8 | | | 1 | | 9 | 5 | 6 | | |
| Feb 4 | (h) | Bradford C | D 1-1 | Crisp | 15,170 | | 2 | | 4 | | 6 | | | 9 | 10 | 11 | 7 | | | | | 3 | | | 8 | | | 1 | | | 5 | | | |
| 25 | (a) | Preston NE | W 3-0 | Morris, A.Smith, Davies | 16,000 | | 2 | | 4 | 5 | 6 | | 8 | | 10 | | 7 | | | | 11 | 3 | | | | | | 1 | | 9 | | | | |
| Mar 4 | (h) | Chelsea | D 2-2 | Davies 2 | 11,026 | | 2 | | 4 | 5 | 6 | | 8 | | 10 | | 7 | | | | 11 | 3 | | | | | | 1 | | 9 | | | | |
| 8 | (a) | Bradford C | D 1-1 | A.Smith | 10,400 | | 2 | | 4 | | 6 | | 8 | | 10 | 11 | 7 | | | | | 3 | | | | | | 1 | | 9 | 5 | | | |
| 11 | (a) | Chelsea | D 1-1 | Morris | 20,000 | | 2 | | 4 | | 6 | | 8 | | 10 | 11 | 7 | | | | | 3 | | | | | | 1 | | 9 | 5 | | | |
| 18 | (a) | Sheffield U | D 0-0 | | 10,900 | | 2 | | 4 | | 6 | | 5 | 9 | 10 | 11 | 7 | | | | | 3 | | | 8 | | | 1 | | | | | | |
| 25 | (a) | Sheffield U | W 3-0 | A.Smith, Richardson, Davies | 12,113 | | 2 | | 4 | | 6 | | 8 | | 10 | 11 | 7 | | | | | 3 | | | | | | 1 | | 9 | 5 | | | |
| 29 | (h) | Preston NE | W 2-0 | Morris, Davies | 12,585 | | 2 | | 4 | 5 | 6 | | 8 | | 10 | 11 | | | | | | 3 | | 7 | | | | 1 | | 9 | | | | |
| Apr 1 | (h) | Burnley | W 2-0 | Morris 2 | 13,304 | | 2 | | 4 | 5 | 6 | | | | 10 | | | | | 8 | 11 | 3 | | 7 | | | | 1 | | 9 | | | | |
| 8 | (a) | Burnley | L 2-4 | Davies 2 | 8,900 | | 2 | 3 | 4 | 5 | 6 | | 8 | | 10 | | 7 | | | | 11 | | | | | | | 1 | | 9 | | | | |
| 15 | (a) | Newcastle U | L 0-3 | | 28,000 | | 2 | 3 | 4 | 5 | 6 | | | | 10 | | 7 | | | | 11 | | | | | | | 1 | | 9 | | | 8 | |
| 17 | (h) | Arsenal | L 0-3 | | 23,997 | | 2 | 3 | 4 | 5 | 6 | | 8 | | 10 | | 7 | | | | 11 | | | | | | | 1 | | 9 | | | | |
| 18 | (a) | Arsenal | D 2-2 | Hutchins (og), Davies | 23,663 | | 2 | 3 | 4 | | 6 | | | | 10 | | 7 | | | | 11 | | | 8 | | | | 1 | | 9 | 5 | | | |
| 22 | (h) | Newcastle U | L 1-2 | Davies | 32,063 | | 2 | | 4 | 5 | 6 | 7 | | | 10 | | | | | | 11 | 3 | | | | | | 1 | | 9 | | | 8 | |
| 29 | (a) | Liverpool | W 2-1 | Gregory 2 | 20,551 | | 2 | | 4 | 5 | 6 | | | | 10 | | 7 | | | | 11 | 3 | | | 8 | | | 1 | | 9 | | | | |
| May 6 | (h) | Liverpool | L 1-4 | Davies | 23,247 | | 2 | | | 5 | 6 | | | | 10 | | 7 | | | | 11 | 3 | | | 8 | | | 1 | | 9 | | | | 4 |
| | | | | **App** | | 14 | 42 | 10 | 38 | 30 | 41 | 4 | 19 | 14 | 38 | 19 | 31 | 1 | 3 | 5 | 28 | 29 | 2 | 4 | 16 | 2 | 2 | 28 | 1 | 25 | 12 | 1 | 2 | 1 |
| | | | | **Goals** | | | | | 1 | | | | 5 | 4 | 11 | 2 | 2 | | | 3 | 4 | | | | 2 | | | | | 14 | 1 | | | |

**Bobby Blood, centre-forward, signed from Port Vale, who actually had one leg shorter than the other but still possessed a cannonball shot – in either foot.**

# 1922-23

## Division 1

| Date | | Opponent | Result | Scorers | Att | Pearson H | Smith J | Adams W | Magee T | Bowser S | McNeal R | Jephcott C | Jones I | Davies S | Morris F | Gregory H | Crisp J | Smith A | Chamberlain H | Fitton A | Glidden T | Carter J | Blood R | Ashmore G | Richardson S | Dutton H | Spencer J | Wilson C | Ford E |
|---|---|---|---|---|---|---|---|---|---|---|---|---|---|---|---|---|---|---|---|---|---|---|---|---|---|---|---|---|---|
| Aug 26 | (a) | Burnley | L 0-3 | | 30,000 | 1 | 2 | 3 | 4 | 5 | 6 | 7 | 8 | 9 | 10 | 11 | | | | | | | | | | | | | |
| 28 | (h) | Preston NE | D 2-2 | Davies, Morris | 25,343 | 1 | 2 | 3 | 4 | 5 | 6 | 7 | 8 | 9 | 10 | 11 | | | | | | | | | | | | | |
| Sep 2 | (h) | Burnley | W 2-1 | Davies 2 | 23,561 | 1 | 2 | 3 | 4 | 5 | 6 | 7 | 8 | 9 | 10 | 11 | | | | | | | | | | | | | |
| 4 | (a) | Preston NE | D 0-0 | | 30,200 | 1 | 2 | 3 | 4 | 5 | 6 | 7 | 8 | 9 | 10 | | 11 | | | | | | | | | | | | |
| 9 | (a) | Aston Villa | L 0-2 | | 40,000 | 1 | 2 | 3 | 4 | 5 | 6 | 7 | 8 | 9 | 10 | | 11 | | | | | | | | | | | | |
| 16 | (h) | Aston Villa | W 3-0 | Davies 2, Morris | 39,576 | 1 | 2 | 3 | 4 | 5 | 6 | | | 9 | 10 | 11 | 7 | 8 | | | | | | | | | | | |
| 23 | (a) | Stoke C | W 2-0 | Davies, A.Smith | 20,000 | 1 | 2 | 3 | 4 | 5 | 6 | | | 9 | 10 | 11 | 7 | 8 | | | | | | | | | | | |
| 30 | (h) | Stoke C | L 0-1 | | 20,385 | 1 | 2 | 3 | 4 | 5 | 6 | | | 9 | 10 | 11 | 7 | 8 | | | | | | | | | | | |
| Oct 7 | (a) | Arsenal | L 1-3 | Gregory | 32,500 | 1 | 2 | 3 | 4 | 5 | 6 | | 8 | 9 | 10 | 11 | 7 | | | | | | | | | | | | |
| 14 | (h) | Arsenal | W 7-0 | Morris 4, Crisp 2, Gregory | 21,730 | 1 | 2 | 3 | 4 | 5 | 6 | | 8 | 9 | 10 | 11 | 7 | | | | | | | | | | | | |
| 21 | (a) | Tottenham H | L 1-3 | Gregory | 35,000 | 1 | | 2 | 4 | 5 | 6 | | 8 | 9 | 10 | 11 | 7 | | 3 | | | | | | | | | | |
| 28 | (h) | Tottenham H | W 5-1 | Jones, Davies 2, Gregory, Crisp | 20,150 | 1 | 2 | 3 | 4 | 5 | 6 | | 8 | 9 | 10 | 11 | 7 | | | | | | | | | | | | |
| Nov 4 | (h) | Manchester C | W 2-0 | Davies, Morris | 17,124 | 1 | 2 | 3 | 4 | 5 | 6 | | 8 | 9 | 10 | 11 | 7 | | | | | | | | | | | | |
| 11 | (a) | Manchester C | D 1-1 | Davies | 25,000 | 1 | 2 | 3 | 4 | 5 | 6 | | 8 | 9 | 10 | | 7 | | | 11 | | | | | | | | | |
| 18 | (h) | Everton | D 0-0 | | 18,539 | 1 | 2 | 3 | 4 | 5 | 6 | | 8 | 9 | 10 | | 7 | | | 11 | | | | | | | | | |
| 25 | (a) | Everton | W 1-0 | Morris | 35,000 | 1 | 2 | 3 | 4 | 5 | 6 | | 8 | 9 | 10 | | | | | 11 | 7 | | | | | | | | |
| Dec 2 | (h) | Bolton W | D 1-1 | Davies | 16,527 | 1 | 2 | | 4 | 5 | 6 | | 8 | 9 | 10 | | | | 3 | 11 | 7 | | | | | | | | |
| 9 | (a) | Bolton W | L 0-3 | | 20,000 | 1 | 2 | | 4 | 5 | 6 | | | 9 | 10 | 11 | | | 3 | | 7 | 8 | | | | | | | |
| 16 | (a) | Sunderland | L 2-3 | Morris, Gregory | 10,000 | 1 | 2 | 3 | 4 | 5 | 6 | | 8 | | 10 | 11 | | | | | 7 | | 9 | | | | | | |
| 23 | (h) | Sunderland | D 1-1 | Morris | 23,092 | 1 | 2 | 3 | 4 | 5 | 6 | | 8 | | 10 | 11 | | | | | 7 | | 9 | | | | | | |
| 26 | (a) | Cardiff C | L 0-3 | | 39,000 | 1 | 2 | 3 | 4 | 5 | 6 | | 8 | | 10 | 11 | | | | | 7 | | 9 | | | | | | |
| 27 | (h) | Cardiff C | W 3-0 | Davies (pen), Morris, Spencer | 14,898 | | 2 | 3 | | 5 | | | 8 | | 10 | 11 | | | | | | | 9 | 1 | 4 | 6 | 7 | | |
| 30 | (a) | Blackburn R | L 1-5 | Morris (pen) | 7,000 | 1 | 2 | 3 | | 5 | | | 8 | | 10 | 11 | | | | | | | 9 | | 4 | 6 | 7 | | |
| Jan 6 | (h) | Blackburn R | W 3-0 | Gregory, Davies, Morris (pen) | 17,024 | 1 | 2 | 3 | 4 | 5 | 6 | | 8 | 9 | 10 | 11 | | | | | | | | | | | 7 | | |
| 20 | (a) | Birmingham | W 2-0 | Davies, Gregory | 32,180 | 1 | 2 | 3 | 4 | 5 | 6 | | 8 | 9 | 10 | 11 | | | | | | | | | | | 7 | | |
| 27 | (h) | Birmingham | W 1-0 | Morris | 25,123 | 1 | 2 | 3 | 4 | 5 | 6 | | 8 | 9 | 10 | 11 | | | | | | | | | | | 7 | | |
| Feb 7 | (a) | Liverpool | L 0-2 | | 26,000 | 1 | 2 | 3 | 4 | 5 | 6 | | 8 | 9 | 10 | 11 | | | | | | | | | | | 7 | | |
| 10 | (h) | Liverpool | D 0-0 | | 20,464 | 1 | 2 | 3 | 4 | 5 | 6 | | 8 | 9 | 10 | 11 | | | | | | | | | | | 7 | | |
| 14 | (a) | Newcastle U | L 0-2 | | 10,000 | 1 | 2 | 3 | 4 | 5 | 6 | | 8 | 9 | 10 | 11 | | | | | | | | | | | 7 | | |
| Mar 3 | (a) | Nottingham F | W 4-0 | Bowser, Blood 3 | 17,134 | 1 | 2 | 3 | 4 | 5 | 6 | | 8 | | | 7 | | | | | | | 9 | | | | 7 | | |
| 10 | (h) | Nottingham F | D 0-0 | | 15,990 | 1 | 2 | 3 | 4 | 5 | 6 | | 8 | | 10 | 11 | | | | | | | 9 | | | | 7 | | |
| 14 | (h) | Newcastle U | W 2-1 | Jones, Blood | 5,520 | 1 | 2 | 3 | 4 | 5 | 6 | | 8 | | 10 | 11 | | | | | | | 9 | | | | 7 | | |
| 17 | (h) | Chelsea | D 0-0 | | 12,242 | 1 | 2 | 3 | 4 | 5 | 6 | | | | | | | 11 | | | | 8 | 9 | | | | 7 | 10 | |
| 31 | (a) | Sheffield U | W 4-0 | Carter, Davies 3 | 15,147 | 1 | 2 | 3 | 4 | 5 | 6 | | | 10 | 9 | | | | | | | 8 | | | | | 7 | | 11 |
| Apr 2 | (h) | Huddersfield T | L 0-2 | | 24,291 | 1 | 2 | 3 | 4 | 5 | 6 | | | 10 | 9 | 11 | | | | | | 8 | | | | | 7 | | |
| 3 | (a) | Huddersfield T | L 1-4 | Carter | 13,000 | 1 | 2 | 3 | 4 | 5 | 6 | | | 10 | 9 | 11 | | | | | | 8 | | | | | 7 | | |
| 7 | (a) | Sheffield U | L 1-3 | Davies | 10,000 | 1 | 2 | 3 | 4 | 5 | 6 | | | 10 | 9 | 11 | | | | | | 8 | | | | | 7 | | |
| 14 | (h) | Oldham A | W 1-0 | Carter | 8,405 | 1 | 2 | 3 | 4 | 5 | 6 | | | 9 | 10 | | | | | | 11 | 8 | | | | | 7 | | |
| 21 | (h) | Oldham A | D 0-0 | | 4,700 | 1 | 2 | 3 | 4 | 5 | 6 | | 8 | 9 | 10 | | | | | | 11 | | | | | | 7 | | |
| 25 | (a) | Chelsea | D 2-2 | Spencer, Jones | 15,000 | | 2 | 3 | 4 | 5 | 6 | | 8 | 9 | 10 | | | | | | 11 | | | 1 | | | 7 | | |
| 28 | (h) | Middlesbrough | W 1-0 | Davies | 10,021 | | 2 | 3 | 4 | 5 | 6 | | 8 | 9 | 10 | | | | | | 11 | | | 1 | | | 7 | | |
| May 5 | (a) | Middlesbrough | W 1-0 | Davies | 9,000 | | 2 | 3 | 4 | 5 | 6 | | | 9 | 10 | | | | | | 11 | 8 | | 1 | | | 7 | | |
| | | | | | App | 38 | 41 | 40 | 40 | 42 | 40 | 5 | 31 | 37 | 40 | 27 | 13 | 3 | 3 | 4 | 11 | 8 | 9 | 4 | 2 | 2 | 20 | 1 | 1 |
| | | | | | Goals | | | | 1 | | | | 3 | 20 | 14 | 7 | 3 | 1 | | | | 3 | 4 | | | | 2 | | |

**Albion's playing staff in 1922-3. Back row (left to right): T.Magee, R.Hunt, S.Richardson, H.Pearson, F.Reed, G.Ashmore, S.Guest (assistant trainer), H.Gregory. Third row: S.Davis, J.Pennington, J.Crisp, R.Blood, J.Smith, W.Telford, J.Blagdon, W.Gopsill (trainer), J.Wallace. Seated: W.Lamus, H.Chamberlain, T.Glidden, I.Jones, R.McNeal, S.Bowser, F.Morris, W.Adams, G.James. On ground: T.Rooke, H.Dutton, C.Wilson, R.Lenny, E.Watson.**

# 1923-24

## Division 1

| Date | | Opponent | Result | Scorers | Att | Ashmore G | Smith J | Adams W | Magee T | Bowser S | McNeal R | Spencer J | Jones I | Davies S | Morris F | Fitton A | Glidden T | Richardson S | Carter J | Pearson H | Blood R | Smith H | Perry A | Reed F | Gregory H | Chamberlain H | Byers J | Dutton H | James G | Wilson C |
|---|---|---|---|---|---|---|---|---|---|---|---|---|---|---|---|---|---|---|---|---|---|---|---|---|---|---|---|---|---|---|
| Aug 25 | (h) | Liverpool | W 2-0 | Davies, Fitton | 25,121 | 1 | 2 | 3 | 4 | 5 | 6 | 7 | 8 | 9 | 10 | 11 | | | | | | | | | | | | | | |
| 27 | (a) | Nottingham F | D 1-1 | Davies | 21,000 | 1 | 2 | 3 | 4 | 5 | 6 | 7 | 8 | 9 | 10 | 11 | | | | | | | | | | | | | | |
| Sep 1 | (a) | Liverpool | D 0-0 | | 40,000 | 1 | 2 | 3 | 4 | 5 | 6 | 7 | 8 | 9 | 10 | 11 | | | | | | | | | | | | | | |
| 3 | (h) | Nottingham F | W 3-2 | Davies 2, Jones | 26,909 | 1 | 2 | 3 | 4 | 5 | 6 | 7 | 8 | 9 | 10 | 11 | | | | | | | | | | | | | | |
| 8 | (h) | Arsenal | W 4-0 | Jones, Davies 2 (2 pens), Fitton | 35,233 | 1 | 2 | 3 | 4 | 5 | 6 | 7 | 8 | 9 | 10 | 11 | | | | | | | | | | | | | | |
| 15 | (a) | Arsenal | L 0-1 | | 36,004 | 1 | 2 | 3 | 4 | 5 | 6 | | 8 | 9 | 10 | 11 | 7 | | | | | | | | | | | | | |
| 22 | (h) | Blackburn R | D 3-3 | Morris 2, Jones | 21,238 | 1 | 2 | 3 | 4 | 5 | 6 | | 8 | 9 | 10 | 11 | 7 | | | | | | | | | | | | | |
| 29 | (a) | Blackburn R | L 0-4 | | 20,209 | 1 | 2 | 3 | | 5 | 6 | | 8 | 9 | 10 | 11 | 7 | 4 | | | | | | | | | | | | |
| Oct 6 | (h) | Huddersfield T | L 2-4 | Davies, Carter | 17,041 | 1 | 2 | 3 | 4 | 5 | 6 | 7 | 10 | 9 | | 11 | | | 8 | | | | | | | | | | | |
| 13 | (a) | Huddersfield T | D 0-0 | | 19,000 | 1 | 2 | 3 | 4 | 5 | 6 | | | 9 | 10 | 11 | 7 | | 8 | | | | | | | | | | | |
| 20 | (h) | Aston Villa | W 1-0 | Morris | 42,096 | 1 | 2 | 3 | 4 | 5 | 6 | | | 9 | 10 | 11 | 7 | | 8 | | | | | | | | | | | |
| 27 | (a) | Aston Villa | L 0-4 | | 52,550 | 1 | 2 | 3 | 4 | 5 | 6 | | | 9 | 10 | 11 | 7 | | 8 | | | | | | | | | | | |
| Nov 3 | (a) | Cardiff C | L 0-3 | | 20,600 | 1 | 2 | 3 | 4 | 5 | 6 | | | 9 | 10 | 11 | 7 | | 8 | | | | | | | | | | | |
| 10 | (h) | Cardiff C | L 2-4 | Blood 2 (1 pen) | 15,143 | | 2 | 3 | 4 | 5 | 6 | 7 | 10 | | | | | | 8 | 1 | 9 | 11 | | | | | | | | |
| 17 | (a) | Everton | L 0-2 | | 28,700 | 1 | 2 | 3 | 4 | 5 | 6 | 7 | 10 | | | | | | 8 | | 9 | 11 | | | | | | | | |
| 24 | (h) | Everton | W 5-0 | Blood 3, Morris, Gregory | 14,387 | 1 | 2 | | 4 | | 6 | 7 | 10 | | | | | | 8 | | 9 | | 3 | 5 | 11 | | | | | |
| Dec 1 | (a) | Tottenham H | D 0-0 | | 28,100 | 1 | 2 | | 4 | | 6 | 7 | 10 | | | | | | 8 | | 9 | | 3 | 5 | 11 | | | | | |
| 8 | (h) | Tottenham H | W 4-1 | Carter 4 | 15,048 | 1 | 2 | | 4 | | 6 | 7 | 10 | | | | | | 8 | | 9 | | 3 | 5 | 11 | | | | | |
| 15 | (h) | Birmingham | D 0-0 | | 24,786 | 1 | 2 | | 4 | | 6 | 7 | 10 | | | | | | 8 | | 9 | | 3 | 5 | 11 | | | | | |
| 22 | (a) | Birmingham | D 0-0 | | 32,000 | 1 | 2 | | 4 | | 6 | 7 | | 9 | 10 | | | | 8 | | | | 3 | 5 | 11 | | | | | |
| 25 | (a) | Bolton W | L 0-2 | | 20,000 | 1 | 2 | | 4 | | 6 | 7 | | | 10 | | | | 8 | | 9 | | 3 | 5 | 11 | | | | | |
| 26 | (h) | Bolton W | L 0-5 | | 12,148 | 1 | 2 | | 4 | | 6 | 7 | | | 10 | | | | | | 9 | | 3 | 5 | 11 | | | | | |
| 29 | (a) | Manchester C | D 3-3 | Carter 2, Bowser | 16,402 | 1 | 2 | | 4 | 9 | 6 | | | 7 | 10 | | | | 8 | | | | | 5 | 11 | 3 | | | | |
| Jan 5 | (h) | Manchester C | W 2-1 | Bowser, Morris | 11,991 | 1 | 2 | | 4 | 9 | 6 | | | 7 | 10 | | | | 8 | | | | 3 | 5 | 11 | | | | | |
| 19 | (h) | Burnley | L 0-3 | | 8,527 | 1 | 2 | | 4 | | 6 | | 8 | 7 | 10 | 11 | | | | | 9 | | 3 | 5 | | | | | | |
| 26 | (a) | Burnley | L 0-4 | | 12,000 | 1 | 2 | | | | 6 | 7 | | 9 | 10 | | | 4 | 8 | | | | 3 | 5 | | | 11 | | | |
| Feb 9 | (a) | Middlesbrough | W 1-0 | Spencer | 15,000 | 1 | 2 | | | | 6 | 7 | | 9 | 10 | | | 4 | 8 | | | | 3 | 5 | | | 11 | | | |
| 16 | (h) | Preston NE | L 1-2 | Carter | 10,024 | 1 | 2 | | | | 6 | 7 | | 9 | 10 | | | 4 | 8 | | | | 3 | 5 | 11 | | | | | |
| Mar 1 | (h) | Chelsea | D 2-2 | Byers, James | 11,485 | | 2 | | | | | 7 | 8 | | | | | 4 | | 1 | | | 3 | 5 | | | 11 | 6 | 9 | 10 |
| 12 | (a) | Chelsea | D 0-0 | | 17,900 | | 2 | | 4 | | | | 10 | | | | | 7 | | 1 | | | 3 | 5 | | | 11 | 6 | 9 | 8 |
| 15 | (a) | Newcastle U | D 1-1 | Reed | 20,000 | | 2 | | 4 | | | | 8 | | | | | 7 | | 1 | | | 3 | 5 | | | 11 | 6 | 9 | 10 |
| 19 | (a) | Preston NE | W 2-1 | Wilson, Dutton | 12,100 | | 2 | | 4 | | | | 8 | | | | | 7 | | 1 | | | 3 | 5 | | | 11 | 6 | 9 | 10 |
| 22 | (h) | Newcastle U | D 0-0 | | 16,053 | | 2 | | | | 6 | | 8 | | | | | | | 1 | | | 3 | 5 | | | 11 | 4 | 9 | 10 |
| 29 | (a) | West Ham U | L 0-1 | | 18,112 | | 2 | | 4 | | | | 8 | | | | | | | 1 | | | 3 | 5 | | | 11 | 6 | 9 | 10 |
| Apr 5 | (h) | West Ham U | D 0-0 | | 13,248 | 1 | 2 | | 4 | | | 7 | 8 | | | | | | | | 9 | | 3 | 5 | | | 11 | 6 | | 10 |
| 9 | (h) | Middlesbrough | D 1-1 | Blood | 14,473 | 1 | 2 | | 4 | | | 7 | 8 | | | | | | | | 9 | | 3 | 5 | | | 11 | 6 | | 10 |
| 12 | (h) | Notts C | W 5-0 | James 2, Wilson 2 (1 pen), Jones | 8,003 | 1 | 2 | | 4 | | | 7 | 8 | | | | | | | | | | 3 | 5 | 11 | | | 6 | 9 | 10 |
| 18 | (a) | Sunderland | L 0-2 | | 13,000 | 1 | 2 | | 4 | | | 7 | 8 | | | | | | | | | | 3 | 5 | 11 | | | 6 | 9 | 10 |
| 19 | (a) | Notts C | L 0-1 | | 20,000 | 1 | 2 | | 4 | | | 7 | 8 | | | | | | | | | | 3 | 5 | | | 11 | 6 | 9 | 10 |
| 21 | (h) | Sunderland | W 3-1 | James, Wilson, Gregory | 12,033 | 1 | 2 | 3 | 4 | | | 7 | | | | | | | | | | | | 5 | 10 | | 11 | 6 | 9 | 8 |
| 26 | (a) | Sheffield U | L 0-2 | | 10,500 | 1 | 2 | | 4 | | | 7 | 8 | | | | | | | | | | 3 | 5 | | | 11 | 6 | 9 | 10 |
| May 3 | (h) | Sheffield U | W 3-1 | Blood 3 (1 pen) | 10,023 | 1 | 2 | | 4 | | | 7 | 8 | | 10 | | | | | | 9 | | 3 | 5 | 11 | | 6 | | | |
| App | | | | | | 35 | 42 | 16 | 36 | 17 | 29 | 27 | 21 | 21 | 30 | 14 | 12 | 5 | 19 | 7 | 11 | 2 | 25 | 27 | 14 | 1 | 13 | 14 | 11 | 13 |
| Goals | | | | | | | | | | 2 | | 1 | 4 | 7 | 5 | 2 | | | 8 | | 9 | | | 1 | 2 | | 1 | 1 | 4 | 4 |

**Albion's popular outside-right, Tommy Glidden, later to skipper the side to that FA Cup and promotion double in 1930-31.**

# 1924-25

## Division 1

| Date | | Opponent | Result | Scorers | Att | Ashmore G | Smith J | Perry A | Magee T | Reed F | Dutton H | Spencer J | Jones I | Blood R | Wilson C | Byers J | McNeal R | Carter J | James G | Glidden T | Richardson S | Fitton A | Davies S | Rooke E | Baugh R | Gregory H | Pearson H | Adams W |
|---|---|---|---|---|---|---|---|---|---|---|---|---|---|---|---|---|---|---|---|---|---|---|---|---|---|---|---|---|
| Aug 30 | (h) | Notts C | L 1-2 | Blood | 21,572 | 1 | 2 | 3 | 4 | 5 | 6 | 7 | 8 | 9 | 10 | 11 | | | | | | | | | | | | |
| Sep 1 | (a) | Bolton W | D 1-1 | Jones | 25,000 | 1 | 2 | 3 | 4 | 5 | 6 | 7 | 8 | 9 | 10 | 11 | | | | | | | | | | | | |
| 6 | (a) | Everton | L 0-1 | | 24,700 | 1 | 2 | 3 | 4 | 5 | | 7 | 8 | 9 | 10 | 11 | 6 | | | | | | | | | | | |
| 8 | (h) | Tottenham H | W 2-0 | Blood, Wilson | 20,880 | 1 | 2 | 3 | 4 | 5 | | 7 | | 9 | 10 | 11 | 6 | 8 | | | | | | | | | | |
| 13 | (h) | Sunderland | W 2-1 | Wilson, James | 24,166 | 1 | 2 | 3 | 4 | 5 | | 7 | | | 10 | 11 | 6 | 8 | 9 | | | | | | | | | |
| 20 | (a) | Cardiff C | W 1-0 | Carter | 21,000 | 1 | 2 | 3 | 4 | 5 | | 7 | | | 10 | 11 | 6 | 8 | 9 | | | | | | | | | |
| 22 | (a) | Tottenham H | W 1-0 | James | 37,000 | 1 | 2 | 3 | 4 | 5 | | 7 | | | 10 | 11 | 6 | 8 | 9 | | | | | | | | | |
| 27 | (h) | Preston NE | D 1-1 | Wilson | 30,183 | 1 | 2 | 3 | 4 | 5 | | 7 | | | 10 | 11 | 6 | 8 | 9 | | | | | | | | | |
| Oct 4 | (a) | Burnley | W 1-0 | Carter | 30,000 | 1 | 2 | 3 | 4 | 5 | | 7 | | | 10 | 11 | 6 | 8 | 9 | | | | | | | | | |
| 11 | (h) | Leeds U | W 3-1 | James 2, Carter | 21,332 | 1 | 2 | 3 | 4 | 5 | | | | | 10 | 11 | 6 | 8 | 9 | 7 | | | | | | | | |
| 18 | (h) | Birmingham | D 1-1 | James | 35,617 | 1 | 2 | 3 | 4 | 5 | | 7 | | | 10 | 11 | 6 | 8 | 9 | | | | | | | | | |
| 25 | (a) | Aston Villa | L 0-1 | | 48,126 | 1 | 2 | 3 | 4 | 5 | | 7 | | | 10 | 11 | 6 | 8 | 9 | | | | | | | | | |
| Nov 1 | (h) | Huddersfield T | W 1-0 | James | 15,683 | 1 | 2 | 3 | 4 | 5 | | | 7 | | 10 | 11 | | 8 | 9 | | 6 | | | | | | | |
| 8 | (a) | Blackburn R | L 0-1 | | 16,000 | 1 | 2 | 3 | 4 | 5 | | | 7 | | 10 | | | 8 | 9 | | 6 | 11 | | | | | | |
| 15 | (h) | West Ham U | W 4-1 | Carter, Wilson 3 | 23,959 | 1 | 2 | 3 | 4 | 5 | | | | | 10 | 11 | | 8 | | 7 | 6 | | 9 | | | | | |
| 22 | (a) | Sheffield U | L 0-2 | | 15,100 | 1 | 2 | 3 | 4 | 5 | | | | | 10 | 11 | 6 | 8 | | 7 | | | 9 | | | | | |
| 29 | (h) | Newcastle U | W 2-0 | Carter, Byers | 13,141 | 1 | 2 | 3 | 4 | 5 | 6 | | | | 10 | 11 | | 8 | 9 | 7 | | | | | | | | |
| Dec 6 | (a) | Liverpool | D 1-1 | James | 18,000 | 1 | 2 | 3 | 4 | 5 | 6 | | | | 10 | 11 | | 8 | 9 | 7 | | | | | | | | |
| 13 | (h) | Nottingham F | W 5-1 | James 4, Carter | 16,227 | 1 | 2 | 3 | 4 | 5 | 6 | | | | 10 | 11 | | 8 | 9 | 7 | | | | | | | | |
| 20 | (a) | Bury | W 2-0 | James 2 | 12,000 | 1 | 2 | 3 | 4 | 5 | 6 | | | | 10 | 11 | | 8 | 9 | 7 | | | | | | | | |
| 25 | (a) | Manchester C | W 2-1 | James, Carter | 20,000 | 1 | 2 | 3 | 4 | 5 | 6 | | | | 10 | 11 | | 8 | 9 | 7 | | | | | | | | |
| 26 | (h) | Manchester C | W 3-1 | James 2, Carter | 41,990 | 1 | 2 | 3 | 4 | 5 | | | | | 10 | 11 | | 8 | 9 | 7 | 6 | | | | | | | |
| 27 | (a) | Notts C | W 2-0 | James, Smith (og) | 12,000 | 1 | 2 | 3 | | | | | | | 10 | 11 | 6 | | 9 | 7 | 4 | | 8 | 5 | | | | |
| Jan 3 | (h) | Everton | W 3-0 | James 2, Wilson | 21,773 | 1 | 2 | 3 | 4 | 5 | | | | | 10 | 11 | | 8 | 9 | 7 | 6 | | | | | | | |
| 17 | (a) | Sunderland | L 0-3 | | 33,000 | 1 | 2 | 3 | 4 | 5 | | | | | 10 | 11 | | 8 | 9 | 7 | 6 | | | | | | | |
| 24 | (h) | Cardiff C | W 1-0 | Wilson | 22,508 | 1 | 2 | 3 | 4 | 5 | | | | | 10 | 11 | | 8 | 9 | 7 | 6 | | | | | | | |
| Feb 7 | (h) | Burnley | L 1-4 | James | 24,492 | 1 | 2 | 3 | 4 | 5 | | | | | 10 | 11 | | 8 | 9 | 7 | 6 | | | | | | | |
| 12 | (a) | Preston NE | W 2-1 | Carter, Wilson | 16,000 | 1 | 2 | | 4 | 5 | | | | | 10 | 11 | | 8 | 9 | 7 | 6 | | | | | 3 | | |
| 14 | (a) | Leeds U | W 1-0 | Carter | 18,500 | 1 | 2 | | 4 | 5 | | | | | 10 | 11 | | 8 | 9 | 7 | 6 | | | | | 3 | | |
| 28 | (h) | Aston Villa | W 4-1 | Davies, James 3 | 22,123 | 1 | 2 | | 4 | 5 | | | | | 10 | 11 | | | 9 | 7 | 6 | 8 | | | | 3 | | |
| Mar 11 | (a) | Huddersfield T | D 1-1 | Carter | 21,000 | 1 | 2 | | 4 | 5 | | | | | 10 | | | 8 | 9 | 7 | 6 | | | | | 3 | 11 | |
| 14 | (h) | Blackburn R | D 1-1 | James | 21,858 | 1 | 2 | | 4 | 5 | 6 | | | | 10 | | | 8 | 9 | 7 | | | | | | 3 | 11 | |
| 16 | (a) | Birmingham | D 0-0 | | 30,000 | 1 | 2 | | 4 | 5 | | | 10 | | | | | 8 | 9 | 7 | 6 | 11 | | | | 3 | | |
| 21 | (a) | West Ham U | L 1-2 | Wilson | 10,900 | | 2 | | 4 | 5 | | | | | 10 | | | 8 | 9 | 7 | 6 | 11 | | | | 3 | 1 | |
| 30 | (h) | Sheffield U | W 2-1 | Glidden, Davies | 9,892 | | | | | | | | | | 8 | 9 | | 7 | 6 | 11 | 10 | 5 | | | | 3 | | |
| Apr 4 | (a) | Newcastle U | W 1-0 | Carter | 25,400 | 1 | 2 | | | 5 | 4 | | | | 10 | 11 | | 8 | 9 | 7 | 6 | | | | | 3 | | |
| 11 | (h) | Liverpool | D 0-0 | | 13,157 | 1 | 2 | | 4 | 5 | | | | | 10 | 11 | | 8 | 9 | 7 | 6 | | | | | 3 | | |
| 13 | (h) | Arsenal | W 2-0 | Glidden, Wilson | 23,285 | 1 | 2 | | 4 | 5 | | | | | 10 | 11 | | 8 | 9 | 7 | 6 | | | | | 3 | | |
| 14 | (a) | Arsenal | L 0-2 | | 21,000 | 1 | 2 | | 4 | 5 | | | | | 10 | | | 8 | 9 | 7 | 6 | 11 | | | | 3 | | |
| 18 | (a) | Nottingham F | W 1-0 | Carter | 6,000 | 1 | 2 | | 4 | 5 | | | | | 10 | | | 8 | 9 | 7 | 6 | 11 | | | | | | 3 |
| 25 | (h) | Bury | D 1-1 | James | 15,277 | 1 | 2 | | 4 | 5 | | | | | 10 | 11 | | 8 | 9 | 7 | 6 | | | | | 3 | | |
| May 2 | (h) | Bolton W | D 0-0 | | 13,383 | 1 | 2 | | 4 | 5 | | | | | 10 | 11 | | 8 | 9 | 7 | 6 | | | | | 3 | | |
| | | | | App | | 41 | 42 | 27 | 40 | 40 | 9 | 11 | 6 | 6 | 4 | 40 | 34 | 12 | 37 | 36 | 29 | 23 | 6 | 5 | 2 | 14 | 2 | 1 |
| | | | | Goals | | | | | | | | | 1 | 2 | 11 | 1 | | 13 | 25 | 2 | | | 2 | | | | | |

**Albion's forward line in 1924-25 – Glidden, Carter, James, Wilson and Byers.**

# 1925-26

## Division 1

| Date | Opponent | Res | Score | Scorers | Att | Ashmore G | Smith J | Baugh R | Magee T | Reed F | Richardson S | Glidden T | Carter J | James G | Wilson C | Byers J | Adams W | Dutton H | Jones I | Davies S | Rooke E | Perry A | Fitton A | Sproson T | Spencer J | Finch R | Evans J | Darnell L |
|---|---|---|---|---|---|---|---|---|---|---|---|---|---|---|---|---|---|---|---|---|---|---|---|---|---|---|---|---|
| Aug 29 (a) | Huddersfield T | D 1-1 | | James | 30,000 | 1 | 2 | 3 | 4 | 5 | 6 | 7 | 8 | 9 | 10 | 11 | | | | | | | | | | | | |
| Sep 2 (h) | Everton | D 1-1 | | Wilson | 29,856 | 1 | 2 | 3 | 4 | 5 | 6 | 7 | 8 | 9 | 10 | 11 | | | | | | | | | | | | |
| 5 (h) | Sunderland | L 2-5 | | Wilson, Jones | 21,520 | 1 | | 3 | | 5 | 4 | 7 | | | 10 | 11 | 2 | 6 | 8 | 9 | | | | | | | | |
| 12 (a) | Blackburn R | W 2-1 | | Dutton, Davies | 25,000 | 1 | 2 | 3 | | | 4 | 7 | | 9 | | 11 | | 6 | 8 | 10 | 5 | | | | | | | |
| 16 (a) | Everton | L 0-4 | | | 40,000 | 1 | 2 | 3 | | | 4 | 7 | | 9 | | 11 | | 6 | 8 | 10 | 5 | | | | | | | |
| 23 (h) | Manchester C | W 4-1 | | Davies 2, Wilson 2 | 8,287 | 1 | 2 | | | 5 | 4 | 7 | | 9 | 8 | | | 6 | | 10 | | 3 | 11 | | | | | |
| 26 (a) | Birmingham | L 0-3 | | | 34,850 | 1 | 2 | | | 5 | 4 | 7 | | 9 | 8 | | | 6 | | 10 | | 3 | 11 | | | | | |
| Oct 3 (h) | Aston Villa | D 1-1 | | Davies | 52,332 | 1 | 2 | 3 | | 5 | 4 | 7 | 8 | | 10 | | | 6 | | 9 | | | 11 | | | | | |
| 10 (h) | Sheffield U | W 2-0 | | Wilson, Davies | 15,973 | 1 | 2 | 3 | | 5 | 4 | 7 | 8 | | 10 | | | 6 | | 9 | | | 11 | | | | | |
| 17 (a) | Leicester C | L 0-3 | | | 20,500 | 1 | 2 | 3 | | 5 | 4 | 7 | 8 | | 10 | | | 6 | | 9 | | | 11 | | | | | |
| 24 (h) | West Ham U | W 7-1 | | Davies 3 (1 pen), Glidden, Wilson, Carter 2 | 20,851 | 1 | 2 | 3 | | 5 | 4 | 7 | 8 | | 10 | | | 6 | | 9 | | | 11 | | | | | |
| 31 (a) | Bolton W | D 2-2 | | Carter, James | 16,000 | | 2 | 3 | | 5 | 4 | 7 | 8 | 9 | 10 | | | 6 | | | | | 11 | 1 | | | | |
| Nov 7 (h) | Notts C | D 4-4 | | Carter 2, Davies, Wilson | 10,406 | 1 | 2 | 3 | | 5 | 4 | 7 | 8 | | 10 | | | 6 | | 9 | | | 11 | | | | | |
| 9 (h) | Bury | W 4-0 | | Davies 2, Fitton, Carter | 10,922 | 1 | 2 | 3 | | 5 | 4 | 7 | 8 | | 10 | | | 6 | | 9 | | | 11 | | | | | |
| 14 (a) | Liverpool | L 0-2 | | | 40,000 | 1 | 2 | 3 | | 5 | 4 | 7 | 8 | | 10 | | | 6 | | 9 | | | 11 | | | | | |
| 21 (h) | Burnley | W 5-3 | | Davies 2, Carter, Glidden, Wilson | 15,133 | 1 | 2 | 3 | | 5 | 4 | 7 | 8 | | 10 | | | 6 | | 9 | | | 11 | | | | | |
| 28 (a) | Leeds U | W 1-0 | | Glidden | 15,200 | 1 | 2 | | | 5 | 4 | 7 | 8 | 9 | 10 | | 3 | 6 | | | | | 11 | | | | | |
| Dec 5 (h) | Newcastle U | W 4-0 | | Davies 2, Wilson, Fitton | 11,260 | 1 | 2 | | | 5 | 4 | 7 | 8 | | 10 | | 3 | 6 | | 9 | | | 11 | | | | | |
| 12 (a) | Arsenal | L 0-1 | | | 35,000 | 1 | 2 | | | 5 | 4 | 7 | 8 | | 10 | | 3 | 6 | | 9 | | | 11 | | | | | |
| 19 (h) | Manchester U | W 5-1 | | Carter, Glidden, Davies 2, James | 16,554 | 1 | 2 | | | 5 | 4 | 7 | 8 | 9 | | | 3 | 6 | | 10 | | | 11 | | | | | |
| 25 (a) | Cardiff C | L 2-3 | | Davies 2 | 15,225 | 1 | 2 | | | 5 | 4 | 7 | 8 | 9 | | | 3 | 6 | | 10 | | | 11 | | | | | |
| 26 (h) | Cardiff C | W 3-0 | | Carter 2, James | 31,554 | 1 | 2 | | | 5 | 4 | 7 | 8 | 9 | | | 3 | 6 | | 10 | | | 11 | | | | | |
| Jan 1 (a) | Manchester C | L 1-3 | | Carter | 23,030 | 1 | 2 | | | 5 | 4 | 7 | 8 | 9 | | | 3 | 6 | | 10 | | | 11 | | | | | |
| 2 (h) | Huddersfield T | D 2-2 | | Reed, Glidden (pen) | 15,000 | 1 | 2 | | | 5 | 4 | 7 | 8 | 9 | | | 3 | 6 | | 10 | | | 11 | | | | | |
| 16 (a) | Sunderland | L 0-4 | | | 20,000 | 1 | | 2 | 4 | 5 | | 7 | 8 | 9 | | 10 | 11 | | 3 | 6 | | | | | | | | |
| 23 (h) | Blackburn R | D 1-1 | | Byers | 11,105 | 1 | | 2 | 4 | 5 | | | 8 | | | 10 | 11 | | 3 | 6 | 9 | | | | 7 | | | |
| Feb 6 (h) | Birmingham | W 5-1 | | James 2, Wilson 3 | 23,104 | 1 | | 2 | 7 | 5 | 4 | | 8 | 9 | 10 | 11 | | | 3 | 6 | | | | | | | | |
| 13 (a) | Aston Villa | L 1-2 | | Byers | 46,200 | 1 | 2 | 3 | 7 | 5 | 4 | | 8 | 9 | 10 | 11 | | | | 6 | | | | | | | | |
| 20 (a) | Sheffield U | L 2-3 | | Carter 2 | 11,400 | | 2 | 3 | 7 | 5 | 4 | | 8 | 9 | 10 | 11 | | | | 6 | | | | 1 | | | | |
| 24 (a) | Bury | L 0-2 | | | 10,000 | 1 | 2 | 3 | 7 | 5 | 4 | | 8 | 9 | 10 | 11 | | | | 6 | | | | | | | | |
| 27 (h) | Leicester C | W 3-1 | | Glidden (pen), James, Byers | 19,532 | 1 | | 3 | 4 | 5 | 6 | 7 | 8 | 9 | | 11 | | | | 10 | | | 2 | | | | | |
| Mar 6 (a) | West Ham U | L 0-3 | | | 25,000 | 1 | | 3 | 4 | | 6 | 7 | 8 | 9 | | 11 | | | | 10 | | | 2 | | 5 | | | |
| 13 (h) | Bolton W | L 0-3 | | | 14,388 | 1 | | 3 | 4 | 5 | | 7 | 8 | 9 | | 11 | | 6 | | 10 | | | 2 | | | | | |
| 20 (h) | Notts C | D 0-0 | | | 12,000 | 1 | | 3 | 4 | 5 | | 7 | 8 | 9 | | 11 | | | | | 6 | | 2 | | | | | 10 |
| 27 (h) | Liverpool | L 0-3 | | | 10,503 | 1 | | 3 | 4 | 5 | | 7 | 8 | 9 | | 11 | | | | | 6 | | 2 | | | | | 10 |
| Apr 2 (a) | Tottenham H | L 2-3 | | James, Wilson | 45,000 | 1 | | 3 | 4 | 5 | | 7 | 8 | 9 | 10 | 11 | | | | | 6 | 2 | | | | | | |
| 3 (a) | Burnley | W 4-3 | | James 2, Wilson, Reed | 21,700 | 1 | | 3 | 4 | 5 | 6 | 7 | 8 | 9 | 10 | 11 | | | | | | 2 | | | | | | |
| 5 (h) | Tottenham H | W 1-0 | | Wilson (pen) | 10,180 | 1 | | 3 | 4 | 5 | 6 | 7 | 8 | 9 | 10 | 11 | | | | | | 2 | | | | | | |
| 10 (h) | Leeds U | W 3-0 | | Hart (og), Carter, Wilson | 13,065 | 1 | | 3 | 4 | 5 | 6 | 7 | 8 | 9 | 10 | 11 | | | | | | 2 | | | | | | |
| 17 (a) | Newcastle U | L 0-3 | | | 12,500 | 1 | | 3 | 4 | 5 | 6 | 7 | 8 | 9 | 10 | 11 | | | | | | 2 | | | | | | |
| 24 (h) | Arsenal | W 2-1 | | James, Wilson | 16,802 | 1 | | 3 | 4 | 5 | 6 | 7 | 8 | 9 | 10 | 11 | | | | | | 2 | | | | | | |
| May 1 (a) | Manchester U | L 2-3 | | James, Magee | 11,198 | 1 | | 3 | 4 | 5 | 6 | 7 | 8 | 9 | 10 | 11 | | | | | | 2 | | | | | | |
| **App** | | | | | | 40 | 26 | 32 | 20 | 39 | 36 | 37 | 37 | 28 | 30 | 23 | 12 | 29 | 3 | 26 | 5 | 9 | 19 | 2 | 1 | 5 | 1 | 2 |
| **Goals** | | | | | | | | | 1 | 2 | | 6 | 14 | 12 | 17 | 3 | | 1 | 1 | 19 | | | 2 | | | | | |

**Albion staff in 1925-26. Back row (left to right): S.Davies, P.Hunt (assistant trainer), T.Gopsill (trainer), H.Pearson, T.Sproson, G.Ashmore, S.Guest (assistant trainer), J.Evans, T.Magee. Third row: E.Smith (assistant secretary), R.McNeal, T.Gliddon, J.Byers, H.Chamberlain, A.Fitton, J.Smith, J.Carter, H.Dutton, W.Adams, Mr F.Everiss (secretary). Seated: R.Finch, E.Rooke, S.Richardson, I.Jones, Mr W.I.Bassett (chairman), F.Reed, G.James, J.Poxton, R.Baugh. On ground: H.Smith, C.Wilson, S.Short, E.Hickman, J.Hallows, H.Gregory.**

# 1926-27

## Division 1

Match details (date, venue, opponent, result, scorers, attendance) followed by the player appearance grid. Player columns, in order: Ashmore G, Perry A, Baugh R, Magee T, Reed F, Howarth N, Glidden T, Carter J, Davies S, Wilson C, Byers J, James G, Dutton H, Short S, Adams W, Fitton A, Sproson T, Rooke E, Richardson S, Evans J, Finch R, Corbett F, Ashurst W, Shaw G, Poxton J.

| Date | | Opponent | Result | Scorers | Att. | Ash | Per | Bau | Mag | Ree | How | Gli | Car | Dav | Wil | Bye | Jam | Dut | Sho | Ada | Fit | Spr | Roo | Ric | Eva | Fin | Cor | Ash | Sha | Pox |
|---|---|---|---|---|---|---|---|---|---|---|---|---|---|---|---|---|---|---|---|---|---|---|---|---|---|---|---|---|---|
| Aug 28 | (h) | Sunderland | W 3-0 | Davies, Carter, Byers | 31,132 | 1 | 2 | 3 | 4 | 5 | 6 | 7 | 8 | 9 | 10 | 11 | | | | | | | | | | | | | | |
| 30 | (a) | Huddersfield T | L 1-4 | Wilson | 32,500 | 1 | 2 | 3 | 4 | 5 | 6 | 7 | 8 | 9 | 10 | 11 | | | | | | | | | | | | | | |
| Sep 4 | (a) | Cardiff C | D 1-1 | Byers | 18,000 | 1 | 2 | 3 | 4 | 5 | 6 | 7 | 8 | | 10 | 11 | 9 | | | | | | | | | | | | | |
| 6 | (h) | Everton | W 3-2 | Davies 2, Carter | 35,330 | 1 | 2 | 3 | 4 | 5 | 6 | 7 | 8 | | 10 | 11 | 9 | | | | | | | | | | | | | |
| 11 | (a) | Bury | L 3-7 | Carter, James 2 | 15,000 | 1 | 2 | 3 | 4 | 5 | 6 | 7 | 8 | | 10 | 11 | 9 | | | | | | | | | | | | | |
| 15 | (a) | Everton | D 0-0 | | 42,000 | 1 | 2 | 3 | 4 | 5 | 6 | 7 | | 10 | 8 | 11 | 9 | | | | | | | | | | | | | |
| 18 | (h) | Birmingham | L 1-2 | Jones (og) | 26,803 | 1 | 2 | 3 | 4 | 5 | | 7 | | 8 | 10 | 11 | 9 | 6 | | | | | | | | | | | | |
| 25 | (a) | Tottenham H | L 0-3 | | 40,003 | 1 | 2 | | 4 | 5 | 6 | 7 | 8 | | 10 | 11 | 9 | | | 3 | | | | | | | | | | |
| Oct 2 | (h) | West Ham U | L 1-3 | Fitton | 24,737 | 1 | 2 | | 4 | 5 | 6 | 7 | 8 | | 10 | | 9 | | | 3 | 11 | | | | | | | | | |
| 9 | (a) | Sheffield W | L 1-2 | Glidden | 18,000 | 1 | 2 | | 4 | 5 | 6 | 7 | 8 | 9 | 10 | | | | | 3 | 11 | | | | | | | | | |
| 16 | (h) | Bolton W | D 1-1 | Glidden | 24,246 | 1 | 2 | | 4 | 5 | 6 | 7 | 8 | 9 | 10 | 11 | | | | 3 | | | | | | | | | | |
| 23 | (a) | Aston Villa | L 0-2 | | 49,952 | | 3 | 2 | 4 | | 6 | 9 | 8 | 7 | 10 | 11 | | | | | | 1 | 5 | | | | | | | |
| 30 | (h) | Burnley | W 4-2 | Carter 2, Byers, Magee | 20,957 | | 3 | 2 | 7 | | 6 | 9 | 8 | | 10 | 11 | | 4 | | | | 1 | 5 | | | | | | | |
| Nov 6 | (a) | Newcastle U | L 2-5 | Glidden, Wilson | 30,000 | | 3 | 2 | 7 | | 6 | 9 | 8 | | 10 | 11 | | 4 | | | | 1 | 5 | | | | | | | |
| 13 | (h) | Leeds U | L 2-4 | James 2 | 15,103 | | 3 | 2 | 7 | | 6 | | 8 | | 10 | 11 | 9 | 4 | | | | 1 | 5 | | | | | | | |
| 20 | (a) | Liverpool | L 1-2 | Wilson | 21,000 | 1 | | | 4 | | 6 | 7 | 8 | | 10 | 11 | 9 | | | | | | 5 | | | | | 2 | 3 | |
| 27 | (h) | Arsenal | L 1-3 | Carter | 16,351 | 1 | | | 4 | | 6 | 7 | 8 | 9 | 10 | 11 | | | | | | | 5 | | | | | 3 | 2 | |
| Dec 4 | (a) | Sheffield U | L 1-2 | James | 20,000 | 1 | | | 4 | 5 | 6 | 7 | 8 | | 10 | | 9 | | 11 | | | | | | | | | 2 | 3 | |
| 11 | (h) | Derby C | W 3-1 | Davies 2, Magee | 19,557 | 1 | | | 4 | 5 | | 7 | 8 | 9 | 10 | | | | 11 | | | | | 6 | | | | 2 | 3 | |
| 18 | (a) | Manchester U | L 0-2 | | 21,489 | 1 | | | 4 | 5 | | 8 | 7 | 9 | 10 | | | | 11 | | | | | 6 | | | | 2 | 3 | |
| 25 | (h) | Leicester C | L 0-5 | | 25,017 | 1 | | | 4 | 5 | 6 | 7 | 8 | 9 | 10 | | | | 11 | | | | | | | | | 2 | 3 | |
| 27 | (h) | Leicester C | L 0-1 | | 31,286 | 1 | | | 4 | | 6 | 7 | 8 | 9 | | | | | 10 | 2 | 11 | | 5 | | | | | | 3 | |
| Jan 1 | (h) | Huddersfield T | D 2-2 | Short 2 | 30,998 | 1 | | | 4 | | 6 | 7 | 8 | 9 | | | | | 10 | 2 | 11 | | 5 | | | | | | 3 | |
| 15 | (a) | Sunderland | L 1-4 | Wilson | 28,500 | 1 | | | 4 | | 6 | 7 | 8 | 9 | 10 | 11 | | | | | | | 5 | | | | | 2 | 3 | |
| 29 | (h) | Bury | W 3-1 | Davies 2, Carter | 10,043 | 1 | | | 4 | | 6 | 7 | 8 | 9 | 10 | 11 | | | | | | | 5 | | | | | 2 | 3 | |
| Feb 5 | (a) | Birmingham | L 0-1 | | 34,000 | 1 | | | 4 | | 6 | 7 | 8 | 9 | 10 | 11 | | | | | | | 5 | | | | | 2 | 3 | |
| 12 | (h) | Tottenham H | W 5-0 | Davies 2, Carter 2, Short | 15,998 | 1 | | | 4 | | | 7 | 8 | 9 | | 11 | | | 10 | | | | 5 | 6 | | | | 2 | 3 | |
| 19 | (a) | West Ham U | W 2-1 | Rooke, Short | 19,849 | 1 | | | 4 | | | 7 | 8 | 9 | | 11 | | | 10 | | | | 5 | 6 | | | | 2 | 3 | |
| 21 | (h) | Cardiff C | L 1-2 | Glidden | 10,068 | 1 | | | 4 | | | 7 | 8 | 9 | | 11 | | | 10 | | | | 5 | 6 | | | | 2 | 3 | |
| 26 | (h) | Sheffield W | D 2-2 | Carter, Short | 12,006 | 1 | | | 4 | | | 7 | 8 | 9 | | 11 | | | 10 | | | | 5 | 6 | | | | 2 | 3 | |
| Mar 5 | (a) | Bolton W | D 1-1 | Carter | 13,076 | 1 | | | 4 | | 6 | 7 | 8 | 9 | | 11 | | | 10 | | | | 5 | | | | | 2 | 3 | |
| 12 | (h) | Aston Villa | W 6-2 | Glidden 2, Carter, Davies 2, Short | 50,392 | 1 | | | 4 | | 6 | 7 | 8 | 9 | | 11 | | | 10 | | | | 5 | | | | | 2 | 3 | |
| 19 | (a) | Burnley | L 1-2 | Davies | 11,408 | 1 | | | 4 | | 6 | 7 | 8 | 9 | | 11 | | | 10 | | | | 5 | | | | | 2 | 3 | |
| 26 | (h) | Newcastle U | W 4-2 | Byers, Davies, Carter, Short (pen) | 22,135 | 1 | | | 4 | | 6 | 7 | 8 | 9 | | 11 | | | 10 | | | | 5 | | | | | 2 | 3 | |
| Apr 2 | (a) | Leeds U | L 1-3 | Carter | 14,898 | 1 | | | 4 | | 6 | 7 | 8 | | | 11 | 9 | | 10 | | | | 5 | | | | | 2 | 3 | |
| 9 | (h) | Liverpool | L 0-1 | | 20,268 | 1 | | | 4 | | 6 | 7 | 8 | 9 | | 11 | | | 10 | | | | 5 | | | | | 2 | 3 | |
| 16 | (a) | Arsenal | L 1-4 | Davies | 27,000 | 1 | | | 4 | | 6 | 7 | 8 | | 10 | 11 | 9 | | | | | | 5 | | | | | 2 | 3 | |
| 18 | (h) | Blackburn R | W 2-0 | Byers, Ashurst | 14,383 | 1 | | | 4 | | 6 | 7 | 8 | | 10 | 11 | 9 | | | | | | 5 | | | | | 2 | 3 | |
| 19 | (h) | Blackburn R | D 0-0 | | 9,965 | 1 | | | 4 | | 6 | 7 | 8 | | | 11 | 9 | | 10 | | | | 5 | | | | 3 | | 2 | |
| 23 | (h) | Sheffield U | W 1-0 | James (pen) | 13,104 | 1 | | | 4 | | 6 | 7 | 8 | | | 11 | 9 | | 10 | | | | 5 | | | | 3 | | 2 | |
| 30 | (a) | Derby C | L 1-2 | Carter | 9,000 | 1 | | | 4 | | 6 | 7 | 8 | | | 11 | 9 | | 10 | | | | 5 | | | | | 2 | 3 | |
| May 7 | (h) | Manchester U | D 2-2 | Magee, Davies | 11,022 | 1 | | | 4 | | 6 | 7 | 8 | 9 | | | | | 10 | | | | 5 | | | | | 2 | 3 | 11 |
| | | | App | | | 38 | 13 | 13 | 42 | 15 | 34 | 41 | 36 | 33 | 18 | 29 | 17 | 3 | 18 | 6 | 12 | 4 | 25 | 7 | 5 | 1 | 4 | 22 | 25 | 1 |
| | | | Goals | | | | | | 3 | | | 6 | 15 | 15 | 4 | 5 | 6 | | 7 | | 1 | | 1 | | | | | 1 | | |

**George Shaw, a big-money signing by Albion in 1926.**

# 1927-28

## Division 2

| Date | | Opponent | Result | Scorers | Att | Sproson T | Baugh R | Shaw G | Magee T | Evans J | Howarth N | Glidden T | Carter J | Cookson J | Wilson C | Byers J | Finch R | Fryer E | Ashmore G | Fitton A | James G | Rooke E | Poxton J | Bytheway G | Pearson H | Short S | Chambers H | Bromage E | Corbett F | Edwards J | Rix J |
|---|---|---|---|---|---|---|---|---|---|---|---|---|---|---|---|---|---|---|---|---|---|---|---|---|---|---|---|---|---|---|
| Aug 27 | (a) | Oldham A | L 1-3 | Cookson | 13,600 | 1 | 2 | 3 | 4 | 5 | 6 | 7 | 8 | 9 | 10 | 11 | | | | | | | | | | | | | | | |
| 31 | (h) | Stoke C | L 2-4 | Cookson, Byers | 20,329 | 1 | 2 | 3 | 4 | 5 | 6 | 7 | 8 | 9 | 10 | 11 | | | | | | | | | | | | | | | |
| Sep 3 | (h) | Grimsby T | W 3-1 | Carter 2, Wilson | 16,615 | 1 | | 3 | 4 | 5 | | 7 | 8 | 9 | 10 | 11 | 2 | 6 | | | | | | | | | | | | | |
| 5 | (a) | Stoke C | D 1-1 | Cookson | 20,000 | | | 3 | 4 | 5 | | 7 | 8 | 9 | 10 | | 2 | 6 | 1 | 11 | | | | | | | | | | | |
| 10 | (a) | Reading | W 4-1 | Cookson, Fitton, Glidden, Wilson | 14,000 | | | 3 | 4 | 5 | | 7 | 8 | 9 | 10 | | 2 | 6 | 1 | 11 | | | | | | | | | | | |
| 17 | (h) | Blackpool | W 6-3 | Cookson 6 (1 pen) | 20,203 | | | 3 | 4 | 5 | | 7 | 8 | 9 | 10 | | 2 | 6 | 1 | 11 | | | | | | | | | | | |
| 24 | (a) | Chelsea | D 1-1 | Carter | 40,098 | | | 3 | 4 | 5 | | 7 | 8 | 9 | 10 | | 2 | 6 | 1 | 11 | | | | | | | | | | | |
| Oct 1 | (h) | Clapton O | W 4-1 | Fitton, Carter, Glidden, Cookson | 21,324 | | | 3 | 4 | 5 | | 7 | 8 | 9 | 10 | | 2 | 6 | 1 | 11 | | | | | | | | | | | |
| 8 | (a) | Wolves | L 1-4 | Evans | 41,000 | | | 3 | 4 | 5 | | 7 | 8 | | 10 | | 2 | 6 | 1 | 11 | 9 | | | | | | | | | | |
| 15 | (a) | Bristol C | W 1-0 | Glidden | 25,000 | | | 3 | 7 | 5 | | | 9 | 8 | 10 | | 2 | 6 | 1 | 11 | 4 | | | | | | | | | | |
| 22 | (h) | Swansea T | W 5-2 | Fitton, Carter 2, Cookson, Wilson | 22,779 | | | 3 | 4 | 5 | | 7 | 8 | 9 | 10 | | 2 | 6 | 1 | 11 | | | | | | | | | | | |
| 29 | (a) | Fulham | L 1-3 | Cookson | 20,500 | | | 3 | 4 | 5 | | 7 | 8 | 9 | 10 | | 2 | 6 | 1 | 11 | | | | | | | | | | | |
| Nov 5 | (h) | Barnsley | D 1-1 | Wilson | 18,350 | | | 3 | 4 | 5 | | 7 | 8 | 9 | 10 | | 2 | | 1 | | | 6 | 11 | | | | | | | | |
| 12 | (a) | Preston NE | D 3-3 | Cookson, Glidden 2 | 11,895 | | | 3 | 4 | 5 | | 7 | 8 | 9 | 10 | | 2 | | 1 | | | 6 | 11 | | | | | | | | |
| 19 | (h) | Hull C | D 1-1 | Glidden | 8,116 | | | 3 | 4 | 5 | | 7 | 8 | 9 | 10 | | 2 | 6 | 1 | | | | 11 | | | | | | | | |
| 26 | (a) | Leeds U | W 2-1 | Carter 2 | 20,014 | | | 3 | 4 | 5 | | | 9 | 8 | 10 | | 2 | 6 | 1 | | | | 11 | 7 | | | | | | | |
| Dec 3 | (h) | Nottingham F | L 2-3 | Carter, Glidden | 10,205 | | | 3 | 4 | 5 | | | 9 | 8 | 10 | | 2 | 6 | 1 | | | | 11 | 7 | | | | | | | |
| 10 | (a) | Manchester C | L 1-3 | Glidden | 40,000 | | | 3 | 4 | 5 | | 10 | 8 | 9 | | | 2 | 6 | 1 | | | | 11 | 7 | | | | | | | |
| 17 | (h) | South Shields | W 3-0 | Glidden, Evans, Cookson | 11,376 | | | 3 | 4 | 5 | | 10 | 8 | 9 | | 11 | 2 | 6 | | | | | | 7 | 1 | | | | | | |
| 24 | (a) | Port Vale | L 1-4 | | 13,560 | | | 3 | 4 | 5 | | 10 | 8 | 9 | | 11 | 2 | 6 | | | | | | 7 | 1 | | | | | | |
| 26 | (h) | Notts C | D 2-2 | Cookson, Poxton | 28,038 | | | 3 | 4 | 5 | 6 | 10 | 8 | 9 | | | 2 | | | | | | 11 | 7 | 1 | | | | | | |
| 27 | (a) | Notts C | L 0-3 | | 16,000 | | | 3 | | 5 | 6 | 7 | 8 | 9 | 10 | | 2 | | 4 | | | | 11 | | 1 | | | | | | |
| 31 | (h) | Oldham A | D 0-0 | | 9,203 | | | 3 | 4 | 5 | 6 | 10 | 8 | 9 | | | 2 | | 1 | 11 | | | | 7 | | | | | | | |
| Jan 7 | (a) | Grimsby T | W 6-0 | Cookson 4, Short, Bytheway | 10,000 | | | 3 | 4 | 5 | 6 | | 8 | 9 | | | 2 | | 1 | 11 | | | | 7 | | 10 | | | | | |
| 21 | (h) | Reading | W 5-3 | Inglis (og), Cookson 4 | 15,014 | | | 3 | 4 | 5 | 6 | | 8 | 9 | | | 2 | | 1 | 11 | | | | 7 | | 10 | | | | | |
| 28 | (a) | Blackpool | L 3-4 | Cookson 2, Short | 12,500 | | | 3 | 4 | 5 | 6 | | 8 | 9 | | | 2 | | 1 | 11 | | | | 7 | | 10 | | | | | |
| Feb 4 | (h) | Chelsea | W 3-0 | Short 2, Carter | 25,865 | | | 3 | 4 | 5 | 6 | 7 | 8 | 9 | | | 2 | | 1 | 11 | | | | | | 10 | | | | | |
| 11 | (a) | Clapton O | D 0-0 | | 11,600 | | | 3 | 4 | 5 | 6 | 7 | 8 | 9 | | | 2 | | 1 | 11 | | | | | | 10 | | | | | |
| 18 | (h) | Wolves | W 4-0 | Cookson 2, Carter, Wilson | 37,342 | | | 3 | 4 | 5 | 6 | 7 | 8 | 9 | 10 | | 2 | | 1 | 11 | | | | | | | | | | | |
| 25 | (h) | Bristol C | D 0-0 | | 32,115 | | | 3 | 4 | 5 | 6 | 7 | 8 | 9 | | | 2 | | | 11 | | | | | 1 | 10 | | | | | |
| Mar 3 | (a) | Swansea T | L 2-3 | Cookson 2 | 16,000 | | | 3 | 4 | 5 | 6 | 7 | 8 | 9 | | | 2 | | | 11 | | | | | 1 | 10 | | | | | |
| 10 | (h) | Fulham | W 4-0 | Cookson, Chambers, Glidden 2 | 17,029 | | | 3 | 4 | 5 | 6 | 7 | 8 | 9 | | | 2 | | 1 | 11 | | | | | | | 10 | | | | |
| 17 | (a) | Barnsley | W 4-2 | Carter, Cookson 2, Glidden | 10,109 | | | 3 | 4 | 5 | 6 | 7 | 8 | 9 | | | 2 | | 1 | | | | | | | | 10 | 11 | | | |
| 24 | (h) | Preston NE | L 2-4 | Carter, Cookson | 28,055 | | | 3 | 4 | 5 | 6 | 7 | 8 | 9 | | | 2 | | 1 | | | | | | | | 10 | 11 | | | |
| 31 | (a) | Hull C | D 1-1 | Bromage | 20,000 | | 2 | | 4 | 5 | 6 | 7 | | 9 | | | | | 1 | | | | | | | | 10 | 11 | 3 | 8 | |
| Apr 7 | (h) | Leeds U | L 0-1 | | 25,180 | | | 3 | 4 | 5 | 6 | 7 | 8 | 9 | | | 2 | | 1 | | | | | | | | 10 | 11 | | | |
| 9 | (a) | Southampton | L 2-3 | Glidden, Carter | 16,800 | | | 3 | 4 | | 6 | 7 | 8 | 9 | | | 2 | | 1 | | | 5 | | | | | 10 | 11 | | | |
| 10 | (h) | Southampton | W 2-1 | Cookson, Short | 20,046 | | | 3 | 4 | | 6 | 7 | 8 | 9 | | | 2 | | | | | 5 | | | 1 | 10 | | 11 | | | |
| 14 | (a) | Nottingham F | W 2-0 | Cookson, Carter | 7,000 | | | 3 | 4 | | 6 | | 8 | 9 | | | 2 | | | | | 5 | | 7 | 1 | 10 | | 11 | | | |
| 21 | (h) | Manchester C | D 1-1 | Chambers | 14,238 | | | 3 | 4 | | 6 | 7 | 8 | 9 | | | 2 | | | | | 5 | | | 1 | | 10 | 11 | | | |
| 28 | (a) | South Shields | W 3-2 | Bromage, Dunn (og), Cookson | 10,700 | | | 3 | 4 | | 6 | | 8 | 9 | | | 2 | | | | | 5 | | 7 | 1 | | 10 | 11 | | | |
| May 5 | (h) | Port Vale | D 0-0 | | 10,095 | | | 3 | 4 | | | | 8 | 9 | | | 2 | | | | | 5 | | 7 | 1 | 10 | | 11 | | | 6 |
| App | | | | | | 3 | 2 | 42 | 41 | 36 | 23 | 39 | 38 | 38 | 19 | 5 | 39 | 17 | 28 | 19 | 1 | 9 | 8 | 13 | 11 | 10 | 8 | 10 | 1 | 1 | 1 |
| Goals | | | | | | | | | 2 | | | 13 | 15 | 38 | 5 | 1 | | | | 3 | | | 1 | 1 | | 5 | 2 | 2 | | | |

Harry Chambers (left), joined Albion from Liverpool in 1928. Jimmy Cookson (right) came from Chesterfield the previous year.

# 1928-29

## Division 2

| Date | | Opponent | Result | Scorers | Att. | Pearson H | Finch R | Shaw G | Magee T | Evans J | Howarth N | Glidden T | Carter J | Cookson J | Chambers H | Fitton A | Ashmore G | Wood S | Darnell L | James G | Corbett F | Rix J | Fryer E | Short S | Bytheway G | Leedham F | Dale R | Richardson W | Webster H | Edwards J |
|---|---|---|---|---|---|---|---|---|---|---|---|---|---|---|---|---|---|---|---|---|---|---|---|---|---|---|---|---|---|---|
| Aug 25 | (h) | Clapton O | W 3-1 | Chambers, Glidden, Carter | 19,756 | 1 | 2 | 3 | 4 | 5 | 6 | 7 | 8 | 9 | 10 | 11 | | | | | | | | | | | | | | |
| 27 | (a) | Notts C | L 1-3 | Howarth | 12,000 | 1 | 2 | 3 | 4 | 5 | 6 | 7 | 8 | 9 | 10 | 11 | | | | | | | | | | | | | | |
| Sep 1 | (a) | Stoke C | L 1-4 | Glidden | 20,103 | | 2 | 3 | 4 | 5 | 6 | 7 | 8 | 9 | 10 | 11 | 1 | | | | | | | | | | | | | |
| 3 | (h) | Notts C | L 1-3 | Cookson | 15,221 | | 2 | 3 | 4 | 5 | 6 | 7 | 8 | 9 | 10 | | 1 | | | 11 | | | | | | | | | | |
| 8 | (h) | Grimsby T | W 1-0 | Glidden (pen) | 15,132 | | 2 | 3 | 4 | 5 | | 7 | 8 | | 10 | | 1 | | | 11 | 6 | 9 | | | | | | | | |
| 15 | (a) | Bradford | L 1-5 | Glidden | 9,014 | | 2 | 3 | 4 | 5 | | 7 | 8 | | 10 | | 1 | | | 11 | 6 | | 9 | | | | | | | |
| 22 | (h) | Swansea T | W 5-1 | Carter 2, Short, James 2 | 12,333 | | 2 | 3 | 4 | | | 7 | 8 | 9 | | | 1 | 6 | 5 | 11 | | | | 10 | | | | | | |
| 29 | (a) | Blackpool | W 2-0 | Short, Wood | 10,516 | | 2 | 3 | 4 | | | 7 | 8 | 9 | | | 1 | 6 | 5 | 11 | | | | 10 | | | | | | |
| Oct 6 | (h) | Chelsea | W 3-0 | Bytheway, Short, Glidden | 16,447 | | 2 | 3 | 4 | | | 7 | 8 | 9 | | | 1 | 6 | 5 | | | | | 10 | 11 | | | | | |
| 13 | (a) | Barnsley | L 0-2 | | 8,689 | | 2 | 3 | 4 | | | 7 | 8 | 9 | | | 1 | 6 | 5 | | | | | 10 | 11 | | | | | |
| 20 | (a) | Millwall | D 2-2 | Short, Glidden | 10,600 | | 2 | 3 | 4 | | | 7 | 8 | 9 | | | 1 | 6 | 5 | 11 | | | | 10 | | | | | | |
| 27 | (h) | Port Vale | W 3-1 | James, Glidden, Short | 12,725 | | 2 | 3 | 4 | | | 7 | 8 | 9 | | | 1 | 6 | 5 | 11 | | | | 10 | | | | | | |
| Nov 3 | (a) | Hull C | L 1-4 | James | 10,007 | | 2 | 3 | 4 | | | 7 | 8 | 9 | | | 1 | 6 | 5 | 11 | | | | 10 | | | | | | |
| 10 | (a) | Wolves | L 0-2 | | 24,902 | | 2 | 3 | 4 | | | 7 | 8 | 9 | | | 1 | 6 | 5 | 11 | | | | 10 | | | | | | |
| 17 | (a) | Reading | L 3-5 | Cookson 3 | 10,715 | | 2 | 3 | 4 | | | 7 | 8 | 9 | | | 1 | 6 | 5 | 11 | | | | 10 | | | | | | |
| 24 | (h) | Preston NE | D 1-1 | Glidden | 8,048 | | 2 | 3 | 4 | | | 7 | 8 | 9 | | | 1 | 6 | 5 | 11 | | | | | | | 10 | | | |
| Dec 1 | (a) | Middlesbrough | D 1-1 | Glidden | 8,200 | | 2 | 3 | 4 | | | 7 | 8 | 9 | 10 | | 1 | 6 | 5 | 11 | | | | | | | | | | |
| 8 | (h) | Oldham A | W 1-0 | Cookson | 6,994 | | 2 | 3 | 4 | | | | 8 | 9 | 10 | | 1 | 6 | 5 | 11 | | | | | | | 7 | | | |
| 15 | (a) | Southampton | D 1-1 | Carter | 13,530 | | 2 | 3 | 4 | | | | 8 | 9 | 10 | | 1 | 6 | 5 | 11 | | | | | | | 7 | | | |
| 22 | (h) | Tottenham H | W 3-2 | Shaw (pen), Cookson, Carter | 11,565 | | 2 | 3 | 4 | | | 7 | 8 | 9 | 10 | | 1 | 6 | 5 | 11 | | | | | | | | | | |
| 25 | (h) | Bristol C | D 1-1 | Glidden | 11,303 | | 2 | 3 | 4 | | | 7 | 8 | 9 | 10 | | 1 | 6 | 5 | 11 | | | | | | | | | | |
| 26 | (a) | Bristol C | W 3-2 | Wood 2, Cookson | 10,812 | | 2 | 3 | 4 | | | 7 | 8 | 9 | 10 | | 1 | 6 | 5 | 11 | | | | | | | | | | |
| 29 | (a) | Clapton O | W 2-0 | Cookson, Glidden | 6,400 | | 2 | 3 | 4 | | | 7 | 8 | 9 | 10 | | 1 | 6 | 5 | 11 | | | | | | | | | | |
| Jan 5 | (h) | Stoke C | L 2-3 | Magee, Cookson | 20,067 | | 2 | 3 | 4 | | | 7 | 8 | 9 | 10 | | 1 | 6 | 5 | 11 | | | | | | | | | | |
| 19 | (a) | Grimsby T | L 1-3 | Cookson | 9,727 | | 2 | 3 | 4 | | | 7 | 8 | 9 | 10 | | 1 | 6 | 5 | 11 | | | | | | | | | | |
| Feb 2 | (a) | Swansea T | L 1-6 | Carter | 10,000 | | 2 | 3 | 4 | | | 7 | 8 | 9 | 10 | | 1 | 6 | 5 | 11 | | | | | | | | | | |
| 9 | (h) | Blackpool | D 2-2 | Carter 2 | 12,094 | | 2 | 3 | 4 | | | 7 | 8 | 9 | 10 | | 1 | 6 | 5 | 11 | | | | | | | | | | |
| 23 | (h) | Barnsley | W 6-2 | Shaw (pen), Glidden 2, Carter, Cookson 2 | 13,810 | | 2 | 3 | 4 | | | 7 | 8 | 9 | 10 | | 1 | 6 | 5 | 11 | | | | | | | | | | |
| Mar 9 | (a) | Port Vale | L 1-8 | James | 8,000 | | 2 | 3 | 7 | | | | 8 | 9 | 10 | | 1 | 6 | 5 | 11 | | | | | | | | 4 | | |
| 11 | (h) | Bradford | L 1-2 | Cookson | 9,952 | | 2 | 3 | | | | 7 | 8 | 9 | | | | 6 | 5 | | | | | | | 11 | | 4 | 1 | 10 |
| 16 | (h) | Hull C | W 2-0 | Cookson, Chambers | 7,138 | 1 | 2 | 3 | | | | 7 | | 9 | 10 | | | 6 | 5 | | | | | | | 11 | | 4 | | 8 |
| 23 | (a) | Wolves | W 1-0 | Cookson | 21,000 | 1 | 2 | 3 | | | | 7 | 8 | 9 | 10 | | | 6 | 5 | 11 | | | | | | | | 4 | | |
| 29 | (a) | Nottingham F | W 2-1 | Cookson 2 | 12,289 | 1 | 2 | 3 | 4 | 5 | | 7 | 8 | 9 | | 11 | | 6 | | | | | | | | | | | | 10 |
| 30 | (h) | Reading | W 5-0 | Cookson 2, Fitton, Edwards, Glidden | 10,382 | 1 | 2 | 3 | 4 | | | 7 | 8 | 9 | | 11 | | 6 | 5 | | | | | | | | | | | 10 |
| Apr 1 | (h) | Nottingham F | W 3-0 | Glidden, Cookson, Fitton | 12,130 | 1 | 2 | 3 | | | | 7 | 8 | 9 | | 11 | | 6 | 5 | | | | | | | | | 4 | | 10 |
| 6 | (a) | Preston NE | D 1-1 | Edwards | 13,100 | 1 | 2 | 3 | | 5 | | 7 | 8 | 9 | | 11 | | 6 | | | | | | | | | | 4 | | 10 |
| 10 | (h) | Millwall | W 3-2 | Edwards, Glidden, Carter | 13,532 | 1 | 2 | 3 | | 5 | | 7 | 8 | 9 | | 11 | | 6 | | | | | | | | | | 4 | | 10 |
| 13 | (h) | Middlesbrough | D 1-1 | Glidden | 14,068 | 1 | 2 | 3 | | 5 | | 7 | 8 | 9 | | 11 | | 6 | | | | | | | | | | 4 | | 10 |
| 17 | (a) | Chelsea | W 5-2 | Glidden 3, Carter, Evans | 20,000 | 1 | 2 | 3 | | 5 | | 7 | 8 | 9 | | 11 | | 6 | | | | | | | | | | 4 | | 10 |
| 20 | (a) | Oldham A | L 0-3 | | 16,000 | 1 | 2 | 3 | | 5 | | 7 | 8 | 9 | | 11 | | 6 | | | | | | | | | | 4 | | 10 |
| 27 | (h) | Southampton | W 3-1 | Cookson, Glidden, Carter | 10,024 | 1 | 2 | 3 | | 5 | | 7 | 8 | 9 | | 11 | | 6 | | | | | | | | | | 4 | | 10 |
| May 4 | (a) | Tottenham H | L 0-2 | | 17,233 | 1 | 2 | 3 | | 5 | | 7 | 8 | 9 | | 11 | | 6 | | | | | | | | | | 4 | | 10 |
| | | | App | | | 14 | 39 | 42 | 31 | 16 | 4 | 40 | 36 | 31 | 32 | 14 | 27 | 27 | 27 | 11 | 3 | 1 | 4 | 11 | 2 | 4 | 10 | 24 | 1 | 11 |
| | | | Goals | | | | | 2 | 1 | 1 | 1 | 21 | 12 | 21 | 2 | 2 | | 3 | | 5 | | | | 5 | 1 | | | | | 3 |

Albion in 1928-29. Back row (left to right): P.Hunt (assistant trainer), Bill Richardson, Jim Edwards, Arthur Parry, Harold Pearson, Len Darnell, George Ashmore, Joe Carter, Herbert Webster, Joe Evans, Stan Wood, Jim Hudson, M.E.Jones (ground assistant). Second row: Mr E.Smith (assistant secretary), Mr F.Everiss (secretary), Ernie Pattison, Mr L.Nurse (director), Mr.H.Keys (director), Mr W.I.Bassett (chairman), Mr J.Round, (director), Mr W.Hackett (director), Tommy Glidden, Sam Guest (assistant trainer), Fred Reed (trainer). Seated: Reg Fryer, George James, Nelson Howarth, Jack Rix, Dickie Baugh, Sammy Short, Enos Bromage, Francis Corbett, Bertram Cope, Bob Finch. On ground: Fred Leedham, Frank White, Jimmy Cookson, Jimmy Murphy, Arthur Fitton, George Shaw, Alf Taylor, George Bytheway, Tommy Magee.

# 1929-30

## Division 2

| Date | Opponent | Result | Scorers | Att. | Pearson H | Finch R | Shaw G | Richardson W | Evans J | Darnell L | Glidden T | Carter J | Cookson J | Cresswell F | Wood S | Ashmore G | Magee T | Edwards J | Adams J | Fitton A | Boston H | Corbett F | Richardson WG | Trentham H | Dale R | Murphy J | Rix J |
|---|---|---|---|---|---|---|---|---|---|---|---|---|---|---|---|---|---|---|---|---|---|---|---|---|---|---|---|
| Aug 31 | (a) Wolves | W 4-2 | Cookson 2, Carter, Shaw | 25,961 | 1 | 2 | 3 | 4 | 5 | 6 | 7 | 8 | 9 | 10 | 11 | | | | | | | | | | | | |
| Sep 2 | (h) Oldham A | L 0-3 | | 25,221 | 1 | 2 | 3 | 4 | 5 | 6 | 7 | 8 | 9 | 10 | 11 | | | | | | | | | | | | |
| 7 | (h) Bradford | W 5-0 | Cresswell, Cookson 3, Evans | 22,997 | 1 | 2 | 3 | 4 | 5 | 6 | 7 | 8 | 9 | 10 | 11 | | | | | | | | | | | | |
| 9 | (a) Southampton | L 2-3 | Cookson 2 | 20,035 | 1 | 2 | 3 | 4 | 5 | 6 | 7 | 8 | 9 | 10 | 11 | | | | | | | | | | | | |
| 14 | (a) Barnsley | D 2-2 | Wood, Glidden | 9,804 | 1 | 2 | 3 | 4 | 5 | 6 | 7 | 8 | 9 | 10 | 11 | | | | | | | | | | | | |
| 21 | (h) Blackpool | W 5-1 | Carter 2, Cookson 2, Glidden | 16,515 | 1 | 2 | 3 | 4 | 5 | 6 | 7 | 8 | 9 | 10 | 11 | | | | | | | | | | | | |
| 28 | (a) Bury | L 2-3 | Cookson, Shaw (pen) | 9,000 | 1 | 2 | 3 | 4 | 5 | 6 | 7 | 8 | 9 | 10 | 11 | | | | | | | | | | | | |
| Oct 5 | (h) Chelsea | W 2-0 | Cookson, Glidden | 19,317 | 1 | 2 | 3 | 4 | 5 | 6 | 7 | 8 | 9 | 10 | 11 | | | | | | | | | | | | |
| 12 | (a) Nottingham F | W 2-0 | Cookson, Glidden | 16,000 | 1 | 2 | 3 | 4 | 5 | 6 | 7 | 8 | 9 | 10 | 11 | | | | | | | | | | | | |
| 19 | (a) Bradford C | D 2-2 | Glidden 2 | 12,000 | 1 | 2 | 3 | 4 | 5 | 6 | 7 | 8 | 9 | 10 | 11 | | | | | | | | | | | | |
| 26 | (h) Swansea T | W 6-2 | Glidden 4, Cresswell, Carter | 21,070 | 1 | 2 | 3 | 4 | 5 | 6 | 7 | 8 | 9 | 10 | 11 | | | | | | | | | | | | |
| Nov 2 | (a) Cardiff C | L 2-3 | Carter, Cresswell | 15,027 | | 2 | 3 | 4 | 5 | 6 | 7 | 8 | 9 | 10 | 11 | 1 | | | | | | | | | | | |
| 9 | (h) Preston NE | W 2-0 | Carter 2 | 18,869 | | 2 | 3 | 5 | | 6 | 7 | 8 | 9 | 10 | 11 | 1 | 4 | | | | | | | | | | |
| 16 | (a) Bristol C | L 1-2 | Shaw (pen) | 20,000 | | 2 | 3 | 4 | 5 | 6 | 7 | 8 | 9 | | 11 | 1 | | 10 | | | | | | | | | |
| 23 | (h) Notts C | W 4-2 | Carter, Glidden, Evans, Cookson | 15,118 | | 2 | 3 | 4 | 5 | 6 | 7 | 8 | 9 | 10 | 11 | | | | 1 | | | | | | | | |
| 30 | (a) Reading | D 2-2 | Cookson 2 | 10,201 | | 2 | 3 | 4 | 5 | 6 | 7 | 8 | 9 | 10 | 11 | | | | 1 | | | | | | | | |
| Dec 7 | (h) Charlton A | D 1-1 | Cookson | 10,886 | | 2 | 3 | 4 | 5 | 6 | 7 | 8 | 9 | 10 | 11 | | | | 1 | | | | | | | | |
| 14 | (a) Hull C | L 2-3 | Cookson, Carter | 16,000 | | 2 | 3 | 4 | 5 | 6 | 7 | 8 | 9 | | | | | 10 | 1 | 11 | | | | | | | |
| 21 | (h) Stoke C | L 2-3 | Boston, Cookson | 11,809 | | 2 | 3 | 5 | | 6 | | 8 | 9 | | 11 | | 4 | 10 | 1 | | 7 | | | | | | |
| 25 | (a) Millwall | L 1-2 | Carter | 18,000 | | 2 | 3 | 5 | | 6 | 7 | 8 | 9 | 10 | 11 | | 4 | | 1 | | | | | | | | |
| 26 | (h) Millwall | W 6-1 | Carter 2, Glidden 2, Richardson, Wood | 24,032 | | | 3 | 6 | 5 | | 7 | 8 | | 10 | 11 | | 4 | | 1 | | | 2 | 9 | | | | |
| 28 | (h) Wolves | W 7-3 | Evans, Cresswell 2, Glidden, Carter 2, Shaw (og) | 20,211 | | | 3 | 6 | 5 | | 7 | 8 | | 10 | 11 | | 4 | | 1 | | | 2 | 9 | | | | |
| Jan 1 | (a) Oldham A | L 0-5 | | 11,000 | | | 3 | 6 | 5 | | 7 | 8 | | 10 | 11 | | 4 | | 1 | | | 2 | 9 | | | | |
| 4 | (a) Bradford | L 1-5 | Carter | 10,450 | | | 3 | 6 | 5 | | 7 | 8 | 9 | 10 | 11 | | 4 | | 1 | 2 | | | | | | | |
| 18 | (h) Barnsley | W 4-2 | Shaw (pen), Richardson, Cresswell, Carter | 8,138 | | 2 | 3 | 4 | 5 | 6 | 7 | 8 | | 10 | | | | | 1 | 11 | | | 9 | | | | |
| Feb 1 | (h) Bury | W 5-1 | Fitton, Evans, Glidden, Carter 2 | 10,445 | | 2 | 3 | 4 | 5 | 6 | 7 | 8 | | 10 | | | | | 1 | 11 | | | 9 | | | | |
| 8 | (a) Chelsea | L 0-2 | | 20,000 | | 2 | 3 | 4 | 5 | 6 | 7 | 8 | | 10 | | | | | 1 | 11 | | | 9 | | | | |
| 22 | (h) Bradford C | W 4-2 | Carter, Glidden, Cookson 2 | 11,770 | | 2 | 3 | 4 | 5 | 6 | 7 | 8 | 9 | 10 | | | | | 1 | 11 | | | | | | | |
| Mar 1 | (a) Swansea T | L 0-1 | | 8,000 | | 2 | 3 | 4 | 5 | 6 | | 8 | 9 | 10 | | | | | 1 | 11 | 7 | | | | | | |
| 5 | (a) Blackpool | L 0-1 | | 7,000 | | 2 | | 6 | | | 7 | | | | 10 | | 4 | | 1 | 11 | | | 9 | 3 | 5 | 8 | |
| 8 | (h) Cardiff C | L 0-2 | | 5,889 | | 2 | | 6 | | | 7 | | | | 10 | 11 | 4 | | 1 | | | | 9 | | 5 | 8 | |
| 15 | (a) Preston NE | D 2-2 | Wood, Glidden | 5,389 | 1 | 2 | 3 | 6 | 5 | 8 | 7 | | 9 | 10 | 11 | | 4 | | | | | | | | | | |
| 19 | (h) Nottingham F | L 1-3 | Wood | 1,495 | 1 | 2 | 3 | 6 | 5 | 8 | 7 | | 9 | 10 | 11 | | 4 | | | | | | | | | | |
| 22 | (h) Bristol C | W 2-0 | Cookson, Evans | 5,060 | 1 | 2 | 3 | 6 | 5 | 4 | | 8 | 9 | | 11 | | | 10 | | | 7 | | | | | | |
| 29 | (a) Notts C | L 1-2 | Cookson | 6,000 | 1 | 2 | 3 | 6 | | | | 8 | 9 | | 11 | | 4 | 10 | | | 7 | | | | 5 | | |
| Apr 5 | (h) Reading | W 1-0 | Edwards | 8,020 | 1 | 2 | 3 | 6 | | | | 8 | 9 | | 11 | | 4 | 10 | | | 7 | | | | 5 | | |
| 12 | (a) Charlton A | W 1-0 | Wood | 12,106 | 1 | 2 | 3 | 6 | | | | 8 | 9 | | 11 | | 4 | 10 | | | 7 | | | | 5 | | |
| 18 | (a) Tottenham H | W 2-0 | Wood, Boston | 12,000 | 1 | 2 | 3 | 6 | | | | 8 | 9 | | 11 | | 4 | 10 | | | 7 | | | | 5 | | |
| 19 | (h) Hull C | W 7-1 | Glidden 2, Cookson 4, Boston | 10,036 | 1 | 2 | 3 | 6 | | | | 8 | 9 | | 11 | | 4 | 10 | | | 7 | | | | 5 | | |
| 21 | (h) Tottenham H | W 4-3 | Cookson, Wood, Reddish (og), Glidden | 12,908 | 1 | 2 | 3 | 6 | | | | 8 | 9 | | 11 | | 4 | 10 | | | 7 | | | | | | |
| 26 | (a) Stoke C | W 3-0 | Cookson 2, Edwards | 8,012 | 1 | 2 | 3 | 5 | | | | 8 | 9 | | 11 | | 4 | 10 | | | 7 | | | | | 6 | |
| May 3 | (h) Southampton | W 5-1 | Cookson 4, Edwards | 14,685 | | 2 | 3 | 5 | | | | | 9 | | 11 | 1 | 4 | 10 | | | 7 | | 8 | | | 6 | |
| | | App | | | 21 | 38 | 41 | 42 | 30 | 28 | 41 | 27 | 34 | 30 | 35 | 12 | 17 | 12 | 9 | 7 | 11 | 4 | 9 | 1 | 9 | 2 | 2 |
| | | Goals | | | | | 4 | | 5 | | 20 | 19 | 33 | 6 | 7 | | 3 | | | 1 | 3 | | 2 | | | | |

**Bob Finch, Harold Pearson and George Shaw, Albion's 1-2-3 in 21 League games this season.**

# 1930-31

## Division 2

| Date | | Opponent | Result | Scorers | Att | Pearson H | Finch R | Shaw G | Magee T | Richardson W | Rix J | Boston H | Glidden T | Cookson J | Edwards J | Wood S | Trentham H | Carter J | Richardson WG | Sandford E | Fitton A | Raw H | Murphy J | Bytheway G |
|---|---|---|---|---|---|---|---|---|---|---|---|---|---|---|---|---|---|---|---|---|---|---|---|---|
| Aug 30 | (h) | Bristol C | W 3-0 | Glidden 2, Edwards | 11,037 | 1 | 2 | 3 | 4 | 5 | 6 | 7 | 8 | 9 | 10 | 11 | | | | | | | | |
| Sep 1 | (a) | Charlton A | W 4-0 | Cookson, Wood, Pitcairn (og), Boston | 13,141 | 1 | | 2 | 4 | 5 | 6 | 7 | 8 | 9 | 10 | 11 | 3 | | | | | | | |
| 6 | (a) | Cardiff C | W 6-3 | Cookson 4, Carter, Boston | 12,088 | 1 | | 2 | 4 | 5 | | 7 | 8 | 9 | 6 | 11 | 3 | 10 | | | | | | |
| 8 | (h) | Bradford C | W 1-0 | Shaw (pen) | 18,126 | 1 | | 2 | 4 | 5 | | 7 | 8 | 9 | 6 | 11 | 3 | 10 | | | | | | |
| 13 | (h) | Everton | L 1-2 | Cookson | 23,517 | 1 | 2 | 3 | 4 | 5 | | 7 | 8 | 9 | 6 | 11 | | 10 | | | | | | |
| 17 | (a) | Bradford C | W 3-2 | Cookson, Glidden, Boston | 15,120 | 1 | 2 | 3 | | 5 | 4 | 7 | 8 | 9 | 6 | 11 | | 10 | | | | | | |
| 20 | (a) | Bury | D 2-2 | Carter 2 | 7,270 | 1 | 2 | 3 | | 5 | 4 | 7 | 8 | 9 | 6 | 11 | | 10 | | | | | | |
| 27 | (h) | Plymouth A | L 1-2 | Cookson | 15,938 | 1 | 2 | 3 | | 5 | 4 | 7 | 8 | 9 | 6 | 11 | | 10 | | | | | | |
| Oct 4 | (a) | Swansea T | D 1-1 | Carter | 19,988 | 1 | | 2 | | 5 | 4 | 7 | 8 | 9 | 6 | 11 | 3 | 10 | | | | | | |
| 11 | (h) | Wolves | W 2-1 | Carter, Cookson | 40,065 | 1 | | 2 | | 5 | 4 | 7 | 8 | 9 | 6 | 11 | 3 | 10 | | | | | | |
| 18 | (a) | Southampton | D 1-1 | Carter | 12,138 | 1 | | 2 | | 5 | 4 | 7 | 8 | 9 | 6 | 11 | 3 | 10 | | | | | | |
| 25 | (h) | Reading | W 1-0 | Wood | 19,112 | 1 | | 2 | | 5 | 4 | 7 | 8 | 9 | 6 | 11 | 3 | 10 | | | | | | |
| Nov 1 | (a) | Millwall | L 0-2 | | 11,875 | 1 | | 2 | | 5 | 4 | 7 | 8 | 9 | 6 | 11 | 3 | 10 | | | | | | |
| 8 | (h) | Oldham A | W 2-0 | Cookson, Carter | 12,880 | 1 | | 2 | 4 | 5 | | 7 | | 9 | 6 | 11 | 3 | 10 | 8 | | | | | |
| 15 | (a) | Preston NE | W 3-2 | Wood, Cookson, Sandford | 15,064 | 1 | | 2 | 4 | 5 | | 7 | | 9 | 6 | 11 | 3 | | 8 | 10 | | | | |
| 22 | (h) | Tottenham H | L 0-2 | | 18,078 | 1 | | 2 | 4 | 5 | | 7 | | 9 | 6 | 11 | 3 | | 8 | 10 | | | | |
| 29 | (a) | Nottingham F | W 6-1 | Wood 2, Carter, Richardson 2, Sandford | 15,207 | 1 | | 2 | 4 | 5 | | | 7 | | 6 | 11 | 3 | 8 | 9 | 10 | | | | |
| Dec 6 | (h) | Burnley | W 2-0 | Wood, Richardson | 17,197 | 1 | | 2 | 4 | 5 | | | 7 | | 6 | 11 | 3 | 8 | 9 | 10 | | | | |
| 13 | (a) | Bradford | L 1-3 | Richardson | 9,005 | 1 | | 2 | 4 | 5 | | | 7 | | 6 | 11 | 3 | 8 | 9 | 10 | | | | |
| 20 | (h) | Stoke C | W 4-0 | Richardson, Glidden 2, Magee | 15,629 | 1 | | 2 | 4 | 5 | | 7 | 8 | | 6 | 11 | 3 | | 9 | 10 | | | | |
| 25 | (a) | Barnsley | D 0-0 | | 10,052 | 1 | | 2 | 4 | 5 | | 7 | 8 | | 6 | 11 | 3 | | 9 | 10 | | | | |
| 26 | (h) | Barnsley | W 5-0 | Richardson, Wood, Glidden 2, Shaw (pen) | 22,981 | 1 | | 2 | 4 | 5 | | | 7 | | 6 | 11 | 3 | 8 | 9 | 10 | | | | |
| 27 | (a) | Bristol C | D 1-1 | Richardson | 20,996 | 1 | | 2 | 4 | 5 | | | 7 | | 6 | 11 | 3 | 8 | 9 | 10 | | | | |
| Jan 3 | (h) | Cardiff C | W 3-2 | Sandford, Carter, Richardson | 24,028 | 1 | | 2 | 4 | 5 | | | 7 | | 6 | 11 | 3 | 8 | 9 | 10 | | | | |
| 17 | (a) | Everton | L 1-2 | Glidden | 33,199 | 1 | | 2 | 4 | 5 | | | 7 | | 6 | 11 | 3 | 8 | 9 | 10 | | | | |
| 26 | (h) | Bury | W 2-0 | Glidden, Sandford | 20,160 | 1 | | 2 | 4 | 5 | | | 7 | | 6 | 11 | 3 | 8 | 9 | 10 | | | | |
| 31 | (a) | Plymouth A | L 1-5 | Wood | 9,560 | 1 | | 2 | 4 | 5 | | | 7 | | 6 | 11 | 3 | 8 | 9 | 10 | | | | |
| Feb 7 | (h) | Swansea T | D 0-0 | | 15,977 | 1 | | 2 | 4 | 5 | 6 | | 7 | | | | 3 | 8 | 9 | 10 | | | | 11 |
| 18 | (a) | Wolves | W 4-1 | Wood 2, Richardson 2 | 36,054 | 1 | | 2 | 4 | 5 | | | 7 | 9 | 6 | 11 | 3 | | 8 | 10 | | | | |
| 21 | (h) | Southampton | L 1-2 | Richardson | 20,682 | 1 | | 2 | 4 | 5 | | | 7 | 9 | 6 | 11 | 3 | | 8 | 10 | | | | |
| Mar 7 | (h) | Millwall | D 0-0 | | 17,763 | 1 | | 2 | 4 | 5 | | | | | 6 | 11 | 3 | 8 | 9 | 10 | 7 | | | |
| 21 | (h) | Preston NE | W 2-0 | Glidden 2 | 26,558 | 1 | | 2 | 4 | 5 | | | 7 | | 6 | 11 | 3 | 8 | 9 | 10 | | | | |
| 23 | (a) | Oldham A | D 2-2 | Raw, Glidden | 6,305 | 1 | | 2 | 4 | 5 | | | 7 | | 6 | 11 | 3 | | 9 | 10 | | 8 | | |
| 28 | (a) | Tottenham H | D 2-2 | Sandford, Glidden | 56,012 | 1 | | 2 | | 5 | | | 7 | | 6 | 11 | 3 | 8 | 9 | 10 | | | 4 | |
| Apr 3 | (a) | Port Vale | L 0-1 | | 13,128 | 1 | | 2 | | 5 | | | 7 | | 6 | 11 | 3 | 8 | 9 | 10 | | | 4 | |
| 4 | (h) | Nottingham F | W 2-1 | Wood 2 | 19,054 | 1 | | 2 | 4 | 5 | | | 7 | | 6 | 11 | 3 | 8 | 9 | 10 | | | | |
| 6 | (h) | Port Vale | W 4-1 | Richardson 2, Glidden, Wood | 23,806 | 1 | | 2 | 4 | 5 | | | 7 | | 6 | 11 | 3 | 8 | 9 | 10 | | | | |
| 11 | (a) | Burnley | L 1-2 | Richardson | 24,133 | 1 | | 2 | 4 | 5 | | | 7 | | 6 | 11 | 3 | | 9 | 10 | | 8 | | |
| 15 | (a) | Reading | W 3-0 | Richardson 2, Sandford | 10,510 | 1 | 2 | 3 | 4 | 5 | | | 7 | | 6 | 11 | | 8 | 9 | 10 | | | | |
| 18 | (h) | Bradford | D 1-1 | Shaw (pen) | 21,176 | 1 | 2 | 3 | 4 | 5 | | | 7 | | 6 | 11 | | 8 | 9 | 10 | | | | |
| 30 | (a) | Stoke C | W 1-0 | Richardson | 35,181 | 1 | | 2 | 4 | 5 | | | 7 | | 6 | 11 | 3 | 8 | 9 | 10 | | | | |
| May 2 | (h) | Charlton A | W 3-2 | Sandford, Glidden, Richardson | 52,415 | 1 | 2 | 3 | 4 | 5 | | | 7 | | 6 | 11 | | 8 | 9 | 10 | | | | |
| | | | | | App | 42 | 8 | 42 | 32 | 42 | 11 | 16 | 39 | 18 | 41 | 41 | 34 | 32 | 29 | 28 | 1 | 3 | 2 | 1 |
| | | | | | Goals | | | 3 | 1 | | | 3 | 15 | 11 | 1 | 13 | | 9 | 18 | 7 | | 1 | | |

**Albion's left-wing duo of Teddy Sandford and Stan Wood, who were partners for three seasons (1930-33).**

# 1931-32

## Division 1

| Date | | Opponent | Res | Scorers | Att | Pearson H | Shaw G | Trentham H | Magee T | Richardson W | Edwards J | Glidden T | Carter J | Richardson WG | Sandford E | Wood S | Foulkes H | Raw H | Murphy J | Boyes W | Cookson J | Rix J | Gale A | Adams J | Finch R | Robbins W |
|---|---|---|---|---|---|---|---|---|---|---|---|---|---|---|---|---|---|---|---|---|---|---|---|---|---|---|
| Aug 29 | (a) | Arsenal | W 1-0 | Wood | 55,380 | 1 | 2 | 3 | 4 | 5 | 6 | 7 | 8 | 9 | 10 | 11 | | | | | | | | | | |
| Sep 2 | (a) | Sunderland | L 1-2 | Richardson | 29,500 | 1 | 2 | | 4 | 5 | 6 | 7 | 8 | 9 | 10 | 11 | 3 | | | | | | | | | |
| 5 | (h) | Blackpool | W 4-0 | Richardson 2, Longden (og), Glidden | 18,506 | 1 | 2 | 3 | 4 | 5 | 6 | 7 | 8 | 9 | 10 | 11 | | | | | | | | | | |
| 7 | (h) | Sunderland | W 1-0 | Wood | 24,950 | 1 | 2 | 3 | 4 | 5 | 6 | 7 | 8 | 9 | 10 | 11 | | | | | | | | | | |
| 12 | (a) | Sheffield W | L 0-1 | | 16,700 | 1 | 2 | 3 | 4 | 5 | 6 | 7 | 8 | 9 | 10 | 11 | | | | | | | | | | |
| 14 | (h) | Manchester C | D 1-1 | Richardson | 19,042 | 1 | 2 | 3 | 4 | 5 | 6 | 7 | 8 | 9 | 10 | 11 | | | | | | | | | | |
| 19 | (h) | Blackburn R | W 4-1 | Edwards, Sandford, Glidden 2 | 25,885 | 1 | 2 | 3 | 4 | 5 | 6 | 7 | 8 | 9 | 10 | 11 | | | | | | | | | | |
| 23 | (a) | Manchester C | W 5-2 | Richardson, Wood, Raw 2, Glidden | 25,000 | 1 | 2 | 3 | 4 | 5 | 6 | 7 | | 9 | 10 | 11 | | 8 | | | | | | | | |
| 26 | (a) | Portsmouth | W 1-0 | Glidden (pen) | 17,937 | 1 | 2 | 3 | 4 | 5 | 6 | 7 | | 9 | 10 | 11 | | 8 | | | | | | | | |
| Oct 3 | (h) | Derby C | W 4-0 | Shaw (pen), Glidden, Sandford, Richardson | 33,192 | 1 | 2 | 3 | 4 | 5 | 6 | 7 | | 9 | 10 | 11 | | 8 | | | | | | | | |
| 10 | (a) | Huddersfield T | D 2-2 | Richardson 2 | 25,000 | 1 | 2 | 3 | 4 | 5 | 6 | 7 | | 9 | 10 | 11 | | 8 | | | | | | | | |
| 17 | (h) | Liverpool | L 1-2 | Glidden | 30,065 | 1 | 2 | 3 | 4 | 5 | 6 | 7 | | 9 | 10 | 11 | | 8 | | | | | | | | |
| 24 | (a) | Bolton W | L 0-1 | | 19,852 | 1 | 2 | | 4 | 5 | 6 | 7 | | 9 | 10 | 11 | 3 | 8 | | | | | | | | |
| 31 | (h) | Sheffield W | D 1-1 | Richardson | 31,334 | 1 | 2 | 3 | 4 | 5 | 6 | 7 | | 9 | 10 | 11 | | 8 | | | | | | | | |
| Nov 7 | (a) | West Ham U | W 5-1 | Richardson 4, Sandford | 18,134 | 1 | 2 | 3 | 4 | 5 | | 7 | | 9 | 10 | 11 | | 8 | 6 | | | | | | | |
| 14 | (h) | Aston Villa | W 3-0 | Glidden, Richardson, Raw | 59,674 | 1 | 2 | 3 | 4 | 5 | 6 | 7 | | 9 | | 11 | | 8 | | 10 | | | | | | |
| 21 | (a) | Newcastle U | L 1-5 | Glidden | 36,000 | 1 | 2 | 3 | 4 | 5 | | 7 | | 9 | 10 | 11 | | 8 | 6 | | | | | | | |
| 28 | (h) | Middlesbrough | D 1-1 | Sandford | 17,824 | 1 | 2 | 3 | 4 | 5 | | 7 | | 9 | 10 | 11 | | 8 | 6 | | | | | | | |
| Dec 5 | (a) | Leicester C | W 3-2 | Richardson, Glidden, Wood | 30,000 | 1 | 2 | 3 | 4 | 5 | | 7 | | 9 | 10 | 11 | | 8 | 6 | | | | | | | |
| 12 | (h) | Chelsea | W 4-0 | Richardson 2, Boyes, Glidden | 24,186 | 1 | 2 | 3 | 4 | 5 | | 7 | | 9 | 10 | 11 | | | 6 | 8 | | | | | | |
| 19 | (a) | Grimsby T | D 0-0 | | 12,000 | 1 | 2 | 3 | 4 | 5 | | 7 | | 9 | 10 | 11 | | | 6 | 8 | | | | | | |
| 25 | (h) | Birmingham | L 0-1 | | 38,053 | 1 | 2 | 3 | 4 | 5 | | 7 | | 9 | 10 | 11 | | | 6 | 8 | | | | | | |
| 26 | (a) | Birmingham | L 0-1 | | 57,806 | 1 | 2 | 3 | | 5 | 6 | 7 | 8 | | 10 | 11 | | 4 | | | 9 | | | | | |
| Jan 2 | (h) | Arsenal | W 1-0 | Glidden | 25,790 | 1 | 2 | 3 | | 5 | 6 | 7 | 8 | 9 | 10 | 11 | | 4 | | | | | | | | |
| 16 | (a) | Blackpool | W 2-1 | Richardson, Sandford | 16,000 | 1 | 2 | 3 | | 5 | | 7 | | 9 | 10 | 11 | | 8 | 4 | | | 6 | | | | |
| 25 | (h) | Sheffield U | L 0-1 | | 11,382 | 1 | 2 | 3 | | 5 | | 7 | 8 | 9 | 10 | 11 | | 4 | | | | 6 | | | | |
| 30 | (a) | Blackburn R | L 0-2 | | 12,502 | 1 | 2 | 3 | | | | 7 | | 9 | 5 | 11 | | 8 | 4 | 10 | | 6 | | | | |
| Feb 6 | (h) | Portsmouth | W 3-0 | Glidden 2, Richardson | 21,065 | 1 | 2 | 3 | | 5 | | 7 | | 9 | 6 | 11 | | 8 | 4 | 10 | | | | | | |
| 17 | (a) | Derby C | L 1-3 | Glidden | 15,000 | 1 | 2 | | | 5 | | 7 | | 9 | 6 | 11 | 3 | 8 | 4 | 10 | | | | | | |
| 20 | (h) | Huddersfield T | W 3-2 | Richardson, Raw, Glidden | 20,105 | 1 | 2 | | | 5 | | 7 | | 9 | 6 | 11 | 3 | 8 | 4 | 10 | | | | | | |
| Mar 2 | (a) | Liverpool | L 1-4 | Richardson | 21,000 | 1 | 2 | | | 5 | | 7 | 10 | 9 | 3 | 11 | | 8 | 4 | 6 | | | | | | |
| 5 | (h) | Bolton W | W 3-0 | Richardson, Glidden, Wood | 16,050 | 1 | 2 | 3 | | 5 | | 7 | 8 | 9 | 10 | 11 | | 4 | 6 | | | | | | | |
| 12 | (a) | Sheffield W | W 5-2 | Carter, Glidden, Richardson, Sandford, Wood | 13,389 | 1 | 2 | 3 | | 5 | | 7 | 8 | 9 | 10 | 11 | | 4 | 6 | | | | | | | |
| 19 | (h) | West Ham U | W 3-1 | Wood, Carter, Richardson | 19,271 | 1 | 2 | 3 | | 5 | | 7 | 8 | 9 | 10 | 11 | | 4 | 6 | | | | | | | |
| 25 | (a) | Everton | L 1-2 | Richardson | 20,000 | 1 | 2 | 3 | | 5 | 6 | 7 | 8 | 9 | 10 | 11 | | 4 | | | | | | | | |
| 26 | (a) | Aston Villa | L 0-2 | | 51,000 | 1 | 2 | 3 | | 5 | | 7 | 8 | 9 | 10 | 11 | | 4 | 6 | | | | | | | |
| 28 | (h) | Everton | D 1-1 | Carter | 31,486 | 1 | 2 | 3 | | 5 | | 7 | 8 | 9 | 10 | 11 | | 4 | 6 | | | | | | | |
| Apr 2 | (h) | Newcastle U | W 2-1 | Davidson (og), Glidden | 18,614 | 1 | 2 | 3 | | 5 | 6 | 7 | | 9 | 10 | | | 4 | 11 | | | | 8 | | | |
| 9 | (a) | Middlesbrough | L 0-1 | | 18,000 | | | 3 | | 5 | 6 | 7 | | 9 | | 11 | | 4 | 10 | | | | 8 | 1 | 2 | |
| 16 | (h) | Leicester C | L 1-2 | Sandford | 15,014 | 1 | 2 | 3 | | 5 | | 7 | 8 | | 10 | 11 | | 4 | 6 | | | | 9 | | | |
| 23 | (a) | Chelsea | W 2-0 | Carter, Richardson | 29,000 | 1 | 2 | 3 | | 5 | 6 | 7 | 8 | 9 | 10 | | | 4 | | | | | | | | 11 |
| 30 | (h) | Grimsby T | L 5-6 | Richardson, Sandford, Carter, Edwards (pen), Glidden | 7,796 | 1 | 2 | 3 | | 5 | 6 | 7 | 8 | 9 | 10 | 11 | | 4 | | | | | | | | |
| **App** | | | | | | 41 | 41 | 37 | 22 | 41 | 22 | 42 | 20 | 40 | 40 | 40 | 4 | 18 | 27 | 17 | 1 | 3 | 3 | 1 | 1 | 1 |
| **Goals** | | | | | | | 1 | | | | 2 | 20 | 5 | 27 | 8 | 7 | | 4 | | 1 | | | | | | |

**W.G.Richardson (in stripes) of West Bromwich Albion, seen here scoring the second of his four goals in five minutes against West Ham at Upton Park on 7 November 1931.**

# 1932-33

## Division 1

| Date | | Opponent | Result | Scorers | Att | Pearson H | Shaw G | Trentham H | Magee T | Richardson W | Edwards J | Glidden T | Carter J | Richardson WG | Sandford E | Wood S | Finch R | Gale A | Robbins W | Murphy J | Rix J | Raw H | Ridyard A |
|---|---|---|---|---|---|---|---|---|---|---|---|---|---|---|---|---|---|---|---|---|---|---|---|
| Aug 27 | (h) | Everton | W 3-1 | Sandford, Carter, Richardson | 31,922 | 1 | 2 | 3 | 4 | 5 | 6 | 7 | 8 | 9 | 10 | 11 | | | | | | | |
| 31 | (a) | Arsenal | W 2-1 | Glidden, John (og) | 40,200 | 1 | 2 | 3 | 4 | 5 | 6 | 7 | 8 | 9 | 10 | 11 | | | | | | | |
| Sep 3 | (a) | Blackpool | W 4-2 | Glidden 3, Richardson | 21,563 | 1 | 2 | 3 | 4 | 5 | 6 | 7 | 8 | 9 | 10 | 11 | | | | | | | |
| 10 | (h) | Derby C | W 2-0 | Richardson, Glidden | 30,715 | 1 | 2 | 3 | 4 | 5 | 6 | 7 | 8 | 9 | 10 | 11 | | | | | | | |
| 14 | (h) | Arsenal | D 1-1 | Carter | 45,038 | 1 | 2 | 3 | 4 | 5 | 6 | 7 | 8 | 9 | 10 | 11 | | | | | | | |
| 17 | (h) | Blackburn R | D 4-4 | Carter 2, Glidden, Wood | 18,400 | 1 | 2 | 3 | 4 | 5 | 6 | 7 | 8 | 9 | 10 | 11 | | | | | | | |
| 24 | (h) | Leeds U | L 0-1 | | 26,497 | 1 | 2 | 3 | 4 | 5 | 6 | 7 | 8 | 9 | 10 | 11 | | | | | | | |
| Oct 1 | (a) | Sheffield W | L 1-3 | Robbins | 21,900 | 1 | | 3 | | 4 | 5 | 6 | 7 | 8 | | 10 | | 2 | 9 | 11 | | | |
| 8 | (h) | Wolves | W 4-1 | Richardson 2, Glidden, Sandford | 30,058 | 1 | 2 | 3 | | 5 | 6 | 7 | 8 | 9 | 10 | 11 | | | | 4 | | | |
| 15 | (h) | Birmingham | W 1-0 | Sandford | 29,145 | 1 | 2 | 3 | | 5 | 6 | 7 | 8 | 9 | 10 | 11 | | | | 4 | | | |
| 22 | (a) | Newcastle U | L 0-3 | | 25,580 | 1 | 2 | 3 | | 5 | 6 | 7 | 8 | 9 | 10 | | | | 11 | 4 | | | |
| 29 | (h) | Aston Villa | W 3-1 | Robbins, Carter, Richardson | 42,093 | 1 | 2 | 3 | | 5 | 6 | 7 | 8 | 9 | 10 | | | | 11 | 4 | | | |
| Nov 5 | (a) | Portsmouth | L 0-3 | | 26,000 | 1 | 2 | 3 | | 5 | 6 | 7 | 8 | 9 | 10 | | | | 11 | 4 | | | |
| 12 | (h) | Chelsea | W 3-2 | Wood, Robbins, Sandford | 21,569 | 1 | 2 | 3 | | 5 | 6 | 7 | 8 | | 10 | 11 | | | 9 | 4 | | | |
| 19 | (a) | Huddersfield T | L 1-2 | Richardson | 27,500 | 1 | 2 | 3 | | | | | 7 | 9 | 5 | | | | 10 | 4 | 6 | 8 | |
| 26 | (h) | Sheffield U | L 0-1 | | 16,882 | 1 | 2 | 3 | | 5 | | 7 | 8 | | 10 | 11 | | | 9 | 4 | 6 | | |
| Dec 3 | (a) | Middlesbrough | L 1-3 | Raw | 16,700 | 1 | 2 | 3 | 4 | 5 | | | 7 | | 10 | 11 | | | 9 | | 6 | 8 | |
| 10 | (h) | Bolton W | W 4-0 | Raw, Robbins 2, Richardson | 12,662 | 1 | 2 | 3 | | 5 | | | 7 | 9 | | 11 | | | 10 | 4 | 6 | 8 | |
| 17 | (a) | Liverpool | L 0-2 | | 32,500 | 1 | 2 | 3 | | 5 | | | 7 | 9 | | 11 | | | 10 | 4 | 6 | 8 | |
| 24 | (h) | Leicester C | W 4-3 | Richardson 3, Sandford | 15,905 | 1 | 2 | 3 | | 5 | 6 | 7 | 8 | 9 | | 11 | | | 10 | 4 | | | |
| 26 | (h) | Sunderland | W 5-1 | Richardson 3, Carter, Robbins | 26,113 | 1 | 2 | 3 | | 5 | 6 | 7 | 8 | 9 | | 11 | | | 10 | 4 | | | |
| 31 | (a) | Everton | W 2-1 | Glidden, Robbins | 34,700 | 1 | 2 | 3 | | 5 | | 7 | 8 | 9 | | 11 | | | 10 | 4 | 6 | | |
| Jan 2 | (a) | Sunderland | D 2-2 | Richardson, Wood | 29,850 | 1 | 2 | 3 | | 5 | | 7 | 8 | 9 | | 11 | | | 10 | 4 | 6 | | |
| 7 | (h) | Blackpool | W 2-1 | Richardson, Wood | 17,280 | 1 | 2 | 3 | | 5 | 6 | 7 | 8 | 9 | | 11 | | | 10 | 4 | | | |
| 21 | (a) | Derby C | D 2-2 | Glidden, Carter | 21,000 | 1 | 2 | 3 | | | 6 | 7 | 8 | 9 | 10 | 11 | | | | 4 | | | 5 |
| Feb 4 | (a) | Leeds U | D 1-1 | Richardson | 24,440 | 1 | 2 | 3 | | | 6 | 7 | 8 | 9 | 10 | 11 | | | | 4 | | | 5 |
| 8 | (h) | Blackburn R | L 1-3 | Richardson | 10,775 | 1 | 2 | 3 | | | 6 | 7 | 8 | 9 | 10 | 11 | | | | 4 | | | 5 |
| 11 | (h) | Sheffield W | W 2-0 | Richardson, Sandford | 20,863 | 1 | 2 | 3 | | 5 | 6 | 7 | 8 | 9 | 10 | 11 | | | | 4 | | | |
| 18 | (a) | Wolves | D 3-3 | Glidden, Richardson, Wood | 29,400 | 1 | 2 | 3 | | 5 | 6 | 7 | 8 | 9 | 10 | 11 | | | | 4 | | | |
| Mar 4 | (h) | Newcastle U | W 3-2 | Richardson 2, Wood | 21,847 | 1 | 2 | 3 | | 5 | 6 | 7 | 8 | 9 | 10 | 11 | | | | 4 | | | |
| 11 | (a) | Aston Villa | L 2-3 | Richardson 2 | 50,600 | 1 | | 3 | | 5 | 6 | 7 | 8 | 9 | 10 | 11 | | 2 | | 4 | | | |
| 18 | (h) | Portsmouth | W 4-2 | Richardson 2, Sandford 2 | 16,356 | 1 | 2 | 3 | | 5 | 6 | | 8 | 9 | 10 | 11 | 7 | | | 4 | | | |
| 25 | (a) | Chelsea | W 2-1 | Gale, Richardson | 21,600 | 1 | 2 | 3 | | 5 | 6 | | 8 | 9 | 10 | | | 7 | 11 | 4 | | | |
| Apr 1 | (h) | Huddersfield T | W 2-1 | Richardson, Carter | 17,610 | 1 | 2 | 3 | | 5 | 6 | | 8 | 9 | 10 | | 7 | | 11 | 4 | | | |
| 8 | (a) | Sheffield U | D 1-1 | Robbins | 20,528 | 1 | 2 | 3 | | 5 | 6 | 7 | 8 | 9 | 10 | | | | 11 | 4 | | | |
| 14 | (a) | Manchester C | L 0-1 | | 28,200 | 1 | 2 | 3 | | 5 | 6 | 7 | 8 | 9 | 10 | | | | 11 | 4 | | | |
| 15 | (h) | Middlesbrough | L 0-1 | | 17,530 | 1 | 2 | 3 | | 5 | 6 | 7 | 8 | 9 | 10 | | | | 11 | 4 | | | |
| 17 | (h) | Manchester C | W 4-0 | Robbins, Carter 3 | 18,988 | 1 | 2 | 3 | | 5 | 6 | 7 | 8 | 9 | 10 | | | | 11 | 4 | | | |
| 22 | (a) | Bolton W | D 2-2 | Robbins, Carter | 14,000 | 1 | 2 | 3 | | 5 | 6 | 7 | 8 | 9 | 10 | | | | 11 | 4 | | | |
| 26 | (a) | Birmingham | D 1-1 | Richardson | 27,000 | 1 | 2 | 3 | | 5 | 6 | 7 | 8 | 9 | 10 | | | | 11 | 4 | | | |
| 29 | (h) | Liverpool | W 2-1 | Carter, Richardson | 8,933 | 1 | 2 | 3 | | 5 | | 7 | 8 | 9 | 10 | | | | 11 | 4 | 6 | | |
| May 6 | (a) | Leicester C | L 2-6 | Carter, Sandford | 19,000 | 1 | 2 | 3 | | 5 | | 7 | 8 | 9 | 10 | | | | 11 | 4 | 6 | | |
| | | | | | App | 42 | 42 | 40 | 9 | 38 | 33 | 39 | 36 | 38 | 39 | 28 | 2 | 4 | 25 | 34 | 6 | 4 | 3 |
| | | | | | Goals | | | | | | | 10 | 14 | 30 | 9 | 6 | | 1 | 10 | | | 2 | |

**Tommy Magee, Bill Richardson and Jim Edwards**

# 1933-34

### Division 1

| Date | Opponent | Result | Scorers | Att | Pearson H | Shaw G | Trentham H | Murphy J | Richardson W | Edwards J | Glidden T | Carter J | Richardson WG | Sandford E | Wood S | Ridyard A | Finch R | Robbins W | Boyes W | Gale A | Crowe E | Magee T | Sankey J | Rix J | Green T | Foulkes H | Trevis B |
|---|---|---|---|---|---|---|---|---|---|---|---|---|---|---|---|---|---|---|---|---|---|---|---|---|---|---|---|
| Aug 26 | (a) Everton | L 0-1 | | 25,760 | 1 | 2 | 3 | 4 | 5 | 6 | 7 | 8 | 9 | 10 | 11 | | | | | | | | | | | | |
| Sep 2 | (h) Middlesbrough | W 3-0 | Glidden, Richardson 2 | 21,152 | 1 | 2 | 3 | 4 | 5 | 6 | 7 | 8 | 9 | 10 | 11 | | | | | | | | | | | | |
| 6 | (a) Arsenal | L 1-3 | Wood | 34,083 | 1 | 2 | 3 | 4 | | 6 | 7 | 8 | 9 | 10 | 11 | 5 | | | | | | | | | | | |
| 9 | (a) Blackburn R | L 0-4 | | 20,595 | 1 | | 3 | 4 | | 6 | 7 | 8 | 9 | 10 | 11 | 5 | 2 | | | | | | | | | | |
| 13 | (h) Arsenal | W 1-0 | Carter | 29,398 | 1 | | 3 | 4 | 5 | 6 | 7 | 8 | 9 | 10 | 11 | | 2 | | | | | | | | | | |
| 16 | (h) Newcastle U | D 1-1 | Glidden | 24,481 | 1 | | 3 | 4 | | 6 | 7 | 8 | 9 | 10 | 11 | 5 | 2 | | | | | | | | | | |
| 23 | (a) Leeds U | L 0-3 | | 21,119 | 1 | 2 | 3 | 4 | 5 | 6 | 7 | 8 | 9 | 10 | 11 | | | | | | | | | | | | |
| 30 | (h) Derby C | W 5-1 | Richardson 4, Glidden | 24,570 | 1 | 2 | 3 | 4 | 5 | 6 | 7 | 8 | 9 | 10 | | | | | 11 | | | | | | | | |
| Oct 7 | (a) Wolves | D 0-0 | | 37,287 | 1 | 2 | 3 | 4 | 5 | 6 | 7 | 8 | 9 | 10 | | | | | 11 | | | | | | | | |
| 14 | (a) Birmingham | W 1-0 | Richardson | 29,103 | 1 | 2 | 3 | 4 | 5 | 6 | 7 | 8 | 9 | 10 | | | | | 11 | | | | | | | | |
| 21 | (h) Stoke C | W 5-1 | Beachill (og), Richardson, Sandford 2, Wood | 22,771 | 1 | 2 | 3 | 4 | 5 | 6 | 7 | | 9 | 10 | 11 | | | 8 | | | | | | | | | |
| 28 | (a) Huddersfield T | L 1-3 | Richardson | 28,531 | 1 | 2 | 3 | 4 | 5 | 6 | 7 | | 9 | 10 | 11 | | | 8 | | | | | | | | | |
| Nov 4 | (h) Tottenham H | L 1-2 | Wood | 32,276 | 1 | 2 | 3 | 4 | 5 | 6 | 7 | | 9 | 10 | 11 | | | 8 | | | | | | | | | |
| 11 | (a) Sunderland | D 2-2 | Glidden, Carter | 27,434 | 1 | 2 | 3 | 4 | 5 | 6 | 7 | 8 | 9 | 10 | 11 | | | | | | | | | | | | |
| 18 | (h) Chelsea | W 3-1 | Richardson, Sandford, Glidden | 12,325 | 1 | 2 | 3 | 4 | 5 | 6 | 7 | 8 | 9 | 10 | 11 | | | | | | | | | | | | |
| 25 | (a) Liverpool | D 1-1 | Carter | 33,089 | 1 | 2 | 3 | 4 | 5 | 6 | 7 | 8 | 9 | 10 | 11 | | | | | | | | | | | | |
| Dec 2 | (h) Sheffield U | W 3-0 | Wood, Richardson, Sandford | 10,493 | 1 | 2 | 3 | 4 | 5 | 6 | 7 | 8 | 9 | 10 | 11 | | | | | | | | | | | | |
| 9 | (a) Leicester C | W 1-0 | Carter | 20,614 | 1 | 2 | 3 | 4 | 5 | 6 | 7 | 8 | 9 | 10 | 11 | | | | | | | | | | | | |
| 16 | (h) Aston Villa | W 2-1 | Richardson, Glidden | 25,503 | 1 | 2 | 3 | 4 | 5 | 6 | 7 | 8 | 9 | 10 | 11 | | | | | | | | | | | | |
| 23 | (a) Portsmouth | D 2-2 | Richardson, Wood | 15,113 | 1 | 2 | 3 | 4 | 5 | 6 | 7 | 8 | 9 | 10 | 11 | | | | | | | | | | | | |
| 26 | (h) Sheffield W | L 1-3 | Glidden | 34,905 | 1 | 2 | 3 | 4 | 5 | 6 | 7 | 8 | 9 | 10 | 11 | | | | | | | | | | | | |
| 27 | (h) Sheffield W | D 1-1 | Carter | 32,660 | 1 | 2 | 3 | | 5 | 6 | 7 | 8 | 9 | 4 | 11 | | | | | | 10 | | | | | | |
| 30 | (h) Everton | D 3-3 | Gale, Richardson, Sandford | 18,876 | 1 | 2 | 3 | | 5 | 6 | 7 | 8 | 9 | 4 | 11 | | | | | 10 | | | | | | | |
| Jan 1 | (a) Manchester C | W 7-2 | Robbins 2, Richardson 3, Carter, Sandford | 20,996 | 1 | 2 | 3 | 4 | 5 | 6 | 7 | 8 | 9 | 10 | | | | 11 | | | | | | | | | |
| 6 | (a) Middlesbrough | L 0-3 | | 13,927 | 1 | 2 | 3 | 4 | 5 | 6 | 7 | 8 | 9 | 10 | | | | 11 | | | | | | | | | |
| 20 | (h) Blackburn R | L 0-1 | | 16,297 | | | 3 | | 5 | | 7 | 8 | 9 | 10 | 11 | | 2 | | | | | 1 | 4 | 6 | | | |
| 27 | (a) Newcastle U | W 2-1 | Gale, Sandford | 21,824 | | 2 | 3 | | 5 | | 7 | 8 | | 10 | | | | | 11 | 9 | | 1 | 4 | 6 | | | |
| Feb 3 | (h) Leeds U | L 0-3 | | 13,343 | | 2 | 3 | 4 | 5 | | 7 | | | 10 | | | | | 11 | 9 | | 1 | | 6 | 8 | | |
| 10 | (a) Derby C | D 1-1 | Richardson | 20,887 | | | | | 5 | | 7 | 8 | 9 | 10 | | | 2 | | 11 | | | 1 | 4 | 6 | 3 | | |
| 17 | (h) Wolves | W 2-0 | Richardson, Sandford | 24,892 | | | | 4 | 5 | | 7 | 8 | 9 | 10 | | | 2 | | 11 | | | 1 | | 6 | 3 | | |
| 24 | (h) Birmingham | L 1-2 | Glidden | 24,525 | | 2 | | 4 | 5 | | 7 | 8 | 9 | 10 | | | | | 11 | | | 1 | | 6 | 3 | | |
| Mar 8 | (a) Stoke C | L 1-4 | Carter | 16,420 | | 2 | | 4 | 5 | | 7 | 8 | 9 | 10 | | | | | 11 | | | 1 | | 6 | 3 | | |
| 10 | (h) Huddersfield T | L 2-3 | Richardson, Sankey | 16,280 | | | | | 5 | | 7 | 8 | 9 | 10 | | | 2 | | 11 | | | 1 | 4 | 6 | 3 | | |
| 17 | (a) Tottenham H | L 1-2 | Boyes | 25,150 | | | 3 | 4 | | | 7 | 8 | 9 | 10 | | 5 | 2 | | 11 | | | 1 | | 6 | | | |
| 24 | (h) Sunderland | W 6-5 | Richardson, Boyes, Glidden 2, Carter, Sandford(pen) | 11,889 | | | 3 | 4 | | | 7 | 8 | 9 | 10 | | 5 | 2 | | 11 | | | 1 | | 6 | | | |
| 31 | (a) Chelsea | L 2-3 | Richardson, Boyes | 20,851 | | | 3 | 4 | 5 | | 7 | 8 | 9 | 10 | | | 2 | | 11 | | | 1 | | 6 | | | |
| Apr 2 | (h) Manchester C | W 4-0 | Carter, Boyes, Richardson 2 | 22,198 | 1 | 2 | 3 | 4 | 5 | | 7 | 8 | 9 | 10 | | | | | 11 | | | | | 6 | | | |
| 7 | (h) Liverpool | D 2-2 | Carter, Sandford (pen) | 15,730 | 1 | 2 | 3 | | 5 | | 7 | 8 | 9 | 10 | | | | | 11 | | | | | 6 | | 4 | |
| 14 | (a) Sheffield U | W 1-0 | Boyes | 10,402 | 1 | 2 | 3 | 4 | 5 | | 7 | 8 | 9 | 10 | | | | | 11 | | | | | 6 | | | |
| 21 | (h) Leicester C | W 2-0 | Richardson, Boyes | 11,309 | 1 | 2 | 3 | 4 | 5 | | 7 | 8 | 9 | 10 | | | | | 11 | | | | | 6 | | | |
| 28 | (a) Aston Villa | D 4-4 | Glidden 2, Richardson, Green | 20,050 | 1 | 2 | 3 | 4 | 5 | | 7 | | 9 | 10 | | | | | 11 | | | | | 6 | 8 | | |
| May 5 | (h) Portsmouth | W 2-1 | Glidden, Green | 10,679 | 1 | 2 | 3 | 4 | 5 | | 7 | | 9 | 10 | | | | | 11 | | | | | 6 | 8 | | |
| | | | App | | 31 | 32 | 37 | 35 | 37 | 25 | 42 | 36 | 40 | 42 | 21 | 5 | 10 | 6 | 19 | 3 | 1 | 11 | 4 | 16 | 3 | 5 | 1 |
| | | | Goals | | | | | | | | 13 | 10 | 26 | 10 | 5 | | | 2 | 6 | 2 | | | 1 | | 2 | | |

**Albion players pictured in the bath at The Hawthorns in 1933.**

# 1934-35

## Division 1

| Date | | Opponent | Res | Score | Scorers | Att | Pearson H | Shaw G | Trentham H | Murphy J | Richardson W | Sankey J | Glidden T | Carter J | Richardson WG | Sandford E | Robbins W | Boyes W | Edwards J | Wood S | Crowe E | Ridyard A | Whitehead N | Gale A | Jones H | Screen J | Finch R | Rawlings S |
|---|---|---|---|---|---|---|---|---|---|---|---|---|---|---|---|---|---|---|---|---|---|---|---|---|---|---|---|---|
| Aug 25 | (h) | Manchester C | D | 1-1 | Richardson | 24,480 | 1 | 2 | 3 | 4 | 5 | 6 | 7 | 8 | 9 | 10 | 11 | | | | | | | | | | | |
| 29 | (h) | Birmingham | L | 1-2 | Richardson | 22,025 | 1 | 2 | 3 | 4 | 5 | 6 | 7 | 8 | 9 | 10 | 11 | | | | | | | | | | | |
| Sep 1 | (a) | Middlesbrough | D | 0-0 | | 15,800 | 1 | 2 | 3 | 4 | 5 | | 7 | 8 | 9 | 10 | | 11 | 6 | | | | | | | | | |
| 3 | (a) | Birmingham | W | 2-1 | Richardson 2 | 25,000 | 1 | 2 | 3 | 4 | 5 | | 7 | 8 | 9 | 6 | | 10 | | | | | 11 | | | | | |
| 8 | (h) | Blackburn R | D | 2-2 | Richardson, Glidden | 19,063 | 1 | 2 | 3 | 4 | 5 | | 7 | 8 | 9 | 10 | | 11 | 6 | | | | | | | | | |
| 15 | (a) | Arsenal | L | 3-4 | Richardson 2, Boyes | 30,100 | 1 | 2 | 3 | 4 | 5 | | 7 | 8 | 9 | 10 | | 11 | 6 | 1 | | | | | | | | |
| 22 | (h) | Portsmouth | W | 4-2 | Richardson 2, Glidden, Sandford | 11,396 | 1 | 2 | 3 | 4 | 5 | | 7 | 8 | 9 | 10 | | 11 | 6 | | | | | | | | | |
| 29 | (a) | Liverpool | L | 2-3 | Sandford 2 | 16,500 | 1 | 2 | 3 | | 5 | 4 | 7 | 8 | 9 | 10 | | 11 | 6 | | | | | | | | | |
| Oct 6 | (h) | Leeds U | W | 6-3 | Richardson 4, Boyes, Carter | 15,843 | 1 | 2 | 3 | 4 | 5 | 6 | 7 | 8 | 9 | 10 | | 11 | | | | | | | | | | |
| 13 | (a) | Wolves | L | 2-3 | Sandford 2 (1 pen) | 45,066 | 1 | 2 | 3 | 4 | 5 | 6 | 7 | 8 | 9 | 10 | | 11 | | | | | | | | | | |
| 20 | (h) | Huddersfield T | W | 4-1 | Boyes 2, Glidden, Richardson | 19,250 | 1 | 2 | 3 | 4 | 5 | 6 | 7 | 8 | 9 | 10 | | 11 | | | | | | | | | | |
| 27 | (a) | Everton | L | 0-4 | | 27,154 | 1 | 2 | 3 | 4 | 5 | 6 | 7 | 8 | 9 | 10 | | 11 | | | | | | | | | | |
| Nov 3 | (h) | Aston Villa | D | 2-2 | Boyes 2 | 44,503 | 1 | 2 | 3 | 4 | 5 | 6 | 7 | 8 | 9 | 10 | | 11 | | | | | | | | | | |
| 10 | (a) | Chelsea | W | 3-2 | Boyes 2, Sandford | 25,828 | 1 | 2 | 3 | 4 | 5 | 6 | 7 | 8 | 9 | 10 | | 11 | | | | | | | | | | |
| 17 | (h) | Tottenham H | W | 4-0 | Sandford, Boyes 2, Richardson | 20,397 | 1 | 2 | 3 | 4 | 5 | 6 | 7 | 8 | 9 | 10 | | 11 | | | | | | | | | | |
| 24 | (a) | Sunderland | W | 1-0 | Carter | 31,223 | 1 | 2 | 3 | 4 | 5 | 6 | 7 | 8 | 9 | 10 | | 11 | | | | | | | | | | |
| Dec 1 | (h) | Leicester C | W | 4-1 | Boyes 2, Glidden 2 | 17,174 | 1 | 2 | 3 | 4 | 5 | 6 | 7 | 8 | 9 | 10 | | 11 | | | | | | | | | | |
| 8 | (a) | Derby C | L | 3-9 | Richardson, Sandford (pen), Glidden | 14,308 | 1 | 2 | 3 | 4 | 5 | 6 | 7 | 8 | 9 | 10 | | 11 | | | | | | | | | | |
| 15 | (h) | Grimsby T | W | 4-2 | Boyes 2, Sandford 2 | 17,098 | 1 | 2 | 3 | 4 | | | 7 | 8 | 9 | 10 | | 11 | 6 | | | 5 | | | | | | |
| 22 | (a) | Preston NE | W | 2-1 | Richardson, Boyes | 15,835 | 1 | 2 | 3 | 4 | | | 7 | 8 | 9 | 10 | | 11 | 6 | | | 5 | | | | | | |
| 25 | (h) | Stoke C | W | 3-0 | Carter 2, Richardson | 38,531 | 1 | 2 | 3 | 4 | 5 | | 7 | 8 | 9 | 10 | | 11 | 6 | | | | | | | | | |
| 26 | (a) | Stoke C | L | 0-3 | | 18,334 | 1 | 2 | 3 | 4 | 5 | | | 8 | 9 | 10 | | 11 | 6 | | | | 7 | | | | | |
| 29 | (a) | Manchester C | L | 2-3 | Gale, Sandford | 23,545 | 1 | 2 | 3 | 4 | 5 | | | 8 | 9 | 10 | | 11 | 6 | | | | | 7 | | | | |
| Jan 1 | (a) | Sheffield W | L | 1-2 | Gale | 17,636 | 1 | 2 | 3 | 4 | 5 | | | 8 | 9 | | | 11 | 6 | | | | | 7 | 10 | | | |
| 5 | (h) | Middlesbrough | W | 6-3 | Richardson, Boyes, Gale, Sandford 2, Carter | 18,952 | 1 | | 3 | 4 | 5 | 6 | | 8 | 9 | 10 | | 11 | | | | | | 7 | | 2 | | |
| 19 | (a) | Blackburn R | L | 0-3 | | 15,320 | 1 | 2 | 3 | 4 | 5 | 6 | | 8 | 9 | 10 | | 11 | | | | | | 7 | | | | |
| 30 | (h) | Arsenal | L | 0-3 | | 30,667 | 1 | 2 | 3 | 4 | 5 | 6 | | 8 | 9 | 10 | | 11 | | | | | | 7 | | | | |
| Feb 2 | (a) | Portsmouth | W | 2-0 | Sandford, Richardson | 18,048 | 1 | 2 | 3 | 4 | 5 | | | 8 | 9 | 10 | | 11 | 6 | | | | | 7 | | | | |
| 9 | (h) | Liverpool | D | 1-1 | Sandford | 20,182 | 1 | 2 | 3 | 4 | 5 | | | 8 | 9 | 10 | | 11 | 6 | | | | | 7 | | | | |
| 20 | (a) | Leeds U | L | 1-4 | Sandford | 20,242 | 1 | 2 | 3 | 4 | 5 | 7 | | 8 | 9 | 10 | | 11 | 6 | | | | | | | | | |
| 23 | (h) | Wolves | W | 5-2 | Sandford, Boyes 2, Richardson 2 | 31,494 | 1 | 2 | 3 | 4 | 5 | | | 8 | 9 | 10 | | 11 | 6 | | | | | 7 | | | | |
| Mar 6 | (a) | Huddersfield T | L | 0-3 | | 24,176 | 1 | | 3 | 4 | 5 | 7 | | 8 | 9 | | | 11 | 6 | | | | | | 10 | 2 | | |
| 9 | (h) | Everton | L | 0-1 | | 20,002 | 1 | 2 | 3 | 4 | 5 | 10 | | 8 | 9 | | | 11 | 6 | | | | | 7 | | | | |
| 23 | (h) | Chelsea | D | 2-2 | Sandford, Jones | 13,721 | 1 | 2 | 3 | 4 | 5 | | | | 9 | 10 | | 11 | 6 | | | | | | 8 | | 7 | |
| 30 | (a) | Tottenham H | W | 1-0 | Richardson | 30,144 | 1 | 2 | 3 | 4 | 5 | | | | 9 | 10 | | 11 | 6 | | | | | | 8 | | 7 | |
| Apr 3 | (a) | Aston Villa | W | 3-2 | Gibson (og), Boyes, Richardson | 55,067 | 1 | | 3 | 4 | 5 | | | | 9 | 10 | | 11 | 6 | | | | | | 8 | 2 | 7 | |
| 6 | (h) | Sunderland | D | 1-1 | Sandford (pen) | 24,510 | 1 | | 3 | 4 | 5 | | | | 9 | 10 | | 11 | 6 | | | | | | 8 | 2 | 7 | |
| 13 | (a) | Leicester C | D | 0-0 | | 21,508 | 1 | 2 | 3 | 4 | 5 | | | | 9 | 10 | | 11 | 6 | | | | | | 8 | | 7 | |
| 20 | (h) | Derby C | W | 4-3 | Sandford, Richardson, Glidden, Jones | 16,464 | 1 | 2 | 3 | 4 | | | 7 | | 9 | 10 | | 11 | 6 | | | 5 | | | 8 | | | |
| 22 | (h) | Sheffield W | D | 1-1 | Boyes | 33,540 | 1 | 2 | 3 | 4 | | 6 | | | 9 | | 10 | 11 | | | | 5 | | | 7 | 8 | | |
| May 1 | (a) | Grimsby T | L | 0-3 | | 16,239 | 1 | 2 | 3 | 4 | 5 | | 7 | | 9 | 8 | 10 | 11 | 6 | | | | | | | | | |
| 4 | (h) | Preston NE | D | 0-0 | | 10,420 | 1 | 2 | 3 | 4 | 5 | | 7 | | 9 | 8 | 10 | 11 | 6 | | | | | | | | | |
| **App** | | | | | | | 41 | 38 | 42 | 41 | 38 | 20 | 24 | 33 | 42 | 38 | 4 | 41 | 25 | 1 | 1 | 4 | 1 | 10 | 9 | 1 | 3 | 5 |
| **Goals** | | | | | | | | | | | | | 7 | 5 | 25 | 20 | | 20 | | | | | | 3 | 2 | | | |

**West Brom in 1934-35. Back row (left to right): Mr F.Everiss (secretary), Fred Reed (trainer), Harry Raw, Harold Pearson, Joe Carter, George Shaw, Mr C.Jephcott (director). Middle row: W.G.Richardson, Teddy Sandford, Bill Richardson, Mr W.I.Bassett (chairman), Tommy Glidden, Jimmy Edwards, Bert Trentham. Front row: Stan Wood, Jack Sankey, Wally Boyes, Harry Jones, Jimmy Murphy.**

# 1935-36

## Division 1

| Date | Opponent | Result | Scorers | Att | Pearson H | Shaw G | Trentham H | Murphy J | Richardson W | Edwards J | Glidden T | Green T | Richardson WG | Sandford E | Boyes W | Rawlings S | Finch R | Robbins W | Sankey J | Wood S | Gale A | Rix J | Mahon J | Jones H | Carter J | Crowe E | Alsop G | Ridyard A | Adams J | Light W | Foulkes H |
|---|---|---|---|---|---|---|---|---|---|---|---|---|---|---|---|---|---|---|---|---|---|---|---|---|---|---|---|---|---|---|---|
| Aug 31 | (a) Manchester C | L 0-1 | | 23,200 | 1 | 2 | 3 | 4 | 5 | 6 | 7 | 8 | 9 | 10 | 11 | | | | | | | | | | | | | | | | |
| Sep 4 | (h) Sunderland | L 1-3 | Rawlings | 24,385 | 1 | 2 | 3 | 4 | 5 | 6 | | 8 | 9 | 10 | 11 | 7 | | | | | | | | | | | | | | | |
| Sep 7 | (h) Stoke C | W 2-0 | Green, Richardson | 24,060 | 1 | 2 | 3 | 4 | 5 | 6 | | 8 | 9 | 10 | 11 | 7 | | | | | | | | | | | | | | | |
| Sep 11 | (a) Sunderland | L 1-6 | Richardson | 29,530 | 1 | 2 | 3 | 4 | 5 | 6 | | 8 | 9 | 10 | 11 | 7 | | | | | | | | | | | | | | | |
| Sep 14 | (a) Blackburn R | L 1-3 | Boyes | 16,421 | 1 | | 3 | 4 | 5 | 6 | | | 9 | 8 | 11 | 7 | 2 | 10 | | | | | | | | | | | | | |
| Sep 18 | (h) Birmingham | D 0-0 | | 18,083 | 1 | | 3 | 4 | 5 | | | | 9 | 10 | 8 | 7 | 2 | | 6 | 11 | | | | | | | | | | | |
| Sep 21 | (h) Chelsea | L 1-2 | Gale | 17,183 | 1 | | 3 | 4 | 5 | | 7 | | | 10 | 8 | | 2 | | 6 | 11 | 9 | | | | | | | | | | |
| Sep 28 | (a) Liverpool | L 0-5 | | 28,301 | 1 | 2 | 3 | | 5 | | | | 9 | 10 | 11 | | | | 4 | | | 6 | 7 | | 8 | | | | | | |
| Oct 5 | (h) Grimsby T | W 4-1 | Richardson, Mahon, Carter 2 | 20,787 | 1 | 2 | 3 | | 5 | | | | 9 | 10 | 11 | | | | 4 | | | 6 | 7 | | 8 | | | | | | |
| Oct 12 | (a) Leeds U | D 1-1 | | 16,560 | 1 | 2 | 3 | | 5 | | | | 9 | 10 | 11 | | | | 4 | | | 6 | 7 | | 8 | | | | | | |
| Oct 19 | (a) Aston Villa | W 7-0 | Richardson 4, Wood, Mahon, Sankey | 38,037 | 1 | 2 | 3 | 4 | 5 | | | | 9 | 10 | | | | | 6 | 11 | | | 7 | | 8 | | | | | | |
| Oct 26 | (h) Wolves | W 2-1 | Richardson, Sandford | 42,402 | 1 | 2 | 3 | 4 | 5 | | | | 9 | 10 | | | | | 6 | 11 | | | 7 | | 8 | | | | | | |
| Nov 2 | (a) Sheffield W | W 5-2 | Wood 2, Sandford, Mahon, Richardson | 15,100 | 1 | 2 | 3 | 4 | 5 | | | | 9 | 10 | | | | | 6 | 11 | | | 7 | | 8 | | | | | | |
| Nov 9 | (h) Portsmouth | W 2-0 | Richardson 2 | 23,055 | 1 | 2 | 3 | 4 | 5 | | | | 9 | 10 | | | | | 6 | 11 | | | 7 | | 8 | | | | | | |
| Nov 16 | (a) Preston NE | L 0-3 | | 20,146 | 1 | 2 | 3 | 4 | 5 | | | | 9 | 10 | | | | | 6 | 11 | | | 7 | | 8 | | | | | | |
| Nov 23 | (h) Huddersfield T | L 1-2 | Richardson | 24,324 | | 2 | 3 | 4 | 5 | | | | | 10 | 11 | | | | 6 | | | | 7 | | 8 | 1 | 9 | | | | |
| Nov 30 | (a) Derby C | L 0-2 | | 18,600 | 1 | 2 | 3 | | 5 | | | | 9 | 10 | | | | | 4 | 11 | | 6 | 7 | | 8 | | | | | | |
| Dec 7 | (h) Everton | W 6-1 | Richardson 2, Mahon 2, Sandford, Carter | 17,151 | 1 | 2 | 3 | | 5 | | | | 9 | 10 | | | | | 4 | 11 | | 6 | 7 | | 8 | | | | | | |
| Dec 14 | (a) Bolton W | L 1-3 | Sandford | 13,400 | 1 | 2 | 3 | | 5 | | | | 9 | 10 | | | | | 4 | 11 | | 6 | 7 | | 8 | | | | | | |
| Dec 21 | (h) Brentford | W 1-0 | Mahon | 14,265 | 1 | 2 | 3 | | 5 | | | | 9 | 10 | | | | | 4 | 11 | | 6 | 7 | | 8 | | | | | | |
| Dec 26 | (h) Middlesbrough | W 5-2 | Shaw (pen), Richardson 4 | 26,049 | 1 | 2 | 3 | 4 | 5 | | | | 9 | | | | | | 10 | 11 | | 6 | 7 | | 8 | | | | | | |
| Dec 28 | (h) Manchester C | W 5-1 | Mahon, Robbins, Glidden, Richardson 2 | 31,012 | 1 | 2 | 3 | | | | 8 | | 9 | | | | | 10 | 4 | 11 | | 6 | 7 | | | | | 5 | | | |
| Jan 1 | (a) Middlesbrough | L 1-3 | Richardson | 18,055 | 1 | 2 | 3 | | | | 8 | | 9 | | | | | 10 | 4 | 11 | | 6 | 7 | | | | | 5 | | | |
| Jan 4 | (a) Stoke C | L 2-3 | Richardson, Mahon | 13,200 | 1 | 2 | 3 | | | | | | 9 | | | | | 10 | 4 | 11 | | 6 | 7 | | 8 | | | 5 | | | |
| Jan 18 | (h) Blackburn R | W 8-1 | Richardson 3, Mahon 3, Robbins, Sankey | 16,464 | | 2 | 3 | | 5 | | | | 9 | 8 | | | | 10 | 4 | 11 | | 6 | 7 | | | | | | | | 1 |
| Feb 1 | (h) Liverpool | W 6-1 | Richardson 3, Mahon, Wood 2 | 23,080 | | | 3 | | 5 | | | | 9 | 10 | | 2 | | | 4 | 11 | | 6 | 7 | | 8 | | | | | | 1 |
| Feb 8 | (a) Grimsby T | L 2-4 | Richardson 2 | 10,247 | | | 3 | 10 | | | | | 9 | 8 | | 2 | | | 4 | 11 | | 6 | 7 | | | | | 5 | 1 | | |
| Feb 19 | (h) Leeds U | W 3-2 | Sandford 2, Wood | 7,893 | | | 3 | | | | | | 9 | 8 | | 2 | | 10 | 4 | 11 | | 6 | 7 | | | | | 5 | 1 | | |
| Feb 29 | (a) Portsmouth | L 1-3 | Richardson | 15,100 | | | 3 | | | 6 | | | 9 | 8 | | 2 | | 10 | 4 | 11 | | | 7 | | | | | 5 | 1 | | |
| Mar 7 | (h) Derby C | L 0-3 | | 18,408 | | 2 | 3 | | 5 | | | 8 | 9 | | | | | 10 | 4 | 11 | | 6 | 7 | | | | | | 1 | | |
| Mar 11 | (a) Chelsea | D 2-2 | Mahon, Richardson | 20,400 | | 2 | 3 | | | 6 | | 8 | 9 | | | | | 10 | 4 | 11 | | | 7 | | | | | 5 | 1 | | |
| Mar 14 | (a) Wolves | L 0-2 | | 25,253 | | 2 | 3 | 4 | | | | 8 | 9 | | | | | 10 | 6 | 11 | | | 7 | | | | | 5 | | 1 | |
| Mar 21 | (h) Preston NE | L 2-4 | Richardson, Mahon | 19,665 | | 2 | 3 | | 5 | | | 8 | 9 | | | | | | 4 | 11 | | 6 | 7 | 10 | | | | | | 1 | |
| Mar 28 | (a) Huddersfield T | W 3-2 | Richardson 2, Boyes | 25,307 | | | | | 5 | | | | 9 | 10 | | 2 | | | 4 | 11 | | 6 | 7 | | 8 | 3 | | | | 1 | |
| Apr 1 | (h) Aston Villa | L 0-3 | | 28,821 | | | | | 5 | | | | 9 | 10 | | 2 | | | 4 | 11 | | 6 | 7 | | 8 | 3 | | | | 1 | |
| Apr 4 | (h) Sheffield W | D 2-2 | Jones 2 | 17,604 | | | 3 | | 5 | | | | 9 | | 11 | 2 | | | 4 | | | 6 | 7 | 10 | 8 | | | | | 1 | |
| Apr 10 | (a) Arsenal | L 0-4 | | 30,176 | | | | | 5 | | | | 9 | 10 | | 2 | | | 4 | 11 | | 6 | 7 | | 8 | 3 | | | | 1 | |
| Apr 11 | (a) Everton | L 3-5 | Jones, Mahon | 24,008 | | | 3 | 4 | 5 | 6 | | | 9 | | 11 | 2 | | | | | | | 7 | 10 | 8 | | | | | 1 | |
| Apr 13 | (h) Arsenal | W 1-0 | Jones | 42,286 | | 2 | 3 | | 5 | 6 | 7 | 8 | 9 | | | | | | 4 | 11 | | | | 10 | | | | | | 1 | |
| Apr 18 | (h) Bolton W | D 2-2 | Glidden, Richardson | 27,398 | | 2 | 3 | | 5 | 6 | 7 | 8 | 9 | | | | | | 4 | 11 | | | | 10 | | | | | | 1 | |
| Apr 25 | (a) Brentford | D 2-2 | Wood, Richardson | 25,692 | | 2 | 3 | | 5 | 6 | | | 9 | 10 | | | | | 4 | 11 | | | 7 | | 8 | | | | | 1 | |
| May 2 | (a) Birmingham | W 3-1 | Mahon, Richardson, Boyes | 28,124 | | 2 | 3 | | 5 | | | | 9 | 10 | | | | | 4 | 11 | | 6 | 7 | | 8 | | | | | 1 | |
| **App** | | | | | 23 | 32 | 37 | 16 | 35 | 11 | 9 | 7 | 41 | 23 | 21 | 5 | 12 | 11 | 36 | 29 | 1 | 22 | 33 | 8 | 19 | 3 | 1 | 8 | 5 | 11 | 3 |
| **Goals** | | | | | | 1 | | | | | 2 | 1 | 39 | 6 | 3 | 1 | | 2 | 2 | 7 | 1 | | 17 | 4 | 3 | | | | | |

**Joe Carter, W.G.Richardson, Teddy Sandford and George Shaw in training in 1935.**

# 1936-37

### Division 1

| Date | | Opponent | Result | Scorers | Att. | Light W | Shaw G | Trentham H | Murphy J | Richardson W | Sankey J | Mahon J | Sandford E | Richardson WG | Robbins W | Wood S | Swinden S | Jones H | Edwards J | Boyes W | Finch R | Pearson H | Prew J | Brockhurst W | Green T | Ridyard A | Gale A | Foulkes W | Shaw C | Adams J | Rix J | Coen L | Heaselgrave S |
|---|---|---|---|---|---|---|---|---|---|---|---|---|---|---|---|---|---|---|---|---|---|---|---|---|---|---|---|---|---|---|---|---|
| Aug 29 | (h) | Derby C | L 1-3 | Richardson | 30,149 | 1 | 2 | 3 | 4 | 5 | 6 | 7 | 8 | 9 | 10 | 11 | | | | | | | | | | | | | | | | | |
| Sep 2 | (h) | Birmingham | W 3-2 | Jones, Richardson, Wood | 26,013 | 1 | | 3 | 4 | 5 | 6 | 7 | 10 | 9 | | 11 | 2 | 8 | | | | | | | | | | | | | | | |
| 5 | (a) | Manchester C | L 2-6 | Boyes, Richardson | 25,070 | 1 | | 3 | | 5 | 4 | 7 | 10 | 9 | | | 2 | 8 | | 6 | 11 | | | | | | | | | | | | |
| 9 | (a) | Birmingham | D 1-1 | Jones | 34,135 | 1 | | 3 | | 5 | 4 | 7 | 10 | 9 | | 11 | 2 | 8 | | 6 | | | | | | | | | | | | | |
| 12 | (h) | Portsmouth | W 3-1 | Wood, Richardson, Sandford | 12,224 | 1 | | 3 | | 5 | 4 | 7 | 10 | 9 | | 11 | 2 | 8 | | 6 | | | | | | | | | | | | | |
| 19 | (a) | Chelsea | L 0-3 | | 25,100 | 1 | | 3 | | 5 | 4 | 7 | 10 | 9 | | 11 | | 8 | | 6 | 2 | | | | | | | | | | | | |
| 26 | (h) | Stoke C | D 2-2 | Richardson, Mahon | 27,086 | 1 | | 3 | | 5 | 4 | 7 | 10 | 9 | | 11 | | 8 | | 6 | 2 | | | | | | | | | | | | |
| Oct 3 | (a) | Charlton A | L 2-4 | Sandford, Jones | 37,430 | 1 | | 3 | | 5 | 4 | 7 | 10 | 9 | | 11 | | 8 | | 6 | 2 | | | | | | | | | | | | |
| 10 | (h) | Grimsby T | W 4-2 | Richardson 3 (1 pen), Sandford | 24,445 | | | 3 | | 5 | 4 | | 10 | 9 | | 11 | | 8 | | 6 | 2 | 1 | 7 | | | | | | | | | | |
| 17 | (h) | Wolves | W 2-1 | W.Richardson, Prew | 33,962 | | | 3 | | 5 | 4 | | 10 | 9 | | 11 | | 8 | | 6 | 2 | 1 | 7 | | | | | | | | | | |
| 24 | (a) | Sunderland | L 0-1 | | 28,700 | | | 3 | | 5 | 4 | | 10 | 9 | | 11 | | 8 | | 6 | 2 | 1 | 7 | | | | | | | | | | |
| 31 | (h) | Huddersfield T | W 2-1 | Jones, Wood | 20,605 | | | 3 | | 5 | 4 | | 10 | 9 | | 11 | | 8 | | 6 | 2 | 1 | 7 | | | | | | | | | | |
| Nov 7 | (a) | Everton | L 2-4 | Richardson, Wood | 20,901 | | | 3 | | 5 | 4 | | 10 | 9 | | 11 | | 8 | | 6 | 2 | 1 | 7 | | | | | | | | | | |
| 14 | (h) | Bolton W | L 0-2 | | 20,110 | | | 3 | | | 4 | | | 9 | | 11 | | 10 | | 6 | 2 | 1 | 7 | 5 | 8 | | | | | | | | |
| 21 | (a) | Brentford | L 1-2 | Jones | 18,044 | | | 3 | | | 4 | 7 | | | 11 | | | 10 | | 6 | 2 | 1 | | | 8 | 5 | 9 | | | | | | |
| 28 | (h) | Arsenal | L 2-4 | Gale, Wood | 27,609 | 1 | | 3 | | | 4 | 7 | | | 11 | | | 10 | | 6 | 2 | | | | 8 | 5 | 9 | | | | | | |
| Dec 5 | (a) | Preston NE | L 2-3 | Mahon 2 | 20,203 | | | 3 | | | 4 | 7 | 10 | 9 | | 11 | | 8 | | 6 | 2 | 1 | | | | | 5 | | | | | | |
| 19 | (a) | Manchester U | D 2-2 | Mahon, Wood | 25,107 | | | 3 | | | 4 | 7 | 10 | 9 | | 11 | | 8 | | 6 | 2 | 1 | | | | | 5 | | | | | | |
| 25 | (h) | Liverpool | W 3-1 | Jones 2, Wood | 23,697 | | | | | | 4 | 7 | 10 | 9 | | 11 | | 8 | | 6 | 2 | 1 | | | | | 5 | 3 | | | | | |
| 26 | (h) | Derby C | L 0-1 | | 18,993 | | | | | 5 | 4 | 7 | 10 | 8 | | 11 | | 9 | | 6 | 2 | 1 | | | | | | 3 | | | | | |
| 28 | (a) | Liverpool | W 2-1 | Sandford, Robbins | 26,500 | | | | | 5 | 4 | 7 | 8 | 9 | 10 | 11 | | | | 6 | 2 | 1 | | | | | | 3 | | | | | |
| Jan 1 | (a) | Middlesbrough | L 1-4 | Robbins | 20,099 | | | | | 5 | 4 | 7 | 8 | 9 | 10 | 11 | | | | 6 | 2 | 1 | | | | | | 3 | | | | | |
| 2 | (h) | Manchester C | D 2-2 | Wood, Mahon | 18,004 | | | | 4 | 5 | | 7 | 10 | 9 | | 11 | | 8 | | 6 | | 1 | | | | | | 3 | 2 | | | | |
| 9 | (a) | Portsmouth | L 3-5 | Jones, Richardson 2 | 14,405 | | | | 4 | 5 | | 7 | 10 | 9 | | 11 | | 8 | | 6 | 2 | 1 | | | | | | 3 | | | | | |
| 23 | (a) | Chelsea | W 2-0 | Jones, Sandford | 9,642 | 1 | | | 4 | 5 | 6 | | 10 | 9 | 11 | | 8 | | | | 2 | | 7 | | | | | 3 | | | | | |
| Feb 4 | (a) | Stoke C | L 3-10 | Richardson, Boyes, Robbins | 15,230 | 1 | | | 4 | 5 | | 7 | 10 | 9 | 11 | | 8 | | 6 | 2 | | | | | | | | 3 | | | | | |
| 6 | (h) | Charlton A | L 1-2 | Mahon | 26,459 | | | | | 5 | | 7 | 10 | 9 | | | 8 | | | 6 | 2 | | | | | | | 3 | 1 | 4 | 11 | | |
| 13 | (a) | Grimsby T | W 3-2 | Richardson, Jones 2 | 12,000 | | | | 4 | | 6 | 7 | 5 | 9 | | | 8 | | 10 | 2 | | | | | | 3 | 1 | | | | 11 | | |
| 27 | (h) | Sunderland | W 6-4 | Richardson, Boyes, Coen, Shaw (pen), Jones 2 | 25,267 | | | | 4 | | 6 | 7 | 5 | 9 | | | 8 | | 10 | 2 | | | | | | 3 | 1 | | | | 11 | | |
| Mar 10 | (a) | Huddersfield T | D 1-1 | Boyes | 23,102 | | | | 4 | | 6 | 7 | 5 | 9 | 11 | | 8 | | 10 | 2 | | | | | | 3 | 1 | | | | | | |
| 13 | (h) | Everton | W 2-1 | Shaw (pen), Richardson | 26,283 | | | | 4 | | 6 | 7 | 5 | 9 | 11 | | 8 | | 10 | 2 | | | | | | 3 | 1 | | | | | | |
| 20 | (a) | Bolton W | L 1-4 | Jones | 12,035 | | | | 4 | 5 | 6 | 7 | | 9 | 11 | | 8 | | 10 | 2 | | | | | | 3 | 1 | | | | | | |
| 22 | (h) | Preston NE | D 0-0 | | 9,068 | | 2 | | 4 | | 6 | 7 | | 9 | 11 | | 8 | | 10 | | | | | | 5 | | 3 | 1 | | | | | | |
| 27 | (h) | Brentford | W 1-0 | Coen | 29,858 | | 2 | | 4 | | 6 | 7 | | 9 | | | | | 10 | | | | | | 5 | | 3 | 1 | | | 11 | 8 | |
| 29 | (h) | Leeds U | W 3-0 | Jones, Mahon, Richardson | 31,251 | | 2 | | 4 | | 6 | 7 | | 9 | | | 8 | | 10 | | | | | | 5 | | 3 | 1 | | | 11 | | |
| 30 | (a) | Leeds U | L 1-3 | Coen | 16,548 | | 2 | | 4 | | 6 | 7 | | 9 | | | | | 10 | | | | | | 5 | | 3 | 1 | | | 11 | 8 | |
| Apr 3 | (a) | Arsenal | L 0-2 | | 24,600 | | | | 4 | | | 7 | | 9 | 11 | | | | 10 | 2 | | | | | 5 | | 3 | 1 | 6 | | 8 | | |
| 14 | (a) | Wolves | L 2-5 | Robbins 2 | 28,486 | | | | 4 | | 6 | 7 | | 9 | 10 | 11 | | 8 | 2 | | | | | | 5 | | 3 | 1 | | | | | |
| 17 | (a) | Sheffield W | W 3-2 | Robbins 2, Mahon | 12,719 | 1 | 2 | | 4 | | 6 | 7 | | 9 | 10 | | 8 | | 11 | | | | | 5 | | | 3 | | | | | | |
| 21 | (h) | Sheffield W | L 2-3 | Robbins 2 | 10,826 | 1 | 2 | | 4 | | 6 | 7 | | 9 | 10 | | 8 | | 11 | | | | | 5 | | | 3 | | | | | | |
| 24 | (h) | Manchester U | W 1-0 | Jones | 16,245 | | 2 | | 4 | | 6 | 7 | | 9 | 10 | | 8 | | 11 | | | | | 5 | | | 3 | 1 | | | | | |
| May 1 | (h) | Middlesbrough | W 3-1 | Jones, Coen, Mahon | 7,022 | | 2 | | 4 | | 6 | 7 | | | 10 | | 8 | | 11 | | | | | 5 | | | 3 | 1 | | | 9 | | |
| | | | | | App | 13 | 9 | 18 | 21 | 22 | 37 | 35 | 28 | 39 | 16 | 23 | 4 | 35 | 1 | 39 | 28 | 15 | 7 | 5 | 3 | 11 | 2 | 3 | 22 | 14 | 2 | 7 | 3 |
| | | | | | Goals | | | | | 1 | | 9 | 5 | 16 | 9 | 8 | | 17 | | 4 | | | 1 | | | | 1 | | 2 | | | 4 | |

**Albion's first goal against Wolves at The Hawthorns on 17 October 1936. It was credited to Bill Richardson.**

# 1937-38

## Division 1

| Date | | Opp | Res | Scorers | Att | Adams J | Shaw G | Shaw C | Murphy J | Sandford E | Sankey J | Mahon J | Jones H | Richardson WG | Richardson W | Robbins W | Boyes W | Rix J | Clarke I | Wood S | Male N | Finch R | Light W | Johnson J | Heaselgrave S | Lowery H | McNab A | Harris W | Baldwin H | Bassett I | Davies C |
|---|---|---|---|---|---|---|---|---|---|---|---|---|---|---|---|---|---|---|---|---|---|---|---|---|---|---|---|---|---|---|
| Aug 28 | (a) | Portsmouth | W 3-2 | Richardson, Mahon | 25,703 | 1 | 2 | 3 | 4 | 5 | 6 | 7 | 8 | 9 | 10 | 11 | | | | | | | | | | | | | | | |
| 30 | (h) | Stoke C | L 0-1 | | 22,113 | 1 | 2 | 3 | 4 | 5 | 6 | 7 | 8 | 9 | 10 | 11 | | | | | | | | | | | | | | | |
| Sep 4 | (h) | Chelsea | W 4-0 | Mahon, Robbins 2, Richardson | 23,097 | 1 | 2 | 3 | 4 | 5 | 6 | 7 | 8 | 9 | 10 | 11 | | | | | | | | | | | | | | | |
| 6 | (a) | Stoke C | L 0-4 | | 16,520 | 1 | 2 | 3 | 4 | 5 | | 7 | 8 | 9 | 10 | 11 | | 6 | | | | | | | | | | | | | |
| 11 | (a) | Charlton A | L 1-3 | Sankey | 25,570 | 1 | 2 | 3 | 4 | 5 | 6 | 7 | | 9 | 10 | | | | 8 | 11 | | | | | | | | | | | |
| 13 | (h) | Middlesbrough | W 3-1 | Richardson, Clarke, Jones | 8,028 | 1 | 2 | 3 | 4 | 5 | | 7 | 8 | 9 | | | | 6 | 10 | 11 | | | | | | | | | | | |
| 18 | (h) | Preston NE | D 1-1 | Mahon | 23,469 | 1 | 2 | 3 | 4 | 5 | 6 | 7 | 8 | 9 | | | | | 10 | 11 | | | | | | | | | | | |
| 25 | (a) | Grimsby T | W 4-1 | Jones 2, Male, Clarke | 9,713 | 1 | | 3 | 4 | 5 | | 7 | 9 | | 10 | | | 6 | 8 | 11 | 2 | | | | | | | | | | |
| Oct 2 | (h) | Leeds U | W 2-1 | Mahon, Robbins | 25,619 | 1 | | 3 | 4 | 5 | | 7 | 9 | | 10 | | | 6 | 8 | 11 | 2 | | | | | | | | | | |
| 9 | (a) | Liverpool | W 1-0 | Wood | 26,505 | 1 | | 3 | 4 | 5 | | 7 | 9 | | 10 | | | 6 | 8 | 11 | 2 | | | | | | | | | | |
| 16 | (a) | Leicester C | L 1-4 | Robbins | 18,772 | 1 | | 3 | 4 | 5 | | 7 | 9 | | 10 | | | 6 | 8 | 11 | 2 | | | | | | | | | | |
| 23 | (h) | Sunderland | L 1-6 | Wood (pen) | 27,705 | 1 | | 3 | 4 | 5 | | 7 | 9 | | 10 | | | 6 | 8 | 11 | 2 | | | | | | | | | | |
| 30 | (a) | Derby C | L 3-5 | Robbins, Mahon, Jones | 18,450 | | | 3 | 4 | 5 | | 7 | 9 | | 10 | 6 | | | 8 | 11 | 2 | 1 | | | | | | | | | |
| Nov 6 | (h) | Bolton W | L 2-4 | Sankey, Jones | 20,281 | | | 3 | 4 | 5 | 6 | 7 | 9 | | | 10 | | | 8 | 11 | 2 | 1 | | | | | | | | | |
| 13 | (a) | Arsenal | D 1-1 | Mahon | 25,790 | 1 | | 3 | 4 | 5 | | 7 | 10 | 9 | | | | 6 | 8 | 11 | 2 | | | | | | | | | | |
| 20 | (h) | Everton | W 3-1 | Mahon 2, Boyes | 20,800 | 1 | | 3 | 4 | 5 | 6 | 7 | 10 | 9 | | | 11 | | 8 | | 2 | | | | | | | | | | |
| 27 | (a) | Brentford | W 2-0 | Richardson 2 | 16,100 | 1 | | 3 | 4 | 5 | 6 | 7 | 10 | 9 | | | 11 | | 8 | | 2 | | | | | | | | | | |
| Dec 11 | (a) | Huddersfield T | L 1-2 | Richardson | 20,669 | 1 | | 3 | 4 | 5 | | 7 | 10 | 9 | | | | 6 | 8 | | 2 | | 11 | | | | | | | | |
| 18 | (h) | Blackpool | L 1-2 | Jones | 18,077 | 1 | | 3 | 4 | 5 | | 7 | 10 | 9 | | | | 6 | 8 | | 2 | | 11 | | | | | | | | |
| 27 | (h) | Wolves | D 2-2 | Clarke 2 | 55,444 | 1 | | 3 | 4 | 5 | | 7 | 9 | | 10 | | | 6 | 8 | | 2 | | 11 | | | | | | | | |
| Jan 1 | (h) | Portsmouth | L 1-2 | Clarke | 19,442 | 1 | | 3 | 4 | 5 | | 7 | 9 | | 10 | | | 6 | 8 | | 2 | | 11 | | | | | | | | |
| 15 | (a) | Chelsea | D 2-2 | Richardson, Johnson | 23,533 | 1 | | 3 | 4 | 5 | 6 | 7 | | 9 | | | | 10 | 8 | | 2 | | 11 | | | | | | | | |
| 26 | (h) | Charlton A | D 0-0 | | 9,579 | 1 | | 3 | 4 | 5 | | | 7 | 9 | | | | 6 | 10 | | 2 | | 11 | 8 | | | | | | | |
| 29 | (a) | Preston NE | D 1-1 | Smith (og) | 10,604 | 1 | | 3 | | 5 | | | 9 | 7 | | | | 6 | 10 | | 2 | | 11 | 8 | 4 | | | | | | |
| Feb 5 | (h) | Grimsby T | W 2-1 | Johnson, Mahon | 19,648 | 1 | | 3 | | 5 | | 7 | 9 | | | | | 6 | 10 | | 2 | | 11 | 8 | 4 | | | | | | |
| 12 | (a) | Leeds U | L 0-1 | | 10,509 | 1 | | 3 | | 5 | | 7 | | 9 | | | | 6 | 10 | | 2 | | 11 | 8 | 4 | | | | | | |
| 19 | (h) | Liverpool | W 5-1 | Richardson 3, Clarke, Johnson | 17,565 | 1 | | 3 | | 5 | | 7 | | 9 | | | | 6 | 10 | | 2 | | 11 | 8 | 4 | | | | | | |
| 26 | (h) | Leicester C | L 1-3 | Johnson | 21,563 | 1 | | 3 | | 5 | | 7 | | 9 | | | | 6 | 10 | | 2 | | 11 | 8 | 4 | | | | | | |
| Mar 9 | (a) | Sunderland | L 0-3 | | 20,887 | 1 | | 3 | | 5 | | 7 | 10 | 9 | | | | 6 | 8 | | 2 | | 11 | | 4 | | | | | | |
| 12 | (h) | Derby C | W 4-2 | Richardson 2, Johnson, Heaselgrave | 25,439 | 1 | | 3 | | 5 | | 7 | 10 | 9 | | | | | | | 2 | | 11 | 8 | 4 | 6 | | | | | |
| 16 | (h) | Manchester C | D 1-1 | Shaw (pen) | 10,792 | 1 | | 3 | | 5 | | 7 | | 9 | 10 | | | | | | 2 | | 11 | 8 | 4 | 6 | | | | | |
| 19 | (a) | Bolton W | L 0-3 | | 13,150 | 1 | | 3 | | 5 | | 7 | | 9 | | | | 6 | 10 | | 2 | | 11 | 8 | 4 | | | | | | |
| 26 | (h) | Arsenal | D 0-0 | | 33,944 | 1 | | 3 | | 5 | | 7 | 10 | 9 | | | | | | | 2 | | 11 | 8 | 4 | 6 | | | | | |
| Apr 2 | (a) | Everton | L 3-5 | Mahon, Shaw (pen), Jones | 24,395 | | | 3 | | 5 | | 7 | 10 | 9 | 11 | | | | | | 2 | 1 | | 8 | 4 | 6 | | | | | |
| 9 | (h) | Brentford | W 4-3 | Mahon, Heaselgrave, Johnson 2 | 23,642 | | | 3 | 10 | 5 | | 7 | 9 | | | | | | | | 2 | 1 | 11 | 8 | 4 | 6 | 1 | | | | |
| 15 | (a) | Birmingham | L 1-2 | Jones | 25,008 | | | 3 | | 5 | | 7 | 10 | 9 | | | | | | | 2 | 1 | 11 | 8 | 4 | 6 | | | | | |
| 16 | (a) | Manchester C | L 1-7 | Shaw (pen) | 16,700 | | | 3 | 4 | 5 | 11 | 7 | 10 | 9 | | | | | | | 2 | 1 | | 8 | 6 | | 10 | | | | |
| 18 | (h) | Birmingham | W 4-3 | Richardson 2, Shaw (pen), Jones | 34,406 | | | 3 | | 5 | 6 | 11 | 9 | 7 | | | | | | | 2 | 1 | | 8 | 4 | 10 | | 1 | | | |
| 23 | (h) | Huddersfield T | W 5-1 | Heaselgrave 2, Jones 2, Richardson | 27,530 | | | 3 | | 5 | 6 | 11 | 9 | 7 | | | | | | | 2 | 1 | | 8 | 4 | 10 | | 1 | | | |
| 30 | (a) | Blackpool | L 1-2 | Mahon | 20,000 | | | 3 | | 5 | 6 | 7 | 9 | | | | | | | | 2 | 1 | 11 | 8 | 4 | 10 | | 1 | | | |
| May 2 | (a) | Wolves | L 1-2 | Sandford | 39,024 | | | 3 | 10 | 4 | 11 | 9 | 7 | | | | | | | | | | | 8 | | 6 | | 1 | 2 | 5 | |
| 7 | (a) | Middlesbrough | L 1-4 | Heaselgrave | 18,025 | | | 3 | 10 | 4 | 11 | 9 | 7 | | | | | | | | | | | 8 | | 6 | | 1 | 2 | 5 | |
| App | | | | | | 31 | 7 | 42 | 23 | 42 | 16 | 40 | 33 | 29 | 18 | 14 | 15 | 27 | 11 | 3 | 30 | 4 | 18 | 19 | 17 | 12 | 2 | 5 | 2 | 2 | |
| Goals | | | | | | | 4 | | | 1 | 2 | 13 | 11 | 15 | 5 | 1 | | | 6 | 2 | 1 | | | 7 | 5 | | | | | | |

Albion squad for season 1937-8. Back row (left to right): J.S.Carpenter (groundstaff), T.Glidden (coach), A.Everiss (clerk), G.Hewitt, W.G.Richardson, W.Tudor, L.Coen, J.Adams, W.Light, W.Harris, A.Newman, W.Robbins, J.Murphy, J.Rix, G.Shaw, H.Jones. Third row: F.Reed (trainer), E.Smith (asst.secretary), S.Guest (asst.trainer), R.Finch, I.Bassett, J.Lewis, H.Lowery, W.Brockhurst, A.Ridyard, C.Davies, N.Male, H.Kinsell, J.Screen, J.Mahon, T.J.Powell (groundstaff), S.Short (trainer). Second row (seated): C.Shaw, H.W.Keys (director), J.Prew, N.W.Bassett (director), I.Clarke, J.S.Round (vice-chairman), E.Sandford, L.J.Nurse (chairman), W.Boyes, W.H.Thursfield (director), H.Ashley, A.C.Jephcott (director), S.Wood, F.Everiss (secretary). Front row (on ground): T.Edmunds, T.Lewis, S.Heaselgrave, C.S.Morgan, B.Clift, G.Spencer, J.Sankey, D.Lapworth.

# 1938-39

## Division 2

### Match results

| Date | | Opponent | Result | Scorers | Attendance |
|---|---|---|---|---|---|
| Aug 27 | (h) | Luton T | W 3-0 | Jones 2, Burgin | 24,377 |
| Sep 1 | (a) | Norwich C | W 3-2 | Burgin 2, Jones | 20,537 |
| Sep 3 | (a) | Plymouth A | L 1-2 | Jones | 15,166 |
| Sep 7 | (h) | Newcastle U | W 5-2 | Burgin, Heaselgrave 2, Jones 2 | 17,016 |
| Sep 10 | (h) | Sheffield U | L 3-4 | Heaselgrave 3 | 25,866 |
| Sep 14 | (a) | Newcastle U | L 1-5 | Jones | 31,054 |
| Sep 17 | (a) | Burnley | W 3-0 | Heaselgrave, Jones, Spencer | 19,222 |
| Sep 24 | (h) | Tottenham H | W 4-3 | Jones 3, Heaselgrave | 25,041 |
| Oct 1 | (a) | Southampton | L 1-2 | Clarke | 15,204 |
| Oct 8 | (h) | Coventry C | W 3-1 | Sandford, Johnson, McNab | 30,943 |
| Oct 15 | (h) | Chesterfield | W 1-0 | Johnson | 23,702 |
| Oct 22 | (a) | Tranmere R | L 1-3 | Johnson | 12,184 |
| Oct 29 | (h) | Manchester C | W 3-1 | Clarke 3, Johnson | 22,274 |
| Nov 5 | (a) | Bury | D 3-3 | Dudley, Shaw (pen), Clarke | 10,109 |
| Nov 12 | (h) | Sheffield W | W 5-1 | Spencer, Burgin 2, Clarke, Witcomb | 18,297 |
| Nov 19 | (a) | Fulham | L 0-3 | | 15,200 |
| Nov 26 | (h) | Blackburn R | W 2-0 | Burgin, Richardson | 22,127 |
| Dec 3 | (a) | Millwall | W 5-1 | McNab, Clarke, Jones 2, Heaselgrave | 35,140 |
| Dec 10 | (h) | West Ham U | W 3-2 | Clarke 2, Jones | 23,909 |
| Dec 17 | (a) | Bradford | D 4-4 | Burgin 2, Clarke, Witcomb | 10,664 |
| Dec 24 | (a) | Luton T | L 1-3 | Johnson | 11,700 |
| Dec 27 | (a) | Swansea T | L 2-3 | Jones, Elliott | 12,532 |
| Dec 31 | (h) | Plymouth A | W 4-2 | Clarke, Heaselgrave, Shaw (pen), Jones | 19,833 |
| Jan 14 | (a) | Sheffield U | D 1-1 | Richardson | 16,490 |
| Jan 28 | (a) | Tottenham H | D 2-2 | Johnson 2 | 38,868 |
| Feb 1 | (h) | Burnley | L 1-2 | Jones | 7,781 |
| Feb 4 | (h) | Southampton | W 2-0 | Johnson, Elliott | 21,757 |
| Feb 11 | (a) | Coventry C | D 1-1 | Johnson | 25,086 |
| Feb 18 | (a) | Chesterfield | L 1-3 | Heaselgrave | 18,135 |
| Feb 25 | (h) | Tranmere R | W 2-0 | Elliott, Shaw (pen) | 17,193 |
| Mar 4 | (a) | Manchester C | D 3-3 | Johnson 2, Clarke | 18,479 |
| Mar 11 | (h) | Bury | W 6-0 | Clarke, Heaselgrave, Johnson 4 | 17,062 |
| Mar 18 | (a) | Sheffield W | L 1-2 | Shaw (pen) | 28,034 |
| Mar 25 | (h) | Fulham | W 3-0 | Jones, Clarke, Dudley | 19,541 |
| Apr 1 | (a) | Blackburn R | L 0-3 | | 11,407 |
| Apr 7 | (a) | Nottingham F | L 0-2 | | 21,056 |
| Apr 8 | (h) | Millwall | D 0-0 | | 19,895 |
| Apr 10 | (h) | Nottingham F | D 0-0 | | 16,058 |
| Apr 15 | (a) | West Ham U | L 1-2 | Clarke | 15,022 |
| Apr 19 | (h) | Swansea T | D 0-0 | | 5,162 |
| Apr 22 | (h) | Bradford | L 0-2 | | 6,885 |
| Apr 29 | (h) | Norwich C | W 4-2 | Banks 2, Richardson 2 | 3,109 |

### Player appearances / team line-ups

| Opponent | Adams J | Bassett I | Shaw C | Sankey J | Davies C | McNab A | Mahon J | Heaselgrave S | Jones H | Burgin M | Johnson J | White H | Robbins W | Tudor W | Hoyland E | Sandford E | Murphy J | Witcomb D | Spencer G | Clarke I | Dudley G | Richardson WG | Elliott W | Saunders W | Pike R | Gripton W | Butler S | Banks G |
|---|---|---|---|---|---|---|---|---|---|---|---|---|---|---|---|---|---|---|---|---|---|---|---|---|---|---|---|---|
| Luton T | 1 | 2 | 3 | 4 | 5 | 6 | 7 | 8 | 9 | 10 | 11 | | | | | | | | | | | | | | | | | |
| Norwich C | 1 | 2 | 3 | 4 | 5 | 6 | 7 | 8 | 9 | 10 | 11 | | | | | | | | | | | | | | | | | |
| Plymouth A | 1 | 2 | 3 | 4 | 5 | 6 | 7 | 8 | 9 | 10 | 11 | | | | | | | | | | | | | | | | | |
| Newcastle U | 1 | 2 | 3 | 4 | 5 | 6 | 7 | 8 | 9 | 10 | 11 | | | | | | | | | | | | | | | | | |
| Sheffield U | 1 | | 3 | 4 | 5 | 6 | 7 | 8 | | 9 | 11 | 2 | 10 | | | | | | | | | | | | | | | |
| Newcastle U | 1 | | 3 | 4 | | 6 | | 8 | 9 | | 11 | 2 | 10 | 5 | 7 | | | | | | | | | | | | | |
| Burnley | 1 | | 3 | 4 | | 6 | | 8 | 9 | | 11 | 2 | 10 | 5 | | | | | 7 | | | | | | | | | |
| Tottenham H | 1 | | 3 | 4 | | 6 | | 8 | 9 | | 11 | 2 | | 5 | | | | 10 | 7 | | | | | | | | | |
| Southampton | 1 | | 3 | 4 | | 6 | | 8 | 9 | | 11 | 2 | | 5 | | | | | 7 | 10 | | | | | | | | |
| Coventry C | 1 | | 3 | 4 | | 6 | | 8 | 9 | | 11 | 2 | | 5 | | 7 | | | | 10 | | | | | | | | |
| Chesterfield | 1 | | 3 | 4 | | 6 | | 8 | 9 | | 11 | 2 | | 5 | | 7 | | | | 10 | | | | | | | | |
| Tranmere R | 1 | | 3 | 4 | | 6 | | 8 | 9 | | 11 | 2 | | 5 | | 7 | | | | 10 | | | | | | | | |
| Manchester C | 1 | | 3 | 4 | | 6 | | 8 | 9 | | 11 | 2 | | 5 | | | | | 7 | 10 | | | | | | | | |
| Bury | 1 | | 3 | 4 | | 6 | | 8 | 9 | | 11 | 2 | | 5 | | | | | | 10 | 7 | | | | | | | |
| Sheffield W | 1 | | 3 | 4 | | 6 | | | | 9 | 11 | 2 | | 5 | | | | 8 | 7 | 10 | | | | | | | | |
| Fulham | 1 | | 3 | 4 | | 6 | | | | 9 | 11 | 2 | | 5 | | | | 8 | 7 | 10 | | | | | | | | |
| Blackburn R | 1 | | 3 | 4 | | 6 | | | | 8 | 11 | 2 | | 5 | | | | | 7 | 10 | | 9 | | | | | | |
| Millwall | 1 | | 3 | 4 | | 6 | | 8 | 9 | | 11 | 2 | | 5 | | | | | 7 | 10 | | | | | | | | |
| West Ham U | 1 | | 3 | 4 | | 6 | | 8 | 9 | | 11 | 2 | | 5 | | | | | 7 | 10 | | | | | | | | |
| Bradford | 1 | | 3 | 4 | | 6 | | | | 9 | 11 | 2 | | 5 | | | | 8 | 7 | 10 | | | | | | | | |
| Luton T | 1 | | 3 | 4 | | 6 | | | | 9 | 11 | 2 | | 5 | | | | 8 | 7 | 10 | | | | | | | | |
| Swansea T | | | 3 | 4 | | 6 | | 8 | 9 | | 11 | 2 | | 5 | | | | | | 10 | | | 7 | 1 | | | | |
| Plymouth A | 1 | | 3 | 4 | | 6 | | 8 | 9 | | 11 | 2 | | 5 | | | | | | 10 | | | 7 | | | | | |
| Sheffield U | 1 | | 3 | 4 | | 6 | | 8 | | | 11 | 2 | | 5 | | | | | | 10 | | 9 | 7 | | | | | |
| Tottenham H | 1 | | 3 | 4 | | 6 | | 8 | 9 | | 11 | 2 | | 5 | | | | | | 10 | | | 7 | | | | | |
| Burnley | 1 | | 3 | 4 | | 6 | | 8 | 9 | | 11 | 2 | | 5 | | | | | | 10 | | | 7 | | | | | |
| Southampton | 1 | | 3 | 4 | | 6 | | 8 | | | 11 | 2 | | 5 | | | | | | 10 | | 9 | 7 | | | | | |
| Coventry C | | | 3 | 4 | | 6 | | 8 | | | 11 | 2 | | 5 | | | | | | 10 | | 9 | 7 | 1 | | | | |
| Chesterfield | 1 | | 3 | 4 | | 6 | | 8 | | | 11 | 2 | | 5 | | | | 10 | | | | 9 | 7 | | | | | |
| Tranmere R | 1 | | 3 | 4 | | 6 | | 8 | 9 | | 11 | 2 | | 5 | | | | | | 10 | | | 7 | | | | | |
| Manchester C | 1 | | 3 | 4 | | 6 | | 8 | 9 | | 11 | 2 | | 5 | | | | | | 10 | | | 7 | | | | | |
| Bury | 1 | 2 | 3 | 4 | | 6 | | 8 | 9 | | 11 | | | 5 | | | | | | 10 | | | 7 | | | | | |
| Sheffield W | 1 | 2 | 3 | 4 | | 6 | | 8 | 9 | | 11 | | | 5 | | | | | | 10 | | | 7 | | | | | |
| Fulham | 1 | | 3 | 4 | | 6 | | 8 | 9 | | | 2 | | 5 | | | | | | 10 | 11 | | 7 | | | | | |
| Blackburn R | 1 | | 3 | 4 | | 6 | | 8 | 9 | | 11 | 2 | | 5 | | | | | | 10 | | | 7 | | | | | |
| Nottingham F | 1 | | 3 | 4 | | 6 | | | | | 11 | 2 | | 5 | | | | 8 | | 10 | | | 7 | | 9 | | | |
| Millwall | 1 | | 3 | 4 | | 6 | | | | 10 | 11 | 2 | | | | | | 8 | | 9 | | | 7 | | | 5 | | |
| Nottingham F | 1 | | 3 | 4 | | 6 | | | | 10 | 11 | 2 | | | | | | 8 | | 9 | | | 7 | | | 5 | | |
| West Ham U | 1 | | 3 | 4 | | 6 | | 8 | | | 11 | 2 | | | | | | 10 | | 9 | | | 7 | | | 5 | | |
| Swansea T | 1 | | 3 | 4 | | 6 | | 8 | | | 11 | 2 | | | | | | 10 | | | | 9 | 7 | | | 5 | | |
| Bradford | 1 | | 3 | 4 | | 6 | | 8 | | | 11 | 2 | | | | | | 10 | | | | 9 | 7 | | | 5 | | |
| Norwich C | 1 | | 3 | 4 | | 6 | | | | | 11 | 2 | | | | | | | | 10 | | 9 | 7 | | | 5 | | 8 |
| **App** | 40 | 6 | 42 | 19 | 5 | 37 | 5 | 27 | 32 | 14 | 34 | 36 | 3 | 31 | 1 | 6 | 3 | 29 | 13 | 32 | 6 | 13 | 17 | 2 | 1 | 6 | 1 | 1 |
| **Goals** | | | 4 | | 2 | | | 11 | 18 | 9 | 15 | | | | | 1 | | 2 | 2 | 14 | 2 | 4 | 3 | | | | | 2 |

The Baggies preparing for training in 1938, showing 'W.G.' Richardson (left) with Harry Jones next to him, Joe Johnson next and then Ike Clarke, Jimmy Murphy, Walter Robbins (Wally Boyes peeping from under him), Cecil Shaw, George Dudley, Bob Finch, Billy Light and Jack Rix.

# 1946-47

## Division 2

| Date | | Opponent | Result | Scorers | Att. | Sanders J | Pemberton J | Kinsell H | Witcomb D | Tranter G | Millard L | Elliott W | Clarke I | Walsh D | Duggan J | Hodgetts F | Hood G | Shaw C | Edwards C | Barlow R | Butler S | Evans C | Drury G | Grimley T | Richards G | Gripton W | Tighe J | Vernon J | Ryan R | Lunn W | Aldridge N | Finch R | Rowley A |
|---|---|---|---|---|---|---|---|---|---|---|---|---|---|---|---|---|---|---|---|---|---|---|---|---|---|---|---|---|---|---|---|---|
| Aug 31 | (a) | Swansea T | W 3-2 | Walsh 2, Hodgetts | 29,186 | 1 | 2 | 3 | 4 | 5 | 6 | 7 | 8 | 9 | 10 | 11 | | | | | | | | | | | | | | | | | |
| Sep 2 | (a) | Coventry C | L 2-3 | Walsh 2 | 26,204 | 1 | 2 | 3 | 4 | 5 | 6 | 7 | 8 | 9 | 10 | 11 | | | | | | | | | | | | | | | | | |
| 7 | (h) | Tottenham H | W 3-2 | Clarke, Walsh, Hodgetts | 38,670 | 1 | 2 | 3 | 4 | 5 | 6 | 7 | 8 | 9 | 10 | 11 | | | | | | | | | | | | | | | | | |
| 14 | (a) | Burnley | W 2-0 | Walsh, Clarke | 20,881 | 1 | 2 | 3 | 4 | 5 | 6 | 7 | 8 | 9 | 10 | 11 | | | | | | | | | | | | | | | | | |
| 18 | (h) | Birmingham C | W 3-0 | Walsh, Elliott 2 | 42,031 | 1 | 2 | 3 | 4 | | | 6 | 7 | 10 | 9 | 8 | 11 | 5 | | | | | | | | | | | | | | | |
| 21 | (h) | Barnsley | L 2-5 | Duggan, Walsh | 24,965 | 1 | 2 | | 4 | | | 6 | 7 | 10 | 9 | 8 | 11 | 5 | 3 | | | | | | | | | | | | | | |
| 25 | (a) | Birmingham C | L 0-1 | | 50,535 | 1 | 2 | 3 | 4 | 5 | | 7 | 10 | 9 | 8 | 11 | | | 6 | | | | | | | | | | | | | | |
| 28 | (a) | Newport C | W 7-2 | Southam (og), Barlow, Elliott, Clarke 4 | 20,521 | 1 | 2 | 3 | 4 | 5 | 6 | 7 | 9 | | 8 | | | | | 10 | 11 | | | | | | | | | | | | |
| Oct 5 | (h) | Southampton | W 2-0 | Clarke, Duggan | 27,122 | 1 | 2 | 3 | 4 | 5 | 6 | 7 | 9 | | 8 | | | | | 10 | 11 | | | | | | | | | | | | |
| 12 | (a) | Nottingham F | D 1-1 | Witcomb | 25,272 | 1 | 2 | 3 | 4 | 5 | 6 | 7 | 9 | | 8 | | | | | 10 | 11 | | | | | | | | | | | | |
| 19 | (a) | Millwall | W 2-1 | Duggan, Walsh | 20,167 | 1 | 2 | 3 | | 5 | 6 | 7 | | 9 | 8 | 11 | | | 4 | 10 | | | | | | | | | | | | | |
| 26 | (h) | Bradford | D 1-1 | Duggan | 20,028 | 1 | 2 | 3 | 4 | 5 | 6 | 7 | | 9 | 10 | 11 | | | | | | | 8 | | | | | | | | | | |
| Nov 2 | (a) | Manchester C | L 0-5 | | 38,821 | 1 | 2 | 3 | 4 | 5 | 6 | 7 | 10 | 9 | | 11 | | | | | | | 8 | | | | | | | | | | |
| 9 | (h) | West Ham U | L 2-3 | Walsh, Millard | 18,076 | 1 | 2 | 3 | 4 | 5 | 6 | 7 | | 9 | | 11 | | | | 10 | | | 8 | | | | | | | | | | |
| 16 | (h) | Sheffield W | D 2-2 | Walsh 2 | 19,245 | 1 | 2 | 3 | 4 | | 5 | 6 | 7 | 8 | 9 | 11 | | | | 10 | | | | | | | | | | | | | |
| 23 | (h) | Fulham | W 6-1 | Clarke 2, Walsh, Barlow 2, Hodgetts | 20,243 | | 2 | | | 4 | 5 | 6 | 7 | 8 | 9 | 11 | | | 3 | 10 | | 1 | | | | | | | | | | | |
| 30 | (a) | Bury | L 0-4 | | 11,146 | | 2 | | | 4 | 5 | 6 | 7 | 8 | 9 | 11 | | | 3 | 10 | | 1 | | | | | | | | | | | |
| Dec 7 | (h) | Luton T | L 1-2 | Richards | 19,867 | | 2 | 3 | 4 | 5 | 6 | | 8 | 9 | | 11 | | | | 10 | | | | 1 | 7 | | | | | | | | |
| 14 | (a) | Plymouth A | L 1-2 | Walsh | 27,495 | | 2 | 3 | 4 | | 6 | 7 | 8 | 9 | | 11 | | | 5 | | | | | 1 | | | | | | | | | |
| 21 | (h) | Leicester C | W 4-2 | Duggan 2, Millard, Walsh | 18,820 | 1 | 2 | 3 | 4 | | 6 | 7 | 8 | 9 | 10 | 11 | | | 5 | | | | | | | | | | | | | | |
| 25 | (a) | Newcastle U | W 4-2 | Walsh 2, Duggan, Elliott | 44,722 | 1 | 2 | 3 | 4 | | 6 | 7 | 8 | 9 | 10 | 11 | | | 5 | | | | | | | | | | | | | | |
| 26 | (h) | Newcastle U | W 3-2 | Walsh 2, Clarke | 31,794 | 1 | 2 | 3 | 4 | | 6 | 7 | 8 | 9 | 10 | 11 | | | 5 | | | | | | | | | | | | | | |
| 28 | (h) | Swansea T | W 2-1 | Hodgetts, Elliott | 24,998 | 1 | 2 | 3 | 4 | | 6 | 7 | 8 | 9 | 10 | 11 | | | 5 | | | | | | | | | | | | | | |
| Jan 4 | (a) | Tottenham H | L 0-2 | | 40,050 | 1 | 2 | 3 | 4 | | 6 | 7 | 8 | 9 | 10 | 11 | | | 5 | | | | | | | | | | | | | | |
| 18 | (h) | Burnley | D 1-1 | Duggan | 40,082 | 1 | 2 | 3 | 4 | | 6 | 7 | | 9 | 8 | 11 | | | | 10 | | | | | | | | | | | | | |
| Feb 1 | (h) | Newport C | D 2-2 | Walsh 2 | 15,104 | | 2 | 3 | 4 | | 6 | 7 | | 9 | 8 | 11 | | | 5 | 10 | | | | 1 | | | | | | | | | |
| 8 | (a) | Southampton | W 1-0 | Elliott | 10,095 | | 2 | 3 | 4 | | 6 | 7 | 8 | 9 | | 11 | | | 5 | 10 | | 1 | | | | | | | | | | | |
| Mar 15 | (a) | West Ham U | L 2-3 | Hodgetts, Elliott | 25,136 | | 2 | 3 | | | 6 | 7 | 8 | 9 | | 11 | | | 4 | | | | 10 | 1 | | | | 5 | | | | | |
| 22 | (h) | Sheffield W | W 2-1 | Drury, Clarke | 35,448 | | 2 | 3 | | | 6 | 7 | 8 | 9 | | 11 | | | 4 | | | | 10 | 1 | | | | 5 | | | | | |
| 29 | (a) | Fulham | W 1-0 | Hodgetts | 22,078 | | 2 | 3 | | | 6 | 7 | 8 | 9 | 10 | 11 | | | 4 | | | | | 1 | | | | 5 | | | | | |
| Apr 4 | (a) | Chesterfield | D 1-1 | Walsh | 16,044 | | 2 | 3 | | | 6 | 7 | 8 | 9 | 10 | 11 | | | 4 | | | | | 1 | | | | 5 | | | | | |
| 5 | (h) | Bury | W 3-0 | Clarke 3 | 27,745 | | 2 | 3 | | | 6 | 7 | 8 | 9 | 10 | 11 | | | 4 | | | | | 1 | | | | 5 | | | | | |
| 7 | (h) | Chesterfield | W 3-2 | Walsh 2, Hodgetts | 21,180 | | 2 | 3 | | | | | 8 | 9 | 10 | 7 | | | 4 | | | | | 1 | | | | 5 | | 6 | 11 | | |
| 12 | (a) | Luton T | L 0-2 | | 20,990 | | 2 | | | 3 | 11 | | 8 | 9 | 10 | 7 | | | 4 | | | | | 1 | | | | 5 | | 6 | | | |
| 19 | (h) | Plymouth A | L 2-5 | Walsh, Clarke | 25,068 | | | | | | | 7 | 8 | 9 | | 11 | | 3 | 4 | | | | | 1 | | | | 5 | | 6 | 2 | 10 | |
| 26 | (a) | Leicester C | D 1-1 | Clarke | 30,017 | | 2 | 3 | | | 6 | 7 | 8 | 9 | | 11 | | | 4 | | | | | 1 | | | | 5 | | 10 | | | |
| May 3 | (h) | Coventry C | D 1-1 | Hodgetts | 23,807 | | 2 | 3 | | | 6 | 7 | 8 | | | 11 | | | 4 | | | | | 1 | | | | 5 | | 10 | | 9 | |
| 10 | (h) | Millwall | L 2-4 | Elliott, Clarke | 10,663 | | 2 | 3 | | | 6 | 7 | 8 | 9 | | 11 | | | 4 | | | | | 1 | | | | 5 | | | | | 10 |
| 17 | (h) | Nottingham F | W 5-1 | Lunn, Millard, Walsh, Elliott, Clarke | 10,506 | | 2 | 3 | | | 6 | 7 | 8 | 9 | | 11 | | | 4 | | | | | 1 | | | | 5 | | 10 | | | |
| 26 | (a) | Barnsley | L 1-2 | Edwards | 15,070 | | 2 | 3 | | | 6 | 7 | 8 | 9 | | 11 | | | 4 | | | | | 1 | | | | 5 | | 10 | | | |
| 27 | (a) | Bradford | W 4-2 | Walsh (pen), Lunn 2, Elliott | 9,990 | | 2 | | | 3 | | 7 | 8 | 9 | | 11 | | | 4 | | | | | 1 | | | | 5 | | 6 | 10 | | |
| 31 | (h) | Manchester C | W 3-1 | Walsh, Clarke, Williams (og) | 21,281 | | 2 | | | 3 | | 7 | 8 | 9 | | 11 | | | 4 | | | | | 1 | | | | 5 | | 6 | 10 | | |
| | | | | **App** | | 21 | 41 | 35 | 26 | 16 | 39 | 40 | 37 | 38 | 25 | 39 | 2 | 4 | 25 | 10 | 3 | 1 | 6 | 20 | 1 | 2 | 1 | 14 | 5 | 5 | 1 | 3 | 2 |
| | | | | **Goals** | | | | | 1 | | 3 | 10 | 19 | 28 | 8 | 8 | | | 1 | 3 | | | 1 | | 1 | | | | | | 3 | | | |

**West Bromwich Albion FC 1946-47. Back row (left to right): D.Bradley, J.Pemberton, D.Walsh, W.Lunn. Second row: D.Banks, W.Gripton, L.Twigg, F.Reed (trainer), J.Sanders, G.Tranter, L.Millard. Seated: C.Evans, I.Clarke, C.Shaw, W.Elliott, D.Witcomb, F.Hodgetts, H.Kinsell. On ground: R.Ryan, J.Duggan, S.Butler.**

# 1947-48

## Division 2

Player columns (left to right): Grimley T, Pemberton J, Millard L, Edwards C, Vernon J, Hood G, Elliott W, Clarke I, Walsh D, Drury G, Hodgetts F, Sanders J, Williams G, Lunn W, Kinsell H, Ryan R, Gripton W, Evans A, Smith D, McKennan P, Heath N, Rowley A, Finch R, Gordon D, Haines J, Richards G, Taylor A.

| Date | | Opponent | Result | | Scorers | Att. |
|---|---|---|---|---|---|---|
| Aug 23 | (h) | Tottenham H | W | 1-0 | Walsh | 32,521 |
| 27 | (h) | Fulham | W | 2-1 | Walsh 2 (1 pen) | 23,064 |
| 30 | (a) | Barnsley | W | 1-0 | Walsh | 24,989 |
| Sep 3 | (a) | Fulham | W | 1-0 | Drury | 21,065 |
| 6 | (h) | Plymouth A | D | 1-1 | Drury | 31,427 |
| 10 | (h) | Coventry C | W | 3-1 | Walsh 2, Drury | 21,421 |
| 13 | (a) | Luton T | D | 1-1 | Drury | 26,155 |
| 15 | (a) | Coventry C | L | 0-1 | | 30,048 |
| 20 | (h) | Brentford | W | 3-2 | Drury 2, Walsh | 29,445 |
| 27 | (a) | Leicester C | D | 1-1 | Elliott | 30,266 |
| Oct 4 | (a) | Leeds U | W | 3-2 | Lunn 2, Elliott | 30,479 |
| 11 | (h) | Millwall | W | 2-1 | Walsh 2 | 32,661 |
| 18 | (a) | Chesterfield | W | 2-0 | Elliott, Walsh | 15,400 |
| 25 | (h) | West Ham U | L | 1-2 | Walsh | 37,764 |
| Nov 1 | (a) | Bury | W | 2-1 | Walsh 2 | 24,179 |
| 8 | (h) | Southampton | W | 1-0 | Smith | 45,985 |
| 15 | (a) | Doncaster R | L | 1-2 | Walsh | 21,774 |
| 22 | (h) | Nottingham F | W | 3-2 | Elliott, Drury, McKennan | 28,568 |
| 26 | (a) | Bradford | L | 1-3 | McKennan | 17,480 |
| Dec 6 | (h) | Cardiff C | L | 2-3 | Walsh, McKennan | 38,914 |
| 13 | (a) | Sheffield W | W | 2-1 | Walsh, Elliott | 31,553 |
| 20 | (a) | Tottenham H | D | 1-1 | Walsh | 52,071 |
| 26 | (h) | Newcastle U | L | 0-1 | | 48,322 |
| Jan 1 | (a) | Newcastle U | L | 1-3 | Walsh | 61,301 |
| 3 | (h) | Barnsley | L | 0-2 | | 25,045 |
| 17 | (a) | Plymouth A | L | 1-2 | Walsh | 18,050 |
| 31 | (h) | Luton T | W | 1-0 | Walsh | 26,979 |
| Feb 7 | (a) | Brentford | L | 0-1 | | 22,140 |
| 14 | (h) | Leicester C | L | 1-3 | McKennan | 29,322 |
| 21 | (a) | Leeds U | L | 1-3 | Rowley | 22,096 |
| 28 | (a) | Millwall | D | 1-1 | Walsh | 17,995 |
| Mar 6 | (h) | Chesterfield | W | 1-0 | Hodgetts | 25,242 |
| 13 | (a) | West Ham U | W | 2-0 | Haines, Elliott | 25,133 |
| 20 | (h) | Bury | D | 3-3 | Walsh, Hodgetts, Rowley | 28,638 |
| 27 | (a) | Southampton | D | 1-1 | Rowley | 27,330 |
| 29 | (a) | Birmingham C | L | 0-4 | | 43,168 |
| 30 | (h) | Birmingham C | D | 1-1 | Elliott | 51,945 |
| Apr 3 | (h) | Doncaster R | L | 1-3 | Squires (og) | 22,076 |
| 10 | (a) | Nottingham F | L | 1-3 | Taylor | 19,713 |
| 17 | (h) | Bradford | W | 6-0 | Haines 3, Taylor 2, Finch | 13,349 |
| 24 | (a) | Cardiff C | W | 5-0 | Taylor 2, Haines 2 (1 pen), Rowley | 25,032 |
| May 1 | (h) | Sheffield W | D | 1-1 | Elliott | 24,818 |

**Appearances:** Grimley 10, Pemberton 42, Millard 42, Edwards 15, Vernon 35, Hood 20, Elliott 39, Clarke 12, Walsh 35, Drury 23, Hodgetts 23, Sanders 19, Williams 7, Lunn 5, Kinsell 18, Ryan 14, Gripton 5, Evans 18, Smith 7, McKennan 11, Heath 13, Rowley 21, Finch 9, Gordon 3, Haines 10, Richards 2, Taylor 4.

**Goals:** Elliott 8, Walsh 22, Drury 7, Hodgetts 2, Lunn 2, Smith 1, McKennan 4, Rowley 4, Finch 1, Haines 6, Taylor 5.

Albion's 1947 first-team squad. Back row (left to right): C.Edwards, P.McKennan, J.Sanders, J.Pemberton, G.Hood. Middle row: D.Walsh, W.Elliott, J.Vernon, A.Evans, D.Smith, L.Millard. Front row: H.Kinsell, R.Ryan.

# 1948-49

## Division 2

| Date | | Opponent | Result | Scorers | Att | Sanders J | Pemberton J | Kinsell H | Millard L | Vernon J | Hood G | Elliott W | Haines J | Walsh D | Barlow R | Smith A | Hodgetts F | Williams C | Finch R | Ryan R | Boyd J | Barker R | Cox S | Rowley A | Morrow H | Wilcox E | Shepherd E | Kennedy J |
|---|---|---|---|---|---|---|---|---|---|---|---|---|---|---|---|---|---|---|---|---|---|---|---|---|---|---|---|---|
| Aug 21 | (a) | Nottingham F | W 1-0 | Walsh | 32,110 | 1 | 2 | 3 | 4 | 5 | 6 | 7 | 8 | 9 | 10 | 11 | | | | | | | | | | | | |
| 25 | (h) | Chesterfield | D 0-0 | | 29,041 | 1 | 2 | 3 | 4 | 5 | 6 | 7 | 8 | 9 | 10 | 11 | | | | | | | | | | | | |
| 28 | (h) | Bury | L 2-3 | Barlow, Walsh | 31,904 | 1 | 2 | 3 | 4 | 5 | 6 | | 8 | 9 | 10 | 11 | | 7 | | | | | | | | | | |
| Sep 1 | (a) | Chesterfield | D 0-0 | | 30,799 | 1 | 2 | 3 | 4 | 5 | 6 | 7 | 10 | 9 | | | | 8 | | 11 | | | | | | | | |
| 4 | (a) | West Ham U | L 0-1 | | 26,528 | 1 | 2 | 3 | 4 | 5 | 6 | 7 | 10 | 9 | | | | 8 | | 11 | | | | | | | | |
| 8 | (h) | Lincoln C | W 5-0 | Haines 2, Walsh 3 | 13,009 | 1 | 2 | 3 | 6 | 5 | | 7 | 10 | 9 | | | | 8 | | 11 | | 4 | | | | | | |
| 11 | (h) | Tottenham H | D 2-2 | Haines, Walsh | 32,279 | 1 | | 3 | 6 | 5 | | 7 | 10 | 9 | | | 11 | 8 | | | | 4 | 2 | | | | | |
| 15 | (a) | Lincoln C | W 3-0 | Walsh, Barker, Ryan | 17,232 | 1 | 2 | 3 | 6 | 5 | | 7 | 10 | 9 | | | | 8 | | 11 | | 4 | | | | | | |
| 18 | (a) | Brentford | D 0-0 | | 33,145 | 1 | | 3 | 2 | 5 | 6 | 7 | 10 | 9 | | | | 8 | | 11 | | 4 | | | | | | |
| 25 | (h) | Leicester C | W 2-1 | Williams, Walsh | 32,517 | 1 | | 3 | | 5 | 6 | 7 | 10 | 9 | | | | 8 | | 11 | | 4 | 2 | | | | | |
| Oct 2 | (a) | Leeds U | W 3-1 | Williams 2, Walsh | 30,068 | 1 | | 3 | 4 | 5 | 6 | 7 | 10 | 9 | | | | 8 | | 11 | | | 2 | | | | | |
| 9 | (a) | Fulham | W 2-1 | Haines, Barker | 22,103 | 1 | 2 | 3 | 6 | 5 | | 7 | 10 | | | | | 8 | | 11 | | 4 | | 9 | | | | |
| 16 | (h) | Plymouth A | W 3-0 | Williams, Haines, Walsh | 32,849 | 1 | 2 | 3 | 4 | 5 | 6 | 7 | 10 | 9 | | | | 8 | | 11 | | | | | | | | |
| 23 | (a) | Blackburn R | D 0-0 | | 28,186 | 1 | 2 | 3 | 4 | 5 | 6 | 7 | 10 | 9 | | | | 8 | | 11 | | | | | | | | |
| 30 | (h) | Cardiff C | W 2-0 | Haines, Williams | 46,036 | 1 | 2 | 3 | 4 | 5 | 6 | 7 | 10 | 9 | | | | 8 | | 11 | | | | | | | | |
| Nov 6 | (a) | Queen's Park R | W 2-0 | Walsh, Hodgetts | 24,200 | 1 | 2 | 3 | 4 | 5 | 6 | 7 | 10 | 9 | | | 11 | 8 | | | | | | | | | | |
| 13 | (h) | Luton T | W 2-1 | Williams, Elliott | 32,589 | 1 | 2 | 3 | 4 | 5 | 6 | 7 | 10 | 9 | | | 11 | 8 | | | | | | | | | | |
| 20 | (a) | Bradford | L 1-4 | Haines | 18,064 | 1 | 2 | 3 | 4 | 5 | 6 | 7 | 10 | 9 | | | 11 | 8 | | | | | | | | | | |
| 27 | (h) | Southampton | W 2-0 | Millard, Elliott | 47,028 | 1 | 2 | 3 | 4 | 5 | 6 | 7 | 10 | 9 | | | | 8 | | | | | | | 11 | | | |
| Dec 4 | (a) | Barnsley | L 0-2 | | 20,864 | 1 | 2 | 3 | 4 | 5 | 6 | 7 | | 9 | 10 | | | 8 | | | | | | | 11 | | | |
| 11 | (h) | Grimsby T | W 5-2 | Williams 3, Haines (pen), Walsh | 22,664 | 1 | 2 | 3 | 4 | 5 | 6 | 7 | 10 | 9 | | | | 8 | | | | | | | 11 | | | |
| 18 | (h) | Nottingham F | W 2-1 | Haines, Elliott | 32,583 | 1 | 2 | 3 | 4 | 5 | 6 | 7 | 10 | 9 | | | | 8 | | | | | | | | | 11 | |
| 25 | (h) | Sheffield W | W 1-0 | Vernon | 34,881 | 1 | 2 | 3 | 4 | 5 | 6 | 7 | 10 | 9 | | | | 8 | | | | | | | | | 11 | |
| 27 | (a) | Sheffield W | L 1-2 | Westlake (og) | 32,513 | 1 | 2 | 3 | 4 | 5 | 6 | 7 | 10 | 9 | | | | 8 | | | | | | | | | 11 | |
| Jan 1 | (a) | Bury | L 0-4 | | 16,861 | 1 | 2 | 3 | 4 | 5 | 6 | 7 | 10 | 9 | | | | 8 | | | | | | | | | 11 | |
| 15 | (h) | West Ham U | W 2-1 | Walsh 2 | 33,100 | 1 | 2 | 3 | 4 | 5 | 6 | 7 | 11 | 9 | 10 | | | 8 | | | | | | | | | | |
| 22 | (a) | Tottenham H | L 0-2 | | 62,556 | 1 | 2 | 3 | 4 | 5 | 6 | 7 | 11 | 9 | 10 | | | 8 | | | | | | | | | | |
| Feb 5 | (h) | Brentford | W 2-0 | Walsh, Smith | 39,482 | 1 | 2 | | 3 | 5 | 6 | 7 | 10 | 9 | 4 | 11 | | 8 | | | | | | | | | | |
| Mar 5 | (h) | Fulham | L 1-2 | Elliott | 27,595 | 1 | 2 | 11 | 3 | 5 | 6 | 7 | 10 | 9 | 4 | | | 8 | | | | | | | | | | |
| 12 | (a) | Plymouth A | W 2-1 | Walsh, Elliott | 26,011 | 1 | 2 | | 3 | 5 | 6 | 7 | 10 | 9 | 4 | | | 8 | | | | 11 | | | | | | |
| 19 | (h) | Blackburn R | W 2-1 | Elliott, Haines | 36,053 | 1 | 2 | | 3 | 5 | 6 | 7 | 10 | 9 | 4 | | | 8 | | | | 11 | | | | | | |
| 26 | (a) | Cardiff C | D 2-2 | Haines, Walsh | 55,177 | 1 | 2 | 3 | 6 | 5 | | 7 | 10 | 9 | 4 | | | 8 | | | | 11 | | | | | | |
| Apr 2 | (h) | Queen's Park R | D 1-1 | Elliott | 35,093 | 1 | 2 | 3 | 6 | 5 | | 7 | 10 | 9 | 4 | | | 8 | | | | 11 | | | | | | |
| 6 | (h) | Leeds U | W 1-0 | Barlow (pen) | 28,562 | 1 | 2 | | 3 | 5 | | 7 | 10 | 9 | 4 | | | 8 | 6 | | | 11 | | | | | | |
| 9 | (a) | Luton T | W 1-0 | Morrow | 16,651 | 1 | 2 | | 3 | 5 | | | 10 | 9 | | | | 8 | 6 | | | 11 | | | 7 | | | 4 |
| 16 | (h) | Bradford | W 7-1 | Walsh 4 (1 pen), Haines 2, Morrow | 39,241 | 1 | 2 | | 3 | 5 | | 7 | 10 | 9 | | | | 8 | 6 | | | | | | 11 | | | 4 |
| 18 | (h) | Coventry C | W 1-0 | Haines | 42,488 | 1 | 2 | | 3 | 5 | | 7 | 10 | 9 | | | | 8 | 6 | | | | | | 11 | | | 4 |
| 19 | (a) | Coventry C | L 0-1 | | 39,480 | 1 | 2 | | 3 | 5 | | 7 | 10 | 9 | | | | 8 | 6 | | | | | | 11 | | | 4 |
| 23 | (a) | Southampton | D 1-1 | Smith | 30,856 | 1 | 2 | | 3 | 5 | | 7 | 8 | 9 | 10 | 11 | | | 6 | | | | | | | | | 4 |
| 30 | (h) | Barnsley | W 2-0 | Barlow, Walsh | 31,966 | 1 | 2 | | 3 | 5 | 6 | 7 | | 9 | 10 | 11 | | | 4 | | | | | | | | | 8 |
| May 5 | (a) | Leicester C | W 3-0 | Walsh, Kennedy, Barlow | 34,585 | 1 | 2 | | 3 | 5 | 6 | 7 | | 9 | 10 | 11 | | | 4 | | | | | | | | | 8 |
| 7 | (a) | Grimsby T | L 0-1 | | 16,056 | 1 | 2 | | 3 | 5 | 6 | 7 | | 9 | 10 | 11 | | | 4 | | | | | | | | | 8 |
| | | | | App | | 42 | 38 | 30 | 41 | 38 | 34 | 40 | 38 | 41 | 22 | 8 | 5 | 31 | 3 | 14 | 1 | 14 | 2 | 1 | 5 | 2 | 4 | 8 |
| | | | | Goals | | | | | 1 | 1 | | 7 | 14 | 23 | 4 | 2 | 1 | 9 | | 1 | | 2 | | | 2 | | | 1 |

Albion's 1948-49 promotion squad. Back row (left to right): F.Reed (trainer), E.Wilcox, J.Kennedy, H.Kinsell, R.Barlow, R.Barker, G.Hood, J.Haines, R.Ryan, 'W.G.' Richardson (coach). Front row: L.Millard, W.Elliott, C.Williams, D.Walsh, J.Vernon, J.Sanders, J.Pemberton, A.Smith, J.Boyd.

# 1949-50

## Division 1

| Date | | Opponent | Result | Scorers | Att | Sanders J | Pemberton J | Millard L | Kennedy J | Vernon J | Barlow R | Elliott W | Williams C | Walsh D | Haines J | Lee G | Hood G | Ryan R | Smith A | Wilcox E | Horne L | Inwood G | Dudley J | Gordon G | Betteridge M | Allen R | Rickaby S |
|---|---|---|---|---|---|---|---|---|---|---|---|---|---|---|---|---|---|---|---|---|---|---|---|---|---|---|---|
| Aug 20 | (h) | Charlton A | W 1-0 | Williams | 49,596 | 1 | 2 | 3 | 4 | 5 | 6 | 7 | 8 | 9 | 10 | 11 | | | | | | | | | | | |
| 24 | (a) | Birmingham C | L 0-2 | | 50,027 | 1 | 2 | 3 | 4 | 5 | | 7 | 8 | 9 | 10 | 11 | | 6 | | | | | | | | | |
| 27 | (a) | Manchester U | D 1-1 | Williams | 44,655 | 1 | 2 | 3 | 4 | 5 | | 7 | 8 | 9 | 10 | 11 | | 6 | | | | | | | | | |
| 31 | (h) | Birmingham C | W 3-0 | Haines 2, Walsh | 50,299 | 1 | 2 | 3 | 4 | 5 | | 7 | 8 | 9 | 10 | 11 | | 6 | | | | | | | | | |
| Sep 3 | (h) | Chelsea | D 1-1 | Williams | 45,337 | 1 | 2 | 3 | 4 | 5 | | 7 | 8 | 9 | 10 | 11 | | 6 | | | | | | | | | |
| 7 | (h) | Arsenal | L 1-2 | Elliott | 43,663 | 1 | 2 | 3 | | 5 | | 7 | 8 | 9 | 10 | | 4 | 6 | 11 | | | | | | | | |
| 10 | (a) | Stoke C | W 3-1 | Haines, Williams 2 | 30,021 | 1 | 2 | 3 | | 5 | | 7 | 8 | | 10 | | 4 | 6 | 11 | 9 | | | | | | | |
| 14 | (a) | Arsenal | L 1-4 | Walsh | 48,073 | 1 | 2 | 3 | | 5 | | 7 | 8 | 9 | 10 | | 4 | 6 | 11 | | | | | | | | |
| 17 | (h) | Burnley | W 3-0 | Elliott (pen), Walsh, Williams | 37,091 | 1 | 2 | 3 | | 5 | | 7 | 8 | 9 | 10 | | 4 | 6 | 11 | | | | | | | | |
| 24 | (a) | Sunderland | L 1-2 | Elliott | 50,896 | 1 | 2 | 3 | | 5 | | 7 | 8 | 9 | 10 | | 4 | 6 | 11 | | | | | | | | |
| Oct 1 | (h) | Liverpool | L 0-1 | | 44,219 | 1 | 2 | 3 | | | | 7 | 8 | 9 | 10 | 11 | 4 | 6 | | 5 | | | | | | | |
| 8 | (h) | Aston Villa | D 1-1 | Wilcox | 53,690 | 1 | 2 | 3 | 4 | 5 | | 7 | 8 | | | 11 | | 6 | 10 | 9 | | | | | | | |
| 15 | (a) | Wolves | D 1-1 | Elliott | 56,661 | 1 | 2 | 3 | 4 | 5 | | 7 | 8 | 9 | | | | 6 | 10 | | | 11 | | | | | |
| 22 | (h) | Portsmouth | W 3-0 | Walsh, Williams, Elliott | 40,808 | 1 | 2 | 3 | 4 | 5 | | 7 | 8 | 9 | | | | 6 | 10 | | | 11 | | | | | |
| 29 | (a) | Huddersfield T | D 1-1 | Walsh | 22,461 | 1 | 2 | 3 | 4 | 5 | | 7 | 8 | 9 | | | | 6 | 10 | | | 11 | | | | | |
| Nov 5 | (h) | Everton | W 4-0 | Walsh 2, Smith, Williams | 29,309 | 1 | 2 | 3 | 4 | 5 | | 7 | 8 | 9 | | | | 6 | 10 | | | 11 | | | | | |
| 12 | (a) | Middlesbrough | L 0-3 | | 28,014 | 1 | 2 | 3 | 4 | 5 | | 7 | 8 | 9 | | | | 6 | 10 | | | 11 | | | | | |
| 26 | (a) | Newcastle U | L 1-5 | Walsh | 32,415 | 1 | 2 | 3 | 4 | 5 | 10 | 7 | 8 | 9 | | | | 6 | | | | 11 | | | | | |
| Dec 3 | (h) | Fulham | W 4-1 | Walsh 2, Elliott, Barlow | 30,883 | 1 | 2 | 3 | 4 | 5 | 10 | 7 | 8 | 9 | | | | 6 | | | | 11 | | | | | |
| 10 | (a) | Manchester C | D 1-1 | Elliott | 29,544 | 1 | 2 | | | 5 | 10 | 7 | 8 | 9 | | 3 | | 6 | | | | 11 | 4 | | | | |
| 17 | (a) | Charlton A | W 2-1 | Walsh 2 | 20,369 | 1 | 2 | 3 | 4 | 5 | 10 | | 8 | 9 | | 11 | | 6 | | | | | | 7 | | | |
| 24 | (h) | Manchester U | L 1-2 | Walsh | 44,885 | 1 | 2 | 3 | 4 | 5 | 10 | 7 | 8 | 9 | | 11 | | 6 | | | | | | | | | |
| 26 | (a) | Bolton W | L 0-3 | | 38,122 | 1 | | 2 | 4 | 5 | 10 | | | 9 | | 3 | 11 | 6 | | | | | | 8 | 7 | | |
| 27 | (h) | Bolton W | W 2-1 | Walsh, Barlow | 41,746 | 1 | 2 | 3 | 4 | 5 | 10 | | 8 | 9 | | | | 6 | | | | 11 | | 7 | | | |
| 31 | (a) | Chelsea | L 1-2 | Gordon | 41,610 | 1 | 2 | 3 | 4 | 5 | 10 | | 8 | 9 | | | | 6 | | | | 11 | | 7 | | | |
| Jan 14 | (h) | Stoke C | D 0-0 | | 34,840 | 1 | 2 | 3 | 8 | 5 | | | 10 | 9 | | 11 | | 6 | | | | | 4 | 7 | | | |
| 21 | (a) | Burnley | D 0-0 | | 26,193 | 1 | 2 | 3 | 8 | 5 | 10 | | | 9 | | 11 | | 6 | | | | | 4 | 7 | | | |
| Feb 4 | (h) | Sunderland | L 0-2 | | 36,101 | 1 | 2 | 3 | 8 | 5 | 10 | | | 9 | | 11 | | 6 | | | | | 4 | 7 | | | |
| 18 | (a) | Liverpool | L 1-2 | Lee | 46,634 | 1 | 2 | 3 | 4 | 5 | 6 | | 8 | 9 | | 11 | | 10 | 7 | | | | | | | | |
| 25 | (a) | Aston Villa | L 0-1 | | 40,132 | 1 | 2 | 3 | 4 | 5 | 6 | | | 9 | | 11 | | 10 | 7 | | | | | 8 | | | |
| Mar 4 | (h) | Wolves | D 1-1 | Allen | 60,945 | 1 | 2 | 3 | 4 | 5 | 10 | | | | | 11 | 6 | | 8 | | 9 | | | | | 7 | |
| 11 | (a) | Blackpool | L 0-3 | | 23,088 | 1 | 2 | 3 | 4 | | 10 | | | | | 11 | 6 | | 8 | 5 | 9 | | | | | 7 | |
| 18 | (h) | Newcastle U | D 1-1 | Walsh | 33,469 | 1 | 2 | 3 | 4 | 5 | 10 | | | 9 | | 11 | 6 | | 8 | | | | | | | 7 | |
| 29 | (a) | Everton | W 2-1 | Allen, Barlow | 18,345 | 1 | 2 | 3 | | 5 | 10 | | | 9 | | 11 | | 6 | 8 | | | | 4 | | | 7 | |
| Apr 1 | (h) | Middlesbrough | L 0-3 | | 32,942 | 1 | 2 | 3 | 4 | 5 | 10 | | | 9 | | 11 | 6 | | 8 | | | | | | | 7 | |
| 7 | (a) | Derby C | L 1-3 | Allen | 25,198 | 1 | 2 | 3 | 4 | 5 | | | | 9 | | 11 | 6 | | | | | | 10 | 7 | | 8 | |
| 8 | (a) | Portsmouth | W 1-0 | Ryan | 33,903 | 1 | 2 | 3 | 4 | 5 | | | | 9 | | 11 | | 6 | 8 | | | | 10 | | | 7 | |
| 10 | (h) | Derby C | W 1-0 | Lee | 31,516 | 1 | 2 | 3 | 4 | 5 | 10 | | | 9 | | 11 | 6 | | | | | | 8 | | | 7 | |
| 15 | (h) | Huddersfield T | D 0-0 | | 28,240 | 1 | 2 | 3 | 4 | 5 | 10 | | | | | 11 | 6 | | | | | | 8 | 9 | | 7 | |
| 22 | (a) | Fulham | W 1-0 | Allen | 34,909 | 1 | 2 | 3 | 4 | 5 | 6 | | | 9 | | 11 | | | | | | | 10 | 8 | | 7 | |
| 26 | (h) | Blackpool | W 1-0 | Allen | 28,858 | 1 | 2 | 3 | 4 | 5 | 6 | | | 9 | | 11 | | | | | | | 10 | 8 | | 7 | |
| 29 | (h) | Manchester C | D 0-0 | | 16,780 | 1 | | 3 | 4 | 5 | 6 | | | 9 | | 11 | | | | | | | 10 | 8 | 7 | | 2 |
| **App** | | | | | | 42 | 40 | 41 | 34 | 40 | 23 | 21 | 26 | 37 | 11 | 25 | 13 | 34 | 21 | 4 | 2 | 10 | 13 | 11 | 2 | 11 | 1 |
| **Goals** | | | | | | | | | | | 3 | 7 | 8 | 15 | 3 | 2 | | 1 | 1 | 1 | | | | 1 | | 5 | |

**Blackpool goalkeeper George Farm saving from Dave Walsh in Albion's 1-0 win on 26 April 1950.**

# 1950-51

### Division 1

| Date | | Opponent | Result | Scorers | Att | Sanders J | Pemberton J | Millard L | Kennedy J | Vernon J | Barlow R | Elliott W | Williams C | Walsh D | Allen R | Lee G | Rickaby S | Richardson F | Smith A | Gordon D | Ryan R | Betteridge M | Heath N | Dudley J | Wilcox E | Guy H | Horne L | McCall A | Griffin F |
|---|---|---|---|---|---|---|---|---|---|---|---|---|---|---|---|---|---|---|---|---|---|---|---|---|---|---|---|---|---|
| Aug 19 | (a) | Aston Villa | L 0-2 | | 65,036 | 1 | 2 | 3 | 4 | 5 | 6 | 7 | 8 | 9 | 10 | 11 | | | | | | | | | | | | | |
| 23 | (a) | Newcastle U | D 1-1 | Elliott | 48,720 | 1 | | 3 | 4 | 5 | 6 | 7 | 8 | 9 | 10 | 11 | 2 | | | | | | | | | | | | |
| 26 | (h) | Stoke C | D 1-1 | Elliott | 33,215 | 1 | | 3 | 4 | 5 | 6 | 7 | 8 | 9 | | 11 | 2 | | 10 | | | | | | | | | | |
| 30 | (h) | Newcastle U | L 1-2 | Walsh | 29,377 | 1 | | 3 | 4 | 5 | 6 | 7 | 8 | 9 | | 11 | 2 | | 10 | | | | | | | | | | |
| Sep 2 | (a) | Everton | W 3-0 | Barlow, Allen, Smith | 46,602 | 1 | | 3 | 4 | 5 | 6 | 7 | 8 | 9 | | 11 | 2 | | | 10 | | | | | | | | | |
| 6 | (a) | Middlesbrough | L 1-2 | Walsh | 28,000 | 1 | | 3 | 4 | 5 | 6 | | 8 | 9 | | 11 | 2 | | | 10 | | 7 | | | | | | | |
| 9 | (h) | Portsmouth | W 5-0 | Walsh, Elliott, Williams, Smith 2 | 34,460 | 1 | | 3 | 4 | 5 | 6 | 7 | 8 | 9 | | 11 | 2 | | | 10 | | | | | | | | | |
| 13 | (h) | Middlesbrough | L 2-3 | Elliott, Allen | 31,530 | 1 | | 3 | 4 | 5 | 6 | 7 | 8 | 9 | | 11 | 2 | | | 10 | | | | | | | | | |
| 16 | (a) | Chelsea | D 1-1 | Walsh | 39,570 | 1 | | 3 | 4 | 5 | 6 | 7 | 8 | 9 | | 11 | 2 | | 10 | | | | | | | | | | |
| 23 | (h) | Burnley | W 2-1 | Lee, Walsh | 32,638 | 1 | | 3 | 4 | 5 | 10 | | 8 | 9 | 7 | 11 | 2 | | | 6 | | | | | | | | | |
| 30 | (a) | Arsenal | L 0-3 | | 53,700 | 1 | | 3 | 4 | 5 | 10 | 7 | | 9 | 8 | 11 | 2 | | | 6 | | | | | | | | | |
| Oct 7 | (a) | Derby C | D 1-1 | Williams | 28,042 | 1 | | 3 | | 5 | 6 | | 8 | 9 | 7 | 11 | 2 | | 10 | 4 | | | | | | | | | |
| 14 | (h) | Liverpool | D 1-1 | Walsh | 35,030 | 1 | | 3 | 4 | 5 | 6 | | 8 | 9 | 7 | 11 | 2 | | | | 10 | | | | | | | | |
| 21 | (a) | Blackpool | L 1-2 | Allen | 32,142 | 1 | | 3 | 4 | 5 | 6 | | 8 | | 7 | 11 | 2 | | 9 | | 10 | | | | | | | | |
| 28 | (h) | Tottenham H | L 1-2 | Barlow | 44,543 | 1 | | 3 | 4 | 5 | 6 | 7 | 8 | | | 11 | 2 | | 9 | | 10 | | | | | | | | |
| Nov 4 | (a) | Fulham | W 1-0 | Richardson | 25,076 | | | 3 | 4 | 5 | 6 | | | | 7 | 11 | 2 | 9 | | | 8 | | 1 | | 10 | | | | |
| 11 | (h) | Bolton W | L 0-1 | | 28,816 | | | 3 | 4 | 5 | 6 | | | | 7 | 11 | 2 | 9 | | | 8 | | 1 | | 10 | | | | |
| 18 | (a) | Charlton A | W 3-2 | Richardson, Allen, Croker (og) | 21,876 | | | 3 | | 5 | 6 | | | | 7 | 11 | 2 | 9 | | | 8 | | 1 | 4 | 10 | | | | |
| 25 | (h) | Manchester U | L 0-1 | | 28,146 | | | 3 | | 5 | 6 | | | | 7 | 11 | 2 | 9 | | | 8 | | 1 | 4 | 10 | | | | |
| Dec 2 | (a) | Wolves | L 1-3 | Ryan | 44,937 | | | 3 | | 5 | 6 | | | | 7 | 11 | 2 | 9 | | | 8 | | 1 | 4 | 10 | | | | |
| 9 | (h) | Sunderland | W 3-1 | Richardson 2, Wilcox | 26,666 | | | 3 | 4 | 5 | 6 | | | | 7 | 11 | 2 | 9 | | | 8 | | 1 | | 10 | | | | |
| 16 | (h) | Aston Villa | W 2-0 | Richardson, Wilcox | 28,796 | | | 3 | 4 | 5 | 6 | | | | 7 | 11 | 2 | 9 | | | 10 | | 1 | | 8 | | | | |
| 23 | (a) | Stoke C | D 1-1 | Allen | 19,198 | | | 3 | 4 | 5 | 6 | | | | 7 | 11 | 2 | 9 | | | 10 | | 1 | | 8 | | | | |
| 25 | (h) | Sheffield W | L 1-3 | Ryan | 28,023 | | | | | 5 | 6 | | | | 7 | 11 | 2 | 9 | | | 10 | | 1 | 4 | 8 | | 3 | | |
| 26 | (a) | Sheffield W | L 0-3 | | 44,819 | | | | | 5 | 6 | | 8 | | 7 | 11 | 2 | 9 | | | 10 | | 1 | 4 | | | | 3 | |
| 30 | (h) | Everton | L 0-1 | | 17,912 | | | 3 | | 5 | 6 | | | | 7 | 11 | 2 | 9 | | | 10 | | 1 | 4 | 8 | | | | |
| Jan 13 | (a) | Portsmouth | D 2-2 | Richardson, Allen | 23,642 | 1 | | 3 | 4 | 5 | 8 | | | | 7 | 11 | 2 | 9 | | | 10 | | | 6 | | | | | |
| 20 | (h) | Chelsea | D 1-1 | Lee | 30,985 | 1 | | 3 | 4 | 5 | 8 | | | | 7 | 11 | 2 | 9 | | | | | | 6 | | | | 10 | |
| Feb 3 | (a) | Burnley | W 1-0 | Allen | 19,104 | 1 | | 3 | 4 | 5 | 6 | | | | 7 | 11 | 2 | 9 | | | 8 | | | | | | | 10 | |
| 17 | (h) | Arsenal | W 2-0 | Richardson 2 | 35,999 | 1 | | 3 | 4 | 5 | 6 | | | | 7 | 11 | 2 | 9 | | | 8 | | | | | | | 10 | |
| 24 | (a) | Derby C | L 1-2 | Dudley | 33,702 | 1 | | 3 | 4 | 5 | 6 | | | | 7 | 11 | 2 | 9 | | | | | | 8 | | | | 10 | |
| Mar 3 | (a) | Liverpool | D 1-1 | McCall | 33,654 | 1 | | 3 | | 5 | 6 | | | | 7 | 11 | 2 | 9 | | 4 | | | | 8 | | | | 10 | |
| 17 | (a) | Tottenham H | L 0-5 | | 45,180 | 1 | | 3 | 4 | 5 | 6 | | | | 7 | 11 | 2 | 9 | | | 8 | | | | | | | 10 | |
| 24 | (h) | Fulham | D 0-0 | | 23,803 | 1 | | 3 | 4 | 5 | 6 | | | | 7 | 11 | 2 | 9 | | | | | | 8 | | | | 10 | |
| 26 | (h) | Huddersfield T | L 0-2 | | 24,360 | 1 | | 3 | 4 | 5 | 6 | | | | 7 | 11 | 2 | 9 | | | | | | 8 | | | | 10 | |
| 27 | (h) | Huddersfield T | W 2-1 | Barlow 2 | 32,401 | 1 | | 3 | 4 | 5 | 9 | | | | | 11 | 2 | 8 | | 7 | 6 | | | | | | | 10 | |
| 31 | (a) | Bolton W | W 2-0 | Barlow, Gordon | 24,898 | 1 | | 3 | 4 | 5 | 9 | | | | | 11 | 2 | | | 7 | 6 | | | 8 | | | | 10 | |
| Apr 4 | (h) | Blackpool | L 1-3 | Barlow (pen) | 39,591 | 1 | | 3 | 4 | 5 | 9 | | | | | 11 | 2 | | | 7 | 6 | | | 8 | | | | 10 | |
| 7 | (h) | Charlton A | W 3-0 | Allen, McCall, Ryan | 26,083 | 1 | | 3 | 4 | 5 | 9 | | 8 | | 7 | 11 | 2 | | | | 6 | | | | | | | 10 | |
| 14 | (a) | Manchester U | L 0-3 | | 24,764 | 1 | | 3 | 4 | 5 | 9 | | | | 7 | 11 | 2 | | | | 6 | | | 8 | | | | 10 | |
| 21 | (h) | Wolves | W 3-2 | Barlow 2, Allen | 39,066 | 1 | | 3 | 4 | 5 | 9 | | 10 | | 7 | 11 | 2 | | | | 6 | | | | | | | 8 | |
| 28 | (a) | Sunderland | D 1-1 | Allen | 20,149 | | | 3 | 4 | 5 | 9 | | 10 | | | 11 | 2 | | | | 6 | | | | | 1 | | 8 | 7 |
| | | | | App | | 31 | 1 | 40 | 35 | 41 | 42 | 13 | 14 | 14 | 40 | 31 | 41 | 24 | 6 | 11 | 24 | 3 | 11 | 16 | 6 | 1 | 1 | 15 | 1 |
| | | | | Goals | | | | | | | 8 | 4 | 2 | 6 | 10 | 2 | | 8 | 3 | 1 | 3 | | | 1 | 2 | | | 2 | |

**Albion in 1950-51. Back row (left to right):** J.Pemberton, R.Floyd, J.Kennedy, J.McIlvenny, G.Jones, M.Betteridge, S.Rickaby, N.Heath, J.Dudley. **Middle:** 'W.G.'Richardson (trainer-coach), K.Hodgkisson, A.Wright, A.Crowshaw, J.Sanders, G.Hood, D.Walsh, J.Vernon, T.Rawlings, C.Williams, F.Richardson. **Front:** R.Barlow, D.Gordon, W.Elliott, R.Allen, J.Smith (manager), A.Smith, L.Millard, P.Hilton, E.Wilcox, R.Ryan, A.Fitton (trainer).

# 1951-52

## Division 1

| Date | Match | Res | Scorers | Att | Sanders J | Rickaby S | Millard L | Dudley J | Vernon J | Ryan R | Allen R | Smith A | Richardson F | McCall A | Lee G | Gordon D | Kennedy J | Heath N | Barlow R | Carter W | Griffin F | Horne L | Williams S | Nicholls J | Cutler R | Corbett G |
|---|---|---|---|---|---|---|---|---|---|---|---|---|---|---|---|---|---|---|---|---|---|---|---|---|---|---|
| Aug 18 | (h) Manchester U | D 3-3 | Allen, Smith 2 | 29,897 | 1 | 2 | 3 | 4 | 5 | 6 | 7 | 8 | 9 | 10 | 11 | | | | | | | | | | | |
| 20 | (a) Stoke C | D 1-1 | Smith | 19,122 | 1 | 2 | 3 | 4 | 5 | 6 | 7 | 8 | 9 | 10 | 11 | | | | | | | | | | | |
| 25 | (a) Tottenham H | L 1-3 | Allen | 51,544 | 1 | 2 | 3 | 4 | 5 | 6 | 7 | 8 | 9 | 10 | 11 | | | | | | | | | | | |
| 29 | (h) Stoke C | W 1-0 | Allen | 18,903 | 1 | 2 | 3 | 4 | 5 | 6 | 7 | 8 | | 10 | 11 | 9 | | | | | | | | | | |
| Sep 1 | (h) Preston NE | D 1-1 | Allen | 27,645 | 1 | 2 | 3 | 4 | 5 | 6 | 7 | 8 | | 10 | 11 | 9 | | | | | | | | | | |
| 5 | (h) Newcastle U | D 3-3 | McMichael (og), McCall, Lee | 29,311 | 1 | 2 | 3 | 4 | | 6 | 7 | 8 | 9 | 10 | 11 | | 5 | | | | | | | | | |
| 8 | (a) Burnley | L 1-6 | Smith | 23,868 | 1 | 2 | 3 | 4 | | 6 | 7 | 8 | 9 | 10 | 11 | | 5 | | | | | | | | | |
| 15 | (h) Charlton A | D 1-1 | Allen | 23,197 | | 2 | 3 | | 5 | 6 | 7 | 8 | | 10 | 11 | | 4 | 1 | 9 | | | | | | | |
| 22 | (a) Fulham | L 0-1 | | 30,025 | | 2 | 3 | | 5 | 6 | 7 | | | 10 | 11 | | 4 | 1 | 9 | 8 | | | | | | |
| 29 | (h) Middlesbrough | L 2-3 | Smith, Allen | 28,961 | | 2 | 3 | | 5 | 10 | 9 | 8 | | | 11 | | 4 | 1 | 6 | | 7 | | | | | |
| Oct 6 | (h) Huddersfield T | D 0-0 | | 24,236 | | 2 | 3 | | 4 | 10 | 9 | 8 | | | 11 | | 5 | 1 | 6 | | 7 | | | | | |
| 13 | (a) Chelsea | W 3-1 | Carter, Allen 2 | 34,917 | | 2 | 3 | | 5 | 10 | 9 | | | | 11 | | 4 | 1 | 6 | 8 | 7 | | | | | |
| 20 | (h) Portsmouth | W 5-0 | Griffin 2, Smith, Kennedy, Allen (pen) | 26,736 | | 2 | 3 | | 5 | 10 | 9 | 8 | | | 11 | | 4 | 1 | 6 | | 7 | | | | | |
| 27 | (a) Liverpool | W 5-2 | Ryan, Lee, Griffin 2, Allen | 34,891 | | 2 | 3 | | 5 | 10 | 9 | 8 | | | 11 | | 4 | 1 | 6 | | 7 | | | | | |
| Nov 3 | (h) Blackpool | D 1-1 | Allen | 43,214 | | 2 | 3 | | 5 | 10 | 9 | 8 | | | 11 | | 4 | 1 | 6 | | 7 | | | | | |
| 10 | (a) Arsenal | L 3-6 | Allen 2, Griffin | 53,432 | | 2 | 3 | | 5 | 10 | 9 | 8 | | | 11 | | 4 | 1 | 6 | | 7 | | | | | |
| 17 | (h) Manchester C | W 3-2 | Lee, Griffin, Allen | 32,126 | 1 | 2 | 3 | | 5 | 10 | 9 | | | 8 | 11 | | 4 | | 6 | | 7 | | | | | |
| 24 | (a) Derby C | L 1-2 | Lee | 21,811 | 1 | 2 | 3 | | 5 | 10 | 9 | | | 8 | 11 | | 4 | | 6 | | 7 | | | | | |
| Dec 1 | (h) Aston Villa | L 1-2 | Allen | 47,782 | 1 | 2 | 3 | | 5 | 10 | 9 | | | 8 | 11 | | 4 | | 6 | | 7 | | | | | |
| 8 | (a) Sunderland | D 3-3 | Lee, Allen, Hall (og) | 26,774 | 1 | 2 | 3 | | 5 | 10 | 9 | | | 8 | 11 | | 4 | | 6 | | 7 | | | | | |
| 15 | (a) Manchester U | L 1-5 | Allen | 27,548 | 1 | 2 | 3 | 6 | 5 | 10 | 9 | | | 8 | 11 | | 4 | | | | 7 | | | | | |
| 22 | (h) Tottenham H | W 3-1 | Dudley 2, Allen | 30,094 | 1 | 2 | 3 | 8 | 5 | 10 | 9 | | | | 11 | | 4 | | 6 | | 7 | | | | | |
| 25 | (a) Bolton W | L 2-3 | Dudley, Rickaby | 33,005 | 1 | 2 | 3 | 8 | 5 | 10 | 9 | | | | 11 | | 4 | | 6 | | 7 | | | | | |
| 26 | (h) Bolton W | W 3-2 | Allen 3 | 37,822 | 1 | 2 | 3 | 8 | 5 | 10 | 9 | | | | 11 | | 4 | | 6 | | 7 | | | | | |
| 29 | (a) Preston NE | L 0-1 | | 31,979 | | 2 | 3 | 8 | | 10 | 9 | | | | 11 | | 4 | 1 | 6 | | 7 | 5 | | | | |
| Jan 5 | (h) Burnley | D 1-1 | Lee | 26,115 | | 2 | 3 | 8 | | 10 | 9 | | | | 11 | | 4 | 1 | 6 | | 7 | 5 | | | | |
| 19 | (a) Charlton A | D 3-3 | Lee, Allen, Griffin | 18,126 | | 2 | 3 | 8 | | 10 | 9 | | | | 11 | | 4 | 1 | 6 | | 7 | 5 | | | | |
| 26 | (a) Fulham | L 0-2 | | 24,375 | | 2 | 3 | 8 | | 10 | 9 | | | | 11 | | 4 | 1 | 6 | | 7 | 5 | | | | |
| Feb 9 | (a) Middlesbrough | W 1-0 | Lee | 20,123 | | 2 | 3 | 8 | | 10 | 9 | | | | 11 | | 4 | 1 | 6 | | 7 | 5 | | | | |
| 16 | (h) Huddersfield T | L 0-3 | | 17,250 | | 2 | 3 | 4 | | 10 | | 8 | | | 11 | | | 1 | 6 | | 7 | 5 | 9 | | | |
| Mar 1 | (h) Chelsea | L 0-1 | | 24,431 | | 2 | | 8 | 5 | 10 | | | | | 11 | | 4 | 1 | | | 7 | 3 | 6 | 9 | | |
| 12 | (a) Portsmouth | D 1-1 | Nicholls | 22,991 | | 2 | 3 | | | 10 | 9 | | | | 11 | | 4 | 1 | 6 | | 7 | 5 | | 8 | | |
| 15 | (h) Liverpool | D 3-3 | Ryan, Allen 2 | 27,183 | | 2 | 3 | | | 10 | 9 | | | | 11 | | 4 | 1 | 6 | | 7 | 5 | | 8 | | |
| 22 | (a) Blackpool | L 0-2 | | 20,128 | | 2 | 3 | | | 10 | 9 | | | | 11 | | 4 | 1 | 6 | | 7 | 5 | | 8 | | |
| Apr 5 | (a) Manchester C | W 2-1 | Nicholls, Allen | 13,842 | | 2 | 3 | 4 | | 10 | 9 | | | | 11 | | 5 | 1 | 6 | | 7 | | | 8 | | |
| 12 | (h) Derby C | W 1-0 | Allen | 27,733 | | 2 | 3 | 4 | | 10 | 9 | | | | | | 5 | 1 | 6 | | 7 | | | 8 | 11 | |
| 14 | (h) Wolves | W 2-1 | Griffin, Nicholls | 33,429 | | 2 | 3 | 4 | | 10 | 9 | | | | | | 5 | 1 | 6 | | 7 | | | 8 | 11 | |
| 15 | (a) Wolves | W 4-1 | Allen 3, Nicholls | 48,120 | | 2 | 3 | 4 | | 10 | 9 | | | | | | 5 | 1 | 6 | | 7 | | | 8 | | 11 |
| 19 | (a) Aston Villa | L 0-2 | | 50,137 | | 2 | 3 | 4 | | 10 | 9 | | | | 11 | | 5 | 1 | 6 | | 7 | | | 8 | | |
| 21 | (h) Arsenal | W 3-1 | Allen, Lee, Ryan | 29,618 | | 2 | 3 | 4 | | 10 | 9 | | | | 11 | | 5 | 1 | 6 | | 7 | | | 8 | | |
| 23 | (a) Newcastle U | W 4-1 | Ryan, Nicholls, Allen, Lee | 31,188 | | 2 | 3 | 4 | | 10 | 9 | | | | 11 | | 5 | 1 | 6 | | 7 | | | 8 | | |
| 26 | (h) Sunderland | D 1-1 | Allen (pen) | 31,154 | | 2 | 3 | 4 | | 10 | 9 | | | | 11 | | 5 | 1 | 6 | | 7 | | | 8 | | |
| **App** | | | | | 15 | 42 | 41 | 26 | 22 | 42 | 40 | 14 | 5 | 16 | 39 | 2 | 36 | 27 | 33 | 2 | 33 | 10 | 2 | 12 | 2 | 1 |
| **Goals** | | | | | | 1 | | 3 | | 4 | 32 | 6 | | 1 | 10 | | 1 | | | 1 | 8 | | | 5 | | |

Albion in 1951-52. Back row (left to right): 'W.G.'Richardson (coach), Williams, Kennedy, Sanders, Rickaby, Heath, Gordon, Lee, Fitton. Seated: Howe, Ryan, Vernon, J.Smith (manager), E.Smith (secretary), Millard, Griffin. On ground: A.Smith, McCall, Allen, Dudley.

# 1952-53

## Division 1

| Date | | Opponent | Result | Scorers | Att. | Heath N | Rickaby S | Millard L | Dudley J | Kennedy J | Barlow R | Griffin F | Nicholls J | Allen R | Ryan R | Lee G | Evans E | Williams S | Cutler R | Dugdale J | Gallagher M | Mountford D | Sanders J | Carter W | Hodgkisson K |
|---|---|---|---|---|---|---|---|---|---|---|---|---|---|---|---|---|---|---|---|---|---|---|---|---|---|
| Aug 23 | (a) | Tottenham H | W 4-3 | Clarke (og), Allen 2, Lee | 56,552 | 1 | 2 | 3 | 4 | 5 | 6 | 7 | 8 | 9 | 10 | 11 | | | | | | | | | |
| 27 | (h) | Newcastle U | W 1-0 | Lee | 46,206 | 1 | 2 | 3 | 4 | 5 | 6 | 7 | 8 | 9 | 10 | 11 | | | | | | | | | |
| 30 | (h) | Burnley | L 1-2 | Allen | 31,543 | 1 | 2 | 3 | 4 | 5 | 6 | 7 | 8 | 9 | 10 | 11 | | | | | | | | | |
| Sep 6 | (a) | Preston NE | L 0-1 | | 34,072 | 1 | 2 | 3 | 4 | 5 | 6 | 7 | 8 | 9 | 10 | 11 | | | | | | | | | |
| 10 | (h) | Cardiff C | W 1-0 | Barlow | 23,494 | 1 | 2 | 3 | 4 | 5 | 6 | 7 | | 9 | 10 | 11 | 8 | | | | | | | | |
| 13 | (h) | Stoke C | W 3-2 | Griffin, Ryan, Allen | 27,409 | 1 | 2 | 3 | 4 | 5 | 6 | 7 | | 9 | 10 | 11 | 8 | | | | | | | | |
| 17 | (a) | Cardiff C | W 2-1 | Dudley, Allen | 32,156 | 1 | 2 | 3 | 4 | 5 | 6 | 7 | | 9 | 10 | 11 | 8 | | | | | | | | |
| 20 | (a) | Manchester C | W 1-0 | Allen | 33,043 | 1 | 2 | 3 | 4 | 5 | 6 | 7 | | 9 | 10 | 11 | 8 | | | | | | | | |
| 27 | (h) | Liverpool | W 3-0 | Griffin 2, Allen | 33,142 | 1 | 2 | 3 | 4 | 5 | 6 | 7 | | 9 | 10 | 11 | 8 | | | | | | | | |
| Oct 4 | (a) | Middlesbrough | L 2-4 | Allen, Evans | 27,065 | 1 | 2 | 3 | 4 | | 6 | 7 | | 9 | 10 | 11 | 8 | 5 | | | | | | | |
| 11 | (a) | Sunderland | L 0-1 | | 40,756 | 1 | 2 | 3 | 4 | 5 | 6 | 7 | | 9 | 10 | 11 | 8 | | | | | | | | |
| 18 | (h) | Wolves | D 1-1 | Lee | 54,480 | 1 | 2 | 3 | 4 | 5 | 6 | 7 | | 9 | 10 | 11 | 8 | | | | | | | | |
| 25 | (a) | Charlton A | D 0-0 | | 24,550 | 1 | 2 | 3 | 4 | 5 | 6 | 7 | 8 | 9 | 10 | 11 | | | | | | | | | |
| Nov 1 | (h) | Arsenal | W 2-0 | Lee, Ryan | 43,041 | 1 | 2 | 3 | 4 | 5 | 6 | 7 | 8 | 9 | 10 | 11 | | | | | | | | | |
| 8 | (a) | Derby C | D 1-1 | Lee | 26,234 | 1 | 2 | 3 | 4 | 5 | 6 | 7 | 8 | 9 | 10 | 11 | | | | | | | | | |
| 15 | (a) | Blackpool | L 0-1 | | 33,869 | 1 | 2 | 3 | 4 | 5 | 6 | 7 | 8 | 9 | | 11 | | | 10 | | | | | | |
| 22 | (a) | Chelsea | W 2-0 | Allen, Nicholls | 34,142 | 1 | 2 | 3 | 4 | 5 | 6 | 7 | 8 | 9 | 10 | 11 | | | | | | | | | |
| 29 | (h) | Manchester U | W 3-1 | Allen, Lee, Griffin | 23,617 | 1 | 2 | 3 | 4 | 5 | 6 | 7 | 8 | 9 | 10 | 11 | | | | | | | | | |
| Dec 6 | (a) | Portsmouth | W 2-1 | Griffin, Allen | 27,365 | 1 | 2 | 3 | 4 | 5 | 6 | 7 | 8 | 9 | 10 | 11 | | | | | | | | | |
| 13 | (h) | Bolton W | L 0-1 | | 16,250 | 1 | 2 | 3 | 4 | | 6 | 7 | 8 | | 10 | 11 | 9 | | | 5 | | | | | |
| 20 | (h) | Tottenham H | W 2-1 | Ryan, Allen | 18,816 | 1 | 2 | 3 | 4 | 5 | 6 | 7 | 8 | 9 | 10 | 11 | | | | | | | | | |
| 26 | (a) | Sheffield W | W 5-4 | Curtis (og), Barlow, Gannon (og), Nicholls, Allen | 59,398 | 1 | 2 | 3 | 4 | 5 | 6 | 7 | 8 | 9 | 10 | 11 | | | | | | | | | |
| 27 | (h) | Sheffield W | L 0-1 | | 52,681 | 1 | 2 | 3 | 4 | 5 | 6 | 7 | 8 | 9 | 10 | 11 | | | | | | | | | |
| Jan 1 | (a) | Newcastle U | W 5-3 | Ryan, Lee, Nicholls, Griffin, Barlow | 48,944 | 1 | 2 | 3 | 4 | 5 | 6 | 7 | 8 | 9 | 10 | 11 | | | | | | | | | |
| 3 | (a) | Burnley | L 0-5 | | 35,780 | 1 | 2 | 3 | 4 | 5 | | 7 | 8 | 9 | 10 | | | 6 | | | 11 | | | | |
| 17 | (h) | Preston NE | W 2-1 | Ryan, Nicholls | 44,763 | 1 | 2 | 3 | 4 | 5 | 6 | 7 | 8 | 9 | 10 | 11 | | | | | | | | | |
| 24 | (a) | Stoke C | L 1-5 | Nicholls | 35,226 | 1 | 2 | 3 | 4 | 5 | 6 | 7 | 8 | 9 | 10 | 11 | | | | | | | | | |
| Feb 7 | (h) | Manchester C | W 2-1 | Allen, Barlow | 27,932 | 1 | 2 | 3 | 4 | 5 | 6 | 7 | 8 | 9 | 10 | 11 | | | | | | | | | |
| 14 | (a) | Liverpool | L 0-3 | | 24,981 | 1 | 2 | | 4 | | 6 | | | 9 | 10 | 11 | 8 | 3 | | 5 | | 7 | | | |
| 21 | (h) | Middlesbrough | W 3-0 | Allen 2, Lee | 24,433 | 1 | 2 | 3 | 4 | | 6 | | | 9 | 10 | 11 | 8 | | | 5 | | 7 | | | |
| 28 | (h) | Sunderland | D 1-1 | Ryan | 31,831 | 1 | 2 | 3 | 4 | | 6 | | | 9 | 10 | 11 | 8 | | | 5 | | 7 | | | |
| Mar 7 | (a) | Wolves | L 0-2 | | 48,247 | 1 | 2 | 3 | 4 | | 6 | | | 9 | 10 | 11 | 8 | | | 5 | | 7 | | | |
| 14 | (h) | Charlton A | W 3-1 | Evans, Griffin 2 | 26,944 | 1 | 2 | 3 | 4 | | 6 | 7 | | 9 | 10 | 11 | 8 | | | 5 | | | | | |
| 21 | (a) | Arsenal | D 2-2 | Evans, Lee | 50,078 | 1 | 2 | 3 | 4 | | 6 | 7 | | 9 | 10 | 11 | 8 | | | 5 | | | | | |
| 28 | (h) | Derby C | D 2-2 | Ryan, Lee | 17,686 | 1 | 2 | 3 | 4 | | 6 | 7 | | 9 | 10 | 11 | 8 | | | 5 | | | | | |
| Apr 4 | (a) | Blackpool | L 0-2 | | 30,502 | 1 | 2 | 3 | 4 | | 6 | 7 | | 9 | 10 | 11 | 8 | | | 5 | | | | | |
| 6 | (h) | Aston Villa | W 3-2 | Allen 2 (1 pen), Griffin | 34,310 | | 2 | 3 | 4 | | 6 | 7 | | 9 | 10 | 11 | | | | 5 | | | 1 | 8 | |
| 7 | (a) | Aston Villa | D 1-1 | Allen | 49,510 | | 2 | 3 | 4 | | 6 | 7 | | 9 | 8 | 11 | | | | 5 | | | 1 | | 10 |
| 11 | (h) | Chelsea | L 0-1 | | 32,703 | | 2 | 3 | 4 | | 6 | 7 | | 9 | 8 | 11 | | | | 5 | | | 1 | | 10 |
| 18 | (a) | Manchester U | D 2-2 | Hodgkisson, Ryan | 31,380 | | 2 | 3 | 4 | | 6 | 7 | | 9 | 10 | 11 | | | | 5 | | | 1 | | 8 |
| 22 | (a) | Bolton W | W 1-0 | Allen | 28,547 | | 2 | 3 | 4 | | 6 | 7 | | 9 | 10 | 11 | | | | 5 | | | 1 | | 8 |
| 25 | (h) | Portsmouth | W 2-0 | Hodgkisson 2 | 24,879 | | 2 | 3 | 4 | | 6 | 7 | | 9 | | 11 | | | | 5 | | | 1 | 8 | 10 |
| App | | | | | | 36 | 42 | 41 | 42 | 26 | 41 | 35 | 23 | 41 | 40 | 41 | 17 | 3 | 1 | 15 | 1 | 4 | 6 | 2 | 5 |
| Goals | | | | | | | | | 1 | | 4 | 9 | 5 | 20 | 8 | 10 | 3 | | | | | | | | 3 |

**Stan Rickaby covers as Norman Heath, Albion's goalkeeper, gathers the ball at White Hart Lane in August 1952.**

# 1953-54

## Division 1

| Date | | Opponent | Result | Scorers | Att | Heath N | Rickaby S | Millard L | Dudley J | Dugdale J | Barlow R | Griffin F | Hodgkisson K | Allen R | Nicholls J | Lee G | Ryan R | Williams S | Cox F | Brookes W | Kennedy J | Carter W | Sanders J | Jones G | Cutler R | Davies R |
|---|---|---|---|---|---|---|---|---|---|---|---|---|---|---|---|---|---|---|---|---|---|---|---|---|---|---|
| Aug 19 | (h) | Arsenal | W 2-0 | Nicholls 2 | 41,812 | 1 | 2 | 3 | 4 | 5 | 6 | 7 | 8 | 9 | 10 | 11 | | | | | | | | | | |
| 22 | (h) | Bolton W | D 1-1 | Barlow | 29,122 | 1 | 2 | 3 | 4 | 5 | 6 | 7 | 8 | 9 | 10 | 11 | | | | | | | | | | |
| 26 | (a) | Manchester U | W 3-1 | Dudley, Nicholls, Lee | 42,000 | 1 | 2 | 3 | 4 | 5 | 6 | 7 | 8 | 9 | 10 | 11 | | | | | | | | | | |
| 29 | (a) | Preston NE | W 2-0 | Nicholls 2 | 32,000 | 1 | 2 | 3 | 4 | 5 | 6 | 7 | 8 | 9 | 10 | 11 | | | | | | | | | | |
| Sep 2 | (h) | Manchester U | W 2-0 | Allen, Hodgkisson | 29,036 | 1 | 2 | 3 | 4 | 5 | 6 | 7 | 8 | 9 | 10 | 11 | | | | | | | | | | |
| 5 | (h) | Tottenham H | W 3-0 | Allen, Nicholls, Ramsey (og) | 43,168 | 1 | 2 | 3 | 4 | 5 | 6 | 7 | | 9 | 10 | 11 | 8 | | | | | | | | | |
| 9 | (h) | Newcastle U | D 2-2 | Ryan, Barlow | 32,953 | 1 | 2 | 3 | 4 | 5 | 6 | 7 | | 9 | 10 | 11 | 8 | | | | | | | | | |
| 12 | (a) | Burnley | W 4-1 | Nicholls 2, Allen, Ryan | 38,948 | 1 | 2 | 3 | 4 | 5 | 6 | 7 | | 9 | 10 | 11 | 8 | | | | | | | | | |
| 16 | (a) | Newcastle U | W 7-3 | Nicholls 3, Allen 2, Griffin, Ryan | 58,075 | 1 | 2 | 3 | 4 | 5 | 6 | 7 | | 9 | 10 | 11 | 8 | | | | | | | | | |
| 19 | (h) | Charlton A | L 2-3 | Barlow, Griffin | 43,809 | 1 | 2 | 3 | 4 | 5 | 6 | 7 | | 9 | 10 | 11 | 8 | | | | | | | | | |
| 26 | (a) | Sheffield W | W 3-2 | Griffin, Nicholls, Lee | 45,503 | 1 | 2 | | 4 | 5 | 6 | 7 | | 9 | 10 | 11 | 8 | 3 | | | | | | | | |
| Oct 3 | (h) | Middlesbrough | W 2-1 | Nicholls, Lee | 37,042 | 1 | 2 | 3 | 4 | 5 | 6 | 7 | | 9 | 10 | 11 | | | 8 | | | | | | | |
| 10 | (h) | Huddersfield T | W 4-0 | Allen 3, Nicholls | 47,043 | 1 | 2 | 3 | 4 | 5 | | 7 | | 9 | 10 | 11 | 8 | | | 6 | | | | | | |
| 17 | (a) | Sheffield U | W 2-1 | Allen, Nicholls | 35,114 | 1 | 2 | 3 | 4 | 5 | 6 | 7 | | 9 | 10 | 11 | 8 | | | | | | | | | |
| 24 | (h) | Chelsea | W 5-2 | Allen 3, Nicholls, Lee | 35,443 | 1 | 2 | 3 | 4 | 5 | 6 | 7 | | 9 | 10 | 11 | 8 | | | | | | | | | |
| 31 | (a) | Blackpool | L 1-4 | Allen | 27,104 | 1 | 2 | 3 | 4 | 5 | 6 | 7 | | 9 | 10 | 11 | 8 | | | | | | | | | |
| Nov 7 | (h) | Sunderland | W 2-0 | Barlow, Lee | 37,704 | 1 | 2 | 3 | 4 | | 6 | 7 | | 9 | 8 | 11 | 10 | | | | 5 | | | | | |
| 14 | (a) | Wolves | L 0-1 | | 56,590 | 1 | 2 | 3 | 4 | | 6 | 7 | | 9 | 8 | 11 | 10 | | | | 5 | | | | | |
| 21 | (h) | Cardiff C | W 6-1 | Allen 4, Nicholls 2 | 39,618 | 1 | | 3 | 4 | | 6 | 7 | | 9 | 10 | 11 | 8 | 2 | | | 5 | | | | | |
| 28 | (a) | Manchester C | W 3-2 | Lee, Allen, Nicholls | 40,753 | 1 | 2 | 3 | 4 | | 6 | 7 | | 9 | 10 | 11 | 8 | | | | 5 | | | | | |
| Dec 5 | (h) | Portsmouth | L 2-3 | Nicholls, Allen | 29,623 | 1 | 2 | 3 | 4 | | 6 | 7 | | 9 | 10 | 11 | 8 | | | | 5 | | | | | |
| 12 | (a) | Arsenal | D 2-2 | Nicholls 2 | 55,269 | 1 | 2 | 3 | 4 | | 6 | 7 | | 9 | 10 | 11 | 8 | | | | 5 | | | | | |
| 19 | (a) | Bolton W | L 1-2 | Ryan | 27,198 | 1 | 2 | 3 | 4 | | 6 | 7 | | 9 | 10 | 11 | 8 | | | | 5 | | | | | |
| 25 | (h) | Liverpool | W 5-2 | Nicholls, Griffin 2, Barlow, Allen | 30,390 | 1 | 2 | 3 | 4 | | 6 | 7 | | 9 | 10 | 11 | 8 | | | | 5 | | | | | |
| 26 | (a) | Liverpool | D 0-0 | | 51,167 | 1 | 2 | 3 | 4 | | 6 | 7 | | 9 | 10 | 11 | 8 | | | | 5 | | | | | |
| Jan 2 | (h) | Preston NE | W 3-2 | Allen 2, Nicholls | 20,306 | 1 | 2 | 3 | 4 | | 6 | 7 | | 9 | 10 | 11 | 8 | | | | 5 | | | | | |
| 16 | (a) | Tottenham H | W 1-0 | Allen | 48,812 | 1 | 2 | 3 | 4 | 5 | 6 | 7 | | 9 | | 11 | 8 | | | | | 10 | | | | |
| 23 | (h) | Burnley | D 0-0 | | 42,850 | 1 | 2 | 3 | 4 | 5 | 6 | 7 | | 9 | 10 | 11 | 8 | | | | | | | | | |
| Feb 6 | (a) | Charlton A | D 1-1 | Allen | 27,553 | 1 | 2 | 3 | 4 | 5 | 6 | 7 | | 9 | | 11 | 8 | | | | | 10 | | | | |
| 13 | (h) | Sheffield W | W 4-2 | Nicholls, Butler (og), Rickaby, Ryan | 38,475 | 1 | 2 | 3 | 4 | 5 | | 7 | | 9 | 10 | 11 | 8 | | | | 6 | | | | | |
| 24 | (a) | Middlesbrough | D 1-1 | Allen | 15,389 | 1 | 2 | 3 | 4 | 5 | 6 | 7 | | 9 | 10 | 11 | 8 | | | | | | | | | |
| 27 | (a) | Huddersfield T | W 2-0 | Ryan, Nicholls | 48,237 | | 2 | 3 | 4 | 5 | 6 | 7 | | 9 | 10 | 11 | 8 | | | | | | 1 | | | |
| Mar 6 | (h) | Sheffield U | D 2-2 | Nicholls, Lee | 37,650 | | 2 | 3 | 4 | 5 | 6 | 7 | | 9 | 10 | 11 | 8 | | | | | | 1 | | | |
| 17 | (a) | Chelsea | L 0-5 | | 46,089 | 1 | 2 | 3 | 4 | 5 | 6 | 7 | | 9 | 10 | 11 | 8 | | | | | | | | | |
| 20 | (h) | Blackpool | W 2-1 | Allen, Ryan | 53,210 | 1 | | 3 | 4 | 5 | 6 | 7 | | 9 | 10 | 11 | 8 | 2 | | | | | | | | |
| 31 | (a) | Sunderland | L 1-2 | Cox | 48,060 | 1 | | | 4 | 5 | 6 | | | | | 11 | 8 | 3 | 9 | | 2 | 10 | | 7 | | |
| Apr 3 | (h) | Wolves | L 0-1 | | 49,884 | | | 3 | 4 | 5 | 9 | | | | | | 8 | 2 | 7 | | 6 | 10 | 1 | | | 11 |
| 10 | (a) | Cardiff C | L 0-2 | | 50,967 | | | 3 | 4 | 5 | | | | 9 | 10 | 11 | 8 | 2 | 7 | | 6 | | 1 | | | |
| 17 | (h) | Manchester C | W 1-0 | Allen (pen) | 38,742 | | | 3 | 4 | 5 | 6 | 7 | | 9 | 10 | 11 | 8 | 2 | | | | | 1 | | | |
| 19 | (h) | Aston Villa | D 1-1 | Nicholls | 45,972 | | | 3 | 4 | 5 | 6 | 7 | | 9 | 10 | 11 | 8 | 2 | | | | | 1 | | | |
| 20 | (a) | Aston Villa | L 1-6 | Griffin | 45,557 | | | 3 | 4 | 5 | 6 | 7 | | 9 | 10 | 11 | 8 | 2 | | | | | 1 | | | |
| 24 | (a) | Portsmouth | L 0-3 | | 28,004 | | | 3 | 4 | 5 | 6 | | | | 10 | 11 | 8 | 2 | | | | | 1 | 9 | 7 | |
| | | | | | App | 34 | 33 | 40 | 42 | 32 | 39 | 38 | 5 | 39 | 38 | 41 | 36 | 10 | 4 | 2 | 13 | 5 | 7 | 2 | 1 | 1 |
| | | | | | Goals | | 1 | | 1 | | 5 | 6 | 1 | 27 | 28 | 7 | 7 | | 1 | | | | | | | |

**Albion in 1953-54, pictured with the FA Cup. Back row (left to right): A.Fitton (trainer), E.Smith (secretary), V.Buckingham (manager), A.Everiss (assistant secretary). Third row: S.Rickaby, J.Kennedy, J.Dugdale, R.Barlow, J.Sanders, J.Dudley, L.Millard, G.Lee, N.Heath. Seated: L.Pritchard (director), S.R.Shephard (director), W.H.Thursfield (vice-chairman), W.H.Keys (chairman), J.W.Gaunt (director), T.W.Glidden (director). On ground: R.Ryan, R.Allen, J.Nicholls, F.Griffin.**

# 1954-55

## Division 1

| Date | | Opponent | Res | Score | Scorers | Att | Sanders J | Rickaby S | Millard L | Dudley J | Dugdale J | Barlow R | Griffin F | Ryan R | Allen R | Nicholls J | Lee G | Kennedy J | Carter W | Williams S | Davies R | Jackson A | Crowshaw A | Barnsley G | Hodgkisson K | Brookes W | Cutler R |
|---|---|---|---|---|---|---|---|---|---|---|---|---|---|---|---|---|---|---|---|---|---|---|---|---|---|---|
| Aug 21 | (a) | Sunderland | L | 2-4 | Ryan, Nicholls | 56,827 | 1 | 2 | 3 | 4 | 5 | 6 | 7 | 8 | 9 | 10 | 11 | | | | | | | | | | |
| 25 | (a) | Newcastle U | L | 0-3 | | 58,548 | 1 | 2 | 3 | 4 | | 6 | 7 | 8 | 9 | 10 | 11 | 5 | | | | | | | | | |
| 28 | (h) | Arsenal | W | 3-1 | Allen, Ryan, Nicholls | 46,247 | 1 | 2 | 3 | 4 | | 6 | 7 | 8 | 9 | 10 | 11 | 5 | | | | | | | | | |
| Sep 1 | (h) | Newcastle U | W | 4-2 | Nicholls 2, Allen, Ryan | 36,414 | 1 | 2 | 3 | 4 | | 6 | 7 | 8 | 9 | 10 | 11 | 5 | | | | | | | | | |
| 4 | (a) | Sheffield U | W | 2-1 | Carter, Allen | 28,005 | 1 | 2 | 3 | 4 | | 6 | 7 | 8 | 9 | | 11 | 5 | 10 | | | | | | | | |
| 8 | (a) | Everton | W | 2-1 | Griffin, Allen | 55,147 | 1 | 2 | 3 | 4 | | 6 | 7 | 8 | 9 | | 11 | 5 | 10 | | | | | | | | |
| 11 | (h) | Preston NE | W | 2-0 | Lee, Allen | 41,125 | 1 | 2 | 3 | 4 | | 6 | 7 | 8 | 9 | | 11 | 5 | 10 | | | | | | | | |
| 15 | (h) | Everton | D | 3-3 | Allen 2, Lee | 32,442 | 1 | 2 | 3 | 4 | | 6 | 7 | 8 | 9 | | 11 | 5 | 10 | | | | | | | | |
| 18 | (a) | Burnley | W | 2-0 | Allen 2 | 29,726 | 1 | 2 | 3 | 4 | | 6 | 7 | 8 | 9 | | 11 | 5 | 10 | | | | | | | | |
| 25 | (h) | Leicester C | W | 6-4 | Allen, Griffin, Nicholls 3, Lee | 48,422 | 1 | 2 | 3 | 4 | | 6 | 7 | 8 | 9 | 10 | 11 | 5 | | | | | | | | | |
| Oct 2 | (a) | Chelsea | D | 3-3 | Allen, Lee, Millard | 67,440 | 1 | 2 | 3 | 4 | 5 | | 7 | 8 | 9 | | 11 | 6 | | | 10 | | | | | | |
| 9 | (a) | Tottenham H | L | 1-3 | Nicholls | 45,547 | 1 | 2 | 3 | 4 | 5 | | 7 | 8 | 9 | 10 | 11 | 6 | | | | | | | | | |
| 16 | (h) | Sheffield W | L | 1-2 | Lee | 35,407 | 1 | 2 | 3 | 4 | | 6 | 7 | | 9 | 10 | 11 | 5 | 8 | | | | | | | | |
| 23 | (a) | Wolves | L | 0-4 | | 55,374 | 1 | 2 | 3 | 4 | | 6 | 7 | 8 | 9 | 10 | 11 | 5 | | | | | | | | | |
| 30 | (h) | Aston Villa | L | 2-3 | Allen, Lee | 51,833 | | 2 | 3 | 4 | | | 7 | 8 | 9 | 10 | 11 | 5 | 6 | | | | 1 | | | | |
| Nov 6 | (a) | Charlton A | W | 3-1 | Jackson, Allen 2 | 36,074 | 1 | 2 | 3 | 4 | | 6 | 7 | | 9 | | | 5 | 8 | | 11 | 10 | | | | | |
| 13 | (h) | Bolton W | D | 0-0 | | 35,136 | 1 | 2 | 3 | 4 | | 6 | 7 | 8 | 9 | | 11 | 5 | | | | 10 | | | | | |
| 20 | (a) | Huddersfield T | D | 3-3 | Nicholls, Lee 2 | 28,372 | 1 | 2 | 3 | 4 | | 6 | 7 | 8 | 9 | 10 | 11 | 5 | | | | | | | | | |
| 27 | (h) | Manchester U | W | 2-0 | Nicholls, Allen | 33,267 | 1 | 2 | 3 | 4 | | 6 | 7 | 8 | 9 | 10 | | 5 | 11 | | | | | | | | |
| Dec 4 | (a) | Portsmouth | L | 1-6 | Allen | 28,027 | 1 | 2 | 3 | 4 | | 6 | 7 | 8 | 9 | 10 | | 5 | 11 | | | | | | | | |
| 11 | (h) | Blackpool | L | 0-1 | | 33,792 | 1 | 2 | 3 | 4 | | 6 | 7 | 8 | 9 | 10 | 11 | 5 | | | | | | | | | |
| 18 | (h) | Sunderland | D | 2-2 | Williams, Nicholls | 27,989 | 1 | 2 | 3 | 4 | 5 | 6 | | | 9 | 10 | 11 | | 7 | 8 | | | | | | | |
| 25 | (a) | Cardiff C | L | 2-3 | Carter, Allen | 25,044 | 1 | 2 | 3 | 4 | 5 | 6 | | | 9 | 10 | 11 | | 7 | 8 | | | | | | | |
| 27 | (h) | Cardiff C | W | 1-0 | Millard | 51,051 | 1 | 2 | 3 | 4 | 5 | 6 | 7 | 10 | 9 | 8 | 11 | | | | | | | | | | |
| Jan 1 | (a) | Arsenal | D | 2-2 | Allen, Nicholls | 40,246 | 1 | 2 | 3 | 4 | 5 | 6 | 7 | | 9 | 10 | 11 | | | 8 | | | | | | | |
| 22 | (a) | Preston NE | L | 1-3 | Williams | 23,464 | | 2 | 3 | 4 | 5 | 6 | 7 | | 9 | 10 | 11 | | | 8 | | | 1 | | | | |
| Feb 5 | (h) | Burnley | D | 2-2 | Ryan, Allen | 22,896 | | 2 | 3 | 4 | 5 | 6 | 7 | 10 | 9 | | 11 | | | 8 | | | 1 | | | | |
| 12 | (a) | Leicester C | L | 3-6 | Carter 2, Lee | 28,786 | | | 3 | 4 | 5 | 6 | 7 | 10 | 9 | | 11 | | 8 | 2 | | | | 1 | | | |
| Mar 5 | (a) | Blackpool | L | 1-3 | Carter | 20,430 | 1 | 2 | 3 | 4 | 5 | 6 | 7 | | 9 | | 11 | | 8 | | | | | | 10 | | |
| 9 | (h) | Chelsea | L | 2-4 | Allen 2 | 7,764 | 1 | 2 | 3 | 4 | 5 | 6 | 7 | | 9 | | 11 | | 8 | | | | | | 10 | | |
| 12 | (h) | Sheffield U | D | 3-3 | Carter 2, Barlow | 22,249 | 1 | 2 | 3 | 4 | 5 | 9 | 7 | | | | 11 | | 8 | | | | | | 10 | 6 | |
| 16 | (h) | Wolves | W | 1-0 | Lee | 28,573 | 1 | | 3 | 4 | | | 7 | 10 | 9 | | 11 | 5 | 8 | 2 | | | | | | 6 | |
| 19 | (a) | Aston Villa | L | 0-3 | | 40,175 | 1 | | 3 | 4 | | | 7 | 10 | 9 | | 11 | 5 | 8 | 2 | | | | | | 6 | |
| 26 | (h) | Charlton A | W | 2-1 | Griffin, Lee | 8,191 | 1 | | 3 | 4 | | | 7 | 10 | 9 | | 11 | 5 | 8 | 2 | | | | | | 6 | |
| Apr 2 | (a) | Bolton W | W | 4-2 | Allen 2, Lee, Carter | 16,714 | 1 | | 3 | 4 | | | 7 | 10 | 9 | | 11 | 5 | 8 | 2 | | | | | | 6 | |
| 8 | (a) | Manchester C | L | 0-4 | | 57,226 | 1 | | 3 | 4 | | | 7 | 10 | 9 | | 11 | 5 | 8 | 2 | | | | | | 6 | |
| 9 | (h) | Portsmouth | W | 3-1 | Carter, Allen, Griffin | 27,696 | 1 | | 3 | 4 | | | 7 | 10 | 9 | | 11 | 5 | 8 | 2 | | | | | | 6 | |
| 11 | (h) | Manchester C | W | 2-1 | Griffin, Lee | 30,303 | 1 | | 3 | 4 | | | 7 | 10 | 9 | | 11 | 5 | 8 | 2 | | | | | | 6 | |
| 16 | (a) | Manchester U | L | 0-3 | | 24,785 | 1 | | 3 | 4 | | | 7 | 10 | 9 | | 11 | 5 | 8 | 2 | | | | | | 6 | |
| 23 | (h) | Huddersfield T | W | 2-1 | Allen 2 | 18,661 | 1 | | 3 | 4 | | | 7 | 10 | 9 | | 11 | 5 | 8 | 2 | | | | | | 6 | |
| 27 | (h) | Tottenham H | L | 1-2 | Allen | 16,743 | 1 | | 3 | 4 | | | 7 | 10 | 9 | | 11 | 5 | 8 | 2 | | | | | | 6 | |
| 30 | (a) | Sheffield W | L | 0-5 | | 16,684 | 1 | | 3 | 4 | | | | 10 | 9 | | 11 | 5 | 8 | 2 | | | | | | 6 | 7 |
| App | | | | | | | 38 | 30 | 42 | 42 | 13 | 32 | 36 | 25 | 42 | 17 | 37 | 32 | 26 | 25 | 3 | 2 | 3 | 1 | 3 | 12 | 1 |
| Goals | | | | | | | | | 2 | | | 1 | 5 | 4 | 27 | 12 | 13 | | 9 | 2 | | 2 | | | | | |

Jimmy Dugdale (far left) had now lost his place to Joe Kennedy, but was recalled when Kennedy was injured. Frank Griffin (left) scored the winner in the 1954 Cup Final but netted only five League goals the following season.

# 1955-56

### Division 1

| Date | V | Opponent | Res | Score | Scorers | Att | Sanders J | Williams S | Millard L | Dudley J | Kennedy J | Barlow R | Griffin F | Carter W | Allen R | Nicholls J | Lee G | Howe D | Kevan D | Jackson A | Hodgkisson K | Perkins E | Dugdale J | Brown F | Brookes W | Crowshaw A | Williams G | Setters M | Summers G | Robson R | Horobin R | Whitehouse B |
|---|---|---|---|---|---|---|---|---|---|---|---|---|---|---|---|---|---|---|---|---|---|---|---|---|---|---|---|---|---|---|---|---|
| Aug 20 | (h) | Wolves | D | 1-1 | Nicholls | 45,306 | 1 | 2 | 3 | 4 | 5 | 6 | 7 | 8 | 9 | 10 | 11 | | | | | | | | | | | | | | | |
| 24 | (h) | Everton | W | 2-0 | Kevan 2 | 24,402 | 1 | | 3 | 4 | 5 | 6 | 7 | 8 | | 10 | 11 | 2 | 9 | | | | | | | | | | | | | |
| 27 | (a) | Manchester U | L | 1-3 | Kevan | 31,994 | 1 | | 3 | 4 | 5 | 6 | 7 | 8 | | 10 | 11 | 2 | 9 | | | | | | | | | | | | | |
| 31 | (a) | Everton | L | 0-2 | | 38,559 | 1 | | 3 | 4 | 5 | 6 | 7 | 8 | | 10 | 11 | 2 | 9 | | | | | | | | | | | | | |
| Sep 3 | (h) | Sheffield U | W | 2-1 | Kevan, Nicholls | 20,061 | 1 | 2 | 3 | 4 | 5 | 6 | 7 | 8 | | 10 | 11 | | 9 | | | | | | | | | | | | | |
| 7 | (h) | Newcastle U | D | 1-1 | Jackson | 20,555 | 1 | 2 | 3 | 4 | 5 | 6 | 7 | | | 8 | 11 | | | 9 | 10 | | | | | | | | | | | |
| 10 | (a) | Preston NE | W | 1-0 | Docherty (og) | 28,202 | 1 | 2 | 3 | 4 | 5 | 6 | 7 | | | 8 | 11 | | | 9 | 10 | | | | | | | | | | | |
| 17 | (h) | Burnley | W | 1-0 | Nicholls | 23,510 | 1 | 2 | 3 | 4 | 5 | 6 | 7 | | 9 | 8 | 11 | | | | 10 | | | | | | | | | | | |
| 24 | (a) | Luton T | W | 2-0 | Griffin, Allen (pen) | 24,440 | 1 | 2 | 3 | 4 | 5 | 6 | 7 | | 9 | 8 | 11 | | | | 10 | | | | | | | | | | | |
| Oct 1 | (h) | Charlton A | D | 3-3 | Allen 2 (1 pen), Kennedy | 31,168 | 1 | 2 | | 4 | 5 | 6 | 7 | | 9 | 8 | 11 | | | | 10 | 3 | | | | | | | | | | |
| 8 | (h) | Aston Villa | W | 1-0 | Nicholls | 37,395 | 1 | 2 | 3 | 4 | 5 | 6 | 7 | | 9 | 8 | 11 | | | | 10 | | | | | | | | | | | |
| 15 | (a) | Sunderland | L | 1-2 | Allen (pen) | 47,094 | 1 | 2 | 3 | 4 | 5 | 6 | 7 | | 9 | 8 | 11 | | | | 10 | | | | | | | | | | | |
| 22 | (h) | Cardiff C | W | 2-1 | Allen 2 | 22,286 | 1 | | 3 | 4 | | 6 | 7 | | 9 | 8 | 11 | 2 | | | 10 | | 5 | | | | | | | | | |
| 29 | (a) | Manchester C | L | 0-2 | | 25,081 | | 2 | 3 | 4 | 5 | | 7 | | 9 | 8 | 11 | | | | 10 | | | 1 | 6 | | | | | | | |
| Nov 5 | (h) | Bolton W | W | 2-0 | Allen 2 | 23,808 | 1 | 2 | 3 | 4 | 5 | | 7 | | 9 | 10 | 11 | | | | | 8 | | | 6 | | | | | | | |
| 12 | (a) | Chelsea | L | 0-2 | | 41,898 | 1 | 2 | 3 | 4 | 5 | | 7 | 8 | 9 | 10 | 11 | | | | | | | | 6 | | | | | | | |
| 19 | (h) | Blackpool | L | 1-2 | Allen | 38,294 | 1 | 2 | 3 | 4 | 5 | 6 | 8 | | 9 | 10 | | | | | | | | | | | 7 | 11 | | | | |
| 26 | (a) | Huddersfield T | L | 0-1 | | 18,731 | 1 | 2 | 3 | 4 | 5 | 6 | 7 | | 9 | 10 | | | | | | | | | | | | 11 | 8 | | | |
| Dec 3 | (h) | Portsmouth | W | 4-0 | Setters 2, Griffin, Lee | 22,949 | 1 | 2 | 3 | 4 | 5 | 6 | 7 | 10 | 9 | | 11 | | | | | | | | | | | | 8 | | | |
| 10 | (a) | Arsenal | L | 0-2 | | 33,217 | 1 | 2 | 3 | 4 | 5 | 6 | 7 | 10 | 9 | | 11 | | | | | | | | | | | | 8 | | | |
| 17 | (a) | Wolves | L | 2-3 | Allen, Carter | 31,068 | 1 | 2 | 3 | 4 | 5 | 6 | 7 | 10 | 9 | | 11 | | | | | | | | | | | | 8 | | | |
| 24 | (h) | Manchester U | L | 1-4 | Lee | 25,286 | 1 | 2 | 3 | 4 | 5 | | 8 | | 9 | 10 | 11 | | | | | | | | | 7 | | | | 6 | | |
| 26 | (a) | Tottenham H | L | 1-4 | Allen (pen) | 32,061 | 1 | | 3 | 4 | 5 | | 8 | | 9 | 10 | 11 | 2 | | | | | | | | 7 | | | | 6 | | |
| 27 | (h) | Tottenham H | W | 1-0 | Lee | 31,522 | 1 | | 3 | 4 | | | 8 | | 9 | 10 | 11 | 2 | | | | | 5 | | | 7 | | | | 6 | | |
| 31 | (h) | Sheffield U | D | 2-2 | Allen, Lee | 23,973 | 1 | | 3 | 4 | | | 8 | | 9 | 10 | 11 | 2 | | | | | 5 | | | 7 | | | | 6 | | |
| Jan 2 | (a) | Newcastle U | W | 3-0 | Allen 3 (1 pen) | 50,768 | 1 | | 3 | 4 | 5 | 9 | 7 | | 10 | | 11 | 2 | | | | | | | | | | | 8 | 6 | | |
| 14 | (h) | Preston NE | W | 3-2 | Crowshaw 2, Lee | 22,471 | 1 | | | 4 | 5 | 9 | | | 10 | | 11 | 2 | | | 3 | | | | | 7 | | | 8 | 6 | | |
| 21 | (a) | Burnley | W | 2-1 | Lee, Griffin | 23,749 | 1 | | 3 | 4 | 5 | 9 | 7 | | 10 | | 11 | 2 | | | | | | | | | | | 8 | 6 | | |
| Feb 4 | (h) | Luton T | W | 3-1 | Griffin, Lee, Williams | 25,310 | 1 | 10 | 3 | 4 | 5 | 9 | 7 | | | | 11 | 2 | | | | | | | | | | | 8 | 6 | | |
| 11 | (a) | Charlton A | L | 1-5 | Nicholls | 13,573 | 1 | | 3 | 4 | 5 | 9 | 7 | | 10 | 8 | 11 | 2 | | | | | | | | | | | | 6 | | |
| 25 | (h) | Sunderland | W | 3-0 | Barlow, Griffin, Lee | 23,620 | 1 | | 3 | 4 | 5 | 9 | 7 | | 10 | | 11 | 2 | | | | | | | | | | | 8 | 6 | | |
| Mar 3 | (a) | Blackpool | L | 1-5 | Allen (pen) | 19,763 | 1 | | 3 | 4 | 5 | 9 | | | 10 | | | 2 | | | | | | | | 7 | | | 8 | 6 | | |
| 10 | (h) | Manchester C | L | 0-4 | | 32,680 | 1 | | 3 | | 5 | | | | 10 | | 11 | 2 | 9 | | | | | | | 7 | 4 | | 8 | 6 | | |
| 17 | (a) | Bolton W | L | 0-4 | | 23,393 | 1 | | 3 | 4 | 5 | 10 | 7 | | 9 | | | 2 | | | | | | | | | | | 8 | 6 | | |
| 24 | (h) | Chelsea | W | 3-0 | Nicholls 2, Griffin | 20,219 | 1 | | 3 | 4 | 5 | | 7 | | 9 | 10 | 11 | 2 | | | | | | | | | | | 8 | 6 | | |
| 31 | (a) | Cardiff C | W | 3-1 | Allen, Robson, Nicholls | 40,126 | 1 | | 3 | 4 | 5 | | | | 9 | 10 | 11 | 2 | | | | | | | | | | | 8 | 6 | 7 | |
| Apr 2 | (a) | Birmingham C | L | 0-2 | | 38,892 | 1 | | 3 | 4 | 5 | | | | 9 | 10 | 11 | 2 | | | | | | | | | | | 8 | 6 | 7 | |
| 3 | (h) | Birmingham C | L | 0-2 | | 35,986 | 1 | | 3 | 4 | 5 | | 7 | | 9 | 10 | 11 | 2 | | | | | | | | | | | 8 | 6 | | |
| 7 | (h) | Huddersfield T | L | 1-2 | Horobin | 16,141 | 1 | 10 | 3 | 4 | 5 | | | | 9 | | 11 | 2 | | | | | | | | | | | 8 | 6 | 7 | |
| 14 | (a) | Portsmouth | D | 1-1 | Lee | 17,520 | 1 | | 3 | 4 | 5 | | | | 9 | | 11 | 2 | | | | | | | | | | | 8 | 6 | 7 | 10 |
| 21 | (h) | Arsenal | W | 2-1 | Lee, Goring (og) | 22,392 | 1 | | 3 | 4 | 5 | | 7 | | 9 | | 11 | 2 | | | | | | | | | | | 8 | 6 | | 10 |
| 28 | (a) | Aston Villa | L | 0-3 | | 45,120 | 1 | | 3 | 4 | 5 | | 7 | | 9 | | 11 | 2 | | | | | | | | | | | 8 | 6 | | 10 |
| App | | | | | | | 41 | 20 | 40 | 41 | 31 | 38 | 31 | 13 | 34 | 24 | 40 | 24 | 7 | 2 | 8 | 2 | 3 | 1 | 4 | 8 | 2 | 11 | 20 | 10 | 4 | 3 |
| Goals | | | | | | | | 1 | | | 1 | 1 | 6 | 1 | 17 | 8 | 10 | | 4 | 1 | | | | | | 2 | | 2 | | 1 | 1 | |

**West Bromwich Albion's great half-back line of the 1950s – Jimmy Dudley, Joe Kennedy and Ray Barlow.**

# 1956-57

### Division 1

| Date | | Opponent | Res | Scorers | Att | Sanders J | Howe D | Williams S | Dudley J | Barlow R | Summers G | Griffin F | Robson R | Allen R | Whitehouse B | Lee G | Brookes W | Kennedy J | Millard L | Kevan D | Setters M | Nicholls J | Horobin R | Carter W | Lee M | Brown F | Jackson A |
|---|---|---|---|---|---|---|---|---|---|---|---|---|---|---|---|---|---|---|---|---|---|---|---|---|---|---|---|
| Aug 18 | (a) | Sheffield W | L 2-4 | Lee, Allen | 22,586 | 1 | 2 | 3 | 4 | 5 | 6 | 7 | 8 | 9 | 10 | 11 | | | | | | | | | | | |
| 22 | (h) | Aston Villa | W 2-0 | Robson, Whitehouse | 37,255 | 1 | 2 | 3 | 4 | 6 | | 7 | 8 | 9 | 10 | 11 | 5 | | | | | | | | | | |
| 25 | (h) | Manchester U | L 2-3 | Allen, Lee | 26,516 | 1 | 2 | 3 | 4 | 6 | | 7 | 8 | 9 | 10 | 11 | | 5 | | | | | | | | | |
| 27 | (a) | Aston Villa | D 0-0 | | 33,052 | 1 | 2 | 3 | 4 | 6 | | 7 | 8 | 9 | 10 | 11 | | 5 | | | | | | | | | |
| Sep 1 | (a) | Arsenal | L 1-4 | Whitehouse | 39,973 | 1 | 2 | 3 | 4 | 6 | | 7 | 8 | 9 | 10 | 11 | | 5 | | | | | | | | | |
| 5 | (h) | Portsmouth | W 2-1 | Robson, Kevan | 15,059 | 1 | 2 | | 4 | 6 | | 7 | 8 | | 10 | 11 | | 5 | 3 | 9 | | | | | | | |
| 8 | (h) | Burnley | D 2-2 | Allen, Griffin | 23,746 | 1 | 2 | | 4 | 6 | | 7 | 8 | 10 | | 11 | | 5 | 3 | 9 | | | | | | | |
| 15 | (a) | Preston NE | L 2-3 | Robson 2 | 28,380 | 1 | 2 | | 4 | 6 | | 7 | 8 | 10 | | 11 | | 5 | 3 | 9 | | | | | | | |
| 22 | (h) | Chelsea | W 2-1 | Griffin, Kevan | 24,684 | 1 | 2 | | | 6 | | 7 | 8 | | | 11 | | 5 | 3 | 9 | 4 | 10 | | | | | |
| 29 | (a) | Cardiff C | D 0-0 | | 28,115 | 1 | 2 | | | 6 | | | 8 | | | 11 | | 5 | 3 | 9 | 4 | 10 | 7 | | | | |
| Oct 6 | (h) | Wolves | D 1-1 | Allen | 34,379 | 1 | 2 | | | 6 | | 7 | 8 | | | 11 | | 5 | 3 | 9 | 4 | 10 | | | | | |
| 13 | (a) | Bolton W | D 1-1 | Griffin | 24,969 | 1 | 2 | | | 6 | | 7 | 10 | 11 | | | | 5 | 3 | 9 | 4 | 8 | | | | | |
| 20 | (h) | Sunderland | W 2-0 | Robson, Allen (pen) | 33,075 | 1 | 2 | | | 6 | | 7 | 10 | 11 | | | | 5 | | 9 | 4 | 8 | 3 | | | | |
| 27 | (a) | Luton T | W 1-0 | Kevan | 16,786 | 1 | 2 | | | 6 | | 7 | 10 | 11 | | | | 5 | 3 | 9 | 4 | 8 | | | | | |
| Nov 3 | (h) | Everton | W 3-0 | Robson, Allen 2 | 23,810 | 1 | 2 | | | 6 | | 7 | 8 | 11 | | | | 5 | 3 | 9 | 4 | 10 | | | | | |
| 10 | (a) | Blackpool | W 1-0 | Robson | 18,839 | 1 | 2 | | 4 | 6 | | 7 | 8 | 11 | | | | 5 | 3 | 9 | | 10 | | | | | |
| 17 | (h) | Manchester C | D 1-1 | Griffin | 26,082 | 1 | 2 | | 4 | 6 | | 7 | 8 | 11 | | | | 5 | 3 | 9 | | 10 | | | | | |
| 24 | (a) | Charlton A | L 2-3 | Barlow, Kevan | 16,361 | 1 | 2 | | 4 | 6 | | 7 | 8 | 11 | | | | 5 | 3 | 9 | | 10 | | | | | |
| Dec 1 | (h) | Leeds U | D 0-0 | | 29,135 | 1 | 2 | | 4 | 6 | | 7 | 8 | 11 | | | | 5 | 3 | 9 | | 10 | | | | | |
| 8 | (a) | Tottenham H | D 2-2 | Kevan 2 | 38,140 | 1 | 2 | | 4 | 6 | | 7 | 8 | 11 | | | | 5 | 3 | 9 | | 10 | | | | | |
| 15 | (a) | Sheffield W | L 1-4 | Kevan | 17,150 | 1 | 2 | | 4 | 6 | | 7 | 8 | | | | | 5 | 3 | 9 | | 10 | 11 | | | | |
| 25 | (h) | Newcastle U | W 1-0 | Barlow | 13,780 | 1 | 2 | | 4 | 6 | | 7 | 10 | 11 | | | | 5 | | 9 | | 8 | 3 | | | | |
| 26 | (a) | Newcastle U | L 2-5 | Kevan, Williams | 20,319 | 1 | 2 | 10 | 4 | 6 | | 7 | | 11 | | | | 5 | | 9 | | 8 | 3 | | | | |
| 29 | (h) | Arsenal | L 0-2 | | 26,162 | 1 | 2 | | 4 | 6 | | 7 | 10 | 11 | | | | 5 | | 9 | | 8 | 3 | | | | |
| Jan 12 | (a) | Burnley | L 0-1 | | 24,249 | 1 | 2 | | 4 | 6 | | 7 | 10 | 11 | | | | 5 | | 9 | | 8 | 3 | | | | |
| 19 | (h) | Preston NE | D 0-0 | | 24,304 | 1 | 2 | | 4 | 6 | | 7 | 10 | | 8 | | | 5 | | 9 | | | 11 | 3 | | | |
| Feb 2 | (a) | Chelsea | W 4-2 | Kevan 2, Allen (pen), Robson | 29,361 | 1 | 2 | | 4 | 6 | | 7 | 8 | 9 | | | | 5 | | 10 | | | 11 | 3 | | | |
| 9 | (h) | Cardiff C | L 1-2 | Kevan | 23,662 | 1 | 2 | | 4 | 6 | | | 8 | 9 | | 11 | | 5 | | 10 | | 7 | | 3 | | | |
| 23 | (h) | Luton T | W 4-0 | Dudley, Whitehouse, Griffin, Kevan | 21,934 | 1 | 2 | | 4 | 6 | | 7 | 8 | | 10 | | | 5 | 3 | 9 | | | 11 | | | | |
| Mar 9 | (h) | Tottenham H | D 1-1 | Whitehouse | 30,739 | 1 | 2 | | 4 | 5 | | 7 | 9 | | 8 | | | | 3 | 10 | 6 | | 11 | | | | |
| 13 | (a) | Sunderland | W 4-1 | Kevan 2, Whitehouse, Allen | 26,336 | 1 | 2 | | | 5 | | 7 | 4 | 9 | 8 | | | | 3 | 10 | 6 | | 11 | | | | |
| 16 | (a) | Everton | W 1-0 | Kevan | 32,606 | 1 | 2 | | | 5 | | 7 | 4 | 9 | 8 | | | | 3 | 10 | 6 | | 11 | | | | |
| 30 | (a) | Manchester C | L 1-2 | Robson | 26,351 | 1 | 2 | | 4 | 6 | | 7 | 9 | | 8 | | | 5 | 3 | 10 | | | 11 | | | | |
| Apr 3 | (h) | Blackpool | L 1-3 | Whitehouse | 6,397 | | 2 | | | 6 | | 7 | 8 | 9 | | | | 5 | 3 | | 4 | 10 | 11 | | | | 1 |
| 6 | (a) | Charlton A | D 2-2 | Setters, Carter (pen) | 15,055 | 1 | 2 | | 4 | | | | | | 8 | | | 5 | 3 | | 6 | 7 | 11 | 9 | 10 | | |
| 13 | (a) | Leeds U | D 0-0 | | 20,535 | 1 | 2 | | | 6 | | | 8 | | 9 | | | 5 | 3 | 10 | 4 | 7 | 11 | | | | |
| 15 | (a) | Wolves | L 2-5 | Robson 2 | 27,942 | 1 | 2 | 3 | | 6 | | | 8 | | 9 | | | 5 | | 10 | 4 | 7 | 11 | | | | |
| 20 | (h) | Bolton W | W 3-2 | Whitehouse, Kevan, Robson | 18,465 | | 2 | | | 6 | | | 8 | | 9 | | | 5 | 3 | 10 | 4 | 7 | 11 | | | | 1 |
| 22 | (h) | Birmingham C | D 0-0 | | 18,828 | | 2 | | 4 | 6 | | | 8 | | 9 | | | 5 | 3 | 10 | | 7 | 11 | | | | 1 |
| 23 | (a) | Birmingham C | L 0-2 | | 33,301 | | 2 | | 4 | 6 | | | 8 | | 9 | | | 5 | 3 | 10 | | 7 | 11 | | | | 1 |
| 27 | (a) | Portsmouth | W 1-0 | Allen | 24,055 | 1 | 2 | | 4 | 5 | | 7 | 8 | 9 | | | | | 3 | 10 | 6 | | 11 | | | | |
| May 1 | (a) | Manchester U | D 1-1 | Millard (pen) | 20,357 | 1 | 2 | | 4 | 5 | | 7 | 8 | 9 | | | | | 3 | 10 | 6 | | 11 | | | | |
| **App** | | | | | | 36 | 41 | 13 | 24 | 40 | 2 | 34 | 39 | 37 | 15 | 9 | 1 | 35 | 28 | 35 | 21 | 17 | 18 | 9 | 1 | 6 | 1 |
| **Goals** | | | | | | | | 1 | 1 | 2 | | 5 | 12 | 10 | 7 | 2 | | | 1 | 16 | 1 | | | 1 | | | |

**West Brom in 1956-57. Back row (left to right):** R.Robson, R.Barlow, S.Williams, J.Sanders, F.Brown, B.Hughes, J.Kennedy, J.Dudley. **Middle row:** D.Howe, B.Whitehouse, G.Summers, L.Millard, R.Horobin, G.Lee, W.Brookes. **Front row:** R.Allen, W.Carter, F.Griffin, J.Nicholls.

# 1957-58

### Division 1

| Date | | Opponent | Result | Scorers | Att | Brown F | Howe D | Williams S | Setters M | Kennedy J | Barlow R | Griffin F | Robson R | Allen R | Kevan D | Lee G | Horobin R | Jackson A | Whitehouse B | Sanders J | Dudley J | Millard L | Burnside D | Drury C | Jackman C | Campbell J | Williams G | Robinson E |
|---|---|---|---|---|---|---|---|---|---|---|---|---|---|---|---|---|---|---|---|---|---|---|---|---|---|---|---|---|
| Aug 24 | (h) | Newcastle U | W 2-1 | Robson, Allen | 31,064 | 1 | 2 | 3 | 4 | 5 | 6 | 7 | 8 | 9 | 10 | 11 | | | | | | | | | | | | |
| 27 | (a) | Arsenal | D 2-2 | Allen 2 (1 pen) | 45,988 | 1 | 2 | 3 | 4 | 5 | 6 | 7 | 8 | 9 | 10 | | 11 | | | | | | | | | | | |
| 31 | (a) | Burnley | D 2-2 | Setters, Lee | 24,003 | 1 | 2 | 3 | 4 | 5 | 6 | 7 | 8 | 9 | | 10 | | 11 | | | | | | | | | | |
| Sep 4 | (h) | Arsenal | L 1-2 | Allen | 26,117 | 1 | 2 | 3 | 4 | 5 | 6 | 7 | 8 | 9 | | 10 | | 11 | | | | | | | | | | |
| 7 | (h) | Preston NE | W 4-1 | Allen, Kevan, Griffin, Horobin | 29,903 | | 2 | 3 | 4 | 5 | 6 | 7 | 8 | 9 | 10 | | 11 | | | 1 | | | | | | | | |
| 11 | (a) | Chelsea | D 2-2 | Allen, Horobin | 29,824 | | 2 | 3 | 4 | 5 | 6 | 7 | 8 | 9 | 10 | | 11 | | | 1 | | | | | | | | |
| 14 | (a) | Sheffield W | W 2-1 | McEvoy (og), Allen (pen) | 27,933 | | 2 | 3 | 4 | 5 | 6 | 7 | 8 | 9 | 10 | | 11 | | | 1 | | | | | | | | |
| 18 | (h) | Chelsea | D 1-1 | Allen (pen) | 36,835 | | 2 | 3 | 4 | 5 | 6 | 7 | 8 | 9 | 10 | | 11 | | | 1 | | | | | | | | |
| 21 | (h) | Manchester C | W 9-2 | Griffin 3, Howe 2 (1 pen), Robson, Horobin, Whitehouse, Kevan (pen) | 26,222 | | 2 | 3 | | 5 | 6 | 7 | 9 | | 10 | | 11 | | 8 | 1 | 4 | | | | | | | |
| 28 | (a) | Nottingham F | W 2-0 | Robson 2 | 41,675 | | 2 | 3 | 4 | 5 | 6 | 7 | 8 | 9 | 10 | | 11 | | | 1 | | | | | | | | |
| Oct 1 | (h) | Birmingham C | D 0-0 | | 39,909 | | 2 | 3 | | 5 | 6 | 7 | 8 | 9 | 10 | | 11 | | | 1 | 4 | | | | | | | |
| 5 | (h) | Portsmouth | W 3-1 | Allen 2, Robson | 32,030 | | 2 | 3 | 4 | 5 | 6 | 7 | 8 | 9 | 10 | | 11 | | | 1 | | | | | | | | |
| 12 | (h) | Bolton W | D 2-2 | Kevan, Allen (pen) | 31,522 | | 2 | 3 | 4 | 5 | 6 | 7 | 8 | 9 | 10 | | 11 | | | 1 | | | | | | | | |
| 19 | (a) | Leeds U | D 1-1 | | 25,507 | | 2 | | | 5 | 6 | 7 | 9 | | | | 11 | | 8 | 1 | 4 | 3 | 10 | | | | | |
| 26 | (h) | Manchester U | W 4-3 | Robson 2, Allen, Kevan | 52,839 | | 2 | 3 | | 5 | 6 | 7 | 8 | 9 | 10 | | 11 | | | 1 | 4 | | | | | | | |
| Nov 2 | (a) | Everton | D 1-1 | Griffin | 53,679 | | 2 | 3 | 4 | 5 | 6 | 7 | 8 | 9 | 10 | | 11 | | | 1 | | | | | | | | |
| 9 | (h) | Aston Villa | W 3-2 | Robson, Allen (pen), Horobin | 41,454 | | 2 | 3 | 4 | 5 | 6 | 7 | 8 | 9 | 10 | | 11 | | | 1 | | | | | | | | |
| 16 | (a) | Wolves | D 1-1 | Kevan | 55,418 | | 2 | 3 | 4 | 5 | 6 | 7 | 8 | 9 | 10 | | 11 | | | 1 | | | | | | | | |
| 23 | (h) | Sunderland | W 3-0 | Kevan, Robson, Setters | 32,682 | | 2 | 3 | 4 | 5 | 6 | 7 | 8 | 9 | 10 | | 11 | | | 1 | | | | | | | | |
| 30 | (a) | Leicester C | D 3-3 | Robson 2, Allen | 33,855 | | 2 | 3 | 4 | 5 | 6 | 7 | 8 | 9 | 10 | | 11 | | | 1 | | | | | | | | |
| Dec 7 | (h) | Blackpool | D 1-1 | Robson | 28,236 | | 2 | 3 | 4 | 5 | 6 | 7 | 8 | 9 | 10 | | 11 | | | 1 | | | | | | | | |
| 14 | (a) | Luton T | L 1-5 | Robson | 15,365 | | 2 | 3 | 4 | 5 | 6 | 7 | 8 | 9 | 10 | | 11 | | | 1 | | | | | | | | |
| 21 | (a) | Newcastle U | L 0-3 | | 31,699 | | 2 | 3 | 4 | 5 | 6 | 7 | 8 | 9 | 10 | 11 | | | | 1 | | | | | | | | |
| 26 | (a) | Birmingham C | W 5-3 | Robson 2, Kevan 2, Allen | 48,396 | | 2 | 3 | 4 | 5 | 6 | 7 | 8 | 9 | 10 | 11 | | | | 1 | | | | | | | | |
| 28 | (h) | Burnley | W 5-1 | Robson 4, Kevan | 38,386 | | 2 | 3 | 4 | 5 | 6 | 7 | 8 | 9 | 10 | 11 | | | | 1 | | | | | | | | |
| Jan 11 | (a) | Preston NE | L 1-3 | Kevan | 25,003 | | 2 | 3 | 4 | 5 | 6 | 7 | 8 | 9 | 10 | | 11 | | | 1 | | | | | | | | |
| 18 | (h) | Sheffield W | W 3-1 | Griffin 2, Setters | 28,963 | | 2 | 3 | 4 | 5 | 6 | 7 | 8 | 9 | 10 | | 11 | | | 1 | | | | | | | | |
| Feb 1 | (a) | Manchester C | L 1-4 | Kevan | 38,702 | | 2 | 3 | | 5 | 6 | 7 | 9 | | 10 | | 11 | | 8 | 1 | 4 | | | | | | | |
| 8 | (h) | Nottingham F | W 3-2 | Kevan 2, Robson | 32,868 | | 2 | 3 | | 5 | 6 | 7 | 9 | | 10 | | 11 | | 8 | 1 | 4 | | | | | | | |
| 22 | (a) | Bolton W | D 2-2 | Kevan 2 | 19,132 | | 2 | 3 | | 5 | | | 8 | 9 | 10 | | 11 | | 7 | 1 | 4 | | | 6 | | | | |
| Mar 8 | (a) | Manchester U | W 4-0 | Allen 2, Greaves (og), Kevan | 63,278 | | 2 | 3 | | 5 | | | 8 | 9 | 10 | | 11 | | 7 | 1 | 4 | | | 6 | | | | |
| 12 | (h) | Leeds U | W 1-0 | Charlton (og) | 16,518 | | 2 | 3 | | 5 | | | 8 | 9 | 10 | | 11 | | 7 | 1 | 4 | | | 6 | | | | |
| 15 | (a) | Everton | W 4-0 | Robson, Kevan 2, Allen (pen) | 28,915 | | 2 | 3 | | 5 | | | 8 | 9 | 10 | | 11 | | 7 | 1 | 4 | | | 6 | | | | |
| 19 | (a) | Portsmouth | D 2-2 | Horobin, Allen | 24,731 | | 2 | 3 | | 5 | 6 | | 8 | 9 | 10 | | 11 | | | | 4 | | | | 1 | 7 | | |
| 22 | (a) | Sunderland | L 0-2 | | 38,323 | | 2 | 3 | | 5 | 6 | | 8 | 9 | 10 | | 11 | | | | 4 | | | | 1 | 7 | | |
| 29 | (h) | Wolves | L 0-3 | | 56,904 | | 2 | 3 | | 5 | 6 | | 8 | 9 | 10 | | 11 | | | | 4 | | | | 1 | 7 | | |
| Apr 4 | (a) | Tottenham H | D 0-0 | | 56,166 | | 2 | 3 | | 5 | | | 8 | 11 | 9 | | 10 | | | | 4 | | | 6 | 1 | 7 | | |
| 5 | (a) | Aston Villa | L 1-2 | Allen | 32,010 | | 2 | | | 5 | | | | 10 | 11 | 9 | 7 | | 8 | | 4 | | | 6 | 1 | | 3 | |
| 7 | (h) | Tottenham H | L 0-2 | | 26,672 | | 2 | 3 | | 5 | | | 9 | 11 | 10 | | | | 8 | | 4 | | | 6 | 1 | 7 | | |
| 12 | (h) | Leicester C | W 6-2 | Robson 3, Whitehouse 2, Kevan | 25,389 | | 2 | | | 5 | | | 8 | 9 | 10 | | 11 | | 7 | | 4 | | | 6 | 1 | | 3 | |
| 19 | (a) | Blackpool | L 0-2 | | 17,442 | | 2 | | | 5 | 6 | | | 9 | | | 11 | | 7 | | 4 | | 10 | | 1 | | 3 | 8 |
| 26 | (h) | Luton T | W 4-2 | Lee 2, Howe, Allen (pen) | 20,289 | | 2 | | 6 | 5 | | | 8 | 9 | | 10 | 11 | | 7 | | 4 | | | | 1 | | 3 | |
| **App** | | | | | | 4 | 39 | 38 | 27 | 34 | 40 | 29 | 41 | 39 | 38 | 8 | 32 | 2 | 14 | 29 | 19 | 1 | 2 | 7 | 9 | 5 | 4 | 1 |
| **Goals** | | | | | | | 3 | | 3 | | | 7 | 24 | 22 | 19 | 3 | 5 | | 3 | | | | | | | | | |

West Brom in 1957-58. Back row (left to right): A.Forrester, A.Jackson, C.Jackman, F.Brown, J.Sanders, J.Kennedy, G.Lee. Middle row: D.Kevan, D.Howe, J.Dudley, S.Williams, B.Whitehouse, F.Griffin. Front row: Vic Buckingham (manager), M.Setters, R.Robson, R.Barlow, R.Horobin, R.Allen, L.Millard.

# 1958-59

## Division 1

| Date | | Opponent | Res | Score | Scorers | Att | Jackman C | Howe D | Williams S | Setters M | Barlow R | Drury C | Campbell J | Robson R | Allen R | Kevan D | Hogg D | Dudley J | Burnside D | Whitehouse B | Williams G | Potter R | Forrester A | Jackson A | Kennedy J | Griffin F |
|---|---|---|---|---|---|---|---|---|---|---|---|---|---|---|---|---|---|---|---|---|---|---|---|---|---|---|
| Aug 23 | (a) | Luton T | D | 1-1 | Kevan | 24,425 | 1 | 2 | 3 | 4 | 5 | 6 | 7 | 8 | 9 | 10 | 11 | | | | | | | | | |
| 27 | (h) | Birmingham C | D | 2-2 | Hogg, Allen (pen) | 46,468 | 1 | 2 | 3 | 4 | 5 | 6 | 7 | 8 | 9 | 10 | 11 | | | | | | | | | |
| 30 | (h) | Bolton W | D | 1-1 | Allen | 37,244 | 1 | 2 | 3 | 6 | 5 | | 7 | 8 | 9 | 10 | 11 | 4 | | | | | | | | |
| Sep 3 | (a) | Birmingham C | W | 6-0 | Burnside 2, Campbell 2, Allen, Kevan | 35,915 | 1 | 2 | 3 | 6 | 5 | | 7 | | 9 | 8 | 11 | 4 | 10 | | | | | | | |
| 6 | (a) | Burnley | W | 3-1 | Burnside 2, Campbell | 22,789 | 1 | 2 | 3 | 6 | 5 | | 7 | | 9 | 8 | 11 | 4 | 10 | | | | | | | |
| 10 | (h) | Portsmouth | L | 1-2 | Campbell | 34,445 | 1 | 2 | 3 | 6 | 5 | | 7 | | 9 | 8 | 11 | 4 | 10 | | | | | | | |
| 13 | (h) | Preston NE | D | 1-1 | Dudley | 36,525 | 1 | 2 | 3 | 6 | 5 | | | | 9 | 8 | 11 | 4 | 10 | 7 | | | | | | |
| 17 | (a) | Portsmouth | W | 6-2 | Allen 2(1 pen), Burnside 2, Kevan, Hayward(og) | 32,972 | 1 | 2 | 3 | 6 | 5 | | 7 | | 9 | 10 | 11 | 4 | 8 | | | | | | | |
| 20 | (a) | Leicester C | D | 2-2 | Allen, Kevan | 38,751 | 1 | 2 | 3 | 4 | 5 | 6 | 7 | | 9 | 10 | 11 | | 8 | | | | | | | |
| 27 | (h) | Everton | L | 2-3 | Campbell, Burnside | 30,721 | 1 | 2 | 3 | 4 | 5 | 6 | 7 | | 9 | 8 | 11 | | 10 | | | | | | | |
| Oct 4 | (a) | Arsenal | L | 3-4 | Kevan 3 | 57,770 | 1 | 2 | | 4 | 5 | 6 | 7 | 8 | 9 | 10 | 11 | | | | | | 3 | | | |
| 11 | (a) | Aston Villa | W | 4-1 | Burnside, Hogg, Robson, Howe (pen) | 47,124 | 1 | 2 | 3 | 4 | 5 | 6 | 7 | 8 | 9 | | 11 | | 10 | | | | | | | |
| 18 | (h) | West Ham U | W | 2-1 | Campbell, Howe (pen) | 36,991 | | 2 | | 4 | 5 | 6 | 7 | 8 | 9 | 10 | 11 | | | | 3 | 1 | | | | |
| 25 | (a) | Manchester U | W | 2-1 | Robson, Kevan | 51,960 | | 2 | 3 | 4 | 5 | 6 | 7 | 8 | 9 | 10 | 11 | | | | | 1 | | | | |
| Nov 1 | (h) | Wolves | W | 2-1 | Campbell, Kevan | 48,898 | | 2 | 3 | 4 | 5 | 6 | 7 | 8 | 9 | 10 | 11 | | | | | 1 | | | | |
| 8 | (a) | Blackpool | D | 1-1 | Burnside | 18,664 | | 2 | 3 | 4 | 5 | 6 | 7 | | 9 | 10 | 11 | | 8 | | | 1 | | | | |
| 15 | (h) | Blackburn R | L | 2-3 | Burnside, Dudley | 31,679 | | 2 | 3 | 4 | 5 | | 7 | | 9 | 10 | 11 | 6 | 8 | | | 1 | | | | |
| 22 | (a) | Newcastle U | W | 2-1 | Kevan, Robson | 51,636 | | 2 | 3 | 4 | 5 | 6 | 7 | 8 | 9 | 10 | 11 | | | | | 1 | | | | |
| 29 | (h) | Tottenham H | W | 4-3 | Howe, Kevan, Forrester, Allen (pen) | 21,861 | | 2 | 3 | 4 | 5 | 6 | | 8 | 9 | 10 | 11 | | | | | 1 | 7 | | | |
| Dec 6 | (a) | Nottingham F | D | 1-1 | Allen (pen) | 34,634 | | 2 | 3 | 4 | 5 | 6 | | 8 | 9 | 10 | 11 | | | | | 1 | 7 | | | |
| 13 | (a) | Chelsea | W | 4-0 | Forrester 2, Allen, Kevan | 19,856 | | 2 | 3 | 4 | 5 | 6 | | 8 | 9 | 10 | 11 | | | | | 1 | 7 | | | |
| 26 | (h) | Leeds U | L | 1-2 | Gibson (og) | 35,020 | | 2 | 3 | 4 | 5 | 6 | | 8 | 9 | 10 | 11 | | | | | 1 | 7 | | | |
| 27 | (a) | Leeds U | W | 1-0 | Kevan | 44,998 | | 2 | 3 | 4 | 5 | 6 | | | 9 | 10 | 11 | | | | | 1 | 7 | 8 | | |
| Jan 3 | (a) | Bolton W | L | 1-2 | Allen | 27,847 | | 2 | 3 | 4 | 5 | 6 | | 8 | 9 | 10 | 11 | | | | | 1 | 7 | | | |
| 31 | (a) | Preston NE | W | 4-2 | Kevan 2, Griffin, O'Farrell (og) | 23,138 | | 2 | 3 | 4 | | 6 | | | 9 | 10 | 11 | | | | | 1 | | 8 | 5 | 7 |
| Feb 7 | (h) | Leicester C | D | 2-2 | Kevan, Allen | 25,375 | | 2 | 3 | 4 | | 6 | | | 9 | 10 | 11 | | | | | 1 | | 8 | 5 | 7 |
| 18 | (a) | Everton | D | 3-3 | Setters, Kevan, Allen | 32,629 | | 2 | 3 | 4 | 5 | 6 | | | 9 | 10 | 11 | | | | | 1 | | 8 | | 7 |
| 21 | (h) | Arsenal | D | 1-1 | Kevan | 32,706 | | 2 | 3 | 4 | 5 | 6 | 7 | | 9 | 10 | 11 | | | | | 1 | | 8 | | |
| Mar 7 | (a) | West Ham U | L | 1-3 | Robson | 30,157 | | 2 | 3 | 4 | 5 | 6 | | 8 | 9 | 10 | 11 | | | | | 1 | 7 | | | |
| 11 | (h) | Burnley | L | 2-4 | Setters, Hogg | 18,824 | | 2 | 3 | 4 | 5 | 6 | | | 9 | 10 | 11 | | | | | 1 | | 8 | | 7 |
| 14 | (h) | Manchester U | L | 1-3 | Kevan | 35,608 | | 2 | 3 | 4 | 5 | | 7 | 8 | 9 | 10 | 11 | | | | | 1 | 6 | | | |
| 21 | (a) | Wolves | L | 2-5 | Kevan 2 | 44,280 | | 2 | 3 | 4 | 5 | | 7 | 8 | 9 | 10 | 11 | | | | | 1 | 6 | | | |
| 28 | (h) | Blackpool | W | 3-1 | Kevan 2, Allen | 29,803 | | 2 | 3 | 4 | | | 7 | 8 | 9 | 10 | 11 | | | | | 1 | 6 | | 5 | |
| 30 | (a) | Manchester C | W | 2-0 | Kevan, Allen | 25,551 | | 2 | 3 | 4 | | | 7 | 8 | 9 | 10 | 11 | | | | | 1 | 6 | | 5 | |
| 31 | (h) | Manchester C | W | 3-0 | Campbell, Allen (pen), Hogg | 32,076 | | 2 | 3 | 4 | | | 7 | 8 | 9 | 10 | 11 | | | | | 1 | 6 | | 5 | |
| Apr 4 | (a) | Blackburn R | D | 0-0 | | 27,200 | | 2 | 3 | 4 | | | 7 | 8 | 9 | 10 | 11 | | | | | 1 | 6 | | 5 | |
| 11 | (h) | Newcastle U | D | 2-2 | Kevan 2 | 23,750 | | 2 | | 4 | | | 7 | 8 | 9 | 10 | 11 | | | | 3 | 1 | 6 | | 5 | |
| 15 | (h) | Luton T | W | 2-0 | Burnside, Allen | 19,293 | | 2 | 3 | 4 | 5 | | 7 | 8 | 9 | 10 | 11 | | | | | 1 | 6 | | | |
| 18 | (a) | Tottenham H | L | 0-5 | | 35,790 | | 2 | 3 | 4 | 5 | | 7 | 8 | 9 | 10 | 11 | | | | | 1 | 6 | | | |
| 22 | (a) | Chelsea | W | 2-0 | Burnside, Hogg | 31,948 | | 2 | | 4 | 5 | | 7 | 8 | 9 | 10 | 11 | | | | 3 | 1 | 6 | | | |
| 25 | (h) | Nottingham F | W | 2-0 | Campbell, Allen | 17,071 | | 2 | 3 | 4 | 5 | | 7 | 8 | 9 | 10 | 11 | | | | | 1 | 6 | | | |
| 29 | (h) | Aston Villa | D | 1-1 | Allen | 48,281 | | 2 | 3 | 4 | | | 7 | 8 | 9 | 10 | 11 | | | | | 1 | 6 | | 5 | |
| App | | | | | | | 12 | 40 | 40 | 41 | 36 | 13 | 26 | 29 | 36 | 41 | 40 | 18 | 27 | 1 | 4 | 30 | 6 | 9 | 10 | 3 |
| Goals | | | | | | | | 3 | | 2 | | | 9 | 4 | 17 | 27 | 5 | 2 | 12 | | | | 3 | | | 1 |

West Bromwich Albion players at marching exercises. From left to right are Ray Potter, Derek Hogg, Bobby Robson, Maurice Setters, Joe Kennedy, Stan Williams and Jimmy Dudley.

# 1959-60

## Division 1

| Date | V | Opponents | Res | Scorers | Att | Potter R | Howe D | Williams S | Setters M | Kennedy J | Barlow R | Allen R | Burnside D | Robson R | Kevan D | Dixon R | Hogg D | Dudley J | Jackson A | Aitken A | Styles A | Wallace J | Cram R | Williams G | Whitehouse B | Drury C | Smith K | Bannister J | Hope R | Carter G |
|---|---|---|---|---|---|---|---|---|---|---|---|---|---|---|---|---|---|---|---|---|---|---|---|---|---|---|---|---|---|---|
| Aug 22 | (h) | Manchester U | W 3-2 | Burnside 2, Foulkes (og) | 40,733 | 1 | 2 | 3 | 4 | 5 | 6 | 7 | 8 | 9 | 10 | 11 | | | | | | | | | | | | | | |
| 26 | (a) | Tottenham H | D 2-2 | Robson, Kevan | 54,114 | 1 | 2 | 3 | 4 | 5 | 6 | 7 | 8 | 9 | 10 | | 11 | | | | | | | | | | | | | |
| 29 | (a) | Preston NE | D 1-1 | Kevan | 24,876 | 1 | 2 | 3 | 4 | 5 | 6 | | 8 | 9 | 10 | 11 | 7 | | | | | | | | | | | | | |
| Sep 2 | (h) | Tottenham H | L 1-2 | Hogg | 35,924 | 1 | 2 | 3 | | 5 | 6 | | | 9 | 10 | 11 | 7 | 4 | 8 | | | | | | | | | | | |
| 5 | (h) | Leicester C | W 5-0 | Dixon, Kevan, Jackson, Robson 2 | 27,259 | 1 | 2 | 3 | 4 | 5 | 6 | | | 9 | 10 | 11 | 7 | | 8 | | | | | | | | | | | |
| 9 | (h) | Newcastle U | D 2-2 | Hogg, Kevan | 27,570 | 1 | 2 | 3 | 4 | 5 | | | 9 | 6 | 10 | 11 | 7 | | 8 | | | | | | | | | | | |
| 12 | (a) | Burnley | L 1-2 | Robson | 23,807 | 1 | 2 | 3 | 4 | 5 | | 7 | 8 | 6 | 9 | | | 11 | 10 | | | | | | | | | | | |
| 16 | (a) | Newcastle U | D 0-0 | | 39,266 | 1 | 2 | 3 | 4 | 5 | 6 | 7 | 8 | 9 | 10 | | | | | 11 | | | | | | | | | | |
| 19 | (h) | Leeds U | W 3-0 | Robson, Allen 2 | 26,369 | 1 | 2 | 3 | 4 | 5 | | 9 | | 6 | 10 | 11 | | | 8 | 7 | | | | | | | | | | |
| 26 | (a) | West Ham U | L 1-4 | Burnside | 30,570 | 1 | 2 | 3 | 4 | 5 | | 9 | 8 | 6 | 10 | | | | 7 | 11 | | | | | | | | | | |
| Oct 3 | (h) | Chelsea | L 1-3 | Jackson | 27,784 | 1 | 2 | 3 | 4 | 5 | | | 8 | 9 | 10 | | 11 | 6 | 7 | | | | | | | | | | | |
| 10 | (h) | Fulham | L 2-4 | Setters 2 | 20,395 | 1 | 2 | 3 | 4 | 5 | | 9 | 8 | | 10 | 11 | 7 | | | 6 | | | | | | | | | | |
| 17 | (a) | Bolton W | D 0-0 | | 22,581 | | | | 4 | 5 | | 9 | | 6 | 10 | 11 | | | 7 | | 8 | 1 | 2 | 3 | | | | | | |
| 24 | (h) | Luton T | W 4-0 | Allen 2, Whitehouse, Kevan | 22,445 | | 2 | 3 | 4 | 5 | | 9 | | 6 | 10 | | | | 7 | 11 | | 1 | | | 8 | | | | | |
| 31 | (a) | Sheffield W | L 0-2 | | 26,178 | | 2 | 3 | 4 | 5 | | 9 | | 6 | 10 | | | | 7 | 11 | | 1 | | | 8 | | | | | |
| Nov 7 | (h) | Blackpool | W 2-1 | Whitehouse, Jackson | 30,568 | | 2 | 3 | 4 | 5 | | 9 | | 6 | 10 | | | | 7 | 11 | | 1 | | | 8 | | | | | |
| 14 | (a) | Blackburn R | L 2-3 | Burnside, Whitehouse | 18,396 | | 2 | 3 | 4 | 5 | | | 9 | 6 | 10 | | | | 7 | 11 | | 1 | | | 8 | | | | | |
| 21 | (h) | Manchester C | W 2-0 | McTavish (og), Burnside | 24,219 | | 2 | 3 | 4 | 5 | | 9 | 8 | 6 | 10 | | 11 | | 7 | | | 1 | | | | | | | | |
| 28 | (a) | Arsenal | W 4-2 | Allen 2 (1 pen), Robson, Kevan | 41,147 | | 2 | 3 | 4 | 5 | | 9 | 8 | 6 | 10 | | 11 | | 7 | | | 1 | | | | | | | | |
| Dec 5 | (h) | Wolves | L 0-1 | | 40,739 | | 2 | 3 | 4 | 5 | | 9 | 8 | 6 | 10 | | 11 | | 7 | | | 1 | | | | | | | | |
| 12 | (a) | Everton | D 2-2 | Kevan, Burnside | 25,769 | | 2 | 3 | | 5 | | 9 | 8 | 6 | 10 | | 11 | | 7 | | | 1 | | | | 4 | | | | |
| 19 | (h) | Manchester U | W 3-2 | Hogg, Allen, Burnside | 33,677 | | 2 | 3 | | 5 | | 9 | 8 | 6 | 10 | | 11 | | 7 | | | 1 | | | | 4 | | | | |
| 26 | (h) | Nottingham F | L 2-3 | Kevan 2 | 28,817 | | 2 | 3 | 4 | 5 | | 9 | 8 | 6 | 10 | | 11 | | 7 | | | 1 | | | | | | | | |
| 28 | (a) | Nottingham F | W 2-1 | Hogg, Jackson | 34,608 | | 2 | | | 5 | | 9 | 8 | 6 | 10 | | 11 | | 7 | | | 1 | | 3 | | 4 | | | | |
| Jan 2 | (h) | Preston NE | W 4-0 | Richardson (og), Jackson, Kevan, Allen | 23,917 | | 2 | | | 5 | | 9 | 8 | 6 | 10 | | 11 | | 7 | | | 1 | | 3 | | 4 | | | | |
| 16 | (a) | Leicester C | W 1-0 | Jackson | 23,802 | | 2 | | | 5 | | 9 | 8 | 6 | 10 | | 11 | | 7 | | | 1 | | 3 | | 4 | | | | |
| 23 | (h) | Burnley | D 0-0 | | 23,512 | | 2 | | | 5 | | 9 | 8 | 6 | 10 | | 11 | | 7 | | | 1 | | 3 | | 4 | | | | |
| Feb 6 | (a) | Leeds U | W 4-1 | Burnside 2, Hogg, Kevan | 23,546 | | 2 | | | 5 | | 9 | 8 | 6 | 10 | | 11 | | 7 | | | 1 | | 3 | | 4 | | | | |
| 24 | (a) | Chelsea | D 2-2 | Kevan, Allen | 26,222 | | 2 | | | 5 | | 9 | 8 | 6 | 10 | | 11 | | 7 | | | 1 | | 3 | | 4 | | | | |
| 27 | (a) | Wolves | L 1-3 | Jackson | 49,791 | | 2 | | 4 | 5 | | 9 | 8 | 6 | 10 | | 11 | | 7 | | | 1 | | 3 | | | | | | |
| Mar 5 | (h) | Bolton W | D 1-1 | Kevan | 23,857 | | 2 | | | 5 | | 9 | 8 | 6 | 10 | | | | 7 | 11 | | 1 | | 3 | | 4 | | | | |
| 9 | (h) | West Ham U | W 3-2 | Kevan 2, Allen (pen) | 12,204 | | 2 | | | 5 | | 9 | 8 | 6 | 10 | | | | 7 | 11 | | 1 | | 3 | | 4 | | | | |
| 12 | (a) | Luton T | D 0-0 | | 18,825 | | 2 | | | 5 | | 9 | 8 | 6 | 10 | | | | 7 | 11 | | 1 | | 3 | | 4 | | | | |
| 19 | (h) | Everton | W 6-2 | Kevan 5, Burnside | 24,887 | | 2 | | | 5 | | 9 | 8 | 6 | 10 | | 11 | | 7 | | | 1 | | 3 | | 4 | | | | |
| 26 | (a) | Blackpool | L 0-2 | | 16,190 | | 2 | | | 5 | | 9 | 8 | 6 | 10 | | 11 | | 7 | | | 1 | | 3 | | 4 | | | | |
| Apr 2 | (h) | Blackburn R | W 2-0 | Kevan, Allen | 24,180 | | 2 | | | 5 | | 9 | | 6 | 10 | | 11 | | 7 | | | 1 | | 3 | | 4 | 8 | | | |
| 9 | (a) | Manchester C | W 1-0 | Jackson | 24,342 | | 2 | | | 5 | | 9 | | | 10 | | 11 | | 7 | | | 1 | | 3 | | 4 | 8 | 6 | | |
| 16 | (h) | Sheffield W | W 3-1 | Burnside, Kevan, Jackson | 27,899 | | 2 | | | 5 | | 9 | 8 | 6 | 10 | | 11 | | 7 | | | 1 | | 3 | | 4 | | | | |
| 18 | (a) | Birmingham C | W 7-1 | Allen 3 (1 pen), Jackson, Kevan 3 | 28,865 | | 2 | | | 5 | | 9 | 8 | 6 | 10 | | 11 | | 7 | | | 1 | | 3 | | 4 | | | | |
| 19 | (h) | Birmingham C | D 1-1 | Kevan | 37,937 | | 2 | | | 5 | | 9 | 8 | 6 | 10 | | 11 | | 7 | | | 1 | | 3 | | 4 | | | | |
| 23 | (a) | Fulham | L 1-2 | Allen | 23,631 | | 2 | | | 5 | | 9 | 8 | 6 | 10 | | 11 | | 7 | | | 1 | | 3 | | 4 | | | | |
| 30 | (h) | Arsenal | W 1-0 | Jackson | 26,380 | | 2 | | | 5 | | 9 | 8 | 6 | | | | | 7 | | | 1 | | 3 | | 4 | | | 10 | 11 |
| | | | | | App | 12 | 41 | 23 | 20 | 41 | 7 | 36 | 31 | 41 | 42 | 7 | 31 | 2 | 31 | 16 | 1 | 30 | 1 | 20 | 4 | 20 | 2 | 1 | 1 | 1 |
| | | | | | Goals | | | | 2 | | | 15 | 11 | 6 | 26 | 1 | 5 | | 11 | | | | | | 3 | | | | | |

**West Brom, 1959-60.** Back row (left to right): R.Dixon, D.Howe, R.Robson, J.Kennedy, M.Setters, B.Hughes. Second row: R.Barlow, R.Cram, J.Crosby, R.Potter, D.Burnside, R.Graham (trainer), D.Hogg, J.Dudley. Seated: A.Styles, J.Lovatt, G.Williams, Mr Gordon Clark (manager), D.Kevan, S.Williams, R.Allen. On ground: R.Hope, A.Jackson, K.Smith, B.Whitehouse, C.Drury.

# 1960-61

## Division 1

| Date | Opp | Result | Scorers | Att | Wallace J | Howe D | Williams G | Drury C | Kennedy J | Robson R | Jackson A | Burnside D | Allen R | Kevan D | Hope R | Billingham P | Jones S | Hogg D | Potter R | Williams S | Smith K | Bannister J | Aitken A | Carter G | Cram R | Macready B | Clark C | Lovatt J | Steele S |
|---|---|---|---|---|---|---|---|---|---|---|---|---|---|---|---|---|---|---|---|---|---|---|---|---|---|---|---|---|---|
| Aug 20 | (a) Sheffield W | L 0-1 | | 34,177 | 1 | 2 | 3 | 4 | 5 | 6 | 7 | 8 | 9 | 10 | 11 | | | | | | | | | | | | | | |
| 24 | (h) Birmingham C | L 1-2 | Jackson | 32,102 | 1 | 2 | 3 | 4 | 5 | 6 | 7 | 10 | 9 | 8 | 11 | | | | | | | | | | | | | | |
| 27 | (h) Fulham | L 2-4 | Jackson, Burnside | 20,609 | 1 | 2 | 3 | 4 | 5 | 6 | 7 | 10 | 9 | 8 | 11 | | | | | | | | | | | | | | |
| 31 | (a) Birmingham C | L 1-3 | Kevan | 37,740 | 1 | 2 | 3 | | | 6 | 7 | 8 | | 9 | 10 | 4 | 5 | 11 | | | | | | | | | | | |
| Sep 3 | (a) Preston NE | L 1-2 | Hogg | 18,476 | | 2 | 3 | 6 | | | 9 | 7 | 8 | | 10 | 4 | 5 | 11 | 1 | | | | | | | | | | |
| 5 | (h) Newcastle U | W 6-0 | Jackson 3, Robson, Kevan, Burnside | 22,548 | | 2 | | 4 | 5 | 6 | 7 | 8 | | 9 | 10 | | | 11 | 1 | 3 | | | | | | | | | |
| 10 | (h) Burnley | L 0-2 | | 26,407 | | 2 | | 4 | 5 | 6 | 7 | 8 | | 9 | 10 | | | 11 | 1 | 3 | | | | | | | | | |
| 14 | (a) Newcastle U | L 2-3 | Smith, Burnside | 16,107 | | 2 | | 4 | 5 | 6 | 7 | 8 | 9 | | | | | 11 | 1 | 3 | 10 | | | | | | | | |
| 17 | (a) Nottingham F | W 2-1 | Allen, Kevan | 22,791 | | 2 | 3 | 4 | 5 | 6 | 7 | 8 | 9 | 10 | | | | 11 | 1 | | | | | | | | | | |
| 24 | (h) Manchester C | W 6-3 | Allen 3, Kevan 2, Burnside | 25,163 | | 2 | 3 | 4 | 5 | 6 | 7 | 8 | 9 | 10 | | | | 11 | 1 | | | | | | | | | | |
| Oct 1 | (a) Arsenal | L 0-1 | | 27,176 | | 2 | 3 | 4 | 5 | 6 | 7 | 8 | 9 | 10 | | | | 11 | 1 | | | | | | | | | | |
| 8 | (a) Bolton W | W 1-0 | Allen | 18,672 | | 2 | 3 | | 5 | | 10 | 8 | 9 | | | 4 | | 11 | 1 | | | 7 | 6 | | | | | | |
| 15 | (h) West Ham U | W 1-0 | Robson | 22,009 | | 2 | 3 | | 5 | 6 | 10 | 8 | 9 | | | 4 | | 11 | 1 | | | 7 | | | | | | | |
| 22 | (a) Leicester C | D 2-2 | Burnside, Aitken | 20,770 | | 2 | | | 5 | 6 | | 8 | 9 | 10 | | 4 | | | 1 | 3 | | | 7 | 11 | | | | | |
| 29 | (h) Aston Villa | L 0-2 | | 41,903 | | 2 | 3 | 4 | 5 | 6 | 7 | 8 | 9 | 10 | | | | | 1 | | | | | 11 | | | | | |
| Nov 5 | (a) Everton | D 1-1 | Jackson | 40,705 | | 2 | 3 | 4 | 5 | 8 | 7 | 10 | 9 | | | | | | 1 | | | | 6 | 11 | | | | | |
| 12 | (h) Blackburn R | L 1-2 | Burnside | 18,701 | | 2 | 3 | 6 | 5 | 8 | 7 | 10 | 9 | | | 4 | | | 1 | | | | | 11 | | | | | |
| 19 | (a) Manchester U | L 0-3 | | 32,756 | 1 | 2 | 3 | 4 | 5 | 6 | 7 | 8 | 9 | | 10 | | | | | | | | | 11 | | | | | |
| 26 | (h) Tottenham H | L 1-3 | Howe | 39,017 | 1 | 8 | 11 | 4 | 5 | 6 | 7 | | 9 | 10 | | | 3 | | | | | | | 2 | | | | | |
| Dec 3 | (a) Chelsea | L 1-7 | Jackson | 19,568 | 1 | 8 | 11 | 4 | 5 | 6 | 7 | | 9 | 10 | | | 3 | | | | | | | 2 | | | | | |
| 10 | (h) Blackpool | W 3-1 | Kevan 2, Jackson | 15,099 | 1 | 2 | 3 | 6 | 5 | 4 | 8 | 10 | | 9 | | | | | | | | 11 | | | | 7 | | | |
| 17 | (h) Sheffield W | D 2-2 | Aitken, Burnside | 17,862 | 1 | 2 | 3 | 6 | 5 | 4 | 8 | 10 | | 9 | | | | | | | | 11 | | | | 7 | | | |
| 26 | (a) Cardiff C | L 1-3 | Macready | 30,103 | 1 | 2 | 3 | 6 | 5 | 4 | 8 | 10 | | 9 | | | | | | | | 11 | | | | 7 | | | |
| 27 | (h) Cardiff C | D 1-1 | Kevan | 30,131 | | 2 | 3 | | 5 | 4 | 10 | | 11 | 9 | | | | | 1 | 8 | 6 | | | | | 7 | | | |
| 31 | (h) Fulham | W 2-1 | Kevan, Burnside | 18,080 | | 2 | 3 | | 6 | 5 | 4 | 11 | 8 | 9 | 10 | | | | 1 | | | | | | | 7 | | | |
| Jan 14 | (h) Preston NE | W 3-1 | Jackson 2, Howe (pen) | 19,639 | | 2 | 3 | | 6 | 5 | 4 | 9 | 8 | 10 | | | | | 1 | | | | | | | 7 | 11 | | |
| 21 | (a) Burnley | W 1-0 | Kevan | 15,305 | | 2 | 3 | | 6 | 5 | 4 | 9 | 8 | 10 | | | | | 1 | | | | | | | 7 | 11 | | |
| 28 | (a) Wolves | L 2-4 | Kevan, Burnside | 31,385 | | 2 | 3 | | 6 | 5 | 4 | 9 | 8 | 10 | | | | | 1 | | | | | | | 7 | 11 | | |
| Feb 4 | (h) Nottingham F | L 1-2 | Burnside | 24,927 | 1 | 2 | 3 | 6 | 5 | 4 | 9 | 8 | | 10 | | | | | | | | 7 | | | | | 11 | | |
| 11 | (a) Manchester C | L 0-3 | | 21,382 | | 2 | 3 | 6 | 5 | 4 | 9 | 8 | | 10 | | | | | 1 | | 10 | | | | | 7 | 11 | | |
| 18 | (h) Arsenal | L 2-3 | Jackson, Robson | 21,962 | | 8 | 3 | 6 | 5 | 4 | 7 | | 9 | 10 | | | | | 1 | | | | | 2 | | | 11 | | |
| 25 | (h) Bolton W | W 3-2 | Allen, Hope, Burnside | 15,171 | 1 | 2 | | 6 | | 4 | 7 | 8 | 9 | | 10 | | 5 | | | | | 3 | | | | | 11 | | |
| Mar 4 | (a) West Ham U | W 2-1 | Lovatt, Hope | 21,607 | 1 | 2 | | 6 | | 4 | 7 | 8 | | | 10 | | 5 | | | | | 3 | | | | | 11 | 9 | |
| 11 | (h) Leicester C | W 1-0 | Clark | 25,168 | 1 | 2 | | 6 | | 4 | 7 | 8 | | | 10 | | 5 | | | | | 3 | | | | | 11 | 9 | |
| 25 | (h) Everton | W 3-0 | Kevan 2, Jackson | 20,590 | 1 | 2 | 3 | 6 | | 4 | 7 | 8 | | 10 | | | 5 | | | | | | | | | | 11 | 9 | |
| 28 | (a) Aston Villa | W 1-0 | Lovatt | 42,800 | 1 | 2 | 3 | 6 | | 4 | 7 | 8 | | 10 | | | 5 | | | | | | | | | | 11 | 9 | |
| Apr 1 | (a) Blackpool | W 1-0 | Lovatt | 20,809 | 1 | 2 | | 6 | | 4 | 7 | 8 | | 10 | | | 5 | | | 11 | | | | | | | | 9 | |
| 3 | (h) Wolves | W 2-1 | Kevan, Burnside | 34,108 | 1 | 2 | | 6 | | 4 | 7 | 8 | | 10 | | | 5 | | | 11 | | | | | | | | 9 | |
| 8 | (h) Manchester U | D 1-1 | Howe | 28,033 | 1 | 2 | 3 | 6 | | 4 | 7 | 8 | | 10 | | | 5 | | | | | | | | | | 11 | 9 | |
| 15 | (a) Blackburn R | L 1-2 | Kevan | 14,600 | 1 | 2 | 3 | 6 | | | 7 | | | 10 | | 4 | 5 | | | | | | | | | | 11 | 9 | 8 |
| 22 | (h) Chelsea | W 3-0 | Kevan 2, Robson | 17,691 | 1 | 2 | | 6 | | 4 | 7 | | | 10 | 8 | | 5 | | | | | 3 | | | | | 11 | 9 | |
| 29 | (a) Tottenham H | W 2-1 | Kevan, Robson | 52,054 | 1 | 2 | | 6 | | 4 | 7 | | | 10 | 8 | | 5 | | | | | | | | | | 11 | 9 | |
| **App** | | | | | 22 | 42 | 31 | 37 | 29 | 40 | 41 | 35 | 20 | 32 | 12 | 7 | 13 | 10 | 20 | 13 | 5 | 5 | 6 | 6 | 6 | 3 | 9 | 15 | 10 |
| **Goals** | | | | | | 3 | | | | 5 | 12 | 12 | 6 | 18 | 2 | | | 1 | | | 1 | | 2 | | | 1 | 1 | 3 | |

**Albion's 1960-61 line-up. Back row (left to right): Gordon Clark (manager), 'Chuck' Drury, Stuart Williams, Don Howe, Jock Wallace, Joe Kennedy, Bobby Robson, Dick Graham (trainer), Graham Williams. Front row: Alec Jackson, Davy Burnside, Ronnie Allen, Derek Kevan, Derek Hogg.**

# 1961-62

### Division 1

| Date | | Opponent | Result | Scorers | Att. | Wallace J | Howe D | Williams S | Robson R | Jones S | Drury C | Jackson A | Burnside D | Lovatt J | Kevan D | Clark C | Hope R | Smith K | Potter R | Millington A | Carter G | Cram R | Bannister J | Williams G |
|---|---|---|---|---|---|---|---|---|---|---|---|---|---|---|---|---|---|---|---|---|---|---|---|---|
| Aug 19 | (h) | Sheffield W | L 0-2 | | 25,464 | 1 | 2 | 3 | 4 | 5 | 6 | 7 | 8 | 9 | 10 | 11 | | | | | | | | |
| 23 | (h) | Everton | W 2-0 | Robson, Kevan | 21,594 | 1 | 2 | 3 | 4 | 5 | 6 | 7 | 8 | 9 | 10 | 11 | | | | | | | | |
| 26 | (a) | Leicester C | L 0-1 | | 20,899 | 1 | 2 | 3 | 4 | 5 | 6 | 7 | 8 | 9 | 10 | 11 | | | | | | | | |
| 30 | (a) | Everton | L 1-3 | Robson | 36,586 | 1 | 2 | 3 | 4 | 5 | 6 | 7 | | 9 | 10 | 11 | 8 | | | | | | | |
| Sep 2 | (h) | Ipswich T | L 1-3 | Jackson | 19,016 | 1 | 2 | 3 | 4 | 5 | 6 | 7 | | | 10 | 11 | 8 | 9 | | | | | | |
| 6 | (h) | Birmingham C | D 0-0 | | 20,541 | 1 | 2 | 3 | 4 | 5 | 6 | 7 | | | 10 | 11 | 8 | 9 | | | | | | |
| 9 | (a) | Burnley | L 1-3 | Burnside | 21,809 | | 2 | 3 | 4 | 5 | 6 | 7 | 9 | | 10 | 11 | 8 | | | 1 | | | | |
| 16 | (h) | Arsenal | W 4-0 | Clark, Jackson, Burnside, Kevan | 20,298 | | 2 | 3 | 4 | 5 | 6 | 7 | 9 | | 10 | 11 | 8 | | | 1 | | | | |
| 20 | (a) | Birmingham C | W 2-1 | Burnside, Kevan | 22,902 | | 2 | 3 | 4 | 5 | 6 | 7 | 9 | | 10 | 11 | 8 | | | 1 | | | | |
| 23 | (a) | Bolton W | L 2-3 | Kevan, Hope | 14,155 | | 2 | 3 | 4 | 5 | 6 | 7 | 9 | | 10 | 11 | 8 | | | 1 | | | | |
| 30 | (h) | Manchester C | D 2-2 | Kevan 2 | 20,820 | | 2 | 3 | 4 | 5 | 6 | 7 | 9 | | 10 | 11 | 8 | | | 1 | | | | |
| Oct 7 | (h) | Manchester U | D 1-1 | Kevan | 25,645 | | 2 | 3 | 4 | 5 | 6 | 7 | 9 | | 10 | 11 | 8 | | | 1 | | | | |
| 18 | (a) | Cardiff C | D 2-2 | Williams, Smith | 20,009 | | 2 | 3 | 4 | 5 | 6 | 7 | 8 | | 10 | 11 | | 9 | | 1 | | | | |
| 21 | (h) | Aston Villa | D 1-1 | Jackson | 39,071 | | 2 | 3 | 4 | 5 | 6 | 7 | 8 | | 10 | 11 | | 9 | | 1 | | | | |
| 28 | (a) | Nottingham F | D 4-4 | Howe (pen), Clark, Kevan, Smith | 20,424 | | 2 | 3 | 4 | 5 | 6 | 7 | 8 | | 10 | 11 | | 9 | | 1 | | | | |
| Nov 4 | (h) | Blackburn R | W 4-0 | Kevan, Jackson, Smith 2 | 17,298 | | 2 | 3 | 4 | 5 | 6 | 7 | 8 | | 10 | 11 | | 9 | | 1 | | | | |
| 11 | (a) | West Ham U | D 3-3 | Jackson, Howe (pen), Kevan | 18,213 | | 2 | 3 | 4 | 5 | 6 | 7 | 8 | | 10 | 11 | | 9 | | 1 | | | | |
| 18 | (h) | Sheffield U | W 3-1 | Kevan 3 | 19,392 | | 2 | 3 | 4 | 5 | 6 | 7 | 8 | | 10 | | | 9 | 11 | 1 | | | | |
| 25 | (a) | Chelsea | L 1-4 | Smith | 25,025 | | 2 | 3 | 4 | 5 | 6 | 7 | 8 | | 10 | 11 | | 9 | | 1 | | | | |
| Dec 2 | (h) | Tottenham H | L 2-4 | Kevan, Smith | 28,701 | | 2 | 3 | 4 | 5 | 6 | 7 | 8 | | 10 | 11 | | 9 | | 1 | | | | |
| 9 | (a) | Blackpool | D 2-2 | Burnside, Kevan | 13,076 | | 2 | 3 | 4 | 5 | 6 | 7 | 8 | | 10 | 11 | | 9 | | 1 | | | | |
| 16 | (a) | Sheffield W | L 1-2 | Smith | 25,168 | | 2 | 3 | 4 | 5 | 6 | 7 | 8 | | 10 | 11 | | 9 | | 1 | | | | |
| 23 | (h) | Leicester C | W 2-0 | Kevan, Smith | 14,286 | | 2 | 3 | 4 | 5 | 6 | 7 | 8 | | 10 | 11 | | 9 | | 1 | | | | |
| 26 | (h) | Wolves | D 1-1 | Kevan | 24,778 | 1 | 2 | 3 | 4 | 5 | 6 | 7 | 8 | | 10 | 11 | | 9 | | | | | | |
| Jan 13 | (a) | Ipswich T | L 0-3 | | 18,378 | 1 | 2 | 3 | 4 | 5 | 6 | 7 | 8 | | 10 | 11 | | 9 | | | | | | |
| 20 | (h) | Burnley | D 1-1 | Smith | 22,141 | 1 | 2 | 3 | 4 | 5 | 6 | 7 | 8 | | 10 | 11 | | 9 | | | | | | |
| Feb 3 | (a) | Arsenal | W 1-0 | Clark | 29,597 | 1 | 2 | 3 | 4 | 5 | 6 | 7 | 8 | | 10 | 11 | | 9 | | | | | | |
| 10 | (h) | Bolton W | W 6-2 | Smith 2, Hope, Williams, Kevan 2 | 20,226 | 1 | 2 | 3 | 4 | 5 | 6 | 7 | 8 | | 10 | | 11 | 9 | | | | | | |
| 21 | (a) | Manchester C | L 1-3 | Kevan | 17,225 | 1 | 4 | 3 | 6 | 5 | | 7 | 8 | | 10 | 11 | | 9 | | | | 2 | | |
| 24 | (a) | Manchester U | L 1-4 | Jackson | 31,456 | | 4 | 3 | | 5 | 6 | 7 | 8 | | 10 | 11 | | 9 | | 1 | | 2 | | |
| Mar 3 | (h) | Cardiff C | W 5-1 | Kevan 2, Clark, Smith, Howe (pen) | 13,894 | | 4 | 3 | | 5 | | 7 | 8 | | 10 | 11 | | 9 | | 1 | | 2 | 6 | |
| 4 | (a) | Aston Villa | L 0-1 | | 35,104 | 1 | 2 | 3 | 4 | 5 | 6 | 7 | 8 | | 10 | 11 | | 9 | | | | | | |
| 17 | (h) | Nottingham F | D 2-2 | Smith 2 | 16,794 | 1 | 2 | 3 | 4 | 5 | 6 | 7 | 8 | | 10 | 11 | | 9 | | | | | | |
| 24 | (a) | Blackburn R | D 1-1 | Jackson | 11,576 | | 4 | 3 | | 5 | 6 | 7 | | | 10 | 11 | 8 | 9 | | 1 | | 2 | | |
| 28 | (a) | Wolves | W 5-1 | Robson, Drury, Smith, Kevan, Thomson (og) | 20,058 | | 2 | | 4 | 5 | 6 | 7 | | | 10 | 11 | 8 | 9 | | 1 | | | | 3 |
| 31 | (h) | West Ham U | L 0-1 | | 16,937 | | 2 | | 4 | 5 | 6 | 7 | | | 10 | 11 | 8 | 9 | | 1 | | | | 3 |
| Apr 7 | (a) | Sheffield U | D 1-1 | Smith | 18,697 | | 2 | | 4 | 5 | 6 | 7 | | | 10 | 11 | 8 | 9 | | 1 | | | | 3 |
| 14 | (h) | Chelsea | W 4-0 | Kevan 2, Smith, Howe | 14,573 | | 2 | | 4 | 5 | 6 | 7 | | | 10 | 11 | 8 | 9 | | 1 | | | | 3 |
| 21 | (a) | Tottenham H | W 2-1 | Kevan 2 | 53,512 | | 2 | | 4 | 5 | 6 | 7 | | | 10 | 11 | 8 | 9 | | 1 | | | | 3 |
| 23 | (a) | Fulham | W 2-1 | Lovatt, Jackson | 29,322 | | 2 | | 4 | 5 | 6 | 7 | | 9 | 10 | 11 | 8 | | | 1 | | | | 3 |
| 24 | (h) | Fulham | W 2-0 | Kevan 2 | 22,022 | | 2 | | 4 | 5 | 6 | 7 | | 9 | 10 | 11 | 8 | | | 1 | | | | 3 |
| 28 | (h) | Blackpool | W 7-1 | Kevan 4, Lovatt, Robson, Howe | 17,462 | | 2 | | 4 | 5 | 6 | 7 | | 9 | 10 | 11 | 8 | | | 1 | | | | 3 |
| **App** | | | | | | 17 | 42 | 34 | 39 | 42 | 40 | 42 | 30 | 7 | 42 | 39 | 20 | 29 | 1 | 24 | 1 | 4 | 1 | 8 |
| **Goals** | | | | | | | 5 | 2 | 4 | | 1 | 8 | 4 | 2 | 33 | 4 | 2 | 17 | | | | | | |

Albion's professional squad in 1961. Back row (left to right): J.Lovatt, P.Billingham, S.Jones, R.Potter, W.Dixon (trainer), J.Wallace, D.Kevan, S.Williams, R.Cram. Middle row: C.Clark, G.Williams, C.Drury, R.Robson, Gordon Clark (manager), D.Howe, A.Jackson, D.Burnside. Front row: K.Smith, G.Carter, R.Hope, C.Brookes, J.Bannister, B.Macready.

# 1962-63

### Division 1

Player columns (left to right): Millington A, Howe D, Williams G, Williams S, Jones S, Drury C, Jackson A, Burnside D, Smith K, Kevan D, Clark C, Potter R, Hope R, Cram R, Foggo K, Carter G, Lovatt J, Bannister J, Murray M, Fenton R, Bradley R, Macready B, Fairfax R

| Date | | Opponent | Result | Scorers | Att. | Mil A | Howe D | Wil G | Wil S | Jon S | Dru C | Jac A | Bur D | Smi K | Kev D | Cla C | Pot R | Hop R | Cra R | Fog K | Car G | Lov J | Ban J | Mur M | Fen R | Bra R | Mac B | Fai R |
|---|---|---|---|---|---|---|---|---|---|---|---|---|---|---|---|---|---|---|---|---|---|---|---|---|---|---|---|---|
| Aug 18 | (a) | Manchester U | D 2-2 | Kevan, Smith | 51,685 | 1 | 2 | 3 | 4 | 5 | 6 | 7 | 8 | 9 | 10 | 11 | | | | | | | | | | | | |
| 22 | (h) | Leyton O | W 2-1 | Smith, Kevan | 22,409 | 1 | 2 | 3 | 4 | 5 | 6 | 7 | 8 | 9 | 10 | 11 | | | | | | | | | | | | |
| 25 | (h) | Burnley | L 1-2 | Smith | 24,040 | | 2 | 3 | 4 | 5 | 6 | 7 | | 9 | 10 | 11 | 1 | 8 | | | | | | | | | | |
| 29 | (a) | Leyton O | W 3-2 | Lewis (og), Jackson, Clark | 17,284 | | 2 | 3 | 4 | 5 | 6 | 7 | | 9 | 10 | 11 | 1 | 8 | | | | | | | | | | |
| Sep 1 | (a) | Sheffield W | L 1-3 | Jackson | 23,042 | | 2 | 3 | 4 | 5 | 6 | 7 | | 9 | 10 | 11 | 1 | 8 | | | | | | | | | | |
| 8 | (h) | Fulham | W 6-1 | Kevan 4, Smith 2 | 19,304 | 1 | 2 | 3 | | 5 | 6 | 7 | | 9 | 10 | 11 | | | 4 | 8 | | | | | | | | |
| 12 | (h) | Birmingham C | W 1-0 | Jackson | 25,499 | 1 | 2 | 3 | | 5 | 6 | 7 | | 9 | 10 | 11 | | | 4 | 8 | | | | | | | | |
| 15 | (a) | Leicester C | L 0-1 | | 21,517 | 1 | 2 | 3 | | 5 | 6 | 7 | | 9 | 10 | 11 | | | 4 | 8 | | | | | | | | |
| 19 | (a) | Birmingham C | D 0-0 | | 28,625 | 1 | 2 | 3 | | 5 | 6 | 7 | | 9 | 10 | | | | 4 | 8 | 11 | | | | | | | |
| 22 | (h) | Bolton W | W 5-4 | Kevan 3, Foggo, Howe (pen) | 18,670 | 1 | 2 | 3 | | 5 | 6 | 7 | | 9 | 10 | | | | 4 | 8 | 11 | | | | | | | |
| 29 | (a) | Everton | L 2-4 | Harris (og), Jackson | 45,471 | 1 | 2 | 3 | | 5 | 6 | 7 | | 9 | 10 | 11 | | | 4 | 8 | | | | | | | | |
| Oct 6 | (a) | Aston Villa | L 0-2 | | 43,613 | 1 | 2 | 3 | | 5 | | 7 | | | 10 | 11 | | | 8 | 4 | 9 | | 6 | | | | | |
| 13 | (h) | Tottenham H | L 1-2 | Jackson | 32,450 | 1 | 2 | 3 | | 5 | | | | 9 | 10 | | | 8 | 4 | 7 | 11 | | 6 | | | | | |
| 20 | (a) | Ipswich T | D 1-1 | Kevan | 19,142 | | 2 | 3 | | 5 | 6 | | | 9 | 10 | | 1 | 8 | 4 | 7 | 11 | | | | | | | |
| 27 | (h) | Liverpool | W 1-0 | Kevan | 17,852 | 1 | 2 | 3 | | 5 | 6 | 7 | | 9 | 10 | 11 | | 8 | 4 | | | | | | | | | |
| Nov 3 | (a) | Blackpool | W 2-0 | Jackson, Hope | 12,865 | 1 | 2 | 3 | | 5 | 6 | 7 | | 9 | 10 | 11 | | 8 | 4 | | | | | | | | | |
| 10 | (h) | Blackburn R | L 2-5 | Carter, Hope | 14,103 | 1 | 2 | 3 | | 5 | 6 | 7 | | 9 | 10 | | | 8 | 4 | | 11 | | | | | | | |
| 17 | (a) | Sheffield U | L 0-1 | | 17,895 | 1 | 2 | 3 | | 5 | 6 | 7 | | 9 | 10 | 11 | | 8 | 4 | | | | | | | | | |
| 24 | (h) | Nottingham F | L 1-4 | Jackson | 18,670 | 1 | 2 | 3 | | 5 | 6 | 7 | | | 10 | 11 | | 8 | 4 | | | | | 9 | | | | |
| Dec 1 | (a) | West Ham U | D 2-2 | Smith 2 | 20,391 | | 2 | 3 | | 5 | 6 | 7 | | 9 | 10 | 11 | 1 | | 4 | | | | | | 8 | | | |
| 8 | (h) | Manchester C | W 2-1 | Smith 2 | 12,402 | | 2 | 3 | | 5 | | 7 | | 9 | 10 | 11 | 1 | | 4 | | 6 | | | | 8 | | | |
| 15 | (h) | Manchester U | W 3-0 | Cram, Smith, Jackson | 17,595 | | 2 | 3 | | 5 | 6 | 7 | | 9 | 10 | 11 | 1 | | 4 | | | | | | 8 | | | |
| Jan 12 | (h) | Sheffield W | L 0-3 | | 15,712 | | 2 | 3 | | 5 | 6 | 7 | | 9 | 10 | 11 | 1 | | 4 | | | | | | 8 | | | |
| Mar 2 | (a) | Tottenham H | L 1-2 | Fenton | 40,590 | | 2 | 3 | | 5 | 6 | | | | 10 | 11 | 1 | | 4 | | | | | 9 | 8 | | | 7 |
| 9 | (h) | Ipswich T | W 6-1 | Kevan 3, Jackson, Clark, Smith | 10,759 | | 2 | 3 | | 5 | 6 | 7 | | 9 | 10 | 11 | 1 | | 4 | | | | | | 8 | | | |
| 16 | (a) | Wolves | L 0-7 | | 22,618 | 1 | 2 | 3 | | 5 | | | | 9 | | 11 | | 10 | 4 | 7 | | | | | 8 | | | 6 |
| 20 | (a) | Liverpool | D 2-2 | Fenton, Smith | 43,987 | | 2 | | | 5 | | | | 9 | | 11 | 1 | 10 | 4 | 7 | | | | | 8 | 3 | | 6 |
| 23 | (h) | Blackpool | L 1-2 | Jones | 15,202 | | 2 | 3 | | 5 | | | | 9 | | 11 | 1 | 10 | 4 | 7 | | | | | 8 | | | 6 |
| 25 | (a) | Bolton W | W 2-1 | Cram, Hope | 14,895 | | | 3 | | 5 | | | | 9 | | 11 | 1 | 10 | 4 | 7 | | | | | 8 | 2 | | 6 |
| Apr 3 | (h) | Wolves | D 2-2 | Cram, Hope | 15,517 | | 2 | | | 5 | | | | 9 | | 11 | 1 | 10 | 4 | 7 | | | | | 8 | 3 | | 6 |
| 6 | (a) | Sheffield U | L 1-2 | Cram | 12,497 | | | 3 | | 5 | | | | 9 | | 11 | 1 | 10 | 4 | 7 | | | | | 8 | 2 | | 6 |
| 12 | (a) | Arsenal | L 2-3 | Hope, Jackson | 28,219 | | 2 | 3 | | 5 | | 8 | | | | 11 | 1 | 10 | 4 | 7 | 6 | | | | 9 | | | |
| 13 | (a) | Blackburn R | L 1-3 | Hope | 11,525 | | | 3 | | 5 | | 8 | | 9 | | 11 | 1 | 10 | 4 | 7 | 6 | | | | | 2 | | |
| 15 | (h) | Arsenal | L 1-2 | Fenton | 16,597 | | | 3 | | 5 | | 8 | | | | 11 | 1 | 10 | 4 | 7 | | | | | 9 | 2 | | 6 |
| 20 | (h) | West Ham U | W 5-1 | Fenton, Foggo 2, Clark, Jackson | 11,192 | | 2 | 3 | | 5 | | 8 | | | | 11 | 1 | 10 | 4 | 7 | | | | | 9 | | | 6 |
| 27 | (a) | Manchester C | W 5-1 | Fenton, Foggo 2, Clark, Jackson | 14,995 | | 2 | 3 | | 5 | | 8 | | | | 11 | 1 | 10 | 4 | 7 | | | | | 9 | | | 6 |
| 30 | (a) | Burnley | L 1-2 | Fenton | 15,971 | | 2 | 3 | | 5 | | 8 | | | | 11 | 1 | 10 | 4 | 7 | | | | | 9 | | | 6 |
| May 4 | (h) | Leicester C | W 2-1 | Fenton, Howe (pen) | 20,564 | | 2 | 3 | | 5 | | 8 | | | | 11 | 1 | 10 | 4 | 7 | | | | | 9 | | | 6 |
| 7 | (h) | Everton | L 0-4 | | 24,730 | | 2 | 3 | | 5 | | 8 | | | | 11 | 1 | 10 | 4 | 7 | | | | | 9 | | | 6 |
| 11 | (h) | Aston Villa | W 1-0 | Jackson | 25,617 | | 2 | 3 | | 5 | 6 | 8 | | | | 11 | 1 | 10 | 4 | 7 | | | | | 9 | | | |
| 14 | (a) | Nottingham F | D 2-2 | Clark 2 | 13,048 | | 2 | 3 | | 5 | 6 | 8 | | | | 11 | 1 | 10 | 4 | 7 | | | | | 9 | | | |
| 18 | (a) | Fulham | D 2-2 | Jackson, Fenton | 17,481 | | 4 | 3 | | 5 | 6 | 8 | | | | 11 | 1 | 10 | | 7 | | | | | 9 | 2 | | |
| App | | | | | | 16 | 38 | 40 | 5 | 40 | 27 | 35 | 2 | 27 | 25 | 36 | 26 | 28 | 36 | 25 | 6 | 1 | 4 | 3 | 21 | 13 | 1 | 7 |
| Goals | | | | | | | 2 | | | 1 | | 14 | | 12 | 14 | 5 | | 6 | 4 | 3 | 1 | | | | 7 | | | |

**Don Howe (left) and 'Chuck' Drury move in to challenge Denis Law during the Manchester United-Albion game at Old Trafford in August 1962.**

# 1963-64

## Division 1

| Date | | Opponent | Result | Scorers | Att | Potter R | Howe D | Williams G | Cram R | Jones S | Simpson T | Foggo K | Fenton R | Kaye J | Hope R | Clark C | Jackson A | Readfern E | Crawford C | Fraser D | Brown T | Fairfax R | Drury C | Macready B | Carter G | Fudge M | Howshall G |
|---|---|---|---|---|---|---|---|---|---|---|---|---|---|---|---|---|---|---|---|---|---|---|---|---|---|---|---|
| Aug 24 | (h) | Leicester C | D 1-1 | Fenton | 23,078 | 1 | 2 | 3 | 4 | 5 | 6 | 7 | 8 | 9 | 10 | 11 | | | | | | | | | | | |
| 27 | (a) | Arsenal | L 2-3 | Clark, Kaye | 31,381 | 1 | 2 | 3 | 4 | 5 | 6 | 7 | 10 | 9 | | 11 | 8 | | | | | | | | | | |
| 31 | (a) | Bolton W | W 2-1 | Williams, Fenton | 14,170 | 1 | 2 | 3 | 4 | 5 | 6 | 7 | 10 | 9 | | 11 | 8 | | | | | | | | | | |
| Sep 4 | (h) | Arsenal | W 4-0 | Foggo 2, Kaye, Clark | 20,258 | 1 | 2 | 3 | 4 | 5 | 6 | 7 | 10 | 9 | | 11 | 8 | | | | | | | | | | |
| 7 | (h) | Fulham | W 3-0 | Jackson, Clark, Foggo | 17,995 | 1 | 2 | 3 | 4 | 5 | 6 | 7 | 10 | 9 | | 11 | 8 | | | | | | | | | | |
| 11 | (a) | Birmingham C | W 1-0 | Foggo | 34,666 | 1 | 2 | 3 | 4 | 5 | 6 | 7 | 10 | | | 11 | 8 | 9 | | | | | | | | | |
| 14 | (a) | Manchester U | L 0-1 | | 50,453 | 1 | 4 | 3 | 8 | 5 | 6 | 7 | 10 | | | 11 | | 9 | 2 | | | | | | | | |
| 18 | (h) | Birmingham C | W 3-1 | Foggo, Clark, Jackson | 29,662 | 1 | 2 | 3 | | 5 | 6 | 7 | 10 | | | 11 | 8 | 9 | | 4 | | | | | | | |
| 21 | (h) | Burnley | D 0-0 | | 24,591 | 1 | 2 | 3 | | 5 | 6 | 7 | 10 | | | 11 | 8 | 9 | | 4 | | | | | | | |
| 28 | (a) | Ipswich T | W 2-1 | Brown, Clark | 13,765 | 1 | 2 | 3 | | 5 | 6 | 7 | | 9 | | 11 | 10 | | | 4 | 8 | | | | | | |
| Oct 2 | (a) | Wolves | D 0-0 | | 37,038 | 1 | 2 | 3 | | 5 | 6 | 7 | 10 | 9 | | 11 | 8 | | | 4 | | | | | | | |
| 5 | (h) | Sheffield W | L 1-3 | Clark | 21,145 | 1 | 2 | 3 | | 5 | 6 | 7 | 10 | 9 | | 11 | 8 | | 2 | 4 | | | | | | | |
| 12 | (h) | Aston Villa | W 4-3 | Cram, Jackson, Brown, Foggo | 28,602 | 1 | | | 9 | 5 | 6 | 7 | | | | 11 | 10 | | 2 | 4 | 8 | 3 | | | | | |
| 19 | (a) | Liverpool | L 0-1 | | 43,009 | 1 | | 3 | 9 | 5 | 6 | 7 | | | | 11 | 10 | | | 4 | 8 | | 2 | | | | |
| 26 | (h) | Stoke C | L 2-3 | Williams, Foggo | 23,973 | 1 | | 3 | 9 | 5 | 6 | 7 | | | | 11 | 10 | | | 4 | 8 | | 2 | | | | |
| Nov 2 | (a) | West Ham U | L 2-4 | Foggo, Cram | 22,888 | 1 | 2 | 3 | 9 | 5 | 6 | 7 | | | | 11 | 10 | | | 4 | 8 | | | | | | |
| 9 | (h) | Chelsea | D 1-1 | Simpson | 16,267 | 1 | | 3 | 9 | 5 | 6 | 7 | 8 | | | 11 | 10 | | 2 | 4 | | | | | | | |
| 16 | (a) | Blackpool | L 0-1 | | 11,047 | 1 | 2 | 3 | | 5 | 6 | 7 | 8 | 9 | 10 | 11 | | | | 4 | | | | | | | |
| 23 | (h) | Blackburn R | L 1-3 | Fenton | 16,441 | 1 | 2 | 3 | | 5 | 6 | | 8 | 9 | 10 | 7 | | | | 4 | | | | | 11 | | |
| 30 | (a) | Nottingham F | W 3-0 | Fenton, Clark, Carter | 19,025 | 1 | 2 | 3 | | 5 | 6 | | 8 | 9 | 10 | 7 | | | | 4 | | | | | 11 | | |
| Dec 7 | (h) | Sheffield U | W 2-0 | Kaye, Clark | 14,149 | 1 | 2 | 3 | | 5 | 6 | | 8 | 9 | | 7 | | | | 4 | | | | 11 | | 10 | |
| 14 | (a) | Leicester C | W 2-0 | Fraser, Foggo | 17,740 | 1 | 2 | 3 | | 5 | 6 | 7 | 8 | 9 | | 11 | | | | 4 | | | | | | 10 | |
| 21 | (h) | Bolton W | D 1-1 | Kaye | 10,715 | 1 | 2 | 3 | | 5 | 6 | 7 | 8 | 9 | | 11 | | | | 4 | | | | | | 10 | |
| 26 | (h) | Tottenham H | D 4-4 | Kaye, Clark, Fudge, Howe | 37,189 | 1 | 2 | 3 | | 5 | 6 | 7 | 8 | 9 | | 11 | | | | 4 | | | | | | 10 | |
| 28 | (a) | Tottenham H | W 2-0 | Fenton, Foggo | 47,325 | 1 | 2 | 3 | | 5 | 6 | 7 | 8 | 9 | | 11 | | | | 4 | | | | | | 10 | |
| Jan 11 | (a) | Fulham | D 1-1 | Clark | 16,398 | 1 | 2 | 3 | | 5 | 6 | 7 | 8 | 9 | | 11 | | | | 4 | | | | | | 10 | |
| 18 | (h) | Manchester U | L 1-4 | Simpson | 25,624 | 1 | 2 | 3 | | 5 | 6 | | 8 | 9 | | 7 | | | | 4 | | | | 11 | | 10 | |
| Feb 1 | (a) | Burnley | L 2-3 | Brown, Clark | 15,840 | 1 | 2 | 3 | | 5 | 6 | 7 | | 9 | | 11 | 10 | | | 4 | 8 | | | | | | |
| 8 | (h) | Ipswich T | W 2-1 | Kaye, Fenton | 13,476 | 1 | 2 | 3 | | 5 | 6 | | 10 | 9 | | 11 | 8 | | | 4 | | 7 | | | | | |
| 15 | (a) | Sheffield W | D 2-2 | Clark, Williams | 19,582 | 1 | 2 | 3 | | 5 | 6 | 7 | | | | 11 | 10 | | | 4 | 9 | | | 8 | | | |
| 22 | (a) | Aston Villa | L 0-1 | | 27,663 | 1 | 2 | 3 | | 5 | 6 | 7 | | 9 | | 11 | | | | | 10 | | | 8 | 4 | | |
| 29 | (h) | Wolves | W 3-1 | Kaye, Clark, Fenton | 19,829 | 1 | 2 | 3 | | 5 | 6 | 7 | 8 | 9 | | 11 | | | | | 10 | | | | 4 | | |
| Mar 7 | (a) | Stoke C | D 1-1 | Kaye | 25,012 | 1 | 2 | 3 | | 5 | 6 | 7 | | 9 | | 11 | 10 | | | 4 | 8 | | | | | | |
| 13 | (h) | Blackpool | W 2-1 | Kaye, Clark | 13,694 | 1 | 2 | 3 | | 5 | 6 | 7 | | 9 | | 11 | 10 | | | 4 | 8 | | | | | | |
| 21 | (a) | Chelsea | L 1-3 | Kaye | 19,829 | 1 | 2 | 3 | | 5 | 6 | 7 | | 9 | | 11 | 10 | | | 4 | 8 | | | | | | |
| 27 | (a) | Everton | D 1-1 | Simpson | 61,187 | 1 | 2 | 3 | | 5 | 6 | 7 | 8 | 9 | | 11 | 10 | | | 4 | | | | | | | |
| 28 | (h) | West Ham U | L 0-1 | | 15,444 | 1 | 2 | 3 | | 5 | 6 | 7 | 8 | 9 | | 11 | 10 | | | 4 | | | | | | | |
| 31 | (h) | Everton | W 4-2 | Williams, Fudge 3 | 27,194 | 1 | 2 | 3 | | 5 | 6 | 7 | | 9 | | 11 | 8 | | | 4 | | | | | | 10 | |
| Apr 4 | (a) | Blackburn R | W 2-0 | Fenton, Clark | 12,052 | 1 | 2 | 3 | | 5 | 6 | 7 | 8 | 9 | | 11 | | | | 4 | | | | | | 10 | |
| 11 | (a) | Nottingham F | L 2-3 | Brown, Foggo | 14,442 | 1 | 2 | 3 | | 5 | 6 | 7 | | 9 | | 11 | | | | 4 | 8 | | | | | 10 | |
| 18 | (a) | Sheffield U | L 1-2 | Brown | 16,605 | | | 3 | 2 | 5 | 6 | 7 | | 9 | | 11 | | | | 4 | 8 | | | | | 10 | 1 |
| 25 | (h) | Liverpool | D 2-2 | Kaye, Clark | 17,833 | | | 3 | 2 | 5 | 6 | 7 | | 9 | | 11 | | | | 4 | 8 | | | | | 10 | 1 |
| App | | | | | | 40 | 35 | 41 | 14 | 42 | 42 | 37 | 31 | 27 | 4 | 42 | 27 | 4 | 4 | 33 | 13 | 1 | 2 | 4 | 4 | 11 | 2 |
| Goals | | | | | | | 1 | 4 | 2 | | 3 | 11 | 8 | 11 | | 16 | 3 | | | 1 | 5 | | | | 1 | 4 | |

West Brom, 1963-64. Back row (left to right): Foggo, Simpson, Jones, Potter, Cram, Williams. Front row: Kaye, Fenton, Howe, Clark, Hope. The mascot is David Winwood.

# 1964-65

## Division 1

| Date | | Opponents | Result | Scorers | Att | Potter R | Cram R | Williams G | Fraser D | Jones S | Simpson T | Foggo K | Brown T | Kaye J | Hope R | Clark C | Collard I | Howshall G | Astle J | Fairfax R | Fenton R | Carter G | Lovett G | Krzywicki R | Fudge M | Williams W | Crawford R |
|---|---|---|---|---|---|---|---|---|---|---|---|---|---|---|---|---|---|---|---|---|---|---|---|---|---|---|---|
| Aug 22 | (a) | Manchester U | D 2-2 | Brown, Foulkes (og) | 52,007 | 1 | 2 | 3 | 4 | 5 | 6 | 7 | 8 | 9 | 10 | 11 | | | | | | | | | | | |
| 26 | (h) | Sunderland | W 4-1 | Brown 3, Clark | 26,139 | 1 | 2 | 3 | 4 | 5 | 6 | 7 | 8 | 9 | 10 | 11 | | | | | | | | | | | |
| 29 | (h) | Fulham | D 2-2 | Williams, Clark | 18,702 | 1 | 2 | 3 | 4 | 5 | 6 | 7 | 8 | 9 | 10 | 11 | | | | | | | | | | | |
| Sep 2 | (a) | Sunderland | D 2-2 | Brown, Clark | 52,177 | 1 | 2 | 3 | 4 | 5 | 6 | 7 | 8 | 9 | 10 | 11 | | | | | | | | | | | |
| 5 | (a) | Nottingham F | D 0-0 | | 28,334 | 1 | 2 | 3 | 4 | 5 | 6 | 7 | 8 | 9 | 10 | 11 | | | | | | | | | | | |
| 9 | (a) | Birmingham C | D 1-1 | Foggo | 26,485 | 1 | 2 | 3 | 4 | 5 | 6 | 7 | 8 | 9 | 10 | 11 | | | | | | | | | | | |
| 12 | (h) | Stoke C | W 5-3 | Foggo, Cram 3 (2 pens), Brown | 24,505 | 1 | 2 | 3 | 4 | 5 | 6 | 7 | 8 | 9 | 10 | 11 | | | | | | | | | | | |
| 16 | (h) | Birmingham C | L 0-2 | | 26,013 | 1 | 2 | 3 | 4 | 5 | 6 | 7 | 8 | 9 | 10 | 11 | | | | | | | | | | | |
| 19 | (a) | Tottenham H | L 0-1 | | 36,525 | 1 | 2 | 3 | 4 | 5 | 6 | 7 | 8 | 9 | 10 | 11 | | | | | | | | | | | |
| 26 | (h) | Burnley | L 1-2 | Cram (pen) | 15,009 | 1 | 2 | 3 | 4 | 5 | 6 | 7 | | 9 | 10 | 11 | | | 8 | | | | | | | | |
| 30 | (a) | Leicester C | L 2-4 | Cram (pen), Williams | 17,218 | 1 | 2 | 3 | | 5 | 6 | 7 | 8 | 9 | | 11 | | | 4 | 10 | | | | | | | |
| Oct 3 | (a) | Sheffield U | D 1-1 | Carter | 17,592 | 1 | 2 | | | 5 | 6 | 7 | 8 | | | | | 4 | 9 | 3 | 10 | 11 | | | | | |
| 10 | (h) | Wolves | W 5-1 | Astle 2, Kaye 2, Cram (pen) | 23,006 | 1 | 2 | 3 | | 5 | 6 | | 8 | 10 | 7 | | | 4 | 9 | | 11 | | | | | | |
| 17 | (a) | Aston Villa | W 1-0 | Howshall | 28,030 | 1 | 2 | 3 | | 5 | 6 | | 8 | 10 | 7 | | | 4 | 9 | | 11 | | | | | | |
| 24 | (h) | Liverpool | W 3-0 | Clark 2, Astle | 22,045 | 1 | 2 | 3 | | 5 | 6 | | 8 | 10 | 7 | | | 4 | 9 | | 11 | | | | | | |
| 31 | (a) | Sheffield W | D 1-1 | Clark | 19,004 | 1 | 2 | 3 | | 5 | 6 | | 8 | 10 | 7 | | | 4 | 9 | | 11 | | | | | | |
| Nov 7 | (h) | Blackpool | L 1-3 | Kaye | 17,504 | 1 | 2 | | | 5 | 6 | | 8 | 10 | 7 | | | 4 | 9 | 3 | 11 | | | | | | |
| 14 | (a) | Blackburn R | L 2-4 | Foggo, Brown | 13,828 | 1 | 2 | 3 | | 5 | 6 | 7 | 8 | | | 11 | | 4 | 9 | | 10 | | | | | | |
| 21 | (h) | Arsenal | D 0-0 | | 18,489 | 1 | 2 | 3 | | 5 | 6 | | 8 | | | 11 | 7 | 4 | 9 | | 10 | | | | | | |
| 28 | (a) | Leeds U | L 0-1 | | 29,533 | 1 | 2 | 3 | 4 | 5 | 6 | 7 | | | 10 | 11 | | | 9 | | 8 | | | | | | |
| Dec 5 | (h) | Chelsea | L 0-2 | | 15,518 | 1 | | 3 | 4 | 5 | | 7 | | | 10 | 11 | | | 9 | 2 | 8 | 6 | | | | | |
| 12 | (h) | Manchester U | D 1-1 | Kaye | 28,504 | 1 | | 3 | 4 | 5 | 6 | 7 | | | 10 | 11 | | | 9 | 2 | 8 | | | | | | |
| 19 | (a) | Fulham | L 1-3 | Jones | 10,390 | 1 | | 3 | 4 | 5 | | | 8 | | 10 | 11 | | | 9 | 2 | | 6 | 7 | | | | |
| 26 | (a) | Everton | L 2-3 | Fenton, Clark | 46,719 | 1 | 2 | 3 | 4 | 5 | 6 | | | | 10 | 11 | | | 9 | | 7 | | 8 | | | | |
| Jan 2 | (h) | Nottingham F | D 2-2 | Fudge, Clark | 16,040 | 1 | 2 | 3 | 4 | | 6 | | | | 10 | 11 | | | 9 | | 7 | | | 8 | 5 | | |
| 16 | (a) | Stoke C | L 0-2 | | 25,405 | 1 | 2 | 3 | 4 | 5 | 6 | 7 | | | 10 | 11 | | | 8 | 9 | | | | | | | |
| 23 | (h) | Tottenham H | W 2-0 | Cram, Clark | 24,233 | 1 | 2 | 3 | 4 | 5 | 6 | 7 | | | 10 | 11 | | | 8 | 9 | | | | | | | |
| Feb 6 | (a) | Burnley | W 1-0 | Foggo | 12,902 | 1 | | 3 | 4 | 5 | 6 | 7 | | | 10 | 11 | | | 8 | 9 | 2 | | | | | | |
| 13 | (h) | Sheffield U | L 0-1 | | 10,511 | 1 | 2 | 3 | 4 | 5 | 6 | 7 | | | 10 | 11 | | | 8 | 9 | | | | | | | |
| 27 | (h) | Aston Villa | W 3-1 | Astle, Cram (pen), Hope | 24,040 | 1 | 2 | 3 | 6 | 5 | | 7 | | | 10 | 11 | | 4 | 8 | | | | | | | | 9 |
| Mar 13 | (h) | Leicester C | W 6-0 | Astle 2, Howshall, Clark, Foggo, Williams | 15,162 | 1 | 2 | 3 | 6 | 5 | | 7 | | | 10 | 11 | | 4 | 8 | | | | | | | | 9 |
| 15 | (a) | Wolves | L 2-3 | Foggo, Harris (og) | 26,722 | 1 | 2 | 3 | 6 | 5 | | 7 | | | 10 | 11 | | 4 | 8 | | | | | | | 9 | |
| 20 | (a) | Blackpool | L 0-3 | | 11,168 | 1 | 2 | 3 | 6 | 5 | 4 | 7 | | 9 | | 11 | | | | 8 | 10 | | | | | | |
| 23 | (h) | Everton | W 4-0 | Astle 2, Foggo, Cram (pen) | 13,013 | 1 | 2 | 3 | 6 | 5 | | 7 | | 9 | 10 | 11 | | 4 | 8 | | | | | | | | |
| 26 | (h) | Blackburn R | D 0-0 | | 17,045 | 1 | 2 | 3 | 6 | 5 | | 7 | | 9 | 10 | 11 | | 4 | 8 | | | | | | | | |
| Apr 3 | (a) | Arsenal | D 1-1 | Hope | 18,797 | 1 | 2 | 3 | 6 | 5 | | 7 | | 9 | 10 | 11 | | 4 | 8 | | | | | | | | |
| 7 | (a) | Liverpool | W 3-0 | Kaye, Hope, Clark | 34,152 | 1 | 2 | 3 | 6 | 5 | | 7 | | 9 | 10 | 11 | | 4 | 8 | | | | | | | | |
| 10 | (h) | Leeds U | L 1-2 | Foggo | 22,010 | 1 | 2 | 3 | 6 | 5 | | 7 | | 9 | 10 | 11 | | 4 | 8 | | | | | | | | |
| 16 | (a) | West Ham U | L 1-6 | Astle | 27,706 | 1 | 2 | 3 | 6 | 5 | | 7 | | 9 | 10 | 11 | | 4 | 8 | | | | | | | | |
| 17 | (a) | Chelsea | D 2-2 | Crawford, Howshall | 30,792 | 1 | 2 | 3 | 6 | 5 | | 7 | | | 10 | | | 4 | 8 | | | 11 | | | | | 9 |
| 19 | (h) | West Ham U | W 4-2 | Foggo, Astle, Brown 2 | 14,018 | 1 | 2 | 3 | 6 | 5 | | 7 | 11 | | 10 | | | 4 | 8 | | | | | | | | 9 |
| 24 | (h) | Sheffield W | W 1-0 | Crawford | 16,002 | 1 | 2 | 3 | 6 | 5 | | 7 | 11 | | 10 | | | 4 | 8 | | | | | | | | 9 |
| **App** | | | | | | 42 | 38 | 40 | 33 | 41 | 28 | 33 | 17 | 25 | 37 | 38 | 1 | 26 | 32 | 6 | 7 | 7 | 2 | 1 | 2 | 1 | 5 |
| **Goals** | | | | | | | 9 | 3 | | 1 | | 9 | 9 | 5 | 3 | 11 | | 3 | 10 | | 1 | 1 | | | 1 | | 2 |

**Bobby Cram (fourth from right) cracks home one of his hat-trick goals against Stoke City at The Hawthorns in September 1964.**

# 1965-66

## Division 1

| Date | | Opponent | Result | Scorers | Att | Potter R | Cram R | Williams G | Lovett G | Jones S | Fraser D | Foggo K | Astle J | Kaye J | Hope R | Clark C | Fairfax R | Howshall G | Brown T | Wilson R | Sheppard R | Crawford R | Collard I | Crawford C | Krzywicki R | Campbell D |
|---|---|---|---|---|---|---|---|---|---|---|---|---|---|---|---|---|---|---|---|---|---|---|---|---|---|---|
| Aug 21 | (h) | West Ham U | W 3-0 | Clark 2, Astle | 19,956 | 1 | 2 | 3 | 4 | 5 | 6 | 7 | 8 | 9 | 10 | 11 | | | | | | | | | | |
| 25 | (a) | Newcastle U | W 1-0 | Kaye | 43,901 | 1 | | 3 | 4 | 5 | 6 | 7 | 8 | 9 | 10 | 11 | 2 | | | | | | | | | |
| 28 | (a) | Nottingham F | L 2-3 | Astle, Foggo | 27,366 | 1 | | 3 | 4 | 5 | 6 | 7 | 8 | 9 | 10 | 11 | 2 | | | | | | | | | |
| Sep 1 | (h) | Newcastle U | L 1-2 | Kaye | 22,043 | 1 | | 3 | 4 | 5 | 6 | 7 | 8 | 9 | 10 | 11 | 2 | | | | | | | | | |
| 4 | (h) | Sheffield W | W 4-2 | Astle 3, Kaye | 15,229 | 1 | 2 | 3 | | 5 | 6 | 7 | 8 | 9 | 10 | 11 | | 4 | | | | | | | | |
| 7 | (a) | Everton | W 3-2 | Brown, Kaye, Astle | 43,468 | 1 | 2 | 3 | | 5 | 6 | 7 | 8 | 9 | 10 | | | 4 | 11 | | | | | | | |
| 10 | (a) | Northampton T | W 4-3 | Hope, Astle 3 | 18,528 | 1 | 2 | 3 | 12 | 5 | 6 | 7* | 8 | 9 | 10 | | | 4 | 11 | | | | | | | |
| 15 | (h) | Everton | D 1-1 | Astle | 25,513 | 1 | 2 | 3 | 10 | 5 | 6 | | 8 | 9 | | 11 | | 4 | 7 | | | | | | | |
| 18 | (h) | Stoke C | W 6-2 | Setters (og), Kaye 3, Cram (pen), Brown | 24,374 | 1 | 2 | 3 | 4 | 5 | 6 | | 8 | 9 | 10 | 11 | | | 7 | | | | | | | |
| 25 | (a) | Burnley | L 0-2 | | 20,489 | 1 | 2 | | 4 | 5 | 6 | | 8 | 9 | 10 | 11 | 3 | | 7 | | | | | | | |
| Oct 2 | (h) | Chelsea | L 1-2 | Fraser | 23,049 | 1 | 2 | | 4 | 5 | 6 | | 8 | 9 | 10 | | 3 | | 7 | 11 | | | | | | |
| 9 | (h) | Sunderland | W 4-1 | Kaye, Cram (pen), Brown 2 | 19,617 | | 2 | 3 | 4 | 5 | 6 | | 8 | 9 | 10 | 11 | | | 7 | | 1 | | | | | |
| 16 | (a) | Aston Villa | D 1-1 | Astle | 41,455 | | 2 | | 4 | 5 | 6 | | 8 | 9 | 10 | 11 | 3 | | 7 | | 1 | | | | | |
| 23 | (h) | Liverpool | W 3-0 | Brown, Kaye, Clark | 29,669 | | 2 | | 4 | 5 | 6 | | | 9 | 10 | 11 | 3 | | 7 | | 1 | 8 | | | | |
| 30 | (a) | Tottenham H | L 1-2 | Crawford | 43,512 | | 2 | | 4 | 5 | 6 | | | 9 | 10 | 11 | 3 | | 7 | | 1 | 8 | | | | |
| Nov 6 | (h) | Fulham | W 6-2 | Wilson, Brown 2, Lovett 2, Clark | 19,858 | | 2 | | 4 | 5 | 6 | | | 9 | 10 | 11 | 3 | | 8 | 11 | 1 | | | | | |
| 13 | (a) | Blackpool | D 1-1 | Brown | 12,642 | | 2 | | 4 | 5 | 6 | | 8 | 9 | 10 | 11 | 3 | | 7 | | 1 | | | | | |
| 20 | (h) | Blackburn R | W 2-1 | Cram (pen), Brown | 17,189 | | 2 | | 4 | 5 | 6 | | 8 | 9 | 10 | 11 | 3 | | 7 | | 1 | | | | | |
| 27 | (a) | Leicester C | L 1-2 | Crawford | 21,124 | | 2 | | 4 | 5 | 6 | | | 9 | 10 | 11 | 3 | | 7 | | 1* | 8 | 12 | | | |
| Dec 4 | (h) | Sheffield U | D 1-1 | Brown | 15,607 | | 2 | | 4 | 5 | 6 | | 8 | 9 | 10 | 11 | 3 | | 7 | | 1 | | | | | |
| 11 | (a) | Leeds U | L 0-4 | | 33,140 | | 2 | | 4 | 5 | 6 | 7 | | 9 | 10 | 11 | 3 | | | | 1 | 8 | | | | |
| 27 | (a) | Manchester U | D 1-1 | Crawford | 54,102 | 1 | 2 | | 4 | 5 | 6 | 7 | | 9 | 10 | 11 | 3 | | | | | 8 | | | | |
| Jan 1 | (a) | Sunderland | W 5-1 | Kaye, Hope, Brown 2, Crawford | 34,938 | 1 | 2 | | 4 | 5 | 6 | 12 | | 9 | 10* | | 3 | | 7 | | | 8 | | | | |
| 8 | (h) | Leeds U | L 1-2 | Wilson | 24,900 | 1 | 2 | | 4 | 5 | 6 | | | 9 | 10 | | 3 | | 7 | 11 | | 8 | | | | |
| 15 | (a) | Liverpool | D 2-2 | Brown, Kaye | 46,687 | 1 | 2 | | 4 | 5 | 6 | | | 9 | 10 | 11 | 3 | | 7 | | | 8 | | | | |
| 29 | (a) | West Ham U | L 0-4 | | 25,500 | 1 | | 3 | 4 | 5 | 6 | | | 9 | 10 | 11 | | | 8 | | | | 2 | 7 | | |
| Feb 5 | (h) | Nottingham F | W 5-3 | Clark, Kaye, Cram (pen), Brown, Hope | 14,054 | 1 | 2 | | 4 | 5 | 6 | 7 | | 9* | 10 | 11 | 3 | 12 | 8 | | | | | | | |
| 11 | (h) | Aston Villa | D 2-2 | Kaye, Brown | 17,089 | 1 | 2 | | 4 | 5 | 6* | 7 | | 9 | 10 | 11 | 3 | 12 | 8 | | | | | | | |
| 19 | (a) | Sheffield W | W 2-1 | Clark, Mobley (og) | 18,358 | 1 | | 3 | 4 | 5 | 6 | | | 9 | 10 | 11 | 2 | 8 | 7 | | | | | | | |
| 26 | (h) | Northampton T | D 1-1 | Clark | 18,923 | 1 | | 3 | 4 | 5 | 6 | | | 9 | | 11 | 2 | 8* | 7 | | | | | 10 | 12 | |
| Mar 12 | (a) | Stoke C | D 1-1 | Clark | 23,261 | 1 | 2 | 6 | 10 | | 4 | | 8 | 9 | | 11 | 3 | | 7 | | | | | | | 5 |
| 19 | (h) | Burnley | L 1-2 | Brown | 18,747 | 1 | 2 | 6 | 10 | | 4 | | 8 | 9 | | 11 | 3 | | 7 | | | | | | | 5 |
| Apr 2 | (a) | Fulham | L 1-2 | Astle | 20,426 | 1 | 2 | | 4 | | 6 | | 8 | 9 | 10 | 11 | 3 | | 7 | | | | | | | 5 |
| 5 | (h) | Arsenal | D 1-1 | Cram (pen) | 8,738 | 1 | 2 | | 4 | | 6 | | 8 | 9 | 10 | 11 | 3 | | 7 | | | | | | | 5 |
| 9 | (h) | Blackpool | W 2-1 | Brown, Foggo | 13,079 | 1 | 2 | | 4 | 5 | 6 | 7 | | 9 | 10* | 11 | 3 | | 8 | | | | 12 | | | |
| 11 | (h) | Arsenal | D 4-4 | Cram 2 (2 pens), Astle, Lovett | 16,094 | 1 | 2 | 4 | 10 | 5 | 6 | | 8 | 9 | | 11 | 3 | | 7 | | | | | | | |
| 16 | (a) | Blackburn R | W 1-0 | Astle | 7,637 | 1 | 2 | 4 | 10 | 5 | 6 | | 8 | 9 | | 11 | 3 | | 7 | | | | | | | |
| 22 | (h) | Leicester C | W 5-1 | Kaye 2, Sjoberg 2 (2 og's), Astle | 15,229 | 1 | 2 | 4 | | 5 | 6 | | 8 | 9 | 10 | 11 | 3 | | 7 | | | | | | | |
| 25 | (h) | Chelsea | W 3-2 | Clark, Astle 2 | 22,804 | 1 | 2 | 4 | 12 | 5 | 6* | | 8 | 9 | 10 | 11 | 3 | | 7 | | | | | | | |
| 30 | (a) | Sheffield U | W 2-0 | Kaye 2 | 16,022 | 1 | | 3 | 4 | 5 | 6 | | 8 | 9 | 10 | 11 | 2 | | 7 | | | | | | | |
| May 4 | (h) | Manchester U | D 3-3 | Clark, Lovett, Kaye | 22,609 | 1 | | 3 | 4 | 5 | 6 | | 8 | 9 | 10 | 11 | 2 | | 7 | | | | | | | |
| 7 | (h) | Tottenham H | W 2-1 | Hope, Astle | 22,586 | 1 | 2 | 4 | | 5 | 6 | | 8 | 9 | 10 | 11 | 3 | | 7 | | | | | | | |
| | | | | | App | 32 | 34 | 22 | 36 | 38 | 42 | 12 | 27 | 42 | 37 | 37 | 34 | 6 | 35 | 3 | 10 | 9 | | 1 | 1 | 4 |
| | | | | | Sub app | | | | 2 | 1 | | | | | | | | 2 | | | | 3 | | | | |
| | | | | | Goals | | 7 | | 4 | | 1 | 2 | 18 | 18 | 4 | 10 | | | 17 | 2 | | 4 | | | | |

**A goal for Jeff Astle in Albion's 4-2 home win over Sheffield Wednesday on 4 September 1965. Astle was on his way to a hat-trick.**

# 1966-67

## Division 1

| Date | | Opponent | Result | Scorers | Att | Potter R | Cram R | Fairfax R | Williams G | Jones S | Fraser D | Brown T | Astle J | Kaye J | Hope R | Clark C | Sheppard R | Collard I | Lovett G | Foggo K | Campbell D | Crawford C | Krzywicki R | Stephens K | Treacy R | Simpson T | Howshall G | Clarke D | Talbot J | Osborne J | Colquhoun E |
|---|---|---|---|---|---|---|---|---|---|---|---|---|---|---|---|---|---|---|---|---|---|---|---|---|---|---|---|---|---|---|
| Aug 20 | (a) | Manchester U | L 3-5 | Hope, Clark 2 | 41,343 | 1 | 2 | 3 | 4 | 5 | 6 | 7 | 8 | 9 | 10 | 11 | | | | | | | | | | | | | | | |
| 24 | (a) | Leeds U | L 1-2 | Astle | 35,102 | 1 | 2 | 3 | 4 | 5 | 6 | 7 | 8 | 9 | 10 | 11 | | | | | | | | | | | | | | | |
| 27 | (h) | Burnley | L 1-2 | Lovett | 21,732 | | 2 | | | 5 | 6 | 7 | 8 | 9 | 10 | 11 | 1 | 3 | 4 | | | | | | | | | | | | |
| 31 | (h) | Leeds U | W 2-0 | Clark, Brown | 22,072 | | 2 | | | 5 | 6 | 7 | 8 | 9 | 10 | 11 | 1 | 3 | 4 | | | | | | | | | | | | |
| Sep 3 | (a) | Nottingham F | L 1-2 | Brown | 21,871 | | 2 | | | 5 | 6 | 7 | 8 | 9 | 10 | 11 | 1 | 3 | 4 | | | | | | | | | | | | |
| 7 | (a) | Newcastle U | W 3-1 | Clark 2, Kaye | 24,748 | | 2 | | | 5 | 6 | 7 | 8 | 9 | 10 | 11 | 1 | 3 | 4 | | | | | | | | | | | | |
| 10 | (h) | Fulham | W 5-1 | Clark 2, Hope 2, Astle | 17,160 | | 2 | | | 5 | 6 | 7 | 8 | 9 | 10 | 11 | 1 | 3 | 4 | | | | | | | | | | | | |
| 17 | (a) | Everton | L 4-5 | Astle, Fraser, Cram (pen), Kaye | 45,165 | | 2 | | | 5 | 6 | | 8 | 9 | 10 | 11 | 1 | 3 | 4 | 7 | | | | | | | | | | | |
| 24 | (h) | Stoke C | L 0-1 | | 24,865 | | 2 | | | 5 | 6 | | 8 | 9 | 10 | 11 | 1 | 3 | 4 | 7 | | | | | | | | | | | |
| Oct 1 | (a) | Sheffield U | L 3-4 | Astle, Fraser, Clark | 15,313 | | 2 | | 4 | | 6 | | 8 | 9 | 10 | 11 | 1 | 3 | | 7 | 5 | | | | | | | | | | |
| 8 | (a) | Sunderland | D 2-2 | Treacy, Clark | 26,632 | 1 | | | 4 | | | | | | 10 | 11 | | 3 | 6 | | 5 | 2 | 7 | 8 | 9 | | | | | | |
| 15 | (h) | Aston Villa | W 2-1 | Astle, Krzywicki | 31,128 | 1 | | | 4 | 5 | 6 | | 8 | 9 | 10* | 11 | | 3 | 12 | | | 2 | 7 | | | | | | | | |
| 22 | (a) | Arsenal | W 3-2 | Hope 2, Clark | 31,036 | 1 | | | | 5 | 6 | | 8 | 9 | 10 | 11 | | 3 | 4 | | | 2 | 7 | | | | | | | | |
| 29 | (h) | Sheffield W | L 1-2 | Astle | 19,335 | 1 | | | 7 | 5 | 6 | | 8 | 9 | 10 | 11 | | 3 | 4 | | | 2 | | | | | | | | | |
| Nov 5 | (a) | Aston Villa | L 2-3 | Kaye, Lovett | 24,018 | 1 | 3 | | 7 | 5 | 6 | | 8 | 9 | 10 | 11 | | | 4 | | | | | | | | | | | | |
| 12 | (h) | Chelsea | L 0-1 | | 28,151 | 1 | 2 | | 4 | 5 | 6 | 7 | 8 | 9 | 10 | 11 | | 3 | | | | | | | | | | | | | |
| 19 | (a) | Leicester C | L 1-2 | Foggo | 25,003 | | 2 | | 4 | 5 | 6* | 10 | 8 | 9 | | 11 | 1 | 3 | | 7 | | | | | | | 12 | | | | |
| 26 | (h) | Liverpool | W 2-1 | Brown, Clark | 25,931 | | 2 | 3 | | 5 | 6 | 8 | | 9 | 10 | 11 | 1 | | 4 | 7 | | | | | | | | | | | |
| Dec 3 | (a) | West Ham U | L 0-3 | | 22,961 | | 2 | 3 | | 5 | 6 | 8 | | 9 | 10 | 11 | 1 | | 4 | 7 | | | | | | | | | | | |
| 10 | (h) | Manchester C | L 0-3 | | 17,299 | | | 3 | | 5 | 6 | 7 | 8 | 9 | 10 | 11 | 1 | | 4 | | | | | | | 2 | | | | | |
| 17 | (h) | Manchester U | L 3-4 | Astle 2, Kaye | 32,080 | 1 | 2 | 12 | | 5 | 6 | 7 | 8 | 9 | 10 | 11 | | 3* | | | | | | | | | | 4 | | | |
| 26 | (h) | Tottenham H | W 3-0 | Brown 3 (1 pen) | 37,969 | 1 | | 3 | | | 6 | 7 | 8 | 9 | 10 | 11 | | | | | | | | | | | 4 | 2 | 5 | | |
| 27 | (a) | Tottenham H | D 0-0 | | 39,002 | 1 | | 3 | | 5 | 6 | 7 | 8 | 9 | 10 | 11 | | | | | | | | | | | 4 | 2 | | | |
| 31 | (a) | Burnley | L 1-5 | Astle | 18,904 | 1 | | 3 | | | 6 | 9 | 8 | | 10 | 11 | | | | 7 | | | | | | | 4 | 2 | 5 | | |
| Jan 7 | (h) | Nottingham F | L 1-2 | Clark | 21,795 | | | 3 | | | 6 | 7 | 8 | 9 | 10 | 11 | | | | | | | | | | | 4 | 2 | 5 | 1 | |
| 14 | (h) | Fulham | D 2-2 | Collard, Cram | 20,680 | | 2 | | | | 6 | 7 | 8 | 9 | 10 | 11 | | 3 | | | | | | | | | 4 | | 5 | 1 | |
| 21 | (h) | Everton | W 1-0 | Clark | 26,104 | | 2 | 3 | | | 6 | | 8 | 9 | 10 | 11 | | | | 7 | | | | | | | 4 | | 5 | 1 | |
| Feb 4 | (a) | Stoke C | D 1-1 | Astle | 26,212 | | 2 | 3 | | | 6 | 7 | 8 | 9 | 10 | 11 | | | | | | | | | | | 4 | 12 | 5* | 1 | |
| 11 | (h) | Sheffield U | L 1-2 | Cram | 20,354 | | 2 | 12 | | 5 | 6 | | 8 | 9* | 10 | 11 | | 3 | | 7 | | | | | | | 4 | | | 1 | |
| 25 | (h) | Sunderland | D 2-2 | Fraser, Astle | 22,296 | | | 3 | | | 6 | 7 | 8 | 9 | 10 | 11 | | | | | | | | | | | 4 | 12 | 5 | 1 | 2* |
| Mar 18 | (h) | Arsenal | L 0-1 | | 16,832 | | 2 | 3 | | 5 | 6 | | 8 | 9 | 10 | 11 | | | | 7 | | | | | | | 4 | | | 1 | |
| 25 | (a) | Manchester C | D 2-2 | Kaye, Fraser | 22,780 | | 2 | 3 | 4 | | 6 | | 8 | 9 | 10 | 11 | | | | 7 | | | | | | | | | 5 | 1 | |
| 27 | (h) | Southampton | W 3-2 | Brown, Clark, Astle | 19,732 | | 2 | 3 | 4 | | 6 | 7 | 8 | 9 | 10 | 11 | | | | | | | | | | | | | 5 | 1 | |
| 28 | (a) | Southampton | D 2-2 | Astle, Clark | 28,870 | | 2 | 3 | 4 | | 6 | 7 | 8 | 9 | 10 | 11 | | | | | | | | 1 | | | | | 5 | | |
| Apr 1 | (h) | Blackpool | W 3-1 | Clark, Williams, Brown | 19,441 | | 2 | 3 | 4 | | 6 | 7 | 8 | 9 | 10 | 11 | | | | | | | | | | | | | 5 | 1 | |
| 10 | (h) | Chelsea | W 2-0 | Clark, Foggo | 18,448 | | 2 | 3 | 4 | | 6 | | 8 | 9 | 10 | 11 | | | | 7 | | | | | | | | | 5 | 1 | |
| 15 | (h) | Leicester C | W 1-0 | Clark | 22,872 | | 2 | 3 | | | 6 | 7 | 8 | 9 | 10 | 11 | | | | | | | | | | | 4 | | 5 | 1 | |
| 19 | (a) | Sheffield W | L 0-1 | | 23,056 | | 2 | 3 | | | 6 | 7 | 8 | 9 | 10 | 11 | | | | | | | | | | | 4 | | 5 | 1 | |
| 22 | (a) | Liverpool | W 1-0 | Astle | 39,883 | | 2 | 3 | | | 6 | 7 | 8 | 9 | 10 | 11 | | | | | | | | | | | 4 | | 5 | 1 | |
| 28 | (h) | West Ham U | W 3-1 | Brown 2 (2 pens), Astle | 23,210 | | 2 | 3 | | | 6 | 7 | 8 | 9 | 10 | 11 | | | | | | | | | | | 4 | | 5 | 1 | |
| May 6 | (a) | Blackpool | W 3-1 | Astle, Williams, Brown (pen) | 9,986 | | 2 | 3 | 4 | | 6 | 7 | 8 | 9* | 10 | 11 | | | | | | | | | | | 12 | | 5 | 1 | |
| 13 | (h) | Newcastle U | W 6-1 | Foggo, Brown 3, Williams, Clark | 20,035 | | 2 | 3 | 4 | | 6 | 7 | 8 | 9 | 10 | 11 | | | | | | | | | | | | | 5 | 1 | |
| | | App | | | | 12 | 11 | 25 | 30 | 23 | 34 | 31 | 38 | 40 | 36 | 42 | 14 | 26 | 15 | 19 | 2 | 5 | 3 | 3 | 1 | 1 | 6 | 5 | 12 | 16 | 12 |
| | | Sub app | | | | | 1 | 1 | 1 | | | | | | | | | | 1 | | | | | | | | 1 | 2 | | | |
| | | Goals | | | | | 3 | | 3 | | 4 | 14 | 16 | 5 | 5 | 19 | | 1 | 2 | 3 | | | 1 | | 1 | | | | | | |

**Astle is on target again, this time against Aston Villa at The Hawthorns in October 1966.**

# 1967-68

### Division 1

| Date | V | Opponent | Result | Scorers | Att | Osborne J | Fraser D | Williams G | Howshall G | Colquhoun E | Talbut J | Foggo K | Astle J | Kaye J | Brown T | Clark C | Collard I | Clarke D | Hope R | Fairfax R | Stephens K | Sheppard R | Campbell D | Treacy R | Krzywicki R | Lovett G | Hartford A | Martin D | Rees R |
|---|---|---|---|---|---|---|---|---|---|---|---|---|---|---|---|---|---|---|---|---|---|---|---|---|---|---|---|---|---|
| Aug 19 | (h) | Chelsea | L 0-1 | | 33,283 | 1 | 2 | 3 | 4 | 5 | 6* | 7 | 8 | 9 | 10 | 11 | 12 | | | | | | | | | | | | |
| 23 | (a) | Wolves | D 3-3 | Foggo, Kaye, Brown | 52,438 | 1 | 2 | 3 | 4 | 5 | 6 | 7 | 8 | 9 | 10 | 11 | | | | | | | | | | | | | |
| 26 | (a) | Southampton | L 0-4 | | 22,714 | 1 | 6 | 3 | 4 | | 5 | | 8 | 9 | 7 | 11 | | | 2 | 10 | | | | | | | | | |
| 30 | (h) | Wolves | W 4-1 | Astle, Clark, Stephens, Kaye | 38,373 | 1 | 4 | 3 | | 5* | 6 | | 9 | 12 | 8 | 11 | | | 10 | 2 | 7 | | | | | | | | |
| Sep 2 | (h) | Liverpool | L 0-2 | | 32,159 | | 4 | 3 | | 5 | 6 | | 9 | 12 | 8* | 11 | | | 10 | 2 | 7 | 1 | | | | | | | |
| 6 | (h) | Arsenal | L 1-3 | Clark | 20,153 | 1 | 4 | 3 | | 5 | 6 | | 9 | 8 | | 11 | | | 10 | 2 | 7* | | | | | | | | |
| 9 | (h) | Stoke C | D 0-0 | | 21,036 | 1 | 2 | 3 | | 5 | 6 | | 12 | 9 | 8 | 11 | 4 | | 10 | | 7* | | | | | | | | |
| 16 | (h) | Nottingham F | W 2-1 | Hope, Stephens | 21,136 | 1 | 2 | | 3 | 5 | | | 9 | | | 11 | 4 | | 10 | | 7 | | 6 | 8 | | | | | |
| 23 | (a) | Coventry C | L 2-4 | Astle, Clark | 31,258 | 1 | | 3 | 2 | 5 | | | 9 | 8 | | 11 | 4* | | 10 | | 7 | | 6 | 12 | | | | | |
| 30 | (h) | Sheffield U | W 4-1 | Astle 3, Brown | 15,186 | 1 | 6 | 3 | 2 | 5 | | | 9 | 8 | 4 | 11 | | | 10 | | 7 | | | | | | | | |
| Oct 7 | (a) | Fulham | W 2-1 | Astle, Brown | 17,758 | 1 | 6 | 3 | 2 | 5 | | | 9 | 8 | 4 | 11 | | | 10 | | 7 | | | | | | | | |
| 14 | (h) | Leeds U | W 2-0 | Astle 2 | 21,024 | 1 | 6 | 3 | 2 | 5 | | | 9 | 8 | 4 | 11 | | | 10 | | 7* | | | | 12 | | | | |
| 21 | (a) | Everton | L 1-2 | Kaye | 44,092 | 1 | 6 | | 2 | 5 | | | 9* | 8 | 4 | | | 3 | 10 | | 11 | | | | 12 | 7 | | | |
| 28 | (h) | Leicester C | D 0-0 | | 20,961 | 1 | 6 | 3 | 2 | 5 | | | 9 | 8 | 4 | 11 | | | 10 | | | | | | 12 | 7* | | | |
| Nov 11 | (h) | Burnley | W 8-1 | Hope 2, Clark 2, Brown, Colquhoun, Kaye, Astle | 18,952 | 1 | 6 | 3 | 2 | 5 | | | 9 | 8 | 4 | 11 | | | 10 | | 7 | | | | | | | | |
| 18 | (h) | Sheffield W | D 2-2 | Clark, Astle | 28,256 | 1 | 6 | 3 | 2 | 5 | | | 9 | 8 | 4 | 11 | | | 10 | | 7 | | | | | | | | |
| 25 | (h) | Tottenham H | W 2-0 | Clark, Hope | 29,033 | 1 | 6 | 3 | 2 | 5 | | | 9 | 8 | 4 | 11 | | | 10 | | 7 | | | | | | | | |
| Dec 2 | (a) | Manchester U | L 1-2 | Kaye | 52,568 | 1 | 6 | 3 | 2 | 5 | | | 9 | 8 | 4 | 11 | | | 10 | | | | | 7 | | | | | |
| 11 | (a) | West Ham U | W 3-2 | Krzywicki, Astle, Hope (pen) | 18,340 | 1 | 6 | 3 | 2 | 5 | | | 9 | 8 | 4 | 11 | | | 10 | | | | | 7 | | | | | |
| 16 | (a) | Chelsea | W 3-0 | Clark, Astle, Krzywicki | 27,739 | 1 | 6 | 3 | 2 | 5 | | | 9 | 8 | 4 | 11 | | | 10 | | | | | 7 | | | | | |
| 23 | (h) | Southampton | D 0-0 | | 24,082 | 1 | 6 | 3 | 2 | 5 | | | 9 | 8 | 4 | 11 | | | 10 | | | | | 7 | | | | | |
| 26 | (h) | Manchester C | W 3-2 | Astle 2, Brown | 44,897 | 1 | 6 | 3 | 2 | 5 | | | 9 | 8 | 4 | 11* | | | 10 | | | | | 7 | 12 | | | | |
| 30 | (a) | Manchester C | W 2-0 | Krzywicki, Brown | 45,754 | 1 | 6 | 3 | 2 | 5 | | | 9 | 8 | 4 | 11 | | | 10 | | | | | 7 | | | | | |
| Jan 6 | (a) | Liverpool | L 1-4 | Brown (pen) | 51,092 | 1 | 6 | 3 | 2 | 5 | | | 9 | 8 | 4 | 11 | | | 10 | | | | | 7 | | | | | |
| 20 | (a) | Nottingham F | L 2-3 | Clark 2 | 34,298 | 1 | 6 | 3 | 2 | 5 | | | 9 | 8 | 4 | 11 | | | 10 | | | | | 7 | | | | | |
| Feb 3 | (a) | Coventry C | L 0-1 | | 28,231 | | 6 | 3 | 2 | 5 | | | 9 | 8 | 4 | 11 | | | 10 | | 12 | 1 | | | 7* | | | | |
| 10 | (a) | Sheffield U | D 1-1 | Astle | 19,281 | | 6 | 3 | 2 | 5 | | | 9 | 8 | 4 | 11 | | | 10 | | | 1 | | | 7 | | | | |
| 24 | (h) | Fulham | W 2-1 | Astle, Brown (pen) | 17,969 | 1 | 6 | 3 | | 5 | | | 9 | 8 | 7 | 11* | 4 | | 2 | 10 | | | | | 12 | | | | |
| Mar 2 | (a) | Tottenham H | D 0-0 | | 31,318 | 1 | 6 | 3 | 2 | 5 | | | 9 | 8 | 7 | 11 | 4 | | 10 | | | | | | | | | | |
| 13 | (h) | Stoke C | W 3-0 | Astle 2 (1 pen), Collard | 20,621 | 1 | 6 | 3 | 2 | 5 | | | 9 | 8 | | | 4 | | | | | | 7 | | 10 | 12 | 11* | | |
| 16 | (h) | Everton | L 2-6 | Collard 2 | 26,481 | 1 | 6 | 3 | 2 | 5 | | | 9 | 8 | | | 4 | | | | | | 7* | | 10 | 12 | 11 | | |
| 23 | (a) | Leicester C | W 3-2 | Clark, Astle | 23,097 | | 6 | 3 | 2* | 5 | | | 9 | 8 | 4 | 11 | 12 | | 10 | | | 1 | | | | | | | 7 |
| Apr 2 | (h) | Sunderland | D 0-0 | | 15,490 | 1 | | 3 | 6 | 5 | | | 9 | 8 | 4 | 11 | 10 | 2 | | | | | | | | | | | 7 |
| 6 | (a) | Burnley | D 0-0 | | 12,204 | 1 | | 3 | 6 | 5 | | | 9 | 8 | 4 | 11 | 10 | 2 | | | | | | | | | | | 7 |
| 12 | (a) | Newcastle U | D 2-2 | Rees 2 | 40,308 | 1 | | 3 | 6* | 5 | | | 9 | 8 | 4 | 11 | 10 | 2 | | | | | 12 | | | | | | 7 |
| 13 | (h) | Sheffield W | D 1-1 | Astle | 20,677 | 1 | 4 | 3 | | 5 | | | 9 | 6 | 8 | | 10 | 2 | | | | | 7 | | 11 | | | | |
| 15 | (h) | Newcastle U | W 2-0 | Brown 2 | 22,194 | 1 | 4 | 3 | | 5 | | | 9 | 6 | 8 | | 12 | 2 | 10 | | | | 7 | | 11* | | | | |
| 20 | (a) | Leeds U | L 1-3 | Lovett | 38,334 | 1 | 6 | 3 | | 5 | | | | | 4 | | 10 | | | | 2 | | 7 | | 11 | 9 | 8 | | |
| 29 | (h) | Manchester U | W 6-3 | Astle 3, Rees, Brown (pen), Hartford | 45,992 | 1 | 6 | 3 | | 5 | | | 9 | | 4 | 8 | 2 | | 10 | | | | | | | 12 | 11 | | 7* |
| May 1 | (h) | West Ham U | W 3-1 | Astle 3 | 25,686 | 1 | 6 | | | 5 | | | 9 | 6 | 8 | | 2 | 3 | 10 | | | | | | | 4 | 11 | | 7 |
| 4 | (a) | Sunderland | D 0-0 | | 31,892 | 1 | 4 | | | 5 | | | 9 | 6 | 11 | | 10 | 2 | 3 | | | | | | | 12 | 8 | | 7* |
| 11 | (a) | Arsenal | L 1-2 | Fraser | 24,896 | | 2 | 3 | | 5 | | | 9 | 6 | 4 | 11 | 8 | | 10 | | | 1 | | | | | | | 7 |
| | | | | App | | 37 | 40 | 35 | 3 | 33 | 42 | 2 | 40 | 37 | 35 | 34 | 17 | 10 | 32 | 6 | 18 | 5 | 2 | 1 | 11 | 7 | 4 | 1 | 10 |
| | | | | Sub app | | | | | | | | | 1 | 2 | | | 3 | | | | 1 | 1 | | | 3 | 2 | 3 | 2 | |
| | | | | Goals | | | 1 | | | 1 | | 1 | 26 | 5 | 11 | 12 | 3 | | 5 | | 2 | | | | 3 | 1 | 1 | | 3 |

**Yet another goal for Jeff Astle, this header going in against Sheffield Wednesday at The Hawthorns in April 1968.**

# 1968-69

## Division 1

| Date | Opponent | Result | Scorers | Att | Sheppard R | Fraser D | Williams G | Brown T | Talbut J | Kaye J | Krzywicki R | Hartford A | Astle J | Hope R | Rees R | Collard I | Wilson R | Clarke D | Osborne J | Lovett G | Clark C | Colquhoun E | Merrick A | Potter R | Hughes L | Martin D | Reed H | Cantello L |
|---|---|---|---|---|---|---|---|---|---|---|---|---|---|---|---|---|---|---|---|---|---|---|---|---|---|---|---|---|
| Aug 10 (h) Sheffield W | | D 0-0 | | 25,031 | 1 | 2 | 3 | 4 | 5 | 6 | 7 | 8 | 9 | 10 | 11 | | | | | | | | | | | | | |
| 14 (h) Manchester U | | W 3-1 | Astle 2, Brown | 38,299 | 1 | 2 | 3 | 4 | 5 | 6 | 7 | | 9 | 10 | 11 | 8 | | | | | | | | | | | | |
| 17 (a) Chelsea | | L 1-3 | Brown | 33,766 | 1 | 2 | 3* | 4 | 5 | 6 | 7 | | 9 | 10 | 11 | 8 | 12 | | | | | | | | | | | |
| 21 (a) Tottenham H | | D 1-1 | Astle | 35,746 | 1 | | 3 | 4 | 5 | 6 | 7 | | 9 | 10 | 11 | 8 | 2 | | | | | | | | | | | |
| 24 (h) Burnley | | W 3-2 | Astle 2, Collard | 21,882 | | | 3 | 4 | 5 | 6 | 7 | | 9 | 10 | 11 | 8* | 12 | 2 | 1 | | | | | | | | | |
| 27 (a) Coventry C | | L 2-4 | Rees, Brown | 36,678 | 1 | 4 | 3 | 8 | 5 | 6 | 7 | | 9 | | 11 | | | 2 | | 10 | | | | | | | | |
| 31 (a) West Ham U | | L 0-4 | | 29,708 | 1 | | 3 | 8 | 5 | 6 | | | 9 | 10 | | 7 | | 2 | | 4 | 11 | | | | | | | |
| Sep 7 (h) Nottingham F | | L 2-5 | Astle, Brown | 23,377 | 1 | 2 | 3 | 4 | 5 | 8 | | | 9 | 10 | 7 | | | | | | 11 | 6 | | | | | | |
| 14 (a) Newcastle U | | W 3-2 | Astle 2, Hartford | 35,128 | 1 | 2 | 3 | 4 | 5 | 6 | | 8 | 9 | 10 | 7 | | | | | | 11 | | | | | | | |
| 21 (h) Wolves | | D 0-0 | | 35,175 | | 2 | 3 | 4 | 5 | 6 | 9* | 10 | | | 7 | | | | 1 | 8 | 11 | 12 | | | | | | |
| 28 (a) Everton | | L 0-4 | | 47,712 | | 2 | 3 | 4 | 5 | 6 | | | 9 | 10* | 7 | | | | 1 | 8 | 11 | | 12 | | | | | |
| Oct 5 (h) Queen's Park R | | W 3-1 | Hartford, Rees, Astle | 22,944 | | 2 | 3 | 4 | 5 | | | 8 | 9 | 10 | 7 | 6 | | | 1 | | 11* | | 12 | | | | | |
| 9 (h) Coventry C | | W 6-1 | Rees, Brown (pen), Astle 2, Hartford, Tudor (og) | 29,255 | | 2 | | 4 | 5 | 6 | | 11 | 9 | 10 | 7 | 8 | 3 | | 1 | | | | | | | | | |
| 12 (a) Leicester C | | W 2-0 | Astle, Hartford | 26,348 | | 2 | | 4 | 5 | 6 | | 11 | 9 | 10 | 7 | 8 | 3 | | 1 | | | | | | | | | |
| 19 (h) Arsenal | | W 1-0 | Brown | 29,324 | | 2 | 12 | 4 | 5 | 6 | | 11 | 9* | 10 | 7 | | | 3 | 1 | | | | | 8 | | | | |
| 26 (a) Leeds U | | D 0-0 | | 33,926 | | 2 | | 4 | 5 | 6 | | 11 | | 10 | 7 | | 8 | 3 | 1 | | | | | 9 | | | | |
| Nov 2 (h) Liverpool | | D 0-0 | | 34,805 | | 2 | | 4 | 5 | 6 | | 11 | 9 | 10 | 7 | | 8 | 3 | 1 | | | | | | | | | |
| 9 (a) Southampton | | L 0-2 | | 19,885 | | 2 | | 4 | 5 | 6 | | 11 | 9 | 10 | 7 | | 8 | 3* | 1 | | | | | 12 | | | | |
| 16 (h) Stoke C | | W 2-1 | Fraser, Hartford | 21,026 | | 2 | | 4 | 5 | 6 | | 11 | 9 | 10 | | 12 | 8 | 3 | 1 | | | | | | 7* | | | |
| 23 (a) Manchester C | | L 1-5 | | 24,667 | 1 | 2 | 12 | 4 | 5 | 6 | | 11 | 9 | 10 | 7 | | 8* | 3 | | | | | | | | | | |
| 30 (h) Sunderland | | W 3-0 | Brown, Rees, Hartford | 19,411 | | 2 | 12 | 4 | 5 | | | 10 | 9 | | | 7 | | 3 | 1 | 8 | 11* | | | 6 | | | | |
| Dec 7 (a) Ipswich T | | L 1-4 | Rees | 20,725 | | 2 | | 4* | 5 | 6 | | 11 | 9 | | 7 | 10 | | 3 | 1 | 8 | | | | | | | | 12 |
| 14 (h) Leicester C | | D 1-1 | Brown (pen) | 16,483 | | 2 | | 4 | 5 | 6 | | 11 | 9 | 10 | 7 | | 8 | 3 | 1 | | | | | | | | | |
| 21 (a) Arsenal | | L 0-2 | | 30,765 | | 2 | | 4 | 5 | 6 | | | 9 | 10 | | | 8 | 3 | 1 | | 7 | | | | 11 | | | |
| 28 (h) Queen's Park R | | W 4-0 | Collard 2, Martin, Rees | 18,649 | | 2 | | 4 | 5 | 6 | | | 9 | | 11 | 10 | | 3 | 1 | 8 | | | | | | 7 | | |
| Jan 11 (a) Liverpool | | L 0-1 | | 45,587 | | 2 | | 4 | 5 | 6 | | 11 | 9 | 7 | | 10 | | 3 | 1 | 8 | | | | | | | | |
| 18 (h) Southampton | | L 1-2 | Brown (pen) | 22,856 | | 2 | | 4 | 5 | | | 12 | 9 | 7 | | 11 | 10* | 3 | 1 | 8 | | | | | | 6 | | |
| Feb 1 (a) Stoke C | | D 1-1 | Astle | 20,567 | | | | 4 | | 6 | 8 | 11 | 9 | 7 | | | | 3 | 1 | 10 | | | 5 | 2 | | | | |
| Mar 5 (a) Sheffield W | | L 0-1 | | 18,690 | 1 | 2 | | 4 | 5 | 6* | 12 | | 9 | 10 | | | | 3 | | 8 | 11 | | | | 7 | | | |
| 8 (a) Chelsea | | L 0-3 | | 25,137 | | | | 4 | 5 | 6 | 8 | 11 | 9 | 10 | | | | 3 | 1 | | | | 2 | | 7 | | | |
| 10 (a) Sunderland | | W 1-0 | Brown | 15,769 | | 2 | | 8 | 4 | | | | | 10 | | | | 3 | 1 | 11 | | | 6 | 5 | 9 | 7 | | |
| 15 (a) Burnley | | D 2-2 | Brown 2 | 12,218 | | 2 | | 4 | 5 | | | | | 10 | | | 6* | 3 | 1 | 8 | 11 | | | | 9 | 12 | 7 | |
| 22 (a) Nottingham F | | L 0-3 | | 20,546 | | 2 | | 4 | 5 | | | | 9 | 10 | | | | 3 | 1 | 8 | 11 | | 6 | | | 7 | | |
| Apr 2 (a) Manchester U | | L 1-2 | Astle | 38,846 | | 2 | | 4 | 5 | 6 | 7 | | 9 | 10 | | | | 3 | 1 | 8 | 11 | | | | | | | |
| 5 (h) Everton | | D 1-1 | Astle | 23,156 | | 2 | | 4 | 5 | 6 | 7 | 12 | 9 | 10* | | | | 3 | 1 | 8 | 11 | | | | | | | |
| 7 (h) Tottenham H | | W 4-3 | Hope, Astle 2, Brown | 24,173 | | 2 | | 4 | 5 | 6 | 7 | 11 | 9 | 10 | | | | 3 | 1 | 8 | | | | | | | | |
| 9 (h) Leeds U | | D 1-1 | Krzywicki | 28,186 | | 2 | | 4 | 5 | 6 | 7 | 11 | 9 | 10 | | | | 3 | 1 | 8 | | | | | | | | |
| 12 (a) Wolves | | W 1-0 | Clark | 37,920 | | 2 | | 4 | 5 | 6 | 7 | 11* | | 10 | | | | 3 | 1 | 8 | 12 | | | | 9 | | | |
| 14 (h) West Ham U | | W 3-1 | Astle 2, Brown | 19,780 | | 2 | 3 | 4 | 5 | 6 | | | 9 | 10 | | | | | 1 | 8 | 11 | | | | 7 | | | |
| 16 (h) Manchester C | | W 2-0 | Krzywicki, Book (og) | 22,717 | | 2 | 3 | 4 | 5 | | 7 | 12 | 9 | 10* | | | | | 1 | 8 | 11 | | | 6 | | | | |
| 19 (h) Newcastle U | | W 5-1 | Kaye, Hartford, Brown (pen), Clark, Astle | 22,481 | | 2 | | 4 | 5 | 6 | 7 | 10 | 9 | | | | | 3 | 1 | 8 | 11 | | | | | | | |
| 23 (h) Ipswich T | | D 2-2 | Astle, Brown | 21,426 | | 2 | | 4 | 5 | 6 | 7 | | 9 | 10 | | | | 3 | 1 | 8 | 11 | | | | | | | |
| App | | | | | 10 | 34 | 17 | 42 | 42 | 34 | 17 | 23 | 37 | 35 | 24 | 19 | 27 | 4 | 32 | 23 | 17 | 1 | 4 | 2 | 5 | 10 | 1 | 2 |
| Sub app | | | | | | 3 | | | 1 | 3 | | 1 | | | | 1 | 2 | | | | 1 | | 1 | 1 | 2 | | 1 | 1 |
| Goals | | | | | | 1 | | 17 | | 1 | 2 | 7 | 21 | 1 | 6 | 3 | | | | | 2 | | | | | 1 | | |

Albion in 1968-69. Back row (left to right): G.Lovett, E.Colquhoun, R.Wilson, R.Sheppard, S.Williams (trainer), J.Kaye, J.Osborne, C.Clark, J.Astle, D.Clarke. Front row: R.Hope, D.Fraser, T.Brown, G.Williams, J.Talbut, I.Collard, R.Rees, R.Hartford.

# 1969-70

## Division 1

| Date | | Venue | Opponent | Result | Scorers | Att. | Osborne J | Williams G | Wilson R | Brown T | Talbut J | Kaye J | Hegan D | Suggett C | Krzywicki R | Hope R | Freeman P | Nisbet G | Astle J | Fraser D | Cumbes J | Hartford A | Merrick A | Hughes L | Potter R | Cantello L | Robertson A | Martin D | Glover A | Lovett G |
|---|---|---|---|---|---|---|---|---|---|---|---|---|---|---|---|---|---|---|---|---|---|---|---|---|---|---|---|---|---|---|
| Aug | 9 | (a) | Southampton | W 2-0 | Suggett 2 | 22,093 | 1 | 2 | 3 | 4 | 5 | 6 | 7 | 8 | 9 | 10 | 11 | | | | | | | | | | | | | |
| | 12 | (a) | Coventry C | L 1-3 | Krzywicki | 37,025 | | 2 | 3* | 4 | 5 | 6 | 7 | 8 | 11 | 10 | | 1 | 9 | 12 | | | | | | | | | | |
| | 16 | (h) | Arsenal | L 0-1 | | 32,215 | | | 3 | 4 | 5 | 6 | 7 | 8 | 11 | 10 | | | 9 | 2 | 1 | | | | | | | | | |
| | 20 | (h) | Coventry C | L 0-1 | | 33,933 | | | 3 | 4 | 5 | 6 | 7 | 8 | 9 | 10 | | | | 2 | 1 | 11 | | | | | | | | |
| | 23 | (a) | West Ham U | W 3-1 | Suggett, Brown, Krzywicki | 29,156 | | | 3 | 4 | 5 | | 7 | 8 | 9 | | | | | 2 | 1 | 11 | 6 | 10 | | | | | | |
| | 26 | (a) | Nottingham F | L 0-1 | | 22,909 | | | 3 | 4 | 5 | 6 | 7* | 8 | 9 | | | | | 2 | 1 | 11 | 12 | 10 | | | | | | |
| | 30 | (h) | Derby C | L 0-2 | | 34,173 | | | | 4 | 5 | 6 | 7 | | 9 | 10 | | | | 2 | 1 | 11 | 3 | 8 | | | | | | |
| Sep | 6 | (a) | Sunderland | D 2-2 | Suggett, Brown | 14,410 | | | | 4 | 5 | 6 | 7* | 9 | 12 | 10 | | | | 2 | 1 | 11 | 3 | 8 | | | | | | |
| | 13 | (h) | Ipswich T | D 2-2 | Astle 2 | 21,173 | | 2 | 3 | 4 | | 6 | 10* | 8 | 7 | 11 | | | 9 | | 1 | 12 | 5 | | | | | | | |
| | 17 | (h) | Stoke C | L 1-3 | Astle | 24,472 | | | 3 | 4 | | 6 | | 8 | 7 | 11 | | | 9 | 2 | 1 | 10 | 5 | | | | | | | |
| | 20 | (a) | Crystal P | W 3-1 | Hegan, Hope, Astle | 27,684 | | | 3 | 7 | 5 | 6 | 10 | 8 | | 11 | | | 9 | 2 | 1 | | 4 | | | | | | | |
| | 27 | (h) | Liverpool | D 2-2 | Astle, Hegan | 34,295 | | | 3 | 7 | 5 | 6 | 10 | 8 | | 11 | | | 9 | 2 | 1 | | 4 | | | | | | | |
| Oct | 4 | (a) | Manchester C | L 1-2 | Pardoe (og) | 34,329 | 1 | 12 | | 7 | 5 | 6 | | 8 | 2 | 11 | | | 9 | 3 | | 10 | 4* | | | | | | | |
| | 7 | (a) | Arsenal | D 1-1 | Astle | 21,165 | 1 | | 3 | | 5 | 6 | | 8 | 7 | 11 | | | 9 | 2 | | 10 | | 4 | | | | | | |
| | 11 | (h) | Leeds U | D 1-1 | Astle | 33,037 | 1 | 3 | | | 5 | 6 | 12 | 8 | 7 | 11 | | | 9 | 2 | | 10 | | 4* | | | | | | |
| | 18 | (a) | Chelsea | L 0-2 | | 34,810 | | 3 | | | 7 | 5 | 6 | | 8 | | 11 | | 9 | 2 | 1 | 10 | | 4 | | | | | | |
| | 25 | (h) | Manchester U | W 2-1 | Brown, Hope | 45,120 | 1 | 3 | | 4 | 5 | | 7 | 8 | 12 | 11 | | | 9 | 2 | | 10* | | | 6 | | | | | |
| Nov | 1 | (a) | Wolves | L 0-1 | | 39,832 | 1 | 3 | | 4 | 5 | 6 | 7 | 8 | | 11 | | | 9* | 2 | | 10 | | 12 | | | | | | |
| | 8 | (h) | Everton | W 2-0 | Astle, Krzywicki | 34,288 | 1 | 3 | | 4 | 5 | 6 | | 8 | 7 | 11 | | | 9 | 2 | | 10 | | | | | | | | |
| | 15 | (a) | Tottenham H | L 0-2 | | 28,340 | 1 | 3 | | 4 | 5 | 6 | | 8 | 7 | 11 | | | 9* | 2 | | 10 | | 12 | | | | | | |
| | 22 | (h) | Sheffield W | W 3-0 | Hope, Suggett, Astle | 20,382 | | 3 | 4 | 5 | 6* | | 7 | 8 | 11 | | | | 9 | 2 | 1 | 10 | | | | 12 | | | | |
| Dec | 6 | (h) | Burnley | L 0-1 | | 18,512 | 1 | 3 | 4 | | | | 8 | 7* | 11 | | | | 9 | 2 | | 10 | | | 5 | 12 | 6 | | | |
| | 13 | (h) | Ipswich T | W 1-0 | Astle | 18,364 | 1 | 12 | 3 | 4 | | 6 | | 8 | | 11 | | | 9* | | | 10 | | 2 | 5 | | 7 | | | |
| | 26 | (h) | West Ham U | W 3-1 | Suggett 2, Astle | 32,246 | 1 | | 3 | 4 | | 6 | | 8 | | 11* | | | 9 | 2 | | 10 | | 12 | 5 | | 7 | | | |
| | 27 | (a) | Derby C | L 0-2 | | 35,581 | 1 | 2 | 3 | 4 | | | 7 | 8 | 12 | | | | 9 | | | 10 | | 6 | 5 | | 11* | | | |
| Jan | 10 | (h) | Crystal P | W 3-2 | Astle 3 | 19,234 | 1 | | 3 | 4 | 5 | 6 | | 8 | 7 | 11 | | | 9 | 2 | | 10 | | | | | | | | |
| | 17 | (h) | Liverpool | D 1-1 | Brown | 43,526 | 1 | | 3 | 4 | 5 | 6 | | 8 | 9 | 11* | | | | 2 | | 10 | | 7 | | | 12 | | | |
| | 28 | (h) | Sunderland | W 3-1 | Astle 2, Brown | 19,024 | 1 | | | 4 | 5 | 6 | | 8 | | 11 | | | 9 | 2 | | 10 | 3 | 7 | | | | | | |
| | 31 | (h) | Manchester C | W 3-0 | Suggett, Astle, Hartford | 30,341 | 1 | | 3 | 4 | 5 | 6 | | 8 | | 11 | | | 9 | 2 | | 10 | | | | 7 | | | | |
| Feb | 6 | (a) | Newcastle U | L 0-1 | | 32,054 | | | 3 | 4 | 5 | 6 | | 8 | | 11 | | | 9 | 2 | 1 | 10 | | | | 7 | | | | |
| | 10 | (a) | Leeds U | L 1-5 | Astle | 31,515 | | | 3 | 4 | 5 | | | 8 | | 11 | | | 9 | 2 | 1 | 10 | | 6 | | 7 | | | | |
| | 20 | (h) | Southampton | W 1-0 | Suggett | 19,453 | 1 | | 3 | 4 | 5 | 6 | | 8 | | 11* | | | 9 | 2 | | 10 | | | | 7 | 12 | | | |
| | 28 | (h) | Wolves | D 3-3 | Astle, Suggett 2 | 37,391 | | | 3 | 4 | 5 | 6 | | 8 | | 11 | | | 9 | 2 | 1 | 10 | | | 7* | | 12 | | | |
| Mar | 10 | (a) | Sheffield W | L 0-2 | | 21,990 | 1 | | 3 | 4 | 5 | | | 8 | | 11 | | | 9 | | | 10 | 2 | | 7 | 6 | | | | |
| | 14 | (h) | Newcastle U | D 2-2 | Astle 2 | 19,322 | 1 | | 3 | 4 | 5 | | | 8 | | 11 | | | 9 | 2* | | 10 | | | 7 | 6 | | | 12 | |
| | 21 | (a) | Burnley | L 1-2 | Brown | 12,821 | 1 | | 3 | 4* | | | | 8 | | 11 | | | 9 | | | 12 | 6 | 2 | 10 | 5 | | | 7 | |
| | 28 | (h) | Tottenham H | D 1-1 | Astle | 24,890 | 1 | | 3 | 4 | | | | 8 | | 11 | | | 9 | | | 12 | 6 | 2 | 10* | 5 | | | 7 | |
| | 30 | (h) | Chelsea | W 3-1 | Brown 2, Astle | 31,207 | 1 | | 3 | 4 | | | | 8 | | 11 | | | 9 | | | 10 | 6 | 2 | | 7 | 5 | | | |
| Apr | 1 | (a) | Everton | L 0-2 | | 58,523 | 1 | | 3 | 10 | | | | 8 | | 11 | | | 9 | 4 | | | 6 | 2 | | 7 | 5 | | | |
| | 4 | (h) | Nottingham F | W 4-0 | Brown 2, Astle, Glover | 20,691 | 1 | | 3 | 10 | | | | 8 | | | 12 | | 9 | 4 | | | 6 | 2 | | 11* | 5 | | 7 | |
| | 8 | (a) | Manchester U | L 0-7 | | 29,396 | 1 | | 3 | 10 | | | | 8 | | 11 | | | 9 | 4 | | | 7 | 6 | 2 | | 5 | | | |
| | 15 | (a) | Stoke C | L 2-3 | Astle, Suggett | 11,804 | 1 | | 3 | 10 | 5 | | | 8 | | 11 | | | 9 | 4 | | | 7 | 6 | 2 | | | | | |
| | | | | | App | | 26 | 14 | 28 | 40 | 30 | 28 | 13 | 42 | 18 | 38 | 2 | 1 | 34 | 33 | 15 | 32 | 11 | 20 | 6 | 15 | 10 | 3 | 1 | 2 |
| | | | | | Sub app | | | 2 | | | | | 1 | | 3 | | 1 | | | 1 | | 3 | 1 | 3 | | 2 | | 2 | 1 | 1 |
| | | | | | Goals | | | | | 10 | | | 2 | 12 | 3 | 3 | | | 25 | | | 1 | | | | | | | 1 | |

**Colin Suggett (8) and Jeff Astle are thwarted by Liverpool's Ray Clemence and Ron Yeats, with Tommy Smith in support. The sides drew 2-2 at The Hawthorns in September 1969.**

# 1970-71

## Division 1

| Date | | Opponent | Result | Scorers | Att | Osborne J | Hughes L | Wilson R | Merrick A | Talbut J | Kaye J | Reed H | Brown T | Astle J | Suggett C | Hope R | Cantello L | Robertson A | Johnson G | Cumbes J | McVitie G | Hartford A | Minton R | Fraser D | Lovett G | Wile J |
|---|---|---|---|---|---|---|---|---|---|---|---|---|---|---|---|---|---|---|---|---|---|---|---|---|---|---|
| Aug 15 | (h) | Crystal P | D 0-0 | | 25,127 | 1 | 2 | 3 | 4 | 5 | 6 | 7 | 8 | 9 | 10 | 11 | | | | | | | | | | |
| 18 | (a) | Nottingham F | D 3-3 | Brown 2, Astle | 24,423 | 1 | 2 | 3 | 4 | 5 | 6 | 7 | 8 | 9 | 10 | 11 | | | | | | | | | | |
| 22 | (a) | Blackpool | L 1-3 | Astle | 22,162 | 1* | 2 | | 3 | 5 | | 7 | 8 | 9 | 10 | 11 | 4 | 6 | 12 | | | | | | | |
| 26 | (h) | Stoke C | W 5-2 | Astle 2, Brown 2, Reed | 22,015 | | 2 | 3 | 4 | 5 | | 12 | 8 | 9 | 10 | 11* | 7 | 6 | | 1 | | | | | | |
| 29 | (h) | Liverpool | D 1-1 | Astle | 31,474 | | 2 | 3 | 4 | 5 | | 12 | 8 | 9 | 10 | 11 | 7* | 6 | | 1 | | | | | | |
| Sep 2 | (h) | Newcastle U | L 1-2 | Astle | 25,112 | | 2 | 3 | 4 | 5 | 6 | | 8 | 9 | 10 | 11 | | | | 1 | 7 | | | | | |
| 5 | (a) | Manchester C | L 1-4 | Hope | 30,549 | | 2 | 3 | | 5 | 6 | | 8* | 9 | 10 | 11 | 4 | 12 | | 1 | 7 | | | | | |
| 12 | (h) | West Ham U | W 2-1 | Suggett 2 | 24,606 | | 2 | | 3 | 5 | 6 | 4 | 9 | 8 | 10 | 11 | | | | 1 | | | | | | |
| 19 | (a) | Arsenal | L 2-6 | Reed, Brown | 33,326 | | 2 | | 3 | 5 | | 7 | 4 | 9 | 8 | | | 6 | | 1 | 11 | 10 | | | | |
| 26 | (h) | Derby C | W 2-1 | McVitie, Brown | 31,216 | | | 3 | 2 | 5 | 6 | | 4 | 9 | 8 | 10 | | | | 1 | 7 | 11 | | | | |
| Oct 3 | (a) | Ipswich T | D 2-2 | Brown, Astle | 17,027 | | | 3 | | 5 | 6 | | 4 | 9 | 8 | 10 | | | | 1 | 7 | 11 | 2 | | | |
| 10 | (h) | Leeds U | D 2-2 | Suggett, McVitie | 37,124 | | | 3 | | 5 | 6 | | 4 | 9 | 8 | 10 | | | | 1 | 7 | 11 | 2 | | | |
| 17 | (a) | Crystal P | L 0-3 | | 28,330 | | | 3 | | 5 | 6 | | 4 | 9 | 8 | 10 | | | | 1 | 7 | 11 | 2 | | | |
| 24 | (a) | Manchester U | L 1-2 | Brown | 43,278 | | | 3 | | 5 | 6 | | 4 | 9 | 10* | 8 | | | | 1 | 7 | 11 | 12 | 2 | | |
| 31 | (h) | Everton | W 3-0 | Astle, Brown, McVitie | 29,628 | | | | | 5 | 6 | | 8 | 9 | 10 | | | 3 | | 1 | 7 | 11 | | 2 | 4 | |
| Nov 7 | (a) | Wolves | L 1-2 | Lovett | 39,670 | | | | | 5 | 6 | | 10 | 9 | 8 | | | 3 | | 1 | 7 | 11 | | 2 | 4 | |
| 14 | (h) | Southampton | W 1-0 | Hartford | 17,824 | | | 5* | | | 6 | | 8 | 9 | 12 | 10 | | 3 | | 1 | 7 | 11 | | 2 | 4 | |
| 21 | (a) | Huddersfield T | L 1-2 | Brown | 18,209 | | | | 6 | 5 | | | 8 | 9 | 12 | 10 | | 3 | | 1 | 7 | 11 | | 2* | 4 | |
| 28 | (h) | Chelsea | D 2-2 | Suggett, Astle | 29,374 | | | | 6 | 5 | | | 4 | 9 | 8 | 10 | | 3 | | 1 | 7 | 11 | | 2* | 12 | |
| Dec 5 | (a) | Burnley | D 1-1 | Brown | 12,437 | | | | 6 | 12 | 5 | | 4 | 9 | 8 | 11 | | 3* | | 1 | 7 | 10 | | 2 | | |
| 12 | (h) | Tottenham H | W 3-1 | Brown 3 (1 pen) | 26,584 | | | | 6 | | 5 | | 4 | 9 | 8 | 10 | | 3 | | 1 | 7 | 10 | | 2 | | |
| 19 | (h) | Blackpool | D 1-1 | Suggett | 17,909 | | | 3 | | | 5 | | 4 | 9 | 8 | 10 | | | | 1 | 7 | 11 | | 2 | 5 | |
| 26 | (a) | Coventry C | D 1-1 | Brown (pen) | 27,526 | | | 3 | 6 | | | | 4 | 9 | 8 | 10 | | | | 1 | 7 | 11 | | 2 | 5 | |
| Jan 9 | (h) | Nottingham F | L 0-1 | | 20,015 | | | 3 | | | 6 | | 4 | 9 | 8 | 10 | | | | 1 | 7 | 11 | | 2 | 5 | |
| 16 | (a) | Stoke C | L 0-2 | | 20,882 | | | 3 | | | 6 | | 4 | 9 | 8 | 10 | | | | 1 | 7 | 11 | | 2 | 5 | |
| 30 | (a) | Chelsea | L 1-4 | Astle | 26,874 | | | 3 | | | 6 | | 4 | 9 | 8 | 10 | | | | 1 | 7 | 11 | | 2 | 5 | |
| Feb 6 | (h) | Burnley | W 1-0 | Brown | 16,982 | | 2 | 3 | | | 6 | | 8 | 9 | | 10 | | | | 1 | 7 | 11 | | | 4 | 5 |
| 17 | (a) | Tottenham H | D 2-2 | Brown 2 | 22,650 | | | 3 | 6 | | 2 | | 8 | 9 | | 10 | | | | 1 | 7 | 11 | | | 4 | 5 |
| 20 | (h) | Huddersfield T | W 2-1 | Brown 2 | 18,254 | 1 | | 3 | 6 | | 2 | | 8 | 9 | | 10 | | | | | 7 | 11 | | | 4 | 5 |
| 27 | (a) | Everton | D 3-3 | Astle, Brown, Wile | 35,965 | | | 3 | 6 | | 2 | | 8 | 9 | | 10 | | | | 1 | 7 | 11 | | | 4 | 5 |
| Mar 6 | (h) | Manchester U | W 4-3 | Brown 3, Wile | 41,134 | | | 3 | 6 | | 2 | | 8 | 9 | | 10 | | | | 1 | 7 | 11 | | | 4 | 5 |
| 13 | (a) | Southampton | L 0-1 | | 19,008 | | | 3 | 6 | | 2 | | 8 | 9 | | 10 | 7 | | | 1 | | 11 | | | 4 | 5 |
| 20 | (h) | Wolves | L 2-4 | McVitie, Brown | 36,754 | | | 3 | 6 | | 2 | | 8 | 9 | | 10 | | | | 1 | 7 | 11 | | | 4 | 5 |
| 27 | (h) | Manchester C | D 0-0 | | 20,363 | | 2 | 3 | | | 6 | | 8 | | 9 | 10 | 4 | | | 1 | 7 | 11 | | | | 5 |
| Apr 2 | (a) | Liverpool | D 1-1 | Brown | 43,580 | | 2 | 3 | | | 6 | | 8 | 9 | | 10 | 4 | | | 1 | 7 | 11 | | | | 5 |
| 9 | (a) | West Ham U | L 1-2 | Astle | 34,981 | | 2 | 3 | | | 6 | | 8 | 9 | 12 | 10 | 4 | | | 1 | 7* | 11 | | | | 5 |
| 10 | (h) | Coventry C | D 0-0 | | 18,726 | | 2 | 3 | | | 6 | | 8 | 9 | 10 | | 4 | | | 1 | 7 | 11 | | | | 5 |
| 12 | (h) | Ipswich T | L 0-1 | | 12,684 | | 2 | 3 | | | 6 | | 8 | 9 | 10 | | 4 | | | 1 | 7 | 11 | | | | 5 |
| 17 | (a) | Leeds U | W 2-1 | Brown, Astle | 36,812 | | 2 | 3 | | | 6 | | 8 | 9 | 7 | 10 | | | | 1 | | 11 | | | 4 | 5 |
| 24 | (h) | Arsenal | D 2-2 | Hartford, Brown | 36,621 | | 2 | 3 | | | 6 | | 8 | 9 | 7 | 10 | | | | 1 | | 11 | | | 4 | 5 |
| 28 | (a) | Newcastle U | L 0-3 | | 18,310 | | 2 | 3 | | | 6 | | 8 | 9 | 7 | 10* | 12 | | | 1 | | 11 | | | 4 | 5 |
| May 1 | (a) | Derby C | L 0-2 | | 33,651 | | 2 | 3 | | | 6 | | 8 | 9 | 7 | | 4 | | | 1 | 11 | 10 | | | | 5 |
| | | App | | | | 4 | 18 | 19 | 34 | 17 | 37 | 4 | 42 | 41 | 30 | 34 | 23 | 3 | | 38 | 33 | 34 | 3 | 6 | 21 | 21 |
| | | Sub app | | | | | | | 1 | | 2 | | | | 3 | | 1 | 1 | 1 | | | | 1 | 1 | | |
| | | Goals | | | | | | | | | | 2 | 28 | 13 | 5 | 1 | | | | | 4 | 2 | | | 1 | 2 |

**Burnley v West Brom in December 1970. A shot by Bobby Hope (not pictured) is turned away for a corner by Peter Mellor.**

# 1971-72

## Division 1

| Date | V | Opponent | Result | Scorers | Att. | Cumbes J | Hughes L | Wilson R | Cantello L | Wile J | Kaye J | Hope R | Suggett C | Astle J | Brown T | Merrick A | Hartford A | Minton R | MacLean H | Gould R | McVitie G | Osborne J | Robertson A | Johnson G | Glover A | Smith G | Nisbet G | Brown A |
|---|---|---|---|---|---|---|---|---|---|---|---|---|---|---|---|---|---|---|---|---|---|---|---|---|---|---|---|---|
| Aug 14 | (a) | West Ham U | W 1-0 | Brown | 27,420 | 1 | 2 | 3 | 4 | 5 | 6 | 7 | 8 | 9 | 10 | 11 | | | | | | • | | | | | | |
| 18 | (h) | Everton | W 2-0 | Wile, Brown | 29,055 | 1 | 2 | 3 | 4 | 5 | 6 | 10 | 7 | 9 | 8 | | 11 | | | | | | | | | | | |
| 21 | (h) | Coventry C | D 1-1 | Brown | 24,692 | 1 | 2 | 3 | 4 | 5 | 6 | 10 | 7 | 9 | 8 | | 11 | | | | | | | | | | | |
| 23 | (a) | Manchester U§ | L 1-3 | Brown | 23,146 | 1 | 2 | 3 | 4 | 5 | 6 | 10 | 7 | 9 | 8 | | 11 | | | | | | | | | | | |
| 28 | (a) | Sheffield U | D 0-0 | | 32,768 | 1 | 2 | 3 | 4 | 5 | 6 | 10 | 7 | | 8 | 9 | 11 | | | | | | | | | | | |
| Sep 1 | (a) | Chelsea | L 0-1 | | 29,931 | 1 | 2 | 3 | 4 | 5 | 6 | 10 | 7 | | 8 | 9 | 11 | | | | | | | | | | | |
| 4 | (h) | Arsenal | L 0-1 | | 29,809 | 1 | 2 | 3 | 4 | 5 | 6 | 10 | 7* | 9 | 8 | 12 | 11 | | | | | | | | | | | |
| 11 | (a) | Huddersfield T | L 0-1 | | 9,938 | 1 | 2 | | 4 | 5 | 6 | | 12 | 7 | | 8 | 11 | 10 | | | 3 | | | | | | | 9* |
| 18 | (h) | Ipswich T | L 1-2 | Brown | 18,885 | 1 | 2 | 3 | 4 | 5 | 6 | | 7 | | | 8 | | 10 | | 9 | 11 | | | | | | | |
| 25 | (a) | Derby C | D 0-0 | | 30,628 | 1 | 2 | 3 | 4 | 5 | 6 | 10 | | | | 8 | | 11 | | 9 | 7 | | | | | | | |
| Oct 2 | (h) | Manchester C | L 0-2 | | 25,834 | 1 | 2 | 3 | 4 | 5 | 6 | 10* | 12 | | | 8 | | 11 | | 9 | 7 | | | | | | | |
| 9 | (a) | Crystal P | W 2-0 | Brown, Gould | 22,399 | | 2 | 3 | 4 | 5 | | | 12 | | 10 | 8 | 11 | | | 9 | 7* | 1 | 6 | | | | | |
| 16 | (h) | West Ham U | D 0-0 | | 20,620 | | 2 | 3 | 4 | 5 | | | 12 | | 9 | 8 | 11 | 7* | | 10 | | 1 | 6 | | | | | |
| 23 | (h) | Leicester C | L 0-1 | | 23,088 | | | 3 | 4 | 5 | | | 7* | | 9 | 8 | 11 | | 2 | 10 | | 1 | 6 | 12 | | | | |
| 30 | (a) | Southampton | D 1-1 | Hartford | 16,972 | | | 3 | 4 | 5 | | | | | | | 11 | 8 | 2 | 9 | | 1 | 6 | 10 | 7 | | | |
| Nov 6 | (h) | Stoke C | L 0-1 | | 19,204 | | | 3 | 4 | 5 | | | | | 8 | | 11 | | 2 | 9 | | 1 | 6 | 10 | 7 | | | |
| 13 | (a) | Nottingham F | L 1-4 | Astle | 20,024 | | | 3 | 4 | 5 | | | | 10 | | | 11 | 8 | 2 | 9 | | 1 | 6 | | 7 | | | |
| 20 | (a) | Tottenham H | L 2-3 | Gould, Brown | 31,895 | | | 3 | 4 | 5 | | 12 | | 9* | | | 11 | 8 | 2 | 10 | | 1 | 6 | | 7 | | | |
| 27 | (h) | Wolves | L 2-3 | Brown (pen), Gould | 37,696 | | | 3 | 4 | 5 | | | | 9 | | | 11 | 8 | 2 | 10 | | 1 | 6 | | 7 | | | |
| Dec 4 | (a) | Leeds U | L 0-3 | | 32,521 | | | 3 | 4 | 5 | | | | 9 | | | 11 | 7 | 2 | 8 | | | 6 | 10 | | 1 | | |
| 11 | (h) | Newcastle U | L 0-3 | | 18,142 | | | 3 | 4 | 5 | | 12 | | 9 | | | 11 | 8 | 2 | 10 | | | 6 | | 7* | 1 | | |
| 18 | (a) | Arsenal | L 0-2 | | 28,177 | | | 3 | 4 | 5 | | | | 8 | 9 | | 10 | 11 | | | 7 | | 6 | | | 1 | 2 | |
| 27 | (h) | Liverpool | W 1-0 | Brown | 43,785 | | | 3 | 4 | 5 | | | | 10 | 8 | | 11 | | | 9 | 7 | | 6 | | | 1 | 2 | |
| Jan 1 | (a) | Ipswich T | W 3-2 | Brown, Gould, McVitie | 17,085 | | | 3 | 4 | 5 | | | | 10 | 8 | | 11 | | | 9 | 7 | | 6 | | | 1 | 2 | |
| 8 | (h) | Sheffield U | D 2-2 | Brown 2 | 21,225 | | | 3 | 4 | 5 | | | | 10 | 8 | | 11 | | | 9 | 7 | | 6 | | | 1 | 2 | |
| 22 | (a) | Everton | L 1-2 | Gould | 36,413 | | | 3 | 4 | 5 | | | 10 | | | 8 | 11 | | | 9 | 7* | 1 | 6 | 12 | | | | |
| 29 | (h) | Manchester U | W 2-1 | Gould, Astle | 46,992 | | | 3 | 4 | 5 | | | 10 | 9 | | 8 | 11 | | | 7 | | 1 | 6 | | | | 2 | |
| Feb 12 | (a) | Leicester C | W 1-0 | Brown | 24,225 | | | 3 | 4 | 5 | | | 10 | 9 | | 8 | 11 | | | 7 | | 1 | 6 | | | | 2 | |
| 19 | (h) | Southampton | W 3-2 | Gould, Cantello, Brown | 17,875 | | | 3 | 4 | 5 | | | 10 | 9 | | 8 | 11 | | | 7 | | 1 | 6 | | | | 2 | |
| Mar 1 | (a) | Manchester C | L 1-2 | Brown (pen) | 25,677 | | | 3 | 4 | 5 | | | 10 | 9 | | 8 | 11 | | | 7 | | 1 | 6 | | | | 2 | |
| 4 | (h) | Nottingham F | W 1-0 | Wile | 16,702 | | | 3 | 4 | 5 | | | 10 | 9 | | 8 | 11 | | | 7 | | 1 | 6 | | | | 2 | |
| 11 | (h) | Crystal P | D 1-1 | A.Brown | 17,105 | | | 3 | 4 | 5 | | | 10 | 9 | | 8 | 11 | | | | | 1 | 6 | | | | 2 | 7 |
| 17 | (a) | Coventry C | W 2-0 | Wile, A.Brown | 22,424 | | | 3 | 4 | 5 | | | | 9 | | 8 | 11 | | | 7 | | 1 | 6 | | | | 2 | 10 |
| 25 | (h) | Huddersfield T | D 1-1 | Gould | 18,373 | | | 3 | 4 | 5 | | | | 9 | | 8 | 11 | | | 7 | | 1 | 6 | | | | 2 | 10 |
| Apr 1 | (a) | Liverpool | L 0-2 | | 46,564 | | | 3 | 4* | 5 | | | | 9 | | 8 | 11 | | | 7 | | 1 | 6 | 12 | | | 2 | 10 |
| 5 | (h) | Derby C | D 0-0 | | 32,439 | | | 3 | | 5 | | 7 | 4 | 9 | | 8 | 11 | | | | | 1 | 6 | | | | 2 | 10 |
| 8 | (h) | Tottenham H | D 1-1 | Hope (pen) | 20,862 | | | 3 | | 5 | | 7 | 4 | 9 | | | 11 | | | 8 | | 1 | 6 | | | | 2 | 10 |
| 15 | (a) | Wolves | W 1-0 | T.Brown | 30,619 | | | 3 | | 5 | | 7 | 4 | 9 | | | 11 | | | 8 | | 1 | 6 | | | | 2 | 10 |
| 22 | (h) | Leeds U | L 0-1 | | 40,675 | | | 3 | | 5 | | 7 | 4 | 9 | | | 11 | | | 8 | | 1 | 6 | | | | 2 | 10 |
| 27 | (h) | Chelsea | W 4-0 | T.Brown, Gould, A.Brown, Cantello | 18,413 | | 11 | | 3 | 5 | | 7 | 4 | 9 | | | | | | 8 | | 1 | 6 | | | | 2 | 10 |
| May 3 | (a) | Newcastle U | L 2-4 | Gould 2 | 20,052 | | | 3 | 4 | 5 | | 7 | 12 | 9 | | | 11 | | | 8 | | 1 | 6 | | | | 2 | 10* |
| 5 | (a) | Stoke C | D 1-1 | Gould | 16,206 | 12 | | 3 | 4* | 5 | | 7 | | 9 | | | 11 | | | 8 | | 1 | 6 | | | | 2 | 10 |
| | | | | App | | 11 | 13 | 40 | 38 | 42 | 11 | 17 | 30 | 22 | 40 | 6 | 39 | 9 | 2 | 31 | 9 | 25 | 31 | 2 | 6 | 6 | 21 | 11 |
| | | | | Sub app | | 1 | | | | | 1 | 5 | 1 | | | | 1 | | | | | | | 1 | 2 | | | |
| | | | | Goals | | | | | 2 | 3 | | 1 | | 2 | 17 | | 1 | | | 12 | 1 | | | | | | | 3 |

§ Played at Victoria Ground, Stoke

**Albion goalkeeper Graham Smith is beaten by Arsenal's John Roberts at Highbury in December 1971.**

# 1972-73

## Division 1

| Date | | Opponent | Result | Scorers | Att | Smith G | Nisbet G | Wilson R | Cantello L | Wile J | Robertson A | Brown T | Brown A | Gould R | Suggett C | Hartford R | Latchford P | MacLean H | Merrick A | Hughes L | Woolgar S | Johnston W | Glover A | Astle J | Shaw D | Osborne J | Minton R |
|---|---|---|---|---|---|---|---|---|---|---|---|---|---|---|---|---|---|---|---|---|---|---|---|---|---|---|---|
| Aug 12 | (h) | West Ham U | D 0-0 | | 22,234 | 1 | 2 | 3 | 4 | 5 | 6 | 7 | 8 | 9 | 10 | 11 | | | | | | | | | | | |
| 16 | (h) | Tottenham H | L 0-1 | | 19,175 | 1 | 2 | 3 | 4 | 5 | 6 | 7 | 8 | 9 | 10 | 11 | | | | | | | | | | | |
| 19 | (a) | Leeds U | L 0-2 | | 36,555 | 1 | 2 | 3 | 4 | 5 | 6 | 7 | 8 | 9 | 10 | 11 | | | | | | | | | | | |
| 23 | (a) | Newcastle U | D 1-1 | A.Brown | 29,010 | 1 | 2 | 3 | 4 | 5 | 6 | 7 | 8 | 9 | 10 | 11 | | | | | | | | | | | |
| 26 | (h) | Sheffield U | L 0-2 | | 15,559 | | 2 | 3 | 4 | 5 | 6 | 7 | 8 | 9* | 10 | 11 | 1 | 12 | | | | | | | | | |
| 30 | (h) | Birmingham C | D 2-2 | Gould, Suggett | 37,108 | | 2 | 3 | | 5 | 6 | | 8 | 9 | 10 | 11 | 1 | | 4 | 7 | | | | | | | |
| Sep 2 | (a) | Everton | L 0-1 | | 36,269 | | 2 | 3 | | 5 | 6 | 10 | 9 | | 7 | 11 | 1 | | 8 | 4 | | | | | | | |
| 9 | (h) | Derby C | W 2-1 | Gould, T.Brown | 17,262 | | 2 | 3 | 4 | 5 | 6 | 8 | 10 | 9 | 7 | 11 | 1 | | | | | | | | | | |
| 16 | (a) | Crystal P | W 2-0 | Gould, Robertson | 17,858 | | 2 | 3 | 4 | 5 | 6 | 8 | 10 | 9 | 7 | 11 | 1 | | | | | | | | | | |
| 23 | (h) | Coventry C | W 1-0 | Suggett | 15,373 | | 2 | | 4 | 5 | 6 | 8 | 10 | 9 | 7 | 11 | 1 | | 3 | | | | | | | | |
| 30 | (a) | Manchester C | L 1-2 | T.Brown | 27,332 | | 2 | 3 | 4 | 5 | 6 | 8 | 10 | 9 | 7 | 11 | 1 | | | | | | | | | | |
| Oct 7 | (h) | Manchester U | D 2-2 | A.Brown 2 | 39,209 | | 2 | 3 | 4* | 5 | 6 | 8 | 10 | 9 | 7 | 11 | 1 | | | | | 12 | | | | | |
| 14 | (a) | Chelsea | L 1-3 | T.Brown (pen) | 28,998 | | 2 | 3 | 4 | 5 | 6 | 8 | 10 | 9 | 7 | 11 | 1 | | | | | | | | | | |
| 21 | (h) | Wolves | W 1-0 | Gould | 30,121 | | 2 | | 4* | 5 | 6 | 8 | 10 | 9 | 7 | 11 | 1 | | 3 | | | 12 | | | | | |
| 28 | (a) | Southampton | L 1-2 | Hartford | 15,810 | | 2 | | | 5 | 6 | 8 | 10 | 9 | 7 | 11 | 1 | | 3 | 4 | | | | | | | |
| Nov 4 | (h) | Newcastle U | L 2-3 | Suggett, Gould | 14,668 | | 2 | 3 | | 5 | 6 | 8 | 10 | 9 | 7 | 11 | 1 | | 4 | | | | | | | | |
| 11 | (a) | Tottenham H | D 1-1 | T.Brown | 25,875 | | 2 | 3 | | 5 | 6 | 8 | 10 | 9 | 7 | 11 | 1 | | 4 | | | | | | | | |
| 18 | (a) | Norwich C | L 0-2 | | 21,874 | | 2 | 3 | 4 | 5 | | 8 | 10 | 9 | 7 | 11 | 1 | | 6 | | | | | | | | |
| 25 | (h) | Stoke C | W 2-1 | T.Brown 2 (1 pen) | 13,332 | | 2 | 3 | 4 | 5 | | 8 | 7 | 9 | 10 | 11 | 1 | | 6 | | | | | | | | |
| Dec 2 | (a) | Leicester C | L 1-3 | Gould | 15,307 | | 2 | 3 | 4* | 5 | | 8 | 10 | 9 | 7 | 11 | 1 | | 6 | | | | | | | | |
| 9 | (h) | Liverpool | D 1-1 | T.Brown | 27,258 | | 2 | 3 | 4* | 5 | 6 | 8 | 7 | 9 | 12 | 10 | 1 | | | | | 11 | | | | | |
| 16 | (a) | Arsenal | L 1-2 | T.Brown | 27,119 | | 2 | 3 | 4 | 5 | | 8 | 9* | | 7 | 10 | 1 | | 6 | | | 11 | 12 | | | | |
| 23 | (h) | Ipswich T | W 2-0 | Glover, Hartford | 12,215 | | 2 | 3 | 4 | 5 | | 8 | | | 7 | 10 | 1 | | 6 | | | 11 | 9 | | | | |
| 26 | (a) | Coventry C | D 0-0 | | 31,493 | | 2 | 3 | 4 | 5 | 6 | 8 | 9 | | | 10 | 1 | | 7 | | | 11 | | | | | |
| Jan 6 | (a) | Sheffield U | L 0-3 | | 16,231 | | 2 | | 4 | 5 | 3 | 8 | 9 | | 7 | 10 | 1 | | 6 | | | 11 | | | | | |
| 27 | (a) | Derby C | L 0-2 | | 28,833 | | 2 | 3 | 4 | 5 | | 8 | 9 | | 7 | 10 | 1 | | 6 | | | 11 | | | | | |
| Feb 10 | (h) | Crystal P | L 0-4 | | 15,163 | | 2 | 3 | 4 | 5 | | 9 | 8 | 12 | 7* | 10 | 1 | | 6 | | | 11 | | | | | |
| 17 | (a) | West Ham U | L 1-2 | T.Brown | 26,071 | | 2 | 3 | 4 | 5 | | 9 | 8 | | | 10 | 1 | | 6 | | 7 | 11* | 12 | | | | |
| 28 | (h) | Arsenal | W 1-0 | T.Brown | 23,308 | | 2 | 3 | 4 | 5 | 6 | 8 | 12 | | | 10 | 1 | | | | 7 | 11 | | 9* | | | |
| Mar 3 | (a) | Manchester U | L 1-2 | Astle | 46,735 | | 2 | 3 | 4 | 5 | 6 | 8 | | | | 10 | 1 | | 7 | | | 11* | | 9 | 12 | | |
| 10 | (h) | Chelsea | D 1-1 | T.Brown | 21,466 | | 2 | 3 | 4 | 5 | 6 | 8 | | | | 10 | | | 7* | | | 11 | | 9 | 12 | 1 | |
| 17 | (a) | Ipswich T | L 0-2 | | 17,619 | | 2 | 3 | 4 | 5 | 6 | 8 | | | | 10 | | | 7* | | | 11 | | 9 | 12 | 1 | |
| 20 | (a) | Wolves | L 0-2 | | 33,520 | | 2 | 3 | 4 | 5 | 6 | 8 | | | | 10 | | | 7 | | | 11 | | 9 | | 1 | |
| 24 | (h) | Southampton | D 1-1 | T.Brown | 12,559 | | 3 | 2 | 4 | 5 | 6 | 8 | | | | 10 | | | 7 | | | 11 | | 9 | | 1 | |
| 28 | (h) | Leeds U | D 1-1 | Shaw | 32,804 | | 3 | 2 | 4 | 5 | 6 | | | | | 10 | | | 7 | | | 11 | | 9 | 8 | 1 | |
| 31 | (a) | Stoke C | L 0-2 | | 21,296 | | 3 | 2 | 4* | 5 | 6 | | | | 12 | 10 | | | 7 | | | 11 | | 9 | 8 | 1 | |
| Apr 7 | (h) | Leicester C | W 1-0 | Astle | 15,235 | | | 3 | 4 | 5 | | 7 | | | | 10 | | | 6 | | | 11 | | 9 | 8 | 1 | 2 |
| 11 | (h) | Everton | W 4-1 | Astle, Hartford, Shaw 2 | 21,375 | | | 3 | 4 | 5 | | 7 | | | | 10 | | | 6 | | | 11 | | 9 | 8 | 1 | 2 |
| 14 | (a) | Liverpool | L 0-1 | | 43,853 | | | 3 | 4 | 5 | | 7 | | | | 10 | | | 6 | | | 11 | | 9 | 8 | 1 | 2 |
| 21 | (h) | Norwich C | L 0-1 | | 23,263 | | | 3 | 4 | 5 | 12 | 7 | | | | 10 | | | 6 | | | 11 | | 9 | 8 | 1 | 2* |
| 25 | (h) | Manchester C | L 1-2 | Astle | 21,480 | | | 3 | 4 | 5 | | 7 | 12 | | | 10 | | | 6 | | | 11* | | 9 | 8 | 1 | 2 |
| 28 | (a) | Birmingham C | L 2-3 | Astle, Wile | 36,784 | | | 3 | 4 | 5 | | 7 | 12 | | | 10 | | | 6 | | | 11 | | 9 | 8 | 1 | 2* |
| App | | | | | | 4 | 33 | 38 | 37 | 40 | 35 | 38 | 26 | 21 | 21 | 41 | 26 | 2 | 30 | 2 | 2 | 22 | 2 | 14 | 10 | 12 | 6 |
| Sub app | | | | | | | | | | | 1 | 1 | 3 | | 1 | | | 2 | 1 | | 2 | | 3 | 2 | | | |
| Goals | | | | | | | | | | 1 | 1 | 12 | 3 | 6 | 3 | 3 | | | | | | | 1 | 5 | 3 | | |

**Jeff Astle is airborne after hitting a tremendous shot which found the net for Albion's goal at Old Trafford in March 1973.**

# 1973-74

## Division 2

| Date | Opponent | Result | Scorers | Att | Latchford P | Minton R | Merrick A | Hughes L | Wile J | Robertson A | Cantello L | Shaw D | Glover A | Brown T | Johnston W | Hartford A | Brown A | Donaghy B | Nisbet G | Mayo J | Wilson R | Thompson T | Astle J |
|---|---|---|---|---|---|---|---|---|---|---|---|---|---|---|---|---|---|---|---|---|---|---|---|
| Aug 25 | (a) Blackpool | W 3-2 | T.Brown 2, Glover | 14,328 | 1 | 2 | 3 | 4 | 5 | 6 | 7 | 8 | 9 | 10 | 11 |  |  |  |  |  |  |  |  |
| Sep 1 | (h) Crystal P | W 1-0 | Glover | 17,898 | 1 | 2 | 3 | 4 | 5 | 6 | 7 | 8 | 9 | 10 | 11 |  |  |  |  |  |  |  |  |
| 8 | (a) Swindon T | L 0-1 |  | 11,583 | 1 | 2* | 3 |  | 5 | 6 | 4 | 8 | 7 | 10 | 11 | 9 | 12 |  |  |  |  |  |  |
| 12 | (a) Sheffield W | L 1-3 | T.Brown | 15,927 | 1 | 2 | 3 | 9 | 5 | 6 | 4 | 10 | 7 | 8 | 11* | 12 |  |  |  |  |  |  |  |
| 15 | (h) Nottingham F | D 3-3 | A.Brown, Minton, T.Brown | 14,779 | 1 | 2 | 3 | 4* | 5 | 6 | 7 |  | 12 | 10 |  | 8 | 9 | 11 |  |  |  |  |  |
| 18 | (h) Preston NE | L 0-2 |  | 11,722 | 1 | 2 | 3* | 8 | 5 | 6 |  | 12 | 7 | 10 |  | 4 | 9 | 11 |  |  |  |  |  |
| 22 | (a) Hull C | D 0-0 |  | 7,089 | 1 |  | 3 | 4* | 5 | 6 |  | 9 | 7 | 10 |  |  | 8 | 11 | 2 | 12 |  |  |  |
| 29 | (h) Sunderland | D 1-1 | A.Brown | 17,024 | 1 |  | 3 |  | 5 | 6 |  | 9 | 7 | 10 |  | 4 | 8 | 11 | 2 |  |  |  |  |
| Oct 1 | (a) Preston NE | L 1-3 | T.Brown | 15,419 | 1 |  | 3 |  | 5 | 6 | 11 | 4 | 9 | 7 | 8 | 10 |  |  | 2 |  |  |  |  |
| 6 | (a) Bristol C | D 1-1 | T.Brown | 14,326 | 1 |  | 3 |  | 5 | 6 | 4 | 10 | 8 | 11 | 7 | 9 |  |  | 2 |  |  |  |  |
| 13 | (h) Carlisle U | D 1-1 | T.Brown | 12,556 | 1 |  | 3 |  | 5 | 6 | 4 | 11 | 9 | 7 | 10 | 8 |  |  | 2 |  |  |  |  |
| 20 | (a) Middlesbrough | D 0-0 |  | 18,997 | 1 |  | 3 |  | 5 | 6 | 4 | 10 | 8 | 11 | 7 | 9 |  |  | 2 |  |  |  |  |
| 24 | (h) Sheffield W | W 2-0 | Shaw 2 | 12,667 | 1 |  | 3 |  | 5 | 6 | 4 | 11 | 9 | 7 | 10 | 8 |  |  | 2 |  |  |  |  |
| 27 | (h) Bolton W | D 0-0 |  | 16,148 | 1 |  | 3 |  | 5 | 6 | 4 | 11 | 9 | 7 | 10 | 8 |  |  | 2 |  |  |  |  |
| Nov 3 | (a) Cardiff C | W 1-0 | T.Brown | 10,668 | 1 |  |  |  | 5 | 6 | 4 |  | 11 | 8 | 7 | 10 | 9 |  | 2 |  | 3 |  |  |
| 10 | (h) Notts C | W 2-1 | T.Brown, Shaw | 15,564 | 1 |  |  |  | 5 | 6 | 4 | 12 | 11 | 8* | 7 | 10 | 9 |  | 2 |  | 3 |  |  |
| 17 | (a) Orient | L 0-2 |  | 11,981 | 1 |  |  |  | 5 | 6 | 4 | 12 | 11* | 8 | 7 | 10 | 9 |  | 2 |  | 3 |  |  |
| 24 | (h) Fulham | W 2-0 | Glover, Hartford | 12,606 | 1 |  |  |  | 5 | 6 | 4 | 12 | 11 | 8 | 7 | 10 | 9* |  | 2 |  | 3 |  |  |
| Dec 1 | (a) Luton T | W 2-0 | Shaw, Hartford | 10,192 | 1 |  |  |  | 5 | 6 | 4 | 12 | 11 | 8 | 7 | 10 | 9* |  | 2 |  | 3 |  |  |
| 8 | (h) Oxford U | W 1-0 | Shaw | 12,277 | 1 |  |  |  | 5 | 6 | 4 | 12 | 11 | 8 | 7 | 10 | 9* |  | 2 |  | 3 |  |  |
| 15 | (h) Portsmouth | L 1-2 | Cantello | 11,574 | 1 |  |  |  | 5 | 6 | 4 | 9 | 11 | 8 | 7 | 10 |  |  | 2 |  | 3 |  |  |
| 22 | (a) Sunderland | D 1-1 | Shaw | 18,389 | 1 | 12 |  |  | 5 | 6 | 4 | 9 | 11* | 8 | 7 | 10 |  |  | 2 |  | 3 |  |  |
| 26 | (h) Aston Villa | W 2-0 | T.Brown 2 | 43,119 | 1 | 10 |  |  | 5 | 6 | 4 | 9 | 11 | 8 | 7 |  |  |  | 2 |  | 3 |  |  |
| 29 | (h) Swindon T | W 2-0 | Merrick, Johnston | 14,969 | 1 | 10 |  |  | 5 | 6 | 4 | 9 | 11 | 8 | 7 |  |  |  | 2 |  | 3 |  |  |
| Jan 1 | (a) Crystal P | L 0-1 |  | 23,338 | 1 | 12 |  |  | 5 | 6 | 4 | 9 | 11 | 8 | 7 | 10 |  |  | 2 |  | 3* |  |  |
| 12 | (a) Nottingham F | W 4-1 | T.Brown 4 | 15,501 | 1 |  |  |  | 5 | 6 | 4 | 9 | 11 | 8 | 7 | 10 |  |  | 2 |  | 3 |  |  |
| 19 | (a) Blackpool | D 1-1 | Wile | 17,808 | 1 |  |  |  | 5 | 6 | 4 | 9 | 11 | 8 | 7 | 10 |  |  | 2 |  | 3 |  |  |
| Feb 3 | (a) Portsmouth | D 1-1 | Glover | 19,769 | 1 |  |  |  | 5 | 6 | 4 | 9 | 11 | 8 | 7 | 10 |  |  | 2 |  | 3 |  |  |
| 23 | (h) Bristol C | D 2-2 | Wile, Astle | 18,928 | 1 |  |  |  | 5 | 6 | 4 |  | 11 | 8 | 7 | 10 |  |  | 2 |  | 3 |  | 9 |
| 25 | (a) Carlisle U | W 1-0 | Johnston | 6,407 | 1 |  |  |  | 5 | 6 | 4 |  | 11 | 8 | 7 | 10* | 12 |  | 2 |  | 3 |  | 9 |
| Mar 2 | (a) Aston Villa | W 3-1 | Wile, T.Brown 2 (1 pen) | 37,323 | 1 | 10 |  |  | 5 | 6 | 4 | 12 | 11 | 8 | 7 |  |  |  | 2 |  | 3 |  | 9* |
| 9 | (h) Bolton W | D 1-1 | T.Brown | 17,760 | 1 | 10 |  |  | 5 | 6 | 4 | 12 | 11 | 8 | 7 |  |  |  | 2 |  | 3 |  | 9* |
| 16 | (h) Middlesbrough | L 0-4 |  | 24,178 | 1 |  |  |  | 5 | 6 | 4 | 12 | 11 | 8 | 7 | 10 |  | 2* |  |  | 3 |  | 9 |
| 19 | (h) Hull C | L 2-3 | Shaw, A.Brown | 13,712 | 1 | 10 |  |  | 5 | 6 | 4 |  | 7 | 11 | 8 |  |  | 9 | 2 |  | 3 |  |  |
| 23 | (a) Notts C | L 0-1 |  | 9,667 | 1 | 10 |  |  | 5 | 6 | 4 |  | 7 | 8 |  | 11 | 9 |  | 2 |  | 3 |  |  |
| 30 | (h) Cardiff C | D 2-2 | Murray (og), Shaw | 11,528 | 1 |  |  |  | 5 | 6 | 4 |  | 7 | 10 | 9* | 8 | 11 |  | 2 |  | 3 | 12 |  |
| Apr 6 | (a) Fulham | D 0-0 |  | 9,494 | 1 |  |  | 6 | 5 |  | 4 |  | 8 | 7 | 9 | 11 | 10 |  |  | 2 | 3 |  |  |
| 12 | (a) Millwall | L 0-1 |  | 8,752 | 1 |  |  | 6 | 5 |  | 4 |  | 8 | 9 | 7 | 11 | 10 |  |  | 2 | 3 |  |  |
| 13 | (h) Orient | W 1-0 | Hartford | 11,456 | 1 |  |  |  | 5 | 6 | 4* | 9 | 11 | 8 | 7 | 10 |  |  | 2 | 12 | 3 |  |  |
| 17 | (h) Millwall | D 1-1 | Glover | 12,346 | 1 |  |  |  | 5 | 6 |  | 8 | 11 | 4 | 7 | 10 |  |  | 2 | 9 | 3 |  |  |
| 20 | (a) Oxford U | L 0-1 |  | 9,256 | 1 |  |  |  | 5 | 6 |  | 9 | 11 | 8 | 7 | 10 |  | 4 | 2 |  | 3 |  |  |
| 27 | (h) Luton T | D 1-1 | T.Brown (pen) | 13,164 | 1 |  |  | 4 | 5 | 6 |  |  | 11 | 8 | 7 | 10 |  |  | 2 | 9 | 3 |  | 8 |
| **App** |  |  |  |  | 42 | 6 | 21 | 8 | 42 | 40 | 35 | 28 | 36 | 41 | 35 | 33 | 13 | 4 | 34 | 9 | 22 | 8 | 5 |
| **Sub app** |  |  |  |  |  | 2 |  |  |  |  |  |  | 9 | 1 |  | 2 | 1 |  |  | 2 |  |  | 1 |
| **Goals** |  |  |  |  |  | 1 | 1 |  | 3 |  | 1 | 8 | 5 | 19 | 2 | 3 | 3 |  |  |  |  |  | 1 |

**A goal for John Wile in Albion's 3-1 win at Villa Park in March 1974.**

# 1974-75

## Division 2

| Date | | Opponent | Result | Scorers | Att | Latchford P | Nisbet G | Wilson R | Cantello L | Robertson A | Merrick A | Glover A | Brown T | Shaw D | Hughes L | Johnston W | Wile J | Mayo J | Donaghy B | Osborne J | Rushbury D | Trewick J | Thompson T | Ward R | Edwards I | Minton R | Brown A | Robson B |
|---|---|---|---|---|---|---|---|---|---|---|---|---|---|---|---|---|---|---|---|---|---|---|---|---|---|---|---|---|
| Aug 17 | (h) | Fulham | L 0-1 | | 11,425 | 1 | 2 | 3 | 4 | 5 | 6 | 7 | 8 | 9 | 10 | 11 | | | | | | | | | | | | |
| 24 | (a) | Hull C | L 0-1 | | 7,864 | 1 | 2 | 3 | 4 | 5 | 6 | 7 | 8 | 9 | 10 | 11 | | | | | | | | | | | | |
| 31 | (h) | Sunderland | W 1-0 | Glover | 12,501 | 1 | 2 | 3 | 4 | 5 | | 7 | 8 | 9 | 10 | 11 | 6 | | | | | | | | | | | |
| Sep 7 | (a) | Portsmouth | W 3-1 | Johnston, Shaw, Merrick | 9,158 | 1 | 2 | 3 | 4 | 5 | 10 | 7 | 8 | 9 | | 11 | 6 | | | | | | | | | | | |
| 14 | (h) | Manchester U | D 1-1 | Merrick | 28,666 | 1 | 2 | 3 | 4 | 6 | 10 | 7 | 8 | 9 | | 11 | 5 | | | | | | | | | | | |
| 18 | (h) | Hull C | D 2-2 | Shaw 2 | 10,038 | 1 | 2 | 3 | 4 | 6 | 10 | 7 | 8 | 9 | | 11 | 5 | | | | | | | | | | | |
| 21 | (a) | Notts C | D 0-0 | | 10,004 | 1 | 2 | 3 | 4 | 6 | 10 | 7 | 8 | 9 | | 11 | 5 | | | | | | | | | | | |
| 25 | (a) | Sheffield W | D 0-0 | | 12,333 | 1 | 2 | 3 | 4 | 6 | 10 | 7 | 8 | 9* | 12 | 11 | 5 | | | | | | | | | | | |
| 28 | (h) | Oxford U | W 3-0 | T.Brown, Merrick, Cantello | 9,667 | 1 | 2 | 3 | 4 | 6 | 10* | 7 | 8 | | 12 | 11 | 5 | 9 | | | | | | | | | | |
| Oct 5 | (h) | York C | W 2-0 | Johnston, Merrick | 11,846 | 1 | 2 | 3 | 4 | 6 | 10 | 7 | 8 | | | 11 | 5 | 9 | | | | | | | | | | |
| 12 | (a) | Cardiff C | W 2-0 | Mayo, Donaghy | 6,723 | 1 | 2 | 3 | 4 | 6 | 10* | 7 | 8 | | | 11 | 5 | 9 | 12 | | | | | | | | | |
| 19 | (h) | Nottingham F | L 0-1 | | 13,948 | 1 | 2 | 3 | 4 | 6 | 10* | 7 | 8 | 12 | | 11 | 5 | 9 | | | | | | | | | | |
| 22 | (a) | Bristol R | L 1-2 | Shaw | 12,101 | 1 | 2 | 3 | 4 | 6 | 10 | 7 | 8 | 9 | | 11 | 5 | | | | | | | | | | | |
| 26 | (a) | Millwall | D 2-2 | Hughes, Kitchener (og) | 8,179 | | 2 | 3 | 4 | | 10 | 7 | 8 | 9* | 11 | | 5 | 12 | | 1 | 6 | | | | | | | |
| Nov 2 | (h) | Norwich C | D 1-1 | Shaw | 12,064 | | 2 | 3 | | | 10 | 7 | 8 | 9* | 4 | 11 | 5 | 12 | | 1 | 6 | | | | | | | |
| 6 | (h) | Bristol R | D 2-2 | T.Brown, Glover | 8,849 | | 2 | 3 | 4 | | 10 | 7 | 8 | 9 | | 11 | 5 | | | 1 | 6 | | | | | | | |
| 9 | (a) | Southampton | L 0-1 | | 15,638 | | 2 | 3 | 4* | | 10 | 7 | 8 | 9 | 12 | 11 | 5 | | | 1 | 6 | | | | | | | |
| 16 | (h) | Bristol C | W 1-0 | Mayo | 11,936 | | 2 | 3 | | | | 7 | | 9 | 10 | 11 | 5 | 8 | | 1 | 6 | | 4 | | | | | |
| 23 | (a) | Orient | W 2-0 | Hughes, Johnston | 6,766 | | 2 | 3 | 4 | | | 7 | | 9 | 10 | 11 | 5 | 8 | | 1 | 6 | | | | | | | |
| 30 | (h) | Oldham A | W 1-0 | T.Brown | 11,399 | | 2 | 3 | 4 | | | 7 | 11 | 9 | 10 | | 5 | 8 | | 1 | 6 | | | | | | | |
| Dec 7 | (a) | Bolton W | W 1-0 | Mayo | 12,315 | | 2 | 3 | 4 | 12 | | 7 | 11* | 8 | 10 | | 5 | 9 | | 1 | 6 | | | | | | | |
| 14 | (a) | Fulham | L 0-1 | | 6,730 | | 2 | 3 | 4 | 12 | | 7 | 11 | 9 | 10 | | 5 | 8* | | 1 | 6 | | | | | | | |
| 21 | (h) | Aston Villa | W 2-0 | Johnston, Mayo | 29,614 | | 2 | | 4 | | | 7 | 8 | | 10 | 11 | 5 | 9 | | 1 | 6 | 3 | | | | | | |
| 26 | (a) | Manchester U | L 1-2 | Cantello | 51,104 | | 2 | 3 | 4 | | | 7 | 8 | | 10 | 11 | 5 | 9 | | 1 | 6 | | | | | | | |
| 28 | (h) | Blackpool | W 2-0 | Johnston, Mayo | 14,839 | | 2 | 3 | 4 | | | 7* | 12 | 8 | 10 | 11 | 5 | 9 | | 1 | 6 | | | | | | | |
| Jan 18 | (a) | Oldham A | D 0-0 | | 11,355 | | 2 | 3 | 4 | | | 7 | 8 | | 10 | 11 | 5 | 9 | | 1 | 6 | | | | | | | |
| Feb 1 | (h) | Southampton | L 0-3 | | 15,763 | | 2 | 3 | 4 | 12 | | 7 | 8* | 10 | 11 | | 5 | 9 | | 1 | 6 | | | | | | | |
| 8 | (a) | Norwich C | L 2-3 | Mayo, Hughes | 34,509 | 2* | | | 4 | | | 7 | 8 | 12 | 10 | 11 | 5 | 9 | | 1 | 6 | 3 | | | | | | |
| 15 | (h) | Orient | W 1-0 | Johnston | 9,388 | 2 | | | 4 | | | 7* | 8 | 12 | 10 | 11 | 5 | 9 | | 1 | 6 | 3 | | | | | | |
| 22 | (a) | Bristol C | L 1-2 | Shaw | 14,180 | | | 3 | 4 | 5 | | 7 | 8 | | 10 | 11 | | 9* | | 1 | 6 | 12 | 2 | | | | | |
| Mar 1 | (a) | Sunderland | L 0-3 | | 28,867 | | 2 | | 4 | 5 | | 7 | 12 | 8 | 10 | 11 | | 9 | 1* | | 6 | 3 | | | | | | |
| 8 | (h) | Sheffield W | W 4-0 | T.Brown 2 (1 pen), Wile, Edwards | 10,330 | | 2 | 3 | 4 | | | 7 | 8 | | 10 | 11 | 5 | | | | 6 | | 1 | 9 | | | | |
| 15 | (h) | Oxford U | D 1-1 | | 7,212 | | 2 | 3 | 4 | | | 7 | 8 | 12 | 10 | 11 | 5 | | | 1 | 6 | | | 9* | | | | |
| 22 | (h) | Portsmouth | W 2-1 | T.Brown, Wilson | 10,017 | | 2 | 3 | 4 | | | 7 | 8 | 12 | | 11 | 5 | | | 6 | 10* | | 1 | 9 | | | | |
| 29 | (a) | Aston Villa | L 1-3 | T.Brown | 47,574 | | 2 | | 4 | 10 | 7 | 8 | | | 11 | 5 | | 1 | 6 | | 3 | | | 9 | | | | |
| 31 | (a) | Blackpool | L 0-2 | | 11,611 | | 2 | | | 4 | 7 | 8 | 10 | | | 11 | 5 | | 1 | 6 | 3* | | | 12 | 9 | | | |
| Apr 2 | (h) | Notts C | W 4-1 | Edwards, T.Brown 2 (1 pen), Cantello | 7,812 | | 2 | | 4 | 6 | 7 | | 8 | | | 10 | 11 | 5 | | 1 | 3 | | | 9 | | | | |
| 5 | (h) | Millwall | W 2-1 | T.Brown 2 | 8,130 | | 2 | | 4 | 6 | 7 | | 8 | 12 | 10* | 11 | 5 | | | | 3 | | 1 | 9 | | | | |
| 8 | (h) | Bolton W | L 0-1 | | 7,957 | | 2 | 3 | 4 | 6 | 7 | | 8 | | | 11 | 5 | | | | 10 | | 1 | 9 | | | | |
| 12 | (a) | York C | W 3-1 | Johnston, Mayo 2 | 7,566 | | 2 | 3 | 4 | 6 | 7 | | | | | 11 | 5 | 9 | | | | | 1 | | | | 8 | 10 |
| 19 | (h) | Cardiff C | W 2-0 | Robson, Robertson | 10,071 | | 2 | 3 | | 6 | 7 | 4 | | | | 11 | 5 | 9 | | | | | 1 | | | | 8 | 10 |
| 26 | (a) | Nottingham F | L 1-2 | Robson | 11,721 | | 2 | 3 | | 6 | 7 | 4 | | | | 11 | 5 | 9 | | | | | 1 | | | | 8 | 10 |
| | | | | App | | 13 | 41 | 34 | 37 | 21 | 24 | 35 | 32 | 27 | 23 | 38 | 38 | 21 | | 22 | 26 | 2 | 7 | 7 | 7 | | 4 | 3 |
| | | | | Sub app | | | | | | 2 | 1 | 2 | 6 | 3 | | | | 2 | 1 | | | 1 | | | | 1 | | |
| | | | | Goals | | | 1 | 3 | 1 | 4 | 2 | 12 | 6 | 3 | 7 | 1 | 8 | 1 | | | | | | 2 | | | 2 | |

**Dave Shaw scores for Albion at Ashton Gate in February 1975.**

# 1975-76

## Division 2

| Date | | Opponent | Result | Scorers | Att | Osborne J | Nisbet G | Wilson R | Cantello L | Wile J | Robertson A | Trewick J | Brown A | Mayo J | Merrick A | Johnston W | Brown T | Hurst G | Giles J | Robson B | Thompson T | Rushbury D | Glover A | Martin M | Mulligan P | Edwards I |
|---|---|---|---|---|---|---|---|---|---|---|---|---|---|---|---|---|---|---|---|---|---|---|---|---|---|---|
| Aug 16 | (a) | Southampton | L 0-3 | | 15,246 | 1 | 2 | 3 | 4 | 5 | 6 | 7 | 8 | 9* | 10 | 11 | 12 | | | | | | | | | |
| 20 | (h) | Chelsea | D 0-0 | | 17,962 | 1 | 2 | 3 | 4 | 5 | 6 | 7 | 8 | 9 | | 11 | | 10 | | | | | | | | |
| 23 | (h) | Luton T | W 1-0 | Trewick | 14,062 | 1 | 2 | 3 | | 5 | 6 | 7 | 8 | 9 | | 11 | | 10 | 4 | | | | | | | |
| 30 | (a) | Fulham | L 0-4 | | 9,910 | 1 | 2 | 3 | 4 | 5 | 6 | 7 | 8* | 9 | | 11 | | 10 | 12 | | | | | | | |
| Sep 6 | (h) | York C | D 2-2 | T.Brown, Hurst | 10,904 | 1 | 2 | | 4 | 5 | 6 | 7 | 8 | 9 | | 11 | | 10 | | 3 | | | | | | |
| 13 | (a) | Sunderland | L 0-2 | | 25,159 | 1 | 2 | | 4 | 5 | 6 | 7 | 8 | 9 | | 11* | | 10 | 12 | 3 | | | | | | |
| 20 | (h) | Charlton A | D 1-1 | Hurst | 10,496 | 1 | | 3 | 4 | 5 | | 12 | 8* | 9 | | 11 | | 10 | | 2 | 6 | 7 | | | | |
| 27 | (a) | Carlisle U | D 1-1 | A.Brown | 6,625 | 1 | | 3 | 4 | 5 | 6 | | 8 | 9* | | 11 | 12 | 10 | | 2 | | 7 | | | | |
| Oct 4 | (h) | Oldham A | D 1-1 | Johnston | 10,668 | 1 | | 3 | 4 | 5 | 6 | | 8 | 9* | | 11 | 12 | | 10 | 2 | | 7 | | | | |
| 11 | (a) | Blackburn R | D 0-0 | | 9,973 | 1 | | 3 | 4 | 5 | 6 | | 8 | 9 | | 11 | | | 10 | | | | | 7 | 2 | |
| 18 | (h) | Plymouth A | W 1-0 | A.Brown | 10,970 | 1 | | 3 | 4 | 5 | 6 | | 8 | 9 | | 11 | | | 10 | | | | | 7 | 2 | |
| 25 | (a) | Bristol C | W 2-0 | A.Brown, T.Brown | 19,132 | 1 | | 3 | 4 | 5 | 6 | | 8 | 9 | | 11 | | | 10 | | | | | 7 | 2 | |
| Nov 1 | (h) | Notts C | D 0-0 | | 12,670 | 1 | | 3 | 4 | 5 | 6 | | 8 | 9 | | 11 | | | 10 | | | | | 7* | 2 | 12 |
| 4 | (a) | Bristol R | D 1-1 | Edwards | 13,105 | 1 | | 3 | 4 | 5 | 6 | | 8 | 9 | | 11 | | | 10* | | | | | 7 | 2 | 12 |
| 8 | (a) | Blackpool | W 1-0 | Johnston | 8,271 | 1 | | 3 | 4* | 5 | 6 | 12 | 8 | 9 | | 11 | | | 10 | | | | | 7 | 2 | |
| 12 | (a) | Oxford U | W 1-0 | Mayo | 5,685 | 1 | | 3 | | 5 | 6 | 4 | 8 | 9 | | 11 | 10 | | | | | | | 7 | 2 | |
| 15 | (h) | Hull C | W 2-0 | Martin, T.Brown | 14,469 | 1 | | 3 | | 5 | 6 | 4 | 8 | 9 | | 11 | 10 | | | | | | | 7 | 2 | |
| 22 | (a) | Plymouth A | L 1-2 | Giles | 17,380 | 1 | | 3 | | 5 | 6 | 4* | 8 | 9 | 11 | | 10 | | | | | | | 7 | 2 | 12 |
| 29 | (a) | Bolton W | W 2-1 | Mayo, Robson | 18,710 | 1 | | 3 | | 5 | 6 | | 8 | 9 | | 11 | 7 | | | 10 | | | | 4 | 2 | |
| Dec 6 | (h) | Portsmouth | W 3-1 | A.Brown 2, T.Brown | 15,325 | 1 | | 3 | | | 6 | | 8 | 9 | | 11 | 4 | | 10 | 5 | | | | 7 | 2 | |
| 13 | (a) | Luton T | L 1-2 | Martin | 10,203 | 1 | | 3 | | | 6 | | 8 | 9 | | 11 | 4 | | 10 | 5 | | | | 7 | 2 | |
| 19 | (h) | Southampton | L 0-2 | | 16,780 | 1 | | | 4 | | 6 | 10 | 9 | | | 11 | 8 | | | 5 | | 3 | | 7 | 2 | |
| 26 | (a) | Nottingham F | W 2-0 | Giles, Johnston | 19,393 | 1 | | | 4 | 5 | 6 | | 9 | 3 | | 11 | 8 | | 10 | | | | | 7 | 2 | |
| 27 | (h) | Orient | D 1-1 | Mayo | 20,601 | 1 | | | 4 | 5 | 6 | | 9 | 3 | | 11 | 7 | | 10 | | | | | 8 | 2 | |
| Jan 10 | (h) | Sunderland | D 0-0 | | 24,383 | 1 | | | 4 | 5 | 6 | | 9 | 3 | | 11 | 7 | | 10 | | | | | 8 | 2 | |
| 17 | (a) | York C | W 1-0 | A.Brown | 5,628 | 1 | | | 4 | 5 | 6 | | 9 | 3 | | 11 | 7 | | 10 | | | | | 8 | 2 | |
| 31 | (a) | Chelsea | W 2-1 | Martin, T.Brown | 15,896 | 1 | | | | 5 | 6 | | 9 | 3 | | 11 | 7 | | 10 | 4 | | | | 8 | 2 | |
| Feb 7 | (h) | Bristol R | W 3-0 | Cantello, Mayo, A.Brown | 16,732 | 1 | | | 8 | 5 | 6 | | 9 | 3 | | 11 | 4 | | 10 | | | | | 7 | 2 | |
| 21 | (a) | Hull C | L 1-2 | Johnston | 6,137 | 1 | | 8* | | 5 | 6 | | 12 | 9 | | 11 | 4 | | 10 | 3 | | | | 7 | 2 | |
| 25 | (h) | Oxford U | W 2-0 | T.Brown, Robertson | 14,412 | 1 | | | 3 | | 6 | | 8 | 9 | | 11 | 4 | | 10 | 5 | | | | 7 | 2 | |
| Mar 6 | (a) | Notts C | W 2-0 | Mayo, Johnston | 20,032 | 1 | | | 8 | 5 | 6 | | | 9 | | 11 | 4 | | 10 | 3 | | | | 7 | 2 | |
| 13 | (h) | Blackburn R | D 2-2 | Mayo, Wile | 16,969 | 1 | | | 8 | 5 | 6 | | | 9 | | 11 | 4 | | 10 | 3 | | | | 7 | 2 | |
| 17 | (h) | Bristol C | L 0-1 | | 26,640 | 1 | | 8* | | 5 | 6 | | 12 | 9 | | 11 | 4 | | 10 | 3 | | | | 7 | 2 | |
| 20 | (h) | Bolton W | W 2-0 | Mayo, Wile | 25,650 | 1 | | | 8 | 5 | 6 | | 12 | 9 | | 11 | 4 | | 10* | 3 | | | | 7 | 2 | |
| 27 | (a) | Portsmouth | W 1-0 | Cantello | 10,617 | 1 | | | 8 | 5 | 6 | | | 9 | | 11 | 4 | | 10 | 3 | | | | 7 | 2 | |
| 31 | (h) | Blackpool | D 0-0 | | 20,257 | 1 | | | 8 | 5 | 6 | | 12 | 9 | | 11 | 4 | | 10 | 3* | | | | 7 | 2 | |
| Apr 3 | (h) | Carlisle U | W 3-0 | A.Brown, Martin, Mayo | 17,133 | 1 | | | 3 | 5 | 6 | | 8 | 9 | | 11 | 4 | | 10 | | | | | 7 | 2 | |
| 9 | (a) | Charlton A | L 1-2 | T.Brown (pen) | 14,252 | 1 | | | 3 | 5 | 6 | | 8 | 9 | | 11 | 4 | | 10 | | | | | 7 | 2 | |
| 14 | (a) | Fulham | W 3-1 | A.Brown 2, Cantello | 18,237 | 1 | | | 3 | 5 | 6 | | 8 | 9 | | 11 | 4 | | 10 | | | | | 7 | 2 | |
| 17 | (h) | Nottingham F | W 2-0 | Martin, Johnston | 26,580 | 1 | | | 3 | 5 | 6 | | 8 | 9 | | 11 | 4 | | 10 | | | | | 7 | 2 | |
| 20 | (a) | Orient | D 0-0 | | 10,857 | 1 | | | 3 | 5 | 6 | | 8 | 9 | | 11 | 4 | | 10 | | | | | 7 | 2 | |
| 24 | (a) | Oldham A | W 1-0 | T.Brown | 22,356 | 1 | | | 3 | 5 | 6 | | 8 | 9 | | 11 | 4 | | 10 | | | | | 7 | 2 | |
| | | | | | App | 42 | 6 | 19 | 34 | 37 | 42 | 10 | 26 | 28 | 1 | 39 | 37 | 10 | 38 | 14 | 5 | 2 | 3 | 34 | 33 | 2 |
| | | | | | Sub app | | | | | | | | | 1 | | 5 | | | 3 | | 2 | | | | | 3 |
| | | | | | Goals | | | | 3 | 2 | 1 | 1 | 10 | 8 | | 6 | 8 | 2 | 2 | 1 | | | | 5 | | 1 |

Albion's staff at the start of 1975-76. Back row (left to right): J.Trewick, T.Thompson, B.Clarke, I.Edwards, R.Ward, J.Osborne, J.Mayo, B.Robson, A.Brown, R.Wilson, T.Brown, B.Whitehouse (coach). Front: L.Cantello, A.Glover, A.Robertson, G.Nisbet, J.Wile, J.Giles (player-manager), D.Rushbury, W.Johnston.

# 1976-77

## Division 1

| Date | Venue | Opponent | Result | Scorers | Att | Osborne J | Mulligan P | Cantello L | Brown T | Wile J | Robertson A | Martin M | Brown A | Mayo J | Giles J | Johnston W | Robson B | Edwards I | Treacy R | Trewick J | Ward R | Cross D | Statham D | Glover A | Godden A | Cunningham L | Hughes W |
|---|---|---|---|---|---|---|---|---|---|---|---|---|---|---|---|---|---|---|---|---|---|---|---|---|---|---|---|
| Aug 21 | (a) | Leeds U | D 2-2 | A.Brown, T.Brown | 40,248 | 1 | 2 | 3 | 4 | 5 | 6 | 7 | 8 | 9 | 10 | 11 | | | | | | | | | | | |
| 25 | (h) | Liverpool | L 0-1 | | 29,735 | 1 | 2 | 3 | 4 | 5 | 6 | 7 | 8 | 9 | 10 | 11 | | | | | | | | | | | |
| 28 | (h) | Norwich C | W 2-0 | A.Brown, T.Brown (pen) | 16,434 | 1 | 2 | 3 | 4 | 5 | 6 | 7 | 8 | 9 | 10 | 11 | | | | | | | | | | | |
| Sep 4 | (a) | Queen's Park R | L 0-1 | | 18,876 | 1 | 2 | 3 | 4 | 5 | 6 | 7 | 8 | 9 | 10* | 11 | 12 | | | | | | | | | | |
| 11 | (a) | Birmingham C | W 1-0 | T.Brown | 38,448 | 1 | 2 | 3* | 4 | 5 | 6 | 7 | | 9 | 12 | 11 | | 8 | 10 | | | | | | | | |
| 17 | (h) | Coventry C | D 1-1 | Wile | 24,474 | 1 | 2 | | 4 | 5 | 6 | 7 | | 9 | 10 | 11 | 3 | 8 | | | | | | | | | |
| 25 | (h) | Derby C | D 2-2 | Treacy 2 | 24,278 | 1 | 2 | | 4 | 5 | 6 | 7 | 11 | 9 | 10 | | 3 | | 8 | | | | | | | | |
| Oct 2 | (h) | Tottenham H | W 4-2 | T.Brown (pen), Martin 2, Treacy | 23,461 | 1 | 2 | 9 | 4 | 5 | 6 | 7 | | 12 | 10 | 11 | 3* | | 8 | | | | | | | | |
| 6 | (a) | Newcastle U | L 0-2 | | 28,757 | 1 | 2 | 3 | 4 | 5 | 6 | 7 | 12 | 9* | 10 | 11 | | | 8 | | | | | | | | |
| 16 | (h) | Manchester U | W 4-0 | Giles, A.Brown, Cantello, Treacy | 36,615 | 1 | 2 | 3 | 4 | 5 | 6 | 7 | 9 | | 10 | 11 | | | 8 | | | | | | | | |
| 23 | (a) | Middlesbrough | L 0-1 | | 23,169 | 1 | 2 | 3 | 4 | 5 | 6 | 7 | 9 | | 10 | | | 11 | 8 | | | | | | | | |
| 30 | (h) | West Ham U | W 3-0 | Martin, A.Brown 2 | 20,396 | 1 | 2 | 3 | 4 | 5 | 6 | 7 | 9 | | 10 | | | 11* | 8 | 12 | | | | | | | |
| Nov 6 | (a) | Ipswich T | L 0-7 | | 26,706 | 1 | 2 | 3 | 4 | 5 | 6 | 7 | 9 | | 10 | | | 8 | 11 | | | | | | | | |
| 10 | (h) | Aston Villa | D 1-1 | Wile | 41,867 | | 2 | 3 | 4 | 5 | 6 | 7 | 11 | 9 | 10 | | | 8 | | | 1 | | | | | | |
| 20 | (a) | Manchester C | L 0-1 | | 36,656 | 1 | 2 | 3 | 4 | 5 | 6 | 7 | 11 | | 10 | | | 8 | | | | 9 | | | | | |
| 27 | (h) | Everton | W 3-0 | T.Brown, Cross, Treacy | 21,078 | 1 | 2 | 3 | 4 | 5 | 6 | 7 | 12 | | 10* | 11 | | 8 | | | | 9 | | | | | |
| Dec 11 | (h) | Leicester C | D 2-2 | Treacy, Cross | 19,049 | 1 | 2 | 3 | 4 | 5 | 6 | 7 | 10 | | | 11 | | 8 | | | | 9 | | | | | |
| 18 | (a) | Stoke C | W 2-0 | Statham, Trewick | 15,989 | | 2 | | 4 | 5 | 6 | 7 | | | | 11 | | | 8 | 10 | 1 | 9 | 3 | | | | |
| 27 | (h) | Bristol C | D 1-1 | Cross | 30,497 | 1 | 2 | | 4 | 5 | 6 | 7 | 12 | | | 11 | 3 | | 8 | 10 | | 9* | | | | | |
| Jan 3 | (a) | West Ham U | D 0-0 | | 25,236 | 1 | 2 | | 4 | 5 | 6 | 7 | | | | 11 | 3 | | 8 | 10 | | 9 | | | | | |
| 15 | (a) | Liverpool | D 1-1 | Cross | 39,195 | 1 | 2* | 3 | 4 | 5 | 6 | 7 | | | | 11 | 12 | | 8 | 10 | | 9 | | | | | |
| 22 | (h) | Leeds U | L 1-2 | T.Brown (pen) | 25,958 | 1 | | 2 | 4 | 5 | 6 | 7 | | | | 10 | 11 | 3 | 8 | | | 9 | | | | | |
| Feb 5 | (a) | Norwich C | L 0-1 | | 19,613 | 1 | 2 | 7 | 4 | 5 | 6 | | | | | 10 | 11* | 3 | 8 | 12 | | 9 | | | | | |
| 12 | (h) | Queen's Park R | D 1-1 | Wile | 18,342 | 1 | 2 | 3 | 4 | 5 | 6 | | | | | 10 | | | 7 | 8 | | 9 | | 11 | | | |
| 22 | (a) | Sunderland | L 1-6 | | 30,317 | 1 | 2 | 3 | 4 | 5 | 6 | | | | | 10 | | | 7 | 8 | | 9 | | | | | |
| 28 | (h) | Birmingham C | W 2-1 | Robson, A.Brown | 28,639 | 1 | 2 | | 4 | 5 | 6 | | 8 | | | 10 | 11 | 7 | | | | 9 | 3 | | | | |
| Mar 5 | (h) | Derby C | W 1-0 | Robson | 19,280 | 1 | 2 | 3 | 4 | 5 | 6 | | 8 | | | 10 | 11 | 7 | | | | 9 | | | | | |
| 8 | (a) | Arsenal | W 2-1 | Cross 2 | 19,517 | 1 | 2 | | 4 | 5 | 6 | | 8 | | | 10 | 11 | 7* | | | 12 | 9 | 3 | | | | |
| 12 | (a) | Tottenham H | W 2-0 | Robson, Cross | 28,834 | | 2 | | 4 | 5 | 6 | | | | | 10 | 11 | 7 | | | | 9 | 3 | | 1 | 8 | |
| 16 | (a) | Ipswich T | W 4-0 | Robson 3, Cunningham | 23,054 | | 2 | | 4* | 5 | 6 | | 12 | | | 10 | 11 | 7 | | | | 9 | 3 | | 1 | 8 | |
| 19 | (h) | Newcastle U | D 1-1 | Cunningham | 23,843 | | 2 | | | 5 | 6 | 4 | | | | 10 | 11 | 7 | | | | 9 | 3 | | 1 | 8 | |
| 23 | (a) | Manchester U | D 2-2 | Cross, Robson | 51,053 | | 2 | | | 5 | 6 | 4 | | | | 10 | 11 | 7 | | | | 9 | 3 | | 1 | 8 | |
| Apr 2 | (h) | Middlesbrough | W 2-1 | Cunningham, Johnston | 18,519 | | 2 | | | 5 | 6 | 4 | | | | 10 | 11 | 7 | | | | 9 | 3 | | 1 | 8 | |
| 5 | (a) | Bristol C | W 2-1 | Hunter (og), Cross | 23,752 | | 2 | | | 5 | 6 | 4 | | | | 10 | 11 | 7 | | | | 9 | 3 | | 1 | 8 | |
| 9 | (h) | Arsenal | L 0-2 | | 24,242 | 1 | 2 | | | 5 | 6 | 4 | | | | 10 | 11 | 7 | | | | 9 | 3 | | | 8 | |
| 16 | (h) | Manchester C | L 0-2 | | 24,899 | 1 | 2 | | 12 | 5 | 6 | 4 | | | | 10 | 11 | 7* | | | | 9 | 3 | | | 8 | |
| 19 | (a) | Coventry C | D 1-1 | Wile | 19,136 | 1 | 2 | | 7 | 5 | 6 | 4 | 9 | | | 10 | 11 | | | | | | 3 | | | 8 | |
| 30 | (h) | Sunderland | L 2-3 | Cunningham, Cross | 21,859 | 1 | 2 | | 7 | 5 | 6 | 4 | | | | 10 | 11 | | | | | 9 | 3 | | | 8 | |
| May 7 | (a) | Leicester C | W 5-0 | Martin 2, Cross, Cunningham, T.Brown | 18,139 | 1 | 2 | | 7 | 5* | 6 | 4 | 11 | | | 10 | | | 12 | | | 9 | 3 | | | 8 | |
| 14 | (h) | Stoke C | W 3-1 | Martin, Cunningham, Cross | 22,754 | 1 | 2 | | 7 | 5 | 6 | 4 | | | | 10 | 11 | | | | | 9 | 3 | | | 8 | |
| 16 | (a) | Everton | D 1-1 | T.Brown | 20,102 | 1 | | | 7 | 5 | 6 | 2 | 4 | | | 10 | 11 | | | | | 9 | 3 | | | 8 | |
| 23 | (a) | Aston Villa | L 0-4 | | 42,532 | 1 | 2 | | 7 | 5 | 6* | 3 | 4 | | | 10 | 11 | | 8 | | | 9 | | | | | 12 |
| **App** | | | | | | 34 | 40 | 21 | 36 | 42 | 42 | 34 | 19 | 9 | 36 | 34 | 21 | 4 | 20 | 5 | 2 | 27 | 16 | 1 | 6 | 13 | |
| **Sub app** | | | | | | | | | | | | | | 4 | 1 | 1 | 2 | | 1 | 3 | 1 | | | | | | 1 |
| **Goals** | | | | | | | | 1 | 8 | 4 | | 6 | 6 | | 1 | 1 | 8 | | 6 | 1 | | 12 | 1 | | | 6 | |

**John Wile heads a magnificent equaliser for Albion against Queen's Park Rangers at The Hawthorns in February 1977.**

# 1977-78

### Division 1

| Date | | Opponent | Result | Scorers | Att | Godden A | Mulligan P | Statham D | Brown T | Wile J | Robertson A | Cantello L | Cunningham L | Cross D | Robson B | Johnston W | Trewick J | Regis C | Martin M | Hughes W | Brown A | Batson B |
|---|---|---|---|---|---|---|---|---|---|---|---|---|---|---|---|---|---|---|---|---|---|---|
| Aug 20 | (h) | Chelsea | W 3-0 | T.Brown 2 (1 pen), Cross | 20,146 | 1 | 2 | 3 | 4 | 5 | 6 | 7 | 8 | 9 | 10 | 11 | | | | | | |
| 24 | (a) | Leeds U | D 2-2 | Cunningham, Cross | 21,846 | 1 | 2 | 3 | 4 | 5 | 6 | 7 | 8 | 9 | 10 | 11 | | | | | | |
| 27 | (a) | Liverpool | L 0-3 | | 48,525 | 1 | 2 | 3 | 4 | 5 | 6 | 7 | 8 | 9* | 10 | 11 | | | 12 | | | |
| Sep 3 | (h) | Middlesbrough | W 2-1 | Robson, Regis | 19,044 | 1 | 2 | 3 | | 5 | 6 | 7 | 8 | | 10 | 11 | 4* | 9 | | 12 | | |
| 10 | (a) | Newcastle U | W 3-0 | Regis, Cunningham, Robson | 23,351 | 1 | 2 | 3 | 4 | 5 | 6 | 7 | 8* | | 10 | 11 | | 9 | 12 | | | |
| 17 | (h) | Wolves | D 2-2 | T.Brown (pen), Cross | 30,395 | 1 | 2 | 3 | 4 | 5 | 6 | 7 | | 8 | 10 | 11 | | 9 | | | | |
| 24 | (h) | Birmingham C | W 3-1 | T.Brown 2 (1 pen), Regis | 29,115 | 1 | 2 | 3 | 4 | 5 | 6 | 7 | | | 10 | 11 | | 9 | | | 8 | |
| Oct 1 | (a) | Coventry C | W 2-1 | T.Brown 2 | 25,707 | 1 | 2 | 3 | 4 | 5 | 6 | 7* | | | 10 | 11 | | 9 | 12 | | 8 | |
| 4 | (a) | Everton | L 1-3 | T.Brown (pen) | 34,582 | 1 | 2 | 3 | 4 | 5 | 6 | 7 | 8 | | 10 | 11 | | 9 | | | | |
| 8 | (h) | Ipswich T | W 1-0 | Robson | 22,970 | 1 | 2 | 3 | 4 | 5 | 6 | 7 | 8 | | 10 | 11 | | 9 | | | | |
| 15 | (a) | Derby C | D 1-1 | Regis | 28,397 | 1 | 2 | 3 | 4 | 5 | 6 | 7 | 8 | | 10 | 11 | | 9 | | | | |
| 22 | (h) | Manchester U | W 4-0 | Cross 2, Wile, Cunningham | 27,649 | 1 | 2 | 3 | 4 | 5 | 6 | 7 | 8 | 9 | 10 | 11 | | | | | | |
| 29 | (a) | Queen's Park R | L 1-2 | Johnston | 18,880 | 1 | 2 | 3 | 4 | 5 | 6 | 7* | 8 | 9 | 10 | 11 | 12 | | | | | |
| Nov 5 | (h) | Leicester C | W 2-0 | T.Brown, Cross | 20,082 | 1 | 2 | 3 | 4 | 5 | 6 | 7 | 8 | 9 | 10 | 11 | | | | | | |
| 12 | (a) | West Ham U | D 3-3 | Wile 2, Cunningham | 23,601 | 1 | 2 | 3 | 4 | 5 | 6 | 7 | 8 | 9 | 10 | 11 | | | | | | |
| 19 | (h) | Manchester C | D 0-0 | | 26,953 | 1 | 2 | 3 | 4 | 5 | 6 | | 8 | 9 | 10 | 11 | | 7 | | | | |
| 26 | (a) | Nottingham F | D 0-0 | | 31,908 | 1 | 2 | 3 | 4 | 5 | 6 | | 8 | 9 | 10 | 11 | | 7 | | | | |
| Dec 3 | (h) | Norwich C | D 0-0 | | 18,137 | 1 | 2 | 3 | 4 | 5 | 6 | | | 11 | 9 | 10 | 8 | 7 | | | | |
| 10 | (a) | Aston Villa | L 0-3 | | 43,196 | 1 | 2 | 3 | 4 | 5 | 6 | 7 | 11* | | 10 | | 8 | 12 | | 9 | | |
| 17 | (h) | West Ham U | W 1-0 | A.Brown | 18,896 | 1 | 2 | 3 | 4 | 5 | 6 | | | | 10 | 11 | 8 | 7 | | 9 | | |
| 26 | (a) | Bristol C | L 1-3 | T.Brown | 29,292 | 1 | 2 | 3 | 4 | 5 | 6 | | 12 | | 10 | 11 | 9* | 7 | | 8 | | |
| 27 | (h) | Arsenal | L 1-3 | Cunningham | 27,876 | 1 | 2 | 3 | 4 | 5 | 6 | | 12 | | 10* | 11 | 9 | 7 | | 8 | | |
| 31 | (h) | Leeds U | W 1-0 | T.Brown (pen) | 24,206 | 1 | 2 | | 4 | 5 | 6 | | | | 3 | 11 | 10 | 8 | 7 | 9 | | |
| Jan 2 | (a) | Chelsea | D 2-2 | A.Brown, T.Brown | 30,302 | 1 | 2* | | 4 | 5 | 6 | | | | 3 | 11 | 10 | 8 | 7 | 12 | 9 | |
| 14 | (h) | Liverpool | L 0-1 | | 36,067 | 1 | 2 | 3 | 4 | 5 | 6 | | | 9 | | 11 | 10 | 8* | 7 | | 12 | |
| 21 | (a) | Middlesbrough | L 0-1 | | 19,172 | 1 | 2 | 3 | 4 | 5 | 6 | | | 8 | | 11 | 10 | 9 | 7 | | | |
| Feb 25 | (h) | Coventry C | D 3-3 | Trewick 2, Wile | 25,269 | 1 | | 3 | 4 | 5 | 6 | | 12 | | 2* | 11 | 10 | 9 | 7 | | 8 | |
| 28 | (a) | Birmingham C | W 2-1 | T.Brown, A.Brown | 26,633 | 1 | | 3 | 4 | 5 | 6 | | | | | 11 | 10 | 9 | 7 | | 8 | 2 |
| Mar 4 | (a) | Ipswich T | D 2-2 | T.Brown 2 (1 pen) | 20,130 | 1 | | 3 | 4 | 5 | 6 | | 12 | | | 11 | 10 | 9 | 7* | | 8 | 2 |
| 14 | (h) | Wolves | D 1-1 | Trewick | 29,757 | 1 | 2 | 3 | 4 | 5 | 6 | | 8 | | | 11 | 10 | 9 | 7 | | | |
| 18 | (a) | Manchester U | D 1-1 | Robertson | 46,329 | 1 | 2 | 3 | 4 | 5 | 6 | | | 8 | 7 | 11 | 10 | 9 | | | | |
| 22 | (h) | Queen's Park R | W 2-2 | A.Brown, Regis | 19,536 | 1 | 2 | 3 | 4 | 5 | 6 | | | | 7 | 11 | 10 | 9 | | | 8 | |
| 25 | (a) | Arsenal | L 0-4 | | 36,763 | 1 | 2 | 3 | 4 | 5 | 6 | | 11 | | 7 | | 10 | 9 | | | 8 | |
| 27 | (h) | Bristol C | W 2-1 | Johnston, T.Brown | 23,741 | 1 | 2 | 3 | 4 | 5 | 6 | | 8 | | | 11 | 10 | 9 | 7 | | | |
| Apr 1 | (a) | Leicester C | W 1-0 | T.Brown | 14,637 | 1 | 2 | 3 | 4 | 5 | 6 | | | | | 11 | 10 | 9 | 7 | | 8 | |
| 12 | (h) | Newcastle U | W 2-0 | Regis, Mulligan | 17,053 | 1 | 2 | 3 | 4 | | 6 | 7 | 11 | | 5 | | 10 | 9 | | | 8 | |
| 15 | (a) | Manchester C | W 3-1 | Regis, Cunningham, A.Brown | 36,521 | 1 | 2 | 3 | 4 | | 6 | 7 | 11 | | 5 | | 10 | 9 | | | 8 | |
| 18 | (h) | Derby C | W 1-0 | T.Brown (pen) | 20,961 | 1 | 2 | 3 | 4 | | 6 | 7 | 11 | | 5 | | 10 | 9 | | | 8 | |
| 22 | (a) | Aston Villa | L 0-3 | | 35,112 | 1 | 2* | 3 | 4 | 12 | 6 | 7 | 11 | | 5 | | 10 | 9 | | | 8 | |
| 25 | (h) | Everton | W 3-1 | Regis 2, Hughes | 20,247 | 1 | | 3 | 4 | 5 | 6 | 7 | 11 | | 8 | | | 9 | | 10 | | 2 |
| 29 | (a) | Norwich C | D 1-1 | Regis | 17,302 | 1 | | 3 | 4 | 5 | 6 | 7 | 11 | | 8 | | | 9 | | 10 | | 2 |
| May 2 | (h) | Nottingham F | D 2-2 | T.Brown, Hughes | 23,523 | 1 | | 3 | 4 | 5 | 6 | 7 | 11 | | 8 | | | 9 | | 10 | | 2 |
| | | | | **App** | | 42 | 36 | 40 | 41 | 38 | 42 | 23 | 29 | 11 | 35 | 32 | 18 | 33 | 16 | 3 | 18 | 5 |
| | | | | **Sub app** | | | | | 1 | | | | 4 | | | | | | 1 | 4 | 2 | 1 |
| | | | | **Goals** | | | | 1 | 19 | 4 | 1 | | 6 | 6 | 3 | 2 | 3 | 10 | | 2 | 5 | |

**Albion in 1977-78. Back row (left to right): D.Statham, R.Ward, T.Godden, J.Osborne, T.Thompson. Middle row: G.Wright (physiotherapist), L.Cunningham, M.Martin, A.Brown, J.Trewick, B.Whitehouse (coach). Front row: P.Mulligan, L.Cantello, J.Wile, Ronnie Allen (manager), B.Robson, W.Johnston, D.Cross.**

# 1978-79

## Division 1

| Date | | Opponent | Result | Scorers | Att | Godden A | Batson B | Statham D | Brown T | Wile J | Robertson A | Robson B | Brown A | Regis C | Cantello L | Cunningham L | Johnston W | Trewick J | Martin M | Mills D | Summerfield K | Bennett M |
|---|---|---|---|---|---|---|---|---|---|---|---|---|---|---|---|---|---|---|---|---|---|---|
| Aug 19 | (h) | Ipswich T | W 2-1 | A.Brown, T.Brown | 23,738 | 1 | 2 | 3 | 4 | 5 | 6 | 7 | 8 | 9 | 10 | 11 | | | | | | |
| 22 | (a) | Queen's Park R | W 1-0 | Howe (og) | 15,481 | 1 | 2 | 3 | 4 | 5 | 6 | 7 | 8 | 9 | 10 | 11 | | | | | | |
| 26 | (h) | Bolton W | W 4-0 | A.Brown 2, Cunningham, Regis | 23,095 | 1 | 2 | 3 | 4 | 5 | 6 | 7 | 8 | 9 | 10 | 11* | 12 | | | | | |
| Sep 2 | (a) | Nottingham F | D 0-0 | | 28,239 | 1 | 2 | 3 | | 5 | 6 | 7 | 8 | 9 | 4 | 10 | 11 | | | | | |
| 9 | (h) | Norwich C | D 2-2 | Cunningham, Robson | 21,893 | 1 | 2 | 3 | | 5 | 6 | 7 | 8 | 9 | 10 | 4 | 11 | | | | | |
| 16 | (a) | Derby C | L 2-3 | Regis, Cunningham | 23,697 | 1 | 2 | 3 | | 5 | 6 | 7 | 8 | 9 | | 4 | 11 | 10 | | | | |
| 23 | (h) | Liverpool | D 1-1 | Cunningham | 33,772 | 1 | 2 | 3 | | 5 | 6 | 7 | 8 | 9 | 10 | 4 | 11 | | | | | |
| 30 | (a) | Chelsea | W 3-1 | Regis, Wile, T.Brown | 21,022 | 1 | 2 | 3 | 11* | 5 | 6 | 7 | 8 | 9 | 10 | 4 | | | 12 | | | |
| Oct 7 | (h) | Tottenham H | L 0-1 | | 33,068 | 1 | 2 | 3 | 11 | 5 | 6 | 7 | 8 | 9 | | 4 | | | 10 | | | |
| 14 | (a) | Leeds U | W 3-1 | T.Brown, Regis 2 | 25,931 | 1 | 2 | 3* | 11 | 5 | 6 | 7 | 8 | 9 | 10 | 4 | 12 | | | | | |
| 21 | (h) | Coventry C | W 7-1 | Cantello, Cunningham 2, Regis 2, T.Brown, Statham | 27,409 | 1 | 2 | 3 | 11 | 5 | 6 | 7 | 8 | 9 | 10* | 4 | 12 | | | | | |
| 28 | (a) | Manchester C | D 2-2 | Regis, Robson | 40,521 | 1 | 2 | 3 | 11 | 5 | 6 | 7 | 8 | 9 | 10 | 4 | | | | | | |
| Nov 4 | (h) | Birmingham C | W 1-0 | Trewick | 32,130 | 1 | 2 | | 4 | 5 | 6 | 7 | 8 | 9 | 10 | 11 | | 3 | | | | |
| 11 | (a) | Ipswich T | W 1-0 | A.Brown | 20,938 | 1 | 2 | | 4 | 5 | 6 | 7 | 8 | 9 | 10 | 11 | | 3 | | | | |
| 18 | (a) | Bolton W | W 1-0 | A.Brown | 22,298 | 1 | 2 | | 4 | 5 | 6 | 7 | 8 | | 10 | 11 | | 3 | 9 | | | |
| 25 | (h) | Aston Villa | D 1-1 | T.Brown (pen) | 35,166 | 1 | 2 | 3 | 4 | 5 | 6 | 7 | 8 | 9 | 10 | 11 | | | | | | |
| Dec 9 | (h) | Middlesbrough | W 2-0 | Regis, Cantello | 19,949 | 1 | 2 | 3 | 4 | 5 | 6 | 7 | 8 | 9 | 10 | 11 | | | | | | |
| 16 | (a) | Wolves | W 3-0 | A.Brown 2, T.Brown | 29,117 | 1 | 2 | 3 | 4 | 5 | 6 | 7 | 8 | 9 | 10 | 11 | | | | | | |
| 26 | (a) | Arsenal | W 2-1 | Robson, A.Brown | 40,055 | 1 | 2 | 3 | 4 | 5 | 6 | 7 | 8 | 9 | 10 | 11 | | | | | | |
| 30 | (a) | Manchester U | W 5-3 | T.Brown 2, Cantello, Cunningham, Regis | 45,091 | 1 | 2 | 3 | 4 | 5 | 6 | 7 | 8 | 9 | 10 | 11 | | | | | | |
| Jan 1 | (h) | Bristol C | W 3-1 | A.Brown 2, Wile | 31,738 | 1 | 2 | 3 | 4 | 5 | 6 | 7 | 8 | 9 | 10 | 11 | | | | | | |
| 13 | (a) | Norwich C | D 1-1 | Regis | 20,972 | 1 | 2 | 3 | 4 | 5 | 6 | 7 | 8 | 9 | | 11 | 10 | | | | | |
| Feb 3 | (a) | Liverpool | L 1-2 | A.Brown | 52,211 | 1 | 2 | 3 | 4 | 5 | 6 | 7 | 8 | 9 | 10* | 11 | | | 12 | | | |
| 24 | (h) | Leeds U | L 1-2 | T.Brown | 27,846 | 1 | 2 | 3 | 4 | 5 | 6 | 7 | 8* | 9 | 10 | 11 | | | 12 | | | |
| Mar 3 | (a) | Coventry C | W 3-1 | Robson, A.Brown, Mills | 25,795 | 1 | 2 | 3 | | 5 | 6 | 7 | 8 | 9 | | 11 | | 4 | | 10 | | |
| 14 | (h) | Chelsea | W 1-0 | A.Brown | 20,472 | 1 | 2 | 3 | 4 | 5 | 6 | | 8 | 9* | | 11 | 12 | 7 | | 10 | | |
| 24 | (h) | Queen's Park R | W 2-1 | A.Brown, Cunningham | 23,678 | 1 | 2 | 3 | 4* | 5 | 6 | 7 | 8 | | 10 | 11 | | 12 | | 9 | | |
| 26 | (h) | Derby C | W 2-1 | Cunningham, A.Brown | 20,010 | 1 | 2 | 3 | | 5 | 6 | 7 | 8* | | 10 | 11 | | 4 | | 9 | 12 | |
| Apr 4 | (h) | Manchester C | W 4-0 | Trewick, Power (og), Mills, Summerfield | 22,314 | 1 | 2* | 3 | | 5 | 6 | 7 | | 9 | 10 | 11 | | 4 | 8 | | 12 | |
| 7 | (h) | Everton | W 1-0 | A.Brown | 29,689 | 1 | | 3 | | 5 | 6 | 7 | 8 | 9 | | 11 | | 4 | | 10 | | 2 |
| 13 | (a) | Southampton | D 1-1 | Regis | 22,063 | 1 | 2 | 3 | 12 | 5 | 6 | 7 | 8 | 9 | | 11 | | 4 | | 10* | | |
| 14 | (h) | Arsenal | D 1-1 | T.Brown | 28,623 | 1 | 2 | 3 | 10 | 5 | 6 | 7 | 8 | 9 | | 11 | | 4 | | | | |
| 17 | (a) | Bristol C | L 0-1 | | 30,191 | 1 | 2 | 3 | | 5 | 6 | 7 | 8 | 9 | 10 | 11 | | 4 | | | | |
| 21 | (h) | Wolves | D 1-1 | Robson | 32,386 | 1 | 2 | 3 | 4 | 5 | 6 | 7 | 8 | 9 | 10 | 11 | | | | | | |
| 24 | (a) | Birmingham C | D 1-1 | Robson | 19,895 | 1 | 2 | 3 | 4 | 5 | 6 | 7 | 8* | 9 | 10 | 11 | | | 12 | | | |
| 28 | (a) | Middlesbrough | D 1-1 | A.Brown | 18,063 | 1 | 2 | 3 | 4 | 5 | 6 | 7 | 8 | 12 | 10 | 11* | | | 9 | | | |
| May 1 | (a) | Everton | W 2-0 | Mills, Robson | 30,083 | 1 | 2 | 3 | 4 | 5 | 6 | 7 | 8 | 9 | 10 | | | | | 11 | | |
| 5 | (h) | Manchester U | W 1-0 | Regis | 28,060 | 1 | 2 | 3 | 4* | 5 | 6 | 7 | 8 | 9 | | 12 | | 10 | | 11 | | |
| 8 | (h) | Southampton | W 1-0 | A.Brown | 17,499 | 1 | 2 | 3 | 12 | 5 | 6 | 7 | 8 | 9 | | 4 | | 10* | | 11 | | |
| 11 | (a) | Aston Villa | W 1-0 | Trewick | 35,991 | 1 | 2 | 3 | | 5 | | 7 | 8 | 9 | 6 | 4 | | 10 | | 11 | | |
| 14 | (a) | Tottenham H | L 0-1 | | 24,789 | 1 | 2 | 3 | | 5 | | 7 | 8 | 9 | 10 | 11 | | 4 | | 6 | | |
| 18 | (h) | Nottingham F | L 0-1 | | 28,210 | 1 | 2 | 3 | 4 | 5 | | 7 | 8 | 9 | 10 | | | 11 | | 6 | | |
| App | | | | | | 42 | 41 | 39 | 29 | 42 | 39 | 41 | 41 | 38 | 32 | 39 | 3 | 19 | 1 | 15 | | 1 |
| Sub app | | | | | | | | | 2 | | | | | | 1 | | 1 | 4 | 2 | 3 | 2 | |
| Goals | | | | | | | 1 | | 10 | 2 | | 7 | 18 | 13 | 3 | 9 | | 3 | | 3 | 1 | |

Albion in 1978-79. Back row (left to right): G.Wright (physiotherapist), P.Mulligan, A.Robertson, A.Brown, J.Osborne, M.Martin, T.Godden, L.Cunningham, B.Batson, C.Regis, R.Atkinson (manager). Front: B.Robson, T.Brown, L.Cantello, J.Wile, D.Statham, J.Trewick, W.Johnston.

# 1979-80

### Division 1

| Date | | Opponent | Result | Scorers | Att | Godden A | Batson B | Statham D | Trewick J | Wile J | Robertson A | Robson B | Brown A | Brown T | Owen G | Barnes P | Mills D | Summerfield K | Deehan J | Pendrey G | Regis C | Bennett M | Moses R | Monaghan D | Cowdrill B |
|---|---|---|---|---|---|---|---|---|---|---|---|---|---|---|---|---|---|---|---|---|---|---|---|---|---|
| Aug 18 | (h) | Derby C | D 0-0 | | 24,727 | 1 | 2 | 3 | 4 | 5 | 6 | 7 | 8 | 9 | 10 | 11 | | | | | | | | | |
| 22 | (a) | Manchester U | L 0-2 | | 53,377 | 1 | 2 | 3 | | 5 | 6 | 7 | 8 | 4 | 10 | 11 | 9 | | | | | | | | |
| 25 | (a) | Liverpool | L 1-3 | Barnes | 48,021 | 1 | 2 | 3 | | 5 | 6 | 7 | 8 | 4 | 10 | 11 | 9* | 12 | | | | | | | |
| Sep 1 | (h) | Nottingham F | L 1-5 | Owen | 26,405 | 1 | 2 | 3 | 12 | 5 | 6 | 7 | | 4 | 10 | 11 | 9* | 8 | | | | | | | |
| 8 | (h) | Bolton W | D 0-0 | | 17,033 | 1 | 2 | 3 | 4 | 5 | 6 | 7 | 8 | 9 | 10 | 11 | | | | | | | | | |
| 15 | (h) | Manchester C | W 4-0 | A.Brown, Owen, Summerfield, Robson | 22,267 | 1 | 2 | 3 | 4 | 5 | 6 | 7 | 8 | 9 | 10 | 11* | | 12 | | | | | | | |
| 22 | (a) | Tottenham H | D 1-1 | A.Brown | 29,914 | 1 | 2 | 3 | 4 | 5 | 6 | 7 | 8 | 12 | 10* | 11 | | | 9 | | | | | | |
| 29 | (h) | Brighton & HA | D 2-2 | Robson, A.Brown | 22,225 | 1 | 2 | 3 | 4 | 5 | 6 | 7 | 8 | | 10 | 11 | | | 9 | | | | | | |
| Oct 6 | (a) | Middlesbrough | L 1-2 | Owen | 16,312 | 1 | 2 | 3 | | 5 | 6 | 7 | 8 | 12 | 10* | 11 | 4 | | 9 | | | | | | |
| 10 | (h) | Manchester U | W 2-0 | Robson, Deehan | 27,811 | 1 | 2 | 3 | | 5 | 6 | 7 | 8 | | 10 | 11 | 4 | | 9 | | | | | | |
| 13 | (a) | Aston Villa | D 0-0 | | 36,007 | 1 | 2 | 3 | | 5 | 6* | 7 | 8 | 12 | 10 | 11 | 4 | | 9 | | | | | | |
| 20 | (h) | Southampton | W 4-0 | Deehan, Owen, Robson, A.Brown | 22,766 | 1 | 2 | 3 | 12 | 5 | | 7 | 8 | 11 | 10* | | 4 | | 9 | 6 | | | | | |
| 27 | (h) | Coventry C | W 4-1 | A.Brown 2, T.Brown 2 (1 pen) | 22,746 | 1 | 2 | 3 | | 5 | 6 | 7 | 8 | 11 | 10 | | 4 | | 9 | | | | | | |
| Nov 3 | (a) | Derby C | L 1-2 | Robson | 21,408 | 1 | 2 | 3 | | 5 | 6 | 7 | 8 | 11* | 10 | | 4 | | 9 | | 12 | | | | |
| 10 | (h) | Norwich C | W 2-1 | Wile, Robson | 20,028 | 1 | 2 | | | 5 | 6 | 7 | 8 | | 10 | 11 | 4 | | 9 | 3 | | | | | |
| 17 | (a) | Leeds U | L 0-1 | | 17,481 | 1 | 2 | | | 5 | 6 | 7 | 8 | 10 | | 11 | 4 | | 9 | 3 | | | | | |
| 24 | (a) | Wolves | D 0-0 | | 32,564 | 1 | 2 | | | 5 | 6 | 7 | 8 | | 10 | | 4 | | 9 | 3 | 11 | | | | |
| Dec 1 | (h) | Everton | D 1-1 | Regis | 21,227 | 1 | 2 | | | 5 | 6 | 7 | 8 | 4 | 10 | 11 | | | | 3 | 9 | | | | |
| 8 | (a) | Stoke C | L 2-3 | Regis, Barnes (pen) | 18,865 | 1 | 2 | | 7 | 5 | 6 | | | | 10* | 11 | 4 | | 12 | 3 | 9 | | | | |
| 15 | (h) | Arsenal | D 2-2 | Robson, Trewick | 18,820 | 1 | 2 | | 10 | 5 | | 7 | 8 | | | 11 | 4 | | | 3 | 9 | 6 | | | |
| 26 | (h) | Bristol C | W 3-0 | Owen, Barnes 2 | 19,590 | 1 | 2 | | 4 | 5 | 6 | 7 | | | 10 | 11 | | | 8 | 3 | 9 | | | | |
| 29 | (h) | Liverpool | L 0-2 | | 35,093 | 1 | 2 | | 4 | 5 | 6 | 7 | | 12 | 10* | 11 | | | 8 | 3 | 9 | | | | |
| Jan 1 | (a) | Ipswich T | L 0-4 | | 22,511 | 1 | 2 | | 4 | 5 | 6 | 7* | 8 | 10 | | 11 | | | 9 | 3 | 12 | | | | |
| 12 | (h) | Nottingham F | L 1-3 | Regis | 27,724 | 1 | 2 | 3 | 4 | 5 | 6 | | | 12 | 10 | 11* | 7 | | 8 | | 9 | | | | |
| 26 | (a) | Crystal P | D 2-2 | Robertson, Regis | 23,869 | 1 | 2 | 3* | | 5 | 6 | 7 | | 12 | 10 | 11 | | | 8 | | 9 | | 4 | | |
| Feb 2 | (a) | Manchester C | W 3-1 | Regis, Barnes 2 | 32,904 | 1 | 2 | | | 5 | 6 | 7 | 8 | | 10 | 11 | | | | 3 | 9 | | 4 | | |
| 9 | (h) | Tottenham H | W 2-1 | Regis 2 | 26,860 | 1 | 2 | | | 5 | | 7 | 8 | | 10 | 11 | | | | 3 | 9 | 6 | 4 | | |
| 16 | (a) | Brighton & HA | D 0-0 | | 22,633 | 1 | 2* | | | 5 | | 7 | 8 | | | 11 | 12 | | 10 | 3 | 9 | 6 | 4 | | |
| 23 | (h) | Aston Villa | L 1-2 | Robson | 33,658 | 1 | 2 | | | 5 | 6 | 7 | 8 | | | 11 | | | 10 | 3 | 9 | | 4 | | |
| Mar 1 | (a) | Southampton | D 1-1 | Regis | 22,138 | 1 | 2 | | | 5 | 6* | 7 | | | 10 | 12 | | | 8 | 3 | 9 | | 4 | 11 | |
| 8 | (a) | Coventry C | W 2-0 | Barnes 2 (1 pen) | 23,287 | 1 | 2 | | | 5 | 6 | 7 | | | 10 | 11 | | | 8 | 3 | 9 | | 4 | | |
| 14 | (h) | Middlesbrough | D 0-0 | | 15,955 | 1 | 2 | | | 5 | 6 | 7 | | | 10 | 11 | | | 8 | 3 | 9 | | 4 | | |
| 18 | (h) | Bolton W | D 4-4 | Barnes 3 (2 pens), Moses | 11,735 | 1 | | | | 5 | 6 | 7 | | | 10 | 11 | 12 | | 8 | 3 | 9* | 2 | 4 | | |
| 22 | (a) | Norwich C | D 1-1 | Bond (og) | 14,811 | 1 | 2 | | | 5 | 6 | 7 | 8 | | 10 | 11 | | | | | 9 | | 4 | | 3 |
| 29 | (h) | Leeds U | W 2-1 | Barnes (pen), Deehan | 19,188 | 1 | 2 | | | 5 | 6 | 7* | | | 10 | 11 | | | 8 | | 9 | | 4 | 12 | 3 |
| Apr 1 | (h) | Crystal P | W 3-0 | Trewick, Barnes 2 | 17,723 | 1 | 2 | | 7 | 5 | 6 | | | | 10 | 11 | | | 8 | | 9 | | 4 | | 3 |
| 5 | (a) | Bristol C | D 0-0 | | 15,677 | 1 | 2 | | | 5 | 6 | 7 | | | 10 | 11 | | | 8 | | 9 | | 4 | | 3 |
| 7 | (h) | Ipswich T | D 0-0 | | 19,888 | 1 | 2 | | 12 | 5 | 6 | 7 | | | 10 | 11 | | | 8* | | 9 | | 4 | | 3 |
| 19 | (h) | Wolves | D 0-0 | | 30,010 | 1 | 2 | | 7 | 5 | 6 | | | 8 | 10 | 11 | | | | | 9 | | 4 | | 3 |
| 26 | (a) | Arsenal | D 1-1 | Barnes | 30,326 | 1 | 2 | | 7 | 5 | 6 | | | 8 | 10 | 11 | | | | | 9 | | 4 | | 3 |
| 28 | (a) | Everton | D 0-0 | | 20,356 | 1 | 2 | | 7 | 5 | 6 | | | | 10 | 11 | | | | | 9 | | 4 | 8 | 3 |
| May 3 | (h) | Stoke C | L 0-1 | | 18,920 | 1 | 2 | | 7 | 5 | 6 | | | | 10 | 11 | | | | | 9 | | 4 | 8 | 3 |
| | | | | App | | 42 | 40 | 16 | 17 | 42 | 38 | 35 | 27 | 12 | 37 | 37 | 15 | 1 | 27 | 18 | 24 | 4 | 18 | 3 | 9 |
| | | | | Sub app | | | | | 3 | | | | 2 | 4 | | | 1 | 2 | 2 | 1 | 2 | | | 1 | |
| | | | | Goals | | | | | 2 | 1 | 1 | 8 | 6 | 2 | 5 | 15 | | 1 | 3 | | 8 | | 1 | | |

Albion in 1979-80. Back row (left to right): A.Robertson, B.Batson, M.Bennett, C.Regis, M.Grew, T.Godden, A.Brown, J.Deehan, G.Pendrey, B.Cowdrill, D.Monaghan. Front: M.Brown (assistant manager-coach), D.Mills, J.Trewick, R.Moses, J.Wile, R.Atkinson (manager), B.Robson, G.Owen, P.Barnes, D.Statham, R.Roberts (physiotherapist).

# 1980-81

## Division 1

| Date | Venue / Opponent | Result | Scorers | Att. | Godden A | Trewick J | Statham D | Moses R | Wile J | Robertson A | Robson B | Deehan J | Regis C | Owen G | Barnes P | Batson B | Brown A | Monaghan D | Mills D | Benjamin I | Cowdrill B | Bennett M | Cross N |
|---|---|---|---|---|---|---|---|---|---|---|---|---|---|---|---|---|---|---|---|---|---|---|---|
| Aug 16 | (h) Arsenal | L 0-1 | | 22,360 | 1 | 2 | 3 | 4 | 5 | 6 | 7 | 8 | 9 | 10 | 11 | | | | | | | | |
| 20 | (a) Stoke C | D 0-0 | | 14,085 | 1 | 2 | 3 | 4 | 5 | 6 | 7 | 8 | 9 | 10 | 11 | | | | | | | | |
| 23 | (h) Wolves | D 1-1 | Regis | 25,409 | 1 | | 3 | 4 | 5* | 6 | 7 | 8 | 9 | 10 | 11 | 2 | 12 | | | | | | |
| 30 | (a) Brighton & HA | W 2-1 | Regis, Owen | 18,162 | 1 | 2 | 3 | 4 | 5 | 6 | 7 | | 9 | 10 | 11 | | 8 | | | | | | |
| Sep 6 | (h) Norwich C | W 3-0 | Barnes (pen), Owen, Brown | 15,414 | 1 | 2 | 3 | 4 | 5 | 6 | 7* | 12 | 9 | 10 | 11 | | 8 | | | | | | |
| 13 | (a) Liverpool | L 0-4 | | 36,792 | 1 | 12 | 3 | 4 | 5 | 6 | 7 | | 9 | 10* | 11 | 2 | 8 | | | | | | |
| 20 | (a) Birmingham C | D 1-1 | Brown | 22,016 | 1 | 10 | 3 | 4 | 5 | 6 | 7 | | 9 | | 11 | 2 | 8 | | | | | | |
| 27 | (h) Southampton | W 2-1 | Brown 2 | 20,845 | 1 | 7 | 3 | 4 | 5 | 6 | | | 9 | 10 | 11 | 2 | 8 | | | | | | |
| Oct 4 | (a) Crystal P | W 1-0 | Regis | 16,081 | 1 | 7 | 3 | 4 | 5 | 6 | | | 9 | 10 | 11 | 2 | 8 | | | | | | |
| 8 | (h) Coventry C | W 1-0 | Barnes | 16,377 | 1 | 12 | 3 | 4* | 5 | 6 | 7 | | | 10 | 11 | 2 | 8 | 9 | | | | | |
| 11 | (a) Manchester C | W 3-1 | Regis, Robson, Trewick | 19,515 | 1 | 4 | 3 | | 5 | 6 | 7 | | 9 | 10 | 11 | 2 | 8 | | | | | | |
| 18 | (a) Nottingham F | L 1-2 | Moses | 25,096 | 1 | 12 | 3 | 4 | 5 | 6 | 7 | | 9 | 10 | 11* | 2 | 8 | | | | | | |
| 21 | (a) Everton | D 1-1 | Wile | 24,076 | 1 | 10 | 3 | 4 | 5 | 6 | 7 | | 9 | | | 2 | 8 | 11 | | | | | |
| 25 | (h) Middlesbrough | W 3-0 | Regis 2, Brown | 16,162 | 1 | 10 | 3 | 4 | 5 | 6 | 7 | | 9 | | | 2 | 8 | 11* | 12 | | | | |
| Nov 1 | (a) Ipswich T | D 0-0 | | 23,043 | 1 | 2 | 3* | 4 | 5 | 6 | 7 | | 9 | | | | 8 | 11 | 10 | 12 | | | |
| 8 | (h) Aston Villa | D 0-0 | | 34,195 | 1 | | | 4 | 5 | 6 | 7 | | 9 | 10 | 11 | 2 | 8 | | | | 3 | | |
| 15 | (a) Arsenal | D 2-2 | Barnes, Owen (pen) | 25,855 | 1 | | | 4 | 5 | 6 | 7 | | 9 | 10 | 11* | 2 | 8 | | | | 3 | | |
| 22 | (h) Leicester C | W 3-1 | Robson, Moses, Owen (pen) | 17,752 | 1 | | | 4 | 5 | 6 | 7 | | 9 | 10 | 11 | 2 | 8 | | 12 | | 3 | | |
| 25 | (h) Stoke C | D 0-0 | | 15,922 | 1 | | | 4 | 5 | 6 | 7 | | 9 | 10 | 11 | 2 | 8 | | | | 3 | | |
| 29 | (a) Tottenham H | W 3-2 | Brown, Robson, Barnes | 27,371 | 1 | 3 | | 4 | 5 | | 7 | | 9 | 10 | 11 | 2 | 8* | | 12 | | | | 6 |
| Dec 6 | (h) Leeds U | L 1-2 | Moses | 17,771 | 1 | | | 4 | 5 | | 7 | | 9 | 10 | 11 | 2 | 8* | | 12 | | 3 | | 6 |
| 13 | (a) Coventry C | L 0-3 | | 16,027 | 1 | | | 4 | 5 | 6 | 7 | 12 | 9 | 10 | 11* | 2 | 8 | | | | 3 | | |
| 26 | (a) Sunderland | D 0-0 | | 28,296 | 1 | | | 4 | 5 | | 7 | | 9 | 10 | 11 | 2 | 8 | | | | 3 | | 6 |
| 27 | (h) Manchester U | W 3-1 | Owen (pen), Barnes, Regis | 30,326 | 1 | | | 4 | 5 | | 7 | | 9 | 10 | 11 | 2 | 8 | | | | 3 | | 6 |
| Jan 10 | (a) Leicester C | W 2-0 | Bennett, Deehan | 17,778 | 1 | | | 4 | 5 | | 7 | 9 | | 10 | 11 | 2 | 8 | | | | 3 | 12 | 6 |
| 17 | (h) Brighton & HA | W 2-0 | Regis, Barnes | 15,643 | 1 | | | 4 | 5 | 2 | 7 | | 9 | 10 | 11 | | 8 | | | | 3 | | 6 |
| 31 | (a) Wolves | L 0-2 | | 29,764 | 1 | | 3 | 4 | 5 | | 7 | | 9 | 10 | 11 | 2 | 8 | | | | | | 6 |
| Feb 7 | (h) Liverpool | W 2-0 | Robson, Regis | 27,905 | 1 | | 3 | 4 | 5 | | 7* | 8 | 9 | 10 | 11 | 2 | 12 | | | | | | 6 |
| 14 | (a) Norwich C | W 2-0 | Regis, Owen (pen) | 15,218 | 1 | | 3 | 4 | 5 | | 7 | 8 | 9 | 10 | 11 | 2 | | | | | | | 6 |
| 21 | (a) Southampton | D 2-2 | Robson, Regis | 21,910 | 1 | | 3 | 4 | 5 | | 7 | 8 | 9 | 10 | 11 | 2 | | | | | | | 6 |
| 28 | (h) Birmingham C | D 2-2 | Moses, Brown | 24,843 | 1 | | 3 | 4 | 5 | | 7 | 8 | 9* | 10 | 11 | 2 | 12 | | | | | | 6 |
| Mar 7 | (h) Crystal P | W 1-0 | Robson | 15,599 | 1 | | 3 | 4 | 5 | | 7 | | 9 | 10 | 11 | 2* | 8 | 12 | | | | | 6 |
| 14 | (a) Manchester C | L 1-2 | Robson | 36,581 | 1 | | 3 | 4 | 5 | 2 | 7 | | 9 | | 11 | | 8 | 12 | 10* | | | | 6 |
| 21 | (h) Nottingham F | W 2-0 | Gunn (og), Deehan | 19,269 | 1 | | 3 | 4 | 5 | | 7 | 8 | 9 | | 11 | 2 | | | 10 | | | | 6 |
| 28 | (a) Middlesbrough | L 1-2 | | 13,288 | 1 | | 3 | 4 | 5 | | 7 | 8* | 9 | | 11 | 2 | 12 | | 10 | | | | 6 |
| 31 | (h) Everton | W 2-0 | Robson, Brown | 14,833 | 1 | | 3 | 4 | 5 | | 7 | 8 | 9 | | 11 | 2 | 12 | | 10 | | 6* | | |
| Apr 4 | (a) Ipswich T | W 3-1 | Brown, Batson, Barnes | 22,216 | 1 | | 3 | 4 | 5 | 6 | 7 | | 9 | 10 | 11 | 2 | 8 | | | | | | |
| 8 | (a) Aston Villa | L 0-1 | | 47,998 | 1 | | 3 | 4 | 5 | 6 | 7 | | 9 | 10 | 11 | 2 | 8 | | | | | | |
| 18 | (a) Manchester U | L 1-2 | Regis | 44,442 | 1 | | 3 | 4 | 5 | 6 | 7 | | 9 | 10 | 11 | 2 | 8* | | | | | 12 | |
| 20 | (h) Sunderland | W 2-1 | Regis 2 | 15,243 | 1 | | 3 | 4 | 5 | 6 | 7 | | 9 | 10 | 11 | 2 | 8 | | | | | | |
| May 2 | (h) Tottenham H | W 4-2 | Brown, Barnes, Robson, Cross | 20,429 | 1 | | 3 | 4 | 5 | 6 | 7 | | 9 | 10* | 11 | 2 | 8 | | | | | 12 | |
| 6 | (a) Leeds U | D 0-0 | | 17,218 | 1 | | 3 | 4 | 5 | 6 | 7 | | 9 | | 11 | 2 | 8 | | | 10 | | | |
| **App** | | | | | 42 | 12 | 31 | 41 | 42 | 28 | 40 | 13 | 38 | 34 | 39 | 35 | 31 | 4 | 5 | 1 | 10 | | 16 |
| **Sub app** | | | | | | 3 | | | | | | 2 | | | | | | 5 | 5 | 1 | | 2 | |
| **Goals** | | | | | | 1 | | 4 | 1 | | 10 | 2 | 14 | 6 | 8 | 1 | 10 | | | | 1 | | 1 |

**Albion take a minute's silence prior to the home game against Southampton on 27 September 1980, in honour of director Tom Silk who was killed in a plane crash on his way to watch Albion in a League Cup tie at Everton. From left to right: John Wile, Cyrille Regis, John Trewick, Gary Owen, Ally Robertson, Derek Statham, Derek Monaghan, Remi Moses, Ally Brown, Peter Barnes, Tony Godden and Brendan Batson.**

# 1981-82

### Division 1

| Date | | Opponent | Result | Scorers | Att | Godden A | Batson B | Statham D | Moses R | Wile J | Bennett M | Robson B | Mills D | Deehan J | Lowery A | Mackenzie S | Cross N | Robertson A | Owen G | Regis C | Brown A | Arthur D | King A | Summerfield K | Jol M | Grew M | Whitehead C | Monaghan D | Lewis M | Childs G | Webb A | Zondervan R | Cowdrill B |
|---|---|---|---|---|---|---|---|---|---|---|---|---|---|---|---|---|---|---|---|---|---|---|---|---|---|---|---|---|---|---|---|---|---|
| Aug 29 | (a) | Manchester C | L 1-2 | Mills (pen) | 36,187 | 1 | 2 | 3 | 4 | 5 | 6 | 7 | 8 | 9 | 10* | 11 | 12 | | | | | | | | | | | | | | | | |
| Sep 2 | (h) | Arsenal | L 0-2 | | 17,104 | 1 | 2 | 3 | 4* | 5 | | 7 | 8 | 9 | | 11 | 12 | 6 | 10 | | | | | | | | | | | | | | |
| 5 | (h) | Swansea C | W 4-1 | Regis 3, Mackenzie | 18,063 | 1 | 2 | 3 | 4 | 5 | | 7 | 8 | | | 11 | | 6 | 10 | 9 | | | | | | | | | | | | | |
| 12 | (a) | Nottingham F | D 0-0 | | 22,618 | 1 | 2 | 3 | 4 | 5 | | 7 | 8 | | | 11 | | 6 | 10 | 9 | | | | | | | | | | | | | |
| 19 | (h) | West Ham U | D 0-0 | | 19,516 | 1 | 2 | 3 | | 5 | | | 8 | 7 | | 11 | 12 | 6 | 10* | 9 | 4 | | | | | | | | | | | | |
| 22 | (a) | Ipswich T | L 0-1 | | 20,542 | 1 | 2 | 3 | | 5 | | | 8 | 7 | | 11 | 10 | 6* | | 9 | 4 | 12 | | | | | | | | | | | |
| 26 | (a) | Everton | L 0-1 | | 23,871 | 1 | 2 | 3 | | 5 | | 7 | 8 | | | 11 | 6 | | 10 | 9 | | | 4 | | | | | | | | | | |
| Oct 3 | (h) | Middlesbrough | W 2-0 | Summerfield, Regis | 12,849 | 1 | 2 | 3 | | 5 | | | | | | 11 | 7 | 6 | 10 | 9 | | | 4 | 8 | | | | | | | | | |
| 10 | (h) | Brighton & HA | D 0-0 | | 13,704 | 1 | 2 | 3 | | 5 | | | 12 | | | 11 | 7* | 6 | 10 | 9 | | | 4 | 8 | | | | | | | | | |
| 17 | (a) | Leeds U | L 1-3 | Mills | 19,164 | 1 | 2 | 3 | | 5 | | | 7 | | | 11 | | 6 | 10 | 9 | 8 | | 4 | | | | | | | | | | |
| 24 | (h) | Southampton | D 1-1 | Brown | 15,730 | 1 | 2 | 3 | | 5 | | | 12 | | | 11 | | 6 | 10 | 9 | 8 | | 4* | 7 | | | | | | | | | |
| 31 | (h) | Birmingham C | D 3-3 | Regis 3 | 21,301 | 1 | 2 | 3 | | 5 | | | 4 | | | 11 | | 6 | 10 | 9 | 8 | | | 7 | | | | | | | | | |
| Nov 7 | (a) | Tottenham H | W 2-1 | Hughton (og), Jol | 32,436 | | 2* | 3 | | 5 | | | | | | 11 | | 6 | 10 | 9 | 8 | | | 12 | 7 | 1 | 4 | | | | | | |
| 14 | (h) | Stoke C | L 1-2 | Smith (og) | 15,787 | | 2* | 3 | | 5 | | | | | | 11 | | 6 | 10 | 9 | 8 | | | 12 | 7 | 1 | 4 | | | | | | |
| 21 | (h) | Liverpool | D 1-1 | Regis | 20,871 | | 2 | 3 | | 5 | | | | | | 11 | | 6 | 10 | 9 | 8* | | | 12 | 7 | 1 | 4 | | | | | | |
| 28 | (a) | Sunderland | W 2-1 | Brown, Regis | 15,897 | | 2 | 3 | | 5 | | | | | | 11 | | 6 | 10 | 9 | 8 | | | | 7 | 1 | 4 | | | | | | |
| Dec 5 | (h) | Wolves | W 3-0 | Regis 2, Whitehead | 23,378 | | 2 | 3 | | 5 | | | | | | 11 | | 6 | 10 | 9 | 8 | | | 12 | 7* | 1 | 4 | | | | | | |
| 26 | (a) | Coventry C | W 2-0 | Owen, Regis | 15,053 | | 2 | | | 5 | 3 | | | | | 11 | | 6 | 10* | 9 | | | 4 | | | 1 | 7 | 8 | 12 | | | | |
| Jan 30 | (a) | West Ham U | L 1-3 | King | 24,423 | | 2 | 3 | | 5 | | | | | | 11 | 12 | 6 | 10 | 9 | | | 4 | | 7 | 1 | 8* | | | | | | |
| Feb 6 | (h) | Nottingham F | W 2-1 | Bennett, Summerfield | 15,006 | | 2 | | | 5 | 6 | | | | | 11 | | 3 | 10 | 9 | | | 4 | 8 | | 1 | 7 | | | | | | |
| 20 | (h) | Everton | D 0-0 | | 14,819 | | | 3 | 2 | 5 | | | | | | 11 | 12 | 6 | 10 | 9 | | | 4 | 8* | | 1 | 7 | | | | | | |
| 27 | (h) | Brighton & HA | D 2-2 | Cross, Bennett | 14,553 | | | 3 | | 5 | 6 | | | | | 11 | 12 | | 10 | 9 | | | | 8 | | 1 | | | 4* | 7 | 2 | | |
| Mar 9 | (a) | Middlesbrough | L 0-1 | | 9,884 | | 2 | 3 | | 5 | 4 | | | | | 11 | | 6 | 10* | 9 | 7 | | | 8 | | 1 | | | | | | 12 | |
| 13 | (a) | Southampton | D 0-0 | | 21,376 | | 2 | | | 5 | 4 | | | | | 11 | | 6 | 10 | 9 | 7 | | | 8 | | 1 | | | | | | 3 | |
| 16 | (a) | Arsenal | D 2-2 | King, Cross | 15,799 | | 2* | 3 | | 5 | 4 | | | | | | 12 | 6 | 10 | | 7 | | | 8 | | 1 | | 9 | | | | 11 | |
| 20 | (h) | Birmingham C | D 1-1 | Robertson | 21,160 | | 2 | 3 | | 5 | 4 | | | | | | 7 | 6 | 10 | 9 | | | | 8 | | 1 | | | | | | 11 | |
| 24 | (h) | Notts C | L 2-4 | Regis, King | 12,759 | | 2 | 3* | | 5 | 4 | | | | | | 7 | 6 | 10 | 9 | 12 | | | 8 | | 1 | | | | | | 11 | |
| 27 | (h) | Tottenham H | W 1-0 | Regis | 20,275 | | 2 | | | 5 | 4 | | | | | | 7 | 6 | 10 | 9 | | | | 8 | | 1 | | | | | 3 | 11 | |
| 30 | (a) | Aston Villa | L 1-2 | King | 28,440 | | 2 | | | 5 | 4 | | | | | 11 | 7 | 6 | 10 | | 9 | | | 8 | | 1 | | | | | 3 | | |
| Apr 6 | (a) | Swansea C | L 1-3 | Mackenzie | 15,744 | | | 3 | | 5 | 4* | | | | | 11 | 8 | 6 | 10 | 9 | 12 | 2 | | | | 1 | | | | | | 7 | |
| 10 | (h) | Coventry C | L 1-2 | Mackenzie | 12,718 | | 2 | 3 | | 5 | 4 | | | | | 11 | 8* | 6 | 10 | 9 | 12 | | | | | 1 | | | | | | 7 | |
| 12 | (a) | Manchester U | L 0-1 | | 38,717 | | 2 | 3 | | 5 | | | | | | 11 | 12 | 6 | 10 | 9 | 8 | | 4 | | | 1 | | | | | | 7* | |
| 17 | (a) | Liverpool | L 0-1 | | 34,286 | | 2 | 3 | | 5 | 7 | | | | | 11 | 12 | 6 | 10 | 9 | 8* | | | | | 1 | | | | | | | 4 |
| 21 | (h) | Manchester C | L 0-1 | | 11,733 | | 2 | 3 | | 5 | | | | | | 11 | | 6 | 10* | 9 | 8 | 4 | | | | 1 | | | | | | 7 | 12 |
| 24 | (h) | Sunderland | L 2-3 | Brown, Owen (pen) | 13,298 | | 2 | 3 | | 5 | 6 | | | | | 11* | | | 10 | 9 | 4 | | | 8 | | 1 | | | 12 | | | 7 | |
| May 1 | (a) | Wolves | W 2-1 | Regis, Monaghan | 19,813 | 1 | 2 | | | 5 | 4 | | | | | 11 | | 6 | 10 | 9 | 8 | | | | | | | 12 | | | | 7* | 3 |
| 5 | (h) | Ipswich T | L 1-2 | Owen | 12,564 | 1 | 2 | | | 5 | 4 | | | | | 11* | | 6 | 10 | 9 | 8 | | | | | | | 12 | | | | 7 | 3 |
| 8 | (h) | Aston Villa | L 0-1 | | 19,650 | 1 | 2 | 3 | | 5 | 4 | | | | | | | 6 | 10 | 9 | 8 | | | | | | | | | | 11 | 7 | |
| 12 | (h) | Manchester U | L 0-3 | | 19,772 | 1 | 2 | 3 | | 5 | 4 | | | | | | 7 | | 10 | 9 | 12 | | | 8* | | | | | | | 11 | | 6 |
| 15 | (a) | Notts C | W 2-1 | Mackenzie, Regis | 8,734 | 1 | 2 | 3 | | 5 | 4 | | | | | | 7 | | 10 | 9 | 12 | | | 11* | | | | | | 6 | | 7 | |
| 18 | (h) | Leeds U | W 2-0 | Regis, Mackenzie | 23,118 | 1 | 2 | 3 | | 5 | 4 | | | | | 11 | | | 10 | 9 | 8 | | | | | | | | | 6 | | 7 | |
| 20 | (a) | Stoke C | L 0-3 | | 19,698 | 1 | 2 | 3 | | 5 | 4 | | | | | | 7 | | 10 | 9 | | | 11 | | | | 8 | | | | | 6* | 12 |
| | | | | | App | 19 | 39 | 35 | 4 | 42 | 23 | 5 | 9 | 4 | 1 | 37 | 11 | 33 | 39 | 37 | 22 | 2 | 21 | 4 | 9 | 23 | 8 | 5 | 3 | 2 | 6 | 13 | 6 |
| | | | | | Sub app | | | | | | | | 2 | | | | 11 | | | | | 3 | 1 | 4 | | | 3 | 1 | | | | 1 | 2 |
| | | | | | Goals | | | | | | 2 | | 2 | | | 5 | 2 | 1 | 3 | 17 | 3 | | 4 | 2 | 1 | | 1 | 1 | | | 1 | | |

West Brom, 1981-82. Back row (left to right): Richard Roberts (physiotherapist), Nicky Cross, Martyn Bennett, Mark Grew, Tony Godden, Bryan Robson, Alistair Robertson, David Mills, Barry Cowdrill. Front row: Cyrille Regis, Peter Barnes, Gary Owen, John Wile, Ronnie Allen (manager), Brendon Batson, Derek Statham, John Deehan.

# 1982-83

## Division 1

| Date | | Venue & Opponent | Result | Scorers | Att. | Grew M | Batson B | Cowdrill B | Zondervan R | Bennett M | Robertson A | Jol M | Brown A | Eastoe P | Mackenzie S | Whitehead C | Webb A | Owen G | Cross N | Regis C | Statham D | Godden A | Wile J | Mills D | Barron P | Lewis M | Thompson G | Perry M | Luke N | Robson G |
|---|---|---|---|---|---|---|---|---|---|---|---|---|---|---|---|---|---|---|---|---|---|---|---|---|---|---|---|---|---|---|
| Aug 28 | (a) | Liverpool | L 0-2 | | 35,652 | 1 | 2 | 3 | 4 | 5 | 6* | 7 | 8 | 9 | 10 | 11 | 12 | | | | | | | | | | | | | |
| Sep 1 | (h) | Brighton & HA | W 5-0 | Cross, Brown 2, Jol, Eastoe | 11,546 | 1 | 2 | | 4 | 5 | 6 | 7 | 8 | 9 | | 3 | | 10 | 11 | | | | | | | | | | | |
| 4 | (h) | Manchester U | W 3-1 | Bennett, Eastoe, Brown | 25,014 | 1 | 2 | | 4 | 5 | 6 | 7 | 8 | 11 | | 3 | | 10 | | 9 | | | | | | | | | | |
| 8 | (a) | Stoke C | W 3-0 | Regis, Eastoe, Brown | 17,446 | 1 | 2 | | 4 | 5 | 6 | 7 | 8 | 11 | | 3 | | 10 | | 9 | | | | | | | | | | |
| 11 | (a) | Watford | L 0-3 | | 17,603 | 1 | 2 | | 4 | 5 | 6 | 7 | 8 | 11 | | 3 | | 10 | | 9 | | | | | | | | | | |
| 18 | (h) | West Ham U | L 1-2 | Eastoe | 15,321 | 1 | 2 | | 4 | 5 | 6 | 7 | 8* | 11 | | 3 | 12 | 10 | | 9 | | | | | | | | | | |
| 25 | (a) | Norwich C | W 3-1 | Regis 3 | 15,130 | 1 | 2 | | 4 | 5 | 6 | 7 | 8 | 11 | | 3 | | 10 | | 9 | | | | | | | | | | |
| Oct 2 | (h) | Aston Villa | W 1-0 | Cross | 25,331 | 1 | 2 | | 4 | 5 | 6 | 7 | 8 | 11 | | 3 | | 10 | | 9 | | | | | | | | | | |
| 9 | (h) | Nottingham F | W 2-1 | Regis, Owen | 13,718 | 1 | 2 | | 4 | 5 | 6 | 7 | 8 | 11* | | 3 | 12 | 10 | | 9 | | | | | | | | | | |
| 16 | (a) | Arsenal | L 0-2 | | 21,666 | 1 | 2 | | 4 | 5 | 6 | 7 | 8 | | | 3 | | 10 | 11* | 9 | 12 | | | | | | | | | |
| 23 | (h) | Luton T | W 1-0 | Whitehead | 16,345 | | 2 | | 4 | 5 | 6 | 7 | 8 | 11 | | | | 10 | | 9 | 3 | 1 | | | | | | | | |
| 30 | (a) | Ipswich T | L 1-6 | Regis | 20,011 | | 2* | | 4 | | 6 | 7 | 8 | 11 | | | | 10 | 12 | 9 | 3 | 1 | 5 | | | | | | | |
| Nov 6 | (a) | Birmingham C | L 1-2 | Eastoe | 18,520 | | 2 | | 4* | | 6 | 7 | 8 | 11 | | | | 10 | 12 | 9 | 3 | 1 | 5 | | | | | | | |
| 13 | (h) | Swansea C | D 3-3 | Cross, Jol, Eastoe | 12,432 | | | | 4 | | 6 | 7 | | 11 | | | 2 | 10 | 8 | 9 | 3 | 1 | 5 | | | | | | | |
| 20 | (a) | Everton | D 0-0 | | 16,001 | | | | 4 | | 6 | 7 | | 11 | | | 2 | 10 | 8 | 9 | 3 | 1 | 5 | | | | | | | |
| 27 | (h) | Coventry C | W 2-0 | Robertson, Regis | 12,115 | | | | 4 | | 6 | 7 | | 11 | | | 2 | 10 | 8 | 9 | 3 | 1 | 5 | | | | | | | |
| Dec 4 | (a) | Tottenham H | D 1-1 | Mills | 26,208 | | | | 4 | | 6 | 7 | | 11* | | | 2 | 10 | 8 | 9 | 3 | 1 | 5 | 12 | | | | | | |
| 11 | (h) | Sunderland | W 3-0 | Robertson, Owen, Zondervan | 11,137 | | | | 4 | | 6 | 7 | | 11 | | | 2 | 10 | 8* | 9 | 3 | 1 | 5 | 12 | | | | | | |
| 18 | (a) | Southampton | L 1-4 | Regis | 16,896 | | | | 4 | | 6 | 7 | | 11 | | | 2 | 10 | 8 | 9 | 3 | 1 | 5 | | | | | | | |
| 27 | (h) | Notts C | D 2-2 | Eastoe, Owen | 17,768 | | | | 4 | | 6 | 7 | | 11 | | | 2 | 10 | 8 | 9 | 3 | 1 | 5 | | | | | | | |
| 28 | (a) | Manchester C | L 1-2 | Brown | 25,172 | | | | 4* | 12 | 6 | 7 | 8 | 11 | | | 2 | 10 | | 9 | 3 | 1 | 5 | | | | | | | |
| Jan 1 | (h) | Everton | D 2-2 | Zondervan, Owen | 15,194 | | | | 4 | | 6 | 7 | | 11 | | | 2 | 10 | 8* | 9 | 3 | 1 | 5 | 12 | | | | | | |
| 3 | (a) | Manchester U | D 0-0 | | 39,123 | | | | 4 | 8 | 6 | 7 | | 11 | | | 2 | 10 | | 9 | 3 | | 5 | | 1 | | | | | |
| 15 | (h) | Liverpool | L 0-1 | | 24,560 | | | | 4 | 8 | 6 | 7 | | 11 | | | 2 | 10 | | 9 | 3 | | 5 | | 1 | | | | | |
| 22 | (a) | West Ham U | W 1-0 | Eastoe | 19,887 | | | | 4 | 8 | 6 | 7 | | 11 | | | 2 | 10 | 12 | 9* | 3 | | 5 | | 1 | | | | | |
| Feb 5 | (h) | Stoke C | D 1-1 | Cross | 11,486 | | | | 4 | 2 | 6 | 7 | 8 | 11 | | | | 10 | | 9 | 3 | | 5 | | 1 | | | | | |
| 12 | (a) | Brighton & HA | D 0-0 | | 9,902 | | | | 4 | | 6 | 7 | 8 | | | 11 | 2 | | | 9 | 3 | | 5 | | 1 | 10 | | | | |
| 19 | (a) | Nottingham F | D 0-0 | | 14,507 | | | | 4 | | 6 | 7 | 8 | | | 11 | 2 | | | 9 | 3 | | 5 | | 1 | 10 | | | | |
| 26 | (h) | Arsenal | D 0-0 | | 16,923 | | | | 4 | 2* | 6 | 7 | | | | 11 | 12 | 10 | 8 | | 3 | | 5 | | 1 | | 9 | | | |
| Mar 5 | (a) | Luton T | D 0-0 | | 10,852 | | | | 4 | 2 | 6 | 7 | | | | 11 | | 10 | 8 | | 3 | | 5 | | 1 | | 9 | | | |
| 12 | (h) | Ipswich T | W 4-1 | Thompson 2, Statham, Gernon (og) | 12,892 | | | | 4 | | 6 | | 12 | | | 7 | 2 | 10 | 11 | 9* | 3 | | 5 | | 1 | | 8 | | | |
| 19 | (h) | Birmingham C | W 2-0 | Regis, Thompson | 20,794 | | | | 4 | | 6 | 7 | | | | | 2 | 10 | 11 | 9 | 3 | | 5 | | 1 | | 8 | | | |
| 26 | (a) | Swansea C | L 1-2 | Thompson | 11,222 | | | | 4 | | 6 | | | | | 11* | 2 | 10 | 12 | 9 | 3 | | 5 | | 1 | | 8 | | | |
| Apr 2 | (h) | Manchester C | L 0-2 | | 13,654 | | | | 4 | | 6 | 7 | | | | 11 | 2 | 10* | | 9 | 3 | | 5 | | 1 | | 8 | | | |
| 4 | (a) | Notts C | L 1-2 | Thompson | 8,692 | | | | 4 | 2 | 6 | 7 | | 9 | | 11 | | | | | 3 | | 5 | | 1 | 10 | 8 | | | |
| 9 | (h) | Watford | L 1-3 | Jol | 11,828 | | | 3 | 4 | | 6 | 7 | 9 | | | | 2 | 10 | 11 | | | | 5 | | 1 | | | 8 | | |
| 16 | (a) | Aston Villa | L 0-1 | | 26,921 | | | | 4 | 2 | 6 | 7 | | | | | | 9 | 11 | | 3 | | 5 | | 1 | 10 | | 8 | | |
| 23 | (h) | Tottenham H | L 0-1 | | 14,940 | | | | 4 | | 6 | 7 | | | | 11* | 2 | 10 | | 9 | 3 | | 5 | | 1 | | 8 | 12 | | |
| 30 | (a) | Coventry C | W 1-0 | Perry | 9,410 | | | | 12 | 4 | 6 | | | | | 7* | 2 | 10 | | | 3 | | 5 | | 1 | | 8 | 9 | | |
| May 2 | (h) | Norwich C | W 1-0 | Thompson | 9,221 | | | | 4 | | 6 | | | | | | 2 | 10 | 11 | | 3 | | 5 | | 1 | 7* | 9 | 8 | 12 | |
| 7 | (h) | Southampton | W 1-0 | Statham | 11,241 | | | | 4 | | 6 | | | | | 7* | 2 | 10 | 11 | | 3 | | 5 | | 1 | | 9 | 8 | | |
| 14 | (a) | Sunderland | D 1-1 | Thompson | 16,375 | | | | 4 | | 6 | | | | | 7 | 2 | 10 | 11 | | 3 | | 5 | | 1 | | 9 | 8* | 12 | |
| | | App | | | | 10 | 12 | 2 | 40 | 22 | 37 | 39 | 16 | 30 | 1 | 35 | 12 | 38 | 26 | 26 | 31 | 12 | 31 | | 20 | 4 | 12 | 6 | | |
| | | Sub app | | | | | 1 | 1 | | | | | 1 | 1 | | | | | 6 | | 1 | | | 3 | | 1 | 1 | 1 | 1 | 2 |
| | | Goals | | | | | | | 2 | 1 | 2 | 3 | 5 | 8 | | 1 | | 4 | 4 | 9 | 2 | | | 1 | | | 7 | 1 | | |

**Albion 1982-83. Back row (left to right):** Cyrille Regis; Martin Jol, Peter Eastoe, Brendon Batson, Tony Godden, Mark Grew, Martyn Bennett, Derek Monaghan, Alistair Brown, Alistair Robertson, Richard Roberts (physiotherapist). **Front row:** Barry Cowdrill, Derek Statham, Alan Webb, Gary Owen, Steve Mackenzie, Ron Wylie (team manager), Clive Whitehead, Nicky Cross, Romeo Zondervan, David Mills.

# 1983-84

## Division 1

| Date | | Opponent | Res | Scorers | Att | Barron P | Webb A | Whitehead C | Zondervan R | McNaught K | Bennett M | Jol M | Thompson G | Regis C | Owen G | Cross N | Robson G | Robertson A | Cowdrill B | Perry M | Lewis M | Childs G | Luke N | Monaghan D | Forsyth M | Mackenzie S | Morley A | Ebanks W | Statham D | Kent K | Hunt S | Grealish A |
|---|---|---|---|---|---|---|---|---|---|---|---|---|---|---|---|---|---|---|---|---|---|---|---|---|---|---|---|---|---|---|---|---|
| Aug 27 | (a) | Aston Villa | L 3-4 | Zondervan, Thompson, Regis | 29,522 | 1 | 2 | 3 | 4* | 5 | 6 | 7 | 8 | 9 | 10 | 11 | 12 | | | | | | | | | | | | | | | |
| 29 | (a) | Stoke C | L 1-3 | Cross | 16,156 | 1 | 2 | 3 | 4 | 5 | 6 | 7 | 8 | 9 | 10 | 11 | | | | | | | | | | | | | | | | |
| Sep 3 | (h) | Leicester C | W 1-0 | Whitehead | 12,016 | 1 | | 3 | 2 | 5 | 6 | 7 | 8 | 9 | 10 | 11 | 4 | | | | | | | | | | | | | | | |
| 7 | (h) | Tottenham H | D 1-1 | Regis | 14,889 | 1 | 2 | | 4 | 5 | 6 | 7* | 8 | 9 | 10 | 11 | | | 3 | 12 | | | | | | | | | | | | |
| 10 | (a) | Everton | D 0-0 | | 15,543 | 1 | 2 | | 4 | 5 | 6 | | 8 | 9 | 10 | 12 | 7* | | 3 | 11 | | | | | | | | | | | | |
| 17 | (h) | West Ham U | W 1-0 | Thompson | 15,161 | 1 | 2 | | 4 | 5 | 6 | | 8 | 9 | 10 | 11* | | | 3 | 12 | 7 | | | | | | | | | | | |
| 24 | (a) | Ipswich T | W 4-3 | Zondervan, Regis, Perry, Thompson (pen) | 16,611 | 1 | 2 | | 4 | 5 | 6 | | 8 | 9 | 11 | 10* | | | 3 | 12 | 7 | | | | | | | | | | | |
| Oct 1 | (h) | Watford | W 2-0 | Regis, Thompson | 14,456 | 1 | 2 | 7 | 4 | 5 | 6 | | 8 | 9 | | 11* | | | 3 | | 10 | 12 | | | | | | | | | | |
| 15 | (a) | Manchester U | L 0-3 | | 42,221 | 1 | 2 | | 4 | 5 | 6 | | 8 | 9 | 10 | 11 | | | 3 | | 7 | | | | | | | | | | | |
| 22 | (a) | Coventry C | W 2-1 | Regis, Perry | 13,441 | 1 | 2 | 7 | | 5 | 6 | | 8 | 9* | 10 | 12 | | | 3 | 11 | 4 | | | | | | | | | | | |
| 29 | (h) | Birmingham C | L 1-2 | Perry | 20,224 | 1 | 2 | | 4 | 5 | 6* | | 8 | 9 | 10 | 12 | | | 3 | 11 | 7 | | | | | | | | | | | |
| Nov 5 | (h) | Notts C | W 2-0 | McNaught, Luke | 10,821 | 1 | 2 | | 4 | 5 | | | 8 | | 10 | | | 6 | 3 | 9 | 7 | | 11 | | | | | | | | | |
| 12 | (a) | Southampton | L 0-1 | | 16,450 | 1 | 2 | 4* | 5 | | 8 | | 10 | 12 | 7 | 6 | | 3 | 9 | | | | 11 | | | | | | | | | |
| 19 | (a) | Norwich C | L 0-2 | | 13,368 | 1 | 2 | | 4 | 5 | 7 | | 8 | | 10 | 12 | | 6 | 3 | 9* | | | 11 | | | | | | | | | |
| 26 | (h) | Wolves | L 1-3 | Thompson | 17,947 | 1 | 2 | | 4 | 5 | | 7 | 8 | | 10 | | | 6 | 3 | 9* | | | 11 | 12 | | | | | | | | |
| Dec 3 | (a) | Arsenal | W 1-0 | Monaghan | 22,271 | 1 | 2 | | 4 | 5 | | | 8 | | 10 | | | | 3 | | | | 7 | 9 | 6 | 11 | | | | | | |
| 10 | (h) | Queen's Park R | L 1-2 | Morley | 11,717 | 1 | 2 | | 4 | 5 | 6 | | 8 | | 10 | | | | 3 | 12 | | | 9 | | | 11* | 7 | | | | | |
| 18 | (a) | Luton T | L 0-2 | | 11,566 | 1 | | | 2 | 5 | | 7 | | 9 | | 10 | | | 3 | | 8 | | 4 | | 6 | | 11 | | | | | |
| 26 | (h) | Liverpool | L 1-2 | Morley | 25,139 | 1 | 2 | | 4 | 5 | | 7 | | 9 | | 8* | | | 3 | 12 | 10 | | | | 6 | | 11 | | | | | |
| 27 | (a) | Sunderland | L 0-3 | | 17,968 | 1 | | | 4 | 5 | | | 8 | 9 | 10 | 12 | | | 3 | | 7 | | | | 6 | | 11 | 2* | | | | |
| 31 | (a) | Leicester C | D 1-1 | Thompson | 15,128 | 1 | | 2 | 4 | 5 | 6 | 7 | 8 | 9 | 10 | | | | 3 | | | | | | | | 11 | | | | | |
| Jan 2 | (h) | Ipswich T | W 2-1 | Owen, Thompson | 11,199 | 1 | 2 | 4* | 5 | 6 | | | 8 | 9 | 10 | 12 | | | 3 | | 7 | | | | | | 11 | | | | | |
| 14 | (h) | Aston Villa | W 3-1 | Thompson 2, Regis | 20,399 | 1 | 2 | 7 | | 5 | 6 | | 8 | 9 | 10 | | | | 3 | | | | 4 | | | | 11 | | | | | |
| 21 | (a) | West Ham U | L 0-1 | | 17,213 | 1 | 2 | 7 | | 5 | | 12 | 8 | 9 | 10* | | 6 | | 3 | | | | 4 | | | | 11 | | | | | |
| Feb 4 | (a) | Watford | L 1-3 | Zondervan | 14,240 | 1 | 2 | | 4 | 5 | | 7 | 8 | 9 | | | | | 3 | | 10 | | | | | | 11 | | | | | |
| 8 | (a) | Nottingham F | L 0-5 | | 11,020 | 1 | 2 | | 4 | 5 | | 7 | 8* | 9 | | | | | | | 10 | | | | 6 | 12 | 11 | | 3 | | | |
| 11 | (h) | Everton | D 1-1 | Perry | 10,313 | 1 | 2 | | 4 | 5 | | 7 | | | 12 | | | | | 9 | | | | | 6* | 10 | 11 | | 3 | 8 | | |
| 25 | (h) | Coventry C | D 1-1 | Cross | 10,929 | 1 | | | 4 | 5 | 6 | 7 | 8 | | 9 | | | | | | | | | | | 10 | 11 | 2 | 3 | | | |
| 28 | (a) | Birmingham C | L 1-2 | Mackenzie | 16,780 | 1 | | | 4 | 5 | 6 | 7 | 8 | | 9 | | | | | | | | | | | 10 | 11 | 2 | 3 | | | |
| Mar 3 | (a) | Notts C | D 1-1 | Cross | 7,373 | 1 | 2 | | 4 | 5 | 6 | 7 | 8 | | 9 | | | | | | | | | | | 10 | 11 | | 3 | | | |
| 17 | (a) | Tottenham H | W 1-0 | Regis | 22,385 | 1 | 2 | | | 5 | 6 | | 8 | 9 | | | | | | | | | | | | 10 | 11 | | 3 | | 4 | 7 |
| 24 | (h) | Stoke C | W 3-0 | Mackenzie, Hunt, Morley | 13,681 | 1 | 2 | | | 5 | 6* | | 8 | 9 | | | | | | | | | | | | 10 | 11 | 12 | 3 | | 4 | 7 |
| 31 | (h) | Manchester U | W 2-0 | Mackenzie, Regis | 27,954 | 1 | 2 | | | 5 | 6 | | 8 | 9 | | | | | | | | | | | | 10 | 11 | | 3 | | 4 | 7 |
| Apr 7 | (a) | Nottingham F | L 1-3 | Thompson | 15,245 | 1 | 2 | | | 5 | 6 | | 8 | 9 | | | | | | | | | | | | 10 | 11 | | 3 | | 4 | 7 |
| 14 | (h) | Norwich C | D 0-0 | | 11,572 | 1 | | | | 5 | 6 | | 8 | 9 | | | | | | | | | | | | 10 | 11 | 2 | 3 | | 4 | 7 |
| 21 | (a) | Liverpool | L 0-3 | | 35,320 | 1 | 2 | | | 5 | 6 | | 8 | 9 | | | | | | | | | | | | 10 | 11 | | 3 | | 4 | 7 |
| 23 | (h) | Sunderland | W 3-1 | Regis, Hunt, Thompson | 11,252 | 1 | 2 | | | 5 | 6 | | 8 | 9 | | 12 | | | | | | | | | | 10 | 11 | 3* | 3 | | 4 | 7 |
| 28 | (a) | Wolves | D 0-0 | | 13,208 | 1 | 2 | | | 5 | 6 | | 8 | 9 | | | | | | | | | | | | 10 | 11 | | 3 | | 4 | 7 |
| May 5 | (h) | Arsenal | L 1-3 | Thompson | 13,566 | 1 | 2 | | | 5 | 6 | | 8 | 9 | | 12 | | | | | | | | | | 10 | 11 | | 3 | | 4 | 7* |
| 7 | (a) | Queen's Park R | D 1-1 | Thompson | 14,418 | 1 | 2 | | | 5 | | | 8 | 9 | | | | | 6 | | | | | | | 10 | 11 | 7 | 3 | | 4 | |
| 12 | (h) | Luton T | W 3-0 | Morley, Regis, Mackenzie | 12,417 | 1 | 2 | | | 5 | 6 | | | 9 | | 8 | | | | | | | | | | 10 | 11 | 3* | | 12 | 4 | 7 |
| 14 | (h) | Southampton | L 0-2 | | 10,365 | 1 | 2 | | | 5 | 6 | | 8 | 9 | | | | | 3 | | 9 | | | | | 10 | 11 | 3* | | | 4 | 7 |
| App | | | | | | 42 | 5 | 34 | 29 | 42 | 29 | 15 | 37 | 30 | 20 | 16 | 5 | 6 | 22 | 8 | 14 | | 8 | 2 | 8 | 18 | 26 | 6 | 16 | 1 | 12 | 11 |
| Sub app | | | | | | | | | 1 | | | | | | 9 | 2 | | | | 5 | | | 1 | 1 | | 1 | 1 | | | 1 | | 2 |
| Goals | | | | | | | | 1 | 3 | 1 | | | 13 | 10 | 1 | 3 | | | | 4 | | | 1 | 1 | | 4 | 4 | | | | 2 | |

**Cyrille Regis side-foots home Albion's second goal against Manchester United in the 2-0 victory at The Hawthorns on 31 March.**

# 1984-85

## Division 1

| Date | | Venue | Opponent | Result | Scorers | Att. | Godden A | Whitehead C | Statham D | Hunt S | Bennett M | Robertson A | Grealish A | Thompson G | Regis C | Mackenzie S | Cross N | Morley A | Robson G | Forsyth M | Valentine C | Cross D | Lewis M | Nicholl J | Barron P | Owen G | Cowdrill B |
|---|---|---|---|---|---|---|---|---|---|---|---|---|---|---|---|---|---|---|---|---|---|---|---|---|---|---|---|
| Aug 25 | (a) | Queen's Park R | L | 1-3 | Mackenzie | 12,802 | 1 | 2 | 3 | 4 | 5 | 6 | 7 | 8 | 9 | 10 | 11 | | | | | | | | | | |
| 27 | (h) | Everton | W | 2-1 | Hunt, Thompson | 13,464 | 1 | 2 | 3 | 4 | 5 | 6 | 7* | 8 | 9 | 10 | 11 | | | | | | | | | | |
| Sep 1 | (h) | Luton T | W | 4-0 | Hunt, Regis, Cross, Thompson | 11,720 | 1 | 2 | 3 | 4 | 5 | 6 | 7 | 8 | 9* | 10 | 12 | 11 | | | | | | | | | |
| 5 | (a) | Norwich C | L | 1-2 | Grealish | 14,234 | 1 | 2 | 3 | 4 | 5 | 6 | 7 | 8 | 9 | 10 | | 11 | | | | | | | | | |
| 8 | (a) | Sunderland | D | 1-1 | Thompson | 18,206 | 1 | 2 | 3 | 4 | 5 | 6 | 7 | 8 | 9 | 10 | | 11 | | | | | | | | | |
| 15 | (h) | Sheffield W | D | 2-2 | Thompson 2 | 16,439 | 1 | 2 | 3 | 4 | 5 | 6 | 7 | 8 | 9 | 10 | | 11 | | | | | | | | | |
| 22 | (a) | Leicester C | L | 1-2 | Cross | 11,960 | 1 | 2 | 3 | 4 | 5 | 6 | 7 | 8 | | 10 | 9 | 11 | | | | | | | | | |
| 29 | (h) | Manchester U | L | 1-2 | Thompson (pen) | 26,401 | 1 | 2 | 3 | 4 | 5 | 6* | 7 | 8 | 9 | 10 | 12 | 11 | | | | | | | | | |
| Oct 6 | (a) | Liverpool | D | 0-0 | | 29,346 | 1 | 2 | 3 | 4 | 5 | 6 | 7 | 8 | | 10 | 9 | 11* | 12 | | | | | | | | |
| 13 | (h) | Nottingham F | W | 4-1 | Mackenzie, Thompson 3 | 12,991 | 1 | 2 | 3 | 4 | 5 | 6 | 7 | 8 | | 10 | 9 | 11 | | | | | | | | | |
| 20 | (a) | Ipswich T | L | 0-2 | | 14,154 | 1 | 2 | 3 | 4 | 5 | 6 | 7 | 8 | 9 | 10 | | | 12 | 11* | | | | | | | |
| 27 | (h) | Southampton | D | 0-0 | | 12,454 | 1 | 2 | 3* | 4 | 5 | 6 | 7 | 8 | 9 | | | | | 12 | | 10 | 11 | | | | |
| Nov 3 | (a) | Tottenham H | W | 3-2 | Statham (pen), Cross, Mackenzie | 24,494 | 1 | 2 | 3 | 4 | 5 | 6 | 7 | 8 | 9 | | | | 12 | 11* | 10 | | | | | | |
| 10 | (h) | Stoke C | W | 2-0 | Hunt, Mackenzie | 12,828 | 1 | 12 | 3 | 4 | 5 | 6 | 7* | 8 | 9 | | | | 11 | | 10 | | | 2 | | | |
| 17 | (a) | Chelsea | L | 1-3 | Thompson | 17,573 | 1 | 11 | 3 | 4* | 5 | 6 | 7 | 8 | 9 | 12 | | | | | 10 | | | 2 | | | |
| 24 | (h) | Coventry C | W | 5-2 | Thompson, Valentine, Mackenzie, Hunt, Statham | 12,742 | 1 | | 3 | 4 | 5 | 6 | 7 | 8 | 9 | 12 | | | | 11 | 10* | | | 2 | | | |
| Dec 1 | (a) | West Ham U | W | 2-0 | Hunt, Thompson | 15,572 | 1 | | 3 | 4 | 5 | 6 | 7 | 8 | 9 | | | | | 11 | 10 | | | 2 | | | |
| 8 | (h) | Watford | W | 2-1 | Thompson, Cross | 13,581 | 1 | | 3 | 4 | | 6 | 7 | 8 | 9 | | | | 5 | 11 | 10 | | | 2 | | | |
| 15 | (a) | Arsenal | L | 0-4 | | 23,728 | 1 | 4 | 3 | | 5 | 6 | 7 | 8 | 9 | 12 | | | | 11 | 10* | | | 2 | | | |
| 18 | (a) | Luton T | W | 2-1 | Thompson, Statham (pen) | 7,286 | 1 | 4 | 3 | | 5 | 6 | 7 | 8 | 9 | 10 | | | | 11 | | | | 2 | | | |
| 26 | (h) | Newcastle U | W | 2-1 | Hunt, Thompson | 20,248 | 1 | | 3 | 4 | 5 | 6 | 7 | 8 | 9 | | | | | 11 | 10 | | | 2 | | | |
| 29 | (h) | Norwich C | L | 0-1 | | 13,406 | 1 | 12 | 3 | 4 | 5 | 6 | 7* | 8 | 9 | | | | | 11 | 10 | | | 2 | | | |
| Jan 1 | (a) | Aston Villa | L | 1-3 | Statham (pen) | 31,710 | 1 | 7 | 3 | 4 | 5 | 6* | | 8 | 9 | 12 | | | | 11 | 10 | | | 2 | | | |
| 12 | (a) | Sheffield W | L | 0-2 | | 24,345 | 1 | 12 | 3 | 4 | 5* | 6 | 7 | 8 | 9 | | | | | 11 | 10 | | | 2 | | | |
| 26 | (h) | Queen's Park R | D | 0-0 | | 9,324 | 1 | 4 | 3 | | 5 | | 7 | 8 | 9 | | | | 6 | 11 | 10 | | | 2 | | | |
| Feb 2 | (a) | Manchester U | L | 0-2 | | 36,681 | | 10 | 3 | 4 | 5 | | 7 | 8 | 9* | | | | 6 | 11 | | | | 2 | 1 | 12 | |
| 23 | (h) | Tottenham H | L | 0-1 | | 17,002 | 1 | 10 | | 4 | 5 | 6 | | 8 | 9 | | | | 3 | 11 | | | | 2 | | 7 | |
| Mar 2 | (a) | Southampton | L | 3-4 | Valentine, Thompson 2 | 15,567 | 1 | 12 | 3 | 4 | 5 | 6 | | 8 | 9* | | | | | 11 | 10 | | | 2 | | 7 | |
| 12 | (a) | Stoke C | D | 0-0 | | 6,885 | 1 | 3* | | 4 | 5 | | | 12 | 8 | 9 | | | 6 | 11 | 10 | | | 2 | | 7 | |
| 16 | (a) | Nottingham F | W | 2-1 | Cross, Owen | 12,663 | 1 | 3 | | 4 | 5 | | | 12 | 8 | 9 | 10 | | 6 | 11 | | | | 2 | | 7* | |
| 23 | (h) | Liverpool | L | 0-5 | | 20,847 | 1 | 12 | 3 | 4 | 5 | 6 | 7 | 8 | 9* | 10 | | | | 11 | | | | 2 | | 7 | |
| 30 | (h) | Leicester C | W | 2-0 | Hunt 2 | 9,347 | 1 | 2 | 3 | 4 | | 6 | 12 | 8 | | 10 | | | 9* | 5 | 11 | | | | | 7 | |
| Apr 3 | (h) | Ipswich T | L | 1-2 | Hunt | 8,112 | 1 | 2 | 3 | 4 | | 6 | 12 | 8 | | 10* | | | 9 | 5 | 11 | | | | | 7 | |
| 6 | (a) | Newcastle U | L | 0-1 | | 22,690 | 1 | | | 4 | 5 | 6 | 12 | 8 | | | | | 9 | 11 | 10 | | | 2 | | 7* | 3 |
| 8 | (h) | Aston Villa | W | 1-0 | Valentine | 21,044 | 1 | | | 4 | 5 | 6 | 10 | 8 | | | 12 | | 9* | 11 | | | | 2 | | 7 | 3 |
| 16 | (a) | Everton | L | 1-4 | Grealish | 29,750 | 1 | 12 | | 4 | 5 | 6* | 10 | 8 | 7 | | | | 9 | 11 | | | | 2 | | 7 | 3 |
| 20 | (h) | Chelsea | L | 0-1 | | 11,196 | 1 | | | 4 | 5 | | 10 | 8 | | 12 | | | 9* | 6 | 11 | | | 2 | | 7 | 3 |
| 24 | (h) | Sunderland | W | 1-0 | Cross | 7,423 | 1 | 12 | | | 5 | 6 | 9* | 8 | | 4 | 10 | | | 11 | | | | 2 | | 7 | 3 |
| 27 | (a) | Coventry C | L | 1-2 | Mackenzie | 10,356 | 1 | 9* | | | 5 | 6 | 12 | 8 | | 4 | 10 | | | 11 | | | | 2 | | 7 | 3 |
| May 4 | (h) | West Ham U | W | 5-1 | Hunt, Mackenzie, Grealish, Cross | 8,878 | 1 | | | 4 | 5 | 6 | 12 | 8 | | 9 | 10 | | | 11 | | | | 2 | | 7* | 3 |
| 7 | (a) | Watford | W | 2-0 | Thompson, Owen | 14,062 | 1 | | | 4 | 5 | 6 | 12 | 8 | | 9 | 10* | | | 11 | | | | 2 | | 7 | 3 |
| 11 | (h) | Arsenal | D | 2-2 | Valentine, Thompson | 13,485 | 1 | | | 4 | 5 | 6 | | 8 | | 9 | 10 | | | 11 | | | | 2 | | 7 | 3 |
| | | | **App** | | | | 41 | 25 | 30 | 37 | 39 | 37 | 30 | 42 | 7 | 37 | 15 | 7 | 9 | 9 | 29 | 16 | 1 | 27 | 1 | 14 | 9 |
| | | | **Sub app** | | | | | 7 | | | | | | 8 | | | 1 | 9 | 2 | 1 | | | | | | 1 | |
| | | | **Goals** | | | | | | 4 | 10 | | | 3 | 19 | 1 | 8 | 5 | | | | 4 | 2 | | | | 2 | |

Albion, 1984-85. Back row (left to right): Michael Perry, Garry Thompson, Martyn Bennett, Paul Barron, Darren Carmel, Tony Godden, Ken McNaught, Barry Cowdrill, Michael Forsyth, Gary Robson. Third row: Gary Leonard, Joe Tortolano, Clive Whitehead, Cyrille Regis, Steve Mackenzie, Nicky Cross, Wayne Ebanks, Michael Lewis. Seated: Nobby Stiles (coach), Alistair Robertson, Derek Statham, Gary Owen, Johnny Giles (manager), Steve Hunt, Tony Grealish, Tony Morley, George Wright (physiotherapist). On ground: Carlton Palmer, Hector Wynter, Mark Housego, Wayne Dobbins, Steven Bell, Andy Thompson, Michael Icke, Ian Hathaway, Karl Addis, Philip Walker.

# 1985-86

## Division 1

Player columns (left to right): Godden A, Nicholl J, Statham D, Whitehead C, Bennett M, Robertson A, Grealish A, Varadi I, Mackenzie S, Valentine C, Crooks G, Cowdrill B, Hunt S, Forsyth M, Anderson C, Robson G, Armstrong G, Dennison R, Palmer C, Thomas M, Bradshaw P, Thompson A, Reilly G, Owen G, Grew M, Naylor S, Dickinson M, Dyson P, Bradley D, Madden C, Bull S, Burrows D, Robinson M

| Date | | Opponent | Result | Scorers | Att. |
|---|---|---|---|---|---|
| Aug 17 | (h) | Oxford U | D 1-1 | Varadi | 14,626 |
| 20 | (a) | Everton | L 0-2 | | 26,788 |
| 24 | (a) | Watford | L 1-5 | Varadi | 14,541 |
| 26 | (h) | Manchester C | L 2-3 | Mackenzie 2 | 12,152 |
| 31 | (a) | Chelsea | L 0-3 | | 15,376 |
| Sep 4 | (h) | Aston Villa | L 0-3 | | 17,077 |
| 7 | (h) | Ipswich T | L 1-2 | Crooks | 7,733 |
| 14 | (a) | Newcastle U | L 1-4 | Mackenzie | 21,855 |
| 21 | (h) | Manchester U | L 1-5 | Crooks | 25,068 |
| 28 | (a) | Coventry C | L 0-3 | | 10,295 |
| Oct 5 | (h) | Tottenham H | D 1-1 | Valentine | 12,040 |
| 12 | (a) | Leicester C | D 2-2 | Crooks 2 | 7,236 |
| 19 | (h) | Birmingham C | W 2-1 | Varadi, Valentine | 14,576 |
| 26 | (a) | Sheffield W | L 0-1 | | 19,873 |
| Nov 3 | (a) | Nottingham F | L 1-2 | Hunt | 19,610 |
| 9 | (h) | Queen's Park R | L 0-1 | | 9,016 |
| 16 | (a) | Liverpool | L 1-4 | Crooks | 28,407 |
| 23 | (h) | Arsenal | D 0-0 | | 9,165 |
| 30 | (a) | West Ham U | L 0-4 | | 16,325 |
| Dec 7 | (h) | Everton | L 0-3 | | 12,206 |
| 14 | (a) | Oxford U | D 2-2 | Hunt, Varadi | 9,020 |
| 22 | (h) | Watford | W 3-1 | Hunt (pen), Dennison, Varadi | 11,092 |
| 26 | (a) | Luton T | L 1-2 | Varadi | 12,508 |
| 28 | (a) | Aston Villa | D 1-1 | Hunt | 18,796 |
| Jan 1 | (a) | Southampton | L 1-3 | Varadi | 13,154 |
| 11 | (h) | Newcastle U | D 1-1 | Varadi | 9,106 |
| 18 | (h) | Chelsea | L 0-3 | | 11,275 |
| Feb 1 | (a) | Manchester C | L 1-2 | Grealish | 20,540 |
| 8 | (a) | Birmingham C | W 1-0 | Bennett | 11,514 |
| 22 | (a) | Manchester U | L 0-3 | | 45,193 |
| Mar 8 | (a) | Tottenham H | L 0-5 | | 10,841 |
| 15 | (h) | Leicester C | D 2-2 | Varadi, Mackenzie | 8,337 |
| 19 | (h) | Coventry C | D 0-0 | | 8,831 |
| 22 | (a) | Ipswich T | L 0-1 | | 12,121 |
| 29 | (h) | Southampton | W 1-0 | Thompson | 7,325 |
| Apr 1 | (a) | Luton T | L 0-3 | | 9,226 |
| 5 | (h) | Nottingham F | D 1-1 | Bennett | 7,901 |
| 12 | (a) | Queen's Park R | L 0-1 | | 11,866 |
| 19 | (h) | Liverpool | L 1-2 | Madden | 22,010 |
| 22 | (h) | Sheffield W | D 1-1 | Reilly | 6,021 |
| 26 | (a) | Arsenal | D 2-2 | Reilly 2 | 14,843 |
| May 3 | (h) | West Ham U | L 2-3 | Madden, Reilly (pen) | 17,831 |

| | App | Sub app | Goals |
|---|---|---|---|
| Godden A | 21 | | |
| Nicholl J | 29 | 2 | |
| Statham D | 37 | | |
| Whitehead C | 22 | | 2 |
| Bennett M | 25 | 2 | 1 |
| Robertson A | 20 | 2 | |
| Grealish A | 14 | 1 | 1 |
| Varadi I | 30 | | 9 |
| Mackenzie S | 30 | | 4 |
| Valentine C | 15 | | 2 |
| Crooks G | 18 | | 5 |
| Cowdrill B | 9 | | |
| Hunt S | 19 | 1 | 4 |
| Forsyth M | 11 | | |
| Anderson C | 7 | 4 | |
| Robson G | 9 | 5 | |
| Armstrong G | 7 | 1 | |
| Dennison R | 16 | 5 | 1 |
| Palmer C | 20 | 4 | |
| Thomas M | 8 | | |
| Bradshaw P | 13 | 2 | |
| Thompson A | 20 | 1 | 1 |
| Reilly G | 3 | | 4 |
| Owen G | 1 | | |
| Grew M | 12 | | |
| Naylor S | 7 | | |
| Dickinson M | 11 | | |
| Dyson P | 10 | | 2 |
| Bradley D | 9 | | |
| Madden C | | 1 | |
| Bull S | | | |
| Burrows D | 1 | | |
| Robinson M | 1 | | |

Albion in 1985-86. Back row (left to right): M.Forsyth, J.Nicholl, M.Bennett, T.Godden, P.Bradshaw, B.Cowdrill, C.Palmer. Middle: G.Wright (physiotherapist), T.Brown (coach), G.Robson, C.Anderson, N.Cross, C.Whitehead, D.Statham, S.Hunt, N.Stiles (assistant manager-coach). Front: C.Valentine, S.Mackenzie, A.Robertson, J.Giles (manager), G.Crooks, I.Varadi, T.Grealish.

# 1986-87

## Division 2

| Date | | Opponent | Result | Scorers | Att. | Naylor S | Whitehead C | Burrows D | Bennett M | Dyson P | Dickinson M | Palmer C | Evans S | Mackenzie S | Williamson R | Madden C | Thompson A | Dennison R | Dobbins W | Bull S | Cowdrill B | Anderson C | Robinson M | Crooks G | Hopkins R | Singleton M | Statham D | Steggles K | Bradley D | Reilly G | Robson G | Lynex S | Goodman D |
|---|---|---|---|---|---|---|---|---|---|---|---|---|---|---|---|---|---|---|---|---|---|---|---|---|---|---|---|---|---|---|---|---|---|
| Aug 23 | (a) | Hull C | L 0-2 | | 8,658 | 1 | 2 | 3 | 4 | 5 | 6 | 7 | 8 | 9 | 10 | 11* | 12 | | | | | | | | | | | | | | | | |
| 25 | (h) | Sheffield U | W 1-0 | Evans | 9,102 | 1 | | 3 | 4 | 5 | 6 | 7 | 8 | 9 | 10 | | 2 | 11* | 12 | | | | | | | | | | | | | | |
| 30 | (h) | Huddersfield T | W 1-0 | Bennett | 9,252 | 1 | 2 | 3 | 4 | 5 | 6 | 7 | 8 | 9 | 10* | | | 11 | 12 | | | | | | | | | | | | | | |
| Sep 2 | (a) | Stoke C | D 1-1 | Palmer | 8,664 | 1 | 2 | 3 | 4 | 5 | 6 | 7 | 8 | 9 | 10 | | | 11 | | | | | | | | | | | | | | | |
| 6 | (a) | Reading | D 1-1 | Madden | 7,537 | 1 | 2 | 3 | 4 | 5 | 6 | 7 | | 10 | 12 | 11* | | | 9 | 8 | | | | | | | | | | | | | |
| 13 | (h) | Ipswich T | L 3-4 | Bull 2, Williamson | 9,034 | 1 | 2 | 3 | 4 | 5 | 6 | 7 | | 9 | 10 | 12 | | | | 8 | 11* | | | | | | | | | | | | |
| 20 | (a) | Brighton & HA | L 0-2 | | 8,766 | 1 | 2 | 3 | 4 | 5 | 6 | 7 | 8 | 9 | 10 | | | 11* | 12 | | | | | | | | | | | | | | |
| 27 | (h) | Derby C | W 2-0 | Mackenzie 2 | 10,847 | 1 | 2 | | | 5 | 6 | 4 | 8 | 9 | 10 | | 12 | | | | 7 | 3 | 11* | | | | | | | | | | |
| Oct 4 | (h) | Oldham A | W 2-0 | Whitehead, Crooks | 9,351 | 1 | 2 | | | 5 | 6 | 4 | 8 | 9 | 10 | | | | | | 7 | 3 | 11* | | | | | | | | | | |
| 11 | (a) | Blackburn R | W 1-0 | Dyson | 5,701 | 1 | 2 | | | 5 | | 4 | 8 | 9 | 10 | | 12 | 6 | | | 7 | 3* | | 11 | | | | | | | | | |
| 18 | (h) | Grimsby T | D 1-1 | Hopkins | 8,851 | 1 | 2 | | | 5 | | 4 | 8 | 9 | 10 | | 6 | | | | 3 | | | 11 | 7 | | | | | | | | |
| 25 | (a) | Portsmouth | L 1-2 | Crooks | 11,608 | 1 | 2 | 9* | | 5 | 6 | 4 | 12 | | 10 | | | | | 8 | 3 | | | 11 | 7 | | | | | | | | |
| Nov 1 | (h) | Birmingham C | W 3-2 | Williamson 2, Crooks | 15,329 | 1 | 2 | | | 5 | 6 | 4 | | 9 | 10 | | | | | | 3 | 8 | | 11 | 7 | | | | | | | | |
| 8 | (a) | Sunderland | W 3-0 | Dickinson, Crooks, Williamson | 16,162 | 1 | 2 | | | 5 | 6 | 4 | | 9 | 10 | | 12 | | | | 3 | 8* | | 11 | 7 | | | | | | | | |
| 15 | (a) | Plymouth A | L 0-1 | | 14,697 | 1 | 2 | | | 5 | 6 | 4 | | 9 | 10 | | | | | | 3 | 8 | | 11 | 7 | | | | | | | | |
| 22 | (h) | Millwall | L 0-1 | | 8,035 | 1 | 2 | | | 5 | 6 | 4 | | 9* | 10 | | | | 12 | | 3 | 8 | | 11 | 7 | | | | | | | | |
| 29 | (a) | Barnsley | D 2-2 | Williamson, Crooks | 5,750 | 1 | 2 | | | 5 | 6 | 4 | | 9 | 10 | | | | 12 | | 3 | 8* | | 11 | 7 | | | | | | | | |
| Dec 6 | (h) | Leeds U | W 3-0 | Whitehead 2, Crooks | 10,433 | 1 | 2 | | | 5 | 6 | 4 | | 9 | 10 | | | | | | 3 | 8 | | 11 | 7 | | | | | | | | |
| 12 | (a) | Bradford C | W 3-1 | Abbott (og), Williamson, Hopkins | 4,580 | 1 | 2 | 12 | | 5 | 6* | 4 | | 9 | 10 | | | | | | 3 | 8 | | 11 | 7 | | | | | | | | |
| 19 | (h) | Reading | L 1-2 | Crooks | 7,888 | 1 | 2 | | | 5 | 12 | 4 | | 9 | 10 | | | | | | 3 | 8* | | 11 | 7 | 6 | | | | | | | |
| 26 | (a) | Shrewsbury T | L 0-1 | | 9,281 | 1 | 2 | | | 5 | 6 | | | 10 | 9 | | 12 | | | | 3 | 8 | | 11* | 7 | 4 | | | | | | | |
| 27 | (h) | Plymouth A | D 0-0 | | 12,879 | 1 | 2 | | | 5 | 6 | | | 9 | 10* | | | | 12 | | 3 | 8 | | 11 | 7 | 4 | | | | | | | |
| Jan 1 | (h) | Crystal P | L 1-2 | Hopkins | 8,424 | 1 | 2 | | | 5 | 6* | 4 | | 10 | 9 | | | | | | 3 | 8 | | 11 | 7 | 12 | | | | | | | |
| 3 | (a) | Sheffield U | D 1-1 | Crooks | 9,240 | 1 | 2 | 6 | | 5 | | 4 | | 9 | 10 | | | | | | 3 | | | 11 | 7 | 8 | | | | | | | |
| 24 | (h) | Hull C | D 1-1 | Reilly | 6,785 | 1 | 2 | | | 5 | | 4 | 8 | 10 | 7* | | | | | | 3 | 11 | | | | | 12 | 6 | | 9 | | | |
| Feb 7 | (a) | Huddersfield T | L 1-2 | Reilly | 5,218 | 1 | 12 | | | 5 | 4 | 2 | 8* | 10 | | | | | | | | 11 | | | 7 | | | 3 | | 6 | 9 | | |
| 14 | (h) | Stoke C | W 4-1 | Crooks 2, Reilly 2 (1 pen) | 12,452 | 1 | 4 | | | 5 | 2 | | | 10 | | | | | | | 8 | | | 11 | 7 | | | 3 | | 6 | 9 | | |
| 21 | (a) | Derby C | D 1-1 | Anderson | 16,237 | 1 | 2 | | | 5 | | 7 | | 10 | | | | | | | | 8 | | 11 | | | | 3 | 4 | 6 | 9 | | |
| 28 | (h) | Brighton & HA | D 0-0 | | 8,395 | 1 | 2 | | | 5 | 8 | | | 7* | | | 12 | | | | 10 | 11 | | | | | | 3 | 4 | 6 | 9 | | |
| Mar 3 | (a) | Ipswich T | L 0-1 | | 9,704 | 1 | 2 | | | 5 | 8 | 12 | | | 10* | | | | | | | 11 | | | 7 | | | 3 | 4 | 6 | | 9 | |
| 14 | (a) | Grimsby T | L 1-3 | Crooks | 5,024 | 1 | | 3 | | 5 | 8 | 2 | | | 10 | | | | | | | | | 11 | 7 | | | | 4 | 6 | 9 | | |
| 21 | (a) | Blackburn R | L 0-1 | | 8,998 | 1 | 3 | 12 | | 5 | 8 | 2 | | | | 11 | | | | | | 10 | | | 7 | | | | 4 | 6 | | 9* | |
| 28 | (a) | Oldham A | L 1-2 | Bradley | 6,944 | 1 | | | 4 | 5 | | 2 | | | | 11 | | | | | 3 | | | | 7 | | | 10 | 6 | 12 | 8 | 9* | |
| Apr 4 | (h) | Sunderland | D 2-2 | Lynex, Bennett | 6,198 | 1 | | | 6 | 5 | | 2 | | | | | | | | | 3 | 11 | | | 7 | | | | 4 | | 9 | 10 | 8 |
| 12 | (a) | Birmingham C | W 1-0 | Reilly | 11,158 | 1 | | | 4 | 5 | | 2 | | | | 11 | | | | | 3 | | | | 7 | | | | 6 | 9 | | 10 | 8 |
| 18 | (a) | Crystal P | D 1-1 | Goodman | 7,127 | 1 | | | | 5 | | 2 | | | | 11 | | | | | 3 | | | | 7 | | | | 4 | 6 | 9 | 10 | 8 |
| 20 | (h) | Shrewsbury T | L 1-2 | Williamson | 7,567 | 1 | | | | 5 | | 2* | | | 11 | 9 | | | | | 3 | 12 | | | 7 | | | | 4 | 6 | | 10 | 8 |
| 25 | (a) | Millwall | W 1-0 | Williamson | 3,912 | 1 | 2 | | | 4 | 5 | | | | 9 | | | | | | 3 | 6 | | | 11 | | 7 | | | | | 10 | 8 |
| 29 | (h) | Portsmouth | W 1-0 | Hopkins | 10,018 | 1 | 2 | | | 4 | 5 | | | 3 | 9 | | | | | | | 11 | | | 7 | | | | 6 | | | 10 | 8 |
| May 2 | (h) | Barnsley | L 0-1 | | 6,496 | 1 | 2 | 12 | | 4 | 5 | | | 3 | 9* | 7 | | | | | | 11 | | | | | | 6 | | | | 10 | 8 |
| 4 | (a) | Leeds U | L 2-3 | Dyson, Burrows | 24,688 | 1 | | 3 | | 4 | 5 | 2 | 7 | | | 11 | | | | | | | | | 6 | | | | | 9 | | 10 | 8 |
| 9 | (h) | Bradford C | D 2-2 | Robson, Goodman | 8,559 | 1 | 2 | 3 | | 4 | 5 | | 7 | | | 6 | 11 | | | | | | | | | | | | | 9 | | 10 | 8 |
| | | App | | | | 42 | 33 | 12 | 15 | 42 | 26 | 36 | 13 | 30 | 30 | 1 | 5 | 2 | 3 | 2 | 28 | 27 | 1 | 21 | 25 | 5 | 6 | 10 | 14 | 9 | 4 | 10 | 10 |
| | | Sub app | | | | | 1 | 3 | | | 1 | 1 | 1 | | 1 | 2 | 4 | 2 | 3 | 1 | 1 | 1 | | | 2 | | | | | | | 1 | |
| | | Goals | | | | | 3 | 1 | 2 | 2 | 1 | 1 | 1 | 2 | 8 | 1 | | | | 2 | | 1 | | 11 | 4 | | | | 1 | 5 | 1 | 1 | 2 |

**West Brom 1986-87. Back row (left to right): D.Burrows, C.Madden, S.Naylor, B.Cowdrill, A.Thompson. Middle: G.Doig (physiotherapsit), M.Dickson, George Reilly, S.Bull, S.Mackenzie, R.Dennison, C.Palmer, K.Leonard (coach). Front: S.Evans, C.Whitehead, M.Bennett, R.Saunders (manager), P.Dyson, D.Bradley, R.Williamson.**

# 1987-88

### Division 2

| Date | | Opponent | Result | Scorers | Att. | Naylor S | Robson G | Statham D | Bennett M | Dickinson M | Kelly A | Hopkins R | Goodman D | Williamson R | Bradley D | Morley A | Palmer C | Burrows D | Reilly G | Dobbins W | Singleton M | Steggles K | Cowdrill B | Gray A | Anderson C | Lynex S | Hogg G | Powell D | North S | Hucker P | Talbot B | Swain K | Phillips S | Dyson P | Hodson S |
|---|---|---|---|---|---|---|---|---|---|---|---|---|---|---|---|---|---|---|---|---|---|---|---|---|---|---|---|---|---|---|---|---|---|---|
| Aug 15 | (h) | Oldham A | D 0-0 | | 8,873 | 1 | 2* | 3 | 4 | 5 | 6 | 7 | 8 | 9† | 10 | 11 | 12 | 14 | | | | | | | | | | | | | | | | | |
| 22 | (a) | Blackburn R | L 1-3 | Sulley (og) | 5,619 | 1 | 10† | | 4 | 5 | 6 | 7 | 8* | | 2 | 11 | 12 | 3 | 9 | 14 | | | | | | | | | | | | | | | |
| 29 | (h) | Swindon T | L 1-2 | Bennett | 7,503 | 1 | 9 | | 4 | 5† | 6 | | 8 | 12 | 14 | 11* | 7 | 3 | | | 2 | 10 | | | | | | | | | | | | | |
| 31 | (a) | Leeds U | L 0-1 | | 19,847 | 1 | 9 | | | 5 | 6 | | 8 | 12 | 2 | 11 | 7* | 3 | | | | 10 | 4 | | | | | | | | | | | | |
| Sep 5 | (h) | Shrewsbury T | W 2-1 | Goodman, Pearson (og) | 8,560 | 1 | 7 | | | 5 | 6 | | 8 | 9 | 12 | 11 | 2 | | | | | 10 | 4* | ·3 | | | | | | | | | | | |
| 8 | (a) | Crystal P | L 1-4 | Williamson | 8,554 | 1 | 7† | | | 5 | 6 | 14 | 8 | 9 | 12 | 11 | 2 | | | | | 10 | 4* | 3 | | | | | | | | | | | |
| 12 | (a) | Plymouth A | D 3-3 | Gray 2, Palmer | 10,578 | 1 | | 4* | 14 | | 7 | | 8† | 12 | 6 | 11 | 2 | | | 5 | | 10 | 3 | 9 | | | | | | | | | | | |
| 16 | (h) | Aston Villa | L 0-2 | | 22,072 | 1 | | 4 | | | 7 | | 8* | 12 | 6 | 11 | 2 | | | 5 | | 10 | 3 | 9 | | | | | | | | | | | |
| 19 | (h) | Bournemouth | W 3-0 | Palmer, Morley 2 | 7,749 | 1 | | 4† | 14 | 6* | 7 | | 8 | 10 | 11 | 2 | 5 | | | 12 | | 3 | 9 | | | | | | | | | | | | |
| 26 | (a) | Millwall | L 0-2 | | 6,564 | 1 | | | 4 | 6 | 7 | | 8 | 12 | 10 | | 2† | | | 5 | | 14 | 3 | 9* | 11 | | | | | | | | | | |
| 30 | (h) | Birmingham C | W 3-1 | Palmer, Gray, Singleton | 15,399 | 1 | | | | 6 | 7 | | 8 | 12 | 2 | | 4 | | | 5 | | 10 | 3 | 9* | 11 | | | | | | | | | | |
| Oct 3 | (a) | Reading | W 2-1 | Gray, Williamson | 5,543 | 1 | | | | 6 | 7 | | 8 | 12 | 2 | 11 | 4 | | | 5 | | 10 | 3 | 9* | | | | | | | | | | | |
| 10 | (h) | Bradford C | L 0-1 | | 12,241 | 1 | | | | 6 | 7 | | 8 | 12 | 2 | 11 | 4 | | | 5 | | 10* | 3 | 9 | | | | | | | | | | | |
| 17 | (a) | Middlesbrough | L 1-2 | Kelly (pen) | 10,684 | 1 | | | | 6 | 7 | | 8 | 11 | 2 | | 4 | | | 5 | 12 | 10 | 3 | 9* | | | | | | | | | | | |
| 21 | (a) | Leicester C | L 0-3 | | 9,262 | 1 | 10 | | | 6 | | | 14 | 8† | 2 | 11 | 4 | | | 5 | 12 | | 3* | 9 | | 7 | | | | | | | | | |
| 24 | (h) | Huddersfield T | W 3-2 | Morley 3 | 8,450 | 1 | 10* | | | 6 | | | 8 | | 2 | 11 | 4 | 3 | 5 | | | | 9 | 12 | 7 | | | | | | | | | | |
| Nov 4 | (h) | Sheffield U | W 4-0 | Gray, Goodman, Williamson, Morley | 8,072 | 1 | | | | 6 | | | 8* | 14 | 10† | 11 | 2 | 3 | 5 | | | | 9 | 12 | 7 | 4 | | | | | | | | | |
| 7 | (a) | Stoke C | L 0-3 | | 9,992 | 1 | 12 | | | 6 | | | 8* | 10† | 11 | 2 | 3 | 5 | | | | 9 | 14 | 7 | 4 | | | | | | | | | | |
| 14 | (h) | Ipswich T | D 2-2 | Gray, Goodman | 8,457 | 1 | | | | 6 | | | 8 | | 11 | 5 | 3 | | 2 | | | | 9 | 10 | 7 | 4 | | | | | | | | | |
| 21 | (a) | Hull C | L 0-1 | | 7,654 | 1 | 12 | | | 6 | | | 8 | | 11 | 2 | 3 | 5 | | | | 9 | 10 | 7* | 4 | | | | | | | | | | |
| 28 | (h) | Manchester C | D 1-1 | Goodman | 15,425 | 1 | | | 5 | | | 7 | 8 | | 11 | 2 | 3 | | 10 | | | | 9 | | 6 | 4 | | | | | | | | | |
| Dec 5 | (a) | Barnsley | L 1-3 | Futcher (og) | 5,395 | 1 | 10 | | | 5 | | 7 | 8 | 12 | 2 | | 14 | 11 | | | | | 9† | 3 | 6* | 4 | | | | | | | | | |
| 12 | (h) | Blackburn R | L 0-1 | | 7,303 | 1 | 14 | | | 5 | | 7 | 8 | 12 | 11 | 2 | 3 | 9 | 10† | | | | | 6* | 4 | | | | | | | | | | |
| 18 | (a) | Aston Villa | D 0-0 | | 24,437 | 1 | 12 | | | 6 | | 7 | 8 | | 11 | 4 | 2 | 9 | | | | 3 | | 10* | 6 | | | | | | | | | | |
| 26 | (h) | Millwall | L 1-4 | Morley (pen) | 9,291 | 1 | 14 | | 7 | 5 | | | 8 | | 11 | 4 | 2 | 9* | | | | 3 | 12 | 10† | 6 | | | | | | | | | | |
| 28 | (a) | Bournemouth | L 2-3 | Goodman, Gray | 8,969 | 1 | 10 | | 2 | 6 | | | 8 | 14 | 11† | 4 | 12 | 5* | | | | 3 | 9 | | 7 | | | | | | | | | | |
| Jan 1 | (a) | Swindon T | L 0-2 | | 12,155 | | 10 | | 2 | 6 | 7 | | 8 | 11 | | 4 | | | | | | 3 | 9 | | | 1 | 5 | | | | | | | | |
| 2 | (h) | Plymouth A | W 1-0 | Goodman | 8,445 | 1 | 10* | | 2 | 6 | 7 | | 8 | 14 | 11† | 4 | | | | | | 3 | 9 | 12 | | 1 | 5 | | | | | | | | |
| 16 | (a) | Oldham A | L 1-2 | Robson | 5,557 | 1 | 10 | | | 6 | 2 | 12 | 8 | 11* | 4 | | | | | | | 3 | 9 | 7 | | | 5 | | | | | | | | |
| 30 | (h) | Leeds U | L 1-4 | Dickinson | 9,008 | | 7 | | 12 | 10* | 2 | 8 | | 11 | 6 | | | | | | | 3 | 9 | | | | 5 | 1 | 4 | | | | | | |
| Feb 6 | (a) | Shrewsbury T | W 1-0 | Anderson | 6,360 | | 10 | | | | 7 | 8 | | | 6 | | | | | | | 3 | 9 | 11 | | | 5 | 1 | 4 | 2 | | | | | |
| 13 | (h) | Crystal P | W 1-0 | Goodman | 8,944 | | 10 | | | | 7 | 8 | | | 6 | | | | | | | 3 | 9 | 11 | | | 5 | 1 | 4 | 2 | | | | | |
| 27 | (h) | Reading | L 0-1 | | 8,509 | | 10 | | | | 8 | 9 | | 11* | 6 | 12 | | | 14 | | | 3 | | 7† | | | 5 | 1 | 4 | 2 | | | | | |
| Mar 5 | (h) | Middlesbrough | D 0-0 | | 8,316 | | 10 | | | | 8 | | | 6 | | | 7 | | | | | 3 | | 11 | | | 5 | 1 | 4 | 2 | 9 | | | | |
| 8 | (a) | Birmingham C | W 1-0 | Hopkins | 12,331 | | 10* | | | | 7 | 8 | | | 6 | 12 | | | | | | 3 | | 11 | | | 5 | 1 | 4 | 2 | 9 | | | | |
| 12 | (a) | Bradford C | L 1-4 | Talbot (pen) | 12,502 | | 10* | | | | 7 | 8 | | | 6 | | | | | | | 3 | 12 | 11 | | | 5 | 1 | 4 | 2 | 9 | | | | |
| 26 | (h) | Huddersfield T | W 3-1 | Gray 2, Swain | 4,503 | 1 | | | | | 7 | 8* | | 11 | | | 12 | | | | | 3 | 9 | 10 | | | 5 | | 4 | 2 | 6 | | | | |
| Apr 2 | (h) | Stoke C | W 2-0 | Gray, Talbot (pen) | 12,144 | 1 | 12 | | | | 7 | | | | 10 | | | | | | | 3 | 9* | 11 | | | 5 | | 4 | | 8 | 6 | 2 | | |
| 4 | (a) | Ipswich T | D 1-1 | Phillips | 10,665 | 2 | | | | | 7 | 12 | | | 10* | | | | | | | 3 | 9 | 11 | | | 5 | | 4 | | 8 | 6 | 2 | | |
| 9 | (h) | Leicester C | D 1-1 | Lynex | 11,013 | 1 | 10 | | | | | 12 | | | | | | | | | | 3 | 9 | 11 | 7* | | 5 | | 4 | | 8 | 6 | 2 | | |
| 23 | (a) | Sheffield U | D 0-0 | | 12,091 | 1 | 10* | | | | | 12 | | | | | | | | | | 3 | 9 | 11 | 7 | | 5 | | 4 | | 8 | 6 | 2 | | |
| 30 | (h) | Hull C | D 1-1 | Dyson | 8,004 | 1 | 10 | | | | 7 | 12 | | | | | | | | | | 3 | 9* | 11 | | | 5 | | 4 | | 8 | 6 | 2 | | |
| May 2 | (a) | Manchester C | L 2-4 | Dyson, Lynex | 16,490 | 1 | 10 | | | | 7† | 9 | 14 | | | | | | | | | 3 | | 11* | 12 | | 5 | | 4 | | 8 | 6 | 2 | | |
| 7 | (h) | Barnsley | D 2-2 | Hopkins, Phillips | 8,483 | 1 | 10 | | | | 7 | | | | | | | | | | | 3 | 9 | 11* | 12 | | 5 | | 4 | | 8 | 6 | 2 | | |
| | | | | App | | 35 | 25 | 1 | 6 | 13 | 26 | 28 | 34 | 10 | 15 | 27 | 36 | 17 | 13 | 5 | 10 | 4 | 32 | 30 | 20 | 16 | 7 | 2 | 18 | 7 | 15 | 7 | 10 | 8 | 7 |
| | | | | Sub app | | | 6 | | 3 | | 1 | 6 | 12 | 4 | 1 | | 2 | 4 | 1 | | 5 | 2 | | | 2 | 3 | 3 | | | | | | | | |
| | | | | Goals | | | 1 | | 1 | 1 | 1 | 2 | 7 | 3 | | 7 | 3 | | | | 1 | | | 10 | 1 | 2 | | | | | 2 | 1 | 2 | 2 | |

**Albion line up before the start of 1987-88. Back row (left to right): J.Paskin, S.North, C.Whyte, M.Bennett, S.Naylor, P.Bradshaw, P.Dyson, C.Palmer, D.Bradley, C.Anderson. Front: G.Doig (physiotherapist), W.Dobbins, G.Robson, D.Goodman, B.Talbot (player-manager), R.Hopkins, S.Hodson, A.Albiston, S.Phillips, S.Pearson (coach).**

# 1988-89

### Division 2

| | | | Att | Naylor S | Bradley D | Albiston A | Talbot B | Dyson P | North S | Hopkins R | Goodman D | Paskin J | Palmer C | Anderson C | Gray A | Hodson S | Burrows D | Robson G | Whyte C | Cork D | Phillips S | Durnin J | Dobbins W | Bradshaw P | Rice B | Cartwright N | Bartlett K | West C | Walford S | Ford T | Banks I | Raven P | Robinson R |
|---|---|---|---|---|---|---|---|---|---|---|---|---|---|---|---|---|---|---|---|---|---|---|---|---|---|---|---|---|---|---|---|---|---|
| Aug 27 | (a) Leicester C | D 1-1 Paskin | 13,082 | 1 | 2 | 3 | 4 | 5 | 6 | 7 | 8 | 9 | 10 | 11 | | | | | | | | | | | | | | | | | | | |
| 29 | (h) Watford | L 0-1 | 10,242 | 1 | 2 | 3 | 4 | 5 | 6 | 7 | | 9 | 10 | 11 | 8 | | | | | | | | | | | | | | | | | | |
| Sep 3 | (h) Swindon T | W 3-1 Dyson, Goodman, Paskin | 7,518 | 1 | 4 | 3 | | 6† | 5 | 7 | 8 | 9* | 10 | 11 | 12 | 2 | 14 | | | | | | | | | | | | | | | | |
| 10 | (a) Shrewsbury T | D 1-1 Robson | 5,851 | 1 | 12† | 3 | | | 6 | 7 | 8 | | 10 | 11 | 9* | 2 | 14 | 4 | 5 | | | | | | | | | | | | | | |
| 17 | (h) Walsall | D 0-0 | 13,977 | 1 | | | 4 | | 6 | 7 | 8 | 9† | 10 | 11 | 2* | 3 | 12 | 5 | 14 | | | | | | | | | | | | | | |
| 21 | (a) Brighton & HA | W 1-0 Goodman | 7,395 | 1 | 2 | | 4 | | 6 | 7 | 8 | 9* | 10 | 11 | 3 | | | 5 | 12 | | | | | | | | | | | | | | |
| 24 | (a) Plymouth A | D 1-1 Phillips | 8,539 | 1 | 2 | | 4 | | 6 | 7 | 8 | 10* | 11 | | 3 | | | 5 | 12 | 9 | | | | | | | | | | | | | |
| Oct 1 | (h) Ipswich T | L 1-2 Whyte | 9,357 | 1 | 2 | | 4 | | 6 | 7 | 8 | | 10 | 11 | 3 | | | 5 | 9 | | | | | | | | | | | | | | |
| 5 | (h) Bournemouth | D 0-0 | 7,248 | 1 | 2 | | 4 | | 6 | 7 | 8 | | 10 | 11 | 3 | | | 5 | 9 | | | | | | | | | | | | | | |
| 8 | (a) Barnsley | L 1-2 Talbot | 5,674 | 1 | 12 | 2 | 4 | | 6 | 7* | | | 10 | 11 | 3 | 14 | | 5 | 8† | 9 | | | | | | | | | | | | | |
| 15 | (a) Birmingham C | W 4-1 Hopkins 2, Phillips, Robson | 10,453 | 1 | 12 | 2 | 4 | | 6 | 7* | | | 10 | 11 | 3 | 8 | | 5 | 9 | | | | | | | | | | | | | | |
| 22 | (h) Bradford C | W 1-0 Talbot | 8,989 | 1 | 2 | 3 | 4 | | 6 | 7 | | | 10 | 11 | | | | 8 | 5 | 9 | | | | | | | | | | | | | |
| 26 | (h) Manchester C | W 1-0 Durnin | 14,258 | 1 | | 3 | 4 | | 6 | 7 | | | 10 | 11 | | | | 8 | 5 | | | 9 | 2 | | | | | | | | | | |
| 29 | (a) Blackburn R | W 2-1 Whyte, Anderson | 9,503 | 1 | | 3 | 4 | | 6 | 7 | 12 | | 10 | 11 | | | | 8 | 5 | | | 9* | 2 | | | | | | | | | | |
| Nov 5 | (h) Oxford U | W 3-2 Anderson, Hopkins, Goodman | 11,643 | 1 | | 3 | 4 | | 6 | 7 | 12 | | 10 | 11 | | | | 8 | 5 | | | 9* | 2 | | | | | | | | | | |
| 12 | (a) Leeds U | L 1-2 Durin | 20,442 | 1 | 2 | 3 | 4 | | 6 | 7 | 11 | 12 | 10 | | | | | 8* | 5 | | | 9 | | | | | | | | | | | |
| 19 | (a) Sunderland | D 1-1 Robson | 18,141 | 1 | 2 | 3 | 4 | | 6 | 7 | 8 | 12 | 10 | 11 | | | | 9* | 5 | | | | | | | | | | | | | | |
| 26 | (h) Crystal P | W 5-3 Goodman 3, Hopkins, Paskin | 11,099 | 1 | 2 | 3 | 4* | | 6 | 7 | 8 | 12 | 10 | 11 | | | | 9 | 5 | | | | | | | | | | | | | | |
| Dec 3 | (a) Portsmouth | D 0-0 | 12,779 | 1 | 7 | 3 | 4 | | 6 | | 8 | 12 | 10 | 11 | 2 | | | 9* | 5 | | | | | | | | | | | | | | |
| 10 | (h) Hull C | W 2-0 Goodman 2 | 10,094 | 1 | 7* | 3 | 4 | | 6 | | 8 | 12 | 10 | 11 | 2 | | | 9 | 5 | | | | | | | | | | | | | | |
| 18 | (h) Stoke C | W 6-0 Robson 2, Goodman 2, Paskin 2 | 17,634 | 1 | | 3 | 4 | | 6 | | 8 | 10 | | 11 | 2 | | | 9 | 5 | | | | 7 | | | | | | | | | | |
| 26 | (a) Oldham A | W 3-1 Goodman, Hopkins, Robson | 9,827 | 1 | | 3 | | | 6 | 7 | 8 | 10 | | 11 | 2 | | | 9 | 5 | | | | 4 | | | | | | | | | | |
| 31 | (a) Chelsea | D 1-1 Anderson | 25,906 | 1 | | 3 | 4 | | 6 | 7 | 8 | 10 | | 11 | 2 | | | 9 | 5 | | | | | | | | | | | | | | |
| Jan 2 | (a) Shrewsbury T | W 4-0 Goodman, Moyes (og), Albiston, Robson | 18,411 | | | 3 | 4 | | 6 | 7 | 8 | 12 | 10 | 11 | 2† | | | 9* | 5 | | | | 14 | 1 | | | | | | | | | |
| 14 | (a) Watford | L 0-2 | 15,168 | | 11 | 3 | 4 | | 6 | 7 | | 8 | 10 | | | | | 9 | 5 | | | | 2* | 1 | 12 | | | | | | | | |
| 21 | (h) Leicester C | D 1-1 Robson | 15,792 | 1 | 2† | 3 | 4 | | 6 | 7 | | 8* | 10 | | | | | 9 | 5 | | | | 14 | | 11 | 12 | | | | | | | |
| Feb 4 | (h) Bournemouth | L 1-2 Albiston | 11,571 | 1 | | 3 | 4 | | 6 | 7 | | 8 | 10 | | | | | 9 | 5 | | | | 2 | | 11 | | | | | | | | |
| 11 | (h) Barnsley | D 1-1 Goodman | 12,650 | 1 | | 3 | 4* | | 6 | 7 | 8 | 12 | 10 | 11 | | | | 9 | 5 | | | | 2 | | | | | | | | | | |
| 18 | (a) Bradford C | L 0-2 | 11,047 | 1 | | 3 | 4 | | 6 | 7 | 8 | | 10 | 11 | | | | 2 | 5 | | | | | | | | 9 | | | | | | |
| 25 | (h) Birmingham C | D 0-0 | 16,148 | 1 | 2 | 3 | 4 | | 6 | 7 | 8* | | 11 | | | | | 10 | 5 | | | | | | | | 12 | 9 | | | | | |
| Mar 1 | (a) Manchester C | D 1-1 Whyte | 25,109 | 1 | 2 | 3* | | | 6 | 7 | 8 | | | 11 | | | | 4 | 5 | | | | 12 | | | | 10 | 9 | | | | | |
| 5 | (h) Leeds U | W 2-1 Goodman 2 | 15,914 | 1 | 7 | 3* | | | 6 | | 8 | 12 | | 11 | | | | 4† | 5 | | | | 2 | | | | 10 | 9 | 14 | | | | |
| 11 | (a) Oxford U | D 1-1 West | 7,581 | 1 | 7 | | | | 6 | | 8 | | | 11 | | | | 4 | 5 | | | | 2 | | | | 10 | 9 | 3 | | | | |
| 15 | (h) Blackburn R | W 2-0 West 2 | 12,821 | 1 | 2 | 3 | 4 | | 6 | | 8 | | | 11 | | | | 7 | 5 | | | | | | | | 10 | 9 | | | | | |
| 18 | (h) Brighton & HA | W 1-0 Bartlett | 11,586 | 1 | 2 | 3 | 4 | | 6 | 12 | 8 | | | 11 | | | | 7* | 5 | | | | | | | | 10 | 9 | | | | | |
| 25 | (a) Swindon T | D 0-0 | 12,240 | 1 | 2 | 3 | 4 | | 6 | | 8* | | | 11 | | | | 10 | | | | | | | | | 12 | 9 | 5 | 7 | | | |
| 27 | (h) Oldham A | W 3-1 West, Bartlett, Anderson (pen) | 13,812 | 1 | 2 | 3 | 4† | | 6 | | 8* | | | 11 | | | | 10 | 5 | | | | | | | | 12 | 9 | | 7 | 14 | | |
| Apr 1 | (a) Walsall | D 0-0 | 9,520 | 1 | 2 | 3 | 4 | | 6 | | | | | 11 | | | | 10 | | | | | | | | | 8 | 9 | 5 | 7 | | | |
| 4 | (a) Stoke C | D 0-0 | 11,151 | 1 | 2 | 3 | 4 | | 6 | | 12 | | | 11 | | | | 10† | 5* | | | | | | | | 8 | 9 | 5 | 7 | 14 | | |
| 8 | (h) Chelsea | L 2-3 Anderson, Ford | 22,858 | 1 | 6 | 3 | 4 | | 5 | | 8* | | | 11 | | | | | | | | | 2 | | | | 12 | 9 | | 7 | 10 | | |
| 15 | (h) Plymouth A | D 2-2 Brown (og), West | 11,358 | 1 | 2* | 3 | 4 | | 6 | | 8 | | | 11 | | | | 10 | 5 | | | | 12 | | | | | 9 | | 7 | | | |
| 22 | (a) Ipswich T | L 1-2 West | 12,047 | 1 | | 3 | | | 6 | | 8* | 12 | | 11 | | | | 10 | 5 | | | | 14 | | | | 7† | 9 | | | 2 | 4 | |
| 29 | (a) Crystal P | L 0-1 | 13,728 | 1 | | 3 | 4 | | 6 | | 12 | 8 | | 11* | | | | 10 | 5 | | | | 2 | | | | | 9 | | 7 | | | |
| May 1 | (h) Portsmouth | W 3-0 Anderson (pen), West 2 | 9,586 | 1 | | 3 | 4 | | 6 | | 14 | 8† | | 11 | | | | 10 | 5 | | | | 12 | | | | 9* | 7 | | | 2 | | |
| 6 | (h) Sunderland | D 0-0 | 10,451 | 1 | | 3 | 4 | | 6 | | 14 | 8* | | 11 | | | | 10† | 5 | | | | 12 | | | | 9 | 7 | | | 2 | | |
| 13 | (a) Hull C | W 1-0 Bartlett | 5,217 | 1 | | | 4† | | 6 | | 14 | 12 | | 11 | | | | 10 | 5 | | | | 8* | | | | 9 | 7 | | | 2 | 3 | |
| **App** | | | | 44 | 23 | 43 | 39 | 3 | 46 | 28 | 30 | 14 | 26 | 42 | 2 | 9 | 7 | 36 | 40 | 1 | 5 | 5 | 12 | 2 | 2 | | 10 | 17 | 3 | 11 | 2 | 3 | 1 |
| **Sub app** | | | | | 3 | | | | | 1 | 6 | 11 | | | 1 | | | 2 | 2 | | | | 3 | | | | 4 | | 1 | 1 | 7 | | 1 | 2 |
| **Goals** | | | | | | 2 | 2 | 1 | | 5 | 15 | 5 | | 6 | | | | 8 | 3 | | 2 | 2 | | | | | 3 | 8 | | 1 | | | |

**Tony Ford (hidden) scoring Albion's second goal against Chelsea at The Hawthorns on 8 April 1989. Albion lost 2-3.**

# 1989-90

## Division 2

| Date | | Venue | Opponent | Result | Scorers | Att. | Bradshaw P | Bradley D | Parkin S | Talbot B | Whyte C | North S | Ford T | Goodman D | West C | McNally B | Anderson C | Robson G | Thomas J | Burgess D | Marriott A | Naylor S | Barham M | Bartlett K | Hodson S | Allardyce S | Harbey G | Bennett M | Raven P | Andersen V | Dobbins W | Cartwright N | Foster A | Shakespeare C | Hackett G | Bannister G |
|---|---|---|---|---|---|---|---|---|---|---|---|---|---|---|---|---|---|---|---|---|---|---|---|---|---|---|---|---|---|---|---|---|---|---|---|
| Aug 19 | (h) | Sheffield U | | L 0-3 | | 14,907 | 1 | 2 | 3 | 4* | 5 | 6 | 7 | 8† | 9 | 10 | 11 | 12 | 14 | | | | | | | | | | | | | | | | | |
| 22 | (a) | Bournemouth | | D 1-1 | Goodman | 8,226 | 1 | 2 | 3 | | 5 | 6 | 7 | 8 | 9* | 10 | 11 | 4 | | 12 | | | | | | | | | | | | | | | | |
| 26 | (a) | Port Vale | | L 1-2 | Whyte | 7,695 | 1 | 6 | 3 | 12 | 5 | | 7 | 8 | 9 | 10* | 11† | 4 | 14 | 2 | | | | | | | | | | | | | | | | |
| Sep 2 | (h) | Sunderland | | D 1-1 | Goodman | 10,885 | 1† | 6 | 3 | 12 | 5 | | 7 | 8* | 9 | 10 | 11 | 4 | 14 | 2 | | | | | | | | | | | | | | | | |
| 9 | (a) | Leicester C | | W 3-1 | West, Whyte, Goodman | 10,700 | | 6 | 3 | 12 | 5 | | 7 | 8 | 9 | 10 | 11 | 4* | | 2 | | 1 | | | | | | | | | | | | | | |
| 16 | (h) | Oxford U | | W 3-2 | Robson, Greenall (og), Bradley | 9,628 | | 6 | 3 | | 5 | 12 | 7 | 8 | 9 | 10 | 11 | 4† | 14 | 2* | | 1 | | | | | | | | | | | | | | |
| 23 | (a) | Oldham A | | L 1-2 | West | 6,907 | | 2 | | | 5 | 6 | 7 | 8 | 9 | 10 | 11* | 4 | 12 | 3 | | 1 | | | | | | | | | | | | | | |
| 27 | (h) | Blackburn R | | D 2-2 | Goodman, Ford | 9,269 | | 2 | | 12 | 5 | 6 | 7 | 8 | 9* | 10 | 11† | 4 | 14 | 3 | | 1 | | | | | | | | | | | | | | |
| 30 | (a) | West Ham U | | W 3-2 | Ford, McNally 2 (1 pen) | 19,739 | | 2 | | 12 | 5 | 6 | 7 | 8 | | 10 | 11 | 4* | 9 | 3 | | 1 | | | | | | | | | | | | | | |
| Oct 7 | (a) | Watford | | W 2-0 | Thomas, Whyte | 10,444 | | 2 | | 4 | 5 | 6 | 11 | | | 10 | | | 9 | 3 | | 1 | 7 | 8 | | | | | | | | | | | | |
| 15 | (h) | Wolves | | L 1-2 | Talbot | 21,316 | | 2* | | 4 | 5 | 6 | 11 | 8 | | 10 | | 12 | 9 | 3 | | 1 | 7 | | | | | | | | | | | | | |
| 17 | (h) | Stoke C | | L 1-2 | Bartlett | 11,991 | | 2 | | 12 | 5 | 6 | 7 | 8 | | 10 | | 4* | 9 | 3 | | 1 | 11† | 14 | | | | | | | | | | | | |
| 21 | (h) | Hull C | | D 1-1 | Parkin | 9,228 | | 2 | | 12 | 5 | 6 | 7 | 8 | | 10 | | 4 | 9 | 3 | | 1 | 11* | | | | | | | | | | | | | |
| 28 | (a) | Middlesbrough | | D 0-0 | | 14,076 | | 2 | | 4 | 5 | 6 | 7 | 8 | | 10 | 11 | | 9 | | | 1 | | | | | 3 | | | | | | | | | |
| Nov 1 | (h) | Newcastle U | | L 1-5 | Goodman | 12,339 | | 2 | | 4 | 5 | 6 | 7 | 8 | | 10 | 11* | | 9† | | | 1 | | 12 | | | 3 | 14 | | | | | | | | |
| 4 | (a) | Ipswich T | | L 1-3 | Goodman | 12,028 | | | | 4 | 5 | 6 | 11 | 8 | | 10 | | 12 | | 2 | | 1 | 7* | 9 | | | 3 | | | | | | | | | |
| 11 | (h) | Barnsley | | W 7-0 | Goodman 3, Ford, Bartlett 2, McNally (pen) | 9,317 | | | 11 | 4 | | 6 | 7 | 8 | | 10 | | 14 | | 2 | | 1 | 12 | 9† | | | 3 | | 5* | | | | | | | |
| 18 | (a) | Portsmouth | | D 1-1 | McNally (pen) | 9,069 | | | 11 | 4 | | 6 | 7 | 8 | | 10 | | | | 2 | | 1 | | 9 | | | 3 | | 5 | | | | | | | |
| 25 | (h) | Leeds U | | W 2-1 | Goodman, Bartlett | 15,116 | | | 11 | 4* | | 6 | 7 | 8 | | 10 | | 12 | | 2 | | 1 | | 9 | | | 3 | | 5 | | | | | | | |
| Dec 2 | (a) | Sheffield U | | L 1-3 | Robson | 14,094 | | | 11 | 4* | | 6 | 7 | 8 | | 10 | | 12 | 14 | 2 | | 1 | | 9† | | | 3 | | 5 | | | | | | | |
| 9 | (h) | Bournemouth | | D 2-2 | Goodman, Bartlett | 8,568 | | | | | | 6 | 7 | 8 | 12 | 10 | 11† | 4 | | 2 | | 1 | | 9* | | | 3 | | 5 | | 14 | | | | | |
| 17 | (a) | Swindon T | | L 1-2 | Goodman (pen) | 9,884 | | | | | | 6 | 12 | 7 | 8 | 9 | 10 | 11† | 4 | 2 | | 1 | | 14 | | | 3 | | 5* | | | | | | | |
| 26 | (a) | Plymouth A | | D 2-2 | Goodman 2 | 9,782 | | | | | | 6 | 5 | 7 | 8 | 9 | 10 | 11† | 4* | | | 1 | | 14 | | | 3 | | | | 2 | 12 | | | | |
| 30 | (a) | Bradford C | | L 0-2 | | 8,560 | | | | | | 6 | 5 | 7 | 8 | 10* | 11† | 4 | 9 | | | 1 | | 14 | | | 3 | | | | 2 | 12 | | | | |
| Jan 1 | (h) | Brighton & HA | | W 3-0 | Robson, Bartlett, West | 9,407 | | | | | | 6 | 5 | 7 | 8 | 9 | 10 | 4 | | | | 1 | | 11 | | | 3 | | | | 2 | | | | | |
| 13 | (h) | Port Vale | | L 2-3 | Goodman, Ford | 13,575 | | | | | | 6 | 5 | 7 | 8 | 9 | 10 | 4 | | | | 1 | | 11 | | | 3 | | 5 | | 2 | | | | | |
| 20 | (a) | Sunderland | | D 1-1 | Robson | 15,583 | | | 14 | | | 6 | 7 | 8 | 9 | 10† | 4 | 12 | | | | 1 | | 11 | | | 3 | | 5 | | 2* | | | | | |
| Feb 3 | (h) | Oldham A | | D 2-2 | Robson, West | 12,237 | | | | | | 6 | 5 | 7* | 9 | 10 | 4 | | | 2 | | 1 | | 11 | | | 3 | | | | | | 12 | 8 | | |
| 10 | (a) | Oxford U | | W 1-0 | Shakespeare | 6,749 | | | | | | 6 | 5 | | 9 | 10 | 4 | | | 2 | | 1 | | 11 | | | 3 | | | | | | 8 | 7 | | |
| 21 | (h) | Leicester C | | L 0-1 | | 10,902 | 14 | | | 4† | 6 | 5 | | 8 | 9* | 10 | | | | 2 | | 1 | | 3 | | | | | | | | | 11 | 12 | 7 | |
| 24 | (h) | Leeds U | | D 2-2 | Goodman, Bartlett | 30,004 | 4 | | | | 5 | 8 | 12 | 10 | 6 | | | 1 | 11 | 2 | | 3 | | | | | | | | | 9* | 7 | | | | |
| Mar 3 | (h) | Portsmouth | | D 0-0 | | 10,502 | 4 | | | | 5 | 8* | 9 | 10 | | 6 | | 1 | 11 | 2 | | 3 | | | | | | | | | 7 | 12 | | | | |
| 10 | (a) | Blackburn R | | L 1-2 | Ford | 8,148 | | | | 14 | 5 | 7 | 9* | 10 | 6† | | | 1 | | 2 | | 3 | | | | | | | | 12 | 4 | 11 | 8 | | |
| 14 | (a) | Bradford C | | W 2-0 | Ford, McNally | 8,017 | 12 | | | | 6 | 5 | 7 | 10* | | | | 2 | | 1 | | 3 | | | | | | | | 9 | 4 | 11 | 8 | | |
| 17 | (h) | Watford | | W 2-0 | Hackett, Whyte | 9,915 | 10 | | | | 6 | 5 | 7 | | | | | 2 | | 1 | | 3 | | | | | | | | 9 | 4 | 11 | 8 | | |
| 20 | (a) | Wolves | | L 1-2 | Foster | 24,475 | 10† | | | | 6 | 5 | 7 | 12 | | | | 2 | | 1 | | 3 | | | | | | | | 14 | 9† | 4 | 11* | 8 | |
| 24 | (h) | Stoke C | | D 1-1 | Ford | 12,771 | 10 | | | | 6 | 5 | 7 | 8 | | | | 2 | | 1 | | 3 | | | | | | | | | 4 | 11 | 9 | | |
| 31 | (a) | Hull C | | W 2-0 | Goodman, Hackett | 5,418 | 10 | | | | 6 | 5 | 7 | 8 | | | | 2* | | 1 | | 3 | | | | | | | | 12 | 4 | 11 | 9 | | |
| Apr 4 | (h) | West Ham U | | L 1-3 | Goodman | 11,556 | 2 | | | | 6 | 5 | 7 | 8 | | | | 1 | | | | 3 | | | | | | | | 10 | 12 | 4 | 11* | 9 | |
| 7 | (h) | Middlesbrough | | D 0-0 | | 9,458 | 2 | | | | 6 | 5 | 7 | 8 | | 10 | | 1 | | | | 3 | | | | | | | | | 4 | 11 | 9 | | |
| 11 | (a) | Newcastle U | | L 1-2 | Goodman | 19,460 | 2 | | | | 6 | 5 | 7 | 8 | | 10 | | 14 | | 1 | | 3 | | | | | | | | 12 | 4 | 11† | 9* | | |
| 14 | (a) | Brighton & HA | | W 3-0 | Goodman, Ford, Bannister | 9,371 | 11 | | | | 6 | 5 | 7 | 8 | | 10 | | 2 | | 1 | | 3 | | | | | | | | 12 | 4 | | 9* | | |
| 16 | (h) | Plymouth A | | L 0-3 | | 9,728 | 11 | | | | 6 | 5 | 7 | 8 | | 10 | | 2* | | 1 | | 3 | | | | | | | | 14 | 4 | 12 | 9† | | |
| 21 | (a) | Swindon T | | L 1-2 | Goodman | 8,495 | 11 | | | | 6 | 5 | 7 | 8 | | 10 | | | | 1 | | 3 | | | | | | 2 | | 9 | 4* | 12 | | | |
| 28 | (a) | Barnsley | | D 2-2 | Tiler (og), Bradley | 10,334 | 11 | | | | 6 | | 7 | 8 | | 10 | | 5 | | 1 | | 3 | | | | | | 2* | | | 4 | 12 | 9 | | |
| May 5 | (h) | Ipswich T | | L 1-3 | Bannister | 11,567 | 2* | | 4† | | 6 | | 6 | 7 | | 10 | | 5 | | 1 | | 3 | | | | | | | | | 14 | 11 | 12 | 9 | |
| App | | | | | | | 4 | 25 | 14 | 12 | 43 | 32 | 42 | 39 | 18 | 41 | 13 | 21 | 8 | 31 | 3 | 39 | 4 | 15 | 10 | | 30 | 1 | 7 | | 5 | 2 | 7 | 18 | 9 | 13 |
| Sub app | | | | | | | 2 | | 8 | 1 | 2 | | 3 | | | 4 | 10 | 3 | | | | 5 | 1 | | | | | 1 | | 5 | 7 | | 5 | | | |
| Goals | | | | | | | | 2 | 1 | 1 | 4 | | 8 | 21 | 4 | 5 | | 5 | 1 | | | | | 7 | | | | | | | | | 1 | 1 | 2 | 2 |

**Action from Albion's visit to Vale Park in August 1989.**

# 1990-91

## Division 2

Player columns (left to right): Naylor S, Hodson S, Harbey G, Robson G, Burgess D, Strodder G, Ford T, Goodman D, Bannister G, Bradley D, Shakespeare C, Hackett G, West C, McNally B, Hawker P, Raven P, Ehiogu U, Anderson C, Foster A, Dobbins W, Palmer L, Roberts G, Parkin S, Rees M, Rogers D, Williams P, White W, Ampadu K

| Date | | Opponent | Result | Scorers | Att | Nay | Hod | Har | Rob | Bur | Str | For | Goo | Ban | Bra | Sha | Hac | Wes | McN | Haw | Rav | Ehi | And | Fos | Dob | Pal | Rob' | Par | Ree | Rog | Wil | Whi | Amp |
|---|---|---|---|---|---|---|---|---|---|---|---|---|---|---|---|---|---|---|---|---|---|---|---|---|---|---|---|---|---|---|---|---|---|
| Aug 25 | (a) | Portsmouth | D 1-1 | Ford | 12,008 | 1 | 2 | 3 | 4* | 5 | 6 | 7 | 8 | 9 | 10 | 11 | 12 | | | | | | | | | | | | | | | | |
| Sep 1 | (h) | Ipswich T | L 1-2 | Bannister | 10,318 | 1 | 2 | 3 | 4 | 5 | 6 | 7 | | 9 | 10 | 11* | 12 | 8 | | | | | | | | | | | | | | | |
| 8 | (a) | Oxford U | W 3-1 | Bannister, West 2 | 5,225 | 1 | 2 | 3 | 4 | 5* | 6 | 7 | | 9 | 10 | 11 | | 8 | 12 | | | | | | | | | | | | | | |
| 15 | (h) | Bristol C | W 2-1 | Bannister, Harbey | 12,081 | 1 | 2 | 3 | 4* | | 6 | 7 | 12 | 9 | 5 | 11 | | 8 | 10 | | | | | | | | | | | | | | |
| 22 | (a) | Hull C | D 1-1 | McNally | 5,953 | 1 | 2 | | 4 | | | 7 | 12† | 9 | 5 | 11 | | 8* | 10 | 3 | 6 | | 14 | | | | | | | | | | |
| 29 | (h) | Oldham A | D 0-0 | | 13,782 | 1 | 2 | 3 | 4 | | 6 | 7 | | 9 | 5 | 11 | | 8 | 10 | | | | | | | | | | | | | | |
| Oct 2 | (a) | Plymouth A | L 0-2 | | 5,617 | 1 | 2 | 3 | 4 | | 6 | 7 | | 9 | 5 | 11* | 12 | 8 | 10 | | | | | | | | | | | | | | |
| 6 | (a) | Millwall | L 1-4 | West | 10,718 | 1 | | 3 | 4 | | 6 | 7* | | 9 | 5 | 11† | 12 | 8 | 10 | | 2 | | 14 | | | | | | | | | | |
| 13 | (h) | Brighton & HA | D 1-1 | Gatting (og) | 9,833 | 1 | | 3 | 4 | 2 | 6 | 7† | | 9* | 5 | | | 8 | 10 | | 11 | | 12 | 14 | | | | | | | | | |
| 20 | (h) | Barnsley | D 1-1 | West (pen) | 9,577 | 1 | | 3 | 4 | 2 | 6 | 7 | | 9 | 5 | | | 8 | 10 | | 11 | | | | | | | | | | | | |
| 22 | (h) | Port Vale | W 2-1 | Bannister, West (pen) | 8,824 | 1 | | 3 | 4 | 2 | 6 | 7 | | 9 | 5 | | | 8 | 10 | | 11 | | | | | | | | | | | | |
| 27 | (a) | Newcastle U | D 1-1 | Anderson | 14,774 | 1 | | 3 | 4 | 2 | 6 | 7 | | 9 | 5 | | | 8 | 10 | | 11* | | 12 | | | | | | | | | | |
| Nov 3 | (h) | Bristol R | W 3-1 | West 2, Anderson | 10,997 | 1 | | 3 | 4 | 2 | 6 | 7 | | 9 | 5* | 14 | | 8 | 10 | | 11† | | 12 | | | | | | | | | | |
| 6 | (h) | Middlesbrough | L 0-1 | | 10,521 | 1 | 12 | | 4* | 2 | 6 | 7 | | 9 | 5 | 11 | | 8 | 10 | | 3 | | | | | | | | | | | | |
| 10 | (a) | Notts C | L 3-4 | Bannister 2, Bradley | 8,162 | 1 | 12 | | 4 | 2 | 6 | 7 | | 9 | 5 | | | 8 | 10 | | 11† | | 3* | 14 | | | | | | | | | |
| 17 | (h) | Blackburn R | W 2-0 | Bannister, West | 6,985 | 1 | | 3 | 2 | | 6 | 7 | 12 | 9* | 5 | | | 8 | 10 | | 11 | | | | | | 4 | | | | | | |
| 24 | (a) | Sheffield W | L 1-2 | Robson | 16,546 | 1 | | 3 | 2 | 14 | 6 | 7 | 12 | 9* | 5 | | | 8 | 10† | | 11 | | | | | | 4 | | | | | | |
| Dec 1 | (a) | West Ham U | L 1-3 | Ford | 24,753 | 1 | | 3 | 2 | | 6 | 7 | 12 | 9 | 5 | | | 8 | | | 11* | | | | | | 4 | 10 | | | | | |
| 5 | (h) | Watford | D 1-1 | Roberts (pen) | 7,657 | 1 | | 3 | 2 | 6 | | 7 | 8* | 9 | 5 | 14 | | 12 | | | 11† | | | | | | 4 | 10 | | | | | |
| 15 | (h) | Portsmouth | D 0-0 | | 7,856 | 1 | 14 | 3 | 2† | | | 7 | 8* | 12 | 5 | | | 9 | 10 | | 6 | | 11 | | | | 4 | | | | | | |
| 22 | (a) | Swindon T | L 1-2 | Roberts (pen) | 7,798 | 1 | 2 | 3 | 9 | | | 7 | 8* | 12 | 5 | | | | 10 | | 6 | | 11† | | | | 4 | 14 | | | | | |
| 26 | (a) | Charlton A | W 1-0 | Goodman | 9,305 | 1 | | 3 | 11† | | 6 | 7 | 8* | 9 | 5 | 2 | | 12 | 10 | | | | | | | | 4 | 14 | | | | | |
| 29 | (h) | Wolves | D 1-1 | Bannister | 28,495 | 1 | | 3 | 11 | | 6 | 7 | | 9 | 5 | 2 | | 8 | 10 | | | | | | | | 4 | | | | | | |
| Jan 1 | (a) | Leicester C | L 1-2 | Ford | 12,210 | 1 | | 3 | 11 | | 6 | 7 | | 9† | 5 | 2 | | 8* | 10 | | | | | | | | 12 | 4 | 14 | | | | |
| 12 | (a) | Ipswich T | L 0-1 | | 11,036 | 14 | | | | | 6 | 7 | | 9 | | 2 | | 12 | 10 | 5† | | | 3 | | | | 11* | 4 | 8 | 1 | | | |
| 19 | (a) | Oxford U | W 2-0 | Bannister, Shakespeare | 8,017 | 2 | | | | | 6 | 7 | | 10 | | 11 | | 9 | | 5 | | | 3 | | | | 4 | 8 | 1 | | | | |
| Feb 2 | (a) | Bristol C | L 0-2 | | 11,492 | 2 | | | | | 5 | 7 | 8 | 9 | | 11 | | | | | 6 | | 3 | | | | 4 | 10 | 1 | | | | |
| 16 | (a) | Blackburn R | W 3-0 | Robson, Goodman 2 | 7,695 | 2 | | | 10* | 5 | 14 | 7 | 8† | 9 | 6 | 11 | | | 12 | | | | | | | | 4 | 3 | 1 | | | | |
| 19 | (h) | Middlesbrough | L 2-3 | Bannister 2 | 15,334 | 2 | | | 10 | 5 | | 7 | 8* | 9 | 6 | 11 | | | 12 | | | | | | | | 4 | 3 | 1 | | | | |
| 23 | (h) | Notts C | D 2-2 | Bannister 2 | 11,068 | 2 | | | 10 | 5 | 14 | 7 | | 9 | 6 | 3 | | | 12 | | | | 11† | | | | 4 | 8* | 1 | | | | |
| Mar 2 | (h) | West Ham U | D 0-0 | | 16,089 | 2 | | | 10 | 5 | | 7 | | 9 | 6 | 3 | | | | | | | 11 | | | | 4 | 8 | 1 | | | | |
| 9 | (a) | Sheffield W | L 0-1 | | 26,934 | 2 | | | | 5 | 14 | 7 | | 9 | | 3* | | 10† | 12 | | | | 11 | 6 | | | 4 | 8 | 1 | | | | |
| 13 | (h) | Plymouth A | L 1-2 | Palmer | 8,673 | 2 | | 3 | 5 | | | 7 | | 9 | | 14 | | | | | 12 | | 11 | 6† | 10* | | 4 | 8 | 1 | | | | |
| 16 | (a) | Oldham A | L 1-2 | Ford | 12,584 | 2 | | 14 | 5 | | | 7 | | 9 | 6 | 3 | | | | | | | | 12 | 11 | 10* | 4† | 8 | 1 | | | | |
| 20 | (a) | Brighton & HA | L 0-2 | | 6,676 | 2† | | | 5 | 10 | 7 | | 9 | 6 | 3 | 12 | | | | | | | 8* | | 11 | 4 | | | 1 | 14 | | | |
| 23 | (a) | Millwall | L 0-1 | | 9,116 | 2 | | | | 5 | 7 | | 9 | 6 | 10 | | 8 | | | | 4† | 14 | 12 | 11* | | | | | | 1 | 3 | | |
| 30 | (a) | Charlton A | L 0-2 | | 5,686 | | | | | 5 | 7 | 10 | | 6 | 3 | | | | | | 4 | | | | | | 8 | 1 | 2 | 9 | 11* | 12 | |
| Apr 1 | (h) | Swindon T | W 2-1 | Parkin, Roberts (pen) | 10,415 | | | | 5* | | 7 | 10 | 8 | 2 | 11 | | | | | | 12 | | 3 | | | | 4 | 6 | 1 | 9 | | | |
| 6 | (a) | Wolves | D 2-2 | Goodman, Ford | 22,982 | 2 | | | 5 | | 7 | 10 | 8* | 14 | 11 | | | | | | | | 3 | | | | 4 | 6 | 1 | 9† | 12 | | |
| 10 | (a) | Hull C | D 1-1 | Roberts | 10,356 | 2 | | | 5 | | 7 | 10† | 8 | | 11 | | 12 | | | | | | 3 | | | | 4 | 6 | 1 | 9 | | | |
| 13 | (a) | Leicester C | W 2-1 | White, Goodman | 13,991 | 2 | | | 5† | | 7 | 12 | 8* | 3 | 11 | | | | | | | | | | | | 4 | 6 | 1 | 9 | 10 | 14 | |
| 20 | (a) | Barnsley | D 1-1 | Strodder | 9,593 | 2 | | | | 14 | 7 | 8* | 12 | 3† | 11 | | | | | | | | | | | | 4 | 6 | 1 | 9 | 10 | 5 | |
| 23 | (a) | Watford | D 1-1 | Goodman | 15,054 | 1 | 2 | | | | 5 | 7 | 8 | | 11 | | | | | | 3 | | | | | | 4 | 6 | | 9 | 10* | 12 | |
| 27 | (h) | Port Vale | D 1-1 | Goodman | 13,650 | 1 | 2 | | 10* | | 5 | 7 | 8 | 12 | 3 | 14 | | | | | | | | | | | 4† | 6 | | 9 | | 11 | |
| May 4 | (h) | Newcastle U | D 1-1 | Goodman | 16,706 | 1 | 2 | | | 4 | 5 | 7 | 8† | 12 | 3 | 10 | | | | | | | 2 | | | | | 6 | | 9 | 14 | 11† | |
| 11 | (a) | Bristol R | D 1-1 | Ampadu | 7,595 | 1 | | | | 5 | 7 | | 12 | 3 | 11 | | | 10* | | | 2 | | | 8 | | | | 6 | | 4† | 9 | | 14 |
| **App** | | | | | | 28 | 26 | 21 | 30 | 24 | 30 | 46 | 16 | 38 | 38 | 32 | | 24 | 20 | 1 | 11 | | 22 | 2 | 5 | 5 | 27 | 22 | 18 | 3 | 10 | 4 | 3 |
| **Sub app** | | | | | | | 4 | | 1 | 1 | 4 | | 6 | 6 | 1 | 4 | 5 | 4 | 5 | | 2 | 2 | 1 | 3 | 3 | 2 | | 3 | | 1 | | 2 | 4 |
| **Goals** | | | | | | | | 1 | 2 | | 1 | 5 | 8 | 13 | 1 | 1 | | 8 | 1 | | | | 2 | | | 1 | 4 | 1 | | | | 1 | 1 |

**Albion's 1990-91 line-up. Back row (left to right): G.Bannister, C.Anderson, S.North, G.Harbey, S.Parkin. Middle: S.Allardyce (coach), D.Burgess, C.West, P.Raven, S.Naylor, D.Bradley, C.Shakespeare, W.Dobbins, S.Pearson (assistant manager-coach). Front: T.Ford, G.Robson, S.Hodson, B.Talbot (manager), B.McNally, D.Goodman, G.Hackett.**

# 1991-92

## Division 2

| Date | | Opponent | Result | Scorers | Att | Miller A | Bradley D | Harbey G | Ford A | Strodder G | Burgess D | Bannister G | Goodman D | Foster A | Shakespeare C | Ampadu K | Williams P | McNally B | Piggott G | Hodson S | Naylor S | Parkin S | Robson G | Bowen S | Pritchard D | Palmer L | Hackett G | West C | White W | Rogers D | Sinclair F | Fereday W | Roberts G | Taylor R | Dibble A | Raven P | Hunter R | Cartwright N |
|---|---|---|---|---|---|---|---|---|---|---|---|---|---|---|---|---|---|---|---|---|---|---|---|---|---|---|---|---|---|---|---|---|---|---|---|---|---|---|
| Aug 17 | (h) | Exeter C | W 6-3 | Shakespeare 2 (2 pens), Goodman 2, Foster, Williams | 12,892 | 1 | 2 | 3 | 4 | 5 | 6 | 7 | 8* | 9 | 10 | 11† | 12 | 14 | | | | | | | | | | | | | | | | | | | | |
| 24 | (a) | Darlington | W 1-0 | Goodman | 5,658 | 1 | 2 | 3 | 4 | 5 | 6 | | 8 | | 10 | 11 | 12 | 7 | 9* | | | | | | | | | | | | | | | | | | | |
| 31 | (h) | Wigan A | D 1-1 | McNally | 12,053 | 1 | 2 | 3 | 4 | 5 | | 8 | | | 12 | 10 | 11 | 9* | 7 | 6 | | | | | | | | | | | | | | | | | | |
| Sep 3 | (a) | Fulham | D 0-0 | | 4,523 | | 2 | 3 | 4 | 5 | 6 | 8 | | | 11* | 10 | 12 | 9 | 7† | | 1 | 14 | | | | | | | | | | | | | | | | |
| 7 | (a) | Bolton W | L 0-3 | | 7,980 | | | 3 | 4 | 5 | 6 | | | 9 | 10 | 11 | 12 | 7 | 8* | | 1 | 2 | | | | | | | | | | | | | | | | |
| 14 | (h) | Stockport C | W 1-0 | Williams | 11,845 | | | 3 | 4 | 5 | 6 | 7* | | | 10 | | 12 | | | | 2 | 1 | 8 | 9 | 11† | 14 | | | | | | | | | | | | |
| 17 | (h) | Peterborough U | W 4-0 | Robson 2, Williams, Bowen | 10,037 | | | 3 | 4 | 5 | 6 | | | | 10† | | 7 | | | | 2 | 1 | 8 | 9 | 11* | | | 12 | 14 | | | | | | | | | |
| 21 | (a) | Chester C | W 2-1 | Robson, Burgess | 3,895 | | 14 | 3 | 4 | 5 | 6 | | | | 10 | | 7 | | | 12 | 2† | 1 | 8 | 9 | 11* | | | | | | | | | | | | | |
| 28 | (h) | Hull C | W 1-0 | Burgess | 11,932 | | | 3 | 4 | 5 | 6 | | | 7 | 10 | | 12 | | | | 2 | 1 | 8 | 9* | 11† | 14 | | | | | | | | | | | | |
| Oct 1 | (a) | Preston NE | L 0-2 | | 5,293 | | | 3 | 4 | 5 | 6 | | | | 10 | | 8* | | | | 2 | 1 | 7 | 9 | 11 | 12 | | | | | | | | | | | | |
| 12 | (h) | Shrewsbury T | W 2-0 | Goodman, West | 12,457 | | | 3 | 4 | 5 | 6 | | 8† | | 10 | | 14 | | | | 2 | 1 | 7 | | 11* | 12 | | 9 | | | | | | | | | | |
| 19 | (a) | Brentford | W 2-1 | Ampadu, Goodman | 8,575 | | 7 | 3 | 4 | 5 | 6* | | 8 | | 10 | 11 | | | 12 | | 2 | 1 | | | | | | 9 | | | | | | | | | | |
| 26 | (h) | Birmingham C | L 0-1 | | 26,168 | 6 | | 3 | 4 | 5 | | | 8 | | 10 | 11* | 12 | 7 | | | 2 | 1 | | | | | | 9 | | | | | | | | | | |
| Nov 2 | (h) | Bury | D 1-1 | Robson | 8,439 | 14 | | 3 | 4 | 5 | 6 | | 8 | | 10 | | | | | | 2 | 1 | 12 | 11† | 7 | | | 9* | | | | | | | | | | |
| 5 | (a) | Hartlepool U | D 0-0 | | 2,810 | 7 | | 3 | 4 | 5 | 6 | 12 | 8 | | 10 | 11* | | | | | 2 | 1 | 9 | | | | | | | | | | | | | | | |
| 9 | (a) | Reading | W 2-1 | Robson, Goodman | 5,826 | 4† | | 3 | | 5 | 6 | 12 | 8 | | 10 | | | | | | 2 | 1 | 9* | | | | | | 14 | | | 11 | | | | | | |
| 23 | (h) | Huddersfield T | W 2-1 | Robson, Harbey | 14,029 | 4 | | 3 | | 5 | 6 | | | | 10 | | 12 | 7 | | | 2 | 1 | 9* | | | | | | 11 | | | | | | | | | |
| 30 | (h) | Stoke C | D 2-2 | Shakespeare, Goodman | 17,207 | 4 | | 3 | | 5† | 6 | | | | 10 | | 12 | 7 | | | 1 | 2 | 9 | | | | | 11* | 14 | | | | | | | | | |
| Dec 14 | (a) | Bradford C | D 1-1 | Bradley | 7,195 | 4 | | 3 | | 5 | | | | | 10 | 12 | 8 | 7 | | 6 | 1 | | 9 | | | | | | | | 2 | 11* | | | | | | |
| 22 | (h) | Darlington | W 3-1 | Strodder, Sinclair, Fereday | 13,261 | 4 | | 3 | | 5 | 6 | 12 | | | 10 | | 8 | 7 | | | 1 | | 9 | | | | | | | | 2 | 11* | | | | | | |
| 26 | (a) | Wigan A | W 1-0 | Shakespeare (pen) | 5,068 | 4* | | 3 | | 5 | 6 | | | | 14 | 10 | 12 | 8 | 7 | | 1 | | 9† | | | | | | | | 2 | 11 | | | | | | |
| 28 | (a) | Exeter C | D 1-1 | Shakespeare (pen) | 5,830 | 4 | | 3 | | 5 | | | | 9* | 10 | 12 | 8 | 7 | | 6 | 1 | | | | | | | 11† | 14 | | 2 | | | | | | | |
| Jan 1 | (h) | Fulham | L 2-3 | Robson, Shakespeare (pen) | 16,422 | 4 | | 3 | | 5† | | | | | 10 | 12 | 8 | 7* | | | 1 | | 9 | | | | | | 11 | 6 | 2 | 14 | | | | | | |
| 4 | (a) | Torquay U | L 0-1 | | 4,159 | 4 | | 3 | | | | | | 9* | 10 | 12 | 8 | 7 | 11† | 1 | | | 9 | | | | | | | 6 | 2 | 14 | 5 | | | | | |
| 11 | (h) | Bournemouth | W 4-0 | Robson, Bannister 2, Williams | 10,932 | 4 | | 3 | | 5 | 6 | | | | 10* | 11† | 12 | | | | 2 | 1 | 9 | | | | | | 14 | | | 7 | | | | | | |
| 18 | (a) | Leyton O | D 1-1 | Bradley | 6,329 | 4 | | 3 | | 5 | 6 | 8 | | | | | | | | | 2 | 1 | 9 | | | | | 11 | | | | 7 | 10 | | | | | |
| 25 | (h) | Swansea C | L 2-3 | Roberts 2 (1 pen) | 10,395 | 4 | | 3 | | 5 | 6 | 8† | | | 12 | | 14 | | | | 2 | 1 | 9 | | | | | 11 | | | | 7* | 10 | | | | | |
| Feb 1 | (h) | Brentford | W 2-0 | Taylor, Fereday | 15,984 | 4 | | 3 | | | 6 | | | | 5 | | 14 | 12 | | | 2 | 1 | 9* | | | | | 11 | | | | 7 | 10 | 8† | | | | |
| 8 | (a) | Birmingham C | W 3-0 | Robson, Taylor 2 | 27,508 | 4 | | 3 | | | 6 | | | | 5 | | | 12 | | | 2 | 1 | 9 | | | | | 11 | | | | 7* | 10 | 8 | | | | |
| 12 | (a) | Stoke C | L 0-1 | | 23,645 | 4 | | 3 | | | 6 | 12 | | | 5 | | | | | | 2* | 1 | 9 | | | | | 11 | | | | 7 | 10 | 8 | | | | |
| 15 | (h) | Bradford C | D 1-1 | Shakespeare | 12,607 | 4† | | 3 | | | 6 | | | | 12 | 5 | | | | | 2 | 1 | 9 | | | | | 11* | | 14 | | 7 | 10 | 8 | | | | |
| 22 | (a) | Bournemouth | L 1-2 | Taylor | 7,721 | 4 | | 3 | | | 6 | | | | 12 | 5 | | | | | 2† | 1 | 9 | 11* | | | | | | 14 | | 7 | 10 | 8 | | | | |
| 29 | (h) | Torquay U | W 1-0 | Hunter | 11,669 | 4 | | 3 | | | 6 | | | | 5 | | 12 | | | | | | 9 | | | | | 11* | | | | 7 | 10† | 8 | 1 | 2 | 14 | |
| Mar 3 | (h) | Leyton O | L 1-3 | Bannister | 11,165 | 4 | 3* | | | 6 | | 9 | | | 5 | | 12 | 11† | | | | | | | | | | | | | | 7 | 10 | 8 | 1 | 2 | 14 | |
| 6 | (a) | Swansea C | D 0-0 | | 5,629 | 4 | 3 | | | 6 | | 9 | | | 5 | | | 11 | | | | | 7 | | | | | | | | | | 10 | 8 | 1 | 2 | | |
| 11 | (h) | Hartlepool U | L 1-2 | Williams | 10,307 | 4 | 3 | | | 5 | | 6 | | | 14 | | 12 | 11* | | | | | 7 | | | | | | | | 2† | | 10 | 8 | 1 | | | |
| 14 | (a) | Bury | D 1-1 | Taylor | 3,810 | | 3 | | 4 | 6 | | | | | 5 | | 9 | | | | 10 | | | | | | | | | | | | 8 | | 1 | 2 | 5 | 7 |
| 21 | (h) | Reading | W 2-0 | Strodder, Raven | 10,707 | 4 | 3 | | | 5 | 6 | | | | | | 12 | | | | | | 7 | | | | | | | | | | 8 | | 1 | 2 | 14 | 9† |
| 28 | (h) | Huddersfield T | L 0-3 | | 7,428 | 4 | 3 | | | 5 | 6 | | | | 10 | | 12 | | | | | 14 | | | | | | 7* | | | | | 8 | | 1 | 2 | | 9† |
| 31 | (a) | Stockport C | L 0-3 | | 6,090 | | 3 | | | 5 | 6 | | | | 10 | 11* | 12 | | | | 2† | | 9 | | | | | 7 | | | | | 8 | | 1 | 14 | 4 | |
| Apr 4 | (h) | Bolton W | D 2-2 | Ampadu, Taylor | 10,287 | 4 | 3 | | | 5 | 6 | | | | 10 | 11 | 9 | | | | | | 7 | | | | | | | | | 12 | 8 | 1* | | 2 | | |
| 11 | (a) | Peterborough U | D 0-0 | | 9,040 | 4 | 3 | | | 5 | 6 | | | | 10 | 11 | 9 | | | 1 | | | 12 | | | | | 7* | | | | 2 | 8 | | | | | |
| 18 | (h) | Chester C | D 1-1 | Rogers | 10,137 | 4 | 3 | | | 5 | | | | | 10 | 11* | | | | 1 | | | 6 | | | | | 7† | 12 | 14 | | 2 | 8 | | | | | |
| 20 | (a) | Hull C | L 0-1 | | 4,815 | 4 | 3 | | | 5 | | | | | 10 | 11† | 9* | | | 1 | | | 6 | | | | | 7 | 12 | 14 | | 2 | 8 | | | | | |
| 25 | (h) | Preston NE | W 3-0 | Taylor, Ampadu, West | 11,318 | 4† | 3 | | | 5 | | | | | | 11 | | | 12 | 1 | | | 10 | | | | | 7 | 9 | 6 | | 2 | 8* | | | | 14 | |
| May 2 | (a) | Shrewsbury T | W 3-1 | Strodder, Shakespeare, Taylor | 7,442 | | 3 | | | 5 | | | | | 4 | 11 | | | 9 | 1 | | | 10 | | | | | 7 | | 6 | | 2 | 8 | | | | | |
| | | App | | | | 3 | 35 | 46 | 15 | 37 | 36 | 11 | 11 | 4 | 42 | 15 | 16 | 17 | 3 | 25 | 34 | 8 | 29 | 8 | 1 | | | 13 | 5 | 9 | 4 | 6 | 19 | 12 | 19 | 9 | 6 | 3 |
| | | Sub app | | | | 2 | | | | 4 | | 4 | 2 | 6 | 18 | 4 | 2 | | 1 | 3 | | 4 | 1 | 2 | 2 | 1 | 6 | | 3 | | | | | | | | 1 | 4 |
| | | Goals | | | | | 2 | 1 | | 3 | 2 | 3 | 7 | 1 | 8 | 3 | 5 | 1 | | | | | 9 | | | | | 2 | | 1 | 1 | 2 | 2 | 8 | | 1 | 1 |

C.Heggs played number-11 against Bury (a), Reading (h) (substituted) and Huddersfield Town (a).

**Don Goodman, who left to join Sunderland in a £900,000 deal midway through the season.**

# 1992-93

## Division 2

| Date | Opponent | Result | Scorers | Att | Naylor S | Fereday W | Lilwall S | Hunter R | Strodder G | Shakespeare C | Garner S | Hamilton I | Taylor R | McNally B | Robson G | Ampadu K | Hodson S | Bradley D | Raven P | Coldicott S | Hackett G | Heggs C | Donovan K | Blissett L | Burgess D | Lange A | Reid N | Dickens A | Darton S | Speedie D | Mellon M | Hunt A |
|---|---|---|---|---|---|---|---|---|---|---|---|---|---|---|---|---|---|---|---|---|---|---|---|---|---|---|---|---|---|---|---|---|
| Aug 15 (h) Blackpool | W 3-1 | Taylor 2, McNally | 16,527 | 1 | 2* | 3 | 4 | 5 | 6 | 7 | 8 | 9 | 10 | 11 | | 12 | | | | | | | | | | | | | | | |
| 22 (a) Huddersfield T | W 1-0 | Garner | 7,947 | 1 | | 3 | | 5 | 6 | 7* | 8 | 9 | 10 | 11 | 12 | 2 | 4 | | | | | | | | | | | | | | |
| 29 (h) Bournemouth | W 2-1 | Taylor, Shakespeare (pen) | 12,563 | 1 | 2 | 3 | | 5 | 6 | 10 | 8 | 9 | | 11 | 12 | | 4† | 14 | | 7* | | | | | | | | | | | |
| Sep 2 (h) Stockport C | W 3-0 | Garner 2, Hamilton | 12,305 | 1 | | 3 | | 5 | | 7 | 8 | 9 | 10 | 11 | | | 4 | 6 | 2 | | | | | | | | | | | | |
| 5 (a) Fulham | D 1-1 | Taylor | 9,143 | 1 | | 3 | | 5 | 12 | 7 | 8 | 9 | 10 | 11* | | | 4 | 6 | 2 | | | | | | | | | | | | |
| 9 (h) Reading | W 3-0 | Garner, Taylor, Shakespeare | 13,164 | 1 | | 3 | | 5 | 6 | 7 | 8 | 9 | | 11 | | | 4 | 10 | 2 | | | | | | | | | | | | |
| 15 (a) Bolton W | W 2-0 | Taylor 2 | 8,531 | 1 | | 3 | | 5* | 6 | 7 | 8 | 9 | 10 | 11† | | | 4 | 2 | 12 | 14 | | | | | | | | | | | |
| 19 (a) Stoke C | L 3-4 | Taylor 2, Garner | 18,764 | 1 | 14 | 3† | | | 6 | 7 | 8 | 9 | 10 | 11 | | | 4 | 5 | 2* | 12 | | | | | | | | | | | |
| 26 (h) Exeter C | W 2-0 | Hamilton, McNally | 14,676 | 1 | 2* | 3 | | | 6 | 7† | 8 | 9 | 10 | 11 | | | 4 | 5 | 12 | | 14 | | | | | | | | | | |
| Oct 3 (a) Burnley | L 1-2 | Garner | 14,816 | 1 | 2* | 3 | | | 6 | 7 | 8 | 9 | 10 | 11† | | | 4 | 5 | 12 | | 14 | | | | | | | | | | |
| 10 (h) Port Vale | L 0-1 | | 17,512 | 1 | 2* | 3 | | | 6 | 7 | 8 | 9 | 10 | 11† | | | 4 | 5 | 2 | | 14 | | | | | | | | | | |
| 17 (a) Wigan A | L 0-1 | | 4,408 | 1 | | 3 | | | 6 | | 8 | 9 | 10 | 11 | 12 | | 4 | 5 | 2 | | | 7* | | | | | | | | | |
| 24 (h) Rotherham U | D 2-2 | Taylor, Donovan | 13,170 | 1 | | 3 | | 12 | 6* | | 8 | 9 | 10 | | 14 | | 4 | 5 | 2 | | | 7 | 11† | | | | | | | | |
| 31 (a) Hull C | W 2-1 | Garner, Bradley | 5,443 | 1 | 12 | 3 | | | 6 | 7† | 8 | 9 | 10 | 14 | 11† | | 4 | 5 | 2 | | | | | | | | | | | | |
| Nov 3 (h) Hartlepool U | W 3-1 | Taylor, Blissett, Robson | 13,046 | 1 | 2† | 3 | | | 6 | 7 | 8 | 9 | 10 | 12 | | | 4 | 5 | | | | | 11† | 14 | | | | | | | |
| 7 (a) Leyton O | L 0-2 | | 8,640 | 1 | | 3 | | | 6 | | 8 | 9 | 10 | 7 | | | 4 | 5 | | | | | 11 | 2 | | | | | | | |
| 21 (h) Bradford C | D 1-1 | Raven | 15,416 | 1 | | 3 | | | 6 | 7 | 8 | 9 | 10 | | | | 4 | 5 | | | | | 11 | 2 | | | | | | | |
| 28 (a) Preston NE | D 1-1 | Robson | 6,306 | 1 | 12 | 3 | | | 6 | 7 | 8 | 9 | 10 | 14 | | | 4 | 5 | 2* | | | | 11† | | | | | | | | |
| Dec 12 (a) Swansea C | D 0-0 | | 5,610 | 1 | | 3 | | | 6 | 7* | 8 | 9 | 10 | 12 | | | 4 | 5 | | | | | | | | 2 | 11 | | | | |
| 20 (h) Mansfield T | W 2-0 | McNally, Dickens | 13,134 | 1 | | 3 | | | 6 | | 8 | 9 | 10 | | | | 4 | 5 | | | | 7 | | | | 2 | 11 | | | | |
| 26 (h) Chester C | W 2-0 | Raven 2 | 15,209 | 1 | | 3 | | | 6 | 12 | 14 | 8 | 9 | 10 | | | 4* | 5 | | | | 7 | | | | 2 | 11† | | | | |
| 28 (a) Plymouth A | D 0-0 | | 11,370 | 1 | | 3 | | | 6 | 4 | 14 | 8 | 9 | 10 | 11 | | | 5 | 12 | | | 7† | | | | 2* | | | | | |
| Jan 9 (h) Bolton W | W 3-1 | Hamilton, Strodder, Taylor | 14,581 | 1 | 2 | 3 | | | 6 | | 8 | 9 | 10 | 12† | | | 4 | 5 | | 7* | 14 | 11 | | | | | | | | | |
| 16 (a) Exeter C | W 3-2 | Heggs, Hackett, Hamilton (pen) | 5,437 | 1 | 2 | 3 | | | 6† | | 8 | 9 | 10 | 12 | | | 4 | 5* | | 7 | 14 | 11 | | | | | | | | | |
| 23 (a) Stoke C | L 1-2 | | 29,341 | 1 | 2 | 3 | | | 6 | 8† | | 9 | 10 | | | | 4 | 5 | | 12 | 14 | 11* | | | | | 7 | | | | |
| 26 (a) Bournemouth | W 1-0 | Speedie | 5,867 | 1 | 2 | 3 | | | 6 | | 8 | 9 | 10 | | | | 4 | 5 | | 11* | 12 | | | | | | 7 | | | | |
| 30 (h) Huddersfield T | D 2-2 | Donovan, Speedie | 13,667 | | 2 | 3 | | | 6 | | 8 | 9 | 10 | | | | 4† | 5 | | | 14 | 12 | 11 | | 1 | | 7* | | | | |
| Feb 6 (a) Blackpool | L 1-2 | Taylor | 9,386 | 1 | 2 | 3 | | | 6 | | 8 | 9 | 10* | | | | 4 | 5 | | 12 | | | 11 | | | | 7 | | | | |
| 13 (h) Fulham | W 4-0 | Taylor (pen), Hamilton, Mellon, Fereday | 12,859 | 1 | 2 | 3 | | | 6 | | 8 | 9† | 10 | | | | 4 | 5 | | | 14 | | 11† | | | | 7 | | | 12 | |
| 20 (a) Stockport C | L 1-5 | | 7,181 | 1 | | 3 | | | 6 | | 8 | 9 | 10 | 2 | 12 | | 4 | 5 | | | | | 11 | | | | 7* | | | | |
| 27 (a) Port Vale | L 1-2 | Hamilton | 13,291 | 1 | | 3 | | | 6 | | 8 | 9 | | 2* | 12 | | 4 | 5 | | | 14 | | 11 | | | | 7† | | | 10 | |
| Mar 6 (h) Burnley | W 2-0 | Garner, Taylor | 15,722 | 1 | | 3 | | | | 7* | 8 | 9 | 4 | | | | | 5 | 2 | | | 12 | 11 | 6 | | | | | | 10 | |
| 10 (a) Brighton & HA | L 1-3 | Taylor (pen) | 7,440 | 1 | | 3 | | | | 7† | 8 | 9 | 4 | | | | 12 | 5 | 2 | | 14 | 11 | 6 | | | | | | 10† | | |
| 13 (h) Leyton O | W 2-0 | Burgess, Donovan | 15,023 | | | 3 | 12 | | | 7* | 8 | 9 | | | | | 4 | 5 | | | | 11 | 6 | 1 | 2 | | | | | 10 | |
| 20 (a) Hartlepool U | D 2-2 | Hamilton, Raven | 4,174 | | | 3 | 12 | | | 7† | 8 | 9 | | 14 | | | 4 | 5 | | | | 11 | 6 | 1 | 2* | | | | | 10 | |
| 24 (h) Preston NE | W 3-2 | Taylor 2, Mellon | 13,270 | | | 3 | | | | 7* | 8 | 9 | | 14 | | | 4 | 5 | | 12 | 11 | | 6 | 1 | 2 | | | | | 10* | |
| 28 (a) Bradford C | D 2-2 | Taylor (pen), Hunt | 6,627 | | | 3 | | | | 7† | 8 | 9 | 10† | | | | 4 | 5 | | | 11 | | 6 | 1 | 2 | | | | | 12 | 14 |
| Apr 3 (h) Brighton & HA | W 3-1 | Hunt 3 | 13,002 | | | | | | | 12 | 8 | 9 | 14 | | | | 4 | 5 | | | 11 | | 6 | 1 | 2† | 3 | | | | 10* | 7 |
| 7 (h) Swansea C | W 3-0 | Taylor 2, Hunt | 13,401 | | | | | | | 12† | 8 | 9* | 2 | | | | 4 | 5 | | | 11 | | 6 | 1 | 14 | 3 | | | | 10 | 7 |
| 10 (a) Chester C | W 3-1 | Hunt, Raven, Donovan | 4,812 | | | 3 | | | | | 8 | 9 | 2 | | | | 4 | 5 | | 12 | 11 | | 6 | 1 | 14 | | | | | 10† | 7* |
| 12 (h) Plymouth A | L 2-5 | Taylor, Donovan | 16,130 | | | 3 | | | | | 8 | 9 | 2 | | | | 4 | 5† | | 12 | 11 | | 6 | 1 | 14 | | | | | 10* | 7 |
| 17 (a) Mansfield T | W 3-0 | Hunt, Taylor, Heggs | 6,659 | | | 3 | | | | 8* | 9 | 4 | | 12 | | | | 5 | | 14 | 11 | | 6 | 1 | 2 | | | | | 10 | 7† |
| 21 (a) Reading | D 1-1 | Taylor | 8,026 | | | 3 | | | | | 8 | 9 | 2 | | | | 4† | 5 | | 12 | 11 | | 6 | 1 | 14 | | | | | 10 | 7* |
| 24 (a) Wigan A | W 5-1 | Taylor 2, Mellon, Donovan, Raven | 14,867 | | | 3 | | | | | 8 | 9 | 2 | | | | 4 | 5 | | 12 | 11 | | 6 | 1 | 14 | | | | | 10 | 7* |
| May 1 (a) Rotherham U | W 2-0 | Raven, Taylor | 8,059 | | | 3 | | | | | 8 | 9 | 2 | | | | 4 | 5 | | 12 | 11 | | 6 | 1 | 14 | | | | | 10† | 7* |
| 8 (h) Hull C | W 3-1 | Taylor, Hunt 2 | 20,122 | | | 3 | | | | | 8 | 9 | 2 | | | | 4 | 5 | | | 11 | | 6 | 1 | | | | | | 10 | 7 |
| | App | | | | 32 | 13 | 44 | 1 | 26 | 12 | 21 | 46 | 46 | 39 | 16 | 1 | 1 | 41 | 43 | 10 | 4 | 30 | 3 | 17 | 14 | 10 | 3 | 2 | 7 | 15 | 9 | |
| | Sub app | | | | 3 | | | | 3 | 2 | 4 | | | | 1 | 6 | 9 | 1 | 1 | | 1 | 4 | 6 | 17 | 2 | | 1 | | 5 | | | 2 | 1 |
| | Goals | | | | 1 | | | | 1 | 2 | 8 | 7 | 30 | 3 | 2 | | | 1 | 7 | | | 1 | 2 | 6 | 1 | 1 | | | | 1 | 2 | 3 | 9 |

## Play-offs

**Semi-final (1st leg)**
**16 May v Swansea City (a) 1-2**
*McFarland (og)*
Lange; McNally, Lilwall, Bradley, Raven, Burgess, Hunt(Reid), Hamilton, Taylor, Mellon(Heggs), Donovan.
Att: 13,917

**Semi-final (2nd leg)**
**19 May v Swansea City (h) 2-0 (agg 3-2)**
*Hunt, Hamilton*
Lange; McNally, Lilwall, Bradley, Raven, Strodder, Hunt, Hamilton, Taylor, Mellon, Donovan.
Att: 26,045

**Final**
**30 May v Port Vale (Wembley) 3-0**
*Hunt, Reid, Donovan*
Lange; Reid, Lilwall, Bradley, Raven, Strodder, Hunt(Garner), Hamilton, Taylor, McNally, Donovan.
Att: 53,471

**Andy Hunt and Dean Glover in action during the play-off Final against Port Vale. Hunt was signed from Newcastle for £100,000 and scored a hat-trick on his home debut.**

This season Albion scored 114 goals, 88 in the Second Division. Only Newcastle United (91) recorded more in the entire League. The average League attendance at The Hawthorns was 15,174 — the highest for ten years. Albion registered 17 home League wins, equalling the club record, set in 1919-20. Bob Taylor scored 37 League and Cup goals, putting himself in third position in the club records for most goals scored in a season, behind W.'G'.Richardson (40) and Jimmy Cookson (38). Thirty of his goals came in Division Two matches — the first Albion player to achieve this tally since Derek Kevan in 1962 and he also set a new post-war scoring record for Albion, beating the total of 35 goals set earlier by Ronnie Allen (1951-52) and Jeff Astle (1967-68).

# Albion in World War One

## 1915-16

| Date | | Opponent | Result | Att | 1 | 2 | 3 | 4 | 5 | 6 | 7 | 8 | 9 | 10 | 11 |
|---|---|---|---|---|---|---|---|---|---|---|---|---|---|---|---|
| Apr 22 | (a) | Aston Villa | D 1-1 Gregory | 15,253 | Pearson | Smith | Shore | Waterhouse | Bowser | McNeal | Wright | Morris | Newall | Gregory | Crisp |
| 24 | (h) | Aston Villa | W 3-1 Wright, Mann, Reed | 8,221 | | | Pennington | | Reed | | Jephcott | Wright | | Mann | Hackett |

## 1916-17

| Date | | Opponent | Result | Att | 1 | 2 | 3 | 4 | 5 | 6 | 7 | 8 | 9 | 10 | 11 |
|---|---|---|---|---|---|---|---|---|---|---|---|---|---|---|---|
| Nov 11 | (n) | Wolves* | L 0-1 | 2,000 | Linden | | | Bowser | Attfield | Seymour | Bore | Shore | | Gregory | Crisp |
| Dec 26 | (h) | Aston Villa | W 5-1 Mann 3, Newall, Gregory | 7,145 | Moorwood | | | Waterhouse | Bowser | McNeal | Jephcott | Mann | | Morris | Gregory |
| Mar 17 | (a) | Birmingham | L 1-3 Newall | 15,000 | Pearson | | | | | | | | | Wright | Shearman |
| Apr 7 | (a) | Aston Villa | W 2-1 Gregory, McNeal | 6,282 | | Bowser | | | Newall | | | Edwards | Wright | Mann | Gregory |
| 9 | (a) | Wolves* | L 2-9 Jephcott, Edgley | 2,200 | Nicholls | Shore | | Richardson | Harrop | | | York | | Davies | Edgley |
| May 15 | (h) | Birmingham | L 0-1 | 7,603 | Pearson | | | Waterhouse | Bowser | | Wright | Edwards | Mann | Gregory | Shearman |

## 1917-18

| Date | | Opponent | Result | Att | 1 | 2 | 3 | 4 | 5 | 6 | 7 | 8 | 9 | 10 | 11 |
|---|---|---|---|---|---|---|---|---|---|---|---|---|---|---|---|
| Dec 24 | (h) | Aston Villa | L 1-2 Mann | 6,882 | | Smith | | | | | Jephcott | | Newall | Mann | Hackett |
| 26 | (a) | Aston Villa | W 2-0 Joyce 2 | 7,500 | | | | | Richardson | Elford | Joyce | | | | Shearman |
| Mar 30 | (h) | Wolves* | L 1-3 Davies | 4,500 | | | Davison | | Holder | Hackett | Jephcott | Wright | | Davies | Merrick |
| Apr 1 | (a) | Wolves | D 3-3 Newall 3 | 3,000 | | | Pennington | | | | | | | | |

## 1918-19

| Date | | Opponent | Result | Att | 1 | 2 | 3 | 4 | 5 | 6 | 7 | 8 | 9 | 10 | 11 |
|---|---|---|---|---|---|---|---|---|---|---|---|---|---|---|---|
| Aug 23 | (h) | Wolves | D 4-4 Roberts 3, Mann | 5,186 | Webb | | | Hackett | Bowser | McNeal | | Hatton | Roberts | Mann | Gregory |
| Sep 5 | (h) | Aston Villa | L 3-4 Roberts, Mann, Bunn | 8,537 | | | | Waterhouse | | | Wright | Newall | | | Bunn |
| 10 | (a) | Wolves | D 3-3 Wright, Mann, Bowser(pen) | 5,000 | | | | | | | | | | | |
| Mar 1 | (h) | Birmingham Wks* | W 4-1 Poulton, Hartland, Hobbs, Aston | 2,000 | Pearson | Robinson | Alexander | Butler | Johnston | Hackett | Poulton | Hartland | Hobbs | Gregory | Aston |
| 22 | (h) | Aston Villa* | W 5-0 Magee 2, Woolley, Wright, Newall | 1,500 | | Cook | | Arch | Barwell | Wall | Jones | Wright | Magee | Newall | Woolley |
| 29 | (a) | Wolves § | L 0-1 | 4,348 | | Smith | Cook | | Waterhouse | Richardson | Crisp | | Sambrook | Gregory | Shearman |
| Apr 5 | (h) | Derby C § | W 3-1 Magee, Sambrook, McNeal | 7,236 | | | | Richardson | Reed | McNeal | Wright | Magee | | Bentley | Gregory |
| 12 | (a) | Derby C § | L 0-1 | 6,500 | | | Pennington | | Newall | | Shearman | Wright | Magee | | |
| 19 | (h) | Aston Villa § | W 5-1 Morris 2, Gregory 2, Magee | 8,218 | | | Cook | Waterhouse | Reed | Richardson | Wright | Magee | Morris | Gregory | Bookman |
| 21 | (a) | Wolves § | D 1-1 Edwards | 6,730 | | | | | Bowser | | | Edwards | Magee | Morris | |
| 22 | (h) | RAF | W 5-3 Magee 3, Bentley, Hartland | 8,056 | | | Adams | | Reed | | | Hartland | | Bentley | Gregory |
| 26 | (a) | Aston Villa § | W 3-0 Gregory, Edwards, Magee | 10,000 | | | Cook | | | | | Edwards (sub Bentley) | | Morris | |

§ Midland Victory League Matches
* Matches played with mixed teams

## Summary of matches:

| P | W | D | L | F | A |
|---|---|---|---|---|---|
| 24 | 10 | 5 | 9 | 57 | 46 |

### APPEARANCES – 1916-1919

Adams W 1, Alexander P S 2, Arch W 2, Aston A 1, Attfield W 1, Barwell R 1, Bentley A 3(1), Bookman L 2, Bore E 1, Bowser S 12, Bunn B 2, Butler E 1, Cook A 6, Crisp J 3, Davies H 3, Davison T 1, Edgley H 1, Edwards E 5, Elford W 1, Gregory H 13, Hackett W 6, Harrop J 1, Hartland H 2, Hatton S 1, Hobbs B 1, Holder H 2, Jephcott C 9, Johnston H 1, Jones A 1, Joyce S 1, Linden J 1, Magee T 7, Mann J F 10, McNeal R 13, Merrick J 2, Moorwood L 1, Morris F 5, Newall J T 14, Nicholls W 1, Pearson H 18, Pennington J 14, Poulton O 1, Reed F 5, Richardson S 9, Roberts S 9, Robinson A E 1, Sambrook C 2, Seymour C 1, Shearman B 5, Shore E W 4, Smith J 19, Wall H 1, Waterhouse F 17, Webb I 3, Woolley H 1, Wright H 18, York R E 1. Total 264(1).

### GOALSCORERS – 1916-1919

8 Magee, Mann, 6 Gregory, Newall, 4 Roberts, 3 Wright, 2 Edwards, Hartland, McNeal, Morris, Joyce, 1 Aston, Bentley, Bunn, Bowser, Davies, Edgley, Hobbs, Jephcott, Poulton, Reed, Sambrook, Woolley. Total 57.

### MIDLAND VICTORY LEAGUE

This was arranged to give clubs competitive matches before the start of the 1919-20 season.
Four teams participated — Albion, Aston Villa, Derby County and Wolves.
The outcome was 'victory' for Albion with this record:

| P | W | D | L | F | A | Pts |
|---|---|---|---|---|---|---|
| 6 | 3 | 1 | 2 | 12 | 5 | 7 |

Derby finished runners-up, Wolves third, Villa fourth.

Albion' average home attendance for this period (1916-1919) was 7,040 — aggregate for nine competitive matches — 63,376.

**Dicky York guested for Albion in 1916.**

# Albion in World War Two.

## 1939-40

| Date | | Opponent | Result | Scorers | Att. | 1 | 2 | 3 | 4 | 5 | 6 | 7 | 8 | 9 | 10 | 11 |
|---|---|---|---|---|---|---|---|---|---|---|---|---|---|---|---|---|
| Aug | 19 | (a) Aston Villa * | D 1-1 | Richardson | 16,007 | Adams | White | C.Shaw | Sankey | Gripton | McNab | E.Jones | Banks | Richardson | Connelly | Johnson |
| | 26 | (a) Swansea T § | W 2-1 | H.Jones 2 | 15,000 | .. | .. | .. | .. | .. | .. | .. | .. | H.Jones | .. | .. |
| | 28 | (a) Coventry § | D 3-3 | E.Jones, Banks, Connelly | 26,000 | | | | | | | | | | | |
| Sept | 2 | (h) Tottenham H § | L 3-4 | E.Jones 3 | 17,008 | | | | | | | | | | | |
| Oct | 21 | (h) Luton T | W 3-1 | Banks 2, Johnson | 5,424 | Saunders | .. | C.Shaw | | | | | | | | |
| | 28 | (a) Coventry C | L 3-6 | Banks, H.Jones, Witcomb | 3,056 | .. | .. | .. | Witcomb | Lowery | | | | | | |
| Nov | 4 | (a) Northampton T | D 1-1 | H.Jones | 4,643 | .. | .. | .. | Sankey | Gripton | Witcomb | Heaselgrave | | | | |
| | 11 | (h) Leicester C | W 1-0 | H.Jones | 4,265 | .. | .. | .. | .. | .. | McNab | Newsome | Bell | | | |
| | 18 | (h) Birmingham | D 2-2 | H.Jones, Sankey(pen) | 8,671 | .. | .. | .. | .. | .. | .. | .. | .. | | | |
| | 25 | (h) Wolves | W 5-0 | H.Jones 2, Bell, Newsome, Johnson | 5,722 | .. | .. | .. | .. | .. | .. | .. | .. | | | |
| Dec | 2 | (a) Walsall | W 2-0 | H.Jones, Newsome | 4,815 | .. | .. | .. | .. | .. | .. | .. | .. | | | |
| | 9 | (a) Luton T | W 5-4 | H.Jones 3, Newsome, Sankey(pen) | 4,000 | .. | .. | .. | .. | .. | .. | .. | .. | | | |
| | 16 | (h) Coventry C | W 3-1 | H.Jones 2, Johnson | 3,802 | .. | .. | .. | .. | .. | .. | .. | .. | | | |
| | 23 | (h) Northampton T | W 4-1 | H.Jones 2, Newsome, Bell | 4,129 | .. | .. | .. | .. | .. | .. | .. | .. | | Banks | .. |
| | 26 | (h) Birmingham | W 3-0 | H.Jones, Johnson, Sankey(pen) | 6,934 | .. | .. | .. | .. | Clarke | .. | .. | .. | | Connelly | .. |
| | 30 | (a) Leicester C | W 5-2 | H.Jones(pen), Connelly, Johnson, Witcomb, Newsome | 1,939 | .. | .. | .. | .. | .. | Witcomb | .. | .. | | .. | .. |
| Jan | 13 | (a) Wolves | L 0-2 | | 9,412 | .. | .. | .. | .. | .. | .. | Newsome | .. | | .. | .. |
| | 20 | (h) Walsall | W 7-2 | H.Jones 3(1 pen), Bell 2, Johnson 2 | 1,831 | .. | .. | .. | .. | C.Davies | .. | .. | .. | | .. | .. |
| Feb | 24 | (h) Birmingham | W 6-1 | H.Jones 2, Newsome, Connelly, Johnson, Bell | 6,799 | .. | Bassett | .. | .. | Gripton | .. | .. | .. | | .. | .. |
| Mar | 2 | (h) Wolves | D 1-1 | Johnson | 8,641 | .. | .. | .. | .. | .. | .. | .. | .. | | .. | .. |
| | 9 | (a) Walsall | D 1-1 | Connelly | 3,012 | .. | White | .. | Lowery | .. | .. | .. | .. | Richardson | .. | .. |
| | 16 | (a) Luton T | W 6-3 | H.Jones 3, Newsome, Heaselgrave, Connelly | 3,224 | .. | Bassett | .. | Sankey | .. | .. | .. | Heaselgrave | H.Jones | .. | .. |
| | 23 | (h) Coventry C | W 3-1 | Sankey 2, Connelly | 6,743 | .. | White | .. | .. | .. | .. | .. | .. | | .. | .. |
| | 25 | (h) Birmingham | W 4-1 | H.Jones 3, Newsome(pen) | 9,986 | .. | .. | .. | .. | .. | .. | .. | .. | | .. | .. |
| | 26 | (h) Leicester C | W 5-1 | H.Jones 2, Newsome 2(1 pen), Connelly | 6,088 | .. | .. | .. | .. | .. | .. | .. | .. | | .. | Butler |
| | 30 | (h) Northampton T | W 4-1 | H.Jones 2, Heaselgrave, Butler | 5,504 | .. | Bassett | .. | .. | C.Davies | .. | .. | .. | | .. | .. |
| Apr | 6 | (a) Leicester C | L 2-5 | H.Jones, Heaselgrave | 5,006 | Adams | White | .. | .. | Bassett | .. | .. | .. | | .. | .. |
| | 13 | (h) Luton T | W 3-1 | H.Jones 3 | 3,398 | Saunders | .. | .. | .. | Gripton | .. | .. | .. | | Clarke | Johnson |
| | 20 | (h) Portsmouth † | W 3-1 | Connelly 2, Heaselgrave | 11,511 | .. | .. | .. | .. | .. | .. | .. | .. | | Connelly | .. |
| | 27 | (a) Portsmouth † | L 2-3 | H.Jones, Summerbee(og) | 9,873 | .. | Bassett | .. | .. | .. | .. | .. | .. | | .. | .. |
| May | 4 | (a) Bournemouth † | W 2-1 | H.Jones 2 | 9,665 | .. | .. | .. | .. | .. | .. | .. | .. | | .. | .. |
| | 11 | (h) Bournemouth † | W 3-1 | H.Jones, Heaselgrave, Connelly | 7,619 | .. | .. | .. | .. | .. | .. | .. | .. | | .. | .. |
| | 13 | (a) Wolves | L 4-5 | H.Jones, Newsome 2(1 pen), Springthorpe(og) | 6,014 | .. | .. | .. | .. | .. | .. | .. | .. | | .. | .. |
| | 14 | (h) Walsall | L 2-3 | Connelly, Newsome | 1,567 | .. | Kinsell | .. | .. | C.Davies | .. | .. | .. | | .. | .. |
| | 18 | (a) Coventry C † | W 1-0 | (a.e.t)Sankey | 8,901 | Adams | Bassett | .. | .. | Lowery | .. | .. | Clarke | | .. | .. |
| | 25 | (a) Blackburn R + | L 1-2 | Richardson | 9,742 | .. | .. | .. | Edwards | Gripton | .. | Elliott | Clarke | Richardson | Chapman | E.Jones |
| Jun | 5 | (h) Northampton T | W 2-1 | Newsome, Heaselgrave | 1,374 | .. | C.Shaw | Kinsell | Sankey | Lowery | McNab | Newsome | Heaselgrave | H.Jones | Connelly | Johnson |
| | 8 | (a) Coventry C | L 0-4 | | 3,998 | .. | .. | .. | .. | .. | .. | .. | .. | | Bell | .. |

## OTHER MATCHES

| Date | | Opponent | Result | Scorers | Att. | 1 | 2 | 3 | 4 | 5 | 6 | 7 | 8 | 9 | 10 | 11 |
|---|---|---|---|---|---|---|---|---|---|---|---|---|---|---|---|---|
| Sep | 23 | (h) Wolves | L 3-5 | C.Shaw(pen), H.Jones, Banks | 5,833 | Adams | White | C.Shaw | Sankey | Gripton | McNab | E.Jones | Banks | H.Jones | Connelly | Johnson |
| | 30 | (h) Stoke C | W 6-0 | H.Jones 3, E.Jones 2, Johnson | 3,696 | Saunders | .. | .. | .. | . | .. | .. | .. | .. | .. | .. |
| Oct | 7 | (a) Chester | W 2-0 | H.Jones 2 | 3,313 | | | | | | | | | | | |
| | 7 | (a) Burton T | W 11-1 | Richardson 4, Clarke 3, Bell 2, Newsome, Butler | 1,126 | Adams | Bassett | Kinsell | Lowery | C.Davies | Witcomb | Newsome | Bell | Richardson | Clarke | Butler |
| | 14 | (h) Coventry C | W 4-2 | H.Jones 2(1 pen), E.Jones 2 | 2,350 | Saunders | White | .. | Sankey | Gripton | McNab | E.Jones | Banks | H.Jones | Connelly | Johnson |
| | 14 | (a) Kidderminster H | W 5-1 | Richardson 2, Heaselgrave, Lowery | 1,190 | Adams | Pemberton | Bassett | Lowery | C.Davies | Witcomb | Elliott‡ | Heaselgrave | Richardson | Clarke | Butler |
| | 21 | (a) Shrewsbury T | W 5-0 | Richardson 2, Newsome, Bell, Dudley | 3,847 | Harris | Bassett | Kinsell | .. | .. | Edwards | Newsome | Burgin | .. | Bell | Dudley |
| Nov | 25 | (a) Worcester C | W 5-0 | Richardson 2, Bassett, Elliott, Witcomb | 2,976 | Adams | .. | .. | .. | .. | Witcomb | Elliott | Heaselgrave | .. | Banks | .. |
| Dec | 2 | (a) Shrewsbury T | W 3-1 | Heaselgrave, Clarke, Witcomb(pen) | 1,816 | Harris | .. | .. | .. | .. | .. | .. | .. | .. | Clarke | Butler |
| | 9 | (a) Bath C | W 7-3 | Heaselgrave 3, Richardson 2, Elliott, Clarke | 1,403 | Adams | .. | .. | .. | .. | .. | .. | .. | .. | .. | .. |
| | 16 | (a) Port Vale | W 4-1 | E.Jones, Pike, Dudley, Burgin | 2,645 | .. | .. | .. | Holder | .. | Clarke | E.Jones | Burgin | Pike | Chapman | Dudley |
| | 26 | (a) Wellington T | L 2-3 | Elliott 2 | 1,985 | .. | .. | .. | Edwards | Lowery | Dudley | Elliott | Heaselgrave | .. | .. | E.Jones |
| | 30 | (a) Notts C | L 0-4 | | 2,251 | .. | .. | .. | .. | .. | Clarke | E.Jones | .. | Richardson | Banks | Butler |
| Jan | 6 | (a) Newport C | W 3-1 | Heaselgrave, Witcomb, Newsome | 2,445 | .. | Pemberton | .. | Lowery | Bassett | Witcomb | Newsome | .. | .. | Clarke | .. |
| | 6 | (h) Sheffield W | L 0-3 | Abandoned after 47 mins(fog) | 1,426 | Saunders | White | C.Shaw | Sankey | Gripton | McNab | E.Jones | Bell | H.Jones | Connelly | Johnson |
| Mar | 2 | (a) Chesterfield | L 0-4 | | 3,142 | Adams | Robinson | Kinsell | Lowery | Britnell | Witcomb | Elliott | Heaselgrave | Richardson | Chapman | Dudley |
| | 9 | (a) Chelmsford | L 1-3 | Elliott | 1,406 | .. | Pemberton | .. | Holder | .. | Edwards | .. | .. | Pike | .. | Butler |
| | 25 | (a) Cardiff C | D 1-1 | Butler | 3,552 | .. | .. | .. | Lowery | Bassett | Witcomb | .. | Bell | Richardson | Dudley | .. |
| Jun | 1 | (a) Birmingham | D 2-2 | Connelly, Johnson | 5,176 | .. | C.Shaw | .. | Sankey | Lowery | McNab | Newsome | Heaselgrave | H.Jones | Connelly | Johnson |

\* Jubilee Fund match.　§ Division 2 matches.　† League Cup matches　　　　　‡ Elliott was substituted by T. Bell

---

### APPEARANCES – DIVISION 2
Adams J 3, Banks G 3, Connelly E 3, Gripton W 3, Johnson J 3, Jones E 3, Jones H 3, McNab A 3, Sankey J 3, Shaw C 3, White H 3 Total 33

### GOALSCORERS – DIVISION 2
4 E.Jones, 2 H.Jones, 1 Banks, Connelly. Total 8

### APPEARANCES – MIDLAND REGIONAL LEAGUE
Adams J 3, Banks G 4, Bassett I 6, Bell T 15, Butler S 3, Clarke I 2, Connelly E 25, Davies C 3, Gripton W 21, Heaselgrave S 12, Johnson J 25, Jones E 2, Jones H 27, Kinsell H 3, Lowery H 4, McNab A 25, Newsome R 25, Richardson WG 1, Sankey J 26, Saunders W 25, Shaw C 28, White H 20, Witcomb D 3. Total 308

### GOALSCORERS – MIDLAND REGIONAL LEAGUE
36 H.Jones, 14 Newsome, 9 Johnson, 7 Connelly, 5 Bell, Sankey, 4 Heaselgrave, 3 Banks, 2 Witcomb, 1 Butler, Opp own goal 1. Total 87

### APPEARANCES – LEAGUE CUP
Adams J 2, Bassett I 5, Chapman G 1, Clarke I 2, Connelly E 5, Edwards C 1, Elliott W 1, Gripton W 5, Heaselgrave S 5, Johnson J 5, Jones E 1, Jones H 4, Lowery H 1, McNab A 5, Newsome R 5, Richardson WG 1, Sankey J 5, Saunders W 4, Shaw C 6, White H 1, Witcomb D 1. Total 66

### GOALSCORERS – LEAGUE CUP
4 H.Jones, 3 Connelly, 2 Heaselgrave, 1 Richardson, Sankey, Opp own goal 1. Total 12

## 1940-41

| Date | | Opponent | Res | Score | Scorers | Att | 1 | 2 | 3 | 4 | 5 | 6 | 7 | 8 | 9 | 10 | 11 |
|---|---|---|---|---|---|---|---|---|---|---|---|---|---|---|---|---|---|
| Aug | 31 | (h) Walsall | W | 3-1 | Price 2, Heaselgrave | 2,966 | Adams | C.Shaw | Kinsell | Sankey | Gripton | Edwards | Newsome | Heaselgrave | Price | Connelly | Dudley |
| Sep | 7 | (a) Walsall | W | 2-0 | Heaselgrave, Johnson | 2,968 | .. | .. | .. | .. | .. | Witcomb | .. | .. | Richardson | .. | Johnson |
| | 14 | (h) Northampton T | W | 4-1 | Richardson 2, Newsome 2(1 pen) | 2,607 | .. | .. | .. | .. | .. | Edwards | .. | Clarke | .. | .. | .. |
| | 21 | (a) Northampton T | D | 1-1 | Newsome (pen) | 3,200 | .. | .. | .. | .. | .. | .. | .. | .. | .. | .. | .. |
| | 28 | (h) Birmingham | L | 1-2 | Richardson | 4,718 | .. | .. | .. | .. | .. | Witcomb | .. | .. | .. | .. | .. |
| Oct | 5 | (a) Birmingham | W | 3-1 | Newsome, Clarke, Johnson | 5,394 | .. | Bassett | C.Shaw | .. | .. | Edwards | .. | .. | .. | .. | .. |
| | 12 | (h) Stoke C | L | 0-1 | | 4,091 | .. | .. | .. | .. | .. | .. | .. | .. | .. | .. | .. |
| | 19 | (h) Stoke C | W | 3-1 | Richardson 2, Johnson | 3,392 | .. | Kinsell | .. | .. | .. | .. | Heaselgrave | .. | .. | .. | .. |
| | 26 | (h) Notts C | W | 3-1 | Richardson 2, Hodgetts | 2,496 | .. | Bassett | .. | .. | .. | .. | Hodgetts | Heaselgrave | .. | .. | Dudley |
| Nov | 2 | (h) Notts C | L | 2-3 | Sankey 2(1 pen) | 2,100 | .. | .. | .. | .. | .. | McNab | .. | .. | .. | .. | .. |
| | 9 | (h) Coventry C | L | 1-4 | Sankey (pen) | 978 | .. | C.Shaw | Kinsell | .. | .. | .. | Newsome | .. | H.Jones | .. | Johnson |
| | 23 | (h) Mansfield T | W | 4-2 | Richardson 2, Heaselgrave, Sankey(pen) | 831 | .. | .. | .. | .. | .. | .. | .. | .. | Richardson | .. | .. |
| | 30 | (a) Mansfield T | D | 3-3 | Richardson 2, Elliott | 2,000 | .. | .. | .. | .. | .. | Edwards | Elliott | .. | .. | .. | .. |
| Dec | 7 | (h) Nottingham F | W | 5-0 | Richardson 3, Heaselgrave, Elliott | 1,261 | Goodall | .. | .. | Lowery | .. | Sankey | .. | .. | .. | .. | Edwards |
| | 14 | (a) Leicester C | L | 3-4 | Heaselgrave 2, Richardson | 939 | Adams | .. | .. | Sankey | .. | Edwards | E.Jones | .. | .. | Clarke | Johnson |
| | 21 | (h) Leicester C | L | 4-5 | Richardson 3, Elliott | 765 | .. | .. | .. | .. | .. | .. | Elliott | .. | .. | .. | .. |
| | 28 | (h) Nottingham F | W | 5-3 | Richardson 2, Elliott 2, Heaselgrave | 1,839 | .. | Bassett | C.Shaw | .. | .. | .. | .. | .. | .. | Chapman | .. |
| Jan | 11 | (h) Notts C * | W | 8-1 | Elliott 2, Heaselgrave 2, Richardson 2, Chapman, Johnson | 1,403 | .. | .. | .. | .. | .. | .. | .. | .. | .. | .. | .. |
| Feb | 8 | (a) Walsall * | L | 3-4 | Johnson 2, Elliott | 3,135 | .. | .. | Kinsell | .. | .. | Witcomb | .. | .. | .. | .. | .. |
| | 15 | (a) Notts C § | L | 0-4 | | 2,700 | .. | .. | C.Shaw | .. | .. | Edwards | .. | .. | Clarke | .. | .. |
| | 22 | (h) Notts C § | W | 5-0 | Heaselgrave 2, Richardson 2, C.Shaw(pen) | 2,581 | .. | .. | .. | .. | .. | .. | .. | .. | Richardson | .. | .. |
| Mar | 1 | (h) Mansfield T § | L | 2-3 | Richardson 2 | 2,132 | .. | .. | Kinsell | .. | .. | .. | .. | .. | .. | .. | .. |
| | 8 | (a) Mansfield T § | L | 2-6 | Gripton 2 | 2,800 | .. | .. | .. | .. | .. | .. | .. | .. | .. | .. | .. |
| | 15 | (h) Stoke C | D | 2-2 | Richardson, Sankey | 2,086 | .. | .. | .. | Lowery | .. | .. | .. | .. | H.Jones | .. | .. |
| | 22 | (a) Stoke C | W | 2-0 | Elliott 2 | 794 | .. | .. | .. | Lowery | Gripton | .. | .. | .. | Chapman | .. | .. |
| | 29 | (h) Walsall | W | 4-1 | H.Jones 2, Elliott, Richardson | 1,412 | .. | .. | .. | Sankey | Lowery | .. | H.Jones | .. | .. | .. | .. |
| Apr | 5 | (a) Walsall | D | 3-3 | Wilkes 2, Heaselgrave | 1,850 | .. | .. | .. | .. | Gripton | .. | Heaselgrave | Wilkes | .. | .. | E.Jones |
| | 12 | (a) Northampton T | L | 1-3 | Elliott | 2,141 | .. | .. | .. | .. | Davies | .. | .. | .. | H.Jones | .. | Johnson |
| | 19 | (h) Northampton T | W | 3-2 | Chapman, Sankey, Hunter(og) | 1,463 | .. | .. | .. | .. | Gripton | McNab | .. | .. | Richardson | .. | Dudley |
| May | 3 | (a) Reading | L | 3-6 | Heaselgrave, Richardson, Wilkes | 4,000 | .. | .. | .. | .. | .. | Edwards | .. | .. | .. | Wilkes | .. |
| | 17 | (a) Cardiff C | D | 4-4 | Elliott 2, Wilkes, C.Evans | 3,009 | .. | Quinton | .. | Lowery | .. | .. | .. | .. | Wilkes | C.Evans | .. |
| | 31 | (a) Walsall | L | 3-10 | Johnson, Elliott, Sankey | 1,512 | Alderwick | Bassett | .. | Sankey | Lowery | McNab | .. | .. | Richardson | .. | Johnson |

## OTHER MATCHES

| Date | | Opponent | Res | Score | Scorers | Att | 1 | 2 | 3 | 4 | 5 | 6 | 7 | 8 | 9 | 10 | 11 |
|---|---|---|---|---|---|---|---|---|---|---|---|---|---|---|---|---|---|
| Apr | 5 | (h) RAF | W | 2-0 | Dudley 2 | 513 | .. | Warrender | Poultney | Lowery | Davies | .. | Hodgetts | Bell | Newsome | Clarke | Dudley |
| | 14 | (h) Aston Villa | W | 4-3 | H.Jones 3, Chapman | 4,549 | Sankey | Robinson | Kinsell | Edwards | Gripton | .. | Elliott | Heaselgrave | H.Jones | Chapman | Johnson |
| | 26 | (h) Aston Villa | L | 1-6 | Sankey | 3,700 | Alderwick | .. | .. | Sankey | .. | .. | .. | .. | .. | .. | .. |
| May | 3 | (h) RAF | W | 4-1 | Bell 2, Newsome, Clarke | 601 | .. | Warrender | Robinson | Lowery | Seeley | .. | Clift | Bell | Newsome | Clarke | A.Evans |
| | 10 | (a) Hednesford T | L | 1-5 | Bell | 1,201 | .. | .. | Kinsell | .. | Lewis | Witcomb | Hodgetts | .. | Ashley | .. | .. |
| | 17 | (h) REVO Sports | L | 2-6 | Clarke, Atkiss | 253 | .. | Robinson | Poultney | Ashley | .. | McNab | Clift | Dutton | Chatterley | .. | Atkiss |
| | 24 | (h) RAF | W | 6-1 | Richardson 6 | 386 | .. | Warrender | Kinsell | Sankey | Lowery | .. | Elliott | Heaselgrave | Richardson | C.Evans | .. |

*Midland Cup matches.   § League Cup matches.

### APPEARANCES – FOOTBALL LEAGUE SOUTH

Adams J 24, Alderwick J 1, Bassett I 13, Chapman G 6, Clarke I 8, Connelly E 14, Davies C 1, Dudley G 6, Edwards C 19, Elliott W 13, Evans C 2, Goodall E 1, Gripton W 22, Heaselgrave S 20, Hodgetts F 2, Johnson J 18, Jones E 2, Jones H 4, Kinsell H 21, Lowery H 6, McNab A 5, Newsome R 9, Price W 1, Quinton W 1, Richardson WG 21, Sankey J 24, Shaw C 17, Wilkes G 3, Witcomb D 2. Total 286

### GOALSCORERS – FOOTBALL LEAGUE SOUTH

23 Richardson, 12 Elliott, 9 Heaselgrave, 7 Sankey, 4 Johnson, Newsome, Wilkes, 2 H.Jones, Price, 1 Clarke, Chapman, Evans, Hodgetts, Opp own goal 1. Total 72

### APPEARANCES – MIDLAND CUP & LEAGUE CUP

Adams J 6, Bassett I 6, Chapman G 6, Clarke I 1, Edwards C 5, Elliott W 6, Gripton W 6, Heaselgrave S 6, Johnson J 6, Kinsell H 3, Richardson WG 5, Sankey J 6, Shaw C 3, Witcomb D 1. Total 66

### GOALSCORERS – MIDLAND CUP & LEAGUE CUP

6 Richardson, 4 Heaselgrave, 3 Elliott, Johnson, 2 Gripton 1 Chapman, Shaw. Total 20

The Albion team which beat Walsall 3-1 at The Hawthorns in August 1940. Back row (left to right): C.Shaw, H.Kinsell, J.Adams, W.Gripton, W.Price. Front row: C.Edwards, R.Newsome, S.Heaselgrave, E.Connelly, G.Dudley, J.Sankey.

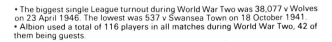

• The biggest single League turnout during World War Two was 38,077 v Wolves on 23 April 1946. The lowest was 537 v Swansea Town on 18 October 1941.
• Albion used a total of 116 players in all matches during World War Two, 42 of them being guests.

## 1941-42

| Date | V | Opponent | Res | Score | Scorers | Att | 1 | 2 | 3 | 4 | 5 | 6 | 7 | 8 | 9 | 10 | 11 |
|---|---|---|---|---|---|---|---|---|---|---|---|---|---|---|---|---|---|
| Aug 30 | (h) | Cardiff C | W | 6-3 | H.Jones 4, Elliott, Johnson | 4,462 | Adams | Bassett | C.Shaw | Sankey | Gripton | Edwards | Elliott | Heaselgrave | H.Jones | Evans | Johnson |
| Sep 6 | (a) | Cardiff C | D | 1-1 | C.Edwards | 4,647 | .. | .. | .. | .. | .. | Witcomb | .. | .. | Dudley | .. | C.Edwards |
| 13 | (h) | Leicester C | W | 4-1 | C.Evans 2, Richardson, Johnson | 3,786 | .. | .. | .. | .. | .. | McNab | .. | .. | Richardson | .. | Johnson |
| 20 | (a) | Leicester C | L | 2-3 | Elliott, Sankey | 3,526 | .. | .. | .. | Edwards | .. | .. | .. | .. | May | .. | .. |
| 27 | (a) | Walsall | L | 1-2 | Elliott | 4,494 | .. | .. | .. | Sankey | .. | Edwards | .. | .. | Banks | .. | .. |
| Oct 4 | (h) | Walsall | W | 4-0 | Elliott, Heaselgrave, Wilkes, Evans | 4,135 | .. | .. | .. | Lowery | .. | .. | .. | .. | Wilkes | .. | Dudley |
| 11 | (a) | Aston Villa | W | 3-2 | H.Jones, Elliott 2 | 5,500 | .. | .. | .. | .. | .. | .. | .. | .. | H.Jones | .. | .. |
| 18 | (h) | Swansea T | W | 8-0 | Richardson 5, Elliott 2, Evans | 537 | .. | .. | .. | Sankey | .. | McNab | .. | .. | Richardson | .. | .. |
| Nov 8 | (a) | Wolves | W | 8-2 | Elliott 3, Evans 3, Johnson Sankey | 6,000 | .. | .. | .. | .. | .. | Edwards | .. | Clarke | .. | .. | Johnson |
| 15 | (h) | Wolves | W | 5-3 | Elliott 2, Richardson 2, Dudley | 3,774 | .. | .. | .. | .. | .. | McNab | .. | .. | .. | .. | Dudley |
| 22 | (h) | Luton T | W | 10-1 | Richardson 6, Evans 2, Elliott, Johnson | 2,618 | .. | .. | .. | .. | .. | Edwards | .. | .. | .. | .. | Johnson |
| 29 | (a) | Luton T | W | 5-4 | Richardson 2, Elliott 2, Clarke | 2,200 | .. | C.Shaw | Kinsell | .. | .. | .. | .. | .. | .. | .. | .. |
| Dec 6 | (h) | Northampton T | W | 7-0 | McKennan 3, Elliott 2, Richardson, Sankey | 1,766 | .. | Bassett | C.Shaw | .. | .. | .. | .. | McKennan | .. | .. | .. |
| 13 | (a) | Northampton T | L | 1-4 | Richardson | 2,000 | .. | .. | .. | .. | .. | .. | .. | Dudley | .. | .. | .. |
| 27 | (h) | Wrexham § | W | 6-4 | Richardson 2, Elliott 2, McKennan, Evans | 4,497 | Willetts | .. | C.Shaw | Edwards | .. | McNab | .. | McKennan | .. | .. | .. |
| Jan 3 | (a) | Wrexham § | D | 5-5 | Richardson 2, McKennan, Dearson, Elliott | 2,500 | Merrick | .. | .. | Dearson | H.Jones | Edwards | .. | .. | .. | .. | .. |
| 10 | (h) | Stoke § | W | 4-0 | Richardson, Elliott, McKennan, Johnson | 7,335 | .. | .. | .. | Sankey | Edwards | McNab | .. | .. | .. | .. | .. |
| 17 | (h) | Stoke § | L | 1-2 | Elliott | 4,578 | .. | .. | .. | .. | .. | .. | .. | .. | .. | .. | .. |
| Feb 14 | (h) | Leicester C § | W | 3-2 | Richardson 2, Elliott | 4,378 | Adams | .. | .. | .. | Gripton | Edwards | .. | .. | .. | .. | Dudley |
| 21 | (h) | Mansfield T § | W | 3-1 | McKennan 2, Richardson | 1,398 | .. | .. | .. | .. | Edwards | McNab | .. | .. | .. | .. | Johnson |
| Mar 7 | (a) | Northampton T § | L | 3-4 | Elliott 2, Evans | 2,000 | .. | Quinton | .. | .. | Gripton | Edwards | .. | .. | .. | .. | .. |
| 14 | (h) | Northampton T § | D | 2-2 | McKennan, Johnson | 3,706 | .. | Bassett | .. | .. | .. | .. | .. | .. | H.Jones | .. | .. |
| 21 | (a) | Leicester C § | L | 2-4 | Sankey, Gripton | 5,685 | .. | .. | Ashley | .. | .. | .. | .. | Heaselgrave | Richardson | .. | .. |
| Apr 4 | (a) | Stoke C § | L | 3-5 | Johnson, Elliott, Evans | 5,000 | .. | .. | C.Shaw | Ashley | Edwards | McNab | .. | .. | .. | .. | .. |
| 6 | (h) | Stoke C § | W | 6-1 | Richardson 2, McKennan 2 (1 pen), Elliott, Sankey | 13,400 | .. | .. | .. | Sankey | Gripton | .. | .. | McKennan | .. | .. | Edwards |
| 11 | (a) | Cardiff C § | D | 1-1 | Richardson | 10,781 | .. | .. | .. | .. | .. | Witcomb | .. | McKennan | .. | .. | Edwards |
| 18 | (h) | Cardiff C § | W | 3-2 | Richardson 2, Elliott | 10,198 | .. | .. | .. | .. | .. | McNab | .. | Edwards | .. | .. | Johnson |
| 25 | (h) | Everton § | W | 3-1 | Evans, Elliott, Edwards | 19,006 | .. | .. | .. | .. | .. | .. | .. | McKennan | .. | .. | Edwards |
| May 2 | (a) | Everton § | W | 5-1 | Elliott 2 McKennan 2, Evans | 34,000 | .. | .. | .. | .. | .. | .. | .. | .. | .. | .. | .. |
| 9 | (h) | Wolves § | L | 0-4 | | 35,000 | .. | .. | .. | .. | .. | .. | .. | .. | .. | .. | .. |
| 16 | (a) | Wolves § | L | 0-3 | | 29,000 | Harris | .. | .. | Witcomb | .. | .. | .. | .. | .. | .. | Johnson |
| 23 | (h) | Walsall | W | 3-1 | Bowen, Elliott, Ashley | 1,695 | .. | .. | .. | Sankey | .. | Edwards | .. | C.Jones | Ashley | .. | Bowen |

## OTHER MATCHES

| Date | V | Opponent | Res | Score | Scorers | Att | 1 | 2 | 3 | 4 | 5 | 6 | 7 | 8 | 9 | 10 | 11 |
|---|---|---|---|---|---|---|---|---|---|---|---|---|---|---|---|---|---|
| Nov 1 | (h) | Czech Army | W | 3-1 | Evans, Elliott, Richardson | 2,638 | Adams | .. | .. | .. | .. | McNab | .. | Heaselgrave | Richardson | .. | Johnson |
| Dec 20 | (h) | Birmingham | W | 4-1 | Richardson 3, Elliott | 1,270 | .. | .. | Kinsell | .. | .. | Edwards | .. | Duggan | .. | .. | .. |
| 25 | (h) | Aston Villa | L | 0-2 | | 5,178 | .. | .. | C.Shaw | Edwards | .. | McNab | .. | McKennan | .. | .. | .. |
| Mar 28 | (h) | Aston Villa | L | 1-2 | Sankey | 4,148 | Harris | .. | .. | Sankey | Edwards | .. | Hodgetts | Heaselgrave | .. | .. | .. |
| May 25 | (h) | Aston Villa | L | 3-4 | Elliott 2, Evans | 2,035 | Adams | .. | .. | C.Edwards | Gripton | .. | Elliott | Sankey | .. | .. | .. |
| 30 | (h) | Birmingham | W | 4-1 | C.Edwards 2(1 pen), G.Edwards, Newsome(pen) | 5,357 | .. | .. | .. | Witcomb | .. | C.Edwards | Newsome | G.Edwards | .. | .. | .. |

§ League Cup matches

### APPEARANCES - FOOTBALL LEAGUE SOUTH

Adams J 13, Ashley H 1, Banks G 1, Bassett I 13, Bowen T 1, Clarke I 4, Dudley G 5, Edwards C 11, Elliott W 14, Evans C 14, Gripton W 14, Harris W 1, Heaselgrave S 7, Johnson J 9, Jones C 1, Jones H 1, Kinsell H 1, Lowery H 1, McKennan P 1, McNab A 4, May G 1, Richardson WG 8, Sankey J 12, Shaw C 14, Wilkes G 1, Witcomb D 1. Total 154

### GOALSCORERS - FOOTBALL LEAGUE SOUTH

18 Richardson, 17 Elliott, 9 Evans, 4 Johnson, H.Jones, 3 McKennan, Sankey, 1 Ashley, Bowen, Clarke, Dudley, Edwards, Heaselgrave, Wilkes. Total 65

### APPEARANCES - LEAGUE CUP

Adams J 12, Ashley H 2, Bassett I 16, Dearson D 1, Dudley G 1, Edwards C 16, Elliott W 17, Evans C 17, Gripton W 12, Harris W 1, Johnson J 11, Jones H 2, McNab A 11, McKennan P 14, Merrick G 3, Quinton W 1, Richardson WG 16, Shaw C 16, Sankey J 13, Willetts J 1, Witcomb D 2. Total 187

### GOALSCORERS - LEAGUE CUP

14 Elliott, 13 Richardson, 10 McKennan, 5 Evans, 3 Johnson, 2 Sankey, 1 Dearson, Edwards, Gripton. Total 50

• In 1939-40 Harry Jones scored in 11 successive games for Albion; Billy Elliott equalled this record in 1941-2.
• Albion scored eight goals in 32 minutes against Luton Town on 22 November 1941. They won the match 10-1.
• The Football League sanctioned a payment of 30 shillings (£1.50) per match to each player for seasons 1939-40 to 1942-3. In 1943-4 it went up to £2 and by 1945-6 it had reached £4.

Albion's team for the game against Cardiff City in August 1941. Back row (left to right): H.Kinsell, H.Jones, I.Bassett, J.Adams, W.Gripton, C.Shaw, E.Jones. Front row: J.Johnson, C.Edwards, S.Heaselgrave, J.Sankey, W.Elliott, C.Evans.

## 1942-43

| | | | 1 | 2 | 3 | 4 | 5 | 6 | 7 | 8 | 9 | 10 | 11 |
|---|---|---|---|---|---|---|---|---|---|---|---|---|---|
| Aug 29 (a) Northampton T | L 0-2 | 4,882 | Adams | Bassett | A.J.Smith | Sankey | Davies | Millard | Elliott | Heaselgrave | Richardson | C.Evans | K.Butler |
| Sep 5 (h) Northampton T | W 6-3 Elliott 3, Sankey 2, Evans | 1,500 | | | | Millard | Gripton | McNab | | | Sankey | | McDonald |
| 12 (h) Leicester C | W 3-2 Millard 3 | 4,000 | | | | Sankey | | | | E.Jones | Millard | | |
| 19 (a) Leicester C | D 0-0 | 4,029 | | Shaw | | | Brown | | Richardson | Clarke | | | |
| 26 (a) Wolves | L 0-2 | 8,382 | | Parker | Shaw | Millard | Sankey | Witcomb | Elliott | Chapman | H.Jones | | |
| Oct 3 (h) Wolves | W 6-2 Millard 3, Elliott 2, Evans | 7,813 | | Shaw | A.J.Smith | Sankey | Davies | McNab | | Heaselgrave | Millard | | Finch |
| 10 (h) Aston Villa | W 6-2 Elliott 2, Shaw, Millard, Evans, Finch | 10,326 | | | | | | | | | | | |
| 17 (a) Aston Villa | L 2-8 Heaselgrave 2 | 12,000 | | | | | | | Hodgetts | | | | |
| 24 (a) Derby C | L 0-4 | 7,810 | | Bassett | | | Gripton | Edwards | Richardson | | | | Dudley |
| 31 (a) Derby C | D 3-3 Heaselgrave 2, Newsome (pen) | 4,571 | | Shaw | | | | Millard | Newsome | | Richardson | | Finch |
| Nov 7 (h) Stoke C | D 0-0 | 4,564 | | Bassett | | | | | | | Simms | | |
| 14 (a) Stoke C | L 1-5 Clarke | 3,331 | | | Kinsell | | | A.Evans | | Clarke | H.Butler | | |
| 21 (h) Walsall | D 0-0 | 2,783 | Harris | | A.Smith | | | Millard | | | McDonald | | |
| 28 (a) Walsall | L 0-2 | 3,412 | Billingsley | | | | | | Hodgetts | Burgin | | | |
| Dec 5 (n) Birmingham | L 0-3 | 3,000 | J.Smith | | | | Edwards | | Elliott | | Richardson | | |
| 12 (h) Birmingham | W 4-3 Ashley 2, Sankey, Dudley | 3,393 | | | | | Gripton | Ashley | | Heaselgrave | | Millard | Dudley |
| 19 (a) Coventry C | L 1-2 Ashley | 5,000 | Adams | | | | | Millard | Hodgetts | Walsh | Ashley | Wood | |
| 25 (h) Coventry C | W 3-0 Ashley 2, Witcomb | 5,199 | | | | Witcomb | | McNab | | Elliott | C.Evans | | |
| 26 (h) Leicester C § | W 5-1 Elliott 3(1 pen), Hodgetts, Dudley | 8,119 | | | | | | | | | | | |
| Jan 2 (a) Leicester C § | L 0-9 | 3,578 | | | | Millard | Sankey | | | | | | |
| 9 (h) Coventry C § | L 2-3 Elliott (pen), Sankey | 3,676 | Marks | Sankey | J.Smith | | Gripton | S.Jones | | | | | Finch |
| 16 (a) Coventry C § | L 0-1 | 8,500 | Adams | Bassett | | Sankey | | Millard | Elliott | Doherty | Richardson | | |
| 23 (a) Aston Villa § | W 5-3 Doherty 2, Green, Elliott, Evans | 12,000 | | | Hapgood | Witcomb | | | | | Green | | |
| 30 (a) Aston Villa § | W 2-1 Elliott (pen), Shaw | 13,200 | | | | Millard | | McNab | | Green | Shaw | | |
| Feb 6 (n) Birmingham § | W 1-0 Green | 8,000 | | Scott | | | | | | Heaselgrave | Green | | |
| 13 (h) Birmingham § | W 2-1 Elliott (pen), Jones | 7,217 | | | A.J.Smith | Sankey | | Millard | | | H.Jones | | Hodgetts |
| 20 (a) Wolves § | L 0-1 | 12,444 | | Bassett | | Millard | | McNab | | | Richardson | | Finch |
| 27 (h) Wolves § | W 2-0 Evans, Shaw | 10,138 | | | | | | | Hodgetts | Sankey | Shaw | | Johnson |
| Mar 6 (a) Coventry C § | D 1-1 Evans | 11,502 | | Shelton | | Sankey | Smalley | Millard | Elliott | Hodgetts | Dearson | | |
| 13 (h) Coventry C § | W 3-0 Lane, Dearson, Elliott | 13,332 | | | Shaw | Millard | Gripton | McNab | | Lane | | | S.Butler |
| 20 (h) Chesterfield § | L 2-3 Elliott 2 | 13,447 | | | A.J.Smith | Sankey | | Millard | | | | | |
| 27 (a) Chesterfield § | D 3-3 Richardson 3 | 13,661 | | | Shaw | Millard | | McNab | | Dearson | Richardson | | Finch |
| Apr 3 (n) Birmingham | L 3-5 Richardson 3 | 4,000 | | | | J.Smith | | Edwards | Dunkley | C.Evans | | A.Evans | |
| 10 (h) Birmingham | L 0-4 | 1,818 | | Parker | Ashley | Davenport | | McNab | Elliott | | Millard | | |
| 17 (h) Walsall | W 4-0 Richardson 2, Jones, A.Evans | 1,575 | | Robinson | J.Smith | Sankey | | Millard | Hodgetts | | Richardson | | E.Jones |
| 24 (a) Walsall | W 2-1 Richardson, Finch | 1,500 | | Ashley | | Bye | | | Elliott | Clarke | | C.Evans | Finch |
| 26 (h) Northampton T | W 6-1 Richardson 3, Clarke 2, A.Evans | 2,468 | | Shaw | | Millard | | McNab | Hodgetts | | | A.Evans | C.Evans |
| May 1 (a) Aston Villa | W 6-2 Richardson 5, Jones | 5,613 | | Ashley | | Sankey | | Millard | | E.Jones | | | |

§ League Cup matches

### APPEARANCES - FOOTBALL LEAGUE NORTH

Adams J 20, Ashley H 6, Bassett I 12, Billingsley G 1, Brown A 1, Burgin M 2, Butler H 1, Butler K 1, Bye J 1, Chapman G 1, Clarke I 5, Davenport A 1, Davies C 4, Dudley G 4, Dunkley M 1, Edwards C 3, Elliott W 11, Evans A 6, Evans C 22, Finch L 12, Gripton W 17, Harris W 1, Heaselgrave S 9, Hodgetts F 7, Jones E 3, Jones H 1, Kinsell H 1, McDonald J 6, McNab A 9, Millard L 22, Newsome R 4, Parker A 2, Richardson WG 11, Robinson E 1, Sankey J 19, Shaw C 7, Simms H 1, Shelton J 1, Smith AJ 21, Smith J 2, Walsh W 1, Witcomb D 2, Wood T 1. Total 264

### GOALSCORERS - FOOTBALL LEAGUE NORTH

14 Richardson, 7 Elliott, Millard, 5 Ashley, 4 Heaselgrave, 3 Clarke, C.Evans, Sankey, 2 A.Evans, E.Jones, Finch, 1 Dudley, Newsome, Shaw, Witcomb. Total 56

### APPEARANCES - LEAGUE CUP

Adams J 13, Ashley H 3, Bassett I 7, Butler S 2, Dearson D 4, Doherty P 2, Dudley G 2, Elliott W 13, Evans C 14, Finch L 7, Green T 3, Gripton W 12, Hapgood E 3, Heaselgrave S 3, Hodgetts F 6, Johnson J 2, Jones H 1, Jones S 1, Lane H 2, McNab A 8, Millard L 13, Marks G 1, Richardson WG 3, Sankey J 7, Scott L 2, Shaw C 4, Shelton J 4, Smalley T 1, Smith AJ 9, Witcomb D 2. Total 154

### GOALSCORERS - LEAGUE CUP

10 Elliott, 3 C.Evans, Richardson, 2 Doherty, Green, Shaw, 1 Dearson, Dudley, Hodgetts, H.Jones, Lane, Sankey. Total 28

**Goalkeeper Billy Harris, who played one game in 1942-43 and kept a clean sheet.**

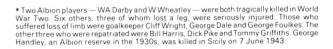

• Two Albion players — WA Darby and W Wheatley — were both tragically killed in World War Two. Six others, three of whom lost a leg, were seriously injured. Those who suffered loss of limb were goalkeeper Cliff Wright, George Dale and George Foulkes. The other three who were repatriated were Bill Harris, Dick Pike and Tommy Griffiths. George Handley, an Albion reserve in the 1930s, was killed in Sicily on 7 June 1943.

## 1943-44

| Date | | Opponent | Result | Scorers | Att | 1 | 2 | 3 | 4 | 5 | 6 | 7 | 8 | 9 | 10 | 11 |
|---|---|---|---|---|---|---|---|---|---|---|---|---|---|---|---|---|
| Aug 28 | (h) | Derby C | W 3-2 | Richardson, Evans, Armstrong | 5,926 | Adams | Bassett | A.J.Smith | Millard | Gripton | McNab | Elliott | E.Jones | Richardson | Armstrong | C.Evans |
| Sep 4 | (a) | Derby C | W 5-1 | Richardson 4, Jones | 6,393 | .. | .. | .. | Sankey | .. | Millard | .. | .. | .. | .. | Duns |
| 11 | (h) | Northampton T | D 4-4 | Elliott 4 (1 pen) | 6,222 | .. | .. | .. | Millard | .. | McNab | .. | Duns | Armstrong | A.Evans | C.Evans |
| 18 | (a) | Northampton T | L 1-2 | Elliott | 3,721 | .. | .. | .. | .. | .. | .. | .. | McCormick | Richardson | Armstrong | Duns |
| 25 | (h) | Wolves | W 4-1 | Richardson 2, Elliott, Duns | 7,363 | Heath | .. | .. | .. | .. | Williams | .. | .. | .. | C.Evans | .. |
| Oct 2 | (a) | Wolves | W 3-2 | Richardson 2 Duns | 8,819 | .. | .. | .. | .. | .. | .. | .. | .. | .. | .. | .. |
| 9 | (a) | Leicester C | W 3-0 | Richardson 2, Hodgetts | 6,971 | .. | .. | .. | .. | .. | McNab | Hodgetts | .. | .. | .. | Finch |
| 16 | (h) | Leicester C | D 2-2 | Richardson 2 | 7,090 | .. | .. | .. | .. | .. | .. | Elliott | .. | Clarke | .. | C.Evans |
| 23 | (a) | Aston Villa | L 1-3 | Richardson | 19,000 | .. | .. | .. | .. | .. | .. | .. | .. | .. | Armstrong | .. |
| 30 | (h) | Aston Villa | W 5-4 | Richardson 2, Elliott 2, Evans | 23,550 | .. | .. | .. | Sankey | .. | Millard | .. | Ball | .. | C.Evans | Hodgetts |
| Nov 6 | (a) | Stoke C | D 3-3 | Richardson, Elliott (pen), Hodgetts | 3,520 | .. | .. | Southam | .. | .. | .. | Armstrong | .. | .. | .. | .. |
| 13 | (h) | Stoke C | W 3-0 | Richardson 2, C.Evans | 6,912 | .. | .. | .. | Witcomb | .. | .. | Hodgetts | C.Evans | .. | A.Evans | Russell |
| 20 | (a) | Walsall | L 0-2 | | 4,297 | .. | .. | .. | Edwards | .. | .. | Elliott | .. | .. | .. | .. |
| 27 | (h) | Walsall | L 1-4 | Duns | 4,556 | .. | .. | .. | Millard | .. | McNab | .. | Edwards | Armstrong | C.Evans | Duns |
| Dec 4 | (h) | Birmingham | L 1-3 | Elliott | 5,494 | .. | Griffiths | A.J.Smith | .. | .. | .. | .. | Wilcoxson | Richardson | A.Evans | .. |
| 11 | (a) | Birmingham | L 0-3 | | 5,156 | .. | Southam | .. | Sankey | .. | Millard | Hodgetts | E.Jones | .. | Armstrong | Finch |
| 18 | (h) | Coventry C | W 3-0 | Elliott 2, Clarke | 2,647 | .. | .. | .. | .. | .. | .. | Elliott | Clarke | Ball | C.Evans | Duns |
| 25 | (a) | Coventry C | L 0-8 | | 7,000 | .. | Ashley | .. | .. | .. | .. | .. | Ball | Richardson | .. | Hodgetts |
| 27 | (h) | Birmingham § | D 1-1 | Elliott (pen) | 14,717 | .. | Southam | .. | Millard | .. | McNab | .. | Clarke | Ball | .. | Finch |
| Jan 1 | (a) | Birmingham § | L 0-4 | | 9,142 | .. | Millard | .. | Witcomb | .. | .. | Duns | Heaselgrave | Richardson | .. | E.Jones |
| 8 | (a) | Walsall § | D 2-2 | Ball 2 | 5,793 | Adams | Southam | .. | Millard | .. | .. | .. | Witcomb | Ball | .. | Finch |
| 15 | (h) | Walsall § | W 7-1 | Ball 3, Elliott 3, Witcomb | 4,800 | .. | .. | .. | .. | .. | .. | Elliott | .. | .. | .. | Hodgetts |
| 22 | (h) | Coventry C § | D 2-2 | Elliott, Witcomb | 5,577 | .. | .. | .. | .. | .. | .. | .. | .. | .. | .. | .. |
| 29 | (a) | Coventry C § | D 3-3 | Elliott 2, Ball | 8,500 | Heath | .. | .. | .. | .. | .. | .. | .. | E.Jones | .. | .. |
| Feb 5 | (a) | Northampton T §L | 0-2 | | 4,381 | .. | .. | .. | .. | .. | .. | .. | .. | .. | .. | .. |
| 12 | (a) | Northampton T §W | 3-1 | Ball 2, Hodgetts | 4,503 | .. | .. | .. | .. | .. | Edwards | Hodgetts | .. | .. | C.Evans | Russell |
| 19 | (h) | Stoke C § | L 2-8 | Duns, Elliott | 5,000 | .. | .. | .. | .. | .. | McNab | Elliott | E.Jones | Duns | .. | Hodgetts |
| 26 | (a) | Stoke C § | L 4-5 | Elliott 3, Duns | 8,030 | .. | .. | .. | .. | .. | Williams | Duns | McNab | Elliott | .. | .. |
| Mar 4 | (h) | Nottingham F * | L 0-1 | | 3,392 | .. | .. | Pemberton | Edwards | .. | .. | .. | Richardson | .. | .. | .. |
| 11 | (a) | Nottingham F * | L 2-3 | Pears, Russell | 6,346 | .. | .. | A.J.Smith | Gripton | McNab | Hodgetts | Heaselgrave | Pears | .. | Russell |
| 18 | (h) | Wolves * | W 5-0 | Elliott 3, Hodgetts, Guest | 4,588 | Adams | .. | .. | .. | .. | Williams | .. | .. | Elliott | .. | Guest |
| 25 | (h) | Wolves * | D 3-3 | Heaselgrave 2, Guest | 6,281 | .. | .. | .. | Bradley | .. | McNab | .. | .. | .. | .. | .. |
| Apr 1 | (a) | Walsall * | D 2-2 | Acquaroff 2 | 2,120 | .. | White | Southam | .. | .. | .. | .. | Acquaroff | .. | Rowley |
| 8 | (h) | Walsall * | W 1-0 | Acquaroff | 5,588 | Heath | .. | A.J.Smith | .. | .. | .. | .. | .. | .. | .. | Guest |
| 10 | (a) | Aston Villa § | L 1-4 | Heaselgrave | 15,000 | .. | Adderley | .. | .. | .. | .. | .. | .. | .. | .. | .. |
| 15 | (h) | Stoke C * | D 1-1 | Elliott | 3,434 | .. | Millard | .. | Williams | .. | Elliott | .. | .. | .. | Hodgetts |
| 22 | (h) | Stoke C * | W 3-1 | Elliott, Heaselgrave, Richardson | 7,202 | .. | Southam | .. | Millard | .. | .. | .. | Richardson | .. | .. |
| 29 | (h) | Nottingham F * | D 2-2 | Richardson, Evans | 8,373 | .. | .. | .. | .. | .. | .. | Hodgetts | .. | .. | Finch |
| May 6 | (a) | Nottingham F * | W 4-3† | Acquaroff 2, Hodgetts, Clarke | 14,438 | .. | .. | .. | .. | .. | Heaselgrave | Acquaroff | Clarke | .. | Hodgetts |

## OTHER MATCHES

| Date | | Opponent | Result | Scorers | Att | 1 | 2 | 3 | 4 | 5 | 6 | 7 | 8 | 9 | 10 | 11 |
|---|---|---|---|---|---|---|---|---|---|---|---|---|---|---|---|---|
| Feb 19 | (a) | Aston Villa | W 4-2 | Heaselgrave 2, Clarke, Russell | 4,067 | Adams | Bradley | Pemberton | Sankey | Tranter | Williams | .. | Clarke | Pears | Bowen | Russell |
| Mar 25 | (h) | Aston Villa | W 8-2 | Clarke 5, Pears 3 | 2,155 | Saunders | Ashley | Adderley | Rollason | .. | Sankey | Yuell | Pears | Clarke | Bell | Ratcliffe |
| Apr 1 | (h) | Wolves | W 3-1 | Clarke 2, Pears | 3,266 | Heath | Davenport | .. | Hampton | .. | Williams | .. | .. | .. | Bowen | .. |
| 15 | (a) | Wolves | W 6-1 | Clarke 4, Bowen, Russell | 3,003 | Adams | .. | .. | Vincent | .. | Ashley | .. | .. | .. | .. | Russell |

§ League Cup matches.   * Midland Cup matches.   † After extra-time.

### APPEARANCES – FOOTBALL LEAGUE NORTH
Acquaroff J 1, Adams J 4, Adderley J 1, Armstrong M 8, Ashley H 1, Ball H 3, Bassett I 14, Clarke I 2, Duns L 8, Edwards C 2, Elliott W 15, Evans A 4, Evans C 15, Finch L 2, Griffiths J 1, Gripton W 19, Guest W 1, Heaselgrave S 1, Heath N 15, Hodgetts F 7, Jones E 3, McCormick J 6, McNab A 9, Millard L 19, Richardson WG 15, Russell T 2, Sankey J 6, Smith AJ 15, Southam J 6, Wilcoxson G 1, Williams G 2, Witcomb D 1. Total 209

### GOALSCORERS – FOOTBALL LEAGUE NORTH
19 Richardson, 12 Elliott, 3 Duns, C.Evans, 2 Hodgetts, 1 Armstrong, Clarke, E.Jones. Total 42

### APPEARANCES – MIDLAND CUP & LEAGUE CUP
Acquaroff J 4, Adams J 6, Ball H 7, Bradley D 1, Clarke I 2, Duns L 5, Edwards C 2, Elliott W 11, Evans C 18, Finch L 3, Gripton L 19, Guest W 3, Heaselgrave S 10, Heath N 14, Hodgetts F 17, Jones E 4, McNab A 18, Millard L 20, Pears W 1, Pemberton J 1, Richardson WG 4, Rowley GA 1, Russell T 2, Smith AJ 17, Southam J 17, White H 2, Williams G 4, Witcomb D 7. Total 220

### GOALSCORERS – MIDLAND CUP & LEAGUE CUP
16 Elliott, 8 Ball, 5 Acquaroff, 4 Heaselgrave, 3 Hodgetts, 2 Duns, Guest, Richardson, Witcomb, 1 Clarke, Evans, Pears, Russell. Total 48

**Frank Hodgetts, star of Albion's Midland Cup-winning team against Nottingham Forest in 1944.**

## 1944-45

| Date | | Venue | Opponent | Result | Score | Goalscorers | Att. | 1 | 2 | 3 | 4 | 5 | 6 | 7 | 8 | 9 | 10 | 11 |
|---|---|---|---|---|---|---|---|---|---|---|---|---|---|---|---|---|---|---|
| Aug | 26 | (a) | Northampton T | W | 4-1 | Evans, Richardson, Elliott(pen), Hodgetts | 5,890 | Adams | Southam | Millard | Sankey | Gripton | McNab | Elliott | Heaselgrave | Richardson | Evans | Hodgetts |
| Sep | 2 | (h) | Northampton T | W | 3-1 | Heaselgrave 2, Hodgetts | 5,998 | .. | .. | .. | Williams | .. | .. | .. | .. | .. | .. | .. |
| | 9 | (h) | Port Vale | W | 2-1 | Rowley, Elliott | 7,749 | .. | .. | .. | .. | .. | .. | Hodgetts | .. | Elliott | .. | Rowley |
| | 16 | (a) | Port Vale | D | 0-0 | | 6,000 | .. | .. | .. | .. | .. | .. | Jones | .. | Richardson | .. | Hodgetts |
| | 23 | (a) | Coventry C | D | 1-1 | Clarke | 8,245 | Heath | Sankey | .. | .. | .. | .. | .. | .. | Clarke | .. | .. |
| | 30 | (h) | Coventry C | W | 4-1 | Clarke 3, Hodgetts | 9,512 | .. | .. | .. | .. | Tranter | .. | Hodgetts | .. | .. | .. | Rowley |
| Oct | 7 | (h) | Leicester C | D | 1-1 | Heaselgrave | 9,970 | .. | .. | Kinsell | Millard | Gripton | .. | .. | .. | .. | .. | Johnson |
| | 14 | (a) | Leicester C | W | 2-0 | Evans, Clarke | 7,201 | .. | Tranter | Millard | Vincent | .. | Lowery | Elliott | .. | .. | .. | Hodgetts |
| | 21 | (a) | Aston Villa | D | 2-2 | Rowley (pen), Clarke | 25,200 | .. | .. | .. | Williams | .. | McNab | Hodgetts | .. | .. | .. | Rowley |
| | 28 | (h) | Aston Villa | L | 1-5 | Clarke | 25,487 | .. | Sankey | .. | .. | .. | .. | .. | .. | .. | .. | .. |
| Nov | 4 | (h) | Stoke C | L | 2-3 | Elliott, Evans | 18,656 | Lewis | Tranter | .. | .. | .. | .. | Elliott | .. | .. | .. | Hodgetts |
| | 11 | (a) | Stoke C | W | 3-2 | Clarke 3 | 8,067 | .. | .. | .. | .. | .. | .. | Hodgetts | .. | .. | .. | Johnson |
| | 18 | (a) | Wolves | L | 2-3 | Clarke, Johnson | 12,485 | .. | .. | .. | .. | .. | .. | .. | .. | .. | .. | .. |
| | 25 | (a) | Wolves | W | 3-2 | Heaselgrave, Evans, Elliott | 5,916 | .. | .. | .. | .. | .. | .. | Elliott | .. | .. | .. | Hodgetts |
| Dec | 2 | (h) | Walsall | W | 3-0 | Elliott 2, Clarke | 8,992 | .. | .. | .. | .. | .. | .. | .. | Ball | .. | .. | .. |
| | 9 | (a) | Walsall | W | 2-1 | Clarke 2 | 5,303 | .. | .. | .. | .. | .. | .. | Hodgetts | .. | .. | .. | Johnson |
| | 16 | (a) | Birmingham | L | 0-2 | | 6,796 | .. | .. | .. | .. | .. | .. | .. | .. | .. | .. | Rowley |
| | 23 | (h) | Birmingham | L | 1-4 | Heaselgrave | 5,000 | .. | Southam | Kinsell | Sankey | .. | Williams | Elliott | Heaselgrave | .. | .. | Hodgetts |
| | 26 | (a) | Aston Villa | W | 4-3 | Clarke 3, McNab | 5,007 | .. | Tranter | Millard | Williams | .. | McNab | Hodgetts | .. | .. | .. | Rowley |
| | 30 | (h) | Coventry C § | D | 1-1 | Heaselgrave | 8,659 | .. | .. | .. | .. | .. | .. | .. | .. | .. | .. | Jones |
| Jan | 6 | (h) | Aston Villa § | L | 1-3 | Ball | 21,995 | .. | .. | .. | Sankey | .. | .. | Elliott | .. | .. | Ball | Hodgetts |
| | 13 | (a) | Aston Villa § | L | 2-6 | McNab, Heaselgrave | 15,000 | .. | .. | .. | .. | .. | .. | .. | .. | Ball | Clarke | .. |
| Feb | 3 | (h) | Walsall § | L | 0-2 | | 6,334 | .. | Millard | Kinsell | Lowery | .. | .. | Hodgetts | Ball | Richardson | Barlow | Johnson |
| | 10 | (a) | Walsall § | D | 0-0 | | 6,376 | .. | Tranter | Millard | .. | .. | .. | .. | Heaselgrave | Clarke | Parkes | .. |
| | 17 | (h) | Birmingham § | W | 4-0 | Clarke 3, Smith | 12,479 | .. | Millard | Hardwick | .. | .. | .. | .. | .. | .. | .. | Smith |
| | 24 | (a) | Birmingham § | D | 1-1 | Heaselgrave | 17,727 | .. | .. | .. | Sankey | .. | .. | .. | .. | .. | .. | .. |
| Mar | 3 | (a) | Coventry C § | W | 3-0 | Hodgetts 2, Smith | 7,048 | .. | .. | .. | Lowery | .. | .. | .. | .. | .. | .. | .. |
| | 10 | (a) | Northampton T § | D | 2-2 | Heaselgrave 2 | 6,200 | .. | Southam | Millard | .. | .. | .. | .. | .. | .. | .. | Johnson |
| | 17 | (h) | Northampton T § | W | 6-0 | Clarke 3, Heaselgrave, Johnson, Coley(og) | 6,938 | .. | Shelton | Male | .. | .. | .. | .. | .. | .. | .. | .. |
| | 24 | (a) | Bristol C § | L | 2-5 | Clarke, Elliott | 21,371 | .. | Southam | Millard | .. | .. | .. | .. | Elliott | Clarke | .. | .. |
| | 31 | (h) | Bristol C § | D | 3-3 | Parker, Heaselgrave, Clarke | 18,315 | .. | Millard | Parker | .. | .. | .. | .. | Clarke | Evans | Dudley | .. |
| Apr | 2 | (h) | Aston Villa | L | 2-4 | Heaselgrave, Evans | 14,378 | Adams | Tranter | Millard | .. | .. | .. | Bowen | .. | .. | .. | Hodgetts |
| | 7 | (h) | Walsall | D | 1-1 | Clarke | 5,227 | W.Saunders | Millard | Kinsell | .. | .. | .. | Elliott | .. | .. | Bowen | .. |
| | 14 | (a) | Walsall | W | 2-1 | Clarke, Bowen | 1,780 | Lewis | .. | .. | .. | .. | .. | Bowen | .. | .. | Finch | .. |
| | 21 | (h) | Leicester C * | W | 1-0 | Clarke | 5,002 | .. | .. | .. | .. | .. | Williams | Elliott | .. | . | .. | .. |
| | 28 | (a) | Leicester C * | L | 0-3 | | 6,166 | .. | .. | .. | .. | .. | McNab | Bowen | .. | .. | .. | .. |
| May | 5 | (a) | Birmingham | L | 1-4 | Clarke | 1,025 | .. | .. | Parker | .. | .. | .. | Jones | .. | .. | .. | .. |
| | 12 | (h) | Birmingham | L | 2-3 | Saunders, Evans | 10,947 | .. | .. | .. | Williams | .. | .. | Hodgetts | .. | .. | Evans | D.Saunders |
| | 19 | (a) | Wolves | L | 0-1 | | 6,702 | .. | Southam | Millard | .. | .. | .. | .. | .. | .. | Finch | .. |
| | 26 | (h) | Wolves | D | 1-1 | Hodgetts | 4,742 | .. | .. | .. | .. | .. | .. | Bowen | .. | .. | .. | .. |

§ League Cup matches.   * Midland Cup matches.   **Note:** Match on 26 December v Aston Villa (a) was abandoned after 81 minutes due to fog but the result was allowed to stand.

## APPEARANCES - FOOTBALL LEAGUE NORTH

Adams J 5, Ball H 3, Bowen T 4, Clarke I 22, Elliott W 9, Evans C 3, Finch R 4, Gripton W 25, Heaselgrave S 22, Heath N 6, Hodgetts F 26, Johnson J 4, Jones E 3, Kinsell H 4, Lewis E 14, Lowery H 5, McNab A 24, Millard L 25, Parker A 2, Richardson WG 3, Rowley GA 6, Sankey J 6, Saunders D 3, Saunders W 1, Southam J 7, Tranter G 12, Vincent E 1, Williams G 19. Total 286

## GOALSCORERS - FOOTBALL LEAGUE NORTH

20 Clarke, 6 Elliott, Evans, Heaselgrave, 4 Hodgetts, 2 Rowley, 1 Bowen, Johnson, McNab, Richardson, D.Saunders. Total 49

## APPEARANCES - MIDLAND CUP & LEAGUE CUP

Ball H 3, Barlow R 1, Bowen T 1, Clarke I 13, Dudley G 1, Elliott W 4, Evans C 4, Finch R 2, Gripton W 14, Hardwick G 3, Heaselgrave S 13, Hodgetts F 14, Johnson J 5, Jones E 1, Kinsell H 3, Lewis E 14, Lowery H 10, McNab A 13, Male N 1, Millard L 13, Parker A 1, Parkes H 6, Richardson WG 1, Sankey J 3, Shelton 1, Smith L 3, Southam J 2, Tranter G 4, Williams G 2. Total 154

## GOALSCORERS - MIDLAND CUP & LEAGUE CUP

9 Clarke, 7 Heaselgrave, 2 Hodgetts, Smith, 1 Ball, Elliott, Johnson, McNab, Parker. Opp own goal 1. Total 26

• Albion's reserve XI beat Smethwick Highfield 17-0 in a friendly match in January 1945, Tommy Bowen (7) and Ray Barlow (6) were the two principal scorers.

• Forty-four hat-tricks were scored by Albion players (all games) between 1939 and 1946. Top of the list was WG Richardson with 10, Ike Clarke hit 9 and Harry Jones and Billy Elliott 8 each.

| Albion's full playing record 1939-46 | | | | | | |
|---|---|---|---|---|---|---|
| **1939-40** | P | W | D | L | F | A |
| Division Two | 3 | 1 | 1 | 1 | 8 | 8 |
| Midland Regional League | 28 | 18 | 4 | 6 | 87 | 51 |
| League Cup | 6 | 4 | 0 | 2 | 12 | 8 |
| Jubilee Fund | 1 | 0 | 1 | 0 | 1 | 1 |
| **1940-41** | | | | | | |
| Football League South | 28 | 13 | 5 | 10 | 83 | 69 |
| League Cup | 4 | 1 | 0 | 3 | 9 | 13 |
| **1941-2** | | | | | | |
| Football League South | 14 | 10 | 1 | 3 | 65 | 27 |
| League Cup | 17 | 8 | 3 | 6 | 50 | 42 |
| **1942-3** | | | | | | |
| Football League North | 24 | 10 | 4 | 10 | 56 | 56 |
| League Cup | 14 | 7 | 2 | 5 | 28 | 27 |
| **1943-4** | | | | | | |
| Football League North | 19 | 8 | 3 | 8 | 43 | 48 |
| League Cup | 10 | 2 | 4 | 4 | 24 | 29 |
| Midland Cup | 10 | 4 | 4 | 2 | 23 | 16 |
| **1944-5** | | | | | | |
| Football League North | 26 | 11 | 6 | 9 | 49 | 48 |
| League Cup | 12 | 3 | 5 | 4 | 25 | 23 |
| Midland Cup | 2 | 1 | 0 | 1 | 1 | 3 |
| **1945-6** | | | | | | |
| Football League South | 42 | 22 | 8 | 12 | 104 | 69 |
| FA Cup | 4 | 1 | 1 | 2 | 6 | 5 |
| **TOTALS** | 264 | 124 | 52 | 88 | 674 | 543 |

Albion also played a total of 40 'other' matches, winning 25, drawing three and losing 12, with a goal average of 138 for and 81 against.

## 1945-46

| | | | | | | 1 | 2 | 3 | 4 | 5 | 6 | 7 | 8 | 9 | 10 | 11 |
|---|---|---|---|---|---|---|---|---|---|---|---|---|---|---|---|---|
| Aug | 25 | (h) Swansea T | W 4-1 | Clarke, Barlow, Millard, Hodgetts | 18,033 | Harris | White | Kinsell | Witcomb | Gripton | Millard | Hodgetts | Barlow | Clarke | Evans | Butler |
| | 29 | (h) Aston Villa | W 1-0 | Millard | 15,898 | | | | | | | | Elliott | | Barlow | |
| Sep | 1 | (a) Swansea T | W 4-2 | Barlow 2, Hodgetts, White (pen) | 8,223 | | | | | | | | | | | |
| | 5 | (a) Aston Villa | D 3-3 | Elliott (pen), Clarke, Saunders | 36,103 | | | | | | | | | | | D.Saunders |
| | 8 | (a) Birmingham | L 0-4 | | 20,068 | | Southam | Bradley | | | | | Heaselgrave | | | Butler |
| | 12 | (h) Luton T | W 3-1 | Clarke, Elliott, Barlow | 14,146 | | | Shaw | | | | | Elliott | | | |
| | 15 | (h) Birmingham | D 0-0 | | 27,745 | | White | | | Tranter | | | Barlow | Pears | Evans | |
| | 22 | (h) Tottenham H | W 5-0 | Barlow 3, Pears, Butler | 26,002 | | N Williams | | | | | | Elliott | | Barlow | |
| | 29 | (a) Tottenham H | L 2-4 | Barlow, Ward (og) | 31,403 | | Shaw | Kinsell | | | | | | | | |
| Oct | 6 | (h) Brentford | L 3-4 | Rowley 2, Barlow | 29,821 | | White | | | | | | | Rowley | | |
| | 13 | (a) Brentford | L 0-2 | | 20,160 | | | Shaw | | | | | Evans | | | |
| | 20 | (a) Chelsea | L 4-7 | Hodgetts, Elliott, Barlow, Butler | 31,061 | W Saunders | | | | Millard | G Williams | | Elliott | | | |
| | 27 | (h) Chelsea | W 8-1 | Clarke 4, Rowley 2, Hodgetts, Witcomb | 21,905 | Harris | Shaw | Kinsell | | Hood | Millard | Elliott | Clarke | | | Hodgetts |
| Nov | 3 | (h) Millwall | W 3-1 | Clarke, Rowley, Hodgetts | 16,046 | W Saunders | | | | Tranter | | | | | | |
| | 10 | (a) Millwall | W 4-1 | Clarke, Rowley, Barlow, Hodgetts | 20,045 | Sanders | | | | | Ryan | | | | | |
| | 17 | (a) Southampton | W 2-1 | Elliott, Clarke | 17,116 | | | Millard | | | | | | | | |
| | 24 | (h) Southampton | W 5-2 | Elliott 3, Hodgetts, Rowley | 18,768 | | White | | | | | | | | | |
| Dec | 1 | (h) Derby C | L 2-3 | Elliott, Rowley | 29,525 | | | | | | | | | | | |
| | 8 | (a) Derby C | D 3-3 | Newsome 2, Barlow | 24,138 | | Millard | Kinsell | | | | | | Newsome | | |
| | 15 | (a) Leicester C | W 3-1 | Elliott, Newsome, Millard | 14,227 | | Shaw | | | | Millard | | | | | |
| | 22 | (h) Leicester C | W 3-2 | Elliott 2, Newsome | 15,107 | | | | | | | | | | | |
| | 24 | (h) Coventry C | D 2-2 | Clarke, Newsome | 18,038 | | | | | | | | | | Evans | |
| | 26 | (a) Coventry C | L 2-3 | Clarke, Newsome | 19,303 | | | | | | Ryan | | | Gomm | Connelly | Newsome |
| | 29 | (a) Luton T | W 2-1 | Connelly, Saunders | 9,146 | | White | Shaw | Millard | | | | | | | D.Saunders |
| Jan | 12 | (a) Arsenal | L 0-2 | | 22,334 | Twigg | Shaw | Kinsell | Witcomb | | Edwards | | Newsome | Millard | | Butler |
| | 19 | (h) Arsenal | L 0-1 | | 26,014 | Sanders | | | | | Millard | Newsome | Clarke | Gomm | | |
| Feb | 2 | (a) Charlton A | D 1-1 | Clarke | 25,083 | | White | Shaw | | | | | Elliott | Newsome | | |
| | 9 | (a) Fulham | W 4-1 | Elliott, Newsome 2, Freeman (og) | 15,139 | | | Kinsell | | | | | | | | |
| | 16 | (a) Fulham | W 3-1 | Elliott 2, Butler | 20,229 | | | Shaw | | | | | | | | |
| | 23 | (h) Plymouth A | W 5-2 | Clarke 2, Elliott, Connelly, Gomm | 13,117 | | | | Millard | | Ryan | | | Gomm | | |
| Mar | 2 | (a) Plymouth A | W 4-0 | Newsome 2, Connelly, Butler | 20,227 | | | | | | | | | Newsome | | |
| | 9 | (a) Portsmouth | L 0-3 | | 15,987 | | | | Witcomb | | | | Barlow | | | |
| | 16 | (h) Portsmouth | W 2-0 | Elliott, Jinks | 15,908 | | | | | | | | | Jinks | Barlow | |
| | 23 | (h) Nottingham F | W 1-0 | Banks | 19,755 | | | | Millard | | | | | Banks | | |
| | 30 | (a) Nottingham F | W 2-0 | Butler, Hodgetts | 21,529 | | | | | | | Hodgetts | | | | |
| Apr | 6 | (a) Newport C | W 3-0 | Clarke, Banks, Butler | 14,014 | | | | Witcomb | | Millard | | | | | |
| | 13 | (h) Newport C | W 6-0 | Clarke 3, Hodgetts, Butler, Millard | 18,690 | | | | | | | | | | | |
| | 15 | (h) Charlton A | L 2-5 | Banks, Elliott | 5,187 | | | | | | | | Elliott | | | Hodgetts |
| | 20 | (a) West Ham U | D 1-1 | Elliott | 24,630 | | Millard | | | | Ryan | | | | | Butler |
| | 22 | (a) Wolves | D 0-0 | | 36,361 | | | | | | | | | | | |
| | 23 | (h) Wolves | D 1-1 | Banks | 38,077 | | | | | | | | | | | |
| | 27 | (h) West Ham U | L 1-2 | Elliott (pen) | 11,821 | | Shaw | | | | | | | Newsome | | |

# 1946 TOUR TO BELGIUM & LUXEMBOURG

| | | | | | | 1 | 2 | 3 | 4 | 5 | 6 | 7 | 8 | 9 | 10 | 11 |
|---|---|---|---|---|---|---|---|---|---|---|---|---|---|---|---|---|
| May | 1 | (n) Belgian XI | L 4-5 | Banks, Elliott (pen), Hodgetts 2 | 15,212 | | Millard | | | | | | Banks | | | |
| | 4 | (n) Fola Jennesse XI | W 5-1 | Hodgetts, Clarke 2, Elliott, Butler | 7,035 | Twigg | Pemberton | * | | Millard | | | | | Hodgetts | Butler |
| | 8 | (n) Anderlecht | D 1-1 | Hodgetts | 8,540 | Sanders | Millard | | | | Ryan | | | | Barlow | Hodgetts § |

* Substituted by Ryan. § Substituted by Butler.

### APPEARANCES – FOOTBALL LEAGUE SOUTH

Banks G 8, Barlow R 32, Bradley D 1, Butler S 25, Clarke I 35, Connelly E 10, Edwards C 1, Elliott W 34, Evans C 4, Gomm B 4, Gripton W 6, Harris W 12, Heaselgrave S 1, Hodgetts F 29, Hood GO 1, Jinks J 1, Kinsell H 31, Millard L 37, Newsome R 12, Pears W 3, Rowley GA 9, Ryan RA 17, Sanders J 27, Saunders D 2, Saunders W 2, Shaw C 29, Southam J 2, Tranter G 34, Twigg L 1, White H 13, Williams G 1, Williams N 1, Witcomb D 37. Total 462

### GOALSCORERS – FOOTBALL LEAGUE SOUTH

19 Clarke, Elliott, 12 Barlow, 10 Newsome, 9 Hodgetts, 8 Rowley, 7 Butler, 4 Banks, Millard, 3 Connelly, 2 D.Saunders, 1 Gomm, Jinks, Pears, White, Witcomb. Opp own goal 2. Total 104

**Players with 50 or more wartime appearances to their credit:**

| | | | |
|---|---|---|---|
| 195 | W.Gripton | 100 | I.Clarke |
| 153 | L.Millard | 92 | I.Bassett |
| 152 | W.Elliott | 90 | W.G.Richardson |
| 134 | A.McNab | 88 | J.Johnson |
| 133 | J.Sankey | 71 | H.Kinsell |
| 131 | C.Shaw | 62 | A.J.Smith |
| 129 | C.Evans | 62 | D.Witcomb |
| 111 | J.Adams | 60 | E.Connelly |
| 111 | S.Heaselgrave | 60 | C.Edwards |
| 109 | F.Hodgetts | 59 | R.Newsome |
| | | 54 | G.Tranter |

Totals include Division Two, FA Cup, League South and North, League Cup and Midland Cup matches, 1939-1946 inclusive.
W.Gripton also played in 13 'other' matches to total 208 in wartime football.

• The two Chelsea-Albion games in 1945-6 produced 20 goals — Albion winning 8-1 at home but losing 7-4 away.

• At the start of 1945-6 season there was a penalty-kick awarded in each of Albion's first five matches — a club record.

• A total of 15 players scored on their debuts for Albion between September 1939 and April 1946.

• Albion's average home wartime attendance — in all major competitions — was around the 9,000 mark. In 1945-6 their average home League gate was 19,992 — aggregate 419,832.

**Bill Saunders made two appearances in goal during 1945-46.**

# Albion in the FA Cup

**1883-84**
**Round 1**
**Nov 10 v Wednesbury Town (h) 0-2**
Roberts; H.Bell, Stanton, E.Horton, Bunn, Swallow, Whitehouse, Aston, Bisseker, Timmins, G.Bell.
*Att: 5,129*

**1884-85**
**Round 1**
**Oct 25 v Junction Street School, Derby (a) 7-1**
*Bayliss 2, G.Bell 2, Aston 2, Loach*
Roberts; H.Bell, H.Green, E.Horton, Bunn, Stanton, Woodall, Aston, Bayliss, Loach, G.Bell.
*Att: 4,000*
**Round 2**
**Dec 6 v Wednesbury Old Athletic (h) 4-2**
*Aston 2, Woodhall, Taylor (og)*
Roberts; J.Horton, H.Green, E.Horton, Bunn, Stanton, Woodhall, Aston, Bayliss, Loach, G.Bell.
*Att: 4,497*
**Round 3**
**Jan 3 v Aston Villa (a) 0-0**
Roberts; H.Bell, H.Green, E.Horton, Bunn, Stanton, Woodhall, Aston, Bayliss, Loach, G.Bell.
*Att: 22,088*
**Replay**
**Jan 10 v Aston Villa (h) 3-0**
*Loach 2, Bayliss*
Roberts; H.Bell, H.Green, E.Horton, Bunn, Stanton, Woodhall, Aston, Bayliss, Loach, G.Bell.
*Att: 10,021*
**Round 4**
**Jan 24 v Druids (h) 1-0**
*Loach*
Roberts; H.Bell, H.Green, E.Horton, Bunn, Stanton, Woodhall, Aston, Bayliss, Loach, G.Bell.
*Att: 5,537*
**Round 5**
Albion received a bye
**Round 6**
**Feb 21 v Blackburn Rovers (h) 0-2**
Matthews; H.Bell, H.Green, E.Horton, Bunn, Timmins, Woodhall, Aston, Bayliss, Loach, G.Bell.
*Att: 16,393*

**1885-86**
**Round 1**
**Oct 31 v Aston Unity (h) 4-1**
*T.Green 2, Woodhall 2*
Roberts; H.Green, H.Bell, E.Horton, Bunn, Timmins, Woodhall, T.Green, Bayliss, Loach, G.Bell.
*Att: 4,027*
**Round 2**
**Nov 21 v Wednesbury Old Athletic (h) 3-2**
*Loach 2, G.Bell*
Roberts; H.Green, H.Bell, E.Horton, Bushell, Timmins, Woodhall, T.Green, Bayliss, Loach, G.Bell.
*Att: 3,578*
**Round 3**
Albion received a bye
**Round 4**
**Jan 2 v Wolverhampton Wanderers (h) 3-1**
*G.Bell, T.Green, Loach*
Roberts; H.Green, H.Bell, E.Horton, Bunn, Timmins, Woodhall, Bayliss, T.Green, Loach, G.Bell.
*Att: 5,196*
**Round 5**
**Jan 23 v Old Carthusians (h) 1-0**
*T.Green*
Roberts; H.Green, H.Bell, E.Horton, Bunn, Timmins, Woodhall, Bayliss, T.Green, Loach, G.Bell.
*Att: 8,137*

**Round 6**
**Feb 13 v Old Westminsters (h) 6-0**
*Bayliss 3, G.Bell 2, Woodhall*
Roberts; H.Green, H.Bell, E.Horton, Bunn, Timmins, Woodhall, Bayliss, T.Green, Loach, G.Bell.
*Att: 5,884*
**Semi-final**
**Mar 6 v Small Heath (at Aston) 4-0**
*Loach 2, Woodhall 2*
Roberts; H.Green, H.Bell, E.Horton, Bunn, Timmins, Woodhall, Bayliss, T.Green, Loach, G.Bell.
*Att: 4,100*
**Final**
**Apr 3 v Blackburn Rovers (at The Oval) 0-0**
Roberts; H.Green, H.Bell, E.Horton, C.Perry, Timmins, Woodhall, T.Green, Bayliss, Loach, G.Bell.
*Att: 15,156*
**Replay**
**Apr 10 v Blackburn Rovers (at Derby) 0-2**
Roberts; H.Green, H.Bell, E.Horton, C.Perry, Timmins, Woodhall, T.Green, Bayliss, Loach, G.Bell.
*Att: 16,144*

**1886-87**
**Round 1**
**Oct 30 v Burton Wanderers (h) 6-0**
*T.Green 2, Bayliss 2, Holden, Paddock*
Roberts; Aldridge, H.Green, E.Horton, C.Perry, Timmins, Woodhall, T.Green, Bayliss, Holden, W.Paddock.
*Att: 5,107*
**Round 2**
**Nov 20 v Derby Junction (a) 2-1**
*G.Bell, Roberts\**
Roberts; Aldridge, Walker, E.Horton, J.Horton, Bayliss, Woodhall, Holden, T.Green, W.Paddock, G.Bell.
*Att: 2,100*
*\*'Roberts, the goalkeeper, punted the ball downfield and, following a scrimmage in the Derby goalmouth, the ball suddenly passed between the posts.'*
**Round 3** Albion received a bye
**Round 4**
**Jan 15 v Mitchell's St George (at Aston) 1-0**
*T.Green*
Roberts; H.Green, Aldridge, E.Horton, C.Perry, Timmins, Woodhall, Holden, Bayliss, T.Green, W.Paddock.
*Att: 4,061*
**Round 5**
**Jan 29 v Lockwood Brothers, Sheffield (a) 1-0\***
*Woodhall*
Roberts; H.Green, Aldridge, E.Horton, C.Perry, Timmins, Woodhall, T.Green, Bayliss, Holden, W.Paddock.
*Att: 6,029*
*\*Following a protest about the goal, the tie was replayed as follows:*
**Feb 12 v Lockwood Brothers, Sheffield (at Derby) 2-1**
*T.Green, Paddock*
Roberts; Aldridge, H.Green, E.Horton, C.Perry, Timmins, Woodhall, Holden, Bayliss, T.Green, W.Paddock.
*Att: 2,120*
**Round 6**
**Feb 19 v Notts County (a) 4-1**
*Bayliss 2, T.Green, Woodhall*
Roberts; Aldridge, H.Green, E.Horton, C.Perry, Timmins, Woodhall, T.Green, Bayliss, Pearson, W.Paddock.
*Att: 15,067*
**Semi-final**
**Mar 5 v Preston North End (at Nottingham) 3-1**
*Pearson 2, Paddock*
Roberts; Aldridge, H.Green, E.Horton, C.Perry, Timmins, Woodhall, T.Green, Bayliss, Pearson, W.Paddock.
*Att: 16,068*

**1887-88**
**Round 1**
**Oct 15 v Wednesbury Old Athletic (h) 7-1**
*Bayliss 3, Wilson 2, Pearson, Horton*
Roberts; Aldridge, H.Green, E.Horton, C.Perry, Timmins, Woodhall, Bassett, Bayliss, Wilson, Pearson.
*Att: 2,484*
**Round 2**
**Nov 5 v Mitchell's St George (a) 1-0**
*Bayliss*
Roberts; Aldridge, H.Green, E.Horton, C.Perry, Timmins, Woodhall, Bassett, Bayliss, Pearson, Wilson.
*Att: 7,800*
**Round 3**
**Nov 26 v Wolverhampton Wanderers (h) 2-0**
*Bassett, Wilson*
Roberts; Aldridge, H.Green, E.Horton, C.Perry, Timmins, Bassett, Woodhall, Bayliss, Askin, Wilson.
*Att: 7,429*
**Round 4**
Albion received a bye
**Round 5**
**Jan 7 v Stoke (h) 4-1**
*Bayliss 4*
Roberts; Aldridge, H.Green, E.Horton, C.Perry, Timmins, Woodhall, Bassett, Pearson, Wilson.
*Att: 9,093*
**Round 6**
**Jan 28 v Old Carthusians (h) 4-2**
*Pearson 2, Wilson 2*
Roberts; Aldridge, H.Green, E.Horton, C.Perry, Timmins, Bassett, Woodhall, Bayliss, Pearson, Wilson.
*Att: 8,818*
**Semi-final**
**Feb 18 v Derby Junction (at Stoke) 3-0**
*Bayliss, Wilson, Woodhall*
Roberts; Aldridge, H.Green, E.Horton, C.Perry, Timmins, Bassett, Woodhall, Bayliss, Pearson, Wilson.
*Att: 5,996*
**Final**
**Mar 24 v Preston North End (at The Oval) 2-1**
*Bayliss, Woodhall*
Roberts; Aldridge, H.Green, E.Horton, C.Perry, Timmins, Woodhall, Bassett, Bayliss, Pearson, Wilson.
*Att: 18,904*

**1888-89**
**Round 1**
**Feb 2 v Small Heath (a) 3-2**
*W.Perry, Wilson, Pearson*
Roberts; Robinson, H.Green, E.Horton, C.Perry, Timmins, Bassett, W.Perry, Bayliss, Pearson, Wilson.
*Att: 3,034*
**Round 2**
**Feb 16 v Burnley (h) 5-1**
*Bayliss 2, Bassett, Wilson, W.Perry*
Roberts; Robinson, H.Green, E.Horton, C.Perry, Timmins, Bassett, W.Perry, Bayliss, Pearson, Wilson.
*Att: 5,104*
**Round 3**
**Mar 2 v Chatham (a) 10-1**
*Wilson 3, Bayliss 2, Bassett 2, Timmins, W.Perry, Conquer (og)*
Roberts; J.Horton, H.Green, E.Horton, C.Perry, Timmins, Bassett, W.Perry, Bayliss, Pearson, Wilson.
*Att: 17,000*
**Semi-final**
**Mar 16 v Preston North End (at Sheffield) 0-1**
Roberts; Robinson, H.Green, E.Horton, C.Perry, Timmins, Bassett, W.Perry, Bayliss, Pearson, Wilson.
*Att: 22,688*

**1889-90**
**Round 1**
**Jan 18 v Accrington (a) 1-3***
*Wilson*
Roberts; J.Horton, H.Green, E.Horton, C.Perry, J.Nicholls, Bassett, Bayliss, Evans, Pearson, Wilson.
*Att: 3,400*
*Albion protested about the ground and the tie was replayed as follows:
**Jan 25 v Accrington (a) 0-3**
Roberts; J.Horton, Powell, E.Horton, C.Perry, J.Nicholls, Bassett, Bayliss, Evans, Pearson, Wilson.
*Att: 5,300*

**1890-91**
**Round 1**
Albion received a bye
**Round 2**
**Jan 31 v Mitchell's St George (a) 3-0**
*Nicholls, Dyer, C.Perry*
Reader; J.Horton, Powell, Bayliss, C.Perry, Dyer, Woodhall, S.Nicholls, Groves, Pearson, J.Burns.
*Att: 7,000*
**Round 3**
**Feb 14 v Sheffield Wednesday (a) 2-0**
*Groves, Pearson*
Reader; Powell, McCulloch, Bayliss, C.Perry, Dyer, Bassett, S.Nicholls, Groves, Pearson, McLeod.
*Att: 16,871*
**Semi-final**
**Feb 28 v Blackburn Rovers (at Stoke) 2-3**
*Groves, Pearson*
Reader; Robinson, Powell, Bayliss, C.Perry, Dyer, Bassett, S.Nicholls, Groves, Pearson, J.Burns.
*Att: 21,774*

**1891-92**
**Round 1**
**Jan 16 v Old Westminsters (a) 3-2**
*McLeod, Pearson, Reynolds*
Reader; Nicholson, McCulloch, Reynolds, C.Perry, Dyer, Bassett, McLeod, Groves, Pearson, Geddes.
*Att: 10,000*
**Round 2**
**Jan 30 v Blackburn Rovers (h) 3-1**
*Pearson 2, Geddes*
Reader; Nicholson, McCulloch, Reynolds, C.Perry, Dyer, Bassett, McLeod, S.Nicholls, Pearson, Geddes.
*Att: 12,135*
**Round 3**
**Feb 13 v Sheffield Wednesday (h) 2-1**
*C.Perry, Nicholls*
Reader; Nicholson, McCulloch, Reynolds, C.Perry, Dyer, Bassett, McLeod, S.Nicholls, Pearson, Geddes.
*Att: 10,477*
**Semi-final**
**Feb 27 v Nottingham Forest (at Molineux) 1-1**
*Geddes*
Reader; Nicholson, McCulloch, Reynolds, C.Perry, Groves, Bassett, McLeod, S.Nicholls, Pearson, Geddes.
*Att: 21,076*
**Replay**
**Mar 5 v Nottingham Forest (at Molineux) 1-1**
*Bassett*
Reader; Nicholson, McCulloch, Reynolds, C.Perry, Groves, Bassett, S.Nicholls, Bayliss, Pearson, Geddes.
*Att: 15,930*
**Second replay**
**Mar 9 v Nottingham Forest (at Derby) 6-2**
*Geddes 3, Bassett, Groves, Perry*
Reader; Nicholson, McCulloch, Reynolds, C.Perry, Groves, Bassett, McLeod, S.Nicholls, Pearson, Geddes.
*Att: 8,024*
**Final**
**Mar 19 v Aston Villa (at The Oval) 3-0**
*Geddes, Nicholls, Reynolds*

Reader; Nicholson, McCulloch, Reynolds, C.Perry, Groves, Bassett, McLeod, S.Nicholls, Pearson, Geddes.
*Att: 32,710*

**1892-93**
**Round 1**
**Jan 21 v Everton (a) 1-4**
*Pearson*
Reader; McCulloch, J.Horton, T.Perry, C.Perry, Groves, Bassett, McLeod, Boyd, Pearson, Geddes.
*Att: 23,867*

**1893-94**
**Round 1**
**Jan 27 v Blackburn Rovers (h) 2-3**
*McLeod 2*
Reader; Nicholson, Crone, T.Perry, C.Perry, Taggart, Bassett, McLeod, Neale, Williams, Geddes.
*Att: 10,243*

**1894-95**
**Round 1**
**Feb 2 v Small Heath (a) 2-1**
*McLeod, Banks*
Reader; C.Perry, Williams, T.Perry, Higgins, Taggart, Bassett, McLeod, W.Richards, Hutchinson, Banks.
*Att: 10,203*
**Round 2**
**Feb 16 v Sheffield United (a) 1-1**
*Bassett*
Reader; C.Perry, Williams, T.Perry, Higgins, Taggart, Bassett, McLeod, W.Richards, Hutchinson, Banks.
*Att: 14,559*
**Replay**
**Feb 20 v Sheffield United (h) 2-1**
*Hutchinson, Foulke (og)*
Reader; C.Perry, Williams, T.Perry, Higgins, Taggart, Bassett, McLeod, W.Richards, Huthinson, Banks.
*Att: 10,025*
**Round 3**
**Mar 2 v Wolverhampton Wanderers (h) 1-0**
*McLeod*
Reader; C.Perry, Williams, T.Perry, Higgins, Taggart, Bassett, McLeod, Hutchinson, W.Richards, Banks.
*Att: 20,977*
**Semi-final**
**Mar 16 v Sheffield Wednesday (at Derby) 2-0**
*Hutchinson, Williams (pen)*
Reader; C.Perry, Williams, T.Perry, Higgins, Taggart, Bassett, McLeod, W.Richards, Hutchinson, Banks.
*Att: 25,013*
**Final**
**Apr 20 v Aston Villa(at The Crystal Palace) 0-1**
Reader; J.Horton, Williams, T.Perry, Higgins, Taggart, Bassett, McLeod, W.Richards, Hutchinson, Banks.
*Att: 42,652*

**1895-96**
**Round 1**
**Feb 1 v Blackburn Rovers (a) 2-1**
*J.Richards, W.Richards*
Reader; J.Horton, Williams, T.Perry, Higgins, Taggart, Bassett, McLeod, Hutchinson, W.Richards, J.Richards.
*Att: 10,035*
**Round 2**
**Feb 15 v Grimsby Town (a) 1-1**
*McLeod*
Reader; J.Horton, Williams, T.Perry, Higgins, Taggart, Bassett, McLeod, Hutchinson, W.Richards, J.Richards.
*Att: 7,108*
**Replay**
**Feb 20 v Grimsby Town (h) 3-0**
*McLeod, W.Richards 2*
Reader; J.Horton, Williams, T.Perry, Higgins, Taggart, Bassett, McLeod, Hutchinson, W.Richards,

Johnson.
*Att: 8,443*
**Round 3**
**Feb 29 v Derby County (a) 0-1**
Reader; J.Horton, Williams, T.Perry, Higgins, Taggart, Bassett, McLeod, Hutchinson, W.Richards, Banks.
*Att: 14,117*

**1896-97**
**Round 1**
**Jan 30 v Luton Town (a) 1-0**
*Flewitt*
Reader; J.Horton, Williams, T.Perry, Higgins, Banks, McLeod, Flewitt, Cameron, W.Richards, Watson.
*Att: 6,898*
**Round 2**
**Feb 13 v Liverpool (h) 1-2**
*Watson*
Reader; Evans, Williams, T.Perry, Higgins, Banks, Dean, Flewitt, Cameron, W.Richards, Watson.
*Att: 16,147*

**1897-98**
**Round 1**
**Jan 29 v New Brighton Tower (h) 2-0**
*Garfield, Flewitt*
Reader; Cave, Williams, T.Perry, Jones, Banks, Bassett, Flewitt, W.Richards, McKenzie, Garfield.
*Att: 15,897*
**Round 2**
**Feb 12 v Sheffield Wednesday (h) 1-0**
*Flewitt*
Reader; Cave, Williams, T.Perry, Jones, Banks, Bassett, Flewitt, Reid, McKenzie, Garfield.
*Att: 16,012*
**Round 3**
**Feb 26 v Nottingham Forest (h) 2-3**
*Williams, Bassett*
Reader; Cave, Williams, T.Perry, Jones, Banks, Bassett, Flewitt, Reid, McKenzie, Garfield.
*Att: 17,483*

**1898-99**
**Round 1**
**Jan 28 v South Shore, Blackpool (h) 8-0**
*Bassett 3, Jones 2, W.Richards, Garfield, Barrow (og)*
Reader; Cave, Williams, T.Perry, Jones, Dunn, Bassett, Simmons, Flewitt, W.Richards, Garfield.
*Att: 5,870*
**Round 2**
**Feb 11 v Bury (h) 2-1**
*W.Richards 2*
Reader; Cave, Williams, T.Perry, Jones, Dunn, Bassett, Simmons, Flewitt, W.Richards, Garfield.
*Att: 14,094*
**Round 3**
**Feb 25 v Liverpool (h) 0-2**
Reader; Cave, Williams, T.Perry, Jones, Dunn, Bassett, Simmons, Richards, McKenzie, Garfield.
*Att: 17,124*

**1899-1900**
**Round 1**
**Jan 27 v Walsall (a) 1-1**
*Roberts*
Reader; Adam, Williams, Dunn, Jones, Hadley, S.Brett, T.Perry, Simmons, W.Richards, Roberts.
*Att: 9,106*
**Replay**
**Feb 1 v Walsall (h) 6-1**
*Jones 2, Brett, Roberts, Richards, Simmons*
Reader; Adams, Williams, Dunn, Jones, Hadley, S.Brett, T.Perry, Simmons, W.Richards, Roberts.
*Att: 4,892*
**Round 2**
**Feb 17 v Liverpool (a) 1-1**
*Simmons*
Reader; Adams, Williams, Dunn, Jones, Hadley, Chadburn, T.Perry, Simmons, W.Richards, Roberts.
*Att: 15,116*

**Replay**
**Feb 21 v Liverpool (h) 2-1**
*Dunn, Chadburn*
Reader; Adams, Williams, Dunn, Jones, Hadley, Chadburn, T.Perry, Simmons, W.Richards, Roberts.
*Att: 8,994*
**Round 3**
**Feb 24 v Southampton (a) 1-2**
*Simmons*
Reader; Adams, Williams, Dunn, Jones, Hadley, Chadburn, T.Perry, Simmons, W.Richards, Roberts.
*Att: 10,067*

**1900-01**
**Round 1**
**Jan 26 v Manchester City (h) 1-0**
*Garfield*
Reader; Adams, Chadburn, T.Perry, G.Williams, Hadley, Roberts, Simmons, Stevenson, Wheldon, Garfield.
*Att: 10,026*
The above was the first FA Cup match to be played at The Hawthorns.
**Round 2**
**Feb 23 v Woolwich Arsenal (a) 1-0**
*Garfield*
Reader; Adams, Chadburn, T.Perry, G.Williams, Hadley, Roberts, Simmons, Stevenson, Wheldon, Garfield.
*Att: 11,024*
**Round 3**
**Mar 23 v Middlesbrough (a) 1-0**
*Buck*
Reader; Adams, Dunn, T.Perry, Jones, Hadley, Roberts, Buck, Stevenson, Smith, Walker.
*Att: 24,769*
**Semi-final**
**Apr 8 v Tottenham Hotspur (at Villa Park) 0-4**
Reader; Adams, Dunn, T.Perry, Jones, Hadley, Roberts, Smith, Stevenson, Wheldon, Walker.
*Att: 34,979*

**1901-02**
**Round 1**
**Jan 25 v Bury (a) 1-5**
*Simmons*
Webb; Kifford, Adams, Nurse, Stevenson, Hadley, McLean, Simmons, Lee, Worton, G.Dorsett.
*Att: 5,622*

**1902-03**
**Round 1**
**Feb 7 v Tottenham Hotspur (a) 0-0**
Webb; Kifford, Adams, Nurse, Stevenson, Hadley, McLean, Buck, Lee, Worton, G.Dorsett.
*Att: 26,125*
**Replay**
**Feb 11 v Tottenham Hotspur (h) 0-2**
Webb; Kifford, Adams, Nurse, Stevenson, Hadley, McLean, Elmore, Lee, Worton, G.Dorsett.
*Att: 32,097*

**1903-04**
**Round 1**
**Feb 6 v Nottingham Forest (h) 1-1**
*Simmons*
Webb; Adams, Pennington, Randle, Stevenson, Hadley, A.Smith, Simmons, Lee, Hobson, G.Dorsett.
*Att: 10,367*
**Replay**
**Feb 13 v Nottingham Forest (a) 1-3**
*Smith*
Webb; Adams, Pennington, Randle, Stevenson, Hadley, A.Smith, Simmons, Lee, Hobson, G.Dorsett.
*Att: 15,084*

**1904-05**
**Intermediate Round**
**Jan 14 v Leicester Fosse (h) 2-5**
*Aston\*, Pheasant*
Cook; Pennington, Brittain, Randle, Pheasant,

Manners, Bell, W.Smith, Jack, Aston, H.Brown.
*Att: 5,230*
*Some reports give Smith as the scorer.

**1905-06**
**Round 1**
**Jan 13 v Everton (a) 1-3**
*Haywood*
Stringer; Williams, Pennington, Randle, Pheasant, Manners, Bradley, Simmons, Shinton, Haywood, Law.
*Att: 18,023*

**1906-07**
**Round 1**
**Jan 12 v Stoke (h) 1-1**
*Broad*
Stringer; Betteley, Pennington, Randle, Pheasant, Timmins, Broad, Buck, Shinton, Haywood, Dilly.
*Att: 32,232*
**Replay**
**Jan 17 v Stoke (a) 2-2 (aet)**
*Rankin, Randle*
Stringer; Betteley, Pennington, Randle, Pheasant, Manners, Broad, Buck, Shinton, Dilly, Rankin.
*Att: 13,545*
**Second replay**
**Jan 21 v Stoke (at Villa Park) 2-0**
*Pheasant, Dilly (pen)*
Stringer; Adams, Pennington, Randle, Pheasant, Manners, Broad, Buck, Bradley, Dilly, Rankin.
*Att: 32,050*
**Round 2**
**Feb 2 v Norwich City (h) 1-0**
*Simmons*
Stringer; Betteley, Pennington, Randle, Pheasant, Manners, Broad, Simmons, Shinton, Dilly, Perkins.
*Att: 25,388*
**Round 3**
**Feb 23 v Derby County (h) 2-0**
*Jordan, Buck*
Stringer; Betteley, Pennington, Randle, Pheasant, Manners, J.Williams, Buck, Jordan, Haywood, Dilly.
*Att: 35,529*
**Round 4**
**Mar 9 v Notts County (h) 3-1**
*Jordan 2, Buck*
Stringer; J.Williams, Pennington, Randle, Pheasant, Manners, Parkes, Buck, Jordan, Haywood, Dilly.
*Att: 27,474*
**Semi-final**
**Mar 23 v Everton (at Bolton) 1-2**
*Haywood*
Stringer; J.Williams, Pennington, Randle, Pheasant, Manners, Parkes, Buck, Jordan, Haywood, Dilly.
*Att: 32,381*

**1907-08**
**Round 1**
**Jan 11 v Birmingham (h) 1-1**
*Wilcox*
Stringer; Pennington, Evans, Young, Pheasant, Timmins, Garratt, Buck, Wilcox, Walker, Brookes.
*Att: 36,727*
**Replay**
**Jan 15 v Birmingham (a) 2-1**
*Wilcox, Jordan*
Pearson; Pennington, Evans, Young, Pheasant, Manners, Parkes, Buck, Wilcox, Jordan, Walker.
*Att: 24,895*
**Round 2**
**Feb 1 v Southampton (a) 0-1**
Pearson; Pennington, Evans, Young, Pheasant, Manners, Parkes, Wilcox, Wright, Walker, Buck.
*Att: 18,728*

**1908-09**
**Round 1**
**Jan 16 v Bolton Wanderers (h) 3-1**
*Garraty, Harris (pen), Buck*
Stringer; Pennington, Harris, Baddeley, Timmins,

Manners, Thompson, Buck, Garraty, Bowser, Davies.
*Att: 19,164*
**Round 2**
**Feb 6 v Bradford City (h) 1-2**
*Garraty*
Stringer; Pennington, Harris, Baddeley, Timmins, Manners, Thompson, Buck, Garraty, Bowser, Davies.
*Att: 32,105*

**1909-10**
**Round 1**
**Jan 15 v Clapton Orient (h) 2-0**
*Pailor 2*
Stringer; Burton, Pennington, Garraty, Timmins, Manners, Davies, Hewitt, Pailor, Bowser, Simpson.
*Att: 7,339*
**Round 2**
**Feb 5 v Bristol City (a) 1-1**
*Pailor*
Pearson; Burton, Pennington, Garraty, Waterhouse, Manners, Hewitt, Bowser, Pailor, Buck, Simpson.
*Att: 16,885*
**Replay**
**Feb 9 v Bristol City (h) 4-2**
*Hewitt 2, Pailor, Simpson*
Pearson; Burton, Pennington, Garraty, Waterhouse, Manners, Hewitt, Bowser, Pailor, Buck, Simpson.
*Att: 14,870*
**Round 3**
**Feb 19 v Barnsley (a) 0-1**
Pearson; Burton, Pennington, Garraty, Waterhouse, Manners, Hewitt, Bowser, Pailor, Buck, Simpson.
*Att: 19,121*

**1910-11**
**Round 1**
**Jan 14 v Fulham (h) 4-1**
*Bowser 2, Wollaston, Lloyd*
Pearson; Smith, Pennington, Baddeley, Waterhouse, McNeal, Wollaston, Bowser, Pailor, Buck, Lloyd.
*Att: 18,034*
**Round 2**
**Feb 4 v Derby County (a) 0-2**
Pearson; Smith, Pennington, Baddeley, Waterhouse, McNeal, Thompson, Bowser, Pailor, Buck, Simpson.
*Att: 20,242*

**1911-12**
**Round 1**
**Jan 13 v Tottenham Hotspur (h) 3-0**
*Bowser, Deacey, Wright*
Pearson; Cook, Pennington, Baddeley, Buck, McNeal, Jephcott, Wright, Deacey, Bowser, Shearman.
*Att: 21,947*
**Round 2**
**Feb 3 v Leeds City (a) 1-0**
*Bowser*
Pearson; Cook, Pennington, Baddeley, Buck, McNeal, Jephcott, Wright, Pailor, Bowser, Shearman.
*Att: 21,320*
**Round 3**
**Feb 21 v Sunderland (a) 2-1**
*Pailor 2*
Pearson; Pennington, Cook, Baddeley, Buck, McNeal, Jephcott, Wright, Pailor, Bowser, Shearman.
*Att: 43,383*
**Round 4**
**Mar 9 v Fulham (h) 3-0**
*Bowser 2, Wright*
Pearson; Cook, Pennington, Baddeley, Buck, McNeal, Jephcott, Wright, Pailor, Bowser, Shearman.
*Att: 41,880*
**Semi-final**
**Mar 30 v Blackburn Rovers (at Liverpool) 0-0**
Pearson; Pennington, Cook, Baddeley, Buck, McNeal, Jephcott, Wright, Pailor, Bowser, Shearman.
*Att: 30,063*

**Replay**
**Apr 3 v Blackburn Rovers (at Sheffield) 1-0 (aet)**
*Pailor*
Pearson; Pennington, Cook, Baddeley, Buck,
McNeal, Jephcott, Wright, Pailor, Allan,
Shearman.
*Att: 20,050*
**Final**
**Apr 20 v Barnsley (at The Crystal Palace) 0-0 (aet)**
Pearson; Cook, Pennington, Baddeley, Buck,
McNeal, Jephcott, Wright, Pailor, Bowser,
Shearman.
*Att: 55,213*
**Replay**
**Apr 24 v Barnsley (at Sheffield) 0-1 (aet)**
Pearson; Cook, Pennington, Baddeley, Buck,
McNeal, Jephcott, Wright, Pailor, Bowser,
Shearman.
*Att: 38,555*

**1912-13**
**Round 1**
**Jan 13 v West Ham United (h) 1-1**
*Wright*
Moorwood; Smith, Cook, Waterhouse, Buck,
McNeal, Jephcott, Morris, Wright, Bowser,
Shearman.
*Att: 19,958*
**Replay**
**Jan 16 v West Ham United (a) 2-2 (aet)**
*Gregory, Bowser*
Moorwood; Smith, Cook, Waterhouse, Buck,
McNeal, Jephcott, Gregory, Morris, Bowser,
Shearman.
*Att: 14,762*
**Second replay**
**Jan 22 v West Ham United (at Chelsea) 0-3**
Moorwood; Smith, Cook, Waterhouse, Buck,
McNeal, Jephcott, Gregory, Morris, Bowser,
Shearman.
*Att: 26,689*

**1913-14**
**Round 1**
**Jan 10 v Grimsby Town (h) 2-0**
*Edwards, Morris*
Pearson; Smith, Pennington, Waterhouse, Buck,
McNeal, Jephcott, Edwards, Bentley, Morris,
Shearman
*Att: 13,976*
**Round 2**
**Jan 31 v Leeds City (a) 2-0**
*Bentley, Jephcott*
Pearson; Smith, Pennington, Waterhouse, Buck,
McNeal, Jephcott, Morris, Bentley, Lewis,
Shearman.
*Att: 29,733*
**Round 3**
**Feb 21 v Aston Villa (a) 1-2**
*Bowser*
Pearson; Smith, Pennington, Waterhouse, Buck,
McNeal, Jephcott, Bowser, Bache, Bentley,
Shearman.
*Att: 57,293*

**1914-15**
**Round 1**
**Jan 9 v Hull City (a) 0-1**
Pearson; Smith, Pennington, Waterhouse,
Bowser, McNeal, Jephcott, Crisp, Bache, Morris,
Shearman.
*Att: 12,142*

**1919-20**
**Round 1**
**Jan 10 v Barnsley (h) 0-1**
Pearson; Smith, Pennington, Richardson,
Bowser, McNeal, Crisp, Magee, Bentley, Morris,
Gregory.
*Att: 32,327*

**1920-21**
**Round 1**
**Jan 8 v Notts County (a) 0-3**
Pearson; Smith, Cook, Richardson, Bowser,
McNeal, Crisp, Bentley, A.W.Smith, Morris,
Gregory.
*Att: 32,995*

**1921-22**
**Round 1**
**Jan 7 v Chelsea (a) 4-2**
*Blagden 2, Davies, Crisp*
Pearson; Smith, Pennington, Richardson, Reed,
McNeal, Magee, Blagden, Davies, Morris, Crisp.
*Att: 36,365*
**Round 2**
**Jan 28 v Liverpool (a) 1-0**
*Davies*
Pearson, Smith, Pennington, Richardson, Reed,
Bowser, Magee, Blagden, Davies, Morris, Crisp.
*Att: 42,118*
**Round 3**
**Feb 18 v Notts County (h) 1-1**
*Davies (pen)*
Pearson; Smith, Pennington, Richardson, Reed,
McNeal, Magee, Blagden, Davies, Morris, Crisp.
*Att: 43,853*
**Replay**
**Feb 22 v Notts County (a) 0-2**
Pearson; Smith, Pennington, Richardson, Reed,
McNeal, Magee, Blagden, Davies, Morris, Crisp.
*Att: 24,278*

**1922-23**
**Round 1**
**Jan 13 v Stalybridge Celtic (h) 0-0**
Pearson; Smith, Adams, Magee, Bowser, McNeal,
Spencer, Jones, Davies, Morris, Gregory.
*Att: 24,008*
**Replay**
**Jan 17 v Stalybridge Celtic (a) 2-0**
*Davies, Morris*
Pearson; Smith, Adams, Magee, Bowser, McNeal,
Spencer, Jones, Davies, Morris, Gregory.
*Att: 9,753*
**Round 2**
**Feb 3 v Sunderland (h) 2-1**
*Morris, Jones*
Pearson; Smith, Adams, Magee, Bowser, McNeal,
Spencer, Jones, Davies, Morris, Gregory.
*Att: 56,474*
**Round 3**
**Feb 24 v Charlton Athletic (a) 0-1**
Pearson; Smith, Adams, Magee, Bowser, McNeal,
Spencer, Jones, Davies, Morris, Gregory.
*Att: 31,489*

**1923-24**
**Round 1**
**Jan 12 v Millwall (a) 1-0**
*Carter*
Ashmore; Smith, Perry, Magee, Reed, McNeal,
Glidden, Carter, Bowser, Morris, Fitton.
*Att: 30,922*
**Round 2**
**Feb 2 v The Corinthians (h) 5-0**
*Morris, Reed, Carter, Davies 2 (1 pen)*
Ashmore; Smith, Perry, Richardson, Reed,
McNeal, Spencer, Carter, Davies, Morris,
Gregory.
*Att: 49,005*
**Round 3**
**Feb 23 v Wolverhampton Wanderers (h) 1-1**
*Wilson*
Ashmore; Smith, Perry, Richardson, Reed,
McNeal, Spencer, Carter, G.James, Wilson,
Gregory.
*Att: 53,649*
**Replay**
**Feb 27 v Wolverhampton Wanderers (a) 2-0**
*Wilson, Gregory*
Ashmore; Smith, Perry, Richardson, Reed,
Dutton, Spencer, Morris, G.James, Wilson,
Gregory.
*Att: 40,283*
**Round 4**
**Mar 8 v Aston Villa (h) 0-2**
Ashmore; Smith, Perry, Magee, Reed, McNeal,
Davies, Wilson, G.James, Morris, Gregory.
*Att: 43,743*

**1924-25**
**Round 1**
**Jan 10 v Luton Town (h) 4-1**
*James 3, Wilson*

Ashmore; Smith, Perry, Magee, Reed,
Richardson, Glidden, Carter, James, Wilson,
Byers.
*Att: 30,287*
**Round 2**
**Jan 31 v Preston North End (h) 2-0**
*James, Wilson*
Ashmore; Smith, Perry, Magee, Reed,
Richardson, Glidden, Carter, James, Wilson,
Byers.
*Att: 39,752*
**Round 3**
**Feb 21 v Aston Villa (h) 1-1**
*Carter*
Ashmore; Smith, Baugh, Magee, Reed,
Richardson, Glidden, Carter, James, Wilson,
Byers.
*Att: 64,612*
**Replay**
**Feb 25 v Aston Villa (a) 2-1**
*Gregory, James*
Ashmore; Smith, Baugh, Magee, Reed,
Richardson, Glidden, Carter, James, Gregory,
Byers.
*Att: 60,015*
**Round 4**
**Mar 7 v Sheffield United (a) 0-2**
Ashmore; Smith, Baugh, Magee, Reed,
Richardson, Glidden, Carter, James, Wilson,
Byers.
*Att: 57,197*

**1925-26**
**Round 3**
**Jan 9 v Bristol City (h) 4-1**
*Glidden 2 (1 pen), Carter, Byers*
Ashmore; Smith, Adams, Magee, Reed, Dutton,
Glidden, Carter, James, Davies, Byers.
*Att: 33,293*
**Round 4**
**Jan 29 v Aston Villa (h) 1-2**
*Carter*
Ashmore; Baugh, Adams, Richardson, Reed,
Dutton, Glidden, Carter, James, Wilson, Byers.
*Att: 52,160*

**1926-27**
**Round 3**
**Jan 8 v Hull City (a) 1-2**
*Howarth*
Ashmore; Ashurst, G.Shaw, Magee, Rooke,
Howarth, Glidden, Carter, Short, Davies, Fitton.
*Att: 24,909*

**1927-28**
**Round 3**
**Jan 14 v Arsenal (a) 0-2**
Ashmore; Finch, Shaw, Magee, Evans, Howarth,
Taylor, Glidden, Cookson, Short, Fitton.
*Att: 41,298*

**1928-29**
**Round 3**
**Jan 12 v Grimsby Town (a) 1-1**
*Cookson*
Ashmore; Finch, Shaw, Magee, W.Richardson,
Dale, Glidden, Carter, Cookson, Chambers,
Wood.
*Att: 12,516*
**Replay**
**Jan 16 v Grimsby Town (h) 2-0**
*Cookson, Chambers*
Ashmore; Finch, Shaw, Magee, W.Richardson,
Dale, Glidden, Carter, Cookson, Chambers,
Wood.
*Att: 20,381*
**Round 4**
**Jan 26 v Middlesbrough (h) 1-0**
*Cookson*
Ashmore; Finch, Shaw, Magee, W.Richardson,
Darnell, Glidden, Carter, Cookson, Chambers,
Wood.
*Att: 33,466*
**Round 5**
**Feb 16 v Bradford (h) 6-0**
*Cookson 4, Glidden, Carter*
Ashmore; Finch, Shaw, Magee, W.Richardson,

Darnell, Glidden, Carter, Cookson, Chambers, Wood.
*Att: 30,307*
**Round 6**
**Mar 2 v Huddersfield Town (a) 1-1**
*Glidden*
Ashmore; Finch, Shaw, Magee, W.Richardson, Darnell, Glidden, Carter, Cookson, Chambers, Wood.
*Att: 52,333*
**Replay**
**Mar 6 v Huddersfield Town (a) 1-2**
*Wood*
Ashmore; Finch, Shaw, Magee, W.Richardson, Darnell, Glidden, Carter, Cookson, Chambers, Wood.
*Att: 36,779*

**1929-30**
**Round 3**
**Jan 11 v Wrexham (a) 0-1**
Ashmore; Finch, Shaw, W.Richardson, Evans, Darnell, Glidden, Carter, Cookson, Cresswell, Wood.
*Att: 16,570*

**1930-31**
**Round 3**
**Jan 10 v Charlton Athletic (h) 2-2**
*Wood, Sandford*
Pearson; Shaw, Trentham, Magee, W.Richardson, Edwards, Glidden, Carter, W.G.Richardson, Sandford, Wood.
*Att: 27,249*
**Replay**
**Jan 14 v Charlton Athletic (a) 1-1 (aet)**
*Carter*
Pearson; Shaw, Trentham, Magee, W.Richardson, Edwards, Glidden, Carter, W.G.Richardson, Sandford, Wood.
*Att: 18,703*
**Second replay**
**Jan 19 v Charlton Athletic (at Villa Park) 3-1**
*Carter, Wood, W.G.Richardson*
Ashmore; Shaw, Trentham, Magee, W.Richardson, Edwards, Glidden, Carter, W.G.Richardson, Sandford, Wood.
*Att: 27,764*
**Round 4**
**Jan 24 v Tottenham Hotspur (h) 1-0**
*Wood*
Pearson; Shaw, Trentham, Magee, W.Richardson, Edwards, Glidden, Carter, W.G.Richardson, Sandford, Wood.
*Att: 40,850*
**Round 5**
**Feb 14 v Portsmouth (a) 1-0**
*W.G.Richardson*
Pearson; Shaw, Trentham, Magee, W.Richardson, Edwards, Glidden, W.G.Richardson, Cookson, Sandford, Wood.
*Att: 30,891*
**Round 6**
**Feb 28 v Wolverhampton Wanderers (h) 1-1**
*W.G.Richardson*
Pearson; Shaw, Trentham, Magee, W.Richardson, Edwards, Glidden, Carter, W.G.Richardson, Sandford, Wood.
*Att: 52,285*
**Replay**
**Mar 4 v Wolverhampton Wanderers (a) 2-1**
*Wood, W.G.Richardson*
Pearson; Shaw, Trentham, Magee, W.Richardson, Edwards, Glidden, Carter, W.G.Richardson, Sandford, Wood.
*Att: 46,860*
**Semi-final**
**Mar 14 v Everton (At Old Trafford) 1-0**
*Glidden*
Pearson; Shaw, Trentham, Magee, W.Richardson, Edwards, Glidden, Carter, W.G.Richardson, Sandford, Wood.
*Att: 69,241*
**Final**
**Apr 25 v Birmingham (at Wembley) 2-1**
*W.G.Richardson 2*

Pearson; Shaw, Trentham, Magee, W.Richardson, Edwards, Glidden, Carter, W.G.Richardson, Sandford, Wood.
*Att: 90,368*

**1931-32**
**Round 3**
**Jan 9 v Aston Villa (h) 1-2**
*W.G.Richardson*
Pearson; Shaw, Trentham, Murphy, W.Richardson, Edwards, Glidden, Raw, W.G.Richardson, Sandford, Wood.
*Att: 49,232*

**1932-33**
**Round 3**
**Jan 14 v Liverpool (h) 2-0**
*Wood, W.G.Richardson*
Pearson; Shaw, Trentham, Murphy, W.Richardson, Edwards, Glidden, Carter, W.G.Richardson, Sandford, Wood.
*Att: 29,329*
**Round 4**
**Jan 28 v West Ham United (a) 0-2**
Pearson; Shaw, Trentham, Murphy, Ridyard, Edwards, Glidden, Carter, W.G.Richardson, Sandford, Wood.
*Att: 37,222*

**1933-34**
**Round 3**
**Jan 13 v Chelsea (a) 1-1**
*Robbins*
Pearson; Shaw, Trentham, Murphy, W.Richardson, Sankey, Glidden, Carter, W.G.Richardson, Sandford, Robbins.
*Att: 51,451*
**Replay**
**Jan 17 v Chelsea (h) 0-1 (aet)**
Pearson; Shaw, Trentham, Murphy, W.Richardson, Sankey, Glidden, Carter, W.G.Richardson, Sandford, Robbins.
*Att: 20,061*

**1934-35**
**Round 3**
**Jan 12 v Port Vale (h) 2-1**
*Gale, W.G.Richardson*
Pearson; Shaw, Trentham, Murphy, W.Richardson, Sankey, Gale, Carter, W.G.Richardson, Sandford, Boyes.
*Att: 18,989*
**Round 4**
**Jan 26 v Sheffield United (h) 7-1**
*W.G.Richardson 3, Sandford 2, Carter, Gale*
Pearson; Shaw, Trentham, Murphy, W.Richardson, Sankey, Gale, Carter, W.G.Richardson, Sandford, Boyes.
*Att: 34,908*
**Round 5**
**Feb 16 v Stockport County (a) 5-0**
*W.G.Richardson 2, Carter, Gale, Boyes*
Pearson; Shaw, Trentham, Murphy, W.Richardson, Edwards, Gale, Carter, W.G.Richardson, Sandford, Boyes.
*Att: 24,684*
**Round 6**
**Mar 2 v Preston North End (h) 1-0**
*Gale*
Pearson; Shaw, Trentham, Murphy, W.Richardson, Edwards, Gale, Carter, W.G.Richardson, Sandford, Boyes.
*Att: 56,227*
**Semi-final**
**Mar 16 v Bolton Wanderers (at Leeds) 1-1**
*W.G.Richardson*
Pearson; Shaw, Trentham, Murphy, W.Richardson, Edwards, Gale, Carter, W.G.Richardson, Sandford, Boyes.
*Att: 49,605*
**Replay**
**Mar 20 v Bolton Wanderers (at Stoke) 2-0**
*W.G.Richardson, Sandford (pen)*
Pearson; Shaw, Trentham, Murphy, W.Richardson, Edwards, Gale, Carter, W.G.Richardson, Sandford, Boyes.
*Att: 49,110*

**Final**
**Apr 27 v Sheffield Wednesday (at Wembley) 2-4**
*Sandford, Boyes*
Pearson; Shaw, Trentham, Murphy, W.Richardson, Edwards, Glidden, Carter, W.G.Richardson, Sandford, Boyes.
*Att: 93,204*

**1935-36**
**Round 3**
**Jan 11 v Hull City (h) 2-0**
*Wood, W.G.Richardson*
Pearson; Finch, Trentham, Sankey, W.Richardson, Rix, Mahon, Sandford, W.G.Richardson, Robbins, Wood.
*Att: 27,505*
**Round 4**
**Jan 29 v Bradford (a) 1-1**
*Robbins*
Crowe; Shaw, Trentham, Sankey, W.Richardson, Rix, Mahon, Sandford, W.G.Richardson, Robbins, Wood.
*Att: 14,958*
**Replay**
**Feb 3 v Bradford (h) 1-1 (aet)**
*Sandford (pen)*
Adams; Finch, Trentham, Sankey, W.Richardson, Rix, Mahon, Glidden, W.G.Richardson, Sandford, Wood.
*Att: 27,503*
**Second replay**
**Feb 10 v Bradford (at Old Trafford) 0-2**
Adams; Finch, Trentham, Sankey, Ridyard, Rix, Mahon, Sandford, W.G.Richardson, Robbins, Wood.
*Att: 11,685*

**1936-37**
**Round 3**
**Jan 16 v Spennymoor United (h) 7-1**
*Sandford 2, W.G.Richardson 2, Wood, Jones, Mahon*
Light; Finch, C.Shaw, Murphy, W.Richardson, Boyes, Mahon, Jones, W.G.Richardson, Sandford, Wood.
*Att: 23,746*
**Round 4**
**Jan 30 v Darlington (h) 3-2**
*W.G.Richardson 3*
Light; Finch, C.Shaw, Murphy, W.Richardson, Sankey, Mahon, Jones, W.G.Richardson, Sandford, Boyes.
*Att: 15,917*
**Round 5**
**Feb 20 v Coventry City (a) 3-2**
*Boyes, Mahon 2*
Adams; Finch, C.Shaw, Murphy, Sandford, Edwards, Mahon, Jones, W.G.Richardson, Boyes, Coen.
*Att: 44,492*
**Round 6**
**Mar 6 v Arsenal (h) 3-1**
*Mahon 2, W.G.Richardson*
Adams; Finch, C.Shaw, Murphy, Sandford, Sankey, Mahon, Jones, W.G.Richardson, Boyes, Coen.
*Att: 64,815*
**Semi-final**
**Apr 10 v Preston North End (at Highbury) 1-4**
*Robbins*
Adams; Finch, C.Shaw, Murphy, Ridyard, Sankey, Mahon, Jones, W.G.Richardson, Boyes, Robbins.
*Att: 42,636*

**1937-38**
**Round 3**
**Jan 8 v Newcastle United (h) 1-0**
*W.G.Richardson*
Adams; Finch, C.Shaw, Murphy, Sandford, Sankey, Mahon, Clarke, W.G.Richardson, Boyes, Johnson.
*Att: 33,932*
**Round 4**
**Jan 22 v York City (a) 2-3**
*W.G.Richardson, Pinder (og)*
Adams; Finch, C.Shaw, Murphy, Robbins,

Sankey, Jones, Clarke, W.G.Richardson, Boyes, Johnson.
*Att: 18,795*

**1938-39**
**Round 3**
**Jan 7 v Manchester United (h) 0-0**
Adams; White, C.Shaw, Witcomb, Tudor, McNab, Heaselgrave, Wilkes, Jones, Clarke, Johnson.
*Att: 23,899*
**Replay**
**Jan 11 v Manchester United (a) 5-1**
*Jones 2, Witcomb, Clarke, W.G.Richardson*
Adams; White, C.Shaw, Witcomb, Tudor, McNab, W.G.Richardson, Heaselgrave, Jones, Clarke, Johnson.
*Att: 17,641*
**Round 4**
**Jan 21 v Portsmouth (a) 0-2**
Adams; White, C.Shaw, Witcomb, Tudor, McNab, W.G.Richardson, Heaselgrave, Jones, Clarke, Johnson.
*Att: 36,661*

**1945-46**
**Round 3 (1st leg)**
**Jan 5 v Cardiff City (a) 1-1**
*Connelly*
Sanders; C.Shaw, Kinsell, Witcomb, Tranter, Millard, Elliott, Clarke, Newsome, Connelly, Saunders.
*Att: 28,928*
**Round 3 (2nd leg)**
**Jan 9 v Cardiff City (h) 4-0 (agg 5-1)**
*Clarke 2, Newsome 2*
Twigg; C.Shaw, Kinsell, Witcomb, Tranter, Millard, Elliott, Clarke, Newsome, Connelly, Hodgetts.
*Att: 18,025*
**Round 4 (1st leg)**
**Jan 26 v Derby County (a) 0-1**
Sanders; C.Shaw, Kinsell, Witcomb, Tranter, Millard, Elliott, Clarke, Newsome, Connelly, Butler.
*Att: 31,440*
**Round 4 (2nd leg)**
**Jan 30 v Derby County (h) 1-3 (agg 1-4)**
*Clarke*
Sanders; C.Shaw, Kinsell, Witcomb, Tranter, Millard, Elliott, Clarke, Newsome, Connelly, Butler.
*Att: 35,882*

**1946-47**
**Round 3**
**Jan 11 v Leeds United (h) 2-1**
*Barlow, Walsh*
Sanders; Pemberton, Kinsell, Witcomb, C.Edwards, Millard, Elliott, Duggan, Walsh, Barlow, Hodgetts.
*Att: 31,007*
**Round 4**
**Jan 25 v Charlton Athletic (h) 1-2**
*Elliott*
Sanders; Pemberton, Kinsell, Witcomb, C.Edwards, Millard, Elliott, Duggan, Walsh, Barlow, Hodgetts.
*Att: 29,996*

**1947-48**
**Round 3**
**Jan 10 v Reading (h) 2-0**
*Finch, Drury*
Sanders; Pemberton, Millard, G.Williams, Vernon, Ryan, Gordon, Finch, Drury, A.Evans, Elliott.
*Att: 30,241*
**Round 4**
**Jan 24 v Tottenham Hotspur (a) 1-3**
*Rowley*
Sanders; Pemberton, Millard, G.Williams, Vernon, Ryan, Elliott, McKennan, Walsh, Drury, Rowley.
*Att: 71,853*

**1948-49**
**Round 3**
**Jan 8 v Lincoln City (a) 1-0**
*Barlow*
Sanders; Pemberton, Kinsell, Millard, Vernon, Hood, Elliott, C.Williams, Walsh, Barlow, Haines.
*Att: 19,602*
**Round 4**
**Jan 29 v Gateshead (a) 3-1 (aet)**
*Walsh 2, A.Smith*
Sanders; Pemberton, Kinsell, Millard, Vernon, Hood, Elliott, C.Williams, Walsh, Barlow, A.Smith.
*Att: 16,885*
**Round 5**
**Feb 12 v Chelsea (h) 3-0**
*Walsh 3*
Sanders; Pemberton, Millard, Barlow, Vernon, Hood, Elliott, C.Williams, Walsh, Haines, A.Smith.
*Att: 57,843*
**Round 6**
**Feb 26 v Wolverhampton Wanderers (a) 0-1**
Sanders; Pemberton, Millard, Barlow, Vernon, Hood, Elliott, C.Williams, Walsh, Haines, A.Smith.
*Att: 55,684*

**1949-50**
**Round 3**
**Jan 7 v Cardiff City (a) 2-2**
*C.Williams, Inwood*
Sanders; Pemberton, Millard, Kennedy, Vernon, Ryan, Gordon, C.Williams, Walsh, Barlow, Inwood.
*Att: 39,980*
**Replay**
**Jan 11 v Cardiff City (h) 0-1**
Sanders; Pemberton, Millard, Kennedy, Vernon, Ryan, Gordon, C.Williams, Walsh, Barlow, Inwood.
*Att: 37,358*

**1950-51**
**Round 3**
**Jan 6 v Derby County (a) 2-2**
*Lee, Barlow*
Sanders; Rickaby, Millard, Kennedy, Vernon, Dudley, Allen, Barlow, F.Richardson, Ryan, Lee.
*Att: 24,807*
**Replay**
**Jan 10 v Derby County (h) 0-1**
Sanders; Rickaby, Millard, Kennedy, Vernon, Dudley, Allen, Barlow, F.Richardson, Ryan, Lee.
*Att: 33,223*

**1951-52**
**Round 3**
**Jan 12 v Bolton Wanderers (h) 4-0**
*Lee 2, Allen, Griffin*
Heath; Rickaby, Millard, Kennedy, Horne, Barlow, Griffin, Dudley, Allen, Ryan, Lee.
*Att: 38,428*
**Round 4**
**Feb 6 v Gateshead (at Newcastle) 2-0**
*Allen 2*
Heath; Rickaby, Millard, Kennedy, Horne, Barlow, Griffin, Dudley, Allen, Ryan, Lee.
*Att: 38,681*
**Round 5**
**Feb 23 v Blackburn Rovers (a) 0-1**
Heath; Rickaby, Millard, Kennedy, Horne, Ryan, Griffin, Dudley, Nicholls, McCall, Lee.
*Att: 51,177*

**1952-53**
**Round 3**
**Jan 10 v West Ham United (a) 4-1**
*Lee, Ryan, Allen, Nicholls*
Heath; Rickaby, Millard, Dudley, Kennedy, S.Williams, Griffin, Nicholls, Allen, Ryan, Lee.
*Att: 35,150*
**Round 4**
**Jan 31 v Chelsea (a) 1-1**
*Nicholls*

Heath; S.Williams, Millard, Dudley, Dugdale, Barlow, Mountford, Nicholls, Allen, Ryan, Lee.
*Att: 58,912*
**Replay**
**Feb 4 v Chelsea (h) 0-0 (aet)**
Heath; S.Williams, Millard, Dudley, Kennedy, Barlow, Griffin, Nicholls, Allen, Ryan, Lee.
*Att: 37,974*
**Second replay**
**Feb 9 v Chelsea (at Villa Park) 1-1 (aet)**
*Dudley*
Heath; Rickaby, Millard, Dudley, Dugdale, Barlow, Griffin, Nicholls, Allen, Ryan, Lee.
*Att: 33,534*
**Third replay**
**Feb 11 v Chelsea (at Highbury) 0-4**
Heath; Rickaby, S.Williams, Dudley, Dugdale, Barlow, Griffin, Nicholls, Allen, Ryan, Lee.
*Att: 27,997*

**1953-54**
**Round 3**
**Jan 9 v Chelsea (h) 1-0**
*Greenwood (og)*
Heath; Rickaby, Millard, Dudley, Dugdale, Barlow, Griffin, Ryan, Allen, Nicholls, Lee.
*Att: 35,294*
**Round 4**
**Jan 30 v Rotherham United (h) 4-0**
*Nicholls 2, Allen, Ryan*
Heath; Rickaby, Millard, Dudley, Dugdale, Barlow, Griffin, Ryan, Allen, Nicholls, Lee.
*Att: 48,242*
**Round 5**
**Feb 20 v Newcastle United (h) 3-2**
*Allen 3*
Heath; Rickaby, Millard, Dudley, Dugdale, Barlow, Griffin, Ryan, Allen, Nicholls, Lee.
*Att: 61,088*
**Round 6**
**Mar 13 v Tottenham Hotspur (h) 3-0**
*Barlow, Nicholls 2*
Heath; Rickaby, Millard, Dudley Dugdale, Barlow, Griffin, Ryan, Allen, Nicholls, Lee.
*Att: 51,049*
**Semi-final**
**Mar 27 v Port Vale (at Villa Park) 2-1**
*Dudley, Allen (pen)*
Heath; Rickaby, Millard, Dudley, Dugdale, Barlow, Griffin, Ryan, Allen, Nicholls, Lee.
*Att: 68,221*
**Final**
**May 1 v Preston North End (at Wembley) 3-2**
*Allen 2 (1 pen), Griffin*
Sanders; Kennedy, Millard, Dudley, Dugdale, Barlow, Griffin, Ryan, Allen, Nicholls, Lee.
*Att: 99,852*

**1954-55**
**Round 3**
**Jan 8 v Bournemouth & BA (a) 1-0**
*Williams*
Sanders; Rickaby, Millard, Dudley, Dugdale, Barlow, Jones, S.Williams, Allen, Nicholls, Lee.
*Att: 19,498*
**Round 4**
**Jan 29 v Charlton Athletic (h) 2-4**
*Williams 2*
Davies; Rickaby, Millard, Dudley, Dugdale, Barlow, Griffin, S.Williams, Allen, Nicholls, Lee.
*Att: 36,264*

**1955-56**
**Round 3**
**Jan 7 v Wolverhampton Wanderers (a) 2-1**
*Griffin, Lee*
Sanders; Howe, Millard, Dudley, Kennedy, Summers, Griffin, Setters, Barlow, Allen, Lee.
*Att: 55,564*
**Round 4**
**Jan 28 v Portsmouth (h) 2-0**
*Lee, Allen (pen)*
Sanders; Howe, Millard, Dudley, Kennedy, Summers, Griffin, Setters, Barlow, Allen, Lee.
*Att: 59,448*

**Round 5**
**Feb 18 v Birmingham City (h) 0-1**
Sanders; Howe, Millard, Dudley, Kennedy, Summers, Griffin, Setters, Barlow, Allen, Lee.
*Att: 57,213*

**1956-57**
**Round 3**
**Jan 5 v Doncaster Rovers (a) 1-1**
*Robson*
Sanders; Howe, Carter, Dudley, Kennedy, Barlow, Griffin, Setters, Kevan, Robson, Allen.
*Att: 25,627*
**Replay**
**Jan 9 v Doncaster Rovers (h) 2-0**
*Allen 2*
Sanders; Howe, Carter, Dudley, Kennedy, Barlow, Griffin, Setters, Kevan, Robson, Allen.
*Att: 18,043*
**Round 4**
**Jan 26 v Sunderland (h) 4-2**
*Kevan 2, Horobin, Allen (pen)*
Sanders; Howe, Carter, Dudley, Kennedy, Barlow, Griffin, Horobin, Allen, Kevan, Lee.
*Att: 42,406*
**Round 5**
**Feb 16 v Blackpool (a) 0-0**
Sanders; Howe, Millard, Dudley, Kennedy, Barlow, Griffin, Whitehouse, Allen, Kevan, Lee.
*Att: 32,707*
**Replay**
**Feb 20 v Blackpool (h) 2-1**
*Kevan, Allen*
Sanders; Howe, Millard, Dudley, Kennedy, Barlow, Griffin, Whitehouse, Allen, Kevan, Horobin.
*Att: 48,054*
**Round 6**
**Mar 2 v Arsenal (h) 2-2**
*Allen, Wills (og)*
Sanders; Howe, Millard, Dudley, Kennedy, Barlow, Griffin, Whitehouse, Allen, Kevan, Horobin.
*Att: 53,459*
**Replay**
**Mar 5 v Arsenal (a) 2-1**
*Whitehouse, Kevan*
Sanders; Howe, Millard, Dudley, Barlow, Setters, Griffin, Whitehouse, Allen, Kevan, Horobin.
*Att: 58,757*
**Semi-final**
**Mar 23 v Aston Villa (at Molineux) 2-2**
*Whitehouse 2*
Sanders; Howe, Millard, Dudley, Kennedy, Barlow, Griffin, Whitehouse, Allen, Kevan, Horobin.
*Att: 55,549*
**Replay**
**Mar 28 v Aston Villa (at St Andrew's) 0-1**
Sanders; Howe, Millard, Dudley, Kennedy, Barlow, Griffin, Whitehouse, Allen, Kevan, Horobin.
*Att: 58,067*

**1957-58**
**Round 3**
**Jan 4 v Manchester City (h) 5-1**
*Allen 2, Griffin, Barlow, Ewing (og)*
Sanders; Howe, S.Williams, Setters, Kennedy, Barlow, Griffin, Robson, Allen, Kevan, Horobin.
*Att: 49,669*
**Round 4**
**Jan 25 v Nottingham Forest (h) 3-3**
*Allen, Kevan, Robson*
Sanders; Howe, S.Williams, Setters, Kennedy, Barlow, Griffin, Robson, Allen, Kevan, Horobin.
*Att: 58,163*
**Replay**
**Jan 28 v Nottingham Forest (a) 5-1**
*Kevan, Whitehouse, Griffin, Robson, Howe (pen)*
Sanders; Howe, S.Williams, Setters, Kennedy, Barlow, Griffin, Whitehouse, Robson, Kevan, Horobin.
*Att: 46,445*

**Round 5**
**Feb 15 v Sheffield United (a) 1-1**
*Allen*
Sanders; Howe, S.Williams, Dudley, Kennedy, Barlow, Griffin, Robson, Allen, Kevan, Horobin.
*Att: 55,847*
**Replay**
**Feb 19 v Sheffield United (h) 4-1**
*Kevan 2, Allen (pen), Robson*
Sanders; Howe, S.Williams, Dudley, Kennedy, Barlow, Griffin, Robson, Allen, Kevan, Horobin.
*Att: 57,503*
**Round 6**
**Mar 1 v Manchester United (h) 2-2**
*Allen, Horobin*
Sanders; Howe, S.Williams, Dudley, Kennedy, Barlow, Whitehouse, Robson, Allen, Kevan, Horobin
*Att: 57,574*
**Replay**
**Mar 5 v Manchester United (a) 0-1**
Sanders; Howe, S.Williams, Dudley, Kennedy, Barlow, Whitehouse, Robson, Allen, Kevan, Horobin.
*Att: 60,523*

**1958-59**
**Round 3**
**Jan 19 v Sheffield Wednesday (a) 2-0**
*Jackson, Hogg*
Potter; Howe, S.Williams, Setters, Barlow, Drury, Griffin, Jackson, Allen, Kevan, Hogg.
*Att: 50,455*
**Round 4**
**Jan 24 v Brentford (h) 2-0**
*Kevan 2*
Potter; Howe, S.Williams, Setters, Barlow, Drury, Griffin, Jackson, Allen, Kevan, Hogg.
*Att: 41,948*
**Round 5**
**Feb 14 v Blackpool (a) 1-3**
*Robson*
Potter; Howe, S.Williams, Setters, Barlow, Drury, Griffin, Robson, Allen, Jackson, Hogg.
*Att: 30,415*

**1959-60**
**Round 3**
**Jan 9 v Plymouth Argyle (h) 3-2**
*Kevan 3*
Wallace; Howe, G.Williams, Drury, Kennedy, Robson, Jackson, Burnside, Allen, Kevan, Hogg.
*Att: 27,548*
**Round 4**
**Jan 30 v Bolton Wanderers (h) 2-0**
*Jackson, Burnside*
Wallace; Howe, G.Williams, Drury, Kennedy, Robson, Jackson, Burnside, Allen, Kevan, Hogg.
*Att: 36,411*
**Round 5**
**Feb 20 v Leicester City (a) 1-2**
*Kennedy*
Wallace; Howe, G.Williams, Drury, Kennedy, Robson, Jackson, Burnside, Allen, Kevan, Hogg.
*Att: 37,753*

**1960-61**
**Round 3**
**Jan 7 v Lincoln City (a) 1-3**
*Burnside*
Potter; Howe, G.Williams, Robson, Kennedy, Drury, Macready, Burnside, Allen, Kevan, Jackson.
*Att: 14,025*

**1961-62**
**Round 3**
**Jan 6 v Blackpool (a) 0-0**
Wallace; Howe, S.Williams, Robson, Jones, Drury, Jackson, Burnside, Smith, Kevan, Clark.
*Att: 19,560*
**Replay**
**Jan 10 v Blackpool (h) 2-1**
*Burnside, Smith*
Wallace; Howe, S.Williams, Robson, Jones, Drury, Jackson, Burnside, Smith, Kevan, Clark.
*Att: 27,781*

**Round 4**
**Jan 27 v Wolverhampton Wanderers (a) 2-1**
*Clark 2*
Wallace; Howe, S.Williams, Robson, Jones, Drury, Jackson, Burnside, Smith, Kevan, Clark.
*Att: 46,411*
**Round 5**
**Feb 17 v Tottenham Hotspur (h) 2-4**
*Kevan, Smith*
Wallace; Howe, S.Williams, Robson, Jones, Drury, Jackson, Burnside, Smith, Kevan, Clark.
*Att: 54,992*

**1962-63**
**Round 3**
**Jan 5 v Plymouth Argyle (a) 5-1**
*Kevan 2, Smith, Cram, Newman (og)*
Potter; Howe, G.Williams, Cram, Jones, Drury, Jackson, Fenton, Smith, Kevan, Clark.
*Att: 21,915*
**Round 4**
**Mar 6 v Nottingham Forest (h) 0-0**
Potter; Howe, G.Williams, Cram, Jones, Drury, Jackson, Fenton, Smith, Kevan, Clark.
*Att: 21,511*
**Replay**
**Mar 11 v Nottingham Forest (a) 1-2 (aet)**
*Smith*
Potter; Howe, G.Williams, Cram, Jones, Drury, Jackson, Fenton, Smith, Kevan, Clark.
*Att: 21,540*

**1963-64**
**Round 3**
**Jan 4 v Blackpool (h) 2-2**
*Clark, Howe (pen)*
Potter; Howe, G.Williams, Fraser, Jones, Simpson, Foggo, Fenton, Readfern, Fudge, Clark.
*Att: 22,459*
**Replay**
**Jan 8 v Blackpool (a) 1-0**
*Fenton*
Potter; Howe, G.Williams, Fraser, Jones, Simpson, Foggo, Fenton, Kaye, Fudge, Clark.
*Att: 21,241*
**Round 4**
**Jan 25 v Arsenal (h) 3-3**
*Fenton, Kaye, Jones*
Potter; Howe, G.Williams, Fraser, Jones, Simpson, Foggo, Fenton, Kaye, Jackson, Clark.
*Att: 39,703*
**Replay**
**Jan 29 v Arsenal (a) 0-2**
Potter; Howe, G.Williams, Fraser, Jones, Simpson, Foggo, Cram, Kaye, Jackson, Clark.
*Att: 57,698*

**1964-65**
**Round 3**
**Jan 9 v Liverpool (h) 1-2**
*Astle*
Potter; Cram, G.Williams, Fraser, Jones, Simpson, Fenton, Fudge, Astle, Hope, Clark.
*Att: 29,851*

**1965-66**
**Round 3**
**Jan 22 v Bolton Wanderers (a) 0-3**
Potter; Cram, Fairfax, Lovett, Jones, Fraser, Brown, R.Crawford, Kaye, Hope, Clark.
*Att: 24,425*

**1966-67**
**Round 3**
**Jan 28 v Northampton Town (a) 3-1**
*Astle, Clark, Brown*
Sheppard; Cram, G.Williams, Collard, Talbut, Fraser, Brown, Astle, Kaye, Hope, Clark.
*Att: 16,899*
**Round 4**
**Feb 18 v Leeds United (a) 0-5**
Sheppard; Cram, G.Williams, Collard, Jones, Fraser, Foggo, Brown, Astle, Hope, Clark.
*Att: 41,329*

**1967-68**
**Round 3**
**Jan 27 v Colchester United (a) 1-1**
*Brown (pen)*
Osborne; Colquhoun, G.Williams, Brown, Talbut, Fraser, Krzywicki(Lovett), Kaye, Astle, Hope, Clark.
*Att: 15,981*
**Replay**
**Jan 31 v Colchester United (h) 4-0**
*Astle 2, Kaye, Clark*
Sheppard; Colquhoun, G.Williams, Brown, Talbut, Fraser, Lovett, Kaye, Astle, Hope, Clark.
*Att: 38,448*
**Round 4**
**Feb 17 v Southampton (h) 1-1**
*Brown*
Sheppard; Clarke, Williams, Brown, Talbut, Fraser, Krzywicki, Kaye, Astle, Hope, Clark.
*Att: 29,957*
**Replay**
**Feb 21 v Southampton (a) 3-2**
*Astle 2, Brown*
Osborne*(Lovett); Clarke, Williams, Collard, Talbut, Fraser, Brown, Kaye, Astle, Hope, Clark.
*Att: 26,036*
*Williams went in goal for the injured Osborne.
**Round 5**
**Mar 9 v Portsmouth (a) 2-1**
*Astle, Clark*
Osborne; Colquhoun, Williams, Collard, Talbut, Fraser, Brown, Kaye, Astle, Hope, Clark.
*Att: 42,642*
**Round 6**
**Mar 30 v Liverpool (h) 0-0**
Osborne; Colquhoun, Williams, Brown, Talbut, Fraser, Krzywicki, Kaye, Astle, Collard, Clark.
*Att: 43,503*
**Replay**
**Apr 8 v Liverpool (a) 1-1 (aet)**
*Astle*
Osborne; Clarke, Williams, Fraser, Talbut, Colquhoun, Kaye, Brown, Astle, Collard (Stephens), Clark.
*Att: 54,273*
**Second replay**
**Apr 18 v Liverpool (at Maine Road) 2-1**
*Astle, Clark*
Osborne; Clarke(Stephens), Williams, Fraser, Talbut, Kaye, Brown, Collard, Astle, Hope, Clark.
*Att: 56,139*
**Semi-final**
**Apr 27 v Birmingham City (at Villa Park) 2-0**
*Astle, Brown*
Osborne; Fraser, Williams, Brown, Talbut, Kaye, Stephens, Collard, Astle, Hope, Clark.
*Att: 60,831*
**Final**
**May 18 v Everton (at Wembley) 1-0 (aet)**
*Astle*
Osborne; Fraser, Williams, Brown, Talbut, Kaye (Clarke), Lovett, Collard, Astle, Hope, Clark.
*Att: 99,665*

**1968-69**
**Round 3**
**Jan 4 v Norwich City (h) 3-0**
*Rees, Astle (pen), Forbes (og)*
Osborne; Fraser, Wilson, Hughes, Talbut, Kaye, Hope, Lovett, Astle, Collard, Rees.
*Att: 30,004*
**Round 4**
**Jan 25 v Fulham (a) 2-1**
*Hartford, Rees*
Osborne; Fraser, Williams, Brown(Rees), Talbut, Kaye, Hope, Lovett, Astle, Collard, Hartford.
*Att: 31,204*
**Round 5**
**Feb 12 v Arsenal (h) 1-0**
*Brown*
Osborne; Fraser, Wilson, Brown, Talbut, Kaye, Martin, Collard, Astle, Lovett, Hartford.
*Att: 45,354*

**FA Cup winners in 1968. The victorious Albion team after their 1-0 Wembley win over Everton.**

**Round 6**
**Mar 1 v Chelsea (a) 2-1**
*Brown, Astle*
Osborne; Fraser, Wilson, Brown, Talbut, Kaye, Martin, Lovett, Astle, Hope, Hartford (Krzywicki).
*Att: 52,285*
**Semi-final**
**Mar 29 v Leicester City (at Hillsborough) 0-1**
Osborne; Fraser, Wilson, Brown, Talbut, Kaye, Martin(Clark), Lovett, Astle, Hope, Hartford.
*Att: 53,207*

**1969-70**
**Round 3**
**Jan 3 v Sheffield Wednesday (a) 1-2**
*Brown*
Osborne; Fraser, Wilson, Brown, Talbut, Kaye, Krzywicki, Hughes, Suggett, Hartford, Martin.
*Att: 29,174*

**1970-71**
**Round 3**
**Jan 2 v Scunthorpe United (h) 0-0**
Cumbes; Lovett, Wilson, Brown, Talbut, Kaye, McVitie, Suggett, Astle, Cantello, Hartford.
*Att: 22,844*
**Replay**
**Jan 11 v Scunthorpe United (a) 3-1**
*Brown 2, Astle*
Cumbes; Lovett, Wilson, Brown, Talbut, Kaye, McVitie, Suggett, Astle, Hope, Hartford.
*Att: 15,926*
**Round 4**
**Jan 23 v Ipswich Town (h) 1-1**
*Suggett*
Cumbes; Lovett, Wilson, Brown, Talbut, Kaye, McVitie, Suggett, Astle, Hope(Merrick), Hartford.
*Att: 27,178*
**Replay**
**Jan 26 v Ipswich Town (a) 0-3**
Cumbes; Lovett, Merrick, Brown, Talbut, Kaye, McVitie, Suggett, Astle, Hope, Hartford.
*Att: 27,015*

**1971-72**
**Round 3**
**Jan 15 v Coventry City (h) 1-2**
*Brown*
Osborne; Nisbet, Wilson, Cantello, Wile, Robertson, McVitie, Brown, Gould, Suggett, Hartford.
*Att: 26,313*

**1972-73**
**Round 3**
**Jan 13 v Nottingham Forest (h) 1-1**
*Winfield (og)*
Latchford; Nisbet, Wilson, Cantello, Wile, Merrick, Suggett, T.Brown, A.Brown, Hartford, Johnston.
*Att: 15,743*
**Replay**
**Jan 16 v Nottingham Forest (a) 1-1***
*Hartford*
Latchford; Nisbet(Robertson), Wilson, Cantello, Wile, Merrick, Suggett, T.Brown, A.Brown, Hartford, Johnston.
*Att: 19,168*
*Tie abandoned after 79 minutes (fog).
**Replay**
**Jan 22 v Nottingham Forest (a) 0-0 (aet)**
Latchford; Nisbet, Wilson, Cantello, Wile, Merrick, Suggett, T.Brown, A.Brown(Robertson), Hartford, Johnston.
*Att: 17,069*
**Second replay**
**Jan 29 v Nottingham Forest (at Leicester) 3-1**
*Cantello, Hartford, Suggett*
Latchford; Nisbet, Wilson, Cantello, Wile, Merrick, Suggett, T.Brown, A.Brown, Hartford, Johnston.
*Att: 12,606*
**Round 4**
**Feb 3 v Swindon Town (h) 2-0**
*T.Brown, Cantello*
Latchford; Nisbet, Wilson, Cantello, Wile, Merrick, Suggett, T.Brown, A.Brown(Robertson), Hartford, Johnston.
*Att: 20,795*

**Round 5**
**Feb 24 v Leeds United (a) 0-2**
Latchford; Nisbet(A.Brown), Wilson, Cantello,
Wile, Robertson, Merrick, T.Brown, Astle,
Hartford, Johnston.
*Att: 39,229*

**1973-74**
**Round 3**
**Jan 5 v Notts County (h) 4-0**
*T.Brown 3, Johnston*
Latchford; Nisbet, Wilson, Cantello, Wile,
Robertson, Johnston, T.Brown, Shaw, Hartford,
Glover.
*Att: 13,123*
**Round 4**
**Jan 27 v Everton (a) 0-0**
Latchford; Nisbet, Wilson, Cantello, Wile,
Robertson, Johnston, T.Brown, Shaw, Hartford,
Glover.
*Att: 53,509*
**Replay**
**Jan 30 v Everton (h) 1-0**
*T.Brown*
Latchford; Nisbet, Wilson, Cantello, Wile,
Robertson, Johnston, T.Brown, Shaw, Hartford,
Glover.
*Att: 27,556*
**Round 5**
**Feb 16 v Newcastle United (h) 0-3**
Latchford; Nisbet, Wilson, Cantello(Merrick),
Wile, Robertson, Johnston, T.Brown, Shaw,
Hartford, Glover.
*Att: 42,747*

**1974-75**
**Round 3**
**Jan 4 v Bolton Wanderers (a) 0-0**
Osborne; Nisbet, Wilson, Cantello, Wile,
Rushbury, T.Brown, Shaw, Mayo, Hughes,
Johnston.
*Att: 17,305*
**Replay**
**Jan 8 v Bolton Wanderers (h) 4-0**
*Cantello, Wile, Shaw, Mayo*
Osborne; Nisbet, Wilson, Cantello, Wile,
Rushbury, T.Brown, Shaw, Mayo, Hughes,
Johnston.
*Att: 21,210*
**Round 4**
**Jan 25 v Carlisle United (a) 2-3**
*T.Brown (pen), Nisbet*
Osborne; Nisbet, Wilson, Cantello, Wile,
Rushbury, T.Brown, Shaw, Mayo, Hughes,
Johnston.
*Att: 14,843*

**1975-76**
**Round 3**
**Jan 3 v Carlisle United (h) 3-1**
*T.Brown 2 (1 pen), A.Brown*
Osborne; Mulligan, Mayo, Cantello, Wile,
Robertson, T.Brown, Martin, A.Brown, Giles,
Johnston.
*Att: 16,159*
**Round 4**
**Jan 24 v Lincoln City (h) 3-2**
*T.Brown, Martin, Robson*
Osborne; Mulligan, Mayo, Robson, Wile,
Robertson, T.Brown, Martin, A.Brown, Giles,
Johnston.
*Att: 26,878*
**Round 5**
**Feb 14 v Southampton (h) 1-1**
*T.Brown*
Osborne; Mulligan, Mayo, T.Brown, Wile,
Robertson, Martin, Cantello, A.Brown, Giles,
Johnston.
*Att: 36,645*
**Replay**
**Feb 17 v Southampton (a) 0-4**
Osborne; Mulligan, Mayo, T.Brown, Wile,
Robertson, Martin, Cantello, A.Brown(Robson),
Giles, Johnston.
*Att: 27,614*

**1976-77**
**Round 3**
**Jan 8 v Manchester City (a) 1-1**
*Johnston*
Osborne; Mulligan, Cantello, T.Brown, Wile,
Robertson, Martin, Treacy, D.Cross, Trewick,
Johnston.
*Att: 38,195*
**Replay**
**Jan 11 v Manchester City (h) 0-1**
Osborne; Mulligan, Cantello(Robson), T.Brown,
Wile, Robertson, Martin, Treacy, D.Cross,
Trewick, Johnston.
*Att: 27,218*

**1977-78**
**Round 3**
**Jan 7 v Blackpool (h) 4-1**
*Johnston 2, Regis, T.Brown (pen)*
Godden; Martin, Statham, T.Brown, Wile,
Robertson, A.Brown, Regis, Cunningham,
Trewick, Johnston.
*Att: 21,379*
**Round 4**
**Jan 28 v Manchester United (a) 1-1**
*Johnston*
Godden; Mulligan, Statham, T.Brown, Wile,
Robson, Martin, Regis, A.Brown, Trewick,
Johnston.
*Att: 57,056*
**Replay**
**Feb 1 v Manchester United (h) 3-2 (a.e.t.)**
*Regis 2, T.Brown*
Godden; Mulligan, Statham, T.Brown, Wile
(W.Hughes), Robson, Martin, Regis, A.Brown,
Trewick, Johnston.
*Att: 37,792*
**Round 5**
**Feb 22 v Derby County (a) 3-2**
*Regis 2, Johnston*
Godden; Mulligan(Cunningham), Statham,
T.Brown, Wile, Robertson, Martin, Regis,
A.Brown, Trewick, Johnston.
*Att: 32,689*
**Round 6**
**Mar 11 v Nottingham Forest (h) 2-0**
*Martin, Regis*
Godden; Mulligan, Statham, T.Brown, Wile,
Robertson, Martin, Regis, A.Brown(Cunningham),
Trewick, Johnston.
*Att: 36,506*
**Semi-final**
**Apr 8 v Ipswich Town (at Highbury) 1-3**
*T.Brown (pen)*
Godden; Mulligan, Statham, T.Brown, Wile
(Cunningham), Robertson, Martin, A.Brown,
Regis, Trewick, Johnston.
*Att: 50,922*

**1978-79**
**Round 3**
**Jan 9 v Coventry City (a) 2-2**
*Cunnigham, A.Brown*
Godden; Batson, Statham, T.Brown, Wile,
Robertson, Robson, A.Brown, Regis, Trewick,
Cunningham
*Att: 38,046*
**Replay**
**Jan 15 v Coventry City (h) 4-0**
*Batson, T.Brown 2, A.Brown*
Godden; Batson, Statham, T.Brown, Wile,
Robertson, Robson, A.Brown, Regis, Cantello,
Cunningham.
*Att: 36,175*
**Round 4**
**Feb 24 v Leeds United (h) 3-3**
*Cunningham, A.Brown, Regis*
Godden; Batson, Statham, T.Brown, Wile,
Robertson, Robson, A.Brown(Mills), Regis,
Cantello, Cunningham.
*Att: 32,424*
**Replay**
**Feb 26 v Leeds United (h) 2-0 (aet)**
*Wile, A.Brown*
Godden; Batson, Statham, T.Brown(Mills), Wile,

Robertson, Robson, A.Brown, Regis, Cantello,
Cunningham.
*Att: 31,143*
**Round 5**
**Mar 10 v Southampton (h) 1-1**
*A.Brown*
Godden; Batson, Statham, T.Brown, Wile,
Robertson, Robson, A.Brown, Regis, Mills,
Cunningham.
*Att: 30,789*
**Replay**
**Mar 12 v Southampton (a) 1-2 (aet)**
*Cunningham*
Godden; Batson, Statham, Trewick, Wile,
Robertson, Mills, A.Brown, Regis(Johnston),
T.Brown, Cunningham.
*Att: 25,755*

**1979-80**
**Round 3**
**Jan 5 v West Ham United (h) 1-1**
*Regis*
Godden; Batson, Statham, Trewick, Wile,
Robertson, Deehan, A.Brown, Regis, Owen,
Barnes.
*Att: 21,321*
**Replay**
**Jan 8 v West Ham United (a) 1-2**
*T.Brown*
Godden; Batson, Statham, Trewick, Wile,
Robertson, Deehan, A.Brown, Regis, Owen
(T.Brown), Barnes.
*Att: 30,869*

**1980-81**
**Round 3**
**Jan 3 v Grimsby Town (h) 3-0**
*Robson, Cowdrill, Barnes*
Godden; Batson, Cowdrill, Moses, Wile, Bennett,
Robson, A.Brown(Mills), Regis, Owen, Barnes.
*Att: 22,477*
**Round 4**
**Jan 24 v Middlesbrough (a) 0-1**
Godden; Robertson, Cowdrill, Moses, Wile,
Bennett, Robson, A.Brown, Regis, Owen, Barnes.
*Att: 28,285*

**1981-82**
**Round 3**
**Jan 2 v Blackburn Rovers (h) 3-2**
*Whitehead, Mackenzie, King (pen)*
Grew; Batson, Statham, Whitehead, Wile,
Robertson, Jol, Monaghan, Regis, King,
Mackenzie.
*Att: 17,892*
**Round 4**
**Jan 23 v Gillingham (a) 1-0**
*Statham*
Grew; Batson, Statham, A.Brown, Wile, Robertson,
Jol, Whitehead, Regis, Owen, Mackenzie.
*Att: 16,038*
**Round 5**
**Feb 13 v Norwich City (h) 1-0**
*Regis*
Grew; Bennett, Statham, Lewis, Wile, Robertson,
N.Cross, King, Regis, Owen, Mackenzie.
*Att: 18,897*
**Round 6**
**Mar 6 v Coventry City (h) 2-0**
*Regis, Owen*
Grew; Batson, Statham, Bennett, Wile, Robertson,
A.Brown, King, Regis, Owen, Mackenzie.
*Att: 28,045*
**Semi-final**
**Apr 3 v Queen's Park Rangers(at Highbury) 0-1**
Grew; Batson, Statham, Zondervan, Wile,
Robertson, Bennett, King(Owen), Regis, N.Cross,
Mackenzie.
*Att: 45,015*

**1982-83**
**Round 3**
**Jan 8 v Queen's Park Rangers (h) 3-2**
*Owen 2 (1 pen), Eastoe*
Barron; Whitehead, Statham, Zondervan, Wile,
Robertson, Jol, Bennett, Regis, Owen, Eastoe.
*Att: 16,528*

**Round 4**
**Jan 29 v Tottenham Hotspur (a) 1-2**
*Whitehead*
Barron; Whitehead(A.Brown); Statham, Zondervan, Wile, Robertson, Jol, Bennett, N.Cross, Owen, Eastoe.
*Att: 38,208*

**1983-84**
**Round 3**
**Jan 3 v Rotherham United (a) 0-0**
Barron; Whitehead, Cowdrill, N.Cross, McNaught, Bennett, Lewis, Thompson, Regis, Owen(Luke), Morley.
*Att: 8,142*
**Replay**
**Jan 11 v Rotherham United (h) 3-0**
*Thompson, Morley 2*
Barron; Whitehead, Cowdrill, Luke, McNaught, Bennett, Lewis, Thompson, Regis, Owen, Morley.
*Att: 12,107*
**Round 4**
**Feb 1 v Scunthorpe United (h) 1-0**
*Forsyth*
Barron; Whitehead, Cowdrill, Luke, McNaught, Forsyth, Zondervan, Thompson, Regis, Lewis, Morley.
*Att: 18,235*
**Round 5**
**Feb 18 v Plymouth Argyle (h) 0-1**
Barron; Whitehead, Statham, Zondervan, McNaught, Bennett, Jol, Thompson, Perry (Luke), Mackenzie, Morley
*Att: 23,795*

**1984-85**
**Round 3**
**Jan 5 v Orient (a) 1-2**
*Cross*
Godden; Nicholl, Statham(Robson), Hunt, Bennett, Forsyth, Grealish, Thompson, Mackenzie, N.Cross, Whitehead.
*Att: 7,061*

**1985-86**
**Round 3**
**Jan 13 v Sheffield Wednesday (a) 2-2**
*Reilly, Statham*
Godden; Nicholl, Statham, Owen, Bennett, Robertson, Thompson, Varadi, Reilly, Thomas, Dennison.
*Att: 17,042*
**Replay**
**Jan 16 v Sheffield Wednesday (h) 2-3**
*Hunt, Thomas*
Godden; Nicholl, Statham, Hunt, Bennett (Owen), Robertson, Thompson, Varadi, Reilly, Thomas, Dennison.
*Att: 11,152*

**1986-87**
**Round 3**
**Jan 10 v Swansea City (a) 2-3**
*Anderson, Lewis (og)*
Naylor; Whitehead, Anderson(Singleton), Palmer, Dyson, Burrows, Hopkins, Statham, Mackenzie, Williamson, Crooks.
*Att: 8,792*

**1987-88**
**Round 3**
**Jan 9 v Wimbledon (a) 1-4**
*Thorn (og)*
Powell; Dickinson, Cowdrell, Palmer, North, Kelly, Hopkins, Goodman, Reilly, Burrows, Williamson.
*Att: 7,252*

**1988-89**
**Round 3**
**Jan 7 v Everton (h) 1-1**
*Anderson*
Bradshaw; Dobbins, Albiston, Talbot, Whyte, North, Hopkins, Goodman, Robson, Palmer, Anderson(Paskin).
*Att: 31,186*
**Replay**
**Jan 11 v Everton (a) 0-1**
Bradshaw; Dobbins, Albiston, Talbot, Whyte, North, Hopkins, Goodman(Paskin), Robson, Palmer, Bradley.
*Att: 31,697*

**1989-90**
**Round 3**
**Jan 6 v Wimbledon (h) 2-0**
*Robson, Bartlett*
Naylor; Dobbins, Harbey, Robson, North, Whyte, Ford, Goodman, West, McNally, Bartlett.
*Att: 12,986*
**Round 4**
**Jan 27 v Charlton Athletic (h) 1-0**
*Ford*
Naylor; Burgess, Harbey, Robson(Talbot), North, Whyte(Foster), Ford, Goodman, West, McNally, Bartlett.
*Att: 18,172*
**Round 5**
**Feb 17 v Aston Villa (h) 0-2**
Naylor; Burgess, Harbey, Robson(Talbot), North, Whyte, Shakespeare, Goodman, West(Foster), McNally, Bartlett.
*Att: 26,585*

**1990-91**
**Round 3**
**Jan 5 v Woking (h) 2-4**
*West, Bradley*
Rees; Shakespeare, Harbey(L.Palmer), Roberts,

Bradley, Strodder, Ford, West, Bannister, McNally, Robson.
*Att: 14,516*

**1991-92**
**Round 1**
**Nov 16 v Marlow (h) 6-0**
*Shakespeare 2 (1 pen), Strodder, McNally, Goodman, Robson*
Naylor; Ford, Harbey, Bradley(Williams), Strodder, Burgess, McNally, Goodman, Robson (Rogers), Shakespeare, White.
*Att: 11,082*
**Round 2**
**Dec 9 v Leyton Orient (a) 1-2**
*Williams*
Naylor; Hodson, Harbey, Bradley, Strodder, Burgess, McNally, Williams, Robson(Bannister), Shakespeare, White.
*Att: 6,189*

**1992-93**
**Round 1**
**Nov 14 v Aylesbury United (h) 8-0**
*Donovan 3, Taylor, Hamilton, McNally, Raven, Robson*
Naylor; Burgess(Coldicott), Lilwall, Bradley, Raven, Strodder, Garner(Robson), Hamilton, Taylor, McNally, Donovan.
*Att: 12,337*
**Round 2**
**Dec 6 v Wycombe Wanderers (a) 2-2**
*Taylor, Bradley*
Naylor; Reid, Lilwall, Bradley(Donovan), Raven, Strodder, Garner, Hamilton, Taylor, McNally, Robson(Williams).
*Att: 6,904*
**Replay**
**Dec 15 v Wycombe Wanderers (h) 1-0**
*Taylor*
Naylor; Reed, Lilwall, Bradley, Raven, Strodder, Donovan, Hamilton, Taylor, McNally, Robson (Heggs).
*Att: 17,640*
**Round 3**
**Jan 2 v West Ham United (h) 0-2**
Naylor; Shakespeare(Fereday), Lilwall, Bradley, Raven, Strodder, Garner, Hamilton, Taylor, McNally, Donovan(Hackett).
*Att: 25,896*

**Neville Southall (Everton) kicking clear as John Paskin moves in during the FA Cup replay at Goodison Park.**

# Albion in the Football League Cup

ALBION entered the Football League Cup for the first time in 1965-66 and since then they have appeared in three Finals, winning in their first season. The competition has changed its name several times since then with various sponsorships but in this section is referred to as the League Cup throughout.

**1965-66**
**Round 1**
Bye
**Round 2**
**Sep 22 v Walsall (h) 3-1**
*Brown 2, Bennett (og)*
Potter; Cram, Fairfax, Lovett, Jones, Fraser, Brown, Astle, Kaye, Hope, Clark.
*Att: 41,188*
**Round 3**
**Oct 13 v Leeds United (a) 4-2**
*Brown, Kaye, Clark, Astle*
Sheppard; Cram, Fairfax, Lovett, Jones, Fraser, Brown, Astle, Kaye, Hope, Clark.
*Att: 13,455*
**Round 4**
**Nov 3 v Coventry City (a) 1-1**
*Kaye*
Sheppard; Cram, Fairfax, Lovett, Jones, Fraser, Brown, Crawford, Kaye, Hope, Clark.
*Att: 38,476*
**Replay**
**Nov 10 v Coventry City (h) 6-1**
*Astle 3, Fraser 2, Brown*
Sheppard; Cram, Fairfax, Lovett, Jones, Fraser, Brown, Astle, Kaye, Hope, Clark.
*Att: 31,956*
**Round 5**
**Nov 17 v Aston Villa (h) 3-1**
*Kaye 2, Brown*
Sheppard; Cram, Fairfax, Lovett, Jones, Fraser, Brown, Astle, Kaye, Hope, Clark.
*Att: 40,694*
**Semi-final (1st leg)**
**Dec 1 v Peterborough United (h) 2-1**
*Brown, Astle*
Sheppard; Cram, Fairfax, Lovett, Jones, Fraser, Brown, Astle, Kaye, Hope, Clark.
*Att: 20,933*
**Semi-final (2nd leg)**
**Dec 15 v Peterborough United (a) 4-2 (agg 6-3)**
*Brown 3, Crawford*
Potter; Cram, Fairfax, Lovett, Jones, Fraser, Brown, Crawford, Kaye, Hope, Clark.
*At: 18,288*
**Final (1st leg)**
**Feb 9 v West Ham United (a) 1-2**
*Astle*
Potter; Cram, Fairfax, Fraser, Campbell, Williams, Brown, Astle, Kaye, Lovett, Clark.
*Att: 28,588*
**Final (2nd leg)**
**Feb 23 v West Ham United (h) 4-1 (agg 5-3)**
*Kaye, Brown, Clark, Williams*
Potter; Cram, Fairfax, Fraser, Campbell, Williams, Brown, Astle, Kaye, Hope, Clark.
*Att: 32,013*

**1966-67**
**Round 1**
Bye
**Round 2**
**Sep 14 v Aston Villa (h) 6-1**
*Hope 3, Fraser 2, Clark*
Sheppard; Cram, Collard, Lovett, Jones, Fraser, Foggo, Astle, Kaye, Hope, Clark.
*Att: 25,039*
**Round 3**
**Oct 5 v Manchester City (h) 4-2**
*Stephens, Krzywicki, Astle, Clark*
Potter; Crawford, Collard, Williams, Campbell, Fraser(Krzywicki), Stephens, Lovett, Astle, Hope, Clark.
*Att: 19,016*
**Round 4**
**Oct 25 v Swindon Town (a) 2-0**
*Astle, Clark*
Potter; Crawford, Collard, Lovett, Jones, Fraser,

Williams, Astle, Kaye, Hope, Clark.
*Att: 16,254*
**Round 5**
**Dec 7 v Northampton Town (a) 3-1**
*Brown, Simpson, Clark*
Sheppard; Simpson, Williams, Lovett, Jones, Fraser, Brown, Astle, Kaye, Hope, Clark.
*Att: 14,706*
**Semi-final (1st leg)**
**Jan 18 v West Ham United (h) 4-0**
*Astle 3, Clark*
Sheppard; Cram, Williams, Collard, Jones, Fraser, Brown, Astle, Kaye, Hope, Clark.
*Att: 30,193*
**Semi-final (2nd leg)**
**Feb 8 v West Ham United (a) 2-2 (agg 6-2)**
*Hope, Clark*
Sheppard; Cram, Williams, Collard, Jones, Fraser, Foggo, Brown, Kaye, Hope, Clark.
*Att: 35,790*
**Final**
**Mar 4 v Queen's Park Rangers(at Wembley) 2-3**
*Clark 2*
Sheppard; Cram, Williams, Collard, Clarke, Fraser, Brown, Astle, Kaye, Hope, Clark.
*Att: 97,952*

**1967-68**
**Round 2**
**Sep 13 v Reading (a) 1-3**
*Collard*
Osborne; Fraser, Williams, Collard, Colquhoun, Talbut, Brown, Astle, Kaye, Hope, Clark.
*Att: 18,910*

**1968-69**
**Round 2**
**Sep 3 v Nottingham Forest(at Meadow Lane) 3-2**
*Astle 2, Rees*
Sheppard; Fraser, Williams, Brown, Talbut, Colquhoun, Rees, Kaye, Astle, Hope, Clark.
*Att: 23,970*
**Round 3**
**Sep 25 v Peterborough United (a) 1-2**
*Brown (pen)*
Osborne; Fraser, Williams, Brown, Talbut, Merrick, Rees, Lovett, Astle, Kaye, Clark.
*Att: 16,510*

**1969-70**
**Round 2**
**Sep 3 v Aston Villa (a) 2-1**
*Suggett, Astle*
Osborne; Fraser, Merrick, Brown, Talbut, Kaye, Suggett, Hughes, Astle, Hope, Hartford.
*Att: 40,202*
**Round 3**
**Sep 24 v Ipswich Town (a) 1-1**
*Suggett*
Osborne; Fraser, Wilson, Hughes, Talbut, Kaye (Krzywicki), Brown, Hegan, Astle, Suggett, Hope.
*Att: 19,261*
**Replay**
**Oct 1 v Ipswich Town (h) 2-0**
*Hope, Astle*
Osborne; Fraser, Wilson(Brown), Hughes, Talbut, Kaye, Krzywicki, Suggett, Astle, Hegan, Hope.
*Att: 24,631*
**Round 4**
**Oct 15 v Bradford City (h) 4-0**
*Cantello, Hope, Brown, Krzywicki*
Osborne; Fraser, Williams, Cantello, Talbut, Kaye, Krzywicki, Brown, Astle, Hartford, Hope.
*Att: 25,343*
**Round 5**
**Oct 29 v Leicester City (a) 0-0**
Osborne; Fraser, Williams, Brown, Talbut, Kaye,

Hegan, Suggett, Astle, Hartford, Hope.
*Att: 35,121*
**Replay**
**Nov 5 v Leicester City (h) 2-1**
*Astle 2*
Osborne; Fraser, Williams, Brown, Talbut, Kaye, Hegan, Suggett, Astle, Hartford, Hope.
*Att: 26,981*
**Semi-final (1st leg)**
**Nov 19 v Carlisle United (a) 0-1**
Osborne; Fraser, Williams, Brown, Talbut, Kaye, Krzywicki, Suggett, Astle, Hartford, Hope.
*Att: 20,322*
**Semi-final (2nd leg)**
**Dec 3 v Carlisle United (h) 4-1 (agg 4-2)**
*Hope, Suggett, Brown, Martin*
Osborne; Fraser, Wilson, Brown, Talbut(Martin), Kaye, Krzywicki, Suggett, Astle, Hartford, Hope.
*Att: 34,835*
**Final**
**Mar 7 v Manchester City (at Wembley) 1-2 (aet)**
*Astle*
Osborne; Fraser, Wilson, Brown, Talbut, Kaye, Cantello, Suggett, Astle, Hartford(Krzywicki), Hope.
*Att: 97,963*

**1970-71**
**Round 2**
**Sep 8 v Charlton Athletic (h) 3-1**
*Kaye, Astle, Suggett*
Cumbes; Hughes, Merrick, Robertson(Glover), Talbut, Kaye, Reed, Suggett, Astle, Hope, Cantello.
*Att: 16,124*
**Round 3**
**Oct 6 v Preston North End (a) 1-0**
*Hartford*
Cumbes; Minton, Merrick, Brown, Talbut, Kaye, McVitie, Suggett, Astle, Hope, Hartford.
*Att: 18,222*
**Round 4**
**Oct 28 v Tottenham Hotspur (a) 0-5**
Cumbes; Fraser, Merrick, Cantello(Lovett), Talbut, Kaye, McVitie, Suggett, Astle, Brown, Hartford.
*Att: 31,598*

**1971-72**
**Round 2**
**Sep 8 v Tottenham Hotspur (h) 0-1**
Cumbes; Hughes, Minton, Cantello, Wile, Kaye, Suggett, Brown, MacLean, Hope, Hartford.
*Att: 26,185*

**1972-73**
**Round 2**
**Sep 6 v Queen's Park Rangers (h) 2-1**
*Evans (og), T.Brown (pen)*
Latchford; Nisbet, Wilson, Hughes, Wile, Robertson, Suggett, T.Brown, Gould, A.Brown, Hartford.
*Att: 10,494*
**Round 3**
**Oct 3 v Liverpool (h) 1-1**
*Hartford*
Latchford; Nisbet, Wilson, Cantello, Wile, Robertson, Suggett, T.Brown, Gould, A.Brown, Hartford.
*Att: 17,661*
**Replay**
**Oct 10 v Liverpool (a) 1-2 (aet)**
*Robertson*
Latchford; Nisbet, Wilson, Cantello (Woolgar), Wile, Robertson, Suggett, T.Brown, Gould, A.Brown, Hartford.
*Att: 26,461*

**Jeff Astle, Clive Clark and Graham Williams celebrate Albion's League Cup Final victory in 1966.**

**1973-74**
**Round 2**
**Oct 8 v Sheffield United (h) 2-1**
*Shaw, Cantello*
Latchford; Nisbet, Merrick, Cantello(Glover), Wile, Robertson, Johnston, A.Brown, T.Brown, Hartford, Shaw.
*Att: 10,482*
**Round 3**
**Oct 31 v Exeter City (h) 1-3**
*Johnston*
Latchford; Nisbet, Merrick, Cantello, Wile, Robertson, Johnston, A.Brown, T.Brown, Hartford, Shaw.
*Att: 10,719*

**1974-75**
**Round 2**
**Sep 10 v Millwall (h) 1-0**
*Cantello*
Latchford; Nisbet, Wilson, Cantello, Wile, Robertson, Glover, T.Brown, Shaw, Merrick, Johnston.
*Att: 8,294*
**Round 3**
**Oct 9 v Norwich City (h) 1-1**
*Stringer (og)*
Latchford; Nisbet, Wilson, Cantello, Wile, Robertson, Glover, T.Brown, Mayo, Merrick, Johnston.
*Att: 11,625*

**Replay**
**Oct 16 v Norwich City (a) 0-2 (aet)**
Latchford; Nisbet, Wilson, Cantello, Wile, Robertson, Glover, Shaw, Mayo(Donaghy), Hughes, Johnston.
*Att: 18,235*

**1975-76**
**Round 2**
**Sep 9 v Fulham (h) 1-1**
*Johnston*
Osborne; Mulligan, Thompson, Cantello, Wile, Robertson, Trewick, T.Brown, Hurst, Giles, Johnston.
*Att: 10,912*

**Replay**
**Sep 24 v Fulham (a) 0-1**
Osborne; Thompson, Wilson, Cantello, Wile, Robertson, Glover, A.Brown, Hurst, Giles, Johnston.
*Att: 10,785*

**1976-77**
**Round 2**
**Aug 31 v Liverpool (a) 1-1**
*Giles*
Osborne; Mulligan, Cantello, T.Brown, Wile, Robertson, Martin, A.Brown, Mayo, Giles, Johnston.
*Att: 22,984*
**Replay**
**Sep 6 v Liverpool (h) 1-0**
*Martin*
Osborne; Mulligan, Cantello, T.Brown, Wile, Robertson, Martin, Robson, Mayo, Edwards, Johnston.
*Att: 22,662*
**Round 3**
**Sep 22 v Brighton & Hove Albion (h) 0-2**
Osborne; Mulligan, Cantello, T.Brown, Wile, Robertson, Martin, Edwards(Robson), Mayo, Giles, Johnston.
*Att: 18,728*

**1977-78**
**Round 2**
**Aug 31 v Rotherham United (h) 4-0**
*Regis 2 (1 pen), Wile, Martin*
Godden; Mulligan(Trewick), Statham, Martin, Wile, Robertson, Cantello, Cunningham, Regis, Robson, Johnston.
*Att: 15,005*
**Round 3**
**Oct 25 v Watford (h) 1-0**
*T.Brown*
Godden; Mulligan, Statham, T.Brown, Wile, Robertson, Cantello, Cunningham, D.Cross, Robson, Johnston.
*Att: 21,985*
**Round 4**
**Nov 29 v Bury (a) 0-1**
Godden; Mulligan, Statham, T.Brown(Regis), Wile, Robertson, Martin, Cunningham, D.Cross, Robson, Johnston.
*Att: 13,898*

**1978-79**
**Round 2**
**Aug 30 v Leeds United (h) 0-0**
Godden; Batson, Statham, Trewick, Wile, Robertson, Robson, A.Brown(Martin), Regis, Cunningham, Johnston.
*Att: 25,188*
**Replay**
**Sep 6 v Leeds United (a) 0-0 (aet)**
Godden; Batson, Statham, Cunningham, Wile, Robertson, Robson, A.Brown, Regis, Cantello, Johnston.
*Att: 29,316*
**Second replay**
**Oct 2 v Leeds United (at Maine Road) 0-1**
Godden; Batson, Statham, Cunningham, Wile, Robertson, Robson, A.Brown, Regis, Cantello, T.Brown.
*Att: 8,164*

**1979-80**
**Round 2 (1st leg)**
**Aug 29 v Fulham (h) 1-1**
*Robson*
Godden; Batson, Statham, T.Brown, Wile, Robertson, Robson, A.Brown, Mills, Owen, Barnes.
*Att: 14,617*
**Round 2 (2nd leg)**
**Sep 5 v Fulham (a) 1-0 (agg 2-1)**
*Robson*
Godden; Batson, Statham, Trewick, Wile, Robertson, Robson, Mills, T.Brown, Owen, Barnes.
*Att: 11,542*
**Round 3**
**Sep 26 v Coventry City (h) 2-1**

*T.Brown (pen), Wile*
Godden; Batson, Statham, Trewick, Wile, Robertson, Robson, T.Brown, Mills, Owen, Barnes.
*Att: 18,058*
**Round 4**
**Oct 31 v Norwich City (h) 0-0**
Godden; Batson, Statham, Mills, Wile, Robertson, Robson, A.Brown, Regis, Owen, T.Brown.
*Att: 24,251*
**Replay**
**Nov 7 v Norwich City (a) 0-3**
Godden; Trewick, Statham(Barnes), Mills, Wile, Robertson, Robson, A.Brown, Regis, Owen, T.Brown.
*Att: 19,677*

**1980-81**
**Round 2 (1st leg)**
**Aug 26 v Leicester City (h) 1-0**
*Barnes*
Godden; Trewick, Statham, Moses, Wile, Robertson, Robson, A.Brown, Regis, Owen, Barnes.
*Att: 13,810*
**Round 2 (2nd leg)**
**Sep 3 v Leicester City (a) 1-0 (agg 2-0)**
*Regis*
Godden; Trewick, Statham, Moses, Wile, Robertson, Bennett, A.Brown, Regis, Owen, Barnes.
*Att: 17,081*
**Round 3**
**Sep 24 v Everton (a) 2-1**
*Moses, Robertson*
Godden; Batson, Statham, Moses, Wile, Robertson, Trewick, A.Brown, Regis, Owen, Barnes(Monaghan).
*Att: 23,546*
**Round 4**
**Oct 29 v Preston North End (h) 0-0**
Godden; Batson, Statham, Moses, Wile, Robertson, Robson, A.Brown, Regis, Trewick, Barnes(Mills).
*Att: 17,579*
**Replay**
**Nov 4 v Preston North End (a) 1-1 (aet)**
*A.Brown*
Godden; Batson, Cowdrill, Moses, Wile, Robertson, Robson, A.Brown, Regis, Owen(Trewick), Mills.
*Att: 14,420*
**Second replay**
**Nov 12 v Preston North End (h) 2-1**
*Regis 2*
Godden; Batson, Cowdrill, Moses, Wile, Robertson, Robson, A.Brown, Regis, Owen, Barnes(Mills).
*Att: 15,218*
**Round 5**
**Dec 5 v Manchester City (a) 1-2**
*Booth (og)*
Godden; Batson, Trewick, Moses, Wile, Bennett, Robson, A.Brown, Regis, Owen, Barnes.
*Att: 35,611*

**1981-82**
**Round 2 (1st leg)**
**Oct 6 v Shrewsbury Town (a) 3-3**
*Regis, Mackenzie, N.Cross*
Godden; Batson, Statham, King, Wile, Robertson, N.Cross, Summerfield, Regis, Owen, Mackenzie.
*Att: 9,291*
**Round 2 (2nd leg)**
**Oct 28 v Shrewsbury Town (h) 2-1 (agg 5-4)**
*A.Brown, Owen*
Godden; Batson, Statham, King, Wile, Robertson, Jol, A.Brown, Regis, Owen, Mackenzie.
*Att: 12,596*
**Round 3**
**Nov 10 v West Ham United (a) 2-2**
*Regis, King*
Grew; Arthur, Statham, King, Wile, Robertson, Jol, A.Brown, Regis, Owen, Mackenzie.
*Att: 24,168*
**Replay**
**Nov 24 v West Ham United (h) 1-1 (aet)**
*Regis*
Grew; Batson, Statham, King, Wile, Robertson, Jol, A.Brown, Regis, Owen, Mackenzie.
*Att: 15,985*

**Second replay**
**Dec 1 v West Ham United (a) 1-0**
*Regis*
Grew; Batson, Statham, King, Wile, Robertson, Jol, A.Brown, Regis, Owen, Mackenzie.
*Att: 24,502*
**Round 4**
**Dec 15 v Crystal Palace (a) 3-1**
*Regis 2, Monaghan*
Grew; Batson, Bennett, King, Wile, Robertson (Lewis), Arthur, Monaghan, Regis, Owen, Mackenzie.
*Att: 10,311*
**Round 5**
**Jan 20 v Aston Villa (a) 1-0**
*Statham*
Grew; Batson, Statham, A.Brown, Wile, Robertson, Jol, King, Regis, Owen, Mackenzie.
*Att: 35,197*
**Semi-final (1st leg)**
**Feb 3 v Tottenham Hotspur (h) 0-0**
Grew; Batson, Statham, King, Wile, Bennett, Jol, Monaghan(N.Cross), Regis, Owen, Mackenzie.
*Att: 32,166*
**Semi-final (2nd leg)**
**Feb 10 v Tottenham Hotspur (a) 0-1 (agg 0-1)**
Grew; Arthur, Statham, Bennett, Wile, Robertson, Jol, Summerfield, Regis, Owen(King), Mackenzie.
*Att: 47,241*

**1982-83**
**Round 2 (1st leg)**
**Oct 6 v Nottingham Forest (a) 1-6**
*Regis*
Grew; Batson, Whitehead, Zondervan, Bennett, Robertson, Jol, A.Brown, Regis, Owen, Eastoe.
*Att: 11,969*
**Round 2 (2nd leg)**
**Oct 27 v Nottingham Forest (h) 3-1 (agg 4-7)**
*Regis, N.Cross, Whitehead*
Godden; Batson, Statham, Zondervan, Wile, Robertson, Jol, A.Brown, Regis(Cowdrill), N.Cross, Whitehead.
*Att: 6,536*

**1983-84**
**Round 2 (1st leg)**
**Oct 4 v Millwall (a) 0-3**
Barron; Whitehead, Cowdrill, Zondervan, McNaught(Mackenzie), Smith, Lewis, Thompson, Regis, Robson, N.Cross.
*Att: 10,721*
**Round 2 (2nd leg)**
**Oct 25 v Millwall (h) 5-1 (agg 5-4)**
*Thompson 2, Regis 2, Owen (pen)*
Barron; Whitehead, Cowdrill, Zondervan, McNaught, Bennett, Lewis, Thompson, Regis, Owen(N.Cross), Perry.
*Att: 13,331*
**Round 3**
**Nov 9 v Chelsea (a) 1-0**
*Thompson*
Barron; Whitehead, Cowdrill, Zondervan, McNaught, Robertson, Lewis, Thompson, Perry, Owen, Luke.
*Att: 22,932*
**Round 4**
**Nov 30 v Aston Villa (h) 1-2**
*Regis*
Barron; Whitehead, Cowdrill, Zondervan, McNaught, Robertson, Jol, Thompson, Regis (Mackenzie), Owen, N.Cross.
*Att: 31,114*

**1984-85**
**Round 2 (1st leg)**
**Sep 25 v Wigan Athletic (a) 0-0**
Godden; Whitehead, Statham, Hunt, Bennett, Robertson, Grealish, Thompson, N.Cross, Mackenzie, Morley.
*Att: 6,209*
**Round 2 (2nd leg)**
**Oct 10 v Wigan Athletic (h) 3-1 (agg 3-1)**
*Hunt, Thompson, N.Cross*
Godden; Whitehead, Statham, Hunt, Bennett,

Forsyth, Grealish, Thompson, N.Cross, Mackenzie, Robson.
*Att: 8,133*
**Round 3**
**Oct 30 v Birmingham City (a) 0-0**
Godden; Whitehead, Cowdrill, Hunt, Bennett, Robertson, Lewis, Thompson, Mackenzie, D.Cross, Robson.
*Att: 17,616*
**Replay**
**Nov 7 v Birmingham City (h) 3-1**
*Thompson, Robertson, D.Cross*
Godden; Whitehead, Statham, Hunt, Bennett, Robertson, Grealish, Thompson, Mackenzie, D.Cross, Valentine(Robson).
*Att: 16,717*
**Round 4**
**Nov 20 v Watford (a) 1-4**
*D.Cross*
Godden; Nicholl, Statham, Hunt, Bennett, Robertson, Grealish, Thompson, Mackenzie, D.Cross, Valentine.
*Att: 16,378*

**1985-86**
**Round 2 (1st leg)**
**Sep 24 v Port Vale (h) 1-0**
*Armstrong*
Godden; Nicholl, Statham, Hunt, Cowdrill, Robertson, Armstrong, Robson, Mackenzie (Anderson), Valentine, Crooks.
*Att: 6,288*
**Round 2 (2nd leg)**
**Oct 7 v Port Vale (a) 2-2 (agg 3-2)**
*Varadi 2*
Bradshaw; Nicholl, Statham, Grealish, Bennett, Robertson, Valentine(Whitehead), Hunt, Varadi, Thomas, Crooks.
*Att: 7,895*
**Round 3**
**Oct 29 v Coventry City (a) 0-0**
Bradshaw; Nicholl, Statham, Hunt, Bennett, Robertson, Valentine, Grealish, Varadi, Thomas, Crooks.
*Att: 9,804*
**Replay**
**Nov 6 v Coventry City (h) 4-3**
*Hunt, Varadi 2, Crooks*
Bradshaw; Nicholl, Statham, Hunt, Bennett, Robertson(Whitehead), Valentine, Grealish, Varadi, Thomas, Crooks.
*Att: 8,987*
**Round 4**
**Nov 20 v Aston Villa (a) 2-2**
*Crooks, Bennett*
Bradshaw; Nicholl, Statham, Hunt, Bennett, Robertson, Armstrong(Palmer), Whitehead, Varadi, Thomas, Crooks.
*Att: 20,204*
**Replay**
**Nov 27 v Aston Villa (h) 1-2**
*Hunt*
Bradshaw; Palmer, Statham, Hunt, Bennett, Robertson, Dennison(Grealish), Whitehead, Varadi, Thomas, Crooks.
*Att: 18,868*

**1986-87**
**Round 2 (1st leg)**
**Sep 24 v Derby County (a) 1-4**
*Bull*
Naylor; Whitehead, Anderson, Bennett(Burrows), Dyson, Dickenson, Palmer, Evans(Robinson), Bull, Williamson, Dobbins.
*Att: 11,304*
**Round 2 (2nd leg)**
**Oct 7 v Derby County (h) 0-1 (agg 1-5)**
Naylor; Whitehead, Anderson, Palmer, Dyson, Dickenson, Cowdrill, Evans, Mackenzie, Williamson, Bull(Thompson).
*Att: 6,765*

**1987-88**
**Round 1 (1st leg)**
**Aug 19 v Walsall (h) 2-3**
*Forbes (og), Bradley*

Naylor; Dobbins, Burrows, Bennett, Steggles (Lynex), Kelly, Hopkins, Goodman, Palmer, Bradley, Morley.
*Att: 9,605*
**Round 1 (2nd leg)**
**Aug 25 v Walsall (a) 0-0 (agg 2-3)**
Naylor; Dobbins, Burrows, Bennett, Dickinson, Kelly, Palmer(Lynex), Goodman, Robson, Singleton, Morley.
*Att: 8,965*

**1988-89**
**Round 1 (1st leg)**
**Aug 31 v Peterborough United (h) 0-3**
Naylor; Bradley, Albiston, Gray(Robson), Dyson, North, Hopkins, Goodman, Paskin, Palmer, Anderson.
*Att: 4,264*
**Round 1 (2nd leg)**
**Sep 7 v Peterborough United (a) 2-0 (agg 2-3)**
*Gray, Palmer*
Naylor; Hodson, Burrows, Bradley, Whyte, North, Hopkins, Goodman, Gray(Easter), Palmer, Anderson.
*Att: 4,216*

**1989-90**
**Round 2 (1st leg)**
**Sep 20 v Bradford City (h) 1-3**
*McNally*
Ward; Bradley, Parkin(Burgess), Robson, Whyte, North, Ford, Goodman, West, McNally, Anderson.
*Att: 7,771*
**Round 2 (2nd leg)**
**Oct 4 v Bradford City (a) 5-3 (aet) (agg 6-6)**
*Thomas 3, Talbot, Whyte*
Naylor; Bradley, Burgess, Talbot, Whyte, North, Barham, Goodman(Foster), Thomas, McNally, Bartlett.
*Att: 5,731*
*Albion won on away-goals rule*
**Round 3**
**Oct 25 v Newcastle United (a) 1-0**
*Whyte*
Naylor; Parkin, Hodson, Talbot, Whyte, North, Ford, Goodman, Thomas, McNally, Robson (Anderson).
*Att: 22,639*
**Round 4**
**Nov 22 v Derby County (a) 0-2**
Naylor; Hodson(Burgess), Harbey, Talbot, Raven, Whyte, Ford, Goodman, Bartlett, McNally, Parkin.
*Att: 21,313*

**1990-91**
**Round 1 (1st leg)**
**Aug 29 v Bristol City (h) 2-2**
*Bannister, Hackett*
Naylor; Hodson, Harbey, Robson, Burgess, Strodder, Ford, Goodman, Bannister, Bradley (Hackett), Shakespeare.
*Att: 8,721*
**Round 2 (2nd leg)**
**Sep 5 v Bristol City (a) 0-1 aet (agg 2-3)**
Naylor; Hodson, Harbey, Robson(Hackett), Burgess, Strodder, Ford, West, Bannister(Foster), Bradley, Shakespeare.
*Att: 9,851*

**1991-92**
**Round 1 (1st leg)**
**Aug 20 v Swindon Town (a) 0-2**
Naylor; Bradley, Harbey, Ford, Strodder, Burgess, Bannister, Goodman, Foster(McNally), Shakespeare, Ampadu(Williams).
*Att: 6,611*
**Round 1 (2nd leg)**
**Aug 28 v Swindon Town (h) 2-2 (agg 2-4)**
*Goodman, Shakespeare*
Naylor; Bradley, Harbey, Ford, Strodder, Burgess (Foster), McNally, Goodman(Bannister), Williams, Shakespeare, Ampadu.
*Att: 8,522*

Imre Varadi scored four League Cup goals in 1985-86.

Andy Gray, scorer at Peterborough in September 1988.

**1992-93**
**Round 1 (1st leg)**
**Aug 19 v Plymouth Argyle (h) 1-0**
*Taylor*
Naylor; Hodson, Lilwall, Bradley, Strodder, Shakespeare, Garner, Hamilton, Taylor(Ampadu), McNally, Robson.
*Att: 8,264*
**Round 1 (2nd leg)**
**Aug 25 v Plymouth Argyle (a) 0-2 (agg 1-2)**
Naylor; Hodson(Coldicott), Lilwall, Bradley, Strodder, Shakespeare, Garner, Hamilton, Taylor, Raven, Robson.
*Att: 7,880*

# Albion's Other Major Matches

## Full Members Cup

**1985-86**
**Oct 2 v Brighton & Hove Albion (a) 1-2**
*Crooks 2*
Bradshaw; Nicholl, Statham, Hunt, Bennett, Robertson, Valentine, Grealish, Varadi, Thomas, Crooks.
*Att: 4,649*
**Group 8**
**Oct 23 v Crystal Palace (h) 2-1**
*Hunt, Nicholl*
Powell; Nicholl, Palmer, Hunt, Bennett, Forsyth, Valentine, Grealish, Armstrong(Robson), Whitehead, Crooks(Bull).
*Att: 3,914*
**Semi-final (Southern area)**
**Nov 13 v Chelsea (h) 2-2 (aet) Lost 4-5 on penalties**
*Valentine, Crooks: penalties by Bull, Hunt, Varadi and Thompson*
Godden; Palmer(Anderson), Statham, Hunt, Bennett, Robertson, Valentine(Bull), Robson, Varadi, Thomspon, Crooks.
*Att: 4,070*

**1986-87**
**Round 1**
**Oct 21 v Millwall (a) 0-2**
Naylor; Whitehead, Cowdrill, Palmer, Dyson, Hayward, Dennison, Bull(A.Thompson), Williamson, Crooks.

## Simod Cup

**1987-88**
**Round 1**
**Nov 10 v Oldham Athletic (a) 3-0**
*Williamson, Lynex, Morley*
Naylor; Steggles, Anderson, C.Palmer, Burrows, Kelly, Lynex, Dobbins, Reilly(Williamson), Robson, Morley.
*Att: 1,841*
**Round 2**
**Dec 1 v Ipswich Town (a) 1-2**
*Lynex (pen)*
Naylor; C.Palmer, Anderson, Hogg, Dickinson, Lynex, Hopkins, Goodman, Reilly, Dobbins, Morley(Robson).
*Att: 5,308*

**1988-89**
**Round 1**
**Nov 9 v West Ham United (a) 2-5**
*Goodman, Robson*
Naylor; Dobbins(Phillips), Albiston, Talbot, Whyte, North, Hopkins, Goodman, Robson (Goodall), C.Palmer, Bradley.
*Att: 5,960*

## Zenith Data Systems Cup

**1989-90**
**Round 1**
**Nov 29 v Derby County (h) 0-5**
Naylor; Burgess(Robson), Harbey, Talbot, Raven, Whyte, Ford, Goodman, Bartlett (Thomas), McNally, Parkin.
*Att: 4,880*

**1990-91**
**Round 1**
**Nov 21 v Barnsley (h) 3-5**
*Bradley, Bannister, Robson*
Naylor; Dobbins, Harbey(Parkin), Roberts, Bradley, Strodder, Goodman, West, Bannister, McNally, Robson(Ford).
*Att: 4,452*

## Autoglass Trophy

**1991-92**
**Preliminary Round**
**Oct 22 v Shrewsbury Town (h) 4-0**
*Shakespeare, West, Ampadu, Rogers*
Naylor; Hodson, Harbey, Ford, Rogers, Bradley,

McNally, Goodman(Robson), West, Shakespeare (Williams), Ampadu.
*Att: 6,992*
**Preliminary Round**
**Dec 4 v Lincoln City (a) 2-1**
*Williams, Robson*
Naylor; Hodson, Harbey, Bradley, Strodder, Burgess, McNally, Williams, Robson, Shakespeare, White(Bannister).
*Att: 1,861*
**Round 1**
**Jan 14 v Exeter City (h) 0-1**
Naylor; Hodson, Harbey, Bradley, Strodder, Burgess, White, Bannister, Robson, Parkin (Williams), Hackett(Cartwright).
*Att: 6,034*

**1992-93**
**Jan 5 v Walsall (h) 4-0**
*Donovan, Taylor, Hamilton, Heggs*
Lange; Fereday, Darton, Bradley, Raven, Shakespeare(Hamilton), Hackett, Donovan, Taylor, Dickens(Heggs), Robson.
*Att: 6,702*
**Jan 12 v Mansfield Town (a) 1-0**
*Taylor*
Lange; Coldicott(Hamilton), Darton, Sinfield, Raven, Shakespeare, Hackett, Hunter, Taylor (McCue), Heggs, Donovan.
*Att: 2,356*
**Round 2**
**Feb 9 v Torquay United (h) 2-1**
*Donovan 2*
Lange; Fereday, Darton, Hackett(Heggs), Hunter(Colditt), Strodder, Speedie, Hamilton, Taylor, McNally, Donovan.
*Att: 5,219*
**Round 3**
**Feb 16 v Stoke City (a) 1-2**
*Taylor*
Naylor; Fereday(Robson), Lilwall, Bradley, Raven, Strodder, Speedie, Hamilton, Taylor, Shakespeare, Donovan.
*Att: 17,568*

## FA Charity Shield

**1920**
**May 15 v Tottenham Hotspur (a) 2-0**
*A.Smith 2*
Pearson; J.Smith, Pennington, S.Richardson, Bowser, McNeal, Crisp, A.Smith, Bentley, Morris, Gregory.
*Att: 38,168*

**1931**
**Oct 7 v Arsenal (at Villa Park) 0-1**
Pearson; Shaw, Trentham, Magee, W.Richardson, Edwards, Glidden, Raw, W.G.Richardson, Sandford, Wood.
*Att: 21,276*

**1954**
**Sept 29 v Wolverhampton Wanderers (a) 4-4**
*Allen 3, Ryan*
Sanders; Rickaby, Millard, Dudley, Kennedy (Dugdale), Brookes, Griffin, Ryan(Hodgkisson), Allen, Carter, Lee.
*Att: 45,035*

**1968**
**Aug 3 v Manchester City (a) 1-6**
*Krzywicki*
Osborne(Merrick); Fraser, Williams, Lovett, Talbot, Kaye, Stephens, T.Brown, Krzywicki, Collard, Hartford.
*Att: 35,510*
Osborne retired injured in this game. Williams moved into goal and Merrick came on as substitute.

## Anglo Italian Tournament

**1969-70**
**Group 2**
**May 2 v Lanerossi Vicenza (h) 0-0**

Osborne; Hughes, Fraser, Lovett(Reed), Talbot, Merrick, T.Brown, Hartford, Suggett, Cantello, Hope.
*Att: 17,655*
**May 8 v AS Roma (h) 4-0**
*T.Brown 2, Hope, Talbot*
Osborne; Hughes, Fraser, Lovett(Glover), Talbot, Merrick, T.Brown, Hartford, Suggett(Martin), Cantello, Hope.
*Att: 11,833*
**May 16 v Lanerossi Vicenza (a) 1-1***
*Glover*
Osborne; Hughes, Fraser, Lovett, Talbot, Merrick, T.Brown, Hartford, Suggett(Martin), Cantello(Glover), Hope.
*Att: 12,000*
*Game abandoned after 76 minutes due to fighting on and off the field.
**May 23 v AS Roma (a) 1-1**
*Suggett*
Osborne; Hughes, Fraser, T.Brown, Talbot, Merrick, Suggett, Kaye, Martin(Lovett), Hartford, Hope.
*Att: 16,000*
Albion failed to qualify.

**1970-71**
**Group 2**
**May 26 v Internazionale (h) 1-1**
*Wile*
Cumbes; Hughes, Wilson, Cantello, Wile, Kaye, Suggett, T.Brown, Astle, Hope, Hartford.
*Att: 17,645*
**May 29 v Cagliari (h) 1-2**
*Astle*
Cumbes; Hughes, Wilson, Cantello, Wile, Kaye, Suggett, T.Brown, Astle, Hope, Hartford.
*Att: 17,620*
**June 1 v Internazionale (a) 0-1**
Osborne; Hughes, Wilson, Lovett, Wile, Kaye, Suggett, T.Brown, Astle, Hope(MacLean), Hartford.
*Att: 15,000*
**June 4 v Cagliari (a) 0-1**
Osborne; Hughes, Wilson, Robertson, Wile, Kaye, MacLean, T.Brown, Suggett, Lovett, Merrick(Glover).
*Att: 30,000*
Albion failed to qualify.

## Texaco Cup

**1970-71**
**Round 1 (1st leg)**
**Sept 14 v Morton (a) 1-2**
*Rankin (og)*
Cumbes; Hughes, Wilson, T.Brown, Kaye, Merrick(Lovett), McVitie, Suggett, Astle, Hartford, Cantello.
*Att: 7,943*
**Round 1 (2nd leg)**
**Sept 30 v Morton (h) 0-1 (agg 1-3)***
Cumbes; Minton, Merrick, T.Brown, Talbot, Kaye, McVitie, Suggett, Astle, Hope, Hartford.
*Att: 16,168*

**1972-73**
**Round 1 (1st leg)**
**Sep 19 v Sheffield United (a) 1-1**
*A.Brown*
Latchford; Nisbet, Wilson, Cantello, Wile, Robertson, Suggett, T.Brown, Gould, A.Brown, Hartford.
*Att: 13,381*
**Round 1 (2nd leg)**
**Sep 26 v Sheffield United (h) 1-0 (agg 2-1)**
*Gould*
Latchford; Nisbet, Merrick, Cantello, Wile, Robertson, Suggett, T.Brown, Gould, A.Brown, Hartford.
*Att: 8,340*
**Round 2 (1st leg)**
**Oct 25 v Newcastle United (h) 2-1**
*T.Brown 2 (1 pen)*

Latchford; Nisbet, Merrick, Woolgar, Wile, Robertson, Suggett, T.Brown, Gould, A.Brown, Hartford.
*Att: 8,425*
**Round 2 (2nd leg)**
**Nov 8 v Newcastle United (a) 1-3 (agg 3-4)**
*Hartford*
Latchford; Nisbet, Wilson, Merrick, Wile, Robertson, Suggett, T.Brown, Gould, A.Brown, Hartford.
*Att: 20,420*

**1974-75**
**Group 1**
**Aug 3 v Birmingham City (h) 0-0**
Osborne; Nisbet, Wilson, Cantello, Wile, Robertson, Hughes, T.Brown, A.Brown(Shaw), Hartford, Johnston.
*Att: 18,317*
**Aug 6 v Norwich City (h) 5-1**
*T.Brown, Shaw, A.Brown, Hughes, Johnston*
Latchford; Nisbet, Wilson, Glover, Wile, Robertson, Hughes, T.Brown(A.Brown), Shaw, Hartford, Johnston.
*Att: 5,393*
**Aug 10 v Peterborough United (a) 1-2**
*Shaw*
Latchford; Nisbet, Wilson, Glover, Wile, Robertson, Hughes, T.Brown, Shaw(A.Brown), Hartford, Johnston.
*Att: 8,083*
Albion failed to qualify.
*The 1970-71 tournament was billed as the 'British Isles Cup'.*

## Watney Cup
**1971-72**
**Round 1**
**July 31 v Wrexham (a) 2-1**
*T.Brown 2 (1 pen)*
Cumbes; Hughes, Wilson, Cantello(Merrick), Wile, Kaye, Suggett, T.Brown, Astle, Hope, Hartford.
*Att: 11,218*
**Semi-final**
**Aug 4 v Halifax Town (a) 2-0**
*Suggett 2*
Cumbes; Hughes, Wilson, Cantello, Wile, Kaye, McVitie(Merrick), T.Brown, Astle, Suggett, Hartford,
*Att: 12,069*
**Final**
**Aug 7 v Colchester United (h) 4-4***
*Astle 2, Cantello, Suggett*
Cumbes; Hughes, Wilson, Cantello, Wile, Kaye, Suggett, T.Brown, Astle, Hope, Hartford.
*Att: 19.009*
*Colchester won 4-3 on penalties. Astle, T.Brown and Hope scored for Albion.

## Anglo-Scottish Cup
**1975-76**
**Group 2**
**Aug 2 v Mansfield Town (h) 1-1**
*Cantello*
Osborne; Nisbet, Wilson, Cantello(Mayo), Wile, Robertson, Robson, T.Brown, A.Brown, Giles, Johnston.
*Att: 5,704*
**Aug 6 v Hull City (a) 2-1**
*A.Brown 2*
Osborne; Nisbet, Wilson, Cantello, Robertson, Robson, Trewick, A.Brown, Mayo, Giles, Johnston.
*Att: 3,094*
**Aug 9 v Leicester City (a) 1-2**
*Giles*
Osborne; Nisbet, Wilson, Cantello, Wile, Robertson, Robson, A.Brown, Mayo, Giles(Trewick), Johnston.
*Att: 8,219*

**1976-77**
**Midland Group**
**Aug 7 v Bristol City (a) 0-1**

Osborne; Mulligan, Cantello, T.Brown, Wile, Robertson, Martin, A.Brown, Mayo, Giles, Johnston.
*Att: 4,941*
**Aug 10 v Nottingham Forest (a) 2-3**
*Mulligan, Mayo*
Ward; Mulligan, Cantello, T.Brown, Wile, Robson, Martin, Edwards, Mayo, Trewick, Johnston.
*Att: 7,018*
**Aug 14 v Notts County (h) 3-1**
*Mayo 2, Johnston*
Osborne; Mulligan, Robson, T.Brown, Wile, Robertson Martin, Edwards, Mayo, Giles, Johnston.
*Att: 6,936*

## Tennent-Caledonian Cup
all games played at Ibrox Park
**1977-78**
**Semi-final**
**Aug 6 v St Mirren 4-3**
*T.Brown 2 (1pen), D.Cross, Robson*
Osborne; Mulligan, Statham, T.Brown, Wile, Robertson, Robson, Cunningham, D.Cross, Cantello, Johnston.
*Att: 40,404*
**Final**
**Aug 7 v Rangers 2-0**
*Cunningham 2*
Godden; Mulligan, Statham, Martin, Wile, Robertson, Robson, Cunningham, A.Brown (D.Cross), Trewick, Johnston.
*Att: 35,066*

**1978-79**
**Semi-final**
**Aug 5 v Southampton 1-1***
*Regis*
Godden; Batson, Statham, T.Brown, Wile, Robertson, Robson, A.Brown(Johnston), Regis, Trewick, Cunningham.
*Att: 25,563*
*Southampton won 3-1 on penalties. T.Brown scored for Albion.
**Third place play-off**
**Aug 6 v Hearts 0-2**
Godden; Batson, Statham, T.Brown, Wile, Robertson, Martin, Robson, Regis (Hughes), Trewick, Cunningham(A.Brown).
*Att: 18,823*

## United Counties League
**1893-94**
**Group A (on League basis)**
**Feb 24 v Small Heath (a) 5-4**
*Pearson 2, McLeod 2, Geddes*
Reader; Nicholson, Crone, T.Perry, C.Perry, Taggart, Bassett, McLeod, Bostock, Pearson, Geddes.
*Att: 3,000*
**Feb 26 v Small Heath (h) 3-1**
*Pearson, McLeod 2*
Reader; J.Horton, Crone, T.Perry, B.Hadley, Taggart, Norman, McLeod, Bostock, Pearson, Geddes.
*Att: 2,700*
**Mar 10 v Stoke (h) 5-0**
*Bostock, McLeod 2, Bassett, Geddes*
Reader; Nicholson, Crone, T.Perry, C.Perry, Taggart, Bassett, McLeod, Bostock, Pearson, Geddes.
*Att: 3,000*
**Mar 19 v Stoke (a) 2-5**
*C.Perry, Geddes*
Reader; Nicholson, Crone, T.Perry, C.Perry, Taggart, Bassett, McLeod, Bostock, Pearson, Geddes.
*Att: 3,000*
**Apr 2 v Wolverhampton Wanderers (a) 2-4**
*Geddes, Pearson*
Reader; J.Horton, Crone, T.Perry, C.Perry, Taggart, Bassett, McLeod, O.Williams, Pearson, Geddes.
*Att: 4,000*

**April 9 v Wolverhampton Wanderers (h) 3-1**
*McLeod, Bassett, Taggart*
Reader; J.Horton, Crone, T.Perry, C.Perry, Taggart, Bassett, McLeod, O.Williams, Bostock, Geddes.
*Att: 5,853*
Albion won their group with 8 points.
**Final**
**April 30 v Derby County (a) 1-1 (aet)**
*Geddes*
Reader; J.Horton, Crone, T.Perry, C.Perry, Taggart, Bassett, McLeod, Bostock, Pearson, Geddes.
*Att: 9,000*
Replay held over until 1894-95, again at Derby.
**Replay**
**Oct 6 v Derby County (a) 1-2**
*McLeod*
Reader; W.Williams, Crone, T.Perry, C.Perry, Taggart, Bassett, McLeod, Hutchinson, O.Williams, Newall.
*Att: 6,000*

## Centenary Match
**1979-80**
**Aug 11 v Ajax Amsterdam (h) 1-0**
*Barnes*
Katalinic; Batson, Statham, Trewick(Mills), Wile, Robertson, Robson, A.Brown, T.Brown, Owen, Barnes.
*Att: 13,334*

## Opening of Floodlights
**1957**
**Oct 29 v CDSA(Russian Red Army Club) (h) 6-5**
*Kevan 2, Allen (pen), Robson, Griffin, Howe*
Sanders; Howe, Setters, Dudley, Kennedy, Barlow, Griffin, Robson, Allen, Kevan, Horobin.
*Att: 52,805*

## Festival of Britain Matches
**1951**
**May 12 v SC Wacker (Austria) (h) 3-4**
*Allen 2, Barlow*
Sanders; Rickaby, Millard, Kennedy, Horne, Dudley, Griffin, McCall, Barlow, Allen, Lee.
*Att: 16,074*
**May 15 v FC Floriana (Malta) (h) 2-0**
*Smith, Barlow*
Sanders; Rickaby, Millard, Kennedy, Vernon, S.Williams, Griffin, Smith, Barlow, Allen, Lee.
*Att: 15,133*

## International Club Match
**1954**
**Oct 13 v Honvéd (in Brussels) 3-5**
*Nicholls 2, Allen*
Sanders; Rickaby, Millard, Dudley, Kennedy, Barlow, Griffin, Ryan, Allen, Nicholls, Lee.
*Att: 55,000*

## Championship of the World
**1888**
**May 19 v Renton (at Hampden Park) 1-4**
*Pearson*
Roberts; Mason, H.Green, E.Horton, C.Perry, Timmins, Woodhall, Bassett, Bayliss, Pearson, Wilson
*Att: 6,000*
Renton were the Scottish Cup holders.

## Bass Charity Vase
**1892-93**
**Final**
**Feb 27 v Stoke (h) 3-3**
*Geddes, Boyd, Reynolds (pen)*
Reader; Nicholson, McCulloch, Reynolds, C.Perry, Groves, Bassett, McLeod, Boyd, Fellows, Geddes.
*Att: 5,150*
**Replay**
**Mar 9 v Stoke (a) 1-1**
*Bassett*
Reader; Sheldon, McCulloch, Reynolds,

T.Perry, Groves, McLeod, Bassett, Boyd, Fellows, Geddes.
*Att: 6,000*
The trophy was shared.

**1893-94**
**Round 1**
**March 21 v Burton Swifts (a) 4-1**
*Bassett 2, Bostock, Geddes*
Reader; J.Horton, Crone, T.Perry, C.Perry, Taggart, Bassett, Bostock, Pearson, McLeod, Geddes.
*Att: 2,000*
**Semi-final**
**April 11 v Aston Villa (a) 2-5**
*O.Williams 2*
Reader; J.Horton, Crone, T.Perry, Banks,

Taggart, Norman, Bostock, O.Williams, Geddes.
*Att: 5,800*
**1987-88**
**Semi-final**
**July 22 v Burton Albion (n) 3-1**
*Bradley 2, Hopkins*
Naylor; Robson, Cowdrill, Bennett, Steggles, Kelly, Hopkins, Goodman, Reilly, C.Palmer, Bradley.
*Att: 1,000*
**Final**
**July 31 v Derby County (n) 0-1**
Naylor; Robson, Statham, Bennett, Steggles, Kelly, Hopkins, Goodman, Reilly, Bradley, Morley.
*Att: 2,500*

## Record Victory (1st XI)
## Birmingham Senior Cup

**1882-83**
**Round 1**
**Nov 11 v Coseley (h) 26-0 (ht 17-0)**
*Aston 5, Bisseker 4, Timmins 4, G.Bell 3, Bunn 2, E.Horton 2, While 2, Whitehouse 2, H.Bell, Stanton.*
Roberts; Stanton, H.Bell, E.Horton, Bunn, While, Whitehouse, Aston, Bisseker, Timmins, G.Bell.
*Att: 2,500*
Every outfield player scored in this game

# Albion in Europe

## European Cup-winners' Cup

**1968-69**
**Round 1 (1st leg)**
**Sep 18 v RFC Bruges (a) 1-3**
*Hartford*
Osborne; Fraser, Williams, Brown, Talbut, Kaye, Rees, Hartford, Astle(Lovett), Hope, Clark.
*Att: 28,000*
**Round 1 (2nd leg)**
**Oct 2 v RFC Bruges (h) 2-0 (agg 3-3)**
*Hartford, Brown*
Osborne; Fraser, Williams, Brown, Talbut, Kaye, Rees, Hartford(Collard), Astle, Hope, Clark.
*Att: 33,747*
Albion won on away-goals rule.
**Round 2 (1st leg)**
**Nov 13 v Dinamo Bucharest (a) 1-1**
*Hartford*
Osborne; Fraser, Wilson, Brown, Talbut, Kaye(Lovett), Rees, Collard, Astle, Hope, Hartford.
*Att: 15,000*
**Round 2 (2nd leg)**
**Nov 27 v Dinamo Bucharest (h) 4-0 (agg 5-1)**
*Brown 2 (1 pen), Lovett, Astle*
Osborne; Fraser, Wilson, Brown, Talbut, Kaye, Clark, Lovett, Astle, Hope, Hartford.
*Att: 33,059*
**Round 3 (1st leg)**
**Jan 15 v Dunfermline Athletic (a) 0-0**
Osborne; Fraser, Wilson, Brown, Talbut, Kaye, Hope, Lovett, Astle, Collard, Hartford (Krzywicki).
*Att: 22,073*
**Round 3 (2nd leg)**
**Feb 19 v Dunfermline Athletic (h) 0-1(agg 0-1)**
Osborne; Fraser, Wilson, Brown, Talbut, Kaye, Martin, Lovett, Astle, Collard, Hartford
*Att: 32,373*

## Fairs Cup

**1966-67**
**Round 1**
Bye
**Round 2 (1st leg)**
**Nov 2 v DOS Utrecht (a) 1-1**
*Hope*
Potter; C.Crawford, Collard, Lovett, Jones, Fraser, Williams, Astle, Kaye, Hope, Clark.
*Att: 5,500*
**Round 2 (2nd leg)**
**Nov 9 v DOS Utrecht (h) 5-2 (agg 6-3)**
*Brown 3 (1 pen), Kaye, Clark*
Potter; C.Crawford, Collard, Williams, Jones, Fraser, Brown, Astle, Kaye, Hope, Clark.
*Att: 19,170*
**Round 3 (1st leg)**
**Feb 1 v Bologna (a) 0-3**
Osborne; Cram, Williams, Collard, Talbut, Fraser, Brown, Astle, Kaye, Hope, Clark.
*Att: 20,100*

**Round 3 (2nd leg)**
**Mar 8 v Bologna (h) 1-3 (agg 1-6)**
*Fairfax*
Osborne; Clarke, Fairfax, Collard, Colquhoun, Fraser, Brown, Astle, Kaye, Hope, Clark.
*Att: 27,401*

## UEFA Cup

**1978-79**
**Round 1**
Bye
**Round 2 (1st leg)**
**Sep 13 v Galatasary (a) 3-1**
*Cunningham 2 Robson*
Godden; Batson, Statham, Cunningham, Wile, Robertson, Robson, A.Brown, Regis, Trewick, Cantello.
*Att: 38,443*
**Round 2 (2nd leg)**
**Sep 27 v Galatasary (h) 3-1 (agg 6-2)**
*Cunningham (pen), Robson, Trewick*
Godden(Grew); Batson, Statham, Cunningham, Wile, Robertson, Robson, A.Brown, Regis, Cantello, Trewick(T.Brown).
*Att: 22,380*
**Round 3 (1st leg)**
**Oct 18 v SC Braga (a) 2-0**
*Regis 2*
Godden; Batson, Statham, Cunningham, Wile, Robertson, Robson, A.Brown, Regis, Cantello, T.Brown.
*Att: 31,383*
**Round 3 (2nd leg)**
**Nov 1 v SC Braga (h) 1-0 (agg 3-0)**
*A.Brown*
Godden; Batson, Statham, Cunningham, Wile, Robertson, Robson(Martin), A.Brown, Regis, Cantello(Trewick), T.Brown.
*Att: 26,036*
**Round 4 (1st leg)**
**Nov 22 v Valencia (a) 1-1**
*Cunningham*
Godden; Batson, Statham, Trewick, Wile, Robertson, Robson, A.Brown, Regis, Cantello, Cunningham.
*Att: 47,746*
**Round 4 (2nd leg)**
**Dec 6 v Valencia (h) 2-0 (agg 3-1)**
*T.Brown 2 (1 pen)*
Godden; Batson, Statham, Trewick, Wile, Robertson, Robson, T.Brown, Regis, Cantello, Cunningham.
*Att: 35,118*
**Round 5 (1st leg)**
**Mar 7 v Red Star Belgrade (a) 0-1**
Godden; Batson, Statham, T.Brown, Wile, Robertson, Robson, A.Brown, Regis, Trewick, Cunningham.
*Att: 95,300*

**Round 5 (2nd leg)**
**Mar 21 v Red Star Belgrade (h) 1-1 (agg 1-2)**
*Regis*
Godden; Batson, Statham, T.Brown, Wile, Robertson, Robson, A.Brown, Regis, Cantello, Cunningham.
*Att: 31,587*

**Cyrille Regis, whose goal against Red Star was not enough to send Albion through.**

**1979-80**
**Round 1**
Bye
**Round 2 (1st leg)**
**Sep 19 v Carl Zeiss Jena (a) 0-2**
Godden; Batson, Statham, Trewick, Wile, Robertson, Robson, A.Brown, T.Brown, Owen, Mills.
*Att: 21,660*
**Round 2 (2nd leg)**
**Oct 3 v Carl Zeiss Jena (h) 1-2 (agg 1-4)**
*Wile*
Godden; Batson, Statham, Trewick(Monaghan), Wile, Robertson(Mills), Robson, A.Brown, T.Brown, Owen, Barnes.
*Att: 19,204*

**1981-82**
**Round 1 (1st leg)**
**Sep 16 v Grasshopper Zürich (a) 0-1**
Godden; Batson, Statham, Moses, Wile, Robertson, Robson, Mills, Regis, Owen, Mackenzie.
*Att: 8,101*
**Round 1 (2nd leg)**
**Sep 30 v Grasshopper Zürich (h) 1-3 (agg 1-4)**
*Robertson*
Godden; Batson, Statham, Robertson(Webb), Wile, Deehan, Robson, Mills(N.Cross), Regis, Owen, Mackenzie.
*Att: 16,745*

# Foreign Tours and Overseas Tournaments

ALL matches played by Albion on overseas tours and in foreign tournaments are recorded in this section with the relevant goalscorers and attendances. Single matches played abroad can be found in the section covering friendly games, etc.

## 1908-09
### Scandinavian Tour
**May 18 v Newcastle United (in Copenhagen) 0-3**
*Att: 5,000*
**May 20* v Hull City (in Stockholm) 2-1**
*Buck, Timmins*
*Att: 4,000*
**May 21 v Gefle FC (in Gefle) 10-0**
*Garraty 6, Buck 2, Harris, Manners*
*Att: 6,500*
**May 23* v Stockholm Select XI(in Stockholm) 8-3**
*Buck 4, Davies 2, Garraty, Harris*
*Att: 10,200*
**May 24* v Hull City (in Gothenburg) 3-4**
*Thompson, Buck, Timmins (pen)*
*Att: 5,500*
**May 26* v Swedish Select XI (in Stockholm) 2-0**
*Garraty, Buck*
*Att: 15,000*
**May 28 v Danish Select XI (in Copenhagen) 1-3**
*Buck*
*Att: 12,000*
*Dates of games not confirmed

## 1931-32
### Irish Tour
**May 2 v Linfield 5-1**
*Wood 2, W.G.Richardson, Carter, Trentham*
*Att: 12,500*
**May 4 v Shelbourne (Dublin) 0-0**
*17,000*

## 1945-46
### Tour to Belgium and Luxembourg
**May 1 v Belgium XI (at Verviers) 4-5**
*Banks, Elliott (pen), Hodgetts 2*
*Att: 15,212*
**May 4 v Fola Jennesse XI(at Esch-sur-Alzette) 5-1**
*Hodgetts, Clarke 2, Elliott, Batler*
*Att: 7,035*
**May 8* v RSC Anderlecht (in Brussels) 1-1**
*Hodgetts*
*Att: 8,540*
*Benefit match for Tubentia FC. See also under Benefits & Testimonials.

## 1952-53
### Irish Tour
**May 10 v Waterford Select XI 5-4**
*Lee 2, Hodgkisson 2, Griffin*
*Att: 5,136*
**May 13 v Bohemians Select XI (Dublin) 5-1**
*Griffin, Hodgkisson, Allen, Millard, Brookes*
*Att: 6,913*

## 1954-55
### Le Soir International Festival
**Oct 13 v Honvéd (in Brussels) 3-5**
*Nicholls 2, Allen*
*Att: 55,000*

## 1956-57
### Tour to Russia

In June 1957, Albion visited the Soviet Union to play three matches against Russian club sides from the First Division. Albion were undefeated and won many admirers.

**Jun 1 v Zenit Leningrad 1-1**
*Kevan*
Brown; Howe, Millard, Setters, Kennedy, Barlow, Griffin, Robson, Allen, Horobin(Kevan), Lee.
*Att: 80,000*

**Jun 7 v Dinamo Tbilisi 3-1**
*Kevan 2, Horobin*
Sanders; Howe, S.Williams, Setters(Dudley), Kennedy, Barlow, Griffin, Robson(Whitehouse), Allen, Kevan, Horobin.
*Att: 35,000*

**Jun 12 v CDSA (Russian Army Side) 4-2**
*Kevan 2, Whitehouse, Griffin*
Brown; Howe, S.Williams, Setters, Kennedy, Barlow(Dudley), Griffin, Whitehouse(Robson), Allen, Kevan, Horobin.
*Att: 80,500*

## 1958-59
### Tour to Canada and USA
**May 22 v Ontario All Stars (in Toronto) 6-1**
*Whitehouse 2, Allen, Hogg, Robson 2*
*Att: 12,000*
**May 24 v Dundee(at Ebbetts Field, New York) 2-2**
*Allen 2*
*Att: 21,312*
**May 27 v Alberta All Stars (at Calgary) 15-0**
*Smith 3, Whitehouse 2, Kennedy, Robson 6, G.Williams 2, Jackson*
*Att: 6,000*
**May 30 v Dundee (in Vancouver) 7-1**
*Jackson 2, Kevan 2, Allen, Hamilton (og), Drury*
*Att: 17,800*
**Jun 1 v British Columbia All Stars(in Vancouver) 2-3**
*Allen, Burnside*
*Att: 15,000*
**Jun 3 v Manitoba All Stars(at Winnipeg) 10-1**
*Whitehouse 2, Allen 3, Robson 2, Kevan, Smith, Kennedy*
*Att: 8,500*
**Jun 6 v Dundee (in Toronto) 4-2**
*Allen, Burnside 3*
*Att: 10,000*
**Jun 8 v Ottowa All Stars (in Ottowa) 9-0**
*Whitehouse 3, Burnside 2, Robson 2, Kevan, Jackson*
*Att: 25,000*
**Jun 10 v Montreal All Stars (in Montreal) 4-0**
*Allen, Hogg, Whitehouse*
*Att: 15,000*
On this tour, Albion scored 59 goals in nine matches, Bobby Robson (12) and Ronnie Allen (11) were top marksmen.

## 1960-61
### Austrian Tour
**May 22 v Lustenau 3-3**
*Kevan, Burnside, Kiesinger (og)*
*Att: 10,000*
**May 24 v Linz ASK 3-2**
*Jackson 2, Clark*
*Att: 12,000*
**May 26 v Graz 2-1**
*Burnside, Cram*
*Att: 12,500*

## 1964-65
### Tour to Holland
**Aug 8 v Alkmaar 1-2**
*Clark*
*Att: 12,000*
**Aug 12 v ADO (The Hague) 2-1**
*Brown, Fraser*
*Att: 8,000*
**Aug 15 v Ajax Amsterdam 1-0**
*Hope*
*Att: 8,100*

## 1965-66
### South American Tour
**May 13 v Alianza Lima (in Lima) 3-2**
*Brown 2, Cram (pen)*
*Att: 20,000*
**May 15 v Sporto Cristal (in Lima) 2-1**
*Brown, Kaye*
*Att: 10,000*
**May 22 v Uruguay Select XI (in Montevideo) 1-1**
*Collard*
*Att: 20,000*

**May 25 v Newell's Old Boys (in Rosario) 0-0**
*Att: 15,700*
**May 29 v Uruguay Select XI(in Montevideo) 0-2**
*15,000*
**Jun 5 v Flamengo (in Río de Janiero) 2-1**
*Cram (pen), Kaye*
*Att: 30,100*

### New York International Tournament (Section 2)
**Jul 7 v Kilmarnock 0-2**
*Att: 2,278*
**Jul 11 v Ferencváros 1-1**
*Astle*
*Att: 6,387*
**Jul 14 v Polonia Bytom 2-2**
*Kaye, Foggo*
*Att: 4,096*
**Jul 18 v Kilmarnock 2-0**
*Kaye, Cram (pen)*
*Att: 10,066*
**Jul 21 v Ferencváros 1-2**
*Clark*
*Att: 5,663*
**Jul 25 v Polonia Bytom 0-6**
*Att: 8,162*
Albion finished third in their section and failed to qualify for the finals.

## 1967-68
### Tour to East Africa
**May 23 v Dar es Salaam Select XI 1-1**
*Astle*
*Att: 20,000*
**May 25 v Tanzania (Dar es Salaam) 1-1**
*Astle*
*Att: 20,000*
**May 29 v Uganda (Kampala) 1-0**
*Hartford*
*Att: 15,000*
**Jun 1 v Kenya (Nairobi) 2-1**
*Brown (2 pens)*
*Att: 11,000*
**Jun 5 v East African XI (Kampala) 2-2**
*Astle, Rees*
*Att: 22,000*
**Jun 8 v Kenya (Nairobi) 4-3**
*Hartford, Brown, Krzywicki, Collard*
*Att: 16,500*

## 1968-69
### Tour to Canada and USA
**May 11 v Vancouver All Stars 2-0**
*Brown 2 (2 pens)*
*Att: 10,000*
**May 14 v Victoria O'Keefes 4-1**
*Kaye, Krzywicki, Brown, Hegan*
*Att: 2,351*
**May 18 v Dukla Prague 2-1**
*Krzywicki 2*
*Att: 5,207*
**May 23 v California Clippers 2-2**
*Brown, Hegan*
*Att: 3,500*
**May 25 v Vitória Setúbal 0-1**
*Att: 6,000*
**May 27 v Edmonton's All Stars 12-0**
*Martin 3, Lovett 2, Hegan 2, Hope 2, Kaye, Krzywicki, Cantello*
*Att: 6,500*
Last four games played in Palo Alto International Tournament.

## 1969-70
### Tour to Norway
**Jul 30 v Norway Under-23 XI (in Bergen) 2-3**
*Hegan 2*
*Att: 6,000*

**Jul 31 v SFK Lyn (Oslo) 6-0**
*Astle 3, Hope 2, Freeman*
*Att: 5,000*

## 1971-72
## Tour to Yugoslavia
**May 9 v Hajduk Split (in Split) 1-2**
*Gould*
*Att: 8,000*
**May 11 v FK Velež (in Mostar) 3-2**
*Suggett, Hartford, Gould*
*Att: 6,000*
**May 15 v FK Sarajevo (in Sarajevo) 1-1**
*Gould (pen)*
*Att: 10,000*

## 1972-73
## Swedish Örenduscupen Tournament
**Jul 28 v Kalmar FF 3-0**
*Gould 2, Nisbet*
*Att: 5,026*
**Jul 30 v Helsingborgs IF 3-1**
*Gould 2, McVitie*
*Att: 7,995*
**Aug 1 v Landskrona BoIS 1-1**
*T.Brown*
*Att: 7,114*

## 1974-75
## Tour to Belgium
**Jul 28 v KV Mechelen 0-1**
*Att: 3,559*
**Aug 1 v Diest 2-1**
*Hughes, Shaw*
*Att: 4,503*

## 1975-76
## Irish Tour
**Jul 25 v Shamrock Rovers (Dublin) 1-0**
*Fagan (og)*
*Att: 2,211*
**Jul 28 v Finn Harps (Ballybofey) 0-1**
*Att: 1,753*

## 1977-78
## Spanish Trofeo Costa Blanca Tournament in Alicante
**Aug 12 v Dinamo Tbilisi 1-0**
*D.Cross*
*Att: 10,000*
**Aug 14 v Hercules CF 1-5**
*Cunningham*
*Att: 4,000*

## Tour to China and Hong Kong

In May 1978 Albion visited the People's Republic of China where they played four games, thus becoming the first British professional club side to set foot in that country. All four games ended in victories for Albion who also defeated Hong Kong on the homeward journey.

**May 16 v Peking XI 3-1**
*A.Brown 2, Regis*
Godden(Grew); Batson, Statham, T.Brown, Wile, Robertson, Martin, Robson, Regis(Hughes), A.Brown(Summerfield), Cunningham(Monaghan).
*Att: 80,000*

**May 19 v China 2-0**
*Regis, A.Brown*
Godden; Batson, Statham, T.Brown(Hughes), Wile, Robertson, Martin(Loveridge), Robson, Regis, A.Brown, Cunningham.
*Att: 89,400*

**May 22 v Shanghai 2-0**
*Regis, Cunningham*
Grew; Batson, Statham, Hughes(Loveridge), Wile, Robertson, Martin(Trewick) Robson, Regis, A.Brown(Summerfield), Cunningham (Monaghan).
*Att: 40,000*

**May 26 v Kwantung Province 6-0**
*Regis 2, Wile, Martin, T.Brown, Cunningham.*
Godden(Grew); Batson(Hughes), Statham, T.Brown, Wile, Robertson, Martin(Loveridge), Robson, Regis(Summerfield), A.Brown, Cunningham(Monaghan).
*Att: 30,500*

**May 28 v Hong Kong Select 3-0**
*Regis, T.Brown, Chi-Keung (og)*
Godden; Batson, Statham, T.Brown, Wile, Robertson, Martin, Robson, Regis, A.Brown, Cunningham.
*Att: 18,000*

Full record:

| P | W | D | L | F | A |
|---|---|---|---|---|---|
| 5 | 5 | 0 | 0 | 16 | 1 |

Top goalscorers: Regis 6, A.Brown 3, T.Brown 2, Cunningham 2.

In August 1979 China played Albion at The Hawthorns in a 'Friendship Friendly' match. A crowd of 11,382 saw Albion win 4-0, Regis, A.Brown, Barnes and an opponent (og) the scorers.

## 1978-79
## Syrian Tour
**Aug 11 v North Territory Provincial XI 1-0**
*A.Brown*
*Att: 10,000*
**Aug 13 v Damascus Police XI 1-1**
*T.Brown*
*Att: 12,500*

## Tour to Denmark
**May 28 v Aalborg Fodbold-Alliancen 0-1**
*Att: 8,300*
**May 29 v Fyn Boldspil-Union Select XI 4-1**
*Regis 2, T.Brown 2*
*Att: 6,600*
**May 31 v IHF (Denmark) 7-0**
*Cunningham 2, Regis 2, A.Brown 2, T.Brown*
*Att: 4,200*

## 1979-80
## Spanish Trofeo Teresa Tournament in La Coruna
**Aug 14 v Sporting Gijon 0-1**
*Att: 25,200*
**Aug 15 v Honvéd 0-1**
*Att: 38,140*

## Tour to Abu Dhabi and Bahrain
**Jan 14 v Al-Amarath 3-0**
*A.Brown 2, Benjamin*
*Att: 5,000*
**Jan 16 v Al-Hala 4-1**
*Regis, Moses, Deehan, Malrahti (og)*
*Att: 5,400*

## 1980-81
## Yugoslavian Trofej Marjan Tournament
**Aug 6 v Hajduk Split 1-5**
*Regis*
*Att: 20,140*
**Aug 6 v FC Zurich 0-0**
*Att: 4,066*

## Tour to Canada and USA
**May 11 v Vancouver Whitecaps 1-2**
*Regis*
*Att: 17,339*
**May 13 v Portland Timbers 1-0**
*Summerfield*
*Att: 10,140*
**May 15 v Edmonton Drillers 2-1**
*Regis, Summerfield*
*Att: 6,820*

## 1981-82
## X Trofeo Futbol Ciudad de Sevilla Tournament in Spain
**Aug 19 v Real Betis 4-1**
*Owen, Mills 2, Moses*
*Att: 35,535*
**Aug 21 v Sevilla FC 2-0**
*Mackenzie, Deehan*
*Att: 46,723*

## 1982-83
## Spanish IX Trofeo Futbol Ciudad de Barcelona Tournament
**Aug 17 v RCD Español 2-3**
*Regis, Jol*
*Att: 9,371*
**Aug 18 v CA Osasuna 1-2**
*Regis*
*Att: 5,035*

## 1983-84
## Tour to Holland
**Aug 10 v FC Den Bosch '67 3-0**
*Robson, Jol, Thompson*
*Att: 1,920*
**Aug 13 v NAC Breda 2-2**
*Jol, Robson*
*Att: 2,034*
**Aug 16 v Go Ahead Eagles (Deventer) 4-3**
*Thompson, Regis, Jol, Cross*
*Att: 2,145*

## 1989-90
## Irish Tour
**Jul 29 v Shelbourne (Dublin) 4-2**
*Bradley, West, Goodman, Talbot*
*Att: 1,100*
**Aug 1 v Cobh Ramblers 4-2**
*Bartlett, Robson, Goodman, West*
*Att: 950*
**Aug 3 v Glentoran 3-2**
*Ford, Whyte, West*
*Att: 2,054*

## 1989-90
## San Jose Cup
**May 18 v Real Madrid 1-6**
*Shakespeare*
*Att: 15,348*
Hugo Sanchez scored 5 goals for Real in this game.
**May 20 v Vasco da Gama 2-4**
*Goodman, Whyte*
*Att: 18,236*

## USA Tour
## 1989-90
**May 22 v Arizona Condors 6-1**
*L.Palmer 3, Shakespeare, Hackett, Cartwright*
*Att: 966*
**May 23 v Los Angeles Heat 1-1**
*Hackett*
*AttL 820*

## Irish Tour
## 1990-91
**Aug 4 v Glentoran 0-0**
*Att: 3,170*
**Aug 7 v Ards 4-0**
*Bannister 2, Raven 2*
*Att: 2,968*
**Aug 9 v Newry Town 3-1**
*Goodman, Bannister 2*
*Att: 1,650*
**Aug 11 v Shelbourne (Dublin) 1-1**
*Goodman*
*Att: 3,065*

# Testimonial and Benefit Matches

Albion's first team have played numerous benefit and testimonial matches for various players and causes down the years and details of these are recorded in this section except for wartime benefit matches which are under the appropriate wartime section. Attendances and goalscorers are listed from 1900 onwards.

**26 Mar 1883 v Wellington (h) 4-0**
(West Bromwich Hospital)

**7 Apr 1883 v Calthorpe (h) 6-1**
(West Bromwich Dartmouth)

**16 Jun 1883 v Wednesbury Old Athletic (a) 2-3**
(J.Roberts)

**15 Dec 1883 v Wellington (h) 5-1**
(West Bromwich Hospital)

**25 Aug 1884 v Aston Villa (a) 2-3**
(A.Hunter)

**16 May 1885 v District XI (a) 1-2**
(J.Stanton)

**19 Apr 1886 v Aston Villa (a) 1-3**
(Villa-WBA players)

**19 July 1886 v Aston Villa (a) 5-1**
(S.Richardson)

**24 July 1886 v Aston Villa (a) 3-6**
(S.Richardson)

**27 Sept 1886 v Birmingham & District XI (h) 0-0**
(Benefit match)

**14 Nov 1887 v Brierley Hill Alliance (a) 3-0**
(Brockmoor Colliery Relief Fund)

**22 May 1888 v Walsall Town Swifts (h) 3-0**
(R.Roberts)

**17 Dec 1888 v WBA 2nd XI (h) 4-4**
(Mrs J. White)

**20 May 1889 v Hednesford Town (a) 5-0**
(Hospital Benefit)

**3 Mar 1890 v Birmingham & District XI (h) 4-1**
(G.Timmins)

**24 May 1890 v Aston Villa (a) 0-1**
(J.Burton, A.Allan)

**1 Nov 1890 v Stoke (a) 0-1**
(A.Edge)

**2 Mar 1891 v Birmingham & District XI (h) 1-1**
(C.Perry)

**19 Oct 1891 v Stoke (a) 1-1**
(A.Underwood)

**25 Apr 1892 v Birmingham & District XI (a) 2-2**
(T.Pearson)

**17 Oct 1892 v Birmingham & District XI (h) 2-1**
(G.Woodhall)

**20 Mar 1893 v Small Heath (a) 0-5**
(C.Jenkins)

**11 Dec 1893 v Dudley & District XI (a) 6-3**
(Hart Hill Unity)

**8 Oct 1894 v Small Heath (a) 3-1**
(F.Wheldon)

**26 Nov 1894 v Blackburn Rovers (h) 3-1**
(S.Nicholls)

**30 Apr 1895 v Oldbury Town (a) 1-4**
(A.Matthews, C.Fluck)

**16 Sept 1895 v Wolverhampton Wanderers (a) 2-2**
(J.Hassall)

**23 Sept 1895 v Aston Villa (a) 1-2**
(A.Hunter)

**18 Nov 1895 v Aston Villa (h) 1-1**
(R.McLeod)

**7 Apr 1896 v Stoke (h) 3-1**
(J.Horton)

**12 Oct 1896 v Wolverhampton Wanderers (a) 2-0**
(H.Wood)

**10 Nov 1896 v Grimsby Town (a) 2-5**
(W.Higgins)

**7 Dec 1896 v Kettering (a) 1-1**
(Draper)

**17 Mar 1897 v Stoke (at Brighton) 2-4**
(Brighton Children Free Dinner Fund)

**28 Apr 1897 v Aston Villa (a) 1-3**
(Villa players)

**27 Sept 1897 v Leicester Fosse (a) 1-4**
(R.McLeod)

**18 Oct 1897 v Aston Villa (h) 2-0**
(J.Reader)

**3 Jan 1898 v Small Heath (a) 3-8**
(A.Leake)

**14 Feb 1898 v Wolverhampton Wanderers (h) 1-1**
(W.Williams)

**5 Sept 1898 v Aston Villa (a) 1-6**
(F.Burton)

**31 Oct 1898 v Aston Villa (h) 4-0**
(T.Perry)

**17 Apr 1899 v Walsall (a) 1-1**
(S.Holmes)

**26 Apr 1899 v Walsall (at Dudley) 1-1**
(Dudley Town FC)

**30 Oct 1899 v Aston Villa (h) 3-2**
(J.Banks)

**29 Oct 1900 v Wolverhampton Wanderers (h) 3-3**
(W.Richards)
*Simmons 2, A.Smith*
*Att: 5,000*

**24 Dec 1900 v WBA Past XI (h) 6-5**
(Family of H.Green)
*Buck 3, Garfield, Simmons 2*
*Att: 5,500*

**2 Dec 1901 v Small Heath (h) 2-0**
(J Paddock)
*Garfield 2*
*Att: 2,000*

**1 May 1902 v Wolverhampton Wanderers (a) 4-0**
(Ibrox Park Disaster Fund)
*Simmons 2, Worton 2*
*Att: 5,000*

**20 Oct 1902 v Aston Villa (h) 1-5**
(H.Hadley)
*Lee*
*Att: 8,560*

**29 Dec 1902 v Aston Villa (a) 1-2**
(W.George)
*Hadley*
*Att: 12,000*

**14 Apr 1903 v Wolverhampton Wanderers(a) 1-5**
(E.Pheasant)
*Tovey*
*Att: 5,000*

**29 Apr 1903 v Small Heath (h) 3-2**
(Warwickshire CCC)
*E.Smith, Hadley, Cole*
*Att: 4,000*

**26 Oct 1903 v Aston Villa (h) 3-3**
(C.Simmons)
*Dorsett, Hobson, Hadley*
*Att: 5,000*

**25 Dec 1903 v Select XI (h) 1-1**
(G.Cave)
*Simmons*
*Att: 4,500*

**29 Dec 1903 v Aston Villa (a) 0-3**
(G.Johnson)
*Att: 6,000*

**25 Jan 1910 v Aston Villa (a) 1-0**
(Birmingham Theatrical Sports)
*Bowser*
*Att: 3,000*

**4 May 1921 v Wolverhampton Wanderers (h) 2-0**
(W.Barber)
*Gregory, Blood*
*Att: 3,106*

**8 May 1924 v Montgomeryshire District XI (a) 2-1**
(Montgomery County Infirmary)
*Davies, James*
*Att: 2,057*

**4 May 1925 v Aston Villa XI (a) 5-5**
(Rowley Regis Ambulance Fund)
*Reed 2, Carter, James, Wilson*
*Att: 2,500*

**6 May 1925 v Lampard Vachell's XI (a) 7-4**
(Dudley Guest Hospital)
*James 5, Carter, Morris*
*Att: 3,500*

**3 May 1926 v Cradley Heath (a) 1-5**
(Rowley Regis Ambulance Fund)
*Davies*
*Att: 5,800*

**5 May 1926 v F.Morris' XI (at Tipton) 9-0**
(Tipton & District Nurses Home)
*James 3, Davies 2, Carter 2, Byers, H.Smith*
*Att: 3,000*

**8 May 1930 v Cardiff City (at Newtown) 2-1**
(Montgomeryshire County Hospital)
*Edwards, Bytheway*
*Att: 5,000*

**4 May 1931 v Winsford United (a) 3-1**
(Cheshire Royal Infirmary)
*Richardson 3*
*Att: 2,500*

**28 Apr 1932 v Mersey-Widnes XI (a) 4-1**
(Widnes Ground Purchase Fund)
*Cookson, Titley, Sankey, Raw*
*Att: 5,000*

**9 May 1932 v Mid-Cheshire XI (a) 4-2**
(Cheshire Royal Infirmary)
*Corkson 2, Bytheway, Sandford*
*Att: 3,000*

**8 May 1933 v Winsford & District XI (a) 8-0**
(Cheshire Royal Infirmary)
*Richardson 3, Spencer 2, Sankey, Robbins, Wood*
*Att: 3,200*

**7 May 1934 v Winsford & District XI (a) 5-1**
(Cheshire Royal Infirmary)
*Boyes, Sandford, Richardson, Raw, Sankey*
*Att: 2,828*

**20 Aug 1938 v Aston Villa (a) 1-1**
(Football League Jubilee Fund)
*Jones*
*Att: 26,640*

**19 Aug 1939 v Aston Villa (a) 1-1**
(Football League Jubilee Fund)
*Richardson*
*Att: 16,007*

**8 May 1946 v RSC Anderlecht (a) 1-1**
(Tubentia FC)
*Hodgetts*
*Att: 8,540*

**23 Apr 1951 v Swindon Town (a) 5-2**
(H.Martin)
*Allen 2, Lee, F.Richardson 2*
*Att: 6,608*

**24 Mar 1953 v Wolverhampton Wanderers (at Hednesford) 2-4**
(Hednesford Town)
*Nicholls 2*
*Att: 7,153*

Also official opening of Hednesford's floodlights

**28 Apr 1953 v King's Lynn (a) 5-4**
(P.Hooper)
*Nicholls 2, Hodgkisson, Ryan, S.Williams*
*Att: 9,200*

**1 Nov 1954 v Hereford United (a) 5-10**
(J.Sankey & R.Bowen)
*Carter 2, Lee 2, Jackson*
*Att: 4,500*

**2 May 1955 v Mansfield Town (a) 4-1**
(D.Bradley and O.Fox)
*Allen 3, Barlow*
*Att: 12,000*

25 Apr 1956 v International XI (h) 5-5
(N.Heath)
*Allen, Whitehouse 2, Robson 2*
*Att: 55,497*

1 May 1958 v Athletic Bilbao (a) 1-0
*Allen*
*Att: 35,051*

28 Apr 1965 v WBA Past XI (h) 4-6
(G.Williams)
*Kaye, Crawford, T.Brown, Cram*
*Att: 10,160*

15 May 1967 v All Stars XI (h) 6-5
(R.Cram)
*Clark 3, Treacy 2, Foggo*
*Att: 3,943*

21 Apr 1971 v Athletic Bilbao (h) 4-2
(R.Hope)
*Merrick, T.Brown 2, Johnson*
*Att: 14,198*

4 May 1971 v Athletic Bilbao (a) 1-1
(Athletic player)
*Brown*
*Att: 26,103*

18 May 1971 v Swansea City (a) 2-2
(W.Robbins)
*MacLean, Astle*
*Att: 3,950*

30 Nov 1971 v Bristol City (a) 0-0
(T.Bush)
*Att: 4,950*

6 May 1974 v Wolves-Birmingham XI (h) 2-1
(T.Brown)
*Hamilton, T.Brown*
*Att: 11,901*
(Albion-Aston Villa Combined XI opposed Wolves-Birmingham XI)

29 Oct 1974 v WBA '68 XI (h) 1-2
(J.Astle)
*Foggo (og)*
*Att: 11,941*

8 May 1975 v Aston Villa (h) 2-2
(R.Wilson)
*Wilson (pen), Mayo*
*Att: 9,133*

22 Oct 1975 v Leeds United (h) 3-1
(J.Giles)
*Dougan, Mulligan, A.Brown*
*Att: 8,652*

26 Apr 1976 v Aston Villa (a) 1-0
(F.Turnbull)
*Johnston*
*Att: 15,808*

30 Apr 1976 v Walsall (a) 4-1
(C.Harrison)
*T.Brown, A.Brown, Edwards 2*
*Att: 6,729*

20 Oct 1976 v Wolverhampton Wanderers (a) 0-3
(M.Bailey)
*Att: 19,733*

18 May 1977 v Swansea City (a) 1-2
(A.Millington)
*Johnston*
*Att: 4,385*

5 May 1978 v Don Rogers XI (at Swindon) 4-4
(D.Rogers)
*A.Brown, Regis 2, Hughes*
*Att: 3,103*

8 May 1978 v J.Giles XI (h) 0-2
(J.Osborne)
*Att: 12,302*

3 Aug 1978 v Motherwell (a) 8-1
(Wark)
*Stevens (og), A.Brown 3, Cunningham 3, T.Brown*
*Att: 7,401*

13 Nov 1978 v Stafford Rangers (a) 2-2
(S.Chapman)
*Cunningham 2*
*Att: 2,443*

11 Dec 1978 v Exeter City (a) 2-2
(A.Beer)

*Regis, Johnston*
*Att: 4,474*

2 Feb 1979 v Nottingham Forest (at Witney Town) 0-0
(T.Stokes)
*Att: 3,558*

May 15 1979 v Cyrille Regis XI (h) 2-3
(L.Cantello)
*A.Brown, Robson*
*Att: 7,023*

21 May 1979 v Birmingham City (a) 0-4
(G.Pendrey)
*Att: 5,963*

22 May 1979 v Bristol Rovers (a) 3-2
(R.Sheppard)
*A.Brown, Cowdrill 2*
*Att: 2,069*

24 May 1979 v Kettering Town (a) 3-1
(R.Clayton)
*Robson 2, Cowdrill*
*Att: 3,474*

3 Aug 1979 v Torquay United (a) 1-0
(F.King)
*A.Brown*
*Att: 4,718*

15 Oct 1979 v Colchester United (a) 0-1
(M.Cook)
*Att: 2,882*

29 Jan 1980 v Oxford United (a) 1-0
(L.Bateman)
*A.Brown*
*Att: 1,437*

21 Apr 1980 v Cambridge United (a) 2-1
(T.Eades)
*Trewick, Barnes*
*Att: 3,794*

29 Apr 1980 v Wolverhampton Wanderers (h) 3-1
(A.Robertson)
*Regis, Barnes, Cowdrill*
*Att: 5,110*

13 Oct 1980 v Norwich City (at Spalding United) 3-2
(P.Kent)
*Deehan 3*
*Att: 4,029*

8 Dec 198 v Barnet (a) 5-0
(R.Clayton)
*Mills, Trewick, Regis, Deehan, T.Brown*
*Att: 1,001*

16 Mar 1981 v Weymouth (a) 5-2
(A.Iannone)
*A.Brown, Owen, Barnes, Benjamin, Deehan*
*Att: 3,124*

14 Apr 1981 v Aldershot (a) 2-0
(M.Brodie)
*Barnes 2 (1 pen)*
*Att: 3,991*

4 May 1981 v International Select XI (h) 2-3
(J.Wile)
*Deehan, M.Robertson*
*Att: 6,960*

24 Feb 1982 v Dudley Town (a) 3-1
(J.Wile)
*Pike, Owen (pen), King*
*Att: 5,524*

15 Mar 1983 v Wigan Athletic (a) 2-1
(R.Ward)
*Luke, Zondervan*
*Att: 784*

26 Apr 1983 v Walsall (a) 3-3
(A.Caswell)
*Webb, Zondervan, Eastoe*
*Att: 1,870*

30 Apr 1984 v Aston Villa (h) 1-2
(B.Batson)
*Morley*
*Att: 4,800*

18 May 1984 v Oxford United (a) 3-3
(W.Jeffrey)
*N.Cross 2, Morley*

3 Aug 1984 v Newport County (a) 1-2
(J.Relish)
*Hunt*
*Att: 1,535*

8 Aug 1984 v Doncaster Rovers (a) 3-3
(W.Boyd)
*G.Thompson 2, Regis*
*Att: 2,535*

17 Sep 1984 v Grimsby Town (a) 2-1
(J.Waters)
*N.Cross, Morley*
*Att: 1,120*

13 May 1985 v Bristol City (a) 4-2
(J.Shaw)
*Whitehead, Thompson, N.Cross, Mackenzie*
*Att: 1,823*

17 May 1985 v Aston Villa (a) 3-3
(Bradford City Fire Disaster Fund)
*Mackenzie (pen), Grealish, Thompson*
*Att: 7,858*

5 May 1986 v WBA '78 XI(h) 1-1
(A.Godden)
*Dyson*
*Att: 2,815*

19 Feb 1988 v Tottenham Hotspur (h) 4-1
(M.Brown)
*Anderson, Goodman 3*
*Att: 3,169*

15 Mar 1988 v Whitby Town (a) 8-0
(D.Mills)
*Goodman 2, Hopkins, Morley 2, Anderson, C.Johnson, Bradley*
*Att: 290*

19 Apr 1988 v Kettering Town (a) 1-1
(P.Caverner)
*Robson*
*Att: 900*

11 May 1988 v Wolverhampton Wanderers (h) 0-1
(A.Robertson)
*Att: 4,451*

21 Mar 1989 v Irthlingborough Diamonds (a) 4-1
(G.Smith)
*West, Anderson, Robson, Paskin*
*Att: 667*

12 Aug 1989 v Coventry City (a) 1-0
(J.Findlay)
*West*
*Att: 3,596*

26 Mar 1990 v Elmore (a) 10-0
(P.Staddon)
*Goodman 5, Bannister, Talbot, Mortimer, Bradley, Pritchard*
*Att: 940*

11 May 1990 v Walsall (a) 1-1
(P.Hart)
*Bannister*
*Att: 2,180*
This was the last game staged at Fellows Park

7 Oct 1992 v Birmingham City (h) 0-1
(M.Bennett)
*2,842*

## Football League Benefit Matches
Several Albion players have been granted home Football League matches as benefits with most of the gate receipts being presented to the player in question:

W.Bassett v Sheffield Wednesday, 27 Nov 1893.
A.Adams v Stockport County, 28 Oct 1905.
A.Randle v Stockport County, 20 Oct 1906.
J.Pennington v Leeds City, 24 Oct 1908.
F.Buck v Woolwich Arsenal, 11 Nov 1911.
H.Pearson v Bradford City, 22 Mar 1913.
G.Baddeley v Bolton Wanderers, 20 Dec 1913.
J.Pennington v Sunderland, 28 Mar 1914.

# Friendly Matches

This section lists friendly matches played by Albion's first team up to the end of the 1992-93 season. Excluded from this list are wartime friendlies, overseas tour games and testimonial and benefit matches which can be found in a separate section. It should be appreciated that prior to 1883 a full record of friendly matches is not available. No official club records seem to have survived from this period and the newspapers of the time did not record every game contested by the infant Albion club. Goalscorers and attendances have been inserted from 1900 onwards, the year in which Albion moved to The Hawthorns. Because of an increase in the number of Football League fixtures Albion's quota of friendlies decreased during the 1900s. During part of that decade and for several seasons in the 1920s no friendlies of any description were undertaken.

## 1878-79
**Nov 23 v Hudson's (h) 0-0**
R.Roberts; G.Bell, J.Stanton, J.Forrester, H.Evans, T.Waterfield, J.Siddons, J.Stokes, S.Evans, E.Evans, W.Jones, S.Jones.
This was an organized game of soccer played by the George Salter Works Cricket team and is believed to be the first by future members of West Bromwich Albion Football Club, which was officially formed in September of the following year.

## 1879-80
**Dec 13 v Black Lake Victoria (h) 1-0**
This is Albion's first recorded game of this season and a crowd of around 500 saw Harry Aston's goal win the match. Albion fielded 12 players: S.Biddlestone; H.Twist, H.Bell, T.Smith, J.Johnstone, J.Stanton, W.Bisseker (capt), J.Stokes, E.Smith, G.Timmins, H.Aston, G.Bell.
**Dec 20 v Bullock's Club (h) 4-0**
**Jan 31 v St Phillip's (h) ***
**Apr 3 v Heart of Oak (h) 5-0**
**May 1 v Christ Church (h) ***
*Score not recorded

## 1880-81
**Oct 30 v British School (a) 4-0**
**Nov 6 v Smethwick Trinity (h) 2-2**
**Nov 20 v Summer Hill works (h) 4-0**
**Dec 25 v Hockley Abbey (a) 2-0**
**Mar 5 v St Saviours (h) ***
**Jan 1 v Aston Napier (a) 0-0**
**Jan 29 v Hockley Belmont (h) 5-0**
Billy Bisseker's three goals in this match gave him the first reported hat-trick by an Albion player.
**Feb 5 v Summer Hill Works (h) 4-0**
**Feb 12 v Hockley Abbey (a) 2-0**
**Feb 19 v Hockley Belmont (a) 5-0**
**Feb 26 v West Bromwich Royal (h) ***
**Mar 12 v West Bromwich Rovers (h) 8-0**
**Mar 26 v Oakfield (h) 14-0**
*Score not recorded

## 1881-82
**Sep 10 v Oldbury (h) 5-1**
**Oct 1 v The Grove (a) 2-3**
**Oct 8 v Milton (h) 12-0**
Billy Bisseker scored five goals.
**Nov 5 v Milton (a) 3-0 (abandoned 35 minutes; ball burst)**
**Nov 19 v Walsall Unity (a) ***
**Nov 26 v The Grove (h) 2-4**
**Dec 3 v Nechells (h) 9-1**
**Dec 17 v Walsall Alma Athletic (h) ***
**Dec 24 v Wednesday Rovers (h) ***
**Jan 7 v Brunswick Wheel Works (a) 2-1**
**Jan 14 v Fallings Heath Rangers (h) ***
**Jan 28 v Stourbridge (h) ***
**Feb 4 v West Bromwich Rovers (h) 6-1**
**Feb 25 v Fallings Heath Rangers (h) 5-0**
**Feb 27 v Walsall Alma Athletic (h) 4-2**
**Mar 4 v St Luke's (h) 10-0**
George Bell scored six goals.
**Mar 11 v Nechells (a) ***
**Mar 18 v Smethwick Windmill (a) ***
**Apr 1 v Walsall Alma Athletic (a) 1-2**
**Apr 7 v Sandwell Road (a) ***
**Apr 8 v Aston Unity (a) 2-3**
*Score not recorded

## 1882-83
**Sep 23 v St George's (a) 1-7**
**Sep 30 Oldbury (a) ***
**Oct 7 v Stourbridge Standard (h) 10-0**

Albion's first game at the Four Acres. Billy Bisseker scored six goals.
**Oct 14 v Aston Unity (h) 1-0**
**Oct 17 v The Grove (a) ***
**Oct 21 v Excelsior (a) 2-2**
**Dec 2 v Excelsior (h) 3-2**
**Dec 16 v Leek (h) 2-0**
**Dec 26 v Wrexham (a) 5-2**
**Dec 27 v Notts Rangers (a) 2-3**
**Jan 6 v Wellington (a) 2-2**
**Jan 13 v Walsall Alma Athletic (h) 4-0**
**Jan 22 v St John's United (h) 11-0**
**Jan 27 v St George's (h) 3-0**
**Feb 10 v Notts Rangers (h) 1-1 (abandoned)**
**Feb 17 v Birmingham Heath (h) 3-0**
**Feb 19 v Birmingham Junior Association (h) 10-1**
Harry Aston scored six goals.
**Mar 17 v Leek (a) 6-3**
**Mar 19 v The Grove (a) 2-1**
**Mar 31 v Wrexham (h) 3-1**
**Apr 25 v All Saints (h) ***
**Apr 28 v Walsall Swifts (a) 1-2**
**May 5 v Small Heath Alliance (a) 5-1**
**May 12 v Nechells (h) ***
*Score not recorded

## 1883-84
**Sep 17 v Forwards XI (a) 3-3**
**Oct 1 v Wednesday Old Athletic (h) 2-5**
**Oct 6 v Preston North End (a) 1-3**
Last Preston goal disputed and so some reports gave the score as 1-2.
**Oct 1 v Wolverhampton Wanderers (h) 4-2**
**Oct 20 v Stoke (h) 1-5**
**Nov 5 v Walsall Swifts (h) 2-2**
**Nov 12 v Stoke (a) 1-1 (abandoned)**
**Nov 17 v Blackburn Rovers (a) 0-1**
**Nov 19 v Bolton Wanderers (a) 1-2**
Some reports give the score as 1-3 after a third Bolton 'goal' was disputed.
**Dec 1 v West Bromwich Sandwell (h) 5-1**
**Dec 26 v Preston North End (h) 2-1**
**Dec 27 v Sheffield Heeley (h) 8-0**
**Dec 29 v Aston Unity (h) 1-0**
**Jan 19 v Aston Unity (h) 5-0**
**Jan 26 v Wednesbury Old Athletic (h) 2-0 (abandoned)**
**Feb 2 v Bolton Great Lever (h) 4-1**
**Feb 16 v West Bromwich Albion 2nd XI (h) 0-2**
**Feb 26 v Wednesbury Town (h) 2-0**
**Mar 1 v Wednesbury Old Athletic (a) 2-2**
**Mar 22 v Walsall Town (h) 3-2**
**Mar 24 v West Bromwich Sandwell (h) 7-0**
**Apr 19 v Burslem Port Vale (a) 6-0**
**Apr 26 v Wolverhampton Wanderers (a) 3-0**
**May 5 v Walsall Swifts (a) 0-1**

## 1884-85
**Jul 28 v Wednesbury Old Athletic (a) 1-0**
**Aug 23 v Small Heath Alliance (a) 2-0**
**Sep 22 v Walsall Swifts (a) 1-4**
**Oct 4 v Burslem Port Vale (h) 3-0**
**Oct 11 v Aston Unity (h) 3-0**
**Nov 1 v Stoke (a) 4-0**
**Nov 3 v Stafford Rangers (h) 5-0**
**Nov 15 v Wednesbury Town (h) 7-1**
**Nov 29 v Aston Villa (h) 2-4**
**Dec 26 v Preston North End (a) 1-1**
**Dec 27 v Bolton Great Lever (a) 0-3**
**Jan 17 v Walsall Swifts (h) 0-0**
**Feb 7 v Burslem Port Vale (a) 3-2**
**Feb 14 v Aston Unity (a) 2-0**
**Mar 7 v St Luke's (h) 3-2**
**Mar 14 v Aston Villa (a) 2-1**
**Mar 16 v West Bromwich Sandwell (h) 6-2**

**Mar 21 v Church (h) 1-1**
**Mar 28 v Church (a) 0-2**
**Apr 4 v Third Lanark Rifle Volunteers (a) 2-2**
**Apr 6 v Wednesbury Old Athletic (h) 3-2**
Last game at the Four Acres, watched by 3,500 spectators.
**Apr 11 v Stoke (a) 1-1**
**Apr 20 v Burslem Port Vale (a) 1-1**
**Apr 25 v Bolton Wanderers (a) 0-1**
**May 25 v Wolverhampton Wanderers (a) 0-2**

## 1885-86
(Albion's first season at Stoney Lane)
**Jul 27 v Wednesbury Old Athletic (a) 0-1**
**Aug 22 v Small Heath Alliance (a) 7-0**
**Sep 5 v Third Lanark Rifle Volunteers (h) 4-1**
Albion's first game at Stoney Lane. A crowd of 2,122 saw Tommy Green score a hat-trick for Albion.
**Sep 12 v Aston Villa (h) 5-0**
**Sep 19 v Birmingham Excelsior (h) 4-2**
**Sep 21 v Walsall Swifts (a) 0-3**
**Sep 16 v Wednesday Old Athletic (h) 2-1**
**Oct 3 v Northwich Victoria (a) 1-2**
**Oct 5 v Great Bridge Unity (a) 4-0**
**Oct 10 v Blackburn Olympic (a) 3-2**
**Oct 17 v Stoke (h) 3-1**
**Nov 2 v Wolverhampton Wanderers (h) 3-0**
**Nov 14 v Notts County (a) 3-4**
**Nov 23 v Burnley (h) 0-3**
**Nov 28 v Aston Villa (a) 5-4**
**Dec 12 v Derby Midland (a) 5-3**
**Dec 19 v Aston Unity (h) 7-0**
**Dec 26 v Blackburn Olympic (h) 4-0**
**Dec 28 v Bolton Wanderers (h) 0-0 (abandoned)**
**Feb 6 v Aston Villa (h) 3-2**
**Feb 20 v Nottingham Forest (h) 1-0**
**Feb 27 v Derby Junction (h) 5-0**
**Mar 20 v Notts County (h) 3-0**
**Mar 27 v Stoke (a) 3-1**
**Mar 26 v Halliwell (h) 7-0**
**May 1 v Blackburn Rovers (h) 2-5**
**May 15 v Preston North End (h) 1-0**
**May 22 v Bolton Wanderers (a) 1-3**
**May 29 v Aston Villa (h) 3-1**

## 1886-87
**Jul 26 v Wednesbury Old Athletic (h) 6-0**
**Sep 4 v Wolverhampton Wanderers (a) 2-0**
**Sep 11 v Stoke (a) 4-0**
**Sep 18 v Third Lanark Rifle Volunteers (a) 2-1**
**Sep 20 v Hibernian (a) 1-1**
**Sep 25 v Northwich Victoria (h) 2-1**
**Oct 2 v Derby Midland (h) 3-1**
**Oct 23 v Bolton Wanderers (a) 0-1**
**Nov 1 v Oxford University (h) 6-1**
**Nov 27 v Old Carthusians (h) 5-1**
**Dec 4 v Preston North End (a) 0-7**
**Dec 18 v Aston Villa (a) 1-1**
**Dec 27 v Preston North End (h) 5-1**
**Dec 28 v Bolton Wanderers (h) 1-2**
**Jan 22 v Nottingham County (a) 1-3**
**Feb 5 v Aston Unity (h) 5-0**
**Feb 7 v Oxford University (a) 3-2**
**Mar 12 v Wolverhampton Wanderers (h) 0-0**
**Mar 26 v Birmingham Excelsior (h) 3-0**
**Apr 11 v Third Lanark Rifle Volunteers (h) 3-1**
**Apr 16 v Darwen (h) 4-0**
**May 14 v Aston Villa (h) 3-1**
**May 16 v Great Bridge Unity (a) 0-0**
**May 21 v Stoke (h) 1-0**
**May 28 v Bolton Wanderers (h) 2-0**
**May 30 v Blackburn Rovers (h) 3-0**
**June 4 v Wolverhampton Wanderers (a) 0-1**
**June 18 South Shore (a) 3-2**
**June 20 Fleetwood Rangers (a) 3-1**

## 1887-88

Aug 27 v Oldbury Town Crosswells (a) 1-0
Sep 3 v Sheffield Wednesday (h) 4-1
Sep 10 v Third Lanark Rifle Volunteers (a) 0-2
Sep 17 v Stoke (h) 4-0
Sep 24 v Bolton Wanderers (a) 1-1
Oct 3 v Nottingham County (h) 5-1
Oct 17 v Walsall Town (h) 8-0
Oct 22 v Blackburn Rovers (a) 6-7
Oct 29 v Lincoln City (h) 4-1
Nov 7 v Bolton Wanderers (h) 6-0
Nov 12 v Preston North End (a) 2-4
Nov 21 v Oxford University (a) 6-2
Dec 3 v Burnley (h) 3-0
Dec 5 v Cambridge University (h) 5-0
Dec 10 v Lincoln City (a) 6-1
Dec 17 v Long Eaton Rangers (h) 3-1
Dec 26 v Wolverhampton Wanderers (h) 1-1
Jan 14 v Nottingham County (a) 3-3
Jan 21 v Wolverhampton Wanderers (a) 5-0
Feb 4 v Oxford University (a) 5-0
Feb 25 v Aston Villa (h) 4-1
Feb 27 v Cambridge University (a) 6-1
Mar 10 v Aston Villa (a) 4-0
Apr 2 v Third Lanark Rifle Volunteers (a) 0-3
Apr 3 v Newcastle West End (a) 5-1
Apr 7 v Everton (a) 1-0
Apr 16 v Burnley (a) 1-0
Apr 21 v Preston North End (h) 2-2
May 5 v Blackburn Rovers (h) 2-1
May 12 v Third Lanark Rifle Volunteers (h) 5-2
May 19 v Renton (at Hampden Park) 1-4
Played to decide the 'Championship of the World'
May 26 v Aston Villa (a) 1-1
May 28 v Preston North End (a) 0-2

## 1888-89

Aug 6 v Preston North End (h) 2-4
Aug 7 v Birmingham & District XI (h) 0-1
Sep 1 v Sheffield Wednesday (a) 3-1
Sep 3 v Wolverhampton Wanderers (h) 4-2
Sep 17 v Studley & District (h) 23-2
Billy Bassett (5), Bill Hendry (3) and Tom Pearson
(3) led the scoring in this game.
Sep 24 v Walsall Town Swifts (a) 2-2
(played under electric lighting)
Oct 22 v London Caledonians (a) 1-0
Oct 27 v Canadian XI (h) 1-0
Dec 3 v Cambridge University (h) 1-1
Dec 8 v Kidderminster Harriers (a) 4-1
Jan 28 v Oxford University (a) 4-2
Feb 9 v Newcastle West End (a) 2-0
Feb 11 v Sunderland Albion (a) 1-1
Feb 18 v Cambridge University (a) 2-3
Mar 9 v Birmingham St George's (a) 3-1
Mar 30 v Grimsby Town (h) 4-0
Apr 13 v Small Heath (h) 4-1
Apr 15 v Kidderminster Harriers (a) 5-2
Apr 22 v Newton Heath (a) 3-1
Apr 23 v Stockton-on-Tees (a) 3-2
Apr 27 v Birmingham St George's (h) 0-3
Apr 29 v Wolverhampton Wanderers (a) 0-2
May 4 v Small Heath (a) 2-1
May 6 v Wolverhampton Wanderers (h) 3-0
May 8 v Burton & District XI (a) 7-1
May 11 v Wednesbury Old Athletic (a) 2-0
May 18 v Hurst (a) 4-0

## 1889-90

Sep 2 v Warwick County (a) 2-0
Sep 7 v Grimsby Town (a) 1-6
Sep 9 v Great Bridge Unity (a) 6-0
Sep 16 v Walsall Town Swifts (h) 2-1
Oct 14 v Walsall Town Swifts (a) 1-1
Nov 2 v Oxford University (h) 2-3
Feb 15 v Aston Villa (a) 1-0
Feb 22 v Chatham (a) 7-1
Mar 29 v Aston Villa (h) 2-2
Apr 7 v West Manchester (a) 3-2
Apr 8 v Middlesbrough Ironopolis (a) 4-3
Apr 14 v Bootle (a) 3-0
Apr 21 v Kidderminster Olympic (a) 1-2
May 3 v Sunderland (a) 5-3
May 10 v Hyde (a) 3-1
May 24 v Aston Villa (a) 0-1
May 26 v Warwick County (a) 2-1
May 31 v Everton (a) 1-4

## 1890-91

Aug 30 v Stoke (a) 2-2
Sep 8 v Wolverhampton Wanderers (a) 4-2
Sep 15 v Small Heath (h) 3-1
Sep 22 v Walsall Town Swifts (a) 2-1
Sep 29 v Burslem Port Vale (a) 2-1
Oct 6 v Chirk (a) 5-1
Oct 9 v Wolverhampton Wanderers (h) 4-1
Oct 20 v Small Heath (a) 3-3
Nov 10 v Warwick County (a) 4-0
Nov 15 v Nottingham Forest (h) 2-2
Dec 8 v Aston Villa (a) 2-4
Dec 26 v Preston North End (h) 2-0*
Jan 1 v Ardwick (a) 2-2
Jan 10 v Blackburn Rovers (h) 0-4*
Jan 12 v Brierley Hill (a) 2-1
Jan 19 v Aston Villa (h) 4-2
Over 5,000 spectators saw three Scots, McCulloch,
McCullum and McLeod make their debuts for
Albion.
Feb 11 v Oxford University (a) 1-1
Feb 21 v Bootle (a) 0-0
Mar 12 v Nottingham Forest (a) 3-2
Mar 16 v Sheffield Wednesday (a) 2-1
Mar 21 v Preston North End (h) 1-2
Mar 28 v Small Heath (a) 1-2
Mar 30 v Everton (a) 1-2
Mar 31 v Kettering (a) 1-2
Apr 4 v Wolverhampton Wanderers (a) 2-4
Apr 25 v Brierley Hill (a) 2-2
Apr 30 v Hednesford Town (a) 1-3
*Originally designated as Football League matches
but replayed after protest.*

## 1891-92

Sep 1 v Birmingham St George's (h) 4-0
Sep 2 v Coles Farm (a) 5-1
Sep 9 v Burton Swifts (a) 2-1
Sep 14 v Small Heath (a) 0-4
Sep 21 v Birmingham St George's (a) 4-1
Sep 26 v Royal Arsenal (a) 1-1
Sep 28 v Chatham (a) 1-2
Sep 30 v Northwich Victoria (a) 5-0
Oct 5 v Wolverhampton Wanderers (a) 3-3
Oct 26 v Wolverhampton Wanderers (a) 1-2
Nov 9 v Wednesday Old Athletic (h) 2-0
Nov 30 v Aston Villa (a) 2-8
Dec 7 v Wednesday Old Athletic (a) 3-1
Dec 25 v Birmingham St George's (h) 1-1
Dec 29 v Kettering Town (a) 2-0
Dec 30 v Luton Town (a) 4-0
Jan 1 v Ardwick (a) 2-4
Jan 11 v Aston Villa (h) 2-1
Feb 20 v Corinthians (a) 4-4
Mar 22 v Wrexham (a) 2-2
Mar 26 v Corinthians (h) 2-0
Apr 2 v Chirk (h) 3-0
Apr 6 v Everton (a) 0-7
Apr 18 v Heart of Midlothian (a) 0-2
Apr 19 v Sheffield United (a) 0-3
Apr 20 v Bristol Association (a) 7-0

## 1892-93

Sep 1 v Coles Farm Unity (a) 6-2
Sep 3 v Aston Villa (h) 0-1
Sep 5 v Bloxwich (a) 3-1
Sep 7 v Middlesbrough (a) 2-7
Sep 12 v Wrexham (a) 3-1
Sep 26 v Aston Villa (a) 2-3
Sep 27 v Walsall Town Swifts (a) 0-3
Nov 14 v Walsall Town Swifts (h) 2-2
Nov 28 v Wolverhampton Wanderers (h) 1-1
Dec 3 v Royal Arsenal (a) 4-2
Dec 5 v Aston Villa (h) 1-1 (abandoned at half-time)
Feb 4 v Aston Villa (h) 4-4
Feb 18 v Corinthians (a) 3-1
Mar 4 v Aston Villa (h) 2-0
Mar 11 v Burslem Port Vale (h) 2-2
Mar 25 v Heart of Midlothian (a) 0-1
Apr 8 v Bury (a) 2-1
Apr 15 v Newcastle United (a) 2-7
Apr 17 v Small Heath (a) 1-4
Apr 24 v Linfield Athletic (in Belfast) 1-3
Apr 25 v Ulster XI (in Belfast) 0-1
Apr 27 v Wolverhampton Wanderers (a) 4-2
Apr 29 v Millwall (a) 0-1

## 1893-94

Sep 4 v Leicester Fosse (a) 0-3
Sep 11 v Wolverhampton Wanderers (h) 1-0
Sep 14 v Coseley (a) 7-1
Sep 18 v Everton (a) 0-3
Oct 2 v Nottingham County (h) 2-0
Oct 16 v Wolverhampton Wanderers(a) 2-2
Dec 2 v Woolwich Arsenal (a) 0-5
Jan 4 v Nottingham County (a) 0-3
Jan 31 v Oxford University (a) 0-2
Feb 10 v Corinthians (a) 2-5
Feb 19 v Oldbury Town (a) 2-1
Mar 31 v Doncaster Rovers (a) 7-1
Apr 28 v Millwall Athletic (a) 0-3

## 1894-95

Sep 13 v Aston Villa (h) 5-4
Sep 17 v Woolwich Arsenal (a) 1-0
Sep 24 v Wolverhampton Wanderers (a) 2-1
Sep 27 v Coseley (a) 3-2
Oct 22 v Wolverhampton Wanderers (h) 0-1
Nov 20 v Oxford University (a) 4-2
Dec 3 v Walsall (a) 5-1
Jan 28 v Aberystwyth (a) 8-2
Billy Richards scored five goals.
Mar 23 v Everton (a) 2-9
Apr 8 v Wrexham (a) 2-0

## 1895-96

Sep 14 v Burton Swifts (a) 1-5
Sep 24 v Walsall (a) 2-1
Sep 25 v Aberystwyth (a) 10-1
Sep 30 v Millwall Athletic (a) 3-0
Oct 14 v Dundee (a) 1-3
Nov 11 v Cambridge University (a) 2-3
Nov 25 v Oxford University (a) 2-2
Feb 8 v Corinthians (a) 2-5
Mar 14 v Liverpool (a) 1-1
Mar 20 v Thames Ironworks (a) 4-2
(played under electric lighting)
Mar 21 v West Norwood (a) 4-0
Mar 23 v Revd A.R.Bourke's XI (a) 4-1
Mar 24 v West Brompton (a) 9-1
Mar 25 v Wickham Wanderers (a) 4-1
Mar 28 v Llandudno (a) 2-1
Apr 13 v Preston North End (h) 2-2

## 1896-97

Sep 21 v Walsall (a) 0-2
Nov 7 v Great Marlow (a) 3-5
Nov 30 v Oxford University (a) 0-2
Jan 9 v Bolton Wanderers (a) 2-2
Feb 27 v Corinthians (a) 1-3
Mar 20 v Swindon Town (a) 1-0
Mar 27 v Dartford (a) 4-1
Mar 29 v Oldbury Town (a) 2-0
Apr 19 v Hereford Town (a) 2-1
Apr 21 v Derby County (at Bristol) 1-2
Apr 24 v Gravesend (a) 4-0
Apr 29 v Small Heath (a) 1-5

## 1897-98

Sep 28 v Walsall (a) 2-1
Nov 22 v Cambridge University (a) 5-3
Dec 6 v Oxford University (a) 1-1
Jan 8 v Queen's Park Rangers (a) 4-1
Apr 16 v Newcastle United (a) 1-1
Apr 23 v Bristol City (a) 1-1
Apr 25 v Chirk (a) 1-0
Apr 27 v Devon County (a) 8-0
Apr 28 v Dorset County (a) 3-0
Apr 29 v Suffolk County (a) 2-1
Apr 30 v Watford (a) 1-1

## 1898-99

Nov 14 v Cambridge University (a) 4-3
Mar 11 v Newton Heath (a) 0-2
Apr 3 v Small Heath (a) 0-1
Apr 4 v Northampton (a) 1-6
Apr 20 v Swansea Town (a) 13-1
One of Albion's goals was credited to the referee.
Apr 29 v Swindon Town (a) 1-2

## 1899-1900

Sep 16 v Burton Swifts (a) 0-0
Nov 22 v Kaffirs XI (h) 11-6

Nov 27 v Cambridge University (a) 2-2
Mar 17 v Leicester Fosse (a) 1-3
Apr 28 v Small Heath (a) 1-1

**1900-01**
(Albion's first season at The Hawthorns)
Nov 13 v Cambridge University (a) 2-6
*Buck, A.Smith*
*Att: 2,500*
Dec 26 v Liverpool (h) 5-2
*Simmons, Stevenson, Buck, Banks, Roberts*
*Att: 10,000*

**1901-02**
Nov 16 v Reading (a) 1-1
*Simmons*
*Att: 4,133*
Nov 30 v Walsall (a) 2-1
*Brett, Harper*
*Att: 2,500*
Mar 25 v New Brompton (a) 3-2
*Simmons 2, A.Smith*
*Att: 5,000*
Apr 9 v Brownhills Albion (a) 5-0
*Simmons 3, Brett 2*
*Att: 2,000*
Apr 26 v Woolwich Arsenal (at Exeter) 1-0
*Stevenson*
*Att: 3,500*
Apr 28 v West Bromwich Albion Reserves (h) 1-2
*Dorsett*
*Att: 807*
Apr 30 v Middlesbrough (a) 1-1
*Lee*
*Att: 6,150*

**1902-03**
Feb 21 v Belfast Distillery (a) 5-5
*McLean, Dorsett 2, Lee, Worton*
*Att: 5,000*

**1903-04**
Dec 3 v Northampton Town (a) 1-2
*Dorsett*
*Att: 3,000*
Apr 27 v Brighton & Hove Albion (a) 2-3
*Dorsett, Aston*
*Att: 5,000*
Apr v Middlesbrough (a) 0-2
*3,400*

**1904-05**
Oct 19 v Clapton Orient (a) 1-1
*Jack*
*Att: 3,000*
Nov 12 v Plymouth Argyle (a) 2-3
*Jack 2*
*Att: 4,350*
Dec 10 v Portsmouth (a) 2-3
*Brown, Bell*
*Att: 1,200*
Feb 4 v Leeds City (a) 5-0
*W.Smith, Aston, Lewis, Manners, Pheasant*
*Att: 2,100*
Apr 29 v Shepherds Bush (a) 3-3
*Williams 3*
*Att: 3,250*

**1907-08**
Sep 9 v Barnsley (a) 1-0
*Shinton*
*Att: 3,000*

**1913-14**
Apr 25 v Corinthians (h) 0-4
*Att: 3,867*

**1919-20**
Jan 31 v Corinthians (h) 4-3
*A.Smith 2, Crisp, Hatton*
*Att: 9,265*

**1920-21**
Mar 5 v Corinthians (h) 3-0
*Gregory, Blood 2*
*Att: 10,134*

**1924-25**
Mar 28 v Corinthians (h) 4-4
*Carter 2, James, Davies*
*Att: 7,227*

**1929-30**
Jan 25 v Crystal Palace (a) 2-1
*Carter 2*
*Att: 5,000*

**1931-32**
Jan 23 v Corinthians (h) 4-0
*Carter 2, Richardson, Fitton*
*Att: 10,000*

**1954-55**
Feb 19 v Leeds United (a) 1-1
*Hodkisson*
*Att: 16,240*

**1957-58**
Oct 29 v CDSA (Russian Red Army) (h) 6-5
*Howe, Kevan 2, Griffin, Robson, Allen (pen)*
*Att: 52,805*
*Official opening of The Hawthorns floodlights*

**1958-59**
Sep 24 v Port Vale (a) 3-5
*Burnside 2, Main*
*Att: 18,795*
*Official opening of Vale Park floodlights*
Nov v Athletic Bilbao (h) 1-2
*Allen (pen)*
*Att: 24,800*
Dec 10 v Bucharest XI (h) 3-0
*Forrester, Allen, Setters.*
*Att: 7,904*

**1959-60**
Oct 5 v Grenchen (h) 0-0
*Att: 10,909*
May 2 v Geo.Salters Works XI (a) 13-2
*Jackson 5, Burnside 3, G.Williams 2, Hope,*
*Wallace, G.Carter*
*Att: 2,103*
*Salters' Works Bi-centennial celebration match*

**1960-61**
Oct 4 v Canadian FA XI (h) 0-1
*Att: 8,724*

**1962-63**
Feb 20 v Aston Villa (at Stourbridge) 3-2
*Jones, Kevan, Hope*
*Att: 1,600*
Feb 22 v Charlton Athletic (a) 0-5
*Att: 2,282*

**1963-64**
Apr 7 v Alkmaar (h) 2-1
*Foggo, Jones*
*Att: 9,411*

**1967-68**
Aug 7 v Bristol City (a) 4-1
*Clark 2, Astle, Foggo*
*Att: 7,719*
Aug 9 v Bournemouth & BA (a) 1-0
*Brown*
*Att: 5,500*
Aug v Portsmouth (a)1-0
*Astle*
*Att: 8,929*

**1968-69**
July 30 v Carlisle United (a) 1-1
*Brown*
*Att: 11,607*

**1969-70**
July 26 v Rotherham United (a) 4-0
*Watson (og), Hegan, Glover, Astle*
*Att: 4,468*
Jan 23 v Birmingham City (a) 2-2
*Astle, Suggett*
*Att: 20,110*

May 20 v US Triestina (a) 1-1
*Suggett*
*Att: 12,345*

**1970-71**
Aug 3 v Heart of Midlothian (h) 2-0
*Reed, Wilson (pen)*
*Att: 8,024*
Aug 8 v Aston Villa (a) 1-1
*Wright (og)*
*Att: 20,893*

**1971-72**
Feb 2 v Queen's Park Rangers (a) 2-1
*T.Brown, Hartford*
*Att: 7,082*
26 Feb v Preston North End (a) 1-2
*T.Brown*
*Att: 5,912*

**1972-73**
July 23 v Feyenoord (a) 1-4
*Gould*
*Att: 26,251*
Aug 8 v Hibernian (a) 2-0
*A.Brown, Gould*
*Att: 10,203*
Dec 30 v Walsall (h) 1-1
*Robertson*
*Att: 5,648*

**1973-74**
Aug 14 v Colchester United (a) 0-3
*Att: 2,840*
Aug 14 v Rhyl (a) 3-1
*A.Brown, Edwards, Williams (og)*
*Att: 1,112*
Aug 16 v Wolverhampton Wanderers (a) 0-3
*Att: 12,928*
Aug 18 v AFC Bournemouth (h) 0-1
*Att: 4,304*

**1975-76**
May v Coventry City (h) 5-1
*T.Brown 2, Johnston, A.Brown, Rushbury*
*Att: 5,777*
Match arranged to celebrate promotion

**1976-77**
Aug 2 v Crewe Alexandra (a) 6-2
*A.Brown 2, Cantello, Mayo, T.Brown (pen) Nisbet*
*Att: 1,089*
**Centenary Match**
Dec 21 v Kettering Town (a) 2-3
*Treacy, Mayo*
*Att: 1,699*
Jan 29 v Sheffield United (a) 0-1
Att: 3,924

**1977-78**
Dec 13 v Saudi Arabia (at Dhahran) 1-0
*T.Brown*
*Att: 5,000*

**1978-79**
Feb 6 v Portsmouth (a) 0-2
*Att: 8,552*
Feb v Birmingham City (in Guernsey) 1-1
*Regis*
*Att: 4,400*

**1979-80**
Aug 1 v China XI (h) 4-0
*Luofeng (og), Regis, A.Brown, Barnes*
*Att: 11,382*
Aug 6 v Bradford City (a) 1-0
*Robson*
*Att: 4,098*
Aug 11 v Ajax Amsterdam (h) 1-0
*Barnes*
*Att: 13,334*
Albion Centenary Match
Mar 3 v Barnet (a) 2-1
*Moses, Mills*
*Att: 3,556*

**1980-81**
**Jul 26 v Reading (a) 2-4**
*Regis, Deehan*
*Att: 1,595*
**Jul 28 v Bradford City (a) 1-0**
*Owen*
*Att: 1,268*
**Aug 2 v Swindon Town (a) 3-1**
*Muzinic, Deehan, Mills*
*Att: 3,054*
**Aug 12 v Hapoel Tel-Aviv (h) 2-1**
*Barnes, Mills*
*Att: 3,445*
**Sept 10 v AC Naples (a) 2-2**
*Mills, Owen*
*Att: 24,000*
**Feb 2 v Red Star Belgrade (h) 4-2**
*Robson, Wile, Deehan, Mills*
*Att: 3,217*
**Feb 23 v Poole Town (a) 4-2**
*Deehan, A.Brown, Regis, Batson*
*Att: 4,103*
**Mar 3 v Linfield (a) 2-0**
*Robson, Barnes*
*Att: 8,092*
**Apr 12 v Kuwait XI (a) 1-1**
*Regis*
*Att: 11,200*
**Apr 29 v Sweden XI (a) 0-2**
*Att: 3,969*

**1981-82**
**Aug 14 v Newcastle United (a) 2-0**
*Regis, N.Cross*
*Att: 4,340*
**Jan 17 v Birmingham City (in Guernsey) 1-2**
*A.Brown*
*Att: 2,658*

**1982-83**
**Aug 7 v Twente Enschede (a) 3-1**
*Jol 2, Mackenzie*
*Att: 7,894*
**Aug 23 v Sheffield Wednesday (a) 2-2**
*Eastoe, Mackenzie*
*Att: 4,518*
**Nov 10 v AEL Limasol (a) 4-0**
*Eastoe 2, N.Cross, Owen (pen)*
*Att: 2,150*
**Feb 13 v Poole Town (a) 1-2**
*N.Cross*
*Att: 1,408*
**Apr 14 v Stourbridge (a) 3-1**
*Perry 2, Zondervan*
*Att: 1,045*
**May 16 v The Army XI (at Aldershot) 5-0**
*Kent 2, Thompson, Robson, N.Cross*
*Att: 1,016*

**1983-84**
**Jul 27 v Dorchester Town (a) 3-1**
*Perry, Eastoe, Luke*
*Att: 1,100*
**Jul 29 v Poole Town (a) 2-0**
*Regis, Perry*
*Att: 550*
**Aug 2 v Rangers (a) 2-4**
*Regis, Luke*
*Att: 21,566*
**Aug 5 v Gloucester City (a) 1-0**
*Thompson*
*Att: 400*
**Aug 19 v Walsall (a) 1-0**
*Jol*
*Att: 1,853*
**Aug 22 v Sheffield Wednesday (a) 0-1**
*Att: 3,331*
**Dec 11 v BSR (Stourbridge) (a) 9-0**
*N.Cross 3, Monaghan 3, Morley, Owen, Thompson*
*Att: 752*

**1984-85**
**Aug 7 v Walsall (a) 1-3**
*Lewis*
*Att: 200*

**Aug 15 v Walsall (h) 2-0**
*Mower (og), Hunt*
*Att: 150*
**Aug 18 v Oldham Athletic (a) 1-0**
*Bennett*
*Att: 3,000*
**Aug 20 v Stockport County (a) 3-2**
*Thompson 2, McNaught*
*Att: 1,792*
**Oct 3 v Örgryte IS (a) 2-2**
*Grealish, Forsyth*
*Att: 2,588*
**Oct 23 v Hong Kong XI (a) 3-0**
*Grealish, G.Thompson 2*
*Att: 2,022*
**Jan 30 v Tunisian XI (in Tunis) 1-1**
*M.Giles*
*Att: 2,550*
**Feb 19 v Scunthorpe United (a) 0-0**
*Att: 387*

**1985-86**
**July 27 v Rotherham United(at Spring Road) 2-1**
*Crooks, Mackenzie*
*Att: 155*
**Aug 3 v Peterborough United (a) 2-0**
*G.Thompson, Mackenzie*
*Att: 1,329*
**Aug 10 v Doncaster Rovers (a) 3-2**
*Whitehead, Mackenzie, Varadi*
*Att: 1,226*
**Aug 12 v Whitby Town (a) 1-2**
*Valentine*
*Att: 908*
**Feb 14 v Oldham Athletic (a) 1-5**
*Grealish*
*Att: 632*
**Apr 28 v Swansea City (a) 2-2**
*Robson, Bradley*
*Att: 1,565*

**1986-87**
**Aug 9 v Bristol City (a) 0-1**
*2,227*
**Aug 12 v Crewe Alexandra (a) 2-0**
*Burke, Macowat (og)*
*Att: 655*
**Aug 15 v Torpedo Moscow (h) 0-2**
*Att: 2,591*
**Aug 18 v Walsall (a) 2-2**
*Evans 2*
*Att: 2,781*

**1987-88**
**Aug 3 v Mansfield Town (a) 1-1**
*Goodman*
*Att: 1,307*
**Aug 7 v Bristol City (a) 0-2**
*Att: 1,497*
**Aug 11 v SC Mazda (h) 1-1**
*Kelly*
*Att: 1,449*
**Oct 27 v Esperanca de Lagos (a) 1-1**
*Goodman*
*Att: 2,084*
**Jan 13 v Stockport County (a) 2-3**
*Goodman, Hopkins*
*Att: 200*
**Jan 26 v Crewe Alexandra (a) 1-0**
*Goodman*
*Att: 100*
**May 18 v Wolverton (a) 5-0**
*Gray 2, Dobbins, C.Johnson 2*
*Att: 256*

**1988-89**
**Aug 6 v Dumbarton (a) 1-2**
*L.Palmer*
*Att: 745*
**Aug 11 v Witney Town (a) 2-1**
*Paskin 2*
*Att: 400*
**Aug 13 v Wolverton Town (a) 9-1**
*Paskin 3, Hopkins, Gray, Kelly, Dobbins, Ingram,*
*Robson*
*Att: 640*

**Aug 17 v Derby County (h) 3-4**
*Paskin 2, Talbot*
*Att: 3,150*
**Aug 20 v Hereford United (a) 0-0**
*Att: 1,300*
**Dec 20 v Newquay Town (a) 0-0**
*Att: 590*
**Jan 25 v SC Caen (h) 2-0**
*Rice, Talbot*
*Att: 2,073*
**Feb 13 v Torquay United (a) 1-2**
*Robson*
*Att: 897*

**1989-90**
**Aug 5 v Newcastle Town (a) 8-0**
*West 2, Goodman 2, Thomas 2, Robson, McNally*
*Att: 805*
**Aug 8 v Shrewsbury Town (a) 1-1**
*Thomas*
*Att: 1,533*
**Feb 6 v Ryde Sports (a) 4-0**
*McNally, Foster 2, Pearson*
*Att: 525*
**May 8 v Cheshunt (a) 6-1**
*McNally, Davies (og), Foster 2, Harbey, Burgess*
*Att: 250*

**1990-91**
**Aug 16 v Swansea City (a) 0-5**
*Att: 1,259*
**Aug 18 v Stoke City (a) 1-1**
*Goodman*
*Att: 3,940*

**1991-92**
**Jul 31 v Derby County (a) 2-0**
*Ampadu, Goodman (pen)*
*Att: 300*
**Aug 3 v Dudley Town (a) 3-0**
*Ampadu, Goodman, Shakespeare*
*Att: 3,564*
**Aug 6 v Walsall (a) 3-0**
*Foster 2, Bannister*
*Att: 4,965*
**Aug 10 v Chelsea (h) 0-3**
*Att: 3,118*

**1992-93**
**Jul 18 v Evesham Town (a) 4-0**
*Robson, Opp own-goal, Taylor, McNally*
*Att: 2,338*
**Jul 22 v Hereford United (a) 1-0**
*Taylor*
*Att: 1,658*
**Jul 25 v St Albans (a) 7-0**
*Robson, Hackett, Taylor 2, McNally 2, Ampadu*
*Att: 1,028*
**Jul 30 v Sheffield Wednesday (h) 2-2**
*Taylor, Ampadu*
*Att: 6,171*
**Aug 3 v Tottenham Hotspur (h) 0-2**
*Att: 8,078*
**Aug 8 v Blackburn Rovers (h) 2-3**
*Robson, Garner*
*Att: 6,698*

# Birmingham Charity Cup

FROM 1884 until 1933 Albion took part intermittently in the Lord Mayor of Birmingham's Charity Cup. The club's first game in the competition, on 5 April 1884, brought a 4-1 defeat at the hands of Aston Villa who repeated the scoreline the following season. The Albion team for that first Birmingham Charity Cup tie was: Roberts; H.Bell, Green, Horton, Bunn, Stanton, Woodhall, Aston, Smith, Timmins, G.Bell.

Albion's complete record in the Birmingham Charity Cup reads:-

|  | Home |  |  |  |  | Away |  |  |  |  |
|---|---|---|---|---|---|---|---|---|---|---|
| P | W | D | L | F | A | W | D | L | F | A |
| 41 | 4 | 1 | 5 | 26 | 26 | 9 | 4 | 18 | 40 | 72 |

Aston Villa were its first winners, in 1882. It was never regarded as a major local event as Albion showed by entering their second team in 1885-86 (they lost in the first round to Wednesbury Old Athletic), and by refusing to take part in 1887-88 because of pressure of fixtures. During the 1886-87 season Albion lost 3-1 to Wolves after two drawn games in the semi-final. An angry crowd of Albion fans besieged the referee after the final whistle and he had to seek refuge in the Stoney Lane grandstand before rescue came in the shape of six policemen and a number of Albion committee members.

Albion's first Birmingham Charity Cup win did not materialize until 13 September 1897 when Small Heath were overcome 7-4 at home in a first round tie. This was Albion's 12th tie at senior level in the competition and was also to be their record victory. The worst defeat came at Aston Villa in the semi-final on 10 April 1893 when Villa won 6-0.

Albion have played in the Final on 16 occasions, winning the trophy four times and sharing it once, between 1899 and 1933.

From 1910 onwards, the Birmingham Charity Cup Final was an invitation match and no preliminary rounds were contested. On 8 May 1926, Albion were due to meet Aston Villa at St Andrew's in the Final but it was postponed because of the General Strike and ultimately cancelled.

---

**1883-84**
**Semi-final**
**Apr 5 v Aston Villa (a) 1-4**
*Riddell (og)*
*Att: 6,000*

**1884-85**
**Semi-final**
**Apr 18 v Aston Villa (at Wednesbury) 1-4**
*Bayliss*
*Att: 5,000*

**1886-87**
**Semi-final**
**Apr 18 v Wolverhampton Wanderers (a) 3-3**
*Pearson, Woodhall, T.Green*
*Att: 8,000*
**Replay**
**Apr 20 v Wolverhampton Wanderers (a) 0-0 (aet)**
*Att: 6,000*
**Second replay**
**Apr 25 v Wolverhampton Wanderers (h) 1-3**
*Paddock*
*Att: 7,200*

**1889-90**
**Semi-final**
**Apr 26 v Wolverhampton Wanderers (h) 0-1**
*Att: 3,000*

**1890-91**
**Semi-final**
**Apr 27 v Wolverhampton Wanderers (a) 1-4**
*Pearson*
*Att: 4,000*

**1891-92**
**Semi-final**
**Apr 27 v Wolverhampton Wanderers (a) 0-3**
*Att: 5,000*

**1892-93**
**Semi-final**
**Apr 10 v Aston Villa (a) 0-6**
*Att: 6,500*

**1893-94**
**Semi-final**
**Apr 16 v Aston Villa (a) 1-3**
*Pearson*
*Att: 7,000*

**1894-95**
**Semi-final**
**Apr 6 v Small Heath (a) 0-4**
*Att: 8,500*

**1897-98**
**Round 1**
**Sep 13 v Small Heath (h) 7-4 (aet)**
*Garfield 4, Flewitt 2, McKenzie*
*Att: 3,000*
**Semi-final**
**Sep 20 v Aston Villa (a) 0-3**
*Att: 8,500*

**1898-99**
**Round 1**
**Sep 12 v Small Heath (a) 4-3**
*Garfield 2, R.Brett, Banks*
*Att: 3,000*

**Semi-final**
**Sep 26 v Walsall (a) 1-3**
*Jones*
*Att: 4,000*

**1899-1900**
**Round 1**
**Sep 11 v Burton Swifts (h) 4-1**
*Richards 2, Parrett, Paddock*
*Att: 2,100*
**Semi-final**
**Sep 25 v Aston Villa (a) 2-2**
*Simmons, Richards*
*Att: 8,250*
**Semi-final**
**Oct 16 v Aston Villa (a) 2-1 (aet)**
*Jones, Walker*
*Att: 12,150*
**Final**
**Nov 13 v Walsall (at Aston) 1-0**
*Walker*
*Att: 8,250*

**1900-01**
**Semi-final**
**Sep 17 v Walsall (h) 6-1**
*Wheldon 2, Simmons, Chadburn, Jones, Roberts*
*Att: 2,500*
**Final**
**Nov 19 v Aston Villa (h) 1-1**
*Wheldon*
*Att: 10,000*
**Replay**
**Dec 17 v Aston Villa (a) 0-2**
*Att: 12,652*

**1901-02**
**Semi-final**
**Oct 28 v Small Heath (a) 1-0**
*Worton*
*Att: 3,000*
**Final**
**Nov 18 v Aston Villa (a) 0-1**
*Att: 10,600*

**1902-03**
**Round 1**
**Sep 3 v Small Heath (a) 3-1**
*Buck 3*
*Att: 5,000*
**Final**
**Nov 24 v Wolverhampton Wanderers (at Aston) 2-3**
*Lee, Simmons*
*Att: 4,500*
Albion went straight into Final after opening round.

**1903-04**
**Semi-final**
**Sep 21 v Small Heath (h) 4-5**
*Worton, Cole, Dorsett 2*
*Att: 5,000*

**1904-05**
**Round 1**
**Sep 19 v Aston Villa (a) 0-2**
*Att: 6,500*

**1905-06**
**Semi-final**
**Sep 18 v Birmingham (h) 2-1**
*Randle, Broad*
*Att: 5,000*

**Final**
**Nov 20 v Aston Villa (at Small Heath) 3-4**
*Bradley, Broad, F.Nicholls*
*Att: 12,000*

**1910-11**
**Final**
**Sep 19 v Aston villa (a) 1-2**
*Lloyd*
*Att: 5,507*

**1911-12**
**Final**
**Sep 18 v Aston Villa (a) 0-4**
*Att: 6,503*

**1912-13**
**Final**
**Oct 2 v Aston Villa (h) 1-5**
*Shearman*
*Att: 8,077*

**1913-14**
**Final**
**Oct 22 v Aston Villa (a) 1-0**
*Morris*
*Att: 6,000*

**1914-15**
**Final**
**Sep 23 v Aston Villa (a) 3-2**
*Morris, Bache 2*
*Att: 5,017*

**1920-21**
**Final**
**May 14 v Birmingham (at Aston) 2-2**
*Morris, Bentley*
*Att: 8,067*
Trophy shared

**1921-22**
**Final**
**May 13 v Birmingham (at Aston) 2-0**
*Wilson, Morris*
*Att: 7,500*

**1922-23**
**Final**
**May 2 v Aston Villa (a) 0-2**
*Att: 2,300*

**1924-25**
**Final**
**May 9 v Birmingham (a) 3-1**
*James 2, Byers*
*Att: 10,000*

**1930-31**
**Final**
**May 9 v Aston Villa (h) 2-3**
*Raw 2*
*Att: 18,189*

**1932-33**
**Final**
**May 13 v Aston Villa (h) 0-4**
*Att: 8,500*

# *Birmingham Cup*

THE BIRMINGHAM CUP was first competed for in 1875-76 when Tipton FC were the winners. In December 1875, the Birmingham County FA had been formed in Birmingham at a meeting convened by the Calthorpe and Aston Unity clubs, and the Cup competition was quickly introduced by the new body. In April 1881, West Bromwich FC were defeated 2-0 in the semi-final by Aston Villa but Albion's first entry into the competition did not materialize until the following season when Calthorpe, Elwells, Fallings Heath Rovers and Notts Rangers were beaten on the way to a semi-final meeting with Wednesbury Old Athletic.

Albion's first Birmingham Cup tie was against Calthorpe (away) on 12 November 1881, when this team brought off a surprise 3-2 victory: Eld; H.Bell, Bunn, Stanton, While, Whitehouse, Aston, Timmins, Bisseker, Kershaw, G.Bell. Albion's display was so pleasing that the referee, Mr J.H.Cofield, who was secretary of the Birmingham FA, wrote them a long letter of congratulation.

In the semi-final, at the Aston Lower Grounds on 25 March 1882, Albion were well supported as the correspondent of the *Midland Advertiser* pointed out: 'The howling, hooting and yelling, indulged in by the West Bromwich contingent of onlookers, was simply horrible. May I be far away when next Athletic meet West Bromwich Albion in another semi-final, for I have scarcely got the din of the discordant yells out of my hearing yet.'

Unfortunately for the vociferous Albionites the 'Old 'Uns' proved just too good for their opponents in winning an exciting game by 3-2.

On 11 November 1882, Albion crushed Coseley 26-0 in a first round tie, having led 17-0 at half-time, and then defeated Wolves 4-2 away, in the first-ever clash between the two clubs, before losing once again to the 'Old 'Uns'. In 1883-84, Albion progressed to the semi-final again after a three-match marathon with Wednesbury Old Athletic. In the semis they lost to Walsall Swifts. It was during the 1885-86 season that Albion won the trophy for the first time. In the first two rounds Albion's reserve team took over the fixtures after which Albion's seniors demolished Notts Rangers, Burslem Port Vale and Walsall Swifts.

In 1894, Albion and Wolves shared the trophy for six months each. Albion were losing semi-finalists in 1881-82, 1883-84, 1890-91 and 1896-97. In nine home ties from 9 October 1886 to 17 January 1891, Albion did not concede a goal and in 34 home Cup ties in 24 years the Baggies scored in all but two of them.

Albion's record victory was the 1881 slaughter of Coseley whilst the heaviest defeat incurred was 7-0 at Stoney Lane on 16 January 1899 when Wolverhampton Wanderers were the visitors. Albion's record in the Birmingham Cup:-

|   | Home | | | | | Away | | | | |
|---|---|---|---|---|---|---|---|---|---|---|
| P | W | D | L | F | A | W | D | L | F | A |
| 80 | 26 | 3 | 5 | 141 | 33 | 22 | 9 | 15 | 99 | 76 |

The Birmingham Cup was one of the major competitions in the earliest days of Midlands football and was taken very seriously, as shown when Albion withdrew Billy Bassett from the Football League team to meet the Football Alliance in 1891 so that he could play in a semi-final replay against Aston Villa.

Three years earlier Albion withdrew from the Birmingham FA (and the Birmingham Cup) because the club's management did not like the attitude of the FA and the Birmingham newspapers towards the club. By the end of the century, however, the competition had lost much of its importance and in 1906-07 the Birmingham FA decreed that local clubs could field their reserve sides in the Birmingham Cup. Albion's last Birmingham Cup tie at senior level was a 5-1 home defeat by Aston Villa on 4 September 1905.

In recent years Albion's reserve XI played in the Birmingham Cup competition and they won the trophy three times in four seasons. They lifted the Cup in 1988 (for the first time since 1895) by beating Bedworth United 3-1, Bobby Williamson (2) and Tony Kelly the scorers. Then they took the prize in successive seasons, 1989-90 and 1990-91, beating Atherstone United 2-0 (after extra-time) in the former when Sam Allerdyce and Dave Barnett were on target, and beating Nuneaton Borough 2-0 in 1991 when Colin West and Bernard McNally found the net. Nuneaton, in fact, prevented the Baggies from recording a hat-trick of victories when they knocked them out of the 1991-92 competition, 2-1.

**1881-82**
**Round 1**
**Nov 12 v Calthorpe (a) 3-2**
*Att: 1,000*
**Round 2**
**Dec 10 v Elwells (a) 2-1**
*Att: 800*
**Round 3**
**Jan 21 v Fallings Heath Rovers (a) 3-1**
*Att: 1,200*
**Round 4**
**Feb 18 v Notts Rangers (a) 5-2**
*Stokes, Bisseker, Whitehouse, Aston 2*
*Att: 500*
**Semi-final**
**Mar 25 v Wednesbury Old Athletic (at Aston) 2-3**
*Bisseker, Aston*
*Att: 1,000*
Goalscorers not listed for Rounds 1, 2 and 3.

**1882-83**
**Round 1**
**Nov 11 v Coseley (h) 26-0**
*Aston 5, Bisseker 4, Timmins 4, G.Bell 3, Bunn 2, Horton 2, Whitehouse 2, White 2, H.Bell, Stanton.*
*Att: 2,500*
**Round 2**
Albion received a bye
**Round 3**
**Jan 20 v Wolverhampton Wanderers (a) 4-2**
*G.Bell, Bisseker, Biddulph, Aston*
*Att: 3,000*
**Round 4**
**Mar 13 v Wednesbury Old Athletic (a) 1-2**
*Aston*
*Att: 2,500*

**1883-84**
**Round 1**
**Oct 27 v Stourbridge Standard (h) 7-0**
*Bisseker 2, Timmins 2, G.Bell, F.Bunn, Aston*
*Att: 2,000*
**Round 2**
**Dec 8 v Walsall Alma Athletic (h) 6-0**
*Timmins 2, G.Bell, Aston, Smith, Loach*
*Att: 2,500*
**Round 3**
**Jan 5 v Wednesbury Old Athletic (h) 1-1**
*G.Bell*
*Att: 3,000*

**Replay**
**Feb 9 v Wednesbury Old Athletic (a) 3-3**
*Timmins 3*
*Att: 700*
**Second replay**
**Feb 18 v Wednesbury Old Athletic (at Aston) 3-1**
*G.Bell, Aston, Kent (og)*
*Att: 3,000*
**Round 4**
**Feb 23 v Wolverhampton Wanderers (at Aston) 1-1**
*Bisseker*
*Att: 5,000*
**Replay**
**Mar 3 v Wolverhampton Wanderers (at Wednesbury) 2-1**
*Aston, Bisseker*
*Att: 3,800*
**Semi-final**
**Mar 10 v Walsall Swifts (at Aston) 0-1**
*Att: 2,000*

**1884-85**
**Round 1**
**Oct 18 v Darlaston All Saints (h) 8-0**
*Aston 3, Bayliss 2, Loach 2, Jacobs (og)*
*Att: 1,200*
**Round 2**
**Nov 22 v Bloxwich Strollers (h) 15-0**
*Bayliss 6\**
Att: 1,500
*\*No other goalscorers listed for this match.*
**Round 3**
**Dec 20 v St George's (h) 2-3**
*Loach, G.Bell*
*Att: 4,000*

**1885-86**
**Round 3**
**Dec 5 v Notts Rangers (a) 7-2**
*Woodhall, T.Green 3, Loach 2, G.Bell.*
*Att: 520*
**Semi-final**
**Jan 16 v Burslem Port Vale (at Aston) 5-0**
*T.Green 2, Timmins, Loach, Bunn*
*Att: 3,000*
**Final**
**Mar 13 v Walsall Swifts (at Aston) 1-1**
*T.Green*
*Att: 4,000*

**Replay**
**Apr 12 v Walsall Swifts (at Aston) 1-0**
*Woodhall*
*Att: 10,000*
Because of pressure of fixtures, Albion's reserve team represented the club in the first two rounds, defeating Sparkhill Alliance 6-0 and Burton Swifts 4-1 to progress into the quarter-finals.

**1886-87**
**Round 1**
**Oct 9 v Aston Villa (h) 1-0**
*T.Green*
*Att: 12,000*
**Round 2**
**Nov 13 v Mitchell's St George (h) 3-0**
*T.Green, Woodhall 2*
*Att: 3,000*
**Round 3**
**Dec 11 v Derby County (h) 6-0**
*Paddock 2, T.Green 2, Bayliss, Woodhall*
*Att: 8,000*
**Round 4**
**Mar 19 v Stoke (h) 3-0**
*Pearson 2, Bayliss*
*Att: 5,100*
**Semi-final**
**Apr 30 v Burslem Port Vale (at Stoke) 5-1**
*Bayliss 3, Woodhall 2*
*Att: 4,000*
**Final**
**May 7 v Long Eaton Rovers (at Perry Barr) 0-1**
*Att: 5,000*

**1887-88**
**Round 1**
**Oct 8 v Small Heath Alliance (h) 2-0**
*Bayliss 2*
*Att: 4,000*
**Round 2**
**Oct 31 v Burslem Port Vale (a) 3-0**
*Askin, Bayliss, J.Horton*
*Att: 2,500*
**Round 3**
**Nov 19 v Aston Shakespeare (h) 3-0**
*G.Bell, Woodhall 2*
*Att: 3,500*
**Round 4**
**Dec 24 v Mitchell's St George (h) 4-0**
*Wilson 2, Pearson, Woodhall*
*Att: 4,500*

**Semi-final**
**Feb 11 v Wolverhampton Wanderers (h) 2-0**
*Wilson, Timmins*
*Att: 5,000*
**Final**
**Mar 3 v Aston Villa (at Aston Lower Grounds) 2-3**
*Pearson 2*
*Att: 12,000*

**1889-90**
**Round 1**
**Jan 23 v Notts Rangers (a) 4-0**
*Pearson, Sauve 3*
*Att: 3,000*
**Round 2**
**Feb 17 v Small Heath (h) 2-0**
*Pearson 2*
*Att: 1,500*
**Semi-final**
**Apr 5 v Walsall Town Swifts (at Wednesbury) 2-1**
*Evans 2*
*Att: 5,500*
**Final**
**Apr 19 v Aston Villa (a) 0-2**
*Att: 8,000*

**1890-91**
**Round 1**
**Jan 17 v Small Heath (h) 3-2**
*Burns, Nicholls, C.Perry*
*Att: 3,000*
**Round 2**
**Mar 16 v Warwick County (h) 6-0**
*Nicholls, T.Perry, Pearson 3, Bassett*
*Att: 2,600*
**Semi-final**
**Apr 11 v Aston Villa (at Edgbaston) 2-2**
*Dyer, Woodhall*
*Att: 12,000*
**Replay**
**Apr 20 v Aston Villa (at Wolverhampton) 1-1 (aet)**
*Haynes*
*Att: 5,000*
**Second replay**
**Apr 22 v Aston Villa (at Wolverhampton) 2-3**
*Woodhall 2*
*Att: 6,700*

**1891-92**
**Round 3**
**Jan 2 v Wednesbury Old Athletic (h) 2-2**
*Nicholls 2*
*Att: 2,500*
**Replay**
**Feb 15 v Wednesbury Old Athletic (a) 2-1**
*Nicholls, Groves*
*Att: 3,500*
**Round 4**
**Mar 28 v Small Heath (h) 4-1**
*C.Perry, Nicholls, McLeod, Geddes*
*Att: 4,000*
**Semi-final**
**Apr 9 v Aston Villa (at Wolverhampton) 2-0**
*Campbell (og), McLeod*
*Att: 8,000*
**Final**
**Apr 30 v Wolverhampton Wanderers (at Perry Barr) 2-5**
*Reynolds, Bassett*
*Att: 6,500*
Albion received a bye in Rounds 1 and 2.

**1892-93**
**Round 1**
**Jan 23 v Stoke (h) 3-0**
*Horton, McLeod, T.Perry*
*Att: 3,500*
**Round 2**
**Mar 27 v Wolverhampton Wanderers (a) 1-3**
*McLeod*
*Att: 4,000*

**1893-94**
**Round 1**
**Jan 29 v Walsall (a) 1-0**
*Bassett*
*Att: 3,150*

**Round 2**
**Feb 12 v Burslem Port Vale (h) 3-1**
*McLeod, Pearson, Bostock*
*Att: 2,100*
**Semi-final**
**Mar 17 v Loughborough (at Aston) 6-1**
*Boston 2, Geddes, McLeod 3*
*Att: 3,000*
**Final**
**Apr 21 v Wolverhampton Wanderers (Perry Barr) 3-3**
*Bostock, Geddes, Bassett*
*Att: 8,000*
Trophy shared

**1894-95**
**Round 1**
**Jan 19 v Walsall (h) 6-2**
*Hutchinson 2, Williams, Bassett 2, Taggart*
*Att: 5,000*
**Round 2**
**Feb 1 v Burton Wanderers (a) 1-1**
*Hutchinson*
*Att: 2,000*
Burton refused to replay
**Semi-final**
**Mar 18 v Small Heath (at Wolverhampton) 3-2 (aet)**
*Hutchinson, McLeod, T.Perry*
*Att: 5,100*
**Final**
**Mar 30 v Aston Villa (at Small Heath) 0-0**
*Att: 12,000*
**Replay**
**Apr 29 v Aston Villa (at Aston) 1-0**
*Hutchinson*
*Att: 14,200*

**1895-96**
**Round 1**
**Jan 20 v Aston Villa (a) 0-3**
*Att: 7,000*

**1896-97**
**Round 2**
**Jan 25 v Aston Villa (h) 2-1**
*Cameron, Watson*
*Att: 4,000*
**Semi-final**
**Feb 20 v Wolverhampton Wanderers (at Perry Barr) 0-3**
*Att: 6,800*
Albion received a bye in Round 1.

**1897-98**
**Round 1**
**Dec 13 v Burslem Port Vale (a) 0-0**
*Att: 6,000*
**Replay**
**Jan 17 v Burslem Port Vale (h) 0-0 (aet)**
*Att: 3,000*
**Second replay**
**Feb 7 v Burslem Port Vale (h) 2-1 (aet)**
*Richards Flewitt*
*Att: 3,500*
Albion withdrew from competition.

**1898-99**
**Round 1**
**Dec 19 v Wellington St George (h) 5-0**
*Bassett 2, Hadley, Nock, S.Brett*
*Att: 750*
**Round 2**
**Jan 16 v Wolverhampton Wanderers (h) 0-7**
*Att: 2,474*

**1899-1900**
**Round 1**
**Dec 11 v Burslem Port Vale (a) 0-5**
*Att: 2,000*

**1900-01**
**Round 1**
**Sep 24 v Small Heath (h) 5-0**
*Wheldon, Chadburn, Walker, Jones, Simmons*
*Att: 3,600*

**Round 2**
**Oct 15 v Stoke (h) 2-3**
*Garfield, Walker*
*Att: 6,000*

**1901-02**
**Round 1**
**Sep 30 v Wolverhampton Wanderers (a) 0-1**
*Att: 3,500*

**1902-03**
**Round 1**
**Sep 29 v Wolverhampton Wanderers (a) 5-1**
*Lee, Simmons 2, Buck, Dorsett*
*Att: 5,000*
**Semi-final**
**Oct 13 v Walsall (a) 7-1**
*Buck, Simmons 4, A.Smith, Kifford*
*Att: 5,000*
**Final**
**Dec 8 v Aston Villa (a) 0-3**
*Att: 16,000*

**1903-04**
**Round 1**
**Sep 28 v Wolverhampton Wanderers (h) 1-2**
*Hadley*
*Att: 5,500*

**1904-05**
**Round 1**
**Sep 26 v Wolverhampton Wanderers (a) 2-0**
*Bell, Jack*
*At: 7,000*
**Semi-final**
**Oct 22 v Burslem Port Vale (h) 2-1**
*Davies, Jack*
*Att: 5,000*
**Final**
**Feb 20 v Small Heath (a) 2-7**
*Aston, Jack*
*Att: 8,500*

**1905-06**
**Round 1**
**Sep 4 v Aston Villa (h) 1-5**
*E.Bradley*
*Att: 5,000*

## Liverpool Charity Cup

In November 1895, Albion contested a match for the Liverpool Charity Cup on the Everton ground, as a gesture towards the Everton Football Club who had kindly played several matches at Stoney Lane in aid of West Bromwich charities. Albion and Everton met under electric lights at night-time and attracted a crowd of over 5,000.

**5 Nov 1895 v Everton (a) 1-4**
*A.Wilson*
*Att: 5,200*

## Coventry Charity Cup

Albion have competed only once in the Coventry Charity Cup, in 1930 when they met their neighbours Coventry City for the first time ever, in the Final at Highfield Road.

**28 Apr 1930 v Coventry City (a) 2-1**
*Edwards, Cookson*
*Att: 8,000*

# Staffordshire Cup

THE STAFFORDSHIRE FA was created in 1877 and a year later the Staffordshire Cup was introduced. Before Albion won the trophy in their first season of entry, 1882-83, Stoke (twice), Wednesbury Old Athletic and Walsall Town had all been Staffordshire Cup winners.

Albion's first Staffordshire Cup tie was at Bloxwich Strollers on 4 November 1882 when they drew 3-3 before winning the replay 4-0 at the Four Acres a fortnight later. In the second round Albion again started with a 3-3 away draw, this time on the Aston Villa ground in what was the very first meeting between the clubs. Albion won the replay 1-0. In the third round Albion drew 2-2 at home with St George's but afterwards protested that the Dragons had fielded two ineligible players, one of whom was Tom Green who subsequently signed for Albion in 1885. The Staffordshire FA upheld the protest and Albion proceeded to a home semi-final where Leek White Star were swept aside 8-0.

There was great excitement in the Black Country

at the prospect of the hitherto relatively unknown Albion team appearing in their very first Final and they did not let their supporters down, beating Stoke 3-2 (see *Match to Remember 1*).

In April 1884, Albion found themselves in the Final again after overcoming Cocknage, Walsall Town and Stoke, but this time St George's pipped them 2-1 after the Throstles had scored first through Arthur Loach. The winning goal was scored by the above mentioned Tom Green. Between 1883 and 1889 Albion appeared in the Staffordshire Cup Final six times and were losing semi-finalists in 1885.

Albion's complete record in the Staffordshire Cup (first team only):-

|   | Home | | | | | Away | | | | |
|---|---|---|---|---|---|---|---|---|---|---|
| P | W | D | L | F | A | W | D | L | F | A |
| 68 | 22 | 4 | 1 | 114 | 20 | 21 | 6 | 14 | 91 | 62 |

Bayliss scored 12 of 23 goals during the 1886-87 competition.

In all but one of 27 home Staffordshire Cup ties, Albion managed to record at least one goal. The record Staffordshire Cup victory was 23-0 against Burton Wanderers on 1 February 1890 when five players each scored three goals or more. In the first round on 10 October 1898, Albion slumped to their heaviest defeat, 6-1 away to Aston Villa.

Albion played their last Staffordshire Cup tie at senior level on 2 October 1905, away to Aston Villa where they lost 4-0. In 1906-07 the Staffordshire FA decreed that reserve teams could take part. The Albion second team won the trophy in 1923-24 (beating Stoke 3-0), 1925-26 (beating Stoke 3-1), 1931-32 (defeating Wolves 3-2), 1932-33 (beating Villa 2-0) and 1950-51 (defeating Wolves 1-0). They were also losing Finalists in 1906-07, 1907-08, 1924-25, 1937-38 and 1952-53. In 1968-69 the Cup was shared with Stoke City when the sides drew 0-0 in the Final which was also treated as a Central League fixture.

## 1882-83
**Round 1**
**Nov 4 v Bloxwich Strollers (a) 3-3**
*G.Bell, Aston, Timmins*
*Att: 650*
**Replay**
**Nov 18 v Bloxwich Strollers (h) 4-0**
*Biddulph 2, G.Bell, Aston*
*Att: 1,200*
**Round 2**
**Dec 9 v Aston Villa (a) 3-3**
*G.Bell 2, Aston*
*Att: 13,900*
**Replay**
**Dec 23 v Aston Villa (h) 1-0**
*Timmins*
*Att: 10,500*
**Round 3**
**Feb 3 v St George's (h) 2-2**
*Timmins, Bisseker*
*Att: 2,000*
*St George's were subsequently disqualified for playing two ineligible players against Albion.
**Semi-final**
**Mar 10 v Leek White Star (h) 8-0**
*G.Bell, Aston 3, Biddulph 2, Bisseker 2*
*Att: 2,000*
**Final**
**Apr 21 v Stoke (a) 3-2**
*Timmins, Bunn, G.Bell*
*Att: 6,150*

## 1883-84
**Round 1**
**Dec 3 v Cocknage (h) 1-0**
*G.Bell*
*Att: 600*
**Round 2**
**Dec 22 v Walsall Town (h) 4-0**
*Aston 4*
*Att: 1,400*
**Semi-final**
**Mar 15 v Stoke (at Wednesbury) 2-0**
*Bisseker, Timmins*
*Att: 3,000*
**Final**
**Apr 12 v St George's (at Stoke) 1-2**
*Loach*
*Att: 5,500*

## 1884-85
**Round 1**
**Nov 8 v Burton Swifts (h) 7-1**
*G.Bell, Loach 2, Aston 2, Bayliss 2*
*Att: 2,000*
**Round 2**
**Dec 13 v Leek (h) 8-0**
*Aston, Bayliss 2, Loach 3, Woodhall, G.Bell*
*Att: 2,000*

**Round 3**
**Jan 31 v Stoke (h) 6-2**
*Bayliss 3, Bettany (og), Aston, G.Bell*
*Att: 2,000*
**Semi-final**
**Feb 28 v Walsall Town (at Stoke) 0-2**
*Att: 6,000*

## 1885-86
**Round 1**
**Oct 24 v Stafford Rangers (h) 0-0**
*Att: 3,000*
**Replay**
**Nov 7 v Stafford Rangers (a) 4-0**
*Loach 2, G.Bell 2*
*Att: 2,500*
**Round 2**
**Jan 9 v Leek (h) 5-2**
*Loach, Woodhall 3, G.Bell*
*Att: 1,000*
**Round 3**
Albion received a bye
**Round 4**
**Jan 30 v Stoke Free Wanderers (h) 5-0**
*G.Bell, Bayliss, Loach, Woodhall 2*
*Att: 800*
**Semi-final**
**Apr 17 v Burton Wanderers (at Stoke) 3-0**
*Bayliss 2, T.Green*
*Att: 6,000*
**Final**
**Apr 24 v Stoke (a) 0-0**
*Att: 9,000*
**Replay**
**May 10 v Stoke (h) 4-2**
*Bayliss 2, T.Green, Woodhall*
*Att: 5,500*

## 1886-87
**Round 1**
**Oct 4 v Hednesford Town (h) 8-0**
*Bayliss 4, G..Bell 2, T.Green 2*
*Att: 3,000*
**Round 2**
**Nov 6 v Stafford Rangers (h) 5-1**
*G.Bell, Timmins, Bayliss 2, Woodhall*
*Att: 2,500*
**Round 3**
**Feb 26 v Leek (h) 3-0**
*Bayliss 2, Woodhall*
*Att: 3,500*
**Semi-final**
**Mar 21 v Wolverhampton Wanderers (at Burslem) 3-0**
*Bayliss 2, Timmins*
*Att: 4,000*
**Final**
**Apr 9 v Walsall Swifts (at Stoke) 4-0**
*Bayliss 2, Woodhall, Paddock*
*Att: 4,000*

## 1887-88
**Round 1**
**Oct 1 v Burton Wanderers (a) 12-2**
*Black (og), Woodhall 3, Pearson 2, Bayliss 3, Wilson, Bassett 2*
*Att: 3,500*
**Round 2**
**Nov 28 v Wednesbury Old Athletic (a) 2-1**
*Woodhall, Bayliss*
*Att: 3,000*
**Round 3**
**Dec 31 v Leek (a) 3-2**
*Woodhall, Pearson, Wilson*
*Att: 2,700*
**Semi-final**
**Mar 17 v Stoke (a) 1-0**
*Wilson*
*Att: 5,500*
**Final**
**Mar 31 v Wolverhampton Wanderers (at Stoke) 0-0**
*Att: 8,000*
**Replay**
**Apr 14 v Wolverhampton Wanderers (at Stoke) 1-1 (aet)**
*Woodhall*
*Att: 8,500*
**Second replay**
**Apr 28 v Wolverhampton Wanderers (h) 1-2**
*Woodhall*
*Att: 7,000*

## 1888-89
**Round 4**
**Mar 23 v Birmingham St George's (a) 3-1**
*Hadley (og), Pearson, Bayliss*
*Att: 5,000*
**Semi-final**
**Apr 6 v Walsall Town Swifts(at Wednesbury) 5-0**
*Woodhall 2, Pearson 2, W.Perry*
*Att: 3,500*
**Final**
**Apr 20 v Leek (at Stoke) 2-0**
*Bayliss, Wilson*
*Att: 5,500*
Albion were exempt until Round 4 because of Football League commitments.

## 1889-90
**Round 1**
**Feb 1 v Burton Wanderers (h) 23-0**
*Pearson 3, Bassett 6, Wilson 2, Woodhall 3, C.Perry 3, Roberts, Evans 3, Green, J.Horton*
*Att: 3,000*
**Round 2**
**Mar 31 v Stoke (h) 4-0**
*Woodhall 2, Evans, Bassett*
*Att: 5,000*

**Semi-final**
**Apr 12 v Walsall Town Swifts(at Wednesbury) 2-3**
*Pearson, Bassett*
*Att: 5,000*

**1890-91**
**Round 2**
**Jan 24 v Wolverhampton Wanderers (a) 1-3**
*Pearson*
*Att: 5,000*

**1893-94**
**Round 1**
**Jan 15 v Walsall (a) 2-4**
*Geddes, Neale*
*Att: 2,500*

**1894-95**
**Semi-final**
**Feb 4 v Aston Villa (a) 0-2**
*Att: 7,600*

**1895-96**
**Round 1**
**Jan 6 v Small Heath (h) 2-1**
*J. Richards 2*
*Att: 1,000*
**Round 2**
**Mar 16 v Aston Villa (a) 2-4**
*W. Richards, Flewitt*
*Att: 6,000*

**1896-97**
**Round 1**
**Oct 19 v Aston Villa (h) 2-1**
*Ford, Garfield*
*Att: 4,000*
**Round 2**
**Jan 11 v Wolverhampton Wanderers (a) 1-5**
*Watson*
*Att: 2,000*

**1897-98**
**Round 1**
**Nov 8 v Aston Villa (h) 2-1**
*Garfield, McKenzie*
*Att: 7,000*

**Round 3**
**Jan 22 v Small Heath (a) 1-0**
*Robertson (og)*
*Att: 4,500*
**Final**
**Mar 5 v Burslem Port Vale (at Stoke) 0-1**
*Att: 10,000*
Albion received a bye in Round 2 and the semi-final stage was declared void.

**1898-99**
**Round 1**
**Oct 10 v Aston Villa (a) 1-6**
*Jones (pen)*
*Att: 7,000*

**1899-1900**
**Round 1**
**Sep 18 v Aston Villa (a) 3-2**
*Paddock, Walker, Garfield*
*Att: 8,200*
**Round 2**
**Oct 9 v Stoke (a) 3-1**
*Walker, Paddock, Garfield*
*Att: 4,350*
**Semi-final**
**Nov 20 v Wolverhampton Wanderers (h) 3-1**
*Simmons, Jones, Paddock*
*Att: 2,150*
**Final**
**Dec 4 v Burslem Port Vale (at Stoke) 1-1**
*Simmons*
*Att: 3,500*
**Replay**
**Apr 26 v Burslem Port Vale (at Aston) 5-0**
*Simmons, Walker 2, Roberts 2*
*Att: 5,000*

**1900-01**
**Round 1**
**Oct 8 v Wolverhampton Wanderers (a) 1-2**
*Walker*
*Att: 5,500*

**1901-02**
**Round 1**
**Sep 23 v Wolverhampton Wanderers (h) 2-1**
*Simmons 2*
*Att: 3,000*

**Semi-final**
**Oct 7 v Small Heath (h) 2-1**
*Simmons, McLean*
*Att: 4,000*
**Final**
**Nov 25 v Stoke (at Burslem) 3-0**
*McLean, Lee, Harper*
*Att: 3,000*

**1902-03**
**Round 1**
**Sep 15 v Burton United (a) 2-0**
*Dorsett, Simmons*
*Att: 3,000*
**Semi-final**
**Oct 6 v Wolverhampton Wanderers (h) 1-1**
*Simmons*
*Att: 6,000*
**Replay**
**Oct 27 v Wolverhampton Wanderers (a) 4-0**
*Simmons, Stevenson, Lee 2*
*Att: 7,500*
**Final**
**Nov 17 v Stoke (at Aston) 2-0**
*Buck 2*
*Att: 10,000*

**1903-04**
**Round 1**
**Sep 14 v Burton United (h) 1-1**
*Cole*
*Att: 3,000*
**Replay**
**Oct 5 v Burton United (a) 1-2**
*Hadley (pen)*
*Att: 4,000*

**1904-05**
**Round 1**
**Oct 3 v Derby County (a) 1-3**
*Dorsett*
*Att:4,000*

**1905-06**
**Round 1**
**Oct 2 v Aston Villa (a) 0-4**
*Att: 8,500*

# *West Bromwich Charity Cup*

ALBION'S senior team took part in the West Bromwich Friendly Societies Charity Cup for the first time in May 1888. Although the two ties Albion contested were for the benefit of local charities, all was not particularly friendly, for when Albion mastered Wednesbury Old Athletic 4-1 in the semi-final there were skirmishes among the rival supporters and in the Final (where Albion overwhelmed Great Bridge Unity 10-1) a Unity player was ordered off for rough play, a very rare occurrence in those days.

Albion's record in the West Bromwich Charity Cup in matches played by the first team:-

| | Home | | | | | Away | | | | |
|---|---|---|---|---|---|---|---|---|---|---|
| P | W | D | L | F | A | W | D | L | F | A |
| 11 | 6 | 2 | 2 | 25 | 11 | 0 | 0 | 1 | 0 | 4 |

During the 1890s, Everton made regular trips to Stoney Lane to play in the Final — they met Albion on six different occasions. Albion's first team won the trophy in 1888, 1895 and 1897 and shared it with Aston Villa in 1890; and the reserve team were winners in 1903, 1904, 1905, 1906, 1912, 1914, 1915, 1921, 1922 and 1923, this being the last year in which Albion competed for the Cup.

**1887-88**
**Semi-final**
**May 7 v Wednesbury Old Athletic (h) 4-1**
*Wilson, Bayliss, Woodhall 2*
*Att: 5,000*
**Final**
**May 21 v Great Bridge Unity (h) 10-1**
*Bayliss 4, Wilson 2, Bassett 2, Woodhall, H.Green*
*Att: 6,500*

**1888-89**
**Final**
**Jun 1 v Wolverhampton Wanderers (h) 2-0**
*Bassett, Wilson*
*Att: 3,000*

**1889-90**
**Final**
**May 17 v Aston Villa (h) 1-1**
*S.Nicholls*
*Att: 4,000*
Trophy shared

**1890-91**
**Final**
**May 30 v Wednesbury Old Athletic (h) 3-2**
*Pearson, C.Perry, Reynolds*
*Att: 5,000*

**1892-93**
**Final**
**Nov 21 v Everton (h) 0-2**
*Att: 3,500*

**1894-95**
**Final**
**Oct 15 v Everton (h) 1-0**
*C.Perry*
*Att: 5,000*

**1895-96**
**Final**
**Jan 13 v Everton (h) 1-2**
*Hayward*
*Att: 3,500*

**1896-97**
**Final**
**Feb 15 v Everton (h) 2-1**
*McManus, W.Williams*
*Att: 3,000*

**1897-98**
**Final**
**Nov 29 v Everton (h) 1-1**
*Garfield*
*Att: 5,000*
**Replay**
**Apr 18 v Everton (a) 0-4**
*Att: 12,000*

# Walsall Cup

ALBION entered their second team for the Walsall Senior Cup in 1885-86 and from then on it was almost exclusively a competition for the reserves except for two occasions when the first team took over the fixtures. On 16 October 1886 the Albion committee chose a strong team to face Crosswell's Brewery (home) because the brewers had included seven former Throstles in their ranks. Albion won 5-2 and then left the

**Albion's 2nd XI, 1897-98. Back row (left to right): T.Brennand (director), F.Everiss (clerk), W.Moore, P.McManus, A.Flavell, W.G.Ford, T.Harris- Spencer (chairman), J.Banks, H.Powell (director), C.Perry (director), R.Brett. Front: A.McKenzie, S.Vigrow, J,Connor, E.Fellows, J.Nock, S.Brett.**

remainder of the ties to the second team who eventually lost to Walsall Town. In 1887-88 Albion reserves drew twice with Oldbury Town (formerly Crosswell's Brewery) in the first round of the Walsall Cup before the Albion first team took over the tie and sent Oldbury Town packing, 5-1 (away). The second team went on to win the trophy for the first time, overwhelming Walsall Swifts 4-1 in the Final.

In 1900-01 the reserves participated again after a long absence and were joint holders of the Cup after drawing 1-1 with Small Heath Reserves. In 1903 they became Cup winners by beating Brierley Hill Alliance 5-0 and in 1904 were losing Finalists, going down 5-0 to Small Heath after a 0-0 draw. They were again losing finalists, to Wolves, in 1906.

**1886-87**
**Round 1**
**Oct 16 v Crosswell's (h) 5-2**
*Holden, Pearson, Horton 2, Moore (og)*
*Att: 2,500*
Remainder of fixtures completed by Albion Reserves.

**1887-88**
**Round 1**
**Second replay**
**Dec 12 v Oldbury Town (a) 5-1**
*Bayliss 3, Askin, H.Green*
*Att: 1,000*
Albion Reserves completed the remaining fixtures, going on to win the trophy.

# Wednesbury Charity Cup

THIS was a short-lived competition which Albion entered for only two seasons, 1882-83 and 1883-84. By overcoming Wednesbury Strollers and Aston Unity, Albion qualified for the 1883 Final against Nottingham Forest but after leading 2-1 they lost 5-3 after captain John While had been taken off with a broken leg which ended his playing career. Albion were dismissed from the 1884 Wednesbury Charity Cup by St George's and the first team did not participate again. In 1887-88 the reserve team accepted an invitation to enter but were removed from the first round by Wednesbury Old Athletic. Albion reserves were losing Finalists in 1889-90 but won the Cup in 1893-94 by defeating Newport 4-0 at Wellington.

**Complete first team record in the Wednesbury Charity Cup:-**

|   |  | Home |  |  |  |  | Away |  |  |  |  |
|---|---|---|---|---|---|---|---|---|---|---|---|
| P | W | D | L | F | A | W | D | L | F | A |  |
| 7 | 1 | 0 | 0 | 7 | 1 | 2 | 2 | 2 | 11 | 13 |  |

**1882-83**
**Round 1**
**Nov 25 v Wednesbury Strollers (a) 3-3**
*G.Bell, Bisseker, Whitehouse*
*Att: 2,000*
**Replay**
**Dec 30 v Wednesbury Strollers (h) 7-1**
*Bisseker 2, Aston, G.Bell 2, Whitehouse 2*
*Att: 2,100*
**Semi-final**
**Feb 24 v Aston Unity (at Perry Barr) 1-0**
*Aston*
*Att: 4,000*
**Final**
**May 19 v Notts Rangers (at Perry Barr) 3-5**
*Aston 2, Bisseker*
*Att: 4,000*

**1883-84**
**Round 1**
**Nov 24 v Aston Unity (a) 3-0**
*G.Bell, Timmins, Aston*
*Att: 2,500*
**Semi-final**
**Jan 12 v St George's (at Aston) 1-1**
*Stevenson (og)*
*Att: 3,700*
**Replay**
**Mar 29 v St George's (at Wednesbury) 0-4**
*Att: 3,500*

# International and Representative Honours

Before 1924 there was only one 'Ireland' team then the Republic of Ireland began separate international matches. England Under-23 ceased to play international matches in 1976-77 when England Under-21 took over.

## FULL, WARTIME & VICTORY INTERNATIONALS

### ENGLAND

**A.Aldridge** (1) 1887-88 v Ireland.

**R.Allen** (5) 1951-52 v Switzerland; 1953-54 v Scotland (1 goal), Yugoslavia; 1954-55 v Wales, West Germany (1 goal).

**G.S.Ashmore** (1) 1925-26 v Belgium.

**J.Astle** (5) 1968-69 v Wales; 1969-70 v Portugal, Scotland, Brazil, Czechoslovakia.

**R.J.Barlow** (1) 1954-55 v Northern Ireland.

**P.S.Barnes** (6) 1979-80 v Denmark, Wales; 1980-81 v Spain (sub), Brazil, Wales, Switzerland (sub).

**W.I.Bassett** (16) 1887-88 v Ireland; 1888-89 v Wales (1 goal), Scotland (1 goal); 1889-90 v Wales, Scotland; 1890-91 v Ireland (1 goal), Scotland; 1891-92 v Scotland; 1892-93 v Wales (1 goal), Scotland; 1893-94 v Scotland; 1894-95 v Ireland (1 goal), Scotland; 1895-96 v Ireland, Wales (1 goal), Scotland (1 goal).

**A.J.Bayliss** (1) 1890-91 v Ireland.

**S.Bowser** (1) 1919-20 v Ireland.

**W.E.Boyes** (2) 1934-35 v Holland; 1935-36 v Scotland (Jubilee).

**A.Brown** (1) 1970-71 v Wales.

**J.H.Carter** (3) 1925-26 v Belgium (1 goal); 1928-29 v Belgium (1 goal), Spain (2 goals).

**L.P.Cunningham** (3) 1978-79 v Wales, Sweden, Austria

**W.B.Elliott** (2) 1943-44 v Wales (Wartime); 1945-46 v Scotland (Victory).

**B.Garfield** (1) 1897-98 v Ireland.

**H.Hadley** (1) 1902-03 v Ireland.

**J.T.W.Haines** (1) 1948-49 v Switzerland (2 goals).

**D.Howe** (23) 1957-58 v Wales, Northern Ireland, France, Scotland, Portugal, Yugoslavia, USSR (3 times), Brazil, Austria; 1958-59 v Northern Ireland, USSR, Wales, Scotland, Italy, Brazil, Peru, Mexico, USA; 1959-60 v Wales, Sweden, Northern Ireland.

**S.Hunt** (2) 1983-84 v Scotland (sub), USSR (sub).

**D.T.Kevan** (14) 1956-57 v Scotland (1 goal); 1957-58 v Wales, Northern Ireland, Scotland (2 goals), Portugal, Yugoslavia, USSR (3 times — 2 goals), Brazil, Austria (1 goal); 1958-59 v Mexico (1 goal), USA (1 goal); 1960-61 v Mexico.

**T.H.Kinsell** (2) 1945-46 v Northern Ireland, Wales (both Victory).

**R.McNeal** (2) 1913-14 v Wales, Scotland.

**T.P.Magee** (5) 1922-23 v Wales, Sweden; 1924-25 v Belgium, Scotland, France.

**F.Morris** (2) 1919-20 v Scotland (1 goal), 1920-21 v Ireland.

**J.Nicholls** (2) 1953-54 v Scotland (1 goal), Yugoslavia.

**H.F.Pearson** (1) 1931-32 v Scotland.

**J.Pennington** (25) 1906-07 v Wales, Scotland; 1907-08 v Ireland, Wales, Scotland, Austria; 1908-09 v Wales, Scotland, Hungary (twice), Austria; 1909-10 v Wales, Scotland; 1910-11 v Ireland, Wales, Scotland; 1911-12 v Ireland, Wales, Scotland; 1912-13 v Wales, Scotland; 1913-14 v Ireland, Scotland; 1919-20 v Wales, Scoland.

**C.Perry** (3) 1889-90 v Ireland; 1890-91 v Ireland; 1892-93 v Wales.

**T.Perry** (1) 1897-98 v Wales.

**J.Reader** (1) 1893-94 v Ireland.

**C.Regis** (4) 1981-82 v Northern Ireland, Wales, Iceland; 1982-83 v West Germany.

**J.Reynolds** (3) 1891-92 v Scotland; 1892-93 v Wales (1 goal), Scotland (i goal).

**W.G.Richardson** (1) 1934-35 v Holland.

**S.Rickaby** (1) 1953-54 v Northern Ireland.

**R.Roberts** (3) 1886-87 v Scotland; 1887-88 v Ireland; 1889-90 v Ireland.

**B.Robson** (13) 1979-80 v Republic of Ireland, Australia; 1980-81 v Norway, Romania (twice), Switzerland (twice), Spain, Brazil, Wales, Scotland, Hungary; 1981-82 v Norway.

**R.W.Robson** (20) 1957-58 v France (2 goals), USSR (twice), Brazil, Austria; 1959-60 v Spain, Hungary; 1960-61 v Northern Ireland, Luxembourg, Spain, Wales, Scotland (1 goal), Mexico (1 goal), Portugal, Italy; 1961-62 v Luxembourg, Wales, Portugal, Northern Ireland, Switzerland.

**E.A.Sandford** (1) 1932-33 v Wales.

**G.E.Shaw** (1) 1931-32 v Scotland.

**J.Smith** (3) 1919-20 v Wales (Victory), Ireland; 1922-23 v Ireland.

**D.Statham** (3) 1982-83 v Wales, Australia (twice).

**W.Williams** (6) 1896-97 v Ireland; 1897-98 v Ireland, Wales, Scotland; 1898-99 v Ireland, Wales.

**G.Woodhall** (2) 1887-88 v Wales (1 goal), Scotland.

### SCOTLAND

**D.M.Fraser** (2) 1967-68 v Holland; 1968-69 v Cyprus.

**R.A.Hartford** (6) 1971-72 v Peru, Wales, England, Yugoslavia, Czechoslovakia, Brazil.

**R.Hope** (2) 1967-68 v Holland; 1968-69 v Denmark.

**W.M.Johnston** (13) 1976-77 v Sweden, Wales, Northern Ireland, England, Chile, Argentina, Brazil; 1977-78 v East Germany, Czechoslovakia, Wales (twice), England, Peru.

**A.McNab** (1) 1938-39 v England.

### WALES

**S.Davies** (11) 1921-22 v Scotland (1 goal), England, Ireland; 1922-23 v Scotland; 1924-25 v Scotland, Northern Ireland; 1925-26 v Scotland, Northern Ireland, England; 1926-27 v Scotland; 1927-28 v Scotland.

**W.C.Davies** (2) 1908-09 v England; 1909-10 v Scotland.

**H.E.Foukes** (1) 1931-32 v Northern Ireland.

**I.Jones** (4) 1922-23 v England, Ireland; 1923-24 v Scotland; 1925-26 v Northern Ireland.

**R.L.Krzywicki** (2) 1969-70 v East Germany, Italy.

**A.H.Millington** (3) 1962-63 v Scotland, Hungary, England.

**J.P.Murphy** (15) 1932-33 v England, Northern Ireland, France; 1933-34 v Scotland, England; 1934-35 v England, Scotland, Northern Ireland; 1935-36 v Scotland, England, Northern Ireland; 1936-37 v Scotland, Northern Ireland; 1937-38 v Scotland, England.

**S.Powell** (2) 1890-91 v England, Scotland; 1891-92 v England, Scotland.

**R.R.Rees** (2) 1967-68 v West Germany; 1968-69 v Italy.

**W.W.Robbins** (6) 1932-33 v Scotland, England, Northern Ireland (2 goals), France; 1933-34 v Scotland (1 goal); 1935-36 v Scotland.

**M.R.Thomas** (2) 1985-86 v Hungary, Saudi Arabia (sub).

**G.E.Williams** (26) 1959-60 v Northern Ireland; 1960-61 v Republic of Ireland, Scotland, England; 1962-63 v Hungary, Northern Ireland; 1963-64 v England, Scotland, Northern Ireland; 1964-65 v Scotland, Denmark, England, Greece (twice), Northern Ireland (1 goal), Italy, USSR; 1965-66 v Northern Ireland, Brazil (twice), Chile; 1966-67 v Scotland, England, Northern Ireland; 1967-68 v Ireland; 1968-69 v Italy.

### NORTHERN IRELAND
### (& IRELAND BEFORE 1924)

**G.J.Armstrong** (4) 1985-86 v Turkey, Romania (sub), England (sub), France (sub).

**D.Hegan** (1) 1969-70 v USSR.

**J.M.Nicholl** (11) 1984-85 v Finland, England, Spain, Turkey; 1985-86 v Turkey, Romania, England, France, Algeria, Spain, Brazil.

**R.A.Ryan** (1) 1949-50 v Wales.

**J.Vernon** (15) 1946-47 v Wales; 1947-48 v Scotland, England, Wales; 1948-49 v England, Scotland, Wales; 1949-50 v Scotland, England; 1950-51 v England, Scotland, Wales, France; 1951-52 v Scotland, England.

**D.J.Walsh** (9) 1946-47 v Scotland, Wales; 1947-48 v Scotland, England (1 goal), Wales; 1948-49 v England (2 goals), Wales; 1949-50 v Wales.

**P.Williams** (1) 1990-91 v Faroe Islands (sub).

### REPUBLIC OF IRELAND

**M.J.Giles** (7) 1975-76 v Turkey; 1976-77 v England, Turkey, France (twice), Poland, Bulgaria.

**A.Grealish** (10) 1983-84 v Poland, China; 1984-85 v Mexico, USSR, Norway, Denmark, Spain (sub), Switzerland; 1985-86 v USSR, Denmark.

**M.P.Martin** (10) 1975-76 v Turkey, Norway, Poland; 1976-77 v England, Turkey, France (twice), Spain, Poland, Bulgaria.

**P.M.Mulligan** (16) 1975-76 v Turkey, Poland; 1976-77 v England, Turkey, France (twice), Poland, Bulgaria; 1977-78 v Bulgaria, Norway, Denmark; 1978-79 v England, Denmark, Bulgaria, West Germany, Argentina.

**R.A.Ryan** (15) 1949-50 v Sweden, Belgium; 1950-51 v Norway (twice), Argentina; 1951-52 v West Germany (twice), Austria, Spain; 1952-53 v France, Austria; 1953-54 v France (twice — 1 goal), Luxembourg (1 goal); 1954-55 v Norway (1 goal).

**R.C.Treacy** (6) 1965-66 v West Germany; 1966-67 v Spain, Czechoslovakia; 1967-68 v Czechoslovakia (1 goal); 1976-77 v France, Poland.

**D.J.Walsh** (14) 1945-46 v Portugal, Spain; 1946-47 v Spain (2 goals), Portugal; 1947-48 v Portugal, Spain (1 goal); 1948-49 v Switzerland, Portugal, Sweden (1 goal), Spain; 1949-50 v England, Finland, Sweden; 1950-51 v Norway (1 goal).

### CANADA

**C.Valentine** (1) 1985-86 v Honduras.

# 'B' INTERNATIONALS

## ENGLAND

R.Allen (2) 1953-54 v Scotland, Switzerland.
J.Astle (2) 1969-70 v Columbia (1 goal), Ecuador XI (3 goals).
R.J.Barlow (2) 1951-52 v France; 1952-53 v Scotland.
P.S.Barnes (1) 1980-81 v USA.
B.M.Batson (3) 1980-81 v USA, Australia, Spain.
L.P.Cunningham (1) 1978-79 v Czechoslovakia.
J.R.Dugdale (3) 1953-54 v Scotland, Yugoslavia, Switzerland.
A.Ford (2) 1988-89 v Switzerland (sub), Norway.
D.Howe (1) 1956-57 v Scotland.
J.P.Kennedy (3) 1951-52 v France; 1955-56 v Yugoslavia, Scotland.
S.Naylor (3) 1988-89 v Switzerland (sub), Iceland, Norway.
J.Nicholls (1) 1953-54 v Switzerland (sub).
C.Regis (3) 1978-79 v Czechoslovakia (sub); 1980-81 v USA, Australia.
B.Robson (2) 1978-79 v Austria; 1979-80 v Spain.
D.J.Statham (2) 1980-81 v USA (1 goal), Spain (1 goal)

## SCOTLAND

J.G.Dudley (1) 1953-54 v England.

# UNDER-23 & UNDER-21 INTERNATIONALS

## ENGLAND

D.G.Burnside (2) 1960-61 v Danish XI; 1961-62 v Turkey
D.Burrows (1) 1988-89 v Sweden (sub).
L.Cantello (8) 1971-72 v East Germany; 1972-73 v Wales, Holland (twice), Denmark, Czechoslovakia; 1973-74 v Poland, Denmark.
C.Clark (1) 1960-61 v Wales.
L.P.Cunningham (6) 1976-77 v Scotland (1 goal), Finland, Norway (sub); 1977-78 v Norway, Finland (1 goal), Italy.
D.Howe (6) 1955-56 v Scotland; 1956-57 v France, Scotland; 1957-58 v Bulgaria, Scotland, Wales.
D.T.Kevan (4) 1956-57 v Bulgaria, Romania, Czechoslovakia; 1957-58 v Bulgaria.
P.W.Latchford (2) 1973-74 v Poland, Wales.
S.Mackenzie (3) 1981-82 v Norway, Scotland (twice).
R.Moses (7) 1980-81 v Norway (sub), Switzerland (twice), Republic of Ireland, Romania, Hungary; 1981-82 v Norway (sub).
J.Nicholls (1) 1953-54 v Italy.
G.J.M.Nisbet (1) 1971-72 v East Germany.
G.A.Owen (12) 1978-79 v Bulgaria, Sweden (sub); 1979-80 v Denmark, Scotland (twice — 1 goal), East Germany; 1980-81 v Switzerland (1 goal), Romania; 1981-82 v Norway (sub), Hungary; 1982-83 v West Germany (twice — 2 goals).
C.Regis (6) 1978-79 v Denmark, Bulgaria (1 goal), Sweden (1 goal); 1979-80 v Scotland, East Germany; 1982-83 v Denmark (1 goal).
B.Robson (7) 1978-79 v Wales, Bulgaria (sub), Sweden (1 goal); 1979-80 v Denmark, Bulgaria (twice — 1 goal).
M.E.Setters (11) 1957-58 v Bulgaria, Romania, Scotland, Wales; 1958-59 v Poland, Czechoslovakia, France, Italy, West Germany; 1959-60 v Hungary, France.
D.J.Statham (6) 1977-78 v Finland; 1978-79 v Wales, Bulgaria, Sweden; 1979-80 v Denmark; 1982-83 v Greece.

## SCOTLAND

E.P.Colquhoun (1) 1967-68 v England.

R.A.Hartford (5) 1969-70 v Wales; 1970-71 v Wales; 1971-72 v England; 1972-73 v England, Wales.
R.Hope (1) 1966-67 v Wales.
R.T.Wilson (1) 1969-70 v Wales.

## WALES

B.W.Hughes (3) 1976-77 v England, Scotland; 1977-78 v Scotland.
R.L.Krzywicki (3) 1966-67 v Scotland, England; 1969-70 v Scotland
A.H.Millington (4) 1961-62 v Scotland, Northern Ireland; 1962-63 v Scotland, Northern Ireland.
G.E.Williams (2) 1959-60 v Scotland; 1960-61 v Wales

## REPUBLIC OF IRELAND

K.Ampadu (1) 1991-92 v Switzerland.
J.Anderson (5) 1977-78 v Northern Ireland; 1978-79 v USSR, Argentina, Hungary, Yugoslavia.
R.C.P.Treacy (1) 1965-66 v France.

# AMATEUR INTERNATIONALS

## ENGLAND

R.Banks (1) 1933-34 v Wales.
L.F.Cooling (1) 1924-25 v Wales.
W.C.Jordan (2) 1907-08 v France (6 goals); 1909-10 v Ireland (2 goals).

# FOOTBALL LEAGUE HONOURS

R.Allen (1) 1957-58 v Scottish League (1 goal).
J.Astle (2) 1969-70 v Scottish League (2 goals); 1970-71 v Irish League (2 goals).
H.G.Bache (1) 1914-15 v Irish League.
R.J.Barlow (5) 1952-53 v League of Ireland, Danish Combination; 1953-54 v League of Ireland; 1954-55 v League of Ireland; 1957-58 v League of Ireland.
W.I.Bassett (3) 1891-92 v Scottish League (1 goal); 1892-93 v Scottish League (1 goal); 1896-97 v Irish League.
W.E.Boyes (1) 1935-36 v Irish League (1 goal).
A.Brown (2) 1970-71 v Irish League (sub) (1 goal), Scottish League.
F.Buck (2) 1911-12 v Southern League, Irish League.
J.H.Carter (1) 1930-31 v Scottish League.
J.Crisp (1) 1919-20 v Irish League.
J.R.Dugdale (1) 1953-54 v League of Ireland.
J.Edwards (1) 1931-32 v Scottish League.
W.Groves (1) 1891-92 v Scottish League.
T.Higgins (2) 1895-96 v Scottish League; 1896-97 v Irish League.
D.Howe (6) 1956-57 v Scottish League; 1957-58 v Scottish League; 1958-59 v League of Ireland; 1959-60 v Irish League; 1960-61 v Scottish League; 1961-62 v Irish League.
A.Jackson (1) 1961-62 v Scottish League.
A.C.Jephcott (2) 1913-14 v Scottish League; 1919-20 v Irish League.
J.Kaye (2) 1965-66 v League of Ireland (2 goals), Scottish League.
D.T.Kevan (1) 1957-58 v Scottish League (3 goals).
R.McNeal (5) 1912-13 v Southern League, Irish League; 1913-14 v Southern League, Scottish League; 1914-15 v Scottish League.
F.Morris (1) 1919-20 v Scottish League (2 goals).
D.G.Nurse (1) 1902-03 v Irish League.
H.Pearson (2) 1914-15 v Irish League; 1922-23 v Irish League.
J.Pennington (9) 1906-07 v Scottish League; 1910-11 v Scottish League; 1911-12 v Southern League, Irish League, Scottish League; 1912-13 v Irish League; 1913-14 v

Irish League, Southern League; 1919-20 v Scottish League.
C.Perry (1) 1892-93 v Scottish League.
T.Perry (3) 1893-94 v Irish League; 1895-96 v Scottish League; 1896-97 v Irish League.
J.Reader (3) 1891-92 v Scottish League; 1893-94 v Irish League; 1896-97 v Irish League.
J.Reynolds (2) 1891-92 v Scottish League; 1892-93 v Scottish League.
S.Richardson (1) 1921-22 v Irish League.
S.Rickaby (1) 1953-54 v League of Ireland.
R.W.Robson (5) 1957-58 v Scottish League; 1959-60 v Scottish League; 1960-61 v Italian League, Scottish League; 1961-62 v League of Ireland.
G.E.Shaw (1) 1963-64 v Scottish League.
B.W.Shearman (2) 1911-12 v Southern League, Irish League.
J.L.Spencer (1) 1924-25 v Irish League.
H.F.Trentham (1) 1933-34 v Irish League.
W.Williams (5) 1895-96 v Scottish League; 1896-97 v Irish League, Scottish League; 1898-99 v Irish League; 1899-1900 v Irish League.
S.Wood (1) 1932-33 v Irish League (1 goal).

## MISCELLANEOUS REPRESENTATIVE HONOURS

**England XI:** J.Astle, W.I.Bassett, D.Howe, D.T.Kevan, C.Perry, C.Regis, R.W.Robson.

**Scotland XI:** E.P.Colquhoun, J.G.Dudley, D.M.Fraser, R.Hope.

**Wales XI:** A.Evans, S.Powell.

**Republic of Ireland:** A.Grealish, M.P.Martin, P.M.Mulligan.

**Great Britain XI:** J.Vernon.

**Rest of United Kingdom:** J.Vernon.

**All British XI:** D.F.Witcomb.

**Football League XI:** W.I.Bassett, A.McNab, R.McNeal, H.Pearson, J.Pennington, T.Perry, J.Reader, G.Robson.

**Young England XI:** A.Brown, M.E.Setters.

**FA XI:** W.Adams, R.Allen, G.S.Ashmore, R.J.Barlow, W.I.Bassett, D.G.Burnside, J.H.Carter, J.Cookson, J.R.Dugdale, W.B.Elliott, D.Howe, C.E.Jackman, J.P.Kennedy, D.T.Kevan, T.H.Kinsell, T.P.Magee, G.J.McVitie, F.Morris, H.Pearson, S.Richardson, S.Rickaby, R.W.Robson, M.E.Setters, G.E.Shaw.

**Scottish FA XI:** A.McNab.

**FA Amateur XI:** N.J.Whitehead.

## INTERNATIONAL TRIALS

The term 'International Trial' used here includes fixtures such as Professionals against Amateurs, Possibles against Probables, North against South, England against The Rest, Whites against Stripes, Whites against Blues, Players against Gentlemen, England against South, England against North.

**England:** W.I.Bassett, A.J.Bayliss, J.H.Carter, J.Crisp, A.Finch, T.W.Glidden, T.Green, G.C.James, A.C.Jephcott, T.P.Magee, F.Morris, H.F.Pearson, J.Pennington, C.Perry, J.Reynolds, S.Richardson, W.Richardson, R.Roberts, E.A.Sandford, G.E.Shaw, J.Simmons, J.Smith, J.L.Spencer, W.Williams.

**Scotland:** J.Stevenson.

## MISCELLANEOUS REPRESENTATIVE HONOURS WITH OTHER CLUBS

**England:** A.Aldridge, W.Ashurst, M.Barham, P.S.Barnes, L.Blissett, W.E.Boyes, H.Chambers, C.C.Charsley, R.Crawford, W.Garraty, G.H.Holden, G.C.Hurst,

J.A.Johnson, C.Mason, A.W.Morley,
W.W.Morris, C.Palmer, J.Reynolds,
G.Roberts, B.Robson, B.E.Talbot,
G.F.Wheldon.

**Scotland:** A.R.Albiston, E.P.Colquhoun,
A.Goram, A.M.Gray, W.Groves,
A.B.Hannah, R.A.Hartford, J.Holton,
W.M.Johnston, A.McNab, J.Millar,
D.R.Speedie, D.Stewart.

**Wales:** A.M.Bostock, J.Butler, W.T.Butler,
V.Crowe, A.Davies, J.Davies, L.C.Davies,
S.Davies, W.C.Davies, A.Dibble,
I.R.Edwards, K.Jones, P.A.Griffiths,
A.Hughes, I.Jones, R.L.Krzywicki, T.Martin,
A.H.Millington, D.Nardiello, S.Powell,
R.R.Rees, W.W.Robbins, R.Roberts,
M.R.Thomas, G.O.Williams, S.G.Williams,
D.F.Witcomb.

**Northern Ireland:** G.J.Armstrong,
L.O.Bookman, D.A.Campbell, J.Connor,
R.Crone, R.Dennison, A.Elleman, D.Hegan,
W.McCabe, B.McNally, J.M.Nicholl,
J.Reynolds, J.Taggart, J.Vernon, D.J.Walsh.

**Republic of Ireland:** M.J.Giles, A.Grealish,
M.P.Martin, P.M.Mulligan, R.A.Ryan,
R.C.P.Treacy, J.Vernon, D.J.Walsh.

**Canada:** L.G.Johnson, C.Valentine.

**USA:** K.Crow, A.Merrick.

**Holland:** M.C.Jol, R.Zondervan.

**Rhodesia:** B.Grobbelaar.

**Zambia:** D.Chabala.

**Zimbabwe:** B.Grobbelaar.

**Yugoslavia:** I.Katalinić, D.Muzinić.

**England 'B':** S.Bull, D.Burrows, M.Eves,
M.E.Forsyth, S.Mackenzie, A.W.Morley,
G.A.Owen, C.Palmer, G.A.Rowley,
B.E.Talbot.

**England XI:** P.S.Barnes, I.Clarke, J.Dorsett,
G.C.Hurst, J.Mahon, A.W.Morley,
B.Robson.

**England 'B' XI:** B.E.Talbot.

**England Under-23:** J.Farmer, G.C.Hurst,
D.J.Mills, A.W.Morley, R.W.Robson,
M.E.Setters, J.Talbut.

**England Under-21:** G.Bannister, P.S.Barnes,
L.Blissett, P.Bradshaw, S.Bull, D.Burrows,
G.A.Crooks, J.M.Deehan, A.Dickens,
P.Dyson, U.Ehiogu, W.Fereday, M.E.Forsyth,
P.Hucker, A.E.King, A.Marriott, A.Miller,
R.Moses, G.A.Owen, C.Palmer, S.Parkin,
N.Reid, B.E.Talbot, G.Thompson, C.Whyte.

**England (amateur):** H.G.Bache, H.Sharratt,
J.G.Shield.

**Young England:** R.A.Gould, J.Talbut.

**England Semi-Professional:** G.Phillips.

**Football League:** W.Ashurst, W.E.Boyes,
T.Broad, D.Burrows, H.Chambers,
R.Crawford, G.Dorsett, A.Evans, A.Flewitt,
B.Grobbelaar, D.Hogg, G.C.Hurst,
J.Reynolds, F.W.Rouse, G.A.Rowley,
C.E.Shaw, G.F.Wheldon.

**Football League XI:** P.S.Barnes, G.C.Hurst,
G.A.Owen, B.Robson.

**Great Britain (amateur):** H.Sharratt.

**Football Alliance:** R.Roberts.

**Third Division (South):** S.F.Steele.

**Third Division (North):** R.V.Cutler, R.A.Ryan.

**Southern League:** E.Bradley, A.Geddes,
A.Lewis, W.Thompson, H.M.Wilcox.

**Southern League XI:** A.Geddes, A.McKenzie.

**FA XI:** W.Ashurst, N.W.Bassett, S.Bull,
I.Clarke, R.Crawford, D.Howe, J.Mahon,
G.Phillips, M.E.Setters, G.T.Summers

**FA International Trials:** W.Ashurst,
H.Chambers, W.Garraty, J.A.Johnson,
B.Rankin, J.Reynolds, B.Robinson.

**Scotland Under-23:** A.M.Gray, J.Holton,
W.M.Johnston, M.Murray, D.Stewart.

**Scotland Under-21:** A.R.Albiston, A.Goram,

R.A.Hartford, G.Hogg, B.Rice, D.R.Speedie,
J.Tortolano.

**Scotland (amateur):** M.Murray.

**Scotland XI:** A.Goram.

**Scottish League:** L.Bell, A.B.Hannah,
W.M.Johnston, P.S.McKennan, J.Millar.

**Scottish League XI:** J.M.B.Wallace.

**Scottish International Trials:** W.Groves,
J.Millar.

**Wales Under-23:** R.R.Rees, M.R.Thomas.

**Wales Under-21:** A.Dibble, I.R.Edwards,
D.Nardiello, M.R.Thomas.

**Wales (amateur):** A.Hughes.

**Welsh FA XI:** W.W.Robbins.

**Welsh League:** I.Jones, W.Taylor.

**Welsh International Trials:** A.Davies,
L.C.Davies.

**UK-Ireland-Denmark XI:** M.J.Giles.

**Ireland-Northern Ireland XI:** G.Armstrong,
J.M.Nicholl, J.Vernon.

**Northern Ireland XI:** G.J.Armstrong,
J.M.Nicholl.

**Northern Ireland Under 21:** J.M.Nicholl.

**Irish League:** S.Bowser, G.B.Drury,
P.S.McKennan, J.Vernon, D.J.Walsh.

**All Ireland XI:** M.J.Giles, M.P.Martin,
P.M.Mulligan.

**Republic of Ireland XI:** M.J.Giles, A.Grealish,
M.P.Martin, P.M. Mulligan, R.C.P.Treacy

**Republic of Ireland Under 23:** M.P.Martin,
P.M.Mulligan.

**Republic of Ireland Under 21:** K.Ampadu,
A.O'Dwyer.

**Republic of Ireland (amateur):** M.P.Martin.

**League of Ireland:** J.Dainty, J.McStay,
M.P.Martin, P.M.Mulligan, R.C.P.Treacy.

**Holland 'B':** M.C.Jol, R.Zonderan.

**Holland Under-23:** M.C.Jol.

**Holland Under-21:** M.C.Jol, R.Zonderan.

**Malaysian FA XI:** R.Crawford.

# INTERNATIONAL &
# REPRESENTATIVE RECORDS

**First International Cap:** Goalkeeper Bob
Roberts, England against Scotland at
Blackburn, 29 March 1887.

**First Major Representative Honour:**
Goalkeeper Bob Roberts, North against
South, in London, 26 January 1884.

**Youngest International:** Billy Bassett (19 years
2 months) against Ireland, 7 April 1888.

**Most Capped Albion Player:** Full-Back Stuart
Williams with 33 Welsh appearances between
1954 and 1962. After leaving Albion for
Southampton he gained a further ten Welsh
caps between 1962 and 1965. He captained
Wales on 14 occasions.

**Most Capped Player to Represent Albion:**
Former Albion midfielder Bryan Robson, up
to the end of the 1991-92 season, had
appeared in a total of 90 full internationals
for England. Right-back Jimmy Nicholl
made 73 appearances for Northern Ireland
(1976-86) and holds the distinction of being
the most capped player ever to wear Albion
colours. Robson left The Hawthorns after
winning 13 full caps (to 1981).

**Most Internationals on Albion's Books:** Nine,
in 1933-34 (Sandford, Pearson, Shaw, Carter
and Magee of England and Robbins,
Foulkes, Griffiths and Murphy of Wales) and
in 1935-36 (Sandford, Pearson, Shaw, Carter,
Boyes and Richardson of England and
Robbins, Foulkes and Murphy of Wales).

**Most Players in an International Team:** Four, in
1976-77 (Giles, Martin, Mulligan and Treacy
for the Republic of Ireland against France at
Dublin and against Poland, also at Dublin).

**International Captains:** Jesse Pennington
(England), Stan Davies, Jimmy Murphy,
Graham Williams and Stuart Williams
(Wales), Jack Vernon (Ireland, and John
Giles, Mick Martin. Paddy Mulligan and
Tony Grealish (Republic of Ireland) have
each captained their respective countries
while on Albion's books. Vernon also
skippered the United Kingdom XI. Jesse
Pennington, Billy Williams, Ray Barlow,
Don Howe and Bobby Robson have
captained the Football League representative
side while Gary Owen and Cyrille Regis have
led out the England Under-21 team. Doug
Fraser was skipper of the Scotland XI which
toured Israel, Hong Kong, Australia, New
Zealand and Canada in 1967. Asa Hartford
captained the Scotland Under-23 team whilst
with Albion, and Don Howe and Maurice
Setters captained England Under-23. Joe
Kennedy was skipper of England 'B' during
the 1950s.

**Debut Goals:** Seven Albion forward have
scored on their first international appearance
— all for England: George Woodhall (1888),
Fred Morris (1920), Joe Carter (1926), Jack
Hines (1948), Johnny Nicholls (1954), Derek
Kevan (1957) and Bobby Robson (1958).
Haines and Robson both scored twice,
Haines against Switzerland in 1948 and
Robson against France in 1957. In an
amateur international in 1908, centre-forward
Billy Jordan scored six goals against France
on his debut. In his first full appearance for
Wales, against Malta in season 1978-79,
former Albion centre-forward Ian Edwards of
Chester scored four goals.

**Most Goals In Representative Football:** Jimmy
Cookson scored 24 times in 11 matches on
the FA tour of Canada in 1931.

**Consecutive Appearances:** Between 1907 and
1920 Jesse Pennington made nine consecutive
appearances against Scotland and between
1889 and 1896, Billy Bassett played for
England against Scotland on eight
consecutive occasions. When England
defeated Scotland for the third successive year
in 1893, Bassett was one of four England
players who were each awarded a special
international cap. Between October 1957 and
November 1959 Don Howe's 23 England
appearances were consecutive.

**Successful Partnerships:** Between March 1907
and April 1914 Sam Hardy (Aston Villa), Bob
Crompton (Blackburn Rovers) and Jesse
Pennington formed a resolute last line of
defence for England in 14 internationals.
Crompton and Pennington played at full-
back together in 23 England internationals.

**Dual Internationals:** Albion's right-half of the
early 1890s, John 'Baldy' Reynolds, was
capped by both Ireland and England. Before
he signed for Albion he had appeared five
times in the Irish national side while with
the Distillery and Ulster clubs but on
arriving at Stoney Lane it was discovered that
he was born at Blackburn and thus eligible to
play for England. He was subsequently
chosen eight times for England while with
Albion and Aston Villa. Other Albion 'dual'
international players were Dave Walsh, Reg
Ryan and Jack Vernon, all whom played for
both Northern Ireland and the Republic of
Ireland.

# Albion Players' Career Records

*The following is a list of all Albion players who have appeared in first-class matches for the club. Club joined from and transferred to are also shown. The League appearances and goals total includes the three games of the abandoned 1939-40 season. The 'others' total includes wartime matches, Full Members' Cup, Anglo-Scottish Cup, Anglo-Italian Tournament, Watney Cup, Texaco Cup, FA Charity Shield and all other first-team competitive games not included in the preceding totals.*

| PLAYER | BIRTHPLACE & YEAR | POS | FROM (year) — TO (year) | League App | League Gls | FA Cup App | FA Cup Gls | Lge Cup App | Lge Cup Gls | Euro App | Euro Gls | Others App | Others Gls | TOTAL App | TOTAL Gls |
|---|---|---|---|---|---|---|---|---|---|---|---|---|---|---|---|
| ADAMS A | West Bromwich 1880 | FB | Springfields 1897 — Retired 1910 | 209 | 3 | 15 | 0 | 0 | 0 | 0 | 0 | 0 | 0 | 214 | 3 |
| ADAMS J | Norton Canes 1908 | G | Cannock T 1929 — Retired 1945 | 103 | 10 | 0 | 0 | 0 | 0 | 0 | 0 | 108 | 0 | 221/33 | 0 |
| ADAMS W | Blackheath 1892 | FB | Rowley V 1919 — Barrow 1928 | 92 | 0 | 6 | 0 | 0 | 0 | 0 | 0 | 0 | 0 | 98 | 0 |
| ADDERLEY JB | Birmingham 1922 | FB | Bournville Youths 1941 — Released 1946 | 0 | 0 | 0 | 0 | 0 | 0 | 0 | 0 | 1 | 0 | 1 | 0 |
| AITKEN AFS | Craigmillar, Edinburgh 1934 | W | Hibernian 1959 — Falkirk 1961 | 22 | 2 | 0 | 0 | 0 | 0 | 0 | 0 | 0 | 0 | 22 | 2 |
| ALBISTON AR | Edinburgh 1957 | FB | Manchester U 1988 — Dundee 1989 | 43 | 2 | 2 | 0 | 1 | 0 | 0 | 0 | 1 | 0 | 47 | 2 |
| ALDERWICK J | Birmingham 1921 | G | New Oscot FC 1940 — Released 1946 | 0 | 0 | 0 | 0 | 0 | 0 | 0 | 0 | 1 | 0 | 1 | 0 |
| ALDRIDGE AJ | Walsall 1864 | FB | Walsall Swifts 1886 — Walsall TS 1888 | 0 | 0 | 15 | 0 | 0 | 0 | 0 | 0 | 0 | 0 | 15 | 0 |
| ALDRIDGE N | Coventry 1921 | FB | Foxford 1945 — Northampton T 1948 | 1 | 0 | 0 | 0 | 0 | 0 | 0 | 0 | 0 | 0 | 1 | 0 |
| ALLAN SJ | Wallsend-on-Tyne 1884 | CF | Newcastle U 1911 — Nottingham F 1912 | 19 | 4 | 1 | 0 | 0 | 0 | 0 | 0 | 0 | 0 | 20 | 4 |
| ALLARDYCE S | Dudley 1954 | D | Preston North End 1989—Preston North End 1991 | 0/1 | 0 | 0 | 0 | 0 | 0 | 0 | 0 | 0 | 0 | 0/1 | 0 |
| ALLEN R | Fenton, Stoke 1929 | CF | Port Vale 1950 — Crystal P 1961 | 415 | 208 | 42 | 23 | 0 | 0 | 0 | 0 | 1 | 3 | 458 | 234 |
| ALSOP G | Frampton Cotterill, Bristol 1908 | CF | Walsall 1935 — Ipswich T 1937 | 1 | 0 | 0 | 0 | 0 | 0 | 0 | 0 | 0 | 0 | 1 | 0 |
| AMPADU K | Bradford 1970 | M | Arsenal 1991— | 19/19 | 4 | 0 | 0 | 2/1 | 0 | 0 | 0 | 1 | 1 | 22/20 | 5 |
| ANDERSON CR | Newcastle 1962 | FB/M | Torquay U 1985 — Walsall 1991 | 131/9 | 10 | 2 | 2 | 5/2 | 0 | 0 | 0 | 2/1 | 0 | 140/12 | 12 |
| ANDERSEN VN | Kristiansand 1964 | D | Lyngby(trial)1989 — Lyngby 1989 | 0/1 | 0 | 0 | 0 | 0 | 0 | 0 | 0 | 0 | 0 | 0/1 | 0 |
| APPLEBY B | Burton upon Trent 1878 | CF | Burton U 1901 — Bristol R 1903 | 1 | 0 | 0 | 0 | 0 | 0 | 0 | 0 | 0 | 0 | 1 | 0 |
| ARMSTRONG GJ | Belfast 1954 | F | Real Mallorca 1985 — Brighton & HA 1986 | 7/1 | 0 | 0 | 0 | 2 | 1 | 0 | 0 | 1 | 0 | 10/1 | 1 |
| ARTHUR DR | Bushbury, Wolverhampton 1960 | FB | School 1976 — Walsall 1982 | 2/1 | 0 | 0 | 0 | 3 | 0 | 0 | 0 | 0 | 0 | 5/1 | 0 |
| ASHLEY H | Smethwick 1913 | F | Smethwick Highfield 1934 — Derby C 1937 | 0 | 0 | 0 | 0 | 0 | 0 | 0 | 0 | 13 | 6 | 13 | 6 |
| ASHMORE GS | Plymouth 1898 | G | Nineveh Wesley 1919 — Chesterfield 1931 | 246 | 0 | 22 | 0 | 0 | 0 | 0 | 0 | 0 | 0 | 268 | 0 |
| ASHURST W | Willington, Co Durham 1894 | FB | Notts C 1926 — Newark T 1928 | 22 | 1 | 1 | 0 | 0 | 0 | 0 | 0 | 0 | 0 | 23 | 1 |
| ASKIN GW | West Bromwich 1861 | IF | Elwells 1882 — Hednesford 1889 | 0 | 0 | 1 | 0 | 0 | 0 | 0 | 0 | 0 | 0 | 1 | 0 |
| ASTLE J | Eastwood, Notts 1942 | CF | Notts C 1964 — Hellenic (South Africa) 1974 | 290/2 | 137 | 23 | 14 | 28 | 19 | 10 | 1 | 8 | 3 | 359/2 | 174 |
| ASTON JH | Redditch 1881 | CF | Durham Light Infantry 1904 — Willenhall Swifts 1905 | 25 | 9 | 1 | 1 | 0 | 0 | 0 | 0 | 0 | 0 | 26 | 10 |
| ASTON H | Bloxwich 1855 | IF | George Salter Works 1879 — Wolves 1885 | 0 | 0 | 7 | 3 | 0 | 0 | 0 | 0 | 0 | 0 | 7 | 3 |
| BACHE HG | Churchhill, Worcs 1889 | CF | Eastbourne 1914 — Killed 1916 | 12 | 4 | 2 | 0 | 0 | 0 | 0 | 0 | 0 | 0 | 14 | 4 |
| BADDELEY G | Fegg Hayes, Staffs 1874 | HB | Stoke 1908 — Retired 1914cs | 145 | 1 | 12 | 0 | 0 | 0 | 0 | 0 | 0 | 0 | 157 | 1 |
| BALDWIN HJA | Birmingham 1920 | G | Sutton T 1937 — Brighton & HA 1939 | 5 | 0 | 0 | 0 | 0 | 0 | 0 | 0 | 0 | 0 | 5 | 0 |
| BALL HG | West Bromwich 1921 | CF | Golds Green Meths 1939 — Darlaston 1946 | 0 | 0 | 0 | 0 | 0 | 0 | 0 | 0 | 16 | 9 | 16 | 9 |
| BAMFORD AE | Weedon, Northants 1880 | OL | Wellingborough T 1905 — Wellingborough T 1906 | 3 | 0 | 0 | 0 | 0 | 0 | 0 | 0 | 0 | 0 | 3 | 0 |
| BANKS GE | Wednesbury 1919 | CF | Brownhills A 1933 — Mansfield T 1947 | 4 | 3 | 0 | 0 | 0 | 0 | 0 | 0 | 13 | 7 | 17 | 10 |
| BANKS IF | Mexborough 1961 | M | Bradford City 1989 — Barnsley 1989 | 2/2 | 0 | 0 | 0 | 0 | 0 | 0 | 0 | 0 | 0 | 2/2 | 0 |
| BANKS J | West Bromwich 1871 | LH | Oldbury Broadwell 1894 — Newton Heath 1901 | 119 | 5 | 12 | 1 | 0 | 0 | 0 | 0 | 3 | 0 | 134 | 6 |
| BANNISTER G | Warrington 1960 | F | Coventry City 1990 — Nottingham Forest 1992 | 62/10 | 18 | 1/1 | 0 | 3/1 | 1 | 0 | 0 | 3 | 1 | 69/12 | 20 |
| BANNISTER J | Chesterfield 1942 | HB | School 1958 — Scunthorpe U 1964 | 9 | 0 | 0 | 0 | 0 | 0 | 0 | 0 | 0 | 0 | 9 | 0 |
| BARHAM MF | Folkestone 1962 | F | Middlesbrough 1989 —Brighton & HA 1989 | 4 | 0 | 0 | 0 | 1 | 0 | 0 | 0 | 0 | 0 | 5 | 0 |
| BARKER RC | Kinglassie, Glenrothes 1927 | OL | Kelty Rangers 1945 — Shrewsbury T 1950 | 14 | 2 | 0 | 0 | 0 | 0 | 0 | 0 | 0 | 0 | 14 | 2 |
| BARLOW RJ | Swindon 1926 | LH | Garrards 1944 — Birmingham C 1960 | 403 | 31 | 46 | 5 | 0 | 0 | 0 | 0 | 33 | 12 | 482 | 48 |
| BARNES PS | Manchester 1957 | OL | Manchester C 1979 — Leeds U 1981 | 76/1 | 23 | 4 | 1 | 9/1 | 1 | 1 | 0 | 0 | 0 | 90/2 | 25 |
| BARNSLEY GR | Bilston 1935 | G | Erdington A 1951 — Plymouth A 1957 | 1 | 0 | 0 | 0 | 0 | 0 | 0 | 0 | 0 | 0 | 1 | 0 |
| BARRON PG | Woolwich 1953 | G | Crystal P 1982 — Queen's Park R 1985 | 63 | 0 | 6 | 0 | 4 | 0 | 0 | 0 | 0 | 0 | 73 | 0 |
| BARTLETT KF | Portsmouth 1962 | F | Cardiff C 1989 — Notts C 1990 | 25/12 | 10 | 3 | 1 | 2 | 0 | 0 | 0 | 1 | 0 | 31/12 | 11 |
| BASSETT ICH | Brithdir 1915 | FB | Sutton T 1936 — Retired 1943 | 8 | 0 | 0 | 0 | 0 | 0 | 0 | 0 | 92 | 0 | 100 | 0 |
| BASSETT WI | West Bromwich 1869 | OR | Old Church Club 1886 — Retired 1899 | 261 | 61 | 40 | 11 | 0 | 0 | 0 | 0 | 10 | 5 | 311 | 77 |
| BATSON BM | Grenada, West Indies 1953 | FB | Cambridge U 1978 — Retired 1984 | 172 | 1 | 13 | 1 | 21 | 0 | 12 | 0 | 2 | 0 | 220 | 2 |
| BAUGH R | Wolverhampton 1898 | FB | Cardiff C 1924 — Exeter C 1928 | 61 | 0 | 4 | 0 | 0 | 0 | 0 | 0 | 0 | 0 | 65 | 0 |
| BAYLISS AEJM | Tipton 1863 | WH/CF | Wednesbury Old Athletic 1884 — Retired 1892 | 56 | 12 | 39 | 24 | 0 | 0 | 0 | 0 | 0 | 0 | 95 | 36 |
| BEDFORD L | Birmingham 1904 | W | School 1920 — Walsall 1922 | 3 | 0 | 0 | 0 | 0 | 0 | 0 | 0 | 0 | 0 | 3 | 0 |
| BELL G | West Bromwich 1861 | OL | George Salter Works 1879 — Kidderminster H 1888 | 0 | 0 | 16 | 7 | 0 | 0 | 0 | 0 | 0 | 0 | 16 | 7 |
| BELL H | West Bromwich 1862 | FB | George Salter Works 1879 — Retired 1888 | 0 | 0 | 15 | 0 | 0 | 0 | 0 | 0 | 0 | 0 | 15 | 0 |
| BELL SLT | Langbank, Strathclyde 1875 | F | Brentford 1904 — Hibernian 1905 | 16 | 6 | 1 | 0 | 0 | 0 | 0 | 0 | 0 | 0 | 17 | 6 |
| BELL T | Airth, Falkirk 1917 | IF | Cambuslang Rangers 1939 — Retired 1946 | 0 | 0 | 0 | 0 | 0 | 0 | 0 | 0 | 15 | 5 | 15 | 5 |
| BENJAMIN IT | Nottingham 1961 | M | Sheffield U 1979 — Peterborough U 1982 | 1/1 | 0 | 0 | 0 | 0 | 0 | 0 | 0 | 0 | 0 | 1/1 | 0 |
| BENNETT M | Birmingham 1961 | D | Streetly FC 1977 — Worcester C 1990 | 180/1 | 9 | 13 | 0 | 20 | 1 | 0 | 0 | 3 | 0 | 216/1 | 10 |
| BENTLEY A | Alfreton 1887 | CF | Bolton W 1913 — Burton Albion 1922 | 97 | 46 | 5 | 1 | 0 | 0 | 0 | 0 | 3/1 | 0 | 105/1 | 4 |
| BETTELEY RH | Bradley, Bilston 1880 | FB | Wolves 1906 — Bilston U 1912 | 85 | 0 | 4 | 0 | 0 | 0 | 0 | 0 | 0 | 0 | 89 | 0 |
| BETTERIDGE RM | Redditch 1924 | W | Warslow Celtic 1948 — Swindon T 1951 | 5 | 0 | 0 | 0 | 0 | 0 | 0 | 0 | 0 | 0 | 5 | 0 |
| BILLINGHAM PA | Fensnett, Nr Dudley 1938 | WH | Walsall 1960 — Worcester C 1962 | 7 | 0 | 0 | 0 | 0 | 0 | 0 | 0 | 0 | 0 | 7 | 0 |
| BISSEKER W | West Bromwich 1863 | CF | George Salter Works 1879 — Retired 1884 | 0 | 0 | 1 | 0 | 0 | 0 | 0 | 0 | 0 | 0 | 1 | 0 |
| BLAGDEN J | Sheffield 1893 | IF | Cresswell Colliery 1921 — Worksop T 1923 | 16 | 2 | 4 | 2 | 0 | 0 | 0 | 0 | 0 | 0 | 20 | 4 |
| BLISSETT LL | Jamaica 1958 | F | Watford(loan) 1992 — Watford 1992 | 3 | 1 | 0 | 0 | 0 | 0 | 0 | 0 | 0 | 0 | 3 | 1 |
| BLOOD R | Harpur Hill, Nr Buxton 1894 | CF | Port Vale 1921 — Stockport C 1924 | 53 | 26 | 0 | 0 | 0 | 0 | 0 | 0 | 0 | 0 | 53 | 26 |
| BOOKMAN LJ | Dolphin Bar 1890 | OL | Bradford C 1914 — Luton T 1919 | 16 | 1 | 0 | 0 | 0 | 0 | 0 | 0 | 2 | 0 | 18 | 1 |
| BOSTOCK AMW | Brecon, mid Wales 1869 | CF | Shrewsbury T 1892 — Burton Swifts 1894 | 26 | 11 | 0 | 0 | 0 | 0 | 0 | 0 | 8 | 2 | 34 | 13 |
| BOSTON HJ | Nantwich 1899 | OR | Bolton W 1929 — Swansea T 1931 | 27 | 6 | 0 | 0 | 0 | 0 | 0 | 0 | 0 | 0 | 27 | 6 |
| BOURNE RA | Roundle 1881 | OL | Clapton O 1907 — Walsall 1908 | 9 | 1 | 0 | 0 | 0 | 0 | 0 | 0 | 0 | 0 | 9 | 1 |
| BOWDEN J | Manchester 1882 | HB | Handsworth R 1904 — Southampton 1906 | 8 | 0 | 0 | 0 | 0 | 0 | 0 | 0 | 0 | 0 | 8 | 0 |
| BOWEN S | West Bromwich 1972 | M | YTS 1988 — Coventry City(trial)1992 | 8 | 1 | 0 | 0 | 0 | 0 | 0 | 0 | 0 | 0 | 8 | 1 |
| BOWEN TH | West Bromwich 1924 | F | West Bromwich Ath 1941 — Newport C 1946 | 0 | 0 | 0 | 0 | 0 | 0 | 0 | 0 | 6 | 2 | 6 | 2 |
| BOWEN WE | Hednesford 1891 | CH | Nuneaton T 1914 — Hednesford T 1915 | 1 | 0 | 0 | 0 | 0 | 0 | 0 | 0 | 0 | 0 | 1 | 0 |
| BOWSER S | Handsworth 1892 | CH/IF | Willenhall 1908 — Belfast Distillery 1913; Belfast Distillery 1914 — Walsall 1924 | 341 | 64 | 28 | 8 | 0 | 0 | 0 | 0 | 2 | 0 | 371 | 72 |
| BOWSER W | Handsworth 1886 | F | Dudley T 1907 — Walsall 1909 | 1 | 0 | 0 | 0 | 0 | 0 | 0 | 0 | 0 | 0 | 1 | 0 |
| BOYD H | Lanchester 1866 | IF | Burnley 1892 — April 1893 | 7 | 1 | 1 | 0 | 0 | 0 | 0 | 0 | 2 | 1 | 10 | 2 |
| BOYD J | Consett 1925 | RB | Sunderland 1948 — Consett T 1949 | 1 | 0 | 0 | 0 | 0 | 0 | 0 | 0 | 0 | 0 | 1 | 0 |
| BOYES WE | Killamarsh, Nr Sheffield 1913 | WH/OL | Woodhouse Mills U 1931 — Everton 1938 | 151 | 35 | 14 | 3 | 0 | 0 | 0 | 0 | 0 | 0 | 165 | 38 |
| BRADLEY CH | Smethwick 1882 | OR | Invention Street Boys 1905 — Dudley T 1905 | 3 | 0 | 0 | 0 | 0 | 0 | 0 | 0 | 0 | 0 | 3 | 0 |
| BRADLEY DM | Birmingham 1965 | M | Aston Villa 1986 — | 201/13 | 7 | 8 | 2 | 10 | 1 | 0 | 0 | 10 | 1 | 229/13 | 11 |
| BRADLEY DJ | Annerley, Notts 1924 | FB | Clipstone Colliery 1942 — Mansfield T 1949 | 0 | 0 | 0 | 0 | 0 | 0 | 0 | 0 | 2 | 0 | 2 | 0 |
| BRADLEY EJ | Dudley 1882 | WH/IF | Dudley T 1905 — Luton T 1908 | 25 | 6 | 2 | 0 | 0 | 0 | 0 | 0 | 0 | 0 | 27 | 6 |
| BRADLEY RJ | Ellingshall, Wolverhampton 1939 | FB | SE Staffordshire Boys 1954 — Norwich C 1964 | 13 | 0 | 0 | 0 | 0 | 0 | 0 | 0 | 0 | 0 | 13 | 0 |
| BRADSHAW PW | Altrincham 1956 | G | Vancouver Whitecaps 1985 — Vancouver Whitecaps 1985; Newport County 1988 — Peterborough 1990 | 14 | 0 | 2 | 0 | 5 | 0 | 0 | 0 | 1 | 0 | 22 | 0 |
| BRETT R | Chester 1878 | F | Army Medical Corps 1898 — Wellingborough T 1899 | 12 | 3 | 0 | 0 | 0 | 0 | 0 | 0 | 0 | 0 | 12 | 3 |
| BRETT SS | St Asaph, North Wales 1879 | F | Southport Central 1898 — Wellingborough T 1902 | 8 | 2 | 2 | 1 | 0 | 0 | 0 | 0 | 0 | 0 | 10 | 3 |
| BRITTAIN JW | Wednesbury 1880 | FB | Wednesbury OA 1902 — Willenhall Swifts 1906 | 9 | 0 | 1 | 0 | 0 | 0 | 0 | 0 | 0 | 0 | 10 | 0 |
| BROAD T | Stalybridge 1887 | OR | Openshaw LC 1905 — Chesterfield 1908 | 11 | 0 | 4 | 1 | 0 | 0 | 0 | 0 | 0 | 0 | 15 | 1 |
| BROCKHURST WJ | Brownhills 1913 | CH | Cannock CC 1935 — Hednesford T 1938 | 5 | 0 | 0 | 0 | 0 | 0 | 0 | 0 | 0 | 0 | 5 | 0 |
| BROMAGE E | Mickleover, Derby 1898 | OL | Gillingham 1928 — Nottingham F 1929 | 10 | 2 | 0 | 0 | 0 | 0 | 0 | 0 | 0 | 0 | 10 | 2 |
| BROOKES WA | Dudley 1931 | WH | Churchfields 1947 — Allen's Cross 1958 | 19 | 0 | 0 | 0 | 0 | 0 | 0 | 0 | 1 | 0 | 20 | 0 |
| BROOKS J | Stairfoot, Yorks 1886 | OL | Barnsley 1907 — Barnsley 1908 | 21 | 1 | 1 | 0 | 0 | 0 | 0 | 0 | 0 | 0 | 22 | 1 |
| BROWN A | Musselburgh, Lothian 1951 | F | Leicester C 1972 — Crystal P 1983 | 254/25 | 72 | 26/2 | 6 | 27 | 2 | 10 | 1 | 14/1 | 4 | 331/28 | 85 |
| BROWN A | Oldham 1945 | WH/F | Manchester Schools 1961 — Torquay U 1981 | 561/13 | 218 | 53/1 | 27 | 46/1 | 17 | 16/1 | 8 | 28 | 9 | 704/16 | 279 |
| BROWN F | Leyton 1931 | G | Aldershot 1955 — Portsmouth 1958 | 11 | 0 | 0 | 0 | 0 | 0 | 0 | 0 | 0 | 0 | 11 | 0 |
| BROWN H | Northampton 1883 | IF | Northampton T 1903 — Southampton 1905 | 35 | 5 | 1 | 0 | 0 | 0 | 0 | 0 | 0 | 0 | 36 | 5 |
| BROWN JF | Brierley Hill 1886 | IF | Stoke 1908 — Kidderminster H 1910 | 8 | 0 | 0 | 0 | 0 | 0 | 0 | 0 | 0 | 0 | 8 | 0 |

**Jeff Astle after scoring the winning goal in the 1968 FA Cup Final.**

| PLAYER | BIRTHPLACE & YEAR | POS | FROM (year) — TO (year) | League App | League Gls | FA Cup App | FA Cup Gls | Lge Cup App | Lge Cup Gls | Euro App | Euro Gls | Others App | Others Gls | TOTAL App | TOTAL Gls |
|---|---|---|---|---|---|---|---|---|---|---|---|---|---|---|---|
| BUCK F | Newcastle-under-Lyme 1880 | CH/IF | Stafford R 1900 — Liverpool 1903<br>Plymouth A 1906 — Swansea T 1914 | 287 | 90 | 32 | 4 | 0 | 0 | 0 | 0 | 0 | 0 | 319 | 94 |
| BULL S | Tipton 1965 | CF | Tipton Town 1984 — Wolverhampton W 1986 | 2/2 | 2 | 0 | 0 | 2 | 1 | 0 | 0 | 1/2 | 0 | 5/4 | 3 |
| BUNN AF | West Bromwich 1861 | CH | George Salter Works 1879 — Crosswell's B 1886 | 0 | 0 | 12 | 1 | 0 | 0 | 0 | 0 | 0 | 0 | 12 | 1 |
| BURGESS D | Birmingham 1971 | D | YTS 1987— | 108/5 | 3 | 5 | 0 | 5/2 | 0 | 0 | 0 | 5 | 0 | 123/7 | 3 |
| BURGIN M | Sheffield 1911 | IF | Nottingham F 1938 — Retired 1942 | 14 | 9 | 0 | 0 | 0 | 0 | 0 | 0 | 2 | 0 | 16 | 9 |
| BURNS JA | Liverpool 1865 | OL | London Cals 1889 — Notts C 1892 | 15 | 5 | 2 | 0 | 0 | 0 | 0 | 0 | 0 | 0 | 17 | 5 |
| BURNS J | Walsall 1871 | IF | Fairfield Villa 1893 — Stafford R 1894 | 1 | 0 | 0 | 0 | 0 | 0 | 0 | 0 | 0 | 0 | 1 | 0 |
| BURNSIDE DG | Bristol 1939 | IF | Bristol C 1955 — Southampton 1962 | 127 | 39 | 8 | 3 | 0 | 0 | 0 | 0 | 0 | 0 | 135 | 42 |
| BURROWS D | West Bromwich 1968 | FB | School 1985 — Liverpool 1988 | 37/9 | 1 | 2 | 0 | 3/1 | 0 | 0 | 0 | 1 | 0 | 43/10 | 1 |
| BURTON EC | Birmingham 1881 | OR | Walsall 1905 — Walsall 1905 | 1 | 0 | 0 | 0 | 0 | 0 | 0 | 0 | 0 | 0 | 1 | 0 |
| BURTON HA | West Bromwich 1872 | FB | Sheffield W 1909 — Scunthorpe U 1911 | 32 | 0 | 4 | 0 | 0 | 0 | 0 | 0 | 0 | 0 | 36 | 0 |
| BUSHELL G | Wednesbury 1864 | F | West Bromwich FC 1883 — Wednesbury Old Ath 1889 | 0 | 0 | 1 | 0 | 0 | 0 | 0 | 0 | 0 | 0 | 1 | 0 |
| BUTLER S | Stellington 1919 | OL | Scunthorpe U 1938 — Southport 1947 | 4 | 0 | 2 | 0 | 0 | 0 | 0 | 0 | 30 | 8 | 36 | 8 |
| BYERS JE | Selby, Yorks 1897 | OL | Blackburn R 1924 — Worcester C 1928 | 104 | 11 | 7 | 1 | 0 | 0 | 0 | 0 | 0 | 0 | 111 | 12 |
| BYTHEWAY G | Shuttlewood, Derbyshire 1908 | W | Staveley T 1927 — Coventry C 1933 | 16 | 2 | 0 | 0 | 0 | 0 | 0 | 0 | 0 | 0 | 16 | 2 |
| CAMERON JR | Currie, Nr Edinburgh 1875 | CF | Everton 1896 — Blackburn R 1897 | 13 | 2 | 2 | 0 | 0 | 0 | 0 | 0 | 0 | 0 | 15 | 2 |
| CAMPBELL D | Manchester 1944 | CH | Droylsden 1961 — Los Angeles W 1968 | 8 | 0 | 0 | 0 | 3 | 0 | 0 | 0 | 0 | 0 | 11 | 0 |
| CAMPBELL JC | St Pancras, London 1937 | OR | Maidenhead 1954 — Portsmouth 1959 | 31 | 9 | 0 | 0 | 0 | 0 | 0 | 0 | 0 | 0 | 31 | 9 |
| CANTELLO L | Newton Heath, Manchester 1951 | M | School 1967 — Bolton W 1979 | 297/4 | 13 | 22 | 3 | 21 | 3 | 7 | 0 | 18 | 2 | 365/4 | 21 |
| CARTER G | Moulton, Cheshire 1943 | OL | Moulton FC 1959 — Bury 1966 | 25 | 3 | 0 | 0 | 0 | 0 | 0 | 0 | 0 | 0 | 25 | 3 |
| CARTER JH | Aston 1901 | IR | Westbourne C 1921 — Tranmere R 1936 | 414 | 145 | 37 | 10 | 0 | 0 | 0 | 0 | 0 | 0 | 451 | 155 |
| CARTER W | Wednesbury 1933 | F | SE Staffordshire Boys 1949 — Plymouth A 1957 | 57 | 12 | 3 | 0 | 0 | 0 | 0 | 0 | 1 | 0 | 61 | 12 |
| CARTWRIGHT N | Stourbridge 1971 | M | YTS 1987 — Kidderminster H 1993 | 5/6 | 0 | 0 | 0 | 0 | 0 | 0 | 0 | 0/1 | 0 | 5/7 | 0 |
| CASTLE J | Birmingham 1871 | WH | Birmingham St George 1891 — Brierley Hill 1892 | 4 | 0 | 0 | 0 | 0 | 0 | 0 | 0 | 0 | 0 | 4 | 0 |
| CAVE GH | Great Bridge 1874 | FB | Great Bridge U 1896 — Retired 1901 | 77 | 0 | 6 | 0 | 0 | 0 | 0 | 0 | 0 | 0 | 83 | 0 |
| CHADBURN J | Mansfield 1873 | RB/OR | Wolves 1900 — Liverpool 1903 | 43 | 3 | 5 | 1 | 0 | 0 | 0 | 0 | 0 | 0 | 48 | 4 |
| CHAMBERLAIN HG | Langley, West Midlands 1901 | FB | Cradley Heath 1922 — Brighton & HA 1926 | 4 | 0 | 0 | 0 | 0 | 0 | 0 | 0 | 0 | 0 | 4 | 0 |
| CHAMBERS H | Willington Quay, Co Durham 1896 | IF | Liverpool 1928 — Oakengates T 1929 | 40 | 4 | 6 | 1 | 0 | 0 | 0 | 0 | 0 | 0 | 46 | 5 |
| CHAPMAN G | Burton upon Trent 1920 | F | Donisthorpe FC 1938 — Brighton & HA 1946 | 0 | 0 | 0 | 0 | 0 | 0 | 0 | 0 | 14 | 2 | 14 | 2 |
| CHARSLEY CC | Leicester 1864 | G | Small Heath A 1891 — Small Heath A 1891 | 1 | 0 | 0 | 0 | 0 | 0 | 0 | 0 | 0 | 0 | 1 | 0 |
| CHILDS GPC | Birmingham 1964 | M | School 1980 — Walsall 1983 | 2/1 | 0 | 0 | 0 | 0 | 0 | 0 | 0 | 0 | 0 | 2/1 | 0 |
| CLARK B | Wednesbury 1900 | OL | Seaforth Highlanders 1919 — Blakenhall 1920 | 1 | 0 | 0 | 0 | 0 | 0 | 0 | 0 | 0 | 0 | 1 | 0 |
| CLARK C | Leeds 1940 | OL | Queen's Park R 1961 — Queen's Park R 1969 | 300/1 | 80 | 25/1 | 7 | 19 | 10 | 7 | 1 | 0 | 0 | 351/2 | 98 |
| CLARKE D | Stockton-on-Tees 1948 | FB | School 1963 — Huddersfield T 1969 | 19 | 0 | 4/1 | 0 | 1 | 0 | 1 | 0 | 0 | 0 | 25/1 | 0 |
| CLARKE I | Tipton 1915 | IF | Toll End Wesley 1937 — Portsmouth 1947 | 108 | 39 | 9 | 4 | 0 | 0 | 0 | 0 | 96 | 55 | 213 | 98 |
| CLEMENTS HW | Worcester 1884 | OR | Worcester C 1903 — Worcester C 1904 | 10 | 0 | 0 | 0 | 0 | 0 | 0 | 0 | 0 | 0 | 10 | 0 |
| COEN RWL | Lowestoft 1914 | OL | Milford Haven 1932 — Coventry C 1938 | 7 | 4 | 2 | 0 | 0 | 0 | 0 | 0 | 0 | 0 | 9 | 4 |
| COLDICOTT S | Worcester 1974 | FB | YTS 1990 — | 10/4 | 0 | 0/1 | 0 | 0/1 | 0 | 0 | 0 | 1/1 | 0 | 11/7 | 0 |
| COLE HJ | Hill Top, West Bromwich 1885 | IR | Bloxwich St 1901 — Wellingborough T 1904 | 9 | 3 | 0 | 0 | 0 | 0 | 0 | 0 | 0 | 0 | 9 | 3 |
| COLLARD I | South Hetton, Co Durham 1947 | M | School 1962 — Ipswich T 1969 | 63/6 | 7 | 12 | 0 | 7 | 1 | 7/1 | 0 | 1 | 0 | 90/7 | 8 |
| COLQUHOUN EP | Prestonpans, Edinburgh 1945 | D | Bury 1967 — Sheffield U 1968 | 46 | 1 | 5 | 0 | 2 | 0 | 1 | 0 | 0 | 0 | 54 | 1 |
| CONNELLY E | Dumbarton 1916 | IF | Luton T 1939 — Luton T 1946 | 3 | 1 | 4 | 1 | 0 | 0 | 0 | 0 | 54 | 13 | 61 | 15 |
| CONNOR JJM | Lochee, Dundee 1880 | OR | Gordon Highlanders 1898 — Walsall 1899 | 10 | 0 | 0 | 0 | 0 | 0 | 0 | 0 | 0 | 0 | 10 | 0 |
| COOK AF | Stafford 1890 | FB | Wrexham 1911 — Swansea T 1922 | 38 | 0 | 12 | 0 | 0 | 0 | 0 | 0 | 5 | 0 | 55 | 0 |
| COOK F | Rugby 1880 | G | Northampton T 1902 — Portsmouth 1905 | 28 | 0 | 1 | 0 | 0 | 0 | 0 | 0 | 0 | 0 | 29 | 0 |
| COOKSON J | Manchester 1904 | CF | Chesterfield 1927 — Plymouth A 1933 | 122 | 103 | 9 | 7 | 0 | 0 | 0 | 0 | 0 | 0 | 131 | 110 |
| CORBETT FJ | Willenhall 1903 | FB | Hednesford T 1926 — Coventry C 1931 | 12 | 0 | 0 | 0 | 0 | 0 | 0 | 0 | 0 | 0 | 12 | 0 |
| CORBETT G | North Warbottle, Co Durham 1925 | FB | Spennymoor 1951 — Workington 1953 | 1 | 0 | 0 | 0 | 0 | 0 | 0 | 0 | 0 | 0 | 1 | 0 |
| CORBETT R | Wolverhampton 1887 | FB | Willenhall SW 1909 — Walsall 1911 | 3 | 0 | 0 | 0 | 0 | 0 | 0 | 0 | 0 | 0 | 3 | 0 |
| CORFIELD S | Tipton 1883 | CH | Toll End W 1902 — Retired 1904 | 8 | 0 | 0 | 0 | 0 | 0 | 0 | 0 | 0 | 0 | 8 | 0 |
| CORK D | Doncaster 1962 | F | Huddersfield T (loan)1988 — Huddersfield T 1988 | 1/3 | 0 | 0 | 0 | 0 | 0 | 0 | 0 | 0 | 0 | 1/3 | 0 |
| COWDRILL BL | Birmingham 1957 | D | Sutton Town 1979 —Bolton Wanderers 1988 | 127/4 | 0 | 6 | 1 | 9/1 | 0 | 0 | 0 | 1 | 0 | 143/5 | 1 |
| COX FJA | Reading 1920 | W | Arsenal 1953 — Bournemouth 1956 | 0 | 0 | 0 | 0 | 0 | 0 | 0 | 0 | 0 | 0 | 4 | 0 |
| COX S | Mexborough 1920 | FB | Denaby U 1948 — Accrington S 1951 | 2 | 0 | 0 | 0 | 0 | 0 | 0 | 0 | 0 | 0 | 2 | 0 |
| CRABTREE FW | West Bromwich 1865 | W | Christ Church 1887 — Old Stephen's 1889 | 1 | 1 | 0 | 0 | 0 | 0 | 0 | 0 | 0 | 0 | 1 | 1 |
| CRAM R | Hetton-le-Hole, Co Durham 1939 | FB/WH | Durham Boys 1955 — Bromsgrove R 1967 | 141 | 25 | 8 | 1 | 13 | 0 | 1 | 0 | 0 | 0 | 163 | 26 |
| CRAWFORD CHR | Alexandria, Dumbarton 1943 | FB | Scotland Boys 1959 — Exeter C 1967 | 10 | 0 | 0 | 0 | 2 | 0 | 2 | 0 | 0 | 0 | 14 | 0 |
| CRAWFORD R | Portsmouth 1936 | CF | Wolves 1965 — Ipswich T 1966 | 14 | 6 | 1 | 0 | 2 | 1 | 0 | 0 | 0 | 0 | 17 | 7 |
| CRESSWELL F | South Shields 1908 | IF | Sunderland 1929 — Chester 1930 | 30 | 6 | 1 | 0 | 0 | 0 | 0 | 0 | 0 | 0 | 31 | 6 |
| CRISP J | Hamstead, Birmingham 1896 | W | Ordnance FC 1914 — Blackburn R 1923 | 115 | 22 | 7 | 1 | 0 | 0 | 0 | 0 | 2 | 0 | 124 | 23 |
| CRONE R | Belfast 1870 | FB | Middlesbrough 1893 — Burton Swifts 1895 | 40 | 0 | 1 | 0 | 0 | 0 | 0 | 0 | 10 | 0 | 51 | 0 |
| CROOKS GA | Stoke-on-Trent 1958 | F | Tottenham H 1985 — Charlton A 1987 | 39 | 16 | 1 | 0 | 6 | 2 | 0 | 0 | 4 | 3 | 50 | 21 |
| CROSS D | Heywood, Lancashire 1950 | CF | Coventry C 1976 — West Ham U 1977<br>Vancouver Whitecaps 1984 — Bolton W 1985 | 54 | 20 | 2 | 0 | 5 | 2 | 0 | 0 | 0/1 | 1 | 61/1 | 23 |
| CROSS NJR | Birmingham 1961 | F | School 1977 — Walsall 1985 | 68/37 | 15 | 5 | 1 | 6/2 | 3 | 0/1 | 0 | 0 | 0 | 79/40 | 19 |
| CROWE E | Stourport, Worcs 1910 | G | Stourport Swifts 1930 — Swansea T 1936 | 15 | 0 | 1 | 0 | 0 | 0 | 0 | 0 | 0 | 0 | 16 | 0 |
| CROWSHAW AA | Willenhall 1932 | W | Bloxwich W 1946 — Derby C 1956 | 11 | 2 | 0 | 0 | 0 | 0 | 0 | 0 | 0 | 0 | 11 | 2 |
| CRUMP A | Smethwick 1886 | D | Reading 1908 — Dudley T 1910 | 1 | 0 | 0 | 0 | 0 | 0 | 0 | 0 | 0 | 0 | 1 | 0 |
| CUMBES J | East Didsbury, Manchester 1944 | G | Tranmere R 1969 — Aston Villa 1971 | 64 | 0 | 4 | 0 | 4 | 0 | 0 | 0 | 7 | 0 | 79 | 0 |
| CUNNINGHAM LP | Archway, London 1956 | F | Orient 1977 — Real Madrid 1979 | 81/5 | 21 | 7/3 | 3 | 6 | 0 | 8 | 4 | 4 | 2 | 106/8 | 30 |
| CUTLER RV | Blackheath 1935 | OL | Schools 1950 — Bournemouth 1956 | 5 | 0 | 0 | 0 | 0 | 0 | 0 | 0 | 0 | 0 | 5 | 0 |
| DALE RA | Willington, Co Durham 1903 | HB | Birmingham 1922 — Tranmere R 1931 | 19 | 0 | 2 | 0 | 0 | 0 | 0 | 0 | 0 | 0 | 21 | 0 |
| DARNELL L | Irchester, Northants 1905 | HB | Rushden 1924 — Reading 1930 | 57 | 0 | 5 | 0 | 0 | 0 | 0 | 0 | 0 | 0 | 62 | 0 |
| DARTON S | Ipswich 1975 | FB | YTS 1991 — | 2 | 0 | 0 | 0 | 0 | 0 | 0 | 0 | 3 | 0 | 5 | 0 |
| DAVENPORT A | Springfield, Wolverhampton 1924 | D | Springfield 1942 — Released 1946 | 0 | 0 | 0 | 0 | 0 | 0 | 0 | 0 | 1 | 0 | 1 | 0 |
| DAVIES A | Bodhovel 1880 | OR | Druids 1904 — Middlesbrough 1904 | 12 | 1 | 0 | 0 | 0 | 0 | 0 | 0 | 0 | 0 | 12 | 1 |
| DAVIES C | West Bromwich 1917 | CH | Kidderminster H 1935 — Stourbridge 1947 | 7 | 0 | 0 | 0 | 0 | 0 | 0 | 0 | 8 | 0 | 15 | 0 |
| DAVIES LC | Bodhovel 1883 | D | Wrexham 1904 — Wrexham 1905 | 3 | 0 | 0 | 0 | 0 | 0 | 0 | 0 | 0 | 0 | 3 | 0 |
| DAVIES RW | Tipton 1933 | G | Palethorpes 1949 — Walsall 1955 | 4 | 0 | 0 | 0 | 0 | 0 | 0 | 0 | 0 | 0 | 4 | 0 |
| DAVIES SC | Chirk 1898 | F | Everton 1921 — Birmingham 1927 | 147 | 77 | 12 | 6 | 0 | 0 | 0 | 0 | 0 | 0 | 159 | 83 |
| DAVIES WC | Rhayadar 1884 | OL | Crystal P 1906 — Crystal P 1910 | 52 | 4 | 3 | 0 | 0 | 0 | 0 | 0 | 0 | 0 | 55 | 4 |
| DAWES J | Smethwick 1881 | OL | Smethwick C 1903 — Smethwick C 1905 | 2 | 0 | 0 | 0 | 0 | 0 | 0 | 0 | 0 | 0 | 2 | 0 |
| DEACEY C | Wednesbury 1888 | CH/CF | Wednesbury Old Athletic 1910 — Hull C 1914 | 18 | 0 | 1 | 1 | 0 | 0 | 0 | 0 | 0 | 0 | 19 | 1 |
| DEAN A | West Bromwich 1878 | OR | Walsall 1896 — Walsall 1898 | 7 | 3 | 1 | 0 | 0 | 0 | 0 | 0 | 0 | 0 | 8 | 3 |
| DEEHAN JM | Solihull 1957 | F | Aston Villa 1979 — Norwich C 1981 | 44/3 | 5 | 2 | 0 | 0 | 0 | 1 | 0 | 0 | 0 | 47/3 | 5 |
| DENNISON R | Banbridge, Northern Ireland 1963 | F | Glenavon 1985 — Wolves 1987 | 9/7 | 1 | 2 | 0 | 1 | 0 | 0 | 0 | 1 | 0 | 13/7 | 1 |
| DIBBLE AG | Cwmbran 1965 | G | Manchester C (loan) 1992 — Manchester C 1992 | 9 | 0 | 0 | 0 | 0 | 0 | 0 | 0 | 0 | 0 | 9 | 0 |
| DICKEN HJ | Wednesbury 1890 | HB | Bilston 1909 — Bilston U 1910 | 1 | 0 | 0 | 0 | 0 | 0 | 0 | 0 | 0 | 0 | 1 | 0 |
| DICKENS AW | Plaistow 1964 | M | Chelsea (loan)1991 — Chelsea 1992 | 3 | 1 | 0 | 0 | 0 | 0 | 0 | 0 | 1 | 0 | 4 | 1 |
| DICKINSON MJ | Leeds 1963 | M | Leeds U 1986 — Sheffield U 1988 | 46/4 | 2 | 1 | 0 | 3 | 0 | 0 | 0 | 1 | 0 | 51/4 | 2 |
| DILLY T | Arbroath 1882 | OL | Everton 1906 — Derby C 1907 | 30 | 9 | 7 | 1 | 0 | 0 | 0 | 0 | 0 | 0 | 37 | 10 |
| DIXON R | Felling-on-Tyne 1936 | OL | Workington 1959 — Hereford U 1960 | 7 | 1 | 0 | 0 | 0 | 0 | 0 | 0 | 0 | 0 | 7 | 1 |
| DOBBINS W | Bromsgrove 1968 | M | Burlish Olympic 1984 —Torquay U 1991 | 30/5 | 0 | 3 | 0 | 3 | 0 | 0 | 0 | 4 | 0 | 40/15 | 0 |
| DONAGHY B | Consett 1956 | OR | School 1971 — Workington 1975 | 4/2 | 1 | 0 | 0 | 0 | 0 | 0 | 0 | 0 | 0 | 4/2 | 1 |
| DONNACHIE C | Invergowrie, Strathmore 1869 | HB | Dundee 1880 — Cambuslang R 1890 | 2 | 0 | 0 | 0 | 0 | 0 | 0 | 0 | 0 | 0 | 2 | 0 |
| DONOVAN K | Halifax 1971 | M | Huddersfield T 1992 — | 30/2 | 6 | 3/1 | 3 | 0 | 0 | 0 | 0 | 7 | 4 | 40/3 | 13 |
| DORSETT G | Brownhills 1881 | OL | Brownhills A 1901 — Manchester C 1904 | 95 | 22 | 5 | 0 | 0 | 0 | 0 | 0 | 0 | 0 | 100 | 22 |
| DORSETT JA | Brownhills 1888 | OL | Brownhills A 1907 — Manchester C 1910 | 18 | 3 | 0 | 0 | 0 | 0 | 0 | 0 | 0 | 0 | 18 | 3 |
| DRURY CE | Darlaston 1937 | WH | FH Lloyds 1954 — Bristol C 1964 | 146 | 1 | 14 | 0 | 0 | 0 | 0 | 0 | 0 | 0 | 160 | 1 |
| DRURY GB | Hucknall, Notts 1914 | IF | Arsenal 1946 — Watford 1948 | 29 | 8 | 2 | 1 | 0 | 0 | 0 | 0 | 0 | 0 | 31 | 9 |
| DUDLEY G | Gartcosh, Glasgow 1916 | F | Vono Sports 1937 — Banbury Sp 1946 | 6 | 2 | 0 | 0 | 0 | 0 | 0 | 0 | 19 | 3 | 25 | 5 |
| DUDLEY JG | Gartcosh, Glasgow 1928 | WH | Albright YC 1944 — Walsall 1959 | 285 | 9 | 34 | 2 | 0 | 0 | 0 | 0 | 1 | 0 | 320 | 11 |
| DUGDALE JR | Liverpool 1932 | CH | Harrowby 1950 — Aston Villa 1956 | 63 | 0 | 11 | 0 | 0 | 0 | 0 | 0 | 0/1 | 0 | 74/1 | 0 |
| DUGGAN J | Droitwich, Worcs 1920 | IF | Droitwich OB 1935 — Hereford U 1947 | 25 | 8 | 2 | 0 | 0 | 0 | 0 | 0 | 0 | 0 | 27 | 8 |
| DUNN A | Bridgton, Glasgow 1878 | FB | Gordon Highlanders 1898 — Bristol R 1901 | 71 | 2 | 10 | 1 | 0 | 0 | 0 | 0 | 0 | 0 | 81 | 3 |
| DURNIN J | Bootle 1965 | F | Liverpool (loan) 1988 — Liverpool 1988 | 5 | 2 | 0 | 0 | 0 | 0 | 0 | 0 | 0 | 0 | 5 | 2 |

| PLAYER | BIRTHPLACE & YEAR | POS | FROM (year) TO (year) | League App | League Gls | FA Cup App | FA Cup Gls | Lge Cup App | Lge Cup Gls | Euro App | Euro Gls | Others App | Others Gls | TOTAL App | TOTAL Gls |
|---|---|---|---|---|---|---|---|---|---|---|---|---|---|---|---|
| DUTTON HR | Edmonton, London 1900 | LH | Schools 1921 — Bury 1927 | 57 | 2 | 3 | 0 | 0 | 0 | 0 | 0 | 0 | 0 | 60 | 2 |
| DYER F | Bishopbriggs, Strathclyde 1870 | HB | Warwick Co 1890 — Woolwich A 1892 | 41 | 2 | 5 | 1 | 0 | 0 | 0 | 0 | 0 | 0 | 46 | 3 |
| DYSON PI | Birmingham 1959 | CH | Stoke C 1986 — Darlington 1989 | 64 | 5 | 1 | 0 | 3 | 0 | 0 | 0 | 1 | 0 | 69 | 5 |
| EASTER G | Epsom 1969 | M | Apprentice 1986 — Crewe Alex 1989 | 0 | 0 | 0 | 0 | 0/1 | 0 | 0 | 0 | 0 | 0 | 0/1 | 0 |
| EASTOE P | Dorden, Tamworth 1953 | F | Everton 1982 — Sporting Farense 1985 | 30/1 | 8 | 2 | 1 | 1 | 0 | 0 | 0 | 0 | 0 | 33/1 | 9 |
| EBANKS MWR | Birmingham 1964 | D | School 1981 — Port Vale 1984 | 6/1 | 0 | 0 | 0 | 0 | 0 | 0 | 0 | 0 | 0 | 6/1 | 0 |
| EDWARDS CI | Chase Terrace, Cannock 1921 | HB | Cannock T 1938 — Bristol C 1948 | 40 | 1 | 2 | 0 | 0 | 0 | 0 | 0 | 60 | 2 | 102 | 3 |
| EDWARDS EJ | Dudley Port, Tipton 1893 | CF | Old Hill U 1913 — Walsall 1920 | 7 | 3 | 1 | 1 | 0 | 0 | 0 | 0 | 2 | 2 | 10 | 6 |
| EDWARDS IR | Wrexham 1955 | CF | Rhyl A 1973 — Chester 1976 | 15/3 | 3 | 0 | 0 | 2 | 0 | 0 | 0 | 2 | 0 | 19/3 | 3 |
| EDWARDS J | Tipton 1905 | IL/LH | Stourbridge 1926 — Norwich C 1937 | 182 | 9 | 19 | 0 | 0 | 0 | 0 | 0 | 1 | 0 | 202 | 9 |
| EDWARDS S | Wolverhampton 1885 | CH | Brades Park 1904 — Stafford R 1905 | 1 | 0 | 0 | 0 | 0 | 0 | 0 | 0 | 0 | 0 | 1 | 0 |
| ELLIOTT WB | Harrington, Cumbria 1919 | OR | Bournemouth & BA 1938 — Bilston U 1951 | 170 | 39 | 12 | 1 | 0 | 0 | 0 | 0 | 148 | 117 | 330 | 157 |
| ELMORE GV | Wednesbury 1884 | IR | Broadheath FC 1902 — Bristol R 1903 | 3 | 1 | 1 | 0 | 0 | 0 | 0 | 0 | 0 | 0 | 4 | 1 |
| EHIOGO UE | London 1917 | D | YTS 1989 — Aston Villa 1991 | 0/2 | 0 | 0 | 0 | 0 | 0 | 0 | 0 | 0 | 0 | 0/2 | 0 |
| EVANS AJ | Barnard Castle, North Yorks 1874 | FB | Aston Villa 1907 — Retired 1909 | 37 | 0 | 3 | 0 | 0 | 0 | 0 | 0 | 0 | 0 | 40 | 0 |
| EVANS AJ | Penrhycadery, South Wales 1922 | IF | Wilden FC 1943 — Retired 1948 | 18 | 0 | 1 | 0 | 0 | 0 | 0 | 0 | 10 | 2 | 29 | 2 |
| EVANS CJ | West Bromwich 1923 | IF | Cordley Vics 1937 — Stafford R 1950 | 1 | 0 | 0 | 0 | 0 | 0 | 0 | 0 | 129 | 31 | 130 | 31 |
| EVANS EE | Ferndale, Glamorgan 1926 | IF | Cardiff C 1952 — Wrexham 1955 | 17 | 3 | 0 | 0 | 0 | 0 | 0 | 0 | 0 | 0 | 17 | 3 |
| EVANS G | Sutton-in-Ashfield 1865 | IF | Derby C 1889 — Brierley Hill A 1890 | 14 | 8 | 2 | 0 | 0 | 0 | 0 | 0 | 0 | 0 | 16 | 8 |
| EVANS JT | Darlaston 1906 | CH | Darlaston 1922 — Retired 1931 | 88 | 8 | 2 | 0 | 0 | 0 | 0 | 0 | 0 | 0 | 90 | 8 |
| EVANS S | Maltby, Yorks 1960 | F | Wimbledon 1986 — Plymouth A 1987 | 13/1 | 1 | 0 | 0 | 2 | 0 | 0 | 0 | 1 | 0 | 16/1 | 1 |
| EVANS TT | Wolverhampton 1872 | FB | Fairfield FC 1896 — Tottenham H 1897 | 21 | 0 | 1 | 0 | 0 | 0 | 0 | 0 | 0 | 0 | 22 | 0 |
| EVENSON I | Manchester 1882 | WH | Clapton Orient 1907 — Plymouth A 1908 | 8 | 1 | 0 | 0 | 0 | 0 | 0 | 0 | 0 | 0 | 8 | 1 |
| FAIRFAX RJ | Smethwick 1941 | FB | School 1959 — Northampton T 1968 | 79/2 | 0 | 1 | 0 | 9 | 0 | 1 | 1 | 0 | 0 | 90/2 | 1 |
| FARRINGTON SG | Burslem, Stoke-on-Trent 1884 | CF | Hanley Swifts 1902 — Bristol C 1903 | 1 | 1 | 0 | 0 | 0 | 0 | 0 | 0 | 0 | 0 | 1 | 1 |
| FELLOWS E | West Bromwich 1870 | F | Cooper's Hill Meths 1892 — Kings Heath 1897<br>Kings Heath 1899 — Studley Rovers 1899 | 12 | 0 | 0 | 0 | 0 | 0 | 0 | 0 | 2 | 0 | 14 | 0 |
| FENTON F | Gainsborough 1878 | W | Preston NE 1903 — Bristol C 1904 | 6 | 1 | 0 | 0 | 0 | 0 | 0 | 0 | 0 | 0 | 6 | 0 |
| FENTON R | South Shields 1940 | IF | Burnley 1962 — Birmingham C 1965 | 59 | 16 | 7 | 2 | 0 | 0 | 0 | 0 | 0 | 0 | 66 | 1 |
| FEREDAY W | Warley 1963 | U | Bournemouth 1991 — | 32/6 | 3 | 0/1 | 0 | 0 | 0 | 0 | 0 | 3 | 0 | 35/7 | 3 |
| FIELDING RA | Stoke 1884 | OR | Stoke 1908 — Stoke 1909 | 10 | 1 | 0 | 0 | 0 | 0 | 0 | 0 | 0 | 0 | 10 | 1 |
| FINCH EAR | Hednesford 1908 | FB | Hednesford T 1925 — Swansea T 1939 | 216 | 0 | 18 | 0 | 0 | 0 | 0 | 0 | 0 | 0 | 234 | 0 |
| FINCH R | Barry Island 1922 | OL | Swansea T 1944 — Lincoln C 1949 | 15 | 1 | 1 | 1 | 0 | 0 | 0 | 0 | 6 | 0 | 22 | 2 |
| FITTON GA | Melton Mowbray 1902 | OL | Kidderminster Harriers 1922 — Manchester U 1932 | 96 | 11 | 3 | 0 | 0 | 0 | 0 | 0 | 0 | 0 | 99 | 11 |
| FLAVELL AE | West Bromwich 1875 | G | West Bromwich Baptists 1896 — Bournbrook 1898 | 2 | 0 | 0 | 0 | 0 | 0 | 0 | 0 | 0 | 0 | 2 | 0 |
| FLETCHER F | Caversham, Berkshire 1874 | IR | Reading 1892 — Grimsby T 1895 | 2 | 0 | 0 | 0 | 0 | 0 | 0 | 0 | 0 | 0 | 2 | 0 |
| FLEWITT AW | Beeston, Notts 1872 | IF | Everton 1896 — Bedminster 1899 | 65 | 18 | 7 | 3 | 0 | 0 | 0 | 0 | 4 | 2 | 80 | 23 |
| FOGGO KT | Perth, Scotland 1943 | OR | Peebles YMCA 1959 — Norwich C 1967 | 128/1 | 29 | 5 | 0 | 2 | 0 | 0 | 0 | 0 | 0 | 135/1 | 29 |
| FOLKS WT | Tottenham, London 1886 | OR | Clapton FC 1904 — Clapton FC 1904 | 1 | 0 | 0 | 0 | 0 | 0 | 0 | 0 | 0 | 0 | 1 | 0 |
| FORD A | Grimsby 1959 | M | Stoke City 1989 — Grimsby Town 1991 | 114 | 14 | 4 | 1 | 7 | 0 | 0 | 0 | 2/1 | 0 | 127/1 | 15 |
| FORD EF | Chingford, Essex 1897 | OL | Ilford FC 1922 — Retired 1923 | 1 | 0 | 0 | 0 | 0 | 0 | 0 | 0 | 0 | 0 | 1 | 0 |
| FORD WG | Dundee 1872 | IF/WH | Dundee 1896 — Hereford T 1896 | 12 | 1 | 0 | 0 | 0 | 0 | 0 | 0 | 0 | 0 | 12 | 1 |
| FORRESTER AC | Parkstone, Bournemouth 1940 | OR | Dorset Boys 1955 — Southend U 1959 | 6 | 3 | 0 | 0 | 0 | 0 | 0 | 0 | 0 | 0 | 6 | 3 |
| FORSYTH ME | Liverpool 1966 | D | Earlswood Juniors 1982 — Derby C 1986 | 28/1 | 0 | 2 | 1 | 1 | 0 | 0 | 0 | 0 | 0 | 31/1 | 1 |
| FOSTER A | Kidderminster 1971 | F | YTS 1987 — Torquay Utd 1992 | 13/14 | 2 | 0/2 | 0 | 1/3 | 0 | 0 | 0 | 0 | 0 | 14/19 | 2 |
| FOSTER J | Darlaston 1879 | OR | Berwick R 1898 — Blackpool 1899 | 1 | 0 | 0 | 0 | 0 | 0 | 0 | 0 | 0 | 0 | 1 | 0 |
| FOULKES HE | Llandudno 1908 | FB | Llandudno T 1930 — Guildford 1937 | 15 | 0 | 0 | 0 | 0 | 0 | 0 | 0 | 0 | 0 | 15 | 0 |
| FRASER DM | Busby, Scotland 1941 | FB/WH | Aberdeen 1963 — Nottingham F 1971 | 255/2 | 8 | 24 | 0 | 29 | 4 | 10 | 0 | 5 | 0 | 323/2 | 12 |
| FREEMAN RP | Newark 1945 | CF | Stourbridge 1968 — Lincoln C 1970 | 2 | 0 | 0 | 0 | 0 | 0 | 0 | 0 | 0 | 0 | 2 | 0 |
| FRYER ER | South Yardley 1904 | WH | Harborne L 1923 — Shrewsbury T 1930 | 21 | 0 | 0 | 0 | 0 | 0 | 0 | 0 | 0 | 0 | 21 | 0 |
| FUDGE MH | Bristol 1945 | IF | Bristol Boys 1961 — Exeter C 1967 | 13 | 5 | 3 | 0 | 0 | 0 | 0 | 0 | 0 | 0 | 16 | 5 |
| GALE AR | Salford 1904 | OR/CF | Chester 1931 — Chester 1936 | 23 | 8 | 6 | 4 | 0 | 0 | 0 | 0 | 0 | 0 | 29 | 12 |
| GALLAGHER M | Cambuslang, Nr Glasgow 1932 | OL | Bolton W 1952 — Selkirk 1953 | 1 | 0 | 0 | 0 | 0 | 0 | 0 | 0 | 0 | 0 | 1 | 0 |
| GARFIELD BW | Burton upon Trent 1872 | OL | Burton W 1896 — Brighton & HA 1902 | 109 | 34 | 8 | 4 | 0 | 0 | 0 | 0 | 0 | 0 | 117 | 38 |
| GARNER S | Boston 1959 | F | Blackburn Rovers 1992 — | 21/4 | 8 | 3 | 0 | 2 | 0 | 0 | 0 | 0/1 | 0 | 26/5 | 8 |
| GARRATT GT | Byker, Newcastle upon Tyne 1884 | OR | Plymouth A 1907 — Crystal P 1908 | 29 | 3 | 1 | 0 | 0 | 0 | 0 | 0 | 0 | 0 | 30 | 3 |
| GARRATY W | Saltley, Birmingham 1878 | F | Leicester Fosse 1908 — Lincoln C 1910 | 53 | 20 | 6 | 2 | 0 | 0 | 0 | 0 | 0 | 0 | 59 | 22 |
| GEDDES AJ | West Bromwich 1871 | OL | Causeway GV 1891 — Clapham 1894<br>Millwall 1895 — Millwall 1895 | 73 | 25 | 9 | 6 | 0 | 0 | 0 | 0 | 11 | 7 | 93 | 38 |
| GILES JM | Cabra, Dublin 1940 | M | Leeds U 1975 — Shamrock R 1977 | 74/1 | 3 | 4 | 0 | 4 | 1 | 0 | 0 | 5 | 1 | 87/1 | 5 |
| GLIDDEN TW | Coxlodge 1902 | OR | Sunderland WE 1922 — Retired 1936 | 445 | 135 | 33 | 5 | 0 | 0 | 0 | 0 | 1 | 0 | 479 | 140 |
| GLOVER AR | Staines, Middlesex 1950 | M | Queen's Park R 1969 — Orient 1977 | 84/8 | 9 | 4 | 0 | 4/2 | 0 | 0 | 0 | 0/3 | 1 | 92/13 | 10 |
| GODDEN AL | Gillingham 1955 | G | Ashford T 1975 — Chelsea 1986 | 267 | 0 | 19 | 0 | 27 | 0 | 12 | 0 | 4 | 0 | 329 | 0 |
| GOLLINGS P | Winson Green, Birmingham 1878 | HB | Hereford Th 1899 — Brierley Hill A 1904 | 5 | 0 | 0 | 0 | 0 | 0 | 0 | 0 | 0 | 0 | 5 | 0 |
| GOMM BA | Castle Cary, Somerset 1918 | CF | Dudley TC 1935 — Released 1946 | 0 | 0 | 0 | 0 | 0 | 0 | 0 | 0 | 4 | 1 | 4 | 1 |
| GOODALL D | Birmingham 1970 | M | YTS 1986 — Walsall 1989 | 0 | 0 | 0 | 0 | 0 | 0 | 0 | 0 | 0/1 | 0 | 0/1 | 0 |
| GOODMAN D | Leeds, May 1966 | F | Bradford C 1987 — Sunderland 1991 | 140/18 | 60 | 7 | 1 | 11 | 1 | 0 | 0 | 5 | 1 | 163/18 | 63 |
| GORDON DW | Wolverhampton 1924 | W | Oxford City 1947 — Brighton & HA 1952 | 27 | 10 | 3 | 0 | 0 | 0 | 0 | 0 | 0 | 0 | 30 | 10 |
| GOULD RA | Coventry 1946 | CF | Wolves 1971 — Bristol C 1972 | 52 | 18 | 1 | 0 | 4 | 0 | 0 | 0 | 3 | 1 | 60 | 19 |
| GRAY AM | Glasgow 1955 | F | Notts County 1987 — G Rangers 1988 | 32/3 | 10 | 0 | 0 | 2 | 1 | 0 | 0 | 0 | 0 | 34/3 | 11 |
| GREALISH AP | Paddington, London 1956 | M | Brighton & HA 1984 — Manchester C 1986 | 55/10 | 5 | 1 | 0 | 7/1 | 0 | 0 | 0 | 0 | 0 | 63/11 | 5 |
| GREEN H | West Bromwich 1860 | FB | George Salter Works 1881 — Old Hill W 1891 | 33 | 0 | 32 | 0 | 0 | 0 | 0 | 0 | 0 | 0 | 65 | 0 |
| GREEN T | Worcester 1863 | IF | Mitchell St George — 1885 — Aston Villa 1887 | 0 | 0 | 16 | 8 | 0 | 0 | 0 | 0 | 0 | 0 | 16 | 8 |
| GREEN T | Droitwich 1913 | IF | Droitwich Com 1931 — West Ham U 1936 | 13 | 3 | 0 | 0 | 0 | 0 | 0 | 0 | 3 | 2 | 16 | 5 |
| GREEN T | Kings Heath, Birmingham 1873 | IF | Coles Farm U 1894 — Small Heath 1895 | 8 | 2 | 0 | 0 | 0 | 0 | 0 | 0 | 0 | 0 | 8 | 2 |
| GREGORY H | Aston Manor, Birmingham 1894 | OL | Birchfield T 1911 — Retired 1926 | 162 | 39 | 13 | 3 | 0 | 0 | 0 | 0 | 6 | 3 | 181 | 45 |
| GREW MS | Bilston 1958 | G | School 1975 — Leicester C 1983 | 34 | 0 | 5 | 0 | 8 | 0 | 0/1 | 0 | 0 | 0 | 47/1 | 0 |
| GRIFFIN FA | Pendlebury 1928 | OR | Shrewsbury T 1951 — Northampton T 1959 | 240 | 47 | 34 | 5 | 0 | 0 | 0 | 0 | 1 | 0 | 275 | 52 |
| GRIMLEY TW | Dinnington 1920 | G | Swallownest 1939 — New Brighton 1948 | 30 | 0 | 0 | 0 | 0 | 0 | 0 | 0 | 0 | 0 | 30 | 0 |
| GRIPTON WE | Princes End, Tipton 1920 | CH | Brownhills A 1935 — Luton T 1948 | 16 | 0 | 0 | 0 | 0 | 0 | 0 | 0 | 192 | 3 | 208 | 3 |
| GROVES W | Leith 1869 | WH/CF | Glasgow Celtic 1890 — Aston Villa 1893 | 58 | 7 | 9 | 3 | 0 | 0 | 0 | 0 | 2 | 0 | 69 | 10 |
| GUY H | Wolverhampton 1932 | CH | Springfield OB 1948 — Peterborough U 1956 | 1 | 0 | 0 | 0 | 0 | 0 | 0 | 0 | 0 | 0 | 1 | 0 |
| HACKETT G | Stourbridge 1962 | W | Stoke City 1990 — | 26/18 | 3 | 0/1 | 0 | 0/2 | 1 | 0 | 0 | 4 | 0 | 30/21 | 4 |
| HADLEY B | West Bromwich 1871 | WH | Hereford Th 1892 — Hereford T 1896 | 7 | 1 | 0 | 0 | 0 | 0 | 0 | 0 | 1 | 0 | 8 | 0 |
| HADLEY H | Barrow-in-Furness 1878 | HB | Halesowen 1897 — Aston Villa 1905 | 167 | 2 | 14 | 0 | 0 | 0 | 0 | 0 | 0 | 0 | 181 | 2 |
| HAINES JTW | Wickhamford 1920 | IF | Leicester C 1948 — Bradford 1949 | 59 | 23 | 3 | 0 | 0 | 0 | 0 | 0 | 0 | 0 | 62 | 2 |
| HAMILTON IR | Stevenage 1967 | M | Scunthorpe Utd 1992 — | 46 | 7 | 4 | 1 | 2 | 0 | 0 | 0 | 5/2 | 2 | 57/2 | 10 |
| HANCOCK H | Levenshulme, Manchester 1878 | IF | Manchester C 1909 — Brierley Hill A 1910 | 2 | 0 | 0 | 0 | 0 | 0 | 0 | 0 | 0 | 0 | 2 | 0 |
| HARBEY GK | Chesterfield 1964 | FB | Ipswich Town 1989 — Stoke City 1992 | 97 | 2 | 6 | 0 | 5 | 0 | 0 | 0 | 5 | 0 | 113 | 2 |
| HARPER WE | Nechells, Birmingham 1876 | OL | Smethwick WR 1899 — Leicester Fosse 1903 | 8 | 1 | 0 | 0 | 0 | 0 | 0 | 0 | 0 | 0 | 8 | 0 |
| HARRIS GA | Halesowen 1878 | LH | Aston Villa 1909 — Coventry C 1910 | 18 | 0 | 2 | 1 | 0 | 0 | 0 | 0 | 0 | 0 | 20 | 1 |
| HARRIS W | Oakham, Dudley 1918 | G | Whiteheath 1936 — Oldham A 1946 | 2 | 0 | 0 | 0 | 0 | 0 | 0 | 0 | 15 | 0 | 17 | 0 |
| HARTFORD RA | Clydebank 1950 | IF | Drumchapel A 1966 — Manchester C 1974 | 206/9 | 18 | 19 | 2 | 15 | 2 | 6 | 3 | 20 | 1 | 266/9 | 26 |
| HATTON S | West Bromwich 1892 | U | West Bromwich Baptists 1912 — Shrewsbury T 1922 | 6 | 0 | 0 | 0 | 0 | 0 | 0 | 0 | 0 | 0 | 6 | 0 |
| HAWKER PN | Solihull 1962 | D | Walsaall (loan) 1990 — Kidderminster H 1990 | 1 | 0 | 0 | 0 | 0 | 0 | 0 | 0 | 0 | 0 | 1 | 0 |
| HAYCOCK FJ | Smethwick 1886 | IF | Coombs Wood 1904 — Crewe A 1907 | 15 | 8 | 0 | 0 | 0 | 0 | 0 | 0 | 0 | 0 | 15 | 8 |
| HAYNES GA | West Bromwich 1865 | IF | WB Sandwell 1887 — Coles Farm U 1892 | 10 | 1 | 0 | 0 | 0 | 0 | 0 | 0 | 0 | 0 | 10 | 1 |
| HAYWARD A | Oldham 1886 | OL | Blackburn R 1896 — Chorley 1897 | 3 | 0 | 0 | 0 | 0 | 0 | 0 | 0 | 0 | 0 | 3 | 0 |
| HAYWARD AB | Horninglow, Burton upon Trent 1875 | IF | Wolves 1905 — Blackpool 1907 | 62 | 25 | 5 | 2 | 0 | 0 | 0 | 0 | 0 | 0 | 67 | 27 |
| HAYWARD S | Bloxwich 1968 | D | School 1985 — Released, May 1987 | 0 | 0 | 0 | 0 | 0 | 0 | 0 | 0 | 1 | 0 | 1 | 0 |
| HAYWOOD T | Walsall 1880 | HB | Aston Villa 1905 — Crewe A 1908 | 15 | 0 | 0 | 0 | 0 | 0 | 0 | 0 | 0 | 0 | 15 | 0 |
| HEASELGRAVE SE | Smethwick 1916 | IF | Brierley Hill A 1934 — Northampton T 1945 | 49 | 16 | 3 | 0 | 0 | 0 | 0 | 0 | 111 | 41 | 163 | 57 |
| HEATH NH | Wolverhampton 1924 | G | H Meadows FC 1942 — Retired 1955 | 121 | 0 | 13 | 0 | 0 | 0 | 0 | 0 | 35 | 0 | 169 | 0 |
| HEGAN D | Coatbridge 1943 | IF | Ipswich T 1969 — Wolves 1970 | 13 | 2 | 0 | 0 | 4 | 0 | 0 | 0 | 0 | 0 | 17 | 2 |
| HEGGS C | Leicester 1970 | F | Leicester Utd 1991 — | 3/17 | 2 | 0/1 | 0 | 0 | 0 | 0 | 0 | 1/3 | 1 | 4/21 | 3 |
| HENDRY WH | Dundee 1864 | CF | Dundee W 1888 — Stoke 1889 | 18 | 4 | 0 | 0 | 0 | 0 | 0 | 0 | 0 | 0 | 18 | 4 |
| HEWITT C | Greatham, Cleveland 1884 | IF | Liverpool 1908 — Spennymoor U 1910 | 60 | 26 | 4 | 2 | 0 | 0 | 0 | 0 | 0 | 0 | 64 | 28 |

| PLAYER | BIRTHPLACE & YEAR | POS | FROM (year) — TO (year) | League App | League Gls | FA Cup App | FA Cup Gls | Lge Cup App | Lge Cup Gls | Euro App | Euro Gls | Others App | Others Gls | TOTAL App | TOTAL Gls |
|---|---|---|---|---|---|---|---|---|---|---|---|---|---|---|---|
| HIBBERT JW | Hebburn-on-Tyne 1890 | IF/WH | Pelaw 1910 — Hartlepool U 1912 | 3 | 0 | 0 | 0 | 0 | 0 | 0 | 0 | 0 | 0 | 3 | 0 |
| HIGGINS T | Halesowen 1874 | HB | Stourbridge 1894 — Retired 1898 | 78 | 4 | 12 | 0 | 0 | 0 | 0 | 0 | 4 | 1 | 94 | 5 |
| HOBSON AF | Tipton 1878 | U | Wednesbury T 1899 — Brentford 1904 | 13 | 4 | 2 | 0 | 0 | 0 | 0 | 0 | 0 | 0 | 15 | 4 |
| HODGETTS F | Oakham, Dudley 1924 | W | Accles & Pollock 1939 — Millwall 1949 | 67 | 11 | 3 | 0 | 0 | 0 | 0 | 0 | 108 | 23 | 178 | 34 |
| HODKISSON WK | West Bromwich 1933 | IF | Greets Green P 1949 — Walsall 1955 | 21 | 4 | 0 | 0 | 0 | 0 | 0 | 0 | 0 | 0 | 21 | 4 |
| HODSON S | Lincoln 1966 | FB | Newport Co 1988 — Mansfield T 1992 | 78/5 | 0 | 1 | 0 | 7 | 0 | 0 | 0 | 3 | 0 | 89/5 | 0 |
| HOGG D | Stockton-on-Tees 1930 | OL | Leicester C 1958 — Cardiff C 1960 | 81 | 11 | 6 | 1 | 0 | 0 | 0 | 0 | 0 | 0 | 87 | 12 |
| HOGG GJ | Aberdeen 1964 | D | Manchester Utd 1987 — Manchester Utd 1987 | 7 | 0 | 0 | 0 | 0 | 0 | 0 | 0 | 1 | 0 | 8 | 0 |
| HOLDEN GH | West Bromwich 1858 | OR | Wednesbury Old Athletic 1886 — Wednesbury Old Ath 1887 | 0 | 0 | 4 | 1 | 0 | 0 | 0 | 0 | 0 | 0 | 4 | 1 |
| HOOD GO | Pen-twyn, Monmouth 1925 | WH | Nuffield FC 1943 — Retired 1951 | 69 | 0 | 4 | 0 | 0 | 0 | 0 | 0 | 1 | 0 | 74 | 0 |
| HOPE R | Bridge of Allan, Perthshire 1943 | IF | Drumchapel A 1959 — Birmingham C 1972 | 331/5 | 33 | 19 | 0 | 29 | 7 | 9 | 1 | 10 | 1 | 398/5 | 42 |
| HOPKINS R | Hall Green, Birmingham 1961 | F | Manchester C 1986 — | 25 | 4 | 1 | 0 | 0 | 0 | 0 | 0 | 0 | 0 | 26 | 4 |
| HORNE LH | Netherton, Dudley 1925 | CH | Netherton W 1944 — Plymouth A 1952 | 13 | 0 | 3 | 0 | 0 | 0 | 0 | 0 | 0 | 0 | 16 | 0 |
| HOROBIN R | Brownhills 1935 | OL | Walsall Wood 1950 — Notts C 1958 | 54 | 6 | 13 | 2 | 0 | 0 | 0 | 0 | 0 | 0 | 67 | 8 |
| HORTON E | West Bromwich 1861 | RH | West Bromwich FC 1882 — Retired 1891 | 47 | 0 | 36 | 1 | 0 | 0 | 0 | 0 | 0 | 0 | 83 | 1 |
| HORTON JH | West Bromwich 1866 | FB | Wednesbury Old Athletic 1882 — Retired 1899 | 129 | 0 | 13 | 0 | 0 | 0 | 0 | 0 | 10 | 0 | 152 | 0 |
| HOWARTH N | I' o' the Heights, Shropshire 1905 | WH | Bolton W 1926 — Retired 1929 | 61 | 1 | 2 | 1 | 0 | 0 | 0 | 0 | 0 | 0 | 63 | 2 |
| HOWE D | Wolverhampton 1935 | RB | Wolverhampton Boys 1950 — Arsenal 1964 | 342 | 17 | 37 | 2 | 0 | 0 | 0 | 0 | 0 | 0 | 379 | 19 |
| HOWSHALL GT | Stoke-on-Trent 1944 | WH | Plymouth A 1960 — Norwich C 1967 | 43 | 3 | 0 | 0 | 0 | 0 | 0 | 0 | 0 | 0 | 43 | 3 |
| HOYLAND E | Thurnscoe, South Yorkshire 1914 | OR | Blackpool 1938 — Lincoln C 1939 | 1 | 0 | 0 | 0 | 0 | 0 | 0 | 0 | 0 | 0 | 1 | 0 |
| HUCKER PI | Hampstead 1959 | G | Oxford Utd (loan) 1988 — Oxford Utd 1988 | 7 | 0 | 0 | 0 | 0 | 0 | 0 | 0 | 0 | 0 | 7 | 0 |
| HUGHES BW | Port Talbot 1958 | M | Brinton Ferry FC 1974 — Cardiff C 1979 | 3/3 | 2 | 0/1 | 0 | 0 | 0 | 0 | 0 | 0/1 | 0 | 3/5 | 2 |
| HUGHES LJ | Smethwick 1950 | WH | Smethwick Boys 1964 — Peterborough U 1975 | 91/9 | 3 | 5 | 0 | 7 | 0 | 0 | 0 | 15 | 1 | 118/9 | 4 |
| HUMPAGE WLF | Birmingham 1870 | G | Wednesbury Old Athletic 1893 — Hereford T 1896 | 4 | 0 | 0 | 0 | 0 | 0 | 0 | 0 | 0 | 0 | 4 | 0 |
| HUNT A | Thurrock 1970 | F | Newcastle Utd (loan) 1993 (signed 1993) | 9/1 | 9 | 0 | 0 | 0 | 0 | 0 | 0 | 3 | 2 | 12/1 | 11 |
| HUNT S | Witton, Birmingham 1956 | M | Coventry C 1984 — Aston Villa 1986 | 68 | 15 | 2 | 1 | 11 | 3 | 0 | 0 | 3 | 1 | 84 | 20 |
| HUNTER R | Saltburn 1973 | U | YTS 1989 — | 3/4 | 1 | 0 | 0 | 0 | 0 | 0 | 0 | 2 | 0 | 5/4 | 1 |
| HURST GC | Ashton-under-Lyne 1941 | IF | Stoke C 1975 — Seattle Sounders 1976 | 10 | 2 | 0 | 0 | 2 | 0 | 0 | 0 | 0 | 0 | 12 | 2 |
| HUTCHINSON T | Glasgow 1872 | CF | Nelson 1894 — Stockport C 1897 | 45 | 19 | 10 | 2 | 0 | 0 | 0 | 0 | 3 | 0 | 58 | 21 |
| INWOOD GF | Kislingbury, Northants 1928 | OL | Rushden T 1946 — Hull C 1950 | 10 | 0 | 2 | 1 | 0 | 0 | 0 | 0 | 0 | 0 | 12 | 1 |
| JACK WR | Grangemouth 1875 | CF | Bristol R — Clyde 1905 | 25 | 13 | 1 | 0 | 0 | 0 | 0 | 0 | 0 | 0 | 26 | 13 |
| JACKMAN CEJ | Aldershot 1936 | G | Aldershot 1957 — Retired 1960 | 21 | 0 | 0 | 0 | 0 | 0 | 0 | 0 | 0 | 0 | 21 | 0 |
| JACKSON A | Tipton 1937 | UF | WG Allen's FC 1954 — Birmingham C 1964 | 192 | 50 | 16 | 2 | 0 | 0 | 0 | 0 | 0 | 0 | 208 | 52 |
| JACKSON WH | Oldbury 1894 | CF | Langley SM 1912 — 1917 Killed during World War One | 3 | 0 | 0 | 0 | 0 | 0 | 0 | 0 | 0 | 0 | 3 | 0 |
| JAMES GC | Oldbury 1899 | CF | Bilston U 1920 — Reading 1929 | 106 | 52 | 10 | 5 | 0 | 0 | 0 | 0 | 0 | 0 | 116 | 57 |
| JAMES RW | Smethwick 1897 | LH | Smethwick H 1919 — Brentford 1922 | 9 | 4 | 0 | 0 | 0 | 0 | 0 | 0 | 0 | 0 | 9 | 4 |
| JEPHCOTT AC | Smethwick 1891 | OR | Brierley Hill A 1911 — Retired 1923 | 174 | 15 | 15 | 1 | 0 | 0 | 0 | 0 | 1 | 0 | 190 | 16 |
| JOHNSON G | West Bromwich 1871 | UF | Wrockwardine W 1895 — Walsall 1896 | 1 | 0 | 1 | 0 | 0 | 0 | 0 | 0 | 1 | 1 | 3 | 1 |
| JOHNSON JA | Grimsby 1911 | OL | Stoke C 1937 — Norwich Victoria 1946 | 55 | 22 | 5 | 0 | 0 | 0 | 0 | 0 | 85 | 25 | 145 | 47 |
| JOHNSON LG | Vancouver, Canada 1951 | CF | Vancouver Sp 1969 — Vancouver R 1972 | 2 | 0 | 0 | 0 | 0 | 0 | 0 | 0 | 0 | 0 | 2 | 0 |
| JOHNSTON WM | Glasgow 1946 | OL | Glasgow Rangers 1972 — Vancouver Whitecaps 1979 | 203/4 | 18 | 24/2 | 6 | 15 | 2 | 0 | 0 | 12/1 | 2 | 254/7 | 28 |
| JOHNSTONE WR | Kirriemuir, Angus 1877 | CF | Dundee Harp 1889 — Alloa 1890 | 3 | 0 | 0 | 0 | 0 | 0 | 0 | 0 | 0 | 0 | 3 | 0 |
| JOL MC | The Hague, Holland 1956 | M | FC Twente Enschede 1981 — Coventry C 1983 | 53/1 | 4 | 5 | 0 | 10 | 0 | 0 | 0 | 0 | 0 | 68/1 | 4 |
| JONES A | Tipton 1875 | CH | Cameron Highlanders 1896 — Middlesbrough 1901 | 104 | 6 | 13 | 4 | 0 | 0 | 0 | 0 | 0 | 0 | 117 | 10 |
| JONES CL | Penn, Wolverhampton 1925 | IF | Penn FC 1941 — Released 1947 | 0 | 0 | 0 | 0 | 0 | 0 | 0 | 0 | 1 | 0 | 1 | 0 |
| JONES EN | Stirchley, Birmingham 1915 | OR | Portsmouth 1939 — Brentford 1945 | 3 | 4 | 0 | 0 | 0 | 0 | 0 | 0 | 19 | 3 | 22 | 7 |
| JONES GA | Nuneaton 1932 | OR | Erdington A 1947 — Wrexham 1955 | 2 | 0 | 1 | 0 | 0 | 0 | 0 | 0 | 0 | 0 | 3 | 0 |
| JONES H | West Bromwich 1881 | G | Brierley Hill A 1902 — Brierley Hill A 1904 / Brierley Hill A 1905 — Shrewsbury T 1907 | 2 | 0 | 0 | 0 | 0 | 0 | 0 | 0 | 0 | 0 | 2 | 0 |
| JONES HJ | Haydock 1911 | UF | Preston North End 1933 — Retired 1943 | 120 | 54 | 9 | 3 | 0 | 0 | 0 | 0 | 40 | 47 | 169 | 104 |
| JONES I | Merthyr 1899 | IF | Swansea T 1922 — Swansea T 1926 | 63 | 9 | 4 | 1 | 0 | 0 | 0 | 0 | 0 | 0 | 67 | 10 |
| JONES SG | Highley, Shropshire 1938 | CH | Walsall 1960 — Walsall 1968 | 239 | 2 | 14 | 1 | 12 | 0 | 2 | 0 | 0 | 0 | 267 | 3 |
| JORDAN WC | Langley, West Midlands 1885 | CF | Langley SM 1904 — Everton 1909 | 31 | 14 | 4 | 4 | 0 | 0 | 0 | 0 | 0 | 0 | 35 | 18 |
| KAYE J | Goole 1940 | LH/IF | Scunthorpe U 1963 — Hull C 1971 | 281/3 | 45 | 25 | 2 | 31 | 6 | 10 | 1 | 11 | 0 | 358/3 | 54 |
| KELSEY AG | Wallingford, Berkshire 1871 | LH/IF | Worcs Regt Aldershot 1895 — Brierley Hill A 1896 | 11 | 0 | 0 | 0 | 0 | 0 | 0 | 0 | 0 | 0 | 11 | 0 |
| KELLY AG | Prescot 1964 | M | Stoke City 1987 — Shrewsbury T 1989 | 26 | 1 | 1 | 0 | 2 | 0 | 0 | 0 | 1 | 0 | 30 | 1 |
| KENNEDY JP | Cleator Moor, Cumberland 1925 | CH | Altrincham 1948 — Chester 1961 | 364 | 3 | 32 | 1 | 0 | 0 | 0 | 0 | 1 | 0 | 397 | 4 |
| KENT K | Stoke-on-Trent 1965 | F | School 1981 — Newport C 1984 | 1/1 | 0 | 0 | 0 | 0 | 0 | 0 | 0 | 0 | 0 | 1/1 | 0 |
| KEVAN DT | Ripon 1935 | F | Bradford 1953 — Chelsea 1963 | 262 | 157 | 29 | 16 | 0 | 0 | 0 | 0 | 0 | 0 | 291 | 173 |
| KIFFORD J | Paisley, Nr Glasgow 1878 | FB | Portsmouth 1901 — Millwall 1905 | 96 | 8 | 3 | 0 | 0 | 0 | 0 | 0 | 0 | 0 | 99 | 8 |
| KING AE | Luton 1956 | M/IF | Queen's Park R 1981 — Everton 1982 | 21/4 | 4 | 4 | 1 | 8/1 | 1 | 0 | 0 | 0 | 0 | 33/5 | 6 |
| KINSELL TH | Cannock 1921 | FB | School 1935 — Bolton W 1949 | 83 | 0 | 8 | 0 | 0 | 0 | 0 | 0 | 67 | 0 | 158 | 0 |
| KNOWLES JW | Wednesbury 1879 | IF | School 1897 — Dudley T 1898 / Dudley T 1900 — Dudley T 1901 | 3 | 0 | 0 | 0 | 0 | 0 | 0 | 0 | 0 | 0 | 3 | 0 |
| KRZYWICKI RL | Penley, Flint 1947 | OR | Leek YC 1962 — Huddersfield T 1970 | 51 | 9 | 4/1 | 0 | 4/3 | 2 | 0 | 0 | 1 | 1 | 60/4 | 12 |
| LATCHFORD PW | Sheldon, Birmingham 1952 | G | Sutton T 1969 — Glasgow Celtic 1975 | 81 | 0 | 9 | 0 | 8 | 0 | 0 | 0 | 6 | 0 | 104 | 0 |
| LANGE AS | West Ham 1964 | G | Wolverhampton W 1992 — | 14 | 0 | 0 | 0 | 0 | 0 | 0 | 0 | 6 | 0 | 20 | 0 |
| LAW A | Wealdstone 1874 | G | Millwall A 1896 — Stafford R 1897 | 1 | 0 | 0 | 0 | 0 | 0 | 0 | 0 | 0 | 0 | 1 | 0 |
| LAW WD | Pleck, Walsall 1882 | OL | Doncaster R 1905 — Watford 1906 | 10 | 0 | 1 | 0 | 0 | 0 | 0 | 0 | 0 | 0 | 11 | 0 |
| LEE GT | York 1920 | OL | Nottingham F 1949 — Lockheed Leamington 1958 | 271 | 59 | 23 | 6 | 0 | 0 | 0 | 0 | 1 | 0 | 295 | 65 |
| LEE JM | Mold, Flint 1938 | OL | Saltney Juniors 1956 — Crewe A 1958 | 1 | 0 | 0 | 0 | 0 | 0 | 0 | 0 | 0 | 0 | 1 | 0 |
| LEE W | West Bromwich 1878 | CF | Bournville A 1901 — Portsmouth 1904 | 71 | 25 | 5 | 0 | 0 | 0 | 0 | 0 | 0 | 0 | 76 | 25 |
| LEEDHAM F | Lye 1909 | OR | Kidderminster H 1926 — Kidderminster H 1929 | 4 | 0 | 0 | 0 | 0 | 0 | 0 | 0 | 0 | 0 | 4 | 0 |
| LEGGE SG | Willenhall 1881 | OL | Willenhall SW 1906 — Worcester C 1907 / Worcester C 1908 — Coventry C 1910 | 9 | 3 | 0 | 0 | 0 | 0 | 0 | 0 | 0 | 0 | 9 | 3 |
| LEWIS AE | Wolverhampton 1884 | IL | Stafford R 1904 — Northampton T 1906 / Northampton T 1913 — South Shields 1914 | 47 | 9 | 1 | 0 | 0 | 0 | 0 | 0 | 0 | 0 | 48 | 9 |
| LEWIS M | Birmingham 1965 | M | School 1981 — Derby C 1984 | 22/2 | 0 | 4 | 0 | 4/1 | 0 | 0 | 0 | 0 | 0 | 30/3 | 0 |
| LIGHT WH | Woolston, Hampshire 1913 | G | Southampton 1936 — Colchester U 1938 | 28 | 0 | 2 | 0 | 0 | 0 | 0 | 0 | 0 | 0 | 30 | 0 |
| LILWALL S | Solihull 1970 | LB | Kidderminster H 1992 — | 44 | 0 | 4 | 0 | 2 | 0 | 0 | 0 | 4 | 0 | 54 | 0 |
| LLOYD JA | Pelsall 1889 | OL | Hednesford T 1910 — Swansea T 1914 | 45 | 8 | 1 | 0 | 0 | 0 | 0 | 0 | 0 | 0 | 46 | 9 |
| LOACH AA | West Bromwich 1863 | IF | George Salter Works 1882 — Aston Villa 1888 | 0 | 0 | 14 | 9 | 0 | 0 | 0 | 0 | 0 | 0 | 14 | 9 |
| LONG WR | Tividale, West Midlands 1899 | OL | Hednesford T 1919 — Hednesford T 1920 | 2 | 0 | 0 | 0 | 0 | 0 | 0 | 0 | 0 | 0 | 2 | 0 |
| LOVATT J | Burton upon Trent 1941 | CF | Erdington A 1956 — Nuneaton B 1963 | 18 | 5 | 0 | 0 | 0 | 0 | 0 | 0 | 0 | 0 | 18 | 5 |
| LOVETT GJ | Sheldon, Birmingham 1947 | M | Sheldon Schools 1964 — Worcester C 1972 | 106/8 | 8 | 12/2 | 0 | 13/1 | 0 | 4/2 | 1 | 6/3 | 0 | 141/15 | 9 |
| LOWE JA | West Bromwich 1876 | G | Coombs Wood 1899 — Willenhall P 1903 | 4 | 0 | 0 | 0 | 0 | 0 | 0 | 0 | 0 | 0 | 4 | 0 |
| LOWERY A | Wallsend-on-Tyne 1961 | M | Ashington 1981 — Mansfield T 1983 | 1 | 0 | 0 | 0 | 0 | 0 | 0 | 0 | 0 | 0 | 1 | 0 |
| LOWERY H | Moor Row, Cumberland 1918 | WH | Moor Celtic 1934 — Northampton T 1945 | 17 | 0 | 0 | 0 | 0 | 0 | 0 | 0 | 27 | 0 | 44 | 0 |
| LUKE NE | Birmingham 1964 | M | School 1980 — Mansfield T 1984 | 8/1 | 1 | 2/2 | 0 | 1 | 0 | 0 | 0 | 0 | 0 | 11/3 | 1 |
| LUNN WJ | Lurgan, Northern Ireland 1923 | IF | Glenavon 1946 — Bournemouth & BA 1948 | 10 | 5 | 0 | 0 | 0 | 0 | 0 | 0 | 0 | 0 | 10 | 5 |
| LYNEX SC | West Bromwich, Jan 1958 | W | Sandwell R 1974 — Shamrock R 1977 / Leicester C 1987 — Cardiff C 1988 | 26/3 | 3 | 0 | 0 | 0/2 | 0 | 0 | 0 | 2 | 2 | 28/5 | 5 |
| McCALL A | Hamilton 1925 | IF | Blackpool 1951 — Leeds U 1952 | 31 | 3 | 1 | 0 | 0 | 0 | 0 | 0 | 0 | 0 | 32 | 3 |
| McCUE J | Glasgow 1970 | F | YTS 1991 — | 0 | 0 | 0 | 0 | 0 | 0 | 0 | 0 | 0/1 | 0 | 0/1 | 0 |
| McCULLOCH T | Strathblane, Stirlingshire 1868 | FB | Glasgow U 1891 — Stirling 1893 | 46 | 0 | 9 | 0 | 0 | 0 | 0 | 0 | 2 | 0 | 57 | 0 |
| McCULLUM WD | Paisley 1870 | FB | Glasgow Celtic 1891 — Dumbarton 1891 | 3 | 0 | 0 | 0 | 0 | 0 | 0 | 0 | 0 | 0 | 3 | 0 |
| McKENNAN PS | Airdrie 1918 | IF | Partick T 1947 — Leicester C 1948 | 11 | 4 | 1 | 0 | 0 | 0 | 0 | 0 | 15 | 13 | 27 | 17 |
| McKENZIE AD | Greenock 1875 | IF | Millwall A 1897 — Dumbarton 1899 | 51 | 9 | 4 | 0 | 0 | 0 | 0 | 0 | 0 | 0 | 55 | 9 |
| MACKENZIE S | Romford 1961 | M | Manchester C 1981 — Charlton Ath 1987 | 153/3 | 23 | 8 | 1 | 16/2 | 1 | 2 | 0 | 0 | 0 | 179/5 | 25 |
| MacLEAN H | Stornoway 1952 | OL | School 1967 — Swindon T 1974 | 4 | 0 | 0 | 0 | 1 | 0 | 0 | 0 | 1/2 | 0 | 6/2 | 0 |
| McLEAN J | Stoke-on-Trent 1877 | OR | Walsall 1901 — Preston North End 1903 | 57 | 10 | 3 | 0 | 0 | 0 | 0 | 0 | 0 | 0 | 60 | 10 |
| McLEOD R | Kilsyth, Dumbarton 1872 | IF | Partick T 1891 — Leicester Fosse 1897 | 149 | 50 | 20 | 7 | 0 | 0 | 0 | 0 | 16 | 8 | 185 | 65 |
| McMANUS P | Winchburgh, West Lothian 1873 | WH | Hibernian 1896 — Warmley 1898 | 28 | 1 | 0 | 0 | 0 | 0 | 0 | 0 | 0 | 0 | 28 | 1 |
| McNAB A | Glasgow 1911 | WH | Sunderland 1938 — Newport C 1946 | 52 | 2 | 3 | 0 | 0 | 0 | 0 | 0 | 131 | 2 | 186 | 4 |
| McNALLY B | Shrewsbury 1963 | M | Shrewsbury T 1989 | 117/10 | 10 | 10 | 2 | 6/1 | 1 | 0 | 0 | 8 | 0 | 141/11 | 13 |
| McNAUGHT K | Kirkcaldy, Fife 1955 | CH | Aston Villa 1983 — Sheffield U 1985 | 42 | 1 | 4 | 0 | 4 | 0 | 0 | 0 | 0 | 0 | 50 | 1 |
| McNEAL R | Hobson, Co Durham 1891 | LH | Hobson W 1910 — Retired 1925 | 370 | 9 | 30 | 0 | 0 | 0 | 0 | 0 | 3 | 1 | 403 | 10 |
| MACREADY BL | Leicester 1942 | OR | Hull C 1959 — Mansfield T 1964 | 14 | 1 | 1 | 0 | 0 | 0 | 0 | 0 | 0 | 0 | 15 | 1 |

| PLAYER | BIRTHPLACE & YEAR | POS | FROM (year) TO (year) | League App | League Gls | FA Cup App | FA Cup Gls | Lge Cup App | Lge Cup Gls | Euro App | Euro Gls | Others App | Others Gls | TOTAL App | TOTAL Gls |
|---|---|---|---|---|---|---|---|---|---|---|---|---|---|---|---|
| McVITIE GJ | Carlisle 1948 | OR | Carlisle U 1970 — Oldham A 1972 | 42 | 5 | 5 | 0 | 2 | 0 | 0 | 0 | 3 | 0 | 52 | 0 |
| MADDEN C | Manchester 1958 | CF/IF | Bury 1986 — Blackpool 1987 | 10/2 | 3 | 0 | 0 | 0 | 0 | 0 | 0 | 0 | 0 | 10/2 | 0 |
| MAGEE TP | Widnes 1899 | IR/RH | Widnes A 1919 — Crystal P 1934 | 394 | 15 | 34 | 0 | 0 | 0 | 0 | 0 | 6 | 3 | 434 | 1 |
| MAHON J | Gillingham 1911 | OR | Leeds U 1935 — Huddersfield T 1938 | 113 | 39 | 10 | 5 | 0 | 0 | 0 | 0 | 0 | 0 | 123 | 4 |
| MALE NA | West Bromwich 1917 | FB | Bush R 1933 — Walsall 1938 | 3 | 1 | 0 | 0 | 0 | 0 | 0 | 0 | 1 | 0 | 4 | 0 |
| MANN JF | West Bromwich 1891 | CF | Great Bridge Juniors 1912 — Newport C 1918 | 2 | 0 | 0 | 0 | 0 | 0 | 0 | 0 | 0 | 0 | 2 | 0 |
| MANNERS JA | Morpeth 1878 | WH | Morpeth H 1904 — Hartlepools U 1913 | 193 | 7 | 16 | 0 | 0 | 0 | 0 | 0 | 0 | 0 | 209 | 0 |
| MARRIOTT A | Sutton-in-Ashfield 1970 | G | Nottingham F(loan) 1989 — Nottingham F | 3 | 0 | 0 | 0 | 0 | 0 | 0 | 0 | 0 | 0 | 3 | 0 |
| MARTIN DW | Edinburgh 1947 | W | Kettering T 1967 — Carlisle U 1970 | 14 | 1 | 4 | 0 | 0/1 | 1 | 1 | 0 | 1/2 | 0 | 20/3 | 0 |
| MARTIN MP | Dublin 1951 | M | Manchester U 1975 — Newcastle U 1978 | 85/4 | 11 | 12 | 2 | 5/1 | 2 | 0/1 | 0 | 6/1 | 0 | 108/7 | 1 |
| MATTHEWS J | West Bromwich 1860 | G | Aston Unity 1883 — Crosswell's B 1885 | 0 | 0 | 1 | 0 | 0 | 0 | 0 | 0 | 0 | 0 | 1 | 0 |
| MAYO J | Tipton 1951 | CF | Walsall 1973 — Orient 1977 | 67/5 | 16 | 7 | 1 | 5 | 0 | 0 | 0 | 5/1 | 3 | 84/6 | 2 |
| MELLON M | Paisley 1972 | M | Bristol City 1993 — | 15/2 | 3 | 0 | 0 | 0 | 0 | 0 | 0 | 2 | 0 | 17/2 | 3 |
| MERRICK AR | Selly Oak, Birmingham 1950 | D | School 1966 — Kiddermisnter H 1976 | 131/8 | 5 | 6/2 | 0 | 9 | 0 | 0 | 0 | 10/3 | 0 | 156/13 | 0 |
| MILLAR J | Annbank, Ayrshire 1870 | CF | Sunderland 1904 — Chelsea 1905 | 1 | 0 | 0 | 0 | 0 | 0 | 0 | 0 | 0 | 0 | 1 | 0 |
| MILLARD A | West Bromwich 1868 | D | West Bromwich Victoria 1888 — Halesowen 1892 | 5 | 0 | 0 | 0 | 0 | 0 | 0 | 0 | 0 | 0 | 5 | 0 |
| MILLARD L | Coseley, West Midlands 1919 | FB | Sunbeam FC 1937 — Stafford R 1958 | 436 | 7 | 40 | 0 | 0 | 0 | 0 | 0 | 149 | 11 | 625 | 1 |
| MILLER A | Epping 1970 | G | Arsenal(loan) 1991 — Arsenal 1991 | 3 | 0 | 0 | 0 | 0 | 0 | 0 | 0 | 0 | 0 | 3 | 0 |
| MILLINGTON AH | Hawarden, Nr Chester 1943 | G | Sutton T 1959 — Crystal P 1964 | 40 | 0 | 0 | 0 | 0 | 0 | 0 | 0 | 0 | 0 | 40 | 0 |
| MILLS DJ | Robin Hood's Bay 1951 | F | Middlesbrough 1979 — Sheffield W 1983 | 44/15 | 6 | 2/3 | 0 | 6/2 | 0 | 3/1 | 0 | 0 | 0 | 55/21 | 0 |
| MINTON RC | Moseley, Birmingham 1951 | FB | Schools 1966 — Dunstable T 1975 | 24/2 | 1 | 0 | 0 | 2 | 0 | 0 | 0 | 1 | 0 | 27/2 | 0 |
| MONAGHAN DJ | Bromsgrove 1959 | F | Astwood Bank 1976 — Port Vale 1984 | 14/5 | 2 | 1 | 0 | 2/1 | 1 | 0/1 | 0 | 0 | 0 | 17/7 | 0 |
| MOORWOOD L | Wednesbury 1888 | G | Bilston U 1909 — Burnley 1920 | 30 | 0 | 3 | 0 | 0 | 0 | 0 | 0 | 0 | 0 | 33 | 0 |
| MORLEY AW | Ormskirk 1954 | W | Aston Villa 1983 — Den Haag 1986<br>Den Haag 1987 — Tampa Bay Rowdies 1989 | 60/1 | 11 | 4 | 2 | 3 | 0 | 0 | 0 | 2 | 1 | 69/1 | 14 |
| MORRIS F | Tipton 1893 | IL | Redditch 1911 — Coventry C 1924 | 263 | 112 | 20 | 4 | 0 | 0 | 0 | 0 | 4 | 2 | 287 | 11 |
| MORROW JHE | Larne, Northern Ireland 1930 | OR | Nuneaton B 1945 — Nuneaton B 1950 | 5 | 2 | 0 | 0 | 0 | 0 | 0 | 0 | 0 | 0 | 5 | 0 |
| MOSES RM | Manchester 1960 | M | Corpus Christi Boys Club 1977 — Manchester U 1981 | 63 | 5 | 2 | 0 | 7 | 1 | 1 | 0 | 0 | 0 | 73 | 0 |
| MOUNTFORD D | Hanley 1931 | UF | Crewe A 1951 — Crewe A 1953 | 4 | 0 | 1 | 0 | 0 | 0 | 0 | 0 | 0 | 0 | 5 | 0 |
| MULLIGAN PM | Dublin 1945 | FB | Crystal P 1975 — Shamrock R 1979 | 109 | 1 | 11 | 0 | 7 | 0 | 0 | 0 | 5 | 1 | 132 | 0 |
| MURPHY JP | Ton Pentre 1908 | WH | Mid Rhondda Boys 1928 — Swindon T 1939 | 209 | 0 | 19 | 0 | 0 | 0 | 0 | 0 | 0 | 0 | 223 | 0 |
| MURRAY M | Falkirk 1935 | CF | Glasgow Rangers 1962 — Third Lanark 1963 | 3 | 0 | 0 | 0 | 0 | 0 | 0 | 0 | 0 | 0 | 3 | 0 |
| NAYLOR SW | Leeds 1962 | G | Lincoln C 1986 — | 266 | 0 | 10 | 0 | 15 | 0 | 0 | 0 | 10 | 0 | 301 | 0 |
| NEALE W | West Bromwich 1872 | CF | Grove Hall Sts 1893 — Brierley Hill A 1894 | 6 | 3 | 1 | 0 | 0 | 0 | 0 | 0 | 0 | 0 | 7 | 0 |
| NEVIN JW | Gosforth, Tyne and Wear 1887 | WH | Hobson W 1910 — Bristol R 1912 | 2 | 0 | 0 | 0 | 0 | 0 | 0 | 0 | 0 | 0 | 2 | 0 |
| NEWALL JT | West Bromwich 1894 | IF | Great Bridge Celtic 1912 — Retired 1922 | 21 | 3 | 0 | 0 | 0 | 0 | 0 | 0 | 1 | 0 | 22 | 0 |
| NEWALL WT | Lye 1869 | OL | Stourbridge 1894 — Worcester R 1895 | 14 | 2 | 0 | 0 | 0 | 0 | 0 | 0 | 1 | 0 | 15 | 0 |
| NEWSOME R | Hebden Bridge, Yorks 1919 | OR/CF | Congleton 1939 — Coventry C 1947 | 0 | 0 | 4 | 2 | 0 | 0 | 0 | 0 | 55 | 28 | 59 | 3 |
| NICHOLL J | Hamilton, Canada 1956 | RB | Toronto Blizzard 1984 — Rangers 1986 | 56 | 0 | 3 | 0 | 6 | 0 | 0 | 0 | 2 | 1 | 67 | 0 |
| NICHOLLS F | Handsworth 1884 | OR | Handsworth R 1904 — Goldenhill W 1906 | 7 | 0 | 0 | 0 | 0 | 0 | 0 | 0 | 0 | 0 | 7 | 0 |
| NICHOLLS HJ | Walsall 1891 | OL | Hednesford T 1913 — Cannock T 1914 | 4 | 0 | 0 | 0 | 0 | 0 | 0 | 0 | 0 | 0 | 4 | 0 |
| NICHOLLS J | West Bromwich 1867 | U | St John's U 1889 — Kidderminster O 1890 | 4 | 0 | 2 | 0 | 0 | 0 | 0 | 0 | 0 | 0 | 6 | 0 |
| NICHOLLS J | Wolverhampton 1931 | IF | Heath TU 1950 — Cardiff C 1957 | 131 | 58 | 14 | 6 | 0 | 0 | 0 | 0 | 0 | 0 | 145 | 6 |
| NICHOLLS S | West Bromwich 1870 | CF | West Brom Victoria 1890 — London CBC 1892<br>London CBC 1893 — Retired 1894 | 41 | 14 | 9 | 3 | 0 | 0 | 0 | 0 | 0 | 0 | 50 | 1 |
| NICHOLSON MD | Oakengates 1871 | FB | Oswestry T 1891 — Luton T 1894 | 56 | 0 | 8 | 0 | 0 | 0 | 0 | 0 | 4 | 0 | 68 | 0 |
| NISBET GJM | Wallsend-on-Tyne 1951 | FB/G | Willington Boys Club 1968 — Hull C 1976 | 136 | 0 | 13 | 1 | 8 | 0 | 0 | 0 | 10 | 0 | 167 | 0 |
| NOCK JF | West Bromwich 1875 | OL | Halesowen T 1897 — Langley R 1899 | 15 | 6 | 0 | 0 | 0 | 0 | 0 | 0 | 0 | 0 | 15 | 0 |
| NORMAN O | West Bromwich 1866 | UF | Wednesbury Old Athletic 1893 — Hereford T 1896 | 18 | 4 | 0 | 0 | 0 | 0 | 0 | 0 | 2 | 0 | 20 | 0 |
| NORTH S | Luton 1964 | D | Luton Town 1987 — Fulham 1990 | 96/2 | 0 | 6 | 0 | 5 | 0 | 0 | 0 | 1 | 0 | 108/2 | 0 |
| NURSE DG | Princes End, Tipton 1873 | RH | Wolves 1901 — Retired 1905 | 85 | 4 | 3 | 0 | 0 | 0 | 0 | 0 | 0 | 0 | 88 | 0 |
| OLIVER HSM | Birmingham 1863 | LB | Small Heath 1888 — Small Heath 1889 | 1 | 0 | 0 | 0 | 0 | 0 | 0 | 0 | 0 | 0 | 1 | 0 |
| OSBORNE J | Barlborough, Derbyshire 1940 | G | Chesterfield 1967 — Shamrock R 1978 | 250 | 0 | 24 | 0 | 16 | 0 | 8 | 0 | 14 | 0 | 312 | 0 |
| OWEN AG | Coalbrookdale, Shropshire 1880 | OI | Ironbridge 1903 — Walsall 1905 | 7 | 1 | 0 | 0 | 0 | 0 | 0 | 0 | 0 | 0 | 7 | 0 |
| OWEN GA | St Helens 1958 | M | Manchester C 1979 — Panionios (Greece) 1986 | 185/2 | 21 | 12/2 | 3 | 24 | 2 | 4 | 0 | 0 | 0 | 225/4 | 2 |
| OWERS EH | Bromley 1889 | CF | Blackpool 1907 — Chesterfield 1909 | 4 | 0 | 0 | 0 | 0 | 0 | 0 | 0 | 0 | 0 | 4 | 0 |
| PADDOCK JW | West Bromwich 1877 | W | School 1894 — Walsall T 1896<br>Brierley Hill 1899 — Halesowen 1900 | 20 | 5 | 0 | 0 | 0 | 0 | 0 | 0 | 0 | 0 | 20 | 0 |
| PADDOCK W | West Bromwich 1862 | OL | West Bromwich U 1886 — Retired 1888 | 0 | 0 | 8 | 3 | 0 | 0 | 0 | 0 | 0 | 0 | 8 | 0 |
| PAILOR R | Stockton-on-Tees 1887 | CF | West Hartlepool 1908 — Newcastle U 1914 | 79 | 40 | 13 | 7 | 0 | 0 | 0 | 0 | 0 | 0 | 92 | 4 |
| PALMER CL | Rowley Regis, West Midlands 1965 | D | YTS 1983 — Sheffield W 1989 | 114/7 | 4 | 4 | 0 | 7/1 | 1 | 0 | 0 | 6 | 0 | 131/8 | 5 |
| PALMER L | Quinton 1971 | F | YTS 1987 — Kidderminster H | 5/3 | 1 | 0/1 | 0 | 0 | 0 | 0 | 0 | 0 | 0 | 5/4 | 1 |
| PARKER AE | Tipton 1925 | FB | School 1942 — Hereford U 1946 | 0 | 0 | 0 | 0 | 0 | 0 | 0 | 0 | 5 | 1 | 5 | 0 |
| PARKES HA | Gorsty Hill, Halesowen 1888 | OR | Halesowen 1906 — Coventry C 1908<br>Coventry C 1914 — Newport C 1919 | 27 | 4 | 4 | 0 | 0 | 0 | 0 | 0 | 0 | 0 | 31 | 0 |
| PARKIN SW | Mansfield 1965 | FB | Stoke C 1989 — Mansfield T 1992 | 44/4 | 2 | 0 | 0 | 3 | 0 | 0 | 0 | 2/1 | 0 | 49/5 | 2 |
| PARRY J | Glan Mule, Montgomeryshire 1871 | OL | Newtown 1895 — Aberystwyth 1895 | 1 | 0 | 0 | 0 | 0 | 0 | 0 | 0 | 0 | 0 | 1 | 0 |
| PASKIN WJ | Cape Town 1962 | F | KV Kortrikj(Belgium) 1988 — Wolverhampton W 1989 | 14/11 | 5 | 0/2 | 0 | 1 | 0 | 0 | 0 | 0 | 0 | 15/13 | 5 |
| PEARS WG | Aston, Birmingham 1922 | CF | Wolseley FC 1943 — Kidderminster H 1947 | 0 | 0 | 0 | 0 | 0 | 0 | 0 | 0 | 4 | 2 | 4 | 2 |
| PEARSON HF | Tamworth 1908 | G | Tamworth Castle 1925 — Millwall 1937 | 281 | 0 | 21 | 0 | 0 | 0 | 0 | 0 | 1 | 0 | 303 | 0 |
| PEARSON H | Kettlebrook, Tamworth 1886 | G | Tamworth Ath 1906 — Retired 1926 | 341 | 2 | 29 | 0 | 0 | 0 | 0 | 0 | 7 | 0 | 377 | 2 |
| PEARSON T | West Bromwich 1866 | IF | WB Sandwell 1886 — Retired 1894 | 138 | 72 | 26 | 12 | 0 | 0 | 0 | 0 | 7 | 4 | 171 | 88 |
| PEMBERTON JHA | Wolverhampton 1916 | RB | Birmingham 1937 — Retired 1951 | 162 | 0 | 10 | 0 | 0 | 0 | 0 | 0 | 0 | 0 | 172 | 0 |
| PEMBERTON JT | Brierley Hill 1925 | LB | Round Oak FC 1943 — Round Oak FC 1944 | 0 | 0 | 0 | 0 | 0 | 0 | 0 | 0 | 1 | 0 | 1 | 0 |
| PENDREY GJS | Lozells Birmingham 1949 | D | Birmingham C 1979 — Torquay U 1981 | 18 | 0 | 0 | 0 | 0 | 0 | 0 | 0 | 0 | 0 | 18 | 0 |
| PENNINGTON J | West Bromwich 1883 | FB | Dudley T 1903 — Retired 1922 | 455 | 0 | 39 | 0 | 0 | 0 | 0 | 0 | 2 | 0 | 496 | 0 |
| PERKINS EE | Astwood Bank, Worcs 1874 | OL | Worcester C 1904 — Worcester C 1907 | 33 | 1 | 1 | 0 | 0 | 0 | 0 | 0 | 0 | 0 | 34 | 1 |
| PERKINS E | West Bromwich 1934 | FB | Hill Top F 1952 — Walsall 1956 | 2 | 0 | 0 | 0 | 0 | 0 | 0 | 0 | 0 | 0 | 2 | 0 |
| PERRY AA | West Bromwich 1897 | FB | West Brom Baptists 1921 — Wellington 1927 | 74 | 0 | 7 | 0 | 0 | 0 | 0 | 0 | 0 | 0 | 81 | 0 |
| PERRY C | West Bromwich 1866 | HB | West Brom Strollers 1884 — Retired 1896 | 171 | 12 | 39 | 3 | 0 | 0 | 0 | 0 | 9 | 1 | 219 | 16 |
| PERRY M | Wimbledon 1964 | F | School 1980 — Torquay U 1984 | 14/6 | 5 | 1 | 0 | 2 | 0 | 0 | 0 | 0 | 0 | 17/6 | 5 |
| PERRY T | West Bromwich 1871 | HB | Stourbridge 1890 — Aston Villa 1901 | 248 | 14 | 29 | 0 | 0 | 0 | 0 | 0 | 14 | 1 | 291 | 15 |
| PERRY W | West Bromwich 1868 | IF | West Brom Excelsior 1886 — Wolves 1889<br>Warwick C 1894 — Burton S 1895 | 11 | 4 | 4 | 3 | 0 | 0 | 0 | 0 | 0 | 0 | 15 | 7 |
| PETERS S | West Bromwich 1886 | WH | Churchfields 1904 — Crewe A 1907 | 6 | 1 | 0 | 0 | 0 | 0 | 0 | 0 | 0 | 0 | 6 | 1 |
| PHEASANT E | Darlaston 1877 | CH/CF | Wolves 1904 — Leicester Fosse 1910 | 140 | 20 | 12 | 2 | 0 | 0 | 0 | 0 | 0 | 0 | 152 | 22 |
| PHILLIPS SG | Halifax 1961 | F | Hereford U 1988 — Swansea C 1989 | 15 | 4 | 0 | 0 | 0 | 0 | 0 | 0 | 0/1 | 0 | 15/1 | 4 |
| PICKEN T | Hednesford 1883 | G | Shrewsbury 1905 — Rood End 1910 | 2 | 0 | 0 | 0 | 0 | 0 | 0 | 0 | 0 | 0 | 2 | 0 |
| PICKERING TG | Wednesbury 1879 | IF | Brierley Hill A 1900 — Kettering T 1901 | 10 | 2 | 0 | 0 | 0 | 0 | 0 | 0 | 0 | 0 | 10 | 2 |
| PIGGOTT G | Stourbridge 1969 | CF | Dudley Town 1991 — Shrewsbury T 1993 | 3/2 | 0 | 0 | 0 | 0 | 0 | 0 | 0 | 0 | 0 | 3/2 | 0 |
| PIKE RSGA | Finchley 1917 | CF | Banbury Sp 1937 — Banbury Sp 1946 | 1 | 0 | 0 | 0 | 0 | 0 | 0 | 0 | 0 | 0 | 1 | 0 |
| PITTAWAY J | West Bromwich 1867 | UF | West Brom Wednesday 1889 — Stourbridge 1890 | 2 | 1 | 0 | 0 | 0 | 0 | 0 | 0 | 0 | 0 | 2 | 1 |
| POTTER RC | Wolverhampton 1948 | CH | School 1964 — Swindon T 1970 | 8 | 0 | 0 | 0 | 0 | 0 | 0 | 0 | 0 | 0 | 8 | 0 |
| POTTER RJ | Beckenham, Kent 1936 | G | Crystal P 1958 — Portsmouth 1967 | 217 | 0 | 13 | 0 | 6 | 0 | 2 | 0 | 0 | 0 | 238 | 0 |
| POULTON A | Wolverhampton 1896 | CF | Priestfield FC 1913 — Merthyr T 1919 | 9 | 1 | 0 | 0 | 0 | 0 | 0 | 0 | 0 | 0 | 9 | 1 |
| POWELL DR | Hednesford 1967 | G | Cherry Valley FC 1984 — retired 1988 | 2 | 0 | 1 | 0 | 0 | 0 | 0 | 0 | 0 | 0 | 3 | 0 |
| POWELL S | Pulford, Clwyd 1865 | FB | Oswestry 1890 — Burton S 1892 | 30 | 0 | 5 | 0 | 0 | 0 | 0 | 0 | 0 | 0 | 35 | 0 |
| POYNTON W | Hill Top, West Bromwich 1883 | OR | Brittania Vics 1902 — Retired 1903 | 2 | 2 | 0 | 0 | 0 | 0 | 0 | 0 | 0 | 0 | 2 | 2 |
| POXTON JH | Staveley 1904 | OI | Staveley T 1924 — Gillingham 1928 | 9 | 1 | 0 | 0 | 0 | 0 | 0 | 0 | 0 | 0 | 9 | 1 |
| PREW JH | Coventry 1914 | OR | Hinckley U 1936 — Walsall 1938 | 7 | 1 | 0 | 0 | 0 | 0 | 0 | 0 | 0 | 0 | 7 | 1 |
| PRICE GW | Wolverhampton 1888 | CF | Chillington R 1910 — Cradley SL 1911 | 1 | 0 | 0 | 0 | 0 | 0 | 0 | 0 | 0 | 0 | 1 | 0 |
| PRITCHARD D | Wolverhampton | F | YTS 1988 — Telford United 1992 | 1/4 | 0 | 0 | 0 | 0 | 0 | 0 | 0 | 0 | 0 | 1/4 | 0 |
| RAMSEY AR | Collington, Hereford 1867 | RB | Kidderminster H 1888 — Kidderminster H 1900 | 1 | 0 | 0 | 0 | 0 | 0 | 0 | 0 | 0 | 0 | 1 | 0 |
| RANDLE A | West Bromwich 1880 | RH | Darlaston 1901 — Leicester Fosse 1908 | 132 | 1 | 11 | 1 | 0 | 0 | 0 | 0 | 0 | 0 | 143 | 2 |
| RANKIN B | Liverpool 1880 | W | Everton 1906 — Manchester C 1907 | 29 | 5 | 2 | 1 | 0 | 0 | 0 | 0 | 0 | 0 | 31 | 6 |
| RAVEN P | Salisbury 1970 | D | Doncaster Rovers 1989 — | 70/4 | 8 | 4 | 1 | 2 | 0 | 0 | 0 | 7 | 0 | 83/4 | 9 |
| RAW H | Tow Law, Co Durham 1903 | WH/IF | Huddersfield T 1931 — Lincoln C 1936 | 25 | 7 | 1 | 0 | 0 | 0 | 0 | 0 | 1 | 0 | 27 | 7 |
| RAWLINGS JDS | Wombwell, Yorks 1913 | OR | Huddersfield T 1935 — Northampton T 1936 | 10 | 1 | 0 | 0 | 0 | 0 | 0 | 0 | 0 | 0 | 10 | 1 |

| PLAYER | BIRTHPLACE & YEAR | POS | FROM (year) TO (year) | League | | FA Cup | | Lge Cup | | Euro | | Others | | TOTAL | |
|---|---|---|---|---|---|---|---|---|---|---|---|---|---|---|---|
| | | | | App | Gls | App | Gls | App | Gls | App | Gls | App | Gls | App | Gls |
| REA JC | Lledrod, Cardigan 1870 | OL | Aberystwyth 1894 — Aberystwyth 1895 | 1 | 0 | 0 | 0 | 0 | 0 | 0 | 0 | 0 | 0 | 1 | 0 |
| READER J | West Bromwich 1866 | G | School 1885 — Retired 1901 | 315 | 0 | 39 | 0 | 0 | 0 | 0 | 0 | 16 | 0 | 370 | 0 |
| READFERN TE | Crook, Co Durham 1944 | CF | Langley Park Juniors 1960 — Kidderminster H 1964 | 4 | 0 | 1 | 0 | 0 | 0 | 0 | 0 | 0 | 0 | 5 | 0 |
| REED FWM | Scotswood-on-Tyne 1894 | CH | Lintz Inst 1913 — Retired 1927 | 138 | 4 | 16 | 1 | 0 | 0 | 0 | 0 | 3 | 0 | 157 | 5 |
| REED HD | Alexandria, Dumbarton 1950 | OR | Drumchapel A 1966 — Plymouth A 1971 | 5/3 | 2 | 0 | 0 | 0 | 0 | 0 | 0 | 0/1 | 0 | 5/4 | 2 |
| REES MJ | Cardiff 1967 | G | Watford 1990 — Sheffield United 1992 | 18 | 0 | 1 | 0 | 0 | 0 | 0 | 0 | 0 | 0 | 19 | 0 |
| REES RR | Ystradgynlais, Brecknock 1944 | OR/OL | Coventry C 1968 — Nottingham F 1969 | 34 | 9 | 1/1 | 2 | 2 | 1 | 3 | 0 | 0 | 0 | 40/1 | 12 |
| REGIS C | Maripiasoula (French Guyana) 1958 | S | Hayes 1977 — Coventry C 1984 | 233/4 | 82 | 25 | 10 | 27/1 | 16 | 10 | 3 | 2 | 1 | 297/5 | 112 |
| REID GA | Handsworth, Sheffield 1872 | CF | Sheffield W 1897 — Walmley 1898 | 11 | 3 | 2 | 0 | 0 | 0 | 0 | 0 | 0 | 0 | 13 | 3 |
| REID NS | Urmston 1960 | D | Blackburn Rovers 1992 — | 10/5 | 0 | 2 | 0 | 0 | 0 | 0 | 0 | 1/1 | 1 | 13/6 | 1 |
| REILLY GG | Bellshill, Lanarkshire 1957 | CF | Newcastle U 1985 — Cambridge U 1988 | 42/1 | 9 | 3 | 1 | 0 | 0 | 0 | 0 | 2 | 0 | 47/1 | 10 |
| REYNOLDS J | Blackburn 1869 | WH | Ulster 1891 — Aston Villa 1893 | 37 | 3 | 7 | 2 | 0 | 0 | 0 | 0 | 2 | 1 | 46 | 6 |
| RICE B | Glasgow 1963 | M | Nottingham For (loan) 1989 — Nottingham Forest 1989 | 2/1 | 0 | 0 | 0 | 0 | 0 | 0 | 0 | 0 | 0 | 2/1 | 0 |
| RICHARDS AJ | Knighton 1888 | RB | New Invention 1910 — Kilnhurst 1911 | 1 | 0 | 0 | 0 | 0 | 0 | 0 | 0 | 0 | 0 | 1 | 0 |
| RICHARDS GM | Bilston 1929 | OR | Albion Works 1943 — Stafford R 1952 | 3 | 1 | 0 | 0 | 0 | 0 | 0 | 0 | 0 | 0 | 3 | 1 |
| RICHARDS J | Martley, Worcester 1873 | OR | City Ramblers (London) 1895 — Loughborough T 1896 | 14 | 0 | 2 | 1 | 0 | 0 | 0 | 0 | 4 | 1 | 20 | 2 |
| RICHARDS W | West Bromwich 1874 | CF | West Brom Standard 1894 — Newton Heath 1901 | 123 | 35 | 21 | 6 | 0 | 0 | 0 | 0 | 4 | 1 | 148 | 42 |
| RICHARDSON F | Middlestone Moor, Durham 1925 | CF | Barnsley 1950 — Chester 1952 | 29 | 8 | 2 | 0 | 0 | 0 | 0 | 0 | 0 | 0 | 31 | 8 |
| RICHARDSON S | West Bromwich 1892 | WH | Great Bridge Celtic 1913 — Newport C 1927 | 191 | 1 | 15 | 0 | 0 | 0 | 0 | 0 | 6 | 0 | 212 | 1 |
| RICHARDSON W'G' | Framwellgate Moor, Durham 1909 | CF | Hartlepool U 1929 — Shrewsbury T 1945 | 320 | 202 | 34 | 26 | 0 | 0 | 0 | 0 | 90 | 100 | 444 | 328 |
| RICHARDSON W | Great Bridge 1908 | CH | G Bridge Celtic 1926 — Swindon T 1937 | 319 | 1 | 32 | 0 | 0 | 0 | 0 | 0 | 1 | 0 | 352 | 1 |
| RICKABY S | Stockton-on-Tees 1924 | RB | Middlesbrough 1950 — Poole T 1955 | 189 | 2 | 15 | 0 | 0 | 0 | 0 | 0 | 1 | 0 | 205 | 2 |
| RIDYARD A | Shafton, South Yorkshire 1908 | CH | Barnsley 1932 — Queen's Park R 1938 | 31 | 0 | 3 | 0 | 0 | 0 | 0 | 0 | 0 | 0 | 34 | 0 |
| RILEY JH | West Bromwich 1869 | UF | Wednesbury Old Athletic 1889 — Walsall TS 1891 | 3 | 1 | 0 | 0 | 0 | 0 | 0 | 0 | 0 | 0 | 3 | 1 |
| RIX J | Lintz, Bursopfield 1908 | WH | Lintz Colliery 1927 — Lincoln C 1939 | 64 | 0 | 4 | 0 | 0 | 0 | 0 | 0 | 0 | 0 | 68 | 0 |
| ROBBINS WW | Cardiff 1910 | OL | Cardiff C 1932 — Newport C 1939 | 84 | 28 | 7 | 3 | 0 | 0 | 0 | 0 | 0 | 0 | 91 | 31 |
| ROBERTS F | West Bromwich 1874 | D | West Brom Standard 1893 — Smethwick C 1895 | 2 | 0 | 0 | 0 | 0 | 0 | 0 | 0 | 0 | 0 | 2 | 0 |
| ROBERTS GP | Southampton 1959 | D | Chelsea 1990 — Enfield 1992 | 39 | 6 | 1 | 0 | 0 | 0 | 0 | 0 | 1 | 0 | 41 | 6 |
| ROBERTS RHC | Marchweil, Wrexham 1870 | OL | Wrexham 1890 — Corwen 1891 | 1 | 0 | 0 | 0 | 0 | 0 | 0 | 0 | 0 | 0 | 1 | 0 |
| ROBERTS RJ | Redditch 1878 | W | West Brom Excelsior 1899 — Newcastle U 1901 | 43 | 8 | 9 | 2 | 0 | 0 | 0 | 0 | 0 | 0 | 52 | 10 |
| ROBERTS RJ | West Bromwich 1859 | G | George Salter Works 1879 — Sunderland Albion 1890<br>Sunderland Albion 1891 — Aston Villa 1892 | 49 | 0 | 35 | 1 | 0 | 0 | 0 | 0 | 0 | 0 | 84 | 1 |
| ROBERTS TF | Smethwick 1868 | FB | School 1890 — Birmingham St George 1891<br>Birmingham St George 1893 — Retired 1895 | 2 | 0 | 0 | 0 | 0 | 0 | 0 | 0 | 0 | 0 | 2 | 0 |
| ROBERTSON AP | Philpstoun, West Lothian 1952 | D | Uphall Saints 1968 — Wolverhampton W 1986 | 504/2 | 8 | 34/2 | 0 | 53 | 3 | 12 | 1 | 19 | 0 | 622/4 | 12 |
| ROBINSON B | Wheelton, Lancashire 1865 | FB | Bolton W 1889 — Bolton W 1890<br>Bolton W 1891 — Hyde U 1891 | 0 | 0 | 4 | 0 | 0 | 0 | 0 | 0 | 0 | 0 | 4 | 0 |
| ROBINSON EV | Walsall 1922 | FB | Hilary Street Old Boys 1938 — Shrewsbury T 1948 | 0 | 0 | 0 | 0 | 0 | 0 | 0 | 0 | 1 | 0 | 1 | 0 |
| ROBINSON EM | Manchester 1935 | IF | Altrincham 1957 — Rotherham U 1959 | 1 | 0 | 0 | 0 | 0 | 0 | 0 | 0 | 0 | 0 | 1 | 0 |
| ROBINSON MJ | Rochdale 1968 | W | School 1985 — Released, May 1987 | 2 | 0 | 0 | 0 | 0/1 | 0 | 0 | 0 | 0 | 0 | 2/1 | 0 |
| ROBINSON R | Sunderland 1966 | D | Doncaster Rovers 1989 — Rotherham Utd 1989 | 1 | 0 | 0 | 0 | 0 | 0 | 0 | 0 | 0 | 0 | 1 | 0 |
| ROBSON B | Witton Gilbert, Co Durham 1957 | M | Schools 1972 — Manchester U 1981 | 194/4 | 39 | 10/2 | 2 | 17/1 | 2 | 12 | 2 | 9 | 1 | 242/7 | 46 |
| ROBSON G | Chester-le-Street 1965 | M | Whitehill 1981 — | 184/34 | 28 | 10/1 | 3 | 12/2 | 0 | 0 | 0 | 7/5 | 3 | 213/42 | 34 |
| ROBSON RW | Sacriston, Co Durham 1933 | IF/WH | Fulham 1956 — Fulham 1962 | 239 | 56 | 18 | 5 | 0 | 0 | 0 | 0 | 0 | 0 | 257 | 61 |
| ROGERS D | Chester-le-Street 1965 | M | Whitehill FC 1981 | 0 | 0 | 0 | 0 | 0 | 0 | 0 | 0 | 0 | 0 | 0 | 0 |
| ROOKE E | Hockley 1899 | CH | Brierley Hill A 1921 — Nuneaton T 1929 | 41 | 1 | 1 | 0 | 0 | 0 | 0 | 0 | 0 | 0 | 42 | 1 |
| ROUSE FW | Bracknell, Berkshire 1885 | CF | Chelsea 1909 — Croydon Common 1910 | 5 | 2 | 0 | 0 | 0 | 0 | 0 | 0 | 0 | 0 | 5 | 2 |
| ROWLEY GA | Wolverhampton 1926 | IF | Blakenhall SL 1944 — Fulham 1948 | 24 | 4 | 1 | 1 | 0 | 0 | 0 | 0 | 16 | 10 | 41 | 15 |
| RUSHBURY DG | Wolverhampton 1956 | D | St Chad's College 1972 — Sheffield W 1977 | 28 | 0 | 3 | 0 | 0 | 0 | 0 | 0 | 0 | 0 | 31 | 0 |
| RUSSELL TJ | Walsall 1924 | F | Brockhouses FC 1943 — Kidderminster H 1948 | 0 | 0 | 0 | 0 | 0 | 0 | 0 | 0 | 4 | 1 | 4 | 1 |
| RYAN RA | Dublin 1925 | WH/IF | Coventry C 1945 — Derby C 1955 | 234 | 28 | 20 | 2 | 0 | 0 | 0 | 0 | 18 | 1 | 272 | 31 |
| SAMBROOK C | Smethwick 1896 | F | Coventry C 1915 — Retired 1920 | 0 | 0 | 0 | 0 | 0 | 0 | 0 | 0 | 2 | 1 | 2 | 1 |
| SANDERS JA | Hackney, London 1920 | G | Charlton A 1945 — Coventry C 1958 | 327 | 0 | 36 | 0 | 0 | 0 | 0 | 0 | 28 | 0 | 391 | 0 |
| SANDFORD EA | Handsworth 1910 | IF | Smethwick Highfield 1929 — Sheffield U 1939 | 286 | 67 | 30 | 8 | 0 | 0 | 0 | 0 | 1 | 0 | 317 | 75 |
| SANKEY J | Moulton, Cheshire 1912 | WH | Winsford U 1930 — Northampton T 1945 | 147 | 5 | 13 | 0 | 0 | 0 | 0 | 0 | 130 | 22 | 290 | 27 |
| SAUNDERS DG | Birmingham 1927 | OL | W.B.Hawthorne 1942 — Banbury Sp 1948 | 0 | 0 | 1 | 0 | 0 | 0 | 0 | 0 | 5 | 3 | 6 | 3 |
| SAUNDERS S | West Bromwich 1872 | OL | Unity Gas 1895 — Birmingham Centinels 1896 | 2 | 0 | 0 | 0 | 0 | 0 | 0 | 0 | 0 | 0 | 2 | 0 |
| SAUNDERS W | Banbury 1916 | G | Banbury Spencer 1938 — Banbury Spencer 1946 | 2 | 0 | 0 | 0 | 0 | 0 | 0 | 0 | 32 | 0 | 34 | 0 |
| SAVAGE G | Birmingham 1903 | F | Willenhall 1921 — Wrexham 1922 | 2 | 0 | 0 | 0 | 0 | 0 | 0 | 0 | 0 | 0 | 2 | 0 |
| SCREEN J | Oldbury 1915 | FB | Smethwick Highfield 1933 — Wrexham 1939 | 1 | 0 | 0 | 0 | 0 | 0 | 0 | 0 | 0 | 0 | 1 | 0 |
| SETTERS ME | Honiton, Devon 1936 | U | Exeter C 1955 — Manchester U 1960 | 120 | 10 | 12 | 0 | 0 | 0 | 0 | 0 | 0 | 0 | 132 | 10 |
| SHAKESPEARE C | Birmingham 1963 | M | Sheffield Wednesday 1990 — | 104/8 | 12 | 5 | 2 | 6 | 1 | 0 | 0 | 5 | 1 | 120/8 | 16 |
| SHAW CE | Mansfield 1911 | FB | Wolves 1936 — Hereford U 1947 | 113 | 10 | 14 | 0 | 0 | 0 | 0 | 0 | 124 | 4 | 251 | 14 |
| SHAW CR | Willenhall 1862 | OL | Walsall TS 1888 — Walsall TS 1888 | 1 | 1 | 0 | 0 | 0 | 0 | 0 | 0 | 0 | 0 | 1 | 1 |
| SHAW GD | Huddersfield 1948 | IF | Oldham Ath 1969 — Oldham A 1975 | 65/17 | 17 | 7 | 1 | 4 | 1 | 0 | 0 | 2/1 | 1 | 78/18 | 20 |
| SHAW GE | Swinton 1899 | FB | Huddersfield T 1926 — Stalybridge C 1938 | 393 | 11 | 31 | 0 | 0 | 0 | 0 | 0 | 1 | 0 | 425 | 11 |
| SHEARMAN BW | Lincoln 1884 | OL | Bristol C 1911 — Nottingham F 1919 | 126 | 18 | 15 | 0 | 0 | 0 | 0 | 0 | 2 | 0 | 143 | 18 |
| SHELDON A | West Bromwich 1871 | FB | Smethwick Carriage Wks 1892 — Worcester R 1893 | 0 | 0 | 0 | 0 | 0 | 0 | 0 | 0 | 1 | 0 | 1 | 0 |
| SHEPHERD E | Wombwell, Yorks 1919 | OL | Fulham 1948 — Hull C 1949 | 4 | 0 | 0 | 0 | 0 | 0 | 0 | 0 | 0 | 0 | 4 | 0 |
| SHEPPARD RJ | Bristol 1945 | G | Gloucester Schools 1960 — Bristol R 1969 | 39 | 0 | 4 | 0 | 11 | 0 | 0 | 0 | 0 | 0 | 54 | 0 |
| SHINTON F | Wednesbury 1883 | CF | Hednesford T 1905 — Leicester Fosse 1907 | 64 | 46 | 4 | 0 | 0 | 0 | 0 | 0 | 0 | 0 | 68 | 46 |
| SHORE EW | Kings Hill, Wednesbury 1891 | FB | Willenhall Swifts 1913 — Stourbridge 1919 | 5 | 0 | 0 | 0 | 0 | 0 | 0 | 0 | 0 | 0 | 5 | 0 |
| SHORT JS | Norbrigg, Chesterfield 1903 | IF | Seamore FC 1923 — Retired 1930 | 39 | 17 | 2 | 0 | 0 | 0 | 0 | 0 | 0 | 0 | 41 | 17 |
| SIMMONS C | West Bromwich 1878 | CF | Worcester Rov 1898 — West Ham U 1904<br>West Ham U 1905 — Chesterfield T 1907 | 178 | 75 | 15 | 6 | 0 | 0 | 0 | 0 | 0 | 0 | 193 | 81 |
| SIMPSON G | Sheffield 1883 | OL | Sheffield W 1909 — North Shields 1910 | 19 | 5 | 5 | 1 | 0 | 0 | 0 | 0 | 0 | 0 | 24 | 6 |
| SIMPSON TJN | Southampton 1938 | WH | Peterborough U 1963 — Walsall 1967 | 71 | 3 | 5 | 0 | 1 | 1 | 0 | 0 | 0 | 0 | 77 | 4 |
| SINCLAIR F | Lambeth 1971 | FB | Chelsea (loan) 1991 — Chelsea 1992 | 6 | 1 | 0 | 0 | 0 | 0 | 0 | 0 | 0 | 0 | 6 | 1 |
| SINFIELD MR | Cheshunt 1974 | D | YTS 1990 — | 0 | 0 | 0 | 0 | 0 | 0 | 0 | 0 | 1 | 0 | 1 | 0 |
| SINGLETON MD | Banbury, Aug 1963 | M | Bradford C 1986 — Northampton T 1987 | 15/4 | 1 | 0/1 | | 1 | 0 | 0 | 0 | 0 | 0 | 16/5 | 1 |
| SMITH AW | Camberwell 1896 | IF/CH | Birmingham 1919 — Stoke 1923 | 79 | 20 | 1 | 0 | 0 | 0 | 0 | 0 | 1 | 2 | 81 | 22 |
| SMITH AW | Slamannan, Stirling 1879 | F | Newton Heath 1900 — Bristol R 1903 | 23 | 8 | 2 | 0 | 0 | 0 | 0 | 0 | 0 | 0 | 25 | 8 |
| SMITH A | West Bromwich 1880 | OR | Worcester C 1903 — Brierley Hill A 1904 | 8 | 1 | 2 | 1 | 0 | 0 | 0 | 0 | 0 | 0 | 10 | 2 |
| SMITH A | West Bromwich 1878 | IF | West Brom Baptists 1898 — Retired 1900 | 6 | 1 | 0 | 0 | 0 | 0 | 0 | 0 | 0 | 0 | 6 | 1 |
| SMITH AE | Whetstone, Leicester 1921 | OL | Leicester C 1948 — Plymouth A 1952 | 49 | 12 | 3 | 1 | 0 | 0 | 0 | 0 | 0 | 0 | 52 | 13 |
| SMITH D | Armadale, Leicester 1921 | OL | Coltness U 1939 — Chesterfield 1948 | 7 | 1 | 0 | 0 | 0 | 0 | 0 | 0 | 0 | 0 | 7 | 1 |
| SMITH E | Old Hill 1880 | IF | Old Hill W 1899 — Brierley Hill A 1900<br>Brierley Hill A 1901 — Brierley Hill A 1904 | 10 | 4 | 0 | 0 | 0 | 0 | 0 | 0 | 0 | 0 | 10 | 4 |
| SMITH GWC | Liverpool 1947 | G | Colchester U 1971 — Cambridge U 1973 | 10 | 0 | 0 | 0 | 0 | 0 | 0 | 0 | 0 | 0 | 10 | 0 |
| SMITH H | Netherton, Dudley 1903 | W | Hingley's FC 1922 — Blackpool 1927 | 2 | 0 | 0 | 0 | 0 | 0 | 0 | 0 | 0 | 0 | 2 | 0 |
| SMITH J | Northfield, Birmingham 1964 | D | School 1980 — Telford U 1984 | 0 | 0 | 0 | 0 | 1 | 0 | 0 | 0 | 0 | 0 | 1 | 0 |
| SMITH J | Darby End, Cradley 1890 | RB | Cradley Heath St Luke's 1910 — Birmingham 1926 | 434 | 0 | 30 | 0 | 0 | 0 | 0 | 0 | 7 | 0 | 471 | 0 |
| SMITH KW | Woodville, Derbyshire 1940 | IF | Coalville Boys 1957 — Peterborough U 1963 | 63 | 30 | 7 | 4 | 0 | 0 | 0 | 0 | 0 | 0 | 70 | 34 |
| SMITH WA | Old Hill 1882 | IF | Worcester C 1902 — Brierley Hill A 1905 | 21 | 3 | 1 | 0 | 0 | 0 | 0 | 0 | 0 | 0 | 22 | 3 |
| SOUTHAM JH | Willenhall 1920 | FB | Shornhill Rec FC 1939 — Newport Co 1946 | 0 | 0 | 0 | 0 | 0 | 0 | 0 | 0 | 34 | 0 | 34 | 0 |
| SPEEDIE DR | Glenrathes, Fife 1960 | F | Southampton (loan) 1993 — West Ham (loan) 1993 | 7 | 2 | 0 | 0 | 0 | 0 | 0 | 0 | 2 | 0 | 9 | 2 |
| SPENCER G | Shavington, Staffs 1913 | OR | Nantwich Vic 1933 — Brighton & HA 1939 | 13 | 2 | 0 | 0 | 0 | 0 | 0 | 0 | 0 | 0 | 13 | 2 |
| SPENCER JL | Masborough 1900 | OR | Beighton YC 1922 — Aston Villa 1927 | 59 | 3 | 7 | 0 | 0 | 0 | 0 | 0 | 0 | 0 | 66 | 3 |
| SPOONER J | West Bromwich 1871 | CF | Hednesford T 1895 — Retired 1896 | 2 | 0 | 0 | 0 | 0 | 0 | 0 | 0 | 0 | 0 | 2 | 0 |
| SPROSON T | Stoke-on-Trent 1903 | G | Audley FC 1922 — Port Vale 1928 | 9 | 0 | 0 | 0 | 0 | 0 | 0 | 0 | 0 | 0 | 9 | 0 |
| STANTON J | West Bromwich 1862 | FB/WH | George Salter Works 1879 — Newton Heath 1885 | 0 | 0 | 6 | 0 | 0 | 0 | 0 | 0 | 0 | 0 | 6 | 0 |
| STATHAM DJ | Whitmore Reams 1959 | LB | School 1975 — Southampton 1987 | 298/1 | 8 | 26 | 2 | 34 | 1 | 12 | 0 | 2 | 0 | 372/1 | 11 |
| STEELE SF | Fenton, Stoke-on-Trent 1937 | IF | Port Vale 1961 — Port Vale 1961 | 14 | 0 | 0 | 0 | 0 | 0 | 0 | 0 | 0 | 0 | 16 | 0 |
| STEGGLES KP | Bungay, Norfolk 1961 | D | Ipswich T 1987 — Port Vale 1987 | 14 | 0 | 0 | 0 | 1 | 0 | 0 | 0 | 1 | 0 | 16 | 0 |
| STEPHENS KJ | Bristol 1946 | OR | Phildown R 1962 — Walsall 1968 | 21/1 | 2 | 1/2 | 0 | 1 | 1 | 0 | 0 | 1 | 0 | 24/3 | 3 |
| STEVENSON J | Bonhill, Dumbarton 1875 | HB/CF | Preston North End 1900 — Dumbarton 1904 | 120 | 9 | 9 | 0 | 0 | 0 | 0 | 0 | 0 | 0 | 129 | 9 |
| STRINGER J | Netherton, Dudley 1878 | G | Wolves 1905 — Dudley T 1910 | 160 | 0 | 12 | 0 | 0 | 0 | 0 | 0 | 0 | 0 | 172 | 0 |
| STRODDER GJ | Cleckheaton 1965 | CH | West Ham Utd 1990 — | 93/7 | 5 | 7 | 1 | 6 | 0 | 0 | 0 | 7 | 0 | 113/7 | 6 |

**Albion's John Wile, injured in the 1978 FA Cup semi-final against Ipswich at Highbury.**

| PLAYER | BIRTHPLACE & YEAR | POS | FROM (year) TO (year) | League App | League Gls | FA Cup App | FA Cup Gls | Lge Cup App | Lge Cup Gls | Euro App | Euro Gls | Others App | Others Gls | TOTAL App | TOTAL Gls |
|---|---|---|---|---|---|---|---|---|---|---|---|---|---|---|---|
| STYLES AJ | Smethwick 1939 | WH | School 1956 — Wrexham 1960 | 1 | 0 | 0 | 0 | 0 | 0 | 0 | 0 | 0 | 0 | 1 | 0 |
| SUGGETT C | Washington, Co Durham 1948 | IF | Sunderland 1969 — Norwich C 1973 | 123/5 | 20 | 10 | 2 | 15 | 4 | 0 | 0 | 17 | 4 | 165/5 | 30 |
| SUMMERFIELD K | Walsall 1959 | F | School 1975 — Birmingham C 1982 | 5/4 | 4 | 0 | 0 | 2 | 0 | 0 | 0 | 0 | 0 | 7/4 | 4 |
| SUMMERS GT | Small Heath 1933 | WH | Erdington Albion 1950 — Sheffield U 1957 | 22 | 0 | 3 | 0 | 0 | 0 | 0 | 0 | 0 | 0 | 25 | 0 |
| SWAIN KM | Birkenhead 1952 | RB | Portsmouth (loan) 1988 — Portsmouth 1988 | 7 | 1 | 0 | 0 | 0 | 0 | 0 | 0 | 0 | 0 | 7 | 1 |
| SWALLOW J | Sheffield 1860 | WH | Oldbury 1883 — Wednesbury T 1884 | 0 | 0 | 1 | 0 | 0 | 0 | 0 | 0 | 0 | 0 | 1 | 0 |
| SWIFT A | West Hartlepool 1892 | CF | Hartlepool Expansion 1913 — Crystal P 1920 | 28 | 11 | 0 | 0 | 0 | 0 | 0 | 0 | 0 | 0 | 28 | 11 |
| SWINDEN SA | Smethwick 1913 | FB | Smethwick Highfield 1931 — Swindon T 1937 | 4 | 0 | 0 | 0 | 0 | 0 | 0 | 0 | 0 | 0 | 4 | 0 |
| TAGGART J | Belfast 1872 | HB | Middlesbrough 1893 — Walsall 1896 | 68 | 4 | 11 | 0 | 0 | 0 | 0 | 0 | 14 | 0 | 93 | 5 |
| TALBOT BE | Ipswich 1953 | M | Stoke City 1988 — Fulham 1991 | 66/8 | 5 | 2/2 | 0 | 3 | 1 | 0 | 0 | 2 | 0 | 73/10 | 6 |
| TALBUT J | Headington, Oxford 1940 | CH | Burnley 1966 — KV Mechelen 1971 | 143/1 | 0 | 21 | 0 | 15 | 0 | 7 | 0 | 6 | 1 | 192/1 | 1 |
| TAYLOR AS | Lozells, Birmingham 1925 | CF | Handsworth Wood 1941 — Retired 1951 | 4 | 5 | 0 | 0 | 0 | 0 | 0 | 0 | 0 | 0 | 4 | 5 |
| TAYLOR GA | Trehaford 1905 | OR | Trehaford 1927 — Leamington T 1929 | 0 | 0 | 1 | 0 | 0 | 0 | 0 | 0 | 0 | 0 | 1 | 0 |
| TAYLOR H | Dudley 1893 | CF | Dudley Bean 1920 — Barrow 1921 | 9 | 2 | 0 | 0 | 0 | 0 | 0 | 0 | 0 | 0 | 9 | 2 |
| TAYLOR O | Wednesfield 1880 | G | Bilston 1901 — Coventry C 1903 | 5 | 0 | 0 | 0 | 0 | 0 | 0 | 0 | 0 | 0 | 5 | 0 |
| TAYLOR R | Hordon 1967 | CF | Bristol City 1992 — | 65 | 38 | 4 | 3 | 2 | 1 | 0 | 0 | 7 | 3 | 78 | 45 |
| THOMAS JW | Wednesday 1958 | CF | Bolton Wds 1989 — Preston North End 1990 | 8/10 | 1 | 0 | 0 | 2 | 3 | 0 | 0 | 0/1 | 0 | 10/11 | 4 |
| THOMAS MR | Mochdre, Montgomeryshire 1954 | M | Chelsea 1985 — Witchita Wings 1986 | 20 | 0 | 2 | 1 | 5 | 0 | 0 | 0 | 1 | 0 | 28 | 1 |
| THOMPSON AR | Wolverhampton 1967 | M | Featherstone FC 1984 — Wolver 1986 | 18/5 | 1 | 2 | 0 | 0/1 | 0 | 0 | 0 | 1/1 | 0 | 21/7 | 1 |
| THOMPSON GL | Birmingham 1959 | CF | Coventry C 1983 — Sheffield W 1985 | 91 | 39 | 5 | 1 | 9 | 5 | 0 | 0 | 0 | 0 | 105 | 45 |
| THOMPSON JT | North Shields 1955 | FB | Northumberland Boys 1970 — Newport C 1978 | 20 | 0 | 0 | 0 | 2 | 0 | 0 | 0 | 0 | 0 | 22 | 0 |
| THOMPSON W | Morpeth, Northumberland 1886 | OR | Morpeth H 1908 — Sunderland 1911 | 54 | 6 | 3 | 0 | 0 | 0 | 0 | 0 | 0 | 0 | 57 | 6 |
| TIGHE J | Aghamore, Northern Ireland 1923 | G | Larkhall Th 1945 — Hednesford T 1948 | 1 | 0 | 0 | 0 | 0 | 0 | 0 | 0 | 0 | 0 | 1 | 0 |
| TIMMINS G | West Bromwich 1858 | WH/IF | George Salter Works 1879 — Old Hill W 1891 | 33 | 0 | 28 | 1 | 0 | 0 | 0 | 0 | 0 | 0 | 61 | 1 |
| TIMMINS S | West Bromwich 1879 | WH | Nottingham F 1906 — Retired 1911 | 111 | 3 | 5 | 0 | 0 | 0 | 0 | 0 | 0 | 0 | 116 | 3 |
| TRANTER GH | Yardley, Birmingham 1915 | CH | Rover Works 1934 — Hereford U 1947 | 16 | 0 | 4 | 0 | 0 | 0 | 0 | 0 | 50 | 0 | 70 | 0 |
| TREACY RCP | Dublin 1946 | CF | Home Farm 1961 — Charlton A 1968<br>Preston North End 1976 — Shamrock R 1977 | 22/4 | 7 | 2 | 0 | 0 | 0 | 0 | 0 | 0 | 0 | 24/4 | 7 |
| TRENTHAM HF | Chirbury, Shropshire 1908 | FB | Hereford U 1929 — Hereford U 1937 | 246 | 0 | 25 | 0 | 0 | 0 | 0 | 0 | 1 | 0 | 272 | 0 |
| TREWICK J | Bedlington, Northumberland 1957 | M/FB | Schools 1972 — Newcastle U 1980 | 83/13 | 11 | 12 | 0 | 10/2 | 0 | 6/2 | 1 | 5/1 | 0 | 116/18 | 12 |
| TREVIS ASSRTBG | Blackheath 1910 | CH | Leamington T 1929 — Chester 1936 | 1 | 0 | 0 | 0 | 0 | 0 | 0 | 0 | 0 | 0 | 1 | 0 |
| TUDOR WH | Shotton, Chester 1918 | CH | Lavender FC 1934 — Wrexham 1946 | 31 | 0 | 3 | 0 | 0 | 0 | 0 | 0 | 0 | 0 | 34 | 0 |
| TURNER I | Netherton, Dudley 1876 | G | Dudley St James 1898 — Stourbridge 1899 | 1 | 0 | 0 | 0 | 0 | 0 | 0 | 0 | 0 | 0 | 1 | 0 |
| TURNER SI | Langley, West Midlands 1882 | IL | Darlaston 1904 — Coventry 1905 | 1 | 0 | 0 | 0 | 0 | 0 | 0 | 0 | 0 | 0 | 1 | 0 |
| TWIGG L | Buxton, Derbyshire 1921 | G | Buxton FC 1945 — Retired 1947 | 0 | 0 | 1 | 0 | 0 | 0 | 0 | 0 | 1 | 0 | 2 | 0 |
| VALENTINE CH | Manchester 1958 | W | Vancouver Whitecaps 1984 — Wichita Wings 1986 | 44 | 6 | 0 | 0 | 6 | 0 | 0 | 0 | 3 | 1 | 53 | 7 |
| VARADI I | Paddington, London 1959 | CF | Sheffield W 1985 — Manchester C 1986 | 30/2 | 9 | 2 | 0 | 5 | 4 | 0 | 0 | 2 | 0 | 39/2 | 13 |
| VARNEY H | Belper, Derbyshire 1885 | OR | Belper T 1905 — Belper T 1907 | 5 | 0 | 0 | 0 | 0 | 0 | 0 | 0 | 0 | 0 | 5 | 0 |
| VARTY JW | Scotswood-on-Tyne 1890 | WH | Scotswood R 1911 — Hartlepools U 1913 | 3 | 0 | 0 | 0 | 0 | 0 | 0 | 0 | 0 | 0 | 3 | 0 |
| VERNON J | Belfast 1919 | CH | Belfast Celtic 1947 — Crusaders 1952 | 190 | 1 | 10 | 0 | 0 | 0 | 0 | 0 | 0 | 0 | 200 | 1 |
| VIGROW S | Muirhead, Angus 1878 | IL | Dundee 1896 — Airdrie 1897 | 1 | 0 | 0 | 0 | 0 | 0 | 0 | 0 | 0 | 0 | 1 | 0 |
| VINCENT EA | Dudley Wood 1922 | WH | Toll End Wesley 1939 — Worcester C 1946 | 0 | 0 | 0 | 0 | 0 | 0 | 0 | 0 | 1 | 0 | 1 | 0 |
| WALFORD SJ | Highgate 1958 | D | West Ham U (loan) 1989 — West Ham Utd 1989 | 3/1 | 0 | 0 | 0 | 0 | 0 | 0 | 0 | 0 | 0 | 3/1 | 0 |
| WALKER D | Oakdene, Walsall 1884 | IL | Bristol R 1907 — Leicester Fosse 1908 | 36 | 15 | 3 | 0 | 0 | 0 | 0 | 0 | 0 | 0 | 39 | 15 |
| WALKER L | West Bromwich 1860 | FB | West Brom Royal 1883 — West Brom Standard 1891 | 18 | 0 | 1 | 0 | 0 | 0 | 0 | 0 | 0 | 0 | 19 | 0 |
| WALKER WW | Horseley Heath, Tipton 1879 | IF | Toll End Wesley 1898 — Brierley Hill 1903 | 32 | 5 | 2 | 0 | 0 | 0 | 0 | 0 | 0 | 0 | 34 | 5 |
| WALKER W | Walsall 1888 | CF | Halesowen 1910 — Willenhall Swifts 1911 | 1 | 1 | 0 | 0 | 0 | 0 | 0 | 0 | 0 | 0 | 1 | 1 |
| WALLACE JMB | Wallyford, Edinburgh 1935 | G | Airdrie 1959 — Bedford T 1962 | 69 | 0 | 7 | 0 | 0 | 0 | 0 | 0 | 0 | 0 | 76 | 0 |
| WALSH DJ | Waterford 1924 | CF | Linfield 1946 — Aston Villa 1950 | 165 | 94 | 9 | 6 | 0 | 0 | 0 | 0 | 0 | 0 | 174 | 100 |
| WARD G | Sutton Coldfield 1970 | G | Shrewsbury T 1989 — Cardiff City 1989 | 0 | 0 | 0 | 0 | 1 | 0 | 0 | 0 | 0 | 0 | 1 | 0 |
| WARD RA | West Bromwich 1953 | G | Imperial Star 1972 — Blackpool 1977 | 9 | 0 | 0 | 0 | 0 | 0 | 0 | 0 | 1 | 0 | 10 | 0 |
| WATERHOUSE F | Langley Green, West Midlands 1889 | HB | Wednesbury Old Athletic 1908 — Derby C 1920 | 172 | 6 | 12 | 0 | 0 | 0 | 0 | 0 | 4 | 0 | 188 | 6 |
| WATSON A | Sheffield 1868 | W | Mansfield T 1896 — Lincoln C 1899 | 28 | 2 | 2 | 1 | 0 | 0 | 0 | 0 | 0 | 0 | 30 | 3 |
| WATSON E | West Bromwich 1901 | RH | Tanfield FC 1922 — Hereford U 1923 | 1 | 0 | 0 | 0 | 0 | 0 | 0 | 0 | 0 | 0 | 1 | 0 |
| WEBB AR | Wrockwardine Wood, Salop 1963 | D | School 1979 — Port Vale 1984 | 23/1 | 0 | 0 | 0 | 0 | 0 | 0/1 | 0 | 0 | 0 | 23/2 | 0 |
| WEBB I | Worcester 1874 | G | Small Heath 1901 — Sunderland 1904 | 96 | 0 | 5 | 0 | 0 | 0 | 0 | 0 | 0 | 0 | 101 | 0 |
| WEBSTER H | Walsall 1909 | G | Burtonwood Villa 1928 — Swindon T 1929 | 1 | 0 | 0 | 0 | 0 | 0 | 0 | 0 | 0 | 0 | 1 | 0 |
| WEST C | Wallsend 1962 | CF | Sheffield Wed 1989 — Swansea City 1992 | 64/9 | 22 | 4 | 1 | 2 | 0 | 0 | 0 | 2 | 72 | /924 | |
| WHELDON GF | Langley Green, West Midlands 1869 | IF | Aston Villa 1900 — Queen's Park R 1901 | 26 | 3 | 3 | 0 | 0 | 0 | 0 | 0 | 0 | 0 | 29 | 3 |
| WHELDON S | Smethwick 1865 | WH | Langley Green Vics 1891 — Walsall 1892 | 1 | 0 | 0 | 0 | 0 | 0 | 0 | 0 | 0 | 0 | 1 | 0 |
| WHITE H | Wednesbury 1916 | RB | Darlaston 1937 — Worcester C 1946 | 39 | 0 | 3 | 0 | 0 | 0 | 0 | 0 | 36 | 1 | 78 | 1 |
| WHITE W | Leicester 1958 | M | Burnley 1991 — Doncaster 1992 | 13/3 | 1 | 2 | 0 | 0 | 0 | 0 | 0 | 1/1 | 0 | 16/2 | 1 |
| WHITEHEAD CR | Northfield, Birmingham 1955 | U | Bristol C 1981 — Portsmouth 1987 | 157/11 | 6 | 10 | 2 | 14/2 | 1 | 0 | 0 | 2 | 0 | 183/13 | 9 |
| WHITEHEAD NJ | Tamworth 1914 | OR | Birmingham University 1932 — Birmingham 1935 | 1 | 0 | 0 | 0 | 0 | 0 | 0 | 0 | 0 | 0 | 1 | 0 |
| WHITEHOUSE B | West Bromwich 1935 | IF | Vono Sports 1950 — Norwich C 1960 | 37 | 13 | 9 | 4 | 0 | 0 | 0 | 0 | 0 | 0 | 46 | 17 |
| WHITEHOUSE JW | West Bromwich 1861 | OR | West Brom Rovers 1880 — Retired 1884 | 0 | 0 | 1 | 0 | 0 | 0 | 0 | 0 | 0 | 0 | 1 | 0 |
| WHYTE C | London 1961 | D | Los Angeles L 1988 — Leeds United 1990 | 83/1 | 7 | 5 | 0 | 5 | 2 | 0 | 0 | 2 | 0 | 95/1 | 9 |
| WILCOX EE | Blaengarw, Glamorgan 1927 | CF | Oxford C 1947 — Worcester C 1951 | 12 | 3 | 0 | 0 | 0 | 0 | 0 | 0 | 0 | 0 | 12 | 3 |
| WILCOX HM | Hockley, Birmingham 1881 | IF | Leicester Fosse 1907 — Plymouth A 1908 | 17 | 5 | 3 | 2 | 0 | 0 | 0 | 0 | 0 | 0 | 20 | 7 |
| WILCOXSON GH | Heanor, Derbyshire 1925 | IF | Heanor Town 1943 — Heanor Town 1946 | 0 | 0 | 0 | 0 | 0 | 0 | 0 | 0 | 1 | 0 | 1 | 0 |
| WILE JD | Sherburn, Co Durham 1947 | CH | Peterborough U 1970 — Peterborough U 1983 | 499/1 | 24 | 42 | 2 | 42 | 2 | 12 | 1 | 23 | 0 | 618/1 | 29 |
| WILKES AG | Hagley, Worcs 1918 | CF | Kidderminster H 1938 — Blackheath 1946 | 0 | 0 | 1 | 0 | 0 | 0 | 0 | 0 | 4 | 5 | 5 | 5 |
| WILLETTS G | West Bromwich 1920 | G | Clanborough FC 1941 — Retired 1946 | 0 | 0 | 0 | 0 | 0 | 0 | 0 | 0 | 1 | 0 | 1 | 0 |
| WILLIAMS CE | Bristol 1921 | IF | Bristol C 1948 — Bristol C 1951 | 71 | 19 | 6 | 1 | 0 | 0 | 0 | 0 | 0 | 0 | 77 | 20 |
| WILLIAMS G | West Bromwich 1925 | WH | Harvills Hawthorn FC 1943 — Banbury Sp 1949 | 7 | 0 | 2 | 0 | 0 | 0 | 0 | 0 | 28 | 0 | 37 | 0 |
| WILLIAMS GE | Hellan, Rhyl 1938 | FB | Rhyl A 1954 — Weymouth 1972 | 308/6 | 10 | 25 | 0 | 15 | 1 | 5 | 0 | 1 | 0 | 354/6 | 11 |
| WILLIAMS GO | Wednesbury 1879 | HB | Wednesbury Old Athletic 1899 — Brierley Hill 1902 | 16 | 0 | 2 | 0 | 0 | 0 | 0 | 0 | 0 | 0 | 18 | 0 |
| WILLIAMS J | Brownhills 1882 | OR | Aston Villa 1905 — Brownhills A 1909 | 31 | 1 | 4 | 0 | 0 | 0 | 0 | 0 | 0 | 0 | 35 | 1 |
| WILLIAMS NE | Wolverhampton 1924 | FB | Featherstone FC 1944 — Released 1946 | 0 | 0 | 0 | 0 | 0 | 0 | 0 | 0 | 1 | 0 | 1 | 0 |
| WILLIAMS O | Smethwick 1874 | IF | Oldbury T 1893 — Oldbury T 1895 | 14 | 7 | 1 | 0 | 0 | 0 | 0 | 0 | 4 | 2 | 19 | 9 |
| WILLIAMS PA | Sheffield 1963 | CF | Stockport Co 1991 — Stockport County 1993 | 26/18 | 5 | 1/1 | 1 | 1/1 | 0 | 0 | 0 | 1/2 | 1 | 29/22 | 7 |
| WILLIAMS SG | Wrexham 1930 | FB | Wrexham 1950 — Southampton 1962 | 226 | 6 | 20 | 3 | 0 | 0 | 0 | 0 | 0 | 0 | 246 | 9 |
| WILLIAMS W | West Smethwick 1875 | FB | Old Hill Wanderers 1894 — Retired 1901 | 180 | 8 | 23 | 2 | 0 | 0 | 0 | 0 | 5 | 2 | 208 | 12 |
| WILLIAMS WT | Esher, Surrey 1942 | CH | Queen's Park R 1963 — Mansfield T 1966 | 1 | 0 | 0 | 0 | 0 | 0 | 0 | 0 | 0 | 0 | 1 | 0 |
| WILLIAMSON R | Glasgow 1961 | CF | Glasgow Rangers 1986 — Rotherham U 1988 | 40/13 | 11 | 2 | 0 | 2 | 0 | 0 | 0 | 1/1 | 1 | 45/14 | 12 |
| WILSON C | Heeley, Sheffield 1905 | IF | Hallam FC 1920 — Sheffield W 1928 | 125 | 41 | 8 | 4 | 0 | 0 | 0 | 0 | 0 | 0 | 133 | 45 |
| WILSON JJ | Handsworth, Birmingham 1861 | OL | Walsall T 1887 — Kidderminster H 1890 | 40 | 8 | 13 | 12 | 0 | 0 | 0 | 0 | 0 | 0 | 53 | 20 |
| WILSON RT | Grangemouth, Stirling 1947 | OL/FB | Woodburn A 1963 — Retired 1977 | 230/2 | 3 | 21 | 0 | 11 | 0 | 4 | 0 | 16 | 0 | 282/2 | 3 |
| WITCOMB D | Cwm, Gwent 1918 | WH | Enfield 1937 — Sheffield W 1947 | 55 | 3 | 9 | 1 | 0 | 0 | 0 | 0 | 58 | 6 | 122 | 10 |
| WOLLASTON W | Willenhall 1886 | OR | Willenhall Pickwick 1910 — Darlaston 1913 | 25 | 2 | 1 | 1 | 0 | 0 | 0 | 0 | 0 | 0 | 26 | 3 |
| WOOD HF | West Bromwich 1870 | IF | Oldbury T 1891 — Walsall 1893 | 1 | 1 | 0 | 0 | 0 | 0 | 0 | 0 | 0 | 0 | 1 | 1 |
| WOOD MC | Hobson, Co Durham 1890 | FB/CH | Hobson W 1911 — Kidderminster H 1922 | 17 | 0 | 0 | 0 | 0 | 0 | 0 | 0 | 0 | 0 | 17 | 0 |
| WOOD S | Winsford, Cheshire 1905 | OL | Winsford U 1928 — Halifax T 1938 | 256 | 58 | 24 | 8 | 0 | 0 | 0 | 0 | 1 | 0 | 281 | 66 |
| WOODHALL G | West Bromwich 1863 | OR/IR | Churchfield For 1883 — Wolves 1892 | 44 | 10 | 30 | 10 | 0 | 0 | 0 | 0 | 0 | 0 | 74 | 20 |
| WOOLGAR S | Chesterfield 1952 | M | School 1968 — Doncaster R 1974 | 2/2 | 0 | 0 | 0 | 0/1 | 0 | 0 | 0 | 1 | 0 | 3/3 | 0 |
| WORTON T | Wolverhampton 1878 | IF | Wolves 1901 — Retired 1905 | 72 | 23 | 3 | 0 | 0 | 0 | 0 | 0 | 0 | 0 | 75 | 23 |
| WRIGHT F | Wednesbury 1872 | D | Wednesbury Old Athletic 1895 — Rowley RS 1896 | 2 | 0 | 0 | 0 | 0 | 0 | 0 | 0 | 0 | 0 | 2 | 0 |
| WRIGHT HF | West Bromwich 1890 | IF | West Brom Wednesbury A 1906 — Stourbridge 1909<br>Stourbridge 1910 — Wolves 1919 | 89 | 17 | 10 | 3 | 0 | 0 | 0 | 0 | 6 | 0 | 105 | 20 |
| YOUNG G | Kirkintilloch, Dumbarton 1880 | FB | Portsmouth 1905 — West Brom Strollers 1906 | 16 | 0 | 0 | 0 | 0 | 0 | 0 | 0 | 0 | 0 | 16 | 0 |
| YOUNG WC | Chadsmoor, Staffs 1884 | RH | Hednesford T 1907 — Hednesford T 1910 | 19 | 2 | 3 | 0 | 0 | 0 | 0 | 0 | 0 | 0 | 22 | 2 |
| ZONDERVAN R | Surinam (Dutch Guinea) 1959 | M | FC Twente Enschede 1982 — Ipswich T 1984 | 82/2 | 5 | 5 | 0 | 6 | 0 | 0 | 0 | 0 | 0 | 93/2 | 5 |